Tax Formula for Individuals

Income (broadly defined)...	$xx,xxx
Less: Exclusions..	(x,xxx)
Gross income...	$xx,xxx
Less: Deductions *for* adjusted gross income......................................	(x,xxx)
Adjusted gross income..	$xx,xxx
Less: The greater of—	
Total itemized deductions	
or standard deduction...	(x,xxx)
Less: Personal and dependency exemptions*.......................................	(x,xxx)
Deduction for qualified business income**..................................	(x,xxx)
Taxable income...	$xx,xxx
Tax on taxable income...	$ x,xxx
Less: Tax credits (including Federal income tax	
withheld and prepaid)..	(xxx)
Tax due (or refund)...	$ xxx

*Exemption deductions are not allowed from 2018 through 2025.
**Only applies from 2018 through 2025.

Basic Standard Deduction Amounts

Filing Status	2017	2018
Single	$ 6,350	$12,000
Married, filing jointly	12,700	24,000
Surviving spouse	12,700	24,000
Head of household	9,350	18,000
Married, filing separately	6,350	12,000

Amount of Each Additional Standard Deduction

Filing Status	2017	2018
Single	$1,550	$1,600
Married, filing jointly	1,250	1,300
Surviving spouse	1,250	1,300
Head of household	1,550	1,600
Married, filing separately	1,250	1,300

Personal and Dependency Exemption

2017	2018*
$4,050	$4,150

*Note: Exemption deductions have been suspended from 2018 through 2025.

Powerful preparation.
Maximum confidence.

The right tools to help prepare you for the Exam

With Becker Professional Education, you get a fully integrated
CPA Exam Review course that helps you:

MOVE BEYOND MEMORIZATION TO APPLICATION
Interactive simulations and videos move you beyond memorization,
helping you apply concepts — a critical component of the CPA Exam.

STUDY SMART
Adapt2U pre-assessment provides you a recommended study path.

TRACK PROGRESS AND BUILD CONFIDENCE
Mock exams, progress tests and a study planner help you focus on where you need the most help.

LEARN WHAT'S NEEDED
Study with a course that replicates the CPA Exam.

CHOOSE FROM 3 FLEXIBLE COURSE FORMATS
Choose from Self-Study, LiveOnline or Live Classroom formats.

CPA SkillMaster Videos
Tackle Task-Based Simulations
with confidence. Our
expert instructors take you
through the most complex
questions step-by-step.
***It's like having your
own CPA coach!***

ProConnect™ Tax Online

Work like a pro.

Get the #1 cloud-based professional tax software for free.[1,2]

Go beyond the basics and connect with the modern tools you need to work efficiently.

- **Work with confidence.**
  Get returns done right the first time with access to all the forms you need, backed by industry-leading calculations and diagnostics.

- **Work smarter.**
  Save time with logical data-entry worksheets instead of traditional forms-based methods. Plus, get quick training resources so it's easy to stay up to speed.

- **Work from anywhere.**
  It's all online, so there's nothing to install or maintain. And whether you're on your mobile phone or laptop, PC or Mac — you're always good to go.

Visit **TaxEducation.Intuit.com** to get started.

Only one sign-up per student. No special code required. If you have trouble accessing or using the software, reach out to us at taxeducation_support@intuit.com anytime for help.

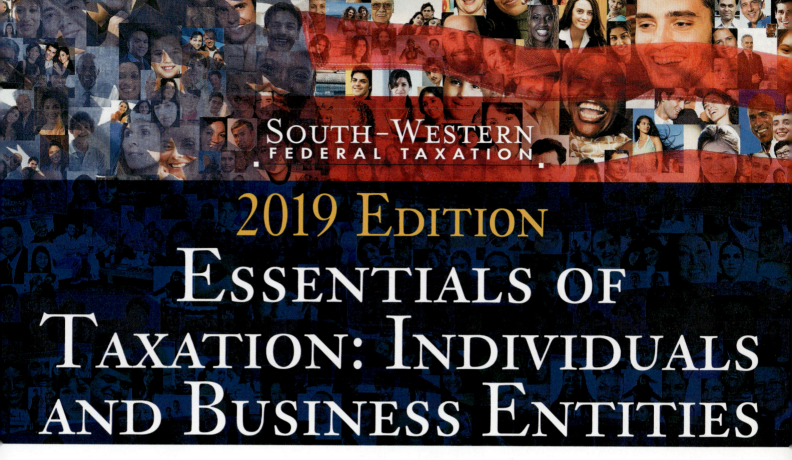

SOUTH-WESTERN FEDERAL TAXATION

2019 EDITION

ESSENTIALS OF TAXATION: INDIVIDUALS AND BUSINESS ENTITIES

General Editors

William A. Raabe
Ph.D., CPA
Madison, Wisconsin

James C. Young
Ph.D., CPA
Northern Illinois University

Annette Nellen
J.D., CPA, CGMA
San Jose State University

David M. Maloney
Ph.D., CPA
University of Virginia

Contributing Authors

Hughlene A. Burton
Ph.D., CPA
University of North Carolina-Charlotte

Gregory Carnes
Ph.D., CPA
University of North Alabama

Andrew Cuccia
Ph.D., CPA
University of Oklahoma

William A. Raabe
Ph.D., CPA
Madison, Wisconsin

Toby Stock
Ph.D.
Ohio University

Kristina Zvinakis
Ph.D.
The University of Texas at Austin

SWFT Series Authors

James H. Boyd
Ph.D., CPA
Arizona State University

D. Larry Crumbley
Ph.D., CPA
Louisiana State University

Steven C. Dilley
J.D., Ph.D., CPA
Michigan State University

Steven L. Gill
Ph.D., CPA
San Diego State University

William H. Hoffman, Jr.
J.D., Ph.D., CPA
University of Houston

David M. Maloney
Ph.D., CPA
University of Virginia

Annette Nellen
J.D., CPA, CGMA
San Jose State University

Mark B. Persellin
Ph.D., CPA, CFP
St. Mary's University

Debra L. Sanders
Ph.D., CPA
Washington State
University, Vancouver

W. Eugene Seago
J.D., Ph.D., CPA
Virginia Polytechnic
Institute and State
University

James C. Young
Ph.D., CPA
Northern Illinois
University

 CENGAGE

Australia • Brazil • Mexico • Singapore • United Kingdom • United States

**South-Western Federal Taxation:
Essentials of Taxation, 2019 Edition**

**William A. Raabe, James C. Young,
Annette Nellen, David M. Maloney**

Senior Vice President, Higher Ed Product, Content,
and Market Development: Erin Joyner

Product Director: Jason Fremder

Sr. Product Manager: John Barans

Sr. Content Manager: Nadia Saloom

Learning Designer: Jonathan Gross

Product Assistant: Aiyana Moore

Marketing Manager: Christopher P. Walz

Sr. Digital Delivery Lead: Tim Richison

Production Service: SPi Global

Senior Designer: Bethany Bourgeois

Text and Cover Designer: Red Hangar Design

Cover Image: John Lund/Blend Images/
Getty Images

Intellectual Property:
Analyst: Reba Frederics
Project Manager: Carly Belcher

Design Images:
Concept Summary, Global Tax Issues,
Bridge Discipline: iStock.com/enot-poloskun
Ethics & Equity: iStock.com/LdF
Problems/Tax Return Problems:
iStock.com/peepo
Financial Disclosure Insights: Vyaseleva Elena/
Shutterstock.com
Tax Planning Strategies: Sergey Nivens/
Shutterstock.com
Tax Fact: carroteater/Shutterstock.com
Digging Deeper: tuulijumala/Shutterstock.com

All tax forms within the text are: Source: Internal Revenue Service
Tax software: Source: Intuit ProConnect
Becker CPA Review: Source: Becker CPA

ISSN: 1544-3590
2019 Annual Edition

Student Edition ISBN: 978-1-337-70297-3
Student Edition with Intuit ProConnect + RIA Checkpoint
ISBN: 978-1-337-70296-6

Cengage
20 Channel Center Street
Boston, MA 02210
USA

Cengage is a leading provider of customized learning solutions with
employees residing in nearly 40 different countries and sales in more than
125 countries around the world. Find your local representative at
www.cengage.com.

Cengage products are represented in Canada by Nelson Education, Ltd.

To learn more about Cengage platforms and services, register or access
your online learning solution, or purchase materials for your course, visit
www.cengage.com.

Printed in the United States of America
Print Number: 01   Print Year: 2018

Preface

COMMITTED TO EDUCATIONAL SUCCESS

South-Western Federal Taxation (SWFT) is the most trusted and best-selling series in college taxation. We are focused exclusively on providing the most useful, comprehensive, and up-to-date tax texts, online study aids, tax preparation tools, and research tools to help instructors and students succeed in their tax courses and beyond.

SWFT is a comprehensive package of teaching and learning materials, significantly enhanced with each edition to meet instructor and student needs and to add overall value to learning taxation.

Essentials of Taxation: Individuals and Business Entities, 2019 Edition provides a dynamic learning experience inside and outside of the classroom. Built with resources and tools that have been identified as the most important, our complete learning system provides options for students to achieve success.

Essentials of Taxation: Individuals and Business Entities, 2019 Edition provides accessible, comprehensive, and authoritative coverage of the relevant tax code and regulations as they pertain to the individual or business taxpayer, as well as coverage of all major developments in Federal Taxation. This edition has been fully updated and revised to reflect changes included in the Tax Cuts and Jobs Act of 2017.

In revising the 2019 Edition, we focused on:

- **Accessibility. Clarity. Substance.** The text authors and editors made this their mantra as they revised the 2019 edition. Coverage has been streamlined to make it more accessible to students, and difficult concepts have been clarified, all without losing the substance that makes up the *South-Western Federal Taxation* series.

- **Developing professional skills.** SWFT excels in bringing students to a professional level in their tax knowledge and skills, to prepare them for immediate success in their careers. In this regard, we include development of speaking and writing communications skills, the use of tax preparation and tax research software, orientation toward success on the CPA exam, consideration of the time value of money in the tax planning process, and facility with advanced applications of spreadsheet construction.

- **CengageNOWv2 as a complete learning system.** Cengage Learning understands that digital learning solutions are central to the classroom. Through sustained research, we continually refine our learning solutions in CengageNOWv2 to meet evolving student and instructor needs. CengageNOWv2 fulfills learning and course management needs by offering a personalized study plan, video lectures, auto-graded homework, auto-graded tests, and a full eBook with features and advantages that address common challenges.

Learning Tools and Features to Help Students Make the Connection

FULL-COLOR DESIGN: We understand that students struggle with learning difficult tax code concepts and applying them to real-world scenarios. The 2019 edition uses color to bring the text to life, capture student attention, and present the tax code in a simple, yet logical format.

❏ Selected **content is streamlined** to guide students in focusing on the most important concepts for the CPA Exam while still providing in-depth coverage of topics.

❏ Examples are clearly labeled and directly follow concepts to assist with student application. An **average of over 40 examples in each chapter** use realistic situations to illustrate the complexities of the tax law and allow students to integrate chapter concepts with illustrations and examples.

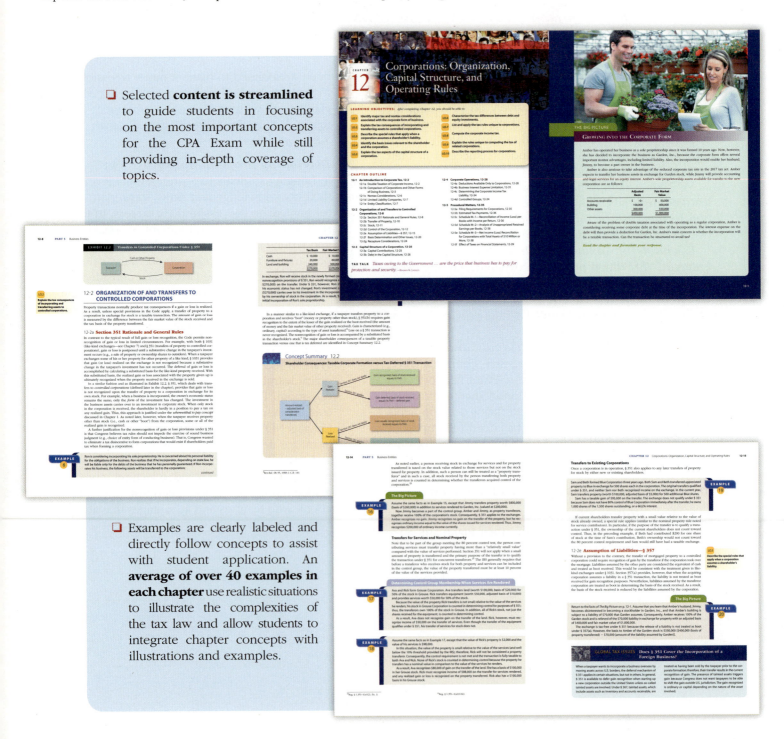

COMPUTATIONAL EXERCISES: Students need lots of practice in areas such as computing tax return problems and adjusting rates. We have developed these exercises to give students practice in calculating the solutions they need to make business decisions.

❏ Found in end-of-chapter section of the textbook

❏ CengageNOWv2 provides algorithmic versions of these problems

Computational Exercises

1. **LO.2** Marie and Ethan form Roundtree Corporation with the transfer of the following. Marie performs personal services for the corporation with a fair market value of $80,000 in exchange for 400 shares of stock. Ethan contributes an installment note receivable (basis $25,000; fair market value $30,000), land (basis $50,000; fair market value $170,000), and inventory (basis $100,000; fair market value $120,000) in exchange for 1,600 shares. Determine Marie and Ethan's current income, gain, or loss; calculate the basis that each takes in the Roundtree stock.

2. **LO.2** Grady exchanges qualified property, basis of $12,000 and fair market value of $18,000, for 60% of the stock of Eadie Corporation. The other 40% of the stock is owned by Pedro, who acquired it five years ago. Calculate Grady 's current income, gain, or loss and the basis he takes in his shares of Eadie stock as a result of this transaction.

3. **LO.3** Jocelyn contributes land with a basis of $60,000 and fair market value of $90,000 and inventory with a basis of $5,000 and fair market value of $8,000 in exchange for 100% of Zion Corporation stock. The land is subject to a $15,000 mortgage. Determine Jocelyn's recognized gain or loss and the basis in the Zion stock received.

BECKER PROFESSIONAL EDUCATION REVIEW QUESTIONS: End-of-chapter CPA review questions from Becker PREPARE STUDENTS FOR SUCCESS. Students review key concepts using proven questions from Becker Professional Education®—one of the industry's most effective tools to prepare for the CPA Exam.

❏ Located in select end-of-chapter sections

❏ Tagged by concept in CengageNOWv2

❏ Similar questions to what students would actually find on the CPA Exam

Becker CPA Review Questions

1. On January 1, year 5, Olinto Corp., an accrual basis, calendar year C corporation, had $35,000 in accumulated earnings and profits. For year 5, Olinto had current earnings and profits of $15,000 and made two $40,000 cash distributions to its shareholders, one in April and one in September of year 5. What amount of the year 5 distributions is classified as dividend income to Olinto's shareholders?

   a. $15,000   c. $50,000
   b. $35,000   d. $80,000

2. Fox Corp. owned 2,000 shares of Duffy Corp. stock that it bought in year 0 for $9 per share. In year 8, when the fair market value of the Duffy stock was $20 per share, Fox distributed this stock to a noncorporate shareholder. Fox's recognized gain on this distribution was:

   a. $40,000   c. $18,000
   b. $22,000   d. $0

v

See how the SWFT series helps students understand the big picture and the relevancy behind what they are learning.

THE BIG PICTURE

TAXES ON THE FINANCIAL STATEMENTS

Raymond Jones, the CEO of Arctic Corporation, would like some help reconciling the amount of income tax expense on Arctic's financial statements with the amount of income tax reported on the company's corporate income tax return for its first year of operations. Mr. Jones does not understand why he can't simply multiply the financial statement income by the company's combined Federal and state 25 percent marginal income tax rate to get the financial tax expense. While the financial statements show book income before tax of $25 million, the reported income tax expense is only $5 million. In addition, the corporate tax return reports taxable income of $19 million and Federal income taxes payable of $3.99 million ($19 million × 21%).

Without knowing the specifics of the company's financial statements, does Arctic's situation look reasonable? Why is Arctic's financial accounting tax expense not equal to $6.25 million ($25 million × 25%)? What causes the $1.01 million difference between the taxes shown on the financial statements and the taxes due on the tax return?

Read the chapter and formulate your response.

THE BIG PICTURE: Tax Solutions for the Real World.
Taxation comes alive at the start of each chapter as The Big Picture Examples give a glimpse into the lives, families, careers, and tax situations of typical individual or business filers. Students will follow the family, individual, or other taxpayer throughout the chapter showing students how the concepts they are learning play out in the real world.

Finally, to solidify student comprehension, each chapter concludes with a **Refocus on the Big Picture** summary and tax planning scenario. These scenarios apply the concepts and topics from the chapter in a reasonable and professional way.

BRIDGE DISCIPLINE BOXES AND END-OF-CHAPTER QUESTIONS:
Bridge Discipline boxes throughout the text present material and concepts from other disciplines such as economics, financial accounting, law, and finance. They help to bridge the gap between taxation issues and issues raised in other business courses. **Bridge Discipline questions**, in the end-of-chapter material, help test these concepts and give students the chance to apply concepts they've learned in the Bridge Discipline boxes.

BRIDGE DISCIPLINE **Bridge to Financial Analysis**

Financial analysts perform an important function for the capital markets in their detailed analyses of companies. The analyst combs through the financial reports and other information about a company to produce an informed opinion on how a company is performing. Analysts' earnings forecasts often constitute an important metric to examine when making decisions about investing in companies.

An experienced financial analyst typically will have a good handle on interpreting financial statement information.

However, even experienced analysts often will "punt" when it comes to interpreting the tax information contained in a financial statement, preferring to look at net income before taxes (or even EBITDA, earnings before interest, taxes, depreciation, and amortization).

A great deal of useful information about a business is contained in its tax footnote, and analysts might have an edge if they work at understanding the mysteries of taxes in the financial statements.

FINANCIAL DISCLOSURE INSIGHTS:
Tax professionals need to understand how taxes affect GAAP financial statements. **Financial Disclosure Insights**, appearing throughout the text, use current data about existing taxpayers to highlight book-tax reporting differences, effective tax rates, and trends in reporting conventions.

FINANCIAL DISCLOSURE INSIGHTS **Tax Losses and the Deferred Tax Asset**

Although a current-year net operating loss (NOL) represents a failure of an entity's business model to some, others see it as an immediate tax refund. But when an NOL hits the balance sheet as a deferred tax asset, the story is not over. The NOL creates or increases a deferred tax asset that may or may not be used in future financial accounting reporting periods. The key question for a financial analyst is whether the entity will generate enough net revenue in future years to create a positive tax liability that can be offset by the NOL carryover amount.

IFRS rules do not allow for a valuation allowance. Under IAS 12, a deferred tax asset is recorded only when it is "probable" (a higher standard than GAAP's "more likely than not") that the deferred tax amount will be realized, and then only to the extent of that probable amount. Thus, no offsetting valuation allowance is needed.

DIGGING DEEPER: Designed
to help students go further in their knowledge of certain topics, **Digging Deeper** links within the text provide more in-depth coverage than the text provides. Digging Deeper materials can be found on the book's website at **www.cengage.com.**

In-depth coverage can be found on this book's companion website: www.cengage.com   1 DIGGING DEEPER

TAX PLANNING FRAMEWORK: To demonstrate the relevance of tax planning for business and individual taxpayers, *Essentials of Taxation: Individuals and Business Entities* presents a unique **tax planning framework.** Introduced in Chapter 1, this framework extends to a series of **Tax Planning Strategies** incorporated throughout the remainder of the text. The inclusion of the tax planning framework, and the planning strategies in each chapter, makes it easier than ever to understand the effects that careful tax planning can have in today's world.

EXHIBIT 1.3	General Framework for Income Tax Planning	
Tax Formula	**Tax Planning Strategy**	**Tax Planning Examples**
Income and exclusions	➤ **Avoid income recognition.**	Compensate employees with nontaxable fringe benefits (see Example 19).
	➤ **Postpone recognition of income to achieve tax deferral.**	Postpone sale of assets (see Example 20).
− Deductions	➤ **Maximize deductible amounts.**	Invest in stock of another corporation (see Example 21).
	➤ **Accelerate recognition of deductions to achieve tax deferral.**	Elect to deduct charitable contribution in year of pledge rather than in year of payment (see Example 22).

TAX PLANNING STRATEGIES   Nexus: To Have or Have Not

FRAMEWORK FOCUS: TAX RATE

Strategy: Shift Net Income from High-Tax Jurisdictions to Low-Tax Jurisdictions.

Most taxpayers try to avoid establishing nexus in a new state, for example, by providing a sales representative with a cash auto allowance rather than a company car, by restricting the location of inventory to only a few states, or by limiting a salesperson's activities to those that are protected by the solicitation standard of P.L. 86–272. This effort to avoid nexus stems in part from the additional compliance burden that falls upon the taxpayer when a new set of income tax returns, information forms, and deadlines must be dealt with in the new state.

Another concern is that the marginal tax rate that applies to the net taxable income generated by the taxpayer may increase. Such a tax increase occurs, of course, only when the applicable tax rate in the new state is higher than the rate that would apply in the home state. If a business already is based in a tax-friendly state such as Florida or Texas or in a no-tax state such as Nevada, its aggregate tax liability is sure to increase.

Still, nexus is not *necessarily* a bad thing. Consider what happens if a business based in California, Maryland, Wisconsin, or another high-tax jurisdiction purposely creates nexus in a low- or no-tax state. If the new state applies a lower marginal rate than is available in the home state or offers special exemptions or exclusions that match the taxpayer's operations, the aggregate tax bill can decrease. Then the planning efforts include determining which activities will *create* nexus in the new jurisdiction and meeting or maintaining that standard.

For instance, an entertainer based in Manhattan is subject to the high income taxes of New York City and New York State. By establishing a permanent office in Tennessee, nexus will be created, and some portion of the taxpayer's income will be subject to taxation there, instead of New York. These are permanent savings, accruing immediately to after-tax income and the share price of the stock of the taxpayer.

TAX PLANNING STRATEGIES: The tax planning framework extends to subsequent chapters as **Tax Planning Strategies boxes** that are tied to the topical coverage of the chapters. Planning Strategies often contain examples to further illustrate the concept for students. Because some tax planning strategies do not fit neatly into the framework, the text also provides tax planning strategies called **Thinking Outside the Framework.**

GLOBAL TAX ISSUES: The **Global Tax Issues** feature gives insight into the ways in which taxation is affected by international concerns and illustrates the effects of various events on tax liabilities across the globe.

GLOBAL TAX ISSUES   **Filing a Joint Return**

John Garth is a U.S. citizen and resident, but he spends much of his time in London, where his employer sends him on frequent assignments. John is married to Victoria, a citizen and resident of the United Kingdom.

Can John and Victoria file a joint return for U.S. Federal income tax purposes? Although § 6013(a)(1) specifically precludes the filing of a joint return if one spouse is a nonresident alien, another Code provision permits an exception. Under § 6013(g), the parties can elect to treat the nonqualifying spouse as a "resident" of the United States. This election would allow John and Victoria to file jointly.

But should John and Victoria make this election? If Victoria has considerable income of her own (from non-U.S. sources), the election could be ill-advised. As a nonresident alien, Victoria's non-U.S. source income *would not* be subject to the U.S. income tax. If she is treated as a U.S. resident, however, her non-U.S. source income *will be subject to U.S. tax.* Under the U.S. worldwide approach to taxation, all income (regardless of where earned) of anyone who is a *resident* or *citizen* of the United States is subject to tax.

Take your students from Motivation to Mastery with CengageNOWv2

MASTERY
APPLICATION
MOTIVATION

CengageNOWv2 is a powerful course management tool and online homework resource that elevates student thinking by providing superior content designed with the entire student workflow in mind.

❏ **MOTIVATION:** engage students and better prepare them for class

❏ **APPLICATION:** help students learn problem-solving behavior and skills to guide them to complete taxation problems on their own

❏ **MASTERY:** help students make the leap from memorizing concepts to actual critical thinking

Motivation —

Many instructors find that students come to class unmotivated and unprepared. To help with engagement and preparedness, CengageNOWv2 for SWFT offers:

❏ **"Tax Drills" test students on key concepts and applications.** With three to five questions per learning objective, these "quick-hit" questions help students prepare for class lectures or review prior to an exam.

Application —

Students need to learn problem-solving behavior and skills, to guide them to complete taxation problems on their own. However, as students try to work through homework problems, sometimes they become stuck and need extra help. To reinforce concepts and keep students on the right track, CengageNOWv2 for SWFT offers the following.

❏ **End-of-chapter homework from the text** is expanded and enhanced to follow the workflow a professional would use to solve various client scenarios. These enhancements better engage students and encourage them to think like a tax professional.

- ❏ **Algorithmic versions** of end-of-chapter homework are available for computational exercises and at least 15 problems per chapter.

- ❏ **"Check My Work" Feedback.** Homework questions include immediate feedback so students can learn as they go. Levels of feedback include an option for "check my work" prior to submission of an assignment.

- ❏ **Post-Submission Feedback.** After submitting an assignment, students receive even more extensive feedback explaining why their answers were incorrect. Instructors can decide how much feedback their students receive and when, including the full solution.

- ❏ **Built-in Test Bank** for online assessment.

Mastery —

- ❏ **Tax Form Problems** give students the option to complete the Cumulative Intuit ProConnect Problems and other homework items found in the end-of-chapter manually or in a digital environment.

- ❏ **"What-If" Questions** allow students to develop a deeper understanding of the material as they are challenged to use their prior knowledge of the tax situations and critically think through new attributes to determine how the outcome will change.

- ❏ **An Adaptive Study Plan** comes complete with an eBook, practice quizzes, crossword puzzle, glossary, and flashcards. It is designed to help give students additional support and prepare them for the exam.

CengageNOWv2 Instant Access Code ISBN:
978-1-337-70376-5

Contact your Cengage Learning Consultant about different bundle options.

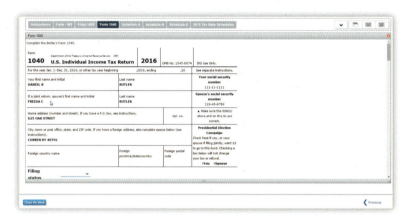

EXTENSIVELY REVISED. DEFINITIVELY UP TO DATE.

Each year the **South-Western Federal Taxation** series is updated with thousands of changes to each text. Some of these changes result from the feedback we receive from instructors and students in the form of reviews, focus groups, web surveys, and personal e-mail correspondence with our authors and team members. Other changes come from our careful analysis of the evolving tax environment. **Every tax law change relevant to the introductory taxation course was considered, summarized, and fully integrated into the revision of text and supplementary materials. This edition is fully updated and revised to reflect changes included in the Tax Cuts and Jobs Act (TCJA) of 2017. (Public Law 115–97; 12/22/17).**

The **South-Western Federal Taxation** authors have made every effort to keep all materials up to date and accurate. All chapters contain the following general changes for the 2019 Edition.

- Updated materials to reflect changes made by Congress through legislative action.
- Streamlined chapter content (where applicable) to clarify material and make it easier for students to understand.
- Revised numerous materials as the result of changes caused by indexing of statutory amounts.
- Revised Problem Materials, Computational Exercises, and CPA Exam problems.
- Updated Chapter Outlines to provide an overview of the material and to make it easier to locate specific topics.
- Revised *Financial Disclosure Insights* and *Global Tax Issues* as to current developments.

In addition, the following materials are available online.

- An appendix that helps instructors broaden and customize coverage of important tax provisions of the Affordable Care Act. (Instructor Companion Website at **www.cengage.com/login**)
- The Depreciation and the Accelerated Cost Recovery System (ACRS) appendix. (Instructor Companion Website at **www.cengage.com/login**)
- The Taxation in the Real World weekly blog posts for instructors. (**https://community.cengage .com/t5/Taxation-in-the-Real-World-Blog/ bg-p/taxationintherealworldblog**)

Chapter 1

- Updated Exhibit 1.1 (Federal Tax Revenues) and Exhibit 1.4 (IRS Audit Types and Rates) with current data.
- Revised text to reflect the TCJA of 2017 and revised various inflation-adjusted information in the chapter.

- Added a new Research Problem to analyze a soda tax or sweetened beverage tax proposal against the AICPA's *Principles of Good Tax Policy*.

Chapter 2

- Created a new fact pattern for the Big Picture.
- Updated the Conference Committee Exhibit 2.2 for the TCJA of 2017.

Chapter 3

- Referenced the revised revenue recognition rules required by GAAP.
- Revised the comments regarding the balance sheet treatment of the deferred tax accounts.
- Updated data for goodwill on the balance sheet for certain U.S. corporations.
- Updated end-of-chapter materials, including Research Problems (including a reference to a recent Institute on Taxation and Economic Policy report).

Chapter 4

- Updated for changes made by the TCJA of 2017, such as to accounting methods and tax rates.
- Added basics of FBAR reporting requirements (Digging Deeper 4).

Chapter 5

- Added new materials related to the TCJA of 2017, including accounting method changes for both accrual and cash method corporations, executive compensation issues (including performance-based compensation now covered by the $1 million limit, changing the definitions of "covered employees" and "publicly held corporation"), expanding the disallowance for fines and penalties, and disallowing deductions for local lobbying expenses.
- Updated material on research and experimental expenditures for changes made by the TCJA of 2017.
- Updated material to reflect TCJA of 2017 changes, including expanded immediate expensing, unlimited bonus depreciation, and changes to listed property rules.
- Added materials and examples related to using immediate expensing and bonus depreciation effectively.
- Modified other existing material to reflect changes dictated by the TCJA of 2017.

Chapter 6

- Added LO 11 and text Section 6-8 on the excess business loss limitation rule added by the TCJA of 2017.
- Updated casualty loss materials to reflect that personal casualty losses only allowed if due to a Federally declared disaster. Updated materials on personal casualty gain and loss netting.
- Revised net operating loss materials updated for changes by the TCJA of 2017.
- Made changes for clarity and simplicity.
- Updated end-of-chapter materials to reflect changes made by the TCJA of 2017.

Chapter 7

- Updated and revised for TCJA of 2017 changes.
- Added communications component to several end-of-chapter problems.
- Identified end-of-chapter problems that include a critical thinking component.

Chapter 8

- Modified the materials related to the definition of capital assets based on TCJA of 2017 changes (related to patents).
- Modified the material on the calculation of the alternative tax on net capital gains and qualified dividend income to reflect changes made by the TCJA of 2017.
- Updated end-of-chapter materials for the TCJA of 2017 and identified critical thinking items.
- Added communications requirements to several end-of-chapter problems.

Chapter 9

- Eliminated learning objective and section on personal exemptions.
- Added new section on AMT and NIIT.
- Updated to reflect changes made by the TCJA of 2017, including tax rates, standard deduction, the child and dependent tax credits, AMT, and the new calculation of the kiddie tax.
- Added information about new Form 1040SR that starts in 2019.
- Updated chapter materials to reflect inflation adjustments.
- Revised and clarified materials as needed throughout the chapter.
- Updated end-of-chapter materials to reflect TCJA of 2017 changes and inflation adjustments.

Chapter 10

- Added a crowdfunding question to the Big Picture.
- Made modifications to remove miscellaneous itemized deduction due to the TCJA of 2017.
- Updated to reflect changes made by the TCJA of 2017, including deductions and the child and dependent tax credits.
- Updated chapter materials to reflect inflation adjustments.
- Revised and clarified materials as needed throughout the chapter.
- Updated end-of-chapter materials to reflect TCJA of 2017 changes and inflation adjustments.

Chapter 11

- Streamlined coverage throughout the chapter; added multiple examples to illustrate text material.
- Updated materials for inflation adjustments.
- Clarified discussion of employee v. contractor issues.
- Explained the effects of TCJA of 2017 on various employee expenses, including meals and entertainment, teachers' expenses, moving costs, and legacy itemized deductions.
- Provided extensive materials concerning the deduction for qualified business income.
- Added material concerning documentation of employee expenditures.

Chapter 12

- Updated for the TCJA of 2017.
- Added new content on the business interest deduction limitation, excessive executive compensation, and restrictions on corporate accumulations.
- Revised end-of-chapter materials extensively to reflect TCJA of 2017 changes; added communications component to several problems; added Microsoft Excel component to one problem.

Chapter 13

- Updated chapter for changes made by the TCJA of 2017, including tax rates and repeal of the § 199 deduction.
- Revised and updated chapter materials as needed; clarified chapter materials when necessary.
- Updated end-of-chapter materials as needed.

Chapter 14

- Clarified definitions of general and limited partners.
- Streamlined discussion of four major types of partnerships.
- Changed from "nonliquidating distribution" to "current distribution" throughout, but kept reference to nonliquidating distributions as an alternative term.
- Integrated a discussion of the deduction for qualified business income as it pertains to partnerships and limited liability entities.
- Clarified and expanded comparisons of partnerships and C corporations (and aggregate and entity theories) throughout.

Chapter 15

- Revised materials affected by the TCJA of 2017, including the application of the § 199A deduction.
- Clarified AAA treatment of unrecognized losses for distributed property.

Chapter 16

- Updated for changes made by the TCJA of 2017 regarding international provisions.

Chapter 17

- Revised business credit materials affected by the TCJA of 2017, including the rehabilitation tax credit, foreign tax credit, and the new family leave credit.
- Revised material affected by the TCJA of 2017, including individual AMT exemption amounts and repeal of corporate AMT.
- Expanded solution and explanations for Microsoft Excel problems.

Chapter 18

- Clarified the availability of limited liability by business entities at the state level.
- Revised materials affected by the TCJA of 2017, including tax rates, distribution policies, the application of the § 199A deduction, and the use of NOLs.

TAX LAW OUTLOOK

From your SWFT Series Editors

Given the significant changes made by the Tax Cuts and Jobs Act of 2017, we are anticipating guidance from the Treasury Department and IRS in many areas, including the qualified business income deduction, excess business losses, net operating losses, and various changes to itemized deductions (including the cap on state and local taxes). Taxpayers and their advisors will be evaluating how all of these changes affect their financial planning strategies and will adjust their plans appropriately.

Small businesses will deliberate about the tax and legal form in which they should organize, taking into account the QBI deduction and other 2017 tax law changes. State and local issues will focus on the forms of interstate transactions and new definitions of nexus, and multinational businesses will deal with the new rules that move toward a territorial approach to cross-border taxation.

The SWFT editors will be monitoring these activities and provide updates to adopters as needed.

SUPPLEMENTS SUPPORT STUDENTS AND INSTRUCTORS

Built around the areas students and instructors have identified as the most important, our integrated supplements package offers more flexibility than ever before to suit the way instructors teach and students learn.

Online and Digital Resources for Students

CengageNOWv2 is a powerful course management and online homework tool that provides robust instructor control and customization to optimize the student learning experience and meet desired outcomes.

CengageNOWv2 Instant Access Code ISBN: 978-1-337-70376-5

Contact your Cengage Learning Consultant about different bundle options.

THOMSON REUTERS
CHECKPOINT™ **Thomson Reuters Checkpoint™** is the leading online tax research database used by professionals. There are three simple ways Checkpoint™ helps introduce students to tax research:

- Intuitive web-based design makes it fast and simple to find what you need.
- Checkpoint™ provides a comprehensive collection of primary tax law, cases, and rulings along with analytical insight you simply can't find anywhere else.
- Checkpoint™ has built-in productivity tools such as calculators to make research more efficient—a resource more tax pros use than any other.

Six months' access to Checkpoint™ (after activation) is packaged automatically with every NEW copy of the textbook.*

 More than software: Put the experience of ProConnect™ Tax Online on your side.

- Get returns done right the first time with access to all the forms you need, backed by industry-leading calculations and diagnostics.
- Save time with logical data-entry worksheets instead of traditional forms-based methods.
- It's all online, so there's nothing to install or maintain.

Online access to ProConnect™ Tax Online software is offered with each NEW copy of the textbook—at no additional cost to students.*

CENGAGE.com Students can use **Cengage.com** to select this textbook and access Cengage Learning content, empowering them to choose the most suitable format and giving them a better chance of success in the course. Buy printed materials, eBooks, and digital resources directly through Cengage Learning and save at **Cengage.com.**

Online Student Resources

Students can go to **www.cengage.com** for free resources to help them study as well as the opportunity to purchase additional study aids. These valuable free study resources will help students earn a better grade:

- Flashcards use chapter terms and definitions to aid students in learning tax terminology for each chapter.
- Online glossary for each chapter provides terms and definitions from the text in alphabetical order for easy reference.
- Learning objectives can be downloaded for each chapter to help keep students on track.
- Tax tables used in the textbook are downloadable for reference.

 The first-of-its-kind digital subscription designed specially to lower costs.
    Students get total access to everything Cengage has to offer on demand—in one place. That's 20,000 eBooks, 2,300 digital learning products, and dozens of study tools across 70 disciplines and over 675 courses. **www.cengage.com/unlimited**

Printed Resources for Students

Looseleaf Edition (978-1-337-70298-0)

This version provides all the pages of the text in an unbound, three-hole punched format for portability and ease of use. Online access to ProConnect™ Tax Online software is included with every NEW textbook as well as Checkpoint™ from Thomson Reuters.*

*NEW printed copies of the textbook are automatically packaged with access to Checkpoint™ and Intuit ProConnect™ Tax Online tax software. If students purchase the eBook, they will not automatically receive access to Checkpoint™ and Intuit ProConnect™ Tax Online software. They must purchase the tax media pack offering both of these products. The ISBN is 978-1-337-70176-1 and can be purchased at **www.cengage.com.**

Comprehensive Supplements Support Instructors' Needs

CengageNOWv2 is a powerful course management and online homework tool that provides robust instructor control and customization to optimize the student learning experience and meet desired outcomes. In addition to the features and benefits mentioned earlier for students, CengageNOWv2 includes these features for instructors:

- **Learning Outcomes Reporting** and the ability to analyze student work from the gradebook. Each exercise and problem is tagged by topic, learning objective, level of difficulty, estimated completion time, and business program standards to allow greater guidance in developing assessments and evaluating student progress.

- **Built-in Test Bank for online assessment.** The Test Bank files are included in CengageNOWv2 so that they may be used as additional homework or tests.

Solutions Manual

Written by the **South-Western Federal Taxation** editors and authors, the Solutions Manual features solutions arranged in accordance with the sequence of chapter material.

Solutions to all homework items are tagged with their Estimated Time to Complete, Level of Difficulty, and Learning Objective(s), as well as the AACSB's and AICPA's core competencies—giving instructors more control than ever in selecting homework to match the topics covered. The Solutions Manual also contains the lettered answers (only) to the end-of-chapter Becker CPA Review Questions. **Available on the Instructor Companion Website at www.cengage.com/login.**

PowerPoint® Lectures with Notes

The Instructor PowerPoint® Lectures contain more than 30 slides per chapter, including outlines and instructor guides, concept definitions, and key points. **Available on the Instructor Companion Website at www.cengage.com/login.**

Test Bank

Written by the **South-Western Federal Taxation** editors and authors, the Test Bank contains approximately 2,200 items and solutions arranged in accordance with the sequence of chapter material.

Each test item is tagged with its Estimated Time to Complete, Level of Difficulty, and Learning Objective(s),

as well as the AACSB's and AICPA's core competencies—for easier instructor planning and test item selection. The 2019 Test Bank is available in Cengage's test generator software, Cognero.

Cengage Learning Testing Powered by Cognero is a flexible, online system that allows you to:

- author, edit, and manage Test Bank content from multiple Cengage Learning solutions

- create multiple test versions in an instant

- deliver tests from your LMS, your classroom, or wherever you want

- create tests from school, home, the coffee shop—anywhere with internet access. (No special installs or downloads needed.)

Test Bank files in Word format as well as versions to import into your LMS are available on the Instructor Companion Website. **Cognero Test Banks available via single sign-on (SSO) account at www.cengage.com/login.**

Other Instructor Resources

All of the following instructor course materials are available online at www.cengage.com/login. Once logged into the site, instructors should select this textbook to access the online Instructor Resources.

- Instructor Guide

- Edition-to-edition correlation grids by chapter

- Detailed answer feedback for the end-of-chapter Becker CPA Review Questions in Word format (Lettered answers only are available in the Solutions Manual.)

- An appendix that helps instructors broaden and customize coverage of important tax provisions of the Affordable Care Act

- The Depreciation and the Accelerated Cost Recovery System (ACRS) appendix

Custom Solutions

Cengage Learning Custom Solutions develops personalized solutions to meet your taxation education needs. Consider the following for your adoption of **South-Western Federal Taxation 2019 Edition.**

- Remove chapters you do not cover or rearrange their order to create a streamlined and efficient text.

- Add your own material to cover new topics or information.

- Add relevance by including sections from Sawyers/Gill's *Federal Tax Research* or your state's tax laws and regulations.

ACKNOWLEDGMENTS

We want to thank all the adopters and others who participated in numerous online surveys as well as the following individuals who provided content reviews and feedback in the development of the **South-Western Federal Taxation** 2019 titles.

William A. Raabe / James C. Young / Annette Nellen / David M. Maloney

Lindsay G. Acker, *University of Wisconsin-Madison*

Deborah S. Adkins, *Nperspective, LLC*

Mark P. Altieri, *Kent State University*

Amy An, *University of Iowa*

Susan E. Anderson, *Elon University*

Henry M. Anding, *Woodbury University*

Jennifer A. Bagwell, *Ohio University*

George Barbi, *Lanier Technical College*

Terry W. Bechtel, *Texas A&M University – Texarkana*

Chris Becker, *LeMoyne College*

John G. Bell

Tamara Berges, *UCLA*

Ellen Best, *University of North Georgia*

Tim Biggart, *Berry College*

Rachel Birkey, *Illinois State University*

Patrick M. Borja, *Citrus College / California State University, Los Angeles*

Dianne H. Boseman, *Nash Community College*

Cathalene Bowler, *University of Northern Iowa*

Madeline Brogan, *Lone Star College – Montgomery*

Darryl L. Brown, *Illinois Wesleyan University*

Timothy G. Bryan, *University of Southern Indiana*

Robert S. Burdette, *Salt Lake Community College*

Ryan L. Burger, *Concordia University Nebraska*

Lisa Busto, *William Rainey Harper College*

Julia M. Camp, *Providence College*

Al Case, *Southern Oregon University*

Machiavelli W. Chao, *Merage School of Business University of California, Irvine*

Eric Chen, *University of Saint Joseph*

Christine Cheng, *Louisiana State University*

James Milton Christianson, *Southwestern University and Austin Community College*

Wayne Clark, *Southwest Baptist University*

Ann Burstein Cohen, *University at Buffalo, The State University of New York*

Ciril Cohen, *Fairleigh Dickinson University*

Dixon H. Cooper, *University of Arkansas*

Rick L. Crosser, *Metropolitan State University of Denver*

John P. Crowley, *Castleton University*

Richard G. Cummings, *University of Wisconsin-Whitewater*

Susan E. M. Davis, *South University*

Dwight E. Denman, *Newman University*

James M. DeSimpelare, *Ross School of Business at the University of Michigan*

John Dexter, *Northwood University*

James Doering, *University of Wisconsin – Green Bay*

Michael P. Donohoe, *University of Illinois at Urbana Champaign*

Deborah A. Doonan, *Johnson & Wales University*

Monique O. Durant, *Central Connecticut State University*

Wayne L. Edmunds, *Virginia Commonwealth University*

Rafi Efrat, *California State University, Northridge*

Charles R. Enis, *The Pennsylvania State University*

Frank J. Faber, *St. Joseph's College*

A. Anthony Falgiani, *University of South Carolina, Beaufort*

Jason Fiske, *Thomas Jefferson School of Law*

John Forsythe, *Eagle Gate College*

Alexander L. Frazin, *University of Redlands*

Carl J. Gabrini, *College of Coastal Georgia*

Kenneth W. Gaines, *East-West University, Chicago, Illinois*

Carolyn Galantine, *Pepperdine University*

Sheri Geddes, *Hope College*

Alexander Gelardi, *University of St. Thomas*

Daniel J. Gibbons, *Waubonsee Community College*

Martie Gillen, *University of Florida*

Charles Gnizak, *Fort Hays State University*

J. David Golub, *Northeastern University*

George G. Goodrich, *John Carroll University*

Marina Grau, *Houston Community College – Houston, TX*

Vicki Greshik, *University of Jamestown College*

Jeffrey S. Haig, *Santa Monica College*

Marcye S. Hampton, *University of Central Florida*

June Hanson, *Upper Iowa University*

Donald Henschel, *Benedictine University*

Susanne Holloway, *Salisbury University*

Susan A. Honig, *Herbert H. Lehman College*

Jeffrey Hoopes, *University of North Carolina*

Christopher R. Hoyt, *University of Missouri (Kansas City) School of Law*

Marsha M. Huber, *Youngstown State University*

Carol Hughes, *Asheville-Buncombe Technical Community College*

Helen Hurwitz, *Saint Louis University*

Richard R. Hutaff, *Wingate University*

Zite Hutton, *Western Washington University*

Brad Van Kalsbeek, *University of Sioux Falls*

John E. Karayan, *Woodbury University*

Carl Keller, *Missouri State University*

Cynthia Khanlarian, *Concord University*

Bob Kilpatrick, *Northern Arizona University*

Gordon Klein, Lecturer, *UCLA Anderson School*

Taylor Klett, *Sam Houston State University*

Aaron P. Knape, *Peru State College*

Cedric Knott, *Colorado State University – Global Campus*

Ausher M. B. Kofsky, *Western New England University*

Emil Koren, *Saint Leo University*

Jack Lachman, *Brooklyn College – CUNY*

Richard S. Leaman, *University of Denver*

Adena LeJeune, *Louisiana College*

Gene Levitt, *Mayville State University*

Teresa Lightner, *University of North Texas*

Sara Linton, *Roosevelt University*

Roger Lirely, *The University of Texas at Tyler*

Jane Livingstone, *Western Carolina University*

Heather Lynch, *Northeast Iowa Community College*

Michael J. MacDonald, *University of Wisconsin-Whitewater*

Mabel Machin, *Florida Institute of Technology*

Maria Alaina Mackin, *ECPI University*

Anne M. Magro, *George Mason University*

Richard B. Malamud, *California State University, Dominguez Hills*

Harold J. Manasa, *Winthrop University*

Barry R. Marks, *University of Houston – Clear Lake*

Dewey Martin, *Husson University*

Anthony Masino, *East Tennessee State University*

Norman Massel, *Louisiana State University*

Bruce W. McClain, *Cleveland State University*

Allison M. McLeod, *University of North Texas*

Meredith A. Menden, *Southern New Hampshire University*

Robert H. Meyers, *University of Wisconsin-Whitewater*

John G. Miller, *Skyline College*

Tracie L. Miller-Nobles, *Austin Community College*
Jonathan G. Mitchell, *Stark State College*
Richard Mole, *Hiram College*
David Morack, *Lakeland University*
Lisa Nash, *CPA, MA, Vincennes University*
Mary E. Netzler, *Eastern Florida State College*
Joseph Malino Nicassio, *Westmoreland County Community College*
Mark R. Nixon, *Bentley University*
Garth Novack, *Pantheon Heavy Industries & Foundry*
Claude R. Oakley, *DeVry University, Georgia*
Al Oddo, *Niagara University*
Sandra Owen, *Indiana University – Bloomington*
Vivian J. Paige, *Old Dominion University*
Carolyn Payne, *University of La Verne*
Ronald Pearson, *Bay College*
Thomas Pearson, *University of Hawaii at Manoa*
Nichole L. Pendleton, *Friends University*
Chuck Pier, *Angelo State University*
Lincoln M. Pinto, *DeVry University*
Sonja Pippin, *University of Nevada – Reno*
Steve Platau, *The University of Tampa*
Walfyette Powell, *Strayer University*
Dennis Price, *Samford University*
Darlene Pulliam, *West Texas A&M University*
John S. Repsis, *University of Texas at Arlington*
John D. Rice, *Trinity University*

Jennifer Hardwick Robinson, *Trident Technical College*
Shani N. Robinson, *Sam Houston State University*
Donald Roth, *Dordt College*
Richard L. Russell, *Jackson State University*
Robert L. Salyer, *Northern Kentucky University*
Rhoda Sautner, *University of Mary*
Bunney L. Schmidt, *Keiser University*
Allen Schuldenfrei, *University of Baltimore*
Eric D. Schwartz, *LaRoche College*
Tony L. Scott, *Norwalk Community College*
Randy Serrett, *University of Houston – Downtown*
Wayne Shaw, *Southern Methodist University*
Paul A. Shoemaker, *University of Nebraska – Lincoln*
Kimberly Sipes, *Kentucky State University*
Georgi Smatrakalev, *Florida Atlantic University*
Randy Smit, *Dordt College*
Leslie S. Sobol, *California State University Northridge*
Marc Spiegel, *University of California, Irvine*
Teresa Stephenson, *University of Wyoming*
Beth Stetson, *Oklahoma City University*
Debra Stone, *Eastern New Mexico University*
Frances A. Stott, *Bowling Green State University*
Todd S. Stowe, *Southwest Florida College*
Julie Straus, *Culver-Stockton College*

Martin Stub, *DeVry University*
James Sundberg, *Eastern Michigan University*
Kent Swift, *University of Montana*
Robert L. Taylor, *Lees-McRae College*
Francis C. Thomas, *Richard Stockton College of New Jersey*
Randall R. Thomas, *Upper Iowa University*
Ronald R. Tidd, *Central Washington University*
MaryBeth Tobin, *Bridgewater State University*
James P. Trebby, *Marquette University*
James M. Turner, *Georgia Institute of Technology*
Anthony W. Varnon, *Southeast Missouri State University*
Adria Palacios Vasquez, *Texas A&M University – Kingsville*
Terri Walsh, *Seminole State College of Florida*
Marie Wang
Natasha R. Ware, *Southeastern University*
Mark Washburn, *Sam Houston State University*
Bill Weispfenning, *University of Jamestown (ND)*
Andrew L. Whitehair
Kent Williams, *Indiana Wesleyan University*
Candace Witherspoon, *Valdosta State University*
Sheila Woods, *DeVry University, Houston, TX*
Xinmei Xie, *Woodbury University*
Thomas Young, *Lone Star College – Tomball*

SPECIAL THANKS

We are grateful to the faculty members who have diligently worked through the problems and test questions to ensure the accuracy of the **South-Western Federal Taxation** homework, solutions manuals, test banks, and comprehensive tax form problems. Their comments and corrections helped us focus on clarity as well as accuracy and tax law currency. We also thank Thomson Reuters for its permission to use Checkpoint™ with the text.

Sandra A. Augustine, *Hilbert College*
Bradrick M. Cripe, *Northern Illinois University*
Stephanie Lewis, *The Ohio State University*
Kate Mantzke, *Northern Illinois University*

Ray Rodriguez, *Murray State University*
George R. Starbuck, *McMurry University*
Donald R. Trippeer, *State University of New York College at Oneonta*

Raymond Wacker, *Southern Illinois University, Carbondale*
Michael Weissenfluh, *Tillamook Bay Community College*

The South-Western Federal Taxation Series

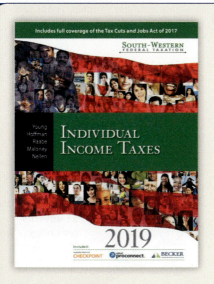

INDIVIDUAL INCOME TAXES, 2019 EDITION

(YOUNG, HOFFMAN, RAABE, MALONEY, NELLEN, Editors)
provides accessible, comprehensive, and authoritative coverage
of the relevant tax code and regulations as they pertain to
the individual taxpayer, as well as coverage of all major
developments in Federal taxation. This edition is fully updated
and revised to reflect changes included in the Tax Cuts and Jobs
Act of 2017.

(ISBN 978-1-337-70254-6)

CORPORATIONS, PARTNERSHIPS, ESTATES & TRUSTS, 2019 EDITION

(RAABE, HOFFMAN, YOUNG, NELLEN, MALONEY, Editors)
covers tax concepts as they affect corporations, partnerships, estates,
and trusts. The authors provide accessible, comprehensive, and
authoritative coverage of relevant tax code and regulations, as well
as all major developments in Federal income taxation. This edition is
fully updated and revised to reflect changes included in the Tax Cuts
and Jobs Act of 2017. This market-leading text is intended for students
who have had a previous course in tax.

(ISBN 978-1-337-70291-1)

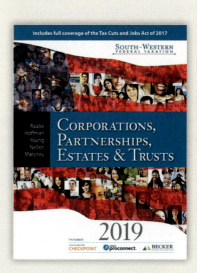

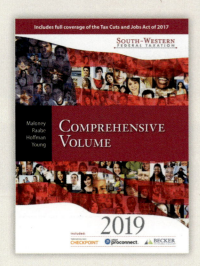

COMPREHENSIVE VOLUME, 2019 EDITION

(MALONEY, RAABE, HOFFMAN, YOUNG, Editors)
Combining the number one individual tax text with the number one corporations text, *Comprehensive Volume, 2019 Edition* is a true winner. An edited version of the first two **South-Western Federal Taxation** textbooks, this book is ideal for undergraduate or graduate levels. This text works for either a one-semester course in which an instructor wants to integrate coverage of individual and corporate taxation or for a two-semester sequence in which the use of only one book is desired.

(ISBN 978-1-337-70301-7)

ESSENTIALS OF TAXATION: INDIVIDUALS AND BUSINESS ENTITIES, 2019 EDITION

(RAABE, YOUNG, NELLEN, MALONEY, Editors)
emphasizes tax planning and the multidisciplinary aspects of taxation. Formerly titled *Taxation of Business Entities*, this text is designed with the AICPA Model Tax Curriculum in mind, presenting the introductory Federal taxation course from a business entity perspective. Its **Tax Planning Framework** helps users fit tax planning strategies into an innovative pedagogical framework. The text is an ideal fit for programs that offer only one course in taxation where users need to be exposed to individual taxation, as well as corporate and other business entity taxation. This text assumes no prior course in taxation has been taken.

(ISBN 978-1-337-70296-6)

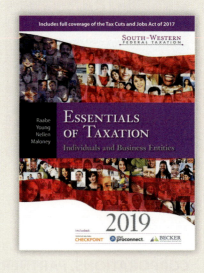

FEDERAL TAX RESEARCH, 11E

(SAWYERS AND GILL) *Federal Tax Research*, Eleventh Edition, offers hands-on tax research analysis and fully covers computer-oriented tax research tools. Also included in this edition is coverage on international tax research, a review of tax ethics, and many new real-life cases to help foster a true understanding of Federal tax law.

(ISBN 978-1-337-28298-7)

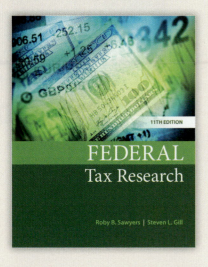

ABOUT THE EDITORS

William A. Raabe, Ph.D., CPA, was the Wisconsin Distinguished Professor of Taxation. He taught at Ohio State, Arizona State, the Capital University (OH) Law School, and the Universities of Wisconsin – Milwaukee and Whitewater. A graduate of Carroll University (Wisconsin) and the University of Illinois, Dr. Raabe's teaching and research interests include international and multistate taxation, technology in tax education, personal financial planning, and the economic impact of sports teams and fine arts groups. Dr. Raabe also writes the PricewaterhouseCoopers Tax Case Studies, an extensive, well-respected set of advanced tax learning resources. Dr. Raabe has been a visiting tax faculty member for a number of public accounting firms, bar associations, and CPA societies. He has received numerous teaching awards, including the Accounting Educator of the Year award from the Wisconsin Institute of CPAs. He has been the faculty adviser for student teams in the Deloitte Tax Case Competition (national finalists at three different schools) and the PricewaterhouseCoopers Extreme Tax policy competition (national finalist).

James C. Young is the Crowe Professor of Accountancy at Northern Illinois University. A graduate of Ferris State University (B.S.) and Michigan State University (M.B.A. and Ph.D.), Jim's research focuses on taxpayer responses to the income tax using archival data. His dissertation received the PricewaterhouseCoopers/American Taxation Association Dissertation Award, and his subsequent research has received funding from a number of organizations, including the Ernst & Young Foundation Tax Research Grant Program. His work has been published in a variety of academic and professional journals, including the *National Tax Journal, The Journal of the American Taxation Association*, and *Tax Notes*. Jim is a Northern Illinois University Distinguished Professor, received the Illinois CPA Society Outstanding Accounting Educator Award in 2012, and has received university teaching awards from Northern Illinois University, George Mason University, and Michigan State University.

Annette Nellen, CPA, CGMA, Esquire, directs San José State University's graduate tax program (MST) and teaches courses in tax research, tax fundamentals, accounting methods, property transactions, employment tax, ethics, leadership, and tax policy. Professor Nellen is a graduate of CSU Northridge, Pepperdine (MBA), and Loyola Law School. Prior to joining SJSU in 1990, she was with a Big 4 firm and the IRS. At SJSU, Professor Nellen is a recipient of the Outstanding Professor and Distinguished Service Awards. Professor Nellen is an active member of the tax sections of the AICPA and American Bar Association, including chairing the AICPA Tax Executive Committee from October 2016 to May 2019. In 2013, she received the AICPA Arthur J. Dixon Memorial Award, the highest award given by the accounting profession in the area of taxation. Professor Nellen is the author of *BloombergBNA Tax Portfolio, Amortization of Intangibles*, and the *BloombergBNA Internet Law Resource Center, Overview of Internet Taxation Issues*. She has published numerous articles in the *AICPA Tax Insider, Tax Adviser, State Tax Notes*, and *The Journal of Accountancy*. She has testified before the House Ways & Means and Senate Finance Committees and other committees on Federal and state tax reform. Professor Nellen maintains the 21st Century Taxation website and blog (www.21stcenturytaxation.com) as well as websites on tax policy and reform, virtual currency, and state tax issues (www.sjsu.edu/people/annette.nellen/).

David M. Maloney, Ph.D., CPA, is the Carman G. Blough Professor of Accounting Emeritus at the University of Virginia's McIntire School of Commerce. He completed his undergraduate work at the University of Richmond and his graduate work at the University of Illinois at Urbana-Champaign. Upon joining the Virginia faculty in January 1984, Dr. Maloney taught Federal taxation in the graduate and undergraduate programs and was a recipient of major research grants from the Ernst & Young and KPMG Foundations. Dr. Maloney has published work in numerous professional journals, including *Journal of Taxation, The Tax Adviser, Tax Notes, Corporate Taxation, Accounting Horizons, Journal of Taxation of Investments*, and *Journal of Accountancy*.

Brief Contents

PART 1: THE WORLD OF TAXATION

CHAPTER 1	INTRODUCTION TO TAXATION	1-1
CHAPTER 2	WORKING WITH THE TAX LAW	2-1
CHAPTER 3	TAXES ON THE FINANCIAL STATEMENTS	3-1

PART 2: STRUCTURE OF THE FEDERAL INCOME TAX

CHAPTER 4	GROSS INCOME	4-1
CHAPTER 5	BUSINESS DEDUCTIONS	5-1
CHAPTER 6	LOSSES AND LOSS LIMITATIONS	6-1

PART 3: PROPERTY TRANSACTIONS

| CHAPTER 7 | PROPERTY TRANSACTIONS: BASIS, GAIN AND LOSS, AND NONTAXABLE EXCHANGES | 7-1 |
| CHAPTER 8 | PROPERTY TRANSACTIONS: CAPITAL GAINS AND LOSSES, SECTION 1231, AND RECAPTURE PROVISIONS | 8-1 |

PART 4: TAXATION OF INDIVIDUALS

CHAPTER 9	INDIVIDUALS AS THE TAXPAYER	9-1
CHAPTER 10	INDIVIDUALS: INCOME, DEDUCTIONS, AND CREDITS	10-1
CHAPTER 11	INDIVIDUALS AS EMPLOYEES AND PROPRIETORS	11-1

PART 5: BUSINESS ENTITIES

CHAPTER 12   CORPORATIONS: ORGANIZATION, CAPITAL
STRUCTURE, AND OPERATING RULES   12-1

CHAPTER 13   CORPORATIONS: EARNINGS & PROFITS
AND DISTRIBUTIONS   13-1

CHAPTER 14   PARTNERSHIPS AND LIMITED LIABILITY ENTITIES   14-1

CHAPTER 15   S CORPORATIONS   15-1

PART 6: SPECIAL BUSINESS TOPICS

CHAPTER 16   MULTIJURISDICTIONAL TAXATION   16-1

CHAPTER 17   BUSINESS TAX CREDITS AND THE
ALTERNATIVE MINIMUM TAX   17-1

CHAPTER 18   COMPARATIVE FORMS OF DOING BUSINESS   18-1

Contents

Part 1: The World of Taxation

CHAPTER 1
INTRODUCTION TO TAXATION — 1-1
The Big Picture: *A Typical Tax Year for a Modern Family* — *1-1*

THE STRUCTURE OF TAX SYSTEMS — 1-4
Tax Rates — 1-4
Tax Fact: *Carrying the Tax Burden* — *1-5*
Tax Bases — 1-5
Incidence of Taxation — 1-6

TYPES OF TAXES — 1-6
Taxes on the Production and Sale of Goods — 1-6
Global Tax Issues: *Why Is Gasoline Expensive? It Depends on Where You Live* — *1-8*
Employment Taxes — 1-9
Taxes at Death — 1-10
Gift Tax — 1-11
Property Taxes — 1-12
Tax Fact: *A Profile of Tax Collections* — *1-13*
Taxes on Privileges and Rights — 1-14
Income Taxes — 1-15
Tax Fact: *What Is the U.S. Tax Burden?* — *1-17*
Concept Summary: *Overview of Taxes in the United States* — *1-18*
Bridge Discipline: *Bridge to Political Science and Sociology* — *1-18*
Financial Disclosure Insights: *What Do You Mean by "Income" Anyway?* — *1-19*

INCOME TAXATION OF BUSINESS ENTITIES — 1-19
Proprietorships — 1-19
C Corporations — 1-19
Partnerships — 1-20
S Corporations — 1-20
Limited Liability Companies and Limited Liability Partnerships — 1-20
Financial Disclosure Insights: *Book-Tax Differences* — *1-21*
Dealings between Individuals and Their Business Entities — 1-21

TAX PLANNING FUNDAMENTALS — 1-22
Overview of Tax Planning and Ethics — 1-22
A General Framework for Income Tax Planning — 1-23
Tax Minimization Strategies Related to Income — 1-23
Tax Minimization Strategies Related to Deductions — 1-24
Tax Minimization Strategies Related to Tax Rates — 1-25

Tax Fact: *The U.S. Federal Income Tax* — *1-27*
Tax Minimization Strategies Related to Credits — 1-28

UNDERSTANDING THE FEDERAL TAX LAW — 1-28
Revenue Needs — 1-28
Economic Considerations — 1-28
Global Tax Issues: *Outsourcing of Tax Return Preparation* — *1-29*
Social Considerations — 1-30
Equity Considerations — 1-30
Political Considerations — 1-31
Influence of the Internal Revenue Service — 1-32
Influence of the Courts — 1-32

SUMMARY — 1-33
Refocus on the Big Picture: *A Typical Tax Year for a Modern Family* — *1-34*

CHAPTER 2
WORKING WITH THE TAX LAW — 2-1
The Big Picture: *Researching Tax Questions* — *2-1*

TAX LAW SOURCES — 2-2
Statutory Sources of the Tax Law — 2-2
Tax Fact: *Scope of the U.S. Tax System* — *2-3*
Administrative Sources of the Tax Law — 2-6
Judicial Sources of the Tax Law — 2-10
Concept Summary: *Federal Judicial System: Trial Courts* — *2-11*
Bridge Discipline: *Bridge to Public Policy* — *2-16*

WORKING WITH THE TAX LAW—TAX RESEARCH — 2-17
Identifying the Problem — 2-18
Refining the Problem — 2-18
Locating the Appropriate Tax Law Sources — 2-18
Bridge Discipline: *Bridge to Business Law* — *2-19*
Assessing Tax Law Sources — 2-20
Arriving at the Solution or at Alternative Solutions — 2-23
Communicating Tax Research — 2-23
Updates — 2-25
Tax Research Best Practices — 2-25
Financial Disclosure Insights: *Where Does GAAP Come From?* — *2-27*

TAX RESEARCH ON THE CPA EXAMINATION — 2-27
Bridge Discipline: *Bridge to Regulation and Oversight* — *2-28*
Refocus on the Big Picture: *Researching Tax Questions* — *2-29*

CHAPTER 3
TAXES ON THE FINANCIAL STATEMENTS   **3-1**
The Big Picture: *Taxes on the Financial Statements*   *3-1*

BOOK-TAX DIFFERENCES   **3-2**
Different Reporting Entities   3-2
Different Taxes   3-4
Different Methods   3-4
Financial Disclosure Insights: *Supersized Goodwill*   *3-6*
Tax Return Disclosures   3-6
Concept Summary: *Income Reporting: Book versus Tax*   *3-7*

INCOME TAXES IN THE FINANCIAL STATEMENTS   **3-8**
GAAP Principles   3-8
Financial Disclosure Insights: *The Book-Tax Income Gap*   *3-9*
Global Tax Issues: *Accounting for Income Taxes in International Standards*   *3-10*
Valuation Allowance   3-12
Tax Planning Strategies: *Releasing Valuation Allowances*   *3-14*
Tax Disclosures in the Financial Statements   3-15
Financial Disclosure Insights: *Tax Losses and the Deferred Tax Asset*   *3-15*
Tax Fact: *Effective Tax Rates for Fortune 100 Companies*   *3-15*
Concept Summary: *Steps in Determining the Book Tax Expense*   *3-16*
Special Issues   3-18
Tax Planning Strategies: *Tax Savings Are Not Always Created Equal*   *3-19*
Concept Summary: *Disclosures Under ASC 740-10*   *3-19*
Summary   3-23

BENCHMARKING   **3-24**
Refining the Analysis   3-24
Bridge Discipline: *Bridge to Financial Analysis*   *3-24*
Sustaining the Tax Rate   3-25
Uses of Benchmarking Analysis   3-26
Concept Summary: *Benchmarking Analysis*   *3-26*
Refocus on the Big Picture: *Taxes on the Financial Statements*   *3-26*

Part 2: Structure of the Federal Income Tax

CHAPTER 4
GROSS INCOME   **4-1**
The Big Picture: *Just What Is Included in Gross Income?*   *4-1*

THE TAX FORMULA   **4-2**
Components of the Tax Formula   4-2

GROSS INCOME—WHAT IS IT?   **4-3**
Concepts of Income   4-3
Financial Disclosure Insights: *What Does "Income" Mean to You?*   *4-4*
Comparing Accounting and Tax Concepts of Income   4-5
Form of Receipt   4-5
Concept Summary: *Gross Income Concepts*   *4-6*

YEAR OF INCLUSION   **4-6**
Taxable Year   4-6
Accounting Methods   4-6
Tax Planning Strategies: *Cash Receipts Method*   *4-8*
Bridge Discipline: *Bridge to Economics and Finance*   *4-9*
Special Rules for Cash Basis Taxpayers   4-10
Special Rules for Accrual Basis Taxpayers   4-11
Tax Planning Strategies: *Prepaid Income*   *4-12*
Concept Summary: *Income Tax Accounting*   *4-13*

INCOME SOURCES   **4-13**
Personal Services   4-13
Income from Property   4-13
Tax Fact: *How Much and What Type of Income?*   *4-14*
Global Tax Issues: *Which Foreign Dividends Get the Discounted Rate?*   *4-15*
Tax Fact: *Business Income and Loss*   *4-16*
Income Received by an Agent   4-16
Tax Planning Strategies: *Techniques for Reducing Investment Income*   *4-17*

SPECIFIC ITEMS OF GROSS INCOME   **4-17**
Gains and Losses from Property Transactions   4-18
Interest on Certain State and Local Government Obligations   4-20
Bridge Discipline: *Bridge to Public Economics*   *4-20*
Life Insurance Proceeds   4-21
Tax Planning Strategies: *Life Insurance*   *4-22*
Income from Discharge of Indebtedness   4-23
Tax Benefit Rule   4-25
Imputed Interest on Below-Market Loans   4-26
Financial Disclosure Insights: *Loans to Executives Prohibited*   *4-27*
Improvements on Leased Property   4-28
Concept Summary: *Income Recognition Rules*   *4-29*
Refocus on the Big Picture: *Just What Is Included in Gross Income?*   *4-29*

CHAPTER 5
BUSINESS DEDUCTIONS   **5-1**
The Big Picture: *Calculating Deductible Expenses*   *5-1*

OVERVIEW OF BUSINESS DEDUCTIONS   **5-2**
Ordinary and Necessary Requirement   5-2
Reasonableness Requirement   5-3
Common Business Deductions   5-3
Tax Planning Strategies: *Unreasonable Compensation*   *5-4*

THE TIMING OF EXPENSE RECOGNITION   **5-4**
Cash Method Requirements   5-4
Tax Planning Strategies: *Time Value of Tax Deductions*   *5-5*
Accrual Method Requirements   5-5
Expenses Accrued to Related Parties   5-6
Prepaid Expenses—The "12-Month Rule"   5-7

DISALLOWANCE POSSIBILITIES **5-8**
Public Policy Limitations 5-8
Global Tax Issues: *Overseas Gun Sales Result in Large Fines* *5-8*
Political Contributions and Lobbying Activities 5-9
Excessive Executive Compensation 5-10
Investigation of a Business 5-11
Transactions between Related Parties 5-12
Expenses and Interest Related to Tax-Exempt Income 5-13
Business Interest 5-14
Expenses Related to Entertainment, Recreation, or Amusement 5-14
Other Disallowance Possibilities 5-15

RESEARCH AND EXPERIMENTAL EXPENDITURES **5-15**
Expense Method 5-16
Deferral and Amortization Method 5-16

OTHER BUSINESS EXPENSES **5-17**
Interest Expense 5-17
Taxes 5-17

CHARITABLE CONTRIBUTIONS **5-18**
Property Contributions 5-19
Limitations Imposed on Charitable Contribution Deductions 5-21

COST RECOVERY ALLOWANCES **5-21**
Overview 5-21
Cost Recovery: In General 5-22
Bridge Discipline: *Bridge to Finance* *5-22*
Modified Accelerated Cost Recovery System (MACRS) 5-24
Concept Summary: *MACRS: Class Lives, Methods, and Conventions* *5-24*
MACRS for Personal Property 5-24
MACRS for Real Estate 5-28
Election to Expense Certain Depreciable Assets (§ 179) 5-29
Financial Disclosure Insights: *Tax and Book Depreciation* *5-32*
Additional First-Year Depreciation (Bonus Depreciation) 5-32
Using § 179 and Bonus Depreciation Effectively 5-33
Bridge Discipline: *Bridge to Economics and the Business Cycle* *5-35*
Concept Summary: *Using § 179 and Bonus Depreciation* *5-35*
Business and Personal Use of Automobiles and Other Listed Property 5-35
Concept Summary: *Listed Property Cost Recovery* *5-39*
Bridge Discipline: *Bridge to Finance and Economics* *5-40*
Alternative Depreciation System (ADS) 5-40
Tax Planning Strategies: *Structuring the Sale of a Business* *5-41*

AMORTIZATION **5-41**

DEPLETION **5-41**
Intangible Drilling and Development Costs (IDCs) 5-42
Depletion Methods 5-42
Tax Planning Strategies: *Switching Depletion Methods* *5-44*

COST RECOVERY TABLES **5-44**
Refocus on the Big Picture: *Calculating Deductible Expenses* *5-48*

CHAPTER 6
LOSSES AND LOSS LIMITATIONS **6-1**
The Big Picture: *Receiving Tax Benefits from Losses* *6-1*

BAD DEBTS **6-2**
Tax Fact: *Just How Good Is Your Credit?* *6-3*
Specific Charge-Off Method 6-3
Concept Summary: *The Tax Treatment of Bad Debts Using the Specific Charge-Off Method* *6-4*
Business versus Nonbusiness Bad Debts 6-4
Loans between Related Parties 6-5

WORTHLESS SECURITIES AND SMALL BUSINESS STOCK LOSSES **6-5**
Worthless Securities 6-5
Small Business Stock (§ 1244 Stock) Losses 6-5
Tax Planning Strategies: *Maximizing the Benefits of Small Business (§ 1244 Stock) Losses* *6-6*

CASUALTY AND THEFT LOSSES **6-7**
Definition of Casualty 6-7
Deduction of Casualty Losses 6-7
Tax Planning Strategies: *Documentation of Related-Taxpayer Loans, Casualty Losses, and Theft Losses* *6-8*
Definition of Theft 6-9
Loss Measurement 6-9
Casualty and Theft Losses of Individuals 6-10
Concept Summary: *Casualty Gains and Losses* *6-12*

NET OPERATING LOSSES **6-13**
Introduction 6-13
General Rules 6-14

THE TAX SHELTER PROBLEM **6-14**
Bridge Discipline: *Bridge to Finance* *6-15*

AT-RISK LIMITATIONS **6-16**
Concept Summary: *Calculation of At-Risk Amount* *6-17*

PASSIVE ACTIVITY LOSS LIMITS **6-17**
Classification and Impact of Passive Activity Income and Loss 6-17
Taxpayers Subject to the Passive Activity Loss Rules 6-21
Rules for Determining Passive Activities 6-22
Material Participation 6-22
Concept Summary: *Tests to Determine Material Participation* *6-23*
Rental Activities 6-24
Concept Summary: *Passive Activity Loss Rules: Key Issues and Answers* *6-25*
Interaction of At-Risk and Passive Activity Loss Limits 6-26
Concept Summary: *Treatment of Losses Subject to the At-Risk and Passive Activity Loss Limitations* *6-27*
Special Rules for Real Estate 6-27
Disposition of Passive Activities 6-29
Tax Planning Strategies: *Utilizing Passive Activity Losses* *6-30*

EXCESS BUSINESS LOSSES — **6-32**

Definition and Rules — 6-32

Computing the Limit — 6-32

Refocus on the Big Picture: *Receiving Tax Benefits from Losses* — *6-33*

Part 3: Property Transactions

CHAPTER 7
PROPERTY TRANSACTIONS: BASIS, GAIN AND LOSS, AND NONTAXABLE EXCHANGES — **7-1**

The Big Picture: *Calculating Basis and Recognized Gain for Property Transactions* — *7-1*

DETERMINATION OF GAIN OR LOSS — **7-2**

Realized Gain or Loss — 7-2

Concept Summary: *Realized Gain or Loss* — *7-3*

Bridge Discipline: *Bridge to Financial Accounting* — *7-7*

Recognized Gain or Loss — 7-7

Concept Summary: *Realized and Recognized Gain or Loss* — *7-8*

Nonrecognition of Gain or Loss — 7-8

BASIS CONSIDERATIONS — **7-9**

Determination of Cost Basis — 7-9

Gift Basis — 7-11

Tax Planning Strategies: *Gift Planning* — *7-12*

Inherited Property — 7-13

Tax Planning Strategies: *Inherited Property* — *7-14*

Disallowed Losses — 7-14

Concept Summary: *Wash Sale Rules* — *7-16*

Tax Planning Strategies: *Avoiding Wash Sales* — *7-16*

Conversion of Property from Personal Use to Business or Income-Producing Use — 7-16

Summary of Basis Adjustments — 7-17

Concept Summary: *Adjustments to Basis* — *7-18*

GENERAL CONCEPT OF A NONTAXABLE EXCHANGE — **7-19**

LIKE-KIND EXCHANGES—§ 1031 — **7-20**

Like-Kind Property — 7-20

Tax Planning Strategies: *Like-Kind Exchanges* — *7-21*

Exchange Requirement — 7-21

Boot — 7-22

Basis and Holding Period of Property Received — 7-23

Bridge Discipline: *Bridge to Economics* — *7-24*

INVOLUNTARY CONVERSIONS—§ 1033 — **7-25**

Involuntary Conversion Defined — 7-27

Replacement Property — 7-27

Concept Summary: *Involuntary Conversions: Replacement Property Tests* — *7-28*

Time Limitation on Replacement — 7-28

Nonrecognition of Gain — 7-29

Tax Planning Strategies: *Recognizing Involuntary Conversion Gains* — *7-30*

OTHER NONRECOGNITION PROVISIONS — **7-31**

Transfer of Assets to Business Entity—§§ 351 and 721 — 7-31

Sale of a Principal Residence—§ 121 — 7-31

Refocus on the Big Picture: *Calculating Basis and Recognized Gain for Property Transactions* — *7-31*

CHAPTER 8
PROPERTY TRANSACTIONS: CAPITAL GAINS AND LOSSES, SECTION 1231, AND RECAPTURE PROVISIONS — **8-1**

The Big Picture: *Capital Gains and Losses, § 1231 Gains and Losses, and Recapture* — *8-1*

GENERAL SCHEME OF TAXATION — **8-2**

Concept Summary: *Recognized Gain or Loss Characteristics* — *8-2*

CAPITAL ASSETS — **8-3**

Definition of a Capital Asset — 8-3

Statutory Expansions — 8-5

SALE OR EXCHANGE — **8-6**

Worthless Securities and § 1244 Stock — 8-7

Retirement of Corporate Obligations — 8-7

Options — 8-7

Concept Summary: *Options: Consequences to the Grantor and Grantee* — *8-9*

Patents — 8-9

Franchises, Trademarks, and Trade Names — 8-10

Lease Cancellation Payments — 8-11

Concept Summary: *Franchises: Consequences to the Franchisor and Franchisee* — *8-12*

HOLDING PERIOD — **8-13**

General Rules — 8-13

Special Holding Period Rules — 8-13

Short Sales — 8-14

Tax Planning Strategies: *Timing Capital Gains* — *8-15*

TAX TREATMENT OF CAPITAL GAINS AND LOSSES OF NONCORPORATE TAXPAYERS — **8-16**

Capital Gains — 8-16

Tax Planning Strategies: *Gifts of Appreciated Securities* — *8-17*

Global Tax Issues: *Capital Gain Treatment in the United States and Other Countries* — *8-17*

Concept Summary: *Capital Gains of Noncorporate Taxpayers* — *8-18*

Capital Losses — 8-18

Capital Gain and Loss Netting Process — 8-19

Tax Planning Strategies: *Matching Gains with Losses* — *8-21*

Small Business Stock — 8-21

TAX TREATMENT OF CAPITAL GAINS AND LOSSES OF CORPORATE TAXPAYERS — **8-23**

SECTION 1231 ASSETS — **8-23**

Relationship to Capital Assets — 8-23

Tax Fact: *Capital Gains for the Wealthy?* — *8-24*

Property Included   8-25

Property Excluded   8-25

Casualty or Theft and Nonpersonal Use Capital Assets   8-25

General Procedure for § 1231 Computation   8-26

Concept Summary: *Section 1231 Netting Procedure*   *8-26*

SECTION 1245 RECAPTURE   **8-29**

Section 1245 Property   8-30

Bridge Discipline: *Bridge to Financial Accounting*   *8-31*

Observations on § 1245   8-31

SECTION 1250 RECAPTURE   **8-31**

Concept Summary: *Comparison of § 1245 and § 1250 Depreciation Recapture*   *8-32*

Unrecaptured § 1250 Gain (Real Estate 25% Gain)   8-33

Additional Recapture for Corporations   8-33

Tax Planning Strategies: *Selling Depreciable Real Estate*   *8-34*

EXCEPTIONS TO §§ 1245 AND 1250   **8-34**

Gifts   8-34

Death   8-35

Charitable Transfers   8-35

Certain Nontaxable Transactions   8-35

Like-Kind Exchanges and Involuntary Conversions   8-36

REPORTING PROCEDURES   **8-36**

Tax Planning Strategies: *Timing of Recapture*   *8-36*

Refocus on the Big Picture: *Capital Gains and Losses, § 1231 Gains and Losses, and Recapture*   *8-37*

Part 4: Taxation of Individuals

CHAPTER 9
INDIVIDUALS AS THE TAXPAYER   9-1

The Big Picture: *A Divided Household*   *9-1*

THE INDIVIDUAL TAX FORMULA   **9-2**

Concept Summary: *Individual Income Tax Formula*   *9-2*

Components of the Tax Formula   9-2

STANDARD DEDUCTION   **9-6**

Basic and Additional Standard Deduction   9-7

Special Limitations on the Standard Deduction for Dependents   9-8

DEPENDENCY STATUS   **9-9**

Qualifying Child   9-9

Concept Summary: *Tiebreaker Rules for Determining Dependency Status*   *9-10*

Qualifying Relative   9-11

Tax Planning Strategies: *Multiple Support Agreements and the Medical Expense Deduction*   *9-14*

Other Rules for Determining Dependency Status   9-14

Tax Planning Strategies: *Problems with a Joint Return*   *9-15*

Comparison of Categories for Dependency Status   9-15

Concept Summary: *Tests for Dependency Status*   *9-16*

FILING STATUS AND FILING REQUIREMENTS   **9-16**

Filing Status   9-16

Bridge Discipline: *Bridge to Equity or Fairness*   *9-18*

Global Tax Issues: *Filing a Joint Return*   *9-19*

Filing Requirements   9-20

TAX DETERMINATION   **9-21**

Tax Table Method   9-21

Tax Rate Schedule Method   9-21

Computation of Net Taxes Payable or Refund Due   9-22

Tax Planning Strategies: *Shifting Income and Deductions across Time*   *9-22*

Kiddie Tax—Unearned Income of Dependent Children   9-23

Tax Planning Strategies: *Income of Certain Children*   *9-24*

ADDITIONAL TAXES FOR CERTAIN INDIVIDUALS   **9-24**

Alternative Minimum Tax   9-25

Net Investment Income Tax and Additional Medicare Tax   9-27

TAX RETURN FILING PROCEDURES   **9-28**

Selecting the Proper Form   9-28

The E-File Approach   9-28

Tax Fact: *What Form of Tax Compliance Is Right for You?*   *9-28*

When and Where to File   9-29

Modes of Payment   9-29

Refocus on the Big Picture: *A Divided Household*   *9-29*

CHAPTER 10
INDIVIDUALS: INCOME, DEDUCTIONS, AND CREDITS   10-1

The Big Picture: *The Tax Implications of Life!*   *10-1*

OVERVIEW OF INCOME PROVISIONS APPLICABLE TO INDIVIDUALS   **10-2**

Bridge Discipline: *Bridge to Economics and Finance*   *10-3*

SPECIFIC INCLUSIONS APPLICABLE TO INDIVIDUALS   **10-3**

Alimony and Separate Maintenance Payments   10-3

Prizes and Awards   10-5

Unemployment Compensation   10-5

Social Security Benefits   10-6

SPECIFIC EXCLUSIONS APPLICABLE TO INDIVIDUALS   **10-6**

Gifts and Inheritances   10-6

Scholarships   10-7

Damages   10-8

Concept Summary: *Taxation of Damages*   *10-9*

Workers' Compensation   10-10

Accident and Health Insurance Benefits   10-10

Educational Savings Bonds   10-10

ITEMIZED DEDUCTIONS   **10-11**

Medical Expenses   10-11

Taxes   10-15

Tax Planning Strategies: *Timing the Payment of Deductible Taxes*   *10-17*

Interest   10-17

Concept Summary: *Deductibility of Personal, Student Loan, Investment, and Mortgage Interest*   *10-21*

Charitable Contributions   10-21

Global Tax Issues: *Choose the Charity Wisely*   *10-23*

Concept Summary: *Determining the Deduction for Contributions of Appreciated Property by Individuals*   *10-24*

Other Itemized Deductions   10-25

Tax Planning Strategies: *Effective Utilization of Itemized Deductions*   *10-27*

INDIVIDUAL TAX CREDITS   **10-27**

Adoption Expenses Credit   10-27

Child and Dependent Tax Credits   10-28

Credit for Child and Dependent Care Expenses   10-28

Education Tax Credits   10-30

Earned Income Credit   10-31

AFFORDABLE CARE ACT PROVISIONS   **10-32**

Individual Shared Responsibility Payment   10-32

Bridge Discipline: *Bridge to the Consequences of the ISRP Penalty Reduction*   *10-33*

Premium Tax Credit   10-33

Refocus on the Big Picture: *The Tax Implications of Life!*   *10-34*

CHAPTER 11
INDIVIDUALS AS EMPLOYEES AND PROPRIETORS   **11-1**

The Big Picture: *Self-Employed versus Employee—What's the Difference?*   *11-1*

EMPLOYEE VERSUS INDEPENDENT CONTRACTOR   **11-2**

Factors Considered in Classification   11-2

Bridge Discipline: *Bridge to Equity or Fairness and Business Law*   *11-3*

Tax Planning Strategies: *Self-Employed Individuals*   *11-4*

EXCLUSIONS AVAILABLE TO EMPLOYEES   **11-4**

Employer-Sponsored Accident and Health Plans   11-5

Medical Reimbursement Plans   11-5

Bridge Discipline: *Bridge to Economic and Societal Needs*   *11-6*

Long-Term Care Insurance Benefits   11-6

Meals and Lodging Furnished for the Convenience of the Employer   11-7

Group Term Life Insurance   11-9

Qualified Tuition Reduction Plans   11-9

Other Employee Fringe Benefits   11-10

Cafeteria Plans   11-11

Flexible Spending Plans   11-11

Concept Summary: *Employee Fringe Benefits*   *11-12*

General Classes of Excluded Benefits   11-12

Concept Summary: *General Classes of Fringe Benefits*   *11-16*

Foreign Earned Income   11-17

EXPENSES RELATING TO TIME AT WORK   **11-18**

Transportation Expenses   11-18

Travel Expenses   11-19

Moving Expenses   11-22

Tax Planning Strategies: *Transportation and Travel Expenses*   *11-22*

Education Expenses   11-22

Tax Planning Strategies: *Education Expenses*   *11-23*

Deduction for Qualified Tuition and Related Expenses   11-24

Entertainment Expenses   11-25

Tax Planning Strategies: *Meal Expenses*   *11-26*

Other Expenses of Work   11-27

Classification of Employee Expenses   11-29

Contributions to Individual Retirement Accounts   11-30

Concept Summary: *Traditional IRAs and Roth IRAs Compared*   *11-33*

INDIVIDUALS AS PROPRIETORS   **11-33**

Accounting Periods and Methods   11-33

Income and Deductions of a Proprietorship   11-34

Retirement Plans for Self-Employed Individuals   11-35

Tax Planning Strategies: *Important Dates Related to IRAs and Keogh Plans*   *11-36*

Tax Planning Strategies: *Factors Affecting Retirement Plan Choices*   *11-37*

Deduction for Qualified Business Income   11-37

Concept Summary: *An Overview of the Qualified Business Income Deduction*   *11-43*

Estimated Tax Payments   11-44

HOBBY LOSSES   **11-45**

General Rules   11-45

Presumptive Rule of Profit-Seeking   11-46

The Deductible Amount   11-47

Refocus on the Big Picture: *Self-Employed versus Employee—What's the Difference?*   *11-48*

Part 5: Business Entities

CHAPTER 12
CORPORATIONS: ORGANIZATION, CAPITAL STRUCTURE, AND OPERATING RULES   **12-1**

The Big Picture: *Growing into the Corporate Form*   *12-1*

AN INTRODUCTION TO CORPORATE TAX   **12-2**

Double Taxation of Corporate Income   12-2

Global Tax Issues: *U.S. Corporate Taxes and International Business Competitiveness*   *12-3*

Comparison of Corporations and Other Forms of Doing Business   12-3

Tax Fact: *Corporations' Reporting Responsibilities*   *12-4*

Bridge Discipline: *Bridge to Finance*   *12-5*

Nontax Considerations   12-6

Concept Summary: *Tax Treatment of Business Forms Compared*   *12-6*

Limited Liability Companies   12-7

Entity Classification   12-7

ORGANIZATION OF AND TRANSFERS TO CONTROLLED CORPORATIONS   **12-8**

Section 351 Rationale and General Rules   12-8

Concept Summary: *Shareholder Consequences: Taxable Corporate Formation versus Tax-Deferred § 351 Transaction*   *12-9*

Transfer of Property   12-10

Stock   12-11

Control of the Corporation   12-12

Tax Planning Strategies: *Utilizing § 351*   *12-13*

Assumption of Liabilities—§ 357   12-15

Global Tax Issues: *Does § 351 Cover the Incorporation of a Foreign Business?*   *12-15*

Concept Summary: *Tax Consequences of Liability Assumption*   *12-18*

Tax Planning Strategies: *Avoiding § 351*   *12-19*

Basis Determination and Other Issues   12-20

Concept Summary: *Tax Consequences to the Shareholders and Corporation: With and Without the Application of § 351 (Based on the Facts of Example 27)*   *12-21*

Recapture Considerations   12-24

Tax Planning Strategies: *Other Considerations When Incorporating a Business*   *12-24*

CAPITAL STRUCTURE OF A CORPORATION   **12-25**

Capital Contributions   12-25

Debt in the Capital Structure   12-26

CORPORATE OPERATIONS   **12-28**

Deductions Available Only to Corporations   12-28

Business Interest Expense Limitation   12-31

Tax Planning Strategies: *Organizational Expenditures*   *12-32*

Determining the Corporate Income Tax Liability   12-34

Controlled Groups   12-34

PROCEDURAL MATTERS   **12-35**

Filing Requirements for Corporations   12-35

Estimated Tax Payments   12-36

Schedule M–1—Reconciliation of Income (Loss) per Books with Income per Return   12-36

Concept Summary: *Conceptual Diagram of Schedule M–1 (Form 1120)*   *12-37*

Schedule M–2—Analysis of Unappropriated Retained Earnings per Books   12-38

Schedule M–3—Net Income (Loss) Reconciliation for Corporations with Total Assets of $10 Million or More   12-38

Bridge Discipline: *Bridge to Financial Accounting*   *12-39*

Effect of Taxes on Financial Statements   12-39

Refocus on the Big Picture: *Growing into the Corporate Form*   *12-40*

CHAPTER 13
CORPORATIONS: EARNINGS & PROFITS AND DISTRIBUTIONS   **13-1**

The Big Picture: *Taxing Corporate Distributions*   *13-1*

CORPORATE DISTRIBUTIONS—OVERVIEW   **13-2**

EARNINGS AND PROFITS (E & P)   **13-2**

Tax Fact: *Who Pays Dividends?*   *13-3*

Computation of E & P   13-3

Summary of E & P Adjustments   13-7

Allocating E & P to Distributions   13-7

Concept Summary: *Computing E & P*   *13-8*

Bridge Discipline: *Bridge to Finance*   *13-11*

Tax Planning Strategies: *Corporate Distributions*   *13-11*

Concept Summary: *Allocating E & P to Distributions*   *13-13*

NONCASH DIVIDENDS   **13-13**

Bridge Discipline: *Bridge to Investments*   *13-13*

Noncash Dividends—Effect on the Shareholder   13-14

Noncash Dividends—Effect on the Corporation   13-14

Bridge Discipline: *Bridge to Finance*   *13-16*

CONSTRUCTIVE DIVIDENDS   **13-16**

Types of Constructive Dividends   13-17

Global Tax Issues: *A Worldwide View of Dividends*   *13-18*

Tax Treatment of Constructive Dividends   13-18

Tax Planning Strategies: *Constructive Dividends*   *13-19*

STOCK DIVIDENDS   **13-21**

STOCK REDEMPTIONS   **13-22**

Bridge Discipline: *Bridge to Finance*   *13-22*

Global Tax Issues: *Non-U.S. Shareholders Prefer Capital Gain Treatment in Stock Redemptions*   *13-23*

Tax Planning Strategies: *Stock Redemptions*   *13-24*

CORPORATE LIQUIDATIONS   **13-24**

The Liquidation Process   13-24

Liquidating and Nonliquidating Distributions Compared   13-24

Tax Planning Strategies: *Corporate Liquidations*   *13-25*

RESTRICTIONS ON CORPORATE ACCUMULATIONS   **13-25**

Refocus on the Big Picture: *Taxing Corporate Distributions*   *13-26*

CHAPTER 14
PARTNERSHIPS AND LIMITED LIABILITY ENTITIES   **14-1**

The Big Picture: *The Tax Consequences of Partnership Formation and Operations*   *14-1*

OVERVIEW OF PARTNERSHIP TAXATION   **14-2**

Forms of Doing Business—Federal Tax Consequences   14-2

TAX FACT: *Partnership Power*   *14-3*

Definition of a Partnership   14-3

Bridge Discipline: *Bridge to Finance*   *14-4*

Partnership Taxation and Reporting   14-4

Partner's Ownership Interest in a Partnership   14-6

Bridge Discipline: *Bridge to Business Law*   *14-7*

FORMATION OF A PARTNERSHIP: TAX EFFECTS   **14-8**

Gain or Loss on Contributions to the Partnership   14-8

Concept Summary: *Partnership/LLC Taxation: Tax Reporting*   *14-9*

Exceptions to Nonrecognition   14-9

Tax Issues Related to Contributed Property   14-11

Inside and Outside Bases   14-12

Tax Accounting Elections   14-12

Concept Summary: *Partnership Formation and Basis Computation*   14-13

Initial Costs of a Partnership   14-13

OPERATIONS OF THE PARTNERSHIP   14-15

Schedules K and K–1   14-15

Partnership Allocations   14-18

Concept Summary: *Tax Reporting of Partnership Activities*   14-18

Basis of a Partnership Interest   14-20

Bridge Discipline: *Bridge to Financial Accounting*   14-21

Tax Fact: *What Do Partnerships Do?*   14-22

Partner's Basis, Gain, and Loss   14-23

Loss Limitations   14-25

Tax Planning Strategies: *Make Your Own Tax Shelter*   14-26

Concept Summary: *Partner's Basis in Partnership Interest*   14-28

TRANSACTIONS BETWEEN PARTNER AND PARTNERSHIP   14-28

Guaranteed Payments   14-29

Other Transactions between a Partner and a Partnership   14-30

Partners as Employees   14-30

Tax Planning Strategies: *Transactions between Partners and Partnerships*   14-31

Concept Summary: *Partner-Partnership Transactions*   14-31

LIMITED LIABILITY COMPANIES   14-32

Taxation of LLCs   14-32

Advantages of an LLC   14-32

Disadvantages of an LLC   14-33

Concept Summary: *Advantages and Disadvantages of the Partnership Form*   14-33

SUMMARY   14-34

Refocus on the Big Picture: *The Tax Consequences of Partnership Formation and Operations*   14-34

CHAPTER 15
S CORPORATIONS   15-1

The Big Picture: *Converting a C Corporation to an S Corporation*   15-1

AN OVERVIEW OF S CORPORATIONS   15-2

QUALIFYING FOR S CORPORATION STATUS   15-3

Definition of a Small Business Corporation   15-3

Bridge Discipline: *Bridge to Business Law*   15-3

Tax Planning Strategies: *When to Elect S Corporation Status*   15-4

Tax Fact: *The Business of S Corporations*   15-5

Tax Planning Strategies: *Beating the 100-Shareholder Limit*   15-6

Making the Election   15-6

Shareholder Consent   15-7

Tax Planning Strategies: *Making a Proper Election*   15-7

Loss of the Election   15-7

Tax Planning Strategies: *Preserving the S Election*   15-9

OPERATIONAL RULES   15-10

Computation of Taxable Income   15-10

Qualified Business Income Deduction   15-12

Allocation of Income and Loss   15-13

Tax Fact: *A "Small" Business Corporation*   15-14

Tax Treatment of Distributions to Shareholders   15-14

Tax Planning Strategies: *Salary Structure*   15-15

Concept Summary: *Distributions from an S Corporation*   15-16

Tax Planning Strategies: *The Accumulated Adjustments Account*   15-19

Tax Treatment of Noncash Distributions by the Corporation   15-19

Concept Summary: *Consequences of Noncash Distributions*   15-20

Shareholder's Basis in S Stock   15-21

Tax Planning Strategies: *Working with Suspended Losses*   15-23

Treatment of Losses   15-23

Concept Summary: *Treatment of S Corporation Losses*   15-24

Tax Planning Strategies: *Loss Considerations*   15-24

Limitation on the Deduction of Excess Business Losses   15-25

Other Operational Rules   15-26

Bridge Discipline: *Bridge to Public Finance*   15-26

ENTITY-LEVEL TAXES   15-27

Tax on Pre-Election Built-In Gain   15-27

Tax Planning Strategies: *Managing the Built-In Gains Tax*   15-28

Tax Fact: *No Double Taxation?*   15-29

Passive Investment Income Penalty Tax   15-29

Tax Fact: *The S Corporation Economy*   15-30

Tax Planning Strategies: *Avoid PII Pitfalls*   15-30

SUMMARY   15-30

Refocus on the Big Picture: *Converting a C Corporation to an S Corporation*   15-31

Part 6: Special Business Topics

CHAPTER 16
MULTIJURISDICTIONAL TAXATION   16-1

The Big Picture: *Going International*   16-1

THE MULTIJURISDICTIONAL TAXPAYER   16-2

U.S. TAXATION OF MULTINATIONAL TRANSACTIONS   16-2

Bridge Discipline: *Bridge to International Law*   16-3

Sources of Law   16-4

Tax Issues   16-5

Tax Fact: *U.S. Income Tax Treaties in Force*   16-6

Tax Fact: *Where Do We Stand?*   16-8

Tax Planning Strategies: *Sourcing Income from Sales of Inventory*   16-9

Tax Planning Strategies: *Utilizing the Foreign Tax Credit*   16-10

Financial Disclosure Insights: *Overseas Operations and Book-Tax Differences*   16-12

Tax Fact: *The Inbound Sector*   16-16

Concept Summary: *U.S. Income Tax Treatment of a Non-U.S. Person's Income*   16-17

CROSSING STATE LINES: STATE AND LOCAL INCOME TAXATION IN THE UNITED STATES   **16-17**

Financial Disclosure Insights: *Tax Rates in Non-U.S. Jurisdictions*   *16-17*

Tax Fact: *State Tax Revenue Sources*   *16-18*

Sources of Law   16-18

Tax Issues   16-19

Tax Planning Strategies: *Nexus: To Have or Have Not*   *16-21*

Financial Disclosure Insights: *State/Local Taxes and the Tax Expense*   *16-24*

Concept Summary: *Corporate Multistate Income Taxation*   *16-24*

Tax Planning Strategies: *Where Should My Income Go?*   *16-25*

COMMON CHALLENGES   **16-25**

Authority to Tax   16-25

Bridge Discipline: *Bridge to Cost Accounting and Executive Compensation*   *16-26*

Division of Income   16-26

Transfer Pricing   16-26

Bridge Discipline: *Bridge to Economic Development and Political Science*   *16-27*

Tax Havens   16-27

Interjurisdictional Agreements   16-28

Refocus on the Big Picture: *Going International*   *16-28*

CHAPTER 17
BUSINESS TAX CREDITS AND THE ALTERNATIVE MINIMUM TAX   **17-1**

The Big Picture: *Dealing With Tax Credits and the AMT*   *17-1*

BUSINESS-RELATED TAX CREDIT PROVISIONS   **17-2**

General Business Credit   17-2

Tax Fact: *Business Tax Credits*   *17-3*

Tax Credit for Rehabilitation Expenditures   17-4

Bridge Discipline: *Bridge to Finance*   *17-5*

Work Opportunity Tax Credit   17-5

Research Activities Credit   17-6

Energy Credits   17-8

Disabled Access Credit   17-8

Credit for Small Employer Pension Plan Startup Costs   17-9

Credit for Employer-Provided Child Care   17-9

Global Tax Issues: *Sourcing Income in Cyberspace—Getting It Right When Calculating the Foreign Tax Credit*   *17-10*

Foreign Tax Credit   17-10

Small Employer Health Insurance Credit   17-11

Credit for Employer-Provided Family and Medical Leave   17-11

Concept Summary: *Tax Credits*   *17-12*

INDIVIDUAL ALTERNATIVE MINIMUM TAX   **17-13**

Alternative Minimum Taxable Income (AMTI)   17-13

AMT Formula: Other Components   17-15

AMT Adjustments   17-16

Tax Planning Strategies: *Control the Timing of Preferences and Adjustments*   *17-26*

Concept Summary: *Summary of AMT Adjustment Provisions*   *17-28*

AMT Preferences   17-28

Tax Planning Strategies: *Avoiding Preferences and Adjustments*   *17-30*

Illustration of the AMT Computation   17-30

AMT Credit   17-31

Tax Planning Strategies: *Other AMT Planning Strategies*   *17-32*

Concept Summary: *Summary of AMT Preference Provisions*   *17-33*

Concept Summary: *AMT Adjustments and Preferences for Individuals*   *17-33*

CORPORATE ALTERNATIVE MINIMUM TAX   **17-33**

Refocus on the Big Picture: *Dealing with Tax Credits and the AMT*   *17-34*

CHAPTER 18
COMPARATIVE FORMS OF DOING BUSINESS   **18-1**

The Big Picture: *Choosing a Business Form and Other Investments*   *18-1*

ALTERNATIVE ORGANIZATIONAL FORMS IN WHICH BUSINESS MAY BE CONDUCTED   **18-2**

NONTAX FACTORS AFFECTING THE CHOICE OF BUSINESS FORM   **18-2**

Limited Liability   18-3

Other Factors   18-3

Tax Fact: *Revenue Relevance of Corporate versus Individual Taxpayers*   *18-4*

Capital Formation   18-4

THE CONDUIT AND ENTITY PERSPECTIVES OF LEGAL BUSINESS FORMS   **18-4**

Effect on the Taxation of Business Operations   18-5

Global Tax Issues: *Do Corporations Pay Taxes?*   *18-5*

Effect on the Ability to Specially Allocate Income among Owners   18-6

Effect on the Tax Treatment of Capital Contributions   18-7

Effect on the Basis of an Ownership Interest   18-7

Tax Fact: *Profitability of Partnerships*   *18-8*

Effect on the Application of the At-Risk and Passive Activity Loss Rules   18-8

Effect on the Tax Treatment of Distributions   18-10

Effect on Other Taxes   18-10

MINIMIZING DOUBLE TAXATION   **18-11**

Making Deductible Distributions   18-11

Deferring Distributions   18-13

Making Return-of-Capital Distributions   18-13

Tax Fact: *Income Tax Returns Filed by Business Entities*   *18-13*

Bridge Discipline: *Bridge to Economics*   *18-14*

Electing S Corporation Status   18-14

DISPOSING OF A BUSINESS   **18-15**

Sole Proprietorships   18-15

Partnerships and Limited Liability Companies   18-16

Tax Planning Strategies: *Selling Stock or Assets*   *18-17*

C Corporations   18-17
S Corporations   18-18
Concept Summary: *Tax Treatment of Disposition of a Business*   *18-18*

CONVERTING TO ANOTHER BUSINESS FORM   **18-20**
Sole Proprietorship   18-20
C Corporation   18-20
Partnership   18-21

OVERALL COMPARISON OF BUSINESS FORMS   **18-21**
Concept Summary: *Tax Attributes of Different Forms of
Doing Business (Assume That Partners and Shareholders
Are All Individuals)*   *18-22*
Refocus on the Big Picture: *Choosing a Business Form and
Other Investments*   *18-25*

APPENDICES

TAX RATE SCHEDULES AND TABLES   A-1

TAX FORMS   B-1

GLOSSARY   C-1

TABLE OF CODE SECTIONS CITED   D-1

TABLE OF REGULATIONS CITED   D-8

TABLE OF REVENUE PROCEDURES AND
REVENUE RULINGS CITED   D-10

TABLE OF CASES CITED   E-1

PRESENT VALUE AND FUTURE VALUE TABLES   F-1

TAX FORMULAS   G-1

INDEX   I-1

Online Appendices

DEPRECIATION AND THE ACCELERATED COST
RECOVERY SYSTEM (ACRS)

AFFORDABLE CARE ACT PROVISIONS

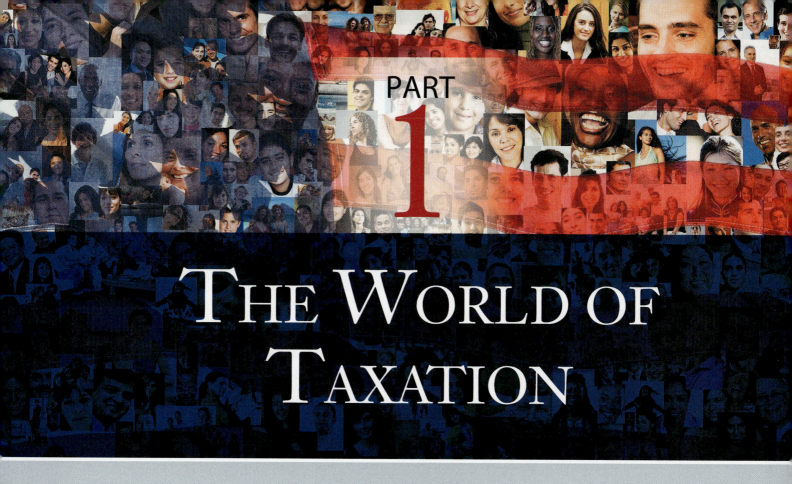

PART

1

THE WORLD OF TAXATION

CHAPTER **1**

Introduction to Taxation

CHAPTER **2**

Working with the Tax Law

CHAPTER **3**

Taxes on the Financial Statements

Part 1 provides an introduction to taxation in the United States. Various taxes imposed by Federal, state, and local governments are discussed. A unique tax planning framework is presented that is applied throughout the book in developing tax planning strategies for both business entities and individual taxpayers. The tax research process, including the relevance of the legislative, administrative, and judicial sources of the tax law, also is discussed. Part 1 concludes with a chapter on accounting for income taxes, as a bridge to materials discussed in other accounting courses and an introduction to the financial disclosure effects of the tax law.

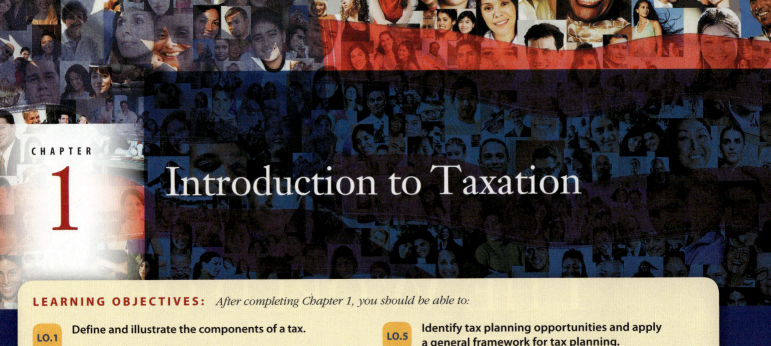

Introduction to Taxation

LEARNING OBJECTIVES: *After completing Chapter 1, you should be able to:*

LO.1 Define and illustrate the components of a tax.

LO.2 Identify the various taxes affecting business entities and individuals.

LO.3 Describe the basic tax formula for individuals and taxable business entities.

LO.4 Identify and explain the tax systems that apply to business entities and their owners.

LO.5 Identify tax planning opportunities and apply a general framework for tax planning.

LO.6 Explain the economic, social, equity, and political considerations that underlie the tax law.

LO.7 Describe the role played by the IRS and the courts in the evolution of the Federal tax system.

CHAPTER OUTLINE

1-1 The Structure of Tax Systems, 1-4
    1-1a Tax Rates, 1-4
    1-1b Tax Bases, 1-5
    1-1c Incidence of Taxation, 1-6

1-2 Types of Taxes, 1-6
    1-2a Taxes on the Production and Sale of Goods, 1-6
    1-2b Employment Taxes, 1-9
    1-2c Taxes at Death, 1-10
    1-2d Gift Tax, 1-11
    1-2e Property Taxes, 1-12
    1-2f Taxes on Privileges and Rights, 1-14
    1-2g Income Taxes, 1-15

1-3 Income Taxation of Business Entities, 1-19
    1-3a Proprietorships, 1-19
    1-3b C Corporations, 1-19
    1-3c Partnerships, 1-20
    1-3d S Corporations, 1-20
    1-3e Limited Liability Companies and Limited Liability Partnerships, 1-20
    1-3f Dealings between Individuals and Their Business Entities, 1-21

1-4 Tax Planning Fundamentals, 1-22
    1-4a Overview of Tax Planning and Ethics, 1-22
    1-4b A General Framework for Income Tax Planning, 1-23
    1-4c Tax Minimization Strategies Related to Income, 1-23
    1-4d Tax Minimization Strategies Related to Deductions, 1-24
    1-4e Tax Minimization Strategies Related to Tax Rates, 1-25
    1-4f Tax Minimization Strategies Related to Credits, 1-28

1-5 Understanding the Federal Tax Law, 1-28
    1-5a Revenue Needs, 1-28
    1-5b Economic Considerations, 1-28
    1-5c Social Considerations, 1-30
    1-5d Equity Considerations, 1-30
    1-5e Political Considerations, 1-31
    1-5f Influence of the Internal Revenue Service, 1-32
    1-5g Influence of the Courts, 1-32

1-6 Summary, 1-33

TAX TALK *How many people were taxed, who was taxed, and what was taxed tell more about a society than anything else.* —CHARLES ADAMS

THE BIG PICTURE

A TYPICAL TAX YEAR FOR A MODERN FAMILY

Travis and Amy Carter are married and live in a state that imposes both a sales tax and an income tax. They have two children, April (age 17) and Martin (age 18). Travis is a mining engineer who specializes in land reclamation. After several years with a mining corporation, Travis established a consulting practice that involves a considerable amount of travel.

Amy is a registered nurse who, until recently, was a homemaker. In November of the current year, she decided to reenter the job market and accepted a position with a medical clinic.

The Carters live only a few blocks from Ernest and Mary Walker, Amy Carter's parents. The Walkers are retired and live on interest, dividends, and Social Security benefits.

The following developments with current year and possible future tax ramifications occurred.

- The ad valorem property taxes on the Carters' residence increased, while those on the Walkers' residence decreased.

- When Travis registered an automobile that was purchased last year in another state, he paid a sales tax to his home state.

- As an anniversary present, the Carters gave the Walkers a recreational vehicle (RV).

- When Travis made a consulting trip to Chicago, the client withheld Illinois state income tax from the payment made to Travis for his services.

- Travis employed his children to draft blueprints and prepare scale models for use in his work. Both April and Martin have had training in drafting and topography.

- Early in the year, the Carters were audited by the state on an income tax return filed a few years ago. Later in the year, they were audited by the IRS on a Form 1040 they filed for the same year. In each case, a tax deficiency and interest were assessed.

- The Walkers were audited by the IRS. Unlike the Carters, they did not have to deal with a revenue agent, but settled the matter by mail.

Explain these developments and resolve any tax issues raised.

Read the chapter and formulate your response.

"Taxes are what we pay for civilized society."

This is a famous quote from U.S. Supreme Court Justice Oliver Wendell Holmes, Jr. It is engraved on the government building at 1111 Constitution Avenue in Washington, D.C.—headquarters of the Internal Revenue Service (IRS). This quote eloquently sums up the primary purpose of taxation—to raise revenue for government operations. Governments at all levels—national, state, and local—require funds for defense, protection (police and fire), education, transportation, the court system, social services, and more. Various types of taxes provide the resources to pay for government services.

In addition, taxation often is used as a tool to influence the behavior of individuals and businesses. For example, an income tax credit (which reduces a taxpayer's tax bill) may be designed to *encourage* people to purchase a fuel-efficient car. A tobacco excise tax may *discourage* individuals from smoking by increasing the cost of tobacco products.

Taxes permeate our society. Various types of taxes, such as income, sales, property, and excise taxes, come into play in many of the activities of individuals, businesses, nonprofit entities (like charities), and governments themselves.

Most directly, individuals are affected by taxes by paying them. Taxes may be paid directly or indirectly. A direct tax is paid to the government by the person who owes the tax. Examples include the personal income tax, which is paid by filing a personal income tax return (Form 1040 at the federal level), and property taxes on one's home (paid to the local government). Individuals also pay many taxes indirectly. For example, when you buy gasoline for your car, the price you pay likely includes some of the income taxes and the gasoline excise taxes seemingly owed by the oil company.

Ultimately, all taxes are paid by individuals. The corporate income tax, for example, is paid directly by the corporation, but it really is paid by individuals in their capacity as customers, investors (owners), or employees; the taxes are passed along to individuals through higher prices for products and services, lower dividends, and/or lower wages.

Taxes also affect the lives of individuals via the ballot box. Federal, state, and local elections often include initiatives that deal with taxation, such as whether Federal income taxes should be raised (or lowered), whether a new tax should be imposed on soda, or whether the sales tax rate should be increased. Candidates running for office often have positions on tax changes they would like to make if they are elected.

The Relevance of Taxation to Accounting and Finance Professionals

The Federal corporate income tax rate is 21 percent. State income taxes constitute, on average, an additional 5 percent. So a large corporation may devote about 25 percent of its net income to pay income taxes. In addition, businesses are subject to employment taxes, property taxes, sales taxes, and various excise taxes. Corporations with international operations are subject to taxation in other countries. Small businesses also pay a variety of taxes that affect profits and cash flows.

Given its significance, taxation is a crucial topic for accounting and finance professionals. They must understand the various types of business taxes to assist effectively with:

- *Compliance:* Ensure that the business files all tax returns and makes all tax payments on time. Mistakes can lead to penalties and interest expense.
- *Planning:* Help a business to apply favorable tax rules, like deferring income and obtaining tax credits, to minimize tax liability (and maximize owner wealth). The time value of money concept also is important here, as is coordinating tax planning with other business goals to maximize earnings per share.
- *Financial reporting:* Financial statements include a variety of tax information, including income tax expense on the income statement, and deferred tax assets and liabilities on the balance sheet. Footnotes to the financial statements report various tax details including the company's effective tax rate. Computation and proper reporting of this information requires knowledge of both tax and the financial reporting rules [including the Financial Accounting Standards Board's Accounting Standards Codification (ASC) 740, *Income Taxes*].

- *Controversy:* Assist when the taxpayer interacts with a tax agency (like the IRS). The IRS and state and local tax agencies regularly audit tax returns that have been filed to verify that taxes were properly computed and paid.
- *Cash management:* Taxes must be paid on time to avoid penalties and interest. Income taxes must be estimated and paid quarterly and reconciled on the annual return. Other taxes may be due weekly, monthly, or semiannually. Businesses must be sure they have the funds ready when the taxes are due and have procedures to track due dates.

The level and depth of tax knowledge needed for any accounting or tax professional depends on his or her specific job. The vice president of tax for a company clearly needs thorough knowledge in all areas of taxation; the same is true of a partner in a CPA firm. In contrast, the corporate treasurer likely focuses more on cash management, working closely with the company's tax advisers.

It is essential to maintain a balanced perspective when working with tax systems. A corporation that is deciding where to locate a new factory does not automatically select the city or state that offers the most generous tax benefits. Nor does the person who is retiring to a warmer climate pick Belize over Arizona because the former has no income tax while the latter does. Tax considerations should not control decisions, but they are one of many factors to be considered (and often, one of the most significant).

How to Study Taxation

The goal of studying taxation is being able to recognize issues (or transactions) that have tax implications, and trying to understand the justification for the related tax rules.

You may have heard that tax is a difficult subject because of the many rules, exceptions, and definitions. You even may have heard that taxation is boring. Taxation *is* a challenging topic, but it is certainly not boring. Taxation is an important and exciting topic due to constant changes made by the three branches of our Federal government (as well as by state and local jurisdictions), the significance of taxes to the bottom line of a company and an individual's finances, and the effects of taxes on our economy and society.

Tax professionals tend to find enjoyment in their chosen field due to the intellectual challenge of dealing with tax rules for compliance and planning purposes, the opportunity to interact with colleagues or clients to help them understand the effects brought about by taxes, and the knowledge that their work affects the financial well-being of individuals and businesses.

For tax professionals, the study of taxation is an ongoing and intriguing process. When Congress changes the tax law, tax professionals must review the new rules to understand how they affect clients or their employer. In addition, decisions rendered by the courts in tax disputes and guidance issued by the Treasury Department and Internal Revenue Service must be understood to ensure correct compliance with the law, and to identify updated tax planning ideas.

In studying taxation, one should focus on understanding the rules and the why(s) behind them, rather than memorizing the many isolated or disconnected rules and terms. The rules become more meaningful by thinking about why the rule exists for the particular type of tax. For example, why do Federal income tax rules allow for a child care credit? Why is tax depreciation different from that used for financial reporting? Aiming for understanding, rather than memorization, will make your journey into the world of taxation interesting and meaningful, and it will prepare you well for dealing with taxation in your accounting or finance career.

Individuals and Taxes

The following diagram illustrates the many ways individuals interact with taxes. For example, as shown in the outer circle, individuals pay taxes and file tax returns (tax compliance). They also engage in tax planning as part of their desire to maximize the present value of after-tax wealth. If their tax return is audited or they do not pay their taxes, taxpayers will deal with the IRS or a state/local tax agency (tax controversy).

Individuals deal with tax rules and planning in their roles as consumers, employees, investors, and business owners. Tax law is designed around these various taxpayer activities. Finally, as shown by the inner circle, individuals have a personal responsibility to comply with tax laws and pay any taxes due. Individuals also have a civic responsibility to understand taxes in their role as citizens and voters. Moreover, individuals need to understand how taxes affect their personal cash flows, consumption, and savings.

Use this diagram as you study the materials in this text, considering where various rules might fit in the circle.

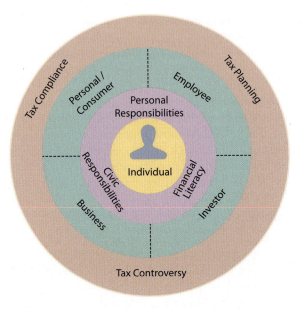

1-1 THE STRUCTURE OF TAX SYSTEMS

LO.1

Define and illustrate the components of a tax.

Most taxes have two components: a tax rate and a tax base (such as income, wages, value, or sales price). Tax liability is computed by multiplying these two components. Taxes vary by the structure of their rates and by the base subject to tax.

1-1a Tax Rates

Tax rates can be progressive, proportional, or regressive. A tax rate is *progressive* if it increases as the tax base increases. The Federal income tax is structured so as to be progressive.

EXAMPLE 1

Refer to the individual Tax Rate Schedule inside the front cover of this text. If Dave and Abby Brown, a married couple filing a joint return, report taxable income of $5,000, their income tax is $500 and their average tax rate is 10% ($500/$5,000, or the ratio of tax liability to the tax base).

If, however, the Browns' taxable income is $200,000, the couple's income tax is $36,579 [$28,179 + .24($200,000 − $165,000)] and their average tax rate is 18.3% ($36,579/$200,000). The tax is *progressive* because the average tax rate increases with increases in the tax base (income).

A tax is *proportional* if the rate of tax is constant, regardless of the size of the tax base. State retail **sales taxes** are proportional.

EXAMPLE 2

Bob purchases an automobile for $6,000. If the sales tax on automobiles is 7% in Bob's state, he will pay a $420 tax. Alternatively, if Bob pays $20,000 for a car, his sales tax will be $1,400 (still 7% of the sales price). Because the average tax rate does not change with the tax base (sales price), the sales tax is *proportional*.

TAX FACT Carrying the Tax Burden

Data from the IRS indicate that the progressive nature of the Federal income tax is quite severe, in that upper-income taxpayers are liable for taxes at a rate that is higher than their share of income reported.

Annual median adjusted gross income (defining the upper and lower one-half of citizens) is about $39,275. Income of about $481,000 puts a taxpayer in the top 1 percent of filers, and effective Federal taxes for the top 10 percent of earners have increased faster than their incomes. The following table shows the share of taxes paid by various income categories.[1]

Income Category	Share of Adjusted Gross Income	Share of Federal Income Taxes Paid
Top 1%	21%	39%
Top 5%	36%	60%
Bottom 50%	11%	3%

Additional observations include the following.

- Individuals earning less than $50,000 per year can pay zero Federal income tax, and their payroll and gasoline taxes may be partly rebated through the earned income credit as well.

- When considering income, sales, payroll, property, and other taxes that are levied by U.S. governmental bodies of all sizes, taxpayers at nearly all income levels pay about 30 percent of their income in taxes.

Finally, *regressive* tax rates decrease as the tax base increases. Federal employment taxes, such as FICA and FUTA, are regressive. When the tax base and the taxpayer's ability to pay generally are positively correlated (i.e., when they move in the same direction), many tax pundits view regressive tax rates as unfair. This is because the tax burden decreases as a *percentage* of the taxpayer's ability to pay.

> **EXAMPLE 3**
>
> In 2018, the combined Social Security and Medicare tax rate levied on the wages of employees is 7.65% up to a maximum of $128,400 and 1.45% on all wages over $128,400. Sarah earns a salary of $30,000. She pays FICA taxes of $2,295, an average tax rate of 7.65%. Alternatively, if Sarah earns $150,000, she pays $10,136 {(.0765 × $128,400) + [.0145 × ($150,000 − $128,400)]}, an average tax rate of 6.75%.
>
> Once the FICA base exceeds the maximum amount subject to the Social Security part of FICA, the FICA tax becomes *regressive* because the average tax rate decreases as the tax base increases.

Under all three tax rate structures, the *amount* of taxes due increases as the tax base increases. The structure of tax rates only affects the *rate* of increase (i.e., progressive taxes increase at an increasing rate, proportional taxes increase at a constant rate, and regressive taxes increase at a decreasing rate).

1-1b Tax Bases

Most taxes are levied on one of four kinds of tax bases.

- Transactions [including sales or purchases of goods and services, and transfers of wealth (e.g., by gift or at death)].
- Property or wealth (including ownership of specific kinds of property).
- Privileges and rights (including the ability to do business as a corporation, the right to work in a certain profession, and the ability to move goods between countries).
- Income on a gross or net-of-expenses basis.

---

[1]Data relate to the 2015 tax year.

Because the Federal income tax usually has the most significant influence when making decisions, it is the principal focus of this text.

DIGGING DEEPER 1 | **In-depth coverage can be found on this book's companion website: www.cengage.com**

1-1c Incidence of Taxation

The degree to which various segments of society share the total tax burden is difficult to assess. Assumptions must be made concerning who absorbs the burden of paying the tax. For example, because dividend payments to shareholders are not deductible by a corporation and generally are taxable to shareholders, the same income is subject to a form of double taxation.

Concern over the potential for double taxation of the same income is valid to the extent that corporations are *not* able to shift the corporate tax to the consumer through higher prices and lower wages. But many research studies have shown that corporations are able to shift the corporate income tax burden (i.e., so that it is borne by both employees and the ultimate purchasers of goods), thereby avoiding any double taxation on the same income.

Tax incidence becomes important in discussions involving the "fair share" of taxation that each party in a society should pay. In measuring the share of tax that each party bears, it usually is best to consider direct and indirect taxes, to include taxes levied by all jurisdictions (e.g., national, state/local, international), and to measure tax liabilities in present value terms.

LO.2

Identify the various taxes affecting business entities and individual.

1-2 TYPES OF TAXES

In many countries, transaction taxes are more important than income taxes. We will discuss three types of transaction taxes: sales and certain excise taxes, employment taxes, and taxes on the transfer of wealth (as gifts and at death).

1-2a Taxes on the Production and Sale of Goods

Sales tax and some excise taxes are imposed on the production, sale, or consumption of commodities or the use of services. Excise taxes and general sales taxes differ by the breadth of their bases. An excise tax base is limited to a specific kind of good or service, while a general sales tax is broad-based (e.g., it might be levied on all retail sales). All levels of government impose excise taxes, while state and local governments (but not the U.S. Federal government) make heavy use of the general sales tax.

Federal Excise Taxes

Together with customs duties, excise taxes served as the principal source of revenue for the United States during its first 150 years of existence. Since World War II, the role of excise taxes in financing the Federal government has decined steadily, falling from about 30 to 40 percent of revenues just prior to the war to about 3 percent now. During this time, the Federal government came to rely upon income and employment taxes as its principal sources of funds.

Despite the decreasing contribution of excise taxes to the Federal government, they continue to have a significant impact on specific industries. Currently, trucks, trailers, tires, liquor, tobacco, firearms, certain sporting equipment, medical devices, and air travel all are subject to Federal excise taxes. In the past, the sale and manufacture of a variety of other goods, including furs, jewelry, boats, luxury automobiles, and theater tickets, have been taxed. Excise taxes extend beyond sales transactions. They also are levied on privileges and rights, as discussed below.

The bases used for Federal excise taxes are as diverse as the goods that are taxed. Fuels are taxed by the gallon, vaccines by the dose, air travel by the price paid for the ticket, water travel by the passenger, coal by the ton extracted or by the sales price, insurance by the premiums paid, and the gas guzzler tax by the mileage rating on the automobile produced. Some of these taxes are levied on producers, some on resellers, and some on consumers. In almost every circumstance, the tax rate structure is proportional.

With the exception of Federal excise taxes on alcohol, tobacco, and firearms, Federal excise taxes are due at least quarterly, when the Federal excise tax return (Form 720) is filed.

State Excise Taxes

Many states levy excise taxes on the same items taxed by the Federal government. For example, most states have excise taxes on gasoline, liquor, and tobacco. However, the tax on specific goods can vary dramatically among states. Compare New York's $4.35 tax on each pack of 20 cigarettes to Missouri's $.17 tax. These differences at the state level can provide ample incentive for smuggling between states and for state-line enterprises specializing in taxed goods.[2]

Other goods and services subject to state and local excise taxes include admission to amusement facilities; hotel occupancy; rental of other facilities; and sales of playing cards, oleomargarine products, and prepared foods. Some counties impose a tax on transfers of property that require recording of documents (such as real estate sales and sales of stock and securities).

Local Excise Taxes

Over the last few years, two types of excise taxes imposed at the local level have become increasingly popular. These are the hotel occupancy tax and the rental car "surcharge." Because they tax the visitor who cannot vote, they are a political windfall and serve as a means of financing special projects that generate civic pride (e.g., convention centers and state-of-the-art sports arenas). A few cities have created excise taxes that apply to digital transactions, like song and movie streams, app downloads, Uber and Lyft fares, and Airbnb rentals.

General Sales Tax

The broad-based general sales tax is a major source of revenue for most state and local governments. It is used in all but five states (Alaska, Delaware, Montana, New Hampshire, and Oregon). The U.S. Federal government does not levy a general sales tax.

While specific rules vary from state to state, the sales tax typically employs a proportional tax rate and includes retail sales of tangible personal property (and occasionally personal services) in the base. Some states exempt medicine and groceries from the base (or tax these items at a lower rate), and sometimes tax rates vary with the good being sold (e.g., the sales tax rate for automobiles may differ from the rate on other goods). The sales tax is collected by the retailer and then paid to the state government.

Local general sales taxes, over and above those levied by the state, are common. It is not unusual to find taxpayers living in the same state who pay different general sales tax rates based on the city or county where they make their purchases.

For various reasons, some jurisdictions suspend the application of a general sales tax. The prevalent justification for these sales tax holidays involves the purchase of back-to-school items. Granted by approximately 15 states, the exemption typically is available in early August and covers modest expenditures for clothing and school supplies. Some states have used sales tax holidays to encourage the purchase of energy-conserving appliances (e.g., Maryland, Missouri, and Texas) and hurricane preparedness items (e.g., Louisiana and Virginia).

---

[2]Some excise taxes are referred to as "sin" taxes (because goods such as liquor, marijuana, and tobacco are subject to the tax). Although it commonly is believed that these taxes are imposed for the purpose of discouraging consumption of the taxed item, evidence frequently fails to show this effect.

GLOBAL TAX ISSUES   **Why Is Gasoline Expensive? It Depends on Where You Live**

In the United States, unlike other countries, the price of gasoline largely is attributable to the cost of crude oil; as U.S. production of crude has increased sharply, gasoline prices have fallen during this decade. In January 2018, the average price per gallon of gasoline in the United States was about $2.35.

In other countries, the real culprit is the amount of tax imposed. Consider the following situations.

Country	Average Price per Gallon (U.S. $)
Hong Kong	$7.12
United Kingdom	6.02
Germany	5.38
China	3.56
Saudi Arabia	2.04
Libya	0.42

While other factors may contribute to the various gasoline prices, the primary factor is the amount of tax charged in those countries. For example, in the United Kingdom, approximately 60 percent of the cost of gasoline is attributable to taxes. The equivalent rate for the United States is 20 percent in most locations.

Use Taxes

One obvious approach to avoiding state and local sales taxes is to purchase goods in a state that has little or no sales tax and then transport the goods back to one's home state. Another alternative is to purchase goods from an out-of-state internet-based vendor (e.g., an Amazon affiliate) that then ships the goods directly to the purchaser. **Use taxes** exist to prevent this tax reduction ploy. The use tax is a value-based tax, usually imposed at the same rate as the sales tax, on the use, consumption, or storage of tangible property. Every state that imposes a general sales tax levied on the consumer also applies a use tax.

The Big Picture

EXAMPLE 4

Return to the facts of *The Big Picture* on p. 1-1. The payment Travis made when he registered the car is probably a use tax. When the car was purchased in another state, likely no (or a lesser) sales tax was levied. The current payment makes up for the amount of sales tax he would have paid had the car been purchased in his home state.

The use tax is difficult to enforce for many purchases; therefore, the purchaser often does not pay it. Most states are taking steps to curtail this loss of revenue, by forcing the purchaser's credit card company to collect the tax, and to add an assessment of the tax to the purchaser's state income tax return.

Value Added Tax

The **value added tax (VAT)** is a variation of a sales tax; it is levied at each stage of production on the value added by the producer. VAT is in widespread use in many countries around the world (most notably in the European Union and in Canada). The tax typically serves as a major source of revenue for governments that use it.[3]

---

[3]Some proposals to reduce the Federal government's reliance on the employment and income taxes have focused on VAT as an alternative tax system.

EXAMPLE 5

Farmer Brown sells wheat to a flour mill for $100. If the wheat cost $65 for Brown to produce and if the VAT rate is 10%, then Brown will owe a VAT of $3.50 [.10($100 − $65)]. If the mill sells the flour for $200 to a baker and if it cost the mill $120 to make the flour (including the cost of Brown's wheat), then it will pay a VAT of $8 [.10($200 − $120)]. If the baker sells the 200 loaves of bread made from the flour for $400 and if it cost the baker $280 to make the bread, then the baker pays a VAT of $12 [.10($400 − $280)].

The consumers who buy the bread will not pay any VAT directly. It is likely, however, that some or all of the total VAT paid of $23.50 ($3.50 + $8 + $12) will be paid by the consumers in the form of higher prices for the bread.

1-2b Employment Taxes

Both Federal and state governments tax the salaries and wages paid to employees. On the Federal side, employment taxes represent a major source of funds. For example, the FICA tax accounts for more than one-third of revenues in the Federal budget, second only to the income tax in its contribution.

The Federal government imposes two kinds of employment tax. The Federal Insurance Contributions Act (FICA) imposes a tax on self-employed individuals, employees, and employers. The proceeds of the tax are used to finance Social Security and Medicare benefits. The Federal Unemployment Tax Act (FUTA) imposes a tax on employers only. The FUTA tax provides funds to state unemployment benefit programs. Most state employment taxes are similar to the FUTA tax, with proceeds used to finance state unemployment benefit payments.

FICA Taxes

The FICA tax has two components: old age, survivors, and disability insurance payments (commonly referred to as Social Security) and Medicare health insurance payments. The Social Security tax rate is 6.2 percent for the employee and 6.2 percent for the employer, and the Medicare tax rate is 1.45 percent for both the employer and the employee. The maximum base for the Social Security tax is $127,200 for 2017 and $128,400 for 2018. There is no ceiling on the base amount for the Medicare tax. The employer withholds the FICA tax from an employee's wages.

Payments usually are made through weekly or monthly electronic payments or deposits to a Federal depository. Employers also file Form 941, Employer's Quarterly Federal Tax Return, by the end of the first month following each quarter of the calendar year (e.g., by July 31 for the quarter ending on June 30) and pay any remaining amount of employment taxes due for the previous quarter. Failure to pay can result in large penalties.

FICA tax is not assessed on all wages paid. For example, wages paid to children under the age of 18 who are employed in a parent's trade or business are exempt from the tax.

The Big Picture

EXAMPLE 6

Return to the facts of *The Big Picture* on p. 1-1. Presuming that April and Martin perform meaningful services for Travis (which the facts seem to imply), they are legitimate employees. April is not subject to Social Security tax because she is under the age of 18. However, Martin is 18, and Travis needs to collect and pay FICA taxes for him.

Furthermore, recall that Amy Carter now is working and is subject to the Social Security and Medicare taxes. Travis, as an independent contractor, is subject to self-employment tax, discussed in the next section.

An additional .9 percent Medicare tax is imposed on earned income (including self-employment income) *above* $200,000 (single filers) or $250,000 (married filing jointly). Unlike the Social Security tax of 6.2 percent and the regular Medicare portion of 1.45 percent, an employer does not match the employees' .9 percent additional Medicare tax.

Similarly, an additional 3.8 percent Medicare tax is assessed on the investment income of individuals whose modified adjusted gross income exceeds $200,000 or $250,000. For this purpose, investment income includes interest, dividends, net capital gains, and income for similar portfolio items.

The Big Picture

EXAMPLE 7

Return to the facts of *The Big Picture* on p. 1-1. The combined income of Travis and Amy Carter may be large enough to trigger one or both of the additional Medicare taxes. The marginal tax rate[4] of "upper-income" taxpayers is higher than that of other individuals because of these taxes. Congress has designated these taxes to cover a portion of Federal health care costs. Betty would have considered these taxes when making her decision to reenter the workforce.

Self-Employment Tax

Self-employed individuals also pay into the FICA system in the form of a self-employment (SE) tax (determined on Schedule SE, filed with Form 1040, U.S. Individual Income Tax Return). Self-employed individuals are required to pay both the employer and the employee portion of the FICA taxes. The 2018 SE tax rate is 15.3 percent on self-employment income up to $128,400 and 2.9 percent on all additional self-employment income. Self-employed individuals deduct half of the SE tax—the amount normally deductible by an employer as a business expense. Self-employment income is discussed in more detail in text Section 11-4b.

Unemployment Taxes

For 2018, FUTA applies at a rate of 6.0 percent on the first $7,000 of covered wages paid during the year to each employee. As with FICA, this represents a regressive rate structure. The Federal government allows a credit for unemployment tax paid (or allowed under a merit rating system)[5] to the state. The credit cannot exceed 5.4 percent of the covered wages. Thus, the amount required to be paid to the U.S. Treasury could be as low as .6 percent (6.0% − 5.4%) of an employee's wages.

FUTA and state unemployment taxes differ from FICA in that the tax is imposed only on the employer.

1-2c **Taxes at Death**

The transfer of property upon the death of the owner may be a taxable event. If the tax is imposed on the transferor at death, it is called an **estate tax**. If the law taxes the recipient of the property, it is termed an **inheritance tax**. As is typical of other types of transaction taxes, the value of the property transferred provides the base for determining the amount of the tax at death.

The Federal government imposes an estate tax. Only a few state governments levy their own additional inheritance taxes, estate taxes, or both.

In a typical year, about 2.5 million U.S. individuals die. At the same time, only about 5,000 estates file a Federal estate tax return showing a taxable estate greater than zero. Total collections of Federal estate and gift tax revenues amount to about $20 billion per year.

---

[4]A taxpayer's *marginal tax rate* (or *marginal tax bracket*) is the rate that would be paid on an additional dollar of taxable income.

[5]States follow a policy of reducing unemployment tax on employers with stable employment. Thus, an employer with no employee turnover might face state unemployment tax rates as low as .1% or, in some cases, zero. This *merit rating system* explicitly accounts for the savings generated by steady employment.

At the time of her death, Wilma lived in a state that imposes an inheritance tax but not an estate tax. Mary, one of Wilma's heirs, lives in the same state. Wilma's estate is subject to the Federal estate tax, and Mary is subject to the state inheritance tax.

The Federal Estate Tax

Never designed to generate a large amount of revenue, the Federal estate tax was intended to prevent large concentrations of wealth from being kept within a family for many generations. Whether this objective has been accomplished is debatable, because estate taxes can be substantially reduced (or deferred for decades) through careful tax planning activities.

Determination of the estate tax base begins with the *gross estate*, which includes property the decedent owned at the time of death. It also includes property interests, such as life insurance proceeds paid to the estate or to a beneficiary other than the estate if the deceased-insured had any ownership rights in the policy. Most property included in the gross estate is valued at fair market value as of the date of death.

Deductions from the gross estate in arriving at the *taxable estate* include funeral and administration expenses, certain taxes, debts of the decedent, and transfers to charitable organizations. A *marital deduction* is available for amounts passing to a surviving spouse (a widow or widower).

When Luis died, he owned $20 million in various securities, real estate, and personal effects. Under his will, Luis gave $1 million to the local art museum and provided $12 million to his surviving wife Angelina. Luis's executor computes a Federal estate tax on the $7 million taxable estate.

Once the taxable estate has been determined and certain taxable gifts have been added to it, one must determine a tentative tax liability. The tentative liability is reduced by a variety of credits to arrive at the amount due.

In most cases, the first $10 million of a U.S. decedent's estate effectively is excluded from the estate tax, with a maximum 40 percent tax rate on any excess. Spouses can share a $20 million estate tax exclusion. The $10 million and $20 million amounts are indexed for inflation.[6]

State Taxes at Death

States usually levy an inheritance tax, an estate tax, or both. The two forms of tax differ according to whether the liability is imposed on the heirs or on the estate.

Typically, an inheritance tax divides the heirs into classes based on their relationship to the decedent. The more closely related the heir, the lower the rates imposed and the greater the exemption allowed. Some states allow a zero rate of tax on amounts passing to a surviving spouse.

1-2d **Gift Tax**

Like estate and inheritance taxes, the Federal **gift tax** is an excise tax levied on the right to transfer property. In this case, however, the tax is imposed on transfers made during the owner's life rather than at death. The tax applies only to transferred amounts that are not supported by full and adequate consideration (i.e., gifts).

Carl sells property worth $20,000 to his daughter, Bryce, for $1,000. Carl has made a $19,000 gift to Bryce.

---

[6]For 2018, the indexed exemption amount for each individual is $11.18 million, and spouses can share a $22.36 million Federal estate tax exclusion.

The Federal gift tax is intended to complement the estate tax. The gift tax base is the sum of all taxable gifts made *during one's lifetime.* Gifts are valued at the fair market value of the property on the date of the gift. To compute the tax due in a year, the tax rate schedule is applied to the sum of all lifetime taxable gifts. The resulting tax is then reduced by gift taxes paid in prior years.

The Federal gift tax and the Federal estate tax are *unified.*[7] The transfer of assets by a decedent at death effectively is treated as a final gift under the tax law. Thus, the $10 million exclusion (as indexed) and the 40 percent top tax rate for the estate tax also is available to calculate the tax liability generated by lifetime gifts. If the exclusion is exhausted during one's lifetime against taxable gifts, it is not available to reduce the estate tax liability. The same tax rate schedule applies to both lifetime gifts and the estate tax.

EXAMPLE 11

Before his death, Ben makes taxable gifts exceeding the $10 million exclusion (as indexed). Because the unified transfer tax exclusion was used up during his life to offset the tax due on these gifts, no further amount is left to reduce Ben's estate tax liability.

Annual taxable gifts are determined by reducing the fair market value of gifts given by an *annual exclusion* of $15,000 per donee; this amount does not use up any of the lifetime exclusion. A married couple can elect *gift splitting*, which enables them to transfer twice the annual exclusion ($30,000) per donee per year, before eroding the lifetime exclusion amount.

Taxable gifts are reduced by deductions for gifts to charity and to one's spouse (the *marital deduction*). Gifts for medical and educational purposes may be exempt from the gift tax as well.

Gift Tax Exclusion and Deductions

EXAMPLE 12

Marco made the following gifts: $500,000 to his wife Irena, $100,000 to their daughter Anita, and $100,000 to the San Mateo Church.

The marital and charitable deductions offset the gifts to Irena and the church. The $15,000 per donee annual exclusion reduces the taxable gift to Anita. Another $15,000 of the taxable gift could be eliminated if Irena agrees to a gift-splitting election.

EXAMPLE 13

On December 31, Vera gives $15,000 to each of her four married children, their spouses, and her eight grandchildren. On January 3 of the following year, she repeats the procedure.

Due to the annual exclusion, Vera has *not* made a taxable gift, although she transferred $240,000 [$15,000 × 16 (the number of donees)] twice, in a matter of days, for a total of $480,000.

If Vera had been married, she could have given twice as much ($960,000) tax-free, by electing gift splitting with her husband.

Unlike death, the timing of which usually is involuntary, the making of a gift is a voluntary parting of ownership. Thus, the ownership of a business or a plot of land can be transferred gradually without incurring drastic and immediate tax consequences.

1-2e **Property Taxes**

A property tax can be a tax on the ownership of property or a tax on wealth, depending on the base used. Any measurable characteristic of the property being taxed can be used as a base (e.g., weight, size, number, or value). Most property taxes in the United States are taxes on wealth; they use value as a base. These value-based property taxes are known as **ad valorem taxes**. Property taxes generally are administered by state and local governments, where they serve as a significant source of revenue.

---

[7]§§ 2010 and 2505.

Federal budget receipts as estimated for fiscal 2018 indicate a dependence to a great extent on payroll and individual income taxes. Corporate income tax collections likely are far below what the general public might expect.

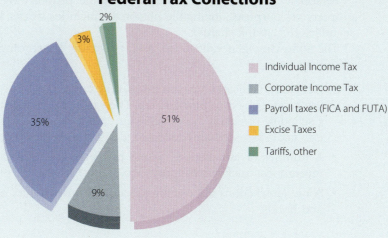

Federal Tax Collections

- 51% Individual Income Tax
- 9% Corporate Income Tax
- 35% Payroll taxes (FICA and FUTA)
- 3% Excise Taxes
- 2% Tariffs, other

Taxes on Realty

Property taxes on **realty** are used chiefly by states and their local political subdivisions such as cities, counties, and school districts. They represent a major source of revenue for local governments, but their importance at the state level is limited.

How realty is defined can have an important bearing on which assets are subject to tax. This is especially true in jurisdictions that do not impose ad valorem taxes on **personalty** (all assets that are not realty, discussed in the next section). Realty generally includes real estate and any capital improvements that are classified as fixtures. A fixture is something so permanently attached to the real estate that its removal will cause irreparable damage. A built-in bookcase might be a fixture, whereas a movable bookcase is not. Certain items such as electrical wiring and plumbing change from personalty to realty when installed in a building.

The following are some of the characteristics of ad valorem taxes on realty.

- Some states partially exempt the homestead, or personal residence, portion of property from taxation.

- Lower taxes may apply to a residence owned by a taxpayer age 65 or older.

- Some jurisdictions extend immunity from tax for a specified period of time (a tax holiday) to new or relocated businesses.

- Some states provide for lower valuations on property dedicated to agricultural use or other special uses (e.g., wildlife sanctuaries).

The Big Picture

EXAMPLE 14

Return to the facts of *The Big Picture* on p. 1-1. Why did the Walkers' taxes decrease while those of the Carters increased?

A likely explanation is that one (or both) of the Walkers achieved senior citizen status, leading to lower tax rates. In the case of the Carters, the assessed value of their property probably increased. Perhaps they made significant home improvements (e.g., kitchen/bathroom renovation, addition of a sundeck).

Taxes on Personality

Personalty includes all assets that are not realty. There is a difference between how property is *classified* (realty or personalty) and how it is *used*. Realty and personalty can be either business use or personal use property. Examples include a residence (personal use realty), an office building (business use realty), surgical instruments (business use personalty), and the family car (personal use personalty).

Personalty also can be classified as tangible property or intangible property. For property tax purposes, intangible personalty includes stocks, bonds, and various other securities (e.g., bank shares).

The following generalizations may be made concerning the property taxes on personalty.

- Generally, vehicles (cars and boats, for example) are the only non-realty personal-use assets subject to property tax. The value of a vehicle typically is established by a schedule based on the vehicle's age and make/model. Usually, any vehicle property tax is assessed and collected along with vehicle license or registration fees.

- A number of jurisdictions assess property taxes on business personalty (e.g., inventories, trucks, machinery, equipment).

- Some jurisdictions impose an ad valorem property tax on intangibles, like stocks and bonds.

DIGGING DEEPER 2   **In-depth coverage can be found on this book's companion website: www.cengage.com**

1-2f Taxes on Privileges and Rights

Taxes on a citizen's privileges and rights usually are considered excise taxes. The most important of these taxes are reviewed here.

Federal Customs Duties

Customs duties or tariffs can be characterized as a tax on the right to move goods across national borders. These taxes, together with selective excise taxes, provided most of the revenues needed by the Federal government during the nineteenth century. For example, tariffs and excise taxes alone paid off the national debt in 1835 and enabled the U.S. Treasury to pay a surplus of $28 million to the states. Today, however, customs duties account for only 1 percent of revenues in the Federal budget.

In recent years, tariffs have acted more as an instrument for carrying out protectionist policies than as a means of generating revenue. Thus, a particular U.S. industry might be saved from economic disaster, so the argument goes, by placing customs duties on the importation of foreign goods that can be sold at lower prices. Protectionists contend that the tariff therefore neutralizes the competitive edge held by the offshore producer of the goods.[8] But tariffs often lead to retaliatory action on the part of the nation or nations affected.

Franchise Taxes and Occupational Taxes

A **franchise tax** is a tax on the privilege of doing business in a state or local jurisdiction. Typically, the tax is imposed by states on corporations, but the tax base varies from state to state. While some states use a measure of corporate net income as part of the base, most states base the tax on the capitalization of the corporation (with or without certain long-term debt).

---

[8]The North American Free Trade Agreement (NAFTA) substantially reduces the tariffs on trade between Canada, Mexico, and the United States.

Closely akin to the franchise tax are **occupational taxes** applicable to various trades or businesses, such as a liquor store license, a taxicab or shared-ride permit, or a fee to practice a profession such as law, medicine, or accounting. Most of these are not significant revenue producers and fall more into the category of licenses than taxes. The revenue derived is used to defray the cost incurred by the jurisdiction to regulate the business or profession for the public good.

The Big Picture

EXAMPLE 15

Return to the facts of *The Big Picture* on p. 1-1. Although the facts do not mention the matter, both Travis and Amy will almost certainly pay occupational fees—Travis for engineering and Amy for nursing.

Severance Taxes

Severance taxes are based on the extraction of natural resources (e.g., oil, gas, iron ore, and coal). They are an important source of revenue for many states; Alaska does not levy either a state-level income or sales/use tax, because the collections from its severance taxes typically are quite large.

1-2g Income Taxes

Income taxes are levied by the Federal government, most states, and some local governments. In recent years, the trend in the United States has been to place greater reliance on this method of taxation, while other countries are relying more heavily on transactions taxes such as the VAT.

Income taxes generally are imposed on individuals, corporations, and certain fiduciaries (estates and trusts). Most jurisdictions attempt to ensure the collection of income taxes by requiring certain pay-as-you-go procedures, including withholding requirements for employees and estimated tax prepayments for all taxpayers.

The Structure of the Federal Income Tax

Although some variations exist, the basic Federal income tax formula is similar for all taxable entities. This formula is shown in Exhibit 1.1.

The income tax is based on the doctrine known as *legislative grace*: all income is subject to tax, and no deductions are allowed unless specifically provided for in the law. Some types of income are excluded on the basis of various economic, social, equity, and political considerations. Examples of such exclusions from the income tax base include gifts, inheritances, life insurance proceeds received by reason of death, and interest income from state and local bonds.

LO.3

Describe the basic tax formula for individuals and taxable business entities.

EXHIBIT 1.1	Basic Formula for Federal Income Tax	
Income (broadly defined)		$xxx,xxx
Less: Exclusions (income that is not subject to tax)		(xx,xxx)
Gross income (income that is subject to tax)		$xxx,xxx
Less: Deductions		(xx,xxx)
Taxable income		$xxx,xxx
Federal income tax on taxable income (see Tax Rate Schedules inside front cover of text)		$ xx,xxx
Less: Tax credits (including Federal income tax withheld and other prepayments of Federal income taxes)		(x,xxx)
Tax due (or refund)		$ xxx

All entities are allowed to deduct business expenses from gross income, but a number of limitations and exceptions are applied. A variety of credits against the tax are also allowed, again on the basis of economic, social, equity, or political goals of Congress.

Individual rates range from 10 percent to 37 percent. Estates and trusts are also subject to income taxation, with rates ranging from 10 percent to 37 percent. Additional Medicare taxes (discussed previously) apply on top of these rates for certain upper-income taxpayers.

Partnerships, qualifying small business corporations, and some limited liability companies are not taxable entities, but must file information returns. Owners of these business entities then are taxed on the net taxable income of the enterprise, proportionate to their holdings. See text Sections 1-3c through 1-3e.

For individuals, deductions are separated into two categories—deductions *for* adjusted gross income (AGI) and deductions *from* AGI. Generally, deductions *for* AGI are related to business activities, while deductions *from* AGI often are personal in nature (e.g., medical expenses, mortgage interest and property taxes on a personal residence, charitable contributions, and personal casualty losses) or are related to investment activities. Deductions *from* AGI take the form of *itemized deductions* and the deduction for qualified business income. Individuals may take a *standard deduction* (a specified amount based on filing status) rather than itemize actual deductions. An overview of the individual income tax formula is provided in Exhibit 1.2.

EXHIBIT 1.2	Federal Income Tax Formula for Individuals	
Income (broadly defined)		$xx,xxx
Less: Exclusions (income that is not subject to tax)		(x,xxx)
Gross income (income that is subject to tax)		$xx,xxx
Less: Certain business and investment deductions (usually referred to as deductions *for* adjusted gross income)		(x,xxx)
Adjusted gross income		$xx,xxx
Less: The greater of certain personal and employee deductions (usually referred to as *itemized deductions*) *or* The standard deduction (including any *additional* standard deduction)		(x,xxx)
Less: Deduction for qualified business income		(x,xxx)
Taxable income		$xx,xxx
Federal income tax on taxable income (see Tax Rate Schedules inside front cover of text)		$ x,xxx
Less: Tax credits (including Federal income tax withheld and other prepayments of Federal income taxes)		(xxx)
Tax owed (or refund)		$ xxx

DIGGING DEEPER 3   **In-depth coverage can be found on this book's companion website: www.cengage.com**

State Income Taxes

Most states (except Alaska, Florida, Nevada, South Dakota, Texas, Washington, and Wyoming) impose a traditional income tax on individuals. Tennessee and New Hampshire tax only certain dividend and interest income. Most states also impose either a corporate income tax or a franchise tax based in part on corporate income.

The following additional points can be made about state income taxes. See also text Section 16-3.

- State income tax laws usually rely on Federal income tax laws to some degree—the states use Federal taxable income (or Federal adjusted gross income) as a base, with a few adjustments (e.g., a few states allow an exclusion for interest income earned on Federal securities).

- Most states require withholding of state income tax from salaries and wages and estimated payments by corporations and self-employed individuals.

- Most states have their own set of rates, exemptions, and credits.

- Many states allow a credit for taxes paid to other states.

- Virtually all state income tax returns provide checkoff boxes for donations to various causes. Many are dedicated to medical research and wildlife programs, but special projects are not uncommon. For example, Oklahoma uses a checkoff to retire the debt incurred for its capitol dome addition, while a Wisconsin checkoff financed part of the renovations of Lambeau Field (home of the Green Bay Packers). These checkoff boxes have been criticized as adding complexity to the returns and misleading taxpayers.

Local Income Taxes

Cities imposing an income tax include Baltimore, Cincinnati, Cleveland, Columbus (OH), Denver, Detroit, Kansas City (MO), New York, Philadelphia, San Francisco, and St. Louis, among others. City income taxes usually apply to anyone who earns income in a city. They are designed to collect contributions for government services from those who live in close-by suburbs but work in the city, as well as from local residents.

Concept Summary 1.1 provides an overview of the major taxes existing in the United States and specifies which political jurisdiction imposes them.

In-depth coverage can be found on this book's companion website: www.cengage.com   **4 DIGGING DEEPER**

TAX FACT What Is the U.S. Tax Burden?

One popular measure of the burden of taxes in the U.S. economy is the Tax Foundation's "Tax Freedom Day." This statistic is a determination of the day upon which an individual has completed the entire year's obligation to governmental units (i.e., if all earnings were paid as taxes to this point, annual taxes would be paid up and one would now begin to "work for his or her own account").

Being "free from taxes" may bring about a feeling of relief, but in reality, tax burdens vary greatly from state to state. And as the U.S. economy has evolved and develops a more complex tax structure, adding emphasis on income and sales/use taxes and reducing the relative reliance on tariffs and excise taxes, year-to-year comparisons become difficult. Nonetheless, as a rough measure of the presence of government in our lives, Tax Freedom Day carries some importance.

If one is in need of consolation, Tax Freedom Day in Canada was June 9, 2017.

Year	Tax Freedom Day
1902	1/31
1930	2/12
1945	4/4
1960	4/15
1970	4/26
1990	5/1
1999	5/11
2000	5/3
2010	4/12
2017	4/23

Concept Summary 1.1

Overview of Taxes in the United States

Type of Tax	Imposed by Jurisdiction		
	Federal	**State**	**Local**
Property taxes:			
Ad valorem on realty	No	Yes	Yes
Ad valorem on personalty	No	Yes	Yes
Transaction taxes:			
Excise	Yes	Yes	Few
General sales	No	Most	Some
Severance	Yes	Some	No
Estate	Yes	Few	No
Inheritance	No	Few	Few
Gift	Yes	Few	No
Income taxes:			
Corporations	Yes	Most	Few
Individuals	Yes	Most	Few
Employment taxes:			
FICA	Yes	No	No
FUTA	Yes	Yes	No
Other taxes			
Customs duties	Yes	No	No
Franchise taxes	No	Yes	No
Occupational taxes or fees	Yes	Yes	Yes

Bridge Discipline   Bridge to Political Science and Sociology

The tax law and its effects on citizens and businesses of the United States are included in many other academic disciplines. Tax burdens are part of American fiction, family studies, and minority issues, as well as economics, finance, and management courses.

In the Bridge feature found in most chapters of this text, we relate the concerns of other disciplines to a more specific review of tax law, as presented here. With the topical knowledge obtained in this text, the reader can better understand the issues raised by other disciplines, sometimes to support beliefs held by others and sometimes to refute them.

For instance, the structure of the U.S. tax system raises many issues of equity and fairness. Politicians and journalists discuss these issues freely, often without the requisite tax knowledge to draw proper conclusions.

- Should the property tax on real estate be used to finance the local public education system? Why should elderly taxpayers with grown children or parents who send their children to private schools continue to pay for public schools through these taxes?

- Would the lack of a charitable contribution deduction impair the ability of charities to raise operating and capital funds?

- Does a regressive sales/use tax fall harder on individuals of color?

- Is the tax law "friendly" to marriage and to families with children?

- How should the tax law be used to encourage investments in "green" energy products? In improving access speeds for the internet?

FINANCIAL DISCLOSURE INSIGHTS · **What Do You Mean by "Income" Anyway?**

Most business taxpayers keep at least "two sets of books," in that they report one amount of "income" for financial accounting purposes and another amount of "taxable income" as required by various taxing jurisdictions—the definition that will be used throughout this book. In fact, "income" might be defined in many different ways, depending on the recipient of the income reports of the enterprise. For instance, a business entity might prepare markedly different income reports for lenders, employee unions, managers in operating divisions, and international agencies.

Financial accounting income guidance is provided for U.S. businesses by the **Financial Accounting Standards Board (FASB)**, using the accumulated **Generally Accepted Accounting Principles (GAAP)** for the reporting period. When an entity conducts business outside the United States,

the **International Financial Reporting Standards (IFRS)** of the **International Accounting Standards Board (IASB)** also may apply.

Throughout this book, we point out some of the effects that Federal income tax provisions can have on the taxpayer's financial accounting results for the tax year. The vast majority of an entity's business transactions receive identical treatment under GAAP, IFRS, and the Federal tax law. But when the applicable provisions differ, "income" can be reported as different amounts—accounting professionals often refer to these as "book-tax differences."

A tax professional must be able to identify and explain the various constructs of "income" so that the business entity's operating results will be accurately reflected in its stock price, loan covenants, and cash-flow demands.

1-3 INCOME TAXATION OF BUSINESS ENTITIES

LO.4

Identify and explain the tax systems that apply to business entities and their owners.

1-3a Proprietorships

The simplest form of business entity is a **proprietorship**, which is not a separate taxable entity. Instead, the proprietor reports the net profit of the business on his or her own individual tax return.

Individuals who own proprietorships (e.g., "Jenny's Fruit Stand") often have specific tax goals with regard to their financial interactions with the business. Because a proprietorship is, by definition, owned by an individual, the individual has great flexibility in structuring the entity's transactions in a way that will minimize his or her marginal income tax rate (or, in some cases, the marginal income tax rates of the family unit).

A proprietorship itself is not a taxpaying entity. The owner of the proprietorship reports the income and deductions of the business on a Schedule C (Profit or Loss from Business) and the net profit (or loss) of the proprietorship on his or her Form 1040 (U.S. Individual Income Tax Return). Specific issues related to the taxation of sole proprietorships are presented in detail in Chapter 11.

1-3b C Corporations

Some corporations pay tax on corporate taxable income, while others pay no tax at the corporate level. Corporations that are separate taxable entities are referred to as **C corporations**, because they are governed by Subchapter C of the Internal Revenue Code. C corporations are addressed in Chapters 12 and 13.

A C corporation files its own tax return (Form 1120) and is subject to the Federal income tax. The shareholders then pay income tax on the dividends they receive when the corporation distributes its profits. Thus, the profits of the corporation can be seen as subject to *double taxation*, first at the corporate level and then at the shareholder level.

Joseph is the president and sole shareholder of Falcon Corporation. Falcon's taxable income is $50,000, and its tax liability is $10,500.

If Joseph has the corporation pay all of its after-tax income to him as a dividend, he will receive $39,500 and pay Federal income tax on that amount as an individual taxpayer. In this case, most of Falcon's $50,000 income has been subjected to Federal income tax twice.

1-3c **Partnerships**

A partnership is not a separate taxable entity. The partnership files a tax return (Form 1065) on which it summarizes the financial results of the business. Each partner then reports his or her share of the net income or loss and other special items that were reported on the partnership return. In Chapter 14, we discuss in more detail the tax requirements that apply to partnerships and similar entities.

Cameron and Connor form a partnership in which they are equal partners. The partnership reports a $100,000 net profit on its tax return, but is not subject to the Federal income tax. Cameron and Connor each report $50,000 net income from the partnership on their separate individual income tax returns.

1-3d **S Corporations**

Corporations that meet certain requirements and pay no tax at the corporate level are referred to as **S corporations**, because they are governed by Subchapter S of the Code. S corporations are discussed in detail in Chapter 15.

An S corporation is treated like a C corporation for all nontax purposes. Shareholders have limited liability, shares are freely transferable, the entity uses centralized management (vested in the board of directors), and there can be an unlimited continuity of life (i.e., the corporation continues to exist after the withdrawal or death of a shareholder).

With regard to tax factors, however, an S corporation is more like a partnership. The S corporation is not subject to the Federal *income tax*. Like a partnership, it does file a tax return (Form 1120S), but the shareholders report their share of net income or loss and other special items on their own tax returns.

Kay and Dawn form a corporation and elect to treat it as an S corporation. Kay owns 60% of the stock of the corporation, and Dawn owns 40%. The S corporation reports a $100,000 net profit on its tax return, but is not subject to the income tax. Kay reports $60,000 net income from the S corporation on her individual income tax return, and Dawn reports $40,000 on her tax return.

1-3e **Limited Liability Companies and Limited Liability Partnerships**

Limited liability companies (LLCs) and limited liability partnerships (LLPs) offer limited liability and some (but not all) of the other nontax features of corporations. Both forms usually are treated as partnerships for tax purposes.

The S corporation, limited liability company, and partnership forms of organization, which are referred to as *flow-through* entities, avoid the double taxation problem associated with the C corporation.

FINANCIAL DISCLOSURE INSIGHTS Book-Tax Differences

"Income" is defined differently for Federal income tax and financial accounting purposes. Financial accounting income (FAI) is designed to indicate the profitability of the business entity for the reporting period, in a fair and understandable way, to shareholders, creditors, and other parties who are interested in the results. Taxable income is a device used by Congress to raise revenue; stimulate or stabilize the economy; and accomplish other economic, social, and political goals in an equitable manner. In general, FAI recognizes *revenue* and *expenses*, while taxable income includes *gross income* and *deductions*.

The taxable income of a business taxpayer is not identical to FAI to the extent that *temporary* and *permanent* book-tax differences exist. Broadly, book-tax differences result when:

- Tax benefits are accelerated or deferred relative to their recognition for book purposes, for example, when cost recovery deductions are claimed earlier than depreciation expenses are allowed.

- Tax benefits are not recognized at all for book purposes (e.g., there is no book expense item corresponding to the domestic production activities deduction).

As a result of temporary book-tax differences, income tax payable (the amount due on the tax return, referred to by many tax professionals as the "cash tax") differs from the income tax expense on the book income statement. The income statement reflects the full income tax burden for the FAI of the reporting period, under the GAAP matching principle, but it is broken into the components *current income tax expense* and *deferred income tax expense*.

When a tax benefit is delayed for book purposes, such as for accelerated cost recovery deductions, a **deferred tax liability** is created on the entity's balance sheet. Taxable income will be greater than FAI in a subsequent year.

When a tax benefit is delayed for tax purposes, such as when a bad debt allowance is used for accounts receivable but is not permissible on the tax return, a **deferred tax asset** is created on the balance sheet. Taxable income will be less than FAI in a subsequent year.

Permanent book-tax differences, such as the exclusion for interest income from a state bond, do not affect the balance sheet. But because FAI and taxable income differ in this amount, the **effective tax rate** of the taxpayer is higher or lower than might be expected. The financial statement footnotes reconcile the statutory and effective tax rates of the entity, in dollar and/or percentage amounts.

The balance sheet accounts for deferred taxes can be sizable. For instance, in most years, Citigroup's deferred tax assets make up about one-third of its tangible equity capital.

1-3f Dealings between Individuals and Their Business Entities

Many of the provisions in the tax law deal with the relationships between owners and the business entities they own. The following are some of the major interactions between owners and business entities.

- Owners put assets into a business when they establish a business entity (e.g., a proprietorship, partnership, or corporation).
- Owners take assets out of the business during its existence in the form of salary, dividends, withdrawals, redemptions of stock, etc.
- Through their entities, owner-employees set up retirement plans for themselves, including IRAs and qualified retirement and pension plans.
- Owners dispose of all or part of a business entity.

Every major transaction that occurs between an owner and a business entity has important tax ramifications. The following are a few of the many tax issues that arise.

- How the tax law applies at both the owner level and the entity level (i.e., the multiple taxation problem), and what effective tax rate is assessed on such income.
- How to move assets into the business with the least adverse tax consequences.
- How to pull accumulated profits and assets out of the business with the least adverse tax consequences.
- How to dispose of the business entity with the least adverse tax consequences.

DIGGING DEEPER **5**   **In-depth coverage can be found on this book's companion website: www.cengage.com**

1-4 TAX PLANNING FUNDAMENTALS

1-4a Overview of Tax Planning and Ethics

Taxpayers generally attempt to minimize their tax liabilities, and it is perfectly acceptable to do so using legal means. It is a long-standing principle that taxpayers have no obligation to pay more than their fair share of taxes. The now-classic words of Judge Learned Hand in *Commissioner v. Newman* reflect the true values a taxpayer should have.

> Over and over again courts have said that there is nothing sinister in so arranging one's affairs as to keep taxes as low as possible. Everybody does so, rich or poor; and all do right, for nobody owes any public duty to pay more than the law demands; taxes are enforced exactions, not voluntary contributions. To demand more in the name of morals is mere cant.[9]

Tax Planning: Avoidance Versus Evasion

Minimizing taxes legally is referred to as **tax avoidance**. On the other hand, some taxpayers attempt to *evade* income taxes through illegal actions. There is a major distinction between tax avoidance and **tax evasion**. Although eliminating or reducing taxes is also a goal of tax evasion, the term *evasion* implies the use of subterfuge and fraud as a means to this end. Tax avoidance is legal, while tax evasion subjects the taxpayer to numerous civil and criminal penalties, including prison sentences.

Clients expect tax professionals to provide advice to help them minimize their tax costs. This part of the tax practitioner's practice is referred to as *tax planning*. To structure a sound tax plan, a practitioner first must have a thorough knowledge of the tax law. Tax planning skill is based on knowledge of tax saving provisions in the tax law, as well as provisions that contain costly pitfalls for the unwary.

Thorough study of the remainder of this text will provide a solid base of the knowledge required to recognize opportunities and avoid pitfalls. Tax planning requires the practitioner to have in mind both a framework for planning and an understanding of the tax planning implications of a client's situation.

The Ethics of Tax Planning

Tax planning (avoidance) is a fully ethical activity by the taxpayer and the tax professional, but tax evasion (fraud) is not. The tax adviser's actions are limited by the codes of conduct of various professional organizations, such as the American Institute of CPAs or the pertinent state bar association.

Other formal restrictions and directives concerning the conduct of the tax professional can be found in two broad forms.

- Penalties and interest may apply to the taxpayer when a tax liability is understated. Examples include penalties for filing a tax return after its due date, understating gross income amounts, and underpaying withholding or estimated taxes that are due.

- Sanctions are used for tax preparers who disregard the tax law. The Treasury issues a regulation known as *Circular 230* to provide guidance to tax return preparers. Tax penalties also apply when the tax preparer fails to sign a tax return that he or she has worked on or takes an improper filing position on a tax return.

 DIGGING DEEPER **6**   **In-depth coverage can be found on this book's companion website: www.cengage.com**

---

[9]47–1 USTC ¶9175, 35 AFTR 857, 159 F.2d 848 (CA–2, 1947).

1-4b A General Framework for Income Tax Planning

★ **Tax Planning Framework**

The primary goal of tax planning is to design a transaction so as to minimize its tax costs, while meeting the other nontax objectives of the client. Generally, this means that the client attempts to maximize the present value of its after-tax income and assets. Selecting a specific form of transaction solely for the sake of tax minimization often leads to a poor business decision. Effective tax planning requires careful consideration of the nontax issues involved in addition to the tax consequences.

Careful analysis of the tax formula (refer to Exhibit 1.1) reveals a series of tax minimization strategies. Through creative tax planning that also takes into consideration a client's nontax concerns, each component of the tax formula can be managed in a way that will help to minimize the client's tax liability. The General Framework for Income Tax Planning in Exhibit 1.3 lists each element in the income tax formula, develops tax planning strategies designed to minimize taxes, and provides brief summaries of specific examples of tax planning. The framework is followed by a discussion of the tax planning strategies, along with detailed examples of how the strategies can be applied. In Chapters 4 through 18 of this book, these strategies and their tax formula components provide the framework for Tax Planning Strategies features.

EXHIBIT 1.3	General Framework for Income Tax Planning	
Tax Formula	**Tax Planning Strategy**	**Tax Planning Examples**
Income and exclusions	➤ **Avoid income recognition.**	Compensate employees with nontaxable fringe benefits (see Example 19).
	➤ **Postpone recognition of income to achieve tax deferral.**	Postpone sale of assets (see Example 20).
− Deductions	➤ **Maximize deductible amounts.**	Invest in stock of another corporation (see Example 21).
	➤ **Accelerate recognition of deductions to achieve tax deferral.**	Elect to deduct charitable contribution in year of pledge rather than in year of payment (see Example 22).
= Taxable income		
× Tax rate	➤ **Shift net income from high-bracket years to low-bracket years.**	Postpone recognition of income to a low-bracket year (see Example 23).
		Postpone recognition of deductions to a high-bracket year (see Example 24).
	➤ **Shift net income from high-bracket taxpayers to low-bracket taxpayers.**	Pay children to work in the family business (see Example 25).
	➤ **Shift net income from high-tax jurisdictions to low-tax jurisdictions.**	Establish subsidiary operations in countries with low tax rates (see Examples 26 and 27).
	➤ **Control the character of income and deductions.**	Hold assets long enough to qualify for long-term capital gain rates before selling them (see Example 28).
	➤ **Avoid double taxation.**	Operate as a flow-through entity rather than a C corporation (see Example 29).
		Maximize deductible expenses paid by a C corporation to a shareholder/employee (see Example 30).
= Federal income tax		
− Tax credits	➤ **Maximize tax credits.**	Make structural changes to a building where the expenditures qualify for the rehabilitation tax credit (see Example 31).
= Tax owed (or refund)		

1-4c Tax Minimization Strategies Related to Income

★ **Framework Focus: Income**

➤ ***Tax Planning Strategy***

➤ ***Avoid Income Recognition.*** Section 61(a) of the Internal Revenue Code, the major source of statutory Federal income tax law, defines gross income as "all income from whatever source derived." However, the Code contains provisions that allow various types of income to be excluded from the tax base. Numerous exclusions are available for individuals, but very few are available for corporations. However, a corporation can provide excludible income for its owners at no tax cost to the corporation.

The average employee of Penguin Corporation is a 25% bracket taxpayer, considering Federal, state, and local income taxes. In negotiations with the employees' union, Penguin proposes that it will increase the amount it spends on nontaxable fringe benefits by an average of $3,000 per employee in lieu of granting a $3,000 average salary increase. The average employee will be better off by $750 if the union accepts Penguin's offer.

	Salary Increase	Fringe Benefit Increase
Value of compensation received	$3,000	$3,000
Tax on employee's compensation	(750)	(–0–)
After-tax increase in compensation	$2,250	$3,000

Although the average employee receives a $750 benefit, there is no tax cost to Penguin because both fringe benefits and salaries are deductible by the corporation.

➤ **Tax Planning Strategy**

➤ *Postpone Recognition of Income to Achieve Tax Deferral.* The tax law requires that both income and expenses be reported in the proper tax year. If not for this requirement, taxpayers could freely shift income and expenses from year to year to take advantage of tax rate differentials, or they could defer tax liabilities indefinitely, thereby achieving a time value of money advantage. Although various rules limit the shifting of income and deductions across time periods, some opportunities still exist.

In 2010, Turquoise Corporation acquired land for investment purposes at a cost of $500,000. In November 2018, Turquoise is negotiating to sell the land to Aqua Corporation for $800,000. Aqua insists that the transaction be completed in 2018, but Turquoise wants to delay the sale until 2019 to defer the tax on the gain. In an effort to compromise, Turquoise agrees to sell the land in November 2018 and asks Aqua to pay for the land in two installments, $400,000 in December 2018 and $400,000 in January 2019. This enables Turquoise to use the installment method for recognizing the gain, under which Turquoise will report $150,000 of the gain in 2018 and the remaining $150,000 in 2019.

By electing the installment method, Turquoise defers the payment of tax on $150,000 of the gain for one year. If the marginal tax rate for Turquoise is 21%, this tax deferral strategy provides $31,500 ($150,000 × 21%) to be invested or used in the business for another year.

★ **Framework Focus: Deductions**

1-4d Tax Minimization Strategies Related to Deductions

➤ **Tax Planning Strategy**

➤ *Maximize Deductible Amounts.* A corporation that owns stock in another corporation is eligible for a *dividends received deduction (DRD)*. The DRD is equal to a specified percentage of the dividends received. The percentage is based on the amount of stock that the investor corporation owns in the investee corporation.

- 50 percent deduction for ownership of less than 20 percent.
- 65 percent deduction for ownership of 20 percent or more but less than 80 percent.
- 100 percent deduction for ownership of 80 percent or more.

Falcon Corporation invests in bonds of Sparrow Corporation and receives interest of $20,000. Red Hawk Corporation acquires 15% of the stock of Pheasant Corporation and receives a $20,000 dividend.

Falcon's taxable income is increased by $20,000 for the interest received. Red Hawk's income is increased by $20,000 in dividend income, but it is allowed a $10,000 dividends received deduction, thus increasing taxable income by only $10,000 for that type of income.

Example 21 demonstrates the *tax* advantage of dividend income versus interest income. However, it is also important to consider *nontax* factors. Is the investment in bonds safer than the investment in stock? Does the potential growth in the value of stock outweigh the possible risk of investing in stock versus bonds?

➤ *Accelerate Recognition of Deductions to Achieve Tax Deferral.* Both corporate and noncorporate taxpayers may deduct charitable contributions if the recipient is a qualified charitable organization. Generally, a deduction is allowed only for the year in which the payment is made. However, an important exception is available for *accrual basis corporations*. They may claim the deduction in the year *preceding* payment if two requirements are met. First, the contribution must be authorized by the board of directors by the end of that year. Second, the contribution must be paid on or before the fifteenth day of the third month of the next year.

➤ *Tax Planning Strategy*

EXAMPLE 22

Blue, Inc., a calendar year, accrual basis corporation, wants to make a $10,000 donation to the Atlanta Symphony Association (a qualified charitable organization), but does not have adequate funds to make the contribution in 2018. On December 28, 2018, Blue's board of directors *authorizes* a $10,000 contribution to the Association. The donation is made on March 14, 2019. Because Blue is an accrual basis corporation, it may claim the $10,000 donation as a deduction for tax year 2018, even though payment is not made until 2019.

Blue was able to take advantage of a tax provision and reduce 2018 taxable income by $10,000. Blue is in the 21% marginal bracket, so the corporation defers payment of $2,100 in Federal income tax. The $2,100 can be invested or used in the business for another tax year.

1-4e Tax Minimization Strategies Related to Tax Rates

➤ *Shift Net Income from High-Bracket Years to Low-Bracket Years.* One objective of shifting income is to defer the payment of income tax (refer to Example 20). A second time-shifting strategy is to shift *net* income from high-tax to low-tax years. This can be accomplished by shifting income from high-bracket years to low-bracket years and by shifting deductions from low-bracket years to high-bracket years.

★ **Framework Focus: Tax Rates**

➤ *Tax Planning Strategy*

Shift Income to Low-Bracket Years

EXAMPLE 23

Allie Singh, a calendar year taxpayer, is in the 35% bracket in 2018, but expects to be in the 24% bracket in 2019. Singh is negotiating a $10,000 service contract with a client, and she decides to wait until 2019 to sign the contract and perform the services. The client is indifferent as to when the contract is completed. Thus, Singh saves $1,100 in income tax by deferring the service contract income to 2019, when she will be taxed at the lower Federal income tax rate.

In this case, the income-shifting strategy is used to accomplish two tax planning objectives. First, shifting the income defers the payment of income tax from 2018 to 2019. Second, the shifting strategy results in the income being taxed at a rate of 24% rather than 35%.

EXAMPLE 24

Kim, a single individual, has been sued for $125,000 damages by a customer, and the parties decided to settle out of court for $100,000. Kim expects to be in the 24% bracket in 2018 and the 35% bracket in 2019. Kim will save $11,000 in income tax if he finalizes the agreement in January 2019 rather than December 2018 [$100,000 × (35% − 24%)].

➤ *Shift Net Income from High-Bracket Taxpayers to Low-Bracket Taxpayers.* Individual income tax rates range from 10 percent to 37 percent (before considering the additional Medicare taxes on certain high-income individuals). Although several provisions in the tax law prevent shifting income from high-bracket taxpayers to low-bracket taxpayers, many opportunities to do so remain. Business entities can be effective vehicles for shifting income to low-bracket taxpayers.

➤ *Tax Planning Strategy*

Bill Gregory is the president and sole shareholder of Grayhawk, Inc., an S corporation. He projects that Grayhawk will earn $400,000 this year. Bill is taxed on this income at a 35% marginal rate. Bill and his wife have four teenage children. The Gregorys record no other taxable income; they file a joint return.

Bill employs the children as part-time workers throughout the year and pays them $11,000 each. This reduces Bill's income from Grayhawk by $44,000 and reduces his Federal income tax by $15,400 ($44,000 × 35%).

The salaries paid to the children will be subject to their lower Federal income tax rates. The salaries also might be exempt from the FICA and other payroll taxes, so the family unit's total tax liability has been reduced by shifting taxable income to the children.

➤ *Tax Planning Strategy*

➤ ***Shift Net Income from High-Tax Jurisdictions to Low-Tax Jurisdictions.*** A choice of the state or country where income is earned (or where a deduction is incurred) can have a large effect on an entity's overall tax liability. Hence, shifting income from high-tax jurisdictions to low-tax jurisdictions or shifting deductions from low-tax jurisdictions to high-tax jurisdictions is an important tax planning strategy.

Shifting Tax Jurisdictions

Patti moves from Utah to Texas, to be closer to the clients she services in her data analysis sole proprietorship. Marginal income tax rates for Patti are 5% in Utah and zero in Texas. Her business generates a $100,000 profit this year, so Patti's state income tax liability is reduced from $5,000 to zero.

Stefano operates his health care management sole proprietorship in several U.S. states. His $50,000 deduction for office supplies is worth $2,875 more to him if it is incurred in North Carolina, where his marginal income tax rate is 5.75%, than it is in Florida, where the tax rate is zero.

➤ *Tax Planning Strategy*

➤ ***Control the Character of Income and Deductions.*** For various policy reasons, Congress has chosen to treat certain categories of income and losses more favorably than others. For instance, the provisions that apply to most individuals and tax long-term capital gains at a maximum rate of 20 percent, compared with a top 37 percent rate on ordinary income, were enacted to encourage individuals to make long-term investments of capital in the economy.

Lisa is the proprietor of Designer Enterprises. Because a proprietorship is a flow-through entity, Lisa reports all of Designer's transactions on her individual income tax return. On October 9, 2018, Lisa invested $25,000 of Designer's excess cash in Lavender Corporation stock. On October 1, 2019, the stock was worth $35,000.

Lisa's marginal tax rate is 34% for ordinary income and 15% for long-term capital gain. She has decided to sell the stock and use the cash to increase Designer's inventory. She must hold the stock until October 10, 2019, for the gain to qualify as long term (held more than a year). If Lisa sells the stock before October 10, 2019, the gain is taxed as short term and she pays 34% tax on the gain. If she sells the stock after October 9, 2019, the gain is long term and she will pay 15% tax on the gain.

➤ *Tax Planning Strategy*

➤ ***Avoid Double Taxation.*** The owners of a corporation can choose between two entity forms. A C corporation is a taxable entity that pays tax on corporate profits. Shareholders also pay tax on dividends received from a C corporation, resulting in what is commonly referred to as *double taxation* (refer to Example 16). Note, however, as discussed in Chapter 4, that the dividends may be eligible for a beneficial tax rate.

TAX FACT **The U.S. Federal Income Tax**

The Federal income tax is pervasive throughout our lives, but how much do we know about where it came from and how it works?

- The current version of the Internal Revenue Code has surpassed its 100th birthday; it was first effective on March 1, 1913.

- A temporary Federal income tax was used to finance the Civil War and the Spanish-American War. The current Federal tax code was adopted after Britain, Germany, France, and other countries in Europe had adopted similar taxing systems.

- The first Form 1040 was four pages long.

- The tax return became Form 1040 because that was the next number sequentially in issued Federal forms.

- The first Form 1040 was due on March 1, 1914. The unextended due date became March 15 for calendar year 1918 returns and April 15 for calendar year 1954 returns.

- Taxes largely are paid today using a withholding system, a creation made necessary to pay for World War II. But at first, no money was sent with the return. A field auditor checked every return and sent a bill to the taxpayer by June 1, payable by June 30.

- A majority of taxpayers at every income level today engage paid tax professionals for assistance in preparing Federal income tax returns.

- More than 85 percent of all Forms 1040 are filed electronically. About 70 percent of Forms 1040 show a refund due to the taxpayer; the average annual refund is about $3,100.

Shareholders can avoid double taxation by electing that a corporate entity become an S corporation. Unlike a C corporation, an S corporation is not a taxable entity. Instead, the profits and losses of the S corporation flow through to the shareholders and are reported on their tax returns (see Chapter 15).

EXAMPLE 29

Chickadee, Inc., a C corporation with net income of $100,000, pays Carl, its sole shareholder, a $79,000 dividend. Chickadee must pay corporate income tax of $21,000 on the net income of $100,000, and Carl must pay Federal income tax on the $79,000 dividend. Sparrow, Inc., an S corporation, also earns $100,000. Sparrow is not a taxable entity, so it pays no income tax on the $100,000 net income. Sam, who is the sole shareholder of Sparrow, includes $100,000 from the S corporation in computing his taxable income.

Other entity choices can be used to avoid double taxation, including partnerships and limited liability companies. Partnerships and limited liability companies, like S corporations, are flow-through entities rather than taxable entities (see Chapter 14).

Choosing to operate as a **flow-through entity** is not the only way to avoid double taxation. Double taxation can be avoided or minimized by having the corporation make tax-deductible payments, such as salaries, rent, and interest to the shareholders.

EXAMPLE 30

Walt is the president and sole shareholder of Meadowlark, Inc., a C corporation. Meadowlark's taxable income before any payment to Walt is $600,000. Walt, a skilled manager, is primarily responsible for the profitability of the corporation. If Meadowlark pays Walt a dividend of $400,000, the corporation must pay Federal income tax on $600,000 and Walt must include the $400,000 dividend in gross income. However, if Meadowlark pays Walt a salary of $400,000, the salary is deductible and the corporation has only $200,000 of taxable income. Walt must include the $400,000 salary in gross income.

In either case, Walt includes $400,000 in gross income (the dividends may be eligible for a beneficial tax rate). Meadowlark, on the other hand, reports $400,000 less taxable income if the payment to Walt is a salary payment rather than a dividend payment.

In considering this plan, Meadowlark should examine the effects of employment taxes on Walt and the corporation as well.

1-4f **Tax Minimization Strategies Related to Credits**

➤ *Maximize Tax Credits.* Congress uses the tax credit provisions of the Internal Revenue Code liberally in implementing tax policy. It is important to understand the difference between a credit and a deduction, both of which reduce a taxpayer's tax liability. A deduction reduces taxable income, which results in a reduction of the tax paid. The tax benefit of the deduction depends on the amount of the qualifying expenditure and the taxpayer's tax rate. A tax credit reduces the tax liability dollar for dollar and is not affected by the taxpayer's tax rate.

EXAMPLE

31

Oriole Corporation, which is in the 21% marginal Federal income tax bracket, has a $6,000 deduction for expenditures made to repair a machine. The deduction reduces taxable income by $6,000 and results in a tax liability reduction of $1,260 ($6,000 deduction × 21% marginal rate).

Oriole also incurred expenditures of $6,000 to rehabilitate a building, which qualifies the corporation for a tax credit of $600 ($6,000 rehabilitation expenditures × 10% rate for the credit). The rehabilitation expenditures credit results in a $600 reduction of Oriole's tax liability.

The tax benefit related to the $6,000 expenditure affects Oriole's tax liability in different ways, depending on whether the expenditure is treated as a deduction or a credit.

LO.6

Explain the economic, social, equity, and political considerations that underlie the tax law.

1-5 UNDERSTANDING THE FEDERAL TAX LAW

The Federal tax law reflects the three branches of our Federal government. It is a mixture of laws passed by Congress, explanations provided by the Treasury Department and the Internal Revenue Service (IRS), and court decisions. For the person who analyzes this information to find the solution to a tax problem, it is good to know that there are reasons behind the law. Recognizing the "whys" of the various rules is the first step toward understanding the Federal tax law.

1-5a **Revenue Needs**

Raising revenues to fund the cost of government operations is the key factor in structuring a tax system. In a perfect world, taxes raised by the government would equal the expenses incurred by government operations. However, this goal has not been achieved at the Federal level. Many states have achieved this objective by passing laws or constitutional amendments precluding deficit spending.

The U.S. Constitution allows deficit spending, and politicians often find it hard to resist the temptation to spend more than the tax system collects currently. Congress uses several approaches to reduce a tax bill's net revenue loss. When tax reductions are involved, the full effect of the legislation can be phased in over a period of years. As an alternative, the tax reduction can be limited to a specified time period. When that period expires, Congress can then renew, modify, or repeal the provision in light of budget considerations.

1-5b **Economic Considerations**

Using the tax system in an effort to accomplish economic objectives has become increasingly popular in recent years. Generally, proponents of this approach use tax legislation to promote measures designed to help control the economy or encourage certain economic activities and businesses.

Encouragement of Certain Activities

Congress often uses the tax law to encourage certain types of economic activity or segments of the economy. For example, the favorable treatment allowed research and development expenditures (immediate deduction vs. capitalization and amortization) can be explained by the desire to foster technological progress. Further, given the time value of money, the tax savings from a current deduction may be preferable to capitalizing the cost with a write-off over the estimated useful life of the asset created.

Similarly, Congress has used the tax depreciation rules as a means of encouraging investment in business capital. Theoretically, shorter asset lives and accelerated methods should encourage additional investment in depreciable property acquired for business use, by speeding up the tax benefits related to the property acquisitions. Conversely, longer asset lives and the required use of the straight-line method of depreciation dampen the tax incentive for capital outlays.

Ecological considerations justify a tax provision that permits a more rapid expensing of the costs of installing pollution control facilities. This provision may aid in maintaining a clean air environment and conserving energy resources; thus, such a tax break also can be justified under social considerations.

Is it wise to stimulate U.S. exports of goods and services? Considering the pressing and continuing problem of a deficit in the U.S. balance of payments, Congress has established incentives for U.S. citizens who accept employment overseas, and for business entities that operate in countries outside the United States.

Is saving desirable for the economy? Saving can lead to capital formation, making funds available to finance home construction and industrial expansion. The tax law encourages saving by according preferential treatment to private retirement plans. Not only are deductions allowed for contributions to certain retirement plans and Individual Retirement Accounts (IRAs), but income on the contributions might not be taxed until withdrawn.

Encouragement of Certain Industries

A sound agricultural base is necessary for a well-balanced national economy. Undoubtedly, this explains why farmers are accorded special treatment under the Federal income tax system. Among the benefits available to farmers are the election to expense rather than capitalize certain soil and water conservation expenditures and fertilizers and the election to defer the recognition of gain on the receipt of crop insurance proceeds.

To stimulate research and production of alternative fuel sources, tax incentives are allowed with respect to operations and sales of solar and wind energy devices, and of autos that do not consume petroleum products.

Encouragement of Small Business

A consensus exists in the United States that what is good for small business is good for the economy as a whole. This belief has led to special provisions in the tax law that favor small business. Several income tax provisions can be explained by the desire to benefit small business, including cost recovery computations that are phased out for larger business entities.

GLOBAL TAX ISSUES **Outsourcing of Tax Return Preparation**

The use of foreign nationals to carry out certain job assignments for U.S. businesses is an increasingly popular practice. Outsourcing such activities as telemarketing to India, for example, usually produces the same satisfactory result but at a much lower cost.

Now outsourcing also is being applied to the preparation of tax returns. Not only can this practice be expected to continue, but it probably will increase in volume. Outsourcing tax return preparation does not violate Federal law, and the practice is compatible with accounting ethical guidelines as long as three safeguards are followed: First, the practitioner must make sure that client confidentiality is maintained. Second, the practitioner must verify the accuracy of the work that has been outsourced. Third, the practitioner must gain the consent of clients when any offshore third-party contractor is used to provide professional services.

Tax professionals justify tax preparation outsourcing as a means of conserving time and effort that can be applied toward more meaningful tax planning on behalf of their clients.

Sources: Reg. § 301.7216–2(c)(2); AICPA Ethics Interpretation 1.700.040.

1-5c **Social Considerations**

Some provisions of the Federal tax law, particularly those dealing with individuals, can be explained by a desire to encourage certain social results.

- Certain benefits provided to employees through accident and health insurance plans financed by employers are nontaxable to employees. It is socially desirable to encourage these plans because they provide medical benefits in the event of an employee's illness or injury.

- A contribution made by an employer to a qualified pension or profit sharing plan for an employee may receive special treatment. The contribution and any income it generates are not taxed to the employee until the funds are distributed. This arrangement also benefits the employer by allowing a tax deduction for its contribution to the qualified plan. Various types of retirement plans are encouraged to supplement the subsistence income level the employee otherwise would obtain under the Social Security system.

- A deduction is allowed for contributions to qualified charities. The deduction shifts some of the financial and administrative burden of socially desirable programs from the public (government) to the private (citizens) sector.

- Various tax incentives are designed to encourage taxpayers to obtain or extend their level of education.

- A tax credit is allowed for amounts spent to furnish care for certain minor or disabled dependents to enable the taxpayer to seek or maintain gainful employment.

- A tax deduction is denied for certain expenditures deemed to be contrary to public policy. Deductions are not allowed for fines, penalties, illegal kickbacks, bribes to government officials, and gambling losses in excess of gains. Social considerations dictate that the tax law should not encourage these activities by permitting a deduction.

1-5d **Equity Considerations**

The concept of equity is relative. Reasonable persons can, and often do, disagree about what is fair or unfair. In the tax area, moreover, equity is most often tied to a particular taxpayer's personal situation. To illustrate, compare the tax positions of those who rent their personal residences with those who own their homes. Renters may not take a Federal income tax deduction for the rent they pay. For some homeowners, however, a large portion of the house payments they make may qualify for the Federal mortgage interest and property tax deductions. Although renters may have difficulty understanding this difference in tax treatment, the encouragement of home ownership can be justified on both economic and social grounds. In many other parts of the law, however, equity concerns are evident.

The Wherewithal to Pay Concept

The **wherewithal to pay** concept recognizes the inequity of taxing a transaction when the taxpayer lacks the means (i.e., funds) to pay the tax when an otherwise taxable transaction has been completed. The wherewithal to pay concept underlies a provision in the tax law dealing with the treatment of gain resulting from an involuntary conversion. An involuntary conversion occurs when property is destroyed by casualty or taken by a public authority through condemnation. If gain results from the conversion, it need not be recognized immediately if the taxpayer replaces the property within a specified time period.

Ron, a rancher, owns some pasture land that is condemned by the state for use as a game preserve. The condemned pasture land cost Ron $120,000, but the state pays him $150,000 (its fair market value). Shortly thereafter, Ron buys more pasture land for $150,000.

Ron has a realized gain of $30,000 [$150,000 (condemnation award) − $120,000 (cost of land)]. It would be inequitable to require Ron to pay a tax on this gain: without selling the new land, Ron would find it difficult to pay the tax (Ron used the condemnation proceeds to purchase more land).

What if Ron reinvests only $140,000 of the award in new pasture land? Now Ron recognizes a $10,000 taxable gain in the current year. Instead of ending up with only replacement property, Ron now holds the new land and $10,000 in cash.

Mitigating the Effect of the Annual Accounting Period Concept

Federal income tax returns are due for every tax year of the taxpayer. The application of this annual accounting period concept can lead to dissimilar tax treatment for taxpayers who are, from a long-range standpoint, in the same economic position.

José and Alicia, both unmarried sole proprietors, experienced the following results during the indicated tax years.

| | Profit (or Loss) | |
Year	José	Alicia
2017	$50,000	$170,000
2018	60,000	60,000
2019	80,000	(40,000)

Although José and Alicia have the same total profit of $190,000 over the three-year period, the annual accounting period concept places Alicia at a disadvantage for tax purposes, both in terms of the time value of money and due to the higher tax rates that will apply to Alicia under the progressive rate structure.

However, the net operating loss deduction generated in 2019 offers Alicia some relief. She can "carry forward" the loss and use it to offset profits in a future tax year. Taxable income cannot be less than zero in a tax year, so the loss is of no immediate use to Alicia.

1-5e **Political Considerations**

A large segment of the Federal tax law is made up of statutory provisions. Because these statutes are enacted by Congress, is it any surprise that political considerations influence tax law?

Special Interest Legislation

Certain provisions of the tax law largely can be explained by the political influence some groups have had on Congress. For example, is there any other realistic reason that prepaid subscription and dues income is not taxed until earned, while prepaid rents are taxed to the landlord in the year received?

State and Local Government Influences

State law has had an influence in shaping our present Federal tax law. One example of this effect is the evolution of Federal tax law in response to states with community property systems. The states with community property systems are Arizona, California, Idaho, Louisiana, Nevada, New Mexico, Texas, Washington, and Wisconsin. Spouses in Alaska can elect community property treatment. The rest of the states are common law jurisdictions.

The difference between common law and community property systems centers around the property rights held by married persons. In a common law system, each spouse owns whatever he or she earns. Under a community property system, one-half of the earnings of each spouse is considered owned by the other spouse.

EXAMPLE 34

Al and Fran are married, and their only income is the $80,000 annual salary Al receives. If they live in New Jersey (a common law state), the $80,000 salary belongs to Al.

If, however, they live in Arizona (a community property state), the $80,000 is divided equally, in terms of ownership, between Al and Fran.

At one time, the tax position of the residents of community property states was so advantageous that many common law states adopted community property systems. Political pressure placed on Congress to correct the disparity in tax treatment was considerable.

To a large extent, this was accomplished when Congress changed the law to extend many of the community property tax advantages to residents of common law jurisdictions. The law change allowed married taxpayers to file joint returns and compute the tax liability as if one-half of the income had been earned by each spouse. This result is automatic in a community property state because half of the income earned by one spouse belongs to the other spouse. The income-splitting benefits of a joint return are incorporated as part of the tax rates applicable to married taxpayers. A similar motivation can be seen for the gift-splitting provisions of the Federal gift tax and the marital deduction of the Federal estate and gift taxes.

LO.7

Describe the role played by the IRS and the courts in the evolution of the Federal tax system.

1-5f **Influence of the Internal Revenue Service**

Some tax laws are created to simplify the task of the IRS in collecting the revenue and administering the law. As to collecting revenue, the U.S. Treasury long has realized the importance of placing taxpayers on a pay-as-you-go basis. Elaborate withholding procedures apply to wages, and accrual basis taxpayers often must pay taxes on prepaid income in the year received and not when earned. A tax prepayment is consistent with the wherewithal to pay concept.

One of the keys to an effective administration of our tax system is the audit process conducted by the IRS. To facilitate the audit process, the IRS is aided by provisions that reduce the chance of taxpayer errors. For example, by increasing the standard deduction amount, the audit function is simplified because there are fewer returns claiming itemized deductions. Tax return preparation software similarly is useful in reducing taxpayer filing errors.

DIGGING DEEPER **7**   **In-depth coverage can be found on this book's companion website: www.cengage.com**

1-5g **Influence of the Courts**

In addition to interpreting statutory provisions and the administrative pronouncements issued by the Treasury Department and the IRS, the Federal courts have influenced tax law in two other ways. First, the courts have developed a number of judicial concepts that help guide the application of various tax provisions, going beyond the strict language of the Internal Revenue Code and Treasury Regulations. Second, certain key court decisions have led to changes in the Code and other sources of tax law.

Judicial Concepts Relating to Tax

Particularly in dealings between related parties, the courts test transactions by looking to whether the taxpayers acted in an arm's length manner. The question to be asked is: Would unrelated parties have handled the transaction in the same way?

EXAMPLE 35

Rex, the sole shareholder of Silver Corporation, leases property to the corporation for a yearly rent of $6,000. To test whether the corporation should be allowed a rent deduction for this amount, the IRS and the courts will apply the arm's length concept. Would Silver have paid $6,000 a year in rent if it had leased the same property from an unrelated party (rather than from Rex)?

Suppose it is determined that an unrelated third party would have charged an annual rent for the property of only $5,000. Under these circumstances, Silver can deduct only $5,000. The other $1,000 it paid for the use of the property represents a *nondeductible dividend*. Rex is treated as having received rent income of $5,000 and dividend income of $1,000.

Judicial Influence on Statutory Provisions

Some court decisions have been of such consequence that Congress has incorporated them into statutory tax law. For example, many years ago, the courts found that stock dividends distributed to the shareholders of a corporation were not gross income and therefore were not subject to tax. This result largely was accepted by Congress, and a provision in the tax statutes now addresses the issue.

1-6 SUMMARY

Tax laws are pervasive in today's global economy. Individuals and businesses must contend with complex rules in planning their personal and professional activities. Taxes can fall on income, wealth, asset transfers, consumer expenditures, and other events.

Tax professionals must be facile in various skills, to deliver expected levels of service to clients and the government.

- Knowledge of technical tax law.
- Productive with technology and data analytics.
- Strengths in business acumen and so-called soft skills, like listening and motivation.
- Functional in problem solving and process improvement.
- Valued contributor in project management and cost-benefit analysis.

Tax planning is a means by which to manage the amount and timing of tax liabilities to accomplish one's long-term objectives. The conduct of tax practitioners is regulated by professional associations, lawmakers, and the taxing agencies.

Taxing systems are designed to provide revenues for governments to accomplish the common goals of citizens. In addition to its necessary revenue-raising objective, the Federal tax law has developed in response to several other factors.

- *Economic considerations.* Tax provisions can help to regulate the economy and encourage certain activities and types of businesses.
- *Social considerations.* Some tax provisions are designed to encourage (or discourage) socially desirable (or undesirable) practices.
- *Equity considerations.* Tax provisions can alleviate the effect of multiple taxation, recognize the wherewithal to pay concept, and mitigate the effect of the annual accounting period concept.

- *Political considerations.* Tax provisions can carry out the desires of special interest groups or reflect the effect of state and local law.

- *Influence of the IRS.* Many tax provisions are intended to aid the IRS in the collection of revenue and the administration of the tax law.

- *Influence of the courts.* Court decisions have established a body of judicial concepts relating to tax law and have, on occasion, led Congress to enact statutory provisions to either clarify or negate their effect.

REFOCUS ON THE BIG PICTURE

A TYPICAL TAX YEAR FOR A MODERN FAMILY

CORBIS/SUPERSTOCK

The explanation given for the difference in the ad valorem property taxes—the Carters' increase and the Walkers' decrease—seems reasonable. It is not likely that the Carters' increase was due to a *general* upward assessment in valuation, as the Walkers' taxes on their residence (located nearby) dropped. More business use of the Carters' residence (presuming that Travis conducts his consulting practice from his home) might be responsible for the increase, but capital improvements appear to be a more likely cause.

The imposition of the use tax when Travis registered the new automobile illustrates one of the means by which a state can preclude the avoidance of its sales tax (see Example 4).

When gifts between family members are material in amount (e.g., an RV) and exceed the annual exclusion, a gift tax return needs to be filed. Even though no gift tax may be due because of the availability of the unified transfer tax exclusion ($11.18 million for 2018, as indexed), the filing of a return starts the running of the statute of limitations.

The imposition of the "jock tax" on nonathletes is unusual but not improper. The Carters must recognize that some of their income is subject to income taxes in two states and take advantage of whatever relief is available to mitigate the result.

Significant Federal income tax savings might be available if Travis were to hire the children to work in the consulting practice.

What If?

Because of the double audit (i.e., both state and Federal) and the deficiency assessed, the Carters need to make sure that future returns do not contain similar errors. As the text suggests, taxpayers with prior deficiencies are among those whose returns may be selected for audit.

Suggested Readings

Ellen Cook, Troy Lewis, and Annette Nellen, "Tax Principles for the Digital Age," *Journal of Accountancy*, May 2017.

Jill Lepore, "Tax Time: Why We Pay," *The New Yorker*, November 26, 2012.

Mark Robyn, Micah Cohen, and Joseph Henchman, "Sales Tax Holidays: Politically Expedient but Poor Tax Policy," July 24, 2013 working paper, **www.taxfoundation.org**.

Joseph J. Thorndike, "The Tenacity of Tax Complexity," December 2001 working paper, **www.taxhistory.org**.

Key Terms

Ad valorem taxes, 1-12	Franchise tax, 1-14	Proprietorship, 1-19
C corporations, 1-19	FUTA tax, 1-9	Realty, 1-13
Deferred tax asset, 1-21	Generally Accepted Accounting Principles (GAAP), 1-19	S corporations, 1-20
Deferred tax liability, 1-21		Sales taxes, 1-4
Effective tax rate, 1-21	Gift tax, 1-11	Tax avoidance, 1-22
Employment taxes, 1-5	Inheritance tax, 1-10	Tax evasion, 1-22
Estate tax, 1-10	International Accounting Standards Board (IASB), 1-19	Use taxes, 1-8
Excise taxes, 1-6		Value added tax (VAT), 1-8
FICA tax, 1-9	International Financial Reporting Standards (IFRS), 1-19	Wherewithal to pay, 1-30
Financial Accounting Standards Board (FASB), 1-19	Occupational taxes, 1-15	
Flow-through entity, 1-27	Personalty, 1-13	

Problems

1. **LO.1, 2, 5** James Corporation believes that it will have a better distribution location for its product if it relocates the corporation to another state. What considerations (both tax and nontax) should James weigh before making a decision on whether to make the move?   *Critical Thinking*

2. **LO.1** Distinguish between taxes that are *proportional* and those that are *progressive*.

3. **LO.2** Several years ago, Ethan purchased the former parsonage of St. James Church to use as a personal residence. To date, Ethan has not received any ad valorem property tax bills from either the city or the county tax authorities.   *Critical Thinking*
   a.   What is a reasonable explanation for this oversight?
   b.   What should Ethan do?

4. **LO.1, 6** In terms of Adam Smith's canon of *economy in collection*, how does the Federal income tax fare?   *Digging Deeper*

5. **LO.2** Jang, a resident of Washington (which imposes a general sales tax), goes to Oregon (which does not impose a general sales tax) to purchase his automobile. Will Jang successfully avoid the Washington sales tax? Explain.   *Critical Thinking*

6. **LO.2** The Irontown Independent School District wants to sell a parcel of unimproved land that it does not need. Its three best offers are as follows: from the State Department of Public Safety (DPS), $4.3 million; from Trinity Lutheran Church, $4.2 million; and from Baker Motors, $3.9 million. DPS would use the property for a new state highway patrol barracks, Trinity would start a church school, and Baker would open a car dealership. As the financial adviser for the school district, which offer would you prefer? Why?   *Critical Thinking*

7. **LO.2** Discuss the application of a general sales tax.
   a.   Do all states impose a general sales tax?
   b.   Does the Federal government impose a general sales tax?

8. **LO.2** Sophia lives several blocks from her parents in the same residential subdivision. Sophia is surprised to learn that her ad valorem property taxes for the year were raised, while those of her parents were lowered. What is a possible explanation for the difference?   *Critical Thinking*

Decision Making
Communications

9. **LO.4, 5** Marco and Cynthia have decided to go into business together. They will operate a burrito delivery business. They expect to generate a loss in the first and second years of the business and then to make a substantial profit.

Marco and Cynthia are concerned about potential liability if a customer ever gets sick after eating one of their products. They have called your office and asked for advice about whether they should run their business as a partnership or as a corporation. Write a letter to Cynthia Clay, at 1206 Seventh Avenue, Fort Worth, TX 76101, describing the alternative forms of business they can select. In your letter, explain what form or forms of business you recommend and why.

Decision Making

10. **LO.4, 5** Ashley runs a small business in Boulder, Colorado, that makes snow skis. She expects the business to grow substantially over the next three years. Because she is concerned about product liability and is planning to take the company public in year 2, she currently is considering incorporating the business. Pertinent financial data are as follows.

	Year 1	Year 2	Year 3
Sales revenue	$150,000	$320,000	$600,000
Tax-free interest income	5,000	8,000	15,000
Deductible cash expenses	30,000	58,000	95,000
Tax depreciation	25,000	20,000	40,000

Ashley expects her combined Federal and state marginal income tax rate to be 25% over the three years before any profits from the business are considered. Her after-tax cost of capital is 12%.

a. Considering only these data, construct a spreadsheet to compute the present value of the future cash flows for the three-year period, assuming that Ashley incorporates the business and pays all after-tax income as dividends (for Ashley's dividends that qualify for the 15% rate).

b. Considering only these data, compute the present value of the future cash flows for the period, assuming that Ashley continues to operate the business as a sole proprietorship.

c. Should Ashley incorporate the business in year 1? Why or why not?

Digging Deeper
Communications

11. **LO.1** A disproportionate amount of the Federal income tax is paid by individuals at upper income levels. Is this a desirable condition? Defend your position in no more than three PowerPoint slides, to be presented to your Business Economics classmates.

Critical Thinking

12. **LO.2** Franklin County is in dire financial straits and is considering a number of sources for additional revenue. Evaluate the following possibilities in terms of anticipated taxpayer compliance.

a. A property tax on business inventories.

b. A tax on intangibles (i.e., stocks and bonds) held as investments.

c. A property tax on boats used for recreational purposes.

13. **LO.6** Discuss the probable non-revenue justifications for each of the following provisions of the tax law.

a. A tax credit allowed for electricity produced from renewable sources.

b. A tax credit allowed for the purchase of a motor vehicle that operates on alternative energy sources (e.g., nonfossil fuels).

c. Favorable treatment accorded to research and development expenditures.

d. The deduction allowed for contributions to qualified charitable organizations.

e. An election that allows certain corporations to avoid the corporate income tax and pass losses through to their shareholders.

14. **LO.6** Discuss the probable non-revenue justifications for each of the following aspects of the tax law.

a. A tax credit is allowed for amounts spent to furnish care for minor children while the parent works.

b. Deductions for interest on home mortgage and property taxes on one's personal residence.

c. The income-splitting benefits of filing a joint return.

d. Civil-law fines and penalties are not deductible.

e. Net operating losses of a current year can be deducted in future profitable years.

f. A taxpayer who sells property on an installment basis can recognize gain on the sale over the period the payments are received.

g. The exclusion from Federal tax of certain interest income from state and local bonds.

h. Prepaid income is taxed to the recipient in the year it is received and not in the year it is earned.

15. **LO.2** Contrast a value added tax (VAT) with a national sales tax in terms of anticipated taxpayer compliance. *Digging Deeper*

16. **LO.2** Go to **www.taxfoundation.org**, and determine Tax Freedom Day for your state and a neighboring state for the years 1950, 1960, 1970, 1980, 1990, 2000, and 2010. Report your results as a line graph. *Communications*

17. **LO.5** Although the Federal income tax law is complex, most individual taxpayers are able to complete their tax returns without outside assistance. Gather data as to the accuracy of this statement. Summarize your comments in an e-mail to your instructor. *Communications*

18. **LO.5** President Franklin D. Roosevelt once said, "I am wholly unable to figure out the amount of tax," and wrote to the Federal Commissioner of Revenue, "may I ask that [the agency] let me know the amount of the balance due." *Ethics and Equity* *Communications*

When a friend of FDR was ordered to pay $420,000 in tax penalties, the President called the Commissioner within earshot of reporters and told him to cut the penalties to $3,000. One listener, journalist David Brinkley, recalled years later: "Nobody seemed to think it was news or very interesting." Evaluate the President's comments and actions, as if you were a content provider for a political blog. Send your comments to your instructor.

19. **LO.2, 5** Mike Barr was an outstanding football player in college and expects to be drafted by the NFL in the first few rounds. Mike has let it be known that he would prefer to sign with an NFL team located in Florida, Texas, or Washington. Is Mike undertaking good income tax planning? Explain. *Critical Thinking*

20. **LO.5** Many state income tax returns contain checkoff boxes that allow taxpayers to make donations to a multitude of local charitable causes. On what grounds can such provisions be criticized? *Ethics and Equity*

BRIDGE DISCIPLINE

1. Discuss with respect to the Federal policy for reducing poverty:

   a. The individual income tax.

   b. The Social Security tax.

Communications

2. Prepare a two-page paper titled "How I Would Apply Federal Income Tax Law to Encourage the Availability of Universal Broadband in This Community" to submit to your economics professor.

Communications

3. Prepare an outline for a 10-minute speech to give to your government class. The speech is titled "If You Don't Pay Federal Taxes, You Can't Vote."

4. When taxes are "too high," taxpayers start to cheat on their taxes and dangerous consequences can result. Evaluate this statement. Give at least two examples to illustrate your conclusions.

5. Some tax rules can be justified on multiple grounds (e.g., economic or social). In this connection, comment on the possible justification for the rules governing the following.

   a. Pension plans.

   b. Education.

   c. Home ownership.

Research Problem

Use internet tax resources to address the following questions. Look for reliable websites and blogs of the IRS and other government agencies, media outlets, businesses, tax professionals, academics, think tanks, and political outlets.

Digging Deeper

Critical Thinking

Research Problem 1. Find a Federal or state proposal for a soda tax or sweetened beverage tax. Apply the AICPA's *Principles of Good Tax Policy* to support your recommendation for or against the bill.

Working with the Tax Law

LEARNING OBJECTIVES: *After completing Chapter 2, you should be able to:*

LO.1 Describe the statutory, administrative, and judicial sources of the tax law and the purpose of each source.

LO.2 Locate and work with the tax law and explain the tax research process.

LO.3 Communicate the results of the tax research process in a client letter and a tax file memorandum.

LO.4 Employ a strategy for applying tax research skills in taking the CPA exam.

CHAPTER OUTLINE

2-1 Tax Law Sources, 2-2
  2-1a Statutory Sources of the Tax Law, 2-2
  2-1b Administrative Sources of the Tax Law, 2-6
  2-1c Judicial Sources of the Tax Law, 2-10

2-2 Working with the Tax Law—Tax Research, 2-17
  2-2a Identifying the Problem, 2-18
  2-2b Refining the Problem, 2-18

  2-2c Locating the Appropriate Tax Law Sources, 2-18
  2-2d Assessing Tax Law Sources, 2-20
  2-2e Arriving at the Solution or at Alternative Solutions, 2-23
  2-2f Communicating Tax Research, 2-23
  2-2g Updates, 2-25
  2-2h Tax Research Best Practices, 2-25

2-3 Tax Research on the CPA Examination, 2-27

TAX TALK *The less people know about how sausages and laws are made, the better they'll sleep at night.* —OTTO VON BISMARCK

MONKEY BUSINESS IMAGES/SHUTTERSTOCK.COM

RESEARCHING TAX QUESTIONS

Early in November 2018, Fred and Megan Martel scheduled a meeting with you to discuss a potential tax problem. Fred and Megan purchased a 40-acre parcel of property in 2013 for $195,000. On it, they built their "dream home" in 2014. In March 2018, while walking on a remote part of their property, they spotted something shiny on the ground. They started digging and eventually unearthed eight metal cans containing more than 1,400 rare gold coins in $5, $10, and $20 denominations dated from 1846 to 1895. The face value of the gold coins is about $28,000, and the coins are in mint condition.

The Martels's delay in coming to you for tax advice was due to state law that required their discovery to be turned over to the state for disposition. The state, for a period of six months, was required to publicize the find and ask if anyone could prove ownership. When no one came forward, the coins were returned to the Martels in October 2018. As they are now the rightful owners of the coins, they want to know the income tax implications (if any) of their discovery.

Read the chapter and formulate your responses.

ederal tax law reflects the three branches of our Federal government. It is a mixture of laws passed by Congress, explanations provided by the Treasury Department and the Internal Revenue Service (IRS), and court decisions. The tax research process allows us to understand, evaluate, and apply the tax law to questions that are raised by taxpayers and tax practitioners.

In addition to being able to locate and interpret the tax law, a tax professional must understand the relative weight of authority that each source carries. The tax law is of little significance, however, until it is applied to a specific set of facts and circumstances. This chapter, therefore, both introduces the statutory, administrative, and judicial sources of the tax law *and* explains how the law is applied to business and individual transactions. It further explains how to apply research techniques effectively.

Tax research is necessary because the application of the law to a specific situation sometimes is not clear. As complicated as the tax rules are, they cannot clearly address every conceivable situation. Accordingly, the tax professional must determine the most likely tax treatment of a transaction through the research process.

Working with such knowledge, a tax professional then can advise the client about the tax consequences of several possible courses of action. Tax research, in other words, is of critical importance not only in properly characterizing completed events but also in planning proposed transactions.

2-1 TAX LAW SOURCES

LO.1

Describe the statutory, administrative, and judicial sources of the tax law and the purpose of each source.

Understanding taxation requires a mastery of the sources of the tax law. These sources include laws passed by Congress, which are accumulated in the Internal Revenue Code, and congressional Committee Reports, as well as Treasury Department Regulations, other Treasury Department and IRS pronouncements, and court decisions. Thus, the *primary sources* of tax law come from all three branches of the Federal government: legislative (statutory), executive, and judicial.

2-1a Statutory Sources of the Tax Law

Statutory sources of law include the Constitution (Article I, Sections 7, 8, and 10), tax treaties (agreements between countries to mitigate the double taxation of taxpayers subject to the tax laws of those countries), and the Internal Revenue Code. The Constitution grants Congress the power to impose and collect taxes, and it authorizes the creation of treaties with other countries. The Internal Revenue Code is the statutory basis for arriving at solutions to all tax questions.

Origin of the Internal Revenue Code

Before 1939, the statutory provisions relating to taxation were contained in the individual revenue acts enacted by Congress every year or two. The inconvenience and uncertainty of dealing with many separate acts led Congress to codify all of the Federal tax laws in 1939. Known as the Internal Revenue Code of 1939, this codification arranged all Federal tax provisions in a logical sequence and placed them in a separate part of the Federal statutes (Title 26 of the U.S. Code). Further rearrangements took place in 1954 and 1986.[1]

Enacted statutory amendments to the tax law are integrated into the existing Code. Congress usually passes one or more laws during the year that have tax provisions and become part of the Internal Revenue Code of 1986. This accumulative process is similar to the methods used by the Financial Accounting Standards Board with respect to its reporting rules.

---

[1]The organization of the Internal Revenue Code of 1986 is not substantively different from the organization of the 1954 Code. In contrast, the numbering scheme of Sections in the 1939 Code differs from that used in the 1954 Code.

TAX FACT Scope of the U.S. Tax System

Although it started out in 1913 as a tax on only the uppermost-income individuals, the tax system today is pervasive in the lives of all U.S. citizens and residents.

- In the typical tax year, the IRS receives about 25 million Forms 1040EZ and about 40 million Forms 1040A.

- The typical Form 1040 requires 7.25 hours to gather records and assemble the return and 6.25 hours to prepare the form and attachments. The estimated cost of complying with tax rules is $425 billion per year.

- The Internal Revenue Code is about 1 million words (2,650 pages) long, and the Regulations require another 4 million words (9,000 pages). Amazingly, these documents are more than twice the combined length of the *Harry Potter* series, *War and Peace*, and the King James Bible.

The Legislative Process

Exhibit 2.1 illustrates the legislative process for enacting changes to the Internal Revenue Code. Federal tax legislation generally originates in the House of Representatives, where it first is considered by the House Ways and Means Committee. (Tax bills also can originate in the Senate if they are attached as riders to other legislative proposals.) Once approved by the Ways and Means Committee, the proposed bill is referred to the

EXHIBIT 2.1	Legislative Process for Tax Bills

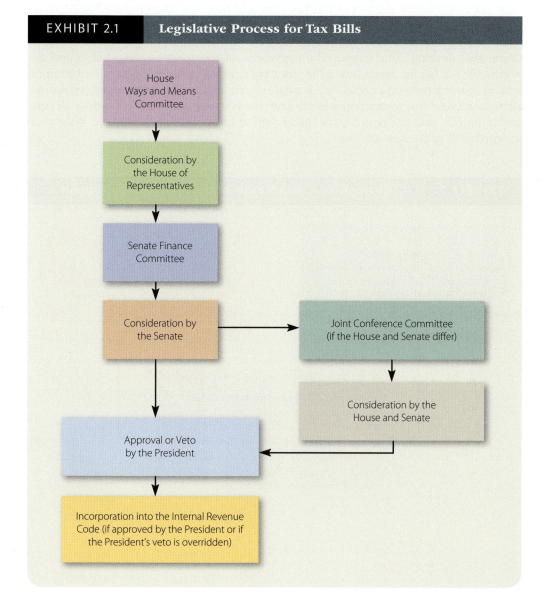

entire House of Representatives for a vote. Approved bills are sent to the Senate, where they initially are considered by the Senate Finance Committee.

After approval by the Finance Committee, the bill is sent to the entire Senate. Assuming no disagreement between the House and Senate, passage by the Senate means referral to the President for approval or veto. If the bill is approved or if the President's veto is overridden, the bill becomes law and part of the Internal Revenue Code.

When the Senate version of the bill differs from that passed by the House, the Conference Committee, which includes members of both the House Ways and Means Committee and the Senate Finance Committee, resolves the differences.

House and Senate versions of major tax bills frequently differ. One reason bills often are changed in the Senate is that, under the usual rules of Congress, each senator has considerable latitude to make amendments when the Senate as a whole is voting on a bill referred to it by the Senate Finance Committee. On the contrary, in most years the entire House of Representatives either accepts or rejects what is proposed by the House Ways and Means Committee, and changes from the floor are rare.

The deliberations of the Conference Committee usually produce a compromise between the two versions, which then is voted on by both the House and the Senate. If both bodies accept the revised bill, it is referred to the President for approval or veto.

The role of the Conference Committee indicates the importance of compromise in the legislative process. Exhibit 2.2 illustrates what happened with amendments to the child tax credit in the drafting of the Tax Cuts and Jobs Act (TCJA) of 2017.

The House Ways and Means Committee, the Senate Finance Committee, and the Conference Committee each typically produce a *Committee Report* for a tax bill. These Committee Reports often explain the provisions of the proposed legislation and are a valuable source for ascertaining the *intent of Congress*. What Congress had in mind when it considered and enacted tax legislation can be a key to interpreting legislation. Because it takes time to develop other primary authority (e.g., from the Treasury Department, the IRS, and the courts), tax researchers rely heavily on Committee Reports to interpret and apply new tax laws.

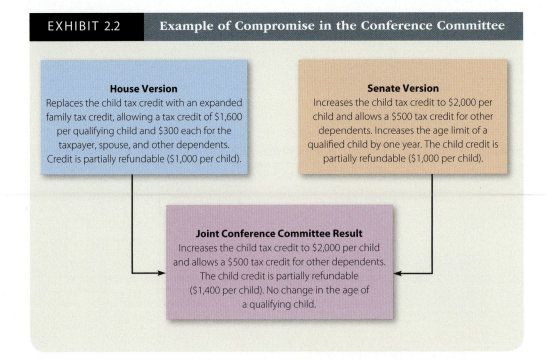

EXHIBIT 2.2   Example of Compromise in the Conference Committee

House Version
Replaces the child tax credit with an expanded family tax credit, allowing a tax credit of $1,600 per qualifying child and $300 each for the taxpayer, spouse, and other dependents. Credit is partially refundable ($1,000 per child).

Senate Version
Increases the child tax credit to $2,000 per child and allows a $500 tax credit for other dependents. Increases the age limit of a qualified child by one year. The child credit is partially refundable ($1,000 per child).

Joint Conference Committee Result
Increases the child tax credit to $2,000 per child and allows a $500 tax credit for other dependents. The child credit is partially refundable ($1,400 per child). No change in the age of a qualifying child.

Arrangement of the Internal Revenue Code

The Internal Revenue Code is found in Title 26 of the U.S. Code. The Code is organized by type of tax and by specific topics; it deals with all Federal taxes, not just income taxes. It also includes procedural rules, such as on due dates and penalties for non-compliance. Here is a partial table of contents.

> Subtitle A. Income Taxes
> > Chapter 1. Normal Taxes and Surtaxes
> > > Subchapter A. Determination of Tax Liability
> > > > Part I. Tax on Individuals
> > > > > Sections 1–5
> > > > Part II. Tax on Corporations
> > > > > Sections 11–12

In referring to a provision of the Code, the tax professional usually cites the Section number. In referring to § 2(a) (dealing with the status of a surviving spouse), for example, it is unnecessary to include Subtitle A, Chapter 1, Subchapter A, and Part I. Merely mentioning § 2(a) suffices, because the Section numbers run consecutively and do not begin again with each new Subtitle, Chapter, Subchapter, or Part. Not all Code Section numbers are used, however. Part I ends with § 5, and Part II starts with § 11 (at present, there are no §§ 6, 7, 8, 9, and 10).[2]

Tax professionals commonly refer to certain areas of income tax law by Subchapter designation. Some of the more common Subchapter designations include Subchapter C ("Corporate Distributions and Adjustments"), Subchapter K ("Partners and Partnerships"), and Subchapter S ("Tax Treatment of S Corporations and Their Shareholders").

Citing the Code

Code Sections often are broken down into subparts.[3] Section 2(a)(1)(A) serves as an example.

Broken down by content, a citation for Code § 2(a)(1)(A) appears as follows.

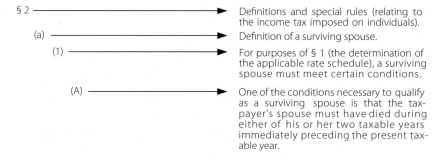

---

[2]When the Code was drafted, some Section numbers were intentionally unassigned, so that later changes could be incorporated into the Code without disrupting its topical organization. When Congress does not leave enough space, subsequent Code Sections are given A, B, C, etc., designations. A good example is the treatment of §§ 280A through 280H.

[3]Some Code Sections do not have subparts. See, for example, §§ 211 and 241.

[4]Some Code Sections omit the subsection designation and use, instead, the paragraph designation as the first subpart. See, for example, §§ 212(1) and 1222(1).

Throughout this text, references to the Code Sections are in the form shown previously. The symbols "§" and "§§" are used in place of "Section" and "Sections," respectively. The following table illustrates the format used in the text.

Complete Reference	Text Reference
Section 2(a)(1)(A) of the Internal Revenue Code of 1986	§ 2(a)(1)(A)
Sections 1 and 2 of the Internal Revenue Code of 1986	§§ 1 and 2
Section 2 of the Internal Revenue Code of 1954	§ 2 of the Internal Revenue Code of 1954
Section 12(d) of the Internal Revenue Code of 1939[5]	§ 12(d) of the Internal Revenue Code of 1939

Effect of Treaties

The United States signs certain tax treaties (sometimes called tax conventions) with foreign countries to render mutual assistance in tax enforcement and to avoid double taxation. These treaties affect transactions involving U.S. persons and entities operating or investing in a foreign country, as well as persons and entities of a foreign country operating or investing in the United States. Although these bilateral agreements are not codified in any one source, they are published at **www.irs.gov**, as well as in various commercial tax services.

Neither a tax law nor a tax treaty automatically takes precedence. When there is a direct conflict, the most recently adopted item prevails. With certain exceptions, a taxpayer must disclose on the tax return any filing position for which a treaty overrides a tax law.[6] There is a $1,000 per *failure to disclose* penalty for individuals and a $10,000 per failure to disclose penalty for C corporations.[7]

2-1b **Administrative Sources of the Tax Law**

The administrative sources of the Federal tax law include Treasury Department Regulations, Revenue Rulings and Revenue Procedures, and various other administrative pronouncements (see Exhibit 2.3). All are issued by either the U.S. Treasury Department or its subsidiary agency, the IRS.

EXHIBIT 2.3	Administrative Sources	
Source	**Location (Selected)**	**Authority**
Regulations	*Federal Register* *Internal Revenue Bulletin*	Force and effect of law. May be cited as precedent.
Temporary Regulations	*Federal Register* *Internal Revenue Bulletin*	May be cited as a precedent.
Proposed Regulations	*Federal Register* *Internal Revenue Bulletin*	Preview of final Regulations. Not yet a precedent.
Revenue Rulings Revenue Procedures Treasury Decisions Actions on Decisions	*Internal Revenue Bulletin*	IRS interpretation only. Weak precedent.
Letter Rulings	Thomson Reuters and CCH tax services	Applicable only to taxpayer addressed. May not be cited as precedent by others, but can be used as authority to avoid certain tax penalties on audit.

---

[5]Section 12(d) of the Internal Revenue Code of 1939 is the predecessor to § 2 of the Internal Revenue Codes of 1954 and 1986.

[6]§ 7852(d).

[7]§ 6712(a).

Treasury Department Regulations

Regulations are issued by the U.S. Treasury Department under authority granted by Congress.[8] Usually interpretive by nature, they provide taxpayers with considerable guidance on the meaning and application of the Code and often include examples. Regulations carry considerable authority as the official interpretation of tax statutes.

Treasury Regulations are arranged in the same sequence as the Code. A number is added at the beginning, however, to indicate the type of tax or other matter to which they relate. For example, the prefix 1 designates the Regulations under the income tax law. Thus, the Regulations under Code § 2 would be cited as Reg. § 1.2, with subparts added for further identification. The numbering pattern of these subparts often has no correlation with the Code subsections. The prefix 20 designates estate tax Regulations, 25 addresses gift tax Regulations, 31 relates to employment taxes, and 301 refers to procedure and administration. This list is not all-inclusive. Reg. § 1.351–1(a)(2) is an example of such a citation.

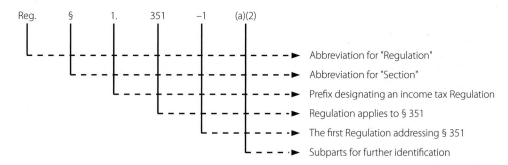

New Regulations and changes in existing Regulations usually are issued in proposed form before they are finalized. The interval between the proposal of a Regulation and its finalization permits taxpayers and other interested parties to comment on the propriety of the proposal. These comments usually are provided in writing, but oral comments can be offered at hearings held by the IRS on the Regulations in question pursuant to a public notice. This practice of notice-and-comment is a major distinction between Regulations and other forms of Treasury guidance such as Revenue Rulings, Revenue Procedures, and the like.

Proposed Regulations under Code § 2, for example, are cited as Prop.Reg. § 1.2. The Tax Court indicates that Proposed Regulations carry little weight in the litigation process.[9]

The Treasury Department issues **Temporary Regulations** relating to matters where immediate guidance is important. These Regulations are issued without the comment period required for Proposed Regulations. Temporary Regulations have the same authoritative value as final Regulations and may be cited as precedents. However, Temporary Regulations also are issued as Proposed Regulations and automatically expire within three years after the date of their issuance.[10]

Proposed, Temporary, and **Final Regulations** are published in the *Federal Register*, the *Internal Revenue Bulletin*, and major tax services.

Regulations also may be classified as *legislative, interpretive,* or *procedural*. These terms are discussed in more detail in text Section 2-2d.

Revenue Rulings and Revenue Procedures

Revenue Rulings are official pronouncements of the National Office of the IRS.[11] Like Regulations, they are designed to provide interpretation of the tax law. However, they do not carry the same legal force and effect as Regulations, but because Rulings are focused on a specific fact pattern, they may provide a more detailed analysis of the law.

---

[8]§ 7805.

[9]*F. W. Woolworth Co.*, 54 T.C. 1233 (1970); *Harris M. Miller*, 70 T.C. 448 (1978); and *James O. Tomerlin Trust*, 87 T.C. 876 (1986).

[10]§ 7805(e).

[11]§ 7805(a).

Both Revenue Rulings and Revenue Procedures serve an important function in providing *guidance* to IRS personnel and taxpayers in handling routine tax matters. Revenue Rulings and Revenue Procedures generally apply retroactively and may be revoked or modified by subsequent rulings or procedures, Regulations, legislation, or court decisions.

Revenue Rulings typically provide one or more examples of how the IRS would apply a law to specific fact situations. Revenue Rulings may arise from other pronouncements by the IRS, court decisions, suggestions from tax practitioner groups, and various tax publications. A Revenue Ruling also may arise from a specific taxpayer's request for a letter ruling (discussed below). If the IRS believes that a taxpayer's request for a letter ruling deserves official publication due to its widespread effect, the letter ruling is converted into a Revenue Ruling and issued for a broader audience.

Revenue Procedures are issued in the same manner as Revenue Rulings, but deal with the internal management practices and procedures of the IRS. Familiarity with these procedures increases taxpayer compliance and helps make the administration of the tax laws more efficient.

Some recent Revenue Procedures dealt with the following matters.

- Treatment of losses incurred in Presidential disaster areas.
- Procedures for requesting a filing date extension when electing S corporation status.
- Inflation-adjusted amounts for various Code provisions.

Revenue Rulings and Revenue Procedures are published weekly by the U.S. Government in the *Internal Revenue Bulletin* (I.R.B.).

The proper form for citing Revenue Rulings is as follows. Revenue Procedures are cited in the same manner, except that "Rev.Proc." is substituted for "Rev.Rul."

Rev.Rul. 2017–16, 2017–35 I.R.B. 215.

Explanation: Revenue Ruling Number 16, beginning at page 215 of the 35th
   weekly issue of the *Internal Revenue Bulletin* for 2017.

Revenue Rulings and other tax resources may be found at **www.irs.gov/tax-professionals/tax-code-regulations-and-official-guidance**.[12]

Letter Rulings

Letter rulings are issued by the IRS National Office for a fee upon a taxpayer's request. They describe how the IRS will treat a *proposed* transaction for tax purposes. Letter rulings can be useful for taxpayers who want to be certain of how a transaction will be taxed before proceeding with it. Letter rulings allow taxpayers to avoid unexpected tax costs.

Requesting a ruling can be quite cumbersome, although it sometimes is the most effective way to carry out tax planning. The IRS limits the issuance of letter rulings to restricted, pre-announced areas of taxation; it generally will not rule on situations that are fact-intensive.[13]

The IRS makes letter rulings available for public inspection after identifying details are deleted.[14] Published digests of private letter rulings are found in Bloomberg BNA's *Daily Tax Reports* and Tax Analysts' *Tax Notes*. *IRS Letter Rulings Reports* (published by CCH) contains both digests and full texts of all letter rulings. In addition, letter rulings are available in electronic, searchable form through several commercial publishers.

---

[12]Commercial sources for Revenue Rulings and Revenue Procedures are available for a subscription fee. Older Revenue Rulings and Revenue Procedures usually were cited as being published in the *Cumulative Bulletin* (C.B.) rather than the *Internal Revenue Bulletin* (I.R.B.).

[13]The first *Internal Revenue Bulletin* issued each year contains a list of areas in which the IRS will not issue rulings. This list may be modified throughout the year. See, for example, Rev.Proc. 2018–3, 2017–1 I.R.B. 118.

[14]§ 6110(c).

Letter rulings are issued multidigit file numbers that indicate the year and week of issuance as well as the number of the ruling during that week. Consider, for example, Ltr.Rul. 201710008, requesting guidance on the tax treatment of the merger of three partnerships.

2017	10	008
Year 2017	10th week of 2017	8th ruling issued during the 10th week

Other Administrative Pronouncements

Treasury Decisions (TDs) are issued by the Treasury Department to announce new Regulations, amend or change existing Regulations, or announce the position of the Government on selected court decisions. Like Revenue Rulings and Revenue Procedures, TDs are published in the *Internal Revenue Bulletin*.

The IRS publishes other administrative communications in the *Internal Revenue Bulletin*, such as Announcements, Notices, Proposed Regulations, Termination of Exempt Organization Status, Practitioner Disciplinary Actions, and Prohibited Transaction Exemptions.

Like letter rulings, **determination letters** are issued at the request of taxpayers and provide guidance on the application of the tax law. They differ from letter rulings in that the issuing source is an IRS executive, rather than the National Office of the IRS. Further, determination letters usually involve *completed* (as opposed to proposed) transactions. Determination letters are not published by the IRS, and they are released officially only to the party making the request.

Letter Rulings and Determination Letters

The shareholders of Red Corporation and Green Corporation want assurance that the consolidation of their corporations into Blue Corporation will be a nontaxable reorganization. The proper approach is to ask the National Office of the IRS to issue a letter ruling concerning the income tax effect of the proposed transaction.

EXAMPLE 1

Chris operates a salon in which he employs eight barbers. To comply with the rules governing income tax and payroll tax withholdings, Chris wants to know whether the barbers working for him are employees or independent contractors. The proper procedure is to request a determination letter on their status from the IRS.

EXAMPLE 2

The National Office of the IRS provides **Technical Advice Memoranda (TAMs)** as needed. TAMs resemble letter rulings in that they give the IRS's determination of an issue. Letter rulings, however, are responses to requests by taxpayers, whereas TAMs are issued by the National Office of the IRS in response to questions raised by IRS field personnel during audits. TAMs deal with completed rather than proposed transactions and are numbered in the same manner as a letter ruling.[15]

In-depth coverage can be found on this book's companion website: www.cengage.com   **1** DIGGING DEEPER

---

[15]Determination letters and technical advice memoranda may constitute substantial authority for purposes of the § 6662 accuracy-related penalty. Notice 90–20, 1990–1 C.B. 328.

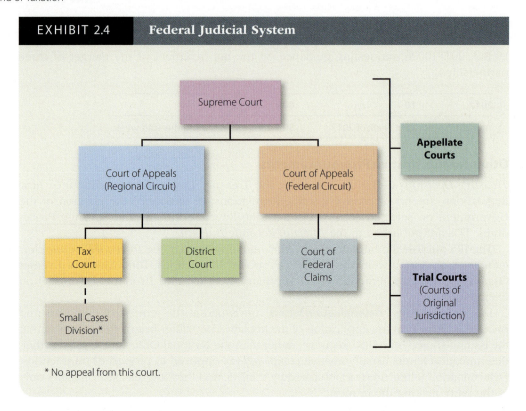

EXHIBIT 2.4   **Federal Judicial System**

* No appeal from this court.

2-1c Judicial Sources of the Tax Law

Once a taxpayer has exhausted the remedies available within the IRS (i.e., no satisfactory settlement has been reached at the agent level or at the Appeals Division level), a dispute can be taken to the Federal courts. The court system for Federal tax litigation is illustrated in Exhibit 2.4. The dispute first is considered by a **court of original jurisdiction** (also known as a trial court). Appeals (either by the taxpayer or the IRS) then are taken to the appropriate appellate court. A taxpayer can choose among four trial courts: a **District Court**, the **Court of Federal Claims**, the **Tax Court**, or the **Small Cases Division** of the Tax Court.

A court decision creates a *precedent*, such that future holdings will be followed in cases with similar facts and applicable law, and in the same jurisdiction. For example, the decisions of an appellate court are binding only on the trial courts within its jurisdiction and not on other trial or appelate courts. Different appellate courts may reach different opinions about the same issue.

The broken line in Exhibit 2.4 between the Tax Court and the Small Cases Division indicates that there is no appeal from the Small Cases Division, by either party to the case. Decisions from the Small Cases Division have no precedential value. They may not be relied upon by other taxpayers or even by the taxpayer itself in subsequent years. The jurisdiction of the Small Cases Division is limited to cases involving tax, interest, and penalty amounts of $50,000 or less.

DIGGING DEEPER 2 | **In-depth coverage can be found on this book's companion website: www.cengage.com**

Here are several terms that are important for the tax professional who is working with court decisions. The plaintiff is the party requesting action in a court, and the defendant is the party against whom the suit is brought. Sometimes a court uses the terms *petitioner* and *respondent*. In general, *petitioner* is a synonym for *plaintiff*, and *respondent* is a synonym for *defendant*. At the trial court level, a taxpayer usually is the petitioner, and the government is the respondent. If the taxpayer wins and the Government appeals as the new petitioner (or appellant), the taxpayer now is the respondent.

Trial Courts

The differences among the various trial courts (courts of original jurisdiction) can be summarized as follows. Concept Summary 2.1 summarizes the characteristics of the trial-level courts with respect to tax cases.

Concept Summary 2.1

Federal Judicial System: Trial Courts

Issue	Tax Court	District Court	Court of Federal Claims
Number of judges per court	19	1 per case	16
Payment of deficiency before trial	No	Yes	Yes
Jury trial available	No	Yes	No
Types of dispute	Tax cases only	Mostly criminal and civil issues	Claims against the United States
Jurisdiction	Nationwide	Location of taxpayer	Nationwide
IRS acquiescence policy	Yes	Yes	Yes
Appeal is to	U.S. Court of Appeals	U.S. Court of Appeals	Court of Appeals for the Federal Circuit

- *Number of courts.* There is only one Court of Federal Claims and only one Tax Court, but there are many District Courts. The taxpayer does not select the District Court that will hear the dispute, but must sue in the one that has jurisdiction where the taxpayer is located.

- *Number of judges.* A case tried in a District Court is heard before only 1 judge. The Court of Federal Claims has 16 judges, and the Tax Court has 19 regular judges. The entire Tax Court, however, reviews a case (the case is heard *en banc*), thereby taking on a more compelling authority, when important or novel tax issues are involved. Most cases, though, are heard and decided by only 1 of the 19 regular judges.

- *Location.* The Court of Federal Claims meets most often in Washington, D.C., while a District Court meets at a prescribed seat for the pertinent location. Each state has at least one District Court, and the more populous states have more than one. Choosing the District Court usually minimizes the inconvenience and expense of traveling for the taxpayer and his or her counsel. The Tax Court is based in Washington, D.C., but its judges regularly travel to different parts of the country and hear cases at predetermined locations and dates.

- *Jurisdiction of the Court of Federal Claims.* The Court of Federal Claims has jurisdiction over any claim against the U.S. government. Thus, the Court of Federal Claims hears nontax litigation as well as tax cases. It is characterized by some as having a pro-business orientation.

- *Jurisdiction of the Tax Court and District Courts.* The Tax Court hears only tax cases and is the most frequently used forum for tax cases. The District Courts hear a wide variety of nontax cases, including drug crimes and other Federal violations, as well as tax cases. For this reason, some suggest that the Tax Court has more expertise in tax matters, while the District Courts can be classified as generalists with respect to the tax law.

- *Jury trial.* A jury trial is available only in a District Court. Juries can decide only questions of fact and not questions of law. If a jury trial is not elected, the judge decides all issues. A District Court decision carries precedential value only in the district where it was issued.

- *Payment of deficiency.* Before the Court of Federal Claims or a District Court can have jurisdiction, the taxpayer must pay the tax deficiency assessed by the IRS and then sue for a refund. If the taxpayer wins (assuming no successful appeal by the Government), the tax paid plus appropriate interest is recovered. Jurisdiction in the Tax Court, however, usually is obtained without first paying the assessed tax deficiency. As a result, whether to pay the tax in advance becomes part of the decision-making process of the taxpayer in selecting a venue.

DIGGING DEEPER 3 | In-depth coverage can be found on this book's companion website: **www.cengage.com**

- *Appeals*. Appeals from a District Court or a Tax Court decision go to the Court of Appeals for the circuit in which the taxpayer resides. Appeals from the Court of Federal Claims go to the Court of Appeals for the Federal Circuit.
- *Bankruptcy*. When a taxpayer files a bankruptcy petition, the IRS, like other creditors, is prevented from taking action against the taxpayer. Sometimes a bankruptcy court settles a tax claim.
- *Gray areas*. Because there are "gray areas" in the tax laws, courts may disagree as to the proper tax treatment of an item. With these differences in possible outcome, the taxpayer must consider how a specific court might rule in choosing the most favorable forum to hear the case.

Appellate Courts

The losing party can appeal a trial court decision to the appropriate **Circuit Court of Appeals**. The 11 geographic circuits, the circuit for the District of Columbia, and the Federal Circuit[16] are shown in Exhibit 2.5.

Process and Outcomes If the government loses at the trial court level (District Court, Tax Court, or Court of Federal Claims), it need not (and frequently does not) appeal. The fact that an appeal is not made, however, does not indicate that the IRS agrees with the result and will not litigate similar issues in the future.

EXHIBIT 2.5   The Federal District Courts and Circuit Courts of Appeals

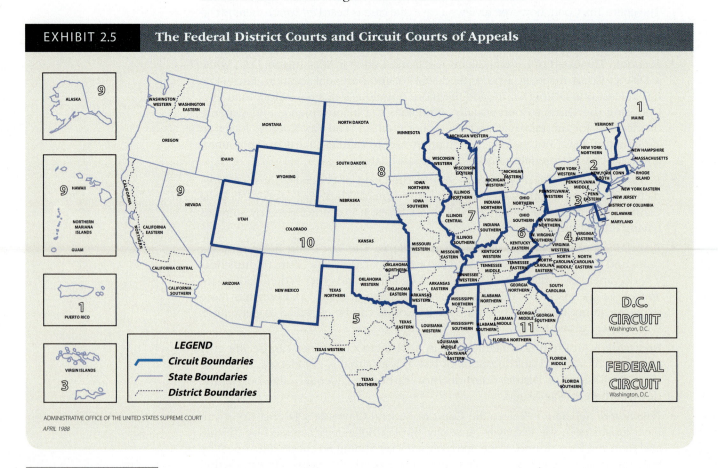

LEGEND
— Circuit Boundaries
— State Boundaries
···· District Boundaries

ADMINISTRATIVE OFFICE OF THE UNITED STATES SUPREME COURT
APRIL 1988

---

[16]The Court of Appeals for the Federal Circuit hears decisions appealed from the Court of Federal Claims.

The IRS may decide not to appeal for a number of reasons. First, its current litigation load may be heavy. As a consequence, the IRS may decide that available personnel should be assigned to other cases. Second, the IRS may not appeal for strategic reasons. For example, the taxpayer may be in a sympathetic position, or the facts may be particularly strong in his or her favor. In that event, the IRS may wait for a different case to test the legal issues involved. Third, if the appeal is from a District Court or the Tax Court, the Court of Appeals of jurisdiction could have some bearing on whether the IRS decides to pursue an appeal. Based on past experience and precedent, the IRS may conclude that the chance for success on a particular issue might be more promising in another Court of Appeals.

The role of appellate courts is limited to a review of the record of the case that was compiled by the trial courts. Thus, the appellate process usually involves a determination of whether the trial court applied the proper law in arriving at its decision, rather than a consideration of the trial court's factual findings.

An appeal can have a number of possible outcomes. The appellate court may let stand (affirm) or overturn (reverse) the lower court's finding, or it may send the case back to the trial court for further consideration (remand). When many issues are involved, a mixed result is not unusual. Thus, the lower court may be affirmed (*aff'd.*) on Issue A and reversed (*rev'd.*) on Issue B, while Issue C is remanded (*rem'd.*) for additional fact finding.

When more than one judge is involved in the decision-making process, disagreements are not uncommon. In addition to the majority view, one or more judges may concur (agree with the result reached but not with some or all of the reasoning) or dissent (disagree with the result). In any decision, the majority view controls. But concurring and dissenting views can influence other courts or, at some subsequent date when the composition of the court has changed, even when involving the same court.

Other Rules and Strategies The Federal Circuit at the appellate level provides a taxpayer with an alternative forum to the Court of Appeals of his or her home circuit. When a particular circuit has issued an adverse decision for a case that is similar in facts, the taxpayer may prefer the Court of Federal Claims, because any appeal will be to the Court of Appeals for the Federal Circuit.

District Courts, the Tax Court, and the Court of Federal Claims must abide by the **precedents** set by the Court of Appeals of their jurisdiction. A particular Court of Appeals need not follow the decisions of another Court of Appeals. All courts, however, must follow decisions of the **Supreme Court**.

This pattern of appellate precedents raises an issue for the Tax Court. Because the Tax Court is a national court, it decides cases from all parts of the country. Appeals from its decisions, however, go to all of the Courts of Appeals except the Court of Appeals for the Federal Circuit. Accordingly, identical Tax Court cases might be appealed to different circuits with different results. As a result of *Golsen,*[17] the Tax Court will not follow its own precedents in a subsequent case if the Court of Appeals with jurisdiction over the taxpayer previously reversed the Tax Court on the issue at hand.

EXAMPLE 3

Emily lives in Texas and sues in the Tax Court on Issue A. The Fifth Circuit Court of Appeals is the appellate court with jurisdiction. The Fifth Circuit already has decided, in a case involving similar facts but a different taxpayer, that Issue A should be resolved in favor of the taxpayer. Although the Tax Court maintains that the Fifth Circuit is wrong, under its *Golsen* policy, the Tax Court will hold for Emily.

Shortly thereafter, in a comparable case, Rashad, a resident of New York, sues in the Tax Court on Issue A. The Second Circuit Court of Appeals, the appellate court with jurisdiction in New York, never has expressed itself on Issue A. Presuming that the Tax Court has not reconsidered its position on Issue A, it will decide against Rashad.

Thus, it is possible for two taxpayers suing in the same court to end up with opposite results merely because they live in different parts of the country.

---

[17]*Jack E. Golsen,* 54 T.C. 742 (1970).

Appeal to the Supreme Court is not automatic. One applies to be heard via a **Writ of Certiorari** . If the Court agrees to hear the case, it will grant the Writ (*Cert. granted*). Most often, it declines to hear the case (*Cert. denied*). In fact, the Supreme Court rarely hears tax cases.

The Court usually grants certiorari to resolve a conflict among the Courts of Appeals (e.g., two or more appellate courts have opposing positions on a particular issue) or where the tax issue is extremely important. The granting of a *Writ of Certiorari* indicates that at least four of the nine members of the Supreme Court believe that the issue is of sufficient importance to be heard by the full Court.

Judicial Citations

Court decisions are an important source of tax law. The ability to locate a case and to cite it is a must in working with the tax law. Judicial citations usually follow a standard pattern: case name, volume number, reporter series, page or paragraph number, court (where necessary), and year of decision. These conventions are based on the legacy of publishing court decisions in hard copy books, but they carry on even in today's electronic research environment.

Judicial Citations—The Tax Court The Tax Court issues two types of decisions: Regular and Memorandum. The Chief Judge decides whether the opinion is issued as a Regular or Memorandum decision. The distinction between the two involves both substance and form. In terms of substance, *Memorandum* decisions deal with situations necessitating only the application of already established principles of law. *Regular* decisions involve novel issues of the tax law that have not previously been resolved by the court. In actual practice, however, this distinction is not always so clear. In any event, both Regular and Memorandum decisions represent the position of the Tax Court and, as such, carry precedential value for others.

Regular and Memorandum decisions issued by the Tax Court also differ in form. Memorandum decisions are not published officially, while Regular decisions are published by the U.S. Government as the *Tax Court of the United States Reports* (T.C.). Each volume of these *Reports* covers a six-month period (January 1 through June 30 and July 1 through December 31) and is given a succeeding volume number. But there is usually a time lag between the date a decision is rendered and the date it appears in official form. A temporary citation often is used to help the researcher locate a recent Regular decision. Consider, for example, the temporary and permanent citations for *Nadine L. Vichich*, a decision filed on April 21, 2016.

Temporary Citation { *Nadine L. Vichich*, 146 T.C. _____, No. 12 (2016).
Explanation: Page number left blank because not yet known.

Permanent Citation { *Nadine L. Vichich*, 146 T.C. 186 (2016).
Explanation: Page number now available.

The temporary citation tells us that the case ultimately will appear in Volume 146 of the *Tax Court of the United States Reports*. Until this volume becomes available to the general public, however, the page number is left blank. Instead, the temporary citation identifies the case as being the 12th Regular decision issued by the Tax Court since Volume 145 ended. With this information, the decision easily can be located at the Tax Court website or in the Tax Court services published by Commerce Clearing House (CCH) and Thomson Reuters *Checkpoint*. Once Volume 146 is released, the permanent citation is substituted, and the number of the case is dropped. Regular decisions and Memorandum decisions are published and searchable at **www.ustaxcourt.gov**.

Before 1943, the Tax Court was called the Board of Tax Appeals, and its decisions were published as the *United States Board of Tax Appeals Reports* (B.T.A.). These 47 volumes cover the period from 1924 to 1942. For example, the citation *Karl Pauli*, 11 B.T.A. 784 (1928) refers to the 11th volume of the *Board of Tax Appeals Reports*, page 784, issued in 1928.

If the IRS loses a decision, it may indicate whether it agrees or disagrees with the results reached by the court by publishing an <mark>acquiescence</mark> ("A" or "*Acq.*") or <mark>nonacquiescence</mark> ("NA" or "*Nonacq.*"), respectively.

The acquiescence or nonacquiescence is published in the *Internal Revenue Bulletin* as an *Action on Decision*. After the announcement is made by the IRS, the acquiescence status of the case is added to the citation for the decision. Examples of such announcements include A.O.D. 2017–04, 2017–15 I.R.B. 1072 (an acquiescence), and A.O.D. 2017–07, 2017–42 I.R.B. 311 (a nonacquiescence). The IRS can revoke an acquiescence retroactively.

In-depth coverage can be found on this book's companion website: www.cengage.com   **4 DIGGING DEEPER**

Tax Court Memorandum decisions are found at **www.ustaxcourt.gov**. Such decisions also are published by CCH and Thomson Reuters. Consider, for example, the ways that a Tax Court Memorandum case can be cited.

Nick R. Hughes, T.C.Memo. 2009–94.
Explanation: The 94th Memorandum decision issued by the Tax Court in 2009.

Nick R. Hughes, 97 TCM 1488 (2009).
Explanation: Page 1488 of Volume 97 of the CCH *Tax Court Memorandum Decisions.*

The second citation requires a parenthetical reference to the year in which the case was published. The first citation does not need this reference, as the publication date is included elsewhere in the citation.

The citation to a decision changes when the IRS issues an acquiescence or a nonacquiescence. For example, a proper citation appears as follows for a case after the A.O.D. is issued.

Estate of Martinez, T.C.Memo. 2004–1501, *nonacq.*, A.O.D. 2015–01.

U.S. Tax Court Summary Opinions relate to decisions of the Tax Court's Small Cases Division. These opinions are published commercially, and on the U.S. Tax Court website, with the warning that they may not be treated as precedent for any other case. For example, a Small Cases decision can be cited as follows.

Charles Edward Fagan, T.C. Summary Opinion 2017–61.

Judicial Citations—The District Courts, Court of Federal Claims, and Courts of Appeals
District Court, Court of Federal Claims, and Court of Appeals decisions dealing with Federal tax matters are reported in both the *U.S. Tax Cases* (USTC) and the *American Federal Tax Reports* (AFTR) series.

District Court decisions, dealing with *both* tax and nontax issues, are also published in the *Federal Supplement Series* (F.Supp.). Volume 999, published in 1998, was the last volume of the Federal Supplement Series. The *Federal Supplement Second Series* (F.Supp.2d) is used for currently issued cases. A District Court case can be cited in three different formats.

Turner v. U.S., 2004–1 USTC ¶60,478 (D.Ct. N.Tex.).

Explanation: Reported in the first volume of the *U.S. Tax Cases* (USTC) for calendar year 2004 (2004–1) and located at paragraph 60,478 (¶60,478).

Turner v. U.S., 93 AFTR 2d 2004–686 (D.Ct. N.Tex.).

Explanation: Reported in the 93rd volume of the second series of the *American Federal Tax Reports* (AFTR 2d) beginning on page 686.

Turner v. U.S., 306 F.Supp.2d 668 (D.Ct. N.Tex., 2004).

Explanation: Reported in the 306th volume of the *Federal Supplement Second Series* (F.Supp.2d) beginning on page 668. The date reference is needed, as it is not found elsewhere in the citation.

BRIDGE DISCIPLINE   Bridge to Public Policy

Sources of the Federal tax law reflect the general construct of the Federal government. The legislative branch issues the statutory tax law sources. The executive branch controls the administrative sources of the tax law, for the most part using the Department of the Treasury. The judicial branch issues various court decisions interpreting the tax law.

Access to the judicial sources of the Federal tax law is prohibitively expensive for most taxpayers. And although the tendency to settle most litigation outside the court system may be cost-effective for all parties, it inhibits the abilities of tax researchers to identify trends in the evolution of the law. Further, the Supreme Court grants certiorari for tax cases so few times each year that the judicial system effectively includes only one trial court and then one appellate opportunity for the taxpayer.

Finally, the political process dictates that wide swings in enforcement initiatives and budgets can occur from year to year. Taxpayers must be able to predict how the law will be administered as they craft and execute their tax plans, but that becomes especially difficult in politically charged times.

Federal tax law is a product of the rest of the governing process as it was designed long ago, but its current operations often make it a creature unto itself.

In all of the preceding citations, the names of both of the parties to the case are listed. This is a common practice in virtually all legal citations, with the name of the plaintiff or petitioner listed first. But in a Tax Court citation, because all such cases are brought by the taxpayer, no reference to the government is needed (i.e., "*v. Commissioner*" is omitted).

Decisions of the Courts of Appeals are published in the USTCs, the AFTRs, and the *Federal Second Series* (F.2d). Volume 999, published in 1993, was the last volume of the *Federal Second Series*. The *Federal Third Series* (F.3d) is used for currently issued cases. Decisions of the Court of Federal Claims are published in the USTCs, the AFTRs, and the *Claims Court Reporter* (abbreviated as Cl.Ct.).

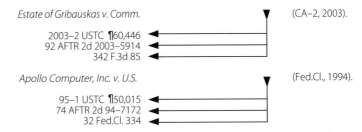

Estate of Gribauskas v. Comm. (CA–2, 2003).

2003–2 USTC ¶60,446
92 AFTR 2d 2003–5914
342 F.3d 85

Apollo Computer, Inc. v. U.S. (Fed.Cl., 1994).

95–1 USTC ¶50,015
74 AFTR 2d 94–7172
32 Fed.Cl. 334

Gribauskas is a decision rendered by the Second Circuit Court of Appeals in 2003 (CA–2, 2003), while *Apollo Computer, Inc.* was issued by the Court of Federal Claims in 1994 (Fed.Cl., 1994), but not published in the USTC until 1995.

DIGGING DEEPER 5   In-depth coverage can be found on this book's companion website: **www.cengage.com**

Judicial Citations—Supreme Court U.S. Supreme Court decisions dealing with Federal tax matters are published in the USTCs and in the AFTRs. The U.S. Government Printing Office publishes all Supreme Court decisions in the *United States Supreme Court Reports* (U.S.). Such decisions also are found in the *Supreme Court Reporter* (S.Ct.) and the *United States Reports, Lawyer's Edition* (L.Ed.).

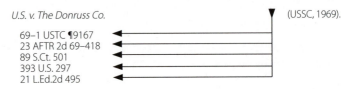

U.S. v. The Donruss Co. (USSC, 1969).

69–1 USTC ¶9167
23 AFTR 2d 69–418
89 S.Ct. 501
393 U.S. 297
21 L.Ed.2d 495

The parenthetical reference (USSC, 1969) identifies the decision as having been rendered by the U.S. Supreme Court in 1969.

2-2 WORKING WITH THE TAX LAW—TAX RESEARCH

LO.2

Locate and work with the tax law and explain the tax research process.

Tax research is undertaken to determine the best available solution to a situation that has tax consequences. In the case of a completed transaction, the objective of the research is to determine the tax result of what has already taken place. For example, is the expenditure incurred by the taxpayer deductible or not deductible for tax purposes? When dealing with proposed transactions, tax research has a different objective: effective tax planning by determining the tax consequences of various alternatives.

Tax research involves the following procedures.

- Identifying and refining the problem.
- Locating the appropriate tax law sources.
- Assessing the tax law sources.
- Arriving at the solution or at alternative solutions, including consideration of nontax factors.
- Effectively communicating the solution to the taxpayer or the taxpayer's representative.
- Updating the solution (where appropriate) in light of new developments.

This process is illustrated in Exhibit 2.6. The broken lines indicate steps of particular interest when tax research is directed toward proposed, rather than completed, transactions.

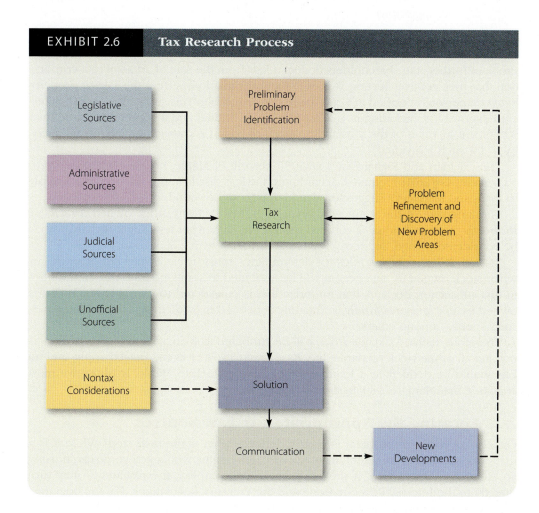

EXHIBIT 2.6   **Tax Research Process**

2-2a **Identifying the Problem**

Problem identification starts with a compilation of the relevant facts involved. In this regard, *all* of the facts that may have a bearing on the problem must be gathered, as any omission could modify the solution reached. To illustrate, consider what appears to be a very simple problem.

EXAMPLE 4

In reviewing their tax and financial situation, Joan and Richard, a married couple, notice that Joan's investment in Airways stock has declined from its purchase price of $8,000 to a current market value of $5,500. Joan wants to sell this stock now and claim the $2,500 loss ($5,500 value − $8,000 cost) as a deduction this year. Richard, however, believes that Airways will yet prosper and does not want to part with the stock. Their daughter Margaret suggests that they sell the Airways stock to Maple, Inc., a corporation owned equally by Joan and Richard. That way, they can claim the deduction this year but still hold the stock through their corporation. Will this suggestion work?

2-2b **Refining the Problem**

Joan and Richard in Example 4 face three choices.

1. Sell the Airways stock through their regular investment broker and get a deduction in the current year (Joan's plan).
2. Continue to hold the Airways stock (Richard's plan).
3. Sell the Airways stock to a corporation owned 50–50 by Joan and Richard (Margaret's suggestion).

The tax consequences of plans (1) and (2) are clear, but the question that Joan and Richard want to resolve is whether plan (3) will work as anticipated. Refining the problem further, can shareholders deduct a loss from the sale of an asset to a corporation that they control? Section 267(a)(1) indicates that losses from the sale of property between persons specified in § 267(b) are not deductible. This subsection lists 12 different relationships, including in § 267(b)(2): "an individual and a corporation more than 50 percent in value of the outstanding stock of which is owned, directly or indirectly, by or for such individual."

Thus, if Joan and Richard each own 50 percent of Maple, neither owns *more than* 50 percent, as § 267(b) requires. Accordingly, the loss disallowance rule would not apply to Joan, and Margaret's suggestion would appear to be sound.

The language of the statute, however, indicates that any stock owned *directly or indirectly* by an individual is counted toward the 50 percent test. Might Richard's stock be considered owned "indirectly" by Joan? Further research is necessary.

Section 267(c) contains rules for determining "constructive ownership of stock," or when stock owned by one person will be attributed to someone else. One of the rules in this subsection declares that an individual is considered to own any stock that is owned by that person's *family*, and family is defined in § 267(c)(4) as including a person's spouse, among others.

Therefore, Richard's Maple stock will be attributed to Joan, so that Joan is treated as owning all of the stock of Maple, Inc. As a result, § 267(a) would indeed apply, and no loss would be deductible if Joan sells the Airways stock to Maple. In short, we must conclude that Margaret's suggestion will not work.

2-2c **Locating the Appropriate Tax Law Sources**

Once a tax research problem is clearly defined, what is the next step? While it is a matter of individual judgment, most tax research begins with a keyword search using an electronic tax service. If the problem is not complex, the researcher may turn directly to the Internal Revenue Code and the Treasury Regulations. For the beginner, the latter procedure saves time and solves many of the more basic problems. If the researcher does not have a personal copy of the Code or Regulations, access to the

BRIDGE DISCIPLINE Bridge to Business Law

U.S. income tax laws change daily by the action of Congress, tax administrators, and the courts. This process matches the three-branch structure of the rest of the government, with the legislative, executive, and judicial branches each having a say in making tax law.

Under the U.S. Constitution, legislation involving government revenues must start in the House of Representatives. This provision likely was included so that the public would have greater control over those who want greater access to their pocketbooks. Several recent pieces of tax legislation, though, have been initiated as bills in the Senate. And most bills introduced in both houses of Congress are required to be "revenue-neutral" (i.e., they must include provisions by which the legislation's new programs will be paid for). In both

houses, this has resulted in amendments to the Internal Revenue Code being attached to legislation involving clean air and water standards, child care programs, and product import and export limitations.

In a few cases, the courts considered a taxpayer challenge to the way that specific tax legislation was crafted. But so far the courts have failed to overturn any tax provisions solely because they were initiated outside of the House and its committee processes. The courts' rationale for this seemingly unconstitutional position typically is that the House and its committees heard a full discussion of the proposal and too much time has passed since adoption of the legislation to easily unwind it and undertake a refund procedure.

appropriate volume(s) of a tax service is necessary.[18] A partial list of the major tax services and their publishers includes:

CCH IntelliConnect, Commerce Clearing House. Includes the *Standard Federal Tax Reporter*.

Thomson Reuters Checkpoint, Research Institute of America. Includes RIA's *Federal Tax Coordinator 2d*.

Parker Tax Pro Library, formerly Kleinrock *Tax Expert*.

Tax Management Portfolios, Bloomberg BNA.

Westlaw services, Thomson Reuters. Includes access to *Federal Tax Coordinator 2d*.

Tax Center, LexisNexis. Mostly primary law sources.

Tax Services

In this text, it is not feasible to explain the use of any particular tax service—this ability can be obtained with further study and professional experience. However, several important observations about the use of tax services cannot be overemphasized. First, always check for current developments. Tax services are updated several times a day, and tax newsletters often feature highlights of recent tax law developments. Second, there is no substitute for the original source. Do not base a conclusion solely on a tax service's commentary. If a Code Section, Regulation, or case is vital to the research, read it.

Tax Commentary

Various tax publications are another source of relevant information. The use of tax editorial commentary in these publications often can shorten the research time needed to resolve a tax issue. If an article or a posting is relevant to the issue at hand, it may provide the references needed to locate the primary sources of the tax law that apply (e.g., citations to judicial decisions, Regulations, and other IRS pronouncements). Thus, the researcher obtains a "running start" in arriving at a solution to the problem.

---

[18]Several of the major tax services publish paperback editions of the Code and Treasury Regulations that can be purchased at modest prices. See also **www.irs.gov/tax-professionals/tax-code-regulations-and-official-guidance**.

The following are some of the more useful tax publications.

Journal of Taxation
Journal of International Taxation
Practical Tax Strategies
Estate Planning
Corporate Taxation
Taxation of Exempts
Real Estate Taxation
Journal of Multistate Taxation and Incentives
ria.thomsonreuters.com/journals

The Tax Executive
www.tei.org

The Tax Adviser
www.thetaxadviser.com

The Tax Lawyer
www.law.georgetown.edu/journals/tax

The ATA Journal of Legal Tax Research
aaajournals.org/loi/jltr

Trusts and Estates
wealthmanagement.com/te-home

Journal of Passthrough Entities
Journal of Tax Practice and Procedure
TAXES—The Tax Magazine
tax.cchgroup.com/books

Tax Notes
State Tax Notes
Tax Notes International
taxnotes.com

2-2d Assessing Tax Law Sources

Once a source has been located, the next step is to assess it in light of the problem at hand. Proper assessment involves careful interpretation of the tax law and consideration of its relevance and significance.

Interpreting the Internal Revenue Code

The language of the Code often is difficult to comprehend fully. The Code is intended to apply more than 320 million citizens, most of whom are willing to exploit any linguistic imprecision to their benefit—to find a "loophole," in popular parlance. Moreover, many of the Code's provisions are limitations or restrictions involving two or more variables. Expressing such concepts algebraically would be more direct; using words to accomplish this task instead is often quite cumbersome.

Nevertheless, the Code usually should be the first source to be consulted by the tax researcher, and often it is the only source needed.

Assessing the Significance of a Treasury Regulation

Treasury Regulations are the official interpretation of the Code and are entitled to great deference. Occasionally, however, a court will invalidate a Regulation or a portion thereof on the grounds that the Regulation is contrary to the intent of Congress. Usually, courts do not question the validity of Regulations. Courts believe that "the first administrative interpretation of a provision as it appears in a new act often expresses the general understanding of the times or the actual understanding of those who played an important part when the statute was drafted."[19]

Keep in mind the following observations when you assess the significance of a Regulation.

- IRS agents *must* give the Code and any related Regulations equal weight when dealing with taxpayers and their representatives.

- Proposed Regulations provide a preview of future final Regulations, but they are not binding on the IRS or taxpayers.

- Taxpayers have the burden of proof to show that a Regulation varies from the language of the statute and is not supported by the related Committee Reports.

---

[19]*Augustus v. Comm.*, 41–1 USTC ¶9255, 26 AFTR 612, 118 F.2d 38 (CA–6, 1941).

- Final Regulations can be classified as procedural, interpretive, or legislative. **Procedural Regulations** often include procedural instructions, indicating information that taxpayers should provide the IRS, as well as information about the internal management and conduct of the IRS itself.

- **Interpretive Regulations** rephrase or elaborate what Congress stated in the Committee Reports that were issued when the tax legislation was enacted. If the language has gone through the public notice and comment procedures discussed earlier in the chapter, interpretive Regulations are *hard and solid* and almost impossible to overturn unless they do not clearly reflect the intent of Congress.

- In some Code Sections, Congress has given the *Treasury Secretary or a delegate* the specific authority to prescribe Regulations to carry out the details of administration or to otherwise create rules not included in the Code. Here, Congress effectively is delegating its legislative powers to the Treasury. Regulations issued under this type of authority possess the force and effect of law and often are called **Legislative Regulations** (e.g., consolidated return Regulations).

The Big Picture

Return to the facts of *The Big Picture* on p. 2-1. Tax law involving the money found by the Martels is found largely in the Internal Revenue Code and Regulations.

EXAMPLE

5

In-depth coverage can be found on this book's companion website: **www.cengage.com**

6 DIGGING DEEPER

Assessing the Significance of Other Administrative Sources of the Tax Law

Revenue Rulings issued by the IRS carry much less weight than Treasury Department Regulations. Revenue Rulings are important for the researcher, however, in that they reflect the position of the IRS on tax matters for specified fact patterns. IRS agents will follow the results reached in applicable Revenue Rulings.

Assessing the Significance of Judicial Sources of the Tax Law

A tax researcher may find that several court cases appear to be relevant for the issue at hand. How much reliance can be placed on a particular decision depends on the following factors.

- *The level of the court.* A decision rendered by a trial court (e.g., a District Court) carries less weight than one issued by an appellate court (e.g., the Fifth Circuit Court of Appeals). Until Congress changes the Code, decisions by the U.S. Supreme Court represent the last word on any tax issue.

- *The legal residence of the taxpayer.* If, for example, a taxpayer lives in Texas, a decision of the Fifth Circuit Court of Appeals means more than one rendered by the Second Circuit Court of Appeals. This is the case because any appeal from a District Court or the Tax Court would be to the Fifth Circuit and not to the Second Circuit.

- *The type of decision.* A Tax Court Regular decision carries more weight than a Memorandum decision; the Tax Court does not consider Memorandum decisions to have precedential value.[20]

- *The weight of the decision.* A decision that is supported by cases from other courts carries more weight than a decision that is not supported by other cases.

- *Subsequent events.* Was the decision affirmed or overruled on appeal?

---

[20]*Severino R. Nico, Jr.*, 67 T.C. 647 (1977).

In connection with the last two factors, a <mark>citator</mark> is helpful to the tax researcher.[21] A citator provides the history of a case to show how it progressed through the court system. Reviewing the references listed in the citator discloses whether the decision was appealed and, if so, with what result (e.g., affirmed, reversed, remanded). It also lists subsequent cases that referred to the earlier case and may indicate how they used that case. If the IRS lost the case, the citator will likely state whether the IRS issued an Action on Decision. In this way, a citator reflects on the currency and validity of a case and may lead to other relevant judicial material. If one plans to rely on a judicial decision to any significant degree, "running" the case through a citator is imperative.

The Big Picture

EXAMPLE 6

Return to the facts of *The Big Picture* on p. 2-1. The Martels need to know if the gold coins are considered taxable income for them. If yes, they also need to know when to report that income and the amount. They share the story with their tax adviser, Jane, a CPA. Jane researches the Martels's questions.

- What if an appellate court ruling issued by the Federal circuit in which they live supports treatment as $28,000 of income in 2018? Is that decision controlling law. If not and the Martels's circuit has not ruled to the contrary on the issue but another circuit has ruled in their favor in a parallel case, the taxpayers could use that decision as support for their side of the argument.

- Assume that a Revenue Ruling also is found that supports treating the coins as income in 2018. How long ago were the Revenue Ruling and appellate decision issued? A legal precedent generally is stronger if it was issued more recently.

- If the Martels's circuit has ruled favorably, have other courts discussed the appellate court holding? What did these courts hold? The more courts that follow a holding and cite it favorably, the stronger the legal precedent of the holding. Information of this sort can be found by reviewing the case history of the decision or by consulting a citator.

Understanding Judicial Opinions

Reading judicial opinions can be more productive if certain conventions of usage are understood. Some courts, including the Tax Court, apply the terms *petitioner* and *respondent* to the plaintiff and defendant, respectively, particularly when the case does not involve an appellate proceeding. Appellate courts often use the terms *appellant* and *appellee* instead.

It also is important to distinguish between a court's final determination, or *holding*, and passing comments made in the course of its opinion. These latter remarks, examples, and analogies, often collectively termed *dicta*, are not part of the court's conclusion and do not have precedential value. Nevertheless, they often facilitate one's understanding of the court's reasoning and can enable a tax adviser to better predict how the court might resolve some future tax case.

DIGGING DEEPER 7 | In-depth coverage can be found on this book's companion website: **www.cengage.com**

Assessing the Significance of Other Sources

Primary sources of tax law include the Constitution, legislative history materials (e.g., Committee Reports), statutes, treaties, Treasury Regulations, IRS pronouncements, and judicial decisions. In general, the IRS regards only primary sources as substantial authority. However, reference to *secondary materials* such as tax publications, treatises, legal opinions, and written determinations may be useful. In general, secondary sources do not constitute tax authority.

---

[21]The major citators are published by CCH, Thomson Reuters Checkpoint™, WESTLAW, and Shepard's Citations, Inc.

Although the statement that the IRS regards only primary sources as substantial authority is generally true, there is one exception. Substantial authority *for purposes of* the accuracy-related penalty in § 6662 includes a number of secondary materials (e.g., letter rulings).[22] "Authority" does not include conclusions reached in treatises, textbooks, and Web postings by tax commentators and written opinions rendered for compensation by tax professionals.

A letter ruling or determination letter can be relied upon *only* by the taxpayer to whom it is issued, except as noted previously with respect to the accuracy-related penalty.

2-2e Arriving at the Solution or at Alternative Solutions

Example 4 raises the question of whether taxpayers would be denied a loss deduction from the sale of stock to a corporation that they own. The solution depends, in part, on the relationship of the corporation's shareholders to each other. Because Richard and Joan are married to each other, § 267(c)(2) attributes Richard's Maple stock to Joan in applying the "more than 50 percent" test of § 267(b)(2). Accordingly, Joan and Maple, Inc., are considered related parties under § 267(a), and a sale between them does not produce a deductible loss. If Richard and Joan were not related to each other, the constructive stock ownership rules would not apply and a loss could be deducted on a sale by Joan to Maple.

If Maple, Inc., were a *partnership* instead of a corporation, § 267 would not apply.[23] However, a different Code Section, namely § 707, produces the same result: no deduction is allowed for the loss from a sale between a "more than 50 percent" partner and the partnership. This additional research prevents the couple from erroneously selling their Airways stock to a related partnership in hopes of obtaining a loss deduction from the sale. Accordingly, Joan still must sell the Airways stock to an unrelated party to deduct the loss.

Because Richard still wants to own Airways stock, he might consider purchasing new Airways Co. stock to replace the stock that Joan sells to the unrelated party. Additional research reveals that for the loss on the sale to be deductible, the "wash sale" rule requires that more than 30 days elapse between the purchase of the new stock and the sale of the old stock.[24] This rule applies to purchases and sales of *substantially identical stock or securities*. As a result, to deduct the loss on the Airways stock, Richard either must wait more than 30 days after Joan sells the shares to buy new Airways stock or acquire stock in a different company at any time. This new company can even be in the same general business as Airways.[25]

2-2f Communicating Tax Research

Once a tax issue has been researched adequately, a memorandum, a letter, or a speech setting forth the result may need to be prepared. The form the communication takes could depend on a number of considerations. For example, does an employer or instructor recommend a particular procedure or format for tax research memos? Is the memo to be given directly to the client, or will it first go to the preparer's employer? If the communication is a speech, who is the audience? How long should one speak?[26] Whatever form it takes, a good research communication should contain the following elements.

- A clear statement of the issue.
- In more complex situations, a short review of the fact pattern that raised the issue.
- A review of the pertinent tax law sources (e.g., Code, Regulations, Revenue Rulings, and judicial authority).
- Any assumptions made in arriving at the solution.
- The solution recommended and the logic or reasoning supporting it.
- The references consulted in the research process.

LO.3

Communicate the results of the tax research process in a client letter and a tax file memorandum.

---

[22]Reg. § 1.6661–3(b)(2).

[23]Reg. § 1.267(b)–1(b)(1).

[24]§ 1091.

[25]Rev.Rul. 59–44, 1959–1 C.B. 205.

[26]See W. A. Raabe and G. E. Whittenburg, "Talking Tax: How to Make a Tax Presentation," *The Tax Adviser*, March 1997, pp. 179–182.

A memo to the tax file is a collection of thoughts resulting from a current tax research project. It is shared with others who have access to the research files so that they do not need to duplicate the current work at a later date. The file memo is written by a tax professional, to be read by another tax professional, so it features citations in good form to the Code, Regulations, and other sources of the law, often hyperlinking directly to the underlying document. A file memo is organized so as to list the pertinent facts, open tax issues, a brief conclusion, and a discussion of the research findings and underlying tax logic.

A letter to the client is written to convey the results of a research engagement and to identify the next steps for the taxpayer to consider. Because most clients have little knowledge or experience in working with tax source documents, citations typically are not used. If the recipient of the letter is a tax executive or other colleague, a more technical approach might be taken in the letter. The letter typically does not exceed a page or two, and it sometimes is supplemented with an attached spreadsheet or chart. It includes various social graces and any needed regulatory language.

Illustrations of the memo for the tax file and the client letter associated with Example 4 appear in Exhibits 2.7 and 2.8.

EXHIBIT 2.7	**Tax File Memorandum**

August 26, 2019

TAX FILE MEMORANDUM

FROM   Gillian J. Jones

SUBJECT   Joan and Richard Taxpayer Engagement

Today I talked with Joan concerning her August 14, 2019 letter requesting tax assistance. Joan wants to know if she can sell some stock in Airways Co. to Maple, Inc., and deduct the $2,500 loss realized.

FACTS Maple, Inc., is owned 50% by Richard and 50% by Joan. Richard wants to continue holding Airways stock in anticipation of a rebound in its value, but Joan wants to sell her shares and deduct the realized loss. They have asked about a proposed sale of this stock to Maple.

ISSUE Can shareholders deduct a loss on the sale of an asset to a corporation, all of whose stock they own?

CONCLUSION Joan should *not* sell the Airways stock to Maple if the couple wants to deduct the realized loss in the current tax year. Instead, Joan should sell this stock to a third party. Then the couple should either acquire new Airways stock more than 30 days before or after the date of sale or acquire stock of a similar company.

ANALYSIS Section 267(a) provides that no loss is deductible on a sale or exchange between certain related parties. One of these relationships involves a corporation and a shareholder who owns "more than 50 percent" of that corporation's stock [see § 267(b)(2)]. Although Richard owns only 50% of Maple, Inc., his wife, Joan, owns the other 50%. The constructive ownership rule of § 267(c)(2) attributes stock held by family members, and a spouse is part of a taxpayer's family for this purpose, according to § 267(c)(4). Consequently, Richard's Maple stock is attributed to Joan, who is then treated as owning 100% of Maple, Inc. The related-party disallowance rule then applies to the loss from Joan's selling the Airways stock to Maple. Accordingly, Joan must sell this stock to an unrelated party to make the realized loss deductible.

Because Richard wants to retain an investment in Airways, he can purchase replacement stock either before or after Joan sells the original Airways stock. Section 1091(a), however, requires that more than 30 days elapse between the purchase and the sale or the sale and the purchase, as the case may be. Moreover, for this purpose, an option to buy the stock is treated as equivalent to the stock itself. As a result, Richard must wait more than 30 days between transactions and cannot utilize stock options in the interim to minimize his stock price exposure.

A final alternative might be to replace the Airways stock with securities of a comparable company in the same industry. Although no two companies are exactly alike, there may be another company whose management philosophy, marketing strategy, and financial data are sufficiently similar to Airways to provide an equivalent return on investment. Under this alternative, Richard could acquire the new company's shares immediately, without waiting the 30 days mandated by § 1091(a). Despite the two companies' investment similarity, they would not be treated as "substantially identical" for this purpose (see Rev.Rul. 59–44, 1959–1 C.B. 205), and the Airways realized loss could be recognized.

EXHIBIT 2.8	Client Letter

Raabe, Young, Nellen, & Maloney, CPAs
5191 Natorp Boulevard
Mason, OH 45040

August 30, 2019

Mr. and Ms. Richard Taxpayer
111 Tragg Boulevard
Williamsburg, VA 23185

Dear Joan and Richard:

It was good to see you last week at our firm's golf outing. I'm glad that your children are doing so well in college and that our work to build up their education funds was so effective in providing the needed cash flow!

I am responding to your request to review your family's financial and tax situation. Our conclusions are based upon the facts as outlined in your August 14 letter. Any change in the facts may affect our conclusions.

Joan owns stock in Airways Co. that has declined in value, but Richard would like to retain this stock in anticipation of a rebound in its value. You have proposed a sale of this stock at its current market value to Maple, Inc., a corporation owned 50–50 by the two of you. Such a sale, however, would not permit the loss to be deducted.

A better approach would be to sell the Airways stock to a third party before year-end and repurchase this stock in the market. Please understand that the loss will not be deductible unless more than 30 days elapse between the sale and the repurchase of the stock. You can sell the old stock first and then buy the new stock, or you can buy the new stock first and then sell the old stock; the ordering of the transactions does not change the result. However, it is essential that more than 30 days elapse between the sale and purchase transactions. Using options during this 30-day period is ineffective and also will prevent the loss from being deducted in the current taxable year.

If the 30-day requirement is unacceptable, you might consider replacing the Airways stock with securities of some other company, perhaps even a company in the same general business as Airways. In that situation, your loss on the Airways stock can be deducted without regard to when you buy the new stock.

Let's meet to discuss this some more—and to allow me to show you our new office. Please e-mail me if I can clarify any of these points or if you have more information for me to consider. My work on this engagement is regulated by Treasury Circular 230.

Sincerely yours,

Gillian J. Jones, CPA
Partner

2-2g Updates

Because tax research may involve a proposed (as opposed to a completed) transaction, a change in the tax law (legislative, administrative, or judicial) could alter the original conclusion. Additional research may be necessary to test the solution in light of current developments (refer to the broken lines at the right in Exhibit 2.6), or to account for additional information that may arise during the research process itself. To the extent that a client has engaged the tax researcher to provide updates to an initial report, new information should be presented in a concise manner.

2-2h Tax Research Best Practices

One's research skills developed in using browsers and apps may not transfer into the tax research setting. The researcher must use the document list that results from a search procedure in a professional manner. Most electronic tax services allow a user to retrieve documents in order of relevance, or in the order listed by database sources. Such a listing seldom will account for the applicability and precedential value of the documents that are found. Reading the primary sources, validating their authority, and checking a citator are essential in reaching a correct answer.

Finding Relevant Materials Effectively

Usually, tax professionals use one of the following strategies when performing computer-based tax research.

- *Search* various databases using keywords that are likely to be found in the underlying documents, as written by Congress, the judiciary, or administrative sources.
- *Link* to tax documents for which all or part of the proper citation is known.
- *Browse* the tax databases, examining various tables of contents and indexes in a traditional manner or using cross-references in the documents to jump from one tax law source to another.

Sometimes a researcher can begin a search process using materials that are available at no direct cost. Such sources include the following.

- *The Web* provides access to a number of sites maintained by accounting and consulting firms, publishers, tax academics and libraries, and governmental bodies. The best sites offer links to other sites and direct contact to the site providers. Exhibit 2.9 lists some of the websites that may be most useful to tax researchers and their internet addresses as of press date.
- *Blogs and newsletters* provide a means by which information related to the tax law can be exchanged among taxpayers, tax professionals, and others who subscribe to the group's services. The tax professional can read the exchanges among other members and offer replies and suggestions to inquiries as desired. Discussions address the interpretation and application of existing law, analysis of proposals and new pronouncements, and reviews of tax software.

While tax information on the internet is plentiful, public domain information never should be relied upon without referring to other, more reliable sources. Always remember that anyone can set up a website and that quality control can be difficult for the tax professional to ascertain.

EXHIBIT 2.9	Tax-Related Websites	
Website	**Web Address at Press Date**	**Description**
Internal Revenue Service	**irs.gov**	News releases, downloadable forms and instructions, tables, Circular 230, and filing advice.
Tax Analysts	**taxanalysts.org**	Policy-oriented readings on tax laws and proposals to change the law moderated bulletins on various tax subjects.
Tax laws online	**law.cornell.edu/cfr**	Treasury Regulations.
	law.cornell.edu/uscode	Internal Revenue Code.
	uscode.house.gov	
Commercial tax publishers	For example, **cchgroup.com** and **tax.thomsonreuters.com**	Information about products and services available by subscription and newsletter excerpts.
Accounting firms and professional organizations	For example, the AICPA's page is at **aicpa.org**, Ernst & Young is at **ey.com**, and KPMG is at **kpmg.com**	Tax planning newsletters, descriptions of services offered and career opportunities, and exchange of data with clients and subscribers.
Cengage Learning	**cengage.com**	Informational updates, newsletters, support materials for students and adopters, and continuing education.

Caution: Web addresses change frequently.

FINANCIAL DISCLOSURE INSIGHTS Where Does GAAP Come From?

Tax law is developed by many entities, including Congress, the legislators of other countries, the courts, the U.S. states, and the IRS. Accounting principles also have many sources. Consequently, in reconciling the tax and financial accounting reporting of a transaction, the tax professional needs to know the hierarchy of authority of accounting principles—in particular, the level of importance to assign to a specific GAAP document. The diagram below presents the sources of GAAP arranged in a general order of authority from highest to lowest.[27] Note how many of these GAAP sources parallel those that have been discussed with respect to the tax law.

Professional research is conducted to find and analyze the sources of accounting reporting standards in much the same way a tax professional conducts research concerning an open tax question. In fact, many of the publishers that provide tax research materials also can be used to find GAAP and IFRS documents. The Financial Accounting Standards Board (FASB) also makes its standards and interpretations available by subscription.

Highest Authority
- Financial Accounting Standards and Interpretations of the FASB.
- Pronouncements of bodies that preceded the FASB, such as the Accounting Principles Board (APB).

- FASB Technical Bulletins.
- Audit and Accounting Guides, prepared by the American Institute of CPAs (AICPA) and cleared by the FASB.
- Practice Bulletins, prepared by the American Institute of CPAs (AICPA) and cleared by the FASB.

- Interpretation Guides of the FASB Staff.
- Accounting Interpretations of the AICPA.
- ASB Accounting Standards.
- FASB Concepts Standards.
- Widely accepted accounting practices, professional journals, accounting textbooks, and treatises.

2-3 TAX RESEARCH ON THE CPA EXAMINATION

LO.4

Employ a strategy for applying tax research skills in taking the CPA exam.

The CPA examination includes tax-oriented questions in the following topical areas. Questions address issues involving tax compliance and tax planning matters.

- Federal tax procedures, ethics, and accounting issues.
- Federal taxation of property transactions.
- Federal taxation—individuals.
- Federal taxation—entities.

Each exam section includes multiple-choice questions and case studies called task-based simulations (TBSs). About 60 multiple-choice tax questions appear in the Regulation section of the exam. TBSs are small case studies designed to test a candidate's tax knowledge and skills using real-life work-related situations. Simulations make available access to certain authoritative literature for the candidate to research in completing the tax items (e.g., Internal Revenue Code, Regulations, IRS publications, and Federal tax forms).

[27]See Chapter 10 of R. B. Sawyers and S. L. Gill, *Federal Tax Research*, 11th ed. (Cengage Learning, 2018), for a discussion of strategies and techniques used in conducting research with financial accounting resources.

BRIDGE DISCIPLINE   Bridge to Regulation and Oversight

The interests of the public are represented by Federal, state, and local governments as they oversee the various economic transactions carried out by individuals and businesses. Control of the financial sector is assigned to the Treasury and the Securities and Exchange Commission, among other agencies.

Most citizens assume that attorneys and CPAs hold broad high-level skills in working with the tax laws. But the nature of today's economy dictates that professionals working in law and accounting instead develop narrower specialties that clients will find valuable in the marketplace. Only a subset of CPAs and attorneys practice regularly with the tax law, but all such professionals must hold and maintain broad-based skills in taxation.

Tax law is the subject of only one of the sections of the CPA exam, and only a portion of those questions relate to specific provisions of the tax law. The exam also tests the candidate's research and communication skills, and because it is administered with computer software, the candidate must have some technological facility as well.

The depth and variety of the skills that are required of an effective tax professional almost certainly are not measured well by the CPA or bar examinations. The integrity of the taxing system may be at risk when one can attain credible professional certification with only entry-level skills. Many observers would prefer that further levels of specialty certifications and rigorous, lifelong knowledge and skill improvement be required of tax professionals.

The typical TBS requires 15–30 minutes to complete. A simulation likely will require that the candidate determine which of the provided information is relevant to the task, and then to complete an analysis that a new CPA is expected to be able to complete. Examples of such simulations follow.

CPA Exam Simulation Example

EXAMPLE 7

The tax *citation type* simulation requires the candidate to research the Internal Revenue Code and enter a Code Section and subsection citation. For example, Amber Company is considering using the simplified dollar-value method of pricing its inventory for purposes of the LIFO method that is available to certain small businesses. What Internal Revenue Code Section is the relevant authority to which you should turn to determine whether the taxpayer is eligible to use this method? To be successful, the candidate must find § 474.

EXAMPLE 8

A *tax form completion* simulation requires the candidate to fill out a portion of a tax form. For example, Red is a limited liability company (LLC). Complete the income section of the Form 1065 for Red Company using the values found and calculated on previous tabs along with the following data.

Ordinary income from other partnerships	$ 5,200
Net gain (loss) from Form 4797	2,400
Management fee income	12,000

The candidate is provided with page 1 of Form 1065 on which to record the appropriate amounts.

Candidates can learn more about the CPA examination at **www.nasba.org/exams/cpaexam**. This online tutorial site reviews the exam's format, navigation functions, and tools. A 30- to 60-minute sample exam will familiarize a candidate with the types of questions on the examination.

RESEARCHING TAX QUESTIONS

In general, the fair market value of the coins that the Martels discovered must be included in 2018 gross income. This conclusion is based on tax research that you conducted, indicating that the taxpayers having "undisputed possession" of the coins (as of October 2018) creates gross income, under § 61 of the Code, and opinions expressed in U.S. Treasury Department regulations and court cases.

Does it make any difference that the couple paid $195,000 for the land where the coins were buried? Since the couple found the gold coins on their own property, the taxpayers could argue that they purchased the coins when they purchased the land. This argument is similar to an individual discovering oil or natural gas on her property. And with natural resources, there must be a realization event (e.g., a sale or exchange) before there is income. Would this notion work for this couple? Unfortunately, no. A decision affirmed by the Sixth Circuit Court of Appeals indicates that the entire value of the couple's discovery would be included in their income in the year of discovery.

Moreover, the "value" of the assets under the tax law is not the $28,000 face value of the coins. Rather, it is the fair market value of the coins.

Given the potential value of this discovery, your letter to the clients would encourage them to seek out a competent appraiser. Once a determination of the value of the assets is made, you then would work with the clients on a plan to pay the related Federal and state income taxes related to this discovery.

What If?

It is not uncommon that you later receive additional information from Fred and Megan about their discovery. This may occur if additional facts occur to them, if Fred and Megan gave you incomplete information because they did not understand which of the facts were relevant in determining the tax outcome, or if your original interviews and data collection from them were incomplete.

If this new information changes the conclusions and recommendations that you already had developed, you should make certain that the clients understand that your original work no longer is valid and that they should not depend on it.

Suggested Readings

Sheldon I. Banoff and Richard M. Lipton, Editors' Shop Talk, "Is Wikipedia Good Authority in the Tax Court?," *Journal of Taxation*, April 2007.

Cara Griffith, "Why Do We Still Have Unpublished Opinions?," *Tax Analysts Blog*, October 30, 2015.

Scott A. Hodge, "The Compliance Costs of IRS Regulations," June 15, 2016, **taxfoundation.org/ compliance-costs-irs-regulations**.

Annette Nellen, "Government Tax Treasures," *The Tax Adviser*, August 2015, **tinyurl.com/ tax-treasures**.

"Writing Skills for the Tax Professional," **www2.gsu.edu/~accerl/home.html**.

Key Terms

Acquiescence, 2-15

Circuit Court of Appeals, 2-12

Citator, 2-22

Court of Federal Claims, 2-10

Court of original jurisdiction, 2-10

Determination letters, 2-9

District Court, 2-10

Final Regulations, 2-7

Interpretive Regulations, 2-21

Legislative Regulations, 2-21

Letter rulings, 2-8

Nonacquiescence, 2-15

Precedents, 2-13

Procedural Regulations, 2-21

Proposed Regulations, 2-7

Revenue Procedures, 2-8

Revenue Rulings, 2-7

Small Cases Division, 2-10

Supreme Court, 2-13

Tax Court, 2-10

Technical Advice Memoranda (TAMs), 2-9

Temporary Regulations, 2-7

Writ of Certiorari, 2-14

Problems

1. **LO.1** What precedents must each of these courts follow?

   a.   U.S. Tax Court.

   b.   U.S. Court of Federal Claims.

   c.   U.S. District Court.

Communications 2. **LO.1, 3** Sonja Bishop operates a small international firm named Tile, Inc. A new treaty between the United States and Spain conflicts with a Section of the Internal Revenue Code. Sonja asks you for advice. If she follows the treaty position, does she need to disclose this on this year's tax return? If she is required to disclose, are there any penalties for failure to disclose? Prepare a letter in which you respond to Sonja. Tile's address is 100 International Drive, Tampa, FL 33620.

3. **LO.1** Distinguish between the following.

   a.   Treasury Regulations and Revenue Rulings.

   b.   Revenue Rulings and Revenue Procedures.

   c.   Revenue Rulings and letter rulings.

   d.   Letter rulings and determination letters.

4. **LO.1, 2** Rank the following items from the lowest to highest authority in the Federal tax law system.

   a.   Interpretive Regulation.

   b.   Legislative Regulation.

   c.   Letter ruling.

   d.   Revenue Ruling.

   e.   Internal Revenue Code.

   f.   Proposed Regulation.

5. **LO.1** Interpret each of the following citations.

   a.   Temp.Reg. § 1.956–2T.

   b.   Rev.Rul. 2012–15, 2012–23 I.R.B. 975.

   c.   Ltr.Rul. 200204051.

6. **LO.1** List an advantage and a disadvantage of using the U.S. Court of Federal Claims as the trial court for Federal tax litigation.

Communications 7. **LO.1, 3** Eddy Falls is considering litigating a tax deficiency of approximately $229,030 in the court system. He asks you to provide him with a short description of his litigation alternatives, indicating the advantages and disadvantages of each. Prepare your response to Eddy in the form of a letter. His address is 200 Mesa Drive, Tucson, AZ 85714.

8. **LO.1** A taxpayer lives in Michigan. In a controversy with the IRS, the taxpayer loses at the trial court level. Describe the appeal procedure for each of the following trial courts.
   a. Small Cases Division of the Tax Court.
   b. Tax Court.
   c. District Court.
   d. Court of Federal Claims.

9. **LO.1** For the Tax Court, the District Court, and the Court of Federal Claims, indicate the following.
   a. Number of regular judges per court.
   b. Availability of a jury trial.
   c. Whether the deficiency must be paid before the trial.

10. **LO.1** A taxpayer living in the following states would appeal a decision of the U.S. District Court to which Court of Appeals?
    a. Wyoming.
    b. Nebraska.
    c. Idaho.
    d. Louisiana.
    e. Illinois.

11. **LO.1** What is meant by the term *petitioner?*

12. **LO.1, 2** In assessing the validity of a prior court decision, discuss the significance of the following on the taxpayer's issue.
    a. The decision was rendered by the U.S. District Court of Wyoming. Taxpayer lives in Wyoming.
    b. The decision was rendered by the Court of Federal Claims. Taxpayer lives in Wyoming.
    c. The decision was rendered by the Second Circuit Court of Appeals. Taxpayer lives in California.
    d. The decision was rendered by the Supreme Court.
    e. The decision was rendered by the Tax Court. The IRS has acquiesced in the result.
    f. Same as part (e), except that the IRS has nonacquiesced in the result.

13. **LO.1** What is the difference between a Regular decision, a Memorandum decision, and a Summary Opinion of the Tax Court?

14. **LO.1** Explain the following abbreviations.
a.	CA–2.	f.	*Cert. denied.*	k.	F.3d.
b.	Fed.Cl.	g.	*acq.*	l.	F.Supp.
c.	*aff'd.*	h.	B.T.A.	m.	USSC.
d.	*rev'd.*	i.	USTC.	n.	S.Ct.
e.	*rem'd.*	j.	AFTR.	o.	D.Ct.

15. **LO.2** Referring to the citation only, determine which tax law source issued these documents.
a.	716 F.2d 693 (CA–9, 1983).	f.	50 AFTR 2d 92–6000 (Cl.Ct., 1992).
b.	92 T.C 400 (1998).	g.	Ltr.Rul. 9046036.
c.	70 U.S. 224 (1935).	h.	111 F.Supp.2d 1294 (S.D.N.Y., 2000).
d.	3 B.T.A. 1042 (1926).	i.	98–50, 1998–1 C.B. 10.
e.	T.C.Memo. 1957–169.		

16. **LO.2** Interpret each of the following citations.

     a.   14 T.C. 74 (1950).

     b.   592 F.2d 1251 (CA–5, 1979).

     c.   95–1 USTC ¶50,104 (CA–6, 1995).

     d.   75 AFTR 2d 95–110 (CA–6, 1995).

     e.   223 F.Supp. 663 (W.D. Tex., 1963).

17. **LO.2** Which of the following items may be found in the *Internal Revenue Bulletin*?

     a.   Action on Decision.

     b.   Small Cases Division of the Tax Court decision.

     c.   Letter ruling.

     d.   Revenue Procedure.

     e.   Final Regulation.

     f.   Court of Federal Claims decision.

     g.   Acquiescences to Tax Court decisions.

     h.   U.S. Circuit Court of Appeals decision.

18. **LO.2** Answer the following questions based upon this citation: *United Draperies, Inc. v. Comm.*, 340 F.2d 936 (CA–7, 1964), *aff'g* 41 T.C. 457 (1963), *cert. denied* 382 U.S. 813 (1965).

     a.   In which court did this decision first appear?

     b.   Did the appellate court uphold the trial court?

     c.   Who was the plaintiff?

     d.   Did the Supreme Court uphold the appellate court decision?

Critical Thinking   19. **LO.2, 4** For her tax class, Yvonne is preparing a research paper discussing the tax aspects of qualified stock options. Explain to Yvonne how she can research the provisions on this topic.

20. **LO.1, 2** Tom, an individual taxpayer, has been audited by the IRS and, as a result, has been assessed a substantial deficiency (which has not yet been paid) in additional income taxes. In preparing his defense, Tom advances the following possibilities.

     a.   Although a resident of Kentucky, Tom plans to sue in a U.S. District Court in Oregon that appears to be more favorably inclined toward taxpayers.

     b.   If part (a) is not possible, Tom plans to take his case to a Kentucky state court where an uncle is the presiding judge.

     c.   Because Tom has found a B.T.A. decision that seems to help his case, he plans to rely on it under alternative (a) or (b).

     d.   If he loses at the trial court level, Tom plans to appeal either to the U.S. Court of Federal Claims or to the U.S. Second Circuit Court of Appeals because he has relatives in both Washington, D.C., and New York. Staying with these relatives could save Tom lodging expense while his appeal is being heard by the court selected.

     e.   Whether or not Tom wins at the trial court or appeals court level, he feels certain of success on an appeal to the U.S. Supreme Court.

Evaluate Tom's notions concerning the judicial process as it applies to Federal income tax controversies.

21. **LO.1** Using the legend provided, classify each of the following statements (more than one answer per statement may be appropriate).

Legend

D = Applies to the District Court
T = Applies to the Tax Court
C = Applies to the Court of Federal Claims
A = Applies to the Circuit Court of Appeals
U = Applies to the Supreme Court
N = Applies to none of the above

a. Decides only Federal tax matters.
b. Decisions are reported in the F.3d Series.
c. Decisions are reported in the USTCs.
d. Decisions are reported in the AFTRs.
e. Appeal is by *Writ of Certiorari*.
f. Court meets most often in Washington, D.C.
g. Offers the choice of a jury trial.
h. Is a trial court.
i. Is an appellate court.
j. Allows appeal to the Court of Appeals for the Federal Circuit and bypasses the taxpayer's own Circuit Court of Appeals.
k. Has a Small Cases Division.
l. Is the only trial court where the taxpayer does not have to first pay the tax assessed by the IRS.

22. **LO.1, 2** Using the legend provided, classify each of the following citations as to the type of court.

Legend

D = District Court
T = Tax Court
C = Court of Federal Claims
A = Circuit Court of Appeals
U = Supreme Court
N = None of the above

a. Rev.Rul. 2009–34, 2009–42 I.R.B. 502.
b. *Joseph R. Bolker*, 81 T.C. 782 (1983).
c. *Magneson*, 753 F.2d 1490 (CA–9, 1985).
d. *Lucas v. Ox Fibre Brush Co.*, 281 U.S. 115 (1930).
e. *Ashtabula Bow Socket Co.*, 2 B.T.A. 306 (1925).
f. *BB&T Corp.*, 97 AFTR 2d 2006–873 (D.Ct. Mid.N.Car., 2006).
g. *Choate Construction Co.*, T.C.Memo. 1997–495.
h. Ltr.Rul. 200940021.
i. *John and Rochelle Ray*, T.C. Summary Opinion 2006–110.

23. **LO.1, 2** Using the legend provided, classify each of the following tax sources.

Legend

P = Primary tax source
S = Secondary tax source
B = Both
N = Neither

---

   a.   Sixteenth Amendment to the U.S. Constitution.
   b.   Tax treaty between the United States and India.
   c.   Revenue Procedure.
   d.   IRS Publication 17.
   e.   U.S. District Court decision.
   f.   *Yale Law Journal* article.
   g.   Temporary Regulations (issued 2017).
   h.   U.S. Tax Court Memorandum decision.
   i.   Small Cases Division of the U.S. Tax Court decision.
   j.   House Ways and Means Committee report.

24. **LO.1** In which Subchapter of the Internal Revenue Code would one find information about corporate distributions?

   a.   Subchapter S.
   b.   Subchapter C.
   c.   Subchapter P.
   d.   Subchapter K.
   e.   Subchapter M.

25. **LO.1, 2** To locate an IRS Revenue Procedure that was issued during the past week, which source would you consult?

   a.   *Federal Register.*
   b.   *Internal Revenue Bulletin.*
   c.   Internal Revenue Code.
   d.   Some other source. Identify it.

26. **LO.1, 2** In the citation *Schuster's Express, Inc.*, 66 T.C. 588 (1976), *aff'd* 562 F.2d 39 (CA–2, 1977), *nonacq.*, to what do the 66, 39, and *nonacq.* refer?

27. **LO.1** Is there an automatic right to appeal to the U.S. Supreme Court? If so, what is the process?

Ethics and Equity   28. **LO.2** An accountant friend of yours tells you that he "almost never" does any tax research because he believes that "research usually reveals that some tax planning idea has already been thought up and shot down." Besides, he points out, most tax returns are never audited by the IRS. Can a tax adviser who is dedicated to reducing his client's tax liability justify the effort to engage in tax research? Do professional ethics *demand* such efforts? Which approach would a client probably prefer?

Communications   29. **LO.1, 4** Go to the U.S. Tax Court website.

   a.   What different types of cases can be found on the site?
   b.   What is a Summary Opinion? Find one.
   c.   What is a Memorandum decision? Find one.
   d.   Find the court's Rules of Practice and Procedures.
   e.   Is the site user-friendly? E-mail suggested improvements to the site's webmaster.

30. **LO.2, 3** Locate the following Code provisions, and give a brief description of each   Communications
    in an e-mail to your instructor.
    a.   § 61(a)(13).
    b.   § 643(a)(2).
    c.   § 2503(g)(2)(A).

BRIDGE DISCIPLINE

1. Comment on these statements.
   a. The tax law is created and administered in the same way as other Federal provisions.
   b. Most taxpayers find it too expensive and time-consuming to sue the government in a tax dispute.

2. Using the title "The Federal Taxing System Operates Outside the U.S. Constitution," write a two-page paper to submit in your Government Policy course. Do not address "tax protester" issues (e.g., that the income tax is unconstitutional or that one's taxes should be measured using only the gold standard). Instead, concentrate on how Federal tax law is made and interpreted and how the process measures up to other governmental standards.   Communications

3. Develop an outline from which you will deliver a 10-minute talk to the local Chamber of Commerce, with the title "Regulation of the Tax Profession in the 21st Century." Use no more than four PowerPoint slides for your talk, and discuss what the business community now needs with respect to oversight of a stable, yet productive revenue-raising system. Include administrative developments of the last two years in your research.   Communications

4. A friend of yours, who is a philosophy major, has overheard the conversation described in Problem 28 and declares that all tax research is "immoral." She says that tax research enables people with substantial assets to shift the burden of financing public expenditures to those who "get up every morning, go to work, play by the rules, and pay their bills." How do you respond?   Ethics and Equity

Research Problems

Note: Solutions to the Research Problems can be prepared by using the Thomson Reuters Checkpoint™ online tax research database, which accompanies this textbook. Solutions can also be prepared by using research materials found in a typical tax library.

THOMSON REUTERS
CHECKPOINT™

Research Problem 1. Locate the following items, and e-mail to your professor a brief   Communications
summary of the results.
a.   *Terrell*, T.C.Memo. 2016–85.
b.   Ltr.Rul. 200231003.
c.   Action on Decision, 2000–004, May 10, 2000.

Research Problem 2. Locate the following Code citations, and list the subchapter, part, and subpart in which it is located. Then give a brief topical description of each.
a.   § 708(a).
b.   § 1371(a).
c.   § 2503(a).

Communications   **Research Problem 3.** Locate the following Regulations, and give a brief topical description of each. Summarize your comments in an e-mail to your instructor.

    a.   Reg. § 1.170A–4A(b)(2)(ii)(C).

    b.   Reg. § 1.672(b)–1.

    c.   Reg. § 20.2031–7(f).

Research Problem 4. Determine the missing data in these court decisions and rulings.

    a.   *Higgins v. Comm.*, 312 U.S.——— (1941).

    b.   *Talen v. U.S.*, 355 F.Supp.2d 22 (D.Ct. D.C., ———).

    c.   Rev.Rul. 2008–18, 2008–13 I.R.B.———.

    d.   *Pahl v. Comm.*, 150 F.3d 1124 (CA–9, ———).

    e.   *Veterinary Surgical Consultants PC*, 117 T.C.——— (2001).

    f.   *Yeagle Drywall Co.*, T.C.Memo. 2001———.

Research Problem 5. Locate the following Tax Court case: *Thomas J. Green, Jr.*, 59 T.C. 456 (1972). Briefly describe the issue in the case, and explain what the Tax Court said about using IRS publications to support a research conclusion.

Research Problem 6. Can a Tax Court Small Cases decision be treated as a precedent by other taxpayers? Explain.

Partial list of research aids:
§ 7463(b).
Maria Antionette Walton Mitchell, T.C. Summary Opinion 2004–160.

Research Problem 7. Find *Kathryn Bernal*, 120 T.C. 102 (2003), and answer the following questions.

    a.   What was the docket number?

    b.   When was the dispute filed?

    c.   Who is the respondent?

    d.   Who was the attorney for the taxpayers?

    e.   Who was the judge who wrote the opinion?

    f.   What was the disposition of the dispute?

Communications   **Research Problem 8.** Find three blogs related to tax practice. In a one-page document, list the URLs for each blog and the general topical areas addressed at each. Pick one posting from one of the blogs and summarize it. Then assess the quality of the blog from the standpoint of how easy it is to find and use. Send your document to the others in your course.

Communications   **Research Problem 9.** Find one instance of each of the following using a nonsubscription site on the Web or an online library at your school. In an e-mail to your professor, give a full citation for the document and describe how you found it.

    a.   Letter Ruling.   f.   Code Section.

    b.   Action on Decision.   g.   Tax Regulation.

    c.   IRS Notice.   h.   Tax treaty.

    d.   Revenue Ruling.   i.   Tax Court Summary Opinion.

    e.   Revenue Procedure.   j.   Tax Court Regular decision.

Taxes on the Financial Statements

LEARNING OBJECTIVES: *After completing Chapter 3, you should be able to:*

LO.1 Identify the differences between book and tax methods of computing income tax expense.

LO.2 Compute a corporation's book income tax expense.

LO.3 Describe the purpose of the valuation allowance.

LO.4 Interpret the disclosure information contained in the financial statements.

LO.5 Identify the GAAP treatment concerning tax uncertainties and tax law changes.

LO.6 Use financial statement income tax information to benchmark a company's tax position.

CHAPTER OUTLINE

3-1 Book-Tax Differences, 3-2
- 3-1a Different Reporting Entities, 3-2
- 3-1b Different Taxes, 3-4
- 3-1c Different Methods, 3-4
- 3-1d Tax Return Disclosures, 3-6

3-2 Income Taxes in the Financial Statements, 3-8
- 3-2a GAAP Principles, 3-8
- 3-2b Valuation Allowance, 3-12

- 3-2c Tax Disclosures in the Financial Statements, 3-15
- 3-2d Special Issues, 3-18
- 3-2e Summary, 3-23

3-3 Benchmarking, 3-24
- 3-3a Refining the Analysis, 3-24
- 3-3b Sustaining the Tax Rate, 3-25
- 3-3c Uses of Benchmarking Analysis, 3-26

TAX TALK *Truth is, figuring out how much tax a company actually pays is impossible.... Tax disclosure is just inscrutable.* —ROBERT WILLENS

TAXES ON THE FINANCIAL STATEMENTS

Raymond Jones, the CEO of Arctic Corporation, would like some help reconciling the amount of income tax expense on Arctic's financial statements with the amount of income tax reported on the company's corporate income tax return for its first year of operations. Mr. Jones does not understand why he can't simply multiply the financial statement income by the company's combined Federal and state 25 percent marginal income tax rate to get the financial tax expense. While the financial statements show book income before tax of $25 million, the reported income tax expense is only $5 million. In addition, the corporate tax return reports taxable income of $19 million and Federal income taxes payable of $3.99 million ($19 million × 21%).

Without knowing the specifics of the company's financial statements, does Arctic's situation look reasonable? Why is Arctic's financial accounting tax expense not equal to $6.25 million ($25 million × 25%)? What causes the $1.01 million difference between the taxes shown on the financial statements and the taxes due on the tax return?

Read the chapter and formulate your response.

T he ultimate result of the many tax planning ideas, advice, and compliance efforts provided by tax professionals to their clients is captured in a simple summary number—income tax expense. A U.S. corporation's tax expense is reported in its annual Federal tax return, its financial statements, and other regulatory filings and is often the starting point for state and local tax returns. As it turns out, however, deriving a corporation's income tax expense (i.e., its "provision" for income taxes) is not so simple.

A corporation may report millions of dollars in tax expense in its financial statements and yet pay virtually nothing to the U.S., state, or foreign governments. Alternatively, a corporation may pay substantial amounts to the U.S., state, and foreign governments and report a very small income tax expense in its financial statements. Why do such differences exist? Which income tax expense is the "correct" number? How can data regarding a corporation's income tax provision provide valuable information for the corporation, its competitors, and tax professionals assisting in the planning function? This chapter addresses these questions.

3-1 BOOK-TAX DIFFERENCES

LO.1

Identify the differences between book and tax methods of computing income tax expense.

A significant difference may exist between a corporation's Federal income tax liability as reported on its Form 1120 (tax) and the corporation's income tax expense as reported on its financial statements (book) prepared using generally accepted accounting principles (GAAP) . This book-tax difference is caused by one or more of the following.

- Different reporting entities included in the calculation.
- Different definition of taxes included in the income tax expense amount.
- Different accounting methods.

A corporation's activities are captured in its accounting records, producing general ledger results. At the end of the year, these records are summarized to produce a trial balance. Adjustments to these accounting data may be necessary to produce both the corporation's financial statements and its corporate income tax return. These book and tax adjustments rarely match. Different entities may be included in the reports, and the book and tax rules can be quite different. For instance, GAAP includes a materiality principle, under which some items can be ignored if they are insignificant in amount. The tax law includes no similar materiality threshold: all items are material in computing taxable income.

On a tax return, Schedule M–1 or M–3 reconciles the differences between an entity's book income and its taxable income, as discussed in text Section 3-1d. See also Exhibit 3.1.

3-1a Different Reporting Entities

Under GAAP, a corporate group must consolidate all U.S. and foreign subsidiaries within a single financial statement when the parent corporation controls more than 50 percent of the voting power of those subsidiaries.[1] In cases where the parent corporation owns between 20 and 50 percent of another corporation, the parent uses the equity method to account for the earnings of the subsidiary. Under the equity method, the parent currently records its share of the subsidiary's income or loss for the year.[2] Corporations that own less than 20 percent of other corporations typically use the *cost method* to account for income from these investments and include income only when actual dividends are received.

---

[1]*Consolidation*, ASC 810. Certain adjustments are made to reduce book income for the after-tax income related to minority shareholders.

[2]*Investments—Equity Method and Joint Ventures*, ASC 323.

EXHIBIT 3.1	Flow of Accounting Data

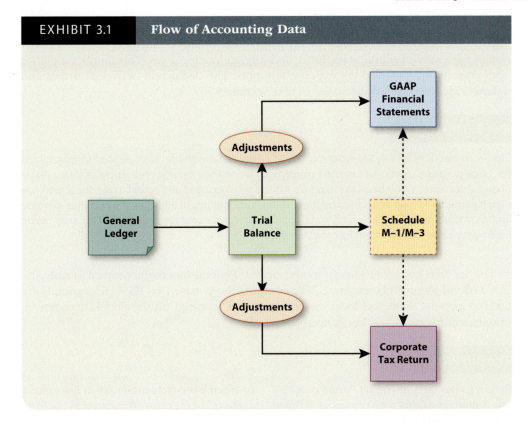

The Big Picture

EXAMPLE 1

Return to the facts of *The Big Picture* on p. 3-1. Arctic Corporation owns 100% of Gator, Inc., a domestic corporation; 100% of Hurricane, Ltd., a foreign corporation; and 40% of Beach, Inc., a domestic corporation. Arctic's combined financial statement includes its own net income and the net income of both Gator and Hurricane. In addition, Arctic's financial statement includes its 40% share of Beach's net income. Arctic's financial statement includes the income of these subsidiaries regardless of whether Arctic receives any actual profit distributions from its subsidiaries.

For Federal income tax purposes, a U.S. corporation may elect to include in its consolidated U.S. tax return any *domestic* subsidiaries that are 80 percent or more owned.[3] On the other hand, the income of non-U.S. subsidiaries and less than 80 percent owned domestic subsidiaries is not included in the consolidated tax return.

The Big Picture

EXAMPLE 2

Return to the facts of *The Big Picture* on p. 3-1. Also assume the facts presented in Example 1. If Arctic elects to include Gator as part of its consolidated Federal income tax return, Arctic's return includes its own taxable income and the taxable income generated by Gator. Hurricane's taxable income is not included in the consolidated return because it is a non-U.S. corporation. Beach, although a domestic corporation, cannot be consolidated with Arctic because Arctic owns only 40% of the stock. Results related to Hurricane and Beach are included in Arctic's U.S. taxable income only when Arctic receives actual or constructive dividends from those two companies.

[3]§§ 1501–1504. An existing election to consolidate an 80% or more owned subsidiary generally can be changed only with the permission of the IRS.

3-1b **Different Taxes**

The income tax amount reported on a corporation's financial statement is the combination of the entity's Federal, state, local, and foreign income taxes. This number includes both current and deferred tax expense amounts. The distinction between current and deferred income taxes is discussed in text Section 3-2a.

The Big Picture

EXAMPLE 3

Return to the facts of *The Big Picture* on p. 3-1. Also assume the facts presented in Example 1. For book purposes, Arctic, Gator, and Hurricane combine their income and expenses into a single financial statement. The book tax expense for the year includes all Federal, state, local, and foreign income taxes paid or accrued by these three corporations. In addition, the book tax expense amount includes any future Federal, state, local, or foreign income tax expenses (or tax savings) on income reported in the current income statement.

The income tax provision computed on the Federal income tax return is only the U.S. *Federal* income tax expense. This computation is based on the U.S. corporation's taxable income. State and local income taxes are reported on the Federal tax return, but as deductions in arriving at taxable income.

The Big Picture

EXAMPLE 4

Return to the facts of *The Big Picture* on p. 3-1. Also assume the facts presented in Examples 1 and 2. Arctic and Gator file a consolidated Federal tax return. The tax expense reported on the Form 1120 is only the U.S. Federal income tax expense for the consolidated taxable income of Arctic and Gator. This tax expense does not include the income taxes that Arctic and its subsidiaries paid to state, local, or foreign governments.

3-1c **Different Methods**

Many differences exist between book and tax accounting methods. Some are **temporary differences**, with income and expenses appearing in *both* the financial statement and the tax return, but in different reporting periods (i.e., a timing difference). Others are **permanent differences**, with items appearing in *either* the financial statement or the tax return, but not both.

Temporary differences include the following.

- *Depreciation on fixed assets.* A taxpayer may use an accelerated depreciation method for tax purposes [e.g., the modified accelerated cost recovery system (MACRS) rules], but adopt the straight-line method for book purposes. Even if identical methods are used, the period over which the asset is depreciated is likely to differ between book and tax; useful lives for tax purposes typically are shorter than those used for book computations, and tax rules can allow the acceleration of the deductions over the asset's life.

- *Compensation-related expenses.* Generally, the tax law does not allow the use of estimates or reserves, as is common under GAAP. For example, under GAAP, corporations accrue the future expenses related to providing postretirement benefits other than pensions (e.g., health insurance coverage). However, these expenses are deductible for tax purposes only when paid.[4]

- *Accrued income and expenses.* Although most income and expense items are recognized for tax and book purposes in the same period, a number of items potentially appear in different periods. For example, warranty expenses are accrued for book purposes but are not deductible for tax purposes until incurred.

---

[4]Exceptions to this rule exist (e.g., concerning stock incentive plans and deferred compensation).

Inventory write-offs are accrued for book but are not deductible for tax until incurred. Similarly, different methods regarding the timing of income recognition may create temporary differences. For instance, GAAP does not follow any of the various income tax deferral methods allowed by the Code for transactions with customers.[5] Similarly, GAAP recognizes income and loss when the *fair value* of most investment assets changes during the year, while tax rules recognize such realized gain or loss only upon a sale or other taxable disposition of the asset.

- *Net operating losses.* Taxable income for the year cannot be less than zero; thus, operating losses from one tax year may be "carried over" (i.e., used to offset taxable income in a future tax year). No such loss carryovers are used under GAAP; GAAP losses are reported as negative income amounts in the year incurred. As a result, the losses incurred in one year for book purposes may be used as a deduction for tax purposes in a different year.

- *Intangible assets.* Goodwill and some other intangibles are not amortizable for book purposes. However, GAAP requires an annual determination of whether the intangible asset has suffered a reduction in value (i.e., impairment). If an intangible has suffered an impairment, a current expense is required to reduce the asset's book value to the lower level. For tax purposes, certain intangibles (including goodwill) can be amortized over 15 years.[6]

Permanent differences include the following.

- *Nontaxable income.* A common example is municipal bond interest, which is income for book purposes but is not taxable.

- *Nondeductible expenses.* A portion of business meals, all entertainment expenses, and certain penalties are not deductible for tax purposes, but they are fully expensed in arriving at book income.

- *Special tax deductions.* GAAP does not allow expenses for certain income tax deductions, such as the dividends received deduction.

- *Tax credits.* Credits such as the research activities credit reduce the Federal income tax liability, but have no corresponding book treatment. Tax credits are discussed in Chapter 17.

In-depth coverage can be found on this book's companion website: www.cengage.com   **1 DIGGING DEEPER**

EXAMPLE 5

Wise, Inc., reported the following results for the current year.

Book income (before tax)	$ 685,000
Tax depreciation in excess of book	(125,000)
Nondeductible warranty expense	65,000
Municipal bond interest income	(35,000)
Taxable income (Form 1120)	$ 590,000

Wise reports net income before tax of $685,000 on its financial statement but must adjust this amount for differences between book and tax income.

Tax depreciation in excess of book is a tax deduction not currently expensed for book purposes, and warranty expense is deductible for book purposes but not yet deductible for tax. Both of these items are temporary differences, because they eventually reverse (with book depreciation eventually exceeding tax depreciation and the warranty expense ultimately deducted for tax when incurred).

The municipal bond interest is a permanent difference because this income will never be subject to tax.

---

[5]ASC 606, *Revenue from Contracts with Customers*; c.f. Rev.Proc. 2004–34, 2004–1 C.B. 991.

[6]See § 197 and *Intangibles—Goodwill and Other*, ASC Topic 350 (formerly *Goodwill and Other Intangible Assets*, Statement of Financial Accounting Standards No. 142).

FINANCIAL DISCLOSURE INSIGHTS   Supersized Goodwill

When a balance sheet includes an asset value for goodwill, the company's total valuation is seen to exceed the aggregate value of its physical assets, such as cash and equipment. Goodwill typically is created as the result of the takeover of a target entity in an acquisition transaction.

GAAP rules concerning goodwill and its impairment evolved in a context of stable market values and managed income. But when goodwill gets to be so large that it is a major asset in itself, are GAAP impairment write-downs sure to follow?

An impairment write-down often is an indication that an acquiror overpaid for the target entity in a takeover transaction. Thus, conglomerates that grow by a series of acquisitions may be doubly exposed to goodwill write-downs. Accordingly, goodwill and its impairment can become an outsized element of the financial statements for many companies.

In a recent year, the following data concerning recorded goodwill were reported.

Company	Goodwill as a Percentage of Balance Sheet Assets
Time Warner	42.1%
Kraft Heinz	36.6%
Frontier Communications	33.3%
Dr Pepper Snapple Group	30.6%
Starbucks	12.0%
Netflix	0.0%

3-1d Tax Return Disclosures

Book-tax differences are reported in the Federal income tax returns of most business entities.

Exhibit 3.2 contains the **Schedule M–1** from Form 1120, the corporate income tax return. The purpose of Schedule M–1 is to reconcile book income to the taxable income as reported on the tax return. Line 1 is the net income or loss per books, and line 2 adds back the book tax expense to get back to book income before tax.[7] The remainder of Schedule M–1 contains adjustments for both temporary and permanent differences, until arriving at taxable income on line 10.[8]

EXHIBIT 3.2	Schedule M–1

Schedule M–1   **Reconciliation of Income (Loss) per Books With Income per Return**

Note: The corporation may be required to file Schedule M-3. See instructions.

1	Net income (loss) per books		7	Income recorded on books this year not included on this return (itemize):
2	Federal income tax per books			Tax-exempt interest $ _____
3	Excess of capital losses over capital gains .			-------------------------------------
4	Income subject to tax not recorded on books this year (itemize):_____			-------------------------------------
	-------------------------------------		8	Deductions on this return not charged against book income this year (itemize):
5	Expenses recorded on books this year not deducted on this return (itemize):		a	Depreciation . . $ _____
a	Depreciation . . . . $ _____		b	Charitable contributions $ _____
b	Charitable contributions . $ _____			-------------------------------------
c	Travel and entertainment . $ _____			-------------------------------------
	-------------------------------------		9	Add lines 7 and 8 . . . .
6	Add lines 1 through 5		10	Income (page 1, line 28)—line 6 less line 9

---

[7]Line 1, "Net income (loss) per books," is not defined in the instructions to the form, and corporations can use various starting points in the Schedule M–1 (e.g., only the book income from U.S. members of the group). The Schedule M–3 is more specific in defining book income.

[8]Form 1120, page 1, line 28 represents corporate taxable income before subtracting the net operating loss and dividends received deductions.

Schedule M–3 is required for a C corporation or consolidated tax group with total year-end assets of at least $10 million. The Schedule M–3 provides the IRS with more detailed information than is provided in the Schedule M–1. In addition, the Schedule M–3 requires identification of whether a book-tax difference is temporary or permanent.

Schedule M–1 or M–3 typically is the starting point for IRS audits of corporations. Identifying large differences between book and taxable income may offer the IRS auditor insights into tax saving strategies (some perhaps questionable) employed by the taxpayer. Concept Summary 3.1 summarizes the sources of typical corporate book-tax differences.

In-depth coverage can be found on this book's companion website: **www.cengage.com**   **2   DIGGING DEEPER**

Concept Summary 3.1

Income Reporting: Book versus Tax

Financial Statement	**U.S. Federal Income Tax Return**
Reporting entities	**Reporting entities**
• 50% or more owned domestic and foreign subsidiaries *must* be consolidated.	• 80% or more owned domestic subsidiaries *may* be consolidated.
• Share of income from 20 to 50% owned domestic and foreign corporations included in current income.	• Share of income from other corporations reported only when actual or constructive dividends are received.
Income tax expense	**Income tax expense**
• Federal income taxes.	• Federal income taxes.
• State income taxes.	• Current only.
• Local income taxes.	
• Non-U.S. income taxes.	
• Current and deferred.	
Methods	**Methods**
• Temporary differences.	• Temporary differences.
• Permanent differences.	• Permanent differences.
• Income tax note reconciliation.	• Schedule M–1 or M–3 reconciliation.

Uncertain Tax Positions

The IRS requires that large corporations list the tax return positions they have taken that may not be fully supported by the law. Schedule UTP ("uncertain tax positions") is added to the Form 1120 for all corporations with assets of at least $10 million.[9]

Disclosures on the Schedule UTP include a list of tax return positions for the current and prior tax years where:

• The taxpayer or a related party recorded a reserve against the Federal income tax expense on its audited financial statements, or

---

[9]Some tax professionals feel that the Schedule UTP alerts the IRS to specific items that will be most vulnerable to audit adjustments. The public does not have access to a corporation's Schedule UTP because tax returns are confidential documents.

- The taxpayer or a related party did *not* record a reserve based on its analysis of expected litigation with the IRS. This means that, in the taxpayer's view, the issue will not be settled with the IRS and, instead, will be litigated. In addition, after analyzing relevant tax law, the taxpayer determines that, if it chooses to take the issue to court, it is *more likely than not* (a greater than 50 percent likelihood) to win the case.

Disclosures are not required for items that are immaterial under GAAP rules, or for which the filing position is sufficiently certain that no financial accounting reserve is required.

The IRS maintains that it will limit releases of the Schedule UTP to other taxing jurisdictions, and that it will not use Schedule UTP data to usurp the attorney-client and tax practitioner privileges of confidentiality or the work-product doctrine. Taxpayers are not required to disclose the amounts of any reserves or the precise nature of the tax planning technique that led to the reserve for the filing position.

For some taxpayers, tax filing positions reported on Schedules UTP are few in number because they are "less aggressive" in making filing decisions, or because they negotiate with the IRS before filing a return as to certain deductions and credits. The most commonly reported uncertain tax positions on a Schedule UTP involve the research credit and transfer pricing computations.

3-2 INCOME TAXES IN THE FINANCIAL STATEMENTS

LO.2

Compute a corporation's book income tax expense.

3-2a GAAP Principles

A corporation's financial statements are prepared in accordance with GAAP. The purpose and objectives of these statements are quite different from the objective of the corporation's income tax return.

The **ASC 740** approach produces a total income tax expense (also called the **income tax provision**) for the income currently reported on a corporation's combined financial statement.[10] This approach follows the *matching principle*, where all of the expenses related to earning income are reported in the same period in which the revenue is reported, without regard to when the expenses actually are paid. If an entity fails to follow GAAP in reporting its tax provision and related accounts, the SEC could respond with a comment letter indicating a material weakness in the financial statements, or the agency might require a full restatement of the statements.

EXAMPLE

6

PanCo, Inc., earns $100,000 in book income before tax and is subject to a 21% marginal Federal income tax rate. PanCo records a single temporary difference. Tax depreciation exceeds book depreciation by $20,000. Accordingly, PanCo's taxable income is $80,000 ($100,000 − $20,000 additional tax deduction).

On its income tax return, PanCo reports a current Federal tax liability of $16,800 ($80,000 × 21%). On its financial statement, PanCo reports a total tax provision of $21,000 ($100,000 × 21%). This $4,200 book-tax difference relates to the difference between the book and tax basis of the depreciable asset times the current corporate tax rate ($4,200 = $20,000 × 21%).

Although PanCo did not actually pay the $4,200 Federal income tax this year, in future years when the book-tax depreciation difference reverses, the $4,200 eventually will be paid. As a result, the *future* income tax expense is matched to the related book income and is reported in the GAAP statements for the current year.

---

[10]*Income Taxes*, ASC 740.

FINANCIAL DISCLOSURE INSIGHTS The Book-Tax Income Gap

According to one study, 115 companies in the Standard and Poor's stock index incurred a Federal and state income tax rate of less than 20 percent. In fact, the rate for 39 of those companies was less than 10 percent.

At least 30 of the Fortune 500 companies paid zero or negative Federal corporate income taxes over a recent three-year period. These companies included General Electric, American Electric Power, FedEx, Honeywell, Pfizer, Verizon, Boeing, and PG&E. Pepco Holdings reported an effective Federal income tax rate of *negative* 57.6 percent!

The firms maintained that they had paid all of their required tax liabilities and that effective income tax planning had resulted in their zero or negative effective tax rates.

Corporations further maintain that the large differences in book and tax income are a function of the different rules and objectives of GAAP for financial statements and the Internal Revenue Code for tax returns.

Low effective tax rates often are traceable to one or more of the following.

- Use of NOL carryovers.

- Large investments in depreciable assets.

- Use of state, local, federal, and international tax incentives (e.g., to encourage new companies and targeted industries such as high-tech, energy, and domestic manufacturing).

- Use of temporary tax provisions (e.g., stimulus, antirecession, or other targeted rules designed to stimulate the economy via tax cuts).

- Negotiations and settlements with revenue agencies.[11]

- Application of legal tax planning techniques.

The total book tax expense under ASC 740 is made up of both current and deferred components. The **current tax expense** represents the theoretical tax liability payable to (or refund receivable from) the governmental authorities for the current period.[12]

One might think of this amount as the actual check the taxpayer writes to the government (or refund received) for the current year; some tax professionals refer to this as the "cash tax" amount. Exhibit 3.3 summarizes the computation of a corporation's current tax expense.

The deferred component of the book tax expense is called the **deferred tax expense** or **deferred tax benefit**. This component represents the future tax cost (or savings) connected with income reported in the current-period financial statement.[13] Deferred tax expense or benefit is created as a result of temporary differences. More technically, ASC 740 adopts a **balance sheet approach** to measuring deferred taxes. Under this approach, the deferred tax expense or benefit is the change from one year to the next in the entity's net, cumulative **deferred tax liability** or **deferred tax asset**.

EXHIBIT 3.3	Current Tax Expense (Simplified)

	Pretax book income
±	Schedule M–1/M–3 adjustments
	Taxable income before NOLs
−	NOL carryforwards
	Taxable income
×	Applicable tax rate
	Current tax expense (provision) before tax credits
−	Tax credits
	Current tax expense (tax provision)

---

[11]For instance, AstraZeneca reduced its effective tax rate after settling an audit with U.S. and U.K. tax authorities about its transfer pricing policies (see text Section 16-4c). The taxpayer's liability after the settlement was less than the tax reserve it had set aside on its GAAP statements with respect to the audit.

[12]ASC 740-10-10-1(a).
[13]ASC 740-10-10-1(b).

A *deferred tax liability* is the expected future tax liability related to current income (measured using enacted tax rates and rules). A deferred tax liability is created in the following situations.

- An item is deductible for tax in the current period but is not expensed for book until some future period.

- Income is includible currently for book purposes but is not includible in taxable income until a future period.

In essence, a deferred tax liability is created when the book basis of an asset exceeds its tax basis. The opposite condition creates a deferred tax asset.

Deferred Tax Expense

EXAMPLE 7

PJ Enterprises earns net income before depreciation of $500,000 in 2018 and $600,000 in 2019. PJ uses equipment acquired in 2018 for $80,000. For tax purposes, assume that PJ uses an accelerated method and deducts $60,000 in depreciation expense for the first year and $20,000 in depreciation expense for the second year. For book purposes, PJ depreciates the asset on a straight-line basis over two years ($40,000 in depreciation expense per year).

2018

	Beginning of Year			End of Year			Change in Basis Difference This Year	Federal and State Income Tax Rate	Change in Deferred Tax Liability
	Book Basis	Tax Basis	Basis Differences, Book to Tax	Book Basis	Tax Basis	Basis Differences, Book to Tax			
Equipment	$—	$—	$—	$40,000	$20,000	$20,000	$20,000	25%	$5,000

A $5,000 deferred tax liability is created in 2018, due to the timing difference for the equipment depreciation.

2019

	Beginning of Year			End of Year			Change in Basis Difference This Year	Federal and State Income Tax Rate	Change in Deferred Tax Liability
	Book Basis	Tax Basis	Basis Differences, Book to Tax	Book Basis	Tax Basis	Basis Differences, Book to Tax			
Equipment	$40,000	$20,000	$20,000	$—	$—	$—	($20,000)	25%	($5,000)

The book-tax difference in the asset basis reverses in 2019, with a resulting reduction of the deferred tax liability account.

---

[14]One can keep up with the FASB and the IASB's work on income tax reporting by visiting the FASB website at **www.fasb.org** and searching for the "Technical Agenda" and "Research" sections under "Projects."

[15]See, for example, Notice 2017–15, 2017–15 I.R.B. 1074, as to the joint FASB and IFRS revenue recognition projects.

Deferred Tax Expense

EXAMPLE 8

Continue with the facts in Example 7. The following journal entries record the book tax expense (provision) for each year. The book total tax expense combines the current amount (income tax payable) and the future amount (deferred tax liability).

2018 Journal Entry

Income tax expense (provision)	$115,000*	
Income tax payable		$110,000**
Deferred tax liability		5,000

2019 Journal Entry

Income tax expense (provision)	$140,000*	
Deferred tax liability	5,000	
Income tax payable		$145,000**

At the end of 2018, the PJ balance sheet reflects a net deferred tax liability of $5,000. At the end of 2019, the PJ balance sheet contains a zero deferred tax liability; the temporary difference that created the deferred tax liability has reversed itself.

*2018: ($500,000 − $40,000) × 25%	**2018: ($500,000 − $60,000) × 25%
2019: ($600,000 − $40,000) × 25%	2019: ($600,000 − $20,000) × 25%

A *deferred tax asset* is the expected future tax benefit related to current book income (measured using enacted tax rates and rules). A deferred tax asset is created in the following situations.

- An expense is claimed for book purposes in the current period but is not deductible for tax until some future period.
- Income is includible in taxable income currently but is not recorded as book income until a future period.

Deferred Tax Assets

EXAMPLE 9

MollCo, Inc., earns net income before warranty expense of $400,000 in 2018 and $450,000 in 2019. In 2018, MollCo records $30,000 in warranty expense for book purposes related to expected warranty repairs. This warranty expense is not deductible for tax purposes until actually incurred. Assume that the $30,000 warranty obligation is paid in 2019 and that this is MollCo's only temporary difference.

2018

	Beginning of Year			End of Year			Change in Basis Difference This Year	Federal and State Income Tax Rate	Change in Deferred Tax Liability
	Book Basis	Tax Basis	Basis Differences, Book to Tax	Book Basis	Tax Basis	Basis Differences, Book to Tax			
Warranty	$—	$—	$—	$—	$30,000	($30,000)	($30,000)	25%	($7,500)

A $7,500 deferred tax asset is created in 2018, due to the timing difference for the warranty obligations.

2019

	Beginning of Year			End of Year			Change in Basis Difference This Year	Federal and State Income Tax Rate	Change in Deferred Tax Liability
	Book Basis	Tax Basis	Basis Differences, Book to Tax	Book Basis	Tax Basis	Basis Differences, Book to Tax			
Warranty	$—	$30,000	($30,000)	$—	$—	$—	$30,000	25%	$7,500

The book-tax difference in the warranty expense payable reverses in 2019, with a resulting reduction of the deferred tax asset account.

Deferred Tax Assets

EXAMPLE 10

Continue with the facts in Example 9. The following journal entries record the book tax expense (provision) for each year. The book total tax expense combines the current amount (income tax payable) and the future amount (deferred tax asset).

2018 Journal Entry

Income tax expense (provision)	$ 92,500	
Deferred tax asset	7,500	
Income tax payable		$100,000

2019 Journal Entry

Income tax expense (provision)	$112,500	
Deferred tax asset		$ 7,500
Income tax payable		105,000

At the end of 2018, the MollCo balance sheet reflects a net deferred tax asset of $7,500. At the end of 2019, the MollCo balance sheet contains a zero deferred tax asset; the temporary difference that created the deferred tax asset has reversed itself.

Deferred tax assets and liabilities are reported on the balance sheet just like any other asset or liability. However, the interpretation of these assets and liabilities is quite different. Typically, an asset is "good" because it represents a claim on something of value, and a liability is "bad" because it represents a future claim against the corporation's assets. In the case of deferred tax assets and liabilities, the interpretation is reversed. Deferred tax liabilities are "good" because they represent an amount that may be paid to the government in the future.

In essence, deferred tax liabilities are like an interest-free loan to the taxpayer from the government with a due date perhaps many years in the future. Deferred tax assets, on the other hand, are future tax benefits, so they are similar to a receivable from the government that may not be received until many years in the future.

3-2b Valuation Allowance

LO.3

Describe the purpose of the valuation allowance.

Much of GAAP is based on the conservatism principle . That is, accounting rules are designed to provide assurance that assets are not overstated and liabilities are not understated. Current recognition of deferred tax liabilities does not require significant professional judgment because future tax liabilities always are expected to be settled in full. However, under ASC 740, deferred tax assets are recognized only when it is *more likely than not* (a greater than 50 percent likelihood) that the future tax benefits will be realized.

Using Future Tax Benefits

EXAMPLE 11

Warren, Inc., reported book income before tax of $2 million in 2017. Warren's taxable income also is $2 million (i.e., there are no temporary or permanent differences). Warren reports a current U.S. income tax liability for the year of $420,000 before tax credits ($2 million × 21%). During the year, Warren earned $100,000 in general business credits that it is not able to use as a credit on its 2019 tax return.

Warren's auditors believe it is *more likely than not* that Warren will be able to use the $100,000 of tax credits within the next 20 years (i.e., in a period before they expire unused). Consequently, the future tax benefit of the tax credits is accounted for in the current-year book tax expense as a $100,000 future tax benefit.

The current and deferred tax expense are calculated as follows.

	Book	Tax
Income tax expense/payable	$320,000	$420,000
Current tax expense	$420,000	
Deferred tax expense (benefit)	($100,000)	

Using Future Tax Benefits

EXAMPLE
12

Warren records the following journal entry for the book income tax expense and deferred tax asset related to the expected use of the FTCs.

Income tax expense (provision)	$320,000	
Deferred tax asset	100,000	
Income tax payable		$420,000

Because Warren can record the benefit of the future tax credits, its effective tax rate is 16% ($320,000 tax expense ÷ $2 million book income before tax).

When a deferred tax asset does not meet the *more likely than not* threshold for recognition, ASC 740 requires that a **valuation allowance** be created. The valuation allowance is a contra-asset account that offsets all or a portion of the deferred tax asset.

Valuation Allowance

EXAMPLE
13

Assume that the auditors in Example 11 believe that Warren will be able to use only $40,000 of the general business credits, with the remaining $60,000 expiring unused. In this case, the future tax benefit recognized currently should be only $40,000 rather than the full $100,000. To implement this reduction in the deferred tax asset, Warren records a valuation allowance of $60,000, resulting in a book tax expense of $380,000.

	Book	Tax
Income tax expense/payable	$380,000	$420,000
Current tax expense	$420,000	
Deferred tax expense (benefit)	($ 40,000)	

EXAMPLE
14

Warren records the following journal entry for the book income tax expense and deferred tax asset related to the expected use of the FTCs.

Income tax expense (provision)	$380,000	
Deferred tax asset	100,000	
Valuation allowance		$ 60,000
Income tax payable		420,000

Warren reduces the deferred tax asset by $60,000, which increases its effective tax rate to 19% ($380,000 tax expense ÷ $2 million book income before tax), compared with the 16% effective tax rate in Example 12.

To determine whether a valuation allowance is required, both positive and negative evidence must be evaluated. Negative evidence (i.e., evidence suggesting that the deferred tax asset will not be realized) includes the following.

- History of losses.
- Expected future losses.
- Short carryback/carryforward periods.
- History of tax credits expiring unused.

Positive evidence (i.e., support for realizing the current benefit of future tax savings) includes the following.

- Strong earnings history.
- Existing contracts.
- Unrealized appreciation in assets.
- Sales backlog of profitable orders.

TAX PLANNING STRATEGIES Releasing Valuation Allowances

FRAMEWORK FOCUS: DEDUCTIONS

Strategy: Maximize Deductible Amounts.

When a corporation records a valuation allowance, it loses the ability to recognize the benefit of future tax savings in the current period. However, all is not lost if the taxpayer can demonstrate that facts and circumstances have changed. For example, if a taxpayer generates a net operating loss (NOL), it records a deferred tax asset for the future tax savings related to using the NOL. However, if the evidence suggests that it is *more likely than not* that all or a portion of the NOL never will be used, a valuation allowance must be recorded.

To reduce this valuation allowance, the taxpayer must demonstrate that there will be enough future taxable income to absorb the NOL in the future. Sources of future taxable income include reversals of temporary differences that will produce future taxable income, demonstrated efficiencies that will reduce future expenses, documented expected increases in sales (and capacity), and any other sources of future profits. Taxpayers also may demonstrate that the adoption of new tax planning strategies will allow the use of deferred tax assets.

For example, assume that Warren, Inc., from Example 13, adopts new planning strategies in 2020 that will allow it ultimately to use all $100,000 of its general business credit carryforward. Warren earns $2.3 million in book income before tax and reports $2.3 million in taxable income in 2020 (i.e., there are no permanent or temporary differences). The current Federal income tax expense is $483,000 ($2.3 million × 21%).

Based on new evidence (implementation of tax planning strategies), the auditors determine that the entire $100,000 in tax credits will be used in the future before they expire. Accordingly, the $60,000 valuation allowance from 2019 is "released," and the tax benefit of this release affects the 2020 financial results as follows.

	Book	Tax
Income tax expense/payable	$423,000	$483,000
Current tax expense	$483,000	
Deferred tax expense	($ 60,000)	

Warren makes the following 2020 journal entry to record the book income tax expense and valuation allowance release related to the expected use of the credits.

Income tax expense (provision)	$423,000	
Valuation allowance	60,000	
Income tax payable		$483,000

Warren's effective tax rate for 2020 is 18.4 percent ($423,000 ÷ $2.3 million). Without the valuation allowance release, Warren's effective tax rate would have been 21 percent ($483,000 ÷ $2.3 million). This tax rate benefit is realized even though the $100,000 in credit carryforwards has yet to be used in Warren's tax return.

The valuation allowance is examined for appropriateness each year. The allowance may be increased or decreased in subsequent reporting periods if facts and circumstances change.

The Big Picture

EXAMPLE 15

Return to the facts of *The Big Picture* on p. 3-1. Arctic Corporation has recorded a $3 million deferred tax asset for an NOL carryforward. The deferred tax asset has been offset by a $1 million valuation allowance, due to doubts over the levels of future sales and profitability.

But this year, Arctic completed improvements to its inventory management system that are likely to increase the contribution margin of every product that Arctic sells. In addition, two of Arctic's largest customers have secured financing that will relieve the financial difficulties that have restricted them. In fact, Arctic just received purchase orders from those customers that will increase unit sales by 20% over the next 18 months. As a result, Arctic's auditors now support a release of $200,000 of the valuation allowance in the current quarter.

DIGGING DEEPER 3   In-depth coverage can be found on this book's companion website: **www.cengage.com**

3-2c **Tax Disclosures in the Financial Statements**

As illustrated earlier, any temporary differences create deferred tax liabilities or deferred tax assets, and these amounts appear in the corporation's balance sheet.

LO.4

Interpret the disclosure information contained in the financial statements.

The Balance Sheet

Deferred tax accounts are treated as noncurrent items on the GAAP balance sheet.[16] A corporation may hold both deferred tax assets and liabilities. The corporation can keep these items separate or report the *net* noncurrent deferred tax assets or liabilities.[17]

The Income Statement

In its GAAP income statement, a corporation reports a total income tax expense that consists of both the current tax expense (or benefit) and the deferred tax expense (or benefit). The tax expense is allocated among income from continuing operations, discontinued operations, extraordinary items, prior-period adjustments, and the cumulative effect of accounting changes. Additional disclosures are required for the tax expense allocated to income from continuing operations (e.g., current versus deferred, benefits of NOL deductions, and changes in valuation allowances).

FINANCIAL DISCLOSURE INSIGHTS **Tax Losses and the Deferred Tax Asset**

Although a current-year net operating loss (NOL) represents a failure of an entity's business model to some, others see it as an immediate tax refund. But when an NOL hits the balance sheet as a deferred tax asset, the story is not over. The NOL creates or increases a deferred tax asset that may or may not be used in future financial accounting reporting periods. The key question for a financial analyst is whether the entity will generate enough net revenue in future years to create a positive tax liability that can be offset by the NOL carryover amount.

IFRS rules do not allow for a valuation allowance. Under IAS 12, a deferred tax asset is recorded only when it is "probable" (a higher standard than GAAP's "more likely than not") that the deferred tax amount will be realized, and then only to the extent of that probable amount. Thus, no offsetting valuation allowance is needed.

TAX FACT **Effective Tax Rates for Fortune 100 Companies**

Here are some recent provisions for income taxes (state, federal, and international) made by selected major corporations, as a percentage of their book income before taxes. These rates were incurred prior to the tax rate changes related to 2017 tax reform.

Allstate	31.8%
Apple	25.6%
Boeing	12.1%
Cisco	16.9%
Citigroup	30.0%
CostCo	34.3%

ExxonMobil	(5.1)%
Ford	32.2%
General Motors	25.7%
Google (Alphabet)	19.4%
IBM	3.6%
JPMorgan Chase	28.4%
Pfizer	13.5%
Starbucks	32.9%
Wal-Mart	30.3%
Walgreens	19.9%

Source: **tinyurl.com/corp-rates.**

---

[16]ASC 740-10-45-4.

[17]ASC 740-10-45-6.

Financial Statement Footnotes

The income tax footnote contains a wealth of information, including the following.

- Breakdown of income between domestic and foreign.
- Analysis of the provision for income tax expense.
- Analysis of deferred tax assets and liabilities.
- Effective tax **rate reconciliation** (dollar amount or percentage).
- Discussion of significant tax matters.

The steps in determining a corporation's income tax expense for book purposes are summarized in Concept Summary 3.2.

Rate Reconciliation

The purpose of the rate reconciliation is to demonstrate how a corporation's actual book effective tax rate relates to its "hypothetical tax rate" (i.e., as if the book income were taxed fully at the top U.S. corporate rate of 21 percent).[18] Although similar to Schedule M–1 or M–3, the tax footnote rate reconciliation generally reports only differences triggered by permanent book-tax differences. An analysis of the rate reconciliation can provide substantial indicators as to the tax planning strategies adopted (or not adopted) by a company; see text Section 3-3.

Concept Summary 3.2

Steps in Determining the Book Tax Expense

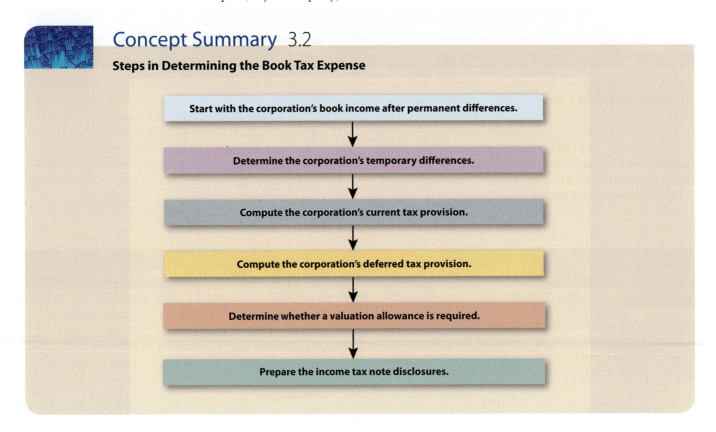

Start with the corporation's book income after permanent differences.

↓

Determine the corporation's temporary differences.

↓

Compute the corporation's current tax provision.

↓

Compute the corporation's deferred tax provision.

↓

Determine whether a valuation allowance is required.

↓

Prepare the income tax note disclosures.

---

[18]ASC 740-10-50-12.

BoxCo, Inc., a domestic corporation, owns 100% of PaperCo, Ltd., an Erasmus corporation. BoxCo's U.S. corporate tax rate is 21%, and its Erasmus rate is 10%. Book income, permanent and temporary differences, and current tax expense are computed as follows.

EXAMPLE

16

	BoxCo	PaperCo
Book income before tax	$300,000	$200,000
Permanent differences		
Business meals expense	20,000	—
Municipal bond interest income	(50,000)	—
Book income after permanent differences	$270,000	$200,000
Temporary differences		
Tax > book depreciation	(50,000)	—
Book > tax bad debt expense	10,000	—
Taxable income	$230,000	$200,000
Tax rate	× 21%	× 10%
Current tax expense	$ 48,300	$ 20,000

Specifically, basis amounts and current deductions for the two assets are reported as follows.

	Book Basis, Beginning of Year	Tax Basis, Beginning of Year	Basis Difference, Beginning of Year	Current-Year Book Expense	Current-Year Tax Deduction
Depreciable assets	$900,000	$750,000	$150,000	$40,000	$90,000
Receivables	800,000	850,000	(50,000)	15,000	5,000

Thus, the beginning-of-the-year deferred tax liability is $21,000 [($150,000 − $50,000) × 21%].

To determine the deferred tax expense (benefit) for the current year, the change in the balance sheet amounts for these temporary differences from the beginning to the end of the year must be determined and then multiplied by the appropriate tax rate.

	Beginning of Year			End of Year			Change in Basis Difference This Year	Tax Rate	Change in Deferred Tax Liability/ (Asset)
	Book Basis	Tax Basis	Basis Differences, Book to Tax	Book Basis	Tax Basis	Basis Differences, Book to Tax			
Depreciation	$900,000	$750,000	$150,000	$860,000	$660,000	$200,000	$ 50,000	21%	$10,500
Receivables	800,000	850,000	(50,000)	785,000	845,000	(60,000)	(10,000)	21%	(2,100)

The deferred tax liability increased by $8,400 for the year. Consequently, BoxCo's total tax provision for book purposes is $76,700.

Current tax expense	
Domestic	$48,300
Foreign	20,000
Deferred tax expense	
Domestic	8,400
Foreign	—
Total tax expense	$76,700

continued

The journal entry to record the book income tax expense is constructed as follows.

Income tax expense (provision)	$76,700	
Income tax payable		$68,300
Deferred tax liability		8,400

BoxCo's book income is $500,000 (the combined book income of both BoxCo and PaperCo). The effective tax rate reconciliation is based on this book income, with the dollar amounts in the table representing the tax expense (benefit) related to the item and the percentage representing the tax expense (benefit) as a percentage of book income. For example, the municipal bond interest of $50,000 reduces tax liability by $10,500 ($50,000 × 21%). This $10,500 as a percentage of the $500,000 book income equals 2.1%.

	Effective Tax Rate Reconciliation	
	$	%
Hypothetical tax at U.S. rate	$105,000	21.0%
Disallowed meals expense	4,200	0.8
Municipal bond interest	(10,500)	(2.1)
Foreign income taxed at less than U.S. rate	(22,000)*	(4.4)
Income tax expense (provision)	$ 76,700	15.3%

*$200,000 × (21% − 10%).

Only permanent differences appear in the rate reconciliation. Temporary differences do not affect the *total* book income tax expense; they simply affect the amount of the tax expense that is current versus deferred.

3-2d Special Issues

LO.5

Identify the GAAP treatment concerning tax uncertainties and tax law changes.

Financial Accounting for Tax Uncertainties

Companies take positions in their tax returns that may not ultimately survive the scrutiny of the IRS or other tax authorities. If a taxpayer loses the benefit of a favorable tax position after an audit, there may be an unfavorable effect on the company's financial statement tax expense in that year. The additional tax cost will become part of the current tax expense, yet the income to which this tax is related would have been reported in a previous year. This result can wreak havoc with a company's effective tax rate.

To avoid such an increase in effective tax rate, companies may record a book reserve (or "cushion") for the uncertain tax position in the year the position is taken. That is, rather than book the entire tax benefit (and thus reduce tax expense in the current year), the company may book only a portion (or none) of the tax benefit. If the company later loses the actual tax benefit upon audit, to the extent the additional tax imposed is charged against the reserve, the additional tax does not affect the future-year tax expense. If the company's tax position is not challenged in the future (or the company successfully defends any challenge), the reserve can be released. This release reduces the current tax expense in the future (release) year, and it lowers the company's effective tax rate in that year.

To add more structure to the accounting for tax reserves, the FASB released an interpretation, "Accounting for Uncertainty in Income Taxes" **(ASC 740-10)** . The approach required under this interpretation results in significantly more disclosure about uncertain tax positions by companies.

When ASC 740-10 applies, uncertain tax positions are defined as those material items that the taxpayer believes, based on the technical merits, it might lose on audit. Such tax positions result in a permanent reduction of income taxes payable, a deferral of income taxes otherwise currently payable to future years, or a change in the expected realizability of deferred tax assets.

Application of the ASC 740-10 rules requires a two-step process—recognition and measurement. These steps are illustrated in Concept Summary 3.3.

First, a tax benefit from an uncertain tax position may be *recognized* in the financial statements only if it is *more likely than not* (a greater than 50 percent likelihood) that the position would be sustained on its technical merits. In this regard, audit or detection risk cannot be considered.

This first step determines whether any of the tax benefit is recognized. If the *more likely than not* standard is failed, the position requires no financial statement disclosure (i.e., the taxpayer cannot book any of the tax benefit related to the issue).

TAX PLANNING STRATEGIES Tax Savings Are Not Always Created Equal

FRAMEWORK FOCUS: THINKING OUTSIDE THE FRAMEWORK

Many different types of tax planning strategies can produce tax savings. Yet, even when planning ideas produce identical current cash-flow effects, some ideas may have an edge. CEOs and CFOs of public companies are focused on the bottom line—the company's net income after tax and related earnings per share. A CFO is likely to be just as interested in an idea's effect on the company's bottom line income as on the cash tax savings.

For example, consider two tax planning ideas that each produce $420,000 of current tax savings. The first idea generates its $420,000 in tax savings by increasing tax depreciation relative to book depreciation by $2 million ($420,000 = $2 million × 21%). The second idea produces

research activities tax credits of $420,000, thus reducing current-year tax by $420,000.

Idea 1 produces its current tax savings via a temporary difference. Accordingly, the book tax expense will not reflect the $700,000 in tax savings. Instead, this $700,000 simply moves from the current tax category to the deferred tax category. Even if the book-tax difference is not expected to reverse in the next 30 years (effectively generating "permanent" savings), the book tax expense does not reflect this savings.

In contrast, idea 2 produces its current tax savings via a permanent difference. Thus, the book tax expense also declines by $420,000. This item appears in the income tax note rate reconciliation.

Concept Summary 3.3

Disclosures Under ASC 740-10

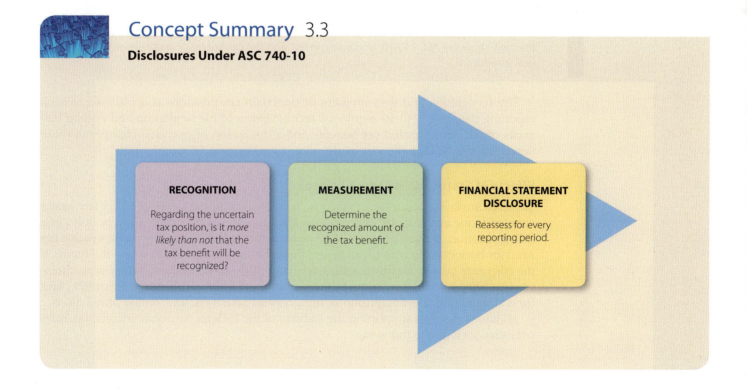

RECOGNITION
Regarding the uncertain tax position, is it *more likely than not* that the tax benefit will be recognized?

MEASUREMENT
Determine the recognized amount of the tax benefit.

FINANCIAL STATEMENT DISCLOSURE
Reassess for every reporting period.

If the uncertain tax position meets the *more likely than not* threshold, the second step is to determine the amount of the tax benefit to report (the *measurement* process). This computation is based on the probabilities associated with the position not being challenged or with it being challenged using a negotiated settlement or litigation.

A probability table is constructed, considering all of the possible post-audit and postsettlement outcomes for the tax benefit from the filing position. The filing position is recorded (i.e., the income or deduction amount is recognized for GAAP purposes) as the largest amount of the related tax benefit that is *more likely than not* (a greater than 50 percent probability) to be agreeable to the taxing authority, assuming that the agency has full knowledge of all relevant information.[19]

EXAMPLE
17

StarksCo has adopted certain aggressive transfer pricing strategies with related parties overseas. StarksCo estimates that it will reduce its Federal income tax liability by $100,000 as a result of these strategies but that the IRS is likely to challenge the pricing structure in an audit. StarksCo estimates that, after an IRS audit and related negotiations, the tax benefit may be reduced (amounts as indicated with related probabilities); StarksCo constructs a table of these probabilities and results.

Resulting Estimated Tax Benefit	Probability of Agreement Between StarksCo and IRS	Cumulative Probability Computed
$100,000	40%	40%
80,000	35%	75%
45,000	20%	95%
–0–	5%	100%

Assume that StarksCo recorded a book tax provision of $250,000, *including* the $100,000 tax benefit from this tax uncertainty. In light of the requirements of ASC 740-10 (FIN 48), StarksCo instead should record an $80,000 tax benefit for this item. That amount is the estimated tax benefit that first exceeds a 50% cumulative probability of agreement with the IRS (here, a 75% chance of acceptance exists).

The journal entry that StarksCo records for this computation is as follows, increasing the tax provision by $20,000, the amount dictated by ASC 740-10 (FIN 48) = $100,000 − $80,000.

Current income tax expense (provision)	$20,000	
ASC 740-10 liability		$20,000

If the taxpayer prevails and the full $100,000 tax benefit is attained in a later year, a journal entry then will show the ASC 740-10 amount reversed, and the current income tax expense in that later year is reduced.

The recognition and measurement of uncertain tax positions is reassessed at each reporting date. ASC 740-10 requires a reconciliation of the beginning and ending balances of the unrecognized tax benefits and a discussion of potential changes in these unrecognized tax benefits that might occur over the next 12 months.

Effects of Statutory Tax Law Changes

Tax rules involving business transactions change only rarely in the Federal tax law; major changes to the taxation of C corporations are described as occurring perhaps only once in a generation. If there are tax policy reasons for this practice, they might involve the need for businesses to plan their tax and budget effects for many years into the future. If the corporate tax law changed almost annually, as do some of the statutory and administrative rules involving individuals, businesses would find it difficult to construct plans for compensation, asset acquisitions, mergers and takeovers, and similar transactions.

Additional reasons supporting the stability of the Federal corporate income tax rules over time include the following.

---

[19]ASC 740-10-30-7.

- State and local income tax rules often are linked to their Federal counterparts. Federal tax law changes sometimes trigger automatic changes at the state and local level, but those jurisdictions have their own budgetary concerns, and a new Federal tax law rule (e.g., to increase the rate of acceleration for cost recovery deductions) might not be adopted (immediately or ever) by all of the states.

- A Federal tax law change may have significant effects on the financial statements of the entities affected, and Congress may be reluctant to make business tax law changes that could trigger changes in stock market valuations for publicly traded corporations.

So-called tax reform legislation was adopted by Congress late in 2017, and those provisions were significant in their scope. Most taxpayers living or doing business in the United States were affected by those changes, which generally were effective beginning in 2018. We will use a few of these revisions to illustrate how changes in the tax law affect GAAP financial statements and other book items that relate to the Federal tax law. Our discussion assumes that taxpayers use a calendar tax year; computations are different for fiscal-year corporations.

Decrease in C Corporation Tax Rate Congress cut the top income tax rate that applies to most C corporations as part of 2017 tax law changes. Previously, the top rate had been 34 or 35 percent, and those were among the highest marginal tax rates in the world as they applied to business income. For many reasons, including to encourage the global competitiveness of the U.S. economy and to provide increased after-tax cash flow for U.S.-based taxpayers, the C corporation tax rate was reduced to 21 percent beginning in 2018.

As a result, adjustments were made to the amounts of tax deferred assets and liabilities that incorporate the enacted Federal income tax rate. For instance, if a GAAP deferred tax liability related to the acceleration of cost recovery deductions over those claimed for book purposes, the deferred tax liability was "worth less" after the lower tax rate was enacted. This resulted in an immediate book gain for the taxpayer, as the deferral account is adjusted downward and financial accounting income increases. Opposite results occurred with respect to deferred tax assets. Because the reduced corporate tax rate is scheduled for all future years, many corporations took an immediate reduction in financial accounting income on their deferred tax assets, in exchange for significant future tax reductions.

Effects of Change in Corporate Tax Rate

EXAMPLE 18

Alpha Corporation generated a temporary book-tax difference before 2018 when it accelerated its cost recovery deductions by $1 million over GAAP amounts. Accordingly, its deferred tax liability account increased by $350,000 ($1 million × 35%).

When the new tax law reduced the applicable Federal corporate income tax rate to 21%, the balance of the deferred tax liability account was adjusted to $210,000, book income tax expense was reduced by $140,000 ($350,000 prior balance − $210,000 new balance), and book income increased by that amount.

EXAMPLE 19

Beta Corporation generated a temporary book-tax difference before 2018 when it incurred a $1 million operating loss for GAAP purposes that it could not deduct immediately under Federal tax law. Accordingly, its deferred tax asset account increased by $350,000.

When the new tax law reduced the applicable Federal corporate income tax rate to 21%, the balance of the deferred tax asset account was adjusted to $210,000, book tax expense increased by $140,000, and book income decreased by that amount.

Treatment of Net Operating Losses and Carryovers Several changes to the provisions concerning net operating losses (NOLs) can affect the related deferred tax asset account. Generally, NOLs generated after 2017 cannot be carried back, and they can offset only 80 percent of future-year taxable income. In addition, NOLs can be carried forward indefinitely, rather than expiring at a future date.

Among other effects, these new provisions may affect the corporation's valuation allowance balances for the losses. However, one cannot assume that the entire NOL now will be deductible in the future, even with the indefinite carryforward of NOLs; the corporation still must demonstrate that corresponding taxable income amounts will arise in the future.

Gamma Corporation holds a $1 million net operating loss carryforward going into 2018. Because of the new rules concerning NOL carryovers, it is more likely that the NOL will be deductible in future tax years. As a result, some (or all) of the valuation allowance related to the loss can be released (see text Section 3-2b), and book income will increase.

Repeal of C Corporation Alternative Minimum Tax Prior law applied an alternative minimum tax (AMT) to C corporations; an additional Federal income tax computation that computed a broader tax base and used a flat 20 percent tax rate. C corporations paid the regular tax liability or the AMT amount, whichever was larger. The corporate AMT was a mere prepayment of tax, though, as a minimum tax credit was available for AMT taxpayers to apply in a future tax year against regular tax liabilities, in the amount of any AMT paid. Only a few C corporations incurred an AMT liability, but the related credit amount was recorded as a deferred tax asset.

The corporate AMT does not exist after 2017, and any AMT credit amount is fully refundable against regular Federal corporate income taxes beginning in 2018. For most corporations, then, any valuation allowance against the AMT credit can be removed. This treatment precludes any conversion of the carryforward amount to a GAAP receivable, though.

Delta Corporation had been subject to the AMT in a few of its tax years prior to 2018. It had generated a $1 million carryforward amount for its minimum tax credit, and it recorded a corresponding deferred tax asset for the credit. Delta placed a $100,000 valuation allowance against the credit, showing uncertainty that enough regular tax liability would be generated in future tax years, against which to apply the credit. For 2018, the valuation allowance can be released in full, and book income increases as a result.

One-Time Transition Tax for Unrepatriated Profits of U.S. Entities Before 2018, U.S. taxpayers with global income were subject to a Federal corporate income tax on their *worldwide* taxable income, with a foreign tax credit allowed against the U.S. tax when income was subject to taxation in more than one country; see text Section 16-2b. For most U.S. taxpayers, this system put them at a competitive disadvantage, as other countries applied tax rates much lower than the U.S. top rate of 35 percent, and they applied a *territorial* approach to the tax base, subjecting to tax only that income generated within the borders of the country, and not on worldwide income.

Prior tax rules allowed U.S. taxpayers to defer the taxation on certain overseas income, though, until the profits were repatriated (paid back as a dividend) to the United States. Effective tax planning, then, encouraged taxpayers to keep profits unrepatriated, so as to reduce the present value of the related income tax liability, and U.S. entities held perhaps $3 trillion of cash profits overseas as a result.

To encourage the return of unrepatriated profits to the United States, and to accomplish other tax goals, U.S. tax rules adopted a modified form of territorial taxation for tax years beginning in 2018; see text Section 16-2b. For many U.S. taxpayers, this new approach to international taxation, combined with the new 21 percent corporate income tax rate, resulted in a projection of significantly lower future Federal income tax liabilities. But Congress accompanied this tax cut with a one-time tax cost: a tax on the balance of unrepatriated profits at a rate of 15.5 percent (if held as cash) or 8 percent (for nonliquid overseas assets).

The tax applied whether or not the profits actually were repatriated. By election, the tax liability could be deferred and paid over as many as eight tax years. The taxpayer could apply certain amounts of NOL and foreign tax credit carryforwards against the tax.

For GAAP purposes, the one-time transition tax was recorded as a 2017 income tax expense. Depending on elections made by the taxpayer, the expenses could be recorded as partly current and noncurrent, but they were not to be discounted to present values. Valuation allowances for the loss and credit carryforwards likely would be adjusted, to reflect the higher probability that they now would be used.

U.S. taxpayer Epsilon Corporation held $1 million cash in overseas accounts from its unrepatriated foreign profits, to defer the related U.S. corporate income tax liability. As of the end of 2017, it owed the one-time transition tax on these profits, even though it retained the cash balance overseas into 2018. After applying NOL carryforwards against the taxable amount, Epsilon owed a tax of $100,000, which it elected to pay over eight years. The valuation allowance against the NOL carryforward was released, increasing book income, and the transition tax liability was divided into its current and noncurrent elements.

3-2e **Summary**

The tax department of a business often is charged with shaping and implementing the entity's tax strategies (*tax planning*) and filing all required tax returns (*tax compliance*) while preparing for subsequent audit and litigation activity (*tax controversy*). Tax professionals often work closely with those who prepare the entity's financial statements, especially concerning the tax footnote, tax deferral accounts, and tax rate reconciliations. Professional tax and accounting research underlies all of this work.

The functions of a modern tax department are depicted in Exhibit 3.4. Tax professionals must be proficient in all of the indicated areas, so that they can meet the demands of the entity and its shareholders, regulators, and taxing agencies. If the tax professional grasps both the tax and financial statement effects of various tax planning and compliance activities, he or she brings great value to the entity through the tax department.

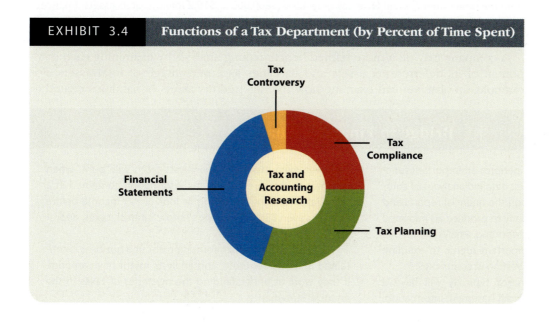

EXHIBIT 3.4   Functions of a Tax Department (by Percent of Time Spent)

LO.6

Use financial statement income tax information to benchmark a company's tax position.

3-3 BENCHMARKING

An entity's income tax expense amount may appear to be of little interest to anyone beyond the taxpayer that makes the payment and the government agencies that collect it. The tax year is over, the transactions are completed, and the final costs have been tallied. Still, this historical tax information may prove valuable. A company's income tax expense is one of the single largest expense items on its income statement, and understanding the components of this expense is a critical activity for the tax professional.

Consider a typical baseball game. Two teams meet, interact following a specific set of rules, and ultimately complete the game, generating a final score. Of course, the final score is of immediate interest to the teams and the fans, but once the game is over, the score and associated statistics (runs, hits, and errors) are relegated to the history books. Yet, these statistics still can be quite useful. A team coach may use the game statistics to evaluate the strengths and weaknesses of the players to assist in improving performance. Other teams may use the data to develop strategies for upcoming games. Players can use this information to "benchmark" themselves against their own performance in prior games or against players on other teams. In short, there is a wealth of information in these historical data.

A taxpayer's reported income tax expense likewise is a valuable source of information for the company, its tax advisers, and its competitors. The reported information provides clues about a company's operational and tax planning strategies.

Companies may benchmark their tax situation to other years' results or to other companies in the same industry. The starting point for a **benchmarking** exercise usually is the data from the income tax note rate reconciliation.

3-3a Refining the Analysis

In addition to comparing effective tax rates, one can analyze entities' levels of deferred tax assets and liabilities.

EXAMPLE 23

Akiko Enterprises reports a net deferred tax liability of $280,000. Erde, Inc., a company in the same industry, reports a net deferred tax liability of $860,000. The presence of deferred tax liabilities on the balance sheet indicates that both companies are benefiting from deferring actual tax payments (essentially, an interest-free loan from the government).

At first glance, it may appear that Erde is doing better in this regard. However, what if Akiko holds total assets of $2.6 million and Erde's assets total $19.2 million? This information indicates that Akiko has 10.8% ($280,000 ÷ $2.6 million) of its total assets "financed" with an interest-free loan from the government, while Erde has only 4.5% ($860,000 ÷ $19.2 million) of its assets "financed" with its deferred tax liabilities.

A company may do a more refined benchmarking analysis by examining each component of its deferred tax assets and liabilities as a percentage of total assets. For example, an observer can examine how the deferred tax assets or liabilities related to

---

BRIDGE DISCIPLINE **Bridge to Financial Analysis**

Financial analysts perform an important function for the capital markets in their detailed analyses of companies. The analyst combs through the financial reports and other information about a company to produce an informed opinion on how a company is performing. Analysts' earnings forecasts often constitute an important metric to examine when making decisions about investing in companies.

An experienced financial analyst typically will have a good handle on interpreting financial statement information.

However, even experienced analysts often will "punt" when it comes to interpreting the tax information contained in a financial statement, preferring to look at net income before taxes (or even EBITDA, earnings before interest, taxes, depreciation, and amortization).

A great deal of useful information about a business is contained in its tax footnote, and analysts might have an edge if they work at understanding the mysteries of taxes in the financial statements.

property, plant, and equipment compare with those of its competitors. The nature of the components of deferred tax liabilities and deferred tax assets becomes important in a benchmarking analysis.

Benchmarking Financial Results

EXAMPLE 24

LinCo reports total book income before taxes of $10 million and a total tax provision of $1.6 million, producing a 16% effective tax rate. TuckCo also reports book income before taxes of $10 million. TuckCo's total tax expense is $1.5 million, producing an effective tax rate of 15%. At first glance, it appears that the entities are similar based on their effective tax rates. The total tax expense divided between current and deferred is as follows.

	LinCo	TuckCo
Current tax expense	$2,500,000	$ 2,600,000
Deferred tax benefit	(900,000)	(1,100,000)
Total tax expense	$1,600,000	$ 1,500,000

Again, it appears that both companies have created deferred tax assets in the current year that are expected to produce tax savings in the future. Knowing the nature of the underlying deferred tax assets will add greatly to one's interpretation of the effective tax rates.

With additional investigation, though, you determine that the deferred tax asset generating LinCo's expected future tax savings is the use of an NOL. The deferred tax asset generating TuckCo's expected future tax savings is generated by different book and tax methods in accounting for warranty expense. This additional information reveals that LinCo previously has incurred losses; to use the NOLs in the coming years, it will be critical for LinCo to generate taxable income.

This is quite different from TuckCo's situation, which reveals only that common differences in accounting methods exist, and that future deductions likely will be used fully. Although the tax positions of LinCo and TuckCo seem very similar on the surface, a closer look reveals a striking difference.

EXAMPLE 25

WageCo and SalaryCo operate in the same industry, and they report the same effective tax rate. Their book income and current, deferred, and total tax expense were reported as follows.

	WageCo	SalaryCo
Book income before tax	$1,500,000	$2,300,000
Current tax expense	$ 680,000	$ 24,000
Deferred tax expense (benefit)	(410,000)	390,000
Total tax expense	$ 270,000	$ 414,000
Effective tax rate	18%	18%

WageCo's total tax expense is highly dependent on the current recognition of future tax savings of $410,000. SalaryCo appears to be deferring a substantial portion of its tax expense to future years. Although both companies report the same effective tax rate, the details indicate that the two companies face very different tax situations. By looking more closely at the financial statements, you should be able to determine why these differences exist.

3-3b **Sustaining the Tax Rate**

It is important in benchmarking exercises to remove the effect of one-time items in comparing sustainable effective tax rates across time or companies. Examples of one-time items include restructuring costs, legal settlements, and IRS or other tax liability settlements. A one-time item may seem beneficial or detrimental to a company's effective tax rate. But the very nature of this item implies that it has little to do with the company's *long-term* sustainable tax costs.

EXAMPLE 26

MetalCo and IronCo operate in the same industry, and they report the following tax rate reconciliations in their tax footnotes.

	MetalCo	IronCo
Hypothetical tax at U.S. rate	21.0%	21.0%
State and local taxes	2.2	2.1
Foreign income taxed at less than U.S. rate	(6.2)	(6.1)
Tax Court settlement on disputed tax issue	(18.6)	—
Effective tax rate	(1.6%)	17.0%

Although it appears that MetalCo has a significantly lower effective tax rate than does IronCo, removing MetalCo's one-time item related to the court settlement indicates that both companies may operate under a similar 17% effective tax rate (18.6% − 1.6% = 17%).

3-3c Uses of Benchmarking Analysis

Benchmarking is part science and part art. A useful analysis requires both an accountant's knowledge of how the underlying financial statements are constructed, including arriving at the appropriate tax expense, and a detective's sense of where to look and what questions to ask. Concept Summary 3.4 summarizes the most typical uses of benchmarking in an analysis of an entity's financial results.

Concept Summary 3.4

Benchmarking Analysis

A benchmarking analysis can be helpful in comparing the tax positions of two or more business entities. One might consider the following aspects of the taxpayers' financial disclosures in this regard. This list is not all-inclusive; benchmarking also includes the judgment and experience of the parties conducting the analysis.

- Compare the effective tax rates of the entities.
- Explain the differences in effective rates. Are these differences sustainable over time?

- Apply the analysis to both the tax dollars involved and the underlying net assets of the entities.
- Discount (but do not ignore) any one-time tax benefits/detriments that are observed.
- Include in your analysis any knowledge of the nontax, competitive strategy and tactics employed and planned by the entity.

REFOCUS ON THE BIG PICTURE

TAXES ON THE FINANCIAL STATEMENTS

Raymond Jones should understand that the tax expense reported on the company's financial statements and the tax payable on the company's income tax returns often differ as a result of differences in the reporting entities used in the calculation and the different accounting methods used for book purposes and tax purposes. The use of different accounting methods may result in both temporary and permanent differences in financial statement income and taxable income. Examples of permanent differences include nontaxable income such as municipal bond interest and tax credits. Temporary differences include depreciation differences and other amounts that are affected by the timing of a deduction or an inclusion, but they ultimately result in the same amount being reflected in the financial statements and income tax returns.

Permanent differences such as municipal bond interest cause Arctic's book income to be greater than its taxable income. In calculating the tax provision shown on the financial statements, Arctic's book income must be adjusted for these permanent differences.

continued

This results in an effective tax rate for financial statement purposes (20 percent) that is below the U.S. statutory corporate income tax rate of 21 percent.

In this case, Arctic's income tax expense of $5 million is higher than the current Federal income tax payable. This results from timing differences and creates a $1.01 million deferred tax liability that is reported on the company's balance sheet. Unlike other liabilities, deferred tax liabilities are "good" in the sense that they represent an amount that may be paid to the government in the future rather than today.

What If?

Mr. Jones is concerned about a newspaper article that said that companies reporting less tax on their tax returns than on their financial statements were cheating the IRS. Is this an accurate assessment?

While differences in income taxes payable to the IRS and financial tax expense can result from aggressive and illegal tax shelters, differences also result from different methods of accounting that are required for financial statement reporting using GAAP and tax laws enacted by Congress.

Suggested Readings

Center on Budget and Policy Priorities, "Actual U.S. Corporate Tax Rates Are in Line with Comparable Countries," October 2017.

Cheryl Anderson, "Creating Value in the Corporate Tax Function Through Benchmarking," *AICPA Tax Adviser*, September 2008.

J. O. Everett, C. J. Hennig, and W. A. Raabe, Schedule M–3 Compliance, 2nd ed., Commerce Clearing House, 2008.

J. Richard Harvey, "Schedule UTP—Why So Few Disclosures?" *Tax Notes*, April 1, 2013.

Key Terms

ASC 740, 3-8	Deferred tax benefit, 3-9	Permanent differences, 3-4
ASC 740-10, 3-18	Deferred tax expense, 3-9	Rate reconciliation, 3-16
Balance sheet approach, 3-9	Deferred tax liability, 3-9	Schedule M–1, 3-6
Benchmarking, 3-24	Equity method, 3-2	Schedule M–3, 3-7
Conservatism principle, 3-12	Generally accepted accounting principles (GAAP), 3-2	Temporary differences, 3-4
Current tax expense, 3-9		Valuation allowance, 3-13
Deferred tax asset, 3-9	Income tax provision, 3-8	

Problems

1. **LO.2** Ovate, Inc., earns $140,000 in book income before tax and is subject to a 21% marginal Federal income tax rate. Ovate records a single temporary difference: Warranty expenses deducted for book purposes are $8,000, of which only $2,000 are deductible for tax purposes. There have been no book-tax differences in prior tax years.

   a. Determine the amount of Ovate's deferred tax asset or liability.

   b. Express your computation as a Microsoft Excel formula.

2. **LO.3** Ion Corporation reports an income tax expense/payable for book purposes of $200,000 and $250,000 for tax purposes. According to Ion's management and financial auditors, Ion only will be able to use $30,000 of any deferred tax asset, with the balance expiring unused. Determine the amount of Ion's deferred tax asset and valuation allowance from this year's activities, and construct Ion's related journal entry for these items.

3. **LO.2** Prance, Inc., earns pretax book net income of $800,000 in 2018. Prance acquires a depreciable asset that year, and first-year tax depreciation exceeds book depreciation by $80,000. Prance reported no other temporary or permanent book-tax differences. The pertinent U.S. tax rate is 21%, and Prance earns an after-tax rate of return on capital of 8%.

    a. Compute Prance's total income tax expense, current income tax expense, and deferred income tax expense.

    b. Determine the end-of-year balance in Prance's deferred tax asset and deferred tax liability balance sheet accounts.

Ethics and Equity
4. **LO.1** Evaluate the following statement: For most business entities, book income differs from taxable income because "income" has different meanings for the users of the data in the income computation.

5. **LO.1** Parent, a domestic corporation, owns 100% of Block, a foreign corporation, and Chip, a domestic corporation. Parent also owns 45% of Trial, a domestic corporation. Parent receives no distributions from any of these corporations. Which of these entities' net income is included in Parent's income statement for current-year financial reporting purposes?

6. **LO.1** Parent, a domestic corporation, owns 100% of Block, a foreign corporation, and Chip, a domestic corporation. Parent also owns 45% of Trial, a domestic corporation. Parent receives no distributions from any of these corporations. Which of these entities' taxable income is included in Parent's current-year Form 1120, U.S. income tax return? Parent consolidates all eligible subsidiaries for Federal income tax purposes.

Communications
7. **LO.1** Marcellus Jackson, the CFO of Mac, Inc., notices that the tax liability reported on Mac's tax return is less than the tax expense reported on Mac's financial statements. Write a letter to Jackson outlining why these two tax expense numbers might differ. Mac's address is 482 Linden Road, Paris, KY 40362.

Critical Thinking
8. **LO.1** Define the terms *temporary difference* and *permanent difference* as they pertain to the financial reporting of income tax expenses. Describe how these two book-tax differences affect the gap between book and taxable income. How are permanent and temporary differences alike? How are they different?

Communications
9. **LO.1** In no more than three PowerPoint slides, list several commonly encountered temporary and permanent book-tax differences. The slides will be used in your presentation next week to your school's Future CPAs Club.

10. **LO.2** Prance, in Problem 3, reports $600,000 of pretax book net income in 2019. Prance's book depreciation exceeds tax depreciation that year by $20,000. Prance reports no other temporary or permanent book-tax differences. Assuming that the pertinent U.S. tax rate is 21%, compute Prance's total income tax expense, current income tax expense, and deferred income tax expense.

11. **LO.2** Using the facts of Problem 10, determine the following.

    a. The 2019 end-of-year balance in Prance's deferred tax asset and deferred tax liability balance sheet accounts.

    b. The value to Prance of the accelerated tax deduction for depreciation, considering the time value of money. Prance earns an after-tax rate of return on capital of 8%.

12. **LO.2** Mini, Inc., earns pretax book net income of $750,000 in 2018. Mini deducted $20,000 in bad debt expense for book purposes. This expense is not yet deductible for tax purposes. Mini records no other temporary or permanent differences. Assuming that the pertinent U.S. tax rate is 21%, compute Mini's total income tax expense, current income tax expense, and deferred income tax expense.

13. **LO.2** Using the facts of Problem 12, determine the 2018 end-of-year balance in Mini's deferred tax asset and deferred tax liability balance sheet accounts.

14. **LO.2** Mini, in Problem 12, reports $800,000 of pretax book net income in 2019. For that year, Mini did not deduct any bad debt expense for book purposes but did deduct $15,000 in bad debt expense for tax purposes. Mini reports no other temporary or permanent differences. Assuming that the U.S. tax rate is 21%, compute Mini's total income tax expense, current income tax expense, and deferred income tax expense.

15. **LO.2** Using the facts of Problem 14, determine the following.
    a. The 2019 end-of-year balance in Mini's deferred tax asset and deferred tax liability balance sheet accounts.
    b. The cost to Mini of the deferral of the bad debt deduction, considering the time value of money. Mini earns an after-tax rate of return on capital of 8%.

16. **LO.3** You saw on the Business News Today blog that YoungCo has "released one-third of its valuation allowances because of an upbeat forecast for sales of its tablet computers over the next 30 months." What effect does such a release likely have on YoungCo's current-year book effective tax rate? Be specific.

17. **LO.6** Jill is the CFO of PorTech, Inc. PorTech's tax advisers have recommended two tax planning ideas that will each provide $5 million of current-year cash tax savings. One idea is based on a timing difference and is expected to reverse in full 10 years in the future. The other idea creates a permanent difference that never will reverse.

    Determine whether these ideas will allow PorTech to reduce its reported book income tax expense for the current year. Illustrate in a table or timeline your preference for one planning strategy over the other. Which idea will you recommend to Jill?   *Decision Making*   *Communications*

18. **LO.6** RoofCo reports total book income before taxes of $20 million and a total tax expense of $8 million. FloorCo reports book income before taxes of $30 million and a total tax expense of $12 million. The companies' breakdown between current and deferred tax expense (benefit) is as follows.

	RoofCo	FloorCo
Current tax expense	$10.0	$13.0
Deferred tax benefit	(2.0)	(1.0)
Total tax expense	$ 8.0	$12.0

    RoofCo's deferred tax benefit is from a deferred tax asset created because of differences in book and tax depreciation methods for equipment. FloorCo's deferred tax benefit is created by the expected future use of an NOL. Compare and contrast these two companies' effective tax rates. How are they similar? How are they different?

19. **LO.6** LawnCo and TreeCo operate in the same industry, and both report a 30% effective tax rate (Federal, state, and global). Their book income and current, deferred, and total tax expense are reported below.   *Communications*

	LawnCo	TreeCo
Book income before tax	$500,000	$650,000
Current tax expense	$200,000	$ 20,000
Deferred tax expense (benefit)	(50,000)	175,000
Total tax expense (Federal, state, global)	$150,000	$195,000
Effective tax rate	30%	30%

ShrubCo is a competitor of both of these companies. Prepare a letter to Laura Collins, VP-Taxation of ShrubCo, outlining your analysis of the other two companies' effective tax rates, using only the preceding information. ShrubCo's address is 9979 West Third Street, Peru, IN 46970.

20. **LO.6** HippCo and HoppCo operate in the same industry and report the following tax rate reconciliations in their tax footnotes. Compare and contrast the effective tax rates of these two companies.

	HippCo	HoppCo
Hypothetical tax at U.S. rate	35.0%	35.0%
State and local taxes	2.7	3.9
Municipal bond interest	(12.5)	(7.8)
Tax Court settlement on disputed tax issue	6.0	—
Effective tax rate	31.2%	31.1%

Ethics and Equity

21. **LO.6** In the current year, Dickinson, Inc., reports an effective tax rate of 36%, and Badger, Inc., reports an effective tax rate of 21%. Both companies are domestic and operate in the same industry. Your initial examination of the financial statements of the two companies indicates that Badger apparently is doing a better job with its tax planning, explaining the difference in effective tax rates. Consequently, all else being equal, you decide to invest in Badger.

In a subsequent year, it comes to light that Badger had used some very aggressive tax planning techniques to reduce its reported tax expense. After an examination by the IRS, Badger loses the tax benefits and reports a very large tax expense in that year. Over this multiple-year period, it turns out that Dickinson had the lower effective tax rate after all.

Do you believe Badger was ethical in not fully disclosing the aggressiveness of its tax positions in its current financial statements? How does ASC 740-10 (FIN 48) affect Badger's disclosure requirement? Does ASC 740-10 (FIN 48) still leave room for ethical decision making by management in determining how to report uncertain tax positions? Explain.

22. **LO.2** Phillips, Inc., a cash basis C corporation, completes $100,000 in sales for year 1, but only $75,000 of this amount is collected during year 1. The remaining $25,000 from these sales is collected promptly during the first quarter of year 2. The applicable income tax rate for year 1 and thereafter is 30%. Compute Phillips's year 1 current and deferred income tax expense.

23. **LO.2** Continue with the results of Problem 22. Prepare the GAAP journal entries for Phillips's year 1 income tax expense.

24. **LO.2** Britton, Inc., an accrual basis C corporation, sells widgets on credit. Its book and taxable income for year 1 totals $60,000 before accounting for bad debts. Britton's book allowance for uncollectible accounts increased for year 1 by $10,000, but none of the entity's bad debts received a specific write-off for tax purposes. The applicable income tax rate for year 1 and thereafter is 30%. Compute Britton's year 1 current and deferred income tax expense.

25. **LO.2** Continue with the results of Problem 24. Prepare the GAAP journal entries for Britton's year 1 income tax expense.

26. **LO.2** Rubio, Inc., an accrual basis C corporation, reports the following amounts for the tax year. The applicable income tax rate is 30%. Compute Rubio's taxable income.

Book income, including the items below	$80,000
Increase in book allowance for anticipated warranty costs	5,000
Interest income from City of Westerville bonds	10,000
Bribes paid to Federal inspectors	17,000

27. **LO.2** Continue with the results of Problem 26.

    a. Determine Rubio's income tax expense and GAAP income for the year.

    b. Express your computations as Microsoft Excel commands.

28. **LO.2** Willingham, Inc., an accrual basis C corporation, reports pretax book income of $1.6 million. At the beginning of the tax year, Willingham reported no deferred tax accounts on its balance sheet. It is subject to a 21% U.S. income tax rate in the current year and for the foreseeable future.

    Willingham's book-tax differences include the following. Compute the entity's current and deferred income tax expense for the year.

Addition to the book reserve for uncollectible receivables (no specific write-offs occurred; therefore, a zero income tax deduction)	$4,000,000
Tax depreciation in excess of book	3,000,000
Book gain from installment sale of nonbusiness asset, deferred for tax	2,000,000
Interest income from school district bonds	200,000

29. **LO.2** Continue with the results of Problem 28. Prepare the GAAP journal entries for Willingham's income tax expense.

30. **LO.2** Relix, Inc., is a domestic corporation with the following balance sheet for book and tax purposes at the end of the year. Based on this information, determine Relix's net deferred tax asset or net deferred tax liability at year-end. Assume a 21% Federal corporate tax rate and no valuation allowance.

	Tax Debit/(Credit)	Book Debit/(Credit)
Assets		
Cash	$ 500	$ 500
Accounts receivable	8,000	8,000
Buildings	750,000	750,000
Accumulated depreciation	(450,000)	(380,000)
Furniture & fixtures	70,000	70,000
Accumulated depreciation	(46,000)	(38,000)
Total assets	$332,500	$410,500
Liabilities		
Accrued litigation expense	$ –0–	($ 50,000)
Note payable	(78,000)	(78,000)
Total liabilities	($ 78,000)	($128,000)
Stockholders' Equity		
Paid-in capital	($ 10,000)	($ 10,000)
Retained earnings	(244,500)	(272,500)
Total liabilities and stockholders' equity	($332,500)	($410,500)

31. **LO.2** Based on the facts and results of Problem 30 and the beginning-of-the-year book-tax basis differences listed below, determine the change in Relix's deferred tax assets for the current year.

	Beginning of Year
Accrued litigation expense	$34,000
Subtotal	$34,000
Applicable tax rate	× 21%
Gross deferred tax asset	$ 7,140

32. **LO.2** Based on the facts and results of Problem 30 and the beginning-of-the-year book-tax basis differences listed below, determine the change in Relix's deferred tax liabilities for the current year.

	Beginning of Year
Building—accumulated depreciation	($57,000)
Furniture & fixtures—accumulated depreciation	(4,200)
Subtotal	($61,200)
Applicable tax rate	× 21%
Gross deferred tax liability	($12,852)

33. **LO.2** Based on the facts and results of Problems 30–32, determine Relix's change in net deferred tax asset or net deferred tax liability for the current year. Provide the journal entry to record this amount.

34. **LO.2** In addition to the temporary differences identified in Problems 30–33, Relix reported two permanent differences between book and taxable income. It earned $2,375 in tax-exempt municipal bond interest, and it incurred $780 in non-deductible business meals expense. Relix's book income before tax is $4,800. With this additional information, calculate Relix's current tax expense.

35. **LO.2** Provide the journal entry to record Relix's current tax expense as determined in Problem 34.

36. **LO.2** Based on the facts and results of Problems 30–35, calculate Relix's total provision for income tax reported in its financial statements, and determine its book net income after tax.

37. **LO.2** Based on the facts and results of Problems 30–36, provide the income tax footnote rate reconciliation for Relix.

38. **LO.2** Kantner, Inc., is a domestic corporation with the following balance sheet for book and tax purposes at the end of the year. Based on this information, determine Kantner's net deferred tax asset or net deferred tax liability at year-end. Assume a 21% Federal corporate tax rate and no valuation allowance.

	Tax Debit/(Credit)	Book Debit/(Credit)
Assets		
Cash	$ 1,000	$ 1,000
Accounts receivable	9,000	9,000
Buildings	850,000	850,000
Accumulated depreciation	(700,000)	(620,000)
Furniture & fixtures	40,000	40,000
Accumulated depreciation	(10,000)	(8,000)
Total assets	$190,000	$272,000
Liabilities		
Accrued warranty expense	$ –0–	($ 40,000)
Note payable	(16,000)	(16,000)
Total liabilities	($ 16,000)	($ 56,000)
Stockholders' Equity		
Paid-in capital	($ 50,000)	($ 50,000)
Retained earnings	(124,000)	(166,000)
Total liabilities and stockholders' equity	($190,000)	($272,000)

39. **LO.2** Based on the facts and results of Problem 38 and the beginning-of-the-year book-tax basis difference listed below, determine the change in Kantner's deferred tax assets for the current year.

	Beginning of Year
Accrued warranty expense	$30,000
Subtotal	$30,000
Applicable tax rate	× 21%
Gross deferred tax asset	$ 6,300

40. **LO.2** Based on the facts and results of Problem 38 and the beginning-of-the-year book-tax basis differences listed below, determine the change in Kantner's deferred tax liabilities for the current year.

	Beginning of Year
Building—accumulated depreciation	($62,000)
Furniture & fixtures—accumulated depreciation	(400)
Subtotal	($62,400)
Applicable tax rate	× 21%
Gross deferred tax liability	($13,104)

41. **LO.2** Based on the facts and results of Problems 38–40, determine Kantner's change in net deferred tax asset or net deferred tax liability for the current year. Provide the journal entry to record this amount.

42. **LO.2** In addition to the temporary differences identified in Problems 38–41, Kantner reported two permanent book-tax differences. It earned $7,800 in tax-exempt municipal bond interest, and it reported $850 in nondeductible business meals expense. Kantner's book income before tax is $50,000. With this additional information, calculate Kantner's current tax expense.

43. **LO.2** Provide the journal entry to record Kantner's current tax expense as determined in Problem 42.

44. **LO.2** Based on the facts and results of Problems 38–43, calculate Kantner's total provision for income tax expense reported on its financial statement and its book net income after tax.

45. **LO.2** Based on the facts and results of Problems 38–44, provide the income tax footnote rate reconciliation for Kantner.

46. **LO.3** Does the taxpayer's effective tax rate increase or decrease when:
    a. It creates a valuation allowance against the deferred tax asset for a net operating loss?
    b. It releases a valuation allowance against the deferred tax asset for a net operating loss?

47. **LO.3** Identify whether each of the following items typically constitutes *positive* or *negative* evidence when a manufacturing entity assesses whether a valuation allowance is required or should be adjusted for its net operating losses.
    a. Product orders are increasing.
    b. Book income for the past three years totals to a negative amount.
    c. Investment assets held by the taxpayer show a realized gain.
    d. The industry in which the taxpayer operates is in a down cycle.
    e. The entity's tax plan includes a switch from MACRS accelerated depreciation to straight-line.

48. **LO.4** KellerCo reports $5 million of U.S. taxable income, the same as its book income, as there are no temporary book-tax differences this year. KellerCo is subject to a 21% Federal income tax rate. Its book-tax differences include the following.

Nondeductible business meals	$ 400,000
Tax depreciation in excess of book depreciation	1,500,000

Construct KellerCo's tax rate reconciliation for its GAAP tax footnote. Use either dollars or percentages in your reconciliation.

49. **LO.5** LaceCo has adopted certain aggressive policies concerning its transfer pricing procedures. The entity estimates that it will reduce its Federal income tax liability by $400,000 as a result of these strategies, but that the IRS is likely to challenge the policies in an audit.

LaceCo estimates that the tax benefit may be reduced after an IRS audit and related negotiations (amounts as indicated with related probabilities); LaceCo constructs a table of these probabilities and results.

Resulting Estimated Tax Benefit	Probability of Agreement Between LaceCo and IRS	Cumulative Probability Computed
$400,000	10%	10%
300,000	35%	45%
250,000	40%	85%
–0–	15%	100%

LaceCo recorded a book-tax provision of $600,000, *including* the $400,000 tax benefit from this tax uncertainty.

a. Determine the amount that LaceCo should record for the tax benefit from this item, under GAAP rules and ASC 740-10.

b. Construct the journal entry that LaceCo should record for these items.

BRIDGE DISCIPLINE

1. Locate summary financial information for two companies in the same industry. Compare and contrast the following items across the two companies: debt-to-equity ratio, return on assets, return on equity, inventory turnover ratio, and effective tax rate.

Communications 2. Locate news or other items reporting financial analysts' forecasts or other information regarding two different companies. Determine whether the analyst appears to use any tax information in the report. For example, does the analyst use pretax or after-tax earnings in the analysis? Draft an e-mail to your instructor describing your findings.

Communications 3. Using the annual reports or 10-Ks of two different public companies in the same industry, locate information regarding the compensation paid to their executives. Prepare a table comparing the compensation levels (cash and noncash) of top executives across the two companies, and send the table to your instructor. Illustrate graphically the relationship between executive compensation and company performance by comparing the compensation to other company information such as net income.

Research Problems

Use internet tax resources to address the following questions. Look for reliable web-sites and blogs of the IRS and other government agencies, media outlets, businesses, tax professionals, academics, think tanks, and political outlets.

Research Problem 1. Locate the most recent financial statements of two compa-nies in the same industry using the companies' websites or the SEC's website (**www.sec.gov**). Perform a benchmarking analysis of the two companies' effective tax rates, components of the effective tax rate reconciliation, levels of deferred tax assets and liabilities, and other relevant data. Summarize this information in an e-mail to your instructor.

Research Problem 2. Locate articles or other discussions regarding the key differences between ASC 740 and International Accounting Standard No. 12 (related to income taxes). Summarize these key differences in an e-mail to your instructor. Make certain you have found the most current information for this comparison. Provide the URL for each of your sources.   *Communications*

Research Problem 3. Locate the financial statements of three different companies that report information in the income tax footnote regarding uncertain tax positions under ASC 740-10. Create a schedule that compares and contrasts the changes in uncertain tax positions reported by the three companies. E-mail the schedule to your instructor.   *Communications*

Research Problem 4. Locate the financial statements of three different companies. Review the income tax footnote information on deferred tax assets (DTAs) and deferred tax liabilities (DTLs). Create a schedule that compares and contrasts the end-of-the-year amounts of DTAs and DTLs, including any valuation allowances. E-mail the schedule to your instructor.   *Communications*

Research Problem 5. Locate summary financial information for two companies in the same industry. Compare and contrast the following items across the two companies: debt-to-equity ratio, return on assets, shareholder yield, return on equity, inventory turnover ratio, and effective tax rate. In your comparison, include the Federal, state/local, and international effective rates for the entities. Summarize in one paragraph the key reasons the effective tax rates are similar (or different).   *Critical Thinking*

Becker CPA Review Questions

1. Two independent situations are described below. Each situation has future deduct-ible amounts and/or future taxable amounts produced by temporary differences.

Situation	1	2
Taxable income	$40,000	$80,000
Amounts at year-end:		
Future deductible amounts	5,000	10,000
Future taxable amounts	–0–	5,000
Balances at beginning of year:		
Deferred tax asset	1,000	4,000
Deferred tax liability	–0–	1,000

The enacted tax rate is 25% for both situations. Determine the income tax expense for the year.

	Situation 1	Situation 2
a.	$10,000	$20,000
b.	$9,000	$21,000
c.	$5,000	$17,000
d.	$–0–	$–0–

2. Two independent situations are described below. Each involves future deductible amounts and/or future taxable amounts produced by temporary differences.

Situation	1	2
Taxable income	$40,000	$80,000
Amounts at year-end:		
Future deductible amounts	5,000	10,000
Future taxable amounts	–0–	5,000
Balances at beginning of year:		
Deferred tax asset	1,000	4,000
Deferred tax liability	–0–	1,000

The enacted tax rate is 25% for both situations. Determine the change in the deferred tax asset balance for the year.

	Situation 1	Situation 2
a.	$5,000	$10,000
b.	$1,250	$1,250
c.	$1,250	$2,500
d.	$–0–	$–0–

3. At the end of year 6, the tax effects of temporary differences reported in Tortoise Company's year-end financial statements were as follows.

	Deferred Tax Assets (Liabilities)
Accelerated tax depreciation	($120,000)
Warranty expense	80,000
NOL carryforward	200,000
Total	$160,000

A valuation allowance was not considered necessary. Tortoise anticipates that $40,000 of the deferred tax liability will reverse in year 7, that actual warranty costs will be incurred evenly in year 8 and year 9, and that the NOL carryforward will be used in year 7. On Tortoise's December 31, year 6 balance sheet, what amount should be reported as a deferred tax asset under U.S. GAAP?

a. $160,000   c. $240,000

b. $200,000   d. $280,000

4. Cavan Company prepared the following reconciliation between book income and taxable income for the current year ended December 31, year 1.

Pretax accounting income	$1,000,000
Taxable income	(600,000)
Difference	$ 400,000
Book-tax differences:	
Interest on municipal income	$ 100,000
Lower financial depreciation	300,000
Total	$ 400,000

Cavan's effective Federal and state income tax rate for year 1 is 30%. The depreciation difference will reverse equally over the next three years at enacted tax rates as follows.

Year	Tax Rate
Year 2	30%
Year 3	25%
Year 4	25%

In Cavan's year 1 income statement, the deferred portion of its provision for income taxes should be:

a. $120,000

b. $80,000

c. $100,000

d. $90,000

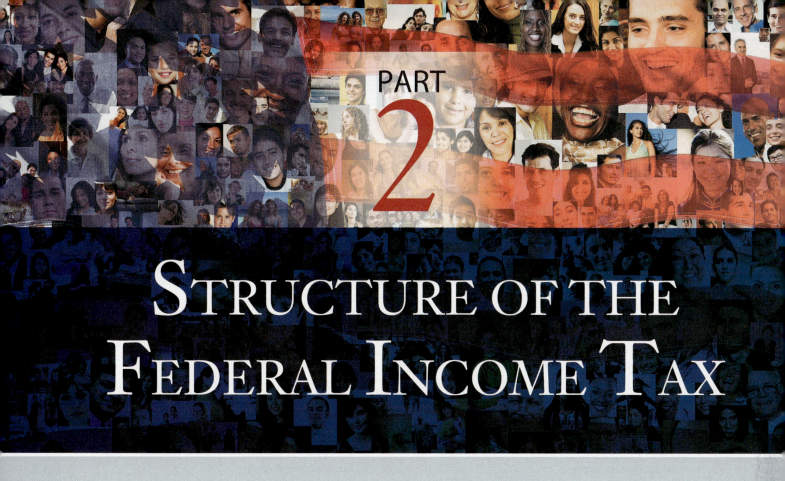

PART 2

STRUCTURE OF THE FEDERAL INCOME TAX

CHAPTER 4
Gross Income

CHAPTER 5
Business Deductions

CHAPTER 6
Losses and Loss Limitations

Part 2 introduces the components of the Federal income tax model. The gross income component, including the effect of exclusions, the accounting period, and accounting methods, is presented. This is followed by an analysis of business deductions, including amounts allowed and disallowed and the proper timing for such deductions. Tax provisions are addressed concerning the amounts and timing of deductions that result from losses, including the use of carryovers and the proper financial accounting treatment of the resulting tax amounts.

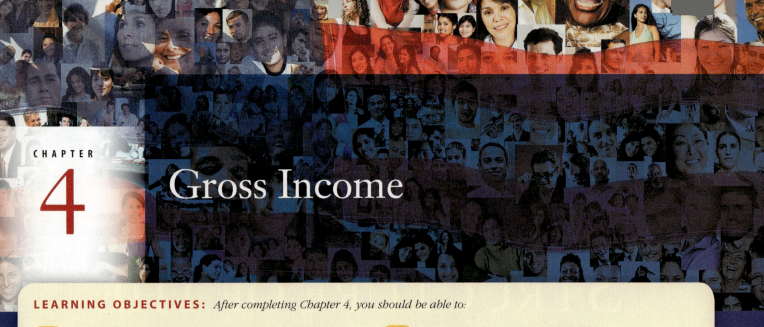

Gross Income

LEARNING OBJECTIVES: *After completing Chapter 4, you should be able to:*

LO.1 Explain the concepts of gross income and realization and distinguish between the economic, accounting, and tax concepts of gross income.

LO.2 Explain when the cash, accrual, and hybrid methods of accounting are used and how they are applied.

LO.3 Identify who should pay the tax on an item of income.

LO.4 Apply the statutory authority as to when to exclude an item from gross income.

LO.5 Describe the general tax consequences of property transactions.

LO.6 Explain and apply the tax provision that excludes interest on state and local government obligations from gross income.

LO.7 Determine the extent to which life insurance proceeds are excluded from gross income.

LO.8 Describe when income must be reported from the discharge of indebtedness.

LO.9 Determine the extent to which receipts can be excluded under the tax benefit rule.

LO.10 Apply the tax provisions on loans made at below-market interest rates.

LO.11 Use the tax rules concerning the exclusion of leasehold improvements from gross income.

CHAPTER OUTLINE

4-1 The Tax Formula, 4-2
    4-1a Components of the Tax Formula, 4-2

4-2 Gross Income—What Is It?, 4-3
    4-2a Concepts of Income, 4-3
    4-2b Comparing Accounting and Tax Concepts of Income, 4-5
    4-2c Form of Receipt, 4-5

4-3 Year of Inclusion, 4-6
    4-3a Taxable Year, 4-6
    4-3b Accounting Methods, 4-6
    4-3c Special Rules for Cash Basis Taxpayers, 4-10
    4-3d Special Rules for Accrual Basis Taxpayers, 4-11

4-4 Income Sources, 4-13
    4-4a Personal Services, 4-13
    4-4b Income from Property, 4-13
    4-4c Income Received by an Agent, 4-16

4-5 Specific Items of Gross Income, 4-17
    4-5a Gains and Losses from Property Transactions, 4-18
    4-5b Interest on Certain State and Local Government Obligations, 4-20
    4-5c Life Insurance Proceeds, 4-21
    4-5d Income from Discharge of Indebtedness, 4-23
    4-5e Tax Benefit Rule, 4-25
    4-5f Imputed Interest on Below-Market Loans, 4-26
    4-5g Improvements on Leased Property, 4-28

TAX TALK *The first nine pages of the Internal Revenue Code define income. The remaining 1,100 pages spin the web of exceptions and preferences.* —WARREN G. MAGNUSON

TYLER OLSON/SHUTTERSTOCK.COM

JUST WHAT IS INCLUDED IN GROSS INCOME?

At the beginning of the year, Dr. Cliff Payne, age 27, opened his new dental practice as a personal service corporation. The entity uses a December 31 year-end and the accrual method of accounting. During the year, the corporation billed patients and insurance companies for $385,000 of dental services. At the end of the year, $52,000 of this amount had not been collected. The entity earned $500 interest on a money market account held at the local bank and another $500 interest on an investment in bonds issued by the Whitehall School District.

Dr. Payne's salary from his corporation is $10,000 per month. However, he did not cash his December payroll check until January. To help provide funds to invest in the new business, Dr. Payne's parents loaned him $150,000 and did not charge him any interest. He also owns stock that has increased in value from $7,000 at the beginning of the year to more than $25,000 at the end of the year.

Although Dr. Payne took several accounting classes in college, he would like your help in calculating the correct amounts of his own gross income and the gross income of the corporation.

Read the chapter and formulate your response.

T he first step in computing an income tax liability is the determination of the amount of income that is subject to tax. In completing that step, some of the following questions must be answered. We will address these and other concerns in this chapter.

- *What:* What is income?
- *When:* In which tax period is the income recognized?
- *Who:* Who is taxed on the income?

4-1 THE TAX FORMULA

The basic income tax formula was introduced in Chapter 1 and summarized in Exhibit 1.1. This chapter, together with Chapters 5 through 8, examines the elements of this formula in detail. However, before embarking on a detailed study of the income tax, a brief introduction of each component of the tax formula, which follows, is provided as an overview.

4-1a Components of the Tax Formula

Income (Broadly Defined)

This includes all of the taxpayer's income, both taxable and nontaxable. Although it essentially is equivalent to gross receipts, it does not include a return of capital or borrowed funds.

Exclusions

For various reasons, Congress has chosen to exclude certain types of income from the income tax base. The principal income exclusions that apply to all entities (e.g., life insurance proceeds received by reason of death of the insured and state and local bond interest) are discussed later in this chapter, while exclusions that are unique to individuals are addressed in Chapters 9 through 11.

Gross Income

Section 61 of the Internal Revenue Code provides the following definition of gross income.

> Except as otherwise provided in this subtitle, gross income means all income from whatever source derived.

This language is based on the Sixteenth Amendment to the Constitution. The "except as otherwise provided" phrase refers to exclusions.

Supreme Court decisions have made it clear that *all* sources of income are subject to tax unless Congress specifically excludes the type of income received.

> The starting point in all cases dealing with the question of the scope of what is included in "gross income" begins with the basic premise that the purpose of Congress was to use the full measure of its taxing power.[1]

While it is clear that income is to be broadly construed, the statutory law fails to provide a satisfactory definition of the term and lists only a small set of items that are specifically included in income, including:

- Compensation for services.
- Business income.

---

[1] *James v. U.S.*, 61–1 USTC ¶9449, 7 AFTR 2d 1361, 81 S.Ct. 1052 (USSC, 1961).

- Gains from sales and other disposition of property.
- Interest.
- Dividends.
- Rents and royalties.
- Certain income arising from discharge of indebtedness.
- Income from partnerships.

Deductions

Generally, all ordinary and necessary trade or business expenses are deductible by taxpaying entities. Such expenses include the cost of goods sold, salaries, wages, operating expenses (such as rent and utilities), research and development expenditures, interest, taxes, depreciation, amortization, and depletion.

As noted in text Section 1-2g, individuals can use two categories of deductions—deductions *for* AGI and deductions *from* AGI. In addition, individuals are unique among taxpaying entities in that they are permitted to deduct a variety of personal expenses (i.e., expenses unrelated to business or investment), they are allowed a standard deduction if this amount exceeds the deductible personal expenses, and they can claim a deduction for personal and dependency exemptions.

Determining the Tax

Taxable income is determined by subtracting deductions (after any applicable limitations) from gross income. The tax rates (located on the inside front cover of this text) then are applied to determine the tax. Finally, tax prepayments (such as Federal income tax withholding on salaries and estimated tax payments) and a wide variety of credits are subtracted from the tax to determine the amount due to the Federal government or the refund due to the taxpayer. This formula is summarized on the inside back cover of this text, and in text Exhibits 1.1 and 1.2.

4-2 GROSS INCOME—WHAT IS IT?

4-2a Concepts of Income

As noted above, Congress failed to provide in the Code a clear definition of income. Instead, it was left to the judicial and administrative branches of government to determine the meaning of the term. As the income tax law developed, two competing models of income were considered by these agencies: economic income and accounting income.

The term **income** is used in the Code and defined broadly. Early in the history of our tax laws, the courts were required to interpret "the commonly understood meaning of the term which must have been in the minds of the people when they adopted the Sixteenth Amendment."[2]

Economists measure income (**economic income**) by determining the change (increase or decrease) in the fair market value of the entity's assets (net of liabilities) from the beginning to the end of the year. This focus on change in *net worth* as a measure of income (or loss) requires no disposition of assets. For *individual* taxpayers, one then adds the value of the year's personal consumption of goods and services (e.g., food, the rental value of owner-occupied housing, etc.).[3]

LO.1

Explain the concepts of gross income and realization and distinguish between the economic, accounting, and tax concepts of gross income.

---

[2]*Merchants Loan and Trust Co. v. Smietanka*, 1 USTC ¶42, 3 AFTR 3102, 41 S.Ct. 386 (USSC, 1921).

[3]See Henry C. Simons, *Personal Income Taxation* (Chicago: University of Chicago Press, 1933), Chapters 2–3.

FINANCIAL DISCLOSURE INSIGHTS   What Does "Income" Mean to You?

Accountants use a definition of income that relies on the realization principle.[4] **Accounting income** is not recognized until it is realized. For realization to occur:

- An exchange of goods or services must take place between the entity and some independent, external party, and

- The goods or services received by the entity must be capable of being objectively valued.[5]

Thus, an increase in the fair market value of an asset before its sale or other disposition is not sufficient to trigger the recognition of accounting income. Similarly, the imputed savings that arise when an entity creates assets for its own use (e.g., feed grown by a farmer for his or her livestock) do not constitute accounting income because no exchange has occurred.

Business taxpayers often reconcile their annual income computations for financial accounting and tax law purposes. Taxpayers required to prepare audited financial statements must explain in the footnotes to the statements (1) the most important accounting principles used in computing book income and (2) the most important tax elections and other consequences of the tax law on earnings per share.

EXAMPLE 1

Helen's economic income is calculated by comparing her net worth at the end of the year (December 31) with her net worth at the beginning of the year (January 1) and adding the amount of her personal consumption.

Fair market value of Helen's assets on December 31	$220,000	
Less liabilities on December 31	(40,000)	
Net worth on December 31		$ 180,000
Fair market value of Helen's assets on January 1	$200,000	
Less liabilities on January 1	(80,000)	
Net worth on January 1		(120,000)
Increase in net worth		$ 60,000
Consumption		
Food, clothing, and other personal expenditures	$ 25,000	
Imputed rental value of the home Helen owns and occupies	12,000	
Total consumption		37,000
Economic income		$ 97,000

The tax law relies to some extent on net worth as a measure of income.[6] Potentially, anything that increases net worth is income, and anything that decreases net worth is deductible (if permitted by statute). Thus, *windfall income* such as buried treasure found in one's backyard is taxable, under the theory that net worth has increased.[7] Likewise, a lender does *not* recognize gross income on receipt of loan principal repayments. The lender's investment simply changes from a loan receivable to cash, so net worth does not change.

Because the strict application of a tax based on economic income would require taxpayers to determine the value of their assets annually, compliance would be burdensome. Controversies between taxpayers and the IRS inevitably would arise under an economic approach to income determination because of the subjective nature of valuation in many circumstances. In addition, using market values to determine income for tax purposes could result in liquidity problems. That is, a taxpayer's assets could increase

---

[4] See the American Accounting Association Committee Report on the "Realization Concept," *The Accounting Review* (April 1965): 312–322.

[5] Valuation is carried out in the local currency of the reporting entity.

[6] *Comm. v. Glenshaw Glass Co.*, 55–1 USTC ¶9308, 47 AFTR 162, 348 U.S. 426 (USSC, 1955).

[7] *Cesarini v. U.S.*, 69–1 USTC ¶9270, 23 AFTR 2d 69–997, 296 F.Supp. 3 (D.Ct. N.Oh., 1969), *aff'd* 70–2 USTC ¶9509, 26 AFTR 2d 70–5107, 428 F.2d 812 (CA-6, 1970); Rev.Rul. 61, 1953–1 C.B. 17.

in value but not be easily converted into the cash needed to pay the resulting tax (e.g., increases in the value of commercial real estate).[8] Thus, the IRS, Congress, and the courts have rejected broad application of the economic income concept as impractical.

The Big Picture

Return to the facts of *The Big Picture* on p. 4-1. Dr. Payne's portfolio has increased in value by more than 250% during the tax year, and that additional value constitutes economic income to him. But the Federal income tax law does not include the value increase in Dr. Payne's gross income, even though the taxpayer could convert some of those gains to cash through, say, a margin loan from his broker.

EXAMPLE 2

4-2b Comparing Accounting and Tax Concepts of Income

Although income tax rules frequently parallel financial accounting measurement concepts, differences do exist. Of major significance, for example, is the fact that unearned (prepaid) income received by an accrual basis taxpayer often is taxed in the year of receipt. For financial accounting purposes, such prepayments are not treated as income until earned. Because of this and other differences, many corporations report financial accounting income that is substantially different from the amounts reported for tax purposes.

The Supreme Court provided an explanation for some of the variations between accounting and taxable income in a decision involving inventory and bad debt adjustments.

> The primary goal of financial accounting is to provide useful information to management, shareholders, creditors, and others properly interested; the major responsibility of the accountant is to protect these parties from being misled. The primary goal of the income tax system, in contrast, is the equitable collection of revenue.... Consistently with its goals and responsibilities, financial accounting has as its foundation the principle of conservatism, with its corollary that "possible errors in measurement [should] be in the direction of understatement rather than overstatement of net income and net assets." In view of the Treasury's markedly different goals and responsibilities, understatement of income is not destined to be its guiding light....
>
> Financial accounting, in short, is hospitable to estimates, probabilities, and reasonable certainties; the tax law, with its mandate to preserve the revenue, can give no quarter to uncertainty.[9]

4-2c Form of Receipt

Gross income is not limited to cash received. "It includes income realized in any form, whether in money, property, or services. Income may be realized [and recognized], therefore, in the form of services, meals, accommodations, stock or other property, as well as in cash."[10]

Form of Receipt

Ostrich Corporation allows Cameron, an employee, to use a company car for his vacation. Cameron realizes income equal to the rental value of the car for the time and mileage.

EXAMPLE 3

---

[8]In text Section 1-5d, this was identified as a justification of the wherewithal to pay concept.

[9]*Thor Power Tool Co. v. Comm.*, 79–1 USTC ¶9139, 43 AFTR 2d 79–362, 99 S.Ct. 773 (USSC, 1979).

[10]Reg. § 1.61–1(a).

Form of Receipt

EXAMPLE 4

Donna is a CPA specializing in individual tax return preparation. Her neighbor, Jill, is a dentist. Each year, Donna prepares Jill's tax return in exchange for two dental checkups. Jill and Donna both have gross income equal to the fair market value of the services they receive.

Concept Summary 4.1

Gross Income Concepts

Taxable income is computed using a specific form of income statement, i.e., one created by Congress. Taxable income can be seen as similar but not identical to both economic income and the income computation that is required by generally accepted accounting principles (GAAP).

1. Economic income is not appropriate for computing taxable income. Economic income depends on annual measures of market value and consumption, both of which would be difficult to apply on a short tax-filing deadline.

2. Many of the same accounting methods that are allowed by GAAP also can be used in computing gross income and tax deductions, as the tax law largely follows the realization principle of financial accounting.

4-3 YEAR OF INCLUSION

4-3a Taxable Year

The annual accounting period or **taxable year** is a basic component of our tax system. Generally, a taxpayer uses the *calendar year* to report gross income. However, a *fiscal year* (a period of 12 months ending on the last day of any month other than December) can be adopted if the taxpayer maintains adequate books and records.[11] In most cases, this fiscal year option generally is not available to partnerships, S corporations, and personal service corporations (i.e., one performing services in health, law, engineering, architecture, accounting, actuarial science, performing arts, or consulting). In most cases, individuals use a calendar tax year, and a business uses a tax year that corresponds with its year-end for financial accounting purposes.

Determining the tax year in which the income is recognized is important in determining the tax consequences of the income.

- With a progressive tax rate system, a taxpayer's marginal tax rate can change from year to year.

- Congress may change the tax rates.

- The relevant rates may change because of a change in the taxpayer's legal form (e.g., a proprietorship may incorporate, or an individual could marry).

- Several provisions in the Code require computations using the taxpayer's income for the year (e.g., the charitable contribution deduction).

- The taxpayer wants to reduce the present value of any tax that is owed. In this regard, income recognition in a later year is preferred; the longer payment of the tax can be postponed, the lower the present value of the tax.

4-3b Accounting Methods

LO.2

Explain when the cash, accrual, and hybrid methods of accounting are used and how they are applied.

The year in which an item of income is subject to tax often depends upon the **accounting method** the taxpayer employs. The three primary methods of accounting are (1) the cash receipts and disbursements method, (2) the accrual method, and (3) the hybrid method. Most individuals and many small businesses use the cash receipts and disbursements

---

[11]§ 441; Reg. § 1.441–1.

method of accounting, while most larger businesses use the accrual method. Generally, the tax law requires the use of the accrual method for determining purchases and sales when inventory is an income-producing factor.[12] Some businesses employ a hybrid method that is a combination of the cash and accrual methods, e.g., using the accrual method for sales and inventories and the cash method for everything else.

In addition to these overall accounting methods, specialized tax accounting methods are available for certain items or transactions. For instance, a taxpayer may spread the gain from an installment sale of property over the collection period by using the *installment method* of income recognition. Contractors may either spread profits from contracts over the period in which the work is done (the *percentage of completion method*) or defer all profit until the year in which the project is completed (the *completed contract method*) in limited circumstances.[13]

The IRS holds broad powers to determine whether the taxpayer's accounting method clearly reflects income, and to have the taxpayer change the method if it does not *clearly reflect income*.

> If no method of accounting has been regularly used by the taxpayer, or if the method used does not clearly reflect income, the computation of taxable income shall be made under such method as, in the opinion of the Secretary . . . does clearly reflect income.[14]

Cash Receipts Method

Under the <mark>cash receipts method</mark>, property or services received are included in the taxpayer's gross income in the year of actual or constructive receipt by the taxpayer, regardless of whether the income was earned in that year.[15] The income received need not be reduced to cash in the same year. All that is necessary for income recognition is that property or services received be measurable by a fair market value.[16]

Thus, a cash basis taxpayer that receives a note in payment for services recognizes gross income in the year of receipt equal to the fair market value of the note. However, a creditor's mere promise to pay (e.g., an account receivable), with no supporting note, usually is not considered to have a fair market value; it is not a cash equivalent.[17] Thus, the cash basis taxpayer defers income recognition until the account receivable is collected.

Finch & Thrush, a CPA firm, uses the cash receipts method of accounting. In 2018, the firm performs an audit for Orange Corporation and bills the client for $5,000, which is collected in 2019. In 2018, the firm also performs an audit for Blue Corporation. Because of Blue's precarious financial position, Finch & Thrush requires Blue to issue an $8,000 secured negotiable note in payment of the fee. The note has a fair market value of $6,000. The firm collects $8,000 on the note in 2019. Finch & Thrush reports the following gross income for the two years.

EXAMPLE
5

	2018	2019
Fair market value of note received from Blue	$6,000	
Cash received		
From Orange on account receivable		$ 5,000
From Blue on note receivable		8,000
Less: Recovery of capital	–0–	(6,000)
Total gross income	$6,000	$ 7,000

---

[12]Reg. § 1.446–1(c)(2)(i); IRC § 471(c) though allows small businesses to use the cash method even though they have inventory.

[13]§§ 453 and 460.

[14]§ 446(b).

[15]*Julia A. Strauss,* 2 B.T.A. 598 (1925). The doctrine of *constructive receipt* holds that if income is unqualifiedly available although not physically in the taxpayer's possession, it is included in gross income. An example is

accrued interest on a savings account. Under the doctrine of constructive receipt, the interest is taxed to a depositor in the year available, rather than the year actually withdrawn. The fact that the depositor uses the cash basis of accounting for tax purposes is irrelevant. Reg. § 1.451–2.

[16]Reg. §§ 1.446–1(a)(3) and (c)(1)(i).

[17]*Bedell v. Comm.,* 1 USTC ¶359, 7 AFTR 8469, 30 F.2d 622 (CA–2, 1929).

Generally, a cash basis taxpayer recognizes gross income when a check is received in payment for goods or services rendered in a business setting. This is true even if the taxpayer receives the check after banking hours. But if the person paying with the check requests that the check not be cashed until a subsequent date, the cash basis income is deferred until the date the check can be cashed.[18]

The cash receipts method could distort taxable income as income, and expenses from the same activity may be recognized in different tax years. Moreover, a taxpayer using the cash receipts method has some degree of control over when income is recognized, such as by delaying the sending of invoices to customers. Thus, the tax law does not allow all businesses to use the cash receipts method. Certain businesses with average annual gross receipts greater than $25 million, computed over the preceding three-year period, must use the accrual method. Businesses with inventory that also have average annual gross receipts in the prior three-year period in excess of $25 million also are required to use the accrual method.[19]

Accrual Method

Under the **accrual method**, an item generally is included in gross income for the year in which it is earned, regardless of when the income is collected.[20] The income is earned when (1) all the events have occurred that fix the right to receive the income and (2) the amount to be received can be determined with reasonable accuracy.[21] Generally, these tests are treated as satisfied no later than when the revenue is included in the taxpayer's financial statements.

Generally, the taxpayer's rights to income accrue when title to property passes to the buyer or the services are performed for the customer or client.[22] If the rights to income have accrued but are subject to a potential refund claim (e.g., under a product warranty), the income is reported in the year of sale and a deduction is allowed in subsequent years when actual claims accrue.[23]

TAX PLANNING STRATEGIES   Cash Receipts Method

FRAMEWORK FOCUS: INCOME

Strategy: Postpone Recognition of Income to Achieve Tax Deferral.

FRAMEWORK FOCUS: TAX RATE

Strategy: Shift Net Income from High-Bracket Years to Low-Bracket Years.

The timing of income from services often can be controlled through the cash method of accounting. The usual lag between billings and collections (e.g., December's billings collected in January) can result in a deferral of some income until the last year of operations.

As another example, before rendering services, a corporate officer approaching retirement may contract with the corporation to defer a portion of his or her compensation to the lower tax bracket retirement years.

---

[18]*Charles F. Kahler*, 18 T.C. 31 (1952); *Bright v. U.S.*, 91–1 USTC ¶50,142, 67 AFTR 2d 91–673, 926 F.2d 383 (CA–5, 1991).

[19]§§ 448, 471(c), and 263A(i). Section 448 requiring certain taxpayers to use the accrual method does not apply to individuals, partnerships without a C corporation partner, S corporations, estates, and trusts. Thus, generally, these types of taxpayers may use the cash receipts method regardless of their gross receipts level. If such entity has inventory and average annual gross receipts in the prior three-year period in excess of $25 million, it will need to use either the accrual method or the hybrid method.

[20]These rules differ from those used for financial accounting purposes.

[21]IRC § 451(b), Reg. § 1.451–1(a).

[22]*Lucas v. North Texas Lumber Co.*, 2 USTC ¶484, 8 AFTR 10276, 50 S.Ct. 184 (USSC, 1930).

[23]*Brown v. Helvering*, 4 USTC ¶1222, 13 AFTR 851, 54 S.Ct. 356 (USSC, 1933).

BRIDGE DISCIPLINE **Bridge to Economics and Finance**

Nontaxable Economic Benefits

Home ownership is the prime example of economic income from capital that is not subject to tax. If the taxpayer uses his or her capital to purchase investments but pays rent on a personal residence, the taxpayer pays tax on the income from the investments but cannot deduct the rent payment.

However, if the taxpayer purchases a personal residence instead of the investments, he or she removes the investment income from the tax return but incurs no other form of gross income. A homeowner "pays rent to himself," but such rent is not subject to income tax. Thus, the home-owner has substituted nontaxable for taxable income.

Tax Deferral

Because deferred taxes are tantamount to interest-free loans to the taxpayer from the government, the deferral of taxes is a worthy goal of the tax planner. However, the tax planner also must consider the tax rates for the years the income is shifted from and to. For example, a one-year deferral of income from a year in which the taxpayer's tax rate was 24 percent to a year in which the tax rate will be 32 percent would not be advisable if the taxpayer expects to earn less than an 8 percent after-tax return on the deferred tax dollars. Text Appendix F provides tables by which to compute the present and future values of gross income, deductions, and tax liabilities.

The taxpayer often can defer the recognition of income from appreciated property by postponing the event triggering realization (e.g., the final closing on a sale or exchange of property). If the tax-payer needs cash, obtaining a loan by using the appreciated property as collateral may be the least costly alternative. When the taxpayer anticipates reinvesting the proceeds, a sale may be inadvisable.

EXAMPLE 6

Ira owns 100 shares of Pigeon Company common stock with a cost of $20,000 and a fair market value of $50,000. Although the stock's value has increased substantially in the past three years, Ira thinks the growth cycle for the stock is over. If he sells the Pigeon stock, Ira will invest the proceeds from the sale in other common stock. Assuming that Ira's marginal tax rate on the sale is 20%, he keeps only $44,000 [$50,000 − .20($50,000 − $20,000)] to reinvest. The alternative investment must substantially outperform Pigeon in the future for the sale to be beneficial.

Where the taxpayer's rights to the income are being contested (e.g., when a contractor fails to meet specifications), gross income is recognized only when payment has been received.[24] If the payment is received before the dispute is settled, however, the court-made **claim of right doctrine** requires the taxpayer to recognize the income in the year of receipt.[25] The taxpayer possesses the funds with which to pay the corresponding tax. Therefore, the government should be allowed to collect the tax rather than waiting until all uncertainty is resolved.

If Finch & Thrush in Example 5 uses the accrual basis of accounting, it recognizes $13,000 ($8,000 + $5,000) income in 2018, the year its rights to the income accrue.

EXAMPLE 7

Tangerine Construction, Inc., completes construction of a building at the end of the year and presents a bill to the customer. The customer refuses to pay the bill and claims that Tangerine has not met specifications. A settlement with the customer is not reached until the next year.

No gross income accrues to Tangerine until the second year.

Hybrid Method

The **hybrid method** is a combination of the accrual and cash methods. Generally, when the hybrid method is used, inventory is an income-producing factor and the taxpayer is

---

[24]*Burnet v. Sanford and Brooks*, 2 USTC ¶636, 9 AFTR 603, 51 S.Ct. 150 (USSC, 1931).

[25]*North American Oil Consolidated Co. v. Burnet*, 3 USTC ¶943, 11 AFTR 16, 52 S.Ct. 613 (USSC, 1932).

not required to use only the accrual method (that is, the taxpayer meets the definition of a small business). The Regulations require use of the accrual method for determining sales of inventory and cost of goods sold. Thus, the taxpayer using the hybrid method accounts for sales of goods and cost of goods sold using the accrual method and uses the cash method for all other income and expense items (e.g., services and interest income). Changes made by the Tax Cuts and Jobs Act (TCJA) of 2017 allow more types of businesses to use the cash method and to not account for inventory. Thus, the hybrid method is not likely to be commonly used.

4-3c Special Rules for Cash Basis Taxpayers

Constructive Receipt

Income that has not actually been received by the taxpayer is taxed as though it had been received—the income is constructively received—under the following conditions.

- The amount is made readily available to the taxpayer.
- The taxpayer's actual receipt is not subject to substantial limitations or restrictions.[26]

The rationale for the **constructive receipt** doctrine is that if the income is available, the taxpayer should not be allowed unilaterally to postpone income recognition. For instance, a taxpayer is not permitted to defer income for December services by refusing to accept payment until January.

Constructive Receipt

Rob, a physician, conducts his medical practice as a sole proprietorship. Rob also is a member of a barter club. This year, Rob provided medical care for other club members and earned 3,000 points. Each point entitles him to $1 in goods and services sold by other members of the club; the points can be used at any time. Rob exchanged his points for a new high-definition TV in the next year, but he recognizes $3,000 gross income in the first year (i.e., when the 3,000 points were credited to his account).[27]

On December 31, an employer issued a bonus check to an employee but asked her to hold it for a few days until the company could make deposits to cover the check. The income was not constructively received on December 31 because the issuer did not have sufficient funds in its account to pay the debt.[28]

Mauve, Inc., an S corporation, owned interest coupons that matured on December 31. The coupons can be converted to cash at any bank at maturity. Thus, the income was constructively received on December 31, even though Mauve failed to cash in the coupons until the following year.[29]

Flamingo Company mails dividend checks on December 31. The checks will not be received by the shareholders until January. The shareholders do not realize gross income until January.[30]

The constructive receipt doctrine does not reach income the taxpayer is not yet entitled to receive, even though the taxpayer could have contracted to receive the income at an earlier date.

[26]Reg. § 1.451–2(a).

[27]Rev.Rul. 80–52, 1980–1 C.B. 100.

[28]*L. M. Fischer*, 14 T.C. 792 (1950).

[29]Reg. § 1.451–2(b).

[30]Reg. § 1.451–2(b).

Murphy offers to pay Peach Corporation (a cash basis taxpayer) $100,000 for land in December 2017. Peach Corporation refuses, but offers to sell the land to Murphy on January 1, 2018, when the corporation will be in a lower tax bracket. If Murphy accepts Peach's offer, the gain is taxed to Peach in 2018, when the sale is completed.[31]

In-depth coverage can be found on this book's companion website: **www.cengage.com**

1 DIGGING DEEPER

Original Issue Discount

Lenders frequently make loans that require a payment at maturity of more than the amount of the original loan. The difference between the amount due at maturity and the amount of the original loan is actually interest, referred to as **original issue discount**. In these circumstances, the original issue discount is reported when earned, regardless of the taxpayer's accounting method.[32] The *interest earned* is calculated by the effective interest rate method.

On January 1, year 1, Blue and White, a cash basis partnership, pays $92,456 for a 24-month certificate of deposit. The certificate is priced to yield 4% (the effective interest rate) with interest compounded annually. No interest is paid until maturity, when Blue and White receives $100,000.

The partnership's gross income from the certificate is $7,544 ($100,000 − $92,456). Blue and White calculates income earned each year as follows.

Year 1 (.04 × $92,456) =	$3,698
Year 2 [.04($92,456 + $3,698)] =	3,846
	$7,544

The original issue discount rules do not apply to U.S. savings bonds or to obligations with a maturity date of one year or less from the date of issue.[33]

Amounts Received under an Obligation to Repay

The receipt of funds with an obligation to repay that amount in the future is the essence of borrowing. The taxpayer's assets and liabilities increase by the same amount, so no income is realized when the borrowed funds are received.

A landlord receives a damage deposit from a tenant. The landlord does not recognize income until the deposit is forfeited because the landlord has an obligation to repay the deposit if no damage occurs.[34] However, if the deposit is in fact a prepayment of rent, it is taxed in the year of receipt.

4-3d Special Rules for Accrual Basis Taxpayers

Prepaid Income

For financial reporting purposes, advance payments received from customers are reflected as prepaid income and as a liability of the seller. For tax purposes, however, the prepaid income often is taxed in the year of receipt.

In December 2018, Jared's sole proprietorship pays its January 2019 rent of $1,000. Jared's calendar year, accrual basis landlord includes the $1,000 in 2018 gross income for tax purposes, although $1,000 unearned rent income is reported as a liability on the landlord's financial accounting balance sheet for December 31, 2018.

---

[31]*Cowden v. Comm.*, 61–1 USTC ¶9382, 7 AFTR 2d 1160, 289 F.2d 20 (CA–5, 1961).

[32]§§ 1272(a)(3) and 1273(a).

[33]§ 1272(a)(2).

[34]*John Mantell*, 17 T.C. 1143 (1952).

Deferral of Advance Payments for Goods

Generally, an accrual basis taxpayer can elect to defer recognition of income from advance payments for goods if the method of accounting for the sale is the same for tax and financial reporting purposes.[35]

EXAMPLE 16

Brown Company ships goods only after payment for the goods has been received. In December 2018, Brown receives a $10,000 payment for goods that are not shipped until January 2019. Assuming that a proper election is in place, Brown reports the income in 2019 for tax purposes, assuming that the company reports the income in that year for financial reporting purposes.

Deferral of Advance Payments for Services, Goods, and Certain Other Items

When payments are received for services that will be performed in a later tax year, an accrual basis taxpayer can defer for one year the recognition of income for the services that will be performed later.[36] This method of accounting may also be used for advance payments received for goods, as well as licensing of intellectual property, and the sale, lease, or license of software.

Advance payments for prepaid rent or prepaid interest, however, always are taxed in the year of receipt, as illustrated in Example 15.

EXAMPLE 17

Yellow Corporation, an accrual basis calendar year taxpayer, sells its computer consulting services under 12-month, 24-month, and 36-month contracts. The corporation provides services to each customer every month. On May 1, year 1, Yellow sold the following contracts.

Length of Contract	Total Proceeds
12 months	$3,000
24 months	4,800
36 months	7,200

Yellow may defer until year 2 all of the income that will be reported on its financial statements after year 1.

Length of Contract	Income Recorded in Year 1	Income Recorded in Year 2
12 months	$2,000 ($3,000 × 8/12)	$1,000 ($3,000 × 4/12)
24 months	1,600 ($4,800 × 8/24)	3,200 ($4,800 × 16/24)
36 months	1,600 ($7,200 × 8/36)	5,600 ($7,200 × 28/36)

TAX PLANNING STRATEGIES   Prepaid Income

FRAMEWORK FOCUS: INCOME

Strategy: Postpone Recognition of Income to Achieve Tax Deferral.

The accrual basis taxpayer who receives advance payments from customers should adopt the available tax accounting income deferral methods. It then should structure the transactions using those rules, so as to avoid a payment of tax on income before the time the income actually is earned.

In addition, both cash and accrual basis taxpayers sometimes can defer income by stipulating that the payments are deposits rather than prepaid income. For example, a tax-savvy landlord might consider requiring an equivalent damage deposit rather than prepayment of the last month's rent.

---

[35]Reg. § 1.451–5(b). The election covers the current and all future tax years, unless the IRS allows the taxpayer to terminate it. See Reg. § 1.451–5(c) for exceptions to this deferral opportunity. The TCJA of 2017 added § 451(c) to allow accrual method taxpayers to elect to defer certain advance payments. This deferral cannot extend beyond the year following the year payment is received.

[36]Rev.Proc. 2004–34, 2004–1 C.B. 991. Per Notice 2018–35, 2018–18 I.R.B. 522, taxpayers may continue to rely on Rev.Proc. 2014–34 until further guidance is issued by the IRS on the changes made to § 451 by the TCJA of 2017.

Concept Summary 4.2

Income Tax Accounting

Tax accounting methods often parallel those used for financial accounting, especially those that affect the timing of the tax recognition of income and deduction items. Certain exceptions do exist, however.

1. Businesses may be able to adopt the cash, accrual, or hybrid method of accounting. The tax law allows certain businesses to use either the cash or hybrid method, while others may be required to use the accrual method. For instance, the accrual method typically is required if the taxpayer holds inventories or is a C corporation with over $25 million of gross receipts (other than a qualified personal service corporation).

2. Other tax accounting methods parallel those of financial accounting, such as the installment method and the treatment of long-term contracts.

3. Special rules apply when the taxpayer has control, but not possession, of funds that have been earned.

4. Tax accounting method rules may allow the deferral of income recognition concerning prepayments for the sale of goods and services.

4-4 INCOME SOURCES

LO.3

Identify who should pay the tax on an item of income.

4-4a Personal Services

It is a well-established principle of taxation that income from personal services must be included in the gross income of the person who performs the services. This principle was first established in a Supreme Court decision, *Lucas v. Earl*.[37] Mr. Earl entered into a binding agreement with his wife under which Mrs. Earl was to receive one-half of Mr. Earl's salary. Justice Holmes used the celebrated **fruit and tree metaphor** to explain that the fruit (income) must be attributed to the tree from which it came (Mr. Earl's services). A mere **assignment of income** to another party does not shift the liability for the tax.

Services of an Employee

Services performed by an employee for the employer's customers are considered performed by the employer. Thus, the employer is taxed on the income from the services provided to the customer, and the employee is taxed on any compensation received from the employer.[38]

The Big Picture

Return to the facts of *The Big Picture* on p. 4-1. Dr. Payne has entered into an employment contract with his corporation and receives a salary. All patients contract to receive their dental services from the corporation, and those services are provided through the corporation's employee, Dr. Payne.

Thus, the corporation earned the income from patients' services and must include the patients' fees in its gross income. Payne includes his salary in his own gross income. The corporation claims a deduction for the reasonable salary paid to Payne.

EXAMPLE 18

In-depth coverage can be found on this book's companion website: www.cengage.com

2 DIGGING DEEPER

4-4b Income from Property

Income earned from property (e.g., interest, dividends, rent) is included in the gross income of the owner of the property. If a shareholder clips interest coupons (the "fruit")

---

[37]2 USTC ¶496, 8 AFTR 10287, 50 S.Ct. 241 (USSC, 1930).

[38]*Sargent v. Comm.*, 91–1 USTC ¶50,168, 67 AFTR 2d 91–718, 929 F.2d 1252 (CA–8, 1991).

from bonds (the "tree") shortly before the interest payment date and transfers the coupons to his or her solely owned corporation, the interest still is taxed to the shareholder.

Often income-producing property is transferred after income from the property has accrued but before the income is recognized under the transferor's method of accounting. The IRS and the courts have developed rules to allocate the income between the transferor and the transferee. These allocation rules are addressed below. Other allocation rules address income in community property states.

DIGGING DEEPER 3 In-depth coverage can be found on this book's companion website: **www.cengage.com**

Interest

According to the tax law, interest accrues daily. Therefore, the interest for the period that includes the date of an asset transfer is allocated between the transferor and the transferee based on the number of days during the period that each owned the property.

EXAMPLE 19

Floyd, a cash basis taxpayer, gives his son, Seth, corporate bonds with a face amount of $12,000 and a 5% stated annual interest rate. The interest is payable on the last day of each quarter. Floyd makes the gift to Seth on February 28. Floyd recognizes $100 interest income at the time of the gift ($12,000 × 5% × 3/12 interest for the quarter × 2/3 months in the quarter earned before the gift).

For the transferor, the timing of the recognition of gross income from the property depends upon the pertinent accounting method and the manner in which the property was transferred. In the case of a gift of income-producing property, the donor's share of the accrued income is recognized at the time it would have been recognized had the donor continued to own the property.[39] If the transfer is a sale, however, the transferor recognizes the accrued income at the time of the sale, because the accrued amount is included in the sales proceeds.

EXAMPLE 20

Mia purchased a corporate bond at its face amount on January 1 for $10,000. The bond paid 5% interest each December 31. On March 31, Mia sold the bond for $10,600. Mia recognizes $125 interest income, accrued as of the date of the sale (5% × $10,000 × 3/12 months before the sale). She also recognizes a $475 capital gain from the sale of the bond, computed as follows.

Amount received from sale	$ 10,600
Accrued interest income already recognized	(125)
Selling price of bond, less interest	$ 10,475
Less cost of the bond	(10,000)
Capital gain recognized on sale	$ 475

---

[39]Rev.Rul. 72–312, 1972–1 C.B. 22.

GLOBAL TAX ISSUES **Which Foreign Dividends Get the Discounted Rate?**

A dividend from a non-U.S. corporation is eligible for qualified dividend status only if one of the following requirements is met: (1) the foreign corporation's stock is traded on an established U.S. securities market or (2) the foreign corporation is eligible for the benefits of a comprehensive income tax treaty or information-sharing agreement between its country of incorporation and the United States.[40]

In-depth coverage can be found on this book's companion website: **www.cengage.com**   **4 DIGGING DEEPER**

Dividends

A corporation is taxed on its earnings, and the shareholders are taxed on the dividends paid to them from the corporation's after-tax earnings.

Partial relief from the double taxation of dividends has been provided in that *qualified dividends* are taxed at the same marginal rate that is applicable to a net capital gain. Generally, net capital gains are subject to a 15 percent rate of Federal income tax. The rate is 0 percent for taxpayers with low taxable income, and 20 percent for upper-income taxpayers. Distributions that are not qualified dividends are taxed at the rates that apply to ordinary income.[41]

Because the beneficial tax rate is intended to mitigate double taxation, only certain dividends are eligible for the beneficial treatment. Excluded are certain dividends from non-U.S. corporations, dividends from tax-exempt entities, and dividends that do not satisfy the holding period requirement.

Corporations that are shareholders (that is, they own stock in another corporation) may be allowed a deduction to offset some or all of their dividend income. See text Section 12-4a.

A holding period requirement must be satisfied for the lower tax rates to apply: the stock that paid the dividend must have been held for more than 60 days during the 121-day period beginning 60 days before the ex-dividend date.[42] The purpose of this requirement is to prevent the taxpayer from buying the stock shortly before the dividend is paid, receiving the dividend, and then selling the stock at a short-term capital loss after the stock goes ex-dividend. A stock's price often declines after the stock goes ex-dividend.

Qualified Dividends

EXAMPLE 21

Green Corporation pays a dividend of $1.50 on each share of its common stock. Madison and Daniel, two unrelated shareholders, each own 1,000 shares of the stock. Consequently, each receives a dividend of $1,500 (1,000 shares × $1.50). Assume that Daniel satisfies the 60/120-day holding period rule, but Madison does not.

The $1,500 that Daniel receives is subject to the lower rates on qualified dividends. The $1,500 that Madison receives, however, is not. Because Madison did not comply with the holding period rule, her dividend is not a *qualified dividend*; it is taxed at ordinary income rates.

---

[40]§§ 1(h)(11)(C)(i), (ii).

[41]§ 1(h)(11). Qualified dividends are not treated as capital gains in the gains and losses netting process; thus, they are *not* reduced by capital losses. For certain high-income individuals, the additional Medicare tax on net investment income also may apply to dividends, interest, net capital gains, and the like. See text Section 9-6d.

[42]The ex-dividend date is the date before the record date on which the corporation finalizes the list of shareholders who will receive the dividends.

TAX FACT Business Income and Loss

Sole proprietors reporting net business income or loss on Form 1040 constitute about 16.5 percent of all returns filed. About 8 percent of all Forms 1040 show income from rentals or farming operations. And more than 1 percent of individuals report winnings from gambling activities.

Qualified Dividends

EXAMPLE 22

Assume that both Madison and Daniel in Example 21 are in the 32% Federal income tax bracket. Consequently, Madison pays a tax of $480 (32% × $1,500) on her dividend, while Daniel pays a tax of $225 (15% × $1,500) on his. The $255 saving that Daniel enjoys underscores the advantages of receiving a qualified dividend.

A distribution by a corporation to its shareholders is classified as a dividend only if it is paid from the entity's *earnings and profits* (E & P). If the distribution is not made from E & P, it is treated as a return of the shareholder's investment and generally is not taxed at the time of the distribution. See text Section 13-2c.

Unlike interest, dividends do not accrue on a daily basis; the declaration of a dividend is at the discretion of the corporation's board of directors. Generally, dividends are taxed to the person who is entitled to receive them—the shareholder of record as of the corporation's record date.[43] Thus, if a taxpayer sells stock after a dividend has been declared but before the record date, the dividend generally is taxed to the purchaser.

If a donor makes a gift of stock to someone (e.g., a family member) after the declaration date but before the record date, the donor does not shift the dividend income to the donee. The *fruit* has ripened sufficiently as of the declaration date to tax the dividend income to the donor of the stock.[44]

EXAMPLE 23

On June 20, the board of directors of Black Corporation declares a $10 per share dividend. The dividend is payable on June 30 to shareholders of record on June 25. As of June 20, Kathleen owns 200 shares of Black stock. On June 21, Kathleen sells 100 of the shares to Jon for their fair market value and gives 100 of the shares to Andrew (her son). Both Jon and Andrew are shareholders of record as of June 25.

Jon (the purchaser) is taxed on $1,000 because he is entitled to receive the dividend. However, Kathleen (the donor) is taxed on the $1,000 received by Andrew (the donee) because the gift was made after the declaration date but before the record date of the dividend.

DIGGING DEEPER 5 | In-depth coverage can be found on this book's companion website: **www.cengage.com**

4-4c Income Received by an Agent

Income received by the taxpayer's agent is considered to be received by the taxpayer. A cash basis principal must recognize the income at the time it is received by the agent.[45]

EXAMPLE 24

Longhorn, Inc., a cash basis corporation, delivers cattle to the auction barn in late December. The auctioneer, acting as the corporation's agent, sells the cattle and collects the proceeds in December. The auctioneer does not pay Longhorn until the following January. Longhorn includes the sales proceeds in its gross income in the year the auctioneer received the funds.

---

[43]Reg. § 1.61–9(c). The record date is the cutoff for determining the shareholders who are entitled to receive the dividend.

[44]*M. G. Anton*, 34 T.C. 842 (1960).

[45]Rev.Rul. 79–379, 1979–2 C.B. 204.

TAX PLANNING STRATEGIES Techniques for Reducing Investment Income

FRAMEWORK FOCUS: INCOME

Strategy: Postpone Recognition of Income to Achieve Tax Deferral.

FRAMEWORK FOCUS: TAX RATE

Strategy: Control the Character of Income

Because no tax is due until a gain has been recognized, the law favors investments that yield appreciation rather than annual income, and it favors capital gains over interest income.

EXAMPLE 25

Chandra can buy a low-rated corporate bond or an acre of land for $10,000. The bond pays $600 of interest (6%) each year, and Chandra expects the land to increase in value 8% each year for the next 10 years. She is in the 40% (combined Federal and state) tax bracket for ordinary income and 26% for qualifying capital gains. If the bond would mature or the land would be sold in 10 years and Chandra would reinvest the interest at a 6% pretax return, she would accumulate the following amounts at the end of 10 years. See text Appendix F for any time value of money factors needed.

		Bond	Land
Original investment		$10,000	$10,000
Annual interest income	$ 600		
Less tax	(240)		
After-tax return	$ 360		
Compound amount reinvested for 10 years at 3.6% after-tax	×11.79	4,244	
Future value		$14,244	
Future value, 10 years at 6%			× 1.79
			$17,900
Less tax on sale 26%($17,900 sale price – $10,000 original cost)			(2,054)
Future value			$15,846

Therefore, the value of the deferral that results from investing in the land rather than in the bond is $1,602 ($15,846 – $14,244).

4-5 SPECIFIC ITEMS OF GROSS INCOME

LO.4

Apply the statutory authority as to when to exclude an item from gross income.

The all-inclusive principles of gross income determination as applied by the IRS and the courts have, on occasion, been expanded or modified by Congress through legislation. This legislation generally provides more specific rules for determining gross income from certain sources. Most of these special rules appear in §§ 71–91 of the Code.

In addition to provisions describing how specific sources of gross income are to be taxed, several specific rules *exclude* items from gross income. Authority for excluding specific items is provided in §§ 101–150 and in various other provisions in the Code.

Many statutory exclusions are unique to *individual taxpayers* (e.g., gifts and inheritances,[46] scholarships,[47] and a variety of fringe benefits paid to *employees*). These exclusions are discussed in Chapters 9 through 11. Other exclusions are broader and apply to all entities. These exclusions include interest on state and local bonds (§ 103), life

---

[46]§ 102.

[47]§ 117.

insurance proceeds received by reason of death of the insured (§ 101), the fair market value of leasehold improvements received by the lessor when a lease is terminated (§ 109),[48] and income from discharge of indebtedness (§ 108).

Taxpayers can recognize gross income when there is a sale or other disposition of a nonbusiness asset. These transactions are discussed in more detail in Chapters 7 and 8, but this section includes an introduction to the tax rules that apply in the most common situations. Some of the broadly applied statutory rules describing inclusions and exclusions are discussed next.

4-5a Gains and Losses from Property Transactions

When property is sold or otherwise disposed of, gain or loss may result. Such gain or loss has an effect on the gross income of the party making the sale or other disposition when the gain or loss is *realized* and *recognized* for tax purposes. The concept of realized gain or loss is expressed as follows.

Amount realized from the sale		Adjusted basis of the property		Realized gain (or loss)

The *amount realized* is the selling price of the property less any costs of disposition (e.g., brokerage commissions) incurred by the seller. The *adjusted basis* of the property is determined as follows.

Cost (or other original basis) at date of acquisition[49]	
Add:	Capital additions
Subtract:	Depreciation (if appropriate) and other capital recoveries (see Chapter 5)
Equals:	Adjusted basis at date of sale or other disposition

Without realized gain or loss, generally, there can be no recognized (taxable) gain or loss. All realized gains are recognized unless some specific part of the tax law provides otherwise. Realized losses may or may not be recognized (deductible) for tax purposes, depending on the circumstances involved. For example, losses realized from the disposition of personal use property (property held by individuals and not used for business or investment purposes) are not recognized.

During the current year, Ted sells his sailboat (adjusted basis of $4,000) for $5,500. Ted also sells one of his personal automobiles (adjusted basis of $8,000) for $5,000. Ted's realized gain of $1,500 from the sale of the sailboat is recognized. The $3,000 realized loss on the sale of the automobile, however, is not recognized. Thus, the gain is taxable, but the loss is not deductible.

Once it has been determined that the disposition of property results in a recognized gain or loss, that amount is included in adjusted gross income. The next step is to classify the gain or loss as capital or ordinary. Although ordinary gain is fully taxable and ordinary loss is fully deductible, the same is not true for capital gains and capital losses.

Capital Gains and Losses

Gains and losses from the disposition of capital assets receive special tax treatment. Capital assets are defined in the Code as any property held by the taxpayer *other than*, among other things, inventory, accounts receivable, and depreciable property or real estate used in a business. The sale or exchange of assets in these categories usually

---

[48]If the tenant made the improvements in lieu of rent payments, the value of the improvements is included in the landlord's gross income.

[49]Cost usually means purchase price plus expenses related to the acquisition of the property and incurred by the purchaser (e.g., brokerage commissions). For the basis of property acquired by gift or inheritance and other basis rules, see text Section 7-2b.

results in ordinary income or loss treatment (see text Sections 8-7 through 8-9). The sale of any other asset generally creates a capital gain or loss.

> Cardinal, Inc., owns a pizza parlor. During the current year, Cardinal sells an automobile. The automobile, which had been used as a pizza delivery car for three years, was sold at a loss of $1,000. Because this automobile was a depreciable asset used in its business, Cardinal reports an ordinary loss of $1,000, rather than a capital loss. Cardinal also sold securities held for investment during the current year. The securities were sold for a gain of $800. The securities are capital assets. Therefore, Cardinal reports a capital gain of $800.
>
> **EXAMPLE 27**

Computing the Net Capital Gain/Loss To ascertain the appropriate tax treatment of capital gains and losses, a netting process first is applied.

1. Capital gains and losses are classified as:
   a. short term, if the sold asset was held for one year or less, or
   b. long term, if the sold asset was held for more than one year.
2. Capital gains and losses then are netted within these two classifications. Specifically, short-term capital losses (STCL) are offset against short-term capital gains (STCG), resulting in either a net short-term capital loss (NSTCL) or a net short-term capital gain (NSTCG).
3. Similarly, long-term capital losses (LTCL) are offset against long-term capital gains (LTCG), resulting in either a net long-term capital gain (NLTCG) or a net long-term capital loss (NLTCL).
4. If the resulting amounts are of opposite signs (i.e., there remains a gain and a loss), those amounts are netted against each other. This produces the taxpayer's net capital gain or loss for the tax year. It is entirely long- or short-term, as dictated by the number that was larger in steps 2 and 3.

> Colin reports the following capital gains (losses) from asset sales during the year.
>
> **EXAMPLE 28**
>
> | | |
> |---|---:|
> | Penguin Corporation stock (held for 7 months) | $ 1,000 |
> | Owl Corporation stock (held for 9 months) | (3,000) |
> | Flamingo Corporation bonds (held for 14 months) | 2,000 |
> | Land (held for 3 years) | 4,000 |
>
> **SHORT TERM:** The Penguin gain of $1,000 is offset by the Owl loss of $3,000. This results in a $2,000 NSTCL.
>
> **LONG TERM:** Netting the results of the sales of the bonds and the land, a $6,000 NLTCG is computed.
>
> **CONTINUE NETTING:** Because there remains a gain and a loss, net these amounts against each other. A $4,000 net long-term capital gain results.

Taxing the Net Capital Gain/Loss Individuals and corporations are taxed differently on their net capital gains and losses. An individual's *net capital gain* is subject to the following *maximum* tax rates.[50] Certain upper-income taxpayers also may incur the additional Medicare tax on net investment income with respect to net capital gains. See text Section 9-6d.

	Maximum Rate[51]
Short-term gains	37%
Long-term gains	20%

---

[50]§ 1(h).

[51]Certain assets, such as collectibles (e.g., art, antiques, stamps, etc.) and some real estate, receive a different treatment. When the 15% or 20% long-term capital gains tax rate otherwise applies, the collectibles gain is taxed at a maximum rate of 28%, and certain real estate gains are taxed at a maximum tax rate of 25%. See text Section 8-5a.

A C corporation's net capital gain does not receive any beneficial tax treatment. It is taxed as ordinary income.

The net capital losses of individuals can be used to offset up to $3,000 of ordinary income each year. Any remaining capital loss is carried forward indefinitely until it is exhausted.

C corporations may deduct capital losses only to the extent of capital gains. Capital losses of C corporations in excess of capital gains may not be deducted against ordinary income. Such unused capital losses are carried back three years and then carried forward five years to offset capital gains in those years.[52]

EXAMPLE 29

Jones records a short-term capital loss of $5,000 during 2017 and no capital gains. If Jones is an individual, she can deduct $3,000 of this amount as an ordinary loss. The remaining $2,000 loss is carried forward to 2018 and thereafter, until it is fully deducted against ordinary income or netted against other capital gains and losses.

If Jones is a C corporation, none of the capital loss is deductible in 2017. All of the $5,000 loss is carried back and offset sequentially against capital gains in 2014, 2015, and 2016 (generating an immediate tax refund). Any remaining capital loss is carried forward and offset against capital gains in tax years 2018 to 2022.

DIGGING DEEPER 6   In-depth coverage can be found on this book's companion website: **www.cengage.com**

LO.6

Explain and apply the tax provision that excludes interest on state and local government obligations from gross income.

4-5b Interest on Certain State and Local Government Obligations

At the time the Sixteenth Amendment was ratified by the states, there was some question as to whether the Federal government possessed the constitutional authority to tax interest on state and local government obligations. Taxing such interest was thought to violate the doctrine of intergovernmental immunity because the tax would impair the ability of state and local governments to finance their operations.[53] Thus, interest on state and local government obligations was specifically exempted from Federal income taxation.[54] However, the Supreme Court has concluded that there is no constitutional prohibition against levying a nondiscriminatory Federal income tax on state and local government obligations.[55] Nevertheless, the statutory exclusion still exists.

The current exempt status applies solely to state and local government bonds. Thus, income received from the accrual of interest on a condemnation award or an overpayment of state tax is fully taxable.[56] Nor does the exemption apply to gains on the sale of tax-exempt securities.

BRIDGE DISCIPLINE **Bridge to Public Economics**

The exclusion granted by the Federal government for interest paid on state and local bonds costs the U.S. Treasury approximately $29 billion per year, according to the Office of Management and Budget. Such forgone revenue is referred to as a "tax expenditure." However, if the capital markets are working properly, the exclusion should produce cost savings to the state and local governments.

If the exclusion were eliminated, state and local governments would pay higher interest rates on their bonds; the investor would demand a higher interest rate to produce the same after-tax yield as that received from taxable bonds of comparable risk. Therefore, the exclusion operates as a form of revenue sharing to the benefit of the state and local governments; it can be seen as a less-visible alternative to a direct grant from the Federal government to the state or local agency. It also is clear that this "expenditure" by the Federal government disproportionately is received by upper-income, high-wealth bondholders.

---

[52]§§ 1211 and 1212.

[53]*Pollock v. Farmer's Loan & Trust Co.*, 3 AFTR 2602, 15 S.Ct. 912 (USSC, 1895).

[54]§ 103(a).

[55]*South Carolina v. Baker III*, 88–1 USTC ¶9284, 61 AFTR 2d 88–995, 108 S.Ct. 1355 (USSC, 1988).

[56]*Kieselbach v. Comm.*, 43–1 USTC ¶9220, 30 AFTR 370, 63 S.Ct. 303 (USSC, 1943); *U.S. Trust Co. of New York v. Anderson*, 3 USTC ¶1125, 12 AFTR 836, 65 F.2d 575 (CA–2, 1933).

Macaw Corporation purchases State of Virginia bonds for $10,000 on July 1. The bonds pay $300 interest each June 30 and December 31. Macaw excludes from gross income the $300 interest received on December 31.

On March 31 of the next year, Macaw sells the bonds for $10,500 plus $150 of accrued interest. Macaw recognizes a $500 taxable gain ($10,500 − $10,000), but the $150 accrued interest still is exempt from Federal income taxation.

EXAMPLE 30

In-depth coverage can be found on this book's companion website: **www.cengage.com**

7 DIGGING DEEPER

The interest exclusion reduces the cost of borrowing for state and local governments. A taxpayer with a 32 percent marginal Federal income tax rate requires only a 3.4 percent yield on a tax-exempt bond to obtain the same after-tax income as a taxable bond paying 5 percent interest [3.4% ÷ (1 − .32) = 5%].

Although the Internal Revenue Code excludes from Federal gross income the interest on state and local government bonds, the interest paid on U.S. government bonds is not excluded from the Federal income tax base. Congress has decided, however, that if the Federal government is not to tax state and local bond interest, the state and local governments are prohibited from taxing interest on U.S. government bonds.[57] While this parity between the Federal and state and local governments exists with regard to taxing each others' obligations, the states are free to tax another's obligations. Thus, some states exempt the interest on the bonds they issue, but tax the interest on bonds issued by other states.

The Big Picture

Return to the facts of *The Big Picture* on p. 4-1. Dr. Payne includes in gross income the $500 of interest income from the bank's money market account, but not the $500 that is earned on the Whitehall School District bonds.

EXAMPLE 31

4-5c Life Insurance Proceeds

LO.7
Determine the extent to which life insurance proceeds are excluded from gross income.

Life insurance proceeds paid to the beneficiary because of the death of the insured are exempt from income tax.[58] Congress chose to exempt life insurance proceeds from gross income for several reasons, including the following.

- For family members, life insurance proceeds serve much the same purpose as a nontaxable inheritance.
- In a business context (as well as in a family situation), life insurance proceeds replace an economic loss suffered by the beneficiary (i.e., from the loss of future sales or of the decedent's professional reputation).

Thus, Congress concluded that, in general, making life insurance proceeds exempt from income tax was a good tax policy.

Sparrow Corporation purchased an insurance policy on the life of its CEO and named itself as the beneficiary. Sparrow paid $174,000 in premiums. When the company's CEO died, Sparrow collected the insurance proceeds of $600,000. The $600,000 is excluded from Sparrow's gross income.

EXAMPLE 32

Exceptions to Exclusion Treatment

The income tax exclusion applies only when the insurance proceeds are received because of the death of the insured. If the owner cancels the policy and receives the

---

[57]31 U.S.C.A. § 742.   [58]*Estate of D. R. Daly*, 3 B.T.A. 1042 (1926).

cash surrender value, he or she must recognize gain to the extent of the excess of the amount received over the cost of the policy.[59]

Another exception to exclusion treatment applies if the policy is transferred after the insurance company issues it. If the policy is transferred for valuable consideration, the insurance proceeds are includible in the gross income of the transferee to the extent the proceeds received exceed the amount paid for the policy by the transferee plus any subsequent premiums paid.

EXAMPLE 33

Platinum Corporation pays premiums of $5,000 for an insurance policy with a face amount of $12,000 on the life of Beth, an officer of the corporation. Subsequently, Platinum sells the policy to Beth's husband, Jamal, for $5,500. On Beth's death, Jamal receives the proceeds of $12,000. Jamal excludes from gross income $5,500 plus any premiums he paid subsequent to the transfer. The remainder of the proceeds constitutes gross income to Jamal, as he acquired the policy for cash consideration.

There are several major exceptions to the consideration rule.[60] These exceptions permit exclusion treatment for transfers to the following parties. The first three exceptions facilitate the use of insurance contracts to fund **buy-sell agreements**.

1. A partner of the insured.
2. A partnership in which the insured is a partner.
3. A corporation in which the insured is an officer or shareholder.
4. A transferee whose basis in the policy is determined by reference to the transferor's basis, such as a gift or a transfer due to a divorce.
5. The insured party under the policy.

EXAMPLE 34

Rick and Sita are equal partners who have a buy-sell agreement that allows either partner to purchase the interest of a deceased partner for $500,000. Neither partner has sufficient cash to buy the other partner's interest, but each holds a life insurance policy on his own life in the amount of $500,000. Rick and Sita could exchange their policies (usually at little or no taxable gain), and upon the death of either partner, the surviving partner could collect tax-free insurance proceeds. The proceeds then could be used to purchase the decedent's interest in the partnership.

Investment earnings arising from the reinvestment of life insurance proceeds generally are subject to income tax. For example, the beneficiary may elect to collect the insurance proceeds in installments that include taxable interest income. The interest portion of each installment is included in gross income.[61]

DIGGING DEEPER 8   **In-depth coverage can be found on this book's companion website: www.cengage.com**

TAX PLANNING STRATEGIES Life Insurance

FRAMEWORK FOCUS: INCOME AND EXCLUSION

Strategy: Avoid Income Recognition.

Life insurance is a tax-favored investment. The annual increase in the cash surrender value of the policy is not taxable because it is subject to substantial restrictions (no income has been actually or constructively received). By borrowing on the policy's cash surrender value, the owner can receive the policy's increase in value in cash without recognizing any current gross income.

---

[59]*Landfield Finance Co. v. U.S.*, 69–2 USTC ¶9680, 24 AFTR 2d 69–5744, 418 F.2d 172 (CA–7, 1969).

[60]§ 101(a)(2).

[61]Reg. §§ 1.72–7(c)(1), 1.101–7T.

4-5d Income from Discharge of Indebtedness

Gross income usually is generated when a creditor cancels a borrower's debt or accepts a payment for less than the amount owed. Foreclosure by a creditor is treated as a sale or exchange of the property and usually triggers gross income.[62]

LO.8

Describe when income must be reported from the discharge of indebtedness.

> **EXAMPLE 35**
>
> Juan owed State Bank $50,000 on a note secured by some investment land. When Juan's basis in the land was $20,000 and the land's fair market value was $50,000, the bank foreclosed on the loan and took title to the land. Juan recognizes a $30,000 gain on the foreclosure, as though he had sold the land directly to State Bank.

A creditor may cancel debt to ensure the viability of the debtor. In such cases, the debtor's net worth is increased by the amount of debt forgiven. Generally, the debtor recognizes gross income equal to the amount of debt canceled.[63]

Debt Cancellation and Gross Income

> **EXAMPLE 36**
>
> Brown Corporation is unable to meet the mortgage payments on its factory building. Both the corporation and the mortgage holder are aware of the depressed market for industrial property in the area. Foreclosure would only result in the creditor obtaining unsellable property.
>
> To improve Brown's financial position and thus improve its chances of obtaining the additional credit necessary for survival from other lenders, the creditor agrees to forgive all amounts past due and to reduce the principal amount of the mortgage. Brown's gross income is increased by the amount of the debt that was forgiven *plus* the reduction in the remaining mortgage balance.

> **EXAMPLE 37**
>
> A corporation issues bonds with a face value of $500,000. Subsequently, the corporation repurchases the bonds in the market for $150,000. It has effectively canceled its $500,000 debt with a $150,000 payment, so it recognizes $350,000 in gross income.[64]

> **EXAMPLE 38**
>
> Keri borrowed $60,000 from National Bank to purchase a warehouse. Keri agreed to make monthly principal and interest payments for 15 years. The interest rate on the note was 3%.
>
> When the balance on the note had been reduced through monthly payments to $48,000, the bank offered to accept $45,000 in full settlement of the note. The bank made the offer because interest rates had increased to 4.5%. Keri accepted the bank's offer. As a result, she recognizes $3,000 ($48,000 − $45,000) gross income.[65]

A discharge of indebtedness generally increases the taxpayer's gross income, but the reduction in debt is excluded in each of the following situations.[66]

1. Creditors' gifts.
2. Discharges that occur when the debtor is insolvent.
3. Discharges under Federal bankruptcy law.
4. Discharge of the farm debt of a solvent taxpayer.
5. Discharge of **qualified real property business indebtedness**.
6. A seller's cancellation of a buyer's indebtedness.
7. A shareholder's cancellation of a corporation's indebtedness.
8. Forgiveness of certain loans to students.

---

[62]*Estate of Delman v. Comm.*, 73 T.C. 15 (1979).

[63]§ 61(a)(12).

[64]See *U.S. v. Kirby Lumber Co.*, 2 USTC ¶814, 10 AFTR 458, 52 S.Ct. 4 (USSC, 1931).

[65]Rev.Rul. 82–202, 1982–1 C.B. 35.

[66]§§ 108 and 1017.

Creditors' Gifts

If the creditor reduces the debt as an act of *love, respect, or generosity*, the debtor has simply received a nontaxable gift (situation 1). Such motivations generally arise only on loans between friends or family members. Rarely will a gift be found to have occurred in a business context. A businessperson may settle a debt for less than the amount due, but only as a matter of business expediency (e.g., high collection costs or disputes as to contract terms) rather than generosity.[67]

Insolvency and Bankruptcy

Cancellation of indebtedness income is excluded when the debtor is insolvent (i.e., the debtor's liabilities exceed the fair market value of the assets) or when the cancellation of debt results from a bankruptcy proceeding (situations 2 and 3). The insolvency exclusion is limited to the amount of insolvency. The tax law permits this exclusion to avoid imposing undue hardship on the debtor (wherewithal to pay) and the debtor's limited resources.

The law imposes a cost for the insolvency and bankruptcy exclusion. More specifically, the debtor must decrease certain tax benefits (capital loss carryforwards, net operating loss carryforwards, some tax credits, and suspended passive activity losses)[68] by the amount of income excluded. In addition, if the amount of excluded income exceeds these tax benefits, the debtor reduces the basis in assets.[69] Thus, excluded cancellation of indebtedness income either accelerates recognition of future income (by reducing tax benefit carryforwards) or is deferred until the debtor's assets are sold (or depreciated).

Before any debt cancellation, Maroon Corporation holds assets with a fair market value of $500,000 and related liabilities of $600,000. A creditor agrees to cancel $125,000 of liabilities. Maroon excludes $100,000 of the debt cancellation income (the amount of insolvency) and is taxed on $25,000. Maroon also reduces any tax benefits and the basis of its assets by $100,000 (the excluded income).

Qualified Real Property Indebtedness

Taxpayers (other than C corporations) can elect to exclude income from cancellation of indebtedness if the canceled debt is secured by real property used in a trade or business (situation 5). The debt must have been used to acquire or improve real property in a trade or business to qualify for the exclusion.[70]

The amount of the exclusion is limited to the *lesser of* (1) the excess of the debt over the fair market value of the real property or (2) the adjusted basis of all depreciable real property held. In addition, the basis of all depreciable real property held by the debtor is reduced by the excluded amount.

Blue, Inc. (an S corporation), owns a warehouse worth $5 million, with a $3 million basis. The warehouse is subject to a $7 million mortgage that was incurred in connection with the acquisition of the warehouse. In lieu of foreclosure, the lender decides that it will reduce the mortgage to $4.5 million. Blue may elect to exclude $2 million from gross income ($7 million debt – $5 million value). If Blue makes the election, it reduces the aggregate basis of its depreciable realty by $2 million.

If the basis of the warehouse had been $1 million, and the warehouse was the only piece of depreciable realty that Blue owned, only $1 million of the debt cancellation income would be excluded.

---

[67]*Comm. v. Jacobson*, 49–1 USTC ¶9133, 37 AFTR 516, 69 S.Ct. 358 (USSC, 1949).

[68]See Chapter 6 for a discussion of net operating loss carryforwards and suspended passive losses. Chapter 8 discusses capital loss carryforwards. Chapter 17 discusses tax credits.

[69]§ 108(b).

[70]§ 108(a)(1)(D).

Seller Cancellation

When a seller of property cancels debt previously incurred by a buyer in a purchase transaction, the cancellation generally does not trigger gross income to the buyer (situation 6). Instead, the reduction in debt is considered to be a reduction in the purchase price of the asset. Consequently, the basis of the asset is reduced in the hands of the buyer.[71]

Snipe, Inc., purchases a truck from Sparrow Autos for $10,000 in cash and a $25,000 note payable. Two days after the purchase, Sparrow announces a sale on the same model truck, with a sales price of $28,000. Snipe contacts Sparrow and asks to be given the sales price on the truck. Sparrow complies by canceling $7,000 of the note payable. The $7,000 is excluded from Snipe's gross income, and the basis of the truck to Snipe is $28,000.

EXAMPLE 41

Shareholder Cancellation

If a shareholder cancels the corporation's indebtedness to him or her (situation 7) and receives nothing in return, the cancellation usually is considered a contribution of capital to the corporation by the shareholder. Thus, the corporation recognizes no gross income. Instead, its paid-in capital is increased, and its liabilities are decreased by the same amount.[72]

In-depth coverage can be found on this book's companion website: **www.cengage.com**   **9** DIGGING DEEPER

Student Loans

Many states make loans to students on the condition that the loan will be forgiven if the student practices a profession in the state upon completing his or her studies. The amount of the loan that is forgiven (situation 8) is excluded from gross income.[73]

4-5e **Tax Benefit Rule**

Generally, if a taxpayer claims a deduction for an item in one year and in a later year recovers all or a portion of the prior deduction, the recovery is included in gross income in the year received.[74]

LO.9

Determine the extent to which receipts can be excluded under the tax benefit rule.

Accrual basis MegaCorp deducted as a loss a $1,000 receivable from a customer when it appeared the amount would never be collected. The following year, the customer paid $800 on the receivable. MegaCorp reports the $800 as gross income in the year it is received.

EXAMPLE 42

However, the <mark>tax benefit rule</mark> limits income recognition when a deduction does not yield a tax benefit in the year it is taken. If MegaCorp in Example 42 reported the same Federal income tax liability in the year that the loss occurred, the $800 receipt would be excluded from gross income in the year of the recovery.

Before deducting a $1,000 loss from an uncollectible business receivable, Tulip Company reported taxable income of $200. The business bad debt deduction yields only a $200 tax benefit (assuming no loss carryback is made). That is, taxable income is reduced by only $200 (to zero) as a result of the bad debt deduction. Therefore, if the customer makes a payment on the previously deducted receivable in the following year, only the first $200 is a taxable recovery of a prior deduction. Any additional amount collected is nontaxable because only $200 of the loss yielded a reduction in taxable income (i.e., a tax benefit).

EXAMPLE 43

---

[71]§ 108(e)(5).
[72]§ 108(e)(6).

[73]§ 108(f).
[74]§ 111(a).

LO.10

Apply the tax provisions on loans made at below-market interest rates.

4-5f Imputed Interest on Below-Market Loans

As discussed earlier in the chapter, generally, no income is recognized unless it is realized. Realization usually occurs when the taxpayer performs services or sells goods, thus becoming entitled to a payment from the other party. It follows that no gross income is realized if the goods or services are provided at no charge. Under this prior-law interpretation of the realization requirement, interest-free loans were used to shift income between taxpayers.

EXAMPLE 44

Brown Corporation is in the 35% tax bracket and has $400,000 in a money market account earning 5% interest. Jack is the sole shareholder of Brown. He is in the 15% tax bracket and has no investment income. In view of the difference in tax rates, Jack believes that it would be better for him to receive and pay tax on the earnings from Brown's $400,000 investment. Jack does not want to receive the $400,000 from Brown as a dividend because that would trigger a tax.

Under prior law, Jack could receive the money market account from Brown in exchange for a $400,000 non-interest-bearing note, payable on Brown's demand. As a result, Jack would receive the $20,000 annual earnings on the money market account, and the combined taxes of Brown and Jack would be decreased every year by $4,000.

Decrease in Brown's tax (.05 × $400,000) × .35	($7,000)
Increase in Jack's tax (.05 × $400,000) × .15	3,000
Overall decrease in tax liability	($4,000)

The Federal income tax law no longer allows this income-shifting result. Brown Corporation in Example 44 is deemed to have received an interest payment from Jack even though no interest was actually paid.[75] This payment of imputed interest is taxable to Brown. Jack may be able to deduct the imaginary interest payment on his return as investment interest if he itemizes deductions. Brown then is deemed to return the interest to Jack in the form of a taxable dividend.

Imputed interest is calculated using rates that the Federal government pays on new borrowings and is compounded semiannually. The Federal rates are adjusted monthly and are published by the IRS.[76] There are three Federal rates: short-term (not over three years and including demand loans), mid-term (over three years but not over nine years), and long-term (over nine years).

If interest is charged on the loan but is less than the Federal rate, the imputed interest is the difference between the amount that would have been charged at the Federal rate and the amount actually charged.

EXAMPLE 45

Assume that the Federal rate applicable to the loan in the preceding example is 3.5% through June 30 and 4% from July 1 through December 31. Brown Corporation made the loan on January 1, and the loan is still outstanding on December 31. Brown recognizes interest income of $15,140, and Jack reports interest expense of $15,140. Brown is deemed to have paid a $15,140 dividend to Jack.

Interest Calculations	
January 1 to June 30 (.035 × $400,000)(½ year)	$ 7,000
July 1 to December 31 [.04($400,000 + $7,000)](½ year)	8,140
	$ 15,140

If Brown had charged 3% interest under the terms of the note, compounded annually, the deemed interest amount would have been $3,140.

Interest at the Federal rate	$ 15,140
Less interest actually charged (.03 × $400,000)	(12,000)
Imputed interest	$ 3,140

---

[75]§ 7872(a)(1).

[76]§§ 7872(b)(2) and (f)(2).

FINANCIAL DISCLOSURE INSIGHTS Loans to Executives Prohibited

Interest-free loans have become a popular form of compensation for executives. Several examples of multimillion-dollar loans have come to light as a result of recent bankruptcies by large corporations. The board of directors often justifies the loans as necessary to enable the executive to be able to purchase a residence or to buy stock in the company.

Loans by publicly held corporations to their executives generally are prohibited by Federal law. The Sarbanes-Oxley provisions generally prohibit loans by corporations to their executives. However, an exception permits corporate loans to finance the acquisition of a personal residence for an executive.

The imputed interest rules apply to the following types of below-market loans.[77]

- Gift loans (made out of love, respect, or generosity).
- Compensation-related loans (employer loans to employees).
- Corporation-shareholder loans (a corporation's loans to its shareholders, as in Example 44).

The effects of these loans on the borrower and lender are summarized in Exhibit 4.1.

Exceptions and Limitations

No interest is imputed on total outstanding *compensation-related loans* or *corporation-shareholder loans* of $10,000 or less unless the purpose of the loan is tax avoidance.[78] This vague tax avoidance standard exposes practically all compensation-related and corporation-shareholder loans to possible imputed interest problems. Nevertheless, the $10,000 exception should apply when an employee's borrowing was necessitated by personal needs (e.g., to meet unexpected expenses) rather than tax considerations.

Similarly, no interest is imputed on outstanding *gift loans* of $10,000 or less between individuals, unless the loan proceeds are used to purchase income-producing property.[79] This exemption eliminates from these complex provisions immaterial amounts that do not result in sizable shifts of income.

On loans of $100,000 or less between individuals, the imputed interest cannot exceed the borrower's net investment income for the year (gross income from all investments less the related expenses).[80] Through the gift loan provision, the imputed interest rules are designed to prevent high-income individuals from shifting income to relatives in a

EXHIBIT 4.1	Effect of Certain Below-Market Loans: Imputed Interest Income and Deductions

Type of Loan		Lender	Borrower
Gift	Step 1	Interest income	Interest expense
	Step 2	Gift made*	Gift received
Compensation related	Step 1	Interest income	Interest expense
	Step 2	Compensation expense	Compensation income
Corporation to shareholder	Step 1	Interest income	Interest expense
	Step 2	Dividend paid	Dividend income

*The gift may be subject to the Federal gift tax (refer to Chapter 1).

---

[77]§ 7872(c). Additional situations exist where these rules apply. See, e.g., §§ 7872(c)(1)(D), (E).

[78]§ 7872(c)(3).

[79]§ 7872(c)(2).

[80]§ 7872(d). The $100,000 provision applies only to gift loans.

EXHIBIT 4.2	**Exceptions to the Imputed Interest Rules for Below-Market Loans**	
Exception	**Eligible Loans**	**Ineligible Loans and Limitations**
De minimis—aggregate loans of $10,000 or less	Gift loans	Proceeds are used to purchase income-producing assets.
	Employer-employee	Principal purpose is tax avoidance.
	Corporation-shareholder	Principal purpose is tax avoidance.
Aggregate loans of $100,000 or less	Gift loans between individuals	Principal purpose is tax avoidance. For all other loans, interest is imputed to the extent of the borrower's net investment income if it exceeds $1,000.

lower marginal bracket. This shifting of investment income is considered to occur only to the extent that the borrower also recognizes net investment income. Thus, the income imputed to the lender is limited to the borrower's net investment income.

If the borrower's net investment income for the year does not exceed $1,000, no interest is imputed on loans of $100,000 or less. However, this exemption does not apply if a principal purpose of a loan is tax avoidance. In such a case, interest is imputed, and the imputed interest is not limited to the borrower's net investment income.[81]

These exceptions to the imputed interest rules are summarized in Exhibit 4.2.

The Big Picture

EXAMPLE 46

Return to the facts of *The Big Picture* on p. 4-1. Dr. Payne's loan from his parents likely is a *gift loan*, as his parents are not shareholders in the personal service corporation. Imputed interest must be computed annually with regard to this loan by both Dr. Payne and his parents, under two different tax rules: (1) the principal amount of the loan exceeds $100,000 and (2) the loan proceeds were invested in an income-producing asset.

EXAMPLE 47

Vicki made interest-free gift loans as follows.

Borrower	Amount	Borrower's Net Investment Income	Purpose
Susan	$ 8,000	$–0–	Education
Dan	9,000	500	Purchase of stock
Mai	25,000	–0–	Purchase of a business
Olaf	120,000	–0–	Purchase of a residence

Tax avoidance is not a principal purpose of any of the loans. The loan to Susan is not subject to the imputed interest rules because the $10,000 exception applies. The $10,000 exception does not apply to the loan to Dan because the proceeds were used to purchase income-producing assets. However, under the $100,000 exception, the imputed interest is limited to Dan's investment income ($500). Because the $1,000 exception also applies to this loan, no interest is imputed.

No interest is imputed on the loan to Mai because the $100,000 exception applies. None of the exceptions apply to the loan to Olaf, because the loan was for more than $100,000; he recognizes imputed interest income related to his loan.

4-5g Improvements on Leased Property

LO.11

Use the tax rules concerning the exclusion of leasehold improvements from gross income.

When a real property lease expires, the landlord regains control of both the real property and any improvements to the property (e.g., buildings and landscaping) made by the tenant during the term of the lease. Any improvements made to the leased property are excluded from the landlord's gross income unless the improvement is made to the property in lieu of rent.[82]

[81] § 7872 (d)(1)(B).   [82] § 109.

Concept Summary 4.3

Income Recognition Rules

Generally, realized income is recognized as gross income by the Federal tax law. Special rules apply for certain taxpayers and transactions.

1. Income from services and the use of property typically are taxed immediately as they are earned to the taxpayer that generated the income item.

2. Interest income is recognized as it is earned, and dividend income is taxed when the corporation makes a distribution to its shareholders from corporate E & P. Dividends can qualify for lower tax rates or offsetting deductions. Long-term capital gains also can qualify for lower tax rates.

3. Income exclusions are available for certain types of income, including life insurance proceeds received and interest income received from the debt of U.S. government agencies at the state and local levels.

4. Generally, gross income results for a borrower when a lender forgives an outstanding debt obligation. Certain taxpayers qualify for an exclusion of such income, though, e.g., in the context of a bankruptcy, a student loan, or a financially distressed residence.

5. Gross income may result when the taxpayer holds a debt investment that pays interest at a rate that is lower than the broader market would pay.

Mahogany Corporation leases office space to Zink and Silver, Attorneys-at-Law. When the law firm took possession of the office space, it added wall partitions, a wireless computer network, and a variety of other improvements to the space. The improvements were not made in lieu of rent payments to Mahogany. When the lease expires and Mahogany regains possession of the space, the value of the improvements is excluded from Mahogany's gross income.

EXAMPLE 48

REFOCUS ON THE BIG PICTURE

JUST WHAT IS INCLUDED IN GROSS INCOME?

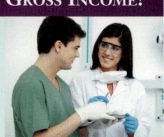

Using the accrual method of accounting, the gross income recognized by Cliff Payne's corporation is $385,500. This includes the entire $385,000 of revenue earned from providing services to patients during the year and the $500 of interest income earned on the money market account. The $500 of school district bond interest is excluded from gross income.

Dr. Payne's own gross income includes $120,000 of salary earned during the year. Even though Cliff did not cash his December paycheck until January, he is considered to have constructively received the income, because it was readily available to him. Dr. Payne may be able to reduce his taxable income with a deduction in the amount of the imputed interest expense on the below-market loan from his parents. The increase in value on his stock does not result in gross income until he sells the stock and realizes a gain or loss.

What If?

Rather than electing the accrual method, what if Dr. Payne had chosen to use the cash method of accounting for his business? Using the cash method is acceptable for certain personal service corporations and small businesses. While using the cash method would reduce the company's gross income from $385,000 to $333,000 ($385,000 amount billed less $52,000 still to be received), this is only part of the picture. Using the cash method also might result in some of the corporation's expenses not being deducted until they are paid in a future year.

TYLER OLSON/SHUTTERSTOCK.COM

Suggested Readings

Kay Bell, "Community Property Effects on Taxes," **tinyurl.com/comm-prop-bell**, August 2012.

Todd D. Keator, "Rental Real Estate and the Net Investment Income Tax," *Journal of Taxation*, August 2013.

Vincenzo Villamena, "Everything You Need to Know about Bitcoin and Your Taxes," **cnbc.com**, February 21, 2018.

Key Terms

Accounting income, 4-4

Accounting method, 4-6

Accrual method, 4-8

Assignment of income, 4-13

Buy-sell agreements, 4-22

Cash receipts method, 4-7

Claim of right doctrine, 4-9

Constructive receipt, 4-10

Economic income, 4-3

Fruit and tree metaphor, 4-13

Gross income, 4-2

Hybrid method, 4-9

Income, 4-3

Life insurance proceeds, 4-21

Original issue discount, 4-11

Qualified real property business indebtedness, 4-23

Tax benefit rule, 4-25

Taxable year, 4-6

Computational Exercises

1. **LO.3** Champ received a $10,000 distribution from NeatCo, a U.S. C corporation. NeatCo's earnings and profits for the year totaled $6,000. How much dividend income does Champ recognize?

2. **LO.5** Lefty completes the following capital asset transactions. By how much does Lefty's AGI increase as a result of these gains/losses?

Long-term gain	$10,000
Short-term gain	4,000
Short-term loss	25,000

3. **LO.8** Before any debt cancellation, the insolvent KuhnCo holds business equipment, its only asset, with a fair market value of $1 million and related liabilities of $1.25 million. The lender agrees to cancel $400,000 of the liabilities. KuhnCo has no other liabilities.

   a. How much gross income does KuhnCo report as a result of the debt cancellation?

   b. How would your answer change, if at all, had the lender canceled $200,000 of the debt?

4. **LO.8** Before any debt cancellation, PeppersCo holds business land with a $2.4 million fair market value, a $1 million tax basis, and a related mortgage of $3 million. In lieu of foreclosure, the lender reduces the mortgage principal by $1.3 million. What are the Federal income tax consequences of the debt cancellation?

5. **LO.9** Leilei operates a sole proprietorship, using the accrual basis of tax accounting. Last year, she claimed a $10,000 bad debt deduction for a receivable from Jackie. But this year, Jackie sent her a check for $7,000, which Leilei accepted in full satisfaction of the receivable. How much gross income does Leilei record for the item this year?

6. **LO.10** Elizabeth makes the following interest-free loans during the year. The relevant Federal interest rate is 5%, and none of the loans are motivated by tax avoidance. All of the loans were outstanding for the last six months of the tax year. Identify the Federal income tax effects of these loans.

Borrower	Amount	Borrower's Other Net Investment Income	Purpose of Loan
Richard	$ 5,000	$800	Gift
Woody	8,000	600	Stock purchase
Irene	105,000	0	Purchase principal residence

Problems

7. **LO.1** Howard buys wrecked cars and stores them on his property. Recently, he purchased a 1990 Ford Taurus for $400. If he can sell all of the usable parts, his total proceeds from the Taurus will be over $2,500. As of the end of the year, he has sold only the radio for $75, and he does not know how many, if any, of the remaining parts will ever be sold. What are Howard's Federal income tax issues?

Critical Thinking

8. **LO.1** Determine the taxpayer's current-year (1) economic income and (2) gross income for tax purposes from the following events.

a. Sam's employment contract as chief executive of a large corporation was terminated, and he was paid $500,000 not to work for a competitor of the corporation for five years.

b. Elliot, a 6-year-old child, was paid $5,000 for appearing in a television commercial. His parents put the funds in a savings account for the child's education.

c. Valery found a suitcase that contained $100,000. She could not determine who the owner was.

d. Winn purchased a lottery ticket for $5 and won $750,000 from it.

e. Larry spent $1,000 to raise vegetables that he and his family consumed. The cost of the vegetables in a store would have been $2,400.

f. Dawn purchased an automobile for $1,500 that was worth $3,500. The seller was in desperate need of cash.

9. **LO.1** The roof of your corporation's office building recently suffered some damage as the result of a storm. You, the president of the corporation, are negotiating with a carpenter who has quoted two prices for the repair work: $600 if you pay in cash ("folding money") and $700 if you pay by check. The carpenter observes that the IRS can more readily discover his receipt of a check. Thus, he hints that he will report the receipt of the check (but not the cash).

Ethics and Equity

The carpenter holds another full-time job and will do the work after hours and on the weekend. He comments that he should be allowed to keep all he earns after regular working hours. Evaluate what you should do.

10. **LO.1** Dolly is a college student who works as a part-time server in a restaurant. Her usual tip is 20% of the price of the meal. A customer ordered a piece of pie and said that he would appreciate prompt service. Dolly fulfilled the customer's request. The customer's bill was $8, but the customer left a $100 bill on the table and did not ask for a receipt. Dolly gave the cashier $8 and pocketed the $100 bill.

Dolly concludes that the customer thought that he had left a $10 bill, although the customer did not return to correct the apparent mistake. The customer had commented about how much he appreciated Dolly's prompt service. Dolly thinks that a $2 tip would be sufficient and that the other $98 is like "found money." How much should Dolly include in her gross income concerning this customer?

11. **LO.2** Determine Amos's gross income in each of the following cases.

   a. In the current year, Amos purchased an automobile for $25,000. As part of the transaction, Amos received a $1,500 rebate from the manufacturer.

   b. Amos sold his business. In addition to the selling price of the stock, he received $50,000 for a covenant not to compete—an agreement that he will not compete directly with his former business for five years.

   c. Amos owned some land he held as an investment. As a result of a change in the zoning rules, the property increased in value by $20,000.

Decision Making 12. **LO.2** The Bluejay Apartments, a new development, is in the process of structuring its lease agreements. The company would like to set the damage deposits high enough that tenants will keep the apartments in good condition. The company actually is more concerned about such damage than about tenants not paying their rent.

   a. Discuss the tax effects of the following alternatives.

   - $1,000 damage deposit with no rent prepayment.
   - $500 damage deposit and $500 rent for the final month of the lease.
   - $1,000 rent for the final two months of the lease and no damage deposit.

   b. Which option do you recommend? Why?

Decision Making 13. **LO.2, 11** Harper is considering three alternative investments of $10,000. Harper is in the 24% marginal tax bracket for ordinary income and 15% for qualifying capital gains in all tax years. The selected investment will be sold at the end of five years. The alternatives are:

   - A taxable corporate bond yielding 5.333% before tax and the interest reinvested at 5.333% before tax.
   - A tax-favored bond that will have a maturity value of $12,200 (a 4% pretax rate of return).
   - Land that will increase in value.

   The gain on the land is classified and taxed as a long-term capital gain. The interest from the bonds is taxed as ordinary income: the interest from the corporate bond as it is earned annually, but that from the tax-favored bond is recognized only upon redemption.

   How much must the land increase in value to yield a greater after-tax return than either of the bonds? Use the future value tables in Appendix F as needed for your calculations and comparisons. Present your answer using Microsoft Excel or another spreadsheet.

14. **LO.1** Determine the taxpayer's gross income for tax purposes in each of the following situations.

   a. Deb, a cash basis taxpayer, traded a corporate bond with accrued interest of $300 for corporate stock with a fair market value of $12,000 at the time of the exchange. Deb's cost of the bond was $10,000. The value of the stock had decreased to $11,000 by the end of the year.

   b. Deb needed $10,000 to make a down payment on her house. She instructed her broker to sell some stock to raise the $10,000. Deb's cost of the stock was $3,000. Based on her broker's advice, instead of selling the stock, she borrowed the $10,000 using the stock as collateral for the debt.

   c. Deb's boss gave her two tickets to the Rabid Rabbits rock concert because Deb met her sales quota. At the time Deb received the tickets, each ticket had a face price of $200 and was selling on eBay for $300 each. On the date of the concert, the tickets were selling for $250 each. Deb and her son attended the concert.

15. **LO.2** Al is a physician who conducts his practice as a sole proprietor. During 2018, he received cash of $280,000 for medical services. Of the amount collected,

$40,000 was for services provided in 2017. At the end of 2018, Al held accounts receivable of $60,000, all for services rendered in 2018. In addition, at the end of the year, Al received $12,000 as an advance payment from a health maintenance organization (HMO) for services to be rendered in 2019. Compute Al's gross income for 2018 using the:

a. Cash basis of accounting.

b. Accrual basis of accounting.

16. **LO.2** Selma operates a contractor's supply store. She maintains her books using the cash method. Selma wants to know whether the accrual basis of accounting would be preferable for her business.

At the end of the year, Selma's accountant computes her accrual basis income that is used on her tax return. For 2018, Selma reported cash receipts of $1.4 million, which included $200,000 collected on accounts receivable from 2017 sales. It also included the proceeds of a $100,000 bank loan. At the end of 2018, she held $250,000 in accounts receivable from customers, all from 2018 sales.

a. Compute Selma's accrual basis gross receipts for 2018.

b. Selma paid cash for all of the purchases. The total amount paid for merchandise in 2018 was $1.3 million. At the end of 2017, she had merchandise on hand with a cost of $150,000. At the end of 2018, the cost of merchandise on hand was $300,000. Compute Selma's gross income from merchandise sales for 2018.

17. **LO.2** Trip Garage, Inc. (459 Ellis Avenue, Harrisburg, PA 17111), is an accrual basis taxpayer that repairs automobiles. In late December 2018, the company repaired Samuel Mosley's car and charged him $1,000. Samuel did not think the problem had been fixed, so he refused to pay; thus, Trip refused to release the automobile.

Communications

In early January 2019, Trip made a few adjustments under the hood; Trip then convinced Samuel that the automobile was working properly. At that time, Samuel agreed to pay only $900 because he did not have the use of the car for a week. Trip said "fine," accepted the $900, and released the automobile to Samuel.

An IRS agent thinks Trip, as an accrual basis taxpayer, should report $1,000 of income in 2018, when the work was done, and then deduct a $100 business loss in 2019. Prepare a memo to Susan Apple, the treasurer of Trip, with your recommended treatment for the disputed income.

18. **LO.1,4** Each Saturday morning, Ted makes the rounds of the local yard sales. He has developed a keen eye for bargains, but he cannot use all of the items he thinks are "real bargains." Ted has found a way to share the benefits of his talent with others. If Ted spots something priced at $40 that he knows is worth $100, for example, he will buy it and list it on eBay for $70.

Ethics and Equity

Ted does not include his gain in his gross income because he reasons that he is performing a valuable service for others (both the original sellers and the future buyers) and sacrificing profit he could receive. "Besides," according to Ted, "the IRS does not know about these transactions." Should Ted's ethical standards depend on his perception of his own generosity and the risk that his income-producing activities will be discovered by the IRS? Discuss.

19. **LO.2** Accounting students understand that the accrual method of accounting is superior to the cash method for measuring the income and expenses from an ongoing business for financial reporting purposes. Often, CPAs advise their clients to use the accrual method of accounting. Yet, CPA firms generally use the cash method to prepare their own tax returns. Are the CPAs being hypocritical? Explain.

Ethics and Equity

20. **LO.2** Drake Appliance Company, an accrual basis taxpayer, sells home appliances and service contracts. Determine the effects of each of the following transactions on the company's 2018 gross income assuming that the company uses any available options to defer its taxes.

a. In December 2017, the company received a $1,200 advance payment from a customer for an appliance that Drake had special ordered from the manufacturer. The appliance did not arrive from the manufacturer until January 2018, and Drake immediately delivered it to the customer. The sale was reported in 2018 for financial accounting purposes.

b. In October 2018, the company sold a 6-month service contract for $240. The company also sold a 36-month service contract for $1,260 in July 2018.

c. On December 31, 2018, the company sold an appliance for $1,200. The company received $500 cash and a note from the customer for $700 and $260 interest, to be paid at the rate of $40 a month for 24 months. Because of the customer's poor credit record, the fair market value of the note was only $600. The cost of the appliance was $750.

Ethics and Equity   21. **LO.2** Dr. Randolph, a cash basis taxpayer, knows that she will be in a lower marginal tax bracket next year. To take advantage of the expected decrease in the marginal tax rate, Randolph instructs her office manager to delay filing the medical insurance claims for services performed in November and December until January of the following year. This will ensure that the receipts will not be included in current gross income. Is Randolph abusing the cash method of accounting rules? Why or why not?

Decision Making   22. **LO.2** Your client is a new partnership, ARP Associates, which is an engineering consulting firm. Generally, ARP bills clients for services at the end of each **Communications** month. Client billings are about $50,000 each month. On average, it takes 45 days to collect the receivables. ARP's expenses are primarily for salary and rent. Salaries are paid on the last day of each month, and rent is paid on the first day of each month.

The partnership has a line of credit with a bank, which requires monthly financial statements. These must be prepared using the accrual method. ARP's managing partner, Amanda Sims, has suggested that the firm also use the accrual method for tax purposes and thus reduce accounting fees by $600.

The partners are in the 35% (combined Federal and state) marginal tax bracket. Write a letter to your client explaining why you believe it would be worthwhile for ARP to file its tax return on the cash basis even though its financial statements are prepared on the accrual basis. ARP's address is 100 James Tower, Denver, CO 80208.

23. **LO.3** Alva received dividends on her stocks as follows.

Amur Corporation (a French corporation whose stock is traded on an established U.S. securities market)	$60,000
Blaze, Inc., a Delaware corporation	40,000
Grape, Inc., a Virginia corporation	22,000

a. Alva purchased the Grape stock three years ago, and she purchased the Amur stock two years ago. She purchased the Blaze stock 18 days before it went ex-dividend and sold it 20 days later at a $5,000 loss. Alva reported no other capital gains and losses for the year. She is in the 32% marginal tax bracket. Compute Alva's tax on her dividend income.

b. Alva's daughter, Veda, who is age 25 and who is not Alva's dependent, reported taxable income of $6,000, which included $1,000 of dividends on Grape stock. Veda purchased the stock two years ago. Compute Veda's tax liability on the dividends.

Digging Deeper   24. **LO.3** Liz and Doug were divorced on July 1, 2018, after 10 years of marriage. Their current year's income received before the divorce included:

Doug's salary	$41,000
Liz's salary	55,000
Rent on apartments purchased by Liz 15 years ago	8,000
Dividends on stock Doug inherited from his mother 4 years ago	1,900
Interest on a savings account in Liz's name funded with her salary	2,400

Allocate the income to Liz and Doug, applying the community property rules of:

a. California.

b. Texas.

25. **LO.4,10** Roy decides to buy a personal residence, and he goes to the bank for a $150,000 loan. The bank tells Roy that he can borrow the funds at 4% if his father will guarantee the debt. Roy's father, Hal, owns a $150,000 CD currently yielding 3.5%. The Federal rate is 3%. Hal agrees to either of the following.   *Decision Making*

- Roy borrows from the bank with Hal's guarantee provided to the bank.
- Cash in the CD (with no penalty) and lend Roy the funds at 2% interest.

Hal is in the 32% marginal tax bracket. Roy, whose only source of income is his salary, is in the 12% marginal tax bracket. The interest that Roy pays on the mortgage will be deductible by him. Which option will maximize the family's after-tax wealth?

26. **LO.6** Determine Hazel's Federal gross income from the following receipts for the year.

Gain on sale of Augusta County bonds	$800
Interest on U.S. government savings bonds	400
Interest on state income tax refund	200
Interest on Augusta County bonds	700

27. **LO.6** Tammy, a resident of Virginia, is considering whether to purchase a North Carolina bond, face amount $100,000, that yields 4.6% before tax. She is in the 35% Federal marginal tax bracket and the 5% state marginal tax bracket.   *Decision Making*

Tammy is aware that State of Virginia bonds of comparable risk are yielding 4.5%. Virginia bonds are exempt from Virginia tax, but the North Carolina bond interest is taxable in Virginia.

Which of the two options will provide the greater after-tax return to Tammy? Tammy can deduct all state taxes paid on her Federal income tax return.

28. **LO.7** Ray and Carin are partners in an accounting firm. The partners have entered into an arm's length agreement requiring Ray to purchase Carin's partnership interest from Carin's estate if she dies before Ray. The price is set at 120% of the book value of Carin's partnership interest at the time of her death.   *Decision Making*

Ray purchased an insurance policy on Carin's life to fund this agreement. After Ray had paid $45,000 in premiums, Carin was killed in an automobile accident, and Ray collected $800,000 of life insurance proceeds. Ray used the life insurance proceeds to purchase Carin's partnership interest.

What amount should Ray include in his gross income from receiving the life insurance proceeds?

29. **LO.7** Laura recently was diagnosed with cancer and has begun chemotherapy treatments. A cancer specialist has given Laura less than one year to live. She has incurred sizable medical bills and other general living expenses and is in need of cash. Therefore, Laura is considering selling stock that cost her $35,000 in 2010 and now has a fair market value of $50,000. This amount would be sufficient to pay her medical bills.   *Digging Deeper*   *Decision Making*

However, she has read about a company (VitalBenefits.com) that would purchase her life insurance policy for $50,000. To date, Laura has paid $30,000 in premiums on the policy.

a. Considering only the Federal income tax effects, would selling the stock or selling the life insurance policy result in more beneficial tax treatment?

b. Assume that Laura is a dependent child and that her mother owns the stock and the life insurance policy, which is on the mother's life. Which of the alternative means of raising the cash would result in more beneficial tax treatment?

30. **LO.8** Vic, who was experiencing financial difficulties, adjusted his debts as follows. Determine the Federal income tax consequences from these events.

    a. Vic is an attorney. Vic owed his uncle $25,000. The uncle told Vic that if he serves as the executor of his estate, Vic's debt will be canceled in the uncle's will.

    b. Vic borrowed $80,000 from First Bank. The debt was secured by land that Vic purchased for $100,000. Vic was unable to pay, and the bank foreclosed when the liability was $80,000, which was also the fair market value of the property.

    c. The Land Company, which had sold land to Vic for $80,000, reduced the mortgage principal on the land by $12,000.

31. **LO.9** How does the tax benefit rule apply in the following cases?

    a. In 2016, the Orange Furniture Store, an accrual method taxpayer, sold furniture on credit for $1,000 to Sammy. Orange's cost of the furniture was $600. In 2017, Orange took a bad debt deduction for the $1,000 because Sammy would not pay his bill.

       In 2018, Sammy inherited some money and paid Orange the $1,000 he owed. Orange was in the 35% marginal tax bracket in 2016, the 15% marginal tax bracket in 2017, and the 35% marginal tax bracket in 2018.

    b. In 2017, Barb, a cash basis taxpayer, was in an accident and incurred $8,000 in medical expenses, which she claimed as an itemized deduction for medical expenses. Because of a limitation, though, the expense reduced her taxable income by only $3,000. In 2018, Barb successfully sued the person who caused the physical injury and collected $8,000 to reimburse her for the cost of her medical expenses. Barb was in the 15% marginal tax bracket in 2017, and in the 12% bracket in 2018.

32. **LO.10** Ridge is a generous individual. During the year, she made interest-free loans to various family members when the Federal interest rate was 3%. What are the Federal tax consequences of the following loans by Ridge?

    a. On June 30, Ridge loaned $12,000 to a cousin, Jim, to buy a used truck. Jim's only source of income was his wages on various construction jobs during the year.

    b. On August 1, Ridge loaned $8,000 to a niece, Sonja. The loan was meant to enable Sonja to pay her college tuition. Sonja reported $1,200 interest income from CDs that her parents had given her.

    c. On September 1, Ridge loaned $25,000 to a brother, Al, to start a business. Al reported only $220 of dividends and interest for the year.

    d. On September 30, Ridge loaned $150,000 to her mother, Joan, so that Joan could pay the entrance fee at a retirement home. Joan's only receipts for the year were $9,000 in Social Security benefits and $500 interest income received.

33. **LO.10** Apply the imputed interest rules in the following situations.

    a. Mike loaned his sister Shonda $90,000 to buy a new home. Mike did not charge interest on the loan. The Federal rate was 4%. Shonda earned $900 of investment income for the year.

    b. Mandeep's employer maintains an emergency loan fund for its employees. During the year, Mandeep's wife Tina was very ill, and he incurred unusually large medical expenses. He borrowed $8,500 from his employer's emergency loan fund for six months. The Federal rate was 4%. Mandeep and Tina earned no investment income for the year.

    c. Jody borrowed $25,000 from her controlled corporation for six months. She used the funds to pay her daughter's college tuition. The corporation charged

Jody 3% interest. The Federal rate was 4%. Jody earned $3,500 of investment income for the year.

d. Kait loaned her son, Jake, $60,000 for six months. Jake used the $60,000 to pay off college loans. The Federal rate was 4%, and Kait did not charge Jake any interest. Jake earned dividend and interest income of $2,100 for the tax year.

BRIDGE DISCIPLINE

1. Find the audited financial statements of a major U.S. corporation.
   a. Summarize its most important financial accounting policies.
   b. Describe two elements of the Federal income tax law that significantly affected the corporation's earnings per share for the operating year.

2. For the same corporation, summarize three key tax accounting applications, and point out how they differ from book income principles. Summarize your findings, and present them to your classmates in no more than five PowerPoint slides.

   Communications

3. The exclusion of state and local bond interest from Federal income tax often is criticized as creating a tax haven for the wealthy. Critics, however, often fail to take into account the effect of market forces. In recent months, the long-term tax-exempt interest rate has been 2.5%, while the long-term taxable rate for bonds of comparable risk was approximately 3.75%. On the other hand, state and local governments do enjoy a savings in interest costs because of the tax-favored status of their bonds.

   To date, Congress has concluded that the benefits gained by the states and municipalities and their residents, such as the access to capital and the creation of jobs to construct and maintain critical infrastructure, outweigh any damages to our progressive income tax system. Do you agree with the proponents of the exclusion? Why or why not?

4. In a two-page paper, separately evaluate each of the following alternative proposals for taxing the income from property.
   a. All assets would be valued at the end of the year, any increase in value that occurred during the year would be included in gross income, and any decrease in value would be deductible from gross income.
   b. No gain or loss would be recognized until the taxpayer sold or exchanged the property.
   c. Increases or decreases in the value of property traded on a national exchange (e.g., the New York Stock Exchange) would be reflected in gross income for the years in which the changes in value occur. For all other assets, no gain or loss would be recognized until the owner disposes of the property.

   Digging Deeper

   Communications

5. Various Federal stimulus provisions were designed to assist state and local governments in borrowing funds, leveraging the gross income exclusion for such bond interest so that such jurisdictions would have increased access to funds. One of the justifications for these provisions was that state and local governments cannot run budget deficits and cannot "print money," so the recent recession put them in a difficult cash-flow position.

   Audits of the use of these borrowed funds showed that some of the bond proceeds were used by the jurisdictions to participate in "public-private partnerships," where government funds were used to assist private entities in expanding in or relocating to the jurisdiction. Specifically, bond proceeds were found to have been used to provide targeted road-building and utility-construction projects to benefit large commercial entities.

   Is this an appropriate use of the gross income exclusion for state and local bond interest? Summarize your comments in an e-mail to your instructor.

   Communications

Research Problems

THOMSON REUTERS
CHECKPOINT™

Note: Solutions to the Research Problems can be prepared by using the Thomson Reuters Checkpoint™ online tax research database, which accompanies this textbook. Solutions can also be prepared by using research materials found in a typical tax library.

Communications

Research Problem 1. Tranquility Funeral Home, Inc., your client, is an accrual basis taxpayer that sells "pre-need" funeral contracts. Under these contracts, the customer pays in advance for goods and services to be provided at the contract beneficiary's death. These payments are refundable at the contract purchaser's request, pursuant to state law, at any time until the goods and services are furnished. Tranquility, consistent with its financial accounting reporting, includes the payments in income for the year the funeral service is provided.

An IRS agent insists that the contract payments constitute prepaid income subject to tax in the year of receipt. Your client believes the amounts involved are tax-deferred customer deposits.

Write a letter to Tranquility that contains your tax advice about how the issue should be resolved. The client's address is 400 Rock Street, Memphis, TN 38152.

Communications
Decision Making

Research Problem 2. Clint, your client, owns a life insurance policy on his own life. He has paid $6,800 in premiums, and the cash surrender value of the policy is $30,000. Clint borrowed $30,000 from the insurance company, using the cash surrender value as collateral. He is considering canceling the policy in payment of the loan. Clint would like to know the Federal income tax consequences of canceling his policy. Summarize your findings in a brief research memo.

Communications

Research Problem 3. Your client, New Shoes Ltd., is a retailer that often issues store gift (debit) cards to customers in lieu of a cash refund. You recall that the IRS issued a revenue procedure that provided that the prepaid income rules in Revenue Procedure 2004–34 could be applied to the income from the gift cards. Locate a more recent revenue procedure that authorizes the deferral of gross income from gift cards. Outline the key points of this document, and send the outline to your instructor.

Research Problem 4. Your friend Hui is an investor in bluecoin, a virtual currency. Indicate whether and how she is subject to Federal income taxation in the following circumstances.

a. Earns $1,000 in bluecoin from mining.

b. Purchases $1,000 in bluecoin from another friend.

c. Sells the purchase in part (b) in the market to a third party for $1,400.

d. Spends $1,000 of bluecoin to acquire an asset worth $1,500.

e. Spends $1,000 of bluecoin to acquire an asset worth $750.

f. Holds bluecoin that she bought in February for $1,000. On December 31, the bluecoin is worth $1,200.

Use internet tax resources to address the following questions. Look for reliable websites and blogs of the IRS and other government agencies, media outlets, businesses, tax professionals, academics, think tanks, and political outlets.

Communications

Research Problem 5. Construct a chart for your state and four of its neighboring states. Provide "Yes/No" entries for each state in the following categories. Send the chart to your classmates by e-mail.

• Does the state exclude interest income from U.S. Treasury bonds?

• Does the state exclude interest income from Fannie Mae bonds?

- Does the state exclude interest income from bonds issued by governments in its own state?

- Does the state exclude interest income from bonds issued by governments in other states?

Research Problem 6. Determine the applicable Federal interest rate as of today for purposes of § 7872 below-market loans. In an e-mail to your professor, describe how the rate is determined and how you discovered the pertinent rules.   Communications

Becker CPA Review Question

1. Danny received the following interest and dividend payments this year. What amount should Danny include in his gross income?

Source	Amount
City of Atlanta bond interest	$1,200
U.S. Treasury bond interest	500
State of Georgia bond interest	1,000
Ellis Company common stock dividend	400
Row Corporation bond interest	600

a. $2,500

b. $1,500

c. $3,700

d. $2,200

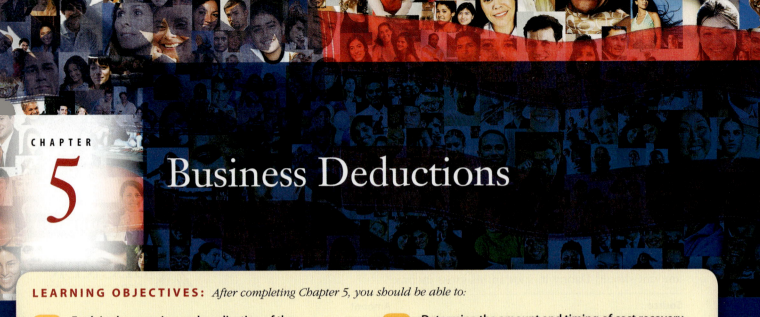

CHAPTER 5

Business Deductions

LEARNING OBJECTIVES: *After completing Chapter 5, you should be able to:*

LO.1 Explain the meaning and application of the ordinary, necessary, and reasonableness requirements for the deduction of business expenses.

LO.2 Describe and apply the cash and accrual methods of accounting for business deductions.

LO.3 Recognize and apply a variety of Internal Revenue Code deduction disallowance provisions.

LO.4 State and calculate the alternative tax treatments of research and experimental expenditures.

LO.5 Identify several other common business deductions.

LO.6 Identify and measure deductible charitable contributions and determine corporate limitations on the contribution deduction.

LO.7 Determine the amount and timing of cost recovery available under MACRS, including additional cost recovery available in the year an asset is placed in service.

LO.8 Identify and apply the cost recovery limitations applicable to automobiles and property used for personal purposes, including listed property.

LO.9 Identify intangible assets that are eligible for amortization and calculate the amount of the deduction.

LO.10 Determine the amount of depletion expense and specify the alternative tax treatments for intangible drilling and development costs.

CHAPTER OUTLINE

5-1 Overview of Business Deductions, 5-2
  5-1a Ordinary and Necessary Requirement, 5-2
  5-1b Reasonableness Requirement, 5-3
  5-1c Common Business Deductions, 5-3

5-2 The Timing of Expense Recognition, 5-4
  5-2a Cash Method Requirements, 5-4
  5-2b Accrual Method Requirements, 5-5
  5-2c Expenses Accrued to Related Parties, 5-6
  5-2d Prepaid Expenses—The "12-Month Rule," 5-7

5-3 Disallowance Possibilities, 5-8
  5-3a Public Policy Limitations, 5-8
  5-3b Political Contributions and Lobbying Activities, 5-9
  5-3c Excessive Executive Compensation, 5-10
  5-3d Investigation of a Business, 5-11
  5-3e Transactions between Related Parties, 5-12
  5-3f Expenses and Interest Related to Tax-Exempt Income, 5-13
  5-3g Business Interest, 5-14
  5-3h Expenses Related to Entertainment, Recreation, or Amusement, 5-14
  5-3i Other Disallowance Possibilities, 5-15

5-4 Research and Experimental Expenditures, 5-15
  5-4a Expense Method, 5-16
  5-4b Deferral and Amortization Method, 5-16

5-5 Other Business Expenses, 5-17
  5-5a Interest Expense, 5-17
  5-5b Taxes, 5-17

5-6 Charitable Contributions, 5-18
  5-6a Property Contributions, 5-19
  5-6b Limitations Imposed on Charitable Contribution Deductions, 5-21

5-7 Cost Recovery Allowances, 5-21
  5-7a Overview, 5-21
  5-7b Cost Recovery: In General, 5-22
  5-7c The Modified Accelerated Cost Recovery System (MACRS), 5-24
  5-7d MACRS for Personal Property, 5-24
  5-7e MACRS for Real Estate, 5-28
  5-7f Election to Expense Certain Depreciable Assets (§ 179), 5-29
  5-7g Additional First-Year Depreciation (Bonus Depreciation), 5-32
  5-7h Using § 179 and Bonus Depreciation Effectively, 5-33
  5-7i Business and Personal Use of Automobiles and Other Listed Property, 5-35
  5-7j Alternative Depreciation System (ADS), 5-40

5-8 Amortization, 5-41
5-9 Depletion, 5-41
  5-9a Intangible Drilling and Development Costs (IDCs), 5-42
  5-9b Depletion Methods, 5-42

5-10 Cost Recovery Tables, 5-44

TAX TALK *Last year I had difficulty with my income tax. I tried to take my analyst off as a business deduction. The Government said it was entertainment. We compromised finally and made it a religious contribution.*—WOODY ALLEN

CALCULATING DEDUCTIBLE EXPENSES

Michael Forney, owner of a small engine service and repair business, operates his business as a C corporation with a December 31 year-end. Mr. Forney owns 80 percent of the corporation's stock, while his wife (Kathleen) and his mother (Terry) each own 10 percent of the stock. Michael is a full-time employee at his business, and his mother helps out with the books for about two hours a week. At this time, Kathleen does not work at the business.

The following expenses, along with $435,000 of gross income, are reported in the corporation's financial statements.

Salaries and wages (including Michael's salary of $55,000 and Terry's salary of $3,000)	$150,000
Building rent	24,000
Depreciation of machinery and equipment*	13,000
Insurance (coverage for all assets of the business)	6,000
Consulting fees	6,000
Utilities	12,000
Taxes and licenses	6,000
Fine paid to city	2,500
Advertising	3,000
Interest expense	3,000
Charitable contributions	3,000
Dues paid to Small Engine Repair Institute	10,000
Political contributions	2,000

*$130,000 of new machinery and equipment were purchased this year. The financial reporting system depreciation is based on straight-line depreciation over 10 years. The MACRS cost recovery period for tax purposes is 7 years. Assume for purposes of this scenario that no depreciation may be claimed this year for assets acquired in prior years because they have been fully depreciated.

Michael would like to know the amount of his deductible expenses for tax purposes.

Michael would also like your advice on another matter. Because his business has been very profitable over the years, it has built up large cash reserves, and its cash flow continues to be strong. Even with the

continued

high levels of cash in the business, it has never paid any dividends to the shareholders. For next year, he is considering paying himself a salary of $140,000 and his mother a salary of $30,000. This would give them more cash to spend for planned vacations and home improvements.

Finally, during the year, Michael purchased another personal residence for $300,000 and converted his original residence to rental property. The original residence cost $250,000 five years ago and has a current market value of $180,000. Also during the year, he purchased a condo for $170,000, which he will rent to tenants. Michael holds these rental properties outside his small engine service and repair business. He would like to know the tax implications, if any, of these transactions.

Read the chapter and formulate your response.

As discussed in the previous chapter, the tax law has an all-inclusive definition of income; that is, income from whatever source derived is includible in gross income. Income cannot be excluded unless the Internal Revenue Code explicitly permits it. The tax law takes a very different approach to deductions. A deduction is allowed only if there is a specific provision in the tax law that permits it. However, the Code goes on to allow a deduction for most expenses incurred in a trade or business. This chapter discusses many of the common business deductions encountered by taxpayers that are specified in the Code.

5-1 OVERVIEW OF BUSINESS DEDUCTIONS

LO.1

Explain the meaning and application of the ordinary, necessary, and reasonableness requirements for the deduction of business expenses.

As just noted, an expense is not deductible under Federal law unless Congress creates a specific provision allowing it.[1] The Code does explicitly allow the deduction of expenses incurred in a trade or business, but only if those expenses are both *ordinary and necessary* and *reasonable* in amount.[2] Generally, a trade or business expense is deductible in full, without limitation or restriction.

5-1a Ordinary and Necessary Requirement

Section 162(a) permits a deduction for all ordinary and necessary expenses paid or incurred in carrying on a trade or business. To understand the scope of this provision, it is critical to understand the meanings of the terms *ordinary* and *necessary*. Since these terms are not defined in the Code or Regulations, the courts have dealt with these terms on numerous occasions.

An expense has been held to be *ordinary* if it is normal, usual, or customary in the type of business conducted by the taxpayer.[3] Note that an expense need not be recurring to be deductible as ordinary. For example, a business may be in a situation that is a very rare occurrence and incur an expense. If other businesses in a similar situation are likely to incur a similar expense, then the expense can be considered ordinary, even though it is not recurring.

EXAMPLE 1

Zebra Corporation was engaged in a mail-order business. The post office judged that Zebra's advertisements were false and misleading. Under a fraud order, the post office stamped "fraudulent" on all letters addressed to Zebra's business and returned them to the senders. Zebra spent $30,000 on legal fees in an unsuccessful attempt to force the post office to stop. The legal fees (although not recurring) were ordinary business expenses because they were normal, usual, or customary under the circumstances.[4]

---

[1] § 161(a).
[2] § 162(a).

[3] *Deputy v. DuPont*, 40–1 USTC ¶9161, 23 AFTR 808, 60 S.Ct. 363 (USSC, 1940).
[4] *Comm. v. Heininger*, 44–1USTC ¶9109, 31 AFTR 783, 64 S.Ct. 249 (USSC, 1943).

An expense has been held to be *necessary* if a prudent businessperson would incur the same expense and the expense is expected to be appropriate and helpful in the taxpayer's business.[5] But as Example 2 shows, no deduction will be allowed unless the expense is also ordinary.

Pat purchased a business that had just been adjudged bankrupt. Because the business had a poor financial rating, Pat wanted to restore its financial reputation. Consequently, he paid off some of the debts owed by the former owners that had been canceled by the bankruptcy court. Because Pat had no legal obligation to make these payments, the U.S. Supreme Court decided that he was trying to generate goodwill. Although the payments were necessary (i.e., appropriate and helpful), they were *not* ordinary and their deduction *was not* allowed.[6]

5-1b Reasonableness Requirement

An expense must also be reasonable to be deductible. Although the Code applies the <mark>reasonableness requirement</mark> solely to salaries and other compensation for services, the courts have held that for any expense to be ordinary and necessary, it must also be reasonable in amount.[7] If an expense is unreasonable, any amount in excess of what is reasonable is not allowed as a deduction.

The question of reasonableness usually arises with respect to closely held corporations where there is no separation of ownership and management. For example, excessive salaries, rent, and other expenses paid by a closely held corporation to its shareholders may be deemed unreasonable. What constitutes reasonableness is a question of fact.[8] For example, the courts will view the reasonableness of a salary paid to a shareholder of a closely held corporation in light of all relevant circumstances and may find that an unusually large salary is reasonable despite its size. If excessive payments for salaries, rent, and other expenses are closely related to the percentage of stock owned by the recipients, the payments are generally treated as dividends.[9] Because dividends are not deductible by the corporation, the disallowance results in an increase in corporate taxable income. Deductions for reasonable salaries will not be disallowed solely because the corporation has paid insubstantial portions of its earnings as dividends to its shareholders.

The Big Picture

EXAMPLE 3

Return to the facts of *The Big Picture* on p. 5-1. The small engine service and repair business, a closely held C corporation, is owned by Michael Forney, his wife (Kathleen) and his mother (Terry). The company has been highly profitable over the years and has never paid dividends. Michael is the key employee of the business, while his mother plays a very minor role. Assuming that their current salaries of $55,000 and $3,000 are comparable to what they could earn at similar companies for the work they do, they are likely to be considered reasonable and, therefore, deductible.

If Mr. Forney's plan to more than double his salary and increase his mother's salary by tenfold is implemented, the amounts in excess of their current salaries may be deemed unreasonable; if that is the case, the excess would be disallowed as deductible salary. The disallowed amounts would then be treated as dividends rather than salary income to Michael and Terry. Salaries are deductible by the corporation, but dividends are not.

5-1c Common Business Deductions

The language of § 162 is broad enough to permit the deduction of many different types of ordinary and necessary business expenses. Some of the more common deductions are listed in Exhibit 5.1.

---

[5]*Welch v. Helvering*, 3 USTC ¶1164, 12 AFTR 1456, 54 S.Ct. 8 (USSC, 1933).

[6]*Welch v. Helvering*, cited in footnote 5.

[7]*Comm. v. Lincoln Electric Co.*, 49–2 USTC ¶9388, 38 AFTR 411, 176 F.2d 815 (CA–6, 1949).

[8]*Kennedy, Jr. v. Comm.*, 82–1 USTC ¶9186, 49 AFTR 2d 82–628, 671 F.2d 167 (CA–6, 1982), *rev'g* 72 T.C. 793 (1979).

[9]Reg. § 1.162–8.

EXHIBIT 5.1	**Partial List of Business Deductions**
Advertising	Pension and profit sharing plans
Bad debts	Rent or lease payments
Commissions and fees	Repairs and maintenance
Depletion	Salaries and wages
Depreciation	Supplies
Employee benefit programs	Taxes and licenses
Insurance	Travel and transportation
Interest	Utilities

TAX PLANNING STRATEGIES   Unreasonable Compensation

FRAMEWORK FOCUS: TAX RATE

Strategy: Avoid Double Taxation.

In substantiating the reasonableness of a shareholder-employee's compensation, an internal comparison test is sometimes useful. If it can be shown that nonshareholder-employees and shareholder-employees in comparable positions receive comparable compensation, it is indicative that compensation is not unreasonable.

Another possibility is to demonstrate that the shareholder-employee has been underpaid in prior years. For example, the shareholder-employee may have agreed to take a less-than-adequate salary during the unprofitable formative years of the business. He or she would expect the "postponed" compensation to be paid in later, more profitable years. The agreement should be documented, if possible, in the corporate minutes.

Keep in mind that in testing for reasonableness, the total pay package must be considered. Compensation includes all fringe benefits or perquisites, such as contributions by the corporation to a qualified pension plan, regardless of when the funds are available to the employee.

For additional discussion of the meaning of reasonable compensation, see Chapter 13.

LO.2

Describe and apply the cash and accrual methods of accounting for business deductions.

5-2 THE TIMING OF EXPENSE RECOGNITION

A taxpayer's accounting method is a major factor in determining taxable income. The method used determines *when* an item is includible in income and *when* an item is deductible. Usually, the taxpayer's normal method of record keeping is used for income tax purposes.[10] The Code and Regulations require that the accounting method used must clearly reflect income and that items be handled consistently.[11] The most common methods of accounting are the cash method and the accrual method. If a taxpayer owns multiple businesses, it may be possible to use the cash method for some and the accrual method for others.[12]

Throughout the portions of the Code dealing with deductions, the phrase *paid or incurred* is used. A cash basis taxpayer is generally allowed a deduction in the year an expense is *paid*. An accrual basis taxpayer is allowed a deduction in the year in which the liability for the expense is *incurred*.

5-2a Cash Method Requirements

The expenses of cash basis taxpayers are deductible only when they are actually paid with cash or other property. Promising to pay or issuing a note does *not* satisfy the actually paid requirement.[13] However, the payment can be made with borrowed funds.

---

[10]§ 446(a).

[11]§§ 446(b) and (e); Reg. § 1.446–1(a)(2).

[12]As discussed in Chapter 4, certain taxpayers, including large C corporations, are prohibited from using the cash method.

[13]*Page v. Rhode Island Trust Co., Exr.,* 37–1 USTC ¶9138, 19 AFTR 105, 88 F.2d 192 (CA–1, 1937).

Taxpayers are allowed to claim the deduction at the time they charge expenses on credit cards. Effectively, they borrowed money from the credit card issuer and simultaneously paid the expenses.[14]

Although the cash basis taxpayer must have actually or constructively paid the expense, payment does not ensure a current deduction. The Regulations require capitalization of any expenditure that creates an asset having a useful life that extends substantially beyond the end of the tax year.[15] The courts have clarified that expenditures that provide a benefit beyond the end of the tax year following the year of payment generally must be capitalized.[16] Thus, cash basis taxpayers cannot take a current deduction for such expenditures except through amortization, depletion, or depreciation over the tax life of the asset.

EXAMPLE 4

Redbird, Inc., a calendar year and cash basis taxpayer, rents property from Bluejay, Inc. On July 1, 2018, Redbird pays $24,000 rent for the 24 months ending June 30, 2020.

The prepaid rent extends 18 months after the close of the tax year—substantially beyond the year of payment. Therefore, Redbird must capitalize the prepaid rent and amortize the expense on a monthly basis. Redbird's deduction for 2018 is $6,000.

Assume that Redbird is required to pay only 12 months' rent in 2018, and pays $12,000 on July 1, 2018. The entire $12,000 is deductible in 2018, as the benefit does not extend beyond the end of 2019.

TAX PLANNING STRATEGIES   Time Value of Tax Deductions

FRAMEWORK FOCUS: DEDUCTIONS

Strategy: Accelerate Recognition of Deductions to Achieve Tax Deferral.

Cash basis taxpayers often have the ability to make early payments for their expenses at the end of the tax year. This may permit the payments to be deducted in the year of payment instead of in the following tax year. Given the time value of money, a tax deduction this year may be worth more than the same deduction next year.

Before employing this strategy, the taxpayer must consider what next year's expected income and tax rates will be and whether a cash-flow problem may develop from early payments. Thus, a variety of considerations must be taken into account when planning the timing of tax deductions.

In-depth coverage can be found on this book's companion website: www.cengage.com   **1 DIGGING DEEPER**

5-2b Accrual Method Requirements

An accrual basis taxpayer can deduct an expense when both the *all events test* and the *economic performance test* are met. The all events test is met when (1) all of the events have occurred to establish the existence of a legal liability and (2) the amount of the liability can be determined with reasonable accuracy. The economic performance test is met when the party obligated to do something (i.e., to perform) to satisfy the liability does so. In situations in which a liability arises as a result of services being provided, or property being transferred, to the taxpayer, economic performance occurs when the service is provided or the property is acquired. If the liability is the result of the taxpayer being required to provide services or transfer property, economic performance occurs when the taxpayer provides the service or transfers the property.[17]

---

[14]Rev.Rul. 78–39, 1978–1 C.B. 73. See also Rev.Rul. 80–335, 1980–2 C.B. 170, which applies to pay-by-phone arrangements.

[15]Reg. § 1.461–1(a).

[16]*Zaninovich v. Comm.*, 80–1 USTC ¶9342, 45 AFTR 2d 80–1442, 616 F.2d 429 (CA–9, 1980), *rev'g* 69 T.C. 605 (1978). Cited by the Supreme Court in

Hillsboro National Bank v. Comm., 83–1 USTC ¶9229, 51 AFTR 2d 83–874, 103 S.Ct. 1134 (USSC, 1983).

[17]§ 461(h).

Robin, Inc., an entertainment business, sponsored a jazz festival in a rented auditorium at City College. Robin is responsible for cleaning up after the festival, which took place on December 22, 2018, and reinstalling the auditorium seats. Because the college is closed over the Christmas holidays, the company hired by Robin to perform the work did not begin these activities until January 3, 2019. Robin cannot deduct its $1,200 labor cost until 2019 when the services are performed.

DIGGING DEEPER 2 | **In-depth coverage can be found on this book's companion website: www.cengage.com**

An important consequence of the economic performance test is that many expenses that are estimated for financial reporting purposes, often by employing reserves or allowance accounts, are not immediately deductible for tax purposes. These expenses typically require estimation precisely because economic performance has not occurred. Instead, deductibility is deferred until economic performance has occurred.

Oriole Airlines is required by Federal law to test its engines after 3,000 flying hours. Aircraft cannot return to flight until the tests have been conducted. An unrelated aircraft maintenance company performs the tests. Oriole estimates that the tests will cost approximately $1,500 per engine.

For financial reporting purposes, the company accrues an expense based upon $.50 per hour of flight ($1,500 ÷ 3,000 hours) and credits an allowance account. The actual amounts paid for maintenance are offset against the allowance account.

For tax purposes, the economic performance test is not satisfied until the work has been done. Therefore, the reserve method cannot be used for tax purposes.

Note that the economic performance test does not require that an expense be paid before it is deductible. In Example 6, the economic performance test is met when the engine tests are performed, even if the expense is not paid until the following year.

5-2c Expenses Accrued to Related Parties

Regardless of the taxpayer's general method of accounting, the Internal Revenue Code places restrictions on the deductibility of expenses accrued to *related parties*. Without these restrictions, related taxpayers who have control over both sides of a transaction would have the ability to enter into transactions that allow the immediate deduction of an expense by an accrual basis taxpayer while allowing the deferral of the related income by a cash basis taxpayer on the other side of the transaction. For example, an accrual basis, closely held corporation might borrow funds from a cash basis individual shareholder. At the end of the year, the corporation would accrue and deduct the interest expense, but the cash basis lender would not recognize interest income because no interest had been paid.

Section 267 specifically addresses related-party transactions, deferring the deduction of an expense accrued to a related party until the related party is required to recognize the item in income. Note that deferral is not required if both parties use the same general method of accounting. Likewise, deferral will not be required if the related party reporting income uses the accrual method and the related party taking the deduction uses the cash method.

Relationships and Constructive Ownership

For purposes of § 267, *related parties* include the following:

- Family members, including brothers and sisters (whether whole, half, or adopted), spouse, ancestors (e.g., parents and grandparents), and lineal descendants (e.g., children and grandchildren) of the taxpayer.

- Corporations and shareholders who own more than 50 percent (directly or indirectly) of the corporation's stock.

- Two corporations that are members of a controlled group (discussed in Chapter 12).

Constructive ownership provisions must be considered when determining whether taxpayers are related for purposes of § 267. Under these provisions, certain taxpayers are treated as if they own the stock directly owned by others. For example, for purposes of applying the tests of § 267, a taxpayer will be treated as owning any stock directly owned by his or her family members.[18]

Related-Party Transactions

The stock of Sparrow Corporation is owned 20% by Ted, 30% by Ted's father, 30% by Ted's mother, and 20% by Ted's sister. Although Ted actually owns only 20% of Sparrow Corporation, he is *deemed* to own the stock owned by his father (30%), mother (30%), and sister (20%).

As a result, he directly and indirectly owns 100% of Sparrow, and Ted and Sparrow are related parties. The same outcome (100% direct and indirect ownership) results for all of the shareholders in this example.

Continue with the facts presented in Example 7. On July 1 of the current year, Ted loaned $10,000 to Sparrow Corporation at 6% annual interest, with principal and interest payable on demand. For tax purposes, Sparrow uses the accrual basis and Ted uses the cash basis. Both report on a calendar year basis.

Because Sparrow and Ted are related parties, Sparrow cannot deduct any interest accrued to Ted until Ted recognizes it as income. Because Ted is a cash basis taxpayer, the deduction is not available to Sparrow until the interest is paid.

5-2d Prepaid Expenses—The "12-Month Rule"

A special rule allows taxpayers, including accrual basis taxpayers, to deduct certain prepaid expenses. A deduction is allowed if the benefit they create doesn't extend beyond the earlier of (1) 12 months after the first date on which the taxpayer realized the benefit, or (2) the end of the tax year following the tax year in which the payment was made (the "12-month rule").[19] Although this rule applies to both cash and accrual method taxpayers, it does not supersede the economic performance test. Therefore, it does not apply to prepayments for services, property, or the use of property for accrual basis taxpayers unless economic performance has occurred. Nor does it apply to other expenses for which special rules regarding their timing exists (e.g., interest and taxes, discussed later in this chapter). Prepaid expenses eligible for the 12-month rule include insurance, dues, and licenses.[20]

"12-Month Rule"

On November 1, 2018, Nada, a calendar year and accrual basis taxpayer, pays $6,000 for a 1-year premium on a catastrophic liability policy that takes effect December 15, 2018. Nada will receive a benefit from this policy from December 15, 2018 through December 14, 2019. Her benefit does not extend beyond 12 months after the benefit begins on December 15. It also does not extend beyond the end of 2019. Therefore, this payment satisfies the requirements of the 12-month rule and Nada can deduct the $6,000 in 2018.

Assume the same facts as in Example 9 except that the benefit from the policy runs from February 1, 2019 through January 31, 2020. Nada's benefit now extends beyond the end of the tax year following the tax year in which the payment was made (December 31, 2019), so the 12-month rule requirements are not met. Nada must capitalize the $6,000 payment in 2018 and amortize it over the benefit period.

[18]While this provision applies to related parties as previously defined, note that it also applies to transactions between any partner (shareholder) and a partnership (S corporation), regardless of the ownership interest held by the partner or shareholder.

[19]Reg. § 1.263(a)-4(f).
[20]Reg. § 1.263(a)-4(f)(6).

LO.3

Recognize and apply a variety of Internal Revenue Code deduction disallowance provisions.

5-3 DISALLOWANCE POSSIBILITIES

Although most ordinary and necessary business expenses are deductible, the tax law contains provisions that disallow a deduction for certain expenditures. The most frequently encountered disallowance provisions are discussed below.

5-3a Public Policy Limitations

Payments considered to be in violation of public policy are not deductible.[21]

Justification for Denying Deductions

The courts initially developed the principle that a payment in violation of public policy is not deductible.[22] Although the payment may be helpful to a business and even contribute to its success, a deduction would, in effect, represent an indirect governmental subsidy for taxpayer wrongdoing.

Under legislation enacted based on this principle, the following expenses are not deductible.

- Bribes and kickbacks illegal under either Federal or state law.
- Two-thirds of the treble damage payments made to claimants resulting from violation of antitrust law.[23]
- Fines and penalties paid to a government for violation of law.

The Big Picture

EXAMPLE

11

Refer to the facts of *The Big Picture* on p. 5-1. Michael Forney had not instituted proper procedures for disposing of used motor oil and other engine fluids from his business. During the current tax year, he was fined $2,500 by the city. Mr. Forney believes the fine should be deducted as an ordinary business expense. However, because the fine was assessed by and paid to a government for a law violation, the $2,500 is not deductible.

DIGGING DEEPER 3   **In-depth coverage can be found on this book's companion website: www.cengage.com**

GLOBAL TAX ISSUES   **Overseas Gun Sales Result in Large Fines**

The Foreign Corrupt Practices Act (FCPA) is intended to punish taxpayers who make illegal payments to foreign officials to obtain economic advantages. Not only are such payments (usually improperly recorded as business expenses) nondeductible for income tax purposes, but serious and consistent violations can lead to the imposition of fines. Severe consequences can result from violating the bribery provisions of the FCPA, as Smith & Wesson recently discovered.

Smith & Wesson is a Massachusetts-based firearms manufacturer that wanted to begin selling firearms in India, Pakistan, and other foreign countries. As a small player in this international market, company officials decided to provide gifts to government officials in these countries to encourage them to do business with Smith & Wesson.

This turned out to be a costly mistake. Smith & Wesson had profits of only $100,000 from this scheme before it was uncovered, and in 2014, it agreed to pay the Securities and Exchange Commission fines of more than $2 million. Of course, the fines are not deductible because they are a violation of public policy.

Source: www.sec.gov/News/PressRelease/Detail/PressRelease/1370542384677#.

---

[21]Beginning in 2018, payments to (or at the direction of) any government in relation to the violation of any law (or a related investigation) are not deductible; § 162(f)(1). This rule does not apply to payments that are restitution for damage caused by the taxpayer or payments for taxes.

[22]*Tank Truck Rentals, Inc. v. Comm.*, 58–1 USTC ¶9366, 1 AFTR 2d 1154, 78 S.Ct. 507 (USSC, 1958).

[23]§§ 162(c), (f), and (g).

Expenses Related to an Illegal Business

Interestingly, the expenses of operating an illegal business (e.g., a money laundering operation) that are not inherently illegal themselves are deductible.[24] While allowing deductions for illegal activity may seem inappropriate, recall that the law taxes net income from a business operation, not gross revenue.

> **EXAMPLE 12**
>
> Grizzly, Inc., owns and operates a restaurant. In addition, Grizzly operates an illegal gambling establishment out of the restaurant's back room. In connection with the illegal activity, Grizzly has the following expenses during the year:
>
> | | |
> |---|---:|
> | Rent | $ 60,000 |
> | Payoffs to police | 40,000 |
> | Depreciation on equipment | 100,000 |
> | Wages | 140,000 |
> | Interest | 30,000 |
> | Criminal fines | 50,000 |
> | Illegal kickbacks | 10,000 |
> | Total | $430,000 |
>
> All of the expenses that are not otherwise disallowed (rent, depreciation, wages, and interest) are deductible; payoffs, fines, and kickbacks are not deductible. Of the $430,000 spent, $330,000 is deductible and $100,000 is not.

An exception applies to expenses incurred in illegal drug trafficking.[25] Drug dealers are not allowed a deduction for ordinary and necessary business expenses incurred in their business, except for cost of goods sold.[26]

5-3b Political Contributions and Lobbying Activities

Political Contributions

No deduction is allowed for direct or indirect payments for political purposes.[27] Historically, Congress has been reluctant to allow deductions for political expenditures even if those expenditures relate to a trade or business. Allowing deductions might encourage abuses and enable businesses to have undue influence on the political process.

> **The Big Picture**
>
> **EXAMPLE 13**
>
> Refer to the facts of *The Big Picture* on p. 5-1. Michael Forney's business made political contributions to the State Senate campaigns of Tom Smith and Virginia White. Mr. Forney made these contributions because he believed these candidates would be sensitive to the needs of small businesses. Therefore, he assumed that these would be deductible business expenses.
>
> However, political contributions are not deductible, so he will receive no tax benefit from them.

Lobbying Expenses

Lobbying expenses incurred in attempting to influence local, state, or Federal legislation or the actions of certain high-ranking individuals are not deductible.[28] The disallowance extends to a pro rata portion of the membership dues of trade associations and other groups that are involved in lobbying activities.

---

[24]*Comm. v. Sullivan*, 58–1 USTC ¶9368, 1 AFTR 2d 1158, 78 S.Ct. 512 (USSC, 1958).

[25]§ 280E.

[26]Reg. § 1.61–3(a). Gross income is defined as sales minus cost of goods sold. Thus, while § 280E prohibits any deductions for drug dealers, it does not modify the normal definition of gross income.

[27]§ 276.

[28]§ 162(e).

There are two special rules related to the disallowance provisions. First, the disallowance provision does not apply to activities devoted solely to *monitoring* legislation. Second, a *de minimis* exception allows the deduction of up to $2,000 of annual *in-house lobbying expenditures* incurred by the taxpayer. In-house lobbying expenditures are those paid or incurred directly by the taxpayer rather than amounts paid to professional lobbyists or other third parties. If in-house expenditures exceed $2,000, none of the in-house expenditures can be deducted.

The Big Picture

EXAMPLE 14

Refer to the facts of *The Big Picture* on p. 5-1. Mr. Forney's business made contributions to the Small Engine Repair Institute, a trade association for owners of similar-type businesses. The trade association estimates that 70% of its dues are allocated to lobbying activities. Thus, the deduction on the corporate tax return is limited to $3,000 ($10,000 × 30%).

5-3c Excessive Executive Compensation

The reasonableness requirement and its relevance to the deductibility of expenses paid by small businesses was discussed above. However, the reasonableness of other expenses, including those paid or incurred by larger businesses, has also gained the attention of Congress as well as the general public. Recall that allowing a deduction indirectly reduces the economic burden of an expense, allowing the taxpayer to share the cost with the larger taxpaying public. In response to concerns over the reasonableness of compensation paid to executives of large corporations, Congress enacted a limitation on the deductibility of such compensation.[29] Specifically, the Code limits the deductibility of the compensation paid to covered employees of publicly traded corporations to $1 million per year. Covered employees are defined as the chief executive officer, chief financial officer, and the three other most highly compensated employees. Any individual who is a covered employee after 2016 will continue to be a covered employee in all future years even if they no longer meet one of the above descriptions. Note that the provision does not limit the amount of compensation that can be paid but only the amount that is deductible.

The limitation does not apply to any compensation that is excludable from the executive's gross income (discussed in Chapter 11) or commissions based on income generated directly by the executive. Before 2018, the $1,000,000 limit excluded performance-based compensation. Contracts in place on November 2, 2017, are grandfathered into pre-2018 law as long as there are no material changes to the contract.

EXAMPLE 15

Johnette became CEO of Lowe's Depot, a home supply store and a publicly traded corporation on May 1, 2018. In 2018, her compensation package consists of:

Cash compensation	$1,800,000
Taxable fringe benefits	100,000
Bonus from a qualified bonus plan	5,000,000

Lowe's Depot can deduct only $1,000,000 of her compensation in 2018 and in all subsequent years that Johnette remains an employee.

---

[29]§ 162(m).

5-3d Investigation of a Business

Recall that § 162 allows a deduction for expenses incurred in carrying on a trade or business. However, expenses may be incurred to investigate the creation or acquisition of a business before the business is actually conducted by the taxpayer. Such costs might include travel, engineering and architectural surveys, marketing reports, and various legal and accounting services. How such expenses are treated for tax purposes depends on the following:

- The current business, if any, of the taxpayer.
- Whether the acquisition actually takes place.

If the taxpayer is in a business that is the *same as or similar* to that being investigated (i.e., the taxpayer is investigating the expansion of an existing trade or business), all investigation expenses are deductible in the year paid or incurred. The tax result is the same whether or not the taxpayer acquires the business being investigated.[30]

The Big Picture

EXAMPLE 16

Return to the facts of *The Big Picture* on p. 5-1. Michael Forney believes that his mechanical and business skills can be used to turn around other small engine businesses whose revenues have been declining. He investigates Southside Small Engine Services LLC, a nearby competitor that is for sale. Expenses paid to consultants and accountants as part of this investigation totaled $6,000. After reviewing various materials, he determined that buying Southside Small Engine Services would not be a good idea.

The $6,000 spent to investigate this business is deductible as a business expense because Mr. Forney is already in the small engine service and repair business. Investigating new business opportunities in one's current trade or business is an ordinary and necessary business expense.

When the taxpayer is *not* in a business that is the same as or similar to the one being investigated, the tax result depends on whether the new business is acquired. If the business is not acquired, the investigation expenses generally are nondeductible.[31]

EXAMPLE 17

Lynn, president and sole shareholder of Marmot Corporation, incurs expenses when traveling from Rochester, New York, to California to investigate the feasibility of acquiring several auto care centers. Marmot is in the residential siding business. If no acquisition takes place, Marmot may not deduct any of the expenses.

If the taxpayer is *not* in a business that is the same as or similar to the one being investigated and actually acquires the new business, the expenses must be capitalized as **startup expenditures**. However, the taxpayer may be able to deduct up to $5,000 of startup expenses in the month in which business begins. This immediate deduction is reduced dollar-for-dollar by the amount total startup expenses exceed $50,000. As a result, the immediate deduction is totally phased out when total startup expenses reach $55,000. Therefore, the immediate deduction primarily benefits smaller businesses. Any expenses not eligible for an immediate deduction are amortized over 180 months, again beginning in the month in which business begins.[32]

---

[30]*York v. Comm.*, 58–2 USTC ¶9952, 2 AFTR 2d 6178, 261 F.2d 421 (CA–4, 1958).

[31]Rev.Rul. 57–418, 1957–2 C.B. 143; *Morton Frank*, 20 T.C. 511 (1953); and *Dwight A. Ward*, 20 T.C. 332 (1953).

[32]§ 195(b).

EXAMPLE 18

Tina, a sole proprietor, owns and operates 10 restaurants located in various cities throughout the Southeast. She travels to Atlanta to discuss the acquisition of an auto dealership. She incurs legal and accounting costs associated with the potential acquisition. After incurring total investigation costs of $52,000, she acquires the auto dealership on October 1, 2018.

Tina may immediately deduct $3,000 [$5,000 − ($52,000 − $50,000)] and amortize the balance of $49,000 ($52,000 − $3,000) over a period of 180 months. For calendar year 2018, therefore, Tina can deduct $3,817 [$3,000 + ($49,000 × 3/180)].

Startup expenses include the following:

- Expenses incurred to investigate the creation or acquisition of a business by the taxpayer (e.g., market studies).

- Expenses incurred in creating or acquiring a business (e.g., professional fees, identifying suppliers, and obtaining licenses).

- Expenses incurred before the day the business begins that would otherwise have been deductible under § 162 (e.g., salaries, utilities, and advertising).

DIGGING DEEPER 4   **In-depth coverage can be found on this book's companion website: www.cengage.com**

5-3e Transactions between Related Parties

As discussed previously, Code § 267 puts restrictions on the deductibility of expenses accrued to related parties. Section 267 also disallows the immediate recognition of any losses from sales or exchanges of property directly or indirectly between those same related parties.[33] Without this restriction, taxpayers would be able to recognize losses on property sales without effectively giving up control of the property itself.

Although the loss realized in a related-party sale is not immediately recognized, it may be used to offset any future gain recognized when the property is subsequently sold to an *unrelated* party (i.e., a right of offset is created). However, this loss offset is only available to the party who subsequently sells the property to an unrelated party, and *not* to the initial seller who realized the loss. Further, the right of offset cannot create or increase a loss. Any right of offset not used by the subsequent seller to offset some or all of the recognized gain is permanently lost.

EXAMPLE 19

Donald owns real estate that he originally purchased in July 2013 for $1 million. In 2018, the property has a fair market value of $600,000. Donald believes the property will appreciate in value when a proposed shopping mall is built nearby and, therefore, does not want to lose control of it. In addition, he has realized a large gain on the sale of a different piece of property and would like to use the loss related to this parcel of real estate to offset the gain. So, at the end of 2018, Donald sells the property to his brother, Ben, for $600,000. In 2020, after the mall is built, Ben sells the land to a developer for $850,000.

Since Ben and Donald are related parties, Donald cannot recognize the $400,000 loss realized on the 2018 sale to Ben. However, when Ben subsequently sells the property to the developer in 2020, his $250,000 realized gain can be reduced, but not below zero, by Donald's $400,000 unrecognized loss. As a result, Ben does not recognize a gain on the sale. The remaining $150,000 loss not used by Ben is permanently lost.

---

[33]§ 267(a)(1).

The Big Picture

EXAMPLE 20

Return to the facts of *The Big Picture* on p. 5-1. Assume that Michael Forney, the 80% shareholder in his small engine service and repair business, sells a stock investment in his personal portfolio with a basis of $10,000 to his corporation for its fair market value of $8,000. Michael's $2,000 loss from the sale of the stock is disallowed because the sale is to a related party. The disallowed loss creates a $2,000 right of offset.

Assume Michael's business sells the stock several years later for $11,000. Although a $3,000 gain is realized ($11,000 selling price − $8,000 basis), only $1,000 must be recognized due to the $2,000 right of offset.

The Big Picture

EXAMPLE 21

Assume the same facts as Example 20, except that the corporation sells the stock for $9,000 to an unrelated party. The corporation's gain of $1,000 ($9,000 selling price − $8,000 basis) is not recognized because of the right of offset of $2,000 from Michael's sale.

The offset may result in only a partial tax benefit upon the subsequent sale (as in this case). If Michael originally had sold the stock to an unrelated party rather than to his corporation, he could have recognized a $2,000 loss. However, aggregating the effect to Michael and his corporation, they can benefit from only $1,000 of loss.

5-3f Expenses and Interest Related to Tax-Exempt Income

In addition to expenses incurred in a trade or business, the law also allows taxpayers to deduct expenses incurred for the production of income (i.e., not generated by a trade or business).[34] However, certain types of income (e.g., interest on municipal bonds) are tax-exempt.[35] Together, these provisions could lead to unintended consequences.

EXAMPLE 22

Oriole, Inc, a corporation in the 35% income tax bracket, borrowed $100,000 to purchase $100,000 of municipal bonds. The bonds pay interest at a rate of 6% but Oriole must pay 8% on the loan. Before considering any potential tax consequences, the net effect of the two transactions is as follows:

Cash paid out on loan	($8,000)
Cash received from bonds	6,000
Net negative cash flow	($2,000)

No tax is due on the municipal interest. If the $8,000 of interest expense were deductible, the deduction would provide a tax benefit of $2,800 (35% × $8,000), turning an arrangement with a negative pretax cash flow into a profitable one due solely to the tax benefits.

To prevent the type of tax arbitrage possibilities illustrated above, the Code generally disallows the deduction of expenses paid or incurred to generate tax-exempt income.[36] The disallowance applies to interest expense that is directly related to purchasing or carrying tax-exempt bonds as well as any other expense allocable to tax-exempt income.

---

[34]§ 212.

[35]§ 103.

[36]§ 265.

EXAMPLE 23

In January of the current year, Crane Corporation borrowed $100,000 at 8% interest. Crane used the loan proceeds to purchase 5,000 shares of stock in White Corporation. In July, Crane sold the stock for $120,000 and reinvested the proceeds in City of Denver bonds, the income from which is tax-exempt.

Assuming that the $100,000 loan remained outstanding throughout the entire year, Crane cannot deduct the interest attributable to the period when the loan was used to carry the bonds.

DIGGING DEEPER 5   **In-depth coverage can be found on this book's companion website: www.cengage.com**

5-3g Business Interest

Beginning in 2018, the Tax Cuts and Jobs Act (TCJA) of 2017 limits the deductibility of business interest for most large corporations. The deduction for net interest expense is limited to business interest income plus 30 percent of adjusted taxable income, taxable income calculated without considering the NOL deduction. For years beginning before 2022, adjusted taxable income is calculated without considering any depreciation, amortization, or depletion deduction. The limitation may impact corporations that are highly leveraged, including those that might have used debt to finance a merger. Any disallowed interest can be carried forward indefinitely. The limitation does not apply to businesses that have annual average gross receipts of $25 million or less during the prior three taxable years.[37]

EXAMPLE 24

In 2018, Corporation NFL has $50,000,000 of adjusted taxable income, $1,000,000 of business interest income, and $20,000,000 of business interest expense. NFL's 2018 deduction for business interest expense is limited to $16,000,000, the sum of its $1,000,000 of business interest income plus 30% of its adjusted taxable income (30% × $50,000,000 = $15,000,000). The $4,000,000 of disallowed interest expense is carried forward to future tax years.

5-3h Expenses Related to Entertainment, Recreation, or Amusement

Taxpayers may incur costs to entertain potential or existing customers, clients, suppliers, or employees. These costs can be incurred either during, or in association with, a business meeting and may reasonably be considered ordinary and necessary trade or business expenses. However, due to the element of personal enjoyment and the related potential for abuse the deductibility of such expense might create, Congress limits the deductibility of these expenses.

Generally, no deduction is allowed for any costs related to entertainment, amusement, or recreation activities. Nor are costs related to any facilities (e.g., airplanes, yachts, stadium boxes, hotel suites, vacation houses) used in such activities deductible. Dues related to membership in any business, social, athletic, or sporting clubs are also nondeductible. Business meals, including those paid in connection with business meetings as well as those paid for employees, are generally deductible as long as they are not lavish or extravagant.[38] However, any deduction is limited to 50 percent of the cost of the meals.[39] The deduction for the cost of meals provided to employees on an employer's business premises is also subject to the 50 percent reduction.[40]

---

[37]§ 163(j); § 448(c).
[38]§ 274(k).

[39]§ 274(n).
[40]These expenses will not be deductible after 2025.

There are several exceptions to the general disallowance of entertainment expenses and the 50 percent cutback on the deductibility of meals, including:[41]

- Expenses for meals or entertainment treated by the recipient as taxable income;
- Expenses for recreational or social activities primarily for the benefit of non-highly compensated employees.

EXAMPLE 25

Peach, Inc., incurred the following expenses during 2018:

Meals with potential customers at various restaurants	$ 20,000
Theater tickets and green fees for activities immediately preceding or following business meals	24,000
Rental of a luxury box at the baseball stadium for entertaining clients	30,000
Memberships in various country clubs and golf clubs	12,000
The costs of maintaining an on-site cafeteria where employees may dine for free so that they are accessible during the workday and can work during lunch	25,000
The costs of maintaining an on-site health facility so employees can work out before or after work, or at lunch	27,000
The costs of an all-day summer party for employees and their families	10,000
	$148,000

Peach may deduct $32,500 of the above expenses (the $10,000 spent on the employee party as well as 50 percent of the $20,000 spent on business meals with potential customers and the $25,000 for the on-site cafeteria). No portion of the $24,000 spent on events preceding or following business meals, the $30,000 to rent the stadium box, the $12,000 spent on club dues, or the $27,000 maintaining the health facility are deductible.

5-3i Other Disallowance Possibilities

Other expenditures that are not deductible include capital expenditures and expenditures for which the taxpayer does not have adequate substantiation.

In-depth coverage can be found on this book's companion website: www.cengage.com | **6 DIGGING DEEPER**

5-4 RESEARCH AND EXPERIMENTAL EXPENDITURES

LO.4

State and calculate the alternative tax treatments of research and experimental expenditures.

Businesses may incur research and experimental expenditures in the development or improvement of products or processes. Taxpayers are allowed several alternatives for handling these expenditures (discussed below).[42] A taxpayer must generally choose the method to be applied to the overall research program (or to a specific research project) when filing the first tax return covering the program or project. Once chosen, a taxpayer may not change methods without the permission of the IRS.[43]

Research and experimental expenditures generally include costs to develop a product or process, the viability of which is uncertain when the costs are paid or incurred. They include expenditures directly related to development, such as salaries and materials, as well as the costs of obtaining a related patent. They do not include the costs of routine quality testing, consumer research, or promotions.[44] Nor do they include the costs of land or depreciable property used in the research, though the depreciation on such property may qualify.[45]

---

[41]§§ 274(e) and 274(n).
[42]§ 174.
[43]§ 174(b)(2).

[44]§ 1.174-2.
[45]§ 174(c).

The law also provides a credit for increasing research expenses over what the expense amount was in a base year or years.[46] The amount otherwise deductible or amortizable is reduced by the available credit to prohibit the taxpayer from benefitting twice from the same expenditure.

5-4a **Expense Method**

In tax years beginning before January 1, 2022, a taxpayer can deduct all research and experimental expenditures in the year in which they are paid or incurred. In certain instances, a taxpayer may incur research and experimental expenditures before actually engaging in any trade or business activity. In such instances, the Supreme Court has applied the liberal standard of deductibility crafted by Congress in § 174 and permitted a deduction in the year paid or incurred.[47]

5-4b **Deferral and Amortization Method**

Alternatively, in tax years beginning before January 1, 2022, research and experimental expenditures may be deferred and amortized. If this election is made, the expenditures are amortized:

1. Over a period of at least 60 months beginning in the month the taxpayer first realizes a benefit from the expenditures (i.e., when the product, process, etc., is first put to use in generating income),[48] or
2. Over a period of 10 years beginning in the year the expenditure is made.[49]

EXAMPLE 26

Gold Corporation decides to develop a new line of adhesives. The project begins in 2018. Gold incurs the following expenses in 2018 and 2019 in connection with the project.

	2018	2019	Total
Salaries	$25,000	$18,000	$43,000
Materials	8,000	2,000	10,000
Depreciation on machinery	6,500	5,700	12,200
Total	$39,500	$25,700	$65,200

The benefits from the project will be realized starting in March 2020.

If Gold Corporation elects a 60-month deferral and amortization period, there is no deduction prior to March 2020, the month benefits from the project begin to be realized. The deduction for 2020 is $10,867, computed as follows:

Salaries ($25,000 + $18,000)	$43,000
Materials ($8,000 + $2,000)	10,000
Depreciation ($6,500 + $5,700)	12,200
Total	$65,200
2020: $65,200 × (10 months/60 months)	$10,867

If Gold elects a 10-year deferral and amortization period, the expenses incurred in 2018 are deducted over 10 years starting in 2018. Similarly, the expenses incurred in 2019 are deducted over 10 years starting in 2019.

Costs that are neither deducted immediately nor treated as deferred expenses must be capitalized. These costs are not deductible until the research project is abandoned or is deemed worthless. Given the time value of money, it is generally preferable to deduct

---

[46]§ 41. See Chapter 17 for a more detailed discussion of the research activities credit.

[47]*Snow v. Comm.*, 74–1 USTC ¶9432, 33 AFTR 2d 74–1251, 94 S.Ct. 1876 (USSC, 1974).

[48]§ 174(b)(2).

[49]§ 59(e).

research and development costs immediately. The deferral of research and experimental expenditures should be considered if the taxpayer expects higher tax rates in the future.

In tax years beginning after December 31, 2021, taxpayers will be *required* to capitalize and amortize all research and development expenditures as described above with two changes. First, the expenditures must be amortized ratably over a 5-year period (15 years for foreign research expenses) rather than ratably over a period of not less than 60 months. Second, amortization will begin at the midpoint of the year the expenses are paid or incurred, rather than the month in which the taxpayer first realizes benefits.[50]

5-5 OTHER BUSINESS EXPENSES

LO.5

Identify several other common business deductions.

In addition to the provisions discussed above, a variety of other expenses are subject to special rules and limitations. Some of these rules are noted briefly in the paragraphs that follow.

5-5a Interest Expense

Generally, taxpayers other than large corporations are not limited in the amount of business interest expense they may deduct. However, the deductibility of expenses (including interest) from certain other activities may be limited.[51] Further, the deductibility of interest by individuals depends on the activity to which the interest relates.[52]

Because the deductibility of interest expense associated with certain activities is limited, the IRS provides rules for allocating interest expense among activities. Under these rules, interest is allocated in the same manner as the debt with respect to which the interest is paid, and debt is allocated by tracing disbursements of the debt proceeds to specific expenditures. The interest tracing rules are complex and depend on whether loan proceeds are commingled with other cash and the length of time the loan proceeds are held before they are spent.

5-5b Taxes

As with interest expense, tax payments in a business or investment context are generally deductible. However, most Federal taxes are not deductible.

State, local, and foreign property taxes are generally deductible. However, the deductibility of real estate taxes in the year in which property is purchased or sold may raise issues. Real estate taxes for the entire year are apportioned between the buyer and seller based on the number of days the property was held by each during the real property tax year. This apportionment is required whether the tax is paid by the buyer or the seller or is prorated according to the purchase agreement. The apportionment determines who is entitled to deduct the real estate taxes in the year of sale. The required apportionment prevents the shifting of the deduction for real estate taxes from buyer to seller, or vice versa. In making the apportionment, the assessment date and the lien date are disregarded. The date of sale counts as a day the property is owned by the buyer.

EXAMPLE 27

A county's real property tax year runs from January 1 to December 31. Nuthatch Corporation, the owner on January 1 of real property located in the county, sells the real property to Crane, Inc., on June 30. Crane owns the real property from June 30 through December 31. The tax for the real property tax year, January 1 through December 31, is $3,650.

Assuming that this is not a leap year, the portion of the real property tax treated as imposed upon Nuthatch, the seller, is $1,800 [(180/365) × $3,650, January 1 through June 29], and $1,850 [(185/365) × $3,650, June 30 through December 31] of the tax is treated as imposed upon Crane, the purchaser.

---

[50]§ 174(a)(2).

[51]See, for example, the discussion of the passive activity limits in Chapter 6.

[52]See Chapter 10 for a more detailed discussion of the deductibility of interest by individuals.

If the actual real estate taxes are not prorated between the buyer and seller as part of the purchase agreement, adjustments are required. The adjustments are necessary to determine the amount realized by the seller and the basis of the property to the buyer. If the buyer pays the entire amount of the tax, it effectively has paid the seller's portion of the real estate tax and has therefore paid more for the property than the actual purchase price. As a result, the amount of real estate tax that is apportioned to the seller (for Federal income tax purposes) and paid by the buyer is added to the buyer's basis. The seller must increase the amount realized on the sale by the same amount.

Seth sells real estate on October 3 for $400,000. The buyer, Winslow Company, pays the real estate taxes of $3,650 for the calendar year, which is the real estate property tax year. Assuming that this is not a leap year, $2,750 (for 275 days) is apportioned to and is deductible by the seller, Seth, and $900 (for 90 days) of the taxes is deductible by Winslow. The buyer has paid Seth's real estate taxes of $2,750 and has therefore paid $402,750 for the property. Winslow's basis is increased to $402,750, and the amount realized by Seth from the sale is increased to $402,750.

The opposite result occurs if the seller (rather than the buyer) pays the real estate taxes. In this case, the seller reduces the amount realized from the sale by the amount that has been apportioned to the buyer. The buyer is required to reduce his or her basis by a corresponding amount.

Finally, the deductibility of state and foreign income taxes may raise at least two issues. The first relates to when these taxes are deductible. A tax is generally defined as a required payment to a government for which there is no direct benefit. The lack of a direct benefit suggests that the liability for income taxes can never meet the economic performance test. Therefore, taxes are generally deductible when paid regardless of a taxpayer's accounting method.[53]

The second issue relates to the state and foreign income taxes of individuals. All income taxes are considered to be the personal liability of the taxpayer. Therefore, even though a portion of an individual's income taxes may be allocable to a business (i.e., a sole proprietorship), an individual's income taxes will never be considered a business expense under § 162.[54]

5-6 CHARITABLE CONTRIBUTIONS

LO.6

Identify and measure deductible charitable contributions and determine corporate limitations on the contribution deduction.

Though charitable contributions are neither ordinary nor necessary business expenses, Congress allows all taxpayers to deduct certain contributions. By allowing a deduction, the government encourages taxpayers to support organizations that provide social welfare needs to communities (while reducing the costs that the government would incur to provide these services).[55] However, as most expenses deductible under § 162 are allowed without limitation or restriction, Congress expressly precludes contributions from falling under § 162 and instead addresses them separately, so as to define precisely what types of contributions are encouraged and how much encouragement will be provided.

A deduction is only available for contributions made to qualified organizations.[56] Qualified organizations include:

- A state or possession of the United States or any subdivisions thereof.

- A corporation, trust, or community chest, fund, or foundation located in the United States and organized and operated exclusively for religious, charitable, scientific, literary, or educational purposes or for the prevention of cruelty to children or animals.

[53]§ 1.461–4(g)(6).

[54]§ 1.162–1T(d); *Douglas H. Tanner* (1965) 45 T.C. 145; Rev.Rul. 70–40, 1970–1 C.B. 50; Rev.Rul. 58–142, 1958–1 C.B. 147.

[55]§ 170.

[56]§ 170(c).

In no case is a deduction allowed for a contribution made to an individual.

In-depth coverage can be found on this book's companion website: www.cengage.com   **7** DIGGING DEEPER

To qualify as a <mark>charitable contribution</mark>, a payment must be made with donative intent and with no expectation of a benefit or consideration being received from the organization. These requirements have potential consequences for the timing of the deduction. Recall that an accrual basis taxpayer may generally only deduct an expense when both the all events and economic performance tests are met. As no consideration results from a contribution, a contribution can never meet the economic performance test. Rather, contributions are usually only deductible when *paid* (regardless of the accounting method used by the taxpayer). However, an *accrual basis corporation* may claim the deduction in the year preceding payment if two requirements are met. First, the contribution must be *authorized* by the board of directors by the end of that year. Second, it must be *paid* on or before the due date of the corporation's tax return (i.e., the fifteenth day of the fourth month following the close of its taxable year).[57]

EXAMPLE 29

On December 28, 2018, Blue Company, a calendar year, accrual basis partnership, authorizes a $5,000 donation to the Atlanta Symphony Association (a qualified charitable organization). The donation is made on April 11, 2019. Because Blue Company is a partnership, the contribution can be deducted only in 2019.[58]

However, if Blue Company is a corporation and the December 28, 2018 authorization was made by its board of directors, Blue may claim the $5,000 donation as a deduction for calendar year 2018.

5-6a **Property Contributions**

A deduction is available for contributions of noncash property as well as cash. How a noncash contribution is measured depends on the type of property contributed. For this purpose, property must be identified as capital gain property or ordinary income property. <mark>Capital gain property</mark> is property that, if sold, would result in a long-term capital gain or § 1231 gain for the taxpayer. <mark>Ordinary income property</mark> is property that, if sold, produces income other than a long-term capital gain for the taxpayer. Examples of ordinary income property include inventory and capital assets held one year or less. Refer to Chapter 4 for a brief introduction to the distinction between capital and ordinary assets and Chapter 8 for a complete discussion of the nature of capital and § 1231 assets.

A contribution of noncash property is generally measured by the property's fair market value. This potentially allows taxpayers to include in the deduction any amount by which the property may have appreciated without also recognizing that appreciation as income. On the other hand, it prevents taxpayers from being able to recognize losses when contributing property that has depreciated. Therefore, rather than contributing depreciated property, taxpayers may want to sell the property, potentially allowing recognition of the loss, and donate the sale proceeds instead.

---

[57]§ 170(a)(2). Previously, the due date was the fifteenth day of the *third* month following the close of the corporation's tax year. In general, the new due date is effective for tax years beginning after 2015.

[58]Each partner will report an allocable portion of the charitable contribution deduction as of December 31, 2019 (the end of the partnership's tax year). See Chapter 14.

EXAMPLE 30

Mallard Corporation is considering making a contribution to Oakland Community College. Mallard owns a parcel of land, a capital asset, which it acquired five years ago for $60,000. If Mallard were to contribute the land to Oakland, Mallard would measure the contribution at the land's fair market value on the contribution date.

If the land's fair market value on the contribution date was $100,000, Mallard would be entitled to a deduction of $100,000, even though the $40,000 of appreciation on the land has never been included in Mallard's income.

Conversely, if the land's fair market on the contribution date was $20,000, Mallard would be entitled to a deduction of only $20,000. The decline in value of $40,000 is not allowed as a loss. In this case, Mallard may want to sell the land, recognize the $20,000 capital loss, and donate the sales proceeds to Oakland.

In some situations, a noncash contribution must be measured at the lesser of its fair market value or its adjusted basis (i.e., it must be measured without regard to any appreciation). These situations include the following:

- Contributions of ordinary income property and
- Contributions of capital gain property that is also tangible and personal, but only if the property is *not* used by the organization in activities related to its tax-exempt purpose.[59]

Contributions of Tangible Personal Property

EXAMPLE 31

White Corporation donates a painting worth $200,000 to Western States Art Museum (a qualified charity), which exhibits the painting. White had acquired the painting in 2001 for $90,000.

Because the museum put the painting to a related use, White is allowed to deduct $200,000, the fair market value of the painting.

EXAMPLE 32

Assume the same facts as in the previous example, except that White Corporation donates the painting to the American Cancer Society, which sells the painting and deposits the $200,000 proceeds in the organization's general fund.

White's deduction is limited to the $90,000 basis because it contributed tangible personal property that was put to an unrelated use by the charitable organization.

EXAMPLE 33

Black Corporation donates a painting worth $90,000 to the American Cancer Society which sells the painting and deposits the $90,000 proceeds into the organization's general fund. Black acquired the painting several years ago for $200,000.

Black's contribution is measured by the fair market value of the painting, but limited to its adjusted basis. As the painting's adjusted basis is greater than its fair market value, Black's contribution is $90,000. Further, Black recognizes no loss on the depreciation of the painting. Rather than contributing a depreciated asset to a qualified charity, a taxpayer should consider selling the asset, recognizing the loss, and donating the proceeds.

DIGGING DEEPER **8**   **In-depth coverage can be found on this book's companion website: www.cengage.com**

---

[59]The measurement of capital gain property contributed to certain private nonoperating foundations (defined in §§ 4942 and 509) is also limited to the basis of the property.

5-6b Limitations Imposed on Charitable Contribution Deductions

Both corporations and individuals are subject to annual limitations on the charitable contribution deduction.[60] The limitations for individual taxpayers are covered in Chapter 10.

For any tax year, a corporate taxpayer's contribution deduction is limited to 10 percent of taxable income. For this purpose, taxable income is computed without regard to the charitable contribution deduction, any net operating loss carryback or capital loss carryback, and the dividends received deduction. Any contributions in excess of the 10 percent limitation may be carried forward to the five succeeding tax years. Any carryforward is combined with the contributions made in the carryforward year with the total subject to the 10 percent limitation. In applying this limitation, the current year's contributions must be deducted first, with carryover amounts from previous years deducted in order of time.[61]

Annual Limitation and Carryover Rules Illustrated

EXAMPLE 34

During 2018, Orange Corporation (a calendar year taxpayer) had the following income and expenses.

Income from operations	$140,000
Expenses from operations	110,000
Dividends received	10,000
Charitable contributions made in May 2018	6,000

For purposes of the 10% limitation only, Orange Corporation's taxable income is $40,000 ($140,000 − $110,000 + $10,000). Consequently, the allowable charitable contribution deduction for 2018 is $4,000 (10% × $40,000). The $2,000 unused portion of the contribution can be carried forward to 2019, 2020, 2021, 2022, and 2023 (in that order) until exhausted.

EXAMPLE 35

Assume the same facts as in the previous example. In 2019, Orange Corporation has taxable income (for purposes of the 10% limitation) of $50,000 and makes a charitable contribution of $4,500. The maximum deduction allowed for 2019 is $5,000 (10% × $50,000). The entire 2019 contribution of $4,500 and $500 of the 2018 charitable contribution carryforward are currently deductible. The remaining $1,500 of the 2018 contribution may be carried over until it is used (or the 5-year carryforward period ends).

5-7 COST RECOVERY ALLOWANCES

LO.7

Determine the amount and timing of cost recovery available under MACRS, including additional cost recovery available in the year an asset is placed in service.

5-7a Overview

Taxpayers may deduct, or recover, the cost of certain assets that are used in a trade or business or held for the production of income. The deduction may take the form of a *cost recovery allowance* (depreciation under prior law), *depletion*, or *amortization*. Generally, the costs of tangible assets, other than natural resources, are recovered through cost recovery allowances. The costs of natural resources are recovered through *depletion*, and the costs of intangible assets are recovered through *amortization*. Generally, no deduction is allowed for an asset that does not have a determinable useful life.

The tax rules for recovering the cost of business assets differ from the financial accounting rules. Several methods are available for determining depreciation for financial accounting purposes, including the straight-line, declining-balance, and sum-of-the-years' digits methods. Historically, *depreciation* for tax purposes was computed using

---

[60]The percentage limitations applicable to individuals and corporations are identified in § 170(b).

[61]The carryover rules relating to all taxpayers are in § 170(d).

variations of these accounting methods. Congress completely revised the ==depreciation== rules in 1981 by creating the ==accelerated cost recovery system (ACRS)==, which shortened the period over which costs are recovered and allowed accelerated methods. In 1986, Congress made substantial modifications to ACRS, which resulted in the ==modified accelerated cost recovery system (MACRS)==.

Although the terms depreciation and ==cost recovery== are often used interchangeably, the former refers to the allocation of costs over the periods they benefit for financial reporting purposes while the latter refers to the recovery of cost for tax purposes. Because most assets whose cost is still being recovered were placed in service after 1986, this portion of the chapter focuses on the MACRS rules.

5-7b Cost Recovery: In General

Cost recovery is available only with respect to qualifying assets used in a business or for the production of income. Thus, identifying the particular assets that qualify and their basis is critical to determining the appropriate cost recovery deduction.

Nature of Property

MACRS provides separate cost recovery periods and methods for realty (real property) and personalty (personal property). *Realty* generally includes land and buildings permanently affixed to the land. *Personalty* is defined as any asset that is not realty. Personalty includes furniture, machinery, equipment, and any other asset that is movable. Personalty should not be confused with personal use property. Personal use property is any property (realty or personalty) that is held for personal use rather than for use in a trade or business or an income-producing activity. Cost recovery deductions are not allowed for personal use assets.

In summary, both realty and personalty can be either business use/income-producing property or personal use property. Examples include:

- A residence (realty that is personal use),
- An office building (realty that is business use),
- A dump truck (personalty that is business use), and
- Common clothing (personalty that is personal use).

Finally, assets used in a trade or business or for the production of income are eligible for cost recovery only if they are subject to wear and tear, decay or decline from

---

BRIDGE DISCIPLINE Bridge to Finance

For many business entities, success in producing goods for sale is dependent on the efficient use of fixed assets, such as machinery and equipment. An important question for such businesses to resolve is how they should gain access to the required complement of fixed assets: that is, whether the assets should be purchased or leased. To answer this question, the taxpayer must determine which alternative is more cost-effective. Critical to this assessment is quantifying the after-tax cost (including the associated tax benefits) of each option.

Purchasing productive assets for business use often necessitates an immediate cash outflow. However, the tax savings resulting from the available depreciation expense deductions mitigate the impact of that outflow by reducing the tax-payer's taxable income and the income tax paid for the year. Consequently, the tax savings from the depreciation calculation associated with the purchase of an asset reduce the after-tax cost of employing the asset. The analysis can be refined further by evaluating the tax savings from the depreciation deductions in present value terms by quantifying the tax savings from the depreciation expense over the life of the asset. The asset's purchase also can be financed with debt.

Taxpayers who lease rather than buy an asset benefit by not giving up the use of funds that otherwise would have gone to purchase the asset. Lessees also forgo the opportunity to claim depreciation deductions; however, they reduce the cost of the leasing option by claiming the lease expense as a deduction against their tax base.

natural causes, or obsolescence. Assets that do not decline in value on a predictable basis or that do not have a determinable useful life (e.g., land, stock, and antiques) are not eligible for cost recovery.

Placed in Service Requirement

An asset becomes eligible for cost recovery when it is placed in service rather than when it is purchased. This distinction is particularly important for an asset that is purchased near the end of the tax year, but not placed in service until the following tax year.

Cost Recovery Allowed or Allowable

To prevent the recovery of the same cost more than once (i.e., through periodic cost recovery during the asset's life and on the sale of the asset), the basis of property is reduced by any cost recovery deductions allowed. Furthermore, the adjusted basis of property is reduced by at least the amount of cost recovery that was allowable, or the amount that could have been taken using the appropriate cost recovery method. Therefore, even if a taxpayer fails to claim any allowable cost recovery in a given year, the basis of the property is still reduced by the amount of cost recovery that should have been claimed.

EXAMPLE

36

On March 15 in year 1, Heron, Inc., purchased, for $10,000, a copier, to use in its business. The copier is 5-year property, and Heron elected to use the straight-line method of cost recovery. Heron made the election because its business was new, and Heron reasoned that in the first few years of the business, a large cost recovery deduction was not needed.

Because the business was doing poorly, Heron did not deduct any cost recovery deductions in years 3 and 4. In years 5 and 6, Heron deducted the proper amount of cost recovery. The *allowed* cost recovery (cost recovery actually deducted) and the *allowable* cost recovery are computed as follows:[62]

	Cost Recovery Allowed	Cost Recovery Allowable
Year 1	$1,000	$ 1,000
Year 2	2,000	2,000
Year 3	–0–	2,000
Year 4	–0–	2,000
Year 5	2,000	2,000
Year 6	1,000	1,000
Totals	$6,000	$10,000

The adjusted basis of the copier at the end of year 6 is $0 ($10,000 cost – $10,000 *allowable* cost recovery). If Heron sells the copier for $800 in year 7, it will recognize an $800 gain ($800 amount realized – $0 adjusted basis).

Cost Recovery Basis for Personal Use Assets Converted to Business or Income-Producing Use

If personal use assets are converted to business or income-producing use, the basis for cost recovery and for loss is the lower of the adjusted basis or the fair market value at the time the property was converted. This rule ensures that any loss in value that occurred when the property was a personal use asset cannot be recognized through cost recovery of the property.

---

[62]The cost recovery allowances are based on the half-year convention, which allows a half-year's cost recovery in the first and last years of the recovery period.

The Big Picture

EXAMPLE 37

Return to the facts of *The Big Picture* on p. 5-1. Five years ago, Michael Forney purchased a personal residence for $250,000. In the current year, Michael found an attractively priced larger home that he acquired for his personal residence. Because of the downturn in the housing market, however, he was not able to sell his original residence and recover his purchase price of $250,000. The residence was appraised at $180,000.

Instead of continuing to try to sell the original residence, he converted it to rental property. The basis for cost recovery of the rental property is $180,000 because the fair market value is less than the adjusted basis. The $70,000 decline in value is deemed to be personal (because it occurred while the property was held for Michael's personal use) and therefore nondeductible.

5-7c Modified Accelerated Cost Recovery System (MACRS)

The IRS issues tables that provide annual cost recovery allowances based on the recovery periods, methods, and conventions specified in the Internal Revenue Code. Those tables are based on depreciation methods and conventions that should be familiar to most accounting students. These methods and conventions are discussed below and summarized in Concept Summary 5.1.

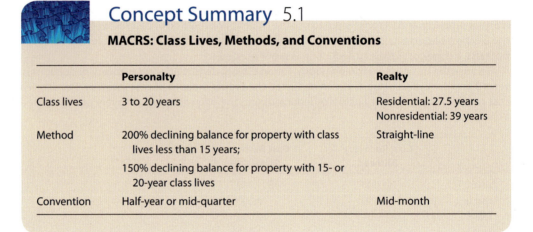

Concept Summary 5.1

MACRS: Class Lives, Methods, and Conventions

	Personalty	Realty
Class lives	3 to 20 years	Residential: 27.5 years Nonresidential: 39 years
Method	200% declining balance for property with class lives less than 15 years; 150% declining balance for property with 15- or 20-year class lives	Straight-line
Convention	Half-year or mid-quarter	Mid-month

5-7d MACRS for Personal Property

MACRS provides that the basis of eligible personalty (and certain realty) is recovered over 3, 5, 7, 10, 15, or 20 years.[63] Property included in the different cost recovery categories is shown in Exhibit 5.2.[64] Notice that the 10-, 15-, and 20-year categories tend to apply to assets used for special purposes or in specific industries. Most general-purpose assets have recovery periods of 5 or 7 years.

Cost recovery of personalty in all but the 15- and 20-year classes is based on double-declining-balance depreciation, switching to straight-line when using straight-line over the asset's remaining recovery period would yield a greater deduction. Cost recovery of property in the 15- and 20-year categories is based on the 150 percent declining-balance method.

Cost recovery of all personalty generally incorporates the **half-year convention**; that is, cost recovery in the year the asset is placed in service, as well as the year it is removed from service, is based on the assumption that the asset was used for exactly one-half of the year, allowing a half-year of cost recovery.[65] Thus, for example, the

---

[63]Personalty is assigned to recovery classes based on asset depreciation range (ADR) midpoint lives provided by the IRS (Rev.Proc. 87–56, 1987–2 C.B. 674). ADR lives generally represent estimates of an asset's useful economic life.

[64]§ 168(e) provides the ADR ranges included in Exhibit 5.2.

[65]§ 168(d)(4)(A).

MACRS recovery period for property with a class life of 3 years begins in the middle of the year the asset is placed in service and ends 3 years later. In practical terms, this means that the cost is actually recovered over 4, 6, 8, 11, 16, or 21 tax years.

As mentioned above, the appropriate methods and conventions are built into the tables provided by the IRS. Therefore, it is generally not necessary for a taxpayer to calculate the appropriate percentages. To determine the amount of the cost recovery allowance, simply identify the asset's MACRS class life and multiply its cost by the recovery percentage from the appropriate table. The only adjustment required is the application of the part-year convention in a year in which an asset is removed from service. The MACRS percentages for personalty are shown in Exhibit 5.4 (MACRS tables are located at the end of the chapter prior to the problem materials).

Taxpayers may *elect* to instead use the straight-line method to compute cost recovery allowances for each of these classes of property. Certain property is not eligible for accelerated cost recovery and must be depreciated under an alternative depreciation system (ADS). Both the straight-line election and ADS are discussed later in the chapter.

EXHIBIT 5.2	Cost Recovery Periods/Classes: Personalty

Class	Generally Includes Assets with the Following ADR Lives	Specific Inclusions
3-year	4 years or less	Tractor units for use over the road
		Any horse that is not a racehorse and is more than 12 years old at the time it is placed in service
		Special tools used in the manufacturing of motor vehicles, such as dies, fixtures, molds, and patterns
5-year	More than 4 years and less than 10 years	Automobiles and taxis
		Light and heavy general-purpose trucks
		Calculators and copiers
		Computers and peripheral equipment
7-year	10 years or more and less than 16 years	Office furniture, fixtures, and equipment
		Agricultural machinery and equipment
10-year	16 years or more and less than 20 years	Vessels, barges, tugs, and similar water transportation equipment
		Assets used for petroleum refining or for the manufacture of grain and grain mill products, sugar and sugar products, or vegetable oils and vegetable oil products
		Single-purpose agricultural or horticultural structures
15-year	20 years or more and less than 25 years	Land improvements
		Qualified improvement property
		Assets used for industrial steam and electric generation and/or distribution systems
		Assets used in the manufacture of cement
20-year	25 years or more	Farm buildings except single-purpose agricultural and horticultural structures
		Water utilities
		Railroad hydraulic and nuclear electric generating equipment

Half-Year Convention

EXAMPLE 38

Robin Corporation acquires a 5-year class asset on April 10, 2018, for $30,000. Robin's cost recovery deduction for 2018 is computed as follows:

MACRS calculation based on Exhibit 5.4 ($30,000 × .20) $6,000

EXAMPLE 39

Assume the same facts as in the previous example. Robin sells the asset on March 5, 2020. Robin's cost recovery deduction for 2020 is $2,880 [$30,000 × ½ × .192 (Exhibit 5.4)].

Mid-Quarter Convention

The half-year convention is based on the simplifying presumption that assets generally will be acquired evenly throughout the tax year. However, Congress was concerned that taxpayers might override that presumption by placing large amounts of property in service toward the end of the taxable year (and, by doing so, still receive a half-year's cost recovery allowance).

To inhibit this behavior, Congress added the **mid-quarter convention**. The mid-quarter convention applies if more than 40 percent of the cost of property other than real estate[66] is placed in service during the last quarter of the year.[67] Under this convention, property acquisitions are grouped by the quarter in which they were acquired for cost recovery purposes. Acquisitions made during the first quarter are allowed 10.5 months (three and one-half quarters) of cost recovery in the year in which they are placed in service; the second quarter, 7.5 months (two and one-half quarters); the third quarter, 4.5 months (one and one-half quarters); and the fourth quarter, 1.5 months. The percentages are shown in Exhibit 5.5.

EXAMPLE 40

Silver Corporation puts into service the following new 5-year class property in 2018.

Acquisition Dates	Cost
February 15	$ 200,000
July 10	400,000
December 5	600,000
Total	$1,200,000

Because more than 40% ($600,000/$1,200,000 = 50%) of the acquisitions are in the last quarter, the mid-quarter convention applies. Silver's cost recovery allowances for the first two years are computed as follows.

2018

	Mid-Quarter Convention Depreciation (Exhibit 5.5)		Total Depreciation
February 15	$200,000 × .35	=	$ 70,000
July 10	$400,000 × .15	=	60,000
December 5	$600,000 × .05	=	30,000
Total			$160,000

continued

---

[66]See MACRS for Real Estate (text Section 5-7e) for a discussion of eligible real estate.

[67]§ 168(d)(3).

	Mid-Quarter Convention Depreciation (Exhibit 5.5)		Total Depreciation
2019			
February 15	$200,000 × .26	=	$ 52,000
July 10	$400,000 × .34	=	136,000
December 5	$600,000 × .38	=	228,000
Total			$416,000

Without the mid-quarter convention, Silver's 2018 cost recovery deduction would have been $240,000 [$1,200,000 × .20 (Exhibit 5.4)]. The mid-quarter convention reduces the taxpayer's available cost recovery in the year an asset is placed in service.

When "mid-quarter" property is sold, the property is treated as though it were sold at the midpoint of the quarter. So in the quarter when sold, cost recovery is allowed for one-half of the quarter.

EXAMPLE 41

Assume the same facts as in the previous example, except that Silver Corporation sells the $400,000 asset on November 30, 2019. The cost recovery deduction for 2019 is computed as follows (Exhibit 5.5):

February 15	$200,000 × .26	=	$ 52,000
July 10	$400,000 × .34 × (3.5/4)	=	119,000
December 5	$600,000 × .38	=	228,000
Total			$399,000

The tax adjusted basis of the $400,000 asset when sold is $221,000 [$400,000 (cost) − $60,000 (2018 cost recovery) − $119,000 (2019 cost recovery)].

Qualified Improvement Property

Nonresidential realty has a 39-year life and any improvements made to this property would normally have a 39-year life. An exception to this general rule is provided for **qualified improvement property**. The cost of qualified improvement property is recovered over a 15-year period, using the half-year convention, and the straight-line method.

Qualified improvement property is any improvement to an interior portion of nonresidential real property made after the property is placed in service, including leasehold improvements.[68] However, it does not include the costs of elevators or escalators, or improvements that enlarge a building or modify its internal framework. The MACRS recovery percentages for qualified improvement property are included in Exhibit 5.7.

EXAMPLE 42

Redbud, Inc., finishes construction of an office building in July 2018. It plans to lease the third floor of the building to a tenant. In January 2019, Crimson Enterprises leases the third floor and immediately builds out the rental space to meet its needs. It spends $50,000 on cubicles, shelving, and other non-permanent additions. These improvements are qualified improvement property and will be cost recovered over 15 years, using the half-year convention and straight-line method.

Crimson's 2019 cost recovery deduction is $1,667 ($50,000 × .03333; see Exhibit 5.7 for cost recovery percentages).

Straight-Line Election

A taxpayer may *elect* to use the straight-line method for depreciable personal property.[69] If the straight-line method is elected, the basis of the property is recovered using the MACRS life of the asset with a half-year convention or a mid-quarter convention,

---

[68]§ 168(e)(6).   [69]§ 168(b)(5).

whichever applies. The election is available on a class-by-class and year-by-year basis. In other words, if the straight-line election is made for any property placed in service during a year, it must be applied to all property with the same class life put into service during that same year. The percentages for the straight-line election with a half-year convention appear in Exhibit 5.7.

Straight-Line Election

EXAMPLE 43

Terry puts into service a new 10-year class asset on August 4, 2018, for $100,000. He elects the straight-line method of cost recovery. Terry's cost recovery deduction for 2018 is $5,000 ($100,000 × .05). His cost recovery deduction for 2019 is $10,000 ($100,000 × .10). (See Exhibit 5.7 for the percentages.)

EXAMPLE 44

Assume the same facts as in the previous example, except that Terry sells the asset on November 21, 2019. His cost recovery deduction for 2019, which is subject to the half-year convention, is $5,000 [$100,000 × .10 × ½ (Exhibit 5.7)].

5-7e MACRS for Real Estate

Under MACRS, the cost of most real property is recovered using the straight-line method. The recovery period for residential rental real estate is 27.5 years. **Residential rental real estate** includes property where 80 percent or more of the gross rental revenues are from residential units (e.g., an apartment building). Therefore, hotels, motels, and similar establishments are not considered residential rental property. The basis of most non-residential real estate is recovered over 39 years.[70]

The cost of most MACRS real estate is recovered using the **mid-month convention**.[71] Under this convention, one-half month's cost recovery is allowed for the month the property is placed in service. If the property is sold before the end of the recovery period, one-half month's cost recovery is allowed for the month of sale (no matter when the property is sold). The cost of qualified improvement property is recovered using the half-year convention described above.

Like personalty, the IRS provides tables to help determine cost recovery on real property. Cost recovery is computed by multiplying the applicable rate by the cost recovery basis. The MACRS real property rates are provided in Exhibit 5.6.

Real Estate Cost Recovery

EXAMPLE 45

Badger Rentals, Inc., acquired a building on April 1, 1999, for $800,000. If the building is classified as residential real estate, the cost recovery deduction for 2018 is $29,088 (.03636 × $800,000).

If the building is sold on October 7, 2018, the cost recovery deduction for 2018 is $23,028 [.03636 × (9.5/12) × $800,000].

If the building is acquired on March 2, 1993, for $1 million and is classified as nonresidential real estate, the cost recovery deduction for 2018 is $31,740 (.03174 × $1,000,000).

If the building is sold on January 5, 2018, the cost recovery deduction for 2018 is $1,323 [.03174 × (.5/12) × $1,000,000]. (See the first two sections of Exhibit 5.6 for the percentages.)

---

[70]§§ 168(b), (c), and (e). A 31.5-year life is used for such property placed in service before May 13, 1993.

[71]§ 168(d)(1).

Real Estate Cost Recovery

EXAMPLE 46

Oakenwood Properties, Inc., acquired a building on November 19, 2018, for $1.2 million. If the building is classified as nonresidential real estate, the cost recovery deduction for 2018 is $3,852 (.00321 × $1,200,000). The cost recovery deduction for 2019 is $30,768 (.02564 × $1,200,000).

If the building is sold on May 21, 2019, the cost recovery deduction for 2019 is $11,538 [.02564 × (4.5/12) × $1,200,000]. (See the last section of Exhibit 5.6 for the percentages.)

In-depth coverage can be found on this book's companion website: **www.cengage.com**

9 DIGGING DEEPER

5-7f Election to Expense Certain Depreciable Assets (§ 179)

Section 179 permits the taxpayer to deduct up to $1,000,000 (in 2018; $510,000 in 2017) of the acquisition cost of specific types of property used in a trade or business. The **§ 179 expensing election** is an annual election that applies to the acquisition cost of property placed in service that year. Property covered by § 179 includes tangible personal property, computer software, qualified improvement property, and certain real property (roofs; heating, ventilation, and air conditioning units; fire protection and alarm systems; security systems). The immediate expense election is not available for property used for the production of income.[72] Amounts that are expensed under § 179 reduce the asset's basis for purposes of calculating additional first-year depreciation (see text Section 5-7g) and cost recovery under MACRS (see text Section 5-7d). As a result, any MACRS cost recovery deduction is calculated on the basis of the asset net of the § 179 expense *and* any additional first-year depreciation.

§ 179 Election and Basis

EXAMPLE 47

Allison acquires and places in service business equipment (a 5-year class asset) on February 1, 2018, at a cost of $1,080,000. It is the only asset she places in service in 2018. Assuming Allison elects § 179, she can deduct $1,000,000 of the asset's cost in 2018. She is also able to use MACRS to recover the remainder of its cost ($80,000) beginning in 2018.

2018	§ 179 deduction	$1,000,000
	MACRS: $80,000 × .20	16,000
	Total 2018 cost recovery	$1,016,000

EXAMPLE 48

Assume the same facts as in Example 47. Allison sells the asset in 2020 for $50,000. Her gain on the sale is $19,280, calculated as follows:

Selling price			$ 50,000
Cost		$1,080,000	
Less: Cost recovery			
2018	$1,016,000		
2019 $80,000 × .32	25,600		
2020 $80,000 × .192 × ½	7,680	(1,049,280)	(30,720)
Realized gain			$ 19,280

---

[72]The annual expense and phaseout amounts ($1 million and $2.5 million, respectively) apply to 2018. These amounts are adjusted for inflation beginning in 2019 and rounded to the nearest $10,000 multiple.

Deduction Limitations

The § 179 expense deduction is subject to three limitations, applied in the following order.

- **Ceiling Amount.** A taxpayer's § 179 deduction cannot exceed an annual ceiling amount ($1,000,000 in 2018; $510,000 in 2017).
- **Property Placed in Service Maximum.** The § 179 deduction ceiling amount is reduced dollar for dollar when § 179 property placed in service during the taxable year exceeds a specified maximum amount ($2,500,000 in 2018; $2,030,000 in 2017). In 2018, a taxpayer who places in service $3,500,000 or more of qualifying property ($1,000,000 + $2,500,000) will be unable to claim a § 179 deduction.
- **Business Income Limitation.** The § 179 deduction allowed for a taxable year cannot exceed the taxpayer's business income for the year.

These limitations are discussed and illustrated below.

Ceiling Amount. A taxpayer can choose to use *all, part, or none* of the annual § 179 amount. If a business expects its marginal tax rate to increase in the future, it may decide *not* to use the § 179 deduction. In such a situation, it may be better to defer deductions to those later years. As discussed below, the business income limitation may also lead a business owner to choose not to expense assets.

EXAMPLE 49

In 2018, Sonya Peters places in service $450,000 of 7-year MACRS assets. Although she could immediately expense all of these assets, she would prefer to use § 179 on just $275,000 of the assets. She knows that combining this $275,000 immediate expense with regular MACRS depreciation effectively reduces her business income to zero, and she wants to defer the remaining deductions to future years when her marginal tax rate will be higher. As a result, Sonya's total cost recovery deduction for 2018 is calculated as follows.

§ 179 expense	$275,000
MACRS depreciation [($450,000 − $275,000) × .1429 (Exhibit 5.4)]	25,008
Total cost recovery deduction	$300,008

Property Placed in Service Maximum. This rule effectively restricts the application of the § 179 deduction to smaller businesses. In 2018, a business that places in service more than $2,500,000 of qualifying property will have its § 179 deduction reduced, and a business that places in service $3,500,000 or more of qualifying property will have its § 179 deduction eliminated.

§ 179: Property Placed in Service Maximum

EXAMPLE 50

During 2018, Madison Sanders places $1,245,000 of § 179 property in service for use in her marketing consultancy. Madison can take a $1,000,000 § 179 expense election; there is no reduction in the § 179 amount since the property placed in service maximum ($2,500,000) was not reached.

EXAMPLE 51

During 2018, George Krull places $3,070,000 § 179 property in service for use in his manufacturing business (all assets are new 7-year MACRS assets). Because George placed in service more than the $2,500,000 maximum, he must reduce his § 179 deduction ($3,070,000 − $2,500,000 = $570,000). As a result, George's maximum § 179 deduction is $430,000 ($1,000,000 − $570,000). This reduction cannot be reclaimed in any way; it is permanently lost. George's total cost recovery deduction for 2018 is calculated as follows.

§ 179 expense	$430,000
MACRS depreciation [($3,070,000 − $430,000) × .1429 (Exhibit 5.4)]	377,256
Total cost recovery deduction	$807,256

continued

George also places in service a $1,500,000 office building during 2018. Will this have any effect on the calculation above? No. The building does not qualify for § 179. Only property qualifying for § 179 is used to determine whether the § 179 ceiling amount ($1,000,000 in 2018) is reduced.

Note: George can also take additional first-year (bonus) depreciation, if he chooses to do so. We will revisit this example after discussing bonus depreciation.

Business Income Limitation. The § 179 deduction allowed for a taxable year cannot exceed the taxpayer's business income for the year. For this purpose, business income is calculated by deducting all business expenses except the § 179 deduction. As a result, a taxpayer's § 179 deduction cannot create (or increase) a net operating loss. A taxpayer's "business income" includes not just income from a sole proprietorship, but also from wages and any allocated business income from a partnership or an S corporation.

During 2018, Lance Smith has a sole proprietorship through which he provides accounting and tax services that generated net income of $68,000. In addition, Lance is a 40% shareholder in a management consultancy operated as an S corporation. The S corporation pays Lance a salary of $40,000, and it recorded taxable income of $50,000. In this case, Lance's business income is $128,000 [$68,000 + $40,000 + $20,000 ($50,000 × 40%)].

Any § 179 amount in excess of taxable income is carried forward to future taxable years and added to other amounts eligible for expensing. Then the various limitations for that carryforward year are applied (i.e., the ceiling amount, the placed in service maximum amount, and the business income limitation).

Jill owns a computer service and repair business and operates it as a sole proprietorship. In 2018, taxable income is $138,000 before considering any § 179 deduction. If Jill spends $2.73 million on new equipment, her § 179 expense deduction for the year is computed as follows.

§ 179 deduction before adjustment	$1,000,000
Less: Dollar limitation reduction ($2,730,000 − $2,500,000)	(230,000)
Remaining § 179 deduction	$ 770,000
Business income limitation	$ 138,000
§ 179 deduction allowed	$ 138,000
§ 179 deduction carryforward ($770,000 − $138,000)	$ 632,000

Effect on Basis

The basis of the property for cost recovery purposes is reduced by the § 179 amount after accounting for the current-year amount of property placed in service in excess of the specified maximum amount ($2,500,000 for 2018). This adjusted amount does not reflect any business income limitation.

Assume the same facts as in Example 53. Jill's adjusted basis in the equipment for cost recovery purposes is $1,960,000 ($2,730,000 cost less the $770,000 § 179 expense amount before the business income limitation). If any portion of the $632,000 carryover (due to the business income limitation) is not deducted before the equipment is sold, this amount may be added back to the basis of the equipment in determining its adjusted basis.

FINANCIAL DISCLOSURE INSIGHTS   Tax and Book Depreciation

A common book-tax difference relates to the depreciation amounts that are reported for GAAP and Federal income tax purposes. Typically, tax depreciation deductions are accelerated; that is, they are claimed in earlier reporting periods than is the case for financial accounting purposes.

Several tax law changes since 1980 have included depreciation provisions that accelerate the related deductions relative to the expenses allowed under GAAP. Accelerated cost recovery deductions represent a means by which the taxing jurisdiction infuses the business with cash flow created by the reduction in the year's tax liabilities.

For instance, approximately one-third of the deferred tax liabilities recently reported by Ford have related to depreciation. Depreciation has recently accounted for approximately 85 percent of the deferred tax liabilities reported by General Motors and all but 1 percent of the deferred tax liabilities reported by trucking company Ryder Systems.

5-7g Additional First-Year Depreciation (Bonus Depreciation)

Congress uses the tax system to stimulate the economy—especially in challenging economic times. An example is **additional first-year depreciation** (also referred to as "bonus depreciation"). This provision allows taxpayers to deduct a percentage of the cost of qualified property in the year it is placed in service. In a significant expansion of this provision, the TCJA of 2017 allows taxpayers to immediately deduct 100 percent of the cost of qualifying property in the year it is placed in service.[73] Qualified property includes:[74]

- Tangible personal property,
- Computer software, and
- Qualified improvement property.

The additional first-year depreciation is taken after any immediate expense (§ 179) deduction is claimed. After the additional first-year depreciation is determined, the regular MACRS cost recovery allowance is calculated by multiplying the cost recovery basis (original cost recovery basis less additional first-year depreciation) by the appropriate MACRS percentage. A taxpayer may elect *not* to claim additional first-year depreciation.

EXAMPLE 55

Kelly acquires equipment (a new 5-year class asset) on February 1, 2018, at a cost of $1,345,000 and elects to expense $1,000,000 under § 179. Kelly also chooses to take bonus depreciation. As a result, her total cost recovery deduction for the year is calculated as follows.

§ 179 expense	$1,000,000
50% additional first-year depreciation [($1,345,000 − $1,000,000) × 100%]	345,000
Total cost recovery deduction	$1,345,000

Alternatively, Kelly could choose not to elect § 179 and still use bonus depreciation to recover the entire cost of the equipment in 2018.

---

[73]§ 168(k). Additional first-year depreciation is allowed for qualified property placed in service after 2011 and before 2027. The additional first-year depreciation percentage, 50% from 2012 to 2017, decreases to 80% in 2023, 60% in 2024, 40% in 2025, and 20% in 2026. No bonus depreciation will be allowed after 2026. Different rules applied between 2008 and 2011.

[74]For property placed in service after September 27, 2017, bonus depreciation applies to both new *and* used property. Prior law restricted bonus depreciation to property that was not used previously by another taxpayer.

5-7h Using § 179 and Bonus Depreciation Effectively

With 100 percent bonus depreciation available from 2018 through 2022, the majority of taxpayers will be able to immediately recover the cost of any MACRS personalty. However, there may be times when the taxpayer will find it better to defer some of these deductions into future years. This would be the case if the taxpayer expects marginal tax rates to increase over time. In addition, the limitations on excess business losses (see text Section 6-8) or the 80% of taxable income limit on net operating losses (see text Section 6-4) might lead a taxpayer to forgo § 179 and/or bonus depreciation.[75] If any of these conditions applies, then other considerations come into play.

Deferring MACRS Deductions to Future Years

Taxpayers may find it better not to use § 179 expensing and/or bonus depreciation to completely write off asset acquisitions. If taxpayers expect their marginal tax rates to increase over time (and in some instances, remain the same), it might be best to forgo § 179 expensing and/or bonus depreciation and instead defer the recovery of the eligible costs to future years using normal MACRS deductions.

EXAMPLE 56

Aditi Moore is married and operates a small business in Fairfax, Virginia. During the year, she purchases $500,000 of equipment (5-year MACRS assets) for use in her business. Aditi and her spouse report $510,000 of taxable income before considering any cost recovery related to the equipment. Their marginal tax rate is 32%.

Aditi is confident that her business will grow significantly over the next few years and expects her marginal tax rate to remain at least 32% during that time.

If Aditi takes $500,000 of bonus depreciation in 2018, she and her spouse will have tax savings of $125,579.* However, much of the bonus depreciation will offset income that would have been taxed at rates lower than 32%.

Another option is to take just enough cost recovery (both bonus depreciation and regular MACRS) to reduce the couple's taxable income from $510,000 to $315,000 (the bottom of the 32% rate bracket). We can determine this combined amount using the following formula.

Bonus depreciation + [($500,000 − Bonus depreciation) × 20% (first-year MACRS)] = $195,000

Solving for bonus depreciation yields $118,750. So, we can reduce the couple's taxable income to $315,000 by taking bonus depreciation of $118,750 and normal MACRS of $76,250 [($500,000 − $118,750) × 20%].

Even if we assume a 5% discount rate on future tax savings, Aditi and her spouse will save $150,036 in taxes by deferring some of the available cost recovery and using it to offset future income that would otherwise be subject to a 32% tax rate.

	2018	2019	2020	2021	2022	2023
Normal MACRS	$381,250	$381,250	$381,250	$381,250	$381,250	$381,250
MACRS factor	× .2000	× .3200	× .1920	× .1152	× .1152	× .0576
MACRS depreciation	$ 76,250	$122,000	$ 73,200	$ 43,920	$ 43,920	$ 21,960
Bonus depreciation	118,750	−0−	−0−	−0−	−0−	−0−
Total MACRS deduction	$195,000	$122,000	$ 73,200	$ 43,920	$ 43,920	$ 21,960
Marginal tax rate	× 32%	× 32%	× 32%	× 32%	× 32%	× 32%
Tax savings	$ 62,400	$ 39,040	$ 23,424	$ 14,054	$ 14,054	$ 7,027
PV factors @ 5% (Appendix F)	× 1.0000	× .9524	× .9070	× .8638	× .8227	× .7835
	$ 62,400	$ 37,182	$ 21,246	$ 12,140	$ 11,562	$ 5,506
Net present value	$150,036					

Overall, the combination of $118,750 bonus depreciation in 2018 plus normal MACRS depreciation in 2018 through 2023 provides a better outcome for Aditi and her spouse, generating $24,457 of tax savings in present value terms over the next six years ($150,036 tax savings by deferring MACRS deductions *less* $125,579 tax savings by using $500,000 of bonus depreciation in 2018).

* Tax on $510,000 = $126,579 {$64,179 + [($510,000 − $315,000) × 32%]}; tax on $10,000 = $1,000 ($10,000 × 10%).

---

[75]In addition, certain assets might not qualify for § 179 expensing or bonus depreciation.

Choosing Assets for Immediate Expensing

The § 179 deduction can be allocated to reduce the basis of qualifying assets in any manner the taxpayer chooses. This allows the deduction to be allocated proportionally across all assets acquired during the year or to specific assets identified by the taxpayer. This flexibility is important.

There are two general rules that might affect this choice. First, taxpayers should not use the § 179 election on automobiles. Automobiles are subject to special cost recovery rules (and annual limits), which are discussed later in this chapter. Second, given the time value of money, taxpayers should accelerate deductions to the earliest year possible. This is accomplished by expensing the assets with the *longest* MACRS lives first.

EXAMPLE
57

During 2018, Dexter purchases equipment (a new 7-year MACRS asset) costing $645,000 and a computer system costing $480,000 (a new 5-year MACRS asset). As the total amount of MACRS assets placed in service for the year ($1,125,000; $645,000 + $480,000) is less than $2,500,000, there is no reduction in the $1,000,000 § 179 deduction.

Dexter chooses not to take bonus depreciation. How should Dexter allocate his $1,000,000 § 179 expense election?

Dexter should expense the longest-lived MACRS asset first (the equipment; the 7-year MACRS asset). If he makes this choice, Dexter's total cost recovery deduction in 2018 is $1,025,000, calculated as follows.

Equipment (7-year MACRS asset)	
§ 179 expense	$ 645,000
Computer system (5-year MACRS asset)	
§ 179 expense ($1,000,000 − $645,000)	355,000
MACRS cost recovery [($480,000 − $355,000) × .2000 (Exhibit 5.4)]	25,000
Total cost recovery deduction	$1,025,000

If Dexter were to allocate the § 179 expense election to the machinery (MACRS 5-year property), his total cost recovery deduction in 2018 would be only $1,017,863, calculated as follows.

Computer system (5-year MACRS asset)	
§ 179 expense	$ 480,000
Equipment (7-year MACRS asset)	
§ 179 expense ($1,000,000 − $480,000)	520,000
MACRS cost recovery [($645,000 − $520,000) × .1429 (Exhibit 5.4)]	17,863
Total cost recovery deduction	$1,017,863

No matter which asset is expensed, after using both § 179 and bonus depreciation, $1,125,000 is subject to MACRS cost recovery. However, if the 7-year MACRS asset is expensed, this $125,000 is recovered over six tax years (here, the $125,000 relates to the 5-year MACRS asset). If the 5-year MACRS asset is expensed, the $125,000 will be recovered over eight tax years (here, the $125,000 relates to the 7-year MACRS asset). Using the § 179 expense election on the longest-lived asset accelerates overall cost recovery deductions to earlier years, gaining a time-value-of-money advantage for the taxpayer.

Using Both § 179 and Bonus Depreciation

In general, in 2018, a business that places in service $1,000,000 or less of qualifying § 179 property will exclusively use § 179 to immediately expense all of those assets, while a business placing in service $3,500,000 or more of qualifying assets (the point at which the § 179 amount is completely phased out; $1,000,000 + $2,500,000) will qualify only for bonus depreciation. Any business placing in service between $1,000,000 and $3,500,000 of qualifying § 179 property will be able to use a combination of both § 179 and bonus depreciation (see Concept Summary 5.2).[76]

---

[76]This general rule applies to the vast majority of taxpayers. However, it would not apply if the § 179 taxable income limitation applies or the taxpayer chooses to defer deductions to later tax years (e.g., if the taxpayer expects marginal tax rates to increase).

Concept Summary 5.2

Using § 179 and Bonus Depreciation

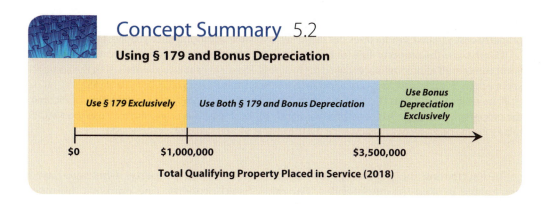

Total Qualifying Property Placed in Service (2018)

EXAMPLE 58

Return to the facts of Example 51. Given that George has placed $3,070,000 of assets in service during 2018, he can use both § 179 and additional first-year depreciation (see Concept Summary 5.2). If George uses both § 179 and bonus depreciation, his total cost recovery deduction will increase to $3,070,000, computed as follows.

§ 179 expense	$ 430,000
Additional first-year depreciation [($3,070,000 − $430,000) × 100%]	2,640,000
Total cost recovery deduction	$3,070,000

As discussed above, George might choose to use only a portion of the § 179 election and/or choose not to use bonus depreciation. However, it is possible for George to deduct all of his 2018 acquisitions immediately.

5-7i **Business and Personal Use of Automobiles and Other Listed Property**

LO.8

Identify and apply the cost recovery limitations applicable to automobiles and property used for personal purposes, including listed property.

Limits exist on cost recovery deductions for automobiles and other **listed property** used for both personal and business purposes.[77] If listed property is not *predominantly used* for business purposes when placed in service, it is not eligible for the accelerated methods built into MACRS, the immediate expense election (§ 179), or bonus depreciation.

If not *predominantly used* for business when first placed in service, the listed property's cost must be recovered using the *straight-line method* (see Exhibit 5.7). Further, the straight-line method must continue to be used even if, at some later date, the property *is* predominantly used for business.

Listed property includes:[78]

- Any passenger automobile.

- Most other property used as a means of transportation (e.g., trucks and airplanes).

---

[77]§§ 280F and 168(k)(2)(D).

[78]§ 280F(d)(4). Listed property also includes any computer or peripheral equipment if placed in service before December 31, 2017.

- Any property of a type generally used for purposes of entertainment, recreation, or amusement.
- Any other property specified in the Regulations.

Automobiles and Other Listed Property Used Predominantly in Business

For listed property to be considered as *predominantly used in business*, its *business use* must exceed 50 percent.[79] The use of listed property for production of income does not qualify as business use for purposes of the more-than-50% test. However, both production-of-income and business use percentages are used to compute the cost recovery deduction.

EXAMPLE 59

On September 1, 2018, Emma acquires and places in service listed 5-year recovery property. The property cost $10,000. Emma does not claim any available additional first-year cost recovery.

If Emma uses the property 40% for business and 25% for the production of income, the property is not considered as predominantly used for business. The asset cost is recovered using the straight-line method. Emma's cost recovery allowance for the year is $650 ($10,000 × .10 × .65).

If, however, Emma uses the property 60% for business and 25% for the production of income, the property is considered as used predominantly for business. Therefore, she may use the MACRS tables. Emma's cost recovery allowance for the year is $1,700 ($10,000 × .20 × .85).

In determining the percentage of business use of listed property, a mileage-based percentage is used for automobiles. For other listed property, one employs the most appropriate unit of time (e.g., hours) for which the property actually is used (rather than its availablility for use).[80]

Limits on Cost Recovery for Automobiles

The law places further limitations on the annual cost recovery deductions for *passenger automobiles*.[81] These dollar limits were imposed because of the belief that the tax system was being used to underwrite automobiles whose cost and luxury features far exceeded what was needed for the taxpayer's business use. Any cost otherwise recoverable but limited by the annual limitation may be recovered in later years subject to the limit applicable to the subsequent year.

The following "luxury auto" depreciation limits apply.[82]

Date Placed in Service	First Year	Second Year	Third Year	Fourth and Later Years
2018*	$10,000	$16,000	$9,600	$5,760
2012–2017	3,160	5,100	3,050	1,875
2010–2011	3,060	4,900	2,950	1,775

*Because the 2019 indexed amounts are not yet available, the 2018 amounts are used in the examples and end-of-chapter problem materials.

If a new passenger automobile otherwise qualifies for additional first-year depreciation, the *luxury auto* limitation increases by $6,400 in 2018.[83] Therefore, for acquisitions made in 2018, the initial-year cost recovery limitation increases from $10,000 to $16,400 ($10,000 + $6,400).[84]

---

[79]§ 280F(b)(3).

[80]Reg. § 1.280F–6T(e).

[81]§ 280F(d)(5). A passenger automobile is any four-wheeled vehicle manufactured for use on public streets, roads, and highways with an unloaded gross vehicle weight (GVW) rating of 6,000 pounds or less. This definition specifically excludes vehicles used directly in the business of transporting people or property for compensation (e.g., taxicabs, ambulances, hearses, and trucks and vans as prescribed by the Regulations).

[82]§ 280F(a)(1); Rev.Proc. 2014–21, 2014–11 I.R.B. 641. Cost recovery limitations for years prior to 2010 are found in IRS Publication 463.

[83]§ 168(k)(2)(F). The $6,400 amount was $8,000 in 2017 and will decrease to $4,800 in 2019. No increase in the first-year recovery limitation will be allowed after 2019.

[84]Different cost recovery limitations apply for trucks and vans, and for electric automobiles.

The luxury auto limits must be reduced proportionally for any personal use of the auto. In addition, the limitation in the first year includes any amount the taxpayer elects to expense under § 179.[85] If the passenger automobile is used partly for personal use, the personal use percentage is ignored for the purpose of determining the unrecovered cost available for deduction in later years.

EXAMPLE 60

On July 1, 2018, Dan acquires and places in service a new automobile that cost $55,000. He does not elect § 179 expensing and he elects not to take any available additional first-year depreciation. The car is used 80% for business and 20% for personal purposes in each tax year. Dan chooses the MACRS 200% declining-balance method of cost recovery (the auto is a 5-year asset; see Exhibit 5.4).

The depreciation computation for 2018 through 2023 is summarized in the table below. The cost recovery allowed is the lesser of the MACRS amount or the recovery limitation.

Year	MACRS Amount	Recovery Limitation	Depreciation Allowed	Depreciation Deferred	Cumulative Deferred Depreciation
2018	$8,800 ($55,000 × .2000 × 80%)	$8,000 ($10,000 × 80%)	$ 8,000	$ 800	$ 800
2019	$14,080 ($55,000 × .3200 × 80%)	$12,800 ($16,000 × 80%)	$12,800	$ 1,280	$2,080
2020	$8,448 ($55,000 × .1920 × 80%)	$7,680 ($9,600 × 80%)	$ 7,680	$ 768	$2,848
2021	$5,069 ($55,000 × .1152 × 80%)	$4,608 ($5,760 × 80%)	$ 4,608	$ 461	$3,309
2022	$5,069 ($55,000 × .1152 × 80%)	$4,608 ($5,760 × 80%)	$ 4,608	$ 461	$3,770
2023	$2,534 ($55,000 × .0576 × 80%)	$4,608 ($5,760 × 80%)	$ 4,608	$(2,074)	$1,696

If Dan continues to use the car after 2023, his cost recovery is limited to the lesser of the deferred depreciation or the recovery limitation (i.e., $5,760 × business use percentage). Thus, the recoverable basis as of January 1, 2024 is $1,696.

If Dan elects to take additional first-year depreciation in 2018, the amount of additional first-year depreciation is $44,000 ($55,000 × 80% × 100%). However, the deduction for the year would be limited to $13,120 [($6,400 + $10,000) × 80%].

Realize the cost recovery limitations are maximum amounts. If the regular MACRS calculation produces a smaller amount of cost recovery, the smaller amount is used.

EXAMPLE 61

On April 2, 2017, Gail places in service a pre-owned automobile that cost $10,000. The car is used 70% for business and 30% for personal use.

The cost recovery allowance for 2017 is $1,400 ($10,000 × .20 × 70%), not $7,000 (the $10,000 passenger auto maximum × 70%).

Limitation for Sport Utility Vehicles

Some sport utility vehicles (SUVs) are not considered passenger automobiles and, therefore, are not subject to the luxury automobile limitations. However, a $25,000 limit applies to the § 179 deduction when the luxury auto limits do not apply to an SUV. The limit is in effect for SUVs with an unloaded gross vehicle weight (GVW) rating of more than 6,000 pounds and not more than 14,000 pounds.[86]

---

[85]§ 280F(d)(1).

[86]§ 179(b)(6).

EXAMPLE 62

During 2018, Jay acquires and places in service a new SUV that cost $70,000 and has a GVW of 8,000 pounds. Jay uses the vehicle 100% of the time for business purposes. The total deduction for 2018 with respect to the SUV is computed as follows:

§ 179 expense, as limited	$25,000
Standard MACRS amount [($70,000 − $25,000) × .20 (Exhibit 5.4)]	9,000
Total cost recovery claimed	$34,000

If Jay chooses to use bonus depreciation on the SUV, then the entire $70,000 cost will be recovered in 2018 ($25,000 § 179 and $45,000 bonus depreciation).

Change from Predominantly Business Use

The cost of automobiles and other listed property not used predominantly (i.e., over 50 percent) in business must be recovered using the alternative depreciation system (i.e., using straight-line recovery over five years; see text Section 5-7j). If the business-use percentage of listed property falls to 50 percent or less after the year the property is placed in service, the property is subject to *cost recovery recapture*. The amount required to be recaptured (i.e., included in the taxpayer's ordinary income) is the excess cost recovery. *Excess cost recovery* is the excess of the cost recovery deductions taken in prior years over the amount that would have been allowed if the straight-line method had been used since the property was placed in service.[87]

EXAMPLE 63

Seth purchased a new car on January 22, 2018, at a cost of $20,000. Business use was 80% in 2018, 70% in 2019, 40% in 2020, and 60% in 2021. Seth elects not to take any available additional first-year depreciation. Seth's excess cost recovery to be recaptured as ordinary income in 2020 is:

2018

MACRS ($20,000 × .20 × 80%) (limited to $10,000 × 80%)	$ 3,200
Straight-line [($20,000 × .10 × 80%) (limited to $10,000 × 80%)]	(1,600)
Excess	$ 1,600

2019

MACRS ($20,000 × .32 × 70%) (limited to $16,000 × 70%)	$ 4,480
Straight-line ($20,000 × .20 × 70%) (limited to $16,000 × 70%)	(2,800)
Excess	$ 1,680

2020

2018 excess	$ 1,600
2019 excess	1,680
Ordinary income recapture	$ 3,280

After the business usage of the listed property drops below the more-than-50% level, the straight-line method must be used for the remaining life of the property.

EXAMPLE 64

Assume the same facts as in Example 63. Seth's cost recovery deduction for 2020 and 2021 is:

2020: $1,600 [($20,000 × .20 × 40%) limited to $9,600 × 40%]
2021: $2,400 [($20,000 × .20 × 60%) limited to $5,760 × 60%]

---

[87]§ 280F(b)(2).

Concept Summary 5.3 illustrates the cost recovery rules for various types of listed property.

Concept Summary 5.3

Listed Property Cost Recovery

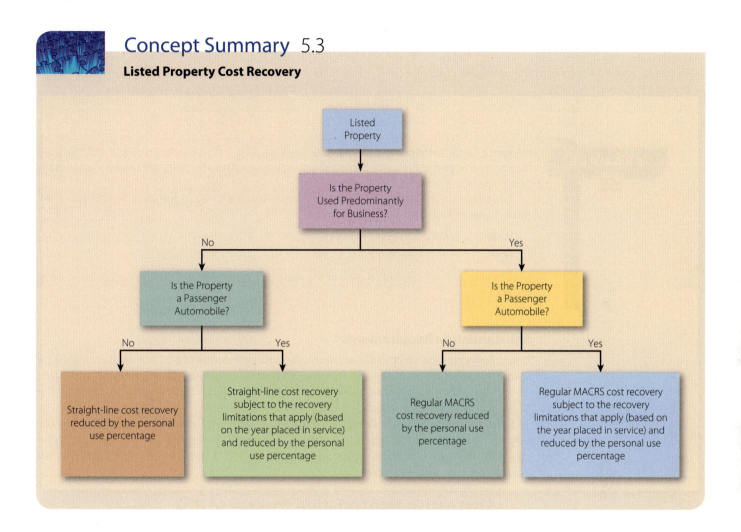

Leased Automobiles

Taxpayers who lease, rather than purchase, a passenger automobile for business purposes are not subject to the luxury auto limits. To prevent taxpayers from circumventing the luxury auto limits by deducting the lease payments associated with a luxury automobile leased for business, the Code requires these taxpayers to report an *inclusion amount* in gross income. The annual inclusion amount, found in tables issued by the IRS, is based on the fair market value of the automobile; it is prorated for the number of days the auto is used during the taxable year. The prorated dollar amount then is multiplied by the business and income-producing use percentage.[88] The taxpayer deducts the lease payments, multiplied by the business and income-producing usage percentage. In effect, the taxpayer's annual deduction for the lease payment is reduced by the inclusion amount.

---

[88]Reg. § 1.280F–7(a).

BRIDGE DISCIPLINE   **Bridge to Finance and Economics**

A new car, on average, loses a much larger portion of its value during the first five years through economic depreciation than it loses during later years. Depreciation accounts for about 35 percent of the ownership costs of a car during this five-year period.

Leasing a car will not eliminate the problem because the monthly lease payments are determined, in part, by the projected value of the car at the end of the lease. Because a new car loses its value faster in the earlier years, the shorter the lease, the higher the economic cost of depreciation.

EXAMPLE 65

On April 1, 2018, Jim leases and places in service a passenger automobile worth $52,400. The lease is to be for a period of five years. During the taxable years 2018 and 2019, Jim uses the automobile 70% for business and 30% for personal use.

Assuming that the inclusion amounts from the IRS table for 2018 and 2019 are $66 and $144, respectively, Jim includes in gross income:

2018: $66 × (274/365) × .70 = $35
2019: $144 × (366/365) × .70 = $101

In each year, Jim still can deduct 70% of the lease payments made, related to his business use of the auto.

Substantiation Requirements

Listed property is subject to the substantiation requirements of § 274. A taxpayer must be able to support for any business use the amount of expense or use, the time and place of use, the business purpose for the use, and the business relationship to the taxpayer of persons using the property.

Substantiation requires adequate records or sufficient evidence corroborating the taxpayer's statement. However, these substantiation requirements do not apply to vehicles that, by reason of their nature, are not likely to be used more than a *de minimis* amount for personal purposes.[89]

5-7j Alternative Depreciation System (ADS)

The **alternative depreciation system (ADS)** must be used:[90]

- For residential and nonresidential real estate and any qualified improvement property placed in service after 2017 by a "real property trade or business" that opts out of the interest expense limitations of § 163(j). In general, the interest expense limitation rules only apply to businesses with annual gross receipts in excess of $25 million.
- To calculate the portion of depreciation treated as an alternative minimum tax (AMT) adjustment (see Chapter 17).[91]
- To compute depreciation allowances as part of earnings and profits (see Chapter 13).

Generally, property is depreciated under the ADS using the straight-line method over a period longer than its MACRS recovery period (e.g., 5–12 years for personal property and 40 years for real property). However, for AMT, depreciation of personal property is computed using the 150 percent declining-balance method with a switch to the straight-line method when appropriate. Exhibits 5.8, 5.9, and 5.10 provide cost recovery rates under the ADS method.

---

[89]§§ 274(d) and (i).

[90]§ 168(g).

[91]This AMT adjustment applies for real and personal property placed in service before 1999. However, it continues to apply for personal property placed in service after 1998 if the taxpayer uses the 200% declining-balance method for regular income tax purposes.

TAX PLANNING STRATEGIES Structuring the Sale of a Business

FRAMEWORK FOCUS: TAX RATE

Strategy: Control the Character of Income and Deductions.

On the sale of a sole proprietorship where the sales price exceeds the fair market value of the tangible assets and stated intangible assets, a planning opportunity may exist for both the seller and the buyer.

The seller's preference is for the excess amount to be allocated to *goodwill* because goodwill is a capital asset whose sale may result in favorably taxed long-term capital gain. Amounts received for a *covenant not to compete*, however, produce ordinary income, which is not subject to favorable long-term capital gain rates.

Because a covenant and goodwill both are amortized over a statutory 15-year period, the tax results of a covenant not to compete versus goodwill are the same for the *buyer*. However, the buyer should recognize that an allocation to goodwill rather than a covenant may provide a tax benefit to the seller. Therefore, the buyer, in negotiating the purchase price, should factor in the tax benefit to the seller of having the excess amount labeled goodwill rather than a covenant not to compete. Of course, if the noncompetition aspects of a covenant are important to the buyer, a portion of the excess amount can be assigned to a covenant.

5-8 AMORTIZATION

LO.9
Identify intangible assets that are eligible for amortization and calculate the amount of the deduction.

Taxpayers can recover the costs of certain intangible assets through an **amortization** deduction. The amount of the deduction is determined by amortizing the adjusted basis of such intangibles ratably over a 15-year period beginning in the month in which the intangible is acquired.[92]

Section 197 covers the amortization of most intangibles. Amortizable *§ 197 intangibles* include most intangibles acquired after August 10, 1993, and acquired in connection with the acquisition of a business including goodwill, going-concern value, franchises, trademarks, copyrights, patents, and covenants not to compete. Generally, self-created intangibles are not § 197 intangibles.

The 15-year amortization period applies regardless of the actual useful life of an amortizable § 197 intangible. No other depreciation or amortization deduction is permitted with respect to any amortizable § 197 intangible except those permitted under the 15-year amortization rules.

On June 1, Sally purchased and began operating the Falcon Café. Of the purchase price, $90,000 is allocated to goodwill.

The year's § 197 amortization deduction is $3,500 [($90,000 ÷ 15) × (7/12)].

EXAMPLE
66

5-9 DEPLETION

LO.10
Determine the amount of depletion expense and specify the alternative tax treatments for intangible drilling and development costs.

Natural resources (e.g., oil, gas, coal, gravel, and timber) are subject to **depletion**, a form of cost recovery that applies to natural resources. Land generally cannot be depleted. Although all natural resources are subject to depletion, oil and gas wells are used as an example in the following paragraphs to illustrate the related costs and issues.

---

[92]§ 197(a).

In developing an oil or gas well, the producer typically makes four types of expenditures:

- Natural resource costs.
- Intangible drilling and development costs.
- Tangible asset costs.
- Operating costs.

Natural resources are physically limited, and the costs to acquire them (e.g., oil under the ground) are, therefore, recovered through depletion. Costs incurred in making the property ready for drilling, such as the cost of labor in clearing the property, erecting derricks, and drilling the hole, are **intangible drilling and development costs (IDCs)**. These costs generally have no salvage value and are a lost cost if the well is not productive (dry).

Costs for tangible assets such as tools, pipes, and engines are capitalized and recovered through depreciation (cost recovery). Costs incurred after the well is producing are operating costs. These costs include expenditures for items such as labor, fuel, and supplies. Operating costs are deductible as trade or business expenses. Intangible drilling and development costs and depletable costs receive different treatment.

5-9a Intangible Drilling and Development Costs (IDCs)

Intangible drilling and development costs can be handled in one of two ways at the option of the taxpayer. They can be either charged off as an expense in the year in which they are incurred or capitalized and written off through depletion. The taxpayer makes the election in the first year such expenditures are incurred, either by taking a deduction on the return or by adding them to the depletable basis.

Once made, the election is binding on both the taxpayer and the IRS for all such expenditures in the future. If the taxpayer fails to elect to expense IDCs, on the original timely filed return for the first year in which such expenditures are incurred, an irrevocable election to capitalize them has been made.

As a general rule, it is more advantageous to expense IDCs. The obvious benefit of an immediate write-off (as opposed to a deferred write-off through depletion) is not the only advantage. Because a taxpayer can use percentage depletion, which is calculated without reference to basis, the IDCs may be completely lost as a deduction if they are capitalized.

5-9b Depletion Methods

There are two methods of calculating depletion. *Cost depletion* can be used on any wasting asset (and is the only method allowed for timber). *Percentage depletion* is subject to a number of limitations, particularly for oil and gas deposits. Depletion should be calculated both ways, and the method that results in the larger deduction should be used. The choice between cost depletion and percentage depletion is an annual decision; the taxpayer can use cost depletion in one year and percentage depletion in the following year.

Cost Depletion

Cost depletion resembles units-of-production depreciation.[93] The basis is divided by the estimated recoverable units of the asset (e.g., barrels and tons) to arrive at the depletion per unit. This amount then is multiplied by the number of units sold (not the units produced) during the year to arrive at the cost depletion allowed.

---

[93]§ 612.

On January 1, 2018, Pablo purchases the rights to a mineral interest for $1 million. At that time, the remaining recoverable units in the mineral interest are estimated to be 200,000. The depletion per unit is $5 [$1,000,000 (adjusted basis) ÷ 200,000 (estimated recoverable units)].

If 60,000 units are mined and 25,000 are sold, the cost depletion is $125,000 [$5 (depletion per unit) × 25,000 (units sold)].

If the taxpayer later discovers that the original estimate was incorrect, the depletion per unit for future calculations is redetermined, using the revised estimate.[94]

Assume the same facts as in the previous example. In 2019, Pablo realizes that an incorrect estimate was made. The remaining recoverable units now are determined to be 400,000. Based on this new information, the revised depletion per unit is $2.1875 [$875,000 (adjusted basis) ÷ 400,000 (estimated recoverable units)]. The adjusted basis is the original cost ($1,000,000) reduced by the depletion claimed in 2018 ($125,000).

If 30,000 units are sold in 2019, the depletion for the year is $65,625 [$2.1875 (depletion per unit) × 30,000 (units sold)].

Percentage Depletion

Percentage depletion (also referred to as statutory depletion) uses a specified percentage provided by the Code. The percentage varies according to the type of mineral interest involved. A sample of these percentages is shown in Exhibit 5.3. The rate is applied to the gross income from the property, but in no event may percentage depletion exceed 50 percent of the taxable income from the property before the allowance for depletion.[95]

CarrolCo reports gross income of $100,000 and other property-related expenses of $60,000 and uses a depletion rate of 22%. CarrollCo's depletion allowance is determined as follows:

Gross income	$100,000
Less: Other expenses	(60,000)
Taxable income before depletion	$ 40,000
Depletion allowance [the lesser of $22,000 (22% × $100,000) or $20,000 (50% × $40,000)]	(20,000)
Taxable income after depletion	$ 20,000

The adjusted basis of CarrollCo's property is reduced by $20,000, the depletion deduction allowed. If the other expenses had been only $55,000, the full $22,000 could have been deducted, and the adjusted basis would have been reduced by $22,000.

Note that percentage depletion is based on a percentage of the gross income from the property and makes no reference to cost. All other cost recovery deductions detailed in this chapter are a function of the adjusted basis (cost) of the property. Thus, when percentage depletion is used, it is possible to claim aggregate depletion deductions that exceed the original cost of the property. If percentage depletion is used, however, the adjusted basis of the property (for computing cost depletion in a future tax year) is reduced by any depletion deducted, until the basis reaches zero.

---

[94]§ 611(a).

[95]§ 613(a). Special rules apply for certain oil and gas wells (e.g., the 50% ceiling is replaced with a 100% ceiling, and the percentage depletion may not exceed 65% of the taxpayer's taxable income from all sources before the allowance for depletion). § 613A.

EXHIBIT 5.3	Selected Percentage Depletion Rates

22% Depletion

Cobalt	Sulfur
Lead	Tin

15% Depletion

Copper	Oil and gas
Gold	Silver

10% Depletion

Coal	Perlite

5% Depletion

Gravel	Sand

TAX PLANNING STRATEGIES Switching Depletion Methods

FRAMEWORK FOCUS: DEDUCTIONS

Strategy: Maximize Deductible Amounts.

As long as the basis of a depletable asset remains above zero, cost depletion or percentage depletion, whichever method the taxpayer elects, is used. When the basis of the asset is exhausted, percentage depletion still can be taken.

EXAMPLE 70

Warbler Company reports the following related to its sulfur mine:

Remaining depletable basis	$ 11,000
Gross income (10,000 units)	100,000
Expenses (other than depletion)	30,000
Percentage depletion rate	22%

Because cost depletion is limited to the remaining depletable basis of $11,000, Warbler would choose percentage depletion of $22,000 [lesser of ($100,000 × 22%) or ($70,000 × 50%)]. The basis in the mine then becomes zero.

In future years, however, Warbler can continue to use percentage depletion; percentage depletion is computed without reference to the remaining asset basis.

5-10 COST RECOVERY TABLES

Summary of Cost Recovery Tables

Exhibit 5.4	Regular MACRS table for personalty.
	Recovery methods: 200 or 150 percent declining-balance switching to straight-line.
	Recovery periods: 3, 5, 7, 10, 15, 20 years.
	Convention half-year.
Exhibit 5.5	Regular MACRS table for personalty.
	Recovery methods: 200 percent declining-balance switching to straight-line.
	Recovery periods: 3, 5, 7 years.
	Convention mid-quarter.

Summary of Cost Recovery Tables (continued)

Exhibit 5.6	MACRS straight-line table for realty. Recovery method: straight-line. Recovery periods: 27.5, 31.5, 39 years. Convention mid-month.
Exhibit 5.7	MACRS straight-line table for personalty (optional) and qualified improvement property. Recovery method: straight-line. Recovery periods: 3, 5, 7, 10, 15, 20 years. Convention half-year.
Exhibit 5.8	ADS for alternative minimum tax: 150 percent declining-balance table for personalty. Recovery method: 150 percent declining-balance switching to straight-line. Recovery periods: 3, 5, 7, 9.5, 10, 12 years. Convention half-year.
Exhibit 5.9	ADS straight-line table for personalty. Recovery method: straight-line. Recovery periods: 5, 10, 12 years. Convention half-year.
Exhibit 5.10	ADS straight-line table for realty. Recovery method: straight-line. Recovery period: 30, 40 years. Convention mid-month.

EXHIBIT 5.4	MACRS Accelerated Depreciation for Personal Property Assuming Half-Year Convention (Percentage Rates)

For Property Placed in Service after December 31, 1986

Recovery Year	3-Year (200% DB)	5-Year (200% DB)	7-Year (200% DB)	10-Year (200% DB)	15-Year (150% DB)	20-Year (150% DB)
1	33.33	20.00	14.29	10.00	5.00	3.750
2	44.45	32.00	24.49	18.00	9.50	7.219
3	14.81*	19.20	17.49	14.40	8.55	6.677
4	7.41	11.52*	12.49	11.52	7.70	6.177
5		11.52	8.93*	9.22	6.93	5.713
6		5.76	8.92	7.37	6.23	5.285
7			8.93	6.55*	5.90*	4.888
8			4.46	6.55	5.90	4.522
9				6.56	5.91	4.462*
10				6.55	5.90	4.461
11				3.28	5.91	4.462
12					5.90	4.461
13					5.91	4.462
14					5.90	4.461
15					5.91	4.462
16					2.95	4.461
17						4.462
18						4.461
19						4.462
20						4.461
21						2.231

*Switchover to straight-line depreciation.

EXHIBIT 5.5	**MACRS Accelerated Depreciation for Personal Property Assuming Mid-Quarter Convention (Percentage Rates)**

For Property Placed in Service after December 31, 1986 (Partial Table*)

3-Year				
Recovery Year	First Quarter	Second Quarter	Third Quarter	Fourth Quarter
1	58.33	41.67	25.00	8.33
2	27.78	38.89	50.00	61.11

5-Year				
Recovery Year	First Quarter	Second Quarter	Third Quarter	Fourth Quarter
1	35.00	25.00	15.00	5.00
2	26.00	30.00	34.00	38.00

7-Year				
Recovery Year	First Quarter	Second Quarter	Third Quarter	Fourth Quarter
1	25.00	17.85	10.71	3.57
2	21.43	23.47	25.51	27.55

*The figures in this table are taken from the official tables that appear in Rev.Proc. 87–57, 1987–2 C.B. 687. Because of their length, the complete tables are not presented.

EXHIBIT 5.6	**MACRS Straight-Line Depreciation for Real Property Assuming Mid-Month Convention***

For Property Placed in Service after December 31, 1986: 27.5-Year Residential Real Property

Recovery Year(s)	The Applicable Percentage Is (Use the Column for the Month in the First Year the Property Is Placed in Service):											
	1	2	3	4	5	6	7	8	9	10	11	12
1	3.485	3.182	2.879	2.576	2.273	1.970	1.667	1.364	1.061	0.758	0.455	0.152
2–18	3.636	3.636	3.636	3.636	3.636	3.636	3.636	3.636	3.636	3.636	3.636	3.636
19–27	3.637	3.637	3.637	3.637	3.637	3.637	3.637	3.637	3.637	3.637	3.637	3.637
28	1.970	2.273	2.576	2.879	3.182	3.485	3.636	3.636	3.636	3.636	3.636	3.636
29	0.000	0.000	0.000	0.000	0.000	0.000	0.152	0.455	0.758	1.061	1.364	1.667

For Property Placed in Service after December 31, 1986, and before May 13, 1993: 31.5-Year Nonresidential Real Property

Recovery Year(s)	The Applicable Percentage Is (Use the Column for the Month in the First Year the Property Is Placed in Service):											
	1	2	3	4	5	6	7	8	9	10	11	12
1	3.042	2.778	2.513	2.249	1.984	1.720	1.455	1.190	0.926	0.661	0.397	0.132
2–19	3.175	3.175	3.175	3.175	3.175	3.175	3.175	3.175	3.175	3.175	3.175	3.175
20–31	3.174	3.174	3.174	3.174	3.174	3.174	3.174	3.174	3.174	3.174	3.174	3.174
32	1.720	1.984	2.249	2.513	2.778	3.042	3.175	3.175	3.175	3.175	3.175	3.175
33	0.000	0.000	0.000	0.000	0.000	0.000	0.132	0.397	0.661	0.926	1.190	1.455

For Property Placed in Service after May 12, 1993: 39-Year Nonresidential Real Property

Recovery Year(s)	The Applicable Percentage Is (Use the Column for the Month in the First Year the Property Is Placed in Service):											
	1	2	3	4	5	6	7	8	9	10	11	12
1	2.461	2.247	2.033	1.819	1.605	1.391	1.177	0.963	0.749	0.535	0.321	0.107
2–39	2.564	2.564	2.564	2.564	2.564	2.564	2.564	2.564	2.564	2.564	2.564	2.564
40	0.107	0.321	0.535	0.749	0.963	1.177	1.391	1.605	1.819	2.033	2.247	2.461

*The official tables contain a separate row for each year. For ease of presentation, certain years are grouped in these tables. In some instances, this will produce a difference of .001 for the last digit when compared with the official tables.

EXHIBIT 5.7	MACRS Straight-Line Depreciation for Personal Property and Qualified Improvement Property Assuming Half-Year Convention*

For Property Placed in Service after December 31, 1986

MACRS Class	% First Recovery Year	Other Recovery Years		Last Recovery Year	
		Years	%	Year	%
3-year	16.67	2–3	33.33	4	16.67
5-year	10.00	2–5	20.00	6	10.00
7-year	7.14	2–7	14.29	8	7.14
10-year	5.00	2–10	10.00	11	5.00
15-year	3.33	2–15	6.67	16	3.33
20-year	2.50	2–20	5.00	21	2.50

*The official table contains a separate row for each year. For ease of presentation, certain years are grouped in this table. In some instances, this will produce a difference of .01 for the last digit when compared with the official table.

Note: The last two rows are used for qualified improvement property (15-year normal MACRS; 20-year ADS).

EXHIBIT 5.8	ADS for Alternative Minimum Tax: 150% Declining-Balance for Personal Property Assuming Half-Year Convention (Percentage Rates)

For Property Placed in Service after December 31, 1986 (Partial Table*)

Recovery Year	3-Year 150%	5-Year 150%	7-Year 150%	9.5-Year 150%	10-Year 150%	12-Year 150%
1	25.00	15.00	10.71	7.89	7.50	6.25
2	37.50	25.50	19.13	14.54	13.88	11.72
3	25.00**	17.85	15.03	12.25	11.79	10.25
4	12.50	16.66**	12.25**	10.31	10.02	8.97
5		16.66	12.25	9.17**	8.74**	7.85
6		8.33	12.25	9.17	8.74	7.33**
7			12.25	9.17	8.74	7.33
8			6.13	9.17	8.74	7.33
9				9.17	8.74	7.33
10				9.16	8.74	7.33
11					4.37	7.32
12						7.33
13						3.66

*The figures in this table are taken from the official table that appears in Rev.Proc. 87–57, 1987–2 C.B. 687. Because of its length, the complete table is not presented.

**Switchover to straight-line depreciation.

EXHIBIT 5.9	ADS Straight-Line for Personal Property Assuming Half-Year Convention (Percentage Rates)

For Property Placed in Service after December 31, 1986 (Partial Table)*

Recovery Year	5-Year Class	10-Year Class	12-Year Class
1	10.00	5.00	4.17
2	20.00	10.00	8.33
3	20.00	10.00	8.33
4	20.00	10.00	8.33
5	20.00	10.00	8.33
6	10.00	10.00	8.33
7		10.00	8.34
8		10.00	8.33
9		10.00	8.34
10		10.00	8.33
11		5.00	8.34
12			8.33
13			4.17

*The figures in this table are taken from the official table that appears in Rev.Proc. 87–57, 1987–2 C.B. 687. Because of its length, the complete table is not presented. The tables for the mid-quarter convention also appear in Rev.Proc. 87–57.

EXHIBIT 5.10	ADS Straight-Line for Real Property Assuming Mid-Month Convention (Percentage Rates)

For Property Placed in Service after December 31, 2017; 30-Year Residential Rental Property

Recovery Year	Month Placed in Service											
	1	2	3	4	5	6	7	8	9	10	11	12
1	3.194	2.917	2.639	2.361	2.083	1.806	1.528	1.250	0.972	0.694	0.417	0.139
2–30	3.333	3.333	3.333	3.333	3.333	3.333	3.333	3.333	3.333	3.333	3.333	3.333
31	0.139	0.417	0.694	0.972	1.250	1.528	1.806	2.083	2.361	2.639	2.917	3.194

For Property Placed in Service after December 31, 1986; 40-Year Nonresidential Real Property*

Recovery Year	Month Placed in Service											
	1	2	3	4	5	6	7	8	9	10	11	12
1	2.396	2.188	1.979	1.771	1.563	1.354	1.146	0.938	0.729	0.521	0.313	0.104
2–40	2.500	2.500	2.500	2.500	2.500	2.500	2.500	2.500	2.500	2.500	2.500	2.500
41	0.104	0.312	0.521	0.729	0.937	1.146	1.354	1.562	1.771	1.979	2.187	2.396

* Also used for residential rental property placed in service before 2018.

REFOCUS ON THE BIG PICTURE

CALCULATING DEDUCTIBLE EXPENSES

In general, the expenses incurred in Michael Forney's small engine service and repair business are deductible as long as they are ordinary and necessary expenses. In addition, the salaries and wages paid must be reasonable. However, his plan to increase salaries radically next year for himself and his mother probably should not be pursued, because most or all of the increase could be considered unreasonable. Charitable contributions generally are limited to 10 percent of taxable income before the charitable

continued

contribution deduction, and political contributions and the fine are not deductible. The dues paid to Small Engine Repair Institute are not fully deductible because 70 percent of the organization's efforts relate to lobbying activities. However, the amount paid to consultants to investigate a new business opportunity is fully deductible as an ordinary and necessary business expense.

Michael can elect to expense the costs of the machinery and equipment under the provisions of § 179. For the current year, assume the § 179 deduction is limited to $1,000,000 and cannot exceed the taxable income derived from the business (before the § 179 deduction). In this case, the entire purchase price of $130,000 is deductible.

Gross income	$ 435,500
Less: Salaries and wages	(150,000)
Building rent	(24,000)
§ 179 deduction	(130,000)
Insurance	(6,000)
Consulting fees	(6,000)
Utilities	(12,000)
Taxes and licenses	(6,000)
Advertising	(3,000)
Interest expense	(3,000)
Dues paid to Small Engine Repair Institute	(3,000)
Taxable income before the charitable contribution deduction	$ 92,500
Less: Charitable contributions	(3,000)
Taxable income	$ 89,500

As to Michael's rental properties, he will be required to report all associated rent income and expenses, including depreciation on the house he converted from personal use to rental use and on the rental condo he purchased.

What If?

Instead assume that Mr. Forney purchased and placed in service this year $142,000 of new machinery and equipment of the type that qualifies for the § 179 deduction. In addition, Michael thinks that he can justify increasing his salary to $115,500 because of special expertise he developed recently, which will increase total salaries and wages to $210,500. Michael still can elect to expense all $142,000 of the cost of the machinery and equipment under § 179. In other words, the machinery and equipment will not be depreciated using the additional first-year depreciation or regular MACRS rules. As a result of the increased salary and § 179 deductions, the charitable contribution deduction now is limited to $2,000. The remainder ($1,000) is carried over to the next tax year.

Gross income	$ 435,500
Less: Salaries and wages	(210,500)
Building rent	(24,000)
§ 179 deduction	(142,000)
Insurance	(6,000)
Consulting fees	(6,000)
Utilities	(12,000)
Taxes and licenses	(6,000)
Advertising	(3,000)
Interest expense	(3,000)
Dues paid to Small Engine Repair Institute	(3,000)
Taxable income before the charitable contribution deduction	$ 20,000
Less: Charitable contributions (limited to 10% of taxable income)	(2,000)
Taxable income	$ 18,000

Suggested Readings

Bradley T. Borden and Cali A. Lieberman, "Section 179(f) Deductions and Recapture of Costs of Qualified Real Property," *Journal of Taxation*, January 2014.

Robert W. Jamison and Christopher W. Hesse, "Controlled Groups and the Sec. 179 Election for S Corporations," *The Tax Adviser*, November 2013.

John M. Malloy, Craig J. Langstraat, and James M. Plečnik, "Major Developments in Cost Segregation," *The Tax Adviser*, April 2014.

Kreig D. Mitchell, "The R&D Tax Credit for Start-Up Companies," *Practical Tax Strategies*, February 2012.

Debra T. Sinclair and Britton A. McKay, "Excess Compensation and the Independent Investor Test," *Practical Tax Strategies*, April 2013.

Christian Wood, "Implementing the New Tangible Property Regulations: The Revised 'Repair Regs' Require Thorough Assessment," *Journal of Accountancy*, January 2014.

Key Terms

Accelerated cost recovery system (ACRS), 5-22

Additional first-year depreciation, 5-32

Alternative depreciation system (ADS), 5-40

Amortization, 5-41

Capital gain property, 5-19

Charitable contribution, 5-19

Cost depletion, 5-42

Cost recovery, 5-22

Depletion, 5-41

Depreciation, 5-22

Half-year convention, 5-24

Intangible drilling and development costs (IDCs), 5-42

Listed property, 5-35

Mid-month convention, 5-28

Mid-quarter convention, 5-26

Modified accelerated cost recovery system (MACRS), 5-22

Ordinary and necessary, 5-2

Ordinary income property, 5-19

Percentage depletion, 5-43

Qualified improvement property, 5-27

Reasonableness requirement, 5-3

Related-party transactions, 5-6

Research and experimental expenditures, 5-15

Residential rental real estate, 5-28

Section 179 expensing election, 5-29

Startup expenditures, 5-11

Computational Exercises

1. **LO.1** Shanna, a calendar year and cash basis taxpayer, rents property from Janice. As part of the rental agreement, Shanna pays $8,400 rent on April 1, 2018, for the 12 months ending March 31, 2019.

    a. How much is Shanna's deduction for rent expense in 2018?

    b. Assume the same facts, except that the $8,400 is for 24 months rent ending March 31, 2020. How much is Shanna's deduction for rent expense in 2018?

2. **LO.3** Vella owns and operates an illegal gambling establishment. In connection with this activity, he has the following expenses during the year:

Rent	$ 24,000
Bribes	40,000
Travel expenses	4,000
Utilities	18,000
Wages	230,000
Payroll taxes	13,800
Property insurance	1,600
Illegal kickbacks	22,000

What are Vella's total deductible expenses for tax purposes?

3. **LO.3** Stanford owns and operates two dry cleaning businesses. He travels to Boston to discuss acquiring a restaurant. Later in the month, he travels to New York to discuss acquiring a bakery. Stanford does not acquire the restaurant but does purchase the bakery on November 1, 2018. Stanford incurred the following expenses:

Total investigation costs related to the restaurant	$28,000
Total investigation costs related to the bakery	51,000

What is the maximum amount Stanford can deduct in 2018 for investigation expenses?

4. **LO.4** Sandstorm Corporation decides to develop a new line of paints. The project begins in 2018. Sandstorm incurs the following expenses in 2018 in connection with the project:

Salaries	$85,000
Materials	30,000
Depreciation on equipment	12,500

The benefits from the project will be realized starting in July 2019. If Sandstorm Corporation chooses to defer and amortize its research and experimental expenditures over a period of 60 months, what are its related deductions in 2018 and 2019?

5. **LO.6** Tabitha sells real estate on March 2 for $260,000. The buyer, Ramona, pays the real estate taxes of $5,200 for the calendar year, which is the real estate property tax year. Assume that this is not a leap year.
   a. Determine the real estate taxes apportioned to and deductible by the seller, Tabitha, and the amount of taxes deductible by Ramona.
   b. Calculate Ramona's basis in the property and the amount realized by Tabitha from the sale.

6. **LO.7** Hamlet acquires a 7-year class asset on November 23, 2018, for $100,000. Hamlet does not elect immediate expensing under § 179. He does not claim any available additional first-year depreciation. Calculate Hamlet's cost recovery deductions for 2018 and 2019.

7. **LO.7** Lopez acquired a building on June 1, 2012, for $1 million. Calculate Lopez's cost recovery deduction for 2018 if the building is:
   a. Classified as residential rental real estate.
   b. Classified as nonresidential real estate.

8. **LO.7** In 2018, McKenzie purchased qualifying equipment for his business that cost $212,000. The taxable income of the business for the year is $5,600 before consideration of any § 179 deduction.
   a. Calculate McKenzie's § 179 expense deduction for 2018 and any carryover to 2019.
   b. How would your answer change if McKenzie decided to use additional first-year (bonus) depreciation on the equipment?

9. **LO.8** On April 5, 2018, Kinsey places in service a new automobile that cost $36,000. He does not elect § 179 expensing, and he elects not to take any available additional first-year depreciation. The car is used 70% for business and 30% for personal use in each tax year.
   Kinsey chooses the MACRS 200% declining-balance method of cost recovery (the auto is a 5-year asset). Assume the following luxury automobile limitations: year 1: $10,000; year 2: $16,000. Compute the total depreciation allowed for 2018 and 2019.

10. **LO.10** Jebali Company reports gross income of $340,000 and other property-related expenses of $229,000 and uses a depletion rate of 14%. Calculate Jebali's depletion allowance for the current year.

Problems

11. **LO.2** Duck, an accrual basis corporation, sponsored a rock concert on December 29, 2018. Gross receipts were $300,000. The following expenses were incurred and paid as indicated:

Expense		Payment Date
Rental of coliseum	$ 25,000	December 21, 2018
Cost of goods sold:		
Food	30,000	December 30, 2018
Souvenirs	60,000	December 30, 2018
Performers	100,000	January 5, 2019
Cleaning of coliseum	10,000	February 1, 2019

Because the coliseum was not scheduled to be used again until January 15, the company with which Duck had contracted did not perform the cleanup until January 8–10, 2019.

Calculate Duck's net income from the concert for tax purposes for 2018.

12. **LO.2** Which of the following are related parties under § 267?

Father
Brother
Niece
Uncle
Cousin
Grandson
Corporation and a 45% shareholder
Corporation and a 55% shareholder

13. **LO.2, 3** Robin Corporation is owned as follows:

Isabelle	26%
Peter, Isabelle's husband	19%
Sonya, Isabelle's mother	15%
Reggie, Isabelle's father	25%
Quinn, an unrelated party	15%

Robin is on the accrual basis, and Isabelle and Peter are on the cash basis. Isabelle and Peter each loaned Robin Corporation $40,000 out of their separate funds. On December 31, 2018, Robin accrued interest at 7% on both loans. The interest was paid on February 4, 2019. What is the tax treatment of this interest expense/income to Isabelle, Peter, and Robin?

Decision Making
Communications
Critical Thinking

14. **LO.2, 3** Brittany Callihan sold stock (basis of $184,000) to her son, Ridge, for $160,000, the fair market value.

a. What are the tax consequences to Brittany?
b. What are the tax consequences to Ridge if he later sells the stock for $190,000? For $152,000? For $174,000?
c. Write a letter to Brittany in which you inform her of the tax consequences if she sells the stock to Ridge for $160,000. Explain how a sales transaction could be structured that would produce better tax consequences for her. Brittany's address is 32 Country Lane, Lawrence, KS 66045.

15. **LO.2, 3** For each of the following independent transactions, calculate the recognized gain or loss to the seller and the adjusted basis to the buyer.

a. Kiera sells Parchment, Inc. stock (adjusted basis $17,000) to Phillip, her brother, for its fair market value of $12,000.

b. Amos sells land (adjusted basis $85,000) to his nephew, Boyd, for its fair market value of $70,000.

c. Susan sells a tax-exempt bond (adjusted basis $20,000) to her wholly owned corporation for its fair market value of $19,000.

d. Sinbad sells a business truck (adjusted basis $20,000) that he uses in his sole proprietorship to his cousin, Agnes, for its fair market value of $18,500.

e. Martha sells her partnership interest (adjusted basis $175,000) in Pearl Partnership to her adult daughter, Kim, for $220,000.

16. **LO.2, 3** Lupe, a cash basis taxpayer, owns 55% of the stock of Jasper Corporation, a calendar year accrual basis C corporation. On December 31, 2018, Jasper accrues a performance bonus of $100,000 to Lupe that it pays to him on January 15, 2019. In which year can Jasper deduct the bonus? In which year must Lupe include the bonus in gross income?

17. **LO.2, 3** Broadbill Corporation, a calendar year C corporation, has two unrelated cash method shareholders: Marcia owns 51% of the stock, and Zack owns the remaining 49%. Each shareholder is employed by the corporation at an annual salary of $240,000. During 2018, Broadbill paid each shareholder-employee $220,000 of his or her annual salary, with the remaining $20,000 paid in January 2019. How much of the 2018 salaries for Marcia and Zack is deductible by Broadbill in 2018 if the corporation is:

a. A cash method taxpayer?

b. An accrual method taxpayer?

18. **LO.3** Angelo, an agent for Waxwing Corporation, which is an airline manufacturer,   **Critical Thinking** is negotiating a sale with a representative of the U.S. government and with a representative of a developing country. Waxwing has sufficient capacity to handle only one of the orders. Both orders will have the same contract price. Angelo believes that if Waxwing authorizes a $500,000 payment to the representative of the foreign country, he can guarantee the sale. He is not sure that he can obtain the same result with the U.S. government. Identify the relevant tax issues for Waxwing.

19. **LO.3** Linda operates an illegal gambling operation and incurs the following expenses. Which of these expenses can reduce her taxable income?

a. Bribes paid to city employees.

b. Salaries to employees.

c. Security cameras.

d. Kickbacks to police.

e. Rent on an office.

f. Depreciation on office furniture and equipment.

g. Tenant's casualty insurance.

h. Utilities.

20. **LO.3** Cardinal Corporation is a trucking firm that operates in the mid-Atlantic states.   **Ethics and Equity** One of Cardinal's major customers frequently ships goods between Charlotte and Baltimore. Occasionally, the customer sends last-minute shipments that are outbound for Europe on a freighter sailing from Baltimore. To satisfy the delivery schedule in these cases, Cardinal's drivers must substantially exceed the speed limit. Cardinal pays for any related speeding tickets. During the past year, two drivers had their licenses suspended for 30 days each for driving at such excessive speeds. Cardinal continues to pay each driver's salary during the suspension periods.

Cardinal believes that it is necessary to conduct its business in this manner if it is to be profitable, maintain the support of the drivers, and maintain the goodwill of customers. Evaluate Cardinal's business practices.

21. **LO.3** Quail Corporation anticipates that being positively perceived by the individual who is elected mayor will be beneficial for business. Therefore, Quail contributes to the campaigns of both the Democratic and Republican candidates. The Republican candidate is elected mayor. Can Quail deduct any of the political contributions it made? Explain.

22. **LO.3** Melissa, the owner of a sole proprietorship, does not provide health insurance for her 20 employees. She plans to spend $1,500 lobbying in opposition to legislation that would require her to provide such insurance. Discuss the tax advantages and disadvantages of paying the $1,500 to a professional lobbyist rather than spending the $1,500 on in-house lobbying expenditures.

Critical Thinking   23. **LO.3** Ella owns 60% of the stock of Peach, Inc. The stock has declined in value since she purchased it five years ago. She is going to sell 5% of the stock to a relative. Ella is also going to make a gift of 10% of the stock to another relative. Identify the relevant tax issues for Ella.

24. **LO.3** Jarret owns City of Charleston bonds with an adjusted basis of $190,000. During the year, he receives interest payments of $3,800. Jarret partially financed the purchase of the bonds by borrowing $100,000 at 5% interest. Jarret's interest payments on the loan this year are $4,900, and his principal payments are $1,100.

  a. Should Jarret report any interest income this year? Explain.
  b. Can Jarret deduct any interest expense this year? Explain.

25. **LO.3** Egret Corporation, a calendar year C corporation, was formed on March 6, 2018, and opened for business on July 1, 2018. After its formation but prior to opening for business, Egret incurred the following expenditures:

Accounting	$ 7,000
Advertising	14,500
Employee payroll	11,000
Rent	8,000
Utilities	1,000

  What is the maximum amount of these expenditures that Egret can deduct in 2018?

26. **LO.3** Henrietta, the owner of a very successful hotel chain in the Southeast, is exploring the possibility of expanding the chain into a city in the Northeast. She incurs $35,000 of expenses associated with this investigation. Based on the regulatory environment for hotels in the city, she decides not to expand. During the year, she also investigates opening a restaurant that will be part of a national restaurant chain. Her expenses for this are $53,000. The restaurant begins operations on September 1. Determine the amount Henrietta can deduct in the current year for investigating these two businesses.

Decision Making   27. **LO.3** Amber, a publicly held corporation, had been paying its chief executive officer
Critical Thinking   (CEO) an annual salary of $900,000. Amber instituted a performance-based
Communications   compensation plan, effective January 1, 2017, that increased the CEO's 2017 compensation by $300,000. It is anticipated that the plan will provide an additional $350,0000 in 2018. Prepare a letter to Amber's board of directors explaining how much of the CEO's 2018 compensation is deductible and the consequences of any changes that might be made to the compensation plan in 2018. Address the letter to the board chairperson, Angela Riddle, whose address is 100 James Tower, Cleveland, OH 44106.

28. **LO.3** In 2018, UNA Corporation has $500,000 of adjusted taxable income, $22,000 of business interest income, and $120,000 of business interest expense. It has average annual gross receipts of more than $25 million over the prior three taxable years.

    a. What is UNA's interest expense deduction?

    b. How much interest expense can be deducted if UNA's adjusted taxable income is $300,000?

29. **LO.4** Blue Corporation, a manufacturing company, decided to develop a new line of merchandise. The project began in 2018. Blue had the following expenses in connection with the project:

	2018	2019
Salaries	$500,000	$600,000
Materials	90,000	70,000
Insurance	8,000	11,000
Utilities	6,000	8,000
Cost of inspection of materials for quality control	7,000	6,000
Promotion expenses	11,000	18,000
Advertising	–0–	20,000
Equipment depreciation	15,000	14,000
Cost of market survey	8,000	–0–

The new product will be introduced for sale beginning in July 2020. Determine the amount of the deduction for research and experimental expenditures for 2018, 2019, and 2020 if:

    a. Blue Corporation elects to expense the research and experimental expenditures.

    b. Blue Corporation elects to amortize the research and experimental expenditures over 60 months.

30. **LO.6** In 2018, Gray Corporation, a calendar year C corporation, holds a $75,000 charitable contribution carryover from a gift made in 2012. Gray is contemplating a gift of land to a qualified charity in either 2018 or 2019. Gray purchased the land as an investment five years ago for $100,000 (current fair market value is $250,000). Before considering any charitable deduction, Gray projects taxable income of $1 million for 2018 and $1.2 million for 2019. Should Gray make the gift of the land to charity in 2018 or in 2019? Provide support for your answer.

Decision Making

31. **LO.6** Dan Simms is the president and sole shareholder of Simms Corporation, 1121 Madison Street, Seattle, WA 98121. Dan plans for the corporation to make a charitable contribution to the University of Washington, a qualified public charity. He will have the corporation donate Jaybird Corporation stock, held for five years, with a basis of $11,000 and a fair market value of $25,000. Dan projects a $310,000 net profit for Simms Corporation in 2018 and a $100,000 net profit in 2019. Dan calls you on December 11, 2018, and asks whether Simms should make the contribution in 2018 or 2019. Write a letter advising Dan about the timing of the contribution.

Decision Making

Communications

32. **LO.6** On December 23, 2018, the directors of Partridge Corporation, an accrual basis calendar year taxpayer, authorized a cash contribution of $10,000 to the American Cancer Association. The payment is made on April 14, 2019. Can Partridge deduct the charitable contribution in 2018? Explain.

Critical Thinking

33. **LO.6** Aquamarine Corporation, a calendar year C corporation, makes the following donations to qualified charitable organizations during the current year:

	Adjusted Basis	Fair Market Value
Painting held four years as an investment, to a church, which sold it immediately	$15,000	$25,000
Apple stock held two years as an investment, to United Way, which sold it immediately	40,000	90,000
Canned groceries held one month as inventory, to Catholic Meals for the Poor	10,000	17,000

Determine the amount of Aquamarine Corporation's charitable deduction for the current year. (Ignore the taxable income limitation.)

Decision Making

Communications

34. **LO.6** Joseph Thompson is president and sole shareholder of Jay Corporation. In December 2018, Joe asks your advice regarding a charitable contribution he plans to have the corporation make to the University of Maine, a qualified public charity. Joe is considering the following alternatives as charitable contributions in December 2018:

	Fair Market Value
(1) Cash donation	$200,000
(2) Unimproved land held for six years ($110,000 basis)	200,000
(3) Maize Corporation stock held for eight months ($140,000 basis)	200,000
(4) Brown Corporation stock held for nine years ($360,000 basis)	200,000

Joe has asked you to help him decide which of these potential contributions will be most advantageous taxwise. Jay Corporation's taxable income is $3.5 million before considering the contribution. Rank the four alternatives and write a letter to Mr. Thompson communicating your advice. The corporation's address is 1442 Main Street, Freeport, ME 04032.

35. **LO.7** On November 4, 2016, Blue Company acquired an asset (27.5-year residential real property) for $200,000 for use in its business. In 2016 and 2017, respectively, Blue took $642 and $5,128 of cost recovery. These amounts were incorrect; Blue applied the wrong percentages (i.e., those for 39-year rather than 27.5-year property). Blue should have taken $910 and $7,272 of cost recovery in 2016 and 2017, respectively.

On January 1, 2018, the asset was sold for $180,000. Calculate the gain or loss on the sale of the asset for that year.

36. **LO.7** Juan, a sole proprietor, acquires a new 5-year class asset on March 14, 2018, for $200,000. This is the only asset Juan acquired during the year. He does not elect immediate expensing under § 179. Juan does not claim any available additional first-year depreciation. On July 15, 2019, Juan sells the asset.
   a.   Determine Juan's cost recovery for 2018.
   b.   Determine Juan's cost recovery for 2019.

37. **LO.7** Debra acquired the following new assets during 2018:

Date	Asset	Cost
April 11	Furniture	$40,000
July 28	Trucks	40,000
November 3	Computers	70,000

Determine Debra's cost recovery deductions for the current year. Debra does not elect immediate expensing under § 179. She does not claim any available additional first-year depreciation.

38. **LO.7** On May 5, 2018, Christy purchased and placed in service a hotel. The hotel cost $10.8 million. Calculate Christy's cost recovery deductions for 2018 and for 2028.

39. **LO.7** Janice acquired an apartment building on June 4, 2018, for $1.6 million. The value of the land is $300,000. Janice sold the apartment building on November 29, 2024.
    a. Determine Janice's cost recovery deduction for 2018.
    b. Determine Janice's cost recovery deduction for 2024.

40. **LO.7** Lori, who is single, purchased 5-year class property for $200,000 and 7-year class property for $420,000 on May 20, 2018. Lori expects the taxable income derived from her business (without regard to the amount expensed under § 179) to be about $550,000. Lori has determined she should elect immediate § 179 expensing in the amount of $520,000, but she doesn't know which asset she should completely expense under § 179. She does not claim any available additional first-year depreciation.   *Decision Making*
    a. Determine Lori's total deduction if the § 179 expense is first taken with respect to the 5-year class asset.
    b. Determine Lori's total deduction if the § 179 expense is first taken with respect to the 7-year class asset.
    c. What is your advice to Lori?
    d. Assume that Lori is in the 24% marginal tax bracket and that she uses § 179 on the 7-year asset. Determine the present value of the tax savings from the depreciation deductions for both assets. See Appendix F for present value factors, and assume a 6% discount rate.
    e. Assume the same facts as in part (d), except that Lori decides not to use § 179 on either asset. Determine the present value of the tax savings under this choice. In addition, determine which option Lori should choose.

41. **LO.7** Olga is the proprietor of a small business. In 2018, the business's income, before consideration of any cost recovery or § 179 deduction, is $250,000.
    Olga spends $620,000 on new 7-year class assets and elects to take the § 179 deduction on them. She does not claim any available additional first-year depreciation. Olga's cost recovery deduction for 2018, except for the cost recovery with respect to the new 7-year assets, is $95,000. Determine Olga's total cost recovery for 2018 with respect to the 7-year class assets and the amount of any § 179 carryforward.

42. **LO.7** On June 5, 2017, Javier Sanchez purchased and placed in service a 7-year class asset costing $560,000 for use in his landscaping business, which he operates as a single member LLC (Sanchez Landscaping LLC). During 2017, his business generated a net income of $945,780 before any § 179 immediate expense election.
    a. Determine the maximum deductions that Javier can claim with respect to this asset in 2017 and 2018.
    b. Complete Javier's Form 4562 (page 1) for 2017. His Social Security number is 123-45-6789.

43. **LO.7** In 2018, Muhammad purchased a new computer for $16,000. The computer is used 100% for business. Muhammad did not make a § 179 election with respect to the computer. He does not claim any available additional first-year depreciation. If Muhammad uses the regular MACRS method, determine his cost recovery deduction for 2018 for computing taxable income and for computing his alternative minimum tax.

44. **LO.7** Jamie purchased $100,000 of new office furniture for her business in June of the current year. Jamie understands that if she elects to use ADS to compute   *Decision Making*

her regular income tax, there will be no difference between the cost recovery for computing the regular income tax and the AMT.

a.   Jamie wants to know the present value of the *tax cost*, after three years, of using ADS rather than MACRS. Assume that Jamie does not elect § 179 expensing, she does not claim any additional first-year depreciation, and her marginal tax rate is 32%. See Appendix F for present value factors, and assume a 6% discount rate.

b.   What is the present value of the *tax savings/costs* that result over the life of the asset if Jamie uses MACRS rather than ADS?

Communications   45. **LO.8** Jabari Johnson is considering acquiring an automobile at the beginning of 2019 that he will use 100% of the time as a taxi. The purchase price of the automobile is $35,000. Johnson has heard of cost recovery limits on automobiles and wants to know the maximum amount of the $35,000 he can deduct in the first year.

Write a letter to Jabari in which you present your calculations. Also prepare a memo for the tax files, summarizing your analysis. Johnson's address is 100 Morningside, Clinton, MS 39058.

46. **LO.8** On October 15, 2018, Jon purchased and placed in service a used car. The purchase price was $25,000. This was the only business use asset Jon acquired in 2018. He used the car 80% of the time for business and 20% for personal use. Jon used the regular MACRS method. Calculate the total deduction Jon may take for 2018 with respect to the car.

47. **LO.8** On June 5, 2017, Leo purchased and placed in service a new car that cost $20,000. The business use percentage for the car is always 100%. Leo claims any available additional first-year depreciation. Compute Leo's cost recovery deduction for 2017 and 2018.

48. **LO.8** On May 28, 2018, Mary purchased and placed in service a new $20,000 car. The car was used 60% for business, 20% for production of income, and 20% for personal use in 2018. In 2019, the usage changed to 40% for business, 30% for production of income, and 30% for personal use. Mary did not elect immediate expensing under § 179. She did not claim any available additional first-year depreciation. Compute Mary's cost recovery deduction and any cost recovery recapture in 2019.

Decision Making   49. **LO.9** Mike Saxon is negotiating the purchase of a business. The final purchase price has been agreed upon, but the allocation of the purchase price to the
Communications   assets is still being discussed. Appraisals on a warehouse range from $1,200,000 to $1,500,000. If a value of $1,200,000 is used for the warehouse, the remainder of the purchase price, $800,000, will be allocated to goodwill. If $1,500,000 is allocated to the warehouse, goodwill will be $500,000.

Mike wants to know what effect each alternative will have on cost recovery and amortization during the first year. Under the agreement, Mike will take over the business on January 1 of next year. Write a letter to Mike in which you present your calculations and recommendation. Then prepare a memo for the tax files. Mike's address is 200 Rolling Hills Drive, Shavertown, PA 18708.

Ethics and Equity   50. **LO.10** Sam Jones owns a granite stone quarry. When he acquired the land, Sam allocated $800,000 of the purchase price to the quarry's recoverable mineral reserves, which were estimated at 10 million tons of granite stone. Based on these estimates, the cost depletion was $.08 per ton. In April of the current year, Sam received a letter from the State Department of Highways notifying him that part of his property was being condemned so that the state could build a new road. At that time, the recoverable mineral reserves had an adjusted basis of $600,000 and 7.5 million tons of granite rock. Sam estimates that the land being condemned contains about 2 million tons of granite. Therefore, for the current year, Sam has computed his cost depletion at $.11 per ton [$600,000/(7,500,000 − 2,000,000)]. Evaluate the appropriateness of what Sam is doing.

51. **LO.10** Wes acquired a mineral interest during the year for $10 million. A geological survey estimated that 250,000 tons of the mineral remained in the deposit. During the year, 80,000 tons were mined, and 45,000 tons were sold for $12 million. Other related expenses amounted to $5 million. Assuming that the mineral depletion rate is 22%, calculate Wes's lowest taxable income, after any depletion deductions.

BRIDGE DISCIPLINE

1. Sparrow Corporation is considering the acquisition of an asset for use in its business over the next five years. However, Sparrow must decide whether it would be better served by leasing the asset or buying it. An appropriate asset could be purchased for $15,000, and it would qualify as a three-year asset under the MACRS classification. Assume that the election to expense assets under § 179 is not available, that any available additional first-year depreciation is not claimed, and that the asset is not expected to have a salvage value at the end of its use by Sparrow. Alternatively, Sparrow could lease the asset for a $3,625 annual cost over the five-year period. If Sparrow is in the 21% tax bracket, would you recommend that Sparrow buy or lease the asset? In your calculations, assume that 10% is an appropriate discount factor.

Decision Making

2. Lark Corporation is considering the acquisition of an asset for use in its business over the next five years. However, Lark must decide whether it would be better served by leasing the asset or buying it. An appropriate asset could be purchased for $15,000, and it would qualify as a three-year asset under the MACRS classification. Assume that the election to expense assets under § 179 is made, but any available additional first-year depreciation is not claimed, and that the asset is not expected to have a salvage value at the end of its use by Lark. Alternatively, Lark could lease the asset for a $3,625 annual cost over the five-year period. If Lark is in the 21% tax bracket, would you recommend that Lark buy or lease the asset? In your calculations, assume that 10% is an appropriate discount factor.

Decision Making

3. Wayside Fruit Company is a sole proprietorship owned by Neil Stephenson. The company's records reflect the following:

Sales revenue	$185,000
Operating expenses	125,000
Depreciation expense for book	13,000
Cost recovery allowance for tax	17,500
Loss on the sale of delivery truck to Neil's brother	5,000
Amount paid to fruit inspector to overlook below-standard fruit shipped to various vendors	3,000

Compute the net income before tax for book purposes and the amount of taxable income for Wayside Fruit Company.

Research Problems

THOMSON REUTERS
CHECKPOINT™

Note: Solutions to the Research Problems can be prepared by using the Thomson Reuters Checkpoint™ online tax research database, which accompanies this textbook. Solutions can also be prepared by using research materials found in a typical tax library.

Communications

Research Problem 1. Gray Chemical Company manufactured pesticides that were toxic. Over the course of several years, the toxic waste contaminated the air and water around the company's plant. Several employees suffered toxic poisoning, and the Environmental Protection Agency cited the company for violations. In court, the judge found Gray guilty and imposed fines of $15 million. The company voluntarily set up a charitable fund for the purpose of bettering the environment and funded it with $8 million. The company incurred legal expenses in setting up the foundation and defending itself in court. The court reduced the fine from $15 million to $7 million.

Gray deducted the $8 million paid to the foundation and the legal expenses incurred. The IRS disallowed both deductions on the grounds that the payment was, in fact, a fine and in violation of public policy.

Gray's president, Ted Jones, has contacted you regarding the deductibility of the $7 million fine, the $8 million payment to the foundation, and the legal fees. Write a letter to Mr. Jones that contains your advice, and prepare a memo for the tax files. Gray's address is 200 Lincoln Center, Omaha, NE 68182.

Partial list of research aids:
§§ 162(a) and (f).
Reg. § 1.162–21(b).

Research Problem 2. In 2014, Jed James began planting a vineyard. The costs of the land preparation, labor, rootstock, and planting were capitalized. The land preparation costs do not include any nondepreciable land costs. In 2018, when the plants became viable, Jed placed the vineyard in service. Jed wants to know whether he can claim a deduction under § 179 on his 2018 income tax return for the 2014 costs for planting the vineyard.

Communications

Research Problem 3. Juan owns a business that acquires exotic automobiles that are high-tech, state-of-the-art vehicles with unique design features or equipment. The exotic automobiles are not licensed, nor are they set up to be used on the road. Rather, the cars are used exclusively for car shows or related promotional photography. With respect to the exotic automobiles, can Juan take a cost recovery deduction on his Federal income tax return? Prepare an outline for your classmates addressing this issue.

Partial list of research aids:
Bruce Selig, 70 TCM 1125, T.C.Memo. 1995–519.

Use internet tax resources to address the following questions. Look for reliable websites and blogs of the IRS and other government agencies, media outlets, businesses, tax professionals, academics, think tanks, and political outlets.

Research Problem 4. Many states that have income taxes "piggyback" onto the Federal income tax calculation. In other words, these states' income tax calculations incorporate many of the Federal calculations and deductions to make both compliance and verification of tax liability easier. However, some state legislatures are concerned that the TCJA of 2017 changes could result in significant revenue losses. Determine how states are reacting to the TCJA of 2017. Be sure to state the sources for your answer.

Research Problem 5. Do depreciation deductions vary by entity type or by industry? Go to the IRS Tax Statistics page (https://www.irs.gov/uac/tax-stats) and review the Excel spreadsheets containing data for corporations, partnerships, and nonfarm proprietorships by sector or industry. You can find these in the Business Tax Statistics section of the IRS site.

Communications

Critical Thinking

Evaluate the depreciation deductions by sector (there are 19 sectors identified in the IRS spreadsheets) and by entity using Excel. E-mail the spreadsheet to your instructor along with a brief summary of your findings.

Becker CPA Review Questions

1. Michael Sima, a sole proprietor craftsman, purchased an amount of equipment in the current year that exceeded the maximum allowable § 179 depreciation election limit by $20,000. Sima's total purchases of property placed in service in the current year did not exceed the limit imposed by § 179. All of the property (including the equipment) was purchased in November of the current year, and Sima elected to depreciate the maximum amount of equipment under § 179. Sima had bottom-line Schedule C income of $50,000 in the current year. Which method may Sima use to depreciate the remaining equipment in the current year?

   a. Sima may not depreciate any additional equipment other than the § 179 maximum in the current year and must carry forward the excess amount to use in the following taxable year.

   b. MACRS half-year convention for personal property.

   c. MACRS mid-quarter convention for personal property.

   d. Straight-line, mid-month convention over 27.5 years for real property.

2. Cox Construction, a company in its 10th year of business, purchased a piece of equipment on April 1, year 9, for $20,000. Cox has used it for business purposes since the initial purchase date. The company depreciated the equipment using the MACRS half-year table for 5-year assets. For tax purposes, what is the amount of accumulated depreciation expense for the equipment as of December 31, year 10?

   a. $6,000
   b. $10,400

   c. $11,600
   d. $12,800

3. Stem Corp. bought a machine in February of year 7 for $20,000. Then Stem bought furniture in November of year 7 for $30,000. Both machines were placed in service for business purposes immediately after purchase. No other assets were purchased during year 7. What depreciation convention must Stem use for the machine purchased in February year 7?

   a. Mid-month
   b. Half year

   c. Mid-quarter
   d. Full year

4. Data, Inc., purchased and placed in service a $5,000 computer on August 24, year 3. This is the only asset purchase during the year. Section 179 expensing was not elected. Using the excerpt of the MACRS half-year convention table below, what is the MACRS depreciation in year 3 for the computer?

Recovery Period	5-Year	7-Year	10-Year
1	20%	14.29%	10%
2	32%	24.49%	18%
3	19.2%	17.49%	14.4%

   a. $500
   b. $715

   c. $960
   d. $1,000

5. Data, Inc., purchased and placed in service a $5,000 computer on August 24, year 3. This is the only asset purchase during the year. Section 179 expensing was not elected. The computer was sold during year 5. Using the excerpt of the MACRS half-year convention table below, what is the MACRS depreciation in year 5 for the computer?

Recovery Period	5-Year	7-Year	10-Year
1	20%	14.29%	10%
2	32%	24.49%	18%
3	19.2%	17.49%	14.4%

a. $360

b. $437

c. $480

d. $960

6. Data, Inc., purchased and placed in service $5,000 of office furniture on August 24, year 3. This is the only asset purchase during the year. Section 179 expensing was not elected. Using the excerpt of the MACRS half-year convention table below, what is the MACRS depreciation in year 3 for the office furniture?

Recovery Period	5-Year	7-Year	10-Year
1	20%	14.29%	10%
2	32%	24.49%	18%
3	19.2%	17.49%	14.4%

a. $500

b. $715

c. $875

d. $1,000

7. Which statement below is correct?

a. Real property is depreciated using the half-year convention.

b. Residential real estate is depreciated over a 39-year life.

c. One-half month of depreciation is taken for the month that real property is disposed of.

d. Salvage value is considered in MACRS depreciation.

CHAPTER

6

Losses and Loss Limitations

LEARNING OBJECTIVES: *After completing Chapter 6, you should be able to:*

LO.1 Determine the amount, classification, and timing of the bad debt deduction.

LO.2 State and illustrate the tax treatment of worthless securities, including § 1244 stock.

LO.3 Identify a casualty and determine the amount, classification, and timing of casualty and theft losses.

LO.4 Describe the impact of the net operating loss carryback and carryover provisions on previous and subsequent years' taxable income.

LO.5 Explain the tax shelter problem and the reasons for at-risk and passive activity loss limitations.

LO.6 Describe how the at-risk limitation and the passive activity loss rules limit deductions for losses and identify taxpayers subject to these restrictions.

LO.7 Discuss the definitions of activity, material participation, and rental activity under the passive activity loss rules.

LO.8 Determine the relationship between the at-risk and passive activity loss limitations.

LO.9 Explain the special treatment available to real estate activities.

LO.10 Determine the consequences of the disposition of passive activities.

LO.11 Describe and compute the excess business loss limitation.

CHAPTER OUTLINE

6-1 Bad Debts, 6-2
    6-1a Specific Charge-Off Method, 6-3
    6-1b Business versus Nonbusiness Bad Debts, 6-4
    6-1c Loans between Related Parties, 6-5

6-2 Worthless Securities and Small Business Stock Losses, 6-5
    6-2a Worthless Securities, 6-5
    6-2b Small Business Stock (§ 1244 Stock) Losses, 6-5

6-3 Casualty and Theft Losses, 6-7
    6-3a Definition of Casualty, 6-7
    6-3b Deduction of Casualty Losses, 6-7
    6-3c Definition of Theft, 6-9
    6-3d Loss Measurement, 6-9
    6-3e Casualty and Theft Losses of Individuals, 6-10

6-4 Net Operating Losses, 6-13
    6-4a Introduction, 6-13
    6-4b General Rules, 6-14

6-5 The Tax Shelter Problem, 6-14

6-6 At-Risk Limitations, 6-16

6-7 Passive Activity Loss Limits, 6-17
    6-7a Classification and Impact of Passive Activity Income and Loss, 6-17
    6-7b Taxpayers Subject to the Passive Activity Loss Rules, 6-21
    6-7c Rules for Determining Passive Activities, 6-22
    6-7d Material Participation, 6-22
    6-7e Rental Activities, 6-24
    6-7f Interaction of At-Risk and Passive Activity Loss Limits, 6-26
    6-7g Special Rules for Real Estate, 6-27
    6-7h Disposition of Passive Activities, 6-29

6-8 Excess Business Losses, 6-32
    6-8a Definition and Rules, 6-32
    6-8b Computing the Limit, 6-32

TAX TALK *The income tax has made more liars out of the American people than golf has. Even when you make a tax form out on the level, you don't know when it's through if you are a crook or a martyr.* —Will Rogers

PRESSMASTER/SHUTTERSTOCK.COM

RECEIVING TAX BENEFITS FROM LOSSES

Robyn, an unmarried, cash basis and calendar year taxpayer, is nearing the end of a year that she would like to forget. Several years ago, she loaned $25,000 to her friend Jamil to enable him to start a business. Jamil had made scheduled payments of $7,000 (including $1,000 of interest) when he suddenly died in January. At the time of his death, he was insolvent, and Robyn's attempts to collect the debt were fruitless.

Last year, Robyn invested $60,000 by purchasing stock in Owl Corporation, a closely held small business corporation started by her brother. However, the company declared bankruptcy in May of this year, and the bankruptcy trustee informed the shareholders that they should not expect to receive anything from the company.

Robyn has owned and operated a bookstore as a sole proprietorship for the past 10 years. The bookstore has been profitable, producing annual taxable income of approximately $75,000. However, due to the growth of online vendors and e-books, the business lost $180,000 this year.

In September, a tornado caused a large oak tree to blow over onto Robyn's bookstore. The cost of removing the tree and making repairs to the property was $32,000. Robyn received a check for $25,000 from her insurance company. Her adjusted basis for the bookstore building was $280,000.

Finally, Robyn invested $20,000 for a 10 percent interest in a limited partnership that owns and operates orange groves in Florida. Due to a hard freeze that damaged much of the fruit, the partnership lost $200,000 and allocated $20,000 of ordinary loss to Robyn.

Robyn has come to you for tax advice and would like to know the tax ramifications of each of the events and transactions listed above.

Read the chapter and formulate your response.

Chapter 5 introduced rules governing the deductibility of trade or business expenses. This chapter extends the notion of deductibility to losses occurring in the course of business operations. In particular, special rules concerning the tax treatment of bad debts, casualty losses, and operating losses are reviewed. In addition, tax shelters and the rules that limit their usefulness as tax avoidance strategies are discussed.

In most situations, financial accounting rules treat losses as "negative gains." As this chapter and the next two chapters will illustrate repeatedly, that is not necessarily true in the tax law. That is, there are frequently different rules for gains and losses under the tax law. This often takes the form of limitations on taxpayers' ability to deduct losses and reduce tax payments. Why would Congress choose to treat gains and losses differently? It appears that there are at least five reasons.

First, Congress often seeks to prevent taxpayers from sheltering certain types of income or gains with other types of deductions or losses. For example, the passive activity loss rules effectively prevent taxpayers from using losses resulting from passive investments (e.g., the taxpayer only contributes money and does not work in that business) from offsetting salary and other types of "active" income. Second, some loss (or deduction) limitations deny deductions to higher-income taxpayers out of a fairness idea. Third, Congress attempts to prevent excessive income shifting across tax years. The net operating loss rules are examples of this motivation. Fourth, holding all else constant, denying losses increases government revenues. This gives Congress some latitude to reduce tax rates or pursue other policy goals that reduce government revenues. Fifth, the measure of taxable income for individuals generally excludes personal losses, such as loss from sale of a personal use car. This prevents possible abuse and simplifies the law. An exception is made for loss due to certain casualties, such as a hurricane.

Taken together, these reasons for limiting losses motivate Congress to enact provisions that treat gains and losses differently—and can also make complying with the rules more difficult and costly for taxpayers. As you read the rules in this chapter, consideration of the five reasons for treating losses and gains differently can help in your understanding of these special tax loss rules.

6-1 BAD DEBTS

LO.1

Determine the amount, classification, and timing of the bad debt deduction.

If a taxpayer lends money or purchases a debt instrument and the debt is not repaid, a **bad debt** deduction is allowed. Similarly, if an accrual basis taxpayer sells goods or provides services on credit and the account receivable subsequently becomes worthless, a bad debt deduction is permitted.[1] No deduction is allowed, however, for a bad debt arising from the sale of a product or service when the taxpayer is on the cash basis because no income is reported until the cash has been collected. Permitting a bad debt deduction for a cash basis taxpayer would amount to a double deduction because the expenses of the product or service rendered are deducted when payments are made to suppliers and to employees or when the sale is made.

EXAMPLE 1

Ella, a sole proprietor, operates a business named Executive Accounting and Tax Services. Last year, Pat hired Ella to help him with the accounting for his small business. Ella also prepared the S corporation income tax return for the business and Pat's personal income tax return. Ella billed Pat $8,000 for the services she performed. Pat has never paid the bill, his business no longer exists, and his whereabouts are unknown.

If Ella is an *accrual basis taxpayer*, she includes the $8,000 in income when the services are performed. When she determines that Pat's account will not be collected, Ella deducts the $8,000 as a bad debt.

If Ella is a *cash basis taxpayer*, she does not include the $8,000 in income until payment is received. When she determines that Pat's account will not be collected, she cannot deduct the $8,000 as a bad debt expense because it was never recognized as income.

---

[1]Reg. § 1.166–1(e). However, some financial institutions are permitted to use the reserve method for computing bad debt deductions (§ 585).

TAX FACT **Just How Good Is Your Credit?**

To be successful, a business must generate sales among customers who are willing and able to pay their obligations. Nonetheless, if a sale is made and it is determined that the related account receivable is uncollectible, an accrual method business is allowed to claim a bad debt deduction.

Recently, corporations claimed bad debt deductions of nearly $194 billion against business receipts of about $26 trillion.

Source: 2012 Corporation Income Tax Returns; Table 2—Balance Sheet, Income Statement, and Selected Other Items, by Size of Total Assets; 2015.

The Big Picture

Return to the facts of *The Big Picture* on p. 6-1. Because Robyn is a cash basis taxpayer, she cannot take as a bad debt deduction any unpaid accrued interest on the loan to her friend, Jamil, because it was never recognized as income.

EXAMPLE

2

6-1a Specific Charge-Off Method

Most taxpayers are required to use the specific charge-off method when accounting for bad debts. A taxpayer using the specific charge-off method may claim a deduction in the year when a specific *business* debt becomes either partially or wholly worthless. If a business debt previously deducted as partially worthless becomes totally worthless in a future year, only the remainder not previously deducted can be deducted in the future year. A *nonbusiness* debt must be wholly worthless to claim a deduction.[2] For either a business or nonbusiness debt, the taxpayer must be able to document the fact and the amount of the partial or complete worthlessness.

In the case of total worthlessness, taxpayers may deduct the entire amount in the year that the debt becomes worthless. The amount of the deduction depends on the taxpayer's basis in the bad debt. If the debt arose from the sale of services or products and the face amount was previously included in income, that amount is deductible. If the taxpayer purchased the debt, the deduction equals the amount the taxpayer paid for the debt instrument.

Determining when a bad debt becomes worthless can be a difficult task. Legal proceedings need not be initiated against the debtor when the surrounding facts indicate that such action will not result in collection.

In 2016, Partridge Company lent $1,000 to Kay, who agreed to repay the loan in two years. In 2018, Kay disappeared after the note became delinquent. If a reasonable investigation by Partridge indicates that Kay cannot be found or that a suit against Kay would not result in collection, Partridge can deduct the $1,000 in 2018.

EXAMPLE

3

Bankruptcy is generally an indication of at least partial worthlessness of a debt. Bankruptcy may create worthlessness before the settlement date. If this is the case, the deduction may be taken in the year of worthlessness.

In Example 3, assume that Kay filed for personal bankruptcy in 2017 and that the debt is a business debt. At that time, Partridge learned that unsecured creditors (including Partridge) were ultimately expected to receive 20 cents on the dollar. In 2018, settlement is made, and Partridge receives only $150. Partridge should deduct $800 ($1,000 loan − $200 expected settlement) in 2017 and $50 in 2018 ($200 balance − $150 proceeds).

EXAMPLE

4

---

[2]§ 166(a).

If a receivable is written off (deducted) as uncollectible and is subsequently collected during the *same* tax year, the write-off entry is reversed. If a receivable has been written off (deducted) as uncollectible, collection in a *later* tax year results in income recognition if the loss deduction yielded a tax benefit in the prior year (the tax benefit rule).

Concept Summary 6.1 provides a summary of the tax treatment of bad debts using the specific charge-off method.

Concept Summary 6.1

The Tax Treatment of Bad Debts Using the Specific Charge-Off Method

	Business Bad Debts	Nonbusiness Bad Debts
Timing of deduction	A deduction is allowed when the debt becomes either partially or wholly worthless.	A deduction is allowed *only* when the debt becomes wholly worthless.
Character of deduction	The bad debt may be deducted as an ordinary loss.	The bad debt is classified as a short-term capital loss, subject to the $3,000 capital loss limitation for individuals.
Recovery of amounts previously deducted	If the account recovered was written off during the current tax year, the write-off entry is reversed. If the account was written off in a previous tax year, income is created subject to the tax benefit rule.	If the account recovered was written off during the current tax year, the write-off entry is reversed. If the account was written off in a previous tax year, income is created subject to the tax benefit rule.

6-1b Business versus Nonbusiness Bad Debts

The nature of a debt depends upon whether the lender is engaged in the business of lending money or whether there is a proximate relationship between the creation of the debt and the *lender's* trade or business. Where either of these conditions is true, a bad debt is classified as a **business bad debt**. If these conditions are not met, a bad debt is classified as a **nonbusiness bad debt**. The use to which the borrowed funds are put is of no consequence when making this classification decision.

The Big Picture

EXAMPLE 5

Return to the facts of *The Big Picture* on p. 6-1. Robyn loaned her friend Jamil $25,000. Jamil used the money to start a business, which subsequently failed. When Jamil died after having made principal payments of $6,000 on the loan, he was insolvent.

Even though the proceeds of the loan were used in a business, the loan is a nonbusiness bad debt because the business was Jamil's, not Robyn's, and Robyn is not in the business of lending money.

The nonbusiness bad debt provisions are *not* applicable to a business entity (e.g., a corporation or partnership). The law assumes that any loans made by a business are related to its trade or business. Therefore, any bad debts resulting from loans made by a business are automatically business bad debts.

EXAMPLE 6

Horace operates a sole proprietorship that sells premium electronic equipment. Horace uses the accrual method to account for sales of the electronic equipment. During the year, he sold $4,000 of equipment to Herbie on credit. Later that year, the account receivable becomes worthless. The loan is a business bad debt, because the debt was related to Horace's business.

The distinction between a business bad debt and a nonbusiness bad debt is important. A business bad debt is deductible as an ordinary loss in the year incurred, whereas a nonbusiness bad debt is always treated as a short-term capital loss. Thus, regardless of the age of a nonbusiness bad debt, the deduction may be of limited benefit due to the $3,000 capital loss limitation for individuals (refer to the discussion in text Section 4-5a and in Chapter 8).

6-1c **Loans between Related Parties**

Loans between related parties raise the issue of whether the transaction was a *bona fide* loan or some other type of transfer, such as a gift, a disguised dividend payment, or a contribution to capital. The Regulations state that a bona fide debt arises from a debtor-creditor relationship based on a valid and enforceable obligation to pay a fixed or determinable sum of money. Thus, individual circumstances must be examined to determine whether advances between related parties are loans. Some considerations are these:

- Was a note properly executed?
- Was there a reasonable rate of interest?
- Was collateral provided?
- What collection efforts were made?
- What was the intent of the parties?

> **EXAMPLE 7**
>
> Ted, who is the sole shareholder of Penguin Corporation, lends the corporation $10,000 so that it can continue business operations. The note specifies a 2% interest rate and is payable on demand. Penguin has shown losses in each year of its five-year existence. The corporation also has liabilities greatly in excess of its assets. It is likely that Ted's transfer to the corporation would be treated as a contribution to capital rather than a liability. Consequently, no bad debt deduction would be allowed upon default by Penguin.

> **DIGGING DEEPER 1**
>
> In-depth coverage can be found on this book's companion website: **www.cengage.com**

6-2 **WORTHLESS SECURITIES AND SMALL BUSINESS STOCK LOSSES**

LO.2

State and illustrate the tax treatment of worthless securities, including § 1244 stock.

6-2a **Worthless Securities**

A loss is allowed for securities that become *completely* worthless during the year (**worthless securities**).[3] Such securities are shares of stock, bonds, notes, or other evidence of indebtedness issued by a corporation or government. The losses generated are treated as capital losses (refer to text Section 4-5a) deemed to have occurred on the last day of the tax year. By treating losses as having occurred on the *last day* of the tax year, a loss that would otherwise have been classified as short term (if the date of worthlessness were used) may be classified as long term.

> **The Big Picture**
>
> **EXAMPLE 8**
>
> Return to the facts of *The Big Picture* on p. 6-1. Robyn owned stock in Owl Corporation that she acquired as an investment on October 1, 2017, at a cost of $60,000. On May 31, 2018, the stock became worthless when the company declared bankruptcy.
>
> Because the stock is deemed to have become worthless as of December 31, 2018, Robyn has a capital loss from an asset held for more than one year (a long-term capital loss). Note that treating the worthless stock as a loss on the last day of the year results in a long-term instead of a short-term capital loss. Alternatively, if the stock is § 1244 small business stock (see the following section), she has a $50,000 ordinary loss and a $10,000 long-term capital loss.

6-2b **Small Business Stock (§ 1244 Stock) Losses**

Congress has enacted tax rules to encourage taxpayers to form and operate small businesses. One such provision is § 1244. The general rule for losses from the sale or exchange of corporate stock is that shareholders receive capital loss treatment. However, it is

---

[3]§ 165(g).

possible to avoid capital loss limitations if the loss is sustained on ==small business stock (§ 1244 stock)==. Such a loss could arise from a sale of the stock or from the stock becoming worthless. Only *individuals*[4] who acquired the stock *from* the issuing corporation qualify for ordinary loss treatment. Section 1244 limits the ordinary loss to $50,000 ($100,000 for married individuals filing jointly) per year. Losses on § 1244 stock in excess of the statutory limits are treated as capital losses.

The issuing corporation must meet certain requirements under § 1244 for the loss on the stock to be treated as an *ordinary*—rather than a capital—loss. The principal requirement is that the total capitalization of the corporation must not exceed $1 million. This limit includes all money and other property received by the corporation for stock and all capital contributions made to the corporation. The $1 million test is made at the time the stock is issued. Section 1244 stock can be either common or preferred.

Section 1244 applies only to losses. If § 1244 stock is sold at a gain, the provision does not apply and the gain is capital gain (which, for individuals, may be subject to preferential tax treatment, as discussed in text Section 4-5a).

EXAMPLE 9

Iris, a single individual, was looking for an investment that would give some diversification to her stock portfolio. A friend suggested that she acquire some stock in Eagle Corporation, a new startup company. On July 1, 2016, Iris purchased 100 shares of Eagle Corporation for $100,000. At the time Iris acquired her stock from Eagle Corporation, the corporation had $700,000 of paid-in capital. As a result, the stock qualified as § 1244 stock. On June 20, 2018, Iris sold all of her Eagle stock to Michael for $20,000, producing an $80,000 loss ($20,000 − $100,000). Because the Eagle stock qualifies as § 1244 stock, Iris recognizes a $50,000 ordinary loss and a $30,000 long-term capital loss.

If Michael sells the stock later for $8,000 in a taxable transaction, the $12,000 loss ($8,000 − $20,000) would not qualify for ordinary loss treatment under § 1244 because Eagle Corporation had not issued the stock to him.

TAX PLANNING STRATEGIES   Maximizing the Benefits of Small Business (§ 1244 Stock) Losses

FRAMEWORK FOCUS: TAX RATE

Strategy: Control the Character of Income and Deductions.

Because § 1244 limits the amount of loss classified as ordinary loss on a yearly basis, a taxpayer might maximize the benefits of § 1244 by selling the stock in more than one taxable year.

EXAMPLE 10

Mitch, a single individual, acquired small business stock in 2016 for $150,000 (150 shares at $1,000 per share). On December 20, 2018, the stock is worth $60,000 (150 shares at $400 per share). Mitch wants to sell the stock at this time. He earns a salary of $80,000 a year, has no other capital transactions, and does not expect any in the future.

If Mitch sells all of the small business stock in 2018, his recognized loss will be $90,000 ($60,000 selling price − $150,000 cost). Section 1244 will result in a $50,000 ordinary loss and a $40,000 long-term capital loss. In computing taxable income for 2018, Mitch could deduct the $50,000 ordinary loss but could deduct only $3,000 of the capital loss (assuming that he has no capital gains). The remainder of the capital loss could be carried over and used in future years subject to the capital loss limitations in those years.

Alternatively, if Mitch sells 82 shares in 2018, he will recognize an ordinary loss of $49,200 [82 × ($400 − $1,000)]. If Mitch then sells the remainder of the shares in 2019, he will recognize an ordinary loss of $40,800 [68 × ($400 − $1,000)], successfully avoiding the capital loss limitation. Mitch could deduct the $49,200 ordinary loss in computing 2018 taxable income and the $40,800 ordinary loss in computing 2019 taxable income and completely avoid any capital loss limitations.

---

[4]The term *individuals* for this purpose does not include a trust or an estate (but could include a partnership or an LLC).

6-3 **CASUALTY AND THEFT LOSSES**

LO.3

Identify a casualty and determine the amount, classification, and timing of casualty and theft losses.

Losses on business property are deductible, whether attributable to casualty, theft, or some other cause (e.g., rust, termite damage). While all *business* property losses are generally deductible, the amount and timing of casualty and theft losses are determined using special rules. Furthermore, for individual taxpayers, who may deduct casualty losses on personal use (nonbusiness) property as well as on business and investment property (held in partnerships and S corporations or in an individual capacity), a set of special limitations applies. Casualty gains are also afforded special consideration in the tax law.

6-3a **Definition of Casualty**

The term *casualty* generally includes *fire, storm, shipwreck,* and *theft.* In addition, losses from *other casualties* are deductible. Such losses generally include any loss resulting from an event that is (1) identifiable; (2) damaging to property; and (3) sudden, unexpected, and unusual in nature. The term also includes accidental loss of property provided the loss qualifies under the same rules as any other casualty.

A *sudden event* is an event that is swift and precipitous and not gradual or progressive. An *unexpected event* is one that is ordinarily unanticipated and occurs without the intent of the taxpayer who suffers the loss. An *unusual event* is an event that is extraordinary and nonrecurring and does not commonly occur during the activity in which the taxpayer was engaged when the destruction occurred.[5] Examples include auto accidents, sonic booms, vandalism, and mine cave-ins. A taxpayer can take a deduction for a casualty loss from an automobile accident if the accident is not attributable to the taxpayer's willful act or willful negligence. Weather that causes damage (e.g., drought) must be unusual and severe for the particular region to qualify as a casualty. Furthermore, damage must be to the *taxpayer's* property to be deductible.

Events That Are Not Casualties

Not all acts of nature are treated as **casualty losses** for income tax purposes. Because a casualty must be sudden, unexpected, and unusual, progressive deterioration (such as erosion due to wind or rain) is not a casualty because it does not meet the suddenness test.

An example of an event that generally does not qualify as a casualty is insect damage. When termites caused damage over a period of several years, some courts have disallowed a casualty loss deduction.[6] On the other hand, some courts have held that termite damage over periods of up to 15 months after infestation constituted a sudden event and was, therefore, deductible as a casualty loss.[7] Despite the existence of some judicial support for the deductibility of termite damage as a casualty loss, the current position of the IRS is that termite damage is not deductible.[8]

Other examples of events that are not casualties are losses resulting from a decline in value rather than an actual loss of the property. For example, a taxpayer was allowed a loss for the actual flood damage to his property but not for the decline in market value due to the property being in a flood-prone area.[9] Similarly, a decline in value of an office building due to fire damage to nearby buildings is not deductible as a casualty.

6-3b **Deduction of Casualty Losses**

Generally, taxpayers can deduct a casualty loss in the year the loss occurs. However, no casualty loss is permitted if a reimbursement claim with a reasonable *prospect of full recovery* exists.[10] If the taxpayer has a partial claim, only part of the loss can be claimed in the year of the casualty and the remainder is deducted in the year the claim is settled.

---

[5]Rev.Rul. 72–592, 1972–2 C.B. 101.

[6]*Fay v. Helvering*, 41–2 USTC ¶9494, 27 AFTR 432, 120 F.2d 253 (CA–2, 1941); U.S. v. Rogers, 41–1 USTC ¶9442, 27 AFTR 423, 120 F.2d 244 (CA–9, 1941).

[7]*Rosenberg v. Comm.*, 52–2 USTC ¶9377, 42 AFTR 303, 198 F.2d 46 (CA–8, 1952); *Shopmaker v. U.S.*, 54–1 USTC ¶9195, 45 AFTR 758, 119 F.Supp. 705 (D.Ct. Mo., 1953).

[8]Rev.Rul. 63–232, 1963–2 C.B. 97.

[9]*S. L. Solomon*, 39 TCM 1282, T.C.Memo. 1980–87.

[10]Reg. § 1.165–1(d)(2)(i).

EXAMPLE 11

Fuchsia Corporation's new warehouse was completely destroyed by fire in 2018. Its cost and fair market value were $250,000. Fuchsia's only claim against the insurance company was on a $70,000 policy and was not settled by year-end. The following year, 2019, Fuchsia settled with the insurance company for $60,000. Fuchsia is entitled to a $180,000 deduction in 2018 and a $10,000 deduction in 2019.

If a taxpayer receives reimbursement for a casualty loss sustained and deducted in a previous year, an amended return is not filed for that year. Instead, the taxpayer must include the reimbursement in gross income on the return for the year in which it is received to the extent the previous deduction resulted in a tax benefit (refer to text Section 4-5e).

EXAMPLE 12

Golden Hawk, Inc., had a deductible casualty loss of $15,000 on its 2017 tax return. Golden Hawk's taxable income for 2017 was $60,000 after deducting the $15,000 loss. In June 2018, the corporation is reimbursed $13,000 for the prior year's casualty loss.

Golden Hawk includes the entire $13,000 in gross income for 2018 because the deduction in 2016 produced a tax benefit.

Disaster Area Losses

An exception to the general rule for the time of deduction is allowed for **disaster area losses**, which are casualties or disaster-related business losses sustained in an area designated as a disaster area by the President of the United States.[11] In such cases, the taxpayer may *elect* to treat the loss as having occurred in the taxable year immediately *preceding* the taxable year in which the disaster actually occurred. The rationale for this exception is to provide immediate relief to disaster victims by accelerating the related tax benefits.

If the extended due date for the prior year's return has not passed, a taxpayer makes the election to claim the disaster area loss on the prior year's tax return. If a disaster area is designated after the prior year's return has been filed, it is necessary to file either an amended return or a refund claim. In any case, the taxpayer must show clearly that such an election is being made.

TAX PLANNING STRATEGIES Documentation of Related-Taxpayer Loans, Casualty Losses, and Theft Losses

FRAMEWORK FOCUS: DEDUCTIONS

Strategy: Maximize Deductible Amounts.

Because the validity of loans between related taxpayers might be questioned, adequate documentation is needed to substantiate a bad debt deduction if the loan subsequently becomes worthless. Documentation should include proper execution of the note (legal form) and the establishment of a bona fide purpose for the loan. In addition, it is desirable to stipulate a reasonable rate of interest and a fixed maturity date.

Because a theft loss deduction is not permitted for misplaced items, a police report and evidence of the

value of the property (e.g., appraisals, pictures of the property, and purchase receipts) are necessary to document a theft.

Similar documentation of the value of property should be provided to support a casualty loss deduction because the amount of loss is measured, in part, by the decline in fair market value of the property.

Casualty loss deductions must be reported on Form 4684.

---

[11]§ 165(i).

The Big Picture

Return to the facts of *The Big Picture* on p. 6-1. On September 28, 2018, a tornado caused an oak tree to fall on Robyn's bookstore. The amount of her uninsured casualty loss was $7,000 ($32,000 loss − $25,000 insurance recovery). Due to the extent of the damage in the area, the President of the United States designated the area a disaster area. Because Robyn's loss is a disaster area loss, she may elect to file an amended return for 2017 and take the loss in that year.

If Robyn forgoes the election, she may take the loss on her 2018 income tax return. The advantage to Robyn of claiming the deduction in 2017 is to receive the tax relief sooner.

EXAMPLE 13

6-3c Definition of Theft

Theft includes, but is not necessarily limited to, larceny, embezzlement, and robbery.[12] Theft does not include misplaced items.[13]

Theft losses are treated like other casualty losses, but the *timing* of recognition of the loss differs. A theft loss is deducted in the *year of discovery*, which may not be the same as the year of the theft. If in the year of the discovery a claim exists (e.g., against an insurance company) and there is a reasonable expectation of recovering the adjusted basis of the asset from the insurance company, no deduction is permitted.[14] If in the year of settlement the recovery is less than the asset's adjusted basis, a deduction may be available. If the recovery exceeds the asset's adjusted basis, *casualty gain* may be recognized.

Sakura, Inc., owned a computer that was stolen from its offices in December 2017. The theft was discovered on June 3, 2018, and the corporation filed a claim with its insurance company that was settled on January 30, 2019.

If Sakura reasonably expected a full recovery from its insurance company, no deduction is allowed in 2018. A deduction may be available in 2019 if the actual insurance proceeds are less than the adjusted basis of the asset. (Loss measurement rules are discussed in the next section.)

EXAMPLE 14

In-depth coverage can be found on this book's companion website: www.cengage.com   **2   DIGGING DEEPER**

6-3d Loss Measurement

The rules for determining the amount of a loss depend in part on whether the loss relates to business, investment, or personal use (nonbusiness) property. Another consideration is whether the property was partially or completely destroyed.

If business property or investment property (e.g., rental property) is *completely destroyed*, the loss equals the adjusted basis[15] (typically cost less depreciation) of the property at the time of destruction.

A different measurement rule applies for *partial destruction* of business and investment property and for *partial* or *complete destruction* of personal use property held by individuals. In these situations, the loss is the lesser of:

- The adjusted basis of the property, or
- The difference between the fair market value of the property before the event and the fair market value immediately after the event.

---

[12]Reg. § 1.165–8(d).

[13]*Mary Francis Allen*, 16 T.C. 163 (1951).

[14]Reg. §§ 1.165–1(d)(2) and 1.165–8(a)(2).

[15]See text Section 7-2 for a detailed discussion of basis rules.

EXAMPLE 15

Wynd and Rain, a law firm, owned an airplane that was used only for business purposes. The airplane was damaged in an accident. On the date of the accident, the fair market value of the plane was $52,000, and its adjusted basis was $32,000. After the accident, the plane was appraised at $24,000.

The law firm's loss deduction is $28,000 (the lesser of the adjusted basis or the decrease in fair market value). If instead the airplane had been completely destroyed in the accident, the loss deduction would have been $32,000 (the adjusted basis of the airplane).

Any insurance recovery reduces the loss for business, investment, and personal-use losses. In fact, a taxpayer may realize a gain if the insurance proceeds exceed the adjusted basis of the property. Chapter 8 discusses the treatment of net gains and losses on business property and income-producing property.

A special rule on insurance recovery applies to *personal use property*. In particular, individuals are not permitted to deduct a casualty loss for damage to insured personal-use property unless an insurance claim is filed. This rule applies whether the insurance provides partial or full reimbursement for the loss.[16]

Generally, an appraisal before and after the casualty is needed to measure the amount of loss. However, the *cost of repairs* to the damaged property generally is acceptable as a method of establishing the loss in value.[17]

DIGGING DEEPER 3   **In-depth coverage can be found on this book's companion website: www.cengage.com**

Multiple Losses

When multiple casualty losses occur during the year, the amount of each loss is computed separately. The rules for computing loss deductions where multiple losses have occurred are illustrated in Example 16.

EXAMPLE 16

During the year, Swan Enterprises had the following business casualty losses:

| | | Fair Market Value of the Asset | | |
Asset	Adjusted Basis	Before the Casualty	After the Casualty	Insurance Recovery
A	$900	$600	$—0—	$400
B	300	800	250	150

The following losses are allowed:

- Asset A: $500. The complete destruction of a business asset results in a deduction of the adjusted basis of the property (reduced by any insurance recovery), regardless of the asset's fair market value.

- Asset B: $150. The partial destruction of a business asset results in a deduction equal to the lesser of the adjusted basis ($300) or the decline in value ($550), reduced by any insurance recovery ($150).

6-3e Casualty and Theft Losses of Individuals

Recall from Chapters 1 and 9 that the individual income tax formula distinguishes between deductions *for* AGI and deductions *from* AGI. Casualty and theft losses incurred by an individual in connection with a business or with rental and royalty activities are deductible *for* AGI and are limited only by the rules previously discussed.[18] Losses from most other investment activities and personal use losses are generally deducted *from*

---

[16]§ 165(h)(4)(E).
[17]Reg. § 1.165–7(a)(2)(ii).

[18]§ 62(a)(1).

AGI. Investment casualty and theft losses (e.g., the theft of a security) are classified as other miscellaneous itemized deductions (not subject to a 2%-of-AGI floor as explained in text Section 10-4e). Casualty and theft losses of personal use property are subject to special limitations discussed next.

Personal Use Property

In addition to the valuation rules discussed previously, individual taxpayers face three limitations on their ability to deduct personal casualty losses. First, after 2017, individuals can only deduct a casualty loss if it occurs in a Federally declared disaster area. Second, taxpayers must reduce each casualty loss by a $100 floor. This applies to all damaged property from a single casualty, and *not* to each asset damaged or destroyed. Third, the individual taxpayer can deduct only the portion of the total of *all* personal casualty losses that exceeds 10 percent of AGI.[19]

> **EXAMPLE 17**
>
> Rocky, who had AGI of $30,000, lost all the furniture in his apartment as a result of a flood in a Federally declared disaster area in 2018. His furniture, which he used only for personal use and had a fair market value of $12,000 and an adjusted basis of $9,000, was completely destroyed. He received $5,000 from his insurance company.
>
> Rocky's casualty loss deduction is $900 [$9,000 basis − $5,000 insurance recovery − $100 floor − $3,000 (.10 × $30,000 AGI)]. The $900 casualty loss is an itemized deduction (*from* AGI).
>
> Had Rocky's loss not related to a Federally declared disaster area, the deduction would have been zero.

Where there are both casualty and theft gains and losses from personal use property, special netting rules apply. Generally, if casualty and theft gains exceed losses during the year, the gains and losses are treated as capital gains and losses. Alternatively, if losses exceed gains, the casualty and theft gains (and losses to the extent of gains) are treated as ordinary gains and losses. Any excess losses are deductible as an itemized deduction but only if they are from a Federally declared disaster.

For the netting of personal casualty gains and losses, there is an exception to the rule that disallows a deduction for personal casualty losses other than those in Federally declared disaster areas.[20] In this case, the taxpayer may use a personal casualty loss (or losses) *not* attributable to a Federally declared disaster to offset any personal casualty gains. After this netting process, if any loss remains, it is not deductible (as it relates to a non-Federally declared disaster area casualty). If, however, a net personal casualty gain remains, it is used to offset any Federally declared disaster area casualty losses.

> **Calculating Personal Casualty Gains and Losses**
>
> **EXAMPLE 18**
>
> During 2018, Emmanuel has AGI of $50,000 and the following personal casualty gains and losses (after deducting the $100 floor):
>
> | Asset | Item | Gain or (Loss) |
> | --- | --- | --- |
> | A | Personal casualty gain | $ 2,500 |
> | B | Personal casualty loss (non-Federally declared disaster area) | (2,000) |
> | C | Personal casualty loss (Federally declared disaster area) | (9,000) |
>
> Emmanuel first offsets the non-Federally declared disaster area losses against the personal casualty gain, resulting in an excess personal casualty gain of $500, computed as follows:
>
> | | |
> | --- | --- |
> | Personal casualty gain | $ 2,500 |
> | Personal casualty loss (non-Federally declared disaster area) | (2,000) |
> | Excess personal casualty gain | $ 500 |
>
> *continued*

---

[19]§§ 165(c)(3) and (h).

[20]§ 165(h)(5)(B); personal casualty gains and losses are defined at § 165(h)(3).

Next, the excess personal casualty gain is used to offset the Federally declared disaster area loss. Emmanuel's overall net personal casualty loss is $8,500, computed as follows:

Personal casualty loss (Federally declared disaster area)	($ 9,000)
Less: Excess personal casualty gain	500
Overall net personal casualty loss	$ 8,500

After this second netting process, because a net personal casualty loss remains and it is from a Federally declared disaster area, Emmanuel can deduct the loss that exceeds the 10%-of-AGI floor. Emmanuel's itemized deduction for casualty losses is $3,500, computed as follows:

Net personal casualty loss	$ 8,500
Less: 10% of AGI (10% × $50,000)	(5,000)
Itemized deduction for casualty loss	$ 3,500

EXAMPLE 19

Refer back to the facts of Example 18. How would the answer change if the casualty loss related to Asset B was $4,000 (rather than $2,500)?

Emmanuel would begin by offsetting the non-Federally declared disaster area losses against the personal casualty gain, resulting in an excess personal casualty loss of $1,500, computed as follows:

Personal casualty gain	$ 2,500
Personal casualty loss (non-Federally declared disaster area)	(4,000)
Excess personal casualty loss	($ 1,500)

Since this net loss relates to a non-Federally declared disaster area, the loss is *not* deductible. Emmanuel's itemized deduction for casualty losses is $4,000, computed as follows:

Personal casualty loss (Federally declared disaster area)	$ 9,000
Less: 10% of AGI (10% × $50,000)	(5,000)
Itemized deduction for casualty loss	$ 4,000

See Concept Summary 6.2 for a review of the tax treatment of casualty gains and losses.

Concept Summary 6.2

Casualty Gains and Losses

	Business Use or Income-Producing Property	Personal Use Property
Event creating the loss	Any event.	Casualty from a Federally declared disaster area.
Amount	The lesser of the decline in fair market value or the adjusted basis, but always the adjusted basis if the property is totally destroyed.	The lesser of the decline in fair market value or the adjusted basis.
Insurance	Insurance proceeds received reduce the amount of the loss.	Insurance proceeds received (or for which there is an unfiled claim) reduce the amount of the loss.
$100 floor	Not applicable.	Applicable per casualty.
Gains and losses	Gains and losses are netted (see detailed discussion in Chapter 8).	Personal casualty and theft gains and losses are netted. An ordering rule requires that gains are first reduced by losses from non-Federally declared disaster, and only then by losses from Federally declared disaster. Only net losses from Federally declared disasters are allowed for 2018 through 2025.
Gains exceeding losses	See Chapter 8.	Treat as gains and losses from the sale of capital assets.

continued

Casualty Gains and Losses—(Continued)

	Business Use or Income-Producing Property	Personal Use Property
Losses exceeding gains	See Chapter 8.	Casualty gain is first offset by personal casualty loss not from a Federally declared disaster. If net gain results, it is then reduced by loss from Federally declared disasters. For personal use property, any loss allowed must be from a Federally declared disaster. The loss is only allowed to the extent it exceeds 10% of AGI and only if the individual itemizes deductions rather than claiming the standard deduction. The losses in excess of gains, to the extent that they exceed 10% of AGI, are itemized deductions (*from* AGI).

In-depth coverage can be found on this book's companion website: **www.cengage.com**   **4**   DIGGING DEEPER

6-4 **NET OPERATING LOSSES**

LO.4

Describe the impact of the net operating loss carryover provisions on previous and subsequent years' taxable income.

Taxpayers who report net operating losses, in which deductions exceed gross income, cannot compute the tax on negative income—taxable income is zero in this case. A <mark>net operating loss (NOL)</mark> in a particular tax year would produce no tax benefits if the Code did not provide for a carryforward of such losses to profitable years to smooth income over time.

6-4a **Introduction**

The requirement that every taxpayer file an annual income tax return (whether on a calendar year or a fiscal year) can lead to inequities for taxpayers who experience uneven income over a series of years. These inequities result from the application of progressive tax rates to taxable income determined on an annual basis.

EXAMPLE

20

Orange, Inc., realizes the following taxable income or loss over a five-year period: year 1, $50,000; year 2, ($30,000); year 3, $100,000; year 4, ($200,000); and year 5, $380,000. Blue Corporation has taxable income of $60,000 every year. Note that both corporations have total taxable income of $300,000 over the five-year period. Assume that there is no provision for carryback or carryover of net operating losses. Orange and Blue would have the following five-year tax liabilities:

Year	Orange's Tax	Blue's Tax
1	$ 10,500	$12,600
2	—0—	12,600
3	21,000	12,600
4	—0—	12,600
5	79,800	12,600
	$111,300	$63,000

Note: The computation of tax is made without regard to any NOL benefit. Rates for 2018 are used to compute the tax.

Even though Orange and Blue realized the same total taxable income ($300,000) over the five-year period, Orange would have to pay taxes of $111,300, while Blue would pay taxes of only $63,000.

To provide partial relief from this inequitable tax treatment, a deduction is allowed for net operating losses (NOLs).[21] This provision permits an NOL for any one year to offset taxable income in future years. The NOL provision provides relief only for losses from the operation of a trade or business or from casualty and theft.

Only C corporations and individuals are permitted an NOL deduction because losses of partnerships and S corporations pass through to their owners. For C corporations, the NOL equals any negative taxable income for the year, with an adjustment for the dividends received deduction (see text Section 12-4a). In addition, deductions for prior-year NOLs are not allowed when determining a current-year NOL.

6-4b General Rules

The mechanism providing a tax benefit from the NOL is the provision that allows a loss deduction in profitable years of the business activity. The loss may be carried over to future years [prior to changes by the Tax Cuts and Jobs Act (TCJA) of 2017, an NOL could also be carried back two years].

NOL Carryforwards

A current-year NOL is carried forward indefinitely following the loss year. When an NOL is carried forward, the current return shows an NOL deduction for the prior year's loss. An NOL deduction is limited to 80 percent of taxable income, determined without regard to the NOL deduction itself. If the NOL carryover is less than the computed limitation, the entire carryover is allowed as a deduction.

6-5 THE TAX SHELTER PROBLEM

LO.5

Explain the tax shelter problem and the reasons for at-risk and passive activity loss limitations.

Before Congress enacted legislation to reduce their effectiveness, tax shelters provided a popular way to avoid or defer taxes, as they could generate losses and other benefits to offset income from other sources. The tax avoidance potential of tax shelters attracted wealthy taxpayers with high marginal tax rates. Many tax shelters merely provided an opportunity for "investors" to buy deductions and credits in ventures that were not expected to generate a profit, even in the long run.

Although it may seem odd that a taxpayer would intentionally invest in an activity that was designed to produce losses, there is a logical explanation. The typical tax shelter operated as a partnership and relied heavily on nonrecourse financing.[22] Accelerated depreciation and interest expense deductions generated large tax losses in the early years of the activity. At the very least, the tax shelter deductions deferred the recognition of any net income until the investor sold the activity. In the best of situations, the investor could realize additional tax savings by offsetting other income (e.g., salary, interest, dividends) with losses flowing from the tax shelter. Ultimately, the sale of the investment would result in *tax-favored* capital gain. The following example illustrates what was possible *before* Congress enacted legislation to curb tax shelter abuses.

EXAMPLE 21

Bob, who earned a salary of $400,000 as a business executive and dividend income of $15,000, invested $20,000 for a 10% interest in a cattle-breeding tax shelter. He did not participate in the operation of the business. Through the use of $800,000 of nonrecourse financing and available cash of $200,000, the partnership acquired a herd of an exotic breed of cattle costing $1 million. Depreciation, interest, and other deductions related to the activity resulted in a loss of $400,000, of which Bob's share was $40,000. Bob was allowed to deduct the $40,000 loss even though he had invested and stood to lose only $20,000 if the investment became worthless. The net effect of the $40,000 deduction from the partnership was that a portion of Bob's salary and dividend income was "sheltered," and as a result, he was required to calculate his tax liability on only $375,000 of income [$415,000 (salary and dividends) − $40,000 (deduction)] rather than $415,000. If this deduction were available under current law and if Bob was in a combined Federal and state income tax bracket of 40%, a tax savings of $16,000 ($40,000 × 40%) would be generated in the first year alone.

---

[21]§ 172.

[22]Nonrecourse debt is an obligation for which the borrower is not personally liable. An example of nonrecourse debt is a liability on real estate acquired by a partnership without the partnership or any of the partners assuming any liability for the mortgage. The acquired property generally is pledged as collateral for the loan.

An important component in wealth maxi-mization is to pay no more tax than the law requires given an investment's before-tax cash flow. Holding constant the before-tax cash flow, one way to reduce the cost of taxation in present value terms is to defer the payment of a tax into the future for as long as possible. This can be accomplished by reducing the taxpayer's tax base (i.e., taxable income) either by deferring the recognition of income or by accelerating the timing of deductions. As a result, to the extent that the tax cost associated with an investment alternative is reduced, the after-tax benefit from that investment and the investor's wealth position are enhanced.

For example, a common attribute of many tax-advantaged investments is the availability of tax losses that investors may claim on their own income tax returns. Many times, these tax losses are the result of investment-level deductions, such as interest and accelerated depreciation deduc-tions, that are bunched in the early years of the life of the investment rather than being due to economic woes of the investment itself.

Through the at-risk limitations and the passive activity loss rules, the tax law works to scale back the ability of tax-payers to claim tax losses flowing from certain investments. These limitations have a direct impact on *when* investors can claim loss deductions flowing from affected investments. The typical result of these provisions is that the loss deductions are deferred. Therefore, when evaluating competing invest-ment alternatives, taxpayers must address the impact of these tax limitations in projecting the after-tax benefits that can be expected to follow.

A review of Example 21 shows that the taxpayer took a two-for-one write-off ($40,000 deduction, $20,000 amount invested). In the heyday of these types of tax shelters, promot-ers often promised tax deductions for the investor well in excess of the amount invested. Later years would often produce similar ordinary loss deductions. Then, at the end of the life of the investment, the investors would sell the assets, possibly producing long-term capital gains that enjoyed significantly lower tax rates. In response to these tax shelter results, in 1986, Congress enacted rules to limit investors' ability to deduct the losses.

The first major law change aimed at reducing the tax benefits from tax shelters is the **at-risk limitation**. Its objective is to limit a taxpayer's deductions to the amount that the taxpayer could actually lose from the investment (the amount "at risk") if it becomes worthless. Thus, in Example 21, the at-risk rule limits Bob's loss to $20,000—the amount at risk.

The second major attack on tax shelters came with the passage of the **passive activity loss** rules. These rules require the taxpayer to segregate all income and losses into three categories: active, portfolio, and passive. (Text Section 6-7 defines these categories.) In general, the passive activity loss limits *disallow* the deduction of passive activity losses against *active or portfolio income* even when the taxpayer is at risk to the extent of the loss. In general, passive activity losses can only offset passive activity income.

The third and most recent tax law change that limits the attractiveness of tax shelters is the "excess business loss" limit. This rule limits the dollar amount of deductible losses of noncorporate taxpayers. Text Section 6-8 covers this rule.

Thus, in Example 21, the passive activity loss rules disallow a current deduction for any of the loss. The loss from the tax shelter is a passive activity loss because Bob does not materially participate in the activity. Therefore, the $20,000 loss that is allowed under the at-risk rules ($40,000 total loss − $20,000 portion not "at risk") is disallowed under the passive activity loss rules because Bob does not report any passive activity income for the year—he reports only active and portfolio income. Consequently, Bob's current-year income must reflect his nonpassive activity income of $415,000. As explained later in the chapter, the disallowed $20,000 passive activity loss is suspended and may be deducted in a future year under certain conditions.

The following two sections explore the nature of the at-risk limits and the passive activity loss rules and their impact on investors. Congress intentionally structured these rules so that investors evaluating potential investments must consider mainly the pretax *economics* of the venture instead of the *tax benefits* or tax avoidance possibilities that an investment may generate.

Describe how the at-risk limitation and the passive activity loss rules limit deductions for losses and identify taxpayers subject to these restrictions.

6-6 **AT-RISK LIMITATIONS**

The at-risk rules limit the deductibility of losses from business and income-producing activities. These rules, which apply to individuals and closely held corporations, are designed to prevent taxpayers from deducting losses that exceed the actual economic investment in an activity. In the case of an S corporation or a partnership, the at-risk limits apply at the owner level. The at-risk rules limit a taxpayer's deductible loss from an activity for any taxable year to the amount the taxpayer could actually lose if the activity fails.

While the amount at risk generally vacillates over time, the initial amount considered at risk consists of the following:[23]

- The amount of cash and the adjusted basis of property contributed to the activity by the taxpayer.
- Amounts borrowed for use in the activity for which the taxpayer is personally liable.
- The adjusted basis of taxpayer property pledged as security that is not used in the activity.

This amount usually is increased each year by the taxpayer's share of income and is decreased by the taxpayer's share of deductible losses and withdrawals from the activity. In addition, because *general partners* are jointly and severally liable for recourse debts of the partnership, their at-risk amounts are increased when the partnership increases its debt and are decreased when the partnership reduces its debt. However, a taxpayer generally is not considered at risk for borrowed amounts if either of the following is true:

- The taxpayer is not personally liable for repayment of the debt (e.g., nonrecourse debt).
- The lender has an interest (other than as a creditor) in the activity.

An important exception provides that in the case of an activity involving the holding of real property, a taxpayer is considered at risk for his or her share of any *qualified non-recourse financing* that is secured by real property used in the activity.[24]

Subject to the passive activity loss rules discussed later in the chapter, a taxpayer may deduct a loss as long as the at-risk amount is positive. However, once the at-risk amount is exhausted, any remaining loss cannot be deducted until a later year. Any losses disallowed for any given taxable year by the at-risk rules may be deducted in the first succeeding year in which the rules do not prevent the deduction—that is, when there is, and to the extent of, a positive at-risk amount.

EXAMPLE 22

In 2018, Sue invests $40,000 in an oil partnership. The partnership incurs a first-year net loss, of which $60,000 is her share. Assume that Sue's interest in the partnership is subject to the at-risk limits but is not subject to the passive activity loss limits. Because Sue has only $40,000 of capital at risk, she cannot deduct more than $40,000 against her other income and must reduce her at-risk amount to zero ($40,000 at-risk amount − $40,000 loss deducted). The nondeductible loss of $20,000 ($60,000 loss generated − $40,000 loss allowed) can be carried over to 2019.

In 2019, Sue has taxable income of $15,000 from the oil partnership and invests an additional $10,000 in the venture. Her at-risk amount is now $25,000 ($0 beginning balance + $15,000 taxable income + $10,000 additional investment). This enables Sue to deduct the $20,000 carryover loss and requires her to reduce her at-risk amount to $5,000 ($25,000 at-risk amount − $20,000 carryover loss allowed).

Complicating the at-risk rules is the fact that previously allowed losses must be recaptured as income to the extent the at-risk amount is reduced below zero.[25] This rule applies in situations such as those when the amount at risk is reduced below zero

---

[23]§ 465(b)(1).

[24]Section 465(b)(6) defines *qualified nonrecourse financing*. See also the related discussion in text Section 14-3e.

[25]§ 465(e).

Concept Summary 6.3

Calculation of At-Risk Amount

Increases to a taxpayer's at-risk amount:

- Cash and the adjusted basis of property contributed to the activity.
- Amounts borrowed for use in the activity for which the taxpayer is personally liable.
- The adjusted basis of property pledged as security that is not used in the activity.
- Taxpayer's share of amounts borrowed for use in the activity that are qualified nonrecourse financing.
- Taxpayer's share of the activity's income.

Decreases to a taxpayer's at-risk amount:

- Withdrawals from the activity.
- Taxpayer's share of the activity's deductible loss.
- Taxpayer's share of any reductions of debt for which recourse against the taxpayer exists or any reductions of qualified non-recourse debt.

by distributions to the taxpayer or when the status of indebtedness changes from recourse to nonrecourse.

Calculation of at-risk amount is reviewed in Concept Summary 6.3.

6-7 PASSIVE ACTIVITY LOSS LIMITS

This section identifies and explains a number of key issues in applying the passive activity loss limits.

- The limits apply only to passive activity losses incurred by certain types of taxpayers.
- Losses are limited under these rules only if they are generated by a passive activity.
- Special rules exist for interests in real estate activities.
- Benefits may arise when a disposition of a passive activity occurs.

6-7a Classification and Impact of Passive Activity Income and Loss

The passive activity loss rules operate by requiring taxpayers to classify their income and losses into three categories. Then the rules limit the extent to which losses in the passive category can be used to offset income in the other categories.

Classification

The passive activity loss rules require income and loss to be classified into one of three categories: *active*, *portfolio*, or *passive*. **Active income** includes:

- Wages, salary, commissions, bonuses, and other payments for services rendered by the taxpayer.
- Profit from a trade or business in which the taxpayer is a material participant (material participation is described later in the chapter).

Portfolio income includes:

- Interest, dividends, annuities, and royalties not derived in the ordinary course of a trade or business.
- Gain or loss from the disposition of property that produces portfolio income or is held for investment purposes.

Passive activity income or loss arises from activities that are treated as passive, which include:

- Any trade or business or income-producing activity in which the taxpayer does not materially participate.
- Subject to certain exceptions (discussed later in the chapter), all rental activities, whether or not the taxpayer materially participates.

General Impact

Losses or expenses generated by passive activities can only be deducted to the extent of income from passive activities. Any excess loss may not be used to offset income from active or portfolio income. Instead, any unused passive activity losses are suspended and carried forward to future years to offset passive activity income generated in those years. Otherwise, suspended losses may be used only when a taxpayer disposes of his or her entire interest in an activity. In that event, generally, all current and suspended passive activity losses related to the activity may offset active and portfolio income.

The Big Picture

EXAMPLE 23

Return to the facts of *The Big Picture* on p. 6-1. Recall that Robyn invested $20,000 in the Florida orange grove limited partnership, which produced an allocable $20,000 loss for her this year. Assume that Robyn earns a salary of $100,000 along with $12,000 in dividends and interest from various portfolio investments. Because her at-risk basis in the partnership is $20,000, the current $20,000 loss is not limited by the at-risk rules. However, because the loss is a passive activity loss, it is not deductible against her other income. The loss is suspended and is carried over to the future. If Robyn has passive activity income from this investment or from other passive activities in the future, she can offset the suspended loss against that passive activity income. If she does not have passive activity income to offset this suspended loss in the future, she will be allowed to offset the loss against other types of income when she eventually disposes of her investment in the passive activity.

Impact of Suspended Losses

The actual economic gain or loss from a passive investment (including any suspended losses) can be determined when a taxpayer disposes of his or her entire interest in the investment. This is why the passive activity loss rules described above allow an overall loss realized from the taxpayer's activity to offset passive, active, and portfolio income. However, there is a strict ordering rule for using suspended passive activity losses, as the next paragraphs describe.

A fully taxable disposition generally involves a sale of the property to a third party at arm's length and thus, presumably, for a price equal to the property's fair market value. As presented in the following example, a gain recognized on the transfer of an interest in a passive activity generally is treated as passive and is first offset by the suspended passive activity losses from that activity.

EXAMPLE 24

Rex sells an apartment building, a passive activity, with an adjusted basis of $100,000 for $180,000. In addition, he has suspended passive activity losses of $60,000 associated with the building. His total gain, $80,000, and his taxable gain, $20,000, are calculated as follows:

Net sales price	$180,000
Less: Adjusted basis	(100,000)
Total gain	$ 80,000
Less: Suspended losses	(60,000)
Taxable gain (passive)	$ 20,000

Second, if current and suspended losses of the passive activity exceed the gain realized from the sale or if the sale results in a realized loss, the amount of

- any loss from the activity for the tax year (including losses suspended in the activity disposed of)

in excess of

- net income or gain for the tax year from all passive activities (without regard to the activity disposed of) is treated as a loss that is not from a passive activity. In computing the loss from the activity for the year of disposition, any gain or loss recognized is included in the calculation.

Dean sells an apartment building, a passive activity, with an adjusted basis of $100,000 for $150,000. In addition, he has current and suspended passive activity losses of $60,000 associated with the building and has no other passive activities. His total gain of $50,000 and his deductible loss of $10,000 are calculated as follows:

Net sales price	$150,000
Less: Adjusted basis	(100,000)
Total gain	$ 50,000
Less: Suspended losses	(60,000)
Deductible loss (not passive)	($ 10,000)

Dean can deduct the $10,000 loss against his active and portfolio income. Even if the building is sold for a loss (i.e., the adjusted basis exceeds the sales price), the total loss, including the suspended losses, is deductible as a nonpassive activity loss.

Carryovers of Suspended Losses

The preceding examples assumed that the taxpayer had an interest in only one passive activity; as a result, the suspended loss related exclusively to the activity just sold. However, taxpayers often own more than one passive activity, in which case any suspended losses must be allocated among those passive activities that generated losses. The allocation to an activity is made by multiplying the disallowed passive activity loss from all activities using the following fraction:

$$\frac{\text{Loss from one passive activity}}{\text{Sum of losses for taxable year from all passive activities having losses}}$$

Diego has investments in three passive activities with the following income and losses for 2017:

Activity A	($30,000)
Activity B	(20,000)
Activity C	25,000
Net passive activity loss	($25,000)
Net passive activity loss of $25,000 allocated to:	
Activity A [$25,000 × ($30,000/$50,000)]	($15,000)
Activity B [$25,000 × ($20,000/$50,000)]	(10,000)
Total suspended losses	($25,000)

Suspended losses are carried over indefinitely and are offset in the future, first against any passive activity income from the activities to which they relate and then against passive activity income from other passive activities.[26] Taxpayers subject to the passive activity loss limitation rule must maintain records to track the suspended losses and the activities to which they belong.

Assume that the facts are the same as in the preceding example and that in 2018, Activity A produces $10,000 of income. Diego may use $10,000 of Activity A's suspended loss of $15,000 from 2017 to offset the $10,000 income from this activity. If Diego sells Activity A in early 2019, the remaining $5,000 suspended loss is used to offset any income from the activity reported by Diego in 2019 and to determine his final gain or loss.

---

[26]§ 469(b).

Passive Activity Credits

Credits (such as the low-income housing credit and rehabilitation credit—discussed in text Section 17-1) that arise from passive activities are limited in much the same way as passive activity losses. Passive activity credits can only offset regular tax attributable to passive activity income,[27] which is calculated by comparing the tax on all income (including passive activity income) with the tax on income excluding passive activity income.

EXAMPLE 28

Sam owes $50,000 of tax, disregarding net passive activity income, and $80,000 of tax, considering both net passive activity and other taxable income (disregarding the credits in both cases). The amount of tax attributable to the passive activity income is $30,000.

In the preceding example, Sam can claim a maximum of $30,000 of passive activity credits; the excess credits are carried over. These passive activity credits can be used only against the *regular* tax attributable to passive activity income. A taxpayer can use no credits if there is a net loss from passive activities during a given year.

Carryovers of Passive Activity Credits

Tax credits attributable to passive activities can be carried forward indefinitely, much like suspended passive activity losses. Unlike passive activity losses, however, passive activity credits are permanently lost when the activity is disposed of in a taxable transaction where a *loss* is recognized. Credits are allowed on dispositions only when there is sufficient tax on passive activity income to absorb them.

Use of Passive Activity Credits upon Disposition of an Activity

EXAMPLE 29

Alicia sells a passive activity for a gain of $10,000. The activity had suspended losses of $40,000 and suspended credits of $15,000. The $10,000 gain is offset by $10,000 of the suspended losses, and the remaining $30,000 of suspended losses is deductible against Alicia's active and portfolio income. The suspended credits are permanently lost because the sale of the activity did not generate any tax after the effect of the suspended losses was considered.

EXAMPLE 30

If Alicia in the preceding example had realized a $100,000 gain on the sale of the passive activity, the suspended credits could have been used to the extent of the regular tax attributable to the net passive activity income.

Gain on sale	$100,000
Less: Suspended losses	(40,000)
Net gain	$ 60,000

If the tax attributable to the net gain of $60,000 is $15,000 or more, the entire $15,000 of suspended credits can be used. If the tax attributable to the gain is less than $15,000, the excess of the suspended credits over the tax attributable to the gain is lost.

When a taxpayer has sufficient regular tax liability from passive activities to trigger the use of suspended credits, the credits lose their character as passive activity credits. They are reclassified as regular tax credits and made subject to the same limits as other credits (see text Section 17-1).

Passive Activity Changes to Active

If a formerly passive activity becomes active, suspended losses are allowed to the extent of income from the now active business.[28] If any of the suspended loss remains, it continues to be treated as a loss from a passive activity. The excess suspended loss can be

---

[27] § 469(d)(2).   [28] § 469(f).

deducted against passive activity income or carried over to the next tax year and deducted to the extent of income from the now active business in the succeeding year(s).

For several years, Rebecca has owned an interest in a passive activity that has produced losses of $80,000 during that period. Because she did not have passive activity income from other sources, she could not deduct any of the activity's passive activity losses. In the current year, she has become a material participant in the activity and her share of the business profits totals $25,000. As a result, she may use $25,000 of the suspended passive activity loss to offset the current business profits. Rebecca's remaining suspended passive activity loss from the activity is $55,000 ($80,000 − $25,000), which is carried over to future years and used to offset income from the formerly passive activity or income from other passive activities.

6-7b Taxpayers Subject to the Passive Activity Loss Rules

The passive activity loss rules apply to individuals, estates, trusts, personal service corporations, and closely held C corporations.[29] Passive activity income or loss from investments in partnerships or S corporations (see Chapters 14 and 15) flows through to the owners, and the passive activity loss rules are applied at the owner level. Consequently, it is necessary to understand how the passive activity rules apply to both entities *and* their owners (including individual taxpayers).

Personal Service Corporations

Determination of whether a corporation is a ==personal service corporation== is based on rather broad definitions. A personal service corporation is a regular (or C) corporation that meets both of the following conditions:

- The principal activity is the performance of personal services.
- Such services are substantially performed by owner-employees.

Generally, personal service corporations include those in the fields of health, law, engineering, architecture, accounting, actuarial science, performing arts, and consulting.[30]

Application of the passive activity loss limitations to personal service corporations is intended to prevent taxpayers from sheltering personal service income by creating personal service corporations and acquiring passive activities at the corporate level.

Two tax accountants who earn an aggregate of $200,000 a year in their individual practices agree to work together in a newly formed personal service corporation. Shortly after its formation, the corporation invests in a passive activity that produces a $200,000 loss during the year. Because the passive activity loss rules apply to personal service corporations, the corporation may not deduct the $200,000 passive activity loss against the $200,000 of active income.

In-depth coverage can be found on this book's companion website: **www.cengage.com**   **5**   DIGGING DEEPER

Closely Held C Corporations

Application of the passive activity loss rules to closely held (nonpersonal service) C corporations is also intended to prevent individuals from incorporating to avoid the passive activity loss limitations. A corporation is classified as a ==closely held C corporation== if at any time during the taxable year, more than 50 percent of the value of its outstanding stock is owned, directly or indirectly, by or for five or fewer individuals. Closely held C corporations (other than personal service corporations) may use passive activity losses to offset *active* income but *not portfolio* income.

---

[29]§ 469(a). [30]§ 448(d)(2)(A).

EXAMPLE 33

Silver Corporation, a closely held (nonpersonal service) C corporation, has a $500,000 passive activity loss from a rental activity, $400,000 of active income, and $100,000 of portfolio income. The corporation may offset $400,000 of the $500,000 passive activity loss against the $400,000 of active business income but may not offset the remainder against the $100,000 of portfolio income. As a result, $100,000 of the passive activity loss is suspended ($500,000 passive activity loss − $400,000 offset against active income).

Application of the passive activity loss limitations to closely held C corporations prevents shareholders from transferring their portfolio investments to such corporations to offset passive activity losses against portfolio income.

LO.7

Discuss the definitions of activity, material participation, and rental activity under the passive activity loss rules.

6-7c Rules for Determining Passive Activities

Identifying what constitutes an activity is a necessary first step in applying the passive activity loss limitation. The rules used to delineate an activity state that in general, a taxpayer can treat one or more trade or business activities or rental activities as a single activity if those activities form an *appropriate economic unit* for measuring gain or loss. The Regulations provide guidelines for identifying appropriate economic units.[31] These guidelines are designed to prevent taxpayers from arbitrarily combining different businesses in an attempt to circumvent the passive activity loss limitation. For example, combining a profitable active business and a passive business generating losses into one activity would allow the taxpayer to offset passive activity losses against active income.

DIGGING DEEPER 6

In-depth coverage can be found on this book's companion website: **www.cengage.com**

To determine which ventures form an appropriate economic unit, all of the relevant facts and circumstances must be considered. However, special rules restrict the grouping of rental and nonrental activities.[32] The following example, adapted from the Regulations, illustrates the application of the activity grouping rules.[33]

EXAMPLE 34

George owns a men's clothing store and an internet café in Chicago. He also owns a men's clothing store and an internet café in Milwaukee. Reasonable methods of applying the facts and circumstances test may result in any of the following groupings:

- All four businesses may be grouped into a single activity because of common ownership and control.

- The clothing stores may be grouped into an activity, and the internet cafés may be grouped into an activity.

- The Chicago businesses may be grouped into an activity, and the Milwaukee businesses may be grouped into an activity.

- Each of the four businesses may be treated as a separate activity.

Once a set of activities has been grouped by the taxpayer using the above rules, the grouping cannot be changed unless a material change in the facts and circumstances occurs or the original grouping was clearly inappropriate. In addition, the Regulations also grant the IRS the right to regroup activities when one of the primary purposes of the taxpayer's grouping is to avoid the passive activity loss limitation and the grouping fails to reflect an appropriate economic unit.[34]

6-7d Material Participation

As indicated previously, if a taxpayer materially participates in a nonrental trade or business activity, any loss from that activity is treated as an active loss that can offset active or portfolio income. (Participation is defined later in the chapter.) If a taxpayer does not

---

[31]Reg. § 1.469–4.
[32]Reg. § 1.469–4(d).

[33]Reg. § 1.469–4(c)(3).
[34]Reg. § 1.469–4(f).

materially participate, however, the loss is treated as a passive activity loss, which can only offset passive activity income. As a result, controlling whether a particular activity is treated as active or passive is an important part of the tax strategy of a taxpayer who owns an interest in one or more businesses. Consider the following examples.

Implications of Material Participation Status

Cameron, a corporate executive, earns a salary of $600,000 per year. In addition, he owns a separate business in which he participates. The business produces a loss of $100,000 during the year. If Cameron materially participates in the business, the $100,000 loss is an active loss that may offset his active income from his corporate employer. If he does not materially participate, the loss is passive and is suspended unless he has other passive activity income. Cameron may use the suspended loss in the future only when he has passive activity income or disposes of the activity.

EXAMPLE
35

Connor, an attorney, earns $350,000 a year in his law practice. In addition, he owns interests in two activities, A and B, in which he participates. Activity A, in which he does not *materially* participate, produces a loss of $50,000. Connor has not yet met the material participation standard, described below, for Activity B, which produces income of $80,000. However, he can meet the material participation standard if he spends an additional 50 hours in Activity B during the year. Should Connor attempt to meet the material participation standard for Activity B?

If he continues working in Activity B and becomes a material participant, the $80,000 of income from the activity is active and the $50,000 passive activity loss from Activity A must be suspended. A more favorable tax strategy is for Connor *not to meet* the material participation standard for Activity B, thus making the income from that activity passive. This enables him to offset the $50,000 passive activity loss from Activity A against most of the passive activity income from Activity B.

EXAMPLE
36

It is possible to devise numerous scenarios in which the taxpayer could control the tax outcome by increasing or decreasing participation in different activities. Examples 35 and 36 demonstrate two of the possibilities. The conclusion reached in most analyses of this type is that taxpayers will benefit by having profitable activities classified as passive so that any passive activity losses can be used to offset that passive activity income. If the activity produces a loss, however, the taxpayer will benefit if it is classified as active so that the loss is not subject to the passive activity loss limitations.

Temporary Regulations[35] provide seven tests (listed in Concept Summary 6.4) that serve to determine when material participation is achieved.

Concept Summary 6.4

Tests to Determine Material Participation

Tests Based on Current Participation

1. The individual participates in the activity for more than 500 hours during the year.

2. The individual's participation in the activity for the taxable year constitutes substantially all of the participation in the activity of all individuals (including nonowner employees) for the year.

3. The individual participates in the activity for more than 100 hours during the year, and this participation is not less than that participation of any other individual (including nonowner employees) for the year.

4. The activity is a significant participation activity (where the person's participation *exceeds* 100 hours during the year), and the hours for all significant participation activities during the year are more than 500 hours.

Tests Based on Prior Participation

5. The individual materially participated in the activity for any 5 taxable years during the 10 taxable years that immediately precede the current taxable year.

6. The activity is a personal service activity, and the individual materially participated in the activity for any three preceding taxable years.

Test Based on Facts and Circumstances

7. Based on all of the facts and circumstances, the individual participates in the activity on a regular, continuous, and substantial basis during the year.

---

[35]Temp.Reg. § 1.469–5T(a).

DIGGING DEEPER 7   **In-depth coverage can be found on this book's companion website: www.cengage.com**

Participation Defined

Participation generally includes any work done by an individual in an activity that he or she owns. Participation does not include work if it is of a type not customarily done by owners *and* if one of its principal purposes is to avoid the disallowance of passive activity losses or credits. Work done in an individual's capacity as an investor (e.g., reviewing financial reports in a nonmanagerial capacity) is not counted in applying the material participation tests. However, participation by an owner's spouse counts as participation by the owner.[36]

EXAMPLE 37

Tom, a partner in a CPA firm, owns a computer store that operated at a loss during the year. To offset this loss against the income from his CPA practice, Tom would like to avoid having the computer business classified as a passive activity. During the year, he worked 480 hours in the business in management and selling activities and 30 hours doing janitorial chores. In addition, Tom's wife participated 40 hours as a salesperson. It is likely that Tom's 480 hours of participation in management and selling activities will count as participation in work customarily done by owners, but the 30 hours spent doing janitorial chores will not. However, the 40 hours of participation by his wife will count. Assuming that none of the participation's principal purposes is to avoid the allowance of passive activity losses or credits, Tom will qualify as a material participant under the more-than-500-hour rule ($480 + 40 = 520$).

Limited Partners

A *limited* partner is a partner whose liability to third-party creditors of the partnership is limited to the amount the partner has invested in the partnership. Such a partnership must have at least one *general* partner who is fully liable in an individual capacity for the debts of the partnership to third parties. Generally, a *limited partner* is not considered a material participant unless he or she qualifies under Test 1, 5, or 6 as shown in Concept Summary 6.4. However, a *general partner* may qualify as a material participant by meeting any of the seven tests. If a general partner also owns a limited interest in the same limited partnership, all interests are treated as a general interest.[37]

Corporations

Personal service corporations and closely held C corporations cannot directly participate in an activity. However, a corporation is deemed to materially participate if its owners materially participate in an activity of the corporation. Together, the participating owners must own directly or indirectly more than 50 percent of the value of the outstanding stock of the corporation.[38] Alternatively, a closely held C corporation may be deemed to materially participate in an activity if, during the entire year, it has at least one full-time employee actively managing the business and at least three full-time nonowner employees working for the business. In addition, the corporation's trade or business expenses must exceed, by 15 percent, the gross income from that business for the year.[39]

6-7e Rental Activities

Subject to certain exceptions, all rental activities are treated as passive activities.[40] A ==rental activity== is defined as any activity where payments are received principally for the use of tangible (real or personal) property.[41] Importantly, an activity classified as a rental activity is subject to the passive activity loss rules even if the taxpayer meets a material participation test.

---

[36]§ 469(h)(5) and Temp.Reg. § 1.469–5T(f)(3).

[37]§ 469(h)(2) and Temp.Reg. § 1.469–5T(e)(3)(ii). Under Prop.Reg. § 1.469–5, however, material participation status for owners of LLCs and LLPs is dependent on the taxpayer's general involvement in the business.

[38]Temp.Reg. § 1.469–1T(g)(3)(i)(A).

[39]Temp.Reg. § 1.469–1T(g)(3)(i)(B).

[40]§ 469(c)(2).

[41]§ 469(j)(8).

Sarah owns a fleet of automobiles that are held for rent, and she spends an average of 60 hours a week in the activity. Assuming that her automobile business is classified as a rental activity, it is automatically subject to the passive activity rules even though Sarah spends more than 500 hours a year in its operation.

EXAMPLE
38

Certain rentals of real and personal property might be classified under the passive activity loss rules as nonrental activities.[42] In these situations, assuming that the activity is a trade or business, the material participation tests shown in Concept Summary 6.4 must be applied to determine whether the activity is a passive activity.

In-depth coverage can be found on this book's companion website: www.cengage.com

8 DIGGING DEEPER

Dan owns a bicycle rental business at a nearby resort. Because the average period of customer use is seven days or less, Dan's business is not treated as a rental activity.

EXAMPLE
39

This exception to the definition of a rental activity is based on the presumption that a person who rents property for seven days or less is generally required to provide significant services to the customer. Providing such services supports a conclusion that the person is engaged in a service business rather than a rental business.

If Dan in Example 39 is a material participant, the business is treated as active. If he is not a material participant, it is treated as a passive activity. For additional discussion of the rental exceptions, see IRS Publication 925 (*Passive Activity and At-Risk Rules*).

The general rules relating to passive activity losses are reviewed in Concept Summary 6.5.

Concept Summary 6.5

Passive Activity Loss Rules: Key Issues and Answers

What is the fundamental passive activity rule?	Passive activity losses may be deducted only against passive activity income and gains. Losses not allowed are suspended and used in future years.
Who is subject to the passive activity rules?	Individuals.
	Estates.
	Trusts.
	Personal service corporations.
	Closely held C corporations.
What is a passive activity?	Trade or business or income-producing activity in which the taxpayer does not materially participate during the year or rental activities, subject to certain exceptions, regardless of the taxpayer's level of participation.
What is an activity?	One or more trades or businesses or rental activities that comprise an appropriate economic unit.
How is an appropriate economic unit determined?	Based on a reasonable application of the relevant facts and circumstances.
What is material participation?	In general, the taxpayer participates on a regular, continuous, and substantial basis. More specifically, when the taxpayer meets the conditions of one of the seven tests provided in the Regulations.
What is a rental activity?	In general, an activity where payments are received for the use of tangible property. Special rules apply to rental real estate.

---

[42]Temp.Reg. § 1.469–1T(e)(3).

LO.8

Determine the relationship between the at-risk and passive activity loss limitations.

6-7f Interaction of At-Risk and Passive Activity Loss Limits

The determination of whether a loss is suspended under the passive activity loss rules is made *after* application of the at-risk rules, as well as other provisions relating to the measurement of taxable income. A loss that is not allowed for the year because the taxpayer is not at risk with respect to it is suspended under the at-risk provisions, not under the passive activity loss rules. Further, a taxpayer's at-risk basis is reduced by the losses (but not below zero) even if the deductions are not currently usable because of the passive activity loss rules. The following examples illustrate these points.

At-Risk and Passive Activity Loss Interactions

EXAMPLE 40

Jack's adjusted basis in a passive activity is $10,000 at the beginning of 2017. His loss from the activity in 2017 is $4,000. Because Jack has no passive activity income, the $4,000 cannot be deducted. At year-end, Jack has an adjusted basis and an at-risk amount of $6,000 in the activity and a suspended passive activity loss of $4,000.

EXAMPLE 41

Jack in the preceding example has a loss of $9,000 in the activity in 2018. Because the $9,000 exceeds his at-risk amount ($6,000) by $3,000, the at-risk rules disallow the $3,000. If Jack has no passive activity income, the passive activity rules suspend the remaining $6,000 loss. At year-end, he has:

- A $3,000 loss suspended under the at-risk rules.
- $10,000 of suspended passive activity losses ($4,000 from 2017 and $6,000 from 2018).
- An adjusted basis and at-risk amount in the activity of zero.

EXAMPLE 42

Jack in Example 41 realizes $1,000 of passive activity income from the activity in 2019. Because the $1,000 increases his at-risk amount, $1,000 of the $3,000 unused loss from 2018 is reclassified as a passive activity loss. If he has no other passive activity income, the $1,000 income is offset by $1,000 of suspended passive activity losses. At the end of 2019, Jack has:

- No taxable passive activity income.
- $2,000 ($3,000 − $1,000) of suspended losses under the at-risk rules.
- $10,000 of (reclassified) suspended passive activity losses ($10,000 + $1,000 of reclassified suspended at-risk losses − $1,000 of passive activity losses offset against passive activity income).
- An adjusted basis and an at-risk amount in the activity of zero.

EXAMPLE 43

In 2020, Jack has no gain or loss from the activity in Example 42. He contributes $5,000 more to the passive activity. Because the $5,000 contribution increases his at-risk amount, the $2,000 of losses suspended under the at-risk rules is reclassified as passive. Jack gets no passive activity loss deduction in 2020. At year-end, he has:

- No suspended losses under the at-risk rules.
- $12,000 of suspended passive activity losses ($10,000 + $2,000 of reclassified suspended at-risk losses).
- An adjusted basis and an at-risk amount of $3,000 ($5,000 additional investment − $2,000 of reclassified losses).

See Concept Summary 6.6 for the interactions of the at-risk and passive activity loss limits.

Concept Summary 6.6

Treatment of Losses Subject to the At-Risk and Passive Activity Loss Limitations

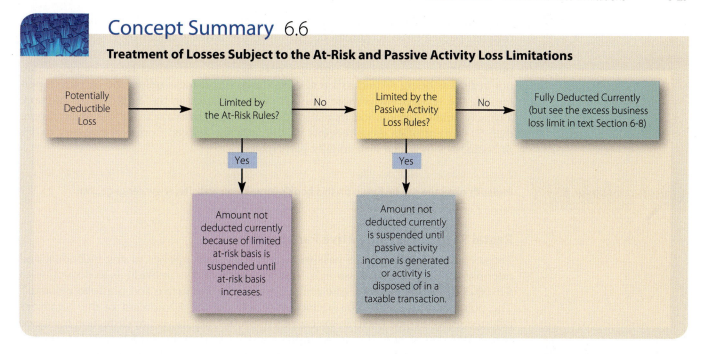

6-7g **Special Rules for Real Estate**

The passive activity loss rules contain two exceptions related to real estate activities. These exceptions allow all or part of real estate rental losses to offset active or portfolio income even though the activity otherwise is defined as a passive activity.

LO.9

Explain the special treatment available to real estate activities.

Real Estate Professionals

The first exception allows certain real estate professionals to avoid passive activity treatment for rental real estate activities.[43] To potentially qualify for nonpassive treatment (of both income and losses), a taxpayer must satisfy both of the following requirements:

- More than half of the personal services that the taxpayer performs in trades or businesses are performed in real property trades or businesses in which the taxpayer materially participates.
- The taxpayer performs more than 750 hours of services in these real property trades or businesses as a material participant.

If these two requirements are met, taxpayers are allowed to apply the material participation tests to their rental real estate activities (that is, the rentals are not per se passive activities). Taxpayers who do not satisfy the above requirements (or who meet them but do not materially participate in their rental real estate activities) must continue to treat income and losses from real estate rental activities as passive activity income and losses.

During the current year, Della performs personal service activities as follows: 900 hours as a personal financial planner, 550 hours in a real estate development business, and 600 hours in a real estate rental activity. Any loss Della incurs in either real estate activity will not be subject to the passive activity loss rules if she meets one of the material participation tests. Being a nonrental business, the real estate development business is deemed active under the more-than-500-hour material participation test. Della meets the two requirements to be a real estate professional [more than 50% of her personal services are devoted to real property trades or businesses (i.e., the development and rental) and these hours exceed 750]. Thus, she is allowed to apply the material participation tests to the real estate rental activity, and she meets one of these tests (the more-than-500-hours test). Hence, any losses from either real estate activity can offset active and portfolio income. Likewise, any income from these activities is nonpassive (active) income.

EXAMPLE 44

---

[43]§ 469(c)(7).

As discussed earlier, a spouse's work is taken into consideration in satisfying the material participation requirement. However, the hours worked by a spouse are not considered in determining whether the two tests are met for hours worked in real property trades or businesses during a year. Services performed by an employee are not treated as being related to a real estate trade or business unless the employee performing the services owns more than a 5 percent interest in the employer. In addition, a closely held C corporation may also qualify for the passive activity loss relief if more than 50 percent of its gross receipts for the year are derived from real property trades or businesses in which it materially participates.[44]

DIGGING DEEPER 9   **In-depth coverage can be found on this book's companion website: www.cengage.com**

Rental Real Estate with Active Participation

The second exception to the passive activity loss limits applies to any individual and not only to real estate professionals. This exception allows individuals to deduct up to $25,000 of losses from real estate rental activities against active and portfolio income.[45] The potential annual $25,000 deduction is reduced by 50 percent of the taxpayer's adjusted gross income (AGI) in excess of $100,000. Thus, the entire deduction is phased out at $150,000 of AGI. If married individuals file separately, the $25,000 deduction is reduced to zero unless they lived apart for the entire year, in which case the loss amount is $12,500 each and the phaseout begins at $50,000 of AGI.

To qualify for the $25,000 exception, a taxpayer must meet both of the following requirements:[46]

- *Actively participate* in the real estate rental activity.
- Own 10 percent or more (in value) of all interests in the activity during the entire taxable year (or shorter period during which the taxpayer held an interest in the activity).

The difference between *active participation* and *material participation* is that the former can be satisfied without regular, continuous, and substantial involvement in operations as long as the taxpayer participates in making management decisions in a significant and bona fide sense. In this context, relevant management decisions include decisions such as approving new tenants, deciding on rental terms, and approving capital or repair expenditures.

The $25,000 allowance is available after all active participation rental losses and gains are netted and applied to other passive activity income. If a taxpayer has a real estate rental loss in excess of the amount that can be deducted under the real estate rental exception, that excess is treated as a passive activity loss, usable in future years.

EXAMPLE 45

Brad has $90,000 of AGI before considering rental activities. Brad also has $85,000 of losses from a real estate rental activity in which he actively participates. He also actively participates in another real estate rental activity from which he has $30,000 of income. He has other passive activity income of $36,000. Of the net rental loss of $55,000 ($30,000 − $85,000), $36,000 is absorbed by the passive activity income, leaving $19,000 that Brad can deduct against active or portfolio income.

The $25,000 offset allowance is an aggregate of both deductions and credits in deduction equivalents. The deduction equivalent of a passive activity credit is the amount of deductions that reduces the tax liability for the taxable year by an amount equal to the credit.[47] A taxpayer with $5,000 of credits and a marginal tax rate of 25 percent would have a deduction equivalent of $20,000 ($5,000 ÷ 25%).

---

[44]§ 469(c)(7)(B) and Reg. § 1.469–9. In *Frank Aragona Trust*, 142 T.C. 165 (2014), the Tax Court found that a trust also could qualify for the real estate professional rule.

[45]§ 469(i).
[46]§ 469(i)(6).
[47]§ 469(j)(5).

If total deductions and deduction equivalents exceed $25,000, the taxpayer must allocate the benefit on a pro rata basis. First, the allowance must be allocated among the losses (including real estate rental activity losses suspended in prior years) and then to credits.

Deduction Equivalent Considerations

Kevin is an active participant in a real estate rental activity that produces $8,000 of income, $26,000 of deductions, and $1,500 of credits. Kevin is a single taxpayer with $85,000 of AGI (before considering this rental activity) and a 25% marginal tax rate. He can deduct the net passive activity loss of $18,000 ($8,000 − $26,000). After deducting the loss, he has an available deduction equivalent of $7,000 ($25,000 − $18,000 passive activity loss). Because the actual credits produce a deduction equivalent ($1,500 ÷ 25% = $6,000) that is less than $7,000, Kevin may claim the entire $1,500 credit.

EXAMPLE
46

Kelly, whose marginal tax rate is 25%, actively participates in three separate real estate rental activities. The relevant tax results for each activity are as follows:

- Activity A: $20,000 of losses.
- Activity B: $10,000 of losses.
- Activity C: $4,200 of credits.

Kelly's deduction equivalent from the credits is $16,800 ($4,200 ÷ 25%). As a result, the total passive activity deductions and deduction equivalents are $46,800 ($20,000 + $10,000 + $16,800), which exceeds the maximum allowable amount of $25,000. Consequently, Kelly must allocate pro rata first from among losses and then from among credits. Deductions from losses are limited as follows:

- Activity A: $25,000 × [$20,000/($20,000 + $10,000)] = $16,667.
- Activity B: $25,000 × [$10,000/($20,000 + $10,000)] = $8,333.

Because the amount of passive activity deductions exceeds the $25,000 maximum, the deduction balance of $5,000 and passive activity credits of $4,200 must be carried forward. Kelly's suspended losses and credits by activity are as follows:

EXAMPLE
47

	Total	Activity		
		A	B	C
Allocated losses	$ 30,000	$ 20,000	$10,000	$ —0—
Allocated credits	4,200	—0—	—0—	4,200
Utilized losses	(25,000)	(16,667)	(8,333)	—0—
Suspended losses	5,000	3,333	1,667	—0—
Suspended credits	4,200	—0—	—0—	4,200

6-7h **Disposition of Passive Activities**

LO.10

Determine the consequences of the disposition of passive activities.

Recall from an earlier discussion that if a taxpayer disposes of an entire interest in a passive activity, any suspended losses (and in certain cases, suspended credits) may be utilized when calculating the final economic gain or loss on the investment. In addition, if a loss ultimately results, that loss can offset other types of income. However, the consequences may differ if the activity is disposed of in a transaction that is not fully taxable. The following sections discuss the treatment of suspended passive activity losses in two such dispositions.

Disposition of a Passive Activity at Death

When a transfer of a taxpayer's interest occurs because of the taxpayer's death, suspended losses are allowed (to the decedent) to the extent they exceed the amount, if any, of the allowed step-up in basis.[48] Suspended losses that are equal to or less than

---

[48]§ 469(g)(2).

the amount of the basis increase are, however, lost. The losses allowed generally are reported on the final return of the deceased taxpayer.

Disposition of Suspended Losses at Death

EXAMPLE 48

Alyson dies with passive activity property having an adjusted basis of $40,000, suspended losses of $10,000, and a fair market value at the date of her death of $75,000. The increase (i.e., step-up) in basis (see text Section 7-2c) is $35,000 (fair market value at date of death in excess of adjusted basis). None of the $10,000 suspended loss is deductible on Alyson's final return or by the beneficiary. The suspended losses ($10,000) are lost because they do not exceed the step-up in basis ($35,000).

EXAMPLE 49

Assume the same facts as in the previous example except that the property's fair market value at the date of Alyson's death is $47,000. Because the step-up in basis is only $7,000 ($47,000 − $40,000), the suspended losses allowed are limited to $3,000 ($10,000 suspended loss at time of death − $7,000 increase in basis). The $3,000 loss available to Alyson is reported on her final income tax return.

Disposition of a Passive Activity by Gift

In a disposition of a taxpayer's interest in a passive activity by gift, the suspended losses are added to the basis of the property.[49]

As such, the suspended losses become permanently nondeductible to both the donor and the donee. Nonetheless, a tax *benefit* may be available to the donee for another reason. Due to the increase in the property's basis, greater depreciation deductions can result and there will be less gain (or more loss) on a subsequent sale of the property.

EXAMPLE 50

Carlton makes a gift to Yolanda of passive activity property having an adjusted basis of $40,000, suspended losses of $10,000, and a fair market value at the date of the gift of $100,000. Carlton cannot deduct the suspended losses in the year of the disposition. However, the suspended losses of $10,000 transfer with the property and are added to the adjusted basis of the property, thus becoming $50,000 in Yolanda's hands. Assuming that Yolanda is able to sell the property for $105,000 soon after she receives the gift, her taxable gain would be $55,000 ($105,000 − $50,000), which reflects the benefit from the increased basis.

TAX PLANNING STRATEGIES   Utilizing Passive Activity Losses

FRAMEWORK FOCUS: TAX RATE

Strategy: Control the Character of Income and Deductions.

Perhaps the biggest challenge individuals face with the passive activity loss rules is to recognize the potential impact of the rules and then to structure their affairs to minimize this impact. Taxpayers who have passive activity losses (PALs) should adopt a strategy of generating passive activity income that can be sheltered by existing passive activity losses. One approach is to buy an interest in a passive activity that is generating income (referred to as a passive income generator, or PIG). Then the PAL can offset income from the PIG. From a tax perspective, it would be foolish to buy a loss-generating passive activity unless one has passive activity income to shelter or the activity is rental real estate that can qualify for the $25,000 exception or the exception available to real estate professionals.

continued

---

[49]§ 469(j)(6).

If a taxpayer invests in an activity that produces losses subject to the passive activity loss rules, the following strategies may help minimize the loss of current deductions:

- If money is borrowed to finance the purchase of a passive activity, the associated interest expense is generally treated as part of any passive activity loss. Consequently, by using more available (i.e., not borrowed) cash to purchase the passive investment, the investor will need less debt and will incur less interest expense. By incurring less interest expense, a possible suspended passive activity loss deduction is reduced.

- If the investor does not have sufficient cash readily available for the larger down payment, cash can be obtained by borrowing against the equity in his or her personal residence. The interest expense on such debt will be deductible under the qualified residence interest provisions (see text Section 10-4c) and will not be subject to the passive activity loss limitations. Thus, the taxpayer avoids the passive activity loss limitation and secures a currently deductible interest expense.

As explained earlier, unusable passive activity losses often accumulate and provide no current tax benefit because the taxpayer has no passive activity income. When the taxpayer disposes of the entire interest in a passive activity, however, any suspended losses from that activity are used to reduce the taxable gain. If any taxable gain still remains, it can be offset by losses from other passive activities. As a result, the taxpayer should carefully select the year in which to dispose of a passive activity. It is to the taxpayer's advantage to wait until sufficient passive activity losses have accumulated to offset any gain recognized on the asset's disposition.

Bill, a calendar year taxpayer, owns interests in two passive activities: Activity A, which he plans to sell in December of this year at a gain of $100,000, and Activity B, which he plans to keep indefinitely. Current and suspended losses associated with Activity B total $60,000, and Bill expects losses from the activity to be $40,000 next year. If Bill sells Activity A this year, the $100,000 gain can be offset by the current and suspended losses of $60,000 from Activity B, producing a net taxable gain of $40,000. However, if Bill delays the sale of Activity A until January of next year, the $100,000 gain will be fully offset by the $100,000 of losses generated by Activity B ($60,000 current and prior losses + $40,000 next year's loss). Consequently, by postponing the sale by one month, he could avoid recognizing $40,000 of gain that would otherwise result.

Taxpayers with passive activity losses should consider the level of their involvement in all other trades or businesses in which they have an interest. If they show that they do not materially participate in a profitable activity, the activity becomes a passive activity. Current and suspended passive activity losses then could shelter any income generated by the profitable business. Family partnerships in which certain members do not materially participate would qualify. The silent partner in any general partnership engaged in a trade or business would also qualify.

Gail has an investment in a limited partnership that produces annual passive activity losses of approximately $25,000. She also owns a newly acquired interest in a convenience store where she works. Her share of the store's income is $35,000. If she works enough to be classified as a material participant, her $35,000 share of income is treated as active income. This results in $35,000 being subject to tax every year, while her $25,000 loss is suspended. However, if Gail reduces her involvement at the store so that she is not a material participant, the $35,000 of income receives passive treatment. Consequently, the $35,000 of income can be offset by the $25,000 passive activity loss, resulting in only $10,000 being subject to tax. Thus, by reducing her involvement, Gail ensures that the income from the profitable trade or business receives passive treatment and can then be used to absorb passive activity losses from other passive activities.

The passive activity loss rules can have a dramatic effect on a taxpayer's ability to claim passive activity losses currently. As a result, it is important to keep accurate records of all sources of income and losses, particularly any suspended passive activity losses and credits and the activities to which they relate, so that their potential tax benefit will not be lost.

The passive activity rules can also affect planning for individuals subject to the Net Investment Income Tax (text Section 9-6b).

6-8 EXCESS BUSINESS LOSSES

A noncorporate taxpayer cannot deduct an **excess business loss**.[50] Instead, taxpayers carry the loss forward and treat it as part of the taxpayer's net operating loss (NOL) carryforward in subsequent years (text Section 6-4 discusses NOLs).

6-8a Definition and Rules

An *excess business loss* is defined as:[51]

> The aggregate deductions for the year attributable to the taxpayer's businesses
>
> Less: The sum of aggregate gross income or gain of the taxpayer
>
> Less: A threshold amount ($500,000 for married taxpayers filing a joint return; $250,000 for all other taxpayers). Beginning in 2019, the threshold amounts are adjusted for inflation each year.

At its core, the purpose of the excess business loss limitation—added by the TCJA of 2017—is to limit the amount of nonbusiness income (e.g., salaries, interest, dividends, and capital gains) that can be "sheltered" from tax as a result of business losses. The excess business loss limitation is applied *after* the application of the § 469 passive loss rules. Given this requirement, losses from *passive* trades or businesses (e.g., a business in which the taxpayer does not materially participate) are limited first by the § 469 passive activity loss rules, and once the losses are allowed under § 469, they are subject to the excess business loss rule.

For a partnership or S corporation, this excess business loss limitation applies at the partner or shareholder level.[52] Each partner's or S corporation shareholder's share of items of income, gain, deduction, or loss of the partnership or S corporation is taken into account in applying the limitation for the tax year of the partner or S corporation shareholder.

6-8b Computing the Limit

The following examples illustrate the operation and effect of the excess business loss limitation.

Computing the Excess Business Loss Limit

EXAMPLE 53

In 2018, Tonya, a single taxpayer, operates a sole proprietorship in which she materially participates. Her proprietorship generates gross income of $320,000 and deductions of $600,000, resulting in a loss of $280,000. The large deductions are due to the acquisition of equipment and the use of immediate expense and additional first-year depreciation to deduct all of the acquisitions. Tonya's excess business loss is $30,000, computed as follows:

Aggregate business deductions	$ 600,000
Less: Aggregate business gross income and gains	(320,000)
Less: Threshold amount	(250,000)
Excess business loss	$ 30,000

So Tonya can deduct $250,000 of the $280,000 proprietorship loss to offset nonbusiness income. The $30,000 excess business loss becomes part of Tonya's NOL carryforward to subsequent years.

EXAMPLE 54

Assume the same facts as in Example 53, except that Tonya is married and files a joint return. In this case, Tonya does not have an excess business loss due to the increased threshold amount.

Aggregate business deductions	$ 600,000
Less: Aggregate business gross income and gains	(320,000)
Less: Threshold amount	(500,000)
Excess business loss	$ None

As a result, Tonya's $280,000 sole proprietorship loss is fully deductible and can offset nonbusiness income (e.g., her spouse's wages or their interest and dividend income).

---

[50]§ 461(l).

[51]§ 461(l)(3).

[52]§ 461(l)(4)(A).

The excess business loss limitation applies to the aggregate gross income and deductions from all of a taxpayer's trades or businesses.[53] So if a married couple files a joint return, information from all of the couple's trades or businesses must be consolidated. Further, as noted in Example 54, if married taxpayers file a joint return, the losses of one spouse can be used to offset the other spouse's nonbusiness income (up to the $500,000 limit in 2018).

The last example illustrates application of the excess business loss limitation in a flow-through entity scenario.

EXAMPLE 55

Jayson, a single taxpayer, is an S corporation shareholder and materially participates in the entity's grocery store business. During 2018, the store had a large depreciation deduction causing a substantial loss. Jayson has a flow-through loss of $345,000 from the S corporation. He also received a $78,000 salary from the corporation. At the beginning of the year, Jayson had a $520,000 basis in his S corporation shares—enough to absorb the S corporation loss. Because he materially participates in the business, it is not a passive activity.

However, Jayson's flow-through loss exceeds the $250,000 excess business loss threshold by $95,000 ($345,000 − $250,000). So Jayson can deduct $250,000 (and use it to offset his salary and other nonbusiness income). The $95,000 excess is not deductible in 2018, but carries forward as a net operating loss.

Assume that in 2019, the grocery store business generates a profit and flows through $210,000 of income to Jayson. Jayson can deduct the 2018 excess business loss of $95,000 against this flow-through income.

REFOCUS ON THE BIG PICTURE

RECEIVING TAX BENEFITS FROM LOSSES

While Robyn's circumstances were unfortunate, the good news is that she will be able to receive some tax benefits from the losses.

- *Bad debt.* Based on the facts provided, it appears that Robyn's loan to her friend, Jamil, was a bona fide nonbusiness bad debt. The amount of the loss deduction is the unpaid principal balance of $19,000 ($25,000 − $6,000). As a nonbusiness bad debt, the loss is classified as a short-term capital loss (see Example 5).

- *Loss from stock investment.* Likewise, the $60,000 loss on the Owl Corporation stock investment is deductible. If Robyn purchased the stock directly from the company, the stock may qualify as small business stock under § 1244. If this is the case, the first $50,000 of the loss is an ordinary loss and the remaining $10,000 loss is treated as a long-term capital loss. If the stock is not § 1244 stock, the entire $60,000 loss is treated as a long-term capital loss (see Example 8).

- *Loss from bookstore.* The $180,000 loss from the bookstore is reported on Schedule C of Robyn's Form 1040. It is an ordinary loss and qualifies for net operating loss (NOL) treatment if she does not have enough other taxable income this year against which the loss could be offset. Robyn can carry the loss forward to reduce taxes owed on taxable income earned in the future.

- *Casualty loss.* The loss from the damage to Robyn's bookstore is a business casualty loss. Using the cost of repairs method, the amount of the casualty loss is $7,000 ($32,000 loss − $25,000 insurance recovery). Robyn deducts this loss above the line (*for* AGI).

continued

---

[53]§ 461(l)(3)(A)(i).

- *Passive activity loss.* The $20,000 loss on the limited partnership is not deductible currently due to the passive activity loss limitation. However, the loss can be carried forward and utilized in the future to offset any passive activity income generated from the venture or other passive activities (see Example 23).

What If?

What if instead of operating orange groves, the partnership was a general partnership that owns and rents apartments to college students and Robyn actively participates in the venture? In this case, Robyn may qualify for a $20,000 ordinary loss deduction under the rental real estate with active participation exception.

Suggested Readings

Sharon Burnett and Darlene Pulliam, "LLC Principal At-Risk Amounts for Guaranteed Debt," *Practical Tax Strategies*, April 2015.

Albert B. Ellentuck, "Deducting Business Bad Debts," *The Tax Adviser*, March 2016.

William C. Hood, "Deducting Ponzi Losses," *Practical Tax Strategies*, March 2014.

David H. Kirk and Vinny Satchit, "Peeling the Onion: Passive Loss Regrouping in Light of Section 1411," *Business Entities*, March/April 2015.

Key Terms

Active income, 6-17	Excess business loss, 6-32	Rental activity, 6-24
At-risk limitation, 6-15	Material participation, 6-23	Significant participation activity, 6-23
Bad debt, 6-2	Net operating loss (NOL), 6-13	Small business stock (§ 1244 stock), 6-6
Business bad debt, 6-4	Nonbusiness bad debt, 6-4	Specific charge-off method, 6-3
Casualty losses, 6-7	Passive activity loss, 6-15	Tax shelters, 6-14
Closely held C corporation, 6-21	Personal service corporation, 6-21	Theft losses, 6-9
Disaster area losses, 6-8	Portfolio income, 6-17	Worthless securities, 6-5

Computational Exercises

1. **LO.1** Last year Aleshia identified $15,000 as a nonbusiness bad debt. In that tax year, before considering the tax implications of the nonbusiness bad debt, Aleshia had $100,000 of taxable income, of which $12,000 consisted of short-term capital gains. This year Aleshia collected $8,000 of the amount she had previously identified as a bad debt. Determine Aleshia's tax treatment of the $8,000 received in the current tax year.

2. **LO.1** Bob owns a collection agency. He purchases uncollected accounts receivable from other businesses at 60% of their face value and then attempts to collect these accounts. During the current year, Bob collected $60,000 on an account with a face value of $80,000. Determine the amount of Bob's bad debt deduction.

3. **LO.2** On May 9, 2016, Calvin acquired 250 shares of stock in Aero Corporation, a new startup company, for $68,750. Calvin acquired the stock directly from Aero, and it is classified as § 1244 stock (at the time Calvin acquired his stock, the corporation had $900,000 of paid-in capital). On January 15, 2018, Calvin sold all of his Aero stock for $7,000. Assuming that Calvin is single, determine his tax consequences as a result of this sale.

4. **LO.3** Noelle's diamond ring was stolen in 2017. She originally paid $8,000 for the ring, but it was worth considerably more at the time of the theft. Noelle filed an insurance claim for the stolen ring, but the claim was denied. Because the insurance claim was denied, Noelle took a casualty loss deduction for the stolen ring on her 2017 tax return. In 2017, Noelle had AGI of $40,000. In 2018, the insurance company had a "change of heart" and sent Noelle a check for $5,000 for the stolen ring. Determine the proper tax treatment of the $5,000 Noelle received from the insurance company in 2018.

5. **LO.3** Determine the treatment of a loss on rental property under the following facts:

Basis	$650,000
FMV before the loss	800,000
FMV after the loss	200,000

6. **LO.6** In the current year, Ed invests $30,000 in an oil partnership. He has taxable income for the current year of $2,000 from the oil partnership and withdraws $10,000. What is Ed's at-risk amount at the end of the year?

7. **LO.6** Lucy sells her partnership interest, a passive activity, with an adjusted basis of $305,000 for $330,000. In addition, she has current and suspended losses of $28,000 associated with the partnership and has no other passive activities. Calculate Lucy's total gain and her current deductible loss. Describe the type of income that the deductible loss may offset.

8. **LO.8** Rhonda has an adjusted basis and an at-risk amount of $7,500 in a passive activity at the beginning of the year. She also has a suspended passive activity loss of $1,500 carried over from the prior year. During the current year, she has a loss of $12,000 from the passive activity. Rhonda has no passive activity income from other sources this year. Determine the following items relating to Rhonda's passive activity as of the end of the year.
   a. Adjusted basis and at-risk amount in the passive activity.
   b. Loss suspended under the at-risk rules.
   c. Suspended passive activity loss.

9. **LO.9** Noah, who has $62,000 of AGI before considering rental activities, has $70,000 of losses from a real estate rental activity in which he actively participates. He also actively participates in another real estate rental activity from which he has $33,000 of income. He has other passive activity income of $20,000. What amount of rental loss can Noah use to offset active or portfolio income in the current year?

10. **LO.10** Rose dies with passive activity property having an adjusted basis of $65,000, suspended losses of $13,000, and a fair market value at the date of her death of $90,000. Of the $13,000 suspended loss existing at the time of Rose's death, how much is deductible on her final return or by the beneficiary?

Problems

11. **LO.1** Several years ago, Loon Finance Company, which is in the lending business, loaned Sara $30,000 to purchase an automobile to be used for personal purposes. In August of the current year, Sara filed for bankruptcy, and Loon was notified that it could not expect to receive more than $4,000. As of the end of the current year, Loon has received $1,000. Loon has contacted you about the possibility of taking a bad debt deduction for the current year.

Communications

Write a letter to Loon Finance Company that contains your advice as to whether it can claim a bad debt deduction for the current year. Also prepare a memo for the tax files. Loon's address is 100 Tyler Lane, Erie, PA 16563.

12. **LO.1** Monty loaned his friend Ned $20,000 three years ago. Ned signed a note and made payments on the loan. Last year, when the remaining balance was $11,000, Ned filed for bankruptcy and notified Monty that he would be unable to pay the balance on the loan. Monty treated the $11,000 as a nonbusiness bad debt. Last year, before considering the tax implications of the nonbusiness bad debt, Monty had capital gains of $9,000 and taxable income of $45,000. During the current year, Ned paid Monty $10,000 in satisfaction of the debt. Determine Monty's tax treatment for the $10,000 received in the current year.

Critical Thinking   13. **LO.2** Many years ago, Jack purchased 400 shares of Canary stock. During the current year, the stock became worthless. It was determined that the company "went under" because several corporate officers embezzled a large amount of company funds. Identify the relevant tax issues for Jack.

Ethics and Equity   14. **LO.1** Jake and Mary Snow are residents of the state of New York. They are cash basis taxpayers and file a joint return for the calendar year. Jake is a licensed master plumber. Two years ago, Jake entered into a contract with New York City to perform plumbing services. During the current year, Jake was declared to be in breach of the contract, and he ceased performing plumbing services. Jake received a Form W–2 that reported $50,000 for wages paid. He also maintains that the city has not paid him $35,000 for work he performed. Jake is considering claiming a $35,000 business bad debt on his tax return. Evaluate Jake's plan.

15. **LO.1, 2** Mable and Jack file a joint return. For the current year, they had the following items:

Salaries	$120,000
Loss on sale of § 1244 stock acquired two years ago	105,000
Gain on sale of § 1244 stock acquired six months ago	20,000
Nonbusiness bad debt	19,000

Determine the impact of the above items on Mable and Jack's income for the current year.

Decision Making   16. **LO.2** Abby, a single taxpayer, purchased 10,000 shares of § 1244 stock several years ago at a cost of $20 per share. In November of the current year, Abby receives an offer to sell the stock for $12 per share. She has the option of either selling all of the stock now or selling half of the stock now and half of the stock in January of next year. Abby's salary is $80,000 for the current year, and it will be $90,000 next year. Abby has long-term capital gains of $8,000 for the current year and will have $10,000 next year. If Abby's goal is to minimize her AGI for the two years, determine whether she should sell all of her stock this year or half of her stock this year and half next year.

Decision Making   17. **LO.3** Olaf lives in the state of Minnesota. A tornado hit the area and damaged his home and automobile. Applicable information is as follows:

Item	Adjusted Basis	FMV Before	FMV After	Insurance Proceeds
Home	$350,000	$500,000	$100,000	$280,000
Auto	60,000	40,000	10,000	20,000

Because of the extensive damage caused by the tornado, the President designated the area a disaster area.

Olaf and his wife, Anna, always file a joint return. Their 2017 tax return shows AGI of $180,000 and taxable income of $140,000. In 2018, their return shows AGI of $300,000 and taxable income (exclusive of the casualty loss deduction) of $215,000.

Determine the amount of Olaf and Anna's loss and the year in which they should take the loss.

18. **LO.3** In 2015, John opened an investment account with Randy Hansen, who held himself out to the public as an investment adviser and securities broker. John contributed $200,000 to the account in 2015. John provided Randy with a power of attorney to use the $200,000 to purchase and sell securities on John's behalf. John instructed Randy to reinvest any gains and income earned. In 2015, 2016, and 2017, John received statements of the amount of income earned by his account and included these amounts in his gross income for these years. In 2018, John discovered that Randy's purported investment advisory and brokerage activity was a fraudulent investment arrangement known as a Ponzi scheme. In reality, John's account balance was zero, the money having been used by Randy in his scheme. Identify the relevant tax issues for John.   **Critical Thinking**

19. **LO.4** Mario, a single taxpayer with two dependent children, has the following items of income and expense during 2018:

Gross receipts from business	$144,000
Business expenses	180,000
Net capital gain	22,000
Interest income	3,000
Itemized deductions (state taxes, residence interest, and contributions)	24,000

    a. Determine Mario's taxable income for 2018.
    b. Determine Mario's NOL for 2018.

20. **LO.6** In 2017, Fred invested $50,000 in a general partnership. Fred's interest is not considered to be a passive activity. If his share of the partnership losses is $35,000 in 2017 and $25,000 in 2018, how much can he deduct in each year?

21. **LO.6** In the current year, Bill Parker (54 Oak Drive, St. Paul, MN 55164) is considering making an investment of $60,000 in Best Choice Partnership. The prospectus provided by Bill's broker indicates that the partnership investment is not a passive activity and that Bill's share of the entity's loss in the current year will likely be $40,000, while his share of the partnership loss next year will probably be $25,000. Write a letter to Bill in which you indicate how the losses would be treated for tax purposes in the current year and the following year.   **Communications**

22. **LO.6** A number of years ago, Kay acquired an interest in a partnership in which she is not a material participant. Kay's basis in her partnership interest at the beginning of 2017 is $40,000. Kay's share of the partnership loss is $35,000 in 2017, while her share of the partnership income is $15,000 in 2018. How much may Kay deduct in 2017 and 2018, assuming that she owns no other passive activities?

23. **LO.6** Jorge owns two passive investments, Activity A and Activity B. He plans to dispose of Activity A in the current year or next year. Juanita has offered to buy Activity A this year for an amount that would produce a taxable passive activity gain to Jorge of $115,000. However, if the sale, for whatever reason, is not made to Juanita, Jorge believes that he could find a buyer who would pay about $7,000 less than Juanita. Passive activity losses and gains generated (and expected to be generated) by Activity B follow: **Decision Making**

Two years ago	($35,000)
Last year	(35,000)
This year	(8,000)
Next year	(30,000)
Future years	Minimal profits

All of Activity B's losses are suspended. Should Jorge close the sale of Activity A with Juanita this year, or should he wait until next year and sell to another buyer? Jorge is in the 32% tax bracket.

24. **LO.6** Sarah has investments in four passive activity partnerships purchased several years ago. Last year, the income and losses were as follows:

Activity	Income (Loss)
A	$ 30,000
B	(30,000)
C	(15,000)
D	(5,000)

In the current year, she sold her interest in Activity D for a $10,000 gain. Activity D, which had been profitable until last year, had a current loss of $1,500. How will the sale of Activity D affect Sarah's taxable income in the current year?

25. **LO.6** Leon sells his interest in a passive activity for $100,000. Determine the tax effect of the sale based on each of the following independent facts:

a. Adjusted basis in this investment is $35,000. Losses from prior years that were not deductible due to the passive activity loss restrictions total $40,000.

b. Adjusted basis in this investment is $75,000. Losses from prior years that were not deductible due to the passive activity loss restrictions total $40,000.

c. Adjusted basis in this investment is $75,000. Losses from prior years that were not deductible due to the passive activity loss restrictions total $40,000. In addition, suspended credits total $10,000.

26. **LO.6** In the current year, White, Inc., earns $400,000 from operations and receives $36,000 of interest income from various portfolio investments. White also pays $150,000 to acquire a 20% interest in a passive activity that produces a $200,000 loss.

a. Assuming that White is a personal service corporation, how will these transactions affect its taxable income?

b. Same as part (a), except that White is closely held but not a personal service corporation.

27. **LO.7** John, an engineer, operates a separate business that he acquired eight years ago. If he participates 85 hours in the business and it incurs a loss of $34,000, under what circumstances can John claim an active loss?

Critical Thinking 28. **LO.7** Rita retired from public accounting after a long and successful career of 45 years. As part of her retirement package, she continues to share in the profits and losses of the firm, albeit at a lower rate than when she was working full-time. Because Rita wants to stay busy during her retirement years, she has invested and works in a local hardware business, operated as a partnership. Unfortunately, the business has recently gone through a slump and has not been generating profits. Identify relevant tax issues for Rita.

Critical Thinking 29. **LO.6, 8** Kristin Graf (123 Baskerville Mill Road, Jamison, PA 18929) is trying to decide how to invest a $10,000 inheritance. One option is to make an additional investment in Rocky Road Excursions in which she has an at-risk basis of $0, suspended losses under the at-risk rules of $7,000, and suspended passive activity losses of $1,000. If Kristin makes this investment, her share of the expected profits this year will be $8,000. If her investment stays the same, her share of profits from Rocky Road Excursions will be $1,000. Another option is to invest $10,000 as a limited partner in the Ragged Mountain Winery; this investment will produce passive activity income of $9,000. Write a letter to Kristin to review the tax consequences of each alternative. Kristin is in the 24% tax bracket.

Communications

Decision Making

Decision Making 30. **LO.8** The end of the year is approaching, and Maxine has begun to focus on ways of minimizing her income tax liability. Several years ago, she purchased an investment in Teal Limited Partnership, which is subject to the at-risk and passive activity loss rules. (Last year, Maxine sold a different investment that was subject

Critical Thinking

to these rules and that produced passive activity income.) She believes that her investment in Teal has good long-term economic prospects. However, it has been generating tax losses for several years in a row. In fact, when she was discussing last year's income tax return with her tax accountant, he said that unless "things change" with respect to her investments, she would not be able to deduct losses this year.

a.   What was the accountant referring to in his comment?

b.   You learn that Maxine's current at-risk basis in her investment is $1,000 and that her share of the current loss is expected to be $13,000. Based on these facts, how will her loss be treated?

c.   After reviewing her situation, Maxine's financial adviser suggests that she invest at least an additional $12,000 in Teal to ensure a full loss deduction in the current year. How do you react to his suggestion?

d.   What would you suggest Maxine consider as she attempts to maximize her current-year deductible loss?

31.   **LO.8** A number of years ago, Lee acquired a 20% interest in the BlueSky Partnership for $60,000. The partnership was profitable through 2017, and Lee's amount at risk in the partnership interest was $120,000 at the beginning of 2018. BlueSky incurred a loss of $400,000 in 2018 and reported income of $200,000 in 2019. Assuming that Lee is not a material participant, how much of his loss from BlueSky Partnership is deductible in 2018 and 2019? Consider the at-risk and passive activity loss rules, and assume that Lee owns no other investments.

32.   **LO.6** Grace acquired an activity four years ago. The loss from the activity is $50,000 in the current year (at-risk basis of $40,000 as of the beginning of the year). Without considering the loss from the activity, she has gross income of $140,000. If the activity is a convenience store and Grace is a material participant, what is the effect of the activity on her taxable income?

33.   **LO.5, 6, 8** Jonathan, a physician, earns $200,000 from his practice. He also receives $18,000 in dividends and interest from various portfolio investments. During the year, he pays $45,000 to acquire a 20% interest in a partnership that produces a $300,000 loss. Compute Jonathan's AGI assuming that:

a.   He does not participate in the operations of the partnership.

b.   He is a material participant in the operations of the partnership.

34.   **LO.5, 6, 8** Five years ago, Gerald invested $150,000 in a passive activity, his sole investment venture. On January 1, 2017, his amount at risk in the activity was $30,000. His shares of the income and losses were as follows:

Year	Income (Loss)
2017	($40,000)
2018	(30,000)
2019	50,000

Gerald holds no suspended at-risk or passive activity losses at the beginning of 2017. How much can Gerald deduct in 2017 and 2018? What is his taxable income from the activity in 2019? Consider the at-risk rules as well as the passive activity loss rules.

35.   **LO.5, 6, 7** You have just met with Scott Myers (603 Pittsfield Drive, Champaign, IL 61821), a successful full-time real estate developer and investor. During your meeting, you discussed his tax situation because you are starting to prepare his current Federal income tax return. During your meeting, Scott mentioned that he and his wife, Susan, went to great lengths to maximize their participation in an apartment complex that they own and manage. In particular, Scott included the following activities in the 540 hours of participation for the current year:

Ethics and Equity

Communications

Digging Deeper

- Time spent thinking about the rentals.
- Time spent by Susan on weekdays visiting the apartment complex to oversee operations of the buildings (i.e., in a management role).
- Time spent by both Scott and Susan on weekends visiting the apartment complex to assess operations. Scott and Susan always visited the complex together on weekends, and both counted their hours (i.e., one hour at the complex was two hours of participation).
- Time spent on weekends driving around the community looking for other potential rental properties to purchase. Again, both Scott's hours and Susan's hours were counted, even when they drove together.

After reviewing Scott's records, you note that the apartment complex generated a significant loss this year. Prepare a letter to Scott describing your position on the deductibility of the loss.

Decision Making   36.   **LO.6, 9** Bonnie and Jake (ages 35 and 36, respectively) are married with no dependents and live in Montana (not a community property state). Because Jake has large medical expenses, they seek your advice about filing separately to save taxes. Their income and expenses for 2018 are as follows:

Bonnie's salary	$ 42,500
Jake's salary	26,000
Interest income (joint)	1,500
Rental loss from actively managed rental property	(23,000)
Jake's unreimbursed medical expenses	8,500
All other itemized deductions:*	
Bonnie	19,000
Jake	6,400

*None subject to limitations.

Determine whether Bonnie and Jake should file jointly or separately for 2018.

37.   **LO.9** During the current year, Gene, a CPA, performs services as follows: 1,800 hours in his tax practice and 50 hours in an apartment leasing operation in which he has a 15% interest. Because of his oversight duties, Gene is considered to be an active participant. He expects that his share of the loss realized from the apartment leasing operation will be $30,000 and that his tax practice will show a profit of approximately $80,000. Gene is single and has no other income. Discuss the character and treatment of the income and losses generated by these activities.

38.   **LO.9** Ida, who has AGI of $80,000 before considering rental activities, is active in three separate real estate rental activities. Ida has a marginal tax rate of 22%. She has $12,000 of losses from Activity A, $18,000 of losses from Activity B, and income of $10,000 from Activity C. She also has $2,100 of tax credits from Activity A. Calculate the deductions and credits that she is allowed and the suspended losses and credits.

39.   **LO.9** Jiu has $105,000 of losses from a real estate rental activity in which she actively participates. She has other rent income of $25,000 and other passive activity income of $32,000. Her AGI before considering these items of income and loss is $95,000. How much rental loss can Jiu deduct against active and portfolio income (ignoring the at-risk rules)? Does she have any suspended losses to carry over? Explain.

40.   **LO.5, 6, 10** In the current year, Abe gives an interest in a passive activity to his daughter, Andrea. The value of the interest at the date of the gift is $25,000, and its adjusted basis to Abe is $13,000. During the time that Abe owned the investment, losses of $3,000 could not be deducted because of the passive activity loss limitations. What is the tax treatment of the suspended passive activity losses to Abe and Andrea?

41. **LO.7** Thomas believes that he has an NOL for the current year and plans to carry it   Critical Thinking
forward, offsetting it against future income. In determining his NOL, Thomas offset his business income by alimony payments he made to his ex-spouse and contributions he made to his traditional Individual Retirement Account (IRA). His reason for using these items in the NOL computation is that each item is a deduction *for* AGI. Identify the relevant tax issues for Thomas.

Bridge Discipline

1. Marketplace, Inc., has recognized over time that a certain percentage of its   Digging Deeper
customer accounts receivable will not be collected. To ensure the appropriate matching of revenues and expenditures in its financial reports, Marketplace uses the reserve method for bad debts. Records show the following pertaining to its treatment of bad debts.

Beginning allowance for bad debts	$120,000
Ending allowance for bad debts	123,000
Bad debts written off during the year	33,000

   a. What was the bad debt expense for financial accounting purposes during the year?

   b. What was the bad debt deduction for income tax purposes during the year?

   c. Assuming that the before-tax net income for financial accounting purposes was $545,000, what is the taxable income for the year if the treatment of bad debts is the only book-tax difference?

2. Heather wants to invest $40,000 in a relatively safe venture and has discovered   Decision Making
two alternatives that would produce the following ordinary income and loss over   Critical Thinking
the next three years:

Year	Alternative 1 Income (Loss)	Alternative 2 Income (Loss)
1	($20,000)	($48,000)
2	(28,000)	32,000
3	72,000	40,000

   She is interested in the after-tax effects of these alternatives over a three-year horizon. Assume that:

   • Heather's investment portfolio produces sufficient passive activity income to offset any potential passive activity loss that may arise from these alternatives.

   • Heather's marginal tax rate is 24%, and her cost of capital is 6% (see Appendix F for the present value factors).

   • Each investment alternative possesses equal growth potential and comparable financial risk.

   • In the loss years for each alternative, there is no cash flow from or to the investment (i.e., the loss is due to depreciation), while in those years when the income is positive, cash flows to Heather equal the amount of the income.

   Based on these facts, compute the present value of these two investment alternatives and determine which option Heather should choose.

continued

Decision Making   3. Emily has $100,000 that she wants to invest and is considering the following two options:

- Option A: Investment in Redbird Mutual Fund, which is expected to produce interest income of $8,000 per year.
- Option B: Investment in Cardinal Limited Partnership (buys, sells, and operates wine vineyards). Emily's share of the partnership's ordinary income and loss over the next three years would be as follows:

Year	Income (Loss)
1	($ 8,000)
2	(2,000)
3	34,000

Emily is interested in the after-tax effects of these alternatives over a three-year horizon. Assume that Emily's investment portfolio produces ample passive activity income to offset any passive activity losses that may be generated. Her cost of capital is 8% (see Appendix F for the present value factors), and she is in the 32% tax bracket. The two investment alternatives possess equal growth potential and comparable financial risk. Based on these facts, compute the present value of these two investment alternatives and determine which option Emily should choose.

Research Problems

THOMSON REUTERS
CHECKPOINT™

Note: Solutions to the Research Problems can be prepared by using the Thomson Reuters Checkpoint™ online tax research database, which accompanies this textbook. Solutions can also be prepared by using research materials found in a typical tax library.

Research Problem 1. Esther owns a large home on the East Coast. Her home is surrounded by large, mature oak trees that significantly increase the value of her home. In August 2017, a hurricane damaged many of the trees surrounding her home; her region was declared a Federal disaster area as a result of the hurricane's damage. In September 2017, Esther engaged a local arborist to evaluate and treat the trees, but five of the largest trees were seriously weakened by the storm. These trees died from disease in 2018. Esther has ascertained that the amount of the casualty loss from the death of the five trees is $25,000; however, she is uncertain in which year to deduct this loss. Discuss whether the casualty loss should be deducted in the calculation of Esther's 2017 or 2018 taxable income.

Partials list of research aids:
Reg. § 1.165–1.
Oregon Mesabi Corporation, 39 B.T.A. 1033 (1939).

Research Problem 2. Five years ago, Bridget decided to purchase a limited partnership interest in a fast-food restaurant conveniently located near the campus of Southeast State University. The general partner of the restaurant venture promised her that the investment would prove to be a winner. During the process of capitalizing the business, $2 million was borrowed from Northside Bank; however, each of the partners was required to pledge personal assets as collateral to satisfy the bank loan in the event that the restaurant defaulted. Bridget pledged shares of publicly traded stock (worth $200,000, basis of $75,000) to satisfy the bank's requirement.

The restaurant did a good business until just recently, when flagrant health code violations were discovered and widely publicized by the media. As a result, business has declined to a point where the restaurant's continued existence is doubtful. In addition, the $2 million loan is now due for payment. Because the restaurant cannot pay, the bank has called for the collateral provided by the partners to be used to satisfy the debt. Bridget sells the pledged stock for $200,000 and forwards the proceeds to the bank. Bridget believes that her share of the restaurant's current and suspended passive activity losses can offset the $125,000 gain from the stock sale. As a result, after netting the passive activity losses against the gain, none of the gain is subject to tax.

How do you react to Bridget's position?

Research Problem 3. During 2018, John was the chief executive officer and a shareholder of Maze, Inc. He owned 60% of the outstanding stock of Maze. In 2015, John and Maze, as co-borrowers, obtained a $100,000 loan from United National Bank. This loan was secured by John's personal residence. Although Maze was listed as a co-borrower, John repaid the loan in full in 2018. On Maze's Form 1120 tax returns, no loans from shareholders were reported. Discuss whether John is entitled to a bad debt deduction for the amount of the payment on the loan.

Partial list of research aids:
U.S. v. Generes, 405 U.S. 93 (1972).
Dale H. Sundby, T.C.Memo. 2003–204.
Arrigoni v. Comm., 73 T.C. 792 (1980).
Estate of Herbert M. Rapoport, T.C.Memo. 1982–584.
Clifford L. Brody and Barbara J. DeClerk, T.C. Summary Opinion, 2004–149.

Use internet tax resources to address the following questions. Look for reliable websites and blogs of the IRS and other government agencies, media outlets, businesses, tax professionals, academics, think tanks, and political outlets.

Research Problem 4. Find a newspaper article that discusses tax planning for casualty losses when a disaster area designation is made. Does the article convey the pertinent tax rules correctly? Then list all of the locations identified by the President as Federal disaster areas in the last two years.

Research Problem 5. Investment advisers and tax professionals are continuously striving to create sophisticated transactions and investment vehicles (i.e., tax-advantaged investments) that are designed to provide economic benefits to investors by reducing their taxes. These professionals might like to patent such schemes. Identify whether patenting a tax shelter is a legal possibility.

Becker CPA Review Questions

1. Which of the following statements regarding passive activity losses is true?

   a. A net passive activity loss may be deducted against wages.
   b. Losses on rental property are always considered passive.
   c. A passive activity is one in which the taxpayer does not materially participate.
   d. Expenses related to passive activities may be deducted from passive activity income and portfolio income.

2. Michael owns a rental house that generated a $10,000 loss this year. Michael manages the rental property, but does not meet the standards for material participation. Michael is a college professor and has wages of $60,000 and $5,000 in dividend income. How is the $10,000 rental real estate loss treated on Michael's tax return?

    a. $5,000 of the loss is deductible against the passive dividend income.
    b. The rental loss is not deductible because Michael does not have any passive income.
    c. $10,000 loss is not deductible because Michael does not materially participate in the rental activity.
    d. $10,000 loss is deductible under the rental real estate exception because Michael actively participates in the rental activity.

3. What is the correct order of applying the loss limitation rules?

    a. Passive loss limits, tax basis, at-risk amount
    b. Tax basis, at-risk amount, passive loss limits
    c. At-risk amount, tax basis, passive loss limits
    d. Passive loss limits, at-risk amount, tax basis

4. Sam rents his second home. During the current year, he reported a $40,000 net loss from the rental. Assume Sam actively participates in the rental activity and no phaseout limitations apply. What is the greatest amount of the rental loss that Sam can deduct against ordinary income in the current year?

    a. $25,000   c. $0
    b. $40,000   d. $5,000

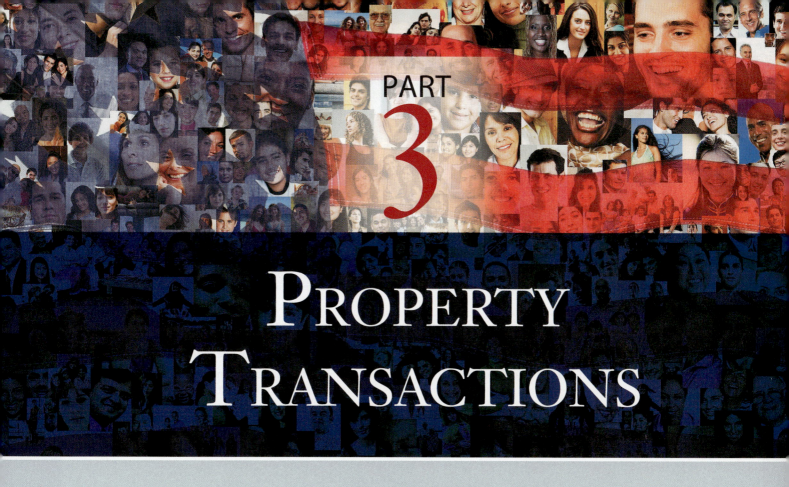

PART 3

PROPERTY TRANSACTIONS

CHAPTER **7**

Property Transactions: Basis, Gain and Loss, and Nontaxable Exchanges

CHAPTER **8**

Property Transactions: Capital Gains and Losses, Section 1231, and Recapture Provisions

Part 3 presents the tax treatment of sales, exchanges, and other dispositions of property. Topics discussed include the determination of the realized gain or loss, recognized gain or loss, and the classification of the recognized gain or loss as capital or ordinary. The topic of basis is evaluated both in terms of its effect on the calculation of the gain or loss, and in the determination of the basis of any other transfers of property.

CHAPTER

7

Property Transactions: Basis, Gain and Loss, and Nontaxable Exchanges

LEARNING OBJECTIVES: *After completing Chapter 7, you should be able to:*

LO.1 State and explain the computation of realized gain or loss on property dispositions.

LO.2 Distinguish between realized and recognized gain or loss.

LO.3 Understand and illustrate how basis is determined for various methods of asset acquisition.

LO.4 Describe various loss disallowance provisions.

LO.5 Apply the nonrecognition provisions and basis determination rules for like-kind exchanges.

LO.6 Explain the nonrecognition provisions available on the involuntary conversion of property.

LO.7 Identify other nonrecognition provisions contained in the Code.

CHAPTER OUTLINE

7-1 Determination of Gain or Loss, 7-2
    7-1a   Realized Gain or Loss, 7-2
    7-1b   Recognized Gain or Loss, 7-7
    7-1c   Nonrecognition of Gain or Loss, 7-8

7-2 Basis Considerations, 7-9
    7-2a   Determination of Cost Basis, 7-9
    7-2b   Gift Basis, 7-11
    7-2c   Inherited Property, 7-13
    7-2d   Disallowed Losses, 7-14
    7-2e   Conversion of Property from Personal Use to Business or Income-Producing Use, 7-16
    7-2f   Summary of Basis Adjustments, 7-17

7-3 General Concept of a Nontaxable Exchange, 7-19

7-4 Like-Kind Exchanges—§ 1031, 7-20
    7-4a   Like-Kind Property, 7-20

    7-4b   Exchange Requirement, 7-21
    7-4c   Boot, 7-22
    7-4d   Basis and Holding Period of Property Received, 7-23

7-5 Involuntary Conversions—§ 1033, 7-25
    7-5a   Involuntary Conversion Defined, 7-27
    7-5b   Replacement Property, 7-27
    7-5c   Time Limitation on Replacement, 7-28
    7-5d   Nonrecognition of Gain, 7-29

7-6 Other Nonrecognition Provisions, 7-31
    7-6a   Transfer of Assets to Business Entity—§§ 351 and 721, 7-31
    7-6b   Sale of a Principal Residence—§ 121, 7-31

TAX TALK *To base all of your decisions on tax consequences is not necessarily to maintain the proper balance and perspective on what you are doing.* —Barber Conable

CALCULATING BASIS AND RECOGNIZED GAIN FOR PROPERTY TRANSACTIONS

Alice owns land that she received from her father 10 years ago as a gift. The land was purchased by her father in 1994 for $2,000 and was worth $10,000 at the time of the gift. Alice's father did not owe gift taxes upon making the transfer. The property is currently worth about $50,000. Alice is considering selling the land and purchasing a piece of undeveloped property in the mountains.

Alice also owns 500 shares of AppleCo stock, 300 of which were acquired as an inheritance when her grandfather died in 1998. Alice's grandfather paid $12,000 for the shares, and the shares were worth $30,000 at the time of his death. The other 200 shares of AppleCo were purchased by Alice two months ago for $28,000. The stock is currently worth $120 per share, and Alice is considering selling the shares.

In addition, Alice owns a house that she inherited from her grandmother two years ago. Her grandmother lived in the house for over 50 years. Alice has many fond memories associated with the house because she spent many summer vacations there, and she has been reluctant to sell the house. However, a developer has recently purchased several homes in the area and has offered Alice $600,000 for the property. Based on the estate tax return, the fair market value of the house at the date of her grandmother's death was $475,000. According to her grandmother's attorney, her grandmother's basis for the house was $275,000. Alice is considering selling the house. She expects any selling expenses to be minimal because she already has identified a buyer for the property.

The building Alice used in her business was destroyed by a fire on October 5, 2018. Fortunately, the building (adjusted basis of $50,000) was insured and on November 17, 2018, she receives an insurance reimbursement of $100,000 for the loss. Alice intends to invest $80,000 in a new building and use the other $20,000 of insurance proceeds to pay off credit card debt.

Alice has come to you for tax advice with respect to the property she owns. What is the recognized gain or loss for the land, stock, and house if they are sold? What tax consequences arise with respect to the involuntary conversion of her business building? Can Alice avoid paying taxes on any of the sales? Alice's objectives are to minimize the recognition of any realized gain and to maximize the recognition of any realized loss.

Read the chapter and formulate your response.

Thⁱs chapter and the following chapter explain the income tax consequences of property transactions, including the sale or other disposition of property. Specifically, the following questions are considered:

- Is there a realized gain or loss?
- If so, is that gain or loss recognized for tax purposes?
- If that gain or loss is recognized, is it ordinary or capital?
- What is the basis of any replacement property that is acquired?

This chapter discusses the determination of realized and recognized gain or loss and the basis of property. The next chapter covers the classification of recognized gain or loss as ordinary or capital.

For the most part, the rules discussed in Chapters 7 and 8 apply to all types of taxpayers. Individuals, partnerships, closely held corporations, limited liability companies, and publicly held corporations all own assets for use in business activities or as investments in entities that themselves conduct business activities. Individuals, however, are unique among taxpayers because they also own assets that are used in daily life, which have no significant business or investment component. Because of that possibility, some property transaction concepts may apply somewhat differently to individual taxpayers. For example, what happens when a married couple sells their family home? Thus, the material that follows pertains to taxpayers generally, except where otherwise noted.

7-1 DETERMINATION OF GAIN OR LOSS

Gains and losses result from "realization events" such as sales, exchanges, or other dispositions of property. Realization events involve a significant change in ownership rights, and once a realization event has occurred, a realized gain or loss can be determined. Many, but not all, *realized* gains and losses are also *recognized* (included in the determination of taxable income) at the time of the realization event. So while realization is an accounting concept, recognition is a tax concept that arises from various tax law provisions.

7-1a Realized Gain or Loss

LO.1

State and explain the computation of realized gain or loss on property dispositions.

For tax purposes, gain or loss is the difference between the *amount realized* from the sale or other disposition of property and the property's *adjusted basis* on the date of disposition. If the amount realized exceeds the property's adjusted basis, the result is a realized gain. Conversely, if the property's adjusted basis exceeds the amount realized, the result is a realized loss.[1] Concept Summary 7.1 summarizes this calculation. The various terms that are part of Concept Summary 7.1 are discussed on the following pages.

EXAMPLE
1

Lavender, Inc., sells Swan Corporation stock with a basis of $3,000 for $5,000. Lavender's realized gain is $2,000. If Lavender had sold the stock for $2,000, it would have had a realized loss of $1,000.

Sale or Other Disposition

The term *sale or other disposition* is defined broadly to include virtually any disposition of property, including: trade-ins, casualties, condemnations, thefts, and bond retirements. The most common disposition of property is a sale or an exchange. Usually, the key factor in determining whether a disposition has taken place is whether an identifiable event has occurred.[2] Fluctuations in the value of the property are not realization events.[3]

---

[1]§ 1001(a) and Reg. § 1.1001–1(a).

[2]Reg. § 1.1001–1(c)(1).

[3]*Lynch v. Turrish*, 1 USTC ¶18, 3 AFTR 2986, 38 S.Ct. 537 (USSC, 1918).

Concept Summary 7.1

Realized Gain or Loss

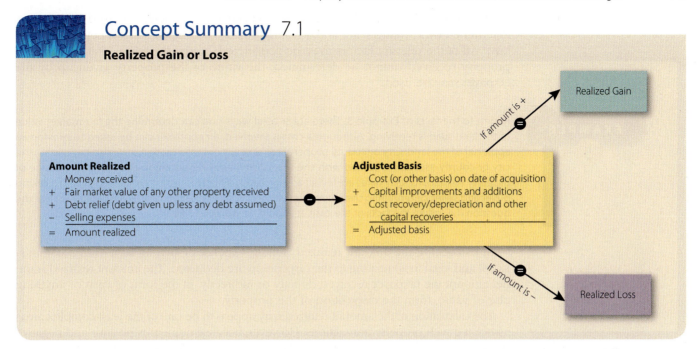

Amount Realized
Money received
+ Fair market value of any other property received
+ Debt relief (debt given up less any debt assumed)
− Selling expenses
_____
= Amount realized

Adjusted Basis
Cost (or other basis) on date of acquisition
+ Capital improvements and additions
− Cost recovery/depreciation and other capital recoveries
_____
= Adjusted basis

Realized Gain

If amount is +

Realized Loss

If amount is −

EXAMPLE 2

Heron & Associates owns Tan Corporation stock that cost $3,000. The stock has appreciated in value and is now worth $5,000. Heron has no realized gain because a change in value is not an identifiable event for tax purposes. Here, Heron has an unrealized gain of $2,000.

The same is true if the stock had declined in value to $1,000. As there was no identifiable event, there is no realized loss. Here, Heron would have an *unrealized* loss of $2,000.

Amount Realized

The **amount realized** from a sale or other disposition of property is the sum of any money received (which includes any debt relief) plus the fair market value of other property received.[4]

Debt relief includes any liability (like a mortgage) assumed by the buyer when the property is sold. Debt relief also occurs if property is sold subject to the mortgage. In addition, debt relief is not limited by the fair market value of the property.[5]

Amount Realized

EXAMPLE 3

Juan sells a machine used in his landscaping business to Peter for $20,000 cash plus four acres of property that Peter owns in a nearby town with a fair market value of $36,000. Juan's amount realized on this sale is $56,000 ($20,000 + $36,000).

EXAMPLE 4

Barry owns property on which there is a mortgage of $20,000. He sells the property to Cole for $50,000 cash and Cole's agreement to assume the mortgage. Barry's amount realized from the sale is $70,000 ($50,000 cash + $20,000 debt relief).

---

[4]§ 1001(b) and Reg. § 1.1001–1(b). The amount realized also includes any real property taxes treated as imposed on the seller that are actually paid by the buyer. The reason for including these taxes in the amount realized is that by paying the taxes, the purchaser is, in effect, paying an additional amount to the seller for the property. Refer to Example 27 in Chapter 5 for a discussion of this subject.

[5]*Crane v. Comm.*, 47–1 USTC ¶9217, 35 AFTR 776, 67 S.Ct. 1047 (USSC, 1947). Although a legal distinction exists between the direct assumption of a mortgage and the taking of property subject to a mortgage, the tax consequences in calculating the amount realized are the same.

In a property transaction, the **fair market value** of property received is the price determined by a willing seller and a willing buyer when neither is compelled to sell or buy.[6] All of the relevant factors must be considered,[7] and if the fair market value of the property received cannot be determined, the value of the property given up by the taxpayer may be used.[8]

EXAMPLE 5

Return to the facts of Example 3. There are several ways one can determine the fair market value of the land Juan is receiving. Although a cost is involved, an appraiser can be asked to provide an appraisal of the land. City or county property tax assessment information may also be helpful; the city or county assessor is tasked with the responsibility of determining the fair market value of property so that property taxes are levied appropriately. Finally, if the exchange is between a willing buyer and seller, determining the fair market value of Juan's landscaping machine could answer the question (i.e., given the facts of the case, it should be worth $56,000).

In calculating the amount realized, selling expenses (such as advertising, commissions, and legal fees) relating to the disposition are deducted. The amount realized is the net amount the taxpayer received directly or indirectly, in the form of cash or anything else of value, from the disposition of the property.

The calculation of the amount realized may appear to be one of the least complex areas associated with property transactions. However, because numerous positive and negative adjustments may be required, this calculation can be complex and confusing. In addition, determining the fair market value of the items received by the taxpayer can be difficult. The following example provides insight into various items that can affect the amount realized.

EXAMPLE 6

Ridge sells an office building and the associated land on October 1, 2018. Under the terms of the sales contract, Ridge is to receive $600,000 in cash. The purchaser is to assume Ridge's mortgage of $300,000 on the property. To assist the purchaser, Ridge agrees to pay $15,000 of the purchaser's closing costs (a "closing cost credit"). The broker's commission on the sale is $45,000. The amount realized by Ridge is determined as follows:

Selling price:		
Cash	$600,000	
Mortgage assumed by purchaser	300,000	
		$900,000
Less:		
Broker's commission	$ 45,000	
Closing cost credit provided by Ridge	15,000	(60,000)
Amount realized		$840,000

Adjusted Basis

The **adjusted basis** of property disposed of is the property's original basis adjusted to the date of disposition.[9] Original basis is the cost or other basis of the property on the date the property is acquired by the taxpayer. Many assets are acquired without purchasing them (for example, via gift or inheritance). Later, this chapter will discuss how to determine basis for these acquisitions. *Capital additions* increase and *capital recoveries* decrease the original basis.[10] As a result, adjusted basis is determined as follows:

> Cost (or other basis) on date of acquisition
> + Capital additions
> − Capital recoveries
> = Adjusted basis on date of disposition

[6]*Comm. v. Marshman,* 60–2 USTC ¶9484, 5 AFTR 2d 1528, 279 F.2d 27 (CA–6, 1960).

[7]*O'Malley v. Ames,* 52–1 USTC ¶9361, 42 AFTR 19, 197 F.2d 256 (CA–8, 1952).

[8]*U.S. v. Davis,* 62–2 USTC ¶9509, 9 AFTR 2d 1625, 82 S.Ct. 1190 (USSC, 1962).

[9]§ 1011(a) and Reg. § 1.1011–1.

[10]§ 1016(a) and Reg. § 1.1016–1.

Capital Additions

Capital additions include the cost of capital improvements and betterments made to the property by the taxpayer. These costs are different from repair and maintenance expenses, which are neither capitalized nor added to the original basis (refer to Chapter 5). Repair and maintenance expenses are deductible in the current taxable year if they are related to business or income-producing property. A buyer's original basis in the property also includes any liability on property that the buyer assumes. The same rule applies if property is acquired subject to a liability.[11]

Bluebird Corporation purchased some manufacturing equipment for $25,000. Whether Bluebird uses $25,000 from the business's cash account to pay for this equipment or uses $5,000 from that account and borrows the remaining $20,000, the basis of this equipment will be the same—namely, $25,000. Moreover, it does not matter whether Bluebird borrowed the $20,000 from the equipment's manufacturer, from a local bank, or from any other lender.

EXAMPLE 7

Capital Recoveries

Capital recoveries decrease the adjusted basis of property. The prominent types of capital recoveries are discussed below.

Depreciation and Cost Recovery The original basis of depreciable property is reduced by the annual depreciation charges (or cost recovery allowances) while the property is held by the taxpayer. The amount of depreciation that is subtracted from the original basis is the greater of the *allowed* or *allowable* cost recovery or depreciation.[12]

EXAMPLE 8

Refer back to Example 3. The machine Juan sold was acquired four years ago for $100,000. It was 7-year MACRS property, and Juan did not take either an immediate expense deduction (§ 179) or bonus depreciation on the property. Juan's adjusted basis is $37,485, computed as follows:

Original cost		$100,000
Cost recovery:		
Year 1 ($100,000 × .1429)	$14,290	
Year 2 ($100,000 × .2449)	24,490	
Year 3 ($100,000 × .1749)	17,490	
Year 4 ($100,000 × .1249 × ½)	6,245	
Total cost recovery		(62,515)
Adjusted basis		$ 37,485

As Juan's amount realized on the sale was $56,000, his realized gain is $18,515, computed as follows:

Amount realized	$ 56,000
− Adjusted basis	(37,485)
Realized gain (loss)	$ 18,515

Casualties and Thefts A casualty or theft may result in the reduction of the adjusted basis of property.[13] The adjusted basis is reduced by the amount of the *deductible* loss. In addition, the adjusted basis is reduced by the amount of insurance proceeds received. However, the receipt of insurance proceeds may result in a recognized gain rather than a deductible loss. The gain increases the adjusted basis of the property.[14]

---

[11]In a similar fashion, amortization of the discount on bonds increases the adjusted basis of the bonds. See Chapter 4 for a discussion of original issue discount.

[12]§ 1016(a)(2) and Reg. § 1.1016–3(a)(1)(i). Allowed depreciation is what a taxpayer has deducted on a tax return. Allowable depreciation is what a

taxpayer could have legally deducted. In most cases, these amounts are the same (refer to Chapter 5).

[13]Refer to Chapter 6 for the discussion of casualties and thefts.

[14]Reg. § 1.1016–6(a).

Capital Recoveries: Casualties and Thefts

EXAMPLE 9

An insured truck owned by Falcon Corporation is destroyed in an accident. At the time of the accident, the adjusted basis was $8,000, and the fair market value was $6,500. Falcon receives insurance proceeds of $6,500.

The amount of the casualty *loss* is $1,500 ($6,500 insurance insurance proceeds − $8,000 adjusted basis). The truck's adjusted basis becomes $0 ($8,000 pre-accident adjusted basis − $1,500 casualty loss − $6,500 of insurance proceeds received).

EXAMPLE 10

How would your answer to Example 9 change if the basis of the truck was $6,000, its fair market value was $9,000, and Falcon received a $9,000 insurance settlement?

Now Falcon has a casualty *gain* of $3,000 ($9,000 insurance proceeds − $6,000 adjusted basis). The truck's adjusted basis is increased by the $3,000 casualty gain and is reduced by the $9,000 of insurance proceeds received ($6,000 basis before casualty + $3,000 casualty gain − $9,000 insurance proceeds = $0 ending adjusted basis).

Certain Corporate Distributions A corporate distribution to a shareholder that is not taxable is treated as a return of capital, and it reduces the basis of the shareholder's stock in the corporation.[15] Corporations normally disclose this information to shareholders. Once the basis of the stock is reduced to zero, the amount of any subsequent distributions is a capital gain if the stock in the hands of the shareholder is a capital asset. See Chapter 13 for additional discussion.

Amortizable Bond Premium The basis in a bond purchased at a premium is reduced by the amortizable portion of the bond premium.[16] Investors in taxable bonds may *elect* to amortize the bond premium annually by taking the amortization as an interest expense deduction.[17] Therefore, the election enables the taxpayer to take an annual interest deduction to offset ordinary income in exchange for a larger capital gain or smaller capital loss on the disposition of the bond (due to the basis reduction).

DIGGING DEEPER 1   **In-depth coverage can be found on this book's companion website: www.cengage.com**

In contrast to the treatment of taxable bonds, the premium on tax-exempt bonds *must* be amortized, and no interest deduction is permitted. Furthermore, the basis of tax-exempt bonds is reduced even though the amortization is not allowed as a deduction. No amortization deduction is permitted on tax-exempt bonds because the interest income is exempt from tax, and the amortization of the bond premium merely represents an adjustment of the tax-exempt income earned on the bond.

EXAMPLE 11

Navy, Inc., purchases Eagle Corporation taxable bonds with a face value of $100,000 for $110,000, thus paying a premium of $10,000. The annual interest rate is 7%, and the bonds mature 10 years from the date of purchase. The annual interest income is $7,000 (7% × $100,000).

If Navy elects to amortize the bond premium, the $10,000 premium is deducted over the 10-year period. Navy's basis for the bonds is reduced each year by the amount of the amortization deduction.

If the bonds were tax-exempt, amortization of the bond premium and the basis adjustment would be mandatory and no deduction would be allowed for the amortization.

---

[15] § 1016(a)(4) and Reg. § 1.1016–5(a).

[16] § 1016(a)(5) and Reg. § 1.1016–5(b). The financial accounting treatment of bond premium amortization is the same as for tax purposes. The amortization results in a decrease in the bond investment account.

[17] § 171(c).

As with financial accounting, when property is traded, we can use the value of the property received to assess the value of the property given up. However, certain property transactions discussed later in this chapter are treated differently for tax purposes than for financial accounting purposes. For example, the category of transactions generally referred to as "nontaxable exchanges," such as like-kind exchanges and involuntary conversions, gives taxpayers the opportunity to defer the recognition of gain on the disposition of property in qualifying transactions. The gains or losses deferred under tax law, however, are not deferred for financial reporting purposes. Instead, the actual gain or loss realized is reflected in the entity's financial reports.

Identifying and calculating the book-tax differences that arise from *taxable* dispositions of certain other property may not be so easy. For example, as discussed in Chapter 5, cost recovery (i.e., depreciation) rules provided by the tax law specify various ways in which an asset's cost may be recovered over time. These methods often differ from the methods used to depreciate an asset for book purposes. Consequently, the annual book-tax differences in these depreciation expense calculations are noted in the financial reports. But in addition, these cumulative differences, as reflected in the accumulated depreciation account, will also produce a book-tax difference on the asset's disposition. That is, because an asset's accumulated depreciation may differ for book and tax purposes, its adjusted basis will also differ. Consequently, when the asset is sold, the amount of gain or loss for book purposes will differ from that recognized for tax purposes.

Easements An easement is the legal right to use another's land for a special purpose. Historically, easements have been used to obtain rights-of-way for utility lines, roads, and pipelines. In recent years, grants of conservation easements have become a popular means of obtaining charitable contribution deductions and reducing the value of real estate for transfer tax (i.e., estate and gift) purposes. For example, a conservation easement on property containing a rare wildlife habitat might prohibit any development, while one on a farm might allow continued farming and the building of additional agricultural structures, but no other development. Although a conservation easement can be sold, typically it is donated to a charitable organization (like the Nature Conservancy). If donated, the difference between the value of the land with and without the easement would be a charitable contribution. Likewise, scenic easements (granted to protect open spaces or scenic views) are used to reduce the value of land as assessed for property tax purposes.

The amount received for granting an easement is subtracted from the basis of the property. If the taxpayer does not retain any right to the use of the land, all of the basis is assigned to the easement. However, if the use of the land is only partially restricted, an allocation of some of the basis to the easement is appropriate. If, however, it is impossible or impractical to separate the basis of the part of the property on which the easement is granted, the basis of the whole property is reduced by the amount received. If the amount received for the easement exceeds the basis, a taxable gain results.[18]

7-1b **Recognized Gain or Loss**

Recognized gain is the amount of the realized gain that is included in the taxpayer's gross income.[19] A **recognized loss**, on the other hand, is the amount of a realized loss that is deductible for tax purposes.[20] As a general rule, the entire amount of a realized gain or loss is recognized when it is realized.[21]

LO.2

Distinguish between realized and recognized gain or loss.

---

[18]See Rev.Rul. 68–291, 1968–1 C.B. 351 and Rev.Rul. 77–414, 1977–2 C.B. 299.

[19]§ 61(a)(3) and Reg. § 1.61–6(a).

[20]§ 165(a) and Reg. § 1.165–1(a).

[21]§ 1001(c) and Reg. § 1.1002–1(a).

Concept Summary 7.2 summarizes the realized gain or loss and recognized gain or loss concepts.

Concept Summary 7.2

Realized and Recognized Gain or Loss

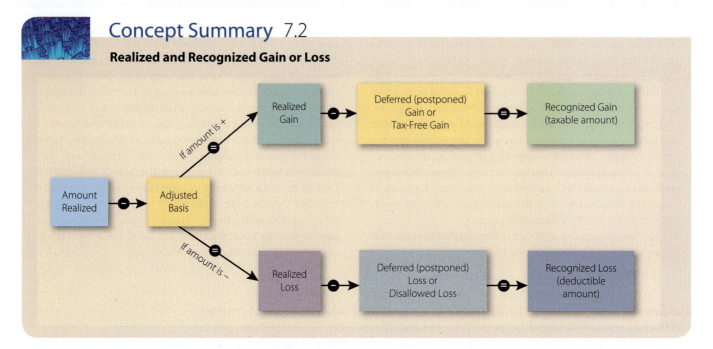

7-1c **Nonrecognition of Gain or Loss**

In certain cases, a realized gain or loss on a property disposition is not recognized. More specifically, the tax law permits or requires gain or loss *deferral* to later tax years for some transactions. Nontaxable exchanges, which are covered later in this chapter, are one example. In addition, there are other instances when the tax law *disallows* or limits deductions for certain tax losses. For example, realized losses from the sale or exchange of property between certain related parties are not recognized.[22] In all of these instances, applying a particular tax rule results in taxpayers not recognizing a realized gain or loss.

Dispositions of Personal Use Assets

For individual taxpayers, special rules apply to *personal use* assets (i.e., assets such as a residence or an automobile that are not used in any business or investment activity). A loss from the sale, exchange, or condemnation of such assets is not recognized for tax purposes. That is, taxpayers cannot deduct losses from their personal garage sale items sold for less than what those items cost them. An exception exists for certain casualty or theft losses from personal use assets (refer to Chapter 6). In contrast, any gain realized from the disposition of personal use assets is generally taxable.

EXAMPLE 12

Freda sells an automobile, which she has held exclusively for personal use, for $6,000. The basis of the automobile is $5,000. Freda has a realized and recognized gain of $1,000.

If she sold this automobile for $4,500, she would have a realized loss of $500, but the loss would not be recognized for tax purposes, because the automobile is a personal use asset.

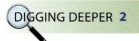

DIGGING DEEPER 2   **In-depth coverage can be found on this book's companion website: www.cengage.com**

---

[22]§ 267(a)(1).

7-2 BASIS CONSIDERATIONS

A key element in calculating gain or loss from a property transaction is the asset's basis at the time of the transaction. Basis is usually unrecovered cost, but can be different, especially if the taxpayer did not purchase the property.

7-2a Determination of Cost Basis

Understand and illustrate how basis is determined for various methods of asset acquisition.

The basis of property is generally the property's cost, which is the amount paid for the property in cash or other property.[23]

A *bargain purchase* of property is an exception to the general rule for determining basis. A bargain purchase results when an employer transfers property to an employee at less than the property's fair market value (as compensation) or when a corporation transfers property to a shareholder at less than the property's fair market value (a dividend). These transfers create taxable income for the purchaser equal to the difference between fair market value and purchase price at the time the property is purchased. The basis of property acquired in a bargain purchase is the property's fair market value.[24] If the basis of the property were not increased by the bargain element, the taxpayer would be taxed on this amount again at disposition.

> Wade buys land from his employer for $10,000. The fair market value of the land is $15,000.
>
> Wade must include the $5,000 difference between the cost and the fair market value of the land in his gross income. The bargain element represents additional compensation to Wade. His basis for the land is $15,000, the land's fair market value.

EXAMPLE 13

Identification Problems

Sometimes it can be difficult to determine the cost of an asset being sold such as when a taxpayer has purchased shares of a company's stock over time at different prices. This problem is frequently encountered in sales of corporate stock, because a taxpayer may purchase separate lots of a company's stock on different dates and at different prices. When the stock is sold, if the taxpayer cannot identify the specific shares being sold (specific identification), the stock sold is determined on a first-in, first-out (FIFO) basis. Thus, the holding period and cost of the stock sold are determined by referring to the purchase date and cost of the first lot of stock acquired, which in times of rising stock markets is lower than current costs, causing higher taxable gains.[25] But, if the stock being sold can be adequately identified, then the basis and holding period of the specific stock sold are used in determining the nature and amount of gain or loss.[26] So, to avoid FIFO treatment when the sold securities are held by a broker, a taxpayer should provide specific instructions and receive written confirmation of the securities being sold. Brokers and others in similar enterprises are now required to provide investors with an annual report on the cost basis of their stocks sold during the year (to be included on Form 1099–B and reported to the IRS).

> Pelican, Inc., purchases 100 shares of Olive Corporation stock on July 1, 2016, for $5,000 ($50 a share) and another 100 shares of Olive stock on July 1, 2017, for $6,000 ($60 a share). Pelican sells 50 shares of the stock on January 2, 2018.
>
> The cost of the stock sold, assuming that Pelican cannot adequately identify the shares, is $50 a share (from shares purchased on July 1, 2016), or $2,500. This is the cost Pelican will compare with the amount realized in determining the gain or loss from the sale.
>
> If Pelican had been able to identify the stock sold as having been from the $60 purchase, the basis deducted from proceeds would have been $3,000.

EXAMPLE 14

---

[23]§ 1012 and Reg. § 1.1012–1(a).

[24]Reg. §§ 1.61–2(d)(2)(i) and 1.301–1(j). See the discussion in Chapter 11 of the circumstances under which what appears to be a taxable bargain purchase is an excludible qualified employee discount (text Section 11-2j).

[25]*Kluger Associates, Inc.*, 69 T.C. 925 (1978).

[26]Reg. § 1.1012–1(c)(1).

Allocation Problems

When a taxpayer acquires *several assets in a lump-sum purchase*, the total cost must be allocated among the individual assets.[27] Allocation is necessary for several reasons:

- Some of the assets acquired may be depreciable (e.g., buildings), while others are not (e.g., land).
- If one of the assets acquired is sold, its basis must be known to compute realized gain or loss.
- Some assets may receive special tax treatment when sold in the future.

The lump-sum cost is allocated on the basis of the fair market values of the individual assets acquired.

Magenta Corporation purchases a building and land for $800,000. Because of the depressed nature of the industry in which the seller was operating, Magenta was able to negotiate a very favorable purchase price. Appraisals of the individual assets indicate that the fair market value of the building is $600,000 and that of the land is $400,000.

Magenta's basis for the building is $480,000 [($600,000/$1,000,000) × $800,000], and its basis for the land is $320,000 [($400,000/$1,000,000) × $800,000].

If a business is purchased and **goodwill** is involved, a special allocation applies. Initially, the purchase price is allocated among the assets acquired, other than goodwill, based on their fair market values. Goodwill is then assigned the residual amount of the purchase price. The allocation is the same for both the buyer and the seller.[28]

Roadrunner, Inc., sells its business to Coyote Corporation. An independent appraisal indicates that the fair market value of the business assets, other than goodwill, are as follows:

Marketable securities	$ 5,000
Inventory	35,000
Building	500,000
Land	200,000

After negotiations, Roadrunner and Coyote agree on a sales price of $1 million. Applying the residual method, the residual purchase price is allocated to goodwill, resulting in the following basis of assets to Coyote Corporation:

Marketable securities	$ 5,000
Inventory	35,000
Building	500,000
Land	200,000
Goodwill	260,000

In the case of *nontaxable stock dividends* on common stock, if the stock dividend is common on common, the cost of the original common shares is allocated to the total shares owned after the dividend.[29]

Yellow, Inc., owns 100 shares of Sparrow Corporation common stock for which it paid $1,100. Yellow receives a 10% common stock dividend, giving it a new total of 110 shares. Before the stock dividend, Yellow's basis was $11 per share ($1,100 ÷ 100 shares). The basis of each share after the stock dividend is $10 ($1,100 ÷ 110 shares).

---

[27]Reg. § 1.61–6(a).

[28]§ 1060. In most cases, the seller's recognized gain associated with the goodwill is classified as capital (as discussed in Chapter 8).

[29]§§ 305(a) and 307(a). The holding period of the new shares includes the holding period of the old shares. § 1223(5) and Reg. § 1.1223–1(e). See Chapter 8 for a discussion of the importance of the holding period.

7-2b Gift Basis

Although business entities can neither make nor receive gratuitous transfers, ownership interests in such entities are frequently gifted. Partnership interests, stock in corporations, and other assets are regularly passed from one generation to another for a variety of family and business reasons. Special basis rules apply to such transfers.

When a taxpayer receives property as a gift, there is no cost to the donee (recipient). When the property is sold, instead of having a realized gain equal to the proceeds received (because the donee has a zero basis in the property), the Code[30] assigns a basis to the property received that depends upon the following:

- The date of the gift.
- The basis of the property to the donor.
- The fair market value of the property.
- The amount of the gift tax paid, if any.

Gift Basis Rules, In General

If a property's fair market value on the date of the gift exceeds the donor's basis in the property (i.e., the property has appreciated in value), the donor's basis carries over to the recipient (donee).[31] This basis is called a *carryover basis* and is used in determining the donee's future gain or loss.

The Big Picture

EXAMPLE 18

Return to the facts of *The Big Picture* on p. 7-1. Alice's father purchased the land in 1994 for $2,000. He gave the land to Alice 10 years ago, when the fair market value was $10,000. No gift tax was paid on the transfer. Alice is considering selling the land, which is currently worth $50,000.

If she sells the property for $50,000, Alice will have a realized gain of $48,000 ($50,000 amount realized − $2,000 basis in the land).

If the property's fair market value on the date of the gift is *lower* than the donor's basis then special *dual basis* rules apply. Here, the donee has one basis for measuring a gain and a different basis for measuring a loss. This special rule is in place to prevent the shifting of losses (typically among family members) to the individual who would receive the greatest benefit. Under this rule, the donee's gain basis is the donor's adjusted basis; the donee's loss basis is the fair market value of the property.

The Big Picture

EXAMPLE 19

Return to the facts of *The Big Picture* on p. 7-1. Instead, assume that Alice's father had purchased the land in 1993 for $12,000. He gave the land to Alice 10 years ago, when the fair market value was $10,000. No gift tax was paid on the transfer.

If Alice sells the property for $50,000, she has a realized gain of $38,000 ($50,000 amount realized − $12,000 basis in the land).

However, if the property has declined in value because of the discovery of contaminants on the property and Alice is able to sell the land for only $7,000, she will realize a loss of $3,000 ($7,000 amount realized − $10,000 basis in the land).

This loss basis rule prevents the donee from receiving a tax benefit from a decline in value that occurred while the donor held the property. Therefore, in the preceding example, Alice has a loss of only $3,000 rather than a loss of $5,000 ($7,000 − $12,000). The $2,000 difference represents the decline in value that occurred while Alice's father

---

[30]§ 1015(a).

[31]§ 1015(a) and Reg. § 1.1015–1(a)(1). See Reg. § 1.1015–1(a)(3) for cases in which the facts necessary to determine the donor's adjusted basis are

unknown. See Example 21 for the effect of depreciation deductions by the donee.

held the property. Ironically, however, a donee might be subject to income tax on the appreciation that occurred while the donor held the property, as illustrated in Example 18.

In any case, the operation of this dual basis rule produces a curious anomaly: if the sales proceeds fall *between* the donor's adjusted basis and the property's fair market value at the date of gift, no gain *or* loss is recognized.

The Big Picture

EXAMPLE

20

Return to the facts of *The Big Picture* on p. 7-1. Instead, assume that Alice's father had purchased the land in 1994 for $12,000. He gave the land to Alice 10 years ago, when the fair market value was $10,000. No gift tax was paid on the transfer. Now Alice plans to sell the property for $11,000.

To calculate gain, she would use a basis of $12,000, her father's basis. But when a $12,000 basis is compared with the $11,000 sales proceeds, a *loss* is produced. Yet in determining loss, Alice must use the property's fair market value at the date of gift—namely, $10,000. When a $10,000 basis is compared to sales proceeds of $11,000, a *gain* is produced. Accordingly, no gain or loss is recognized on this transaction.

Adjustment for Gift Tax

Because of the size of the unified estate and gift tax exemption ($11.18 million in 2018), basis adjustments for gift taxes paid are rare. If, however, gift taxes are paid by the donor, the portion of the gift tax paid that is related to any appreciation is taken into account in determining the donee's gain basis.[32]

TAX PLANNING STRATEGIES   Gift Planning

FRAMEWORK FOCUS: TAX RATE

Strategy: Shift Net Income from High-Bracket Taxpayers to Low-Bracket Taxpayers.

FRAMEWORK FOCUS: DEDUCTIONS

Strategy: Maximize Deductible Amounts.

Gifts of *appreciated property* can produce tax savings if the donee is in a lower tax bracket than the donor. The carryover basis rule effectively shifts the tax on the property's appreciation to the new owner, even if all of the appreciation arose while the property was owned by the donor.

On the other hand, donors should generally avoid making gifts of property that are worth less than the donor's adjusted basis (loss property). The operation of the basis rule

for losses may result in either (1) a realized loss that is not deductible by either the donor or the donee or (2) reduced tax benefits when the loss is recognized by a donee facing lower marginal tax rates. Unless the property is expected to rebound in value before it is sold, a donor would be better advised to sell the property that has declined in value, deduct the resulting loss, and then transfer the proceeds to the prospective donee.

Holding Period

The **holding period** for property acquired by gift begins on the date the donor acquired the property,[33] unless the special circumstance requiring use of the property's fair market value at the date of gift applies. If so, the holding period starts on the date of the gift.[34] The significance of the holding period for capital assets is discussed in Chapter 8.

---

[32]§ 1015(d)(6) and Reg. § 1.1015–5(c)(2). For *gifts made before 1977*, the full amount of the gift tax paid is added to the donor's basis, with basis capped at the donor's fair market value at the date of the gift. Examples illustrating these rules can be found in Reg. § 1.1015–5(c)(5) and IRS Publication 551 (*Basis of Assets*), p. 9.

[33]§ 1223(2) and Reg. § 1.1223–1(b).
[34]Rev.Rul. 59–86, 1959–1 C.B. 209.

Vito gave a machine to Tina earlier this year. At that time, the adjusted basis was $32,000 (cost of $40,000 − accumulated depreciation of $8,000), and the fair market value was $26,000. No gift tax was due. Tina's basis for determining gain is $32,000, and her loss basis is $26,000. During this year, Tina deducts depreciation (cost recovery) of $6,400 ($32,000 × 20%). (Refer to Chapter 5 for the cost recovery tables.) At the end of this year, Tina's basis determinations are calculated as follows:

EXAMPLE 21

	Gain Basis	Loss Basis
Donor's basis or fair market value	$32,000	$26,000
Depreciation	(6,400)	(6,400)
	$25,600	$19,600

Basis for Depreciation

The basis for depreciation on depreciable gift property is the donee's basis for determining gain.[35] This rule is applicable even if the donee later sells the property at a loss and uses the property's fair market value at the date of gift in calculating the amount of the realized loss.

7-2c Inherited Property

Special basis rules apply for inherited property (property acquired from a decedent). Typically, these rules are favorable to the taxpayer receiving this property.

General Rules

The basis of inherited property is generally the property's fair market value at the date of death (referred to as the *primary valuation amount*).[36] The administrator of the estate may elect to value the property at its fair market value six months after the date of death. This amount is referred to as the *alternate valuation amount*.

In-depth coverage can be found on this book's companion website: **www.cengage.com**   **3 DIGGING DEEPER**

Linda and various other family members inherited stock in a closely held corporation from Linda's father, who died earlier this year. At the date of death, her father's basis for the stock Linda inherited was $35,000. The stock's fair market value at the date of death was $50,000. The alternate valuation date was not elected.

EXAMPLE 22

Linda's basis for income tax purposes is $50,000. This is commonly referred to as a *stepped-up basis*.

If, instead, the stock's fair market value at the date of death was $20,000, Linda's basis would be $20,000. This is commonly referred to as a *stepped-down basis*.

The Big Picture

Return to the facts of *The Big Picture* on p. 7-1. Alice owns 500 shares of AppleCo stock, 300 of which were inherited from her grandfather. Her grandfather's cost basis in the stock was $12,000 (i.e., its purchase price), but the shares were worth $30,000 at the time of his death. Alice purchased the other 200 shares for $28,000.

EXAMPLE 23

Therefore, the basis in her 500 AppleCo shares is $58,000: the 300 shares received as an inheritance take a stepped-up basis of $30,000, and the 200 shares purchased take a cost basis of $28,000.

---

[35]§ 1011 and Reg. §§ 1.1011–1 and 1.167(g)–1.   [36]§ 1014(a) and § 1022.

The alternate valuation date and amount are only available to estates for which an estate tax return must be filed (generally, estates with a valuation in excess of $11.18 million in 2018). Even if an estate tax return is filed and the executor elects the alternate valuation date, the six-months-after-death date is available only for property that the executor has not distributed before this date.[37]

The alternate valuation date can be elected *only if*, as a result of the election, *both* the value of the gross estate and the estate tax liability are lower than they would have been if the primary valuation date had been used.[38]

 DIGGING DEEPER 4 | In-depth coverage can be found on this book's companion website: **www.cengage.com**

TAX PLANNING STRATEGIES   Inherited Property

FRAMEWORK FOCUS: INCOME

Strategy: Avoid Income Recognition.

FRAMEWORK FOCUS: DEDUCTIONS

Strategy: Maximize Deductible Amounts.

If a taxpayer *retains appreciated property* until death, the property's basis will be "stepped up" to its fair market value at that time. So, no income tax will be paid on the property's appreciation by either the former owner (the decedent) or the new owner (the heir).

Alternatively, *depreciated property should be sold* prior to death. Otherwise, the property's basis in the heir's hands will be its declined fair market value, and neither the decedent nor the heir will be able to deduct the loss that occurred while the property was owned by the decedent.

Holding Period of Inherited Property

The holding period of inherited property is *deemed to be long term* regardless of when the property was acquired by the decedent and whether the property is disposed of at a gain or at a loss.[39]

7-2d **Disallowed Losses**

In certain situations, losses that normally would be recognized are disallowed. Transactions between related parties and wash sales are two of these situations.

Related Taxpayers

LO.4

Describe various loss disallowance provisions.

Without rules limiting losses on related-party transactions, family members could collude to avoid much of their taxes. However, § 267 provides that realized losses from sales or exchanges of property between certain related parties are not recognized. This loss disallowance rule applies to several types of related-party transactions.[40] The most common involve (1) members of a family, and (2) an individual and a corporation (where the individual owns, directly or indirectly, more than 50 percent in value of the corporation's outstanding stock). Section 707 provides a similar loss disallowance provision where the

---

[37]§ 2032(a)(1) and Rev.Rul. 56–60, 1956–1 C.B. 443. For any property distributed by the executor during the six-month period preceding the alternate valuation date, the basis to the beneficiary will equal the fair market value on the date of distribution.

[38]§ 2032(c). This provision prevents the alternate valuation election from being used to increase the basis of the property to the beneficiary for

income tax purposes without simultaneously increasing the estate tax liability (because of estate tax deductions or credits).

[39]§ 1223(11).

[40]§ 267(b).

related parties are a partner and a partnership in which the partner owns, directly or indirectly, more than 50 percent of the capital interests or profits interests in the partnership. Neither provision, however, prevents the recognition of *gains* between related parties. The rules governing the relationships covered by § 267 were discussed in Chapter 5.

If income-producing or business property is transferred to a related party and a loss is disallowed, the basis of the property to the recipient is what the recipient paid for it (i.e., a cost basis). However, the recipient can use the disallowed loss to offset a gain (down to, but not below, zero) on the later sale of that asset to an unrelated party. See Examples 19 through 21 in Chapter 5.

In-depth coverage can be found on this book's companion website: **www.cengage.com**   **5 DIGGING DEEPER**

Wash Sales

The ==wash sale== rules (§ 1091) are designed to eliminate a taxpayer ploy to sell stock at a loss and replace the stock sold by buying identical shares shortly before or after the sale. If § 1091 applies, a realized loss on the sale or exchange of stock or securities is not recognized. Recognition of the loss is disallowed because the taxpayer is considered to be in substantially the same economic position after the sale and repurchase as before the sale and repurchase. The wash sale rule applies if a taxpayer sells or exchanges stock or securities at a loss, and within 30 days before *or* after the date of the sale or exchange acquires *substantially identical* stock or securities.[41] An option to purchase substantially identical securities is treated the same as actually buying the stock. Corporate bonds and preferred stock normally are not considered substantially identical to a corporation's common stock.[42] Attempts to avoid the application of the wash sale rules by having a related taxpayer repurchase the securities have been unsuccessful.[43] The wash sale provisions do *not* apply to gains. Concept Summary 7.3 provides an overview of the wash sale rules.

A realized loss that is not recognized is added to the *basis* of the substantially identical stock or securities whose acquisition resulted in the nonrecognition of loss.[44] In other words, the basis of the replacement stock or securities is increased by the amount of the unrecognized loss. If the loss were not added to the basis of the newly acquired stock or securities, the taxpayer would never recover the entire basis of the old stock or securities. As a result, the wash sale rule operates to *defer* the recognition of the taxpayer's loss.

EXAMPLE 24

Oriole Manufacturing Company sold 50 shares of Green Corporation stock (basis of $10,000) for $8,000. Ten days later, Oriole purchased 50 shares of the same stock for $7,000.

Oriole's realized loss of $2,000 ($8,000 amount realized − $10,000 basis) is not recognized because it resulted from a wash sale. Oriole's basis in the newly acquired stock is $9,000 ($7,000 purchase price + $2,000 unrecognized loss from the wash sale).

Because the basis of the new stock or securities includes the unrecovered portion of the basis of the formerly held stock or securities, the *holding period* of the new stock or securities begins on the date of acquisition of the old stock or securities.[45]

A taxpayer may acquire fewer shares than the number sold in a wash sale. In this case, the loss from the sale is prorated between recognized and unrecognized loss on the basis of the ratio of the number of shares acquired to the number of shares sold.[46] This disallowance rule does not apply to taxpayers engaged in the business of buying and selling securities.[47]

---

[41]§ 1091(a) and Reg. §§ 1.1091–1(a) and (f).

[42]Rev.Rul. 56–406, 1956–2 C.B. 523. However, if the bonds and preferred stock are convertible into common stock, they may be considered substantially identical under certain circumstances.

[43]*McWilliams v. Comm.*, 47–1 USTC ¶9289, 35 AFTR 1184, 67 S.Ct. 1477 (USSC, 1947).

[44]§ 1091(d) and Reg. § 1.1091–2(a).

[45]§ 1223(4) and Reg. § 1.1223–1(d).

[46]§ 1091(b) and Reg. § 1.1091–1(c).

[47]Reg. § 1.1091–1(a).

Concept Summary 7.3

Wash Sale Rules

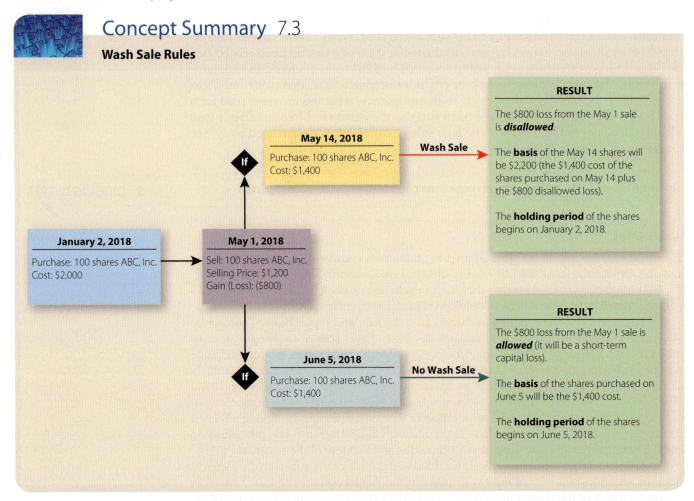

January 2, 2018	May 1, 2018
Purchase: 100 shares ABC, Inc. Cost: $2,000	Sell: 100 shares ABC, Inc. Selling Price: $1,200 Gain (Loss): ($800)

May 14, 2018
Purchase: 100 shares ABC, Inc.
Cost: $1,400

Wash Sale →

RESULT

The $800 loss from the May 1 sale is **disallowed**.

The **basis** of the May 14 shares will be $2,200 (the $1,400 cost of the shares purchased on May 14 plus the $800 disallowed loss).

The **holding period** of the shares begins on January 2, 2018.

June 5, 2018
Purchase: 100 shares ABC, Inc.
Cost: $1,400

No Wash Sale →

RESULT

The $800 loss from the May 1 sale is **allowed** (it will be a short-term capital loss).

The **basis** of the shares purchased on June 5 will be the $1,400 cost.

The **holding period** of the shares begins on June 5, 2018.

TAX PLANNING STRATEGIES   Avoiding Wash Sales

FRAMEWORK FOCUS: DEDUCTIONS

Strategy: Maximize Deductible Amounts.

The wash sale rules can be avoided by replacing the sold security with a *similar* but not "substantially identical" security. For example, if AT&T common stock is sold to claim an unrealized loss, the taxpayer could immediately acquire Verizon common stock without triggering the wash sale rule, even though both entities are telecommunication companies.

Nontax considerations must also come into play, however, because AT&T and Verizon are two different companies with different investment prospects. Although both securities will be affected by many of the same factors, they will also be subject to different factors that may be even more significant than the ones they share.

7-2e Conversion of Property from Personal Use to Business or Income-Producing Use

As discussed previously, losses from the sale of personal use assets are not recognized for tax purposes, but losses from the sale of business and income-producing assets are deductible. Can a taxpayer convert a personal use asset that has declined in value to business or income-producing use and then sell the asset to recognize a business or income-producing loss?

The tax law prevents this practice by specifying that the *basis for determining loss* on personal use assets converted to business or income-producing use is the *lower* of the property's adjusted basis or its fair market value on the date of conversion.[48] The *gain basis* for converted property is the property's adjusted basis on the date of conversion, regardless of whether the property's use is business, income-producing, or personal in nature.

Diane's personal residence has an adjusted basis of $175,000 and a fair market value of $160,000. When she converts the personal residence to residential rental property on January 1, her basis for determining loss is $160,000 (lower of $175,000 adjusted basis and fair market value of $160,000). The $15,000 decline in value is a personal loss and can never be recognized for tax purposes. Diane's basis for determining gain is $175,000.

The basis for determining loss is also the *basis for depreciating* the converted property.[49] This is an exception to the general rule that the basis for depreciation is the basis for determining gain (e.g., property received by gift). This exception prevents the taxpayer from recovering a personal loss indirectly through depreciation of the higher original basis. Once property is converted, both its basis for loss and its basis for gain are adjusted for depreciation deductions from the date of conversion to the date of disposition.

Assume the same facts as in Example 25. The MACRS cost recovery deduction for the current year is $5,576 ($160,000 × 3.485%). Thus, at the end of the current year, Diane's adjusted basis for gain for the rental property is $169,424 ($175,000 − $5,576), and her adjusted basis for loss is $154,424 ($160,000 − $5,576).

In-depth coverage can be found on this book's companion website: **www.cengage.com**   **6, 7** DIGGING DEEPER

7-2f Summary of Basis Adjustments

Some of the more common items that either increase or decrease the basis of an asset appear in Concept Summary 7.4.

There are a number of techniques for determining basis for tax purposes, with the method dependent on the manner in which the asset was acquired. In summary, the basis of an asset can be determined by:

- Its cost.
- The basis of another asset.
- Its fair market value.
- The basis of the asset in the hands of another taxpayer.

---

[48]Reg. § 1.165–9(b)(2).   [49]Reg. § 1.167(g)–1.

Concept Summary 7.4

Adjustments to Basis

Item	Effect	Refer to Chapter	Explanation
Amortization of bond discount	Increase	7	Amortization is mandatory for certain taxable bonds and elective for tax-exempt bonds.
Amortization of bond premium	Decrease	7	Amortization is mandatory for tax-exempt bonds and elective for taxable bonds.
Amortization of covenant not to compete	Decrease	5	Covenant must be for a definite and limited time period. The amortization period is a statutory period of 15 years.
Amortization of intangibles	Decrease	5	Intangibles are amortized over a 15-year period.
Bad debts	Decrease	6	Most taxpayers must use the specific charge-off method.
Capital additions	Increase	7	Certain items, at the taxpayer's election, can be capitalized or deducted.
Casualty	Decrease	7	For a casualty loss, the amount of the adjustment is the sum of the deductible loss and the insurance proceeds received. For a casualty gain, the amount of the adjustment is the insurance proceeds received reduced by the recognized gain.
Condemnation	Decrease	7	See casualty explanation.
Cost recovery	Decrease	5	Section 168 is applicable to tangible assets placed in service after 1980 whose useful life is expressed in terms of years.
Depletion	Decrease	5	Use the greater of cost or percentage depletion. Percentage depletion can be deducted even when the basis is zero.
Depreciation	Decrease	5	Section 167 is applicable to tangible assets placed in service before 1981 and to tangible assets not depreciated in terms of years.
Easement	Decrease	7	If the taxpayer does not retain any use of the land, all of the basis is allocable to the easement transaction. However, if only part of the land is affected by the easement, only part of the basis is allocable to the easement transaction.
Improvements by lessee to lessor's property	Increase	4	Adjustment occurs only if the lessor is required to include the fair market value of the improvements in gross income under § 109.
Imputed interest	Decrease		Amount deducted is not part of the cost of the asset.
Inventory: lower of cost or market	Decrease		Not available if the LIFO method is used.
Limited expensing under § 179	Decrease	5	Occurs only if the taxpayer elects § 179 treatment.
Medical capital expenditure deducted as a medical expense	Decrease	10	Adjustment is the amount of the deduction (the effect on basis is to increase it by the amount of the capital expenditure net of the deduction).
Real estate taxes: apportionment between the buyer and seller	Increase or decrease	5	To the extent the buyer pays the seller's pro rata share, the buyer's basis is increased. To the extent the seller pays the buyer's pro rata share, the buyer's basis is decreased.
Rebate from manufacturer	Decrease		Because the rebate is treated as an adjustment to the purchase price, it is not included in the buyer's gross income.
Stock dividend	Decrease	7	Adjustment occurs only if the stock dividend is nontaxable. While the basis per share decreases, the total stock basis does not change.
Stock rights	Decrease	13	Adjustment to stock basis occurs only for nontaxable stock rights and only if the fair market value of the rights is at least 15% of the fair market value of the stock, or if less than 15%, the taxpayer elects to allocate the basis between the stock and the rights.
Theft	Decrease	6	See casualty explanation.

7-3 GENERAL CONCEPT OF A NONTAXABLE EXCHANGE

A taxpayer who is going to replace a business asset (e.g., a building and land) may decide to sell the old asset and purchase a new asset. In this case, any realized gain or loss on the sale of the old asset is recognized. The basis of the new asset is its cost. Alternatively, the taxpayer may be able to trade the old asset (e.g., land and building) for a new asset (e.g., a large parcel of land on which the taxpayer will construct a new manufacturing plant). This exchange of assets might qualify as a nontaxable exchange.

The tax law recognizes that nontaxable exchanges result in a change in the *form* but not the *substance* of a taxpayer's relative economic position. Effectively, the replacement property received in the exchange is viewed as a continuation of the old investment.[50] In addition, a nontaxable exchange often does not provide the taxpayer with the *wherewithal to pay* the tax on any realized gain that would be recognized (i.e., the taxpayer does not have the cash that would have been received in a sale).

A nontaxable exchange *postpones* (i.e., defers) recognition of gains or losses until the new property received in the nontaxable exchange is subsequently sold in a taxable transaction. This "deferral" is accomplished by assigning a carryover basis to the replacement property.

> **EXAMPLE 27**
>
> Starling Management Company completes a *nontaxable exchange* of property with an adjusted basis of $10,000 and a fair market value of $12,000 for property with a fair market value of $12,000.
>
> Starling has a realized gain of $2,000 ($12,000 amount realized − $10,000 adjusted basis). Its recognized gain is $0. Starling's basis in the replacement property is a carryover basis of $10,000.
>
> Assume that the replacement property is nondepreciable and that Starling subsequently sells it for $13,000. The realized and recognized gain will be the $3,000 gain that was postponed (deferred) in the nontaxable transaction. If the replacement property is depreciable, the carryover basis of $10,000 is used in calculating depreciation.

In some nontaxable exchanges, only some of the property involved in the transaction qualifies for nonrecognition treatment. If the taxpayer receives cash or other nonqualifying property, part or all of the realized gain from the exchange is recognized, since the taxpayer has the wherewithal to pay tax. Here, the basis of the replacement property is adjusted to reflect only the deferred gain (gain realized, but not recognized).

It is important to distinguish between a nontaxable disposition (or nonrecognition transaction, as the term is used in the statute) and a tax-free transaction. As previously mentioned, the term *nontaxable* refers to postponement of recognition via some version of carryover basis. In a *tax-free* transaction, the nonrecognition is a permanent exclusion of gain (e.g., see the discussion later in this chapter of excluding gain from the sale of a principal residence).

Either way, nontaxable and tax-free transactions are exceptions to the Code's general rule that gains and losses are recognized when they are realized. These exceptions have their own sets of requirements, limitations, and restrictions, all of which must be satisfied for a transaction to be characterized as nontaxable or tax-free. Otherwise, the general rule of recognition applies to the gain or loss at hand.

---

[50]Reg. § 1.1002–1(c).

7-4 **LIKE-KIND EXCHANGES—§ 1031**

LO.5

Apply the nonrecognition provisions and basis determination rules for like-kind exchanges.

Section 1031 requires nontaxable exchange treatment if the following requirements are satisfied:[51]

- The property is like-kind property.
- The form of the transaction is an exchange.
- Both the property given up and the property received are either "used in a trade or business" *or* "held for investment."

Qualifying <mark>like-kind exchanges</mark> only apply to *real property* used for business or investment purposes.[52] No other type of property qualifies under the like-kind exchange provisions. As a result, the purpose for which the property is held by the taxpayer in question is critical. For example, if Janet uses a building in her trade or business, it may qualify for like-kind treatment, but if she uses a building as her personal home, it is ineligible for nonrecognition treatment under § 1031.

If a taxpayer exchanges like-kind property solely for like-kind property, gain or loss realized is not recognized (it is deferred) and the basis and holding period from the old property attaches (or carries over) to the new property.

EXAMPLE 28

During the current year, Andy exchanged 40 acres of unimproved land in Illinois (fair market value $200,000; basis $70,000) for 10 acres of unimproved land in California (fair market value $200,000).

Although Andy has a realized gain of $130,000 on this transaction ($200,000 amount realized − $70,000 basis), none of the gain is recognized since the transaction qualifies as a like-kind exchange. Andy's basis in the new property is $70,000. This carryover basis reflects the realized gain which is deferred ($200,000 California property fair market value − $130,000 gain deferred).

If Andy were to sell the California property, he would have a realized and recognized gain of $130,000. The like-kind exchange rules also acknowledge that Andy—after the exchange—would not have the wherewithal to pay tax if the realized gain were recognized.

One final point: the like-kind exchange rules are applied independently to each taxpayer in the exchange; one taxpayer may qualify for like-kind treatment, and the other may not.

7-4a **Like-Kind Property**

The Regulations explain the term *like-kind* as follows: "The words 'like-kind' refer to the nature or character of the property and not to its grade or quality. One kind or class of property may not … be exchanged for property of a different kind or class."[53] The Regulations go on to explain that although real estate can be exchanged only for other real estate, the definition of real estate is quite broad. *Real estate* (or realty) includes principally rental buildings, office and store buildings, manufacturing plants, warehouses, and land. It is immaterial whether real estate is improved or unimproved. Thus, unimproved land can be exchanged for an apartment house. Alternatively, real property located in the United States exchanged for foreign real property (and vice versa) does not qualify as like-kind property. In any case, real estate cannot be exchanged in a like-kind transaction for personal property.

---

[51]§ 1031(a) and Reg. § 1.1031(a)–1(a).

[52]Before January 1, 2018, business and investment *personal property* also qualified for like-kind exchange treatment. This includes machines, equipment, furniture and fixtures, trucks, and automobiles.

[53]Reg. § 1.1031(a)–1(b).

TAX PLANNING STRATEGIES Like-Kind Exchanges

FRAMEWORK FOCUS: DEDUCTIONS

Strategy: Maximize Deductible Amounts.

The nonrecognition provision for like-kind exchanges is *mandatory* rather than elective. A taxpayer who wants to recognize a realized gain or loss will have to structure the transaction in a way that fails the like-kind exchange requirements. For example, a taxpayer may want to avoid like-kind treatment to recognize a realized loss.

EXAMPLE 29

During the current year, Stephanie exchanged her rental condo in Vail, worth $250,000 (basis of $325,000), plus $80,000 cash for a rental condo in Malibu worth $330,000. Although Stephanie has a realized loss of $75,000 on this transaction ($250,000 amount realized − $325,000 basis), none of the loss is recognized since the transaction qualifies as a like-kind exchange.

Stephanie would likely be better off by selling her Vail condo (and recognizing the loss) and then buying the Malibu property.

Even if *disposition would result in a gain*, a taxpayer might want to recognize this gain in the current taxable year. If so, a like-kind exchange should be avoided. Circumstances suggesting this strategy include:

- Unused capital loss carryovers, especially if the taxpayer is a corporation for which such carryovers are limited in duration (see Chapters 4 and 8).
- Unused net operating loss carryovers (see Chapter 6).
- Unused general business credit carryovers (see Chapter 17).
- Suspended or current passive activity losses (see Chapter 6).

EXAMPLE 30

Pheasant, Inc., made the following exchanges during the taxable year:

(a) Inventory for a machine used in business.
(b) Land held for investment for a building used in business.
(c) Stock held for investment for equipment used in business.
(d) A light-duty business truck for a light-duty business truck.
(e) Land held for investment in New York for land held for investment in London.

Only exchange (b), investment real property for business real property, qualifies as an exchange of like-kind property.

The other exchanges do not qualify because they involve (a), inventory; (c), stock; (d), personal property; and (e), U.S. and foreign real estate.

In-depth coverage can be found on this book's companion website: **www.cengage.com**   **8** DIGGING DEEPER

7-4b Exchange Requirement

The transaction must generally involve a direct exchange of property to qualify as a like-kind exchange. The sale of old property and the purchase of new property, even though like kind, is not an exchange. However, the Code does provide a limited procedure for real estate to be exchanged for qualifying property that is acquired subsequent to the exchange.[54]

7-4c **Boot**

It is unusual to find like-kind transactions where the value of the property given up is equal to the value of the property received. In most situations, one party normally provides some other property (e.g., cash) to "even out" the exchange. And, if a taxpayer in a like-kind exchange gives or receives some property that is *not* like-kind property, gain or loss recognition may occur. Property that is not like-kind property, including cash, is often referred to as **boot**. Although the term *boot* does not appear in the Code, tax practitioners commonly use it rather than saying "property that does not qualify as like-kind property."

The *receipt* of boot will trigger recognition of gain if there is realized gain. The amount of the recognized gain is the *lesser* of the boot received or the realized gain (realized gain serves as the ceiling on recognition). If a taxpayer recognizes gain in a like-kind exchange, the character of the gain depends on the character of the asset given up (and depreciation recapture rules can apply; see Chapter 8).

Implications of Boot Received

EXAMPLE 31

Blue, Inc., and White Corporation exchange land and the exchange qualifies as like kind under § 1031. Because Blue's land (with an adjusted basis of $20,000) is worth $24,000 and White's land has a fair market value of $19,000, White also gives Blue cash of $5,000.

Blue's recognized gain is $4,000, the lesser of the realized gain of $4,000 ($24,000 amount realized − $20,000 adjusted basis) or the fair market value of the boot received of $5,000.

EXAMPLE 32

Assume the same facts as in the preceding example, except that White's land is worth $21,000 (not $19,000). Under these circumstances, White gives Blue cash of $3,000 to make up the difference.

Blue's recognized gain is $3,000, the lesser of the realized gain of $4,000 ($24,000 amount realized − $20,000 adjusted basis) or the fair market value of the boot received of $3,000.

The receipt of boot does not result in recognition if there is realized loss. That is, taxpayers never recognize a realized loss on like-kind property.

Implications of Boot Received

EXAMPLE 33

Assume the same facts as in Example 31, except that the adjusted basis of Blue's land is $30,000.

Blue's realized loss is $6,000 ($24,000 amount realized − $30,000 adjusted basis). The receipt of the boot of $5,000 does not trigger recognition of Blue's loss.

The *giving* of boot does not trigger recognition if the boot consists solely of cash.

[54]§ 1031(a)(3).

Implications of Boot Given

EXAMPLE 34

Flicker, Inc., and Gadwall Corporation exchange land in a like-kind exchange. Flicker receives land with a fair market value of $75,000 and transfers land worth $63,000 (adjusted basis of $45,000) and cash of $12,000.

Flicker's realized gain is $18,000 ($75,000 amount realized − $45,000 adjusted basis of land transferred − $12,000 cash), none of which is recognized.

If, however, the boot given is appreciated or depreciated property, gain or loss is recognized to the extent of the difference between the adjusted basis and the fair market value of the boot. For this purpose, *appreciated or depreciated property* is property with an adjusted basis that differs from fair market value.

Implications of Boot Given

EXAMPLE 35

Assume the same facts as in the preceding example, except that Flicker transfers land worth $30,000 (adjusted basis of $36,000) and boot worth $45,000 (adjusted basis of $27,000). Flicker's net gain on this exchange is $12,000 [$75,000 amount realized − adjusted basis of $63,000 ($36,000 + $27,000)]. But Flicker is transferring two pieces of property: land (like-kind property) with a built-in realized loss of $6,000 ($30,000 fair market value − $36,000 adjusted basis) and non-like-kind property (boot) with a built-in realized gain of $18,000 ($45,000 fair market value − $27,000 adjusted basis).

In this case, the $6,000 realized loss on the like-kind property is *deferred* (not recognized) and the $18,000 realized gain on the non-like-kind property is recognized. In other words, the realized loss on the like-kind property *cannot* be used to offset the realized gain on the boot given up as part of the transaction.

7-4d Basis and Holding Period of Property Received

If an exchange qualifies as nontaxable under § 1031, the basis of property received must be adjusted to reflect any postponed (deferred) gain or loss. The *basis of like-kind property* received in the exchange is the property's fair market value less postponed gain or plus postponed loss. The *basis* of any *boot* received is the boot's fair market value.

Basis of Like-Kind Property Received

EXAMPLE 36

Vireo Property Management Company exchanges a building (used in its business) with an adjusted basis of $300,000 and a fair market value of $380,000 for land with a fair market value of $380,000. The land is to be held as an investment. The exchange qualifies as like kind (an exchange of business real property for investment real property).

The basis of the land is $300,000 (land's fair market value of $380,000 − $80,000 postponed gain on the building). If the land is later sold for its fair market value of $380,000, the $80,000 postponed gain is recognized.

EXAMPLE 37

Assume the same facts as in the preceding example, except that the building has an adjusted basis of $480,000 and a fair market value of only $380,000.

The basis in the newly acquired land is $480,000 (fair market value of $380,000 + $100,000 postponed loss on the building). If the land is later sold for its fair market value of $380,000, the $100,000 postponed loss is recognized.

The Code provides an alternative approach for determining the basis of like-kind property received:

> Adjusted basis of like-kind property surrendered
> + Adjusted basis of boot given
> + Gain recognized
> − Fair market value of boot received
> − Loss recognized
> = *Basis of like-kind property received*

This approach is logical in terms of the recovery of capital doctrine. That is, the unrecovered cost or other basis is increased by additional cost (boot given) or decreased by cost recovered (boot received). Any gain recognized is included in the basis of the new property. The taxpayer has been taxed on this amount and is now entitled to recover it tax-free. Any loss recognized is deducted from the basis of the new property because the taxpayer has already received a tax benefit on that amount.

The holding period of the property surrendered in the exchange carries over and *tacks on* to the holding period of the like-kind property received.[55] This rule stems from the basic concept that the new property is a continuation of the old investment. The boot received has a new holding period (from the date of exchange) rather than a carryover holding period.

Depreciation recapture potential carries over to the property received in a like-kind exchange.[56] See Chapter 8 for a discussion of this topic.

DIGGING DEEPER 10 | **In-depth coverage can be found on this book's companion website: www.cengage.com**

If the taxpayer assumes a liability (or takes property subject to a liability), the amount of the liability is treated as boot given. For the taxpayer whose liability is assumed (or whose property is taken subject to the liability), the amount of the liability is treated as boot received. The following example illustrates the effect of such a liability. In addition, the example illustrates the tax consequences for both parties involved in the like-kind exchange.

BRIDGE DISCIPLINE **Bridge to Economics**

One can assert that the "tax variable" is neutralized in nontaxable exchanges when taxable gains or losses do not arise. Neutralizing potential tax consequences can have a positive result given that tax costs tend to dampen economic activity. For example, in a like-kind exchange, a taxpayer can exchange one asset for another asset of like kind without having to recognize a gain or pay a tax. The justification for the tax deferral is that the taxpayer is viewed as having an equivalent economic investment after the transaction as before the transaction. But the tax-neutral result changes when the taxpayer receives property that is not "like kind" because the taxpayer's economic standing has changed.

If, for example, the taxpayer receives investment land *and* cash in exchange for investment land, her ownership in the land given up has, at least in part, been converted to cash, and to that degree, her investment has substantively changed. That is, the taxpayer's economic investment has changed from an ownership exclusively in land to ownership in land *and* cash. Alternatively, if the taxpayer gives up her investment in land for corporate stock in a high-tech venture, the nature of her investment also would substantively change as a result of the transaction. These differences in the taxpayer's economic position after the transaction lead to the transactions being taxed.

---

[55]§ 1223(1) and Reg. § 1.1223–1(a). For like-kind exchanges after March 1, 1954, the tacked-on holding period applies only if the like-kind property surrendered was either a capital asset or § 1231 property.

[56]Reg. §§ 1.1245–2(a)(4) and 1.1250–2(d)(1).

Jaeger & Company and Lark Enterprises, Inc., exchange real estate investments. Jaeger gives up property with an adjusted basis of $250,000 (fair market value of $420,000) that is subject to a mortgage of $80,000 (assumed by Lark). In return for this property, Jaeger receives property with a fair market value of $340,000 (Lark's adjusted basis in the property is $200,000). Jaeger's and Lark's realized and recognized gains and their basis in the like-kind property received are computed as follows:[57]

	Jaeger	Lark
Amount realized:		
Like-kind property received	$ 340,000	$ 420,000
Boot received:		
Mortgage assumed by Lark	80,000	
	$ 420,000	$ 420,000
Adjusted basis:		
Like-kind property given	(250,000)	(200,000)
Boot given:		
Mortgage assumed by Lark		(80,000)
Realized gain	$ 170,000	$ 140,000
Recognized gain	80,000*	–0–**
Deferred gain	$ 90,000	$ 140,000
Basis of property transferred:		
Like-kind property	$ 250,000	$ 200,000
Mortgage assumed		80,000
	$ 250,000	$ 280,000
Plus: Gain recognized	80,000	
Less: Boot received	(80,000)	
Basis of new property	$ 250,000	$ 280,000

*Lesser of boot received ($80,000 mortgage assumed) or realized gain ($170,000).
**No boot received. Therefore, no gain is recognized.

7-5 INVOLUNTARY CONVERSIONS—§ 1033

LO.6

Explain the nonrecognition provisions available on the involuntary conversion of property.

In most cases, taxpayers sell property (or exchange it) when they need to do so. There are times, however, when the taxpayer *involuntarily* (i.e., outside the taxpayer's control) disposes of property. When this happens, the taxpayer usually receives some sort of compensation, like insurance proceeds or a condemnation award from a government entity. Section 1033 provides that a taxpayer who suffers an involuntary conversion of property may postpone recognition of *gain* realized from the conversion (provided the § 1033 rules are met). The objective of this provision is to provide relief to the taxpayer who has suffered hardship and does not have the wherewithal to pay the tax on any gain realized from the conversion.

Postponement of realized gain is permitted to the extent that the taxpayer *reinvests* the amount realized from the conversion in replacement property. If the amount reinvested in replacement property is *less than* the amount realized, realized gain *is recognized* to the extent of the deficiency.

---

[57]Example (2) of Reg. § 1.1031(d)–2 illustrates a special situation where both the buyer and the seller transfer liabilities that are assumed by the other party (or both parties acquire property that is subject to a liability).

By its terms, § 1033 generally is *elective*. A taxpayer need not postpone recognition of gain, even if replacement property is acquired. In essence, a taxpayer has three options:

- Reinvest the proceeds and elect § 1033's nonrecognition of gain.
- Reinvest the proceeds and not elect § 1033, thereby triggering recognition of realized gain under the usual rules applicable to property transactions.
- Not reinvest the proceeds and recognize the realized gain accordingly.

Involuntary Conversions: General Rules

EXAMPLE 39

Jason operates a charter fishing business in Port St. Lucie, Florida, taking customers out in the Atlantic Ocean on daylong fishing trips. Unfortunately, his boat was completely destroyed when Hurricane Matthew hit the Florida coast. His boat had a basis of $78,000 ($120,000 cost − $42,000 of accumulated depreciation). Fortunately, Jason had insurance (which included a replacement cost rider). He filed an insurance claim the week after he lost his boat and received $175,000 in insurance proceeds three weeks later.

Jason has a realized gain of $97,000, computed as follows:

Amount realized (insurance proceeds)	$175,000
Less: Adjusted basis	(78,000)
Realized gain	$ 97,000

Jason can defer the entire gain provided he uses all of the insurance proceeds to purchase a new boat.

EXAMPLE 40

Refer to the facts of Example 39, and assume that Jason buys a new boat for $180,000. He uses the entire insurance settlement as part of the purchase.

In this case, Jason's $97,000 realized gain is deferred, and the basis of his new boat must reflect that deferral. As a result, his new boat's basis is $83,000 ($180,000 cost − $97,000 deferred gain).

EXAMPLE 41

Continuing with the facts of Example 39, assume that Jason is able to negotiate an excellent price for his new boat. In fact, he is able to replace his old boat for only $168,000 and uses the $7,000 remaining from the insurance settlement to pay for other business expenses. What is the outcome?

In this case, Jason must recognize a gain of $7,000, the difference between the $175,000 insurance settlement and the amount he paid for the new boat (the amount of the insurance proceeds he reinvested in replacement property).

The balance of the realized gain is deferred, and the basis of his new boat must reflect that deferral. As a result, his new boat's basis is $78,000 ($168,000 cost − $90,000 deferred gain).

If a *loss* occurs on an involuntary conversion, § 1033 does not apply and the general rules for loss recognition are effective. See Chapter 6 for the discussion of the deduction of losses.

EXAMPLE 42

Refer to the facts of Example 39, but assume that Jason had only partial coverage on his boat, and his insurance settlement is only $50,000. In this case, Jason has a loss of $28,000, computed as follows:

Amount realized (insurance proceeds)	$50,000
Less: Adjusted basis	(78,000)
Realized loss	($28,000)

In this case, § 1033 will not apply to the transaction, and Jason's realized loss of $28,000 is recognized.

With this background, we will now explore the various terms (and related definitions) that are part of § 1033, the reinvestment timing required to secure gain deferral, and the related reporting requirements.

7-5a Involuntary Conversion Defined

An **involuntary conversion** results from the complete or partial destruction, theft, seizure, condemnation, or sale or exchange under threat of condemnation (e.g., a city seizing property under its right of eminent domain) of the taxpayer's property.[58] This description includes fires (other than arson),[59] tornadoes, hurricanes, earthquakes, floods, and other natural disasters. In these circumstances, *gain* can result from insurance proceeds received in an amount that exceeds the taxpayer's historical cost of the property, especially if the property had replacement value insurance or if depreciation deductions have lowered the property's adjusted basis.

For condemnations, the amount realized includes the compensation paid by the public authority acquiring the taxpayer's property. Government seizures are unique events (and, as a result, a unique set of rules have developed under § 1033). In general, for § 1033 to apply, the government entity must have made a decision to acquire the property for public use, and the taxpayer must have reasonable grounds to believe the property will be taken.[60]

In-depth coverage can be found on this book's companion website: **www.cengage.com**   **11** DIGGING DEEPER

7-5b Replacement Property

The requirements for replacement property under the involuntary conversion rules generally are more restrictive than those for like-kind property under § 1031. The basic requirement is that the replacement property be *similar or related in service* or use to the involuntarily converted property.[61]

Different interpretations of the phrase *similar or related in service or use* apply depending on whether the involuntarily converted property is held by an *owner-user* or by an *owner-investor* (e.g., lessor). For an owner-investor, the *taxpayer use test* applies, and for an owner-user, the *functional use test* applies. Furthermore, a special test applies in the case of involuntary conversions that result from condemnations.

Functional Use Test

Under this test, a taxpayer's use of the replacement property and of the involuntarily converted property must be the same. Replacing a manufacturing plant with a wholesale grocery warehouse does not meet this test. Instead, the plant must be replaced with another facility of similar functional use.

Taxpayer Use Test

The taxpayer use test for owner-investors provides much more flexibility in terms of what qualifies as replacement property than the functional use test. Essentially, the properties must be used by the taxpayer (the owner-investor) in similar endeavors. For example, rental property held by an owner-investor qualifies if replaced by other rental

---

[58]§ 1033(a) and Reg. §§ 1.1033(a)–1(a) and −2(a).

[59]Rev.Rul. 82–74, 1982–1 C.B. 110.

[60]Rev.Rul. 63–221, 1963–2 C.B. 332 and *Joseph P. Balistrieri*, 38 TCM 526, T.C.Memo. 1979–115.

[61]§ 1033(a) and Reg. § 1.1033(a)–1.

property, regardless of the type of rental property involved. The test is met when an investor replaces a manufacturing plant (being rented) with a wholesale grocery warehouse (also being rented).[62] The replacement of a rental residence with a personal residence does *not* meet the test.[63]

Special Rule for Condemnations

In addition to the functional and taxpayer use tests, the Code provides a special rule for business or investment real property that is *condemned*. This rule applies the broad like-kind classification for real estate to such circumstances. Accordingly, improved real property can be replaced with unimproved real property.

The rules concerning the nature of replacement property are illustrated in Concept Summary 7.5.

Concept Summary 7.5

Involuntary Conversions: Replacement Property Tests

Type of Property and User	Taxpayer Use Test	Functional Use Test	Special Rule for Condemnations
An investor's rented shopping mall is destroyed by fire; the mall may be replaced with other rental properties (e.g., an apartment building).	X		
A manufacturing plant is destroyed by fire; replacement property must consist of another manufacturing plant that is functionally the same as the property converted.		X	
Personal residence of a taxpayer is condemned by a local government authority; replacement property must consist of another personal residence.		X	
Land used by a manufacturing company is condemned by a local government authority.			X
Apartment and land held by an investor are sold due to the threat or imminence of condemnation.			X

*Applies the same test as in the case of like-kind exchanges.

7-5c **Time Limitation on Replacement**

In general, the taxpayer must acquire replacement property within a two-year period after the close of the taxable year in which gain is realized.[64] Typically, gain is realized when insurance proceeds or damages are received.

---

[62]*Loco Realty Co. v. Comm.*, 62–2 USTC ¶9657, 10 AFTR 2d 5359, 306 F.2d 207 (CA–8, 1962).

[63]Rev.Rul. 70–466, 1970–2 C.B. 165.

[64]§§ 1033(a)(2)(B) and (g)(4) and Reg. § 1.1033(a)–2(c)(3). The two-year period is extended to a four-year period if the property is located in a Presidentially declared disaster area. A taxpayer can apply for an extension of this time period anytime before its expiration [Reg. § 1.1033(a)–2(c)(3)]. Also, the period for filing the application for extension can be extended if a taxpayer shows reasonable cause.

Magpie, Inc.'s building is destroyed by fire on December 16, 2017. The adjusted basis is $325,000. Magpie receives $400,000 from the insurance company on February 2, 2018. The company is a calendar year and cash method taxpayer.

The latest date for replacement is December 31, 2020 (the end of the taxable year in which realized gain occurred plus two years). The critical date is not the date the involuntary conversion occurred, but rather the date of gain realization (when the insurance proceeds are received).

In the case of a condemnation of real property used in a trade or business or held for investment, the Code substitutes a three-year period for the normal two-year period.

Assume the same facts as in the previous example, except that Magpie's building is condemned. On November 1, 2017, Magpie receives notification of the future condemnation, which occurs on December 16, 2017. The condemnation proceeds are received on February 2, 2018.

The latest date for replacement is December 31, 2021 (the end of the taxable year in which realized gain occurred plus three years).

The *earliest date* for replacement typically is the date the involuntary conversion occurs. However, if the property is condemned, it is possible to replace the condemned property before this date. In this case, the earliest date is the date of the threat of condemnation of the property. This rule allows the taxpayer to make an orderly replacement of the condemned property.

7-5d Nonrecognition of Gain

Nonrecognition of gain can be either mandatory or elective, depending on whether the conversion is direct (into replacement property) or indirect (into money).

Direct Conversion

If the conversion is directly into replacement property rather than into money, nonrecognition of realized gain is *mandatory*. In this case, the basis of the replacement property is the same as the adjusted basis of the converted property. Direct conversion is rare in practice and usually involves condemnations.

Oak, Inc.'s property, with an adjusted basis of $20,000, is condemned by the state. Oak receives property with a fair market value of $50,000 as compensation for the property taken.

Because the nonrecognition of realized gain is mandatory for direct conversions, Oak's realized gain of $30,000 is not recognized and the basis of the replacement property is $20,000 (adjusted basis of the condemned property).

Conversion into Money

If the conversion is into money, the realized gain is recognized only to the extent the amount realized from the involuntary conversion exceeds the cost of the qualifying replacement property.[65] This is the usual case, and nonrecognition (postponement) is *elective*. If the election is not made, the realized gain is recognized.

The basis of the replacement property is the property's cost less any postponed (deferred) gain.[66] If the election to postpone gain is made, the holding period of the replacement property includes the holding period of the converted property.

Section 1033 applies *only to gains* and *not to losses*. Losses from involuntary conversions are recognized if the property is held for business or income-producing purposes. Personal casualty losses are recognized (subject to the limitations discussed in Chapter 6), but condemnation losses related to personal use assets (e.g., a personal residence) are neither recognized nor postponed.

---

[65]§ 1033(a)(2)(A) and Reg. § 1.1033(a)–2(c)(1).   [66]§ 1033(b).

The Big Picture

EXAMPLE 46

Return to the facts of *The Big Picture* on p. 7-1. Alice's building (used in her trade or business), with an adjusted basis of $50,000, is destroyed by a fire on October 5, 2018. Alice is a calendar year taxpayer. On November 17, 2018, she receives an insurance reimbursement of $100,000 for the loss. Assume that Alice goes ahead with her plan to invest $80,000 in a new building and to use the other $20,000 of insurance proceeds to pay off credit card debt.

- Alice has until December 31, 2020, to make the new investment and qualify for the nonrecognition election.
- Alice's realized gain is $50,000 ($100,000 insurance proceeds received − $50,000 adjusted basis of old building).
- Assuming that the replacement property qualifies as similar or related in service or use, Alice's recognized gain is $20,000. Because she reinvested $20,000 less than the insurance proceeds received ($100,000 proceeds − $80,000 reinvested), her realized gain is recognized to that extent.
- Alice's basis in the new building is $50,000. This is the building's cost of $80,000 less the postponed gain of $30,000 (realized gain of $50,000 − recognized gain of $20,000).

The Big Picture

EXAMPLE 47

Return to the facts of *The Big Picture* on p. 7-1. Assume the same facts as in the previous example, except that Alice receives only $45,000 of insurance proceeds. She has a realized and recognized loss of $5,000. The basis of the new building is the building's cost of $80,000.

TAX PLANNING STRATEGIES   Recognizing Involuntary Conversion Gains

FRAMEWORK FOCUS: TAX RATE

Strategy: Shift Net Income from High-Bracket Years to Low-Bracket Years.

FRAMEWORK FOCUS: DEDUCTIONS

Strategy: Maximize Deductible Amounts.

Sometimes, a taxpayer may prefer to *recognize a gain from an involuntary conversion* and will choose not to elect § 1033, even though replacement property is acquired. Circumstances suggesting this strategy would include:

- The taxpayer realized the gain in a low-bracket tax year, quite possibly because of the events that caused the involuntary conversion, such as a flood and its aftermath that seriously disrupted the business.
- The taxpayer has an expiring loss carryover that can offset most, if not all, of the gain from the involuntary conversion.
- The replacement property is depreciable, and the taxpayer would prefer an unreduced basis for this asset to maximize depreciation deductions in future years.

Nontax considerations might also come into play, perhaps suggesting that the property not be replaced at all. Even before the event that produced the involuntary conversion, the taxpayer might have been wanting to downsize the business or terminate it outright. In any case, the taxpayer might prefer to recognize the gain, pay the tax involved, and thereby free up the remaining proceeds for other uses—business, investment, or even personal—especially if the gain is small compared to the amount of proceeds received.

7-6 OTHER NONRECOGNITION PROVISIONS

LO.7

Identify other nonrecognition provisions contained in the Code.

Two other nonrecognition provisions are discussed below.

7-6a Transfer of Assets to Business Entity—§§ 351 and 721

Taxpayers can transfer assets to corporations in exchange for stock without recognizing gain or loss on the transfer according to § 351. See Chapter 12 for the applicable restrictions and corresponding basis adjustments for the stock acquired. A similar provision (§ 721) allows the nontaxable transfer of assets to a partnership in exchange for an interest in that partnership. See Chapter 14 for a description of § 721.

7-6b Sale of a Principal Residence—§ 121

Section 121 allows individual taxpayers to exclude gain from the sale of a *principal residence*. This provision applies to the first $250,000 of realized gain, or $500,000 on certain joint returns. For this purpose, the residence must have been owned and used by the taxpayer as the primary residence for at least two of the five years preceding the date of sale, and the exclusion can only be used once every two years. This exclusion can be prorated, however, if a taxpayer failed to meet one or more of these time period requirements due to a change in his or her place of employment or health. Moreover, a surviving spouse counts the ownership and usage periods of the decedent spouse in meeting the two-year test. This provision applies only to gains; losses on residences, like those of other personal use assets, are not recognized for tax purposes.

In-depth coverage can be found on this book's companion website: www.cengage.com   **12, 13, 14** DIGGING DEEPER

REFOCUS ON THE BIG PICTURE

CALCULATING BASIS AND RECOGNIZED GAIN FOR PROPERTY TRANSACTIONS

Alice's basis in the land acquired as a gift is a carryover basis of $2,000. If Alice sells the land outright, she will realize and recognize a gain of $48,000. However, if she replaces the property with other real property, she should be able to qualify for favorable like-kind exchange treatment under § 1031 and defer the gain on the property disposition. If Alice receives any cash as a part of the exchange transaction, realized gain would be recognized to the extent of the cash (boot) received.

Alice's basis in the 300 shares of stock received as an inheritance is the property's $30,000 fair market value at the date of her grandfather's death. If Alice sells the 300 shares, she will realize and recognize a $6,000 gain [$36,000 sales price (300 shares × $120) − $30,000 basis].

Alice's basis in the 200 shares of stock purchased is her purchase price of $28,000. Those shares are currently worth $24,000 (200 shares × $120). Consequently, if she sells those shares, she will realize and recognize a $4,000 loss.

You advise Alice that her basis in the house is its $475,000 fair market value on the date of her grandmother's death. If Alice sells the house for $600,000, her realized and recognized gain would be $125,000.

Regarding the fire-related involuntary conversion of Alice's business building, a $50,000 realized gain occurs upon the receipt of the $100,000 of insurance proceeds. Because she intends to invest only $80,000 of the insurance proceeds in a qualifying property, Alice's recognized gain will be $20,000 ($100,000 proceeds − $80,000 reinvested). Therefore, her realized gain would be recognized to that extent (see Example 46).

continued

ISTOCK.COM/NICOLAMARGARET

What If?

Alice is leaning toward selling the house. However, she knows that her grandmother would not want her to have to pay income taxes on the sale. Alice asks whether there is any way she could avoid paying taxes on the sale.

You inform Alice of the exclusion provision under § 121. Alice can qualify for this exclusion of up to $250,000 of realized gain if she owns and occupies the house as her principal residence for at least two of the five years prior to a sale.

From a tax planning perspective, what can Alice do so that none of the $50,000 of realized gain from the involuntary conversion is recognized? To have full postponement of the $50,000 realized gain, Alice would have to reinvest all of the $100,000 of insurance proceeds received in another qualified building. Under this circumstance, the basis of the replacement building would be $50,000 ($100,000 cost of replacement building − $50,000 deferred gain).

Suggested Readings

Paul Bonner, "Estate Basis Consistency and Reporting: What Practitioners Need to Know," *The Journal of Accountancy*, June 2016.

Mary Cunningham, "Accomplishing Section 1031 Tax-Deferred Exchanges," *Practical Tax Strategies*, August 2014.

Mary B. Foster, "A Checklist for Like-Kind Real Estate Exchanges," *Journal of Real Estate Taxation*, Second Quarter 2015.

James R. Hamill, "Preserving the Residence Sale Exclusion for Mixed Use Property," *Practical Tax Strategies*, June 2013.

Christian J. Kenefick, "What Is a $10 Gold Coin Worth? Basis, FMV, and Realization Issues Abound," *Journal of Taxation*, February 2013.

Edward J. Schnee, "Like-Kind Exchange Rules: Continued Evolution," *The Tax Adviser*, July 2014.

Timothy M. Todd, "Whose Goodwill Is It? The Taxation of Goodwill in Owner-Entity Transactions," *Journal of Taxation*, February 2015.

Key Terms

Adjusted basis, 7-4	Holding period, 7-12	Realized loss, 7-2
Amount realized, 7-3	Involuntary conversion, 7-27	Recognized gain, 7-7
Boot, 7-22	Like-kind exchanges, 7-20	Recognized loss, 7-7
Fair market value, 7-4	Nontaxable exchange, 7-19	Wash sale, 7-15
Goodwill, 7-10	Realized gain, 7-2	

Computational Exercises

1. **LO.3** Luciana, a nonshareholder, purchases a condominium from her employer for $85,000. The fair market value of the condominium is $120,000. What is Luciana's basis in the condominium and the amount of any income as a result of this purchase?

2. **LO.3** Sebastian purchases two pieces of equipment for $100,000. Appraisals of the equipment indicate that the fair market value of the first piece of equipment is

$72,000 and that of the second piece of equipment is $108,000. What is Sebastian's basis in these two assets?

3. **LO.2, 4** Lisa sells business property with an adjusted basis of $130,000 to her son, Alfred, for its fair market value of $100,000.

a. What is Lisa's realized and recognized gain or loss?

b. What is Alfred's recognized gain or loss if he subsequently sells the property for $138,000? For $80,000?

4. **LO.4** Arianna's personal residence has an adjusted basis of $230,000 and a fair market value of $210,000. Arianna converts the personal residence to rental property. What is Arianna's gain basis? What is her loss basis?

5. **LO.1, 4** Peyton sells an office building and the associated land on May 1 of the current year. Under the terms of the sales contract, Peyton is to receive $1,600,000 in cash. The purchaser is to assume Peyton's mortgage of $950,000 on the property. To enable the purchaser to obtain adequate financing, Peyton is to pay the $9,000 in points charged by the lender. The broker's commission on the sale is $75,000. What is Peyton's amount realized? **Critical Thinking**

6. **LO.2, 5** Logan and Johnathan exchange land, and the exchange qualifies as like kind under § 1031. Because Logan's land (adjusted basis of $85,000) is worth $100,000 and Johnathan's land has a fair market value of $80,000, Johnathan also gives Logan cash of $20,000.

a. What is Logan's recognized gain?

b. Assume instead that Johnathan's land is worth $90,000 and he gives Logan $10,000 cash. Now what is Logan's recognized gain?

7. **LO.2, 6** Camilo's property, with an adjusted basis of $155,000, is condemned by the state. Camilo receives property with a fair market value of $180,000 as compensation for the property taken.

a. What is Camilo's realized and recognized gain?

b. What is the basis of the replacement property?

8. **LO.2, 7** Constanza, who is single, sells her current personal residence (adjusted basis of $165,000) for $450,000. She has owned and lived in the house for 30 years. Her selling expenses are $22,500. What is Constanza's realized and recognized gain? **Critical Thinking**

Problems

9. **LO.1** If a taxpayer sells property for cash, the amount realized consists of the net proceeds from the sale. For each of the following, indicate the effect on the amount realized:

a. The property is sold on credit.

b. A mortgage on the property is assumed by the buyer.

c. A mortgage on the property of the buyer is assumed by the seller.

d. The buyer acquires the property subject to a mortgage of the seller.

e. Stock that has a basis to the purchaser of $6,000 and a fair market value of $10,000 is received by the seller as part of the consideration.

10. **LO.1, 2** Pam owns a personal use boat that has a fair market value of $35,000 and an adjusted basis of $45,000. Pam's AGI is $100,000. Calculate the realized and recognized gain or loss if:

a. Pam sells the boat for $35,000.

b. Pam exchanges the boat for another boat worth $35,000.

c. The boat is stolen and Pam receives insurance proceeds of $35,000.

d. Would your answer in part (a) change if the fair market value and the selling price of the boat were $48,000?

11. **LO.1, 2** Yancy's personal residence is condemned as part of an urban renewal project. His adjusted basis for the residence is $480,000. He receives condemnation proceeds of $460,000 and invests the proceeds in stocks and bonds.

a. Calculate Yancy's realized and recognized gain or loss.

b. If the condemnation proceeds are $505,000, what are Yancy's realized and recognized gain or loss?

c. What are Yancy's realized and recognized gain or loss in part (a) if the house was rental property?

12. **LO.1, 2, 3** Kevin purchases 1,000 shares of Bluebird Corporation stock on October 3, 2018, for $300,000. On December 12, 2018, Kevin purchases an additional 750 shares of Bluebird stock for $210,000. According to market quotations, Bluebird stock is selling for $285 per share on December 31, 2018. Kevin sells 500 shares of Bluebird stock on March 1, 2019, for $162,500.

a. What is the adjusted basis of Kevin's Bluebird stock on December 31, 2018?

b. What is Kevin's recognized gain or loss from the sale of Bluebird stock on March 1, 2019, assuming that the shares sold are from the shares purchased on December 12, 2018?

c. What is Kevin's recognized gain or loss from the sale of Bluebird stock on March 1, 2019, assuming that Kevin cannot adequately identify the shares sold?

Communications   13. **LO.2, 3** Rod Clooney purchases Agnes Mitchell's sole proprietorship for $990,000 on August 15, 2018. The assets of the business are as follows:

Asset	Agnes's Adjusted Basis	FMV
Accounts receivable	$ 70,000	$ 70,000
Inventory	90,000	100,000
Equipment	150,000	160,000
Furniture and fixtures	95,000	130,000
Building	190,000	250,000
Land	25,000	75,000
Total	$620,000	$785,000

a. Calculate Agnes's realized and recognized gain.

b. Determine Rod's basis for each of the assets.

c. Write a letter to Rod informing him of the tax consequences of the purchase. His address is 300 Riverview Drive, Delaware, OH 43015.

14. **LO.1, 2, 3** Roberto has received various gifts over the years. He has decided to dispose of several of these assets. What is the recognized gain or loss from each of the following transactions, assuming that no gift tax was paid when the gifts were made?

a. In 1981, he received land worth $32,000. The donor's adjusted basis was $35,000. Roberto sells the land for $95,000 in 2018.

b. In 1986, he received stock in Gold Company. The donor's adjusted basis was $19,000. The fair market value on the date of the gift was $34,000. Roberto sells the stock for $40,000 in 2018.

c. In 1992, he received land worth $15,000. The donor's adjusted basis was $20,000. Roberto sells the land for $9,000 in 2018.

d. In 2013, he received stock worth $30,000. The donor's adjusted basis was $42,000. Roberto sells the stock for $38,000 in 2018.

e.   Build a spreadsheet-based solution that provides the solution to parts (a) through (d) above and uses only the donor's basis, the fair market value at the time of the gift, and the selling price as inputs. You may want to use the IF and AND functions together.

15. **LO.1, 2, 3** Nicky receives a car from Sam as a gift. Sam paid $48,000 for the car. He had used it for business purposes and had deducted $10,000 for depreciation up to the time he gave the car to Nicky. The fair market value of the car is $33,000.

a.   Assuming that Nicky uses the car for business purposes, what is her basis for depreciation?

b.   Assume that Nicky deducts depreciation of $6,500 and then sells the car for $32,500. What is her recognized gain or loss?

c.   Assume that Nicky deducts depreciation of $6,500 and then sells the car for $20,000. What is her recognized gain or loss?

16. **LO.3** Simon owns stock that has declined in value since acquired. He has decided either to give the stock to his nephew, Fred, or to sell it and give Fred the proceeds. If Fred receives the stock, he will sell it to obtain the proceeds. Simon is in the 12% tax bracket, while Fred's bracket is 22%. In either case, the holding period for the stock will be short-term. Identify the tax issues relevant to Simon in deciding whether to give the stock or the sale proceeds to Fred.   *Critical Thinking*

17. **LO.3** On September 18, 2018, Gerald received land and a building from Frank as a gift. Frank's adjusted basis and the fair market value at the date of the gift are as follows:

Asset	Adjusted Basis	FMV
Land	$100,000	$212,000
Building	80,000	100,000

No gift tax was paid on the transfer.

a.   Determine Gerald's adjusted basis for the land and building.

b.   Assume instead that the fair market value of the land was $87,000 and that of the building was $65,000. Determine Gerald's adjusted basis for the land and building.

18. **LO.3** Dan bought a hotel for $2,600,000 in January 2014. In May 2018, he died and left the hotel to Ed. While Dan owned the hotel, he deducted $289,000 of cost recovery. The fair market value in May 2018 was $2,800,000. The fair market value six months later was $2,850,000.

a.   What is the basis of the property to Ed?

b.   What is the basis of the property to Ed if the fair market value six months later was $2,500,000 (not $2,850,000) and the objective of the executor was to minimize the estate tax liability?

19. **LO.4** Sheila sells land to Elane, her sister, for the fair market value of $40,000. Six months later when the land is worth $45,000, Elane gives it to Jacob, her son. (No gift tax resulted.) Shortly thereafter, Jacob sells the land for $48,000.

a.   Assuming that Sheila's adjusted basis for the land is $24,000, what are Sheila's and Jacob's recognized gain or loss on the sales?

b.   Assuming that Sheila's adjusted basis for the land is $60,000, what are Sheila's and Jacob's recognized gain or loss on the sales?

20. **LO.1, 2, 3, 4** Tyneka inherited 1,000 shares of Aqua, Inc. stock from Joe. Joe's basis was $35,000, and the fair market value on July 1, 2018 (the date of death), was $45,000. The shares were distributed to Tyneka on July 15, 2018. Tyneka sold the stock on July 30, 2019, for $33,000. After giving the matter more thought,   *Decision Making*
Critical Thinking

she decides that Aqua is a good investment and purchases 1,000 shares for $30,000 on August 20, 2019.

   a.   What is Tyneka's basis for the 1,000 shares purchased on August 20, 2019?

   b.   Could Tyneka have obtained different tax consequences in part (a) if she had sold the 1,000 shares on December 27, 2018, and purchased the 1,000 shares on January 5, 2019? Explain.

Ethics and Equity   21. **LO.4** Sam owns 1,500 shares of Eagle, Inc., stock that he purchased over 10 years ago for $80,000. Although the stock has a current market value of $52,000, Sam still views the stock as a solid long-term investment. He has sold other stock during the year with overall gains of $30,000, so he would like to sell the Eagle stock and offset the $28,000 loss against these gains—but somehow keep his Eagle investment. He has devised a plan to keep his Eagle investment by using funds in his traditional IRA to purchase 1,500 Eagle shares immediately after selling the shares he currently owns. Evaluate Sam's treatment of these stock transactions. Can his plan work? Explain.

22. **LO.1, 2, 4** Abby's home had a basis of $360,000 ($160,000 attributable to the land) and a fair market value of $340,000 ($155,000 attributable to the land) when she converted 70% of it to business use by opening a bed-and-breakfast. Four years after the conversion, Abby sells the home for $500,000 ($165,000 attributable to the land).

   a.   Calculate Abby's basis for gain, loss, and cost recovery for the portion of her personal residence that was converted to business use.

   b.   Calculate the cost recovery deducted by Abby during the four-year period of business use assuming that the bed-and-breakfast is opened on January 1 of year 1 and the house is sold on December 31 of year 4.

   c.   What is Abby's recognized gain or loss on the sale of the business use portion?

Critical Thinking   23. **LO.4** Surendra's personal residence originally cost $340,000 (ignore land). After liv-
Decision Making   ing in the house for five years, he converts it to rental property. At the date of conversion, the fair market value of the house is $320,000. As to the rental property,
Communications   calculate Surendra's basis for:

   a.   Loss.

   b.   Depreciation.

   c.   Gain.

   d.   Could Surendra have obtained better tax results if he had sold his personal residence for $320,000 and then purchased another house for $320,000 to hold as rental property? Explain.

   e.   Summarize your answer to this problem in an e-mail to your instructor.

24. **LO.5** In 2018, Sue exchanges a sport-utility vehicle (adjusted basis of $16,000; fair market value of $19,500) for cash of $2,000 and a pickup truck (fair market value of $17,500). Both vehicles are for business use. Sue believes that her basis for the truck is $17,500. Is Sue correct?

Critical Thinking   25. **LO.6** A warehouse owned by M&S (a partnership) and used in its business (i.e., to store inventory) is being condemned by the city to provide a right-of-way for a highway. The warehouse has appreciated by $180,000 based on an estimate of fair market value. In the negotiations, the city is offering $35,000 less than what M&S believes the property is worth. Alan, a real estate broker, has offered to purchase the property for $20,000 more than the city's offer. The partnership plans to invest the proceeds it will receive in an office building that it will lease to various tenants.

   a.   Identify the relevant tax issues for M&S.

   b.   Would the answer in part (a) change if M&S's warehouse was property being held for investment rather than being used in its business? Explain.

26. **LO.5** Tanya Fletcher owns undeveloped land (adjusted basis of $80,000 and fair market value of $92,000) on the East Coast. On January 4, 2018, she exchanges it with Lisa Martin (an unrelated party) for undeveloped land on the West Coast and $3,000 cash. Lisa has an adjusted basis of $72,000 for her land, and its fair market value is $89,000. As the real estate market on the East Coast is thriving, on September 1, 2019, Lisa sells the land she acquired for $120,000.

    a. What are Tanya's recognized gain or loss and adjusted basis for the West Coast land on January 4, 2018?

    b. What are Lisa's recognized gain or loss and adjusted basis for the East Coast land on January 4, 2018?

    c. What is Lisa's recognized gain or loss from the September 1, 2019 sale?

    d. What effect does Lisa's 2019 sale have on Tanya?

    e. Write a letter to Tanya advising her of the tax consequences of this exchange. Her address is The Corral, El Paso, TX 79968.

Decision Making
Communications
Critical Thinking

27. **LO.5** Sarah exchanges a building and land (used in its business) for Tyler's land and building and some equipment (used in its business). The assets have the following characteristics:

	Adjusted Basis	Fair Market Value
Sarah's real property	$120,000	$300,000
Tyler's real property	60,000	220,000
Equipment	50,000	80,000

    a. What are Sarah's recognized gain or loss and basis for the land and building and equipment acquired from Tyler?

    b. What are Tyler's recognized gain or loss and basis for the land and building acquired from Sarah?

28. **LO.5** Maple Company owns land (adjusted basis of $90,000; fair market value of $125,000) that it uses in its business. Maple exchanges it for another parcel of land (worth $100,000) and stock (worth $25,000). Determine Maple's:

    a. Realized and recognized gain or loss on the exchange.

    b. Basis in the new land.

    c. Basis in the stock Maple received.

29. **LO.5** Tulip, Inc., would like to dispose of some land it acquired four years ago because the land will not continue to appreciate. Its value has increased by $50,000 over the four-year period. The company also intends to sell stock that has declined in value by $50,000 during the six months since its purchase. Tulip has four offers to acquire the stock and land:

Critical Thinking

Buyer 1: Exchange land.
Buyer 2: Purchase land for cash.
Buyer 3: Exchange stock.
Buyer 4: Purchase stock for cash.

Identify the tax issues relevant to Tulip in disposing of this land and stock.

30. **LO.5** What is the basis of the new property in each of the following exchanges?

    a. Apartment building held for investment (adjusted basis of $145,000) for office building to be held for investment (fair market value of $225,000).

    b. Land and building used as a barbershop (adjusted basis of $190,000) for land and building used as a grocery store (fair market value of $350,000).

    c. Office building (adjusted basis of $45,000) for bulldozer (fair market value of $42,000), both held for business use.

    d. IBM common stock (adjusted basis of $20,000) for ExxonMobil common stock (fair market value of $28,000).

e. Rental house (adjusted basis of $90,000) for mountain cabin to be held for rental use (fair market value of $225,000).

f. General partnership interest (adjusted basis of $400,000) for a limited partnership interest (fair market value of $580,000).

31. **LO.1, 2, 5** Steve owns real estate (adjusted basis of $12,000 and fair market value of $15,000), which he uses in his business. Steve sells the real estate for $15,000 to Aubry (a dealer) and then purchases a new parcel of land for $15,000 from Joan (also a dealer). The new parcel of land qualifies as like-kind property.

a. What are Steve's realized and recognized gain on the sale of the land he sold to Aubry?

b. What is Steve's basis for the land he purchased from Joan?

c. What factors would motivate Steve to sell his land to Aubry and purchase the land from Joan rather than exchange one parcel of land for the other?

d. Assume that the adjusted basis of Steve's original parcel of land is $15,000 and the fair market value of both parcels of land is $12,000. Respond to parts (a) through (c).

32. **LO.5** Cardinal Properties, Inc., exchanges real estate used in its business along with stock for real estate to be held for investment. The stock transferred has an adjusted basis of $45,000 and a fair market value of $50,000. The real estate transferred has an adjusted basis of $85,000 and a fair market value of $190,000. The real estate acquired has a fair market value of $240,000.

a. What is Cardinal's realized gain or loss?

b. Its recognized gain or loss?

c. The basis of the newly acquired real estate?

Decision Making 33. **LO.5** Tom Howard and Frank Peters are good friends (and former college roommates). Each owns investment property in the other's hometown (Tom lives in Kalamazoo, MI; Frank lives in Austin, TX). To make their lives easier, they decide to exchange the investment properties. Under the terms of the exchange, Frank will transfer realty (20 acres of unimproved land; adjusted basis of $52,000; fair market value of $80,000) and Tom will exchange realty (25 acres of unimproved land; adjusted basis of $60,000; fair market value of $92,000). Tom's property is subject to a mortgage of $12,000 that will be assumed by Frank.

a. What are Frank's and Tom's recognized gains?

b. What are their adjusted bases?

c. As an alternative, Frank has proposed that rather than assuming the mortgage, he will transfer cash of $12,000 to Tom. Tom would use the cash to pay off the mortgage. In an e-mail, advise Tom on whether this alternative would be beneficial to him from a tax perspective.

d. Assuming Tom and Frank proceed with the original exchange (rather than the alternative), complete Form 8824 (Parts I and III) for Tom. Assume that the exchange occurs on September 19, 2017 (Tom acquired his 25-acre parcel on February 15, 2009). Tom's Social Security number is 123-45-6789.

34. **LO.5** Determine the realized, recognized, and postponed gain or loss and the new basis for each of the following like-kind exchanges:

	Adjusted Basis of Old Asset	Boot Given	Fair Market Value of New Asset	Boot Received
a.	$ 7,000	$ –0–	$12,000	$4,000
b.	14,000	2,000	15,000	–0–
c.	3,000	7,000	8,000	500
d.	15,000	–0–	29,000	–0–
e.	10,000	–0–	11,000	1,000
f.	17,000	–0–	14,000	–0–

35. **LO.5** Turquoise Realty Company owns an apartment house that has an adjusted basis of $760,000 but is subject to a mortgage of $192,000. Turquoise transfers the apartment house to Dove, Inc., and receives from Dove $120,000 in cash and an office building with a fair market value of $780,000 at the time of the exchange. Dove assumes the $192,000 mortgage on the apartment house.

    a. What is Turquoise's realized gain or loss?

    b. What is its recognized gain or loss?

    c. What is the basis of the newly acquired office building?

36. **LO.5** Randall owns an office building (adjusted basis of $250,000) that he has been renting to a group of physicians. During negotiations over a new seven-year lease, the physicians offer to purchase the building for $900,000. Randall accepts the offer with the stipulation that the sale be structured as a delayed § 1031 transaction. Consequently, the sales proceeds are paid to a qualified third-party intermediary on the closing date of September 30, 2018. On October 2, 2018, Randall properly identifies an office building that he would like to acquire. Unfortunately, on November 10, 2018, the property Randall selected is withdrawn from the market. Working with the intermediary, on November 12, 2018, Randall identifies another office building that meets his requirements. The purchase of this property closes on December 15, 2018, and the title is transferred to Randall. Randall treats the transaction as a § 1031 like-kind exchange. Even though the original office building identified was not acquired, Randall concludes that in substance, he has satisfied the 45-day rule. He identified the acquired office building as soon as the negotiations ceased on his first choice. Should the IRS accept Randall's attempt to comply? Explain.

    Critical Thinking

    Ethics and Equity

37. **LO.6** Howard's roadside vegetable stand (adjusted basis of $275,000) is destroyed by a tractor-trailer accident. He receives insurance proceeds of $240,000 ($300,000 fair market value − $60,000 coinsurance). Howard immediately uses the proceeds plus additional cash of $45,000 to build another roadside vegetable stand at the same location. What are the tax consequences to Howard?

38. **LO.6** For each of the following involuntary conversions, indicate whether the property acquired qualifies as replacement property, the recognized gain, and the basis for the property acquired.

    a. Frank owns a warehouse that is destroyed by a tornado. The space in the warehouse was rented to various tenants. The adjusted basis was $470,000. Frank uses all of the insurance proceeds of $700,000 to build a shopping mall in a neighboring community where no property has been damaged by tornadoes. The shopping mall is rented to various tenants.

    b. Ivan owns a warehouse that is destroyed by fire. The adjusted basis is $300,000. Because of economic conditions in the area, Ivan decides not to rebuild the warehouse. Instead, he uses all of the insurance proceeds of $400,000 to build a warehouse for use in his business in another state.

    c. Ridge's personal residence is condemned as part of a local government project to widen the highway from two lanes to four lanes. The adjusted basis is $170,000. Ridge uses all of the condemnation proceeds of $200,000 to purchase another personal residence.

    d. Swallow Fashions, Inc., owns a building that is destroyed by a hurricane. The adjusted basis is $250,000. Because of an economic downturn in the area caused by the closing of a military base, Swallow decides to rent space for its retail outlet rather than replace the building. It uses all of the insurance proceeds of $300,000 to buy a four-unit apartment building in another city. A realtor in that city will handle the rental of the apartments.

e.   Susan and Rick's personal residence is destroyed by a tornado. They had owned it for 15 months. The adjusted basis was $170,000. Because they would like to travel, they decide not to acquire a replacement residence. Instead, they invest all of the insurance proceeds of $200,000 in a duplex, which they rent to tenants.

f.   Ellen and Harry's personal residence (adjusted basis of $245,000) is destroyed in a flood. They had owned it for 18 months. Of the insurance proceeds of $350,000, they reinvest $342,000 in a replacement residence four months later.

39. **LO.6** Mitchell, a calendar year taxpayer, is the sole proprietor of a fast-food restaurant. His adjusted basis for the building and the related land is $450,000. On March 12, 2018, state authorities notify Mitchell that his property is going to be condemned so that the highway can be widened. On June 20, Mitchell's property is officially condemned, and he receives an award of $625,000. Because Mitchell's business was successful in the past, he would like to reopen the restaurant in a new location.

a.   What is the earliest date Mitchell can acquire a new restaurant and qualify for § 1033 postponement?

b.   On June 30, Mitchell purchases land and a building for $610,000. Assuming that he elects postponement of gain under § 1033, what is his recognized gain?

c.   What is Mitchell's adjusted basis for the new land and building?

d.   If he does not elect § 1033, what are Mitchell's recognized gain and adjusted basis?

e.   Suppose he invests the $625,000 condemnation proceeds in the stock market on June 30. What is Mitchell's recognized gain?

40. **LO.6** Edith's warehouse (adjusted basis of $450,000) is destroyed by a hurricane in October 2018. Edith, a calendar year taxpayer, receives insurance proceeds of $525,000 in January 2019. Calculate Edith's realized gain or loss, recognized gain or loss, and basis for the replacement property if she:

a.   Acquires a new warehouse for $550,000 in January 2019.

b.   Acquires a new warehouse for $500,000 in January 2019.

c.   Does not acquire replacement property.

Critical Thinking   41. **LO.7** Wesley, who is single, listed his personal residence with a real estate agent on March 3, 2018, at a price of $390,000. He rejected several offers in the $350,000 range during the summer. Finally, on August 16, 2018, he and the purchaser signed a contract to sell for $363,000. The sale (i.e., closing) took place on September 7, 2018. The closing statement showed the following disbursements:

Real estate agent's commission	$ 21,780
Appraisal fee	600
Exterminator's certificate	300
Recording fees	800
Mortgage to First Bank	305,000
Cash to seller	34,520

Wesley's adjusted basis for the house is $200,000. He owned and occupied the house for seven years. On October 1, 2018, Wesley purchases another residence for $325,000.

a.   Calculate Wesley's recognized gain on the sale.

b.   What is Wesley's adjusted basis for the new residence?

c.   Assume instead that the selling price is $800,000. What is Wesley's recognized gain? His adjusted basis for the new residence?

BRIDGE DISCIPLINE

1. In April of the current year, Blue Corporation purchased an asset to be used in its manufacturing operations for $100,000. Blue's management expects the asset to ratably provide valuable services in the production process for eight years and have a salvage value of $12,000. The asset is a five-year asset for tax purposes. Blue has adopted the half-year convention for book purposes in the year of acquisition and disposition; Blue uses MACRS for tax purposes.
   a. Compute the depreciation expense in the year of acquisition for book and tax purposes.
   b. Identify the book-tax difference related to the depreciation expense in the year of acquisition.

2. Refer to the facts in the preceding problem. Assume that Blue Corporation disposes of the manufacturing asset at the beginning of year 7 for $40,000. Compute the amount of gain or loss recognized for book and tax purposes. What is the book-tax difference in the year of disposition?

3. Identify whether the taxpayer's economic position has changed in the following exchanges such that they are subject to current taxation. That is, identify whether the following qualify as like-kind exchanges under § 1031.
   a. Improved for unimproved real estate.
   b. Vending machine (used in business) for inventory.
   c. Rental house for personal residence.
   d. Business equipment for securities.
   e. Warehouse for office building (both used for business).
   f. Truck for computer (both used in business).
   g. Rental house for land (both held for investment).
   h. Ten shares of stock in Blue Corporation for 10 shares of stock in Red Corporation.
   i. Office furniture for office equipment (both used in business).
   j. Unimproved land in Jackson, Mississippi, for unimproved land in Toledo, Spain.
   k. General partnership interest for a general partnership interest.

Research Problems

Note: Solutions to the Research Problems can be prepared by using the Thomson Reuters Checkpoint™ online tax research database, which accompanies this textbook. Solutions can also be prepared by using research materials found in a typical tax library.

Research Problem 1. Ruth Ames died on January 10, 2018. In filing the estate tax return, her executor, Melvin Sims, elects the primary valuation date and amount (fair market value on the date of death). On March 12, 2018, Melvin invests $30,000 of cash that Ruth had in her money market account in acquiring 1,000 shares of Orange, Inc. ($30 per share). On January 10, 2018, Orange was selling for $29 per share. The stock is distributed to a beneficiary, Annette Rust, on June 1, 2018, when it is selling for $33 per share. Melvin wants you to determine the amount at which the Orange shares should appear on the estate tax return and the amount of Annette's adjusted basis for the stock. Write a letter to Melvin in which you respond to his inquiry, and prepare a memo for the tax files. His address is 100 Center Lane, Miami, FL 33124.

Communications

Research Problem 2. Terry owns real estate with an adjusted basis of $600,000 and a fair market value of $1.1 million. The amount of the nonrecourse mortgage on the property is $2.5 million. Because of substantial past and projected future losses associated with the real estate development (occupancy rate of only 37% after three years), Terry deeds the property to the creditor.

a.   What are the tax consequences to Terry?

b.   Assume that the data are the same, except that the fair market value of the property is $2,525,000. Therefore, when Terry deeds the property to the creditor, she also receives $25,000 from the creditor. What are the tax consequences to Terry?

Critical Thinking   **Research Problem 3.** Ted and Marvin Brown purchased an apartment building in 2007 as equal tenants in common. After a hectic decade of co-ownership, the brothers decided that their business association should be terminated. This led to the sale of the apartment building and a division of the proceeds.

The realized gain on the sale of the apartment building for each brother was $350,000. Ted recognized gain on his share and used the net proceeds to invest in stock. Marvin wanted to defer any recognized gain, so he worked with a realtor to identify property that would be eligible for § 1031 like-kind exchange treatment. After one prospect failed, the realtor identified a single-family home on Lake Tahoe that was currently being rented by the owner. Marvin agreed with the choice and acquired the single-family house, using the proceeds from the apartment building. Because the single-family house qualified as like-kind property, Marvin deferred all of his realized gain.

After attempting to rent the property for eight months without success, Marvin concluded that he could not continue to make the mortgage payments on his primary residence and this rental property. To ease his financial liquidity problem, Marvin sold his principal residence for a realized gain of $190,000 and moved into the Lake Tahoe house. He reported no recognized gain on the sale of his principal residence as the sale qualified for § 121 exclusion treatment.

The IRS issued a deficiency notice to Marvin associated with the sale of the apartment building. The position of the IRS was that Marvin did not hold the single-family residence for investment purposes as required by § 1031. Instead, his intention was personal—to use it as a replacement for his current residence that he planned on selling.

Who should prevail?

Use internet tax resources to address the following questions. Look for reliable websites and blogs of the IRS and other government agencies, media outlets, businesses, tax professionals, academics, think tanks, and political outlets.

Research Problem 4. Many see the "step-up in basis at death" rule of § 1014 as an expensive tax loophole enjoyed by the wealthy. Find the latest estimates of the revenue loss to the Treasury that is attributable to this rule.

a.   How does Canada's tax law determine the basis of property acquired from a decedent?

b.   Send an e-mail to a member of the House Ways and Means Committee expressing a preference for the preservation of the current § 1014 rule or the modifications made to it by the Tax Relief Reconciliation Act of 2001 and the Tax Relief Act of 2010.

Research Problem 5. In general, the 45-day identification period and the 180-day exchange period for like-kind exchanges cannot be extended. Does this rule change if the like-kind property or the taxpayer involved in the exchange is located in a Presidentially declared disaster area? Use the IRS's website (**www.irs.gov**) to find the answer.

Becker CPA Review Questions

1. Alice gifted stock to her son, Bob, in year 5. Alice bought the stock in year 1 for $8,300. The value of the stock on the date of gift was $6,400. Bob sold the stock in year 7 for $15,800. What is Bob's recognized gain or loss on the sale in year 7?

   a. $0

   b. $7,500 gain

   c. $9,400 gain

   d. $15,800 gain

2. Jerry inherits an asset from his uncle, who purchased the asset five days before he died. Which of the following statements is correct?

   a. If Jerry sells the asset a few days after receiving it, any gain or loss on the sale will be short term.

   b. Jerry's basis in the asset is the carryover basis from his uncle.

   c. Jerry's basis is the FMV on the alternate valuation date or date it is distributed to him.

   d. Jerry's basis is the FMV on his uncle's date of death.

3. Rick purchased 100 shares of XYZ stock on April 4, year 4, for $8,600. He sold 50 shares on February 8, year 5, for $3,000. He then bought another 50 shares of XYZ on March 1, year 5, for $3,200. How much loss will Rick realize in year 5?

   a. $0

   b. $1,300

   c. $3,000

   d. $5,600

4. Agnes sold 50 shares of ABC stock to her son, Steve, in year 4 for $42,000. She bought the stock eight years ago for $50,000. Steve sold the stock to an unrelated party in year 6 for $60,000. How much gain will Steve recognize from the sale in year 6?

   a. $0

   b. $10,000

   c. $18,000

   d. $60,000

5. Chad owned an office building that was destroyed in a tornado. The adjusted basis of the building at the time was $890,000. After the deductible, Chad received an insurance check for $850,000. He used the $850,000 to purchase a new building that same year. How much is Chad's recognized loss, and what is his basis in the new building?

	Recognized Loss	New Basis
a.	$0	$850,000
b.	$0	$890,000
c.	$40,000	$850,000
d.	$40,000	$890,000

6. Chad owned an office building that was destroyed in a tornado. The adjusted basis of the building at the time was $890,000. After the deductible, Chad received an insurance check for $950,000. He used $900,000 of the insurance proceeds to purchase a new building that same year. How much is Chad's recognized gain, and what is his basis in the new building?

	Recognized Loss	New Basis
a.	$0	$890,000
b.	$0	$900,000
c.	$50,000	$890,000
d.	$60,000	$900,000

7. Marsha exchanged land in Florida with an FMV of $72,700 and an adjusted basis of $40,000 for land in Iowa with an FMV of $57,700. Marsha also paid $5,000 cash in the transaction and received an automobile worth $20,000. What is Marsha's recognized gain on the transaction?

    a. $0

    b. $15,000

    c. $20,000

    d. $32,700

8. Marsha exchanged land in Florida with an FMV of $72,700 and an adjusted basis of $40,000 for land in Iowa with an FMV of $57,700. Marsha also assumed a $5,000 liability on the land received in the transaction and was relieved of a $20,000 liability on the land that was given up. What is Marsha's recognized gain on the transaction?

    a. $0

    b. $15,000

    c. $20,000

    d. $32,700

CHAPTER

8

Property Transactions: Capital Gains and Losses, Section 1231, and Recapture Provisions

LEARNING OBJECTIVES: *After completing Chapter 8, you should be able to:*

LO.1 Explain the general scheme of taxation for capital gains and losses and distinguish capital assets from ordinary assets.

LO.2 State and explain the relevance of a sale or exchange to classification as a capital gain or loss.

LO.3 Determine the applicable holding period for a capital asset.

LO.4 Describe the tax treatment of capital gains and losses for noncorporate taxpayers.

LO.5 Describe the tax treatment of capital gains and losses for corporate taxpayers.

LO.6 Distinguish § 1231 assets from ordinary and capital assets and calculate § 1231 gain or loss.

LO.7 Determine when recapture provisions apply and derive their effects.

CHAPTER OUTLINE

8-1 General Scheme of Taxation, 8-2

8-2 Capital Assets, 8-3
  8-2a Definition of a Capital Asset, 8-3
  8-2b Statutory Expansions, 8-5

8-3 Sale or Exchange, 8-6
  8-3a Worthless Securities and § 1244 Stock, 8-7
  8-3b Retirement of Corporate Obligations, 8-7
  8-3c Options, 8-7
  8-3d Patents, 8-9
  8-3e Franchises, Trademarks, and Trade Names, 8-10
  8-3f Lease Cancellation Payments, 8-11

8-4 Holding Period, 8-13
  8-4a General Rules, 8-13
  8-4b Special Holding Period Rules, 8-13
  8-4c Short Sales, 8-14

8-5 Tax Treatment of Capital Gains and Losses of Noncorporate Taxpayers, 8-16
  8-5a Capital Gains, 8-16
  8-5b Capital Losses, 8-18
  8-5c Capital Gain and Loss Netting Process, 8-19
  8-5d Small Business Stock, 8-21

8-6 Tax Treatment of Capital Gains and Losses of Corporate Taxpayers, 8-23

8-7 Section 1231 Assets, 8-23
  8-7a Relationship to Capital Assets, 8-23
  8-7b Property Included, 8-25
  8-7c Property Excluded, 8-25
  8-7d Casualty or Theft and Nonpersonal Use Capital Assets, 8-25
  8-7e General Procedure for § 1231 Computation, 8-26

8-8 Section 1245 Recapture, 8-29
  8-8a Section 1245 Property, 8-30
  8-8b Observations on § 1245, 8-31

8-9 Section 1250 Recapture, 8-31
  8-9a Unrecaptured § 1250 Gain (Real Estate 25% Gain), 8-33
  8-9b Additional Recapture for Corporations, 8-33

8-10 Exceptions to §§ 1245 and 1250, 8-34
  8-10a Gifts, 8-34
  8-10b Death, 8-35
  8-10c Charitable Transfers, 8-35
  8-10d Certain Nontaxable Transactions, 8-35
  8-10e Like-Kind Exchanges and Involuntary Conversions, 8-36

8-11 Reporting Procedures, 8-36

TAX TALK *Governments likely to confiscate wealth are unlikely to find much wealth to confiscate in the long run.* —THOMAS SOWELL

8-2 CAPITAL ASSETS

A variety of different investments, property, and other assets can be categorized as *capital assets*. Capital assets can be held by individuals, partnerships, corporations, and other entities. Investments are the most well-known category of capital assets and include corporate stocks and bonds, mutual funds, partnership interests, government securities, and vacant land. Many capital assets are owned by individuals as part of their daily life, such as residences, automobiles, furniture, and artwork. Recall from text Section 7-1c that losses on the sale of personal use assets are generally not deductible. As a result, the classification of personal use assets as capital assets is relevant only when their disposition produces a recognized gain. Because the intended use of an asset is important for classification as capital or noncapital, a business may have goodwill as its only capital asset. Classification of capital versus noncapital (e.g., ordinary) can make a significant difference in the tax effects of a gain or loss. For example, as discussed later in this chapter, long-term capital gains generally benefit from advantageous lower rates, while net capital losses can be subject to limitations on deductibility.

In-depth coverage can be found on this book's companion website: www.cengage.com **1** DIGGING DEEPER

8-2a Definition of a Capital Asset

Capital assets are not directly defined in the Code. Instead, § 1221(a) defines what is *not* a capital asset. In general, a capital asset is property *other than* inventory, accounts and notes receivable, supplies, and most fixed assets of a business.

Specifically, the Code defines a capital asset as property held by the taxpayer that is *not* any of the following.

- Inventory or property held primarily for sale to customers in the ordinary course of a business.[1]
- Accounts and notes receivable generated from the sale of goods or services in a business.
- Depreciable property or real estate used in a business.
- A patent, invention, model, or design (whether or not patented); a secret formula or process; certain copyrights; literary, musical, or artistic compositions; or letters, memoranda, or similar property created by or for the taxpayer.[2]
- Certain U.S. government publications.
- Supplies used in a business.

Inventory

What constitutes inventory is determined by reference to the taxpayer's business.

Inventory Determination

Green Company buys and sells used automobiles. Its automobiles are inventory. Therefore, Green's gains from the sale of the cars are ordinary income.

EXAMPLE 1

Soong sells her personal use automobile at a $500 gain. The automobile is a personal use asset and, therefore, a capital asset. Soong's gain is a capital gain.

EXAMPLE 2

---

[1]The Supreme Court, in *Malat v. Riddell* 66–1 USTC ¶9317, 17 AFTR 2d 604, 86 S.Ct. 1030 (USSC, 1966), defined *primarily* as meaning "of first importance or principally."

[2]§ 1221(b)(3).

No asset is inherently capital or ordinary. If Soong in Example 2 sells her capital asset automobile to Green Company in Example 1, that very same automobile loses its capital asset status, because it is inventory to Green Company. Similar transformations can occur if, for example, an art dealer sells a painting (inventory, *not* a capital asset) to a private collector (now a capital asset). Whether an asset is capital or ordinary, therefore, depends entirely on the relationship of *that asset* to the taxpayer who sold it. This classification dilemma is but one feature of capital asset treatment that makes this area so confusing and perennially complicated.

Accounts and Notes Receivable

Accounts and notes receivable are often created as part of a business transaction. These assets may be collected by the creditor, be sold by the creditor, or become completely or partially worthless. Also, the creditor may be on the accrual or cash basis of accounting.

Collection of an *accrual basis* account or note receivable does not result in a gain or loss because the amount collected equals the receivable's basis. If sold, an ordinary gain or loss is generated if the receivable is sold for more or less than its basis (the receivable is an ordinary asset). If the receivable is partially or wholly worthless, the creditor has a "bad debt" that may result in an ordinary deduction (see text Section 6-1).

Collection of a *cash basis* account or note receivable does not result in a gain or loss because the amount collected is ordinary income. In addition, a cash basis receivable has a zero basis since no revenue is recorded until the receivable is collected. If sold, an ordinary gain is generated (the receivable is an ordinary asset). There is no bad debt deduction for cash basis receivables because they have no basis. See text Section 8-3 for more details on "sale or exchange."

EXAMPLE 3

Oriole Company, an *accrual basis taxpayer*, has accounts receivable of $100,000. Gross income of $100,000 was recorded, and a $100,000 basis was established when the receivable was created. Because Oriole needs working capital, it sells the receivables for $83,000 to a financial institution. Accordingly, it has a $17,000 ordinary loss.

If Oriole is a *cash basis taxpayer*, it has $83,000 of ordinary income because it would not have recorded any income earlier and the receivable would have no tax basis.

Business Fixed Assets

Depreciable personal property and real estate (both depreciable and nondepreciable) used by a business are *not* capital assets. As a result, *business fixed assets* are not capital assets. However, gains from the sale of business fixed assets can sometimes be treated as capital gains via § 1231, as discussed later in this chapter.

Inventions and Processes

A patent, invention, model, or design (whether or not patented) and a secret formula or process are excluded from being a capital asset. These are *ordinary* assets. The assets may be held either by the taxpayer who created the property or by a taxpayer who received the asset from the taxpayer who created the property (or for whom the property was created). As a result, gains or losses from the sale or exchange of these assets do *not* receive capital gain treatment. In limited circumstances, patents may be treated as capital assets. Those special rules are discussed in text Section 8-3d.

EXAMPLE 4

Abigail invents a multifunctional case for a popular brand of cell phones. She has a manufacturer produce them for her and sells them via the internet. Her cost is $2.30 per case, and she sells each one for $10. To her surprise, she quickly achieves $45,000 in total sales. She has not capitalized any of the costs of developing the invention and has not patented it.

She sells all of her rights to the invention for $350,000 to a company that is in the business of producing cell phone cases. Her profit from sales of the cases is ordinary income because the cases are inventory. The $350,000 gain from selling the rights to the invention is an ordinary gain because the invention is not a capital asset.

Copyrights and Creative Works

Generally, the person whose efforts led to the copyright or creative work has an ordinary asset, not a capital asset. This rule makes the creator comparable to a taxpayer whose customary activity (salary, business profits) is taxed as ordinary income. *Creative works* include the works of authors, composers, and artists. Also, the person for whom a letter, a memorandum, or another similar property was created has an ordinary asset. Finally, a person receiving a copyright, creative work, a letter, a memorandum, or similar property by lifetime gift from the creator or the person for whom the work was created also has an ordinary asset. A taxpayer may elect to treat the sale or exchange of a musical composition or a copyright of a musical work as the disposition of a capital asset.

Creative Works

Wanda is a part-time music composer. A music publisher purchases one of her songs for $5,000.

Wanda has a $5,000 ordinary gain from the sale of an ordinary asset unless she elects to treat the gain as a capital gain.

EXAMPLE 5

Ed received a letter from the President of the United States in 1995. In the current year, Ed sells the letter to a collector for $300.

Ed has a $300 ordinary gain from the sale of an ordinary asset (because the letter was created for Ed).

EXAMPLE 6

Isabella gives her son a song she composed. Her son sells the song to a music publisher for $5,000.

Her son has a $5,000 ordinary gain from the sale of an ordinary asset unless he elects to treat the gain as a capital gain.

If he inherits the song from Isabella, his basis for the song is its fair market value at Isabella's death. In this situation, the song is a capital asset because the son's basis is not related to Isabella's basis for the song (i.e., the song was not a *lifetime* gift).

EXAMPLE 7

U.S. Government Publications

U.S. government publications received from the U.S. government (or its agencies) for a reduced price (i.e., below that at which it is available to the general public) are *not* capital assets. This prevents a taxpayer from later donating the publications to charity and claiming a charitable contribution deduction equal to the fair market value of the publications.

In-depth coverage can be found on this book's companion website: **www.cengage.com**   **2** DIGGING DEEPER

8-2b Statutory Expansions

In several instances, Congress has clarified its general definition of what is *not* a capital asset.

Dealers in Securities

As a general rule, securities (stocks, bonds, and other financial instruments) held by a dealer are considered to be inventory and are, therefore, not subject to capital gain or loss treatment. A *dealer in securities* is a merchant (e.g., a brokerage firm) that regularly engages in the purchase and resale of securities to customers.

In-depth coverage can be found on this book's companion website: **www.cengage.com**   **3** DIGGING DEEPER

Real Property Subdivided for Sale

Substantial real property development activities may result in the owner being considered a dealer for tax purposes. If so, income from the sale of real estate property lots will be taxed as ordinary income. However, § 1237 allows real estate investors to claim capital gain treatment if they engage *only* in *limited* development activities. To be eligible for § 1237 treatment, the following requirements must be met.

- The taxpayer is not a corporation.

- The taxpayer is not a real estate dealer.

- No substantial improvements have been made to the lots sold. *Substantial* generally means more than a 10 percent increase in the value of a lot. Shopping centers and other commercial or residential buildings are considered substantial, while filling, draining, leveling, and clearing operations are not.

- The taxpayer has held the lots sold for at least 5 years, except for inherited property. The substantial improvements test is less stringent if the property is held at least 10 years.

If these requirements are met, all gain is capital gain until the taxable year in which the *sixth* lot is sold. Sales of contiguous lots to a single buyer in the same transaction count as the sale of one lot. Beginning with the taxable year in which the *sixth* lot is sold, 5 percent of the revenue from lot sales is potential ordinary income. That potential ordinary income is offset by any selling expenses from the lot sales. Practically, sales commissions often are at least 5 percent of the sales price, so usually none of the gain is treated as ordinary income.

Section 1237 does not apply to losses. A loss from the sale of subdivided real property is ordinary loss unless the property qualifies as a capital asset under § 1221. The following example illustrates the application of § 1237.

EXAMPLE 8

Ahmed owns a large tract of land and subdivides it for sale. Assume that Ahmed meets all of the requirements of § 1237 and during the tax year sells the first 10 lots to 10 different buyers for $10,000 each. Ahmed's basis in each lot sold is $3,000, and he incurs total selling expenses of $4,000 on the sales. Ahmed's gain is computed as follows.

Selling price (10 × $10,000)	$100,000	
Less: Selling expenses	(4,000)	
Amount realized		$ 96,000
Basis (10 × $3,000)		(30,000)
Realized and recognized gain		$ 66,000
Classification of recognized gain:		
Ordinary income		
Five percent of selling price (5% × $100,000)	$ 5,000	
Less: Selling expenses	(4,000)	
Ordinary gain		1,000
Capital gain		$ 65,000

A portion of the gain recognized is given ordinary treatment because the *sixth* lot is sold in the current year.

8-3 SALE OR EXCHANGE

LO.2

State and explain the relevance of a sale or exchange to classification as a capital gain or loss.

Recognition of capital gain or loss usually requires a sale or exchange of a capital asset. The Code uses the term *sale or exchange*, but does not define it. Generally, a property sale involves the receipt of money by the seller and/or the assumption by the purchaser of the seller's liabilities. An exchange involves the transfer of property for other property. Thus, an involuntary conversion (casualty, theft, or condemnation) is not a sale or exchange. In several situations, the determination of whether or when a sale or exchange has taken place has been clarified by the enactment of Code Sections that specifically provide for sale or exchange treatment. These situations are discussed below.

Recognized gains or losses from the cancellation, lapse, expiration, or any other termination of a right or obligation with respect to personal property (other than stock) that is or would be a capital asset in the hands of the taxpayer are capital gains or losses.[3] See the discussion under Options (text Section 8-3c) for more details.

8-3a Worthless Securities and § 1244 Stock

Occasionally, securities such as stocks and bonds may become worthless due to the insolvency of their issuer. If the security is a capital asset, the loss is deemed to have occurred as the result of a sale or exchange on the *last day* of the tax year.[4] This last-day rule may have the effect of converting a short-term capital loss into a long-term capital loss. Section 1244 allows an *ordinary* deduction on disposition of stock at a loss. The stock must be that of a small business corporation, and the ordinary deduction is limited to $50,000 ($100,000 for married individuals filing jointly) per year. See Chapter 6 (and text Sections 6-2a and 6-2b) for a more complete discussion of these rules.

8-3b Retirement of Corporate Obligations

A debt obligation (e.g., a bond or note payable) may have a tax basis different from its redemption value because it may have been acquired at a premium or discount (see Chapter 7 for a discussion of bond amortization). Consequently, the collection of the redemption value may result in a loss or a gain. Generally, the collection of a debt obligation is treated as a sale or exchange.[5] Therefore, any loss or gain is capital because a sale or exchange has taken place.

Osprey, Inc., purchases $1,000 of Golden Eagle Corporation bonds for $1,020 in the open market. If the bonds are held to maturity and the bond premium is not amortized, the $20 difference between Osprey's collection of the $1,000 redemption value and its cost of $1,020 is treated as capital loss.

EXAMPLE 9

In-depth coverage can be found on this book's companion website: **www.cengage.com**

4 DIGGING DEEPER

8-3c Options

Frequently, a potential buyer of property wants to defer a final purchase decision, but wants to control the sale and/or the sale price in the meantime. **Options** are used to achieve this kind of control. The potential purchaser (the grantee) pays the property owner (the grantor) for an option on the property. The grantee then becomes the option holder. An option, which usually sets the price at which a grantee can buy the property, expires after a specified period of time.

Sale of an Option

In addition to exercising an option or letting it expire, a grantee can often sell or exchange it. This generally results in capital gain or loss if the option property is (or would be) a capital asset to the grantee.[6]

---

[3]§ 1234A.
[4]§ 165(g)(1).

[5]§ 1271.
[6]§ 1234(a) and Reg. § 1.1234–1(a)(1).

EXAMPLE 10

Robin & Associates wants to buy some vacant land for investment purposes. However, the firm cannot afford the full purchase price at the present time. Instead, Robin & Associates (grantee) pays the landowner (grantor) $3,000 for an option to buy the land for $100,000 anytime in the next two years. The option is a capital asset to Robin because if it actually purchased the land (the option property), the land would be a capital asset.

Three months after purchasing the option, Robin sells it to a third party for $7,000. The firm has a $4,000 ($7,000 − $3,000) capital gain on this sale.

Failure to Exercise Options

If an option holder (grantee) fails to exercise the option, the lapse of the option is considered a sale or exchange on the option expiration date. Thus, the resulting loss is a capital loss if the property subject to the option is (or would be) a capital asset in the hands of the grantee.

The grantor of an option on *stocks, securities, commodities, or commodity futures* receives short-term capital gain treatment upon the expiration of the option.[7] For example, an individual investor who owns stock (a capital asset) may sell a call option, entitling the buyer of the option to acquire the stock at a specified price higher than the stock's value at the date the option is granted. The writer of the call (the grantor) receives a premium for writing the option. If the price of the stock does not increase during the option period, the option will expire unexercised. Upon the expiration of the option, the grantor must recognize a short-term capital gain equal to the premium received (whereas the grantee recognizes a loss, the character of which depends on the underlying asset). These provisions do not apply to options held for sale to customers (the inventory of a securities dealer).

Options on property *other than* stocks, securities, commodities, or commodity futures (for instance, vacant land) result in ordinary income to the grantor when the option expires. For instance, the landowner in the preceding example would have ordinary income of $3,000 if Robin (the grantee) had allowed the option to expire.

Exercise of Options by Grantee

If an option is exercised, the amount paid for the option is added to the optioned property's selling price. This increases the gain (or reduces the loss) to the grantor resulting from the sale of the property. The grantor's gain or loss is capital or ordinary depending on the tax status of the property. The grantee adds the cost of the option to the basis of the property purchased.

The Big Picture

EXAMPLE 11

Return to the facts of *The Big Picture* on p. 8-1. On February 1, 2018, Alice purchases 100 shares of Eagle Company stock for $5,000. On April 1, 2018, she writes a call option on the stock, giving the grantee the right to buy the stock for $6,000 during the following six-month period. Alice (the grantor) receives a call premium of $500 for writing the call.

- If the call is exercised by the grantee on August 1, 2018, Alice has $1,500 ($6,000 + $500 − $5,000) of short-term capital gain from the sale of the stock. The grantee has a $6,500 basis for the stock ($500 option premium + $6,000 purchase price).

- Investors sometimes get nervous and want to "lock in" gains or losses.
  - Assume that, prior to the grantee's exercise of the call, Alice decides to sell her stock for $6,000 and enters into a closing transaction by purchasing a call on 100 shares of Eagle Company stock for $5,000.
  - Because the Eagle stock is selling for $6,000, Alice must pay a call premium of $1,000.

continued

---
[7]§ 1234(b)(1).

- She recognizes a $500 short-term capital loss [$500 (call premium received) − $1,000 (call premium paid)] on the closing transaction.

- On the actual sale of the Eagle stock, Alice has a short-term capital gain of $1,000 [$6,000 (selling price) − $5,000 (cost)].

- The original grantee is not affected by Alice's closing transaction. The original option is still in existence, and the grantee's tax consequences depend on what action the grantee takes—exercising the option, letting the option expire, or selling the option.

- Assume that the original option expired unexercised. Alice has a $500 short-term capital gain equal to the call premium received for writing the option. This gain is not recognized until the option expires. The grantee has a loss from expiration of the option. The nature of the loss will depend upon whether the option was a capital asset or an ordinary asset.

Concept Summary 8.2 identifies the consequences of various transactions involving options, to both the grantor and grantee.

Concept Summary 8.2

Options: Consequences to the Grantor and Grantee

Event	Effect on	
	Grantor	**Grantee**
Option is granted.	Receives value and has a contract obligation (a liability).	Pays value and has a contract right (an asset).
Option expires.	Has a short-term capital gain if the option property is stocks, securities, commodities, or commodity futures. Otherwise, gain is ordinary income.	Has a loss (capital loss if option property would have been a capital asset for the grantee).
Option is exercised.	Amount received for option increases proceeds from sale of the option property.	Amount paid for option becomes part of the basis of the option property purchased.
Option is sold or exchanged by grantee.	Result depends upon whether option later expires or is exercised (see above).	Could have gain or loss (capital gain or loss if option property would have been a capital asset for the grantee).

8-3d Patents

Transfer of a **patent** is treated as the sale or exchange of a long-term capital asset when *all substantial rights* to the patent are transferred by a *holder*.[8] The transferor/holder may receive payment in virtually any form, including contingent payments based on the transferee/purchaser's productivity, use, or disposition of the patent. If the transfer meets these requirements, any gain or loss is *automatically a long-term* capital gain or loss. Whether the asset was a capital asset for the transferor, whether a sale or exchange occurred, and how long the transferor held the patent are all irrelevant.

Substantial Rights

To receive favorable capital gain treatment, *all substantial rights* to the patent must be transferred. All substantial rights have not been transferred when the transfer is limited geographically within the issuing country or when the transfer is for a period less than the remaining legal life of the patent. All the facts and circumstances of the transaction, not just the language of the transfer document, are examined when making this determination.[9]

Example 12 illustrates the special treatment for patents.

---

[8]§ 1235.   [9]Reg. § 1.1235–2(b)(1).

EXAMPLE
12

Return to the facts of *The Big Picture* on p. 8-1. Kathy transfers her remaining 50% share of the rights in the battery patent to the Green Battery Company in exchange for a lump-sum payment of $1 million plus $.50 for each battery sold.

Assuming that Kathy has transferred all substantial rights, the question of whether the transfer is a sale or exchange of a capital asset is not relevant. Kathy automatically has a long-term capital gain from both the lump-sum payment received and the per battery royalty to the extent that those proceeds exceed her basis for the patent.

Kathy also had an automatic long-term capital gain when she sold the other 50% of her rights in the patent to Alice, because Kathy transferred an undivided interest that included all substantial rights in the patent.

Whether Alice gets long-term capital gain treatment on a transfer to Green Battery will depend on whether she is a holder (see the following discussion and Example 13).

Holder Defined

The *holder* of a patent must be an *individual* (usually the invention's creator or an individual who purchases the patent rights from the creator). However, the creator's employer is not eligible for long-term capital gain treatment. Normally, the employer will have an ordinary asset because the patent was developed as part of its business.

The Big Picture

EXAMPLE
13

Continuing with the facts of Example 12, Kathy is clearly a holder of the patent because she is the inventor and was not an employee when she invented the battery. When Alice purchased a 50% interest in the patent nine months ago, she became a holder if the patent had not yet been "reduced to practice." Because batteries were apparently not being manufactured at the time of the purchase, the patent had not been reduced to practice.

Consequently, Alice is also a holder, and she has an automatic long-term capital gain or loss when she transfers all substantial rights in her interest in the patent to Green Battery Company. Alice's basis for her share of the patent is $50,000, and the proceeds from the transfer of her share of the patent are $1 million plus $.50 for each battery sold. Thus, Alice will have a long-term capital gain even though she has not held her interest in the patent for more than one year.

Compare the results here to those in Example 4. There, Abigail sold all substantial rights, but she had no patent and the invention had been "reduced to practice" because it was being manufactured and sold.

8-3e Franchises, Trademarks, and Trade Names

A mode of operation, a widely recognized brand name (trade name), and a widely known business symbol (trademark) are all valuable assets. These assets may be licensed (commonly known as *franchising*) by their owner for use by other businesses. Many fast-food restaurants (such as McDonald's and Taco Bell) are franchises. The franchisee usually pays the owner (franchisor) an initial fee plus a contingent fee. The contingent fee is often based upon the franchisee's sales volume.

For Federal income tax purposes, a **franchise** is an agreement that gives the franchisee the right to distribute, sell, or provide goods, services, or facilities within a specified area.[10] A franchise transfer includes the grant of a franchise, a transfer by one franchisee to another person, or the renewal of a franchise.

Section 1253 provides that a transfer of a franchise, trademark, or trade name is *not* a sale or exchange of a capital asset when the transferor retains any significant power, right, or continuing interest in the property transferred.

DIGGING DEEPER 5   In-depth coverage can be found on this book's companion website: **www.cengage.com**

---

[10]§ 1253(b)(1).

Significant Power, Right, or Continuing Interest

In most franchising operations, the transferor retains some powers or rights. As a result, the transaction is *not* a capital asset transfer. *Significant powers, rights, or continuing interests* include control over franchise assignment, quality of products and services, sale or advertising of products or services, the requirement that substantially all supplies and equipment be purchased from the transferor, and the right to terminate the franchise.

In the unusual case where the transferor does not retain any significant power, right, or continuing interest, a capital gain or loss may occur. For capital gain or loss treatment to be available, the asset transferred must qualify as a capital asset.

The Big Picture

Return to the facts of *The Big Picture* on p. 8-1. Alice sells for $101,000 to Mauve, Inc., the franchise purchased from Orange, Inc., nine months ago. The $101,000 received by Alice is not contingent, and all significant powers, rights, and continuing interests are transferred.

The $1,000 gain ($101,000 proceeds − $100,000 basis) is a short-term capital gain because Alice has held the franchise for only nine months.

EXAMPLE 14

Franchise Payments

In most franchise settings, when the transferor retains significant power or rights, both contingent (e.g., based on sales) and noncontingent payments occur.

Noncontingent Payments Any noncontingent payments made by the franchisee to the franchisor are ordinary income to the franchisor. The franchisee capitalizes the payments and amortizes them over 15 years. If the franchise is sold, the amortization is subject to recapture under § 1245.

Grey Company signs a 10-year franchise agreement with DOH Donuts. Grey (the franchisee) makes payments of $3,000 per year for the first 8 years of the franchise agreement—a total of $24,000. Grey cannot deduct $3,000 per year as the payments are made. Instead, Grey must amortize the $24,000 total over 15 years. Thus, Grey may deduct $1,600 per year for each of the 15 years of the amortization period.

The same result would occur if Grey had made a $24,000 lump-sum payment at the beginning of the franchise period. Assuming that DOH Donuts (the franchisor) retains significant powers, rights, or a continuing interest, it will have ordinary income when it receives the payments from Grey.

EXAMPLE 15

Contingent Payments Any contingent franchise payments are ordinary income for the franchisor and an ordinary deduction for the franchisee. Contingent payments must meet the following requirements:

- The payments are made at least annually throughout the term of the transfer agreement.
- The payments are substantially equal in amount or are payable under a fixed formula.

TAK, a spicy chicken franchisor, transfers an eight-year franchise to Egret Corporation. TAK retains a significant power, right, or continuing interest. Egret, the franchisee, agrees to pay TAK 15% of sales. This contingent payment is ordinary income to TAK and a business deduction for Egret as the payments are made.

EXAMPLE 16

Concept Summary 8.3 reviews the effects of transactions involving franchises on both the franchisor and franchisee.

8-3f Lease Cancellation Payments

The tax treatment of payments received for canceling a lease depends on whether the recipient of the payments is the **lessor** or the **lessee** and whether the lease is a capital asset.

Concept Summary 8.3

Franchises: Consequences to the Franchisor and Franchisee

	Effect on	
Event	**Franchisor**	**Franchisee**
Franchisor Retains Significant Powers and Rights		
Noncontingent payment	Ordinary income.	Capitalized and amortized over 15 years as an ordinary deduction; if franchise is sold, amortization is subject to recapture under § 1245.
Contingent payment	Ordinary income.	Ordinary deduction.
Franchisor Does Not Retain Significant Powers and Rights		
Noncontingent payment	Ordinary income if franchise rights are an ordinary asset; capital gain if franchise rights are a capital asset (unlikely).	Capitalized and amortized over 15 years as an ordinary deduction; if the franchise is sold, amortization is subject to recapture under § 1245.
Contingent payment	Ordinary income.	Ordinary deduction.

Lessee Treatment

Lease cancellation payments received by a lessee are treated as an exchange.[11] The treatment of these payments depends on the underlying use of the property and how long the lease has existed.[12]

- If the property was used personally (e.g., an apartment used as a residence), the payment results in a capital gain (and long term if the lease existed for more than one year).
- If the property was used for business and the lease existed for one year or less, the payment results in ordinary income.
- If the property was used for business and the lease existed for more than one year, the payment results in a § 1231 gain.

EXAMPLE 17

Merganser, Inc., owns an apartment building that it is going to convert into an office building. Vicki is one of the apartment tenants who receives $1,000 from Merganser to cancel the lease.

Vicki has a capital gain of $1,000 (which is long term or short term depending upon how long she has held the lease). Merganser has an ordinary deduction of $1,000.

Lessor Treatment

Payments received by a lessor (the landlord) for a lease cancellation are always ordinary income because they are considered to be in lieu of rental payments.[13]

EXAMPLE 18

Finch & Company owns an apartment building near a university campus. Hui-Fen is one of the tenants. Hui-Fen is graduating early and offers Finch $800 to cancel the apartment lease. Finch accepts the offer.

Finch has ordinary income of $800. Hui-Fen has a nondeductible payment because the apartment was personal use property.

---

[11]§ 1241 and Reg. § 1.1241–1(a).

[12]Reg. § 1.1221–1(b) and PLR 200045019. If the lease was held for more than one year before cancellation, it is a § 1231 asset.

[13]Reg. § 1.61–8(b).

8-4 HOLDING PERIOD

8-4a General Rules

Property must be held more than one year to qualify for long-term capital gain or loss treatment.[14] Property held for one year or less results in short-term capital gain or loss. To compute the <mark>holding period</mark>, start counting on the day *after* the property was acquired and include the day of disposition.

The Big Picture

Return to the facts of *The Big Picture* on p. 8-1. Assume that Alice purchased the 200 shares of AppleCo stock on January 15, 2018. If she sells them on January 16, 2019, Alice's holding period is more than one year and the gain or loss is long term.

If instead Alice sells the stock on January 15, 2019, the holding period is exactly one year and the gain or loss is short term.

EXAMPLE 19

To be held for more than one year, a capital asset acquired on the last day of any month must not be sold until on or after the first day of the thirteenth succeeding month.[15]

Purple, Inc., purchases a capital asset on March 31, 2018. If Purple sells the asset on March 31, 2019, the holding period is one year and Purple will have a short-term capital gain or loss.

If Purple sells the asset on April 1, 2019, the holding period is more than one year and it will have a long-term capital gain or loss.

EXAMPLE 20

8-4b Special Holding Period Rules

There are several special holding period rules.[16] The application of these rules varies depending upon the type of asset involved and how it was acquired.

Nontaxable Exchanges

The holding period of property received in a like-kind exchange (and certain other qualified nontaxable exchanges) includes the holding period of the former asset if the property that was exchanged was either a capital asset or a § 1231 asset.

Holding Period Rules

Red Manufacturing Corporation exchanges some vacant real estate it owns (a capital asset) for land closer to its factory.

The transaction is a like-kind exchange, so the holding period of the new land includes the holding period of the old land.

EXAMPLE 21

A lightning strike destroyed Vireo Company's generator (a § 1231 asset) in March. Vireo uses all of the insurance proceeds it received to acquire a comparable generator.

The holding period of the new generator includes the holding period of the old generator because this is a nontaxable involuntary conversion.

EXAMPLE 22

---

[14]§ 1222(3).
[15]Rev.Rul. 66–7, 1966–1 C.B. 188.

[16]§ 1223.

Gifts

When a gift occurs, if the donor's basis carries over to the recipient, the donor's holding period is tacked on to the recipient's holding period. This will occur when the property's fair market value at the date of the gift is greater than the donor's adjusted basis. See the discussion of these items in text Section 7-2b.

Carryover Basis

EXAMPLE 23

Kareem acquired 100 shares of Robin Corporation stock for $1,000 on December 31, 2014. He transferred the shares by gift to Megan on December 31, 2017, when the stock was worth $2,000. Kareem's basis of $1,000 becomes the basis for determining gain or loss on a subsequent sale by Megan. Megan's holding period begins with the date the stock was acquired by Kareem.

EXAMPLE 24

Assume the same facts as in the preceding example, except that the fair market value of the shares was only $800 on the date of the gift. If Megan sells the stock for a loss, its value on the date of the gift is her basis. Accordingly, the tacked-on holding period rule does not apply, and Megan's holding period begins with the date of the gift.

So if she sells the shares for $500 on April 1, 2018, Megan has a $300 recognized capital loss, the holding period is from December 31, 2017, to April 1, 2018, and the loss is short term.

Disallowed Loss Transactions

Under several Code provisions, the recognition of a realized loss is disallowed. When a loss is disallowed, there is no carryover of holding period. Losses can be disallowed under § 267 (sale or exchange between related taxpayers) and § 262 (sale or exchange of personal use assets) as well as other Code sections. Taxpayers who acquire property in a disallowed loss transaction begin a new holding period and have a basis equal to the purchase price.

EXAMPLE 25

Janet sells her personal automobile at a loss. She may not deduct the loss because it arises from the sale of personal use property. Janet purchases a replacement automobile for more than the selling price of her former automobile. Janet has a basis equal to the cost of the replacement automobile, and her holding period begins when she acquires the replacement automobile.

Inherited Property

The holding period for inherited property is treated as long term no matter how long the property is actually held by the heir. The holding period of the decedent or the decedent's estate is not relevant to the heir's holding period.

EXAMPLE 26

Shonda inherits Blue Company stock from her father, who died in 2018. She receives the stock on April 1, 2018, and sells it on November 1, 2018. Even though Shonda did not hold the stock for more than one year, she receives long-term capital gain or loss treatment on the sale.

8-4c Short Sales

A **short sale** occurs when a taxpayer sells borrowed property and repays the lender with substantially identical property either held on the date of the sale or purchased after the sale. Short sales typically involve corporate stock. The seller's objective is to make a profit in anticipation of a decline in the stock's price. If the price declines, the seller in a short sale recognizes a profit equal to the difference between the (higher) sales price of the borrowed stock and the (lower) price paid for its replacement.

Section 1233 provides that a short sale gain or loss is a capital gain or loss to the extent the short sale property constitutes a capital asset of the taxpayer. This gain or loss is not recognized until the short sale is closed. Generally, the holding period of the short sale property is determined by how long the property used to close the short sale was held.

Short Sales

On January 4, Green & Associates sold short 100 shares of Osprey Corporation for $1,500. Green closed the transaction on July 28 of the same year by purchasing 100 shares of Osprey for $1,000 and delivering them to the broker from whom the securities were borrowed. Because this stock was held less than one year (actually, less than a day), Green's $500 gain ($1,500 sale price − $1,000 basis) is short term.

Assume the same facts as in the preceding example, except that the January 4 short sale was not closed until January 28 of the *following* year. The result is the same, because the stock was acquired and used to close the transaction on the same day; that is, it was not held more than a year.

If a taxpayer owns securities that are "substantially identical" to those sold short, § 1259 subjects the short sale to potential *constructive sale treatment*, and the taxpayer recognizes gain (but not loss) as of that date. If the taxpayer has not closed the short sale by delivering the short sale securities to the broker from whom the securities were borrowed before January 31 of the year following the short sale, the short sale is deemed to have closed on the short sale date. The holding period in such circumstances is determined by how long the securities in question were held.

Assume the same facts as in Example 27, except that Green & Associates owned 100 shares of Osprey Corporation when it sold short 100 shares on January 4. Green does not close the short sale before January 31 of the following year. Green must recognize any gain on its 100 shares of Osprey as of January 4 of the current year. If Green owned those shares more than one year as of that date, the gain is long term.

TAX PLANNING STRATEGIES Timing Capital Gains

FRAMEWORK FOCUS: INCOME AND EXCLUSIONS

Strategy: Postpone Recognition of Income to Achieve Tax Deferral.

FRAMEWORK FOCUS: DEDUCTIONS

Strategy: Maximize Deductible Amounts.

Taxpayers have considerable control over the timing of their capital gains through the mechanism of realization. Accordingly, a taxpayer might want to defer recognizing a large capital gain in a year with *substantial itemized deductions*, such as large personal casualty losses or miscellaneous itemized deductions. In so doing, the taxpayer minimizes the loss of such deductions due to AGI limitations. See additional discussion in Chapter 10.

Nontax considerations, of course, often dictate when assets are sold. If a particular stock is peaking in popularity, selling it might be a wise investment strategy, even if the taxpayer's current tax situation is not optimal.

Similarly, if a taxpayer needs cash to start a business, purchase a home, or pay for a child's education or medical costs, the capital asset might need to be sold at a time when investment *and* tax considerations counsel otherwise. In these circumstances, however, a taxpayer might choose to *borrow* the money required and use the capital asset as collateral for the loan, rather than sell the asset. A loan does not trigger tax consequences, and the taxpayer can continue to hold the asset until a more opportune time—albeit at the cost of paying interest, which may be nondeductible.

In-depth coverage can be found on this book's companion website: www.cengage.com

6 DIGGING DEEPER

LO.4

Describe the tax treatment of capital gains and losses for noncorporate taxpayers.

8-5 TAX TREATMENT OF CAPITAL GAINS AND LOSSES OF NONCORPORATE TAXPAYERS

This section discusses how capital gains and losses are taxed to noncorporate taxpayers; that is, individuals, trusts, and estates. The rules applicable to corporations are considered in the following section of this chapter.

8-5a Capital Gains

Gains from the sale or exchange of capital assets are taxed at various rates, depending upon the holding period, the taxpayer's regular tax rate, and the type of asset involved.

Short-Term Gains

Gains on capital assets held one year or less are taxed as *ordinary income*. Accordingly, the applicable tax rates vary from 10 percent to 37 percent. Although short-term capital gains receive no preferential tax treatment compared to ordinary income, they do have one advantage: they can absorb capital losses without limit. As discussed later in this section, *capital losses* are deducted first against capital gains (without limit) and then against ordinary income, but only up to $3,000 per year.[17] Thus, someone with a large capital loss will find short-term capital gains attractive, even though such gains do not qualify for lower tax rates.

EXAMPLE

30

Kay generated a $50,000 long-term capital loss on the sale of her employer's stock (not a small business stock) that she had acquired over the previous 10 years. Kay is also holding a number of short-term appreciated stock positions that she is thinking about selling (as she thinks the prices are going to decline). Rather than wait for long-term capital gain treatment, Kay decides to sell the short-term positions; she is able to shelter these short-term gains by using the large long-term loss.

Long-Term Gains

Gains on capital assets held more than one year are classified as *long-term* gains and are eligible for special (lower) tax rates. A taxpayer qualifies for a 0 percent rate on these gains if the taxpayer is in the 10 percent or the majority of the 12 percent regular tax bracket, after taxing other taxable income. In 2018, the 0 percent alternative rate applies only through $77,200 of taxable income for married taxpayers filing jointly or surviving spouses, $51,700 for heads of household, and $38,600 for single taxpayers and married taxpayers filing separately.

This means that in 2018, the last $200 (married, filing jointly and surviving spouses) or $100 (single, head of household, and married, filing separately) in the 12 percent bracket is subject to the 15 percent alternative rate. As the normal tax rate (12 percent) is less than the alternative tax rate (15 percent), this means that for these $200 or $100 ranges, any net capital gain or QDI will be taxed at 12 percent (rather than 15 percent). These threshold amounts are adjusted annually for inflation.

A taxpayer qualifies for a 15 percent rate on these gains if the taxpayer is in the 22 percent, 24 percent, and 32 percent brackets or a portion of the 35 percent regular rate bracket after taxing other taxable income. In 2018, the 15 percent tax rate applies until taxable income exceeds $479,000 for married taxpayers filing jointly, $452,400 for heads of household, $425,800 for single taxpayers, and $239,500 for married taxpayers filing separately. These threshold amounts are adjusted annually for inflation.

A taxpayer qualifies for a 20 percent rate on these gains if taxable income exceeds the maximum taxable income thresholds for the 15 percent alternative tax rate. Thus, the benefit of these long-term capital gain tax rates can be significant.

---

[17]§ 1211(b).

TAX PLANNING STRATEGIES Gifts of Appreciated Securities

FRAMEWORK FOCUS: TAX RATE

Strategy: Shift Net Income from High-Bracket Taxpayers to Low-Bracket Taxpayers.

Persons with appreciated securities that have been held over one year may reduce the tax due on their sale by giving the securities to someone (often a child) who is in the *lowest tax bracket*. The donor's holding period carries over, along with his or her basis, and the donee's lower tax rate applies when the securities are sold. As a result, the gain could be taxed at the donee's 0 percent, rather than the donor's 15 or 20 percent. The donee should be at least age 19 (or 24 in the case of a full-time student) by year-end, however, or

the *kiddie tax* will nullify most of the tax advantage being sought. The kiddie tax subjects the gain to the parents' tax rate. See Chapter 9.

Such gifts usually bear no gift tax due to the $14,000 annual exclusion. But once the property is transferred by the donor, it belongs to the donee. It is not available to the donor, nor may it be used to pay a parent's essential support obligations. Moreover, these assets may affect a child's eligibility for need-based financial aid when applying to college.

Relatively few capital gains are realized by persons in the 10 or 12 percent tax bracket. In addition, there are few taxpayers who are in the highest income tax bracket and subject to the 20 percent rate. Thus, the tax rate that generally applies to long-term capital gains is 15 percent.

There are two major exceptions, however, to this general treatment. The first exception relates to so-called *28% property*, which consists of the following items.

- **Collectibles** (works of art, rugs, antiques, gems, coins, stamps, and alcoholic beverages) held more than one year.[18]

- The taxable portion of the gain on sales of *qualified small business stock* (see the end of this section).

These assets are labeled *28% property*, because the gains they produce are taxed at 28 percent. But this 28 percent rate is a *maximum* rate, so a taxpayer in a lower tax bracket would pay at that lower rate. As a result, the benefit of the applicable tax rates for gains on *28% property* is as follows.

Ordinary Income Tax Rates	Applicable Tax Rates	Differential (Percentage Points)
10%	10%	None
12%	12%	None
22%	22%	None
24%	24%	None
32%	28%	4%
35%	28%	7%
37%	28%	9%

GLOBAL TAX ISSUES Capital Gain Treatment in the United States and Other Countries

Few other countries apply an alternative tax rate or other incentive to long-term capital gains. Instead, those gains are taxed in the same manner as other income. Consequently, even though

the U.S. system of identifying and taxing capital assets is complex, it may be preferable because of the lower tax rates and because the lower rates are available to taxpayers in all tax brackets.

---

[18]§ 408(m) and Reg. § 1.408–10(b).

Note that gains on *28% property* receive preferential tax treatment only when realized by taxpayers in the top three tax brackets.

Taxation of Collectibles Gains

EXAMPLE 31

Kelsey is in the 12% tax bracket due to her income. She generates $2,000 of gains on the sale of a coin collection she has had since she was a child. Although collectibles are 28% property, her gains will be taxed at only 12%, consistent with her lower ordinary income tax bracket.

EXAMPLE 32

Ashley is in the top ordinary tax bracket (37%). She sells her stamp collection for a $3,000 gain. The stamps are 28% property and will be taxed at the preferential 28% tax rate since Ashley's ordinary tax rate exceeds 28%.

The second major exception involves depreciable real estate that has been held more than one year. Some—but not all—of the gain attributable to depreciation deductions on real estate such as apartments, office buildings, shopping centers, and warehouses is taxable at 25 percent rather than 0, 15, or 20 percent. The amount that is taxed in this manner depends upon how much depreciation is "recaptured" as ordinary income under § 1250, as explained later in this chapter. Accordingly, these gains are called *unrecaptured § 1250 gain*. The 25 percent rate is a *maximum* rate; so the benefit of this tax rate for gains from the sale of depreciable real estate really only impacts taxpayers in the 32 percent to 37 percent tax brackets, and saves them from 7 percentage points to a maximum of 12 percentage points.

Concept Summary 8.4 reviews the tax treatment given to capital gains recognized by noncorporate taxpayers.

Concept Summary 8.4

Capital Gains of Noncorporate Taxpayers

Type of Asset	Applicable Rate
Held not more than one year (short-term).	10%–37%, same as ordinary income.
Collectibles held more than one year (*28% property*).	10%/12%/22%/24% for lowest-bracket taxpayers, 28% for all others.
Taxable portion (50%, 25%, or 0%) of gain on qualified small business stock held more than five years (*28% property*; see text Section 8-5d for a detailed explanation of the special treatment given to "qualified small business stock").	10%/12%/22%/24% for lowest-bracket taxpayers, 28% for all others.
Unrecaptured § 1250 gain on depreciable real estate held more than one year.	10%/12%/22%/24% for four lowest-bracket taxpayers, 25% for all others.
Other capital assets held more than one year (regular long-term).	0%, 15%, or 20% depending on specific taxable income thresholds.

8-5b Capital Losses

As explained previously, capital gains can be classified into four general categories.

- Short term—taxed as ordinary income.
- *28% property*—taxed at no more than 28 percent.
- *Unrecaptured § 1250 gain*—taxed at no more than 25 percent.
- Regular long term—taxed at 0 percent, 15 percent, or 20 percent.

A taxpayer can also have losses from capital assets in *three* of these four categories. The *unrecaptured § 1250 gain* category applies only to gain.

8-5c **Capital Gain and Loss Netting Process**

When both gains and losses occur in the year, they must be netted against each other in the following order.

Step 1. Group all gains and losses into short-term, *28% property, unrecaptured § 1250*, and regular long-term categories.

Step 2. Net the gains and losses within each category to obtain net short-term, net *28% property,* net *unrecaptured § 1250,* and net regular long-term gain or loss.

Step 3. Offset the net *28% property and unrecaptured § 1250* amounts if they are of opposite sign. Add them if they have the same sign. Then offset the resulting amount against the regular net long-term amount if they are of opposite sign, or add the amounts if they have the same sign.

Step 4. Offset the result of Step 3 with the net short-term gain *or loss* from Step 2 if they are of opposite sign.

These netting rules offset net short-term capital loss against the *highest-taxed gain first.* Consequently, if there is a net short-term capital loss, it first offsets any net *28% property gain,* any remaining loss offsets *unrecaptured § 1250 gain,* and then any remaining loss offsets regular long-term gain.

If the result of Step 4 is *only* a short-term capital gain, the taxpayer is not eligible for a reduced tax rate. If the result of Step 4 is a loss, a ==net capital loss== exists and the taxpayer may be eligible for a *capital loss deduction* (discussed later in this chapter). If there was no offsetting in Step 4 because the short-term and Step 3 results were both gains *or* if the result of the offsetting is a *28% property,* an *unrecaptured § 1250 property,* and/or a regular long-term gain, a ==net capital gain== exists and the taxpayer may be eligible for a reduced tax rate. The net capital gain may consist of regular long-term gain, *unrecaptured § 1250 gain,* and/or *28% property gain.* Each of these gains may be taxed at a different rate.

Special Tax Rates and Capital Gain and Loss Netting Process

EXAMPLE 33

Joe is in the 35% Federal income tax bracket, with taxable income that does not exceed $425,800. He is taxed as follows.

Ordinary income	35%
Unrecaptured § 1250 gain	25%
28% gain	28%
Short-term capital gain	35%
Other long-term capital gain	15%

EXAMPLE 34

This example shows how a *net long-term capital loss* is applied. Joe sold assets resulting in a $3,000 short-term capital gain, a $1,000 collectibles capital gain, a $3,000 long-term capital gain, and an $8,000 long-term capital loss.

Step	Short-Term	28% Gain	Unrecaptured § 1250 Gain	Regular Long-Term	Comment
1	$ 3,000	$ 1,000		$ 3,000	
				(8,000)	
2	$ 3,000	$ 1,000		($ 5,000)	Net each category of gains and losses.
3		(1,000)	→	1,000	Netted because of opposite sign.
		$ –0–		($ 4,000)	
4	(3,000)	→	→	3,000	The net short-term gain is netted against the net regular long-term loss, and the remaining loss is eligible for the capital loss deduction.
	$ –0–			($ 1,000)	

Special Tax Rates and Capital Gain and Loss Netting Process

This example shows how *net short-term* and *regular long-term capital losses* are applied. Joe sold assets resulting in a $3,000 short-term capital gain, a $5,000 short-term capital loss, a $15,000 collectibles capital gain, a $7,000 collectibles loss, a $4,000 unrecaptured § 1250 gain, a $3,000 long-term capital gain, and an $8,000 long-term capital loss.

Step	Short-Term	28% Gain	Unrecaptured § 1250 Gain	Regular Long-Term	Comment
1	$ 3,000	$15,000	$4,000	$ 3,000	
	(5,000)	(7,000)		(8,000)	
2	($ 2,000)	$ 8,000	$4,000	($ 5,000)	Net each category of gains and losses.
3		(5,000)	←	5,000	Net regular long-term loss is netted against *28% gain first*. There is no remaining long-term loss to offset against the unrecaptured § 1250 gain.
		$ 3,000		$ –0–	
4	2,000 →	(2,000)			Short-term loss is netted against *28% gain* next.
	$ –0–	$ 1,000	$4,000		
		Net *28% gain*	Net *25% gain*		

If a net loss remains after applying these rules for offsetting losses, a noncorporate taxpayer may deduct up to $3,000 of that loss against ordinary income.[19] Losses in excess of $3,000 are carried over to future years where they are applied first against capital gains and then deducted up to $3,000 per year. Capital loss carryovers expire, however, when the taxpayer dies.

Use of Capital Loss Carryovers

James incurred a $10,000 loss on his only capital asset transaction in 2018. If he has no other capital asset transactions from that point on, his $10,000 loss is deducted as follows.

Year	Deduction
2018	$3,000
2019	3,000
2020	3,000
2021	1,000

Assume the same facts as in the preceding example, except that James realizes a capital gain of $4,500 in 2020. At that time, his remaining capital loss carryover is $4,000 ($10,000 − $6,000 deducted previously). Because his capital gain in 2020 (i.e., $4,500) exceeds this loss carryforward, James can deduct the entire $4,000 against that year's capital gain.

Assume the same facts as in Example 36, except that James died in late 2019. His remaining capital loss carryforward of $4,000 ($10,000 − $6,000 deducted in 2018 and 2019) expires unused.

When a taxpayer's capital loss exceeds $3,000 and derives from more than one category, it is used in the following order: first, short-term; then, *28% property*; then,

---

[19] § 1211(b)(1). Married persons filing separate returns are limited to a $1,500 deduction per tax year.

TAX PLANNING STRATEGIES Matching Gains with Losses

FRAMEWORK FOCUS: INCOME AND EXCLUSIONS

Strategy: Avoid Income Recognition.

A taxpayer who has already realized a large capital gain may want to *match this gain* with an *offsetting capital loss*. Doing so will shelter the capital gain from taxation and will also free up an asset that has declined in value. Without the capital gain, after all, the taxpayer might hesitate to sell a loss asset, because the resulting capital loss may be deductible only in $3,000 annual increments.

Similarly, a taxpayer with a large realized capital loss might use the occasion to sell some appreciated assets. Doing so would enable the taxpayer to use the capital loss immediately and at the same time realize the benefit of the asset appreciation at little or no tax cost.

On the other hand, matching capital losses and long-term capital gains means that the taxpayer utilizes the capital loss

against income that would otherwise qualify for a preferential tax rate of 0, 15, or 20 percent. If the taxpayer's ordinary income is taxed at a higher rate, he or she might prefer to deduct the loss against that higher taxed income, even on a schedule of $3,000 per year. However, the *time value of money* must be considered; a current-year deduction at 0, 15, or 20 percent might be worth more than a series of annual deductions at higher rates spread over several years.

Nontax considerations, such as investment prospects for the assets in question, are also important. Future investment prospects are often unknowable or at least highly speculative, while tax effects can be determined with relative certainty—which explains some of the late December selling activity in publicly traded securities and mutual funds.

unrecaptured § 1250 property; and finally, regular long-term. Unused losses are carried forward as follows: short-term losses carry forward as short-term losses, and long-term losses carry forward as long-term losses.

> **EXAMPLE 39**
>
> Nancy incurs a long-term capital loss of $8,500 this year, of which $3,000 is deducted against her ordinary income. The remaining $5,500 ($8,500 loss − $3,000 deducted) carries forward as a long-term capital loss.

In-depth coverage can be found on this book's companion website: www.cengage.com   **7** DIGGING DEEPER

8-5d Small Business Stock

A special *exclusion* is available to noncorporate taxpayers who derive capital gains from the sale or exchange of **qualified small business stock**.[20] Any amount not excluded from income is taxed at a maximum rate of 28 percent (as noted earlier). The exclusion amount varies, depending on when the qualified small business stock was acquired:

- 100 percent of the gain is excluded for qualified stock acquired after September 27, 2010.

- 75 percent of the gain is excluded for qualified stock acquired after February 17, 2009, and before September 28, 2010.

- 50 percent of the gain is excluded for qualified stock acquired before February 18, 2009.

As a result, the maximum effective tax rate on gains from the sale of qualified small business stock is 0 percent (28% × 0%), 7 percent (28% × 25%), or 14 percent (28% × 50%).

---

[20]§ 1202(a).

Yolanda realized a $100,000 gain on the sale of qualified small business stock that she acquired in 2008. Yolanda's marginal tax rate is 32% without considering this gain. As the stock was acquired before February 18, 2009, $50,000 of this gain (50%) is excluded from gross income, and the other $50,000 is taxed at the maximum rate of 28%. As a result, Yolanda owes Federal income tax of $14,000 on the stock sale ($50,000 × 28%), for an effective tax rate of 14% on the entire $100,000 gain.

If, instead, Yolanda acquired the stock any time after September 27, 2010, she would exclude 100% of the gain.

Given this very favorable treatment, Congress wanted to ensure that the gain exclusion only applied in very specific situations. As a result, they imposed the following restrictions:

- The stock must have been newly issued *after* August 10, 1993.
- The taxpayer must have held the stock *more than five years*.
- The issuing corporation must use at least 80 percent of its assets, determined by their value, in the *active conduct* of a trade or business.
- When the stock was issued, the issuing corporation's assets must not have exceeded $50 million, at adjusted basis, including the proceeds of the stock issuance.
- The corporation does not engage in banking, financing, insurance, investing, leasing, farming, mineral extraction, hotel or motel operations, restaurant operations, or any business whose principal asset is the *reputation or skill* of its employees (such as accounting, architecture, health, law, engineering, or financial services).

Even if each of these requirements is met, the amount of gain eligible for the exclusion is limited to the *greater* of 10 times the taxpayer's basis in the stock or $10 million per taxpayer per company,[21] computed on an aggregate basis.

Rachel purchased $100,000 of qualified small business stock when it was first issued in October 2003. This year, she sold the stock for $4 million. Her gain is $3.9 million ($4,000,000 − $100,000). Although this amount exceeds 10 times her basis ($100,000 × 10 = $1,000,000), it is *less* than $10 million. As a result, the entire $3.9 million gain is eligible for a 50% exclusion.

Transactions that fail to satisfy *any one* of the applicable requirements are taxed as capital gains (and losses) realized by noncorporate taxpayers generally.

Gains are also eligible for *nonrecognition* treatment if the sale proceeds are invested in other qualified small business stock within 60 days.[22] To the extent that the sale proceeds are not so invested, gain is recognized, but the exclusion still applies. To be eligible for this treatment, the stock sold must have been held more than six months.

Assume the same facts as in the preceding example, except that Rachel sold her stock in January 2019 and used $3.5 million of the sale proceeds to purchase other qualified small business stock one month later. Rachel's gain is recognized to the extent that the sale proceeds were not reinvested—namely, $500,000 ($4,000,000 sale proceeds − $3,500,000 reinvested). A 50% exclusion will apply, however, to the $500,000.

DIGGING DEEPER 8   In-depth coverage can be found on this book's companion website: **www.cengage.com**

---

[21]For married persons filing separately, the limitation is $5 million.   [22]§ 1045(a).

8-6 TAX TREATMENT OF CAPITAL GAINS AND LOSSES OF CORPORATE TAXPAYERS

LO.5
Describe the tax treatment of capital gains and losses for corporate taxpayers.

The treatment of a corporation's net capital gain or loss differs dramatically from the rules for noncorporate taxpayers discussed in the preceding section. Briefly, the differences are as follows.

- Net capital gains are taxed at the ordinary income tax rates.
- Capital losses offset only capital gains. Corporations cannot deduct net capital losses against other taxable income.
- There is a three-year carryback and a five-year carryforward period for net capital losses.[23] Capital loss carrybacks and carryforwards are always treated as short-term, regardless of their original nature.

Note that with the treatment given to corporate capital gains and losses, no substantive advantage results to the taxpayer. In fact, capital asset designation often can lead to a detriment (e.g., a delay or the ultimate loss of a capital loss deduction).

EXAMPLE

43

Sparrow Corporation has a $15,000 long-term capital loss for the current year and $57,000 of other taxable income. Sparrow may not offset the $15,000 long-term capital loss against its other income by taking a capital loss deduction.

The $15,000 long-term capital loss becomes a $15,000 short-term capital loss for carryback and carryforward purposes. This amount may offset capital gains in the three-year carryback period or, if not absorbed there, offset capital gains in the five-year carryforward period. Any amount remaining after this carryforward period expires is permanently lost.

8-7 SECTION 1231 ASSETS

LO.6
Distinguish § 1231 assets from ordinary and capital assets and calculate § 1231 gain or loss.

Businesses own many assets that are used in the business rather than held for resale. In financial accounting, such assets are known as "fixed assets." For example, a foundry's 15-ton stamping machine is a fixed asset. It is also a depreciable asset. The building housing the foundry is another fixed asset. Chapter 5 discussed how to depreciate such assets. Chapter 7 discussed how to determine the adjusted basis and the amount of gain or loss from their disposition. The remainder of this chapter largely deals with how to *classify* the gains and losses from the disposition of fixed assets. This classification determines the *character* of the gain or loss. Gain or loss character, along with the netting process of gains and losses, determine their taxation.

8-7a Relationship to Capital Assets

At first glance, the *classification of fixed assets* ought to be straightforward. Section 1221(a)(2) specifically excludes from the capital asset definition any property that is depreciable or that is real estate "used in a trade or business." Accordingly, the foundry's stamping machine and the building housing the foundry described earlier are not capital assets. Therefore, one would expect gains to be taxed as ordinary income and losses to be deductible as ordinary losses. Since World War II, however, certain business assets have received more favorable treatment.

Section 1231 provides that business assets held for more than one year can receive "the best of both worlds" treatment: capital gain treatment on gains and ordinary loss treatment on losses. More specifically, this provision requires that gains and losses from **§ 1231 property** be aggregated at the end of the taxable year; the *net result* is then

---

[23]§ 1212(a)(1).

TAX FACT Capital Gains for the Wealthy?

Economists and other observers of society often accuse the Code of favoring those with higher levels of income and wealth, despite a fairly substantial progressivity in the Federal income tax rate structure. The claim is that the wealthy are the primary owners of capital assets and that capital gains and qualified dividends from those assets are subject to highly favorable tax treatment. Most recently available tax return data may confirm those assertions.

Source: Based on Justin Bryan, "Individual Income Tax Returns, 2011," *SOI Bulletin*, Fall 2013, Figure F.

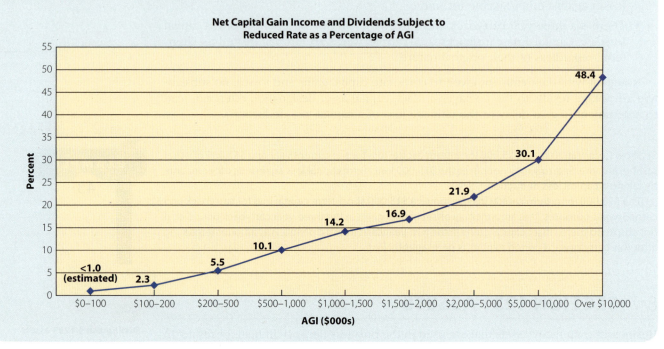

Net Capital Gain Income and Dividends Subject to Reduced Rate as a Percentage of AGI

classified as capital gain if a net gain is produced, or as ordinary loss if a net loss is produced.[24] As a result, a particular disposition's character as capital or ordinary is not determined until the taxable year has concluded and all of the taxpayer's **§ 1231 gains and losses** are tabulated.

Section 1231 Treatment

EXAMPLE 44

Brown & Co. sells a building at a $5,000 gain and equipment at a $3,000 loss. Both properties were § 1231 assets because they were used in Brown's trade or business and held for the long-term holding period (more than one year). Brown's net gain is $2,000, and that net gain *may* (depending on various recapture rules discussed later in this chapter) be treated as a long-term capital gain under § 1231.

EXAMPLE 45

Chickadee, Inc., sells equipment at a $10,000 loss and business land at a $2,000 gain. Both properties were held for more than one year and, therefore, are § 1231 assets. Chickadee's net loss of $8,000 is treated as an ordinary loss under § 1231.

---

[24]In text Sections 8-8 and 8-9, the recapture of some of the beneficial capital gain treatment through the imposition of § 1245 and § 1250 is discussed.

In-depth coverage can be found on this book's companion website: www.cengage.com   **9** DIGGING DEEPER

8-7b Property Included

Section 1231 property includes the following.

- Depreciable personal property used in a business (e.g., machinery or equipment).
- Real property used in a business (e.g., buildings and land).
- Property held for the production of income if it has been involuntarily converted (see discussion of this topic in Chapter 6).
- Certain *purchased* intangible assets (such as patents and goodwill) that are eligible for amortization.
- Certain natural resources (e.g., timber), livestock, and unharvested crops.

In-depth coverage can be found on this book's companion website: www.cengage.com   **10, 11** DIGGING DEEPER

8-7c Property Excluded

Section 1231 property generally does *not* include the following.

- Property not held more than one year.
- Business use property, where casualty losses exceed casualty gains for the taxable year. If a taxpayer has a net casualty loss, the casualty gains and losses are treated as ordinary gains and losses.
- Inventory and property held primarily for sale to customers.
- A patent, invention, model, or design (whether or not patented); a secret formula or process; certain copyrights; literary, musical, or artistic compositions, etc.; and certain U.S. government publications.
- Accounts receivable and notes receivable arising in the ordinary course of the trade or business.

8-7d Casualty or Theft and Nonpersonal Use Capital Assets

When § 1231 assets are disposed of by casualty or theft, a special netting rule is applied. For simplicity, the term *casualty* is used to mean both casualty and theft dispositions. First, the casualty gains and losses from § 1231 assets *and* the casualty gains and losses from **long-term nonpersonal use capital assets** are determined. For business entities, virtually any capital asset is a nonpersonal use capital asset, because partnerships, limited liability companies, and corporations are incapable of using assets *personally*. This classification, therefore, is most significant to individual taxpayers who might use certain capital assets as part of their daily life.

Recall from Chapter 6 that casualties and thefts are *involuntary conversions* and gains from such conversions need not be recognized if the proceeds are timely reinvested in similar property. Thus, the netting process described in the next section ignores casualty and theft gains deferred under § 1033 (see Chapter 7). Section 1231, in other words, has no effect on the amount of *realized* or recognized gain or loss. Instead, § 1231 determines the character of these gains and losses.

This special netting process for casualties and thefts does not apply to *condemnation* gains and losses. As a result, if a § 1231 asset is disposed of by condemnation, any resulting gain or loss will get § 1231 treatment.

8-7e General Procedure for § 1231 Computation

Most of the time, § 1231 gains and losses result from sales of business assets. However, as we have already discussed, disposition by casualty and/or theft can also be part of the § 1231 discussion. Consequently, the tax treatment of § 1231 gains and losses depends on the results of a complex netting procedure. When there are no casualties and/or thefts (the usual case), Step 1 (in Concept Summary 8.5 below) can be skipped and the procedure is simpler. The steps that need to be followed are presented in Concept Summary 8.5 (and in the text that follows).

Concept Summary 8.5

Section 1231 Netting Procedure

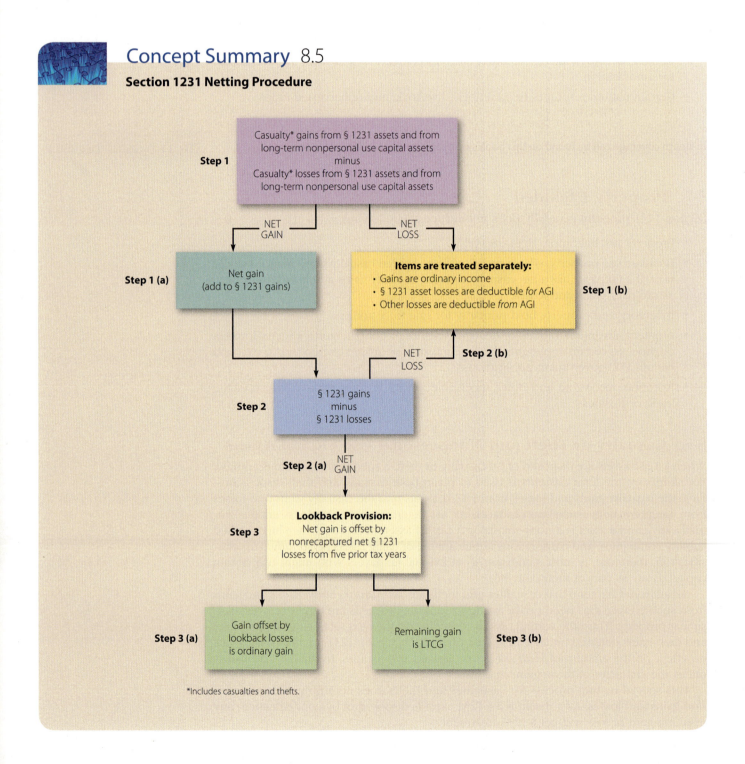

Step 1
Casualty* gains from § 1231 assets and from long-term nonpersonal use capital assets
minus
Casualty* losses from § 1231 assets and from long-term nonpersonal use capital assets

NET GAIN   NET LOSS

Step 1 (a)
Net gain
(add to § 1231 gains)

Step 1 (b)
Items are treated separately:
• Gains are ordinary income
• § 1231 asset losses are deductible *for* AGI
• Other losses are deductible *from* AGI

NET LOSS   **Step 2 (b)**

Step 2
§ 1231 gains
minus
§ 1231 losses

Step 2 (a) NET GAIN

Step 3
Lookback Provision:
Net gain is offset by nonrecaptured net § 1231 losses from five prior tax years

Step 3 (a)
Gain offset by lookback losses is ordinary gain

Step 3 (b)
Remaining gain is LTCG

*Includes casualties and thefts.

Step 1: Casualty Netting

Net all recognized long-term gains and losses from casualties of § 1231 assets and nonpersonal use capital assets. This casualty netting is beneficial because if there is a net gain, the gain may receive long-term capital gain treatment. If there is a net loss, it receives ordinary loss treatment.

a. If the casualty gains exceed the casualty losses, add the net gain to the other § 1231 gains for the taxable year.
b. If the casualty losses exceed the casualty gains, exclude all casualty losses and gains from further § 1231 computation. The casualty gains are ordinary income, and the casualty losses are deductible. For individual taxpayers, the casualty losses must be classified further. For individual taxpayers, § 1231 asset casualty losses are deductible *for* AGI, while other casualty losses may be deductible *from* AGI (see Chapter 10).

Step 2: § 1231 Netting

After adding any net casualty gain from Step 1(a) to the other § 1231 gains and losses (including *recognized* § 1231 asset condemnation gains and losses), net all § 1231 gains and losses.

a. If the gains exceed the losses, the net gain is offset by the "lookback" nonrecaptured § 1231 losses (see Step 3).
b. If the losses exceed the gains, the net loss is deducted against ordinary income. For individual taxpayers only, the gains are ordinary income, the § 1231 asset losses are deductible *for* AGI, and the other casualty losses may be deductible *from* AGI.

Section 1231 Computations

EXAMPLE 46

Falcon Management, Inc., recognized the following gains and losses this year.

Capital Gains and Losses	
Long-term capital gain	$3,000
Long-term capital loss	(400)
Short-term capital gain	1,000
Short-term capital loss	(200)

Casualties	
Gain from insurance recovery on fire loss to building, owned five years	$ 1,200
Loss from theft of computer (uninsured), owned two years	(1,000)

§ 1231 Gains and Losses from Sale of Depreciable Business Assets Held Long Term	
Asset A	$ 300
Asset B	1,100
Asset C	(500)

Gains and Losses from Sale of Depreciable Business Assets Held Short Term	
Asset D	$ 200
Asset E	(300)

continued

Falcon had no net § 1231 losses in prior tax years.

Falcon's gains and losses receive the following tax treatment. [The gains on the business building and Assets A and B are *after* any depreciation recapture (discussed later in the chapter).]

- **Step 1:** The casualty netting of the § 1231 and nonpersonal use capital assets contains two items—the $1,200 gain from the business building and the $1,000 loss from the computer. Consequently, there is a $200 net gain and that gain is treated as a § 1231 gain (added to the § 1231 gains).

- **Step 1 (a):** The gains from § 1231 transactions (Assets A and B and the § 1231 asset casualty gain) exceed the losses (Asset C) by $1,100 ($1,600 − $500). This excess is a long-term capital gain and is added to Falcon's other long-term capital gains.

- **Step 2:** Falcon's net long-term capital gain is $3,700 ($3,000 + $1,100 from § 1231 transactions − $400 long-term capital loss). Its net short-term capital gain is $800 ($1,000 − $200). The result is capital gain income of $4,500, which will be taxed at ordinary rates. If Falcon were an individual rather than a corporation, the $3,700 net long-term capital gain portion would be eligible for preferential capital gain treatment and the $800 net short-term capital gain would be taxed as ordinary income.

- Falcon treats the gain and loss from Assets D and E as ordinary gain and loss because § 1231 does not apply unless the assets have been held more than one year.[25]

Results of the Gains and Losses on Falcon's Tax Computation	
Net long-term capital gain	$3,700
Net short-term capital gain	800
Ordinary gain from sale of Asset D	200
Ordinary loss from sale of Asset E	(300)
Gross income	$4,400

Section 1231 Computations

EXAMPLE 47

Assume the same facts as in the preceding example, except that the loss from Asset C was $1,700 instead of $500.

- The treatment of the casualty gains and losses is the same.

- **Step 1 (b):** The losses from § 1231 transactions now exceed the gains by $100 ($1,700 − $1,600). As a result, the net loss is deducted in full as an ordinary loss.

- Capital gain income is $3,400 ($2,600 long-term + $800 short-term).

Results of the Gains and Losses on Falcon's Tax Computation	
Net long-term capital gain	$2,600
Net short-term capital gain	800
Net ordinary loss on Assets A, B, and C and § 1231 casualty gain	(100)
Ordinary gain from sale of Asset D	200
Ordinary loss from sale of Asset E	(300)
Gross income	$3,200

Step 3: § 1231 Lookback Provision

The net § 1231 gain from Step 2(a) is offset by the "nonrecaptured net § 1231 losses" for the five preceding taxable years.[26] For transactions in 2018, the lookback years are 2013, 2014, 2015, 2016, and 2017. Congress added this rule to § 1231 to make it difficult

---

[25]§ 1231(b)(1).   [26]§ 1231(c).

for taxpayers to group § 1231 losses in one year (and take ordinary loss treatment on these net losses) and then group § 1231 gains in a later year (and take long-term capital gain treatment on these net gains).

a. To the extent of the nonrecaptured net § 1231 loss, the current-year net § 1231 gain is ordinary income. The *nonrecaptured net § 1231 losses* are losses that have not already been used to offset net § 1231 gains in a later tax year.

b. Only the net § 1231 gain exceeding this net § 1231 loss carryforward is given long-term capital gain treatment. In this way, the **§ 1231 lookback** provision reduces the taxpayer's ability to gain a tax advantage by "timing" sales artificially. The § 1231 lookback provision does not change the amount of the gain, only its character.

Section 1231 Lookback Provision

EXAMPLE 48

Komodo Manufacturing Corporation sold used equipment and some business real estate during 2018 for a net § 1231 gain of $25,000. During 2017, Komodo had no § 1231 transactions, but in 2016, it had a net § 1231 loss of $17,000. This loss causes $17,000 of the 2018 gain to be classified as ordinary income. The remaining 2018 gain of $8,000 ($25,000 of § 1231 gain − $17,000 nonrecaptured loss) survives as a net § 1231 gain.

EXAMPLE 49

Assume the same facts as in the preceding example, except that Komodo had a net § 1231 loss of $37,000 in 2016 and a net § 1231 gain of $10,000 in 2017.

- The 2016 net § 1231 loss of $37,000 would cause the net § 1231 gain of $10,000 in 2017 to be classified as ordinary income, and $27,000 ($37,000 loss − $10,000 recaptured) would carry over to 2018.

- The remaining nonrecaptured § 1231 loss of $27,000 from 2016 completely offsets the § 1231 gain of $25,000 from 2018, making that entire gain ordinary income.

- The remaining nonrecaptured § 1231 loss from 2016 is $2,000 ($27,000 nonrecaptured § 1231 loss carried to 2018 − $25,000 recaptured in 2018). This recapture potential carries over to 2019.

8-8 SECTION 1245 RECAPTURE

LO.7

Determine when recapture provisions apply and derive their effects.

As explained earlier, when Congress determined that § 1231 was unduly generous, it chose to *recapture* some of § 1231's benefits rather than repeal that section altogether. The lookback rule just discussed recaptures some or all of the *net* § 1231 gain as ordinary income. In contrast, the depreciation recapture rules reclassify § 1231 gains from selling an *individual asset* as ordinary income.

This recapture phenomenon applies exclusively to the gain side of § 1231; the ordinary loss feature applicable to § 1231 property is not affected by the Code's recapture provisions. In essence, recapture takes part—often all—of the gain from the sale or exchange of a § 1231 asset and classifies it as *ordinary income* before the netting process of § 1231 begins. Accordingly, recaptured gain is computed *first*, without considering the other § 1231 transactions that occurred during the taxable year. This section discusses the § 1245 recapture rules, and text Section 8-9 discusses the § 1250 recapture rules.

Section 1245 requires taxpayers to treat all gain as ordinary gain unless the property is sold for more than its original cost. This result is accomplished by requiring that all gain be treated as ordinary gain to the extent of the depreciation taken on the disposed property. Section 1231 gain results only if the property is disposed of for more than its original cost. The excess of the sales price over the original cost is § 1231 gain. As described more completely in the next section, § 1245 applies primarily to personalty like machinery, trucks, and office furniture.

The Big Picture

EXAMPLE 50

Return to the facts of *The Big Picture* on p. 8-1. Recall that Alice's husband, Jeff, had purchased, for $50,000, depreciable equipment for use in his business and had deducted $35,000 of depreciation.

If Jeff sold the equipment for $45,000, his gain would be $30,000 [$45,000 amount realized − $15,000 adjusted basis ($50,000 cost − $35,000 depreciation taken)]. Section 1245 treats as ordinary income (not as § 1231 gain) any gain to the extent of depreciation taken. In this example, the entire $30,000 gain would be ordinary income.

The Big Picture

EXAMPLE 51

Continue with the facts of *The Big Picture* on p. 8-1. If Jeff sold the business equipment for $60,000, he would have a gain of $45,000 ($60,000 amount realized − $15,000 adjusted basis). The § 1245 gain would be $35,000 (equal to the depreciation taken), and the remaining gain of $10,000 (equal to the excess of the sales price over the original cost) would be § 1231 gain.

The Big Picture

EXAMPLE 52

Continue with the facts of Example 51, except that Jeff sold the equipment for $8,000 instead of $45,000. Jeff would have a loss of $7,000 ($8,000 amount realized − $15,000 adjusted basis). Because there is a loss, there is no depreciation recapture. All of the loss is § 1231 loss.

Section 1245 recapture applies to the portion of *recognized* gain from the sale or other disposition of § 1245 property that represents depreciation.[27] Section 1245 merely *classifies* gain as ordinary income; it does not change the *amount* of recognized gain. Thus, in Example 50, Jeff recaptures as ordinary income only the $30,000 of actual gain, not the entire $35,000 of depreciation taken. In other words, § 1245 recaptures the *lesser* of the depreciation taken or the gain recognized.

The method of depreciation (e.g., accelerated or straight-line) does not matter. Because all depreciation taken is potentially subject to recapture, § 1245 recapture is often referred to as *full recapture*. Any remaining gain after subtracting the amount recaptured as ordinary income will usually be § 1231 gain. The remaining gain is casualty gain, however, if the asset is disposed of in a casualty event. For example, if the equipment in Example 51 had been disposed of by casualty and the $60,000 received had been an insurance recovery, Jeff would still have a gain of $45,000, and $35,000 of that gain would still be recaptured by § 1245 as ordinary gain. The other $10,000 of gain, however, would be casualty gain.

If § 1245 property is disposed of in a transaction other than a sale, exchange, or involuntary conversion, the maximum amount recaptured is the excess of the property's fair market value over its adjusted basis. See the discussion under Exceptions to §§ 1245 and 1250 in text Section 8-10.

8-8a **Section 1245 Property**

Generally, **§ 1245 property** includes all depreciable personal property (e.g., machinery and equipment), including livestock. Buildings and their structural components usually are not § 1245 property. The following property is *also* subject to § 1245 treatment.

- Amortizable personal property such as goodwill, patents, copyrights, and leaseholds of § 1245 property.
- Professional baseball and football player contracts.

---

[27]The term *depreciation* includes § 167 depreciation, § 168 cost recovery, § 179 immediate expensing, § 168(k) additional first-year depreciation, and § 197 amortization.

- Certain depreciable tangible real property (other than buildings and their structural components) employed as an integral part of certain activities such as manufacturing and production. For example, a natural gas storage tank where the gas is used in the manufacturing process is § 1245 property.

- Single-purpose agricultural and horticultural structures and petroleum storage facilities (e.g., a greenhouse or silo).

8-8b Observations on § 1245

- In most instances, the total depreciation taken will exceed the recognized gain. It is uncommon for machinery, equipment, or furniture to sell for more than its original cost. Therefore, the disposition of § 1245 property usually results in ordinary income rather than § 1231 gain (refer to Example 50).

- Recapture applies to the total amount of depreciation allowed or allowable regardless of the depreciation method used (i.e., full recapture).

- Recapture applies regardless of the holding period of the property. Of course, the entire recognized gain would be ordinary income if the property was not held more than one year, because then § 1231 would not apply.

- Section 1245 does not apply to losses, which receive § 1231 treatment.

- Gains from the disposition of § 1245 assets may also be treated as passive activity gains (refer to Chapter 6).

8-9 SECTION 1250 RECAPTURE

Some depreciable property that is not subject to § 1245 recapture faces a separate recapture computation mechanism in § 1250. For the most part, § 1250 applies to *depreciable real property* (principally buildings and their structural components), such as apartments, office buildings, factories, stores, and warehouses. Intangible real property, such as leaseholds of § 1250 property, also is included.

Section 1250 recapture is less onerous than § 1245 recapture. Section 1250 recaptures only a property's *additional depreciation*, which is the excess of the depreciation actually deducted over the amount that would have been allowed under the straight-line method of depreciation. For this reason, § 1250 recapture is often referred to as *partial recapture*, in contrast to § 1245's full recapture.

Because § 1250 recaptures only the additional depreciation, the concept does not apply to properties that were depreciated using the straight-line method (unless they were held for one year or less). Real property placed in service *after 1986* can only be depreciated using the straight-line method, so there is *no § 1250 recapture* upon the disposition of such properties that are held for longer than one year. As a result of the use of straight-line depreciation on most real property for over 30 years, § 1250 is rendered ineffective except in very limited circumstances. However, gains on § 1250 property do *not* escape any recharacterization to ordinary as described in text Sections 8-9a and 8-9b. Finally, § 1250 does not affect the § 1231 treatment of realized losses.

Sanjay Enterprises, Ltd., acquires a residential rental building on January 1, 2017, for $300,000. Sanjay receives an offer of $450,000 for the building and sells it on December 23, 2018.

- Sanjay takes $20,909 [($300,000 × .03485) + ($300,000 × .03636 × $^{11.5}/_{12}$) = $20,909] of total depreciation for 2017 and 2018. The adjusted basis of the property is $279,091 ($300,000 − $20,909).

- Sanjay's recognized gain is $170,909 ($450,000 − $279,091).

- Since all of the depreciation is straight-line, none of the gain will be recaptured under § 1250. All of the gain survives as § 1231 gain.

Concept Summary 8.6 compares and contrasts the § 1245 and § 1250 depreciation recapture rules.

Concept Summary 8.6

Comparison of § 1245 and § 1250 Depreciation Recapture

	§ 1245	§ 1250
Property affected	All depreciable personal property, including items such as § 179 expense and § 197 amortization of intangibles such as goodwill, patents, and copyrights.	Nonresidential real property acquired after 1969 and before 1981, on which accelerated depreciation was taken. Residential rental real property acquired after 1975 and before 1987, on which accelerated depreciation was taken.
Depreciation recaptured	Potentially all depreciation taken. If the selling price is greater than or equal to the original cost, all depreciation is recaptured. If the selling price is between the adjusted basis and the original cost, only some depreciation is recaptured.	Normally, there is no depreciation recapture, but in the special situations listed above, there can be § 1250 depreciation recapture of additional depreciation (the excess of accelerated depreciation over straight-line depreciation). All depreciation taken if property disposed of in first year.
Limit on recapture	Lesser of depreciation taken or gain recognized.	Lesser of additional depreciation or gain recognized.
Treatment of gain exceeding recapture gain	Usually § 1231 gain.	Usually § 1231 gain.
Treatment of loss	No depreciation recapture; loss is usually § 1231 loss.	No depreciation recapture; loss is usually § 1231 loss.

8-9a Unrecaptured § 1250 Gain (Real Estate 25% Gain)

As noted previously in the chapter, *noncorporate taxpayers* pay tax at a maximum rate of 25 percent on their **unrecaptured § 1250 gain**. This gain represents that part of the gain on § 1250 property that is attributable to depreciation that was not recaptured by § 1250.

The procedure for computing this amount involves three distinct steps.

Step 1. Determine the part of the recognized gain that is attributable to *depreciation deductions* claimed in prior years.

Step 2. Apply § 1250 to determine the portion of the gain calculated in Step 1 that is recaptured as ordinary income (if any).

Step 3. Subtract the gain recaptured under § 1250 (Step 2) from the gain derived in Step 1. This amount is the *unrecaptured § 1250 gain*.

Recall that for property placed in service after 1986, § 1250 generally does not apply, because such property is depreciated using the straight-line method under MACRS. As a result, *all* of the gain attributable to depreciation on such assets is *unrecaptured § 1250 gain*.

EXAMPLE
54

Linda, a noncorporate taxpayer, placed two apartment buildings in service at an original cost of $100,000 each. On each building, she claimed depreciation deductions of $78,000. Thus, her adjusted basis for each building is $22,000 ($100,000 cost − $78,000 depreciation deducted). Because the buildings were depreciated using the straight-line method, there is no § 1250 recapture. She now sells these buildings for $96,000 and $110,000, respectively, and computes her gain as follows.

	Building A	Building B
Amount realized	$ 96,000	$110,000
Adjusted basis	(22,000)	(22,000)
Recognized gain	$ 74,000	$ 88,000
Depreciation recaptured by § 1250	(–0–)	(–0–)
Remaining gain	$ 74,000	$ 88,000
Unrecaptured § 1250 gain	(74,000)	(78,000)
§ 1231 gain	None	$ 10,000

8-9b Additional Recapture for Corporations

Although depreciation recapture is generally the same for all taxpayers, *corporate taxpayers* that sell depreciable real estate face an additional amount of depreciation recapture. Section 291(a)(1) requires recapture of 20 percent of the excess of the amount that would be recaptured under § 1245 (had § 1245 applied) over the amount actually recaptured under § 1250.

EXAMPLE
55

Red Corporation purchases nonresidential real property on May 1, 2003, for $800,000. Straight-line depreciation is taken in the amount of $316,239 before the property is sold on October 8, 2018, for $1.2 million.

First, determine the recognized gain:

Sales price		$1,200,000
Less: Adjusted basis—		
Cost of property	$ 800,000	
Less: Cost recovery	(316,239)	(483,761)
Recognized gain		$ 716,239

continued

Second, determine the § 1245 recapture potential. This is the lesser of $716,239 (recognized gain) or $316,239 (cost recovery claimed).

Third, determine the normal § 1250 recapture amount:

Cost recovery taken	$ 316,239
Less: Straight-line cost recovery	(316,239)
§ 1250 ordinary income	$ –0–

Fourth, because the taxpayer is a corporation, determine the additional § 291 amount:

§ 1245 recapture potential	$ 316,239
Less: § 1250 recapture amount	(–0–)
Excess § 1245 recapture potential	$ 316,239
Apply § 291 percentage	× 20%
Additional ordinary income under § 291	$ 63,248

Red Corporation's recognized gain of $716,239 is accounted for as follows:

Ordinary income under § 1250	$ –0–
Ordinary income under § 291	63,248
§ 1231 gain	652,991
Total recognized gain	$ 716,239

TAX PLANNING STRATEGIES Selling Depreciable Real Estate

FRAMEWORK FOCUS: DEDUCTIONS

Strategy: Maximize Deductible Amounts.

FRAMEWORK FOCUS: TAX RATE

Strategy: Control the Character of Income and Deductions.

A building depreciated on an accelerated method eventually generates annual allowances that are smaller than the amount the straight-line method would have produced. Beyond that "cross-over" point, the *cumulative* amount of "additional depreciation" is reduced every year the asset is used. Doing so effectively converts gain for an individual taxpayer that would otherwise be subject to § 1250 recapture into "*unrecaptured § 1250 gain*," enabling the taxpayer to save the difference between the applicable tax rate on ordinary income and 25 percent.

Continuing to use the building, however, brings forth an array of important *nontax considerations*. Each year a building is used subjects it to additional maintenance expenses to keep it in operating condition. Moreover, a building's appeal to current and prospective tenants tends to decline over time as newer structures appear offering more modern amenities, such as wireless high-speed internet access, and other conveniences. Finally, local real estate developments might produce lower resale prices that offset much, if not all, of the tax advantage obtained by holding the property for the additional time.

8-10 EXCEPTIONS TO §§ 1245 AND 1250

Recapture under §§ 1245 and 1250 does not apply to the following transactions.

8-10a Gifts

Depreciation recapture potential carries over to the donee.[28]

---

[28]§§ 1245(b)(1) and 1250(d)(1) and Reg. §§ 1.1245–4(a)(1) and 1.1250–3(a)(1).

Wade gives his daughter, Helen, § 1245 property with an adjusted basis of $1,000. The amount of recapture potential is $700. Helen uses the property in her business and claims further depreciation of $100 before selling it for $1,900.

Helen's recognized gain is $1,000 [$1,900 amount realized − $900 adjusted basis ($1,000 carry-over basis − $100 depreciation taken by Helen)], of which $800 is recaptured as ordinary income ($100 depreciation taken by Helen + $700 recapture potential carried over from Wade). The remaining gain of $200 is § 1231 gain. Even if Helen had used the property for personal purposes, the $700 recapture potential would have carried over.

8-10b Death

Although not an attractive tax planning approach, death eliminates all recapture potential.[29] Depreciation recapture potential is eliminated when property passes from a decedent to an estate or an heir.

Assume the same facts as in the preceding example, except that Helen receives the property as a result of Wade's death and the property has a fair market value of $1,700 when Wade dies. The $700 recapture potential from Wade is extinguished at his death. Helen has a basis in the property equal to its fair market value at Wade's death ($1,700).

Helen will have a $300 gain when the property is sold because the selling price ($1,900) exceeds the property's adjusted basis of $1,600 ($1,700 basis to Helen − $100 depreciation) by $300. Because of § 1245, Helen has ordinary income of $100. The remaining gain of $200 is § 1231 gain.

8-10c Charitable Transfers

Depreciation recapture potential reduces the amount of any charitable contribution deduction.[30]

Bullfinch Corporation donates to a museum § 1245 property with a fair market value of $10,000 and an adjusted basis of $7,000. Assume that the depreciation recapture potential associated with this property is $2,000 (the amount of recapture that would occur if the property were sold).

The company's charitable contribution deduction (subject to the limitations discussed in Chapter 5) is $8,000 ($10,000 fair market value − $2,000 recapture potential).

8-10d Certain Nontaxable Transactions

In certain transactions, the transferor's adjusted basis for the property carries over to the transferee. If this is the case, any depreciation recapture potential also carries over to the transferee.[31] Included in this category are the following transfers of property:

- Nontaxable incorporations under § 351 (see Chapter 12).
- Certain subsidiary liquidations under § 332 (see Chapter 13).
- Nontaxable contributions to a partnership under § 721 (see Chapter 14).
- Nontaxable corporate reorganizations.

Gain may be recognized in these transactions if boot is received. If gain is recognized, it is treated as ordinary income to the extent of the recapture potential or the recognized gain, whichever is lower.[32]

---

[29]§§ 1245(b)(2) and 1250(d)(2).

[30]§ 170(e)(1)(A) and Reg. § 1.170A–4(b)(1). In certain circumstances, § 1231 gain also reduces the amount of the charitable contribution. See § 170(e)(1)(B).

[31]§§ 1245(b)(3) and 1250(d)(3); Reg. §§ 1.1245–2(a)(4) and (c)(2), 1.1245–4(c) and 1.1250–2(d)(1) and (3).

[32]§§ 1245(b)(3) and 1250(d)(3); Reg. §§ 1.1245–4(c) and 1.1250–3(c).

8-10e Like-Kind Exchanges and Involuntary Conversions

As explained in Chapter 7, realized gain is recognized to the extent of boot received in a like-kind exchange. Realized gain is also recognized to the extent the proceeds from an involuntary conversion are not reinvested in similar property. Any recognized gain is subject to recapture as ordinary income under §§ 1245 and 1250. However, since only real property can be the subject of a like-kind exchange, § 1245 recapture is not likely because it generally only applies to tangible personal property. Section 1250 recapture is also not likely because it infrequently applies to dispositions of real property. On the other hand, unrecaptured § 1250 gain (25% gain) is likely to be present if depreciable real property was the subject of the exchange. Any remaining recapture potential carries over to the property received in the exchange.

Crane Corporation exchanges § 1245 property with an adjusted basis of $300 for § 1245 property with a fair market value of $6,000 plus $1,000 cash (boot). The exchange qualifies as a like-kind exchange under § 1031. Crane's realized gain is $6,700 ($7,000 amount realized − $300 adjusted basis of property).

Because Crane received boot of $1,000, it recognizes gain to this extent. Assuming that the recapture potential is $7,500, Crane recognizes § 1245 gain of $1,000. The remaining recapture potential of $6,500 carries over to the like-kind property received.

DIGGING DEEPER 12   In-depth coverage can be found on this book's companion website: **www.cengage.com**

8-11 REPORTING PROCEDURES

Noncapital gains and losses are reported on Form 4797 (Sales of Business Property). However, before Form 4797 is filled out, Part B of Form 4684 (Casualties and Thefts) must be completed to determine whether any casualties will enter into the § 1231 computation procedure. Recall that recognized gains from § 1231 asset casualties may be recaptured by § 1245 or § 1250. These gains do not appear on Form 4684. The § 1231 gains and nonpersonal use long-term capital gains are netted against § 1231 and nonpersonal use long-term capital losses on Form 4684 to determine whether there is a net gain to transfer to Form 4797, Part I.

DIGGING DEEPER 13   In-depth coverage can be found on this book's companion website: **www.cengage.com**

TAX PLANNING STRATEGIES Timing of Recapture

FRAMEWORK FOCUS: TAX RATE

Strategy: Shift Net Income from High-Bracket Years to Low-Bracket Years.
Shift Net Income from High-Bracket Taxpayers to Low-Bracket Taxpayers.

Because recapture is usually not triggered until the property is sold or disposed of, it may be possible to plan for recapture in low-bracket or loss years. If a taxpayer has net operating loss carryovers that are about to expire, the recognition of ordinary income from recapture may be advisable to absorb the loss carryovers.

continued

**EXAMPLE
60**

Angel Corporation has a $15,000 net operating loss carryover that will expire this year. It owns a machine that it plans to sell in the early part of next year. The expected gain of $17,000 from the sale of the machine will be recaptured as ordinary income under § 1245. Angel sells the machine before the end of this year and offsets $15,000 of the ordinary income by the net operating loss carryover.

It is also possible to postpone recapture or to shift the burden of recapture to others. For example, recapture is avoided upon the disposition of a § 1231 asset if the taxpayer replaces the property by entering into a like-kind exchange. In this instance, recapture potential is merely carried over to the newly acquired property (refer to Example 59).

Recapture can be shifted to others through the gratuitous transfer of § 1245 or § 1250 property to family members. A subsequent sale of such property by the donee will trigger recapture to the donee rather than the donor (refer to Example 56). This technique is advisable when the donee is in a lower income tax bracket than the donor.

REFOCUS ON THE BIG PICTURE

CAPITAL GAINS AND LOSSES, § 1231 GAINS AND LOSSES, AND RECAPTURE

The land, stock, franchise, and home owned by Alice are all capital assets and will produce capital gain or loss when sold. Accordingly, Alice will have a long-term capital gain of $48,000 from the sale of the land, a long-term capital gain of $6,000 from the sale of 300 shares of inherited AppleCo stock, a short-term capital loss of $4,000 from the sale of the other 200 shares of AppleCo stock, a short-term capital gain of $1,000 from the sale of the franchise, and a $125,000 long-term capital gain from the sale of the house. The treatment given to the Eagle stock will depend on the nature of its disposition (see Example 11).

For the patent, because Alice is a "holder" of the patent, it will qualify for the beneficial capital gain rate regardless of the holding period if the patent should produce income in excess of her $50,000 investment. However, if Alice loses money on the investment, she will be able to deduct only $3,000 of the loss per year against her ordinary income (assuming that there are no offsetting capital gains in the year of a sale).

The depreciable property owned by Alice's husband is § 1231 property. The $45,000 gain from the sale of the property ($60,000 amount realized − $15,000 adjusted basis) is subject to depreciation recapture under § 1245. Accordingly, the first $35,000 of the gain (up to the amount of depreciation taken on the property) is taxed as ordinary income. The remaining $10,000 is § 1231 gain and is given long-term capital gain treatment.

As a result of these transactions where the amount of gain or loss is determined, Alice and her husband have a net long-term capital gain of $189,000 ($48,000 + $6,000 + $125,000 + $10,000) and a net short-term capital loss of $3,000 ($1,000 gain − $4,000 loss). The long-term capital gain and short-term capital loss are netted, so the final result is a net capital gain of $186,000, which is taxed at the 15 or 20 percent tax rate. Alice and her husband also report $35,000 of ordinary income on their joint income tax return because of the depreciation recapture provisions. Note that the total gain reported is $221,000 ($186,000 + $35,000). This equals the sum of the individual gains and losses realized ($48,000 + $6,000 − $4,000 + $1,000 + $125,000 + $45,000). This result will occur as long as there is no net capital loss that exceeds the $3,000 limit for individual taxpayers.

What If?

What if the depreciable business property was worth only $10,000 when it was sold? In this case, there is no depreciation recapture, and the $5,000 loss is deductible as an ordinary loss under § 1231.

Suggested Readings

Paul L. Caron and Jay A. Soled, "New Prominence of Basis in Estate Planning," *Tax Notes Today*, March 28, 2016.

Tom Crice, "The Perils of Winning: Settlement Payments, Trade Secrets, and Taxes," *Practical Tax Strategies*, September 2012.

Melanie James, "Factors Influencing Reduction in Value for Potential Capital Gains Tax," *Practical Tax Strategies*, April 2014.

John Przybylski, "Managing Capital Gain to Minimize the Pain," *Practical Tax Strategies*, July 2015.

Richard L. Schmalbeck and Jay A. Soled, "Reforming Real Estate Depreciation Recapture," *Tax Notes Today*, Feburary 17, 2015.

Key Terms

Capital assets, 8-2	Long-term nonpersonal use capital assets, 8-25	Section 1231 lookback, 8-29
Capital gains, 8-2	Net capital gain, 8-19	Section 1231 property, 8-23
Capital losses, 8-2	Net capital loss, 8-19	Section 1245 property, 8-30
Collectibles, 8-17	Options, 8-7	Section 1245 recapture, 8-30
Franchise, 8-10	Patent, 8-9	Section 1250 property, 8-31
Holding period, 8-13	Qualified small business stock, 8-21	Section 1250 recapture, 8-32
Lessee, 8-11	Sale or exchange, 8-6	Short sale, 8-14
Lessor, 8-11	Section 1231 gains and losses, 8-24	Unrecaptured § 1250 gain, 8-33

Computational Exercises

1. **LO.1** Dexter owns a large tract of land and subdivides it for sale. Assume that Dexter meets all of the requirements of § 1237 and during the tax year sells the first eight lots to eight different buyers for $22,000 each. Dexter's basis in each lot sold is $15,000, and he incurs total selling expenses of $900 on each sale. What is the amount of Dexter's capital gain and ordinary income?

Digging Deeper 2. **LO.2** Shelia purchases $50,000 of newly issued Gingo Corporation bonds for $45,000. The bonds have original issue discount (OID) of $5,000. After Sheila amortized $2,300 of OID and held the bonds for four years, she sold the bonds for $48,000. What is the amount and character of her gain or loss?

3. **LO.2** Olivia wants to buy some vacant land for investment purposes. She currently cannot afford the full purchase price. Instead, Olivia pays the landowner $8,000 to obtain an option to buy the land for $175,000 anytime in the next four years. Fourteen months after purchasing the option, Olivia sells the option for $10,000. What is the amount and character of Olivia's gain or loss?

4. **LO.4** Coline has the following capital gain and loss transactions for 2018.

Short-term capital gain	$ 5,000
Short-term capital loss	(2,100)
Long-term capital gain (28%)	6,000
Long-term capital gain (15%)	2,000
Long-term capital loss (28%)	(10,500)

After the capital gain and loss netting process, what is the amount and character of Coline's gain or loss?

5. **LO.4** Elliott has the following capital gain and loss transactions for 2018.

Short-term capital gain	$ 1,500
Short-term capital loss	(3,600)
Long-term capital gain (28%)	12,000
Long-term capital gain (25%)	4,800
Long-term capital gain (15%)	6,000
Long-term capital loss (28%)	(4,500)
Long-term capital loss (15%)	(9,000)

After the capital gain and loss netting process, what is the amount and character of Elliott's gain or loss?

6. **LO.6, 7** Renata Corporation purchased equipment in 2016 for $180,000 and has taken $83,000 of regular MACRS depreciation. Renata Corporation sells the equipment in 2018 for $110,000. What is the amount and character of Renata's gain or loss?

7. **LO.6, 7** Jacob purchased business equipment for $56,000 in 2015 and has taken $35,000 of regular MACRS depreciation. Jacob sells the equipment in 2018 for $26,000. What is the amount and character of Jacob's gain or loss?

8. **LO.6, 7** Sissie owns two items of business equipment. Both were purchased in 2014 for $100,000, both have a 7-year MACRS recovery period, and both have an adjusted basis of $37,490. Sissie is considering selling these assets in 2018. One of them is worth $60,000, and the other is worth $23,000. Because both items were used in her business, Sissie simply assumes that the loss on one will offset the gain from the other and that the net gain or loss will increase or reduce her business income. What is the amount and character of Sissie's gain or loss?

9. **LO.7** An apartment building was acquired in 2009 by an individual taxpayer. The depreciation taken on the building was $123,000, and the building was sold for a $34,000 gain. What is the maximum amount of *25% gain?*

10. **LO.7** In a § 1031 like-kind exchange, Rafael exchanges a business building that originally cost $200,000. On the date of the exchange, the building given up has an adjusted basis of $85,000 and a fair market value of $110,000. Rafael pays $15,000 and receives a building with a fair market value of $125,000. What is the amount and character of Rafael's gain or loss?

11. **LO.7** Gaston Corporation distributes § 1245 property as a dividend to its shareholders. The property's fair market value is $580,000, and the adjusted basis is $560,000. In addition, the amount of the recapture potential is $55,000. What is the amount and character of Gaston's gain or loss?

Digging Deeper

Problems

12. **LO.1** An individual taxpayer sells some used assets at a garage sale. Why are none of the proceeds taxable in most situations?

Critical Thinking

13. **LO.1** Alison owns a painting that she received as a gift from her aunt 10 years ago. The aunt created the painting. Alison has displayed the painting in her home and has never attempted to sell it. Recently, a visitor noticed the painting and offered Alison $5,000 for it. If Alison decides to sell the painting, what tax issues does she face?

Critical Thinking

14. **LO.1** During the year, Eugene had the four property transactions summarized below. Eugene is a collector of antique glassware and occasionally sells a

piece to get funds to buy another. What are the amount and nature of the gain or loss from each of these transactions?

Property	Date Acquired	Date Sold	Adjusted Basis	Sales Price
Antique vase	06/18/07	05/23/18	$37,000	$42,000
Blue Growth Fund (100 shares)	12/23/09	11/22/18	22,000	38,000
Orange bonds	02/12/10	04/11/18	34,000	42,000*
Green stock (100 shares)	02/14/18	11/23/18	11,000	13,000

*The sales price included $750 of accrued interest income.

Decision Making
Critical Thinking

15. **LO.1** Rennie owns a video game arcade. He buys vintage video games from estates, often at much less than the retail value of the property. He usually installs the vintage video games in a special section of his video game arcade that appeals to players of "classic" video games. Recently, Rennie sold a classic video game that a customer "just had to have." Rennie paid $11,250 for it, owned it for 14 months, and sold it for $18,000. Rennie had suspected that this particular classic video game would be of interest to collectors; so he had it refurbished, put it on display in his video arcade, and listed it for sale on the internet. No customers in the arcade had played it other than those testing it before considering it for purchase. Rennie would like the gain on the sale of the classic video game to be a long-term capital gain. Did he achieve that objective? Why or why not?

16. **LO.1** George is the owner of numerous classic automobiles. His intention is to hold the automobiles until they increase in value and then sell them. He rents the automobiles for use in various events (e.g., antique automobile shows) while he is holding them. In 2018, he sold a classic automobile for $1.5 million. He had held the automobile for five years, and it had a tax basis of $750,000.

   a. Was the automobile a capital asset? Why or why not?

   b. Assuming a rate of return of 7%, how much would he have had to invest five years ago (instead of putting $750,000 into the car) to have had $1.5 million this year? See Appendix G for the present value factors.

Communications

17. **LO.1** Faith Godwin is a dealer in securities. She has spotted a fast-rising company and would like to buy and hold its stock for investment. The stock is currently selling for $2 per share, and Faith thinks it will climb to $40 a share within two years. Faith's coworkers have told her that there is "no way" she can get long-term capital gain treatment when she purchases stock because she is a securities dealer. Faith has asked you to calculate her potential gain and tell her whether her coworkers are right. Draft a letter to Faith responding to her request. Her address is 200 Catamon Drive, Great Falls, MT 59406.

18. **LO.1** Eagle Partners meets all of the requirements of § 1237 (subdivided realty). In 2018, Eagle Partners begins selling lots and sells four separate lots to four different purchasers. Eagle Partners also sells two contiguous lots to another purchaser. The sales price of each lot is $30,000. The partnership's basis for each lot is $15,000. Selling expenses are $500 per lot.

   a. What are the realized and recognized gain?

   b. Explain the nature of the gain (i.e., ordinary income or capital gain).

   c. Would your answers change if, instead, the lots sold to the fifth purchaser were not contiguous? If so, how?

Digging Deeper

19. **LO.1, 2** Benny purchased $400,000 of Peach Corporation face value bonds for $320,000 on November 13, 2017. The bonds had been issued with $80,000 of original issue discount because Peach was in financial difficulty in 2017. On December 3, 2018, Benny sold the bonds for $283,000 after amortizing $1,000 of the original issue discount. What are the nature and amount of Benny's gain or loss?

20. **LO.2** Carla was the owner of vacant land that she was holding for investment. She paid $2 million for the land in 2016. Raymond was an investor in vacant land. He thought Carla's land might be the site of an exit ramp from a new freeway. Raymond gave Carla $836,000 for an option on her land in 2017. The option was good for two years and gave Raymond the ability to purchase Carla's land for $4,765,000. The freeway was not approved by the government, and Raymond's option expired in 2018. Does Carla have $836,000 of long-term capital gain upon the expiration of the option? Explain.

21. **LO.2, 3, 4** Mac, an inventor, obtained a patent on a chemical process to clean old aluminum siding so that it can be easily repainted. Mac has a $50,000 tax basis in the patent. Mac does not have the capital to begin manufacturing and selling this product, so he has done nothing with the patent since obtaining it two years ago.

    Decision Making

    Critical Thinking

    Communications

    Now a group of individuals has approached him and offered two alternatives. Under one alternative, they will pay Mac $600,000 (payable evenly over the next 15 years) for the exclusive right to manufacture and sell the product. Under the other, they will form a business and contribute capital to it to begin manufacturing and selling the product; Mac will receive 20% of the company's shares of stock in exchange for all of his patent rights. Discuss which alternative is better for Mac. Share your analysis and conclusions in an e-mail to your instructor.

22. **LO.2** Blue Corporation and Fuchsia Corporation are engaged in a contract negotiation over the use of Blue's trademarked name, DateSiteForSeniors. For a one-time payment of $45,000, Blue licensed Fuchsia to use the name DateSiteForSeniors, and the license requires that Fuchsia pay Blue a royalty every time a new customer signs up on Fuchsia's website. Blue is a developer of "website ideas" that it then licenses to other companies such as Fuchsia. Did Fuchsia purchase a franchise right from Blue, or did Fuchsia purchase the name DateSiteForSeniors from Blue?

23. **LO.2** Freys, Inc., sells a 12-year franchise to Reynaldo. The franchise contains many restrictions on how Reynaldo may operate its store. For instance, Reynaldo cannot use less than Grade 10 Idaho potatoes; must fry the potatoes at a constant 410 degrees; must dress store personnel in Freys-approved uniforms; and must have a Freys sign that meets detailed specifications on size, color, and construction. When the franchise contract is signed, Reynaldo makes a noncontingent $160,000 payment to Freys. During the same year, Reynaldo pays Freys $300,000—14% of Reynaldo's sales. How does Freys treat each of these payments? How does Reynaldo treat each of the payments?

24. **LO.3** Maria held vacant land that qualified as an investment asset. She purchased the vacant land on April 10, 2014. She exchanged the vacant land for a rental house in a qualifying like-kind exchange on January 22, 2018. Maria was going to hold the house for several years and then sell it. However, she got an "offer she could not refuse" and sold it on November 22, 2018, for a substantial gain. What was Maria's holding period for the house?

25. **LO.3** Dennis sells short 100 shares of ARC stock at $20 per share on January 15, 2018. He buys 200 shares of ARC stock on April 1, 2018, at $25 per share. On May 2, 2018, Dennis closes the short sale by delivering 100 of the shares purchased on April 1.

    Digging Deeper

    a. What are the amount and nature of Dennis's loss upon closing the short sale?
    b. When does the holding period for the remaining 100 shares begin?
    c. If Dennis sells (at $27 per share) the remaining 100 shares on January 20, 2019, what will be the nature of his gain or loss?

Communications   26. **LO.1, 3, 4** Elaine Case (single with no dependents) has the following transactions in 2018:

AGI (exclusive of capital gains and losses)	$240,000
Long-term capital gain	22,000
Long-term capital loss	(8,000)
Short-term capital gain	19,000
Short-term capital loss	(23,000)

What is Elaine's net capital gain or loss? Draft a letter to Elaine describing how the net capital gain or loss will be treated on her tax return. Assume that Elaine's income from other sources puts her in the 37% bracket. Elaine's address is 300 Ireland Avenue, Shepherdstown, WV 25443.

Decision Making   27. **LO.4** Sally has taxable income of $160,000 as of November 30 of this year. She wants to sell a Rodin sculpture that has appreciated $90,000 since she purchased it six years ago, but she does not want to pay more than $15,000 of additional tax on the transaction. Sally also owns various stocks, some of which are currently worth less than their basis. How can she achieve her desired result?

28. **LO.5** Platinum, Inc., has determined its taxable income as $215,000 before considering the results of its capital gain or loss transactions. Platinum has a short-term capital loss of $24,000, a long-term capital loss of $38,000, and a short-term capital gain of $39,000. What is Platinum's taxable income? What (if any) are the amount and nature of its capital loss carryover?

Ethics and Equity   29. **LO.1, 4** The taxpayer is an antiques collector and is going to sell an antique purchased many years ago for a large gain. The facts and circumstances indicate that the taxpayer might be classified as a dealer rather than an investor in antiques. The taxpayer will save $40,000 in taxes if the gain is treated as long-term capital gain rather than as ordinary income. The taxpayer is considering the following options as ways to ensure the $40,000 tax savings.

- Give the antique to his daughter, who is an investment banker, to sell.
- Merely assume that he has held the antique as an investment.
- Exchange the antique in a like-kind exchange for another antique he wants.

One of the tax preparers the taxpayer has contacted has said that he would be willing to prepare the return under the second option. Would you? Why or why not? Evaluate the other options.

Communications   30. **LO.1, 4** In 2018, Bertha Jarow had a $28,000 loss from the sale of a personal residence. She also purchased from an individual inventor for $7,000 (and resold in two months for $18,000) a patent on a rubber bonding process. The patent had not yet been reduced to practice. Bertha purchased the patent as an investment. In addition, she had the following capital gains and losses from stock transactions:

Long-term capital loss	($ 6,000)
Long-term capital loss carryover from 2017	(12,000)
Short-term capital gain	21,000
Short-term capital loss	(7,000)

What is Bertha's net capital gain or loss? Draft a letter to Bertha explaining the tax treatment of the sale of her personal residence. Assume that Bertha's income from other sources puts her in the 24% bracket. Bertha's address is 1120 West Street, Ashland, OR 97520.

Critical Thinking   31. **LO.1, 3, 4** Bridgette is known as the "doll lady." She started collecting dolls as a child, always received one or more dolls as gifts on her birthday, never sold any dolls, and eventually owned 600 dolls. She is retiring and moving to a small apartment and has decided to sell her collection. She lists the dolls on an internet auction site and, to her great surprise, receives an offer from another doll collector of $45,000 for the entire collection. Bridgette sells the entire collection, except for five dolls she purchased during the last year. She had owned all of the dolls sold for more than a year. What tax factors should Bridgette consider in deciding how to report the sale?

32. **LO.1, 2, 4** Harriet, who is single, is the owner of a sole proprietorship. Two years ago, Harriet developed a process for preserving doughnuts that gives the doughnut a much longer shelf life. The process is not patented or copyrighted, and only Harriet knows how it works. Harriet has been approached by a company that would like to buy the process. Harriet insists that she receive a long-term employment contract with the acquiring company as well as be paid for the rights to the process. The acquiring company offers Harriet a choice of two options: (1) $650,000 in cash for the process and a 10-year covenant not to compete at $65,000 per year or (2) $650,000 in cash for a 10-year covenant not to compete and $65,000 per year for 10 years in payment for the process. Which option should Harriet accept? What is the tax effect on the acquiring company of each approach?

Digging Deeper

Decision Making

33. **LO.6** A sculpture that Korliss Kane held for investment was destroyed in a flood. The sculpture was insured, and Korliss had a $60,000 gain from this casualty. He also had a $17,000 loss from an uninsured antique vase that was destroyed by the flood. The vase was also held for investment. Korliss had no other property transactions during the year and has no nonrecaptured § 1231 losses from prior years. Both the sculpture and the vase had been held more than one year when the flood occurred (i.e., both are long-term nonpersonal use capital assets). Compute Korliss's net gain or loss, and identify how it would be treated. Also write a letter to Korliss, explaining the nature of the gain or loss. Korliss's address is 2367 Meridian Road, Hannibal, MO 63401.

Communications

34. **LO.6** Harold, a CPA, has a new client who recently moved to town. Harold prepares the client's current-year tax return, which shows a net § 1231 gain. Harold calls the client to request copies of the returns for the preceding five years to determine if there are any § 1231 lookback losses. The client says that the returns are "still buried in the moving mess somewhere" and cannot be found. The client also says that he does not remember any § 1231 net losses on the prior year returns. What should Harold do? Justify your answer.

Ethics and Equity

35. **LO.6** Geranium, Inc., has the following net § 1231 results for each of the years shown. What is the nature of the net gain in 2017 and 2018?

Tax Year	Net § 1231 Loss	Net § 1231 Gain
2013	$18,000	
2014	33,000	
2015	42,000	
2016		$41,000
2017		30,000
2018		41,000

36. **LO.6** Jinjie owns two parcels of land (§ 1231 assets). One parcel can be sold at a loss of $60,000, and the other parcel can be sold at a gain of $70,000. Jinjie has no nonrecaptured § 1231 losses from prior years. The parcels could be sold at any time because potential purchasers are abundant. Jinjie has a $35,000 short-term capital loss carryover from a prior tax year and no capital assets that could be sold to generate long-term capital gains. Both land parcels have been held more than one year. What should Jinjie do based upon these facts? (Assume that tax rates are constant, and ignore the present value of future cash flows.)

Decision Making

37. **LO.6, 7** Siena Industries (a sole proprietorship) sold three § 1231 assets on October 10, 2018. Data on these property dispositions are as follows.

Asset	Cost	Acquired	Depreciation	Sold for
Rack	$100,000	10/10/14	$62,000	$85,000
Forklift	35,000	10/16/15	23,000	5,000
Bin	87,000	03/12/17	34,000	60,000

a. Determine the amount and the character of the recognized gain or loss from the disposition of each asset.

b. Assuming that Siena has no nonrecaptured net § 1231 losses from prior years, analyze these transactions and determine the amount (if any) that will be treated as a long-term capital gain.

Communications 38. **LO.6, 7** On December 1, 2016, Lavender Manufacturing Company (a corporation) purchased another company's assets, including a patent. The patent was used in Lavender's manufacturing operations; $49,500 was allocated to the patent, and it was amortized at the rate of $275 per month. On July 30, 2018, Lavender sold the patent for $95,000. Twenty months of amortization had been taken on the patent. What are the amount and nature of the gain Lavender recognizes on the disposition of the patent? Write a letter to Lavender, discussing the treatment of the gain. Lavender's address is 6734 Grover Street, Boothbay Harbor, ME 04538. The letter should be addressed to Bill Cubit, Controller.

39. **LO.6, 7** Larry is the sole proprietor of a trampoline shop. During 2018, the following transactions occurred.

- Unimproved land adjacent to the store was condemned by the city on February 1. The condemnation proceeds were $15,000. The land, acquired in 1986, had an allocable basis of $40,000. Larry has additional parking across the street and plans to use the condemnation proceeds to build his inventory.

- A truck used to deliver trampolines was sold on January 2 for $3,500. The truck was purchased on January 2, 2014, for $6,000. On the date of sale, the adjusted basis was zero.

- Larry sold an antique rowing machine at an auction. Net proceeds were $4,900. The rowing machine was purchased as used equipment 17 years ago for $5,200 and is fully depreciated.

- Larry sold an apartment building for $300,000 on September 1. The rental property was purchased on September 1, 2015, for $150,000 and was being depreciated over a 27.5-year MACRS life using the straight-line method. At the date of sale, the adjusted basis was $124,783.

- Larry's personal yacht was stolen on September 5. The yacht had been purchased in August at a cost of $25,000. The fair market value immediately preceding the theft was $19,600. Larry was insured for 50% of the original cost, and he received $12,500 on December 1.

- Larry sold a Buick on May 1 for $9,600. The vehicle had been used exclusively for personal purposes. It was purchased on September 1, 2014, for $20,800.

- Larry's trampoline stretching machine (owned two years) was stolen on May 5, but the business's insurance company will not pay any of the machine's value because Larry failed to pay the insurance premium. The machine had a fair market value of $8,000 and an adjusted basis of $6,000 at the time of theft.

- Larry had AGI of $102,000 from sources other than those described above.

- Larry has no nonrecaptured § 1231 lookback losses.

a. For each transaction, what are the amount and nature of recognized gain or loss?

b. What is Larry's 2018 AGI?

40. **LO.6, 7** A business building owned by an individual taxpayer on which straight-   *Digging Deeper*
line depreciation of $13,000 was taken is sold on the installment basis for
$100,000 with $20,000 down and four yearly installments of $20,000 plus interest.
The adjusted basis for the building is $35,000 at the time of the sale. The building
had been held for more than 12 months. What are the amount and nature of the
recognized gain?

41. **LO.7** Nicholas owns business equipment with a $155,000 adjusted basis; he paid
$200,000 for the equipment, and it is currently worth $173,000. Nicholas dies
suddenly, and his son Alvin inherits the property. What is Alvin's basis for the property? What happens to the § 1245 depreciation recapture potential?

BRIDGE DISCIPLINE

1. Using an online research service, find the audited financial statements of a major
   U.S. corporation.
   a. List some of the items that the corporation reports as having different treat-
      ment for tax and financial accounting purposes. These items often are men-
      tioned in the footnotes to the statements.
   b. List two or more such items that seem to increase the taxpayer's after-tax
      income and two or more that seem to decrease it.

Research Problems

**Note: Solutions to the Research Problems can be prepared by using the Thomson
Reuters Checkpoint™ online tax research database, which accompanies this
textbook. Solutions can also be prepared by using research materials found in a
typical tax library.**

THOMSON REUTERS
CHECKPOINT™

Research Problem 1. Clyde had worked for many years as the chief executive of Red
Industries, Inc., and had been a major shareholder. Clyde and the company had a
falling out, and Clyde was terminated. Clyde and Red executed a document under
which Clyde's stock in Red would be redeemed and Clyde would agree not to compete against Red in its geographic service area. After extensive negotiations between
the parties, Clyde agreed to surrender his Red stock in exchange for $600,000. Clyde's
basis in his shares was $143,000, and he had held the shares for 17 years. The agree-
ment made no explicit allocation of any of the $600,000 to Clyde's agreement not
to compete against Red. How should Clyde treat the $600,000 payment on his 2018
tax return?

Research Problem 2. Ali owns 100 shares of Brown Corporation stock. He purchased   *Decision Making*
the stock at five different times and at five different prices per share as indicated.

Share Block	Number of Shares	Per-Share Price	Purchase Date
A	10	$60	10/10/2000
B	20	20	08/11/2001
C	15	15	10/24/2002
D	35	30	04/23/2003
E	20	25	07/28/2003

On April 28, 2018, Ali will sell 40 shares of Brown stock for $40 per share. All of
Ali's shares are held by his stockbroker. The broker's records track when the shares
were purchased. May Ali designate the shares he sells? If so, which shares should

he sell? Assume that Ali wants to maximize his gain because he has a capital loss carryforward.

Research Problem 3. Siva Nathaniel owns various plots of land in Fulton County, Georgia. He acquired the land at various times during the last 20 years. About every fourth year, Siva subdivides into lots one of the properties he owns. He then has water, sewer, natural gas, and electricity hookups put in each lot and paves new streets. Siva has always treated his sales of such lots as sales of capital assets. His previous tax returns were prepared by an accountant whose practice you recently purchased. Has the proper tax treatment been used on the prior tax returns? Explain.

Partial list of research aids:
§§ 1221 and 1237.
Jesse W. and Betty J. English, 65 TCM 2160, T.C.Memo. 1993–111.

Use internet tax resources to address the following questions. Look for reliable websites and blogs of the IRS and other government agencies, media outlets, businesses, tax professionals, academics, think tanks, and political outlets.

Research Problem 4. Find a website, other than the IRS website, that discusses the taxation of short sales of securities.

Research Problem 5. Perform a Google search to find information about capital gains tax rates worldwide (and across U.S. states). Try searching for "capital gains rate by country (state)." What jurisdiction has the highest capital gains tax rate? What U.S. states have high capital gains tax rates?

Becker CPA Review Questions

1. A gain on the sale of which of the following assets will not result in a capital gain?
   a. Stock in a public company
   b. A home used as a personal residence
   c. Goodwill of a corporation
   d. Inventory of a corporation

2. Conner purchased 300 shares of Zinco stock for $30,000 in year 1. On May 23, year 6, Conner sold all the stock to his daughter Alice for $20,000, its then fair market value. Conner realized no other gain or loss during year 6. On July 26, year 6, Alice sold the 300 shares of Zinco for $25,000. What was Alice's recognized gain or loss on her sale?
   a. $0
   b. $5,000 long-term gain
   c. $5,000 short-term loss
   d. $5,000 long-term loss

3. Brad and Angie are married and file a joint return. For year 14, they had income from wages in the amount of $100,000 and had the following capital transactions to report on their income tax return:

Carryover of capital losses from year 13	$200,000
Loss on sale of stock purchased in March year 14, sold on October 10, year 14, and repurchased on November 2, year 14	20,000
Gain on the sale of stock purchased 5 years ago and sold on March 14, year 14	15,000
Gain on the sale of their personal residence (all qualifications have been met for the maximum allowable gain exclusion)	675,000
Loss on the sale of their personal automobile	10,000
Gain on the sale of their personal furniture	5,000
Loss on the sale of investment property (land only)	150,000

What is the amount of capital loss carryover to year 15?

a. ($155,000)   c. ($132,000)
b. ($152,000)   d. ($125,000)

4. A piece of depreciable machinery is sold. It has been held for three years and qualifies as Section 1231 property. The selling price is greater than the adjusted basis but less than the original purchase price. Which statement below is correct?

   a. All of the gain will be subject to Section 1245 recapture.
   b. Only a portion of the gain will be subject to Section 1245 recapture.
   c. None of the gain will be subject to Section 1245 recapture.
   d. Section 1245 recapture will not apply because there is a loss on the sale.

5. Wally, Inc., sold the following three personal property assets in year 6:

Asset	Purchase Date	Cost	Accumulated Depreciation	Selling Price
A	5/1/year 3	$5,000	$3,000	$2,300
B	8/13/year 4	1,200	500	2,000
C	2/18/year 4	3,800	1,800	1,500

What is Wally's net Section 1231 gain or loss in year 6?

a. $500 loss   c. $800 gain
b. $300 gain   d. $1,600 gain

6. Net Section 1231 losses are:

   a. Deducted as a capital loss against other capital gains and nothing against ordinary income.
   b. Deducted as a capital loss against other capital gains and up to $3,000 against ordinary income.
   c. Not allowed as a deduction.
   d. Deducted as an ordinary loss.

7. Section 1245 recapture applies to which of the following?

   a. Section 1231 real property sold at a gain with accumulated depreciation in excess of straight line.
   b. Section 1231 personal property sold at a gain with accumulated depreciation.
   c. Section 1231 real property sold at a gain with accumulated depreciation equal to straight-line depreciation.
   d. Section 1231 personal property sold at a loss.

8. Section 1250 recapture applies to which of the following?

   a. Section 1231 real property sold at a gain with accumulated depreciation in excess of straight line.
   b. Section 1231 personal property sold at a gain with accumulated depreciation.
   c. Section 1231 real property sold at a gain with accumulated depreciation equal to straight-line depreciation.
   d. Section 1231 personal property sold at a loss.

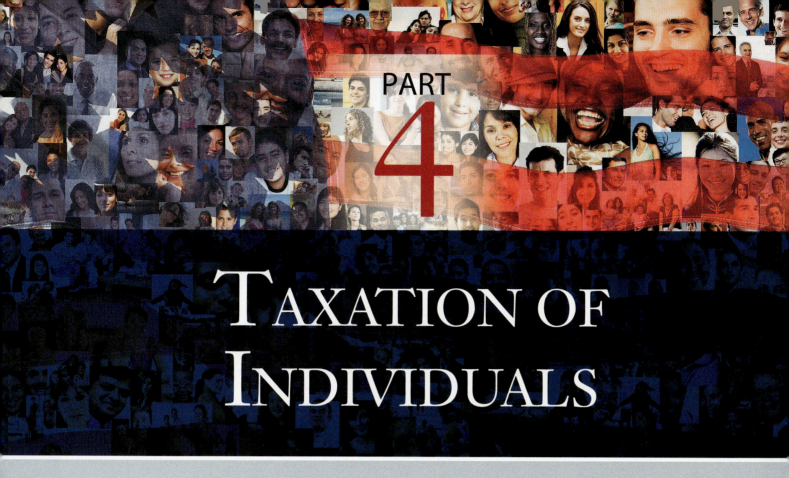

PART 4

TAXATION OF INDIVIDUALS

CHAPTER **9**

Individuals as the Taxpayer

CHAPTER **10**

Individuals: Income, Deductions, and Credits

CHAPTER **11**

Individuals as Employees and Proprietors

Part 4 focuses on numerous tax concepts and rules for individuals. The topics are unique to individual taxpayers, including filing status, itemized deductions, sole proprietorship provisions, and the kiddie tax. Then we discuss various education credits, the earned income credit, and relevant provisions of the Affordable Care Act.

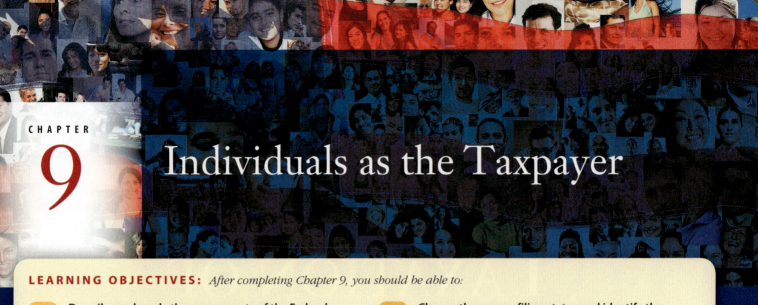

CHAPTER

9

Individuals as the Taxpayer

LEARNING OBJECTIVES: *After completing Chapter 9, you should be able to:*

LO.1 Describe and apply the components of the Federal income tax formula for individuals.

LO.2 Explain the standard deduction and evaluate its choice in arriving at taxable income.

LO.3 Explain the rules for determining dependency status.

LO.4 Choose the proper filing status and identify the related filing requirements.

LO.5 Demonstrate the proper procedures for determining the tax liability.

LO.6 Identify and report kiddie tax situations.

CHAPTER OUTLINE

9-1 The Individual Tax Formula, 9-2
    9-1a   Components of the Tax Formula, 9-2

9-2 Standard Deduction, 9-6
    9-2a   Basic and Additional Standard Deduction, 9-7
    9-2b   Special Limitations on the Standard Deduction for Dependents, 9-8

9-3 Dependency Status, 9-9
    9-3a   Qualifying Child, 9-9
    9-3b   Qualifying Relative, 9-11
    9-3c   Other Rules for Determining Dependency Status, 9-14
    9-3d   Comparison of Categories for Dependency Status, 9-15

9-4 Filing Status and Filing Requirements, 9-16
    9-4a   Filing Status, 9-16
    9-4b   Filing Requirements, 9-20

9-5 Tax Determination, 9-21
    9-5a   Tax Table Method, 9-21
    9-5b   Tax Rate Schedule Method, 9-21
    9-5c   Computation of Net Taxes Payable or Refund Due, 9-22
    9-5d   Kiddie Tax—Unearned Income of Dependent Children, 9-23

9-6 Additional Taxes for Certain Individuals, 9-24
    9-6a   Alternative Minimum Tax, 9-25
    9-6b   Net Investment Income Tax and Additional Medicare Tax, 9-27

9-7 Tax Return Filing Procedures, 9-28
    9-7a   Selecting the Proper Form, 9-28
    9-7b   The E-File Approach, 9-28
    9-7c   When and Where to File, 9-29
    9-7d   Modes of Payment, 9-29

TAX TALK *I'm proud of paying taxes in the United States. The only thing is—I could be just as proud for half the money.* —ARTHUR GODFREY

ATNOYDOR/GETTY IMAGES

A DIVIDED HOUSEHOLD

Polly maintains a household in which she lives with her unemployed husband (Nick), stepdaughter (Paige), and a family friend (Maude). She provides more than half of the support for both Paige and Maude. Maude was fatally injured in an automobile accident in February, and Polly paid for her hospitalization and funeral expenses. Paige, an accomplished gymnast, graduated from high school last year. Paige has a part-time job but spends most of her time training and looking for an athletic scholarship to the "right" college. In March, Nick left for parts unknown and has not been seen or heard from since. Polly was more surprised than distressed over Nick's unexpected departure.

Based on these facts, what are Polly's income tax concerns for the current year?

Read the chapter and formulate your response.

The individual income tax accounts for approximately 40 percent of Federal revenue, compared with approximately 8 percent for the corporate income tax. The tax laws affecting individuals have become increasingly complex in recent years as the government adds new laws to protect or increase this important source of revenue. Taxpayers respond to each new tax act with techniques to exploit loopholes, and the government responds with loophole-closing provisions, making the individual income tax law even more complex.[1]

Describe and apply the components of the Federal income tax formula for individuals.

9-1 THE INDIVIDUAL TAX FORMULA

Individuals are subject to Federal income tax based on taxable income. This chapter explains generally how taxable income and the income tax of an individual taxpayer are determined. To compute taxable income, it is necessary to understand the tax formula in Concept Summary 9.1.

Concept Summary 9.1

Individual Income Tax Formula

Income (broadly defined)	$xx,xxx
Less: Exclusions	(x,xxx)
Gross income	$xx,xxx
Less: Deductions *for* adjusted gross income	(x,xxx)
Adjusted gross income (AGI)	$xx,xxx
Less: The greater of—	
Total itemized deductions *or* standard deduction	(x,xxx)
Less: Personal and dependency exemptions*	(x,xxx)
Less: Deduction for qualified business income**	(x,xxx)
Taxable income	$xx,xxx
Tax on taxable income (see Tax Tables or Tax Rate Schedules)	$ x,xxx
Less: Tax credits (including income taxes withheld and prepaid)	(xxx)
Tax due (or refund)	$ xxx

  *Exemption deductions are not allowed from 2018 through 2025.

** Only applies from 2018 through 2025 (see text Section 11-4d).

Although this formula is rather simple, determining an individual's taxable income can be quite complex because of the numerous provisions that govern the determination of gross income and allowable deductions.

After taxable income is computed, an individual's filing status must be determined because different tax rates apply for single, married, and heads of household taxpayers. The individual tax rate structure is progressive, with rates for 2018 ranging from 10 percent to 37 percent.[2] For comparison, the lowest rate structure, which was in effect from 1913 to 1915, ranged from 1 to 7 percent, and the highest, in effect during 1944 to 1945, ranged from 23 to 94 percent.

Once the individual's tax has been computed, prepayments and credits are subtracted to determine whether the taxpayer owes additional tax or is entitled to a refund.

9-1a Components of the Tax Formula

Before the components of the tax formula are covered in detail, a brief discussion of each is helpful.

---

[1]Refer to the discussion of tax complexity in Chapter 1.

[2]The current Tax Rate Schedules that apply to individuals are shown on the inside front cover of the text.

Income (Broadly Defined)

As discussed in Chapter 4, "income" is broadly defined and includes all of the taxpayer's income, both taxable and nontaxable. In general, the courts have defined "income" as any realized increase in wealth.[3] Income does not include a return of capital, receipt of borrowed funds, or unrealized appreciation in the value of a taxpayer's assets.

EXAMPLE
1

When Dan's apartment lease ends, he decides to buy a house. Consequently, the owner of the apartment building returns to Dan the $600 damage deposit he previously made. To make a down payment on the house, Dan sells stock for $50,000 (original cost of $28,000) and borrows $200,000 from a bank.

Only the $22,000 gain from the sale of the stock is income to Dan. The $600 damage deposit and the $28,000 cost of the stock are a return of capital. The $200,000 bank loan is not income as Dan has an obligation to repay that amount (the loan does not increase his wealth).

Gross Income

The Internal Revenue Code defines gross income broadly as "except as otherwise provided …, all income from whatever source derived."[4] The "except as otherwise provided" phrase refers to exclusions. Gross income includes, but is not limited to, the items in Exhibit 9.1.

Exclusions

For various reasons, Congress has chosen to exclude certain types of income from the income tax base. The principal income exclusions are listed in Exhibit 9.2. The exclusions most commonly encountered by individual taxpayers (employee fringe benefits) are discussed in detail in Chapter 11.

EXHIBIT 9.1	Partial List of Gross Income Items
Alimony received (related to divorces before 2019)	Interest
Bargain purchase from employer	Jury duty fees
Bonuses	Partnership income
Breach of contract damages	Pensions
Business income	Prizes (with some exceptions)
Commissions	Professional fees
Compensation for services	Punitive damages
Debts forgiven (with some exceptions)	Rents
Dividends	Rewards
Embezzled funds	Royalties
Farm income	Salaries
Fees	Severance pay
Gains from illegal activities	Strike and lockout benefits
Gains from sale of property	Tips and gratuities
Gambling winnings	Treasure trove (found property)
Hobby receipts	Wages

---

[3]*Comm. v. Glenshaw Glass Co.*, 55–1 USTC ¶9308, 47 AFTR 162, 348 U.S. 426 (USSC, 1955).

[4]§ 61(a).

EXHIBIT 9.2	**Partial List of Exclusions from Gross Income**

Accident and health insurance proceeds

Alimony received (related to divorces after 2018)

Annuity payments (to the extent proceeds represent a recovery of the taxpayer's investment)

Child support payments

Damages for personal injury or sickness

Fringe benefits of employees:

- Educational assistance payments provided by employer
- Employer-provided accident and health insurance
- Group term life insurance (for coverage up to $50,000)
- Meals and lodging (if furnished for convenience of employer)
- Tuition reductions for employees of educational institutions
- Miscellaneous benefits

Gains from sale of principal residence (subject to statutory ceiling)

Gifts and inheritances received

Interest from state and local bonds

Life insurance paid upon death of insured

Scholarship grants (to a limited extent)

Social Security benefits (to a limited extent)

Workers' compensation benefits

EXAMPLE 2

Beth received the following amounts during the year:

Salary	$30,000
Interest on savings account	900
Gift from her aunt	10,000
Prize won in state lottery	1,000
Alimony from ex-husband (divorced in 2015)	12,000
Child support from ex-husband	6,000
Damages for injury in auto accident	25,000
Ten $50 bills in an unmarked envelope found in an airport lounge (airport authorities could not locate anyone who claimed ownership)	500
Federal income tax refund for last year's tax overpayment	120

In addition, her stock investments increased in value by $5,000.

Review Exhibits 9.1 and 9.2 to determine the amount Beth must include in the computation of taxable income and the amount she may exclude. Then check your answer in footnote 5.[5]

Deductions *for* Adjusted Gross Income

Individual taxpayers have two categories of deductions: (1) deductions *for* adjusted gross income (deductions from gross income to arrive at adjusted gross income) and (2) deductions *from* adjusted gross income. Deductions *for* adjusted gross income (AGI) include the following:[6]

- Ordinary and necessary expenses incurred in a trade or business.
- Part of the self-employment tax paid.

---

[5]Beth must include $44,400 in computing taxable income ($30,000 salary + $900 interest + $1,000 lottery prize + $12,000 alimony + $500 found property). She can exclude $41,000 ($10,000 gift from aunt + $6,000 child support + $25,000 damages). The $120 Federal income tax refund is excluded because it represents an adjustment (i.e., overpayment) of a nondeductible expenditure made in the previous year. The unrealized gain of $5,000 on the stock held for investment is not included in gross income.

[6]See § 62 for a comprehensive list of items that are deductible *for* AGI. Deductions *for* AGI are sometimes known as *above-the-line* deductions because on the tax return, they are taken before the "line" designating AGI.

- Alimony payments related to divorces prior to 2019.
- Certain payments to traditional Individual Retirement Accounts and Health Savings Accounts.
- The capital loss deduction (limited to $3,000).

The effect on AGI of deductions *for* AGI is illustrated below.

Mason, age 45, earned a salary of $78,000 in the current year. He contributed $4,000 to his traditional Individual Retirement Account (IRA), sold stock held as an investment for a short-term capital loss of $2,000, and paid $4,600 in alimony to his ex-wife (the couple divorced in 2016). His AGI is determined as follows:

Gross income		
Salary		$ 78,000
Less: Deductions *for* AGI		
IRA contribution	$4,000	
Capital loss	2,000	
Alimony paid	4,600	(10,600)
AGI		$ 67,400

EXAMPLE 3

Deductions *from* Adjusted Gross Income

As a general rule, personal expenses are not allowed as deductions in computing taxable income; however, Congress allows specified personal expenses as deductions *from* AGI (commonly referred to as **itemized deductions**). Itemized deductions are discussed in Chapter 10.

Distinguishing deductions for AGI and itemized deductions is important for at least two reasons. First, AGI is an important subtotal that serves as the basis for computing percentage limitations on certain itemized deductions such as medical expenses, charitable contributions, and certain casualty losses. For example, medical expenses are deductible only to the extent they exceed 7.5 percent of AGI, and charitable contribution deductions may not exceed 50 percent of AGI (60 percent for certain cash donations). These limitations might be described as a percentage *floor* under the medical expense deduction and a percentage *ceiling* on the charitable contribution deduction. Thus, whether a deduction is available for AGI or from AGI affects the amount of other deductions.

Second, as discussed further below, taxpayers may choose to deduct the greater of their total itemized deductions or the standard deduction. Therefore, even though a taxpayer may incur an expense that qualifies as an itemized deduction, it may not reduce taxable income if total itemized deductions do not exceed the standard deduction. Expenses that qualify as deductions for AGI, however, are available to reduce taxable income whether the taxpayer uses the standard deduction or not. In addition, the deduction for qualified business income added by the Tax Cuts and Jobs Act (TCJA) of 2017 is deductible from AGI whether or not the taxpayer itemizes deductions or claims the standard deduction (see text Section 11-4d).

Assume the same facts as in Example 3, except that Mason also had unreimbursed medical expenses of $8,000. Medical expenses may be included in his itemized deductions to the extent they exceed 7.5% of AGI. In computing his itemized deductions, Mason may include medical expenses of $2,945 [$8,000 medical expenses − $5,055 (7.5% × $67,400 AGI)]

EXAMPLE 4

Standard Deduction

In lieu of claiming itemized deductions, taxpayers will use the **standard deduction**. As discussed later in the chapter, the standard deduction amount varies depending on filing status, age, and blindness. Each year, as required by law, the IRS adjusts the standard deduction amount for the effects of inflation.

Personal and Dependency Exemptions

Prior to 2018, deductions for personal and dependency exemptions were also allowed. A deduction, equal to the exemption allowance amount, was allowed for each taxpayer as well as for each of the taxpayer's dependents. Under the TCJA of 2017, exemption deductions are suspended from 2018 through 2025.

Qualified Business Income Deduction

From 2018 through 2025, a deduction for qualified business income is allowed. In general, this deduction relates to business income generated by noncorporate businesses (e.g., sole proprietorships, S corporations, partnerships, and LLCs) and included in the taxpayer's individual taxable income. Generally, the deduction allowed is the *lesser* of (1) 20 percent of qualified business income or (2) 20 percent of modified taxable income. This deduction is discussed further in Chapter 11.

Taxable Income

The determination of taxable income is illustrated in Example 5.

EXAMPLE
5

Grace, age 25, is single and has her disabled and dependent mother living with her. This qualifies Grace for head-of-household filing status and a standard deduction of $18,000 in 2018. In 2018, Grace earned a $44,000 salary as a high school teacher. Her other income consisted of $1,100 interest on a certificate of deposit (CD) and $500 of nontaxable interest on municipal bonds she had received as a graduation gift in 2012. During 2018, she sold stock that resulted in a deductible capital loss of $1,000. Her itemized deductions are $11,000. Grace's taxable income for the year is computed as follows:

Income (broadly defined)		
Salary		$44,000
Interest on a CD		1,100
Interest on municipal bonds		500
Total income		$45,600
Less: Exclusion—		
Interest on municipal bonds		(500)
Gross income		$45,100
Less: Deduction *for* adjusted gross income—capital loss		(1,000)
Adjusted gross income (AGI)		$44,100
Less: The *greater* of—		
Total itemized deductions	$11,000	
or the standard deduction for head of household	18,000	(18,000)
Less: Deduction for qualified business income		(–0–)
Taxable income		$26,100

The exclusion of $500 (i.e., interest from municipal bonds) is subtracted in determining gross income, while the capital loss of $1,000 is classified as a deduction *for* AGI. Grace chose to itemize her deductions *from* AGI as they exceed the standard deduction (see Exhibit 9.3). Grace's income tax is determined later in this chapter in Example 36.

LO.2

Explain the standard deduction and evaluate its choice in arriving at taxable income.

9-2 STANDARD DEDUCTION

The effect of the standard deduction is to exempt part of a taxpayer's income from Federal income tax liability, making it available to pay for basic living expenses before any income tax is imposed. The allowance of a standard deduction also reduces the number of taxpayers who itemize, reducing compliance complexity for taxpayers as well as the audit effort required of the IRS.

EXHIBIT 9.3	Basic Standard Deduction Amounts		
Filing Status		**2017**	**2018**
Single		$ 6,350	$12,000
Married, filing jointly		12,700	24,000
Surviving spouse		12,700	24,000
Head of household		9,350	18,000
Married, filing separately		6,350	12,000

9-2a Basic and Additional Standard Deduction

The standard deduction is the sum of two components: the *basic* standard deduction and the *additional* standard deduction.[7] Exhibit 9.3 lists the basic standard deduction allowed for taxpayers in each filing status. All taxpayers allowed a *full* standard deduction are entitled to the applicable amount listed in Exhibit 9.3. The standard deduction amounts are subject to adjustment for inflation each year.

Certain taxpayers are not allowed to claim *any* standard deduction, and the standard deduction is *limited* for others. These provisions are discussed later in the chapter.

A taxpayer who is age 65 or over *or* blind in 2018 qualifies for an *additional standard deduction* of $1,300 or $1,600, depending on filing status (see amounts in Exhibit 9.4). Two additional standard deductions are allowed for a taxpayer who is age 65 or over *and* blind. The additional standard deduction provisions also apply for a qualifying spouse who is age 65 or over or blind, but a taxpayer may not claim an additional standard deduction for a dependent.

To determine whether to itemize, the taxpayer compares the *total* standard deduction (the sum of the basic standard deduction and any additional standard deductions) with total itemized deductions. Taxpayers are allowed to deduct the *greater* of itemized deductions or the standard deduction. The choice is elective and may be changed each year. For example, a taxpayer who buys a home may change from using the standard deduction to itemizing deductions (because of mortgage interest and property tax deductions). The taxpayer's age can also make a difference. For 2018, it is expected that about 87 percent of individual tax returns filed will use the standard deduction (rather than itemized deductions). Prior to changes made by the TCJA of 2017, about 69 percent of individual filers used the standard deduction.

Standard versus Itemized Deduction

Juan and Lisa Fernandez have been renting an apartment while saving money for a down payment on a house. Early in 2018, they purchased a house. Interest paid on their home mortgage in 2018 amounted $9,800, and they paid property taxes of $5,500. In addition, they had charitable contributions of $6,000 and paid state income taxes of $4,000. In total, their itemized deductions amount to $25,300, and they will compute their taxable income using this amount rather than the $24,000 standard deduction.

EXAMPLE 6

Prior to 2018, Sara, who is single, had always chosen to itemize. In 2018, however, she reaches age 65. Her itemized deductions for 2018 are $6,500, but her total standard deduction is $13,600 [$12,000 (basic standard deduction) + $1,600 (additional standard deduction)].

Sara should compute her taxable income for 2018 using the standard deduction ($13,600) because it exceeds her itemized deductions ($6,500).

EXAMPLE 7

In-depth coverage can be found on this book's companion website: www.cengage.com   **1** DIGGING DEEPER

---

[7]§ 63(c)(1).

EXHIBIT 9.4	Amount of Each Additional Standard Deduction		
Filing Status		**2017**	**2018**
Single		$1,550	$1,600
Married, filing jointly		1,250	1,300
Surviving spouse		1,250	1,300
Head of household		1,550	1,600
Married, filing separately		1,250	1,300

9-2b Special Limitations on the Standard Deduction for Dependents

Special rules apply to the standard deduction of an individual who can be claimed as a dependent on another person's tax return.

When filing his or her own tax return, a *dependent's* basic standard deduction in 2018 is limited to the greater of $1,050 or the sum of the individual's earned income for the year plus $350.[8] However, if the sum of the individual's earned income plus $350 exceeds the normal standard deduction, the standard deduction is limited to the appropriate amount shown in Exhibit 9.3. These limitations apply only to the basic standard deduction. A dependent who is 65 or over or blind or both is also allowed the additional standard deduction amount on his or her own return (refer to Exhibit 9.4).

Dependent Standard Deduction

EXAMPLE 8

Susan, who is 17 years old and single, qualifies as a dependent of her parents. During 2018, she received $1,200 of interest (unearned income) on a savings account. She also earned $400 from a part-time job. When Susan files her own tax return, her standard deduction is $1,050 (the greater of $1,050 or the sum of earned income of $400 plus $350).

EXAMPLE 9

Assume the same facts as in Example 8, except that Susan is 67 years old and qualifies as her son's dependent. In this case, when Susan files her own tax return, her standard deduction is $2,650 [$1,050 (see Example 8) + $1,600 (the additional standard deduction allowed because Susan is age 65 or over)].

EXAMPLE 10

Peggy, who is 16 years old and single, earned $800 from a summer job and had no unearned income during 2018. She qualifies as a dependent of her parents. Her standard deduction is $1,150 (the greater of $1,050 or the sum of earned income of $800 plus $350).

EXAMPLE 11

Jack, who is 20 years old, single, and a full-time college student, qualifies as a dependent of his parents. He worked as a musician during the summer of 2018, earning $12,250. Jack's standard deduction is $12,000 (the greater of $1,050 or the sum of earned income of $12,250 plus $350, but limited to the $12,000 standard deduction for a single taxpayer).

---

[8] § 63(c)(5). Both the $1,050 amount and the $350 amount are subject to adjustment for inflation each year. In 2016, the amounts were $1,050 and $350.

9-3 DEPENDENCY STATUS

LO.3

Explain the rules for determining dependency status.

As discussed above, the standard deduction ensures taxpayers a given level of income to meet basic living expenses before an income tax is imposed. Historically, taxpayers have also been allowed exemptions to adjust the level of untaxed income allowed to cover basic expenses for the number of individuals supported by the taxpayer. Exemption deductions have been allowed for the taxpayer (**personal exemptions**) as well as for eligible dependents (**dependency exemptions**). The TCJA of 2017, however, suspended the deduction for exemptions and increased the standard deduction amount.

Even though the exemption deduction has been suspended through 2025, understanding when someone qualifies as a "dependent" remains important. For example, the definition of a dependent is used for a variety of purposes including determining eligibility for the child credit and the dependent credit and the deductibility of medical expenses (all discussed in Chapter 10). The exemption amount, still used in the definition of certain dependents, is $4,150 in 2018 ($4,050 in 2017). A person may qualify as another's dependent by meeting the definition of either a qualifying child or a qualifying relative.[9]

9-3a Qualifying Child

Congress has adopted a uniform definition of a qualifying child. The definition applies to the following tax provisions:

- Head-of-household filing status (discussed below).
- Earned income tax credit (discussed in Chapter 10).
- Child and dependent tax credits (discussed in Chapter 10).
- Credit for child and dependent care expenses (discussed in Chapter 10).

A **qualifying child** must meet the relationship, residence, age, and support tests.[10]

Relationship Test

To be considered a qualifying child of a taxpayer, someone must be the taxpayer's child (son or daughter), adopted child, step-child, eligible foster child, brother, sister, half brother, half sister, stepbrother, stepsister, or a *descendant* of any of these parties (e.g., grandchild, nephew, and niece). Note that *ancestors* of any of these parties (e.g., uncles and aunts) and in-laws (e.g., son-in-law and brother-in-law) *are not included*.

An adopted child includes a child placed with the taxpayer even though the adoption is not final. An eligible foster child is a child who is placed with the taxpayer by an authorized placement agency or by a judgment decree or other order of any court of competent jurisdiction.

Residence Test

A qualifying child must live with the taxpayer for more than half of the year. Temporary absences (e.g., school, vacation, medical care, military service, detention in a juvenile facility) are disregarded. Special rules apply in the case of certain kidnapped children.[11]

Age Test

By the end of the tax year, a qualifying child must be under age 19 or under age 24 in the case of a student. A student is a child who, during any part of five months of the year, is enrolled full-time at a school or government-sponsored on-farm training course.[12]

---

[9] § 152.
[10] § 152(c).

[11] § 152(f)(6).
[12] § 152(f)(2).

Also, an individual cannot be older than the taxpayer claiming him or her as a qualifying child (e.g., a brother cannot claim his older sister as a qualifying child). The age test does not apply to a child who is disabled during any part of the year.[13]

The Big Picture

EXAMPLE 12

Return to the facts of *The Big Picture* on p. 9-1. Does Paige meet the requirements of a qualifying child as to Polly? Paige satisfies the relationship and residence tests, but the answer to the age test remains unclear. Because she is not a full-time student or disabled, she must be under 19 to meet the age test. Unfortunately, the facts given do not provide Paige's age.

Support Test

To be a qualifying child, the individual must not be self-supporting (i.e., provide more than one-half of his or her own support). In the case of a child who is a full-time student, scholarships are not considered to be support.[14]

EXAMPLE 13

Shawn, age 23, is a full-time student and lives with his parents and an older cousin. During 2018, Shawn receives his support from the following sources: 30% from a part-time job, 30% from a scholarship, 20% from his parents, and 20% from the cousin.

Shawn is not self-supporting and is a dependent of his parents even though his parents contribute only 20% of his support. (Note: Shawn cannot be his cousin's qualifying child due to the relationship test.)

Tiebreaker Rules

In some situations, a child may be a qualifying child of more than one person. In this event, the tax law specifies the person for whom the child will qualify.[15] Called "tiebreaker rules," these rules are summarized in Concept Summary 9.2.

Concept Summary 9.2

Tiebreaker Rules for Determining Dependency Status

Persons Eligible to Treat Qualified Child as Dependent	Person Prevailing
Only one of the persons is the parent.	Parent
Both persons are the parents, and the child lives longer with one parent.	Parent with the longer period of residence
Both persons are the parents, and the child lives with each the same period of time.	Parent with the higher adjusted gross income (AGI)
None of the persons are the parent.	Person with highest AGI

DIGGING DEEPER 2   In-depth coverage can be found on this book's companion website: **www.cengage.com**

---

[13]Within the meaning of § 22(e)(3) for purposes of the credit for the elderly or disabled.

[14]§ 152(f)(5).

[15]§ 152(c)(4).

9-3b **Qualifying Relative**

Someone may also be considered a dependent of a taxpayer by being designated as a qualifying relative .

A qualifying relative must meet the following relationship, gross income, and support tests.[16]

Relationship Test

The relationship test for a qualifying relative is more expansive than for a qualifying child. In addition to the relatives included in the qualified child test, the following will meet the test for a qualified relative:

- Lineal ascendants (e.g., parents and grandparents).
- Collateral ascendants (e.g., uncles and aunts).
- Certain in-laws (e.g., son-, daughter-, father-, mother-, brother-, and sister-in-law).[17]

Children who do not satisfy the qualifying child definition may meet the qualifying relative criteria.

Inez provides more than half of the support of her son, James. James is age 20, is not disabled or a full-time student, and generates income of $2,400 from a part-time job. James is not a qualifying child due to the age test, but is a qualifying relative. Consequently, Inez may claim a dependency exemption for James.

EXAMPLE 14

The relationship test also includes individuals who are "members of the household" (i.e., live with the taxpayer for the entire year) whether or not they are otherwise related to the taxpayer. For example, cousins are not "qualifying relatives" (cousins are not on the list above), but a cousin can meet the relationship test if a "member of the household." Member-of-the-household status is not available for anyone whose relationship with the taxpayer violates local law or anyone who was a spouse during any part of the year.[18] However, an ex-spouse can qualify as a member of the household in a year following the divorce.

As the relationship test indicates, the category designation of "qualifying relative" is somewhat misleading since persons other than relatives can qualify. Furthermore, not all relatives will qualify (although relatives that are not listed could be a "member of the household").

The Big Picture

Return to the facts of *The Big Picture* on p. 9-1. Although Maude is unrelated to Polly, she qualifies as Polly's dependent by being a member of the household. Because Maude is a dependent, Polly can also deduct the medical expenses she paid on Maude's behalf.

EXAMPLE 15

Gross Income Test

A dependent's gross income must be *less* than the exemption amount—$4,150 in 2018 and $4,050 in 2017. As described in the tax formula, gross income includes any income

---

[16]§ 152(d).

[17]Once established by marriage, in-law status continues to exist and survives divorce.

[18]§§ 152(d)(2)(H) and (f)(3).

that is taxable. In the case of scholarships, for example, any amount that is taxable (e.g., received for room and board) is included in gross income and any amount that is excludable (e.g., used for books and tuition) is not. See the discussion of scholarships in Chapter 10.

Gross Income Test

EXAMPLE 16

Elsie provides more than half of the support of her son, Tom, who does not live with her. Tom, age 26, is a full-time student in medical school, earns $3,000 from a part-time job, and receives a $12,000 scholarship covering his tuition.

Tom is Elsie's dependent because he meets the gross income test and is a qualifying relative. (Note: Tom is not a qualifying child; he fails both the residence and the age test.)

EXAMPLE 17

Aaron provides more than half of the support of his widowed aunt, Myrtle, who does not live with him. Myrtle's income for the year is as follows: dividend income of $1,100, earnings from pet sitting of $1,200, nontaxable Social Security benefits of $6,000, and nontaxable interest from City of Milwaukee bonds of $8,000.

Because Myrtle's gross income is only $2,300 ($1,100 + $1,200), she meets the gross income test and is Aaron's dependent.

The Big Picture

EXAMPLE 18

Return to the facts of *The Big Picture* on p. 9-1. Assuming that Paige is not a qualifying child (see Example 12), can she be a qualifying relative? She meets the relationship and support tests, but what about the gross income test?

If her income from her part-time job is less than $4,150 (the 2018 exemption amount), she does qualify and would be Polly's dependent.

Support Test

The taxpayer must furnish over half of the qualifying relative's support. As with a qualifying child, support includes food, shelter, clothing, toys, medical and dental care, education, and similar items. However, a scholarship (both taxable and nontaxable portions) received by a student is not included for purposes of computing whether the taxpayer furnished more than half of the relative's support.

EXAMPLE 19

Hal contributed $3,400 (consisting of food, clothing, and medical care) toward the support of his nephew, Sam, who lives with him. Sam earned $1,300 from a part-time job and received $2,000 from a student loan to attend a local university. Assuming that the other dependency tests are met, Hal is Sam's dependent because Hal has contributed more than half of Sam's support (i.e., Hal contributed $3,400 and Sam contributed $3,300).

If an individual does not spend funds that have been received from any source, the unspent amounts are not counted for purposes of the support test.

EXAMPLE 20

Emily contributed $3,000 to her father's support during the year. In addition, her father received $2,400 in Social Security benefits, $200 of interest, and wages of $600. Her father deposited the Social Security benefits, interest, and wages in his own savings account and did not use any of the funds for his support. Thus, the Social Security benefits, interest, and wages are not considered to be support provided by Emily's father. Emily's father is Emily's dependent if the other tests are met.

An individual's own funds, however, must be taken into account if applied toward support. The source of the funds is not relevant.

Frank contributes $8,000 toward his parents' total support of $20,000. The parents, who do not live with Frank, obtain the other $12,000 from savings and a home equity loan on their residence. Although the parents have no income, their use of savings and borrowed funds are counted as part of their support. Because Frank does not satisfy the support test, his parents are not considered his dependents.

EXAMPLE 21

Capital expenditures for items such as furniture, appliances, and automobiles are included for purposes of the support test if the item does, in fact, constitute support.

Norm purchased a television costing $950 and gave it to his mother, who lives with him. The television was placed in the mother's bedroom and was used exclusively by her. Norm should include the cost of the television in determining the support of his mother.

EXAMPLE 22

Multiple Support Agreements An exception to the support test involves a <mark>multiple support agreement</mark>. A multiple support agreement allows a group of taxpayers—none of whom provide more than 50 percent of the support of a potential qualifying relative—to designate one member of the group to be treated as passing the support test.[19] Collectively, the group must provide more than 50 percent of the support. Any person who contributed more than 10 percent of the support may be treated as passing the support test. This provision is often used by the children of aged dependent parents when none of the children meet the support test.

The person designated to meet the support test under a multiple support agreement must meet all other requirements to treat the relative as a qualifying relative. For example, a person who does not meet the relationship or member-of-the-household requirement cannot be considered a qualified relative simply by virtue of a multiple support agreement. It does not matter if he or she contributes more than 10 percent of the individual's support.

Wanda, who resides with her son, Adam, received $12,000 from various sources during the year. This constituted her entire support for the year. She received support from the following individuals:

EXAMPLE 23

	Amount	Percentage of Total
Adam, a son	$ 5,760	48%
Bob, a son	1,200	10
Carol, a daughter	3,600	30
Diane, a friend	1,440	12
	$12,000	100%

If Adam and Carol file a multiple support agreement, Wanda can be considered a dependent of either. Wanda cannot be considered a dependent of Bob because Bob did not contribute *more than 10%* of her support. Bob's consent is not required for Adam and Carol to file a multiple support agreement. Diane does not meet the relationship or member-of-the-household test and cannot be a party to the agreement. The decision as to who claims Wanda rests with Adam and Carol. It is possible for Carol to claim Wanda, even though Adam furnished more of Wanda's support.

---

[19]§ 152(d)(3).

DIGGING DEEPER 3   In-depth coverage can be found on this book's companion website: www.cengage.com

TAX PLANNING STRATEGIES Multiple Support Agreements and the Medical Expense Deduction

FRAMEWORK FOCUS: DEDUCTIONS

Strategy: Maximize Deductible Amounts.

Generally, medical expenses are deductible only if they are paid on behalf of the taxpayer, his or her spouse, and their dependents.[20] Because deductibility may rest on dependency status, planning is important in arranging multiple support agreements.

EXAMPLE 24

During the year, Suzanne will be supported by her two sons (Gary and Alan) and her daughter (Maria). Each will furnish approximately one-third of the required support. If the parties decide that the dependency exemption should be claimed by Maria under a multiple support agreement, any medical expenses incurred by Suzanne should be paid by Maria.

In planning a multiple support agreement, take into account which of the parties is most likely to have total medical expenses that exceed the 10%-of-AGI limitation. In Example 24, for instance, Maria might be a poor choice if she and her family do not expect to incur many medical expenses of their own.

Children of Divorced or Separated Parents Another exception to the support test applies when parents with children are divorced or separated. Unmarried parents living apart for the last six months of the year are also covered by these rules. This exception applies if the parents meet the following conditions:

- They would have been entitled to claim the child as a dependent had they been married and filed a joint return.
- They have custody (either jointly or singly) of the child for more than half of the year.

In general, the parent having custody of a child for the greater part of the year (i.e., the custodial parent) is entitled to claim the child as a dependent. However, the custodial parent can sign a waiver that allows the noncustodial parent to claim the child as a dependent.[21]

DIGGING DEEPER 4   In-depth coverage can be found on this book's companion website: www.cengage.com

9-3c Other Rules for Determining Dependency Status

In addition to fitting into either the qualifying child or the qualifying relative category, a dependent must meet the joint return and the citizenship tests.

---

[20]See the discussion of medical expenses in Chapter 10.

[21]See Reg. § 1.152–4T and §§ 152(e)(2) and (5).

Joint Return Test

If an individual is married and files a joint return with his or her spouse, the individual will not be considered a dependent of any taxpayer.[22] The joint return rule does not apply, however, if the following conditions are met:[23]

- The reason for filing is to claim a refund for tax withheld.
- No tax liability would exist for either spouse on separate returns.
- Neither spouse is required to file a return.

Paul provides over half of the support of his son, Quinn. He also provides over half of the support of Vera, who is Quinn's wife. During the year, both Quinn and Vera had part-time jobs. To recover the taxes withheld, they file a joint return. If Quinn and Vera have income low enough that they are not *required* to file a return, both will be considered Paul's dependents.

EXAMPLE 25

TAX PLANNING STRATEGIES **Problems with a Joint Return**

FRAMEWORK FOCUS: DEDUCTIONS

Strategy: Maximize Deductible Amounts.

A married person who files a joint return generally will not be considered a dependent of another taxpayer. If a joint return has been filed, dependency status may still be established if separate returns are substituted on a timely basis (on or before the due date of the return).

While preparing a client's 2017 income tax return on April 2, 2018, a tax practitioner discovered that the client's daughter had filed a joint return with her husband in late January 2018. Presuming that the daughter otherwise qualifies as the client's dependent, dependency status is not lost if she and her husband file separate returns on or before April 17, 2018.

EXAMPLE 26

Citizenship Test

To claim the $500 dependent credit, the dependent must be a U.S. citizen or national or a U.S. resident.[24]

9-3d Comparison of Categories for Dependency Status

Concept Summary 9.3 identifies the tests for the two categories of dependents. In contrasting the two categories, here are some observations:

- As to the relationship tests, the qualifying relative category is considerably more expansive. In addition to those identified under the qualifying child grouping, other relatives are added. Nonrelated persons who are members of the household are also included.
- The support tests are entirely different. In the case of a qualifying child, the key is that the child is not self-supporting.
- The qualifying child category has no gross income limitation, whereas the qualifying relative category has no age restriction.

---

[22]§ 152(b)(2).

[23]Prop Reg § 1.152–1(a)(2).

[24]§ 152(b)(3) read with the modification at § 24(h)(4)(B) added by the TCJA of 2017.

Concept Summary 9.3

Tests for Dependency Status

Test	Qualifying Child	Qualifying Relative
Relationship:		
• Children (natural, step, or adopted) and their *descendants*, and siblings and stepsiblings and their *descendants*.	X	
• Children (natural, step, or adopted) and their *descendants*, siblings and their children, parents and their *ascendants*, uncles and aunts, stepparents and stepsiblings, and certain in-laws.		X
• Member of the household (live with taxpayer for *entire* year; relative or non-relative).		X
Residence	X	
Age	X	
Support:		
• Not self-supporting ("child" furnishes one-half or less of his or her support).	X	
• Taxpayer furnishes over one-half of the support of potential dependent.		X
Gross income *less* than the exemption amount		X
Joint return (potential dependent cannot file joint return)	X	X
Citizenship or residency (potential dependent must meet test)	X	X

Note: The $2,000 child tax credit for a qualifying child under age 17 is only available if the child has a Social Security number before the due date of the return. If the child does not have the number, the $500 dependent credit can be claimed if all of the requirements are met.

LO.4

Choose the proper filing status and identify the related filing requirements.

9-4 FILING STATUS AND FILING REQUIREMENTS

Once taxable income has been calculated, a two-step process is used in determining income tax due (or refund available). First, the taxpayer's filing status and then whether a tax return must be filed must be determined. Second, the tax has to be computed and adjusted for available tax credits—see Concept Summary 9.1 and the tax formula. This section deals with the filing status and filing requirements. Text Section 9-5 covers the tax computation procedures. Text Section 9-6 covers additional taxes that may be owed. Text Section 9-7 covers tax return filing procedures (including selecting the correct form and determining when and how the tax return should be filed).

9-4a Filing Status

Every year, taxpayers must determine their **filing status**. Filing status is used, in part, to capture differences in taxpayers' relative abilities to pay that are not captured by their incomes. The taxpayer's filing status is used to determine:

- The taxpayer's standard deduction;
- Whether the taxpayer must file a tax return;
- The taxpayer's tax liability; and
- Reductions of exemptions, itemized deductions, and certain tax credits.
- Eligibility for certain provisions (e.g., some credits are not available when the married, filing separately status is used).

The five available filing statuses are:

- Single
- Married, filing jointly
- Married, filing separately

- Surviving spouse (qualifying widow or widower)
- Head of household.

The amount of tax varies considerably depending on which filing status is used. This is illustrated in the following example.

The following amounts of tax are computed using the 2018 Tax Rate Schedules for a taxpayer (or taxpayers in the case of a joint return) with $60,000 of taxable income (see Appendix A).

Filing Status	Amount of Tax
Single	$9,140
Married, filing jointly	6,819
Married, filing separately	9,140
Head of household	7,748

Besides the effect from the tax rates that will apply, filing status also has an impact on the amount of the standard deduction that is allowed—see Exhibits 9.3 and 9.4 earlier in the chapter.

Single Taxpayers

A taxpayer who is unmarried (including a taxpayer who is legally separated or divorced) and does not qualify for head-of-household status (discussed below) will file as a single taxpayer.

Married Individuals

The joint filing status was originally enacted to establish equity between married taxpayers in common law states and those in community property states. Before the joint filing status was established, taxpayers in community property states had an advantage relative to taxpayers in common law states because their incomes were split evenly between them in determining their separate taxable incomes, allowing them to take maximum advantage of the lower tax rates.

Taxpayers in common law states did not have this income-splitting option, so their taxable income was subject to higher marginal rates. This inconsistency in treatment was remedied by the joint filing status. The joint return Tax Rate Schedule is constructed based on the assumption that income is earned equally by the two spouses.

A same-sex couple who is legally married in a state or jurisdiction that recognizes same-sex marriage is treated as married for Federal tax purposes (no matter where they live). According to the IRS, registered domestic partners or partners in civil unions, though, are not "spouses" under Federal law. Therefore, they cannot file Federal tax returns using married filing jointly or married filing separately status.[25] Taxpayers need to be aware that some states (e.g., California) recognize certain registered domestic partners as married for tax purposes and thus taxpayers may have a different filing status for Federal and state tax purposes.

If married individuals elect to file separate returns, each reports only his or her own income, exemptions, deductions, and credits, and each must use the married, filing separately tax rates. In a community property state, each individual must report his or her half of the community property income.[26] Most married couples file a joint return because the combined amount of tax is lower. However, special circumstances (e.g., significant medical expenses incurred by one spouse subject to the 10%-of-AGI limitation) may warrant the election to file separate returns. It may be necessary to compute

---

[25]Rev.Rul. 2013–17, 2013–38 I.R.B. 201 and *U.S. v. Windsor*, 2013–2 USTC ¶50,400, 111 AFTR 2d 2013–2385, 133 S.Ct. 2675.

[26]Form 8958 (Allocation of Tax Amounts Between Certain Individuals in Community Property States) is used for this purpose.

the tax under both assumptions to determine the most advantageous filing status. Filing a joint return carries the potential disadvantage of joint and several liability. This means that the IRS can pursue the collection of the tax due for that year against either spouse.

Marriage Penalty When Congress enacted the rate structure available to those filing joint returns, it generally favored married taxpayers. In certain situations, however, the parties would incur less tax if they were not married and filed separate returns. The additional tax that a joint return caused, commonly called the <mark>marriage penalty</mark>, usually developed when spouses had relatively similar levels of income.

DIGGING DEEPER 5 | **In-depth coverage can be found on this book's companion website: www.cengage.com**

Surviving Spouse The joint return rates also apply for two years following the death of one spouse if the surviving spouse maintains a household for a dependent child. The child must be a son, stepson, daughter, or stepdaughter who qualifies as a dependent of the taxpayer. This is referred to as <mark>surviving spouse</mark> status.[27]

Head of Household

Unmarried individuals who maintain a household for a dependent can file as a <mark>head of household</mark>. The tax rates applicable to a head of household are lower than those applicable to a single person but not as low as those applicable to a married couple filing jointly.[28] Head-of-household status is reserved for taxpayers who meet three requirements:

1. the taxpayer is considered unmarried at the end of the year,
2. the taxpayer pays more than one-half the cost of maintaining a home, and
3. a qualifying person lived with the taxpayer in the home for more than one-half of the year.

A qualifying person includes a qualifying child and a qualifying relative (other than someone who qualifies as a relative under the member-of-the-household classification). An important exception to the qualifying person rules permits the parent of a taxpayer to meet the definition of a qualifying person even when that parent does not live in the home for more than one-half of the year.

BRIDGE DISCIPLINE   Bridge to Equity or Fairness

Much has been made in the press and in political circles over the years concerning the so-called marriage penalty. This marriage penalty refers to the additional income tax that married couples pay over and above the aggregate amount two single individuals would pay with equal amounts of income. The marriage penalty arose because of the nature of the income tax rate structure that applies to individual taxpayers.

Relevant policy and ethical issues related to this dilemma are:

• Should the income tax system contain a bias against marriage?

• Should the income tax system require two people of economic means equal to that of two other people to pay a different amount of income taxes?

• Should the income tax system encourage two individuals to cohabit outside the commitment of marriage?

Long aware of the inequity of the marriage penalty, Congress reduced the effect of the problem by increasing the standard deduction available to married filers to 200 percent of that applicable to single persons and increasing the 15 percent bracket for joint filers to 200 percent of the size of that bracket applicable to single filers.

---

[27]§ 2(a). The IRS label for surviving spouse status is "qualifying widow(er) with dependent child."

[28]§ 2(b).

Head-of-Household Status

Tam's 18-year-old unmarried son lived with her all year. He did not provide more than half of his own support and does not meet the tests to be a qualifying child of anyone else. Because he is a qualifying child and is single, he is a qualifying person for head-of-household filing status.

EXAMPLE 28

Haukea's boyfriend and her boyfriend's 10-year-old daughter live with Haukea all year in her home. Even though her boyfriend may be a qualifying relative if the gross income and support tests are met, he is not a qualifying person for head-of-household purposes because he is not related to Haukea. The boyfriend's 10-year-old daughter is not a qualifying child, and because she is the boyfriend's qualifying child, she is not Haukea's qualifying relative. As a result, she is not Haukea's qualifying person for head-of-household purposes.

EXAMPLE 29

The Big Picture

Return to the facts of The Big Picture on p. 9-1. Assuming that Polly can be treated as single (i.e., not married), can Maude qualify Polly for head-of-household filing status? The answer is no. Even though Maude can be claimed as Polly's dependent (see Example 15), she does not meet the relationship test.

EXAMPLE 30

In-depth coverage can be found on this book's companion website: **www.cengage.com**

6 DIGGING DEEPER

Abandoned Spouse Rules

Congress has enacted provisions that allow married taxpayers, commonly referred to as abandoned spouses, to file as a head of household if the following conditions are satisfied:

- The taxpayer does not file a joint return.
- The taxpayer paid more than one-half the cost of maintaining his or her home for the tax year.

GLOBAL TAX ISSUES **Filing a Joint Return**

John Garth is a U.S. citizen and resident, but he spends much of his time in London, where his employer sends him on frequent assignments. John is married to Victoria, a citizen and resident of the United Kingdom.

Can John and Victoria file a joint return for U.S. Federal income tax purposes? Although § 6013(a)(1) specifically precludes the filing of a joint return if one spouse is a nonresident alien, another Code provision permits an exception. Under § 6013(g), the parties can elect to treat the nonqualifying spouse as a "resident" of the United States. This election would allow John and Victoria to file jointly.

But should John and Victoria make this election? If Victoria has considerable income of her own (from non-U.S. sources), the election could be ill-advised. As a nonresident alien, Victoria's non-U.S. source income *would not* be subject to the U.S. income tax. If she is treated as a U.S. resident, however, her non-U.S. source income *will be subject to U.S. tax*. Under the U.S. worldwide approach to taxation, all income (regardless of where earned) of anyone who is a *resident* or *citizen* of the United States is subject to tax.

- The taxpayer's spouse did not live in the home during the last six months of the tax year.
- The home was the principal residence of the taxpayer's son, daughter, stepson, stepdaughter, foster child, or adopted child for more than half the year, and the child can be claimed as a dependent.[29]

The resulting tax burden using the relatively favorable head-of-household status is lower than when using the married filing separately rate schedule.

The Big Picture

EXAMPLE 31

Return to the facts of The Big Picture on p. 9-1. Can Polly qualify as an abandoned spouse? Yes, if she can claim Paige as a dependent—either as a qualifying child (see Example 12) or as a qualifying relative (see Example 18). If so, Polly can use head-of-household filing status. If not, her filing status is married filing separately.

9-4b Filing Requirements

General Rules

In general, from 2018 through 2025, an individual must file a tax return if gross income equals or exceeds the applicable standard deduction.[30] For example, a single taxpayer under age 65 must file a tax return in 2018 if gross income equals or exceeds $12,000. Because the standard deduction amount is subject to an annual inflation adjustment, the gross income thresholds for determining whether a tax return must be filed normally change every year.

DIGGING DEEPER 7   In-depth coverage can be found on this book's companion website: **www.cengage.com**

The additional standard deduction for those age 65 or older is considered in determining the gross income filing requirements. For example, the 2018 filing requirement for a single taxpayer age 65 or older is $13,600 ($12,000 basic standard deduction + $1,600 additional standard deduction).

A self-employed individual with net earnings of $400 or more from a business or profession must file a tax return regardless of the amount of gross income.

Even though an individual has gross income below the filing level amounts and therefore does not owe any tax, he or she must file a return to obtain a tax refund of amounts withheld. A return is also necessary to obtain the benefits of the earned income credit (see Chapter 10) allowed to taxpayers with little or no tax liability. In addition, an individual who needs to reconcile the amount of premium tax credit received in advance during the year or owed to them (to help pay for health insurance obtained through the Marketplace) must file a return (see Chapter 10).

Filing Requirements for Dependents

Computation of the gross income filing requirement for an individual who is a dependent of another taxpayer is subject to more complex rules. For example, such an individual must file a return if he or she has either earned income in excess of the standard deduction amount or unearned income in excess of the greater of $1,050 or the sum of unearned income plus $350.

DIGGING DEEPER 8   In-depth coverage can be found on this book's companion website: **www.cengage.com**

---

[29]§ 7703(b).   [30]§ 6012(a)(1).

9-5 TAX DETERMINATION

LO.5

Demonstrate the proper procedures for determining the tax liability.

The computation of income tax due (or refund) involves applying the proper set of tax rates to taxable income and then adjusting the liability for available credits. In certain cases, however, the application of the kiddie tax will cause a modification of the means by which the tax is determined.

9-5a Tax Table Method

The tax liability is computed using either the Tax Table method or the Tax Rate Schedule method. Most taxpayers compute their tax using the Tax Table . Eligible taxpayers compute taxable income (as shown in Concept Summary 9.1) and *must* determine their tax by reference to the Tax Table.

In-depth coverage can be found on this book's companion website: **www.cengage.com**   **9 DIGGING DEEPER**

Although the Tax Table is derived from the Tax Rate Schedules (discussed next), the tax calculated using the two methods may vary slightly. This variation occurs because the tax for a particular income range in the Tax Table is based on the midpoint amount.

Linda is single and has taxable income of $30,000 for calendar year 2017. To determine Linda's tax using the Tax Table (see Appendix A), find the $30,000 to $30,050 income line. The tax of $4,038 is actually the tax the Tax Rate Schedule for 2017 (see Appendix A) would yield on taxable income of $30,025 (i.e., the midpoint amount between $30,000 and $30,050).

EXAMPLE 32

9-5b Tax Rate Schedule Method

Taxpayers who do not use the Tax Tables use the Tax Rate Schedules . The 2018 rate schedule for single taxpayers is reproduced in Exhibit 9.5.[31] This schedule is used to illustrate the tax computations in Examples 33 and 34.

Pat is single and had $5,870 of taxable income in 2018. His tax is $587 ($5,870 × 10%).

EXAMPLE 33

EXHIBIT 9.5	2018 Tax Rate Schedule for Single Taxpayers		

If Taxable Income Is			
Over	**But Not Over**	**The Tax Is:**	**Of the Amount Over**
$ –0–	$ 9,525	10%	$ –0–
9,525	38,700	$ 952.50 + 12%	9,525
38,700	82,500	4,453.50 + 22%	38,700
82,500	157,500	14,089.50 + 24%	82,500
157,500	200,000	32,089.50 + 32%	157,500
200,000	500,000	45,689.50 + 35%	200,000
500,000		150,689.50 + 37%	500,000

---

[31]Individual tax rates are found in § 1.

Several terms are used to describe tax rates. The rates in the Tax Rate Schedules are often referred to as *statutory* (or nominal) rates. The *marginal* rate is the tax rate that would be assessed on the next dollar of income for a particular taxpayer. In Example 33, the statutory rate and the marginal rate are both 10 percent.

EXAMPLE
34

Chris is single and had taxable income of $102,000 in 2018. Her tax is $18,769.50 [$14,089.50 + 24% ($102,000 − $82,500)].

The *average* rate is equal to the tax liability divided by taxable income. In Example 34, Chris has statutory rates of 10 percent, 12 percent, 22 percent, and 24 percent and a marginal rate of 24 percent. Chris's average rate is 18.4 percent ($18,769.50 tax liability ÷ $102,000 taxable income).

A tax is *progressive* (or graduated) if a higher rate of tax applies as the tax base increases. The progressive nature of the Federal income tax on individuals is illustrated by computing the tax in Example 34 utilizing each rate bracket.

Tax on first $9,525 at 10%	$ 952.50
Tax on $38,700 − $9,525 at 12%	3,501.00
Tax on $82,500 − $38,700 at 22%	9,636.00
Tax on $102,000 − $82,500 at 24%	4,680.00
Total tax on taxable income of $102,000	$18,769.50

A special computation limits the effective tax rate on qualified dividends (see Chapter 4) and net long-term capital gains (see Chapter 8).

9-5c Computation of Net Taxes Payable or Refund Due

The pay-as-you-go feature of the Federal income tax system requires payment of all or part of the taxpayer's income tax liability during the year. These payments take the form of Federal income tax withheld by employers or estimated tax paid by the taxpayer or both.[32] The payments are applied against the tax liability to determine whether the taxpayer will get a refund or pay additional tax.

Employers are required to withhold income tax on compensation paid to their employees and to pay this tax to the government. The employer must provide each employee a Form W–2 (Wage and Tax Statement), which documents wages and taxes withheld (including income, Social Security, and Medicare taxes). The employee should receive this form by January 31 after the year in which the income tax is withheld.

TAX PLANNING STRATEGIES **Shifting Income and Deductions across Time**

FRAMEWORK FOCUS: TAX RATE

Strategy: Shift Net Income from High-Bracket Years to Low-Bracket Years.

It is natural for taxpayers to be concerned about the tax rates that apply to them. What might a tax practitioner suggest to clients about tax rate planning? There are several possibilities. For example, a taxpayer who is in the 12 percent bracket this year and expects to be in the 24 percent bracket next year should, if possible, defer payment of deductible expenses until next year to maximize the tax benefit of the deduction.

A note of caution is in order with respect to shifting income and expenses between years. Congress has recognized the tax planning possibilities of such shifting and has enacted many provisions to limit a taxpayer's ability to do so. Some of these limitations on the shifting of income and deductions are discussed in Chapters 4 through 6.

---

[32]See § 3402 for withholding and § 6654 for estimated payments.

If taxpayers receive income that is not subject to withholding or income from which not enough tax is withheld, they may have to pay estimated tax. Form 1040–ES (Estimated Tax for Individuals) is used for these payments, and estimates are due quarterly.

The income tax liability is reduced by any available tax credits (which are different from tax deductions). Tax credits (including tax withheld) reduce the tax liability dollar for dollar. Tax deductions reduce taxable income on which the tax liability is based.

Gail is a taxpayer in the 24% tax bracket. As a result of incurring $1,000 in child care expenses, she is entitled to a $200 credit for child and dependent care expenses ($1,000 child care expenses × 20% credit rate). She also contributed $1,000 to the American Cancer Society and included this amount in her itemized deductions.

The credit for child and dependent care expenses results in a $200 reduction of Gail's tax liability for the year. The contribution to the American Cancer Society reduces taxable income by $1,000 and results in a $240 reduction in Gail's tax liability ($1,000 reduction in taxable income × 24% tax rate).

Selected tax credits for individuals are discussed in Chapter 10. Following are some of the more common credits available to individuals:

- Child tax credit (generally, $2,000 per child under age 17).
- Dependent credit ($500 per dependent unless qualified for the child tax credit).
- Credit for child and dependent care expenses.
- Earned income credit.
- Premium tax credit.

The computation of net taxes payable or refund due can be illustrated by returning to the facts of Example 5.

Grace is single and has her disabled and dependent mother living with her. Recall that Example 5 established that Grace has taxable income of $26,100. Further assume that she has the following income tax withheld, $2,500; estimated tax payments, $600; and a dependent tax credit, $500. Grace's net taxes payable (refund due) is computed as follows:

Income tax (from 2018 Tax Rate Schedule for head of household)		2,860
Less: Tax credits and prepayments—		
Dependent tax credit	$ 500	
Income tax withheld	2,500	
Estimated tax payments	600	(3,600)
Net taxes payable (refund due, if negative)		($ 740)

9-5d Kiddie Tax—Unearned Income of Dependent Children

LO.6

Identify and report kiddie tax situations.

Most individuals compute taxable income using the tax formula shown in Concept Summary 9.1. Special provisions govern the computation of taxable income and the tax liability for certain children who have **unearned income** in excess of specified amounts.

Current tax law reduces or eliminates the possibility of saving taxes by shifting income from parents to children by taxing the net unearned income of these children using special rules. Unearned income includes taxable interest, dividends, capital gains, rents, royalties, the taxable portion of scholarships, pension and annuity income, and income (other than earned income) received as the beneficiary of a trust.

This provision, commonly referred to as the **kiddie tax**, applies to any child who is under age 19 (or under age 24 if a full-time student) and has unearned income of more

Strategy: Shift Net Income from High-Bracket Taxpayers to Low-Bracket Taxpayers

Taxpayers can use several strategies to avoid or minimize the effect of the kiddie tax. With the cutoff age being 19 (under 24 for full-time students), many children are vulnerable to the application of the kiddie tax. Parents should consider giving a younger child assets that defer the inclusion in gross income until the child reaches a nonvulnerable age. For example, U.S. government Series EE savings bonds can be used to defer income until the bonds are cashed in.

Growth stocks typically pay little in the way of dividends. However, the unrealized appreciation on an astute investment may more than offset the lack of dividends. The child can hold the growth stock until he or she reaches a safe age. If the stock is sold then at a profit, the profit is taxed at the child's low rates.

Taxpayers in a position to do so can employ their children in their business and pay them a reasonable wage for the work they actually perform (e.g., light office help such as filing). The child's earned income is sheltered by the standard deduction, and the parents' business is allowed a deduction for the wages. The kiddie tax rules have no effect on earned income, even if it is earned from the parents' business.

than $2,100 in 2018 (same as in 2017).[33] The kiddie tax does not apply if the child has earned income that exceeds half of his or her support, if the child is married and files a joint return, or if both parents are deceased.

Net Unearned Income

In 2018, net unearned income of a dependent child is computed as follows:

> Unearned income
>
> Less: $1,050
>
> Less: The *greater* of:
>
>> $1,050 of the standard deduction, *or*
>>
>> The amount of allowable itemized deductions directly connected with the production of the unearned income
>
> Equals: Net unearned income

All amounts above are adjusted yearly for inflation. If net unearned income is not a positive amount, the child's tax is computed using the appropriate tax rate schedule (likely single). If the amount of net unearned income (regardless of source) is positive, the net unearned income is taxed using the rates applicable to estates and trusts (see Appendix A). The child's remaining taxable income is taxed at the child's rate.

DIGGING DEEPER 10 | In-depth coverage can be found on this book's companion website: **www.cengage.com**

9-6 ADDITIONAL TAXES FOR CERTAIN INDIVIDUALS

An individual may owe income-based taxes in addition to the income tax. These other taxes include the following:

- Alternative minimum tax (see discussion in Chapter 17)
- Self-employment tax (see discussion in Chapter 11)
- Net Investment Income Tax and Additional Medicare tax

---

[33]§ 1(g)(2).

9-6a **Alternative Minimum Tax**

Regular taxable income includes many items intended more to influence behavior in order to accomplish certain economic and social objectives than to measure income. Taxpayers vary in their ability to take advantage of these incentives, with some potentially able to reduce their tax liabilities significantly as a result. The **alternative minimum tax (AMT)** is intended to ensure that all taxpayers with economic income pay some minimum level of tax regardless of their ability to utilize these incentives. In general, the AMT imposes a tax on a broader tax base than regular taxable income, determined without many of the incentives incorporated in the regular income tax. In theory, all individual taxpayers are subject to the AMT. Taxpayers calculate the tax due under both the regular income tax and the AMT and are liable for whichever is greater. In recent years, approximately 4 million individual taxpayers annually report an AMT liability, paying approximately $25 billion in taxes over their regular tax liabilities.

Although the AMT is conceptually distinct from the regular income tax, most items that impact regular taxable income impact **alternative minimum taxable income (AMTI)** in the same way. Practically, therefore, AMTI is determined by making a series of adjustments to taxable income. The AMT Formula is illustrated in Exhibit 9.6.

Alternative Minimum Taxable Income

Some items that impact regular taxable income are not considered in the determination of AMTI and vice versa. These types of items, referred to preferences, include the exclusion for interest on private activity bonds (a form of tax-free state and municipal bonds) and the deduction for percentage depletion in excess of cost depletion.

Other items are taken into account in different periods for AMT purposes than for regular income tax purposes, potentially reducing some of the benefits otherwise available from deferring the recognition of income or accelerating the deductibility of expenses. Examples of these adjustments include the following:

- Cost recovery is generally calculated over a longer period (for real property) or using a less accelerated method (for personal property)[34,35]

- The completed contract method of accounting for long-term contracts is not allowed.

- The difference between the fair market value of stock and the amount paid for it on the exercise of incentive stock options must be recognized as income when the option is recognized rather than being deferred until the stock is sold.

The standard deduction and certain itemized deductions (such as state and local taxes) also represent AMT adjustments.

EXHIBIT 9.6	Alternative Minimum Tax Formula

Taxable income

± Adjustments

+ Preferences

Alternative Minimum Taxable Income (AMTI)

(Exemption)

Alternative minimum tax base

× 26% and 28% rates

Tentative minimum tax before foreign tax credit

(AMT foreign tax credit)

Tentative minimum tax

(Regular tax liability)

AMT

---

[34]Property on which additional first-year (bonus) depreciation is elected (discussed in Chapter 5) requires no adjustments for AMT purposes.

[35]Using a different recovery method for AMT and regular tax purposes will also result in a different gain or loss being recognized when the taxpayer disposes of the property.

Finally, because AMTI represents a measure of income distinct from regular taxable income, any net operating loss included in the calculation of AMTI must be determined using the rules covering AMTI and not those used to determine regular taxable income. Further, the NOL deducted in determining current-year AMTI is limited to 90 percent of current-year AMTI calculated before the deduction.

AMT Exemption

An exemption is allowed against AMTI to arrive at the AMT base. The exemption protects taxpayers with relatively small amounts of preferences and adjustments from being subject to the AMT. The initial exemption amount is reduced by 25 percent of the amount by which AMTI exceeds a base amount. Both the exemption amount and the base differ by filing status as illustrated below.[36]

		Phaseout	
Filing status	Exemption	Begins at	Ends at
Married, joint	$109,400	$1,000,000	$1,437,600
Single or head of household	70,300	500,000	781,200
Married, separate	54,700	500,000	718,800

The AMT Credit

As discussed above, many differences between regular taxable income and AMTI are due to timing differences. However, because taxpayers always pay the higher of their regular tax and AMT liabilities, those timing differences may never "reverse." To address this issue, taxpayers are allowed an **alternative minimum tax credit** for AMT triggered by timing differences. The credit may be carried forward indefinitely and used against future regular tax liability.

AMT Tax Rate

A graduated, two-tier rate structure applies to the AMT. A 26 percent rate applies to the tax base up to $191,100 ($95,550 for married taxpayers filing separately) and a 28% rate to amounts over that base. Any net capital gains or qualified dividends remain eligible for the favorable rates normally applicable to them (i.e., 0, 15, 20 percent).

The calculation of AMTI and AMT is illustrated in the following example.

EXAMPLE 37

Molly, single and 56 years old, had taxable income in 2018 as follows.

Salary		$92,000
Interest income		8,000
Adjusted gross income		100,000
Less itemized deductions		
State income taxes	8,050	
Interest		
Home mortgage interest	26,000	
Investment interest	3,800	
Charitable contributions	6,000	
Casualty loss in excess of 10% of AGI	4,000	(47,850)
Taxable income		$52,150

continued

---

[36]The exemption amount and phaseout thresholds are both indexed for inflation. Both were temporarily raised by the TCJA of 2017 until 2025 after which they will return to their pre-TCJA levels (e.g., $86,200 and $164,100 for married taxpayers filing jointly).

In addition, Molly earned $40,000 of interest income on private activity bonds issued in 2014. She also exercised ISOs in 2018. The option spread (the difference between the exercise price and the fair market value of the stock on the date of exercise) was $35,000. Molly's regular tax liability in 2018 is $7,413, and her AMT is $9,461 for a total tax liability of $16,874. Molly's AMTI and AMT are calculated as follows.

Taxable income	$ 52,150
Adjustments	
State income taxes	8,050
Incentive stock options	35,000
Preferences: interest on private activity bonds	40,000
AMTI	135,200
Exemption	(70,300)
Minimum tax base	64,900
AMT tax rate	× 26%
Tentative minimum tax	16,874
Regular tax liability	(7,413)
AMT	$ 9,461

9-6b Net Investment Income Tax and Additional Medicare Tax

The Net Investment Income Tax and Additional Medicare Tax were created as part of the Affordable Care Act to increase the Medicare tax and extend it to the unearned investment income of higher-income taxpayers. The Additional Medicare Tax is computed at a rate of .9 percent on wages and self-employment income in excess of threshold amounts. The threshold amount is $250,000 for married taxpayers ($125,000 if married filing separately) and $200,000 for all other taxpayers. An employer must withhold the .9% tax on wages paid to any employee that exceed $200,000 for the year (regardless of the employee's filing status). Unlike the base Medicare tax, the Additional Medicare Tax is imposed only on the employee, not also the employer. The net result of the Additional Medicare Tax is to increase the marginal rate of the Medicare tax on the earned income of higher-income taxpayers to 3.8 percent (2.9 percent basic tax + .9 percent additional tax).

The Net Investment Income Tax (NIIT) extends the Medicare tax to the unearned investment income of higher-income taxpayers. The tax is imposed at a rate of 3.8 percent of the lesser of:

- Net investment income, or
- The excess of modified adjusted gross income (MAGI) over $250,000 for married taxpayers filing a joint return ($125,000 if married filing separately) and $200,000 for all other taxpayers.

In general, "net investment income" includes interest, dividends, annuities, royalties, rents, income from passive activities, and net gains from the sale of investment property, reduced by deductions allowed in generating such income. For purposes of computing the NIIT, MAGI is defined as AGI increased by any foreign earned income exclusion (adjusted for related deductions). See Chapter 11 for discussion of the foreign earned income exclusion.

EXAMPLE 38

Rajiv is single and has the following income for 2018: wages of $220,000, interest income of $6,000, and capital gain of $28,000. Rajiv owes Additional Medicare Tax of $180 [.9% × ($220,000 − $200,000)]. In addition, he owes NIIT of $1,292 computed as follows:

3.8% × the lesser of:

- Net investment income of $34,000 ($6,000 + $28,000), or
- Modified adjusted gross income of $254,000 ($220,000 + $6,000 + $28,000) over $200,000, or $54,000

Unlike many threshold amounts, the ones for the NIIT and the Additional Medicare Tax are not adjusted annually for inflation. These additional taxes must be paid during the year through income tax withholdings or estimated tax payments.

9-7 TAX RETURN FILING PROCEDURES

9-7a Selecting the Proper Form

Although a variety of forms are available to individual taxpayers, the use of some of these forms is restricted. For example, Form 1040–EZ cannot be used if:

- Taxpayer claims any dependents,
- Taxpayer (or spouse) is 65 or older or blind,
- Taxable income is $100,000 or more,
- Taxpayer has taxable Social Security benefits or taxpayer claims credits other than the earned income tax credit.

Taxpayers who want to itemize deductions *from* AGI cannot use Form 1040–A, but must file Form 1040.

Starting in 2019, a new tax form will exist for individuals age 65 by the last day of the year. Form 1040SR allows seniors to use a simpler form (like the Form 1040EZ) if they only report Social Security benefits, retirement plan distributions, interest, dividends, and capital gains or losses. If they have other types of income, Form 1040 or Form 1040A is used.

9-7b The E-File Approach

The **e-file** program is used by the vast majority of individual taxpayers (and is mandatory for most tax return preparers). The required tax information is transmitted to the IRS electronically either directly from the taxpayer (i.e., an "e-file online return") or indirectly through an "Authorized e-file Provider." These providers are tax professionals who have been accepted into the electronic filing program by the IRS. Providers often are the preparers of the return as well.

Taxpayers can also use IRS Free File (with online fillable forms) or use commercial software to file a tax return at no cost. A number of software providers offer free e-filing services. These services are generally available only to taxpayers who have AGI of $62,000 or less. Eligibility requirements and a list of the software providers are available on the IRS website: **www.irs.gov/filing/e-file-options**.

All taxpayers and tax return preparers must attest to the returns they file. For most taxpayers, this is done through an electronic return signature using a personal identification number (a Self-Select PIN). Or the taxpayer can authorize a tax preparer to generate a PIN by signing Form 8879 (IRS e-file Signature Authorization). If certain paper documents must be submitted, a one-page form must be completed and filed

---

TAX FACT   What Form of Tax Compliance Is Right for You?

Based on recent projections from the IRS, when preparing about 155 million individual income tax returns expected to be filed in 2018, taxpayers will be using relatively fewer paper Forms 1040, 1040A, and 1040–EZ. As a result, the IRS expects the level of electronically filed returns to be at or near an all-time high.

	Percentage
Paper individual returns	11%
Electronically filed individual returns	89
	100%

Source: Fiscal Year Return Projections for the United States: 2015–2022, IRS, Document 6292, Fall 2016 Update, Table 1.

when the return is e-filed. Form 8453 (U.S. Individual Income Tax Transmittal for an IRS e-file Return) is used to submit required attachments for both self- and practitioner-prepared electronic returns.

The e-file approach has two major advantages over paper filing. First, it eliminates many reporting errors. Second, it reduces the time required for processing a refund to three weeks or less.

9-7c **When and Where to File**

Tax returns of individuals are due on or before the fifteenth day of the fourth month following the close of the tax year. For the calendar year taxpayer, the usual filing date is on or before April 15 of the following year.[37] When the due date falls on a Saturday, Sunday, or legal holiday, the filing deadline is the next business day.

If a taxpayer is unable to file the return by the specified due date, a six-month extension of time can be obtained by filing Form 4868 (Application for Automatic Extension of Time to File U.S. Individual Income Tax Return).[38]

Although obtaining an extension excuses a taxpayer from a penalty for failure to file, it does not insulate against the penalty for failure to pay. If more tax is owed, the filing of Form 4868 should be accompanied by an additional payment to cover the balance due. The return should be sent or delivered to the IRS Regional Service Center listed in the instructions for each type of return or contained in software applications.[39]

9-7d **Modes of Payment**

Payments of taxes due can be made by check, money order, IRS Direct Pay (electronic funds withdrawal from a bank account), the Electronic Federal Tax Payment System (EFTPS), and a number of major credit cards. The use of a credit or debit card results in a charge to the taxpayer.

REFOCUS ON THE BIG PICTURE

A DIVIDED HOUSEHOLD

Of major concern to Polly is her filing status. If she qualifies as an abandoned spouse, she is entitled to file as head of household. If not, she is considered to be a married person filing separately. Moreover, to be an abandoned spouse, Polly must be able to consider Paige as a dependent. To be a dependent, Paige must meet the requirements of a qualifying child or a qualifying relative.

For qualifying child purposes, Paige must meet either the age (i.e., under age 19) or the full-time student (under age 24) test. (A disabled child exception seems highly unlikely.) Because Paige currently is not a full-time student, is she under age 19? If so, she is a qualifying child (see Example 12). If Paige is not a qualifying child, is she a qualifying relative? Here, the answer depends on meeting the gross income test (see Example 18). How much did Paige earn from her part-time job? If her earnings are under $4,150, she satisfies the gross income test. Thus, if Paige can be claimed as a dependent under either the qualifying child or the qualifying relative category, Polly is an abandoned spouse entitled to head-of-household filing status (see Example 31). If not, she is a married person filing separately.

continued

---

[37]§ 6072(a).

[38]Reg. § 1.6081–4. See also *Your Federal Income Tax* (IRS Publication 17).

[39]The appropriate Regional Service Center address can be found at **www.irs.gov/uac/where-to-file-paper-tax-returns-with-or-without-a-payment**.

Maude will be considered to be Polly's dependent because she is a member of the household. It does not matter that she died in February. Because Maude is her dependent, Polly can claim the medical expenses she paid on Maude's behalf. The funeral expenses, however, are not deductible (see Example 15).

Does Maude qualify Polly for head-of-household filing status? No—although she is a dependent, Maude does not meet the relationship test (see Example 30).

What If?

Assume that Nick left for parts unknown in August (not March). Now Polly cannot qualify as an abandoned spouse. Her spouse lived in the home during part of the last six months of the year. Consequently, Polly is treated as married and cannot qualify for head-of-household filing status. She must file as a married person filing separately.

Suggested Readings

David R. Baldwin, Robert Caplan, Valrie Chambers, Edward A. Gershman, Jennifer S. Korten, Darren Neuschwander, Jeffrey A. Porter II, Kenneth L. Rubin, David E. Taylor, and Donald J. Zidik Jr. "Individual Taxation: Report of Recent Developments," *The Tax Adviser*, March 2018.

Andrew Lafond and Bruce A. Leauby, "Help Wanted: Hire Your Kids for Tax Savings," *Practical Tax Strategies*, October 2013.

Michaele L. Morrow, Mitchell Franklin, and Tomothy A. Gagnon "Tax Considerations for Marriage: I do…or do not," 149 Tax Notes 1059.

Key Terms

Alternative minimum tax (AMT), 9-25

Alternative minimum taxable income (AMTI), 9-25

Alternative minimum tax credit, 9-26

Dependency exemption, 9-9

E-file, 9-28

Filing status, 9-16

Head of household, 9-18

Itemized deductions, 9-5

Kiddie tax, 9-23

Marriage penalty, 9-18

Multiple support agreement, 9-13

Personal exemptions, 9-9

Qualifying child, 9-9

Qualifying relative, 9-11

Standard deduction, 9-5

Surviving spouse, 9-18

Tax Rate Schedules, 9-21

Tax Table, 9-21

Unearned income, 9-23

Computational Exercises

Issue ID 1. **LO.2** Sam and Abby are dependents of their parents, and each has income of $2,100 for the year. Sam's standard deduction for the year is $1,050, while Abby's is $2,450. As their income is the same, what causes the difference in the amount of the standard deduction?

2. **LO.2** Compute the 2018 standard deduction for the following taxpayers.
   a. Margie is 15 and claimed as a dependent by her parents. She has $800 in dividend income and $1,400 in wages from a part-time job.
   b. Ruby and Woody are married and file a joint tax return. Ruby is age 66, and Woody is 69. Their taxable retirement income is $10,000.

c. Shonda is age 68 and single. She is claimed by her daughter as a dependent. Her earned income is $500, and her interest income is $125.

d. Frazier, age 55, is married but is filing a separate return. His wife itemizes her deductions.

3. **LO.4** Paul and Sonja, who are married, had itemized deductions of $13,200 and $400, respectively, during 2018. Paul suggests that they file separately—he will itemize his deductions *from* AGI, and she will claim the standard deduction.   Issue ID

a. Evaluate Paul's suggestion.

b. What should they do?

4. **LO.5** Compute the 2018 tax liability and the marginal and average tax rates for the following taxpayers (use the 2018 tax rate schedules in Appendix A for this purpose).

a. Chandler, who files as a single taxpayer, has taxable income of $94,800.

b. Lazare, who files as a head of household, has taxable income of $57,050.

5. **LO.5** George and Aimee are married. George has wage income of $190,000, and Aimee has a sole proprietorship that generated net income of $85,000. They also have interest and dividend income of $21,000. Compute any NIIT and Additional Medicare Tax they owe for the current year.

6. **LO.6** In 2018, Simon, age 12, has interest income of $4,800 and no earned income. He has no investment expenses. Determine Simon's net unearned income and total tax liability.   Digging Deeper

Problems

7. **LO.1, 4** During the year, Addison is involved in the following transactions: Issue ID

a. Lost money gambling on a recent trip to a casino.

b. Helped pay for her neighbor's dental bills. The neighbor is a good friend who is unemployed.

c. Received from the IRS a tax refund due to Addison's overpayment of last year's Federal income taxes.

d. Paid a traffic ticket received while double parking to attend a business meeting.

e. Contributed to the mayor's reelection campaign. The mayor had promised Addison to have some of her land rezoned. The mayor was reelected and got Addison's land rezoned.

f. Borrowed money from a bank to make a down payment on an automobile.

g. Sold a houseboat and a camper on eBay. Both were personal use items, and the gain from one offset the loss from the other.

h. Paid for dependent grandfather's funeral expenses.

i. Paid premiums on her dependent son's life insurance policy.

What are the possible income tax ramifications of these transactions?

8. **LO.1** Which of the following items are *inclusions* in gross income?

a. During the year, stock that the taxpayer purchased as an investment doubled in value.

b. Amount an off-duty motorcycle police officer received for escorting a funeral procession.

c. While his mother was in the hospital, the taxpayer sold her jewelry and gave the money to his girlfriend.

d. Child support payments received.

e.   A damage deposit the taxpayer recovered when he vacated the apartment he had rented.

f.   Interest received by the taxpayer on an investment in general purpose bonds issued by IBM.

g.   Amounts received by the taxpayer, a baseball "Hall of Famer," for autographing sports equipment (e.g., balls and gloves).

h.   Tips received by a bartender from patrons. (Taxpayer is paid a regular salary by the cocktail lounge that employs him.)

i.   Taxpayer sells his Super Bowl tickets for three times what he paid for them.

j.   Taxpayer receives a new BMW from his grandmother when he passes the CPA exam.

9.   **LO.1** Which of the following items are *exclusions* from gross income?

a.   Alimony payments received from a divorce settlement in 2016.

b.   Damages award received by the taxpayer for personal physical injury—none were for punitive damages.

c.   A new golf cart won in a church raffle.

d.   Amount collected on a loan previously made to a college friend.

e.   Insurance proceeds paid to the taxpayer on the death of her uncle—she was the designated beneficiary under the policy.

f.   Interest income on City of Chicago bonds.

g.   Jury duty fees.

h.   Stolen funds the taxpayer had collected for a local food bank drive.

i.   Reward paid by the IRS for information provided that led to the conviction of the taxpayer's former employer for tax evasion.

j.   An envelope containing $8,000 found (and unclaimed) by the taxpayer in a bus station.

Decision Making   10.   **LO.1** In late 2018, the Polks come to you for tax advice. They are considering selling some stock investments for a loss and making a contribution to a traditional IRA. In reviewing their situation, you note that they have large medical expenses and a casualty loss (in a Federally declared disaster area), neither of which is covered by insurance. What advice would you give the Polks?

11.   **LO.1, 2, 3, 4** Compute the taxable income for 2018 in each of the following independent situations:

a.   Drew and Meg, ages 40 and 41, respectively, are married and file a joint return. In addition to four dependent children, they have AGI of $125,000 and itemized deductions of $27,000.

b.   Sybil, age 40, is single and supports her dependent parents, who live with her, as well as her grandfather, who is in a nursing home. She has AGI of $80,000 and itemized deductions of $8,000.

c.   Scott, age 49, is a surviving spouse. His household includes two unmarried stepsons who qualify as his dependents. He has AGI of $75,000 and itemized deductions of $10,100.

d.   Amelia, age 33, is an abandoned spouse who maintains a household for her three dependent children. She has AGI of $58,000 and itemized deductions of $9,500.

e.   Dale, age 42, is divorced but maintains the home in which he and his daughter, Jill, live. Jill is single and qualifies as Dale's dependent. Dale has AGI of $64,000 and itemized deductions of $9,900.

12. **LO.1, 2, 3** Compute the taxable income for 2018 for Emily on the basis of the following information. Her filing status is single.

Salary	$85,000
Interest income from bonds issued by Xerox	1,100
Alimony payments received (divorce occurred in 2014)	6,000
Contribution to traditional IRA	5,500
Gift from parents	25,000
Short-term capital gain from stock investment	2,000
Amount lost in football office pool	500
Age	40

13. **LO.1, 2, 3** Compute the taxable income for 2018 for Aiden on the basis of the following information. Aiden is married but has not seen or heard from his wife since 2016.

Salary	$80,000
Interest on bonds issued by the City of Boston	3,000
Interest on CD issued by Wells Fargo Bank	2,000
Cash dividend received on Chevron common stock	2,200
Life insurance proceeds paid on death of aunt (Aiden was the designated beneficiary of the policy)	200,000
Inheritance received upon death of aunt	100,000
Jackson (a cousin) repaid a loan Aiden made to him in 2009 (no interest was provided for)	5,000
Itemized deductions (state income tax, property taxes on residence, interest on home mortgage, and charitable contributions)	9,700
Number of dependents (children, ages 17 and 18, and mother-in-law, age 70)	3
Age	43

14. **LO.2** In choosing between the standard deduction and itemizing deductions   Issue ID
from AGI, what effect, if any, does each of the following have?
  a. The age of the taxpayer(s).
  b. The health (i.e., physical condition) of the taxpayer.
  c. Whether taxpayers rent or own their residence.
  d. Taxpayer's filing status (e.g., single, married, filing jointly).
  e. Whether married taxpayers decide to file separate returns.
  f. The taxpayer's uninsured personal residence was recently destroyed by a wildfire (the region was declared a disaster area by the Federal government).
  g. The number of dependents supported by the taxpayer.

15. **LO.2, 3, 4** In 2018, David is age 78, is a widower, and is a dependent of his son. How does this situation affect the following?
  a. David's own individual filing requirement.
  b. The standard deduction allowed to David.
  c. The availability of any additional standard deduction.

16. **LO.2** Determine the amount of the standard deduction allowed for 2018 in the following independent situations. In each case, assume that the taxpayer is the dependent of another taxpayer.
  a. Curtis, age 18, has income as follows: $700 interest from a certificate of deposit and $12,200 from repairing cars.
  b. Mattie, age 18, has income as follows: $600 cash dividends from a stock investment and $4,700 from handling a paper route.
  c. Jason, age 16, has income as follows: $675 interest on a bank savings account and $800 for painting a neighbor's fence.

d. Ayla, age 15, has income as follows: $400 cash dividends from a stock investment and $500 from grooming pets.

e. Sarah, age 67 and a widow, has income as follows: $500 from a bank savings account and $3,200 from babysitting.

17. **LO.3** Analyze each of the characteristics in considering the indicated test for dependency as a qualifying child or qualifying relative. In the last two columns, after each listed test (e.g., gross income), state whether the particular test is Met, Not Met, or Not Applicable (NA).

Characteristic	Qualifying Child Test	Qualifying Relative Test
a. Taxpayer's son has gross income of $7,000	Gross income	Gross income
b. Taxpayer's niece has gross income of $3,000	Gross income	Gross income
c. Taxpayer's uncle lives with him	Relationship	Relationship
d. Taxpayer's daughter is 25 and disabled	Age	Age
e. Taxpayer's daughter is age 18, has gross income of $8,000, and does not live with him	Residence, Gross income	Gross income
f. Taxpayer's cousin does not live with her	Relationship, Residence	Relationship
g. Taxpayer's brother does not live with her	Residence	Relationship
h. Taxpayer's sister has dropped out of school, is age 17, and lives with him	Relationship, Residence, Age	Relationship
i. Taxpayer's older nephew is age 23 and a full-time student	Relationship, Age	Relationship
j. Taxpayer's grandson lives with her and has gross income of $7,000	Relationship, Residence	Relationship, Gross income

18. **LO.3** Caden and Lily are divorced on March 3, 2017. For financial reasons, however, Lily continues to live in Caden's apartment and receives her support from him. Caden does not claim Lily as a dependent on his 2017 Federal income tax return but does so on his 2018 return. Explain.

19. **LO.3** For tax year 2018, determine who is considered a dependent of another taxpayer in each of the following independent situations:

a. Leo and Amanda (ages 48 and 46, respectively) are husband and wife and furnish more than 50% of the support of their two children, Elton (age 18) and Trista (age 24). During the year, Elton earns $4,500 providing transportation for elderly persons with disabilities, and Trista receives a $5,000 scholarship that is used entirely for tuition at the law school she attends.

b. Audry (age 45) was divorced this year. She maintains a household in which she, her ex-husband (Clint), and his mother (Olive) live and furnishes more than 50% of their support. Olive is age 91 and blind.

20. **LO.3** Wesley and Camilla (ages 90 and 88, respectively) live in an assisted care facility and for 2017 and 2018 received their support from the following sources:

	Percentage of Support
Social Security benefits	16%
Son	20
Niece	29
Cousin	12
Brother	11
Family friend (not related)	12

a. Which persons are eligible to treat Wesley and Camilla as dependents under a multiple support agreement?

b. Must Wesley and Camilla be claimed by the same person(s) for both 2017 and 2018? Explain.

c. Who, if anyone, can claim their medical expenses?

21. **LO.2, 3** Taylor, age 18, is a dependent of her parents. For 2018, she has the follow-   *Digging Deeper*
ing income: $4,000 of wages from a summer job, $1,800 of interest from a
money market account, and $2,000 of interest from City of Boston bonds.
   a.   What is Taylor's taxable income for 2018?
   b.   What is Taylor's tax for 2018?

22. **LO.1, 3, 5** Charlotte (age 40) is a surviving spouse and provides all of the support
of her four minor children who live with her. She also maintains the
household in which her parents live and furnished 60% of their support. Besides
interest on City of Miami bonds in the amount of $5,500, Charlotte's father received
$2,400 from a part-time job. Charlotte has a salary of $80,000, a short-term capital
loss of $2,000, a cash prize of $4,000 from a church raffle, and itemized deductions
of $10,500. Using the Tax Rate Schedules, compute Charlotte's 2018 tax liability.

23. **LO.1, 2, 3, 4, 5** Morgan (age 45) is single and provides more than 50% of the support of Rosalyn (a family friend), Flo (a niece, age 18), and Jerold
(a nephew, age 18). Both Rosalyn and Flo live with Morgan, but Jerold (a French
citizen) lives in Canada. Morgan earns a salary of $95,000, contributes $5,000 to a
traditional IRA, and receives sales proceeds of $15,000 for an RV that cost $60,000
and was used for vacations. She has $8,200 in itemized deductions. Using the Tax
Rate Schedules, compute Morgan's 2018 tax liability.

24. **LO.4** Bob and Carol have been in and out of marital counseling for the past few   *Ethics and Equity*
years. Early in 2018, they decide to separate. However, because they are
barely able to get by on their current incomes, they cannot afford separate housing or the legal costs of a divorce. So Bob moves out of their house in March and
takes up residence in their detached garage (which has an enclosed workshop and
bathroom). Carol stays in the house with their two children and pays more than
half of the costs of maintaining their residence. Bob does not enter the house for
the remainder of the year. Can Carol qualify as an abandoned spouse? Explain.

25. **LO.4** Which of the following individuals are required to file a tax return for 2018?
Should any of these individuals file a return even if filing is not required? Why
or why not?
   a.   Patricia, age 19, is a self-employed single individual with gross income of $5,200
from an unincorporated business. Business expenses amounted to $4,900.
   b.   Mike is single and is 67 years old. His gross income from wages was $10,800.
   c.   Ronald is a dependent child under age 19 who received $6,800 in wages from
a part-time job.
   d.   Sam is married and files a joint return with his spouse, Lana. Both Sam and Lana
are 67 years old. Their combined gross income was $24,250.
   e.   Quinn, age 20, is a full-time college student who is claimed as a dependent
by his parents. For 2018, Quinn has taxable interest and dividends of $2,500.

26. **LO.4, 5** Roy and Brandi are engaged and plan to get married. During 2018, Roy is   *Decision Making*
a full-time student and earns $9,000 from a part-time job. With this income,
student loans, savings, and nontaxable scholarships, he is self-supporting. For the
year, Brandi is employed and has wages of $61,000. How much income tax, if any,
can Brandi save if she and Roy marry in 2018 and file a joint return?

27. **LO.5** Jayden calculates his 2018 income tax by using both the Tax Tables and the
Tax Rate Schedules. Because the Tax Rate Schedules yield a slightly lower tax
liability, he plans to pay this amount.
   a.   Why is there a difference?
   b.   Is Jayden's approach permissible? Why or why not?

28. **LO.1, 6** Paige, age 17, is a dependent of her parents in 2018. During 2018, Paige   *Digging Deeper*
earned $3,900 pet sitting and $4,100 in interest on a savings account. What
are Paige's taxable income and tax liability for 2018?

Digging Deeper   29. **LO.1, 3, 6** Terri, age 16, is a dependent of her parents in 2018. During the year, Terri earned $5,000 in interest income and $3,000 from part-time jobs.

    a.   What is Terri's taxable income?

    b.   What is Terri's net unearned income?

    c.   What is Terri's tax liability?

Comprehensive Tax Return Problems

1. Lance H. and Wanda B. Dean are married and live at 431 Yucca Drive, Santa Fe, NM 87501. Lance works for the convention bureau of the local Chamber of Commerce, while Wanda is employed part-time as a paralegal for a law firm.

    During 2018, the Deans had the following receipts:

Salaries ($60,000 for Lance, $41,000 for Wanda)		$101,000
Interest income—		
City of Albuquerque general purpose bonds	$1,000	
Ford Motor Company bonds	1,100	
Ally Bank certificate of deposit	400	2,500
Child support payments from John Allen		7,200
Annual gifts from parents		26,000
Settlement from Roadrunner Touring Company		90,000
Lottery winnings		600
Federal income tax refund (for tax year 2017)		400

Wanda was previously married to John Allen. When they divorced several years ago, Wanda was awarded custody of their two children, Penny and Kyle. (Note: Wanda has never issued a Form 8332 waiver.) Under the divorce decree, John was obligated to pay alimony and child support—the alimony payments were to terminate if Wanda remarried.

    In July, while going to lunch in downtown Santa Fe, Wanda was injured by a tour bus. As the driver was clearly at fault, the owner of the bus, Roadrunner Touring Company, paid her medical expenses (including a one-week stay in a hospital). To avoid a lawsuit, Roadrunner also transferred $90,000 to her in settlement of the personal injuries she sustained.

    The Deans had the following expenditures for 2018:

Medical expenses (not covered by insurance)		$7,200
Taxes—		
Property taxes on personal residence	$3,600	
State of New Mexico income tax (includes amount withheld from wages during 2018)	4,200	7,800
Interest on home mortgage (First National Bank)		6,000
Charitable contributions		3,600
Life insurance premiums (policy on Lance's life)		1,200
Contribution to traditional IRA (on Wanda's behalf)		5,000
Traffic fines		300
Contribution to the reelection campaign fund of the mayor of Santa Fe		500
Funeral expenses for Wayne Boyle		6,300

The life insurance policy was taken out by Lance several years ago and designates Wanda as the beneficiary. As a part-time employee, Wanda is excluded from coverage under her employer's pension plan. Consequently, she provides for her own retirement with a traditional IRA obtained at a local trust company. Because the mayor is a member of the local Chamber of Commerce, Lance felt compelled to make the political contribution.

The Deans' household includes the following, for whom they provide more than half of the support:

	Social Security Number*	Birth Date
Lance Dean (age 42)	123-45-6786	12/16/1976
Wanda Dean (age 40)	123-45-6787	08/08/1978
Penny Allen (age 19)	123-45-6788	10/09/1999
Kyle Allen (age 16)	123-45-6789	05/03/2001
Wayne Boyle (age 75)	123-45-6785	06/15/1943

*In the interest of privacy and to protect against taxpayer identification misuse, Social Security numbers used throughout the textbook have been replaced with fictitious numbers.

Penny graduated from high school on May 9, 2018, and is undecided about college. During 2018, she earned $8,500 (placed in a savings account) playing a harp in the lobby of a local hotel. Wayne is Wanda's widower father, who died on January 20, 2018. For the past few years, Wayne qualified as a dependent of the Deans.

Federal income tax withheld is $4,200 (Lance) and $2,100 (Wanda). The proper amount of Social Security and Medicare tax was withheld.

Determine the Federal income tax for 2018 for the Deans on a joint return by completing the appropriate forms. They do not want to contribute to the Presidential Election Campaign Fund. All members of the family had health care coverage for all of 2018. If an overpayment results, it is to be refunded to them. Suggested software: H&R BLOCK Tax Software.

2. Logan B. Taylor is a widower whose wife, Sara, died on June 6, 2016. He lives at 4680 Dogwood Lane, Springfield, MO 65801. He is employed as a paralegal by a local law firm. During 2018, he had the following receipts:

Tax Return Problem

Decision Making

Communications

Salary		$ 80,000
Interest income—		
Money market account at Omni Bank	$ 300	
Savings account at Boone State Bank	1,100	
City of Springfield general purpose bonds	3,000	4,400
Inheritance from Daniel		60,000
Life insurance proceeds		200,000
Amount from sale of St. Louis lot		80,000
Proceeds from estate sale		9,000
Federal income tax refund (for 2017 tax overpayment)		700

Logan inherited securities worth $60,000 from his uncle, Daniel, who died in 2018. Logan also was the designated beneficiary of an insurance policy on Daniel's life with a maturity value of $200,000. The lot in St. Louis was purchased on May 2, 2013, for $85,000 and held as an investment. As the neighborhood has deteriorated, Logan decided to cut his losses and sold the lot on January 5, 2018, for $80,000. The estate sale consisted largely of items belonging to Sara and Daniel (e.g., camper, boat, furniture, and fishing and hunting equipment). Logan estimates that the property sold originally cost at least twice the $9,000 he received and has declined or stayed the same in value since Sara and Daniel died.

Logan's expenditures for 2018 include the following:

Medical expenses (including $10,500 for dental)		$11,500
Taxes—		
State of Missouri income tax (includes withholdings during 2018)	$4,200	
Property taxes on personal residence	4,500	8,700
Interest on home mortgage		5,600
Contribution to church (paid pledges for 2018 and 2019)		4,800

Logan and his dependents are covered by his employer's health insurance policy for all of 2018. However, he is subject to a deductible, and dental care is not included. The $10,500 dental charge was for Helen's implants. Helen is Logan's widowed mother, who lives with him (see below). Logan normally pledges $2,400 ($200 per month) each year to his church. On December 5, 2018, upon the advice of his pastor, he prepaid his pledge for 2019.

Logan's household, all of whom he supports, includes the following:

	Social Security Number	Birth Date
Logan Taylor (age 48)	123-45-6787	08/30/1970
Helen Taylor (age 70)	123-45-6780	01/13/1948
Asher Taylor (age 23)	123-45-6783	07/18/1995
Mia Taylor (age 22)	123-45-6784	02/16/1996

Helen receives a modest Social Security benefit. Asher, a son, is a full-time student in dental school and earns $4,500 as a part-time dental assistant. Mia, a daughter, does not work and is engaged to be married.

Part 1—Tax Computation
Using the appropriate forms and schedules, compute Logan's income tax for 2018. Federal income tax of $4,500 was withheld from his wages. If Logan has any overpayment on his income tax, he wants the refund sent to him. Assume that the proper amounts of Social Security and Medicare taxes were withheld. Logan does not want to contribute to the Presidential Election Campaign Fund. Suggested software: H&R BLOCK Tax Software.

Part 2—Follow-Up Advice
In early 2017, the following take place:

- Helen decides that she wants to live with one of her daughters and moves to Arizona.
- Asher graduates from dental school and joins an existing practice in St. Louis.
- Mia marries, and she and her husband move in with his parents.
- Using the insurance proceeds he received on Daniel's death, Logan pays off the mortgage on his personal residence.

Logan believes that these events may have an effect on his tax position for 2019. Therefore, he requests your advice.

Write a letter to Logan explaining in general terms the changes that will occur for tax purposes. Assume that Logan's salary and other factors not mentioned (e.g., property and state income taxes) will remain the same. Use the 2018 Tax Rate Schedules in projecting Logan's tax for 2019.

Research Problems

Note: Solutions to the Research Problems can be prepared by using the Thomson Reuters Checkpoint™ online tax research database, which accompanies this textbook. Solutions can also be prepared by using research materials found in a typical tax library.

Communications   **Research Problem 1.** Kathy and Brett Ouray married in 2000. They began to experience marital difficulties in 2014 and, in the current year, although they are not legally separated, consider themselves completely estranged. They have contemplated getting a divorce. However, because of financial concerns and because they both want to remain involved in the lives of their three sons, they have not yet filed for divorce. In addition, their financial difficulties have meant that Kathy and Brett cannot afford to live in separate residences. So although they consider themselves emotionally estranged, they and their three sons all reside in a single-family home in Chicago, Illinois.

Although Brett earns significantly more than Kathy, both contribute financially to maintaining their home and supporting their teenage sons. In one of their few and brief conversations this year, they determined that Brett had contributed far more than Kathy to the maintenance of their home and the support of their sons. Thus, Brett has decided that for the current tax year, they will file separate Federal income tax returns and that he will claim head-of-household filing status. While they live under the same roof, Brett believes that he and Kathy should maintain separate households. Given this fact and the fact that he provides significantly more for the support of his and Kathy's sons, he believes that he is eligible for head-of-household filing status. Advise Brett on which filing status is most appropriate for him in the current year. His address is 16 Lahinch, Chicago, IL 60608.

Use internet tax resources to address the following questions. Look for reliable websites and blogs of the IRS and other government agencies, media outlets, businesses, tax professionals, academics, think tanks, and political outlets.

Research Problem 2. Locate IRS Form 2120 (at **www.irs.gov**), and answer the following questions.

    a.   Who must sign the form?

    b.   Who must file the form?

    c.   Can it be used for someone who is not related to the taxpayer? Explain.

Research Problem 3. What purpose is served by Form 8857? Read the directions to the form, and see IRS Publication 971 for additional information.

Research Problem 4. A nonresident alien earns money in the United States that is subject to Federal income tax. What guidance does the IRS provide about what tax form needs to be used and when it should be filed? In terms of the proper filing date, does it matter whether the earnings were subject to income tax withholding? Explain.

Becker CPA Review Questions

1. Bob provides more than half of his mother's support. His mother earns $6,000 per year as a hairdresser. She lives in an apartment across town. Bob is unmarried and has no children. What is Bob's most advantageous filing status?

    a. Single

    b. Head of household

    c. Qualifying single

    d. Supporting single

2. Jane is 20 years old and is a sophomore at Lake University. She is a full-time student and does not have any gross income. Jane spends the holidays and summers at home with her parents. Her total support for the current tax year is $30,000, including a scholarship for $5,000 to cover her tuition. Jane used $12,000 of her savings, and her grandparents provided $13,000. Which of the following statements regarding the exemption for Jane is true?

    a. If Jane's parents (rather than her grandparents) provided the $13,000, then they would not be able to claim Jane as a dependent because Jane provided more than half of her own support.

    b. Jane's grandparents can claim her as a dependent because Jane did not provide more than half of her own support.

    c. Jane's grandparents cannot claim her as a dependent because Jane provided more than half of her own support.

    d. Jane can claim an exemption for herself because she provided more than half of her own support.

3. In the current tax year, Blake Smith provided more than half of the support for his cousin, niece, and a close family friend. Blake lives alone and sends a monthly support check to each person. None of the individuals whom Blake supports has any income or files a tax return. All three individuals are U.S. citizens. Which of the three people Blake supports can he claim as a dependent on his tax return?

    a. Cousin   c. Family friend
    b. Niece   d. None

CHAPTER 10

Individuals: Income, Deductions, and Credits

LEARNING OBJECTIVES: *After completing Chapter 10, you should be able to:*

LO.1 Identify specific income inclusions and exclusions applicable to individuals.

LO.2 Determine an individual's allowable itemized deductions.

LO.3 Explain and illustrate the adoption expenses credit, child tax credit, education tax credits, credit for child and dependent care expenses, and earned income credit.

LO.4 Explain some of the key tax provisions of the Affordable Care Act.

CHAPTER OUTLINE

10-1 Overview of Income Provisions Applicable to Individuals, 10-2

10-2 Specific Inclusions Applicable to Individuals, 10-3
10-2a Alimony and Separate Maintenance Payments, 10-3
10-2b Prizes and Awards, 10-5
10-2c Unemployment Compensation, 10-5
10-2d Social Security Benefits, 10-6

10-3 Specific Exclusions Applicable to Individuals, 10-6
10-3a Gifts and Inheritances, 10-6
10-3b Scholarships, 10-7
10-3c Damages, 10-8
10-3d Workers' Compensation, 10-10
10-3e Accident and Health Insurance Benefits, 10-10
10-3f Educational Savings Bonds, 10-10

10-4 Itemized Deductions, 10-11
10-4a Medical Expenses, 10-11
10-4b Taxes, 10-15
10-4c Interest, 10-17
10-4d Charitable Contributions, 10-21
10-4e Other Itemized Deductions, 10-25

10-5 Individual Tax Credits, 10-27
10-5a Adoption Expenses Credit, 10-27
10-5b Child and Dependent Tax Credits, 10-28
10-5c Credit for Child and Dependent Care Expenses, 10-28
10-5d Education Tax Credits, 10-30
10-5e Earned Income Credit, 10-31

10-6 Affordable Care Act Provisions, 10-32
10-6a Individual Shared Responsibility Payment, 10-32
10-6b Premium Tax Credit, 10-33

TAX TALK *A tax loophole is something that benefits the other guy. If it benefits you, it is tax reform.* —RUSSELL B. LONG

THE TAX IMPLICATIONS OF LIFE!

Donna and David Steele, ages 35 and 37, respectively, recently married and have come to you for tax advice. They have several questions about their tax situation. Both are employed, and they expect to have combined wages from all sources of $70,000 for the current year.

In the current year, Donna enrolled in the masters of accounting program at State University. She would like to become a CPA, but will need to complete additional accounting coursework to achieve this goal. As a result of her previous accounting work experience and undergraduate business degree, Donna was appointed as a teaching assistant for an introductory accounting course. In addition to a $450 monthly salary, the position also provides for a waiver of $4,500 of her tuition for the semester. Donna also paid $250 of interest during the year on student loans still outstanding from her undergraduate education.

Donna and David received a wedding gift of $10,000 from her grandmother, and the couple earned $250 of interest on a savings account they opened with the money. David sold stock for $1,000 that was purchased two years ago for $5,000.

Early in the year, David was crossing a street in the pedestrian crosswalk when a delivery van struck him. The driver of the truck was intoxicated. David suffered a severe injury to his right arm that required him to miss work for a month. The delivery company's insurance company settled the case by paying damages as follows:

Compensatory damages:	
Medical expenses	$ 30,000
Injury to David's right arm	100,000
Pain and suffering	50,000
Loss of income	10,000
Legal fees	25,000
Punitive damages	160,000
	$375,000

David and Donna initially thought that they would have to sue the delivery company in order to be compensated for the expenses incurred associated with the accident. After many meetings and negotiations,

continued

they received the settlement referenced previously very late in the year. Shortly after the accident, given their medical expenses and the fact that David couldn't work for a month, a friend set up a GoFundMe page to raise money for the family. The initial request was for $8,000. Through the generosity of friends and family, the request raised $12,500. David and Donna used the money to pay medical expenses, their mortgage, and the remaining balance of Donna's tuition.

This is David's second marriage, and he pays alimony to his ex-wife (they divorced in 2015). He has custody of his 15-year-old son, Stephen, who lives with Donna and David for nine months each year. The Steeles rent their home, paid $3,500 of state income taxes, paid a $412 motor vehicle registration tax on their personal car, incurred additional medical expenses of $20,000, and made $2,500 of charitable contributions.

Without calculating Donna and David's tax liability, what are the tax implications of the transactions noted above? Are there other tax deductions or credits for which they may qualify or other tax issues about which they should be made aware?

Read the chapter and formulate your response.

This chapter focuses on the computation of taxable income for individual taxpayers. Recall that taxable income is the base on which the tax liability is calculated. In the simplest of terms, taxable income is determined by reducing *gross income* by allowable *tax deductions*. Prior chapters discussed these terms in a general sense. This chapter explains rules that apply specifically to individual taxpayers, with respect to both income and deduction amounts. In addition, the chapter discusses individual tax credits that may further reduce an individual's tax liability. The chapter concludes by describing elements of the Affordable Care Act that could impact an individual's tax computation.

LO.1

Identify specific income inclusions and exclusions applicable to individuals.

10-1   OVERVIEW OF INCOME PROVISIONS APPLICABLE TO INDIVIDUALS

The definition of gross income is broad enough to include almost all receipts of money, property, or services. However, the tax law provides for exclusion of certain types of income.[1] The following income *inclusions* and *exclusions*, which apply to all taxpayers (including individuals), were discussed in Chapter 4:

- Interest from state and local bonds (exclusion).
- Life insurance paid on death of the insured (exclusion).
- Imputed interest on below-market loans (inclusion).
- Income from discharge of indebtedness (inclusion unless a specific exclusion applies).
- Income included under the tax benefit rule (inclusion).

Many *exclusions* available only to individuals are for *fringe benefits* received by *employees* (refer to Exhibit 9.2 in Chapter 9). Fringe benefits are discussed in Chapter 11. Other inclusions and exclusions for individuals are discussed next.

---

[1]See §§ 101–140.

BRIDGE DISCIPLINE Bridge to Economics and Finance

As is the case for business entities, a primary financial goal for individual taxpayers should entail maximizing the *after-tax value* of their assets over time. This approach requires not only selecting the best investment alternatives but also choosing those investments with the most favorable tax attributes. Fundamental to this notion is recognizing the key role the government plays in all economic activity through its taxing authority. As a result, an investor should consider economically sound strategies that minimize the extent to which the government can stake a claim to his or her success. For example, taxpayers can reduce the government's share of their wealth accumulations by deferring the payment of taxes until future years and by taking advantage of investment strategies for which tax incentives are available. Taxpayers should choose the investment alternatives that provide the best after-tax return over time and not necessarily those that lead to the least amount of taxation.

These points can be illustrated by examining two classic strategies. One of the best ways for individuals to maximize their personal wealth is to invest to the extent possible in qualified retirement savings programs [e.g., Individual Retirement Accounts, § 401(k) plans]. Contributions to such accounts provide a current tax deduction. In addition, earnings in the account are not subject to taxation until they are withdrawn, which, in most cases, is in retirement. Postponing the tax in these two ways reduces the present value of the tax cost, which increases the after-tax value of the investment. Another strategy involves investing in tax-free municipal bonds, which produce interest income that is free of Federal income tax. However, the return on a municipal bond should be compared with the after-tax returns on comparable taxable bonds. For example, a relevant question is how the implicit tax (in the form of a lower return) associated with a municipal bond compares with the explicit tax (in the form of taxable interest) associated with a taxable bond.

10-2 SPECIFIC INCLUSIONS APPLICABLE TO INDIVIDUALS

The general principles governing the determination of gross income have occasionally yielded results that Congress found unacceptable. Thus, Congress has provided more specific rules for determining the amount of gross income from certain sources. The following provisions applicable to individuals are covered in this chapter:

- Alimony and separate maintenance payments.
- Prizes and awards.
- Unemployment compensation.
- Social Security benefits.

10-2a Alimony and Separate Maintenance Payments

When a married couple divorce or legally separate, state law generally requires a division of the property accumulated during the marriage. In addition, one spouse may have a legal obligation to support the other spouse. The Code distinguishes between the support payments (alimony or separate maintenance) and the property division in terms of the tax consequences. Further, if payments are made that are intended to provide for the support of a child, the tax law provides that these payments are distinguishable from both alimony and property settlements.

Alimony and separate maintenance payments made under an agreement entered into before 2019 are deductible by the party making the payments and are includible in the gross income of the party receiving the payments.[2] Thus, income is shifted from the income earner to the income beneficiary, who is better able to pay the tax on the amount received. The Tax Cuts and Jobs Act (TCJA) of 2017 changes the tax treatment of alimony. For divorce agreements executed after 2018, alimony paid is not deductible. As a result, any alimony received is not included in the recipient's gross income.

---

[2] §§ 71 and 215.

Pete and Tina were divorced in 2018, and Tina is required to pay Pete $15,000 of alimony each year. Tina earns $61,000 a year. The tax law presumes that because Pete receives the $15,000, he is better able than Tina to pay the tax on that amount. Therefore, Pete must include the $15,000 in his gross income. While Tina is required to include the $61,000 in her gross income, she is allowed to deduct $15,000 from her gross income. If their divorce had been finalized in 2019 (or later), Pete would not be required to include the alimony in his income and Tina would not be allowed a deduction for the alimony paid.

Property Settlements

A transfer of property other than cash to a former spouse under a divorce decree or agreement is not a taxable event. The transferor is not entitled to a deduction and does not recognize gain or loss on the transfer. The transferee does not recognize income and takes a cost basis equal to the transferor's basis.[3]

Paul transfers stock to Rosa this year as part of a divorce settlement. The cost of the stock to Paul was $12,000, and the stock's fair market value at the time of the transfer is $15,000. Rosa later sells the stock for $16,000. Paul is not required to recognize gain from the transfer of the stock to Rosa, and Rosa has a realized *and* recognized gain of $4,000 ($16,000 − $12,000) when she sells the stock.

Requirements for Alimony

To classify payments as alimony rather than property settlements or child support obligations, Congress developed the following objective rules. Payments made under agreements and decrees are *classified as alimony* only if the following conditions are satisfied:

- The payments are in cash. (This clearly distinguishes alimony from a property division.)

- The agreement or decree does not specify that the payments are not alimony. (This allows the parties to determine by agreement whether the payments will be alimony.)

- The payor and payee are not members of the same household at the time the payments are made. (This ensures the payments are for maintaining two households.)

- There is no liability to make the payments for any period after the death of the payee. (Payments due after death would be a property interest that could be transferred to the heirs.)[4]

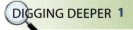

In-depth coverage can be found on this book's companion website: **www.cengage.com**

Child Support

A taxpayer does *not* realize income from the receipt of child support payments made by his or her former spouse. This result occurs because the money is received subject to the duty to use the money for the child's benefit. The payor is not allowed to deduct the child support payments because the payments are made to satisfy the payor's legal obligation to support the child.

In many cases, it may be difficult to determine whether the payments are intended to be alimony or child support. This issue is often resolved by applying the following rule: If the amount of the payments would be reduced upon the occurrence of a

---

[3]§ 1041 was added to the Code in 1984 to repeal the rule in *U.S. v. Davis*, 62–2 USTC ¶9509, 9 AFTR 2d 1625, 82 S.Ct. 1190 (USSC, 1962). Under the *Davis* rule, which applied to pre-1985 divorces, a property transfer incident to divorce was a taxable event.

[4]See *Divorced or Separated Individuals* (IRS Publication 504) for additional information about the tax consequences of divorce.

contingency related to a child (e.g., the child attains age 21 or dies), the amount of the future reduction in the payment is deemed child support. In addition, to the extent a taxpayer's alimony and child support obligations are not met in full in a year, any payments received are categorized first as child support and then any excess is categorized as alimony.[5] These rules are applied even though the divorce agreement specifies other amounts for the support of the child.[6]

Under their divorce agreement, Grace is required to make monthly alimony payments of $500 to Matt. However, when Matt and Grace's child reaches age 21, marries, or dies (whichever occurs first), the payments will be reduced to $300 per month. Matt has custody of the child. Because the required contingency is the cause for the reduction in the payments, from $500 to $300, child support payments are $200 per month and alimony is $300 per month.

EXAMPLE 3

10-2b **Prizes and Awards**

The fair market value of prizes and awards (other than scholarships) must be included in gross income.[7] Therefore, lottery winnings, magazine publisher prizes, door prizes, and awards from an employer to an employee in recognition of performance are fully taxable to the recipient.

A narrow exception permits a prize or an award to be excluded from gross income if *all* of the following requirements are satisfied:

- The prize or award is received in recognition of religious, charitable, scientific, educational, artistic, literary, or civic achievement (e.g., Nobel Prize, Pulitzer Prize, or faculty teaching award).

- The recipient was selected without taking any action to enter the contest or proceeding.

- The recipient is not required to render substantial future services as a condition for receiving the prize or award.

- The recipient transfers the prize or award to a qualified governmental unit or nonprofit organization.[8]

A taxpayer can also avoid including prizes and awards in gross income by refusing to accept the prize or award.[9]

Another exception allows the exclusion of certain employee achievement awards in the form of tangible personal property (e.g., a smart watch) but not cash or cash equivalents (e.g., gift certificates, meals, lodging, or tickets to theatre or sporting events). The awards must be made in recognition of length of service or safety achievement. Generally, the ceiling on the excludible amount for an employee is $400 per taxable year. However, if the award is a *qualified plan award*, the ceiling on the exclusion is $1,600 per taxable year.[10]

10-2c **Unemployment Compensation**

The unemployment compensation program is sponsored and operated by the Federal and state governments to provide a source of income for people who have been employed and are temporarily out of work. In a series of rulings over a period of 40 years, the IRS exempted unemployment benefits from tax. These payments were considered social benefit programs for the promotion of the general welfare. In 1986, in order to reduce the unemployment compensation recipient's potential disincentive to work, Congress amended the Code to make these benefits taxable.[11]

[5]§§ 71(c)(2) and (c)(3).

[6]*Johnson v. Comm.*, T.C.Memo. 2014–67.

[7]§ 74.

[8]§ 74(b).

[9]See Rev.Rul. 57–374, 1957–2 C.B. 69 and Rev.Proc. 87–54, 1987–2 C.B. 669.

[10]§ 74(c). Qualified plan awards are defined in § 274(j) and explained in *Business Expenses*, Chapter 2 (IRS Publication 535).

[11]§ 85.

10-2d Social Security Benefits

If a taxpayer's income exceeds a specified base amount, as much as 85 percent of Social Security retirement benefits must be included in gross income. The taxable amount of benefits is determined through the application of one of two formulas described in § 86.

DIGGING DEEPER 2   **In-depth coverage can be found on this book's companion website: www.cengage.com**

10-3 SPECIFIC EXCLUSIONS APPLICABLE TO INDIVIDUALS

If an income item is within the all-inclusive definition of gross income, the item can be excluded from gross income only if the taxpayer can locate specific authority for doing so. The discussion that follows focuses on common exclusion items available to individual taxpayers.

10-3a Gifts and Inheritances

Beginning with the Income Tax Act of 1913 and continuing to the present, Congress has allowed the recipient of a gift to exclude the value of the property from gross income. The exclusion applies to gifts made during the life of the donor (*inter vivos* gifts) and transfers that take effect upon the death of the donor (bequests and inheritances).[12] However, the recipient of a gift of income-producing property is subject to tax on the income subsequently earned from the property. Also, the donor or the decedent's estate may be subject to gift or estate taxes on such transfers.

In numerous cases, "gifts" are made in a business setting. For example, a salesperson gives a purchasing agent free samples, an employee receives cash from his or her employer upon retirement, or a corporation makes payments to employees who were victims of a natural disaster. In these and similar instances, it is frequently unclear whether the payment was a gift or represents compensation for past, present, or future services.

The courts have defined a gift as "a voluntary transfer of property by one to another without adequate (valuable) consideration or compensation therefrom."[13] If the payment is intended to be for services rendered, it is not a gift, even though the payment is made without legal or moral obligation and the payor receives no economic benefit from the transfer. To qualify as a gift, the payment must be made "out of affection, respect, admiration, charity or like impulses."[14] Thus, the cases on this issue have been decided on the basis of the donor's intent.[15]

In the case of cash or other property received by an employee from his or her employer, Congress has eliminated any ambiguity. Transfers from an employer to an employee cannot be categorized as a gift.[16]

Amounts received as a result of a crowdfunding campaign may meet the definition of a gift. Crowdfunding involves raising funds, often a small amount from a large group of people, for artistic or technology projects, as well as for personal or charitable undertakings. Under the broad definition of gross income provided in the tax law, crowdfunded amounts received would be included in the recipient's income. However, if such funds are given without an expectation of receiving anything in return (e.g., as payment for someone's medical expenses rather than as payment for a future music album), then such amounts could meet the criterion to be considered a gift and, as such, could be excluded from income.

---

[12]§ 102.

[13]*Estate of D. R. Daly*, 3 B.T.A. 1042 (1926).

[14]*Robertson v. U.S.*, 52–1 USTC ¶9343, 41 AFTR 1053, 72 S.Ct. 994 (USSC, 1952).

[15]See, for example, *Comm. v. Duberstein*, 60–2 USTC ¶9515, 5 AFTR 2d 1626, 80 S.Ct. 1190 (USSC, 1960).

[16]§ 102(c). But see § 139 for qualified disaster situations.

The Big Picture

Return to the facts of *The Big Picture* on p. 10-1. The $12,500 received by David and Donna as a result of their GoFundMe campaign could likely be categorized as a gift and, as such, excluded from their income. The contributers to the campaign do not seem to have been motivated by the expectation of receiving anything in return; the contributions resulted from the generosity of their friends and family, as well as strangers. As a result, the payments meet the tax law definition of a gift.

If any of the campaign amounts were contributed by David's employer, those amounts would likely not meet the definition of a gift because David provides services to his employer.

EXAMPLE
4

In-depth coverage can be found on this book's companion website: **www.cengage.com**

3   DIGGING DEEPER

10-3b **Scholarships**

General Information

Payments or benefits received by a student at an educational institution may be categorized as (1) scholarships, (2) compensation for services, or (3) a gift.

The scholarship rules are intended to provide exclusion treatment for education-related benefits that cannot qualify as gifts but are not compensation for services. According to the Regulations, "a scholarship is an amount paid or allowed to, or for the benefit of, an individual to aid such individual in the pursuit of study or research."[17] To be eligible for this beneficial tax treatment, the recipient must be a candidate for a degree at an educational institution.[18] Only the portion of a scholarship used for tuition and fees required for enrollment, as well as books, supplies, and equipment required for classes, qualifies for the scholarship exclusion. In contrast, a portion of a scholarship covering room and board is taxable (not excluded).

If the payments or benefits are received as compensation for services (past or present), the fact that the recipient is a student generally does not mean the amounts can be excluded from gross income.[19] Thus, a university teaching or research assistant is usually considered an employee, and his or her stipend is taxable compensation for services rendered. However, an exception allows nonprofit educational institutions to provide qualified tuition reduction plans for their employees; the tuition reduction amount can be excluded from the employee's gross income. The exclusion also applies to tuition reductions granted to the employee's spouse and dependent children.[20] In contrast, athletic scholarships can generally be excluded from gross income as long as the individual is not required to participate in the sport.[21]

The Big Picture

Return to the facts of *The Big Picture* on p. 10-1. State University waives a portion of tuition for all graduate teaching assistants. The tuition waived is intended as compensation for services and is therefore included in the teaching assistant's gross income. Therefore, the $4,500 Donna receives in the form of a tuition waiver each semester as well as the $450 she receives each month are considered compensation for services. The fact that she uses the funds for educational expenses does not change the tax treatment of the amounts received.

EXAMPLE
5

---

[17]Prop.Reg. § 1.117–6(c)(3)(i).

[18]§ 117(a).

[19]Reg. § 1.117–2(a). See *C. P. Bhalla,* 35 T.C. 13 (1960), for a discussion of the distinction between a scholarship and compensation. See also *Bingler v. Johnson,* 69–1 USTC ¶9348, 23 AFTR 2d 1212, 89 S.Ct. 1439 (USSC, 1969).

For potential exclusion treatment, see the discussion of qualified tuition reductions in text Section 11-2f.

[20]§ 117(d).

[21]Rev.Rul. 77–263, 1977–2 C.B. 47.

Finally, amounts received to be used for educational purposes (other than amounts received from family members) cannot be excluded as gifts because conditions attached to the receipt of the funds mean that the payments were not made out of "detached generosity."

EXAMPLE 6

Terry enters a contest sponsored by a local newspaper. Each contestant is required to submit an essay on local environmental issues. The prize is one year's tuition at State University. Terry wins the contest. The newspaper has a legal obligation to Terry (as the contest winner). Thus, the benefit is not a gift. However, because the tuition payment aids Terry in pursuing her studies and is not compensation for services, the payment is a scholarship.

A scholarship recipient may exclude from gross income the amount used for tuition and related expenses (fees, books, supplies, and equipment required for courses), provided the conditions of the grant do not require that the funds be used for other purposes.[22]

EXAMPLE 7

Kelly received an athletic scholarship from State University. The scholarship pays her tuition, $9,000, and books and supplies, $2,400. She also received $4,500 a year for costs of attendance, which she uses to pay for housing, food, laundry, and transportation. The tuition and the cost of books and supplies are excluded from gross income as a scholarship. The $4,500 received as costs of attendance does not qualify for the scholarship exclusion; therefore, Kelly must include that amount in her gross income.

Timing Issues

Frequently, the scholarship recipient is a cash basis taxpayer who receives the money in one tax year but pays the educational expenses in a subsequent year. The amount eligible for exclusion may not be known at the time the money is received. In that case, the transaction is held open until the educational expenses are paid.[23]

EXAMPLE 8

In August 2018, Sanjay received $10,000 as a scholarship for the academic year 2018–2019. Sanjay's expenditures for tuition, books, and supplies were as follows:

August–December 2018	$3,000
January–May 2019	4,500
	$7,500

Sanjay's gross income for 2019 includes $2,500 ($10,000 − $7,500) that is not excludible as a scholarship. None of the scholarship is included in his gross income in 2018.

Disguised Compensation

Some employers make scholarships available solely to the children of key employees. The tax objective of these plans is to provide a nontaxable fringe benefit to the executives by making the payment to the child in the form of an excludible scholarship. However, the IRS has ruled that the payments are generally includible in the gross income of the parent-employee.[24]

10-3c Damages

A person who suffers harm caused by another is often entitled to **compensatory damages**. The tax consequences of the receipt of damages depend on the type of harm the taxpayer has experienced. The taxpayer may seek recovery for (1) a loss of income, (2) expenses incurred, (3) property destroyed, or (4) personal injury.

Generally, reimbursement for a loss of income is taxed in the same manner as the income replaced (see the exception under Personal Injury on the following page).

---

[22]§ 117(b). See also **https://www.irs.gov/newsroom/tax-benefits-for-education-information-center**.

[23]Prop.Reg. § 1.117–6(b)(2).

[24]Rev.Rul. 75–448, 1975–2 C.B. 55 and *Richard T. Armantrout*, 67 T.C. 996 (1977).

Damages that are a recovery of expenses previously deducted by the taxpayer are generally taxable under the tax benefit rule (refer to text Section 4-5e).

A payment for damaged or destroyed property is treated as an amount received in a sale or exchange of the property. Thus, the taxpayer has a realized gain if the damages received exceed the property's basis. Damages for personal injuries receive special treatment under the Code.

Personal Injury

The legal theory of personal injury damages is that the amount received is intended "to make the plaintiff (the injured party) whole as before the injury."[25] It follows that if the damages received were subject to tax, the after-tax amount received would be less than the actual damages incurred and the injured party would not be "whole as before the injury." With regard to personal injury damages, a distinction is made between compensatory damages and **punitive damages**.

Compensatory damages are intended to compensate the taxpayer for the damages incurred. Only those compensatory damages received on account of *physical personal injury or physical sickness* can be excluded from gross income.[26] Such exclusion treatment includes amounts received for loss of income associated with the physical personal injury or physical sickness. Compensatory damages awarded on account of emotional distress are not received on account of physical injury or sickness and thus cannot be excluded from gross income (except to the extent of any amount received for medical care). Likewise, any amounts received for age discrimination or injury to one's reputation cannot be excluded.

Punitive damages are amounts the party that caused the harm must pay to the victim as punishment for outrageous conduct. Punitive damages are not intended to compensate the victim, but rather to punish the party who caused the harm. It follows that amounts received as punitive damages may actually place the victim in a better economic position than before the harm was experienced. Thus, punitive damages are included in gross income.

These rules are set forth in Concept Summary 10.1.

Concept Summary 10.1

Taxation of Damages

Type of Claim	Taxation of Award or Settlement
Breach of contract (generally loss of income)	Taxable.
Property damages	Gain to the extent damages received exceed basis. A loss is deductible for business property and investment property to the extent of basis over the amount realized. A loss may be deductible for personal use property (see discussion of casualty losses in text Section 6-3).
Personal injury	
Physical	All compensatory amounts are excluded unless previously deducted (e.g., medical expenses). Amounts received as punitive damages are included in gross income.
Nonphysical	Compensatory damages and punitive damages are included in gross income.

The Big Picture

Return to the facts of *The Big Picture* on p. 10-1. The damages David received were awarded as a result of a physical personal injury. Therefore, all of the compensatory damages can be excluded. Note that even the compensation for the loss of income of $10,000 can be excluded. The punitive damages David received, however, must be included in his gross income.

EXAMPLE

9

---

[25]*C. A. Hawkins*, 6 B.T.A. 1023 (1928).   [26]§ 104(a)(2).

10-3d **Workers' Compensation**

State workers' compensation laws require the employer to pay fixed amounts for specific job-related injuries. The state laws were enacted so that the employee would not have to go through the ordeal of a lawsuit (and possibly not collect damages because of some defense available to the employer) to recover the damages. Although the payments are intended, in part, to compensate for a loss of future income, Congress has specifically exempted workers' compensation benefits from inclusion in gross income.[27]

10-3e **Accident and Health Insurance Benefits**

The income tax treatment of accident and health insurance benefits depends on whether the policy providing the benefits was purchased by the taxpayer or the taxpayer's employer. Benefits collected under an accident and health insurance policy purchased by the taxpayer are excludible even though the payments are a substitute for income.[28]

EXAMPLE 10

Bonnie purchases a medical and disability insurance policy. The insurance company pays Bonnie $1,000 per week to replace wages she loses while in the hospital. Although the payments serve as a substitute for income, the amounts received are tax-exempt benefits collected under Bonnie's insurance policy.

A different set of rules applies if the accident and health insurance protection was purchased by the individual's employer, as discussed in text Section 11-2a.

10-3f **Educational Savings Bonds**

Because of the rising cost of attending college, Congress has attempted to assist low- to middle-income parents in saving for their children's college education with specific tax benefits for such saving. One such benefit is an interest income exclusion on educational savings bonds.[29] The interest on U.S. government Series EE savings bonds may be excluded from gross income if the bond proceeds are used to pay qualified higher education expenses.

Qualified higher education expenses consist of tuition and fees paid to an eligible educational institution for the taxpayer, spouse, or dependent. If the redemption proceeds (both principal and interest) exceed the qualified higher education expenses, only a pro rata portion of the interest will qualify for exclusion treatment.

EXAMPLE 11

Tracy's redemption proceeds from qualified savings bonds during the taxable year are $6,000 (principal of $4,000 and interest of $2,000). Tracy's qualified higher education expenses are $5,000. Because the redemption proceeds exceed the qualified higher education expenses, only $1,667 [($5,000/$6,000) × $2,000] of the interest is excludible.

The exclusion is limited by the application of the wherewithal to pay concept. That is, once the modified adjusted gross income exceeds a threshold amount, the phaseout of the exclusion begins. *Modified adjusted gross income (MAGI)* is adjusted gross income prior to the foreign earned income exclusion and the educational savings bond exclusion. The threshold amounts are adjusted for inflation each year. For 2018, the phaseout begins at $79,550. The phaseout is completed when MAGI exceeds the threshold amount by more than $15,000. The otherwise excludible interest is reduced by the amount calculated as follows:

---

[27]§ 104(a)(1).

[28]§ 104(a)(3).

[29]§ 135.

On a joint return, $119,300 is substituted for $79,550 (in 2018), and $30,000 is substituted for $15,000.[30]

Assume the same facts as in Example 11, except that Tracy's MAGI for 2018 is $82,000. Tracy is single. The phaseout results in Tracy's interest exclusion being reduced by $272 {[($82,000 − $79,550)/$15,000] × $1,667}. Therefore, Tracy's exclusion is $1,395 ($1,667 − $272).

EXAMPLE
12

10-4 ITEMIZED DEDUCTIONS

LO.2

Determine an individual's allowable itemized deductions.

Taxpayers are allowed to deduct *from* AGI specified expenditures as itemized deductions. Itemized deductions, which are reported on Schedule A, can be classified as follows:

- Expenses that are purely *personal* in nature.
- Expenses related to (1) the *production or collection of income* and (2) the *management of property* held for the production of income.[31]

Expenses in the second category are sometimes referred to as *nonbusiness expenses*. While trade or business expenses (discussed previously) must be incurred in connection with a trade or business, nonbusiness expenses are expenses incurred in connection with an income-producing activity that does not qualify as a trade or business. If the nonbusiness expense is incurred in connection with rent or royalty property, it is classified as a deduction *for* AGI (similar to trade or business expenses). Otherwise, it is classified as a deduction *from* AGI. Itemized deductions include, but are not limited to, the expenses listed in Exhibit 10.1.

The election to itemize is appropriate when total itemized deductions exceed the standard deduction associated with the taxpayer's filing status (see text Section 9-2). The more commonly encountered itemized deductions are discussed next.

10-4a Medical Expenses

Medical expenses paid for the care of the taxpayer, spouse, and dependents are allowed as an itemized deduction to the extent the expenses are not reimbursed. The medical expense deduction is limited to the amount by which such expenses exceed a threshold percentage of the taxpayer's AGI. Under current law, the threshold percentage is 7.5 percent (10 percent for 2019 and later years).[32]

EXHIBIT 10.1	Partial List of Itemized Deductions

Personal Expenditures

Medical expenses in excess of 7.5% of AGI (10% of AGI for 2019 and later)

State and local income taxes or sales taxes

Real estate taxes

Personal property taxes

Interest on home mortgage

Charitable contributions (limited to a maximum of 60% or 50% of AGI)

Casualty losses incurred in a Federally declared disaster area (in excess of 10% of AGI)

Expenditures Related to Income-Producing Activities

Investment interest (to the extent of net investment income)

---

[30]The indexed amounts for 2017 were $78,150 and $117,250.

[31]§ 212.

[32]§ 213(f).

EXAMPLE 13

Return to the facts of *The Big Picture* on p. 10-1. In addition to the medical expenses incurred associated with David's accident that were later reimbursed by the delivery company's insurance company, the Steeles had other qualifying medical expenses. Assuming that their AGI for the year is $200,000, they will need to itemize their deductions and have more than $15,000 ($200,000 × 7.5%) in unreimbursed medical expenses to receive a tax benefit from those expenses. Thus, their itemized deduction for medical expenses would equal whatever qualifying medical expenses were incurred that exceeded the $15,000 threshold.

Medical Expenses Defined

The term *medical care* includes expenditures incurred for the "diagnosis, cure, mitigation, treatment, or prevention of disease, or for the purpose of affecting any structure or function of the body."[33] Medical expense also includes premiums paid for health care insurance, prescribed drugs and insulin, and lodging while away from home for the purpose of obtaining medical care. Examples of deductible and nondeductible medical expenses appear in Exhibit 10.2.

Cosmetic Surgery

Amounts paid for cosmetic surgery are not deductible medical expenses unless the surgery is medically necessary. Cosmetic surgery is necessary when it ameliorates the effects of (1) a deformity arising from a congenital abnormality, (2) a personal injury, or (3) a disfiguring disease.

Nursing Home Care

The cost of care in a nursing home or home for the aged, including meals and lodging, can be included in deductible medical expenses if the primary reason for being in the home is to get medical care. If the primary reason for being there is personal, any costs

EXHIBIT 10.2	Examples of Deductible and Nondeductible Medical Expenses Paid by Taxpayer
Deductible	**Nondeductible**
Medical (including dental, mental, and hospital) care	Funeral, burial, or cremation expenses
Prescription drugs and insulin	Nonprescription drugs (except insulin)
Special equipment:	Bottled water
Wheelchairs	Toiletries, cosmetics
Crutches	Diaper service, maternity clothes
Artificial limbs	Programs for the general improvement of health:
Eyeglasses (including contact lenses)	Weight reduction
Hearing aids	Health spas
Transportation for medical care	Social activities (e.g., dancing and swimming lessons)
Medical and hospital insurance premiums	Elective cosmetic surgery
Long-term care insurance premiums (subject to limitations)	
Cost of alcohol and drug rehabilitation	
Certain costs to stop smoking	
Weight reduction programs related to obesity	

---

[33]§ 213(d)(1)(A).

for medical or nursing care can be included in deductible medical expenses, but the cost of meals and lodging must be excluded.

Capital Expenditures

When capital expenditures are incurred for medical purposes, they must be deemed medically necessary by a physician, the facility must be used primarily by the patient, and the expense must be reasonable in order to be deductible. Examples of such expenditures include dust elimination systems,[34] elevators,[35] and vans specially designed for wheelchair-bound taxpayers. Other examples of expenditures that may qualify are swimming pools if the taxpayer does not have access to a neighborhood pool and air conditioners if they do not become permanent improvements (e.g., window units).[36]

Both a capital expenditure for a permanent improvement and expenditures made for the operation or maintenance of the improvement may qualify as medical expenses. The allowable cost of such qualified medical expenditures is deductible in the year incurred. Although depreciation is required for most other capital expenditures, it is not required for those qualifying for medical purposes (in other words, the entire cost of a qualifying capital expenditure is immediately deductible).

Medical Expenses for Spouse and Dependents

In computing the medical expense deduction, a taxpayer may include medical expenses for a spouse and for a person who was a dependent at the time the expenses were paid or incurred. Of the requirements that normally apply in determining dependency status, neither the gross income nor the joint return test applies in determining dependency status for medical expense deduction purposes.

Transportation, Meals, and Lodging

Payments for transportation to and from a point of treatment for medical care are also considered deductible medical expenses. These costs include bus, taxi, train, or plane fare; charges for ambulance service; and out-of-pocket expenses for the use of an automobile. A mileage allowance of 18 cents per mile for 2018 may be used instead of actual out-of-pocket automobile expenses.[37] Whether the taxpayer chooses to claim out-of-pocket automobile expenses or the 18 cents per mile automatic mileage option, related parking fees and tolls can also be deducted. Also included are transportation expenditures for someone such as a parent or nurse who must accompany the patient. The cost of meals while en route to obtain medical care is not deductible as a medical expense.

In-depth coverage can be found on this book's companion website: www.cengage.com | **4 DIGGING DEEPER**

Health Savings Accounts

Qualifying individuals may make deductible contributions to a <mark>Health Savings Account (HSA)</mark>. An HSA is a qualified trust or custodial account administered by a qualified HSA trustee, which can be a bank, an insurance company, or another IRS-approved trustee.[38] A taxpayer can use an HSA in conjunction with a high-deductible medical insurance policy to help reduce the overall cost of medical coverage. The high-deductible policy provides coverage for extraordinary medical expenses (in excess of the deductible), and expenses not covered by the policy can be paid with funds withdrawn tax-free from the HSA.

---

[34]Ltr.Rul. 7948029.

[35]*Riach v. Frank*, 62–1 USTC ¶9419, 9 AFTR 2d 1263, 302 F.2d 374 (CA–9, 1962).

[36]Reg. § 1.213–1(e)(1)(iii).

[37]This amount is adjusted periodically; see Notice 2018–3, 2018–2 I.R.B. 285. The allowance was 17 cents per mile for 2017.

[38]§ 223.

EXAMPLE

14

Sanchez, who is married and has three dependent children, carries a high-deductible medical insurance policy with a deductible of $4,400. He establishes an HSA and contributes the maximum allowable amount to the HSA in 2018. During 2018, the Sanchez family incurs medical expenses of $7,000. The high-deductible policy covers $2,600 of the expenses ($7,000 expenses − $4,400 deductible). Sanchez may withdraw $4,400 from the HSA to pay the medical expenses not covered by the high-deductible policy.

High-Deductible Plans High-deductible policies are less expensive than low-deductible policies, so taxpayers with low medical costs can benefit from the lower premiums and use funds from the HSA to pay costs not covered by the high-deductible policy. A plan must meet two requirements to qualify as a high-deductible plan in 2018.[39]

1. The annual deductible is not less than $1,350 for self-only coverage ($2,700 for family coverage).
2. The annual limit on total out-of-pocket costs (excluding the premiums) under the plan does not exceed $6,650 for self-only coverage ($13,300 for family coverage).

Tax Treatment of HSA Contributions and Distributions To establish an HSA, a taxpayer contributes funds to a custodial account.[40] As illustrated in the preceding example, funds can be withdrawn from an HSA to pay medical expenses that are not covered by the high-deductible policy. The following general tax rules apply to HSAs:

1. Contributions made by the taxpayer to an HSA are deductible from gross income to arrive at AGI (deduction *for* AGI). Thus, the taxpayer does not need to itemize to take the deduction.
2. Earnings on HSAs are not subject to taxation unless distributed, in which case taxability depends on how the funds are used.[41]

   • Distributions from HSAs are excluded from gross income if they are used to pay for medical expenses not covered by the high-deductible policy.

   • Distributions that are not used to pay for medical expenses are included in gross income and are subject to an additional 20 percent penalty if made before age 65, death, or disability. Any distributions made by reason of death or disability or distributions made after the HSA beneficiary becomes eligible for Medicare are taxed but not subject to the penalty.

HSAs have at least two other attractive features. First, an HSA is portable. Taxpayers who switch jobs can take their HSAs with them. Second, anyone under age 65 who has a high-deductible plan and is not covered by another policy that is not a high-deductible plan can establish an HSA.

Deductible Amount The annual deduction for contributions to an HSA is limited to an amount that depends on whether the taxpayer has self-only coverage or family coverage. The annual limit for an individual who has self-only coverage in 2018 is $3,450, while the annual limit for an individual who has family coverage in 2018 is $6,900. These amounts are subject to annual cost-of-living adjustments.[42] An eligible taxpayer who has attained the age of 55 by the end of the tax year may make an additional annual (catch-up) contribution in 2018 of up to $1,000. A deduction is not allowed after the individual becomes eligible for Medicare coverage.

---

[39]§ 223(c)(2).

[40]§ 223(d).

[41]§ 223(f).

[42]§ 223(b)(2). The annual limits were $3,400 and $6,750 in 2017.

Determining the Maximum HSA Contribution Deduction

Liu (age 45), who is married and self-employed, carries a high-deductible medical insurance policy with family coverage and an annual deductible of $4,000. In addition, he has established an HSA. In 2018, Liu's maximum annual contribution to the HSA is $6,900.

EXAMPLE
15

During 2018, Adam, who is self-employed, made 12 monthly payments of $1,200 for an HSA contract that provides medical insurance coverage with a $3,600 deductible. The plan covers Adam, his wife, and their two children. Of the $1,200 monthly fee, $675 was for the high-deductible policy, and $525 was deposited into an HSA.

Because Adam is *self-employed*, he can deduct $8,100 of the amount paid for the high-deductible policy ($675 per month × 12 months) as a deduction *for* AGI (refer to text Section 11-4 b). In addition, he can deduct the $6,300 ($525 × 12) paid to the HSA as a deduction *for* AGI. Note that the $6,300 HSA deduction does not exceed the $6,900 ceiling.

EXAMPLE
16

10-4b **Taxes**

A deduction is allowed for certain state and local taxes paid or accrued by a taxpayer.[43] However, deductible taxes must be distinguished from nondeductible fees. Fees for special privileges or services are not deductible as taxes if they are expenditures that are personal in nature. Examples include fees for dog licenses, automobile inspections, automobile titles and registration, hunting and fishing licenses, bridge and highway tolls, drivers' licenses, parking meter deposits, and postage. These items, however, could be deductible if incurred as a business expense or for the production of income. Deductible and nondeductible taxes for purposes of computing itemized deductions are summarized in Exhibit 10.3. Note that Federal income taxes are not deductible.

From 2018 through 2025, the TCJA of 2017 limits the maximum itemized deduction for the nonbusiness state and local taxes discussed next [personal and real property taxes, income (or sales) taxes] to $10,000. This maximum is the same for taxpayers filing individually and jointly. A $5,000 maximum applies for married taxpayers filing separately.

EXHIBIT 10.3	Deductible and Nondeductible Taxes
Deductible*	**Nondeductible**
State, local, and foreign real property taxes	Federal income taxes
State and local personal property taxes	FICA taxes imposed on employees
State and local income taxes *or* sales/use taxes	Employer FICA taxes paid on domestic household workers
Foreign income taxes	Estate, inheritance, and gift taxes
	Federal, state, and local excise taxes (e.g., gasoline, tobacco, and spirits)
	Foreign income taxes if the taxpayer chooses the foreign tax credit option
	Taxes on real property to the extent such taxes are to be apportioned and treated as imposed on another taxpayer
	Special assessments for streets, sidewalks, curbing, and other similar improvements

*Per § 164(b)(6), from 2018 through 2025, the aggregate itemized deduction for these four taxes cannot exceed $10,000.

---

[43]Most deductible taxes are listed in § 164, while nondeductible amounts are included in § 275.

Personal Property Taxes

Deductible personal property taxes must be *ad valorem* (assessed in relation to the value of the property). Therefore, a motor vehicle tax based on weight, model, year, or horsepower is not an ad valorem tax. In contrast, a motor vehicle tax based on the value of the car is deductible.

The Big Picture

EXAMPLE 17

Return to the facts of *The Big Picture* on p. 10-1. Assume that the government imposes a motor vehicle registration tax equal to 2% of the value of the vehicle plus 40 cents per hundred pounds in Donna and David's state of residence. The Steeles own a car having a value of $20,000 and weighing 3,000 pounds in Donna and David's state of residence. They pay an annual registration tax of $412. Of this amount, $400 (2% × $20,000 of value) is deductible as a personal property tax if they itemize their deductions. The remaining $12, based on the weight of the car, is not deductible.

Real Estate Taxes

Real estate taxes of individuals are generally deductible. Taxes on personal use property and investment property are deductible as itemized deductions. Taxes on business property are deductible as business expenses. Real property taxes on property that is sold during the year must be allocated between the buyer and the seller (refer to text Section 5-5b).

State and Local Income Taxes and Sales Taxes

State and local *income* taxes paid by an individual are deductible only as itemized deductions, even if the taxpayer's sole source of income is from a business, rents, or royalties.

Cash basis taxpayers are entitled to deduct state income taxes in the year in which the payment is made. This includes taxes withheld by the employer, amounts paid with the state income tax return when filed, and estimated state income tax payments.[44] If the taxpayer overpays state income taxes, the refund received is included in gross income in the year received to the extent the deduction reduced the taxable income in the prior year.

EXAMPLE 18

Leona, a cash basis, unmarried taxpayer, had $800 of state income tax withheld from her paychecks during 2018. Also in 2018, Leona paid $100 that was due when she filed her 2017 state income tax return and made estimated payments of $300 toward her 2018 state income tax liability. When Leona files her 2018 Federal income tax return in April 2019, she elects to itemize deductions, which amount to $14,500, including the $1,200 of state income tax payments and withholdings, all of which reduce her taxable income.

As a result of overpaying her 2018 state income tax, Leona receives a refund of $200 early in 2019. She will include this amount in her 2019 gross income in computing her Federal income tax. It does not matter whether Leona received a check from the state for $200 or applied the $200 toward her 2019 state income tax.

Individuals can elect to deduct either their state and local income taxes *or* their sales/use taxes paid as an itemized deduction on Schedule A of Form 1040. This election is intended to provide equity to taxpayers living in states that do not have a state income tax (but do have sales taxes). Taxpayers making this election can either deduct actual sales/use tax payments *or* the amount specified in an IRS table. The amount in the table can be increased by sales tax paid on the purchase of motor vehicles, boats, and other specified items.

---

[44]Rev.Rul. 71–190, 1971–1 C.B. 70. See also Rev.Rul. 82–208, 1982–2 C.B. 58, where a deduction is not allowed when the taxpayer cannot, in good faith, reasonably determine that there is additional state income tax liability.

TAX PLANNING STRATEGIES **Timing the Payment of Deductible Taxes**

FRAMEWORK FOCUS: DEDUCTIONS

Strategy: Accelerate Recognition of Deductions to Achieve Tax Deferral.

It is sometimes possible to defer or accelerate the payment of certain deductible taxes, such as state income tax, real property tax, and personal property tax. For instance, the final installment of estimated state income tax is generally due after the end of a given tax year. However, accelerating the payment of the final installment could result in larger itemized deductions for the current year, as long as consideration is given to the $10,000 itemized deduction maximum.

10-4c **Interest**

For Federal income tax purposes, whether interest expense is tax deductible is dictated by the context in which the interest expense is incurred. Business interest is fully deductible as an ordinary and necessary expense. Most personal (consumer) interest such as interest paid on credit cards and car loans is not deductible. However, interest on qualified student loans, investment interest, and qualified residence (home mortgage) interest is deductible, subject to the limits discussed below.

Interest on Qualified Student Loans

Taxpayers who pay interest on a qualified student loan may be able to deduct the interest as a deduction *for* AGI. The deduction is allowable only to the extent the proceeds of the loan are used to pay qualified education expenses. The maximum annual deduction is $2,500. However, in 2018, the deduction is phased out for taxpayers with modified AGI (MAGI) between $65,000 and $80,000 ($135,000 and $165,000 on joint returns). The deduction is not available for taxpayers who are claimed as dependents or for married taxpayers filing separately.[45]

EXAMPLE 19

In 2018, Curt and Rita, who are married and file a joint return, paid $3,000 of interest on a qualified student loan. Their MAGI was $142,500. Their maximum potential deduction for qualified student loan interest is $2,500, but it must be reduced by $625 as a result of the phaseout rules.

$$\$2{,}500 \text{ interest} \times \frac{\$142{,}500 \text{ (MAGI)} - \$135{,}000 \text{ (phaseout floor)}}{\$30{,}000 \text{ (phaseout range)}} = \$625 \text{ reduction}$$

Curt and Rita are allowed a student loan interest deduction of $1,875 ($2,500 maximum deduction − $625 reduction = $1,875 deduction *for* AGI).

Investment Interest

Years ago, wealthy taxpayers used the interest deduction in the tax law to create wealth. By borrowing to purchase investments that would appreciate in the future, the interest on the debt was claimed as an ordinary deduction when paid. Later, when the asset was sold at a gain, only a capital gains tax was due on the appreciation. Thus, today's interest deduction could lead to tomorrow's capital gain.

In response, Congress limited the deductibility of **investment interest**, which is interest paid on debt borrowed for the purpose of purchasing or continuing to hold investment property. The deduction for investment interest allowed during the tax year is limited to the lesser of the investment interest paid or net investment income.[46]

---

[45]§ 221. See § 221(b)(2)(C) for the definition of MAGI. For 2017, the MAGI threshold amounts were the same as in 2018.

[46]§ 163(d)(1).

Net investment income, which serves as the ceiling on the deductibility of investment interest, is the excess of investment income over investment expenses. Investment income includes gross income from interest, annuities, and royalties not derived in the ordinary course of a trade or business.

Investment expenses are those deductible expenses directly connected with the production of investment income, such as property taxes on investment holdings, brokerage charges, and investment counsel fees. Investment expenses do not include interest expense.

After net investment income is determined, the allowable deductible investment interest expense is calculated.

EXAMPLE 20

Ethan's financial records for the year reflect the following:

Interest income from bank savings account	$10,000
Taxable annuity receipts	5,500
Local ad valorem property tax on investments	200
Investment interest expense	17,000

Ethan's investment income amounts to $15,500 ($10,000 + $5,500), and investment expenses total $200. Therefore, his net investment income is $15,300 ($15,500 − $200). Consequently, the investment interest deduction is limited to $15,300, the lesser of investment interest expense ($17,000) or net investment income.

The amount of investment interest disallowed is carried over to future years. In Example 20, the amount that is carried over to the following year is $1,700 ($17,000 investment interest expense − $15,300 deduction allowed). No limit is placed on the length of the carryover period.

DIGGING DEEPER 5 | In-depth coverage can be found on this book's companion website: **www.cengage.com**

Qualified Residence Interest

Qualified residence interest is interest paid or accrued during the taxable year on indebtedness (subject to limitations) secured by any property that is a qualified residence of the taxpayer. Qualified residence interest falls into two categories: (1) interest on **acquisition indebtedness** and (2) interest on **home equity loans**. Before each of these categories is discussed, however, the term *qualified residence* must be defined.

A qualified residence includes the taxpayer's principal residence and one other residence of the taxpayer or spouse. The principal residence is one that meets the requirement for nonrecognition of gain upon sale under § 121 (see text Section 7-6b). The one other residence, or second residence, refers to one that is used as a residence if not rented or, if rented, meets the requirements for a personal residence under the rental of vacation home rules of § 280A. A taxpayer who has more than one second residence can choose the qualified second residence each year (i.e., the taxpayer can select a different second residence each year). A residence includes, in addition to a house in the ordinary sense, cooperative apartments, condominiums, and mobile homes and boats that have living quarters (sleeping accommodations, toilet and cooking facilities).

Although in most cases interest paid on a home mortgage is fully deductible, there are limitations.[47] A deduction is allowed for interest paid or accrued during the tax year on aggregate acquisition indebtedness. *Acquisition indebtedness* refers to amounts incurred in acquiring, constructing, or substantially improving a qualified residence of the taxpayer. The amount of acquisition indebtedness is limited based on when the debt was incurred. If the debt is incurred after December 15, 2017, and before January 1, 2026, acquisition indebtedness is limited to $750,000 ($375,000 for married taxpayers

---

[47]§ 163(h)(3).

filing separate returns). Debt incurred on or before December 15, 2017, is limited to $1 million ($500,000 for married taxpayers filing separate returns). The higher limits will apply to all homeowners after 2025, regardless of the date the debt was incurred.

Prior to 2018, qualified residence interest also included interest on home equity loans. Such loans utilize the personal residence of the taxpayer as security, typically in the form of a second mortgage. Because home equity loan proceeds can be used for personal purposes (e.g., auto purchases and medical expenses), what would otherwise have been nondeductible personal interest was converted to deductible qualified residence interest.

Under the TCJA of 2017, from 2018 through 2025, qualified residence interest includes only interest on acquisition indebtedness.[48] Thus, interest paid on a home equity loan is not deductible unless the loan is used to build or substantially improve the taxpayer's primary residence.[49] For example, assume a taxpayer takes out a home equity loan secured by their primary residence to improve that residence. All of the interest paid on both loans is fully deductible as long as the home equity loan does not exceed the fair market value of the residence reduced by the acquisition indebtedness and the acquisition indebtedness, in aggregate, does not exceed $750,000. However, if the taxpayer took out the home equity loan to pay for a vacation and pay down credit card balances, the home equity loan interest would not be deductible. If proceeds of a home equity loan were used to pay for business expenses, the interest would be deductible business interest.

> **EXAMPLE 21**
>
> Larry owns a personal residence with a fair market value of $950,000 and an outstanding mortgage of $500,000. The mortgage is secured by his personal residence. In February 2018, Larry took out a $225,000 home equity loan to buy a vacation home. This loan is secured by his personal residence. While the total amount of acquisition indebtedness does not exceed $750,000, the interest on the home equity loan is not deductible because the loan is not used to improve the taxpayer's personal residence (the residence which secures the loan).
>
> If Larry had instead borrowed the $225,000 with a loan that was secured by and used to acquire the vacation home, he could deduct the interest assuming that home is Larry's second home (the loan would then be considered acquisition indebtedness).

Prior to 2018, mortgage insurance premiums (subject to a phaseout based on AGI) paid by the taxpayer on a qualified residence could also be treated as qualified residence interest.[50]

Interest Paid for Services Mortgage loan companies commonly charge a fee, often called a loan origination fee, for finding, placing, or processing a mortgage loan. Loan origination fees are typically nondeductible amounts included in the basis of the acquired property. Other fees, sometimes called **points** and expressed as a percentage of the loan amount, are paid to reduce the interest rate charged over the term of the loan. Essentially, the payment of points is a prepayment of interest and is considered compensation to a lender solely for the use of money. To be deductible, points must be in the nature of interest and cannot be a form of service charge or payment for specific services.[51]

In general, points are capitalized and are amortized and deductible ratably over the life of the loan. However, the purchaser of a principal residence may deduct qualifying points in the year of payment.[52] This exception also covers points paid to obtain funds for home improvements.

Points paid to refinance acquisition indebtedness (i.e., an existing home mortgage) cannot be immediately deducted, but must be capitalized and amortized as an interest deduction over the life of the new loan.[53]

---

[48]§ 163(h)(3)(F)(i)(I).
[49]IR-2018-32 (February 21, 2018).
[50]§§ 163(h)(3)(E)(i) and (ii).

[51]Rev.Rul. 69–188, 1969–1 C.B. 54.
[52]§ 461(g)(2).
[53]Rev.Rul. 87–22, 1987–1 C.B. 146.

EXAMPLE 22

Sandra purchased her residence many years ago, obtaining a 30-year mortgage at an annual interest rate of 6%. In the current year, Sandra refinances the mortgage to reduce the interest rate to 4%. To obtain the refinancing, she has to pay points of $2,600. Therefore, the $2,600, which is considered prepayment of interest, must be capitalized and amortized over the remaining life of the mortgage.

Prepayment Penalty

When a mortgage or loan is paid off in full in a lump sum before its term (i.e., paid off early), the lending institution may require an additional payment from the borrower (normally, a specific percentage of the loan balance). This is known as a prepayment penalty and is considered to be interest (e.g., personal, investment, or qualified residence) in the year paid. The general rules for deductibility of interest also apply to prepayment penalties.

Interest Paid to Related Parties

Nothing prevents the deduction of interest paid to a related party as long as the payment actually took place and the interest meets the requirements for deductibility. However, a special rule applies for related taxpayers when the debtor is on the accrual basis and the related creditor is on the cash basis. If this rule applies, interest that has been accrued but not paid at the end of the debtor's tax year is not deductible until payment is made and the income is reportable by the cash basis recipient.

Tax-Exempt Securities

The tax law provides that no deduction is allowed for interest on debt incurred to purchase or carry tax-exempt securities.[54] The meaning of the phrase *to purchase or carry* has been examined in many court cases.

Prepaid Interest

Accrual method reporting is imposed on cash basis taxpayers for interest prepayments that extend beyond the end of the taxable year.[55] Such payments must be allocated to the tax years to which the interest payments relate. These provisions are intended to prevent cash basis taxpayers from accelerating tax deductions by prepaying interest.

Classification of Interest Expense

Whether interest is deductible *for* AGI or as an itemized deduction (*from* AGI) depends on whether the indebtedness has a business, investment, or personal purpose. If the indebtedness is incurred in relation to a business (other than performing services as an employee) or for the production of rent or royalty income, the interest is deductible *for* AGI. If the indebtedness is incurred for personal use, such as qualified residence interest, any deduction allowed is taken *from* AGI and is reported on Schedule A of Form 1040 (thus, the taxpayer must itemize deductions to receive the benefit of this deduction). Note, however, that interest on a student loan is deductible *for* AGI. If the taxpayer is an employee who incurs debt in relation to his or her employment, the interest is considered to be personal interest and is not deductible. Business expenses appear on Schedule C of Form 1040, and expenses related to rents or royalties are reported on Schedule E. Concept Summary 10.2 reviews the tax treatment of the various types of interest expense incurred by individual taxpayers.

---

[54]§ 265(a)(2).   [55]§ 461(g)(1).

Concept Summary 10.2

Deductibility of Personal, Student Loan, Investment, and Mortgage Interest

Type	Deductible	Comments
Personal (consumer) interest	No	Includes any interest that is not qualified residence interest, qualified student loan interest, investment interest, or business interest. Examples include interest on car loans and credit card debt.
Qualified student loan interest	Yes	Deduction *for* AGI; subject to limitations.
Investment interest (*not* related to rental or royalty property)	Yes	Itemized deduction; limited to net investment income for the year; disallowed interest can be carried over to future years.
Investment interest (related to rental or royalty property)	Yes	Deduction *for* AGI; limited to net investment income for the year; disallowed interest can be carried over to future years.
Qualified residence interest (acquisition indebtedness)	Yes	Itemized deduction; limited to indebtedness of $750,000 (up to $1 million if incurred on or before December 15, 2017).
Qualified residence interest (home equity indebtedness)	Potentially	From 2018 to 2025, interest on home equity indebtedness is not deductible. However, such interest expense could be deductible depending on the use of the proceeds of the loan (e.g., acquisition indebtedness or business expenses).

10-4d **Charitable Contributions**

As discussed in text Section 5-6, § 170 allows individuals to deduct contributions made to qualified domestic organizations. Such contributions serve certain social welfare needs and thus relieve the government of the cost of providing these needed services to the community.

Criteria for a Gift

A **charitable contribution** is defined as a gift made to a qualified organization.[56] The major elements needed to qualify a contribution as a gift are a donative intent, the absence of consideration, and acceptance by the donee. Consequently, the taxpayer has the burden of establishing that the transfer was made from motives of disinterested generosity as established by the courts.[57] This test can be subjective and has led to problems of interpretation (refer to the discussion of gifts earlier in this chapter).

Benefit Received Rule

When a donor derives a tangible benefit from a contribution, the value of the benefit is not deductible.

Ralph purchases a ticket at $100 for a special performance of the local symphony (a qualified charity). If the price of a ticket to a symphony concert is normally $35, Ralph is allowed only $65 as a charitable contribution. Even if Ralph does not attend the concert, his deduction is limited to $65.

If, however, he does *not* accept the ticket from the symphony (or returns it prior to the event), he can deduct the full $100.

EXAMPLE 23

Contribution of Services

No deduction is allowed for the value of one's services contributed to a qualified charitable organization. However, unreimbursed expenses related to the services rendered may be deductible. For example, the cost of a uniform (without general utility) that is

---

[56]§ 170(c).

[57]*Comm. v. Duberstein*, 60–2 USTC ¶9515, 5 AFTR 2d 1626, 80 S.Ct. 1190 (USSC, 1960).

required to be worn while performing services may be deductible, as are certain out-of-pocket transportation costs incurred for the benefit of the charity. In lieu of these out-of-pocket costs for an automobile, a standard mileage rate of 14 cents per mile is allowed.[58] Deductions are also permitted for transportation, reasonable expenses for lodging, and the cost of meals while away from home that are incurred in performing the donated services. Such travel expenses are not deductible if the travel involves a significant element of personal pleasure, recreation, or vacation.[59]

Nondeductible Items

In addition to the benefit received rule and the restrictions placed on the contribution of services, the following items may not be deducted as charitable contributions:

- Dues, fees, or bills paid to country clubs, lodges, fraternal orders, or similar groups.
- Cost of raffle, bingo, or lottery tickets.
- Cost of tuition.
- Payment for the right to purchase tickets for seating at an athletic event in a university stadium.[60]
- Value of blood given to a blood bank.
- Payments to homeowners associations.
- Gifts to individuals.
- Rental value of property used by a qualified charity.

EXAMPLE 24

Sarah's neighbor, Dylan, is very ill and has been in the hospital for several weeks. Dylan's insurance will not cover all of his medical bills. As a result, a neighborhood friend set up a crowdfunding website, to allow friends and family to contribute money that will be used to help Dylan pay his medical bills. Sarah contributed $700 to the crowdfunding campaign.

Sarah may not deduct the $700 as a charitable contribution because the payment was made for the benefit of an individual rather than to a (qualified) charitable organization (see text Section 10-4d).

Time of Deduction

A charitable contribution generally is deducted in the year the payment is made. This rule applies to both cash and accrual basis individuals. A contribution is ordinarily deemed to have been made on the date of delivery of the property to the donee. For example, if a gift of common stock is made to a qualified charitable organization, the gift is considered complete on the day of delivery or mailing. However, if the donor delivers the stock certificate to her bank, broker, or the issuing corporation, the gift is considered complete on the date the stock is transferred on the books of the corporation.

A contribution made by check is considered delivered on the date of mailing. Thus, a check mailed on December 31, 2018, is deductible on the taxpayer's 2018 tax return. If the contribution is charged on a credit card, the date the charge is made determines the year of deduction.

Record-Keeping Requirements

In order to claim a charitable contribution deduction, the taxpayer must have appropriate documentation. The specific type of documentation required depends on the amount of the contribution and whether the contribution is made in cash or noncash property.[61] For example, for a single contribution of $250 or more, no charitable deduction is allowed unless the taxpayer receives written acknowledgment of the donation from the

---

[58]§ 170(i).

[59]§ 170(j).

[60]§ 170(l). Prior to 2018, 80% of these payments were allowed as a charitable contribution.

[61]The specific documentation thresholds and requirements are provided in § 170(f).

charity that notes the donation and states whether the donor received anything in return from the donee. In addition, special rules may apply to gifts of certain types of property (e.g., used cars, boats, and airplanes) where Congress has found taxpayer abuse of the rules in the past. Further, for certain gifts of noncash property, Form 8283 (Noncash Charitable Contributions) must be attached to the taxpayer's return.

The taxpayer must have the required documentation before the tax return with the claimed contribution is filed (and no later than the due date, including extensions, of that tax return). Failure to comply with the reporting rules may result in disallowance of the charitable contribution deduction. In addition, substantial penalties may apply if the taxpayer significantly overvalues any contributed property.

Valuation Requirements

Property donated to a charity is generally valued at fair market value at the time the gift is made. Little guidance is provided about the measurement of the fair market value. IRS guidance states that "The fair market value is the price at which the property would change hands between a willing buyer and a willing seller, neither being under any compulsion to buy or sell and both having reasonable knowledge of relevant facts."

Generally, charitable organizations do not attest to the fair market value of the donated property. Nevertheless, the taxpayer must maintain reliable, written evidence of the value of the donation. For certain donations, a qualified appraisal is required.

In-depth coverage can be found on this book's companion website: www.cengage.com   **6   DIGGING DEEPER**

Limitations on Charitable Contribution Deduction

The potential charitable contribution deduction is the total of all donations, both money and property, that qualify for the deduction. However, the charitable contribution deduction is subject to a number of limitations (based on the taxpayer's AGI, the type of property contributed, and the charity receiving the property). In general:

- If the qualifying contributions for the year total 20 percent or less of AGI, they are fully deductible.

- If the qualifying contributions are more than 20 percent of AGI, the deductible amount may be limited to 20 percent, 30 percent, 50 percent, or 60 percent of AGI, depending on the type of property given and the type of organization to which the donation is made.

- In any case, the maximum charitable contribution deduction may not exceed 60 percent of AGI for the tax year.

To correctly calculate the amount of a charitable contribution deduction, it is also necessary to understand the distinction between **capital gain property** and **ordinary income property**. These rules, which were discussed in text Section 5-6, are summarized in Concept Summary 10.3.

The following sections explain when the various percentage limitations apply.

Concept Summary 10.3

Determining the Deduction for Contributions of Appreciated Property by Individuals

If the Type of Property Contributed Is:	And the Property Is Contributed to:	The Contribution Is Measured by:	But the Deduction Is Limited to:
Capital gain property	A 50% organization	Fair market value of the property	30% of AGI
Ordinary income property	A 50% organization	The basis of the property*	50% of AGI
Capital gain property (and the property is tangible personal property put to an unrelated use by the donee)	A 50% organization	The basis of the property*	50% of AGI
Capital gain property	A private nonoperating foundation that is not a 50% organization	The basis of the property*	The lesser of: 1. 20% of AGI 2. 50% of AGI minus other contributions to 50% organizations
Cash	A 50% organization	The amount of cash	60% of AGI

*If the fair market value of the property is less than the adjusted basis (i.e., the property has declined in value instead of appreciating), the fair market value is used.

Fifty Percent Ceiling

Contributions made to public charities may not exceed 50 percent of an individual's AGI for the year. The 50 percent ceiling on contributions applies to public charities such as churches; schools; hospitals; and Federal, state, or local governmental units. The 50 percent ceiling also applies to contributions to private operating foundations and certain private nonoperating foundations.

In the remaining discussion of charitable contributions, public charities and private foundations (both operating and nonoperating) that qualify for the 50 percent ceiling will be referred to as 50 percent organizations.

Temporary Sixty Percent Ceiling

From 2018 through 2025, the TCJA of 2017 increases the deduction limit for *cash dona-tions* made to 50 percent organizations to 60 percent of AGI (from 50 percent of AGI). The TCJA of 2017's higher standard deduction in combination with the elimination and scaling back of many individual itemized deductions will result in fewer individuals itemizing their deductions. This explains the rationale for the increase in the charitable contribution deduction percentage; the increase is intended to offset the potential decrease in charitable donations that could result from fewer individuals itemizing their deductions. Many charitable organization are concerned that this increase will not offset the expected decline in individual giving to charitable organizations.

Thirty Percent Ceiling

A 30 percent ceiling applies to contributions of cash and ordinary income property to private nonoperating foundations that are not 50 percent organizations. The 30 percent ceiling also applies to contributions of appreciated capital gain property to 50 percent organizations.[62]

In the event the contributions for any one tax year involve a combination of 60, 50, and 30 percent property, the allowable deduction comes first from the 60 percent property and next from the 50 percent property.[63]

---

[62]Under a special election, a taxpayer may choose to permanently forgo a deduction of the appreciation on capital gain property. Referred to as the reduced deduction election, this enables the taxpayer to move from the 30% limitation to the 50% limitation. See § 170(b)(1)(C)(iii).

[63]§ 170(b)(1)(G)(iii)(II).

EXAMPLE 25

During the year, Lisa makes the following donations to her church: cash of $2,000 and unimproved land worth $30,000. Lisa purchased the land four years ago for $22,000 and held it as an investment. Therefore, it is capital gain property. Lisa's AGI for the year is $60,000. Disregarding percentage limitations, Lisa's potential charitable contribution deduction is $32,000 [$2,000 (cash) + $30,000 (fair market value of land)].

In applying the percentage limitations, however, the current deduction for the land is limited to $18,000 [30% (limitation applicable to capital gain property) × $60,000 (AGI)]. Thus, the total current deduction is $20,000 ($2,000 cash + $18,000 land). Note that the total deduction does not exceed $30,000, which is 50% of Lisa's AGI.

Twenty Percent Ceiling

A 20 percent ceiling applies to contributions of appreciated capital gain property to private nonoperating foundations that are not 50 percent organizations. In addition, only the basis of the contributed property is allowed as a deduction.

In-depth coverage can be found on this book's companion website: **www.cengage.com**   **7 DIGGING DEEPER**

Contribution Carryovers

Contributions that exceed the percentage limitations for the current year can be carried over for five years.[64] In the carryover process, such contributions do not lose their identity for limitation purposes. Thus, if the contribution originally involved 30 percent property, the carryover will continue to be classified as 30 percent property in the carryover year.

EXAMPLE 26

Assume the same facts as in Example 25. Because only $18,000 of the $30,000 value of the land (the deductible amount) is deducted in the current year, the balance of $12,000 may be carried over to the following year. The carryover will still be treated as a donation of capital gain property and will be subject to the 30%-of-AGI limitation in the carryover year.

In applying the percentage limitations, current charitable contributions must be claimed first before any carryovers can be considered. If carryovers involve more than one year, they are utilized in a first-in, first-out order.

10-4e Other Itemized Deductions

In general, no deduction is allowed for personal, living, or family expenses.[65] Prior to the TCJA of 2017, employment-related expenses of a taxpayer that were not reimbursed by an employer were deductible as itemized deductions, subject to a 2%-of-AGI floor. The TCJA of 2017 suspended such deductions. However, employee business expenses that are reimbursed as part of an accountable plan are not categorized as itemized deductions, but are deducted for AGI. These expenses are discussed in text Section 11-3.

The following expenses and losses are deductible on Schedule A as "Other Miscellaneous Deductions."

- Gambling losses and gambling expenses up to the amount of gambling winnings.
- Impairment-related work expenses of a handicapped person.
- Federal estate tax on income earned or received by a person after their death (e.g., a bonus, interest income).[66]

---

[64]§ 170(d); Reg. § 1.170A–10.
[65]§ 262.

[66]These deductions are addressed in § 165 (gambling losses), § 67 (impairment-related work expenses), and § 691 (estate tax deduction).

EXAMPLE

27

Jean is single and had the following transactions in 2018:

Medicines that required a prescription	$ 830
Doctor and dentist bills paid and not reimbursed	3,120
Medical insurance premium payments	9,200
Contact lenses	370
Transportation for medical purposes on March 1, 2018 (294 miles × 18 cents/ mile + $10 parking)	63
State income tax withheld (exceeds the sales tax from the sales tax table)	7,900
Real estate taxes paid	6,580
Interest paid on qualified residence mortgage (acquisition indebtedness)	4,340
Qualifying charitable contributions (paid by check); proper documentation exists	2,160
Transportation in performing charitable services	119
Unreimbursed employee business expenses	1,870
Tax return preparation fee	450
Safe deposit box (used for keeping investment documents and tax records)	170

Jean's AGI is $120,000. The total of her itemized deductions is $21,202, as calculated below. This amount is greater than her 2018 standard deduction of $12,000. At the time this textbook went to print, the 2018 Schedule A (Form 1040) was not available. Search the IRS website to see if it is currently available.

Medical and Dental Expenses		
Total	$13,583	
Less: 7.5% of AGI	(9,000)	
Deductible amount		$ 4,583
Taxes Paid		
State and local income taxes	$ 7,900	
Real estate taxes	6,580	
Total	$14,480	
Deduction limited to $10,000		10,000
Interest Paid		
Home mortgage interest		4,340
Gifts to Charity		
Gifts by cash or check	$ 2,160	
Other than by cash or check	119	
Total deduction		2,279
Total Itemized Deductions		$21,202

Note: Jean's unreimbursed employee expenses, tax return preparation fee, and safe deposit box rental cost are miscellaneous itemized deductions. From 2018 through 2025, the deduction for these items has been suspended. In 2017, the total of these expenses ($2,490) would have been deductible to the extent they exceeded 2% of Jean's AGI.

As noted above, the TCJA of 2017 both increased the standard deduction amounts for taxpayers in all filing statuses and eliminated or limited a number of itemized deductions. Going forward, these changes are expected to reduce the number of taxpayers who itemize deductions. The total amount of itemized deductions could also decrease substantially, given the limitations on such deductions imposed by the TCJA of 2017.

TAX PLANNING STRATEGIES   Effective Utilization of Itemized Deductions

FRAMEWORK FOCUS: DEDUCTIONS

Strategy: Maximize Deductible Amounts.

An individual may use the standard deduction in one year and itemize deductions in another year. Therefore, it is possible to obtain tax benefits by shifting itemized deductions from one year to another. For example, if a taxpayer's itemized deductions and the standard deduction are approximately the same for each year of a two-year period, the taxpayer should use the standard deduction in one year and shift itemized deductions (to the extent permitted by law) to the other year. The individual could, for example, prepay a church pledge for a particular year or avoid paying end-of-the-year medical expenses to shift the deduction to the following year.

10-5 INDIVIDUAL TAX CREDITS

A tax credit should not be confused with an income tax deduction. Recall from the discussion of the individual income tax formula in Chapter 1 that the tax benefit received from a tax deduction depends on the taxpayer's tax rate, while a tax credit is not affected by the tax rate. Instead, a credit is a dollar-for-dollar reduction in a taxpayer's tax liability. Several commonly encountered tax credits available to individuals are discussed in this section.

LO.3

Explain and illustrate the adoption expenses credit, child tax credit, education tax credits, credit for child and dependent care expenses, and earned income credit.

10-5a Adoption Expenses Credit

The **adoption expenses credit** assists taxpayers who incur nonrecurring costs directly associated with the adoption process, such as adoption fees, attorney fees, court costs, social service review costs, and transportation costs.[67]

In 2018, up to $13,810 of costs incurred to adopt an eligible child qualify for the credit. An eligible child is either:

- Under 18 years of age at the time of the adoption, or
- Physically or mentally incapable of taking care of himself or herself.

In general, taxpayers claim the credit in the year the adoption is completed. If the adoption is not completed, the credit can be claimed in the following year. A married couple must file a joint return to claim the credit.

In late 2017, Sam and Martha pay $4,000 in legal fees, adoption fees, and other expenses directly related to the adoption of an infant daughter, Susan. In 2018, the year in which the adoption is completed, they pay an additional $10,000. Sam and Martha are eligible for a $13,810 credit in 2018 (for expenses of $14,000, paid in 2017 and 2018, and limited by the $13,810 ceiling in 2018).

EXAMPLE 28

The amount of the credit that is otherwise available is subject to phaseout for taxpayers whose AGI (modified for this purpose) exceeds $207,140 in 2018, and it is phased out completely when AGI reaches $247,140. The resulting credit is calculated by reducing the allowable credit (determined without this reduction) by the amount determined using the following formula:

$$\text{Allowable credit} \times \frac{\text{AGI} - \$207,140}{\$40,000}$$

---

[67]§ 23.

Assume the same facts as in the previous example, except that Sam and Martha's AGI is $232,140 in 2018. As a result, their available credit in 2018 is reduced from $13,810 to $5,179 {$13,810 − [$13,810 × ($25,000/$40,000)]}.

The credit is nonrefundable. However, any unused adoption expenses credit may be carried forward for up to five years, utilized on a first-in, first-out order.

10-5b Child and Dependent Tax Credits

The **child tax credit** and the **dependent tax credit** allow individual taxpayers to claim a tax credit based solely on the *number* of their qualifying children and dependents. These credits are among several "family-friendly" provisions that currently are part of the tax law. To be eligible for the child tax credit, the child must be under age 17, must be a U.S. citizen, must have a Social Security number before the return due date, and must be a dependent of the taxpayer.

The child tax credit is $2,000 per child; the dependent tax credit is $500 for dependents other than children for whom the child tax credit is claimed.[68] The child tax credit phases out as AGI exceeds $400,000 (for married taxpayers filing jointly) or $200,000 (for all other taxpayers).[69] The child tax credit is partially refundable; up to $1,400 per child, but no more than 15 percent of earned income in excess of $2,500. The dependent tax credit is not refundable. Per the TCJA of 2017, these increased credits are in place until 2025 and are intended, in part, to offset the loss of the personal and dependency exemptions.

10-5c Credit for Child and Dependent Care Expenses

The **credit for child and dependent care expenses** mitigates the inequity experienced by working taxpayers who must pay for child care services to work outside the home.[70] This credit is a specified percentage of expenses incurred to enable the taxpayer to work or to seek employment. The credit percentage varies based on the taxpayer's AGI, and expenses are capped at a maximum of $6,000.

Eligibility

To be eligible for the credit, an individual must have either:

- A dependent under age 13, or
- A dependent or spouse who is physically or mentally incapacitated and who lives with the taxpayer for more than one-half of the year.

Generally, married taxpayers must file a joint return to obtain the credit.

Eligible Employment-Related Expenses

Eligible expenses include amounts paid for household services and care of a qualifying individual that are incurred to enable the taxpayer to be employed. The care can be provided in the home (e.g., by a nanny) or outside the home (e.g., at a day-care center).

Out-of-the-home expenses incurred for an older dependent or spouse who is physically or mentally incapacitated qualify for the credit if that person regularly spends at least eight hours each day in the taxpayer's household. This makes the credit available to taxpayers who keep handicapped older children and elderly relatives in the home instead of an institution.

Child care payments to a relative are eligible for the credit unless the relative is a child (under age 19) of the taxpayer.

---

[68]§ 24.

[69]AGI is modified for purposes of this calculation. The threshold amounts are *not* indexed for inflation. See §§ 24(a) and (b).

[70]§ 21.

Earned Income Ceiling

Qualifying employment-related expenses are limited to an individual's earned income. For married taxpayers, this limitation applies to the spouse with the lesser amount of earned income. Special rules are provided for taxpayers with nonworking spouses who are disabled or are full-time students. If a nonworking spouse is physically or mentally disabled or is a full-time student, he or she is deemed to have earned income for purposes of this limitation. The deemed amount is $250 per month if there is one qualifying individual in the household (e.g., a dependent child under age 13) or $500 per month if there are two or more qualifying individuals in the household. In the case of a student-spouse, the student's income is treated as earned only for the months the student is enrolled on a full-time basis at an educational institution.[71]

Calculation of the Credit

In general, the credit is equal to a percentage of unreimbursed employment-related expenses up to $3,000 for one qualifying individual and $6,000 for two or more individuals. The credit rate varies between 20 percent and 35 percent, depending on the taxpayer's AGI (see Exhibit 10.4).

EXAMPLE

30

Nancy, who has two children under age 13, worked full-time while her spouse, Ron, attended college for 10 months during the year. Nancy earned $22,000 and incurred $6,200 of child care expenses. Ron is deemed to be fully employed and to have earned $500 for each of the 10 months (or a total of $5,000).

Because Nancy and Ron report AGI of $22,000, their credit rate is 31%. Nancy and Ron are limited to $5,000 in qualified child care expenses ($6,000 maximum expenses, limited to Ron's deemed earned income of $5,000). Therefore, they are entitled to a tax credit of $1,550 (31% × $5,000) for the year.

EXHIBIT 10.4	Child and Dependent Care Credit Computations

Adjusted Gross Income		
Over	**But Not Over**	**Applicable Rate of Credit**
$ 0	$15,000	35%
15,000	17,000	34%
17,000	19,000	33%
19,000	21,000	32%
21,000	23,000	31%
23,000	25,000	30%
25,000	27,000	29%
27,000	29,000	28%
29,000	31,000	27%
31,000	33,000	26%
33,000	35,000	25%
35,000	37,000	24%
37,000	39,000	23%
39,000	41,000	22%
41,000	43,000	21%
43,000	No limit	20%

---

[71]§ 21(d).

10-5d **Education Tax Credits**

The American Opportunity credit and the lifetime learning credit [72] are available to help qualifying low- and middle-income individuals defray the cost of higher education. The credits are available for qualifying tuition and related expenses incurred by students pursuing undergraduate or graduate degrees or vocational training. Books and other course materials are eligible for the American Opportunity credit (but not the lifetime learning credit).[73] Room and board are ineligible for both credits.

Maximum Credit

The American Opportunity credit permits a maximum credit of $2,500 per year (100 percent of the first $2,000 of tuition expenses plus 25 percent of the next $2,000 of tuition expenses) for the *first four years* of postsecondary education. The lifetime learning credit permits a credit of 20 percent of qualifying expenses (up to $10,000 per year) incurred in a year in which the American Opportunity credit is not claimed with respect to a given student. Generally, the lifetime learning credit is used for individuals who are beyond the first four years of postsecondary education.

Eligible Individuals

Both education credits are available for qualified expenses incurred by a taxpayer, taxpayer's spouse, or taxpayer's dependent. The American Opportunity credit is available per eligible student, while the lifetime learning credit is calculated per taxpayer. To be eligible for the American Opportunity credit, a student must take at least one-half of the full-time course load for at least one academic term at a qualifying educational institution. No comparable requirement exists for the lifetime learning credit. Therefore, taxpayers who are seeking new job skills or maintaining existing skills through graduate training or continuing education are eligible for the lifetime learning credit. Taxpayers who are married must file a joint return to claim either education credit. To claim these education credits, the individual must have received Form 1098–T, Tuition Statement, from the educational institution.

Income Limitations and Refundability

Both education credits are subject to income limitations, which differ between the two credits. Forty percent of the American Opportunity credit is refundable, and it can be used to offset a taxpayer's alternative minimum tax (AMT) liability (the lifetime learning credit is neither refundable nor an AMT liability offset).[74]

The American Opportunity credit amount is phased out beginning when the taxpayer's AGI (modified for this purpose) reaches $80,000 ($160,000 for married taxpayers filing jointly).[75] The credit is phased out proportionally over a $10,000 ($20,000 for married taxpayers filing jointly) phaseout range. As a result, the credit is eliminated when modified AGI reaches $90,000 ($180,000 for married taxpayers filing jointly).

For 2018, the lifetime learning credit amount is phased out beginning when the taxpayer's AGI (modified for this purpose) reaches $57,000 ($114,000 for married taxpayers filing jointly). The credit is phased out proportionally over a $10,000 ($20,000 for married taxpayers filing jointly) range. The credit equals zero when AGI reaches $67,000 ($134,000 for married filing jointly).

---

[72]§ 25A.

[73]§ 25A(i)(3).

[74]If the credit is claimed for a taxpayer subject to § 1(g) (the "kiddie tax"), the credit is not refundable.

[75]These amounts are not adjusted for inflation.

American Opportunity Credit: Calculation and Limitation

Tom and Jennifer are married; file a joint tax return; have modified AGI of $158,000; and have two children, Lora and Sam. Tom and Jennifer paid $7,500 of tuition and $8,500 for room and board for Lora (a freshman) and $8,100 of tuition plus $7,200 for room and board for Sam (a junior). Both Lora and Sam are full-time students and are Tom and Jennifer's dependents.

Lora's tuition and Sam's tuition are qualified expenses for the American Opportunity credit. For 2018, Tom and Jennifer may claim a $2,500 American Opportunity credit for both Lora's and Sam's expenses [(100% × $2,000) + (25% × $2,000)]; in total, they qualify for a $5,000 American Opportunity credit.

Assume the same facts as in Example 31, except that Tom and Jennifer's modified AGI for 2018 is $172,000, instead of $158,000. In this case, Tom and Jennifer can claim a $2,000 American Opportunity credit for 2018 (rather than a $5,000 credit).

The potential $5,000 American Opportunity credit is reduced because their modified AGI exceeds the $160,000 limit for married taxpayers. The reduction is computed as the amount by which modified AGI exceeds the limit, expressed as a percentage of the phaseout range, or [($172,000 − $160,000)/$20,000], resulting in a 60% reduction. Therefore, the maximum available credit for 2018 is $2,000 ($5,000 × 40% allowable portion).

Taxpayers are prohibited from receiving a double tax benefit associated with qualifying educational expenses. Therefore, taxpayers who claim an education credit may not deduct the expenses, nor may they claim the credit for amounts that are otherwise excluded from gross income (e.g., scholarships and employer-paid educational assistance).

In-depth coverage can be found on this book's companion website: www.cengage.com   8   DIGGING DEEPER

10-5e **Earned Income Credit**

The **earned income credit** provides income tax equity to the working poor. In addition, the credit has been designed to help offset the cost of other Federal taxes, such as the gasoline tax, that impose a relatively larger burden on low-income taxpayers. Further, the credit is designed to encourage and reward work. As discussed below, a taxpayer's EITC increases as earnings increase (until reaching the maximum). This creates an incentive for people to seek employment or to increase their work hours.[76]

Eligibility Requirements

Eligibility for the credit depends not only on whether the taxpayer meets the earned income and AGI thresholds but also on whether he or she has a *qualifying child*. The term qualifying child generally has the same meaning here as it does for purposes of determining who qualifies as a dependent.

In addition to being available for taxpayers with qualifying children, the earned income credit is also available to certain workers without children. However, this provision is available only to such taxpayers ages 25 through 64 who cannot be claimed as a dependent on another taxpayer's return.

---

[76]§ 32. The earned income credit is not available if the taxpayer's unearned income (e.g., interest and dividends) exceeds $3,500 in 2018 ($3,450 in 2017). See § 32(i).

Amount of the Credit

The earned income credit is determined by multiplying a maximum amount of earned income by the appropriate credit percentage. Generally, earned income includes employee compensation and net earnings from self-employment; it excludes items such as interest, dividends, pension benefits, nontaxable employee compensation, and alimony. If a taxpayer has children, the credit percentage used in the calculation depends on the number of qualifying children.

In 2018, the maximum earned income credit is $3,461 ($10,180 × 34%) for a taxpayer with one qualifying child, $5,716 ($14,290 × 40%) for a taxpayer with two qualifying children, and $6,431 ($14,290 × 45%) for a taxpayer with three or more qualifying children. However, the maximum earned income credit is phased out completely if the taxpayer's earned income or AGI exceeds certain thresholds. To the extent the greater of earned income or AGI exceeds $24,350 in 2018 for married taxpayers filing a joint return ($18,660 for other taxpayers), the difference, multiplied by the appropriate phaseout percentage, is subtracted from the maximum earned income credit.

It is not necessary for the taxpayer to actually compute the earned income credit. To simplify the compliance process, the IRS issues an Earned Income Credit Table for the determination of the appropriate amount of the credit. This table and a worksheet are included in the instructions for the Form 1040.

10-6 AFFORDABLE CARE ACT PROVISIONS

LO.4

Explain some of the key tax provisions of the Affordable Care Act.

The Affordable Care Act (ACA) was enacted to increase the quality and affordability of health insurance, reduce the number of uninsured individuals in the United States by expanding public and private insurance coverage, and lower health care costs for individuals and the government. Included in the ACA are a number of tax provisions, two of which are discussed briefly below. Additional information on ACA tax provisions is also included in an online appendix to this textbook.

10-6a Individual Shared Responsibility Payment

The ACA's "individual mandate"—which has been deemed a "tax" by the U.S. Supreme Court[77]—requires all individuals not covered by an employer-sponsored health plan, Medicare, Medicaid, or other public insurance programs to secure a private insurance policy or pay a penalty for each month they do not have health coverage. The penalty is the **individual shared responsibility payment (ISRP)**.[78]

Under this provision, in 2017, individuals without coverage pay an ISRP of the greater of a flat amount of $695 per adult and $347.50 per child up to a maximum of $2,085 per family, or 2.5 percent of household income. The ISRP cannot be greater than the national average cost of a bronze-level health plan.[79]

Exemptions are granted for financial hardship, religious objections, Native Americans, those without coverage for less than three consecutive months, undocumented immigrants, incarcerated individuals, those for whom the lowest cost plan option exceeds a specified percentage of household income, and those with incomes below the tax filing threshold (in 2017, the percentage is 8.16 percent and the income threshold for taxpayers under age 65 is $10,400 for singles and $20,800 for couples).[80] As a result of the TCJA of 2017, after 2018, the ISRP is reduced to $0.

---

[77] *National Federation of Independent Business v. Sebelius*, 132 S.Ct. 2566 (2012).

[78] § 5000A.

[79] 2018 information was not available at press date.

[80] Rev.Proc. 2016–24, 2016–18 I.R.B. 677. Individuals eligible for an exemption are to report it on Form 8965 (Health Coverage Exemptions). This form also includes worksheets for calculating any ISRP owed.

BRIDGE DISCIPLINE   **Bridge to the Consequences of the ISRP Penalty Reduction**

As noted above, the individual mandate provision in the ACA requires most U.S. citizens and noncitizens who lawfully reside in the country to have health insurance meeting specific standards. The ISRP penalty is imposed on those who do not meet an exemption and who do not comply with the requirement to purchase insurance.

While the TCJA of 2017 did not repeal the individual mandate, the legislation provides that the ISRP penalty is reduced to $0 beginning in 2019. Without a penalty to ensure compliance with the individual mandate, fewer people are expected to purchase health insurance. The Congressional Budget Office (CBO) estimates that the number of people with health insurance will decrease by 4 million in 2019 and 13 million in 2027. This will also likely result in increased premiums for those seeking insurance, as healthier people will be less likely to obtain insurance as a result of the lack of a penalty. The CBO estimates that insurance premiums will increase by about 10 percent in most of the remaining years of the decade.

Are there other consequences of the reduction in the ISRP penalty? The reduction of the penalty significantly reduces the strength of the individual mandate requirement. Thus, the CBO also estimates that Federal budget deficits will be reduced by about $338 billion between 2018 and 2027. Why is the deficit expected to decrease as a result of this change? While the Treasury will lose the revenue generate by the ISRP penalty, the Federal government will spend less to subsidize the cost of insurance because fewer individuals (estimates above) will have Federally subsidized insurance policies [that is, fewer qualifying individuals will purchase insurance that qualifies them for the premium tax credit (see text Section 10-6b)].

Sources: https://www.cbo.gov/publication/53300 and https://www.washingtonpost.com/news/wonk/wp/2017/11/14/why-repealing-obamacares-individual-mandate-is-so-crucial-for-tax-reform/?noredirect=on&utm_term=.71c0d910ce8e.

10-6b **Premium Tax Credit**

Individuals and families whose household incomes are at least 100 percent but no more than 400 percent of the Federal poverty level (also called the Federal poverty line; FPL) may be eligible to receive a Federal subsidy [the **premium tax credit (PTC)**] if they purchase insurance via the Health Insurance Marketplace (the Marketplace).[81] Individuals whose income exceeds 400 percent of the FPL are not eligible for a PTC. For 2017 tax returns, the FPL for claiming a PTC is $11,880 for a single person (an additional $4,160 is added to that amount for each person in the household).[82]

Individuals can choose to receive their PTC in advance; the Marketplace will send the money directly to the insurer to reduce the monthly insurance payments. Alternatively, individuals can receive the PTC as a refundable credit when they file their income tax return for the year. In either case, however, taxpayers will be required to complete Form 8962 (Premium Tax Credit) when their tax return is filed. Taxpayers who claim the premium tax credit cannot use Form 1040EZ (they must use either Form 1040A or Form 1040).

Taxpayers who enroll in health care coverage via the Marketplace will receive information necessary to complete Form 8962 by the end of January each year [Form 1095–A (Health Insurance Marketplace Statement)]. Included in this information statement are monthly health insurance premium payments and any PTC received in advance. This information also is reported to the IRS.

Taxpayers who received the credit in advance must reconcile the actual credit based on their actual income for the year with the amounts that were subsidized through the Marketplace. They will receive a refund (if the advance credit was too low) or owe an additional tax obligation (if the advance credit was too large).

---

[81]§ 36B. Also see Rev.Proc. 2017–36, 2017–21 I.R.B 1251.

[82]Instructions for Form 8962 (2017); 2018 amounts were not available at the time of publication. Different amounts apply for Alaska and Hawaii.

THE TAX IMPLICATIONS OF LIFE!

While Donna and David's wages and salaries of $70,000 are taxable, they should be aware that their employers may have provided them with a number of tax-free fringe benefits. In addition, if Donna and David paid monthly premiums for accident and health care plans or contributed to a flexible spending account, those amounts may reduce their taxable income (these items are discussed more fully in text Section 11-2i). The good news is that the $10,000 gift received from Donna's grandmother can be excluded from gross income. However, the $250 of interest earned on the money is included in income.

Donna's tuition waiver of $4,500 and the related payments of $450 per month are intended as a form of compensation. Therefore, both of these amounts are included in the couple's gross income. With respect to the damages awards, all of the compensatory damages of $215,000 can be excluded from gross income because they relate to personal physical injury or sickness. However, the punitive damages of $160,000 must be included in their gross income. The amounts received from the crowdfunding campaign can be excluded from gross income as these amounts were given to David and Donna with no expectation of receiving anything in return from the couple.

Donna and David have several deductions *for* adjusted gross income. In addition to the alimony paid by David, $3,000 of the capital loss from the stock sale is deductible *for* AGI and interest on the qualified student loan is deductible *for* AGI (subject to a phaseout).

While medical expenses, state income taxes, personal property taxes, and charitable contributions are deductible *from* AGI, Donna and David should claim the standard deduction for a married couple as it appears to exceed their itemized deductions.

Donna and David will determine their tax liability using the tax rate schedule for married couples filing a joint return.

Donna and David may be eligible for one or more tax credits, including the child tax credit and an education tax credit related to the tuition paid by Donna. If Stephen has unearned income in excess of certain thresholds, Donna and David should be made aware of the potential application of the "kiddie" tax.

If Donna and David did not have affordable health coverage from their employers and purchased insurance in the Marketplace, they might be eligible for the PTC (if their household income is no more than 400 percent of the FPL). If they did not have health insurance for any portion of the year and did not meet any exemption, they will owe the ISRP. One of the questions on the Federal income tax form is whether they had health coverage for every month of the year (line 61 of the 2017 Form 1040).

What If?

What if Donna and David purchase a house in the current year? What are the likely tax implications of owning a new home? If Donna and David purchase a new home, mortgage interest and property taxes paid on the home are treated as additional itemized deductions. Depending on the amount of these deductions, Donna and David's itemized deductions might then exceed the standard deduction amount, giving them a larger tax deduction and reducing their tax liability even more.

Suggested Readings

Sheldon I. Banoff, "Bug Bounty Brings Miles, But Taxes Bite: What Value Is Reportable?" *Journal of Taxation*, October 2015.

Seth M. Colwell, "What's New? Pell Grants and the American Opportunity Tax Credit," *Practical Tax Strategies*, December 2015.

J. Russell Hardin and Thomas G. Noland, "The Tax Impact of Home Mortgage Modification Programs," *Practical Tax Strategies*, August 2014.

Neil D. Katz and Gina M. DiGaudio, "The Tax Implications of Divorce Part One—Alimony," *Journal of Taxation*, November 2017.

R. Michael Sorrells, "Challenging Contributions Create Issues for Financial Managers and Advisors," *Journal of Taxation*, January 2018.

Key Terms

Accident and health insurance benefits, 10-10

Acquisition indebtedness, 10-18

Adoption expenses credit, 10-27

Alimony and separate maintenance payments, 10-3

American Opportunity credit, 10-30

Capital gain property, 10-23

Charitable contribution, 10-21

Child tax credit, 10-28

Compensatory damages, 10-8

Credit for child and dependent care expenses, 10-28

Dependent tax credit, 10-28

Earned income credit, 10-31

Educational savings bonds, 10-10

Health Savings Account (HSA), 10-13

Home equity loans, 10-18

Individual shared responsibility payment (ISRP), 10-32

Investment interest, 10-17

Lifetime learning credit, 10-30

Medical expenses, 10-11

Net investment income, 10-18

Ordinary income property, 10-23

Points, 10-19

Premium tax credit (PTC), 10-33

Punitive damages, 10-9

Qualified residence interest, 10-18

Scholarship, 10-7

Computational Exercises

1. **LO.1** Casper and Cecile divorced in 2018. As part of the divorce settlement, Casper transferred stock to Cecile. Casper purchased the stock for $25,000, and it had a market value of $43,000 on the date of the transfer. Cecile sold the stock for $40,000 a month after receiving it. In addition, Casper is required to pay Cecile $1,500 a month in alimony. He made five payments to her during the year. What are the tax consequences for Casper and Cecile regarding these transactions?

    a.   How much gain or loss does Casper recognize on the transfer of the stock?

    b.   Does Casper receive a deduction for the $7,500 alimony paid?

    c.   How much income does Cecile have from the $7,500 alimony received?

    d.   When Cecile sells the stock, how much gain or loss does she report?

2. **LO.1** Sally was an all-state soccer player during her junior and senior years in high school. She accepted an athletic scholarship from State University. The scholarship provided the following:

Tuition and fees	$15,000
Housing and meals	6,000
Books and supplies	1,500
Transportation	1,200

Determine the effect of the scholarship on Sally's gross income.

3.   **LO.1** Jarrod receives a scholarship of $18,500 from Riggers University to be used to pursue a bachelor's degree. He spends $12,000 on tuition, $1,500 on books and supplies, $4,000 for room and board, and $1,000 for personal expenses. How much may Jarrod exclude from his gross income?

4.   **LO.2** Pierre, a cash basis, unmarried taxpayer, had $1,400 of state income tax withheld during 2018. Also in 2018, Pierre paid $455 that was due when he filed his 2017 state income tax return and made estimated payments of $975 toward his 2018 state income tax liability. When Pierre files his 2018 Federal income tax return in April 2019, he elects to itemize deductions, which amount to $15,650, including the state income tax payments and withholdings, all of which reduce his taxable income.

   a.   What is Pierre's 2018 state income tax deduction?

   b.   As a result of overpaying his 2018 state income tax, Pierre receives a refund of $630 early in 2019. The standard deduction for single taxpayers for 2018 was $12,000. How much of the $630 will Pierre include in his 2019 gross income?

5.   **LO.2** Troy's financial records for the year reflect the following:

Interest income from bank savings account	$ 900
Taxable annuity receipts	1,800
City ad valorem property tax on investments	125
Investment interest expense	3,200

   Calculate Troy's net investment income and his current investment interest deduction. How is any potential excess investment interest deduction treated?

6.   **LO.2** Miller owns a personal residence with a fair market value of $195,000 and an outstanding first mortgage of 157,500, which was entirely used to acquire the residence. This year, Miller gets a home equity loan of $10,000 to purchase new jet skis. How much of this mortgage debt is treated as qualified residence indebtedness?

7.   **LO.2** Donna donates stock in Chipper Corporation to the American Red Cross on September 10, 2018. She purchased the stock for $18,100 on December 28, 2017, and it had a fair market value of $27,000 when she made the donation.

   a.   What is Donna's charitable contribution deduction?

   b.   Assume instead that the stock had a fair market value of $15,000 (rather than $27,000) when it was donated to the American Red Cross. What is Donna's charitable contribution deduction?

8.   **LO.2** Barbara incurred the following expenses during the year:

Membership dues at a health club Barbara joined at the suggestion of her physician to improve her general physical condition	$ 840
Multiple vitamins and antioxidant vitamins	240
Smoking cessation program	500
Nonprescription nicotine gum	250
Insulin	600
Funeral expenses for Barbara's mother who passed away in June	7,200

   Before considering the AGI limitation, what amount may Barbara include in computing her medical expense deduction?

9.   **LO.2** Thomas purchased a personal residence from Rachel. To sell the residence, Rachel agreed to pay $5,500 in points related to Thomas's mortgage. Discuss the deductibility of the points.

10. **LO.3** In late 2017, Randy and Rachel Erwin paid $7,000 in legal fees, adoption fees, and other expenses directly related to the adoption of an infant son, Jameson.

In 2018, the year in which the adoption becomes final, they pay an additional $8,000. Their AGI in 2018 is $135,000.

a. Determine the amount of the Erwins' adoption tax credit in 2018.

b. Instead, assume that the Erwins' 2018 AGI is $210,000. Determine the amount of the Erwins' adoption tax credit in 2018.

11. **LO.3** Santiago and Amy are married and file a joint tax return claiming their three children, ages 12, 14, and 18, as dependents. Their AGI is $140,000. Determine the amount of the couple's child and dependent tax credit.

12. **LO.3** Ivanna, who has three children under age 13, worked full-time while her spouse, Sergio, attended college for nine months during the year. Ivanna earned $28,000, and the couple incurred $9,100 of child care expenses. Determine Ivanna and Sergio's child and dependent care credit.

Problems

13. **LO.1** William and Abigail, who live in San Francisco, have been experiencing problems in their marriage. They have a 3-year-old daughter, April, who stays with William's parents during the day because both William and Abigail are employed. Abigail worked to support William while he attended medical school, and now she has been accepted by a medical school in Mexico. Abigail has decided to divorce William and attend medical school. April will stay in San Francisco because of her strong attachment to her grandparents and because they can provide her with excellent day care. Abigail knows that William will expect her to contribute to the cost of raising April. Abigail also believes that to finance her education, she must receive cash for her share of the property they accumulated during their marriage. In addition, she believes that she should receive some reimbursement for her contribution to William's support while he was in medical school. She expects the divorce proceedings to take several months. Identify the relevant tax issues for Abigail.

Critical Thinking

14. **LO.1** Patrick and Eva are planning to divorce in 2018. Patrick has offered to pay Eva $12,000 each year until their 11-year-old daughter reaches age 21. Alternatively, Patrick will transfer to Eva common stock that he owns with a fair market value of $100,000. What factors should Eva and Patrick consider in deciding between these two options?

Decision Making

15. **LO.1** For each of the following, determine the amount that should be included in gross income:

a. Peyton was selected the most valuable player in the Super Bowl. In recognition of this, he was awarded an automobile with a value of $60,000. Peyton did not need the automobile, so he asked that the title be put in his parents' names.

b. Jacob was awarded the Nobel Peace Prize. When he was presented the check for $1.4 million, Jacob said, "I do not need the money. Give it to the United Nations to use toward the goal of world peace."

c. Linda won sixth place in the collegiate Crossfit Games championship. She received a $10,000 scholarship that paid her $6,000 for tuition and $4,000 for meals and housing for the academic year.

16. **LO.1** Herbert was employed for the first six months of 2018 and earned $90,000 in salary. During the next six months, he collected $8,800 of unemployment compensation, borrowed $12,000 (using his personal residence as collateral), and withdrew $2,000 from his savings account (including $60 of interest earned this year).

He received dividends of $550. In December, he won $1,500 in the lottery on a $5 ticket. Calculate Herbert's gross income.

17. **LO.1** Adrian was awarded an academic scholarship to State University for the 2018–2019 academic year. He received $6,500 in August and $7,200 in December 2018. Adrian had enough personal savings to pay all expenses as they came due. Adrian's expenditures for the relevant period were as follows:

Tuition, August 2018	$3,700
Tuition, January 2019	3,750
Room and board	
August–December 2018	2,800
January–May 2019	2,500
Books and educational supplies	
August–December 2018	1,000
January–May 2019	1,200

Determine the effect on Adrian's gross income for 2018 and 2019.

18. **LO.1** Determine the effect on gross income in each of the following cases:
   a. Eloise received $150,000 in settlement of a sex discrimination case against her former employer.
   b. Nell received $10,000 for damages to her personal reputation. She also received $40,000 in punitive damages.
   c. Beth received $10,000 in compensatory damages and $30,000 in punitive damages in a lawsuit she filed against a tanning parlor for severe burns she received from using its tanning equipment.
   d. Joanne received compensatory damages of $75,000 and punitive damages of $300,000 from a cosmetic surgeon who botched her nose job.

Communications   19. **LO.2** Emma Doyle is employed as a corporate attorney. For calendar year 2018, she had AGI of $100,000 and paid the following medical expenses:

Medical insurance premiums	$3,700
Doctor and dentist bills for Bob and April (Emma's parents)	6,800
Doctor and dentist bills for Emma	5,200
Prescription medicines for Emma	400
Nonprescription insulin for Emma	350

Bob and April would qualify as Emma's dependents, except that they file a joint return. Emma's medical insurance policy does not cover them. Emma filed a claim for reimbursement of $2,800 of her own expenses with her insurance company in December 2018 and received the reimbursement in January 2019. What is Emma's maximum allowable medical expense deduction for 2018? Prepare a memo for your firm's tax files in which you document your conclusions.

20. **LO.2** Reba, who is single, does a lot of business entertaining at home. Lawrence, Reba's 84-year-old dependent grandfather, lived with Reba until this year, when he moved to Lakeside Nursing Home because he needs medical and nursing care. During the year, Reba made the following payments on behalf of Lawrence:

Room at Lakeside	$11,000
Meals for Lawrence at Lakeside	2,200
Doctor and nurse fees at Lakeside	1,700
Cable TV service for Lawrence's room at Lakeside	380
Total	$15,280

Lakeside has medical staff in residence. Disregarding the AGI floor, how much, if any, of these expenses qualify for a medical expense deduction by Reba?

21. **LO.2** Paul suffers from emphysema and severe allergies and, upon the recommen-
    dation of his physician, has a dust elimination system installed in his per-
    sonal residence. In connection with the system, Paul incurs and pays the following
    amounts during 2018.

Doctor and hospital bills	$ 2,500
Dust elimination system	10,000
Increase in utility bills due to the system	450
Cost of certified appraisal	300

    In addition, Paul pays $750 for prescribed medicines.
       The system has an estimated useful life of 20 years. The appraisal was to deter-
    mine the value of Paul's residence with and without the system. The appraisal states
    that his residence was worth $350,000 before the system was installed and $356,000
    after the installation. Paul's AGI for the year was $50,000. How much of the medical
    expenses qualify for the medical expense deduction in 2018?

22. **LO.2** Norma, who is single and uses the cash method of accounting, lives in a state
    that imposes an income tax. In April 2018, she files her state income tax return
    for 2017 and pays an additional $1,000 in state income taxes. During 2018, her with-
    holdings for state income tax purposes amount to $7,400, and she pays estimated
    state income tax of $700. In April 2019, she files her state income tax return for 2018,
    claiming a refund of $1,800. Norma receives the refund in August 2019. Norma has
    no other state or local tax expenses.

    a. Assuming that Norma itemized deductions in 2018, how much may she claim
       as a deduction for state income taxes on her Federal return for calendar year
       2018 (filed in April 2019)?
    b. Assuming that Norma itemized deductions in 2018 (which totaled $20,000),
       how will the refund of $1,800 that she received in 2019 be treated for Federal
       income tax purposes?
    c. Assume that Norma itemized deductions in 2018 (which totaled $20,000) and
       that she elects to have the $1,800 refund applied toward her 2019 state income
       tax liability. How will the $1,800 be treated for Federal income tax purposes?
    d. Assuming that Norma did not itemize deductions in 2018, how will the refund
       of $1,800 received in 2019 be treated for Federal income tax purposes?

23. **LO.2** In 2018, Kathleen Tweardy incurs $30,000 of interest expense related to her   Decision Making
    investments. Her investment income includes $7,500 of interest, $6,000 of quali-   Communications
    fied dividends, and a $12,000 net capital gain on the sale of securities. Kathleen asks
    you to compute the amount of her deduction for investment interest, taking into con-
    sideration any options she might have. In addition, she would like your suggestions
    about any tax planning alternatives that are available. Write a letter to her that con-
    tains your advice. Kathleen lives at 11934 Briarpatch Drive, Midlothian, VA 23113.

24. **LO.2** Helen Derby borrowed $150,000 to acquire a parcel of land to be held for
    investment purposes. During the current year, she reported AGI of $90,000
    and paid interest of $12,000 on the loan. Other items related to Helen's investments
    include the following:

Interest and annuity income	$11,000
Long-term capital gain on sale of stock	3,500
Real estate tax on the investment land	800

    a. Determine Helen's investment interest deduction for the current year.
    b. Discuss the treatment of the portion of Helen's investment interest that is disal-
       lowed in the current year.
    c. Complete Helen's Form 4952 using whatever version of the form is available
       on **www.irs.gov**. For this purpose, assume that she chooses not to include
       the long-term capital gain as investment income. Her Social Security number
       is 123-45-6789.

25. **LO.2** The Wilmoths plan to purchase a house and would like to determine the after-tax cost of financing its purchase. Given their projected taxable income, the Wilmoths are in the 24% Federal income tax bracket and the 8% state income tax bracket (i.e., an aggregate marginal tax bracket of 32%). Assume that the Wilmoths will benefit from itemizing their deductions for both Federal and state tax purposes. The total cash outlay during the first year of ownership will be $23,400 ($1,200 principal payments, $22,200 qualified residence interest payments). Determine the initial year after-tax cost of financing the purchase of the home.

Decision Making

Communications

Digging Deeper

26. **LO.2** In December of each year, Eleanor Young contributes 10% of her gross income to the United Way (a 50% organization). Eleanor, who is in the 24% marginal tax bracket, is considering the following alternatives for satisfying the contribution.

	Fair Market Value
(1) Cash donation	$23,000
(2) Unimproved land held for six years ($3,000 basis)	23,000
(3) Blue Corporation stock held for eight months ($3,000 basis)	23,000
(4) Gold Corporation stock held for two years ($28,000 basis)	23,000

Eleanor has asked you to help her decide which of the potential contributions listed above will be most tax advantageous. Evaluate the four alternatives, and write a letter to Eleanor to communicate your advice. Her address is 2622 Bayshore Drive, Berkeley, CA 94709.

Decision Making

Digging Deeper

27. **LO.2** Ramon had AGI of $180,000 in 2018. He is considering making a charitable contribution this year to the American Heart Association, a qualified charitable organization. Determine the current allowable charitable contribution deduction in each of the following independent situations, and indicate the treatment for any amount that is not deductible currently.

a.   A cash gift of $95,000.

b.   A gift of OakCo stock worth $95,000 on the contribution date. Ramon acquired the stock as an investment two years ago at a cost of $84,000.

c.   A gift of a painting worth $95,000 that Ramon purchased three years ago for $60,000. The charity has indicated that it would sell the painting to generate cash to fund medical research.

d.   Assume that Ramon has decided to donate cash to the American Heart Association of $113,000. However, he is considering delaying his donation until next year, when his AGI will increase to $300,000 and he will be in the 32% income tax bracket, an increase from his current-year income tax bracket of 24%. Ramon asks you to determine the tax savings from the tax deduction in present value terms if he were to make the donation this year, rather than delaying the donation until next year. See Appendix F for the present value factors, and assume a 6% discount rate.

28. **LO.2** Linda, age 37, who files as a single taxpayer, had AGI of $280,000 for 2018. She incurred the following expenses and losses during the year:

Medical expenses (before the 7.5%-of-AGI limitation)	$33,000
State and local income taxes	4,800
State sales tax	1,300
Real estate taxes	6,000
Home mortgage interest	5,000
Automobile loan interest	750
Credit card interest	1,000
Charitable contributions	7,000
Casualty loss (before 10% limitation but after $100 floor; not in a Federally declared disaster area)	34,000
Unreimbursed employee business expenses	7,600

Calculate Linda's allowable itemized deductions for the year.

29. **LO.3** Ann and Bill were on the list of a local adoption agency for several years, seeking to adopt a child. Finally, in 2017, good news comes their way, and an adoption seems imminent. They paid qualified adoption expenses of $5,000 in 2017 and $11,000 in 2018. Assume that the adoption becomes final in 2018. Ann and Bill always file a joint income tax return.

    a. Determine the amount of the adoption expenses credit available to Ann and Bill, assuming that their combined annual income is $120,000. In what year(s) will they benefit from the credit?

    b. Assuming that Ann and Bill's modified AGI in 2017 and 2018 is $220,000, calculate the amount of the adoption expenses credit.

30. **LO.3** Paul and Karen Kent are married, and both are employed (Paul earns $44,000 and Karen earns $9,000 during 2018). Paul and Karen have two dependent children, both under the age of 13 (Samuel and Joy). So they can work outside the home, Paul and Karen pay $3,800 ($1,900 for each child) to Sunnyside Day Care Center (422 Sycamore Road, Ft. Worth, TX 76028; Employer Identification Number: 11-2345678) to care for their children while they are working.

    a. Assuming that Paul and Karen file a joint return, what, if any, is their tax credit for child and dependent care expenses?

    b. Complete Form 2441 for Paul and Karen; their AGI is $53,750, and their tax liability before any available child care credit is $2,825. Relevant Social Security numbers are as follows: Paul (123-45-6789); Samuel (123-45-6788); Joy (123-45-6787). Neither Paul nor Karen received any child care benefits from their employers.

31. **LO.3** Jim and Mary Jean are married and have two dependent children under the age of 13. Both parents are employed outside the home and, during 2018, earn salaries as follows: $16,000 (Jim) and $5,200 (Mary Jean). To care for their children while they work, they pay Eleanor (Jim's mother) $5,600. Eleanor does not qualify as a dependent of Jim and Mary Jean. Assuming that Jim and Mary Jean file a joint tax return, what, if any, is their credit for child and dependent care expenses?

32. **LO.3** Jenna, a longtime client of yours, is an architect and the president of the local Rotary chapter. To keep up to date with the latest developments in her profession, she attends continuing education seminars offered by the architecture school at State University. During 2018, Jenna spends $2,000 on course tuition to attend such seminars. She also spends another $400 on architecture books during the year.

    Communications

    Digging Deeper

    Jenna's daughter, Caitlin, is a senior majoring in engineering at the University of the Midwest. During the 2018 calendar year, Caitlin incurs the following expenses: $8,200 for tuition ($4,100 per semester) and $750 for books and course materials. Caitlin, who Jenna claims as a dependent, lives at home while attending school full-time. Jenna is married, files a joint return, and reports a combined AGI with her husband of $116,000.

    a. Calculate Jenna's education tax credit for 2018.

    b. In her capacity as president of the local Rotary chapter, Jenna has asked you to make a 30- to 45-minute speech outlining the different ways the tax law helps defray (1) the cost of higher education and (2) the cost of continuing education once someone is in the workforce. Prepare an outline of possible topics for presentation. A tentative title for your presentation is "How Can the Tax Law Help Pay for College and Continuing Professional Education?"

33. **LO.3** Mark and Lisa are approaching an exciting time in their lives as their oldest son, Austin, graduates from high school and moves on to college. What are some of the tax issues Mark and Lisa should consider as they think about paying for Austin's college education?

    Critical Thinking

Decision Making   34.   **LO.3** Joyce, a widow, lives in an apartment with her two minor children (ages 8 and 10), whom she supports. Joyce earns $33,000 during 2018. She uses the standard deduction.

    a.   Calculate the amount, if any, of Joyce's earned income credit.

    b.   During the year, Joyce is offered a new job that has greater future potential than her current job. If she accepts the job offer, her earnings for the year will be $39,000; however, she is afraid she will not qualify for as much of the earned income credit. Using after-tax cash-flow calculations, determine whether Joyce should accept the new job offer. As the child tax credit will be the same under either scenario, you can ignore it for purposes of this analysis.

Comprehensive Tax Return Problems

Decision Making   1.   Alice J. and Bruce M. Byrd are married taxpayers who file a joint return. Their Social Security numbers are 123-45-6789 and 111-11-1112, respectively. Alice's birthday is September 21, 1971, and Bruce's is June 27, 1970. They live at 473 Revere Avenue, Lowell, MA 01850. Alice is the office manager for Lowell Dental Clinic, 433 Broad Street, Lowell, MA 01850 (Employer Identification Number 98-7654321). Bruce is the manager of a Super Burgers fast-food outlet owned and operated by Plymouth Corporation, 1247 Central Avenue, Hauppauge, NY 11788 (Employer Identification Number 11-1111111).

    The following information is shown on their Wage and Tax Statements (Form W–2) for 2018.

Line	Description	Alice	Bruce
1	Wages, tips, other compensation	$58,000	$62,100
2	Federal income tax withheld	4,500	5,300
3	Social Security wages	58,000	62,100
4	Social Security tax withheld	3,596	3,850
5	Medicare wages and tips	58,000	62,100
6	Medicare tax withheld	841	900
15	State	Massachusetts	Massachusetts
16	State wages, tips, etc.	58,000	62,100
17	State income tax withheld	2,950	3,100

The Byrds provide over half of the support of their two children, Cynthia (born January 25, 1994, Social Security number 123-45-6788) and John (born February 7, 1998, Social Security number 123-45-6786). Both children are full-time students and live with the Byrds except when they are away at college. Cynthia earned $6,200 from a summer internship in 2018, and John earned $3,800 from a part-time job.

    During 2018, the Byrds provided 60% of the total support of Bruce's widower father, Sam Byrd (born March 6, 1942, Social Security number 123-45-6787). Sam lived alone and covered the rest of his support with his Social Security benefits. Sam died in November, and Bruce, the beneficiary of a policy on Sam's life, received life insurance proceeds of $1,600,000 on December 28.

    The Byrds had the following expenses relating to their personal residence during 2018:

Property taxes	$5,000
Qualified interest on home mortgage (acquisition indebtedness)	8,700
Repairs to roof	5,750
Utilities	4,100
Fire and theft insurance	1,900

The Byrds had the following medical expenses for 2018:

Medical insurance premiums	$4,500
Doctor bill for Sam incurred in 2017 and not paid until 2018	7,600
Operation for Sam	8,500
Prescription medicines for Sam	900
Hospital expenses for Sam	3,500
Reimbursement from insurance company, received in 2018	3,600

The medical expenses for Sam represent most of the 60% that Bruce contributed toward his father's support.

Other relevant information follows:

- When they filed their 2017 state return in 2018, the Byrds paid additional state income tax of $900.
- During 2018, Alice and Bruce attended a dinner dance sponsored by the Lowell Police Disability Association (a qualified charitable organization). The Byrds paid $300 for the tickets. The cost of comparable entertainment would normally be $50.
- The Byrds contributed $5,000 to Lowell Presbyterian Church and gave used clothing (cost of $1,200 and fair market value of $350) to the Salvation Army. All donations are supported by receipts, and the clothing is in very good condition.
- Via a crowdfunding site (**gofundme.com**), Alice and Bruce made a gift to a needy family who lost their home in a fire ($400). In addition, they made several cash gifts to homeless individuals downtown (estimated to be $65).
- In 2018, the Byrds received interest income of $2,750, which was reported on a Form 1099–INT from Second National Bank, 125 Oak Street, Lowell, MA 01850 (Employer Identification Number 98-7654322).
- The home mortgage interest was reported on Form 1098 by Lowell Commercial Bank, PO Box 1000, Lowell, MA 01850 (Employer Identification Number 98-7654323). The mortgage (outstanding balance of $425,000 as of January 1, 2018) was taken out by the Byrds on May 1, 2014.
- Alice's employer requires that all employees wear uniforms to work. During 2018, Alice spent $850 on new uniforms and $566 on laundry charges.
- Bruce paid $400 for an annual subscription to the *Journal of Franchise Management* and $741 for annual membership dues to his professional association.
- Neither Alice's nor Bruce's employer reimburses for employee expenses.
- The Byrds do not keep the receipts for the sales taxes they paid and had no major purchases subject to sales tax.
- All members of the Byrd family had health care coverage for all months of 2018.
- This year the Byrds gave each of their children $2,000, which was then deposited into their Roth IRAs.
- Alice and Bruce paid no estimated Federal income tax. Neither Alice nor Bruce wants to designate $3 to the Presidential Election Campaign Fund.

Part 1—Tax Computation

Compute net tax payable or refund due for Alice and Bruce Byrd for 2018. If they have overpaid, they want the amount to be refunded to them. If you use tax forms for your computations, you will need Form 1040 and Schedules A and B.

Part 2—Tax Planning

Alice and Bruce are planning some significant changes for 2019. They have provided you with the following information and asked you to project their taxable income and tax liability for 2019.

The Byrds will invest the $1,600,000 of life insurance proceeds in short-term certificates of deposit (CDs) and use the interest for living expenses during 2019. They expect to earn total interest of $32,000 on the CDs.

Bruce has been promoted to regional manager, and his salary for 2019 will be $88,000. He estimates that state income tax withheld will increase by $4,000 and the Social Security tax withheld will be $5,456.

Alice, who has been diagnosed with a serious illness, will take a leave of absence from work during 2019. The estimated cost for her medical treatment is $15,400, of which $6,400 will be reimbursed by their insurance company in 2019. Their medical insurance premium will increase to $9,769. Property taxes on their residence are expected to increase to $5,100. The Byrds' home mortgage interest expense and charitable contributions are expected to be unchanged from the prior year.

John will graduate from college in December 2018 and will take a job in New York City in January 2019. His starting salary will be $46,000.

Assume that all of the information reported in 2018 will be the same in 2019 unless other information has been presented.

2. Paul and Donna Decker are married taxpayers, ages 44 and 42, respectively, who file a joint return for 2018. The Deckers live at 1121 College Avenue, Carmel, IN 46032. Paul is an assistant manager at Carmel Motor Inn, and Donna is a teacher at Carmel Elementary School. They present you with W–2 forms that reflect the following information:

	Paul	Donna
Salary	$68,000	$56,000
Federal tax withheld	6,770	6,630
State income tax withheld	1,400	1,100
FICA (Social Security and Medicare) withheld	5,202	4,284
Social Security numbers	111-11-1112	123-45-6789

Donna is the custodial parent of two children from a previous marriage who reside with the Deckers through the school year. The children, Larry and Jane Parker, reside with their father, Bob, during the summer. Relevant information for the children follows:

	Larry	Jane
Age	17	18
Social Security numbers	123-45-6788	123-45-6787
Months spent with Deckers	9	9

Under the divorce decree, Bob pays child support of $150 per month per child during the nine months the children live with the Deckers. Bob says that he spends $200 per month per child during the three summer months they reside with him. Donna and Paul can document that they provide $2,000 of support per child per year. The divorce decree is silent as to which parent can claim the exemptions for the children.

In August, Paul and Donna added a suite to their home to provide more comfortable accommodations for Hannah Snyder (Social Security number 123-45-6786), Donna's mother, who had moved in with them in February 2017 after the death of Donna's father. Not wanting to borrow money for this addition, Paul sold 300 shares of Acme Corporation stock for $50 per share on May 3, 2018, and used the proceeds of $15,000 to cover construction costs. The Deckers had purchased the stock on April 29, 2013, for $25 per share. They received dividends of $750 on the jointly owned stock a month before the sale.

Hannah, who is 66 years old, received $7,500 in Social Security benefits during the year, of which she gave the Deckers $2,000 to use toward household expenses and deposited the remainder in her personal savings account. The Deckers determine that they have spent $2,500 of their own money for food, clothing, medical expenses, and other items for Hannah. They do not know what the rental value of Hannah's suite would be, but they estimate it would be at least $300 per month.

Interest paid during the year included the following:

Home mortgage interest (paid to Carmel Federal Savings and Loan)	$7,890
Interest on an automobile loan (paid to Carmel National Bank)	1,660
Interest on Citibank Visa card	620

In July, Paul hit a submerged rock while boating. Fortunately, he was uninjured after being thrown from the boat and landing in deep water. However, the boat, which was uninsured, was destroyed. Paul had paid $25,000 for the boat in June 2017, and its value was appraised at $18,000 on the date of the accident.

The Deckers paid doctor and hospital bills of $10,700 and were reimbursed $2,000 by their insurance company. They spent $640 for prescription drugs and medicines and $5,904 for premiums on their health insurance policy. They have filed additional claims of $1,200 with their insurance company and have been told they will receive payment for that amount in January 2019. Included in the amounts paid for doctor and hospital bills were payments of $380 for Hannah and $850 for the children. All members of the Decker family had health insurance coverage for all of 2018.

Additional information of potential tax consequence follows:

Real estate taxes paid	$6,850
Sales taxes paid (per table)	1,379
Contributions to their church	2,600
Appraised value of books donated to public library	740
Refund of state income tax for 2017 (the Deckers itemized on their 2017 Federal tax return)	1,520

Compute net tax payable or refund due for the Deckers for 2018. Ignore the child tax credit in your computations. If the Deckers have overpaid, the amount is to be credited toward their taxes for 2019.

BRIDGE DISCIPLINE

1. George comes to you asking for your advice. He wants to invest $10,000 either in a debt security or in an equity investment. His choices are shown below.

   - Redbreast Corporation bond, annual coupon rate of 7.5%.
   - City of Philadelphia general obligation bond, coupon rate of 6.0%.
   - Blue Corporation 7.5% preferred stock (produces qualified dividend income).

   These alternatives are believed to carry comparable risk. Assuming that George is in the 35% marginal tax bracket, which investment alternative could be expected to produce the superior annual after-tax rate of return?

2. Assume the same facts as in Problem 1, except that George is a C corporation rather than an individual and is in the 25% marginal tax bracket (combined Federal and state rate). Which investment strategy would maximize George, Inc.'s annual return?

Research Problems

THOMSON REUTERS

Note: Solutions to the Research Problems can be prepared by using the Thomson Reuters Checkpoint™ online tax research database, which accompanies this textbook. Solutions can also be prepared by using research materials found in a typical tax library.

Research Problem 1. Jane suffers from a degenerative spinal disorder. Her physician said that swimming could help prevent the onset of permanent paralysis and recommended the installation of a swimming pool at her residence for her use. Jane's residence had a market value of approximately $500,000 before the swimming pool was installed. The swimming pool was built, and an appraiser estimated that the value of Jane's home increased by $98,000 because of the addition.

The pool cost $194,000, and Jane claimed a medical expense deduction of $96,000 ($194,000 − $98,000) on her tax return. Upon audit of the return, the IRS determined that an adequate pool should have cost $70,000 and would increase the value of her home by only $31,000. Thus, the IRS claims that Jane is entitled to a deduction of only $39,000 ($70,000 − $31,000).

a. Is there any ceiling limitation on the amount deductible as a medical expense? Explain.

b. Can capital expenditures be deductible as medical expenses? Explain.

c. What is the significance of a "minimum adequate facility"? Should aesthetic or architectural qualities be considered in the determination? Why or why not?

Research Problem 2. Ken and Mary Jane Blough, your neighbors, have asked you for advice after receiving correspondence in the mail from the IRS. You learn that the IRS is asking for documentation in support of the itemized deductions the Bloughs claimed on a recent tax return. The Bloughs tell you that their income in the year of question was $75,000. Because their record-keeping habits are poor, they felt justified in claiming itemized deductions equal to the amounts that represent the average claimed by other taxpayers in their income bracket. These averages are calculated and reported by the IRS annually based on actual returns filed in an earlier year. Accordingly, they claimed medical expenses of $7,102, taxes of $6,050, interest of $10,659, and charitable contributions of $2,693. What advice do you give the Bloughs?

Partial list of research aids:
Cheryl L. de Werff, T.C. Summary Opinion, 2011–29.

Research Problem 3. Ashby and Curtis are married and have a 2-year-old son, Jason. Curtis works full-time as an electrical engineer, but Ashby has not worked outside the home since Jason was born. As Jason is getting older, Ashby thinks that Jason would benefit from attending nursery school several times a week, which would give her an opportunity to reinvigorate her love of painting at a nearby art studio. Ashby thinks that if she is lucky, the proceeds from the sale of her paintings will pay for the nursery school tuition. In addition, she is planning to claim the credit for child and dependent care expenses because the care provided Jason at the nursery school is required for her to pursue her art career. Can Ashby and Curtis claim the credit for child and dependent care expenses for the nursery school expenditure? Why or why not?

Use internet tax resources to address the following questions. Look for reliable websites and blogs of the IRS and other government agencies, media outlets, businesses, tax professionals, academics, think tanks, and political outlets.

Research Problem 4. The Federal government incurs a cost for every item that is deductible in the computation of taxable income. These costs, which take the form of forgone tax revenue, are often referred to as "tax expenditures." The Joint Committee on Taxation regularly estimates the current and projected tax expenditures associated with of a long list of provisions in the tax law. Locate the Joint Committee on Taxation's most recent analysis, and identify the current tax expenditure associated with the deductions for medical expenses, interest on student loans, mortgage interest, and charitable contributions. How are these costs expected to change over the next five years? How is the concept of tax expenditures helpful to tax policy analysts and lawmakers?

Research Problem 5. One income exclusion that some states allow that the Federal government does not is for lottery winnings. Does your state have an exclusion for lottery winnings? If so, how does it work? Why do you think a state might allow winnings from its own state lottery to be excluded from state income taxes?

Research Problem 6. Taxpayers who purchase health insurance coverage through the Health Insurance Marketplace may be eligible for the premium tax credit under § 36B. Use the IRS's website (**www.irs.gov**) to read about this provision and determine which taxpayers are eligible for the credit.

Becker CPA Review Questions

1. Stephen is a graduate student at West University. He works part time at the campus coffee shop earning $5,000 this year. Stephen also receives a $25,000 scholarship that pays for his tuition, fees, and books. What amount does Stephen include in his gross income?

   a. $25,000
   b. $5,000
   c. $30,000
   d. $0

2. Kim was seriously injured at her job. As a result of her injury, she received the following payments.

   - $5,000 reimbursement from employer-provided health insurance for medical expenses paid by Kim. The premiums this year paid by Kim's employer totaled $6,000.

   - $15,000 disability pay. Kim has disability insurance provided by her employer as a nontaxable fringe benefit. Kim's employer paid $6,000 in disability premiums this year on behalf of Kim.

   - $10,000 received for damages for personal physical injury.

   - $200,000 in punitive damages.

   What amount is taxable to Kim?

   a. $215,000
   b. $225,000
   c. $236,000
   d. $0

3. In the current year, Wells paid the following expenses:

Premiums on an insurance policy against loss of earnings due to sickness or accident	$3,000
Physical therapy after spinal surgery	2,000
Premium on an insurance policy that covers reimbursement for the cost of prescription drugs	500

   In the current year, Wells recovered $1,500 of the $2,000 that she paid for physical therapy through insurance reimbursement from a group medical policy paid for by her employer. Disregarding the adjusted gross income percentage threshold, what amount could be claimed on Wells's current-year income tax return for medical expenses?

   a. $4,000
   b. $3,500
   c. $1,000
   d. $500

4. Which of the following credits is considered "refundable"?

    a. Child and dependent care credit

    b. Retirement plan contribution credit

    c. Child tax credit

    d. Credit for elderly

5. Jim spent four years earning his undergraduate degree at a local university. He began his first year of law school in January of the current year. Assuming he is under the phaseout limitation, what education tax credit is Jim eligible for in the current year?

    a. American Opportunity credit

    b. Earned income credit

    c. Lifetime learning credit

    d. Professional education and training credit

6. Which of the following statements is true regarding the taxation of Social Security benefits?

    a. 85% is the maximum amount of taxable Social Security benefits.

    b. 50% is the maximum amount of taxable Social Security benefits.

    c. If a taxpayer's only source of income is $10,000 of Social Security benefits, then 50% of the benefits are taxable.

    d. If a taxpayer's only source of income is $10,000 of Social Security benefits, then 85% of the benefits are taxable.

7. Bill and Jane Jones were divorced on January 1, 2018. They have no children. In accordance with the divorce decree, Bill transferred the title of their house over to Jane. The home had a fair market value of $250,000 and was subject to a $100,000 mortgage. Under the divorce agreement, Bill is to make $1,000 monthly mortgage payments on the home for the remainder of the mortgage. In the current year, Bill made 12 mortgage payments. What amount is taxable to Jane in the current year?

    a. $12,000   c. $100,000

    b. $250,000   d. $0

8. Jake pays the following amounts to his former spouse during the current year:

Regular alimony payments	$ 12,000
Child support	10,000
Residence as part of a property settlement	115,000

    What amount can Jake deduct as alimony for the current year? Assume the divorce occurred before 2019.

    a. $0   c. $22,000

    b. $12,000   d. $137,000

CHAPTER 11

Individuals as Employees and Proprietors

LEARNING OBJECTIVES: *After completing Chapter 11, you should be able to:*

LO.1 Distinguish between employee and independent contractor status.

LO.2 State and explain the exclusions from income available to employees who receive fringe benefits.

LO.3 Apply the rules for computing deductible expenses of work, including transportation, travel, moving, education, and entertainment expenses.

LO.4 Explain the difference between accountable and nonaccountable employee plans.

LO.5 Understand the opportunities available to build wealth through Individual Retirement Accounts.

LO.6 State and explain the tax provisions applicable to proprietors.

LO.7 Distinguish between business and hobby activities and apply the rules limiting the deduction of hobby losses.

CHAPTER OUTLINE

11-1 Employee versus Independent Contractor, 11-2
11-1a Factors Considered in Classification, 11-2

11-2 Exclusions Available to Employees, 11-4
11-2a Employer-Sponsored Accident and Health Plans, 11-5
11-2b Medical Reimbursement Plans, 11-5
11-2c Long-Term Care Insurance Benefits, 11-6
11-2d Meals and Lodging Furnished for the Convenience of the Employer, 11-7
11-2e Group Term Life Insurance, 11-9
11-2f Qualified Tuition Reduction Plans, 11-9
11-2g Other Employee Fringe Benefits, 11-10
11-2h Cafeteria Plans, 11-11
11-2i Flexible Spending Plans, 11-11
11-2j General Classes of Excluded Benefits, 11-12
11-2k Foreign Earned Income, 11-17

11-3 Expenses Relating to Time at Work, 11-18
11-3a Transportation Expenses, 11-18
11-3b Travel Expenses, 11-19
11-3c Moving Expenses, 11-22
11-3d Education Expenses, 11-22
11-3e Deduction for Qualified Tuition and Related Expenses, 11-24
11-3f Entertainment Expenses, 11-25
11-3g Other Expenses of Work, 11-27
11-3h Classification of Employee Expenses, 11-29
11-3i Contributions to Individual Retirement Accounts, 11-30

11-4 Individuals as Proprietors, 11-33
11-4a Accounting Periods and Methods, 11-33
11-4b Income and Deductions of a Proprietorship, 11-34
11-4c Retirement Plans for Self-Employed Individuals, 11-35
11-4d Deduction for Qualified Business Income, 11-37
11-4e Estimated Tax Payments, 11-44

11-5 Hobby Losses, 11-45
11-5a General Rules, 11-45
11-5b Presumptive Rule of Profit-Seeking, 11-46
11-5c The Deductible Amount, 11-47

TAX TALK *The taxpayer—that's someone who works for the Federal government but doesn't have to take a civil service examination.*—RONALD REAGAN

ISTOCK.COM/NEUSTOCKIMAGES

SELF-EMPLOYED VERSUS EMPLOYEE—WHAT'S THE DIFFERENCE?

Mark and Mary Herman come to you for tax advice. Mark is a self-employed consultant. Last year, Mark's business generated revenue of $165,000 and incurred expenses of $18,000 for rent and utilities for an office. Mark also spent $8,000 purchasing depreciable equipment used in the business and paid a part-time assistant $12,000 for work performed during the year. He hired Ellen to help him in his consulting practice. Mark paid Ellen $40,000 for her work during the year.

Mark paid $3,000 for his own health insurance and $500 for term life insurance; he did not contribute to any retirement plans. Mary (Mark's wife) also works as a consultant, but is employed by a large firm. Her salary last year was $85,000. Mary's employer paid $3,000 of premiums for her health insurance and provided $50,000 of group term life insurance to each of its employees. Mary is not covered by a qualified retirement plan at work, but she contributed $5,500 to a traditional IRA.

Mary routinely travels for her job and was reimbursed by her employer for all travel expenses. In addition, Mary spent $500 on other employee business expenses that were not reimbursed by her employer.

What are the tax consequences of these items? Can Mark and Mary deduct the expenses they incurred? Are there other tax planning opportunities the couple may be missing or tax issues of which they should be aware?

Read the chapter and formulate your response.

Generally, individuals earn business income as employees or through self-employment. Self-employed individuals are commonly referred to as independent contractors but are also described as freelancers, external consultants, micro-business owners, entrepreneurs, proprietors, or individuals who work in the "gig economy."

In many cases, properly categorizing an individual as an employee or as self-employed for tax purposes is a complex determination. This chapter begins with a discussion of the factors that must be considered in determining whether an individual is an employee or is self-employed. This is followed by a discussion of tax provisions applicable to employees and then by a discussion of tax provisions related to self-employed individuals.

11-1 EMPLOYEE VERSUS INDEPENDENT CONTRACTOR

LO.1

Distinguish between employee and independent contractor status.

When one person performs services for another person or for an entity, the person performing the services either is an employee or is self-employed (i.e., an independent contractor). Globalization, advances in technology, and economic factors have led to increases in self-employment. Some individuals view self-employment as a way to be their own boss, have a flexible work schedule, and do work they truly love. Employers often see hiring self-employed individuals (rather than employees) as a means to achieve greater workforce flexibility and control costs. As a result, the proper determination of employment status is important and is often scrutinized.

From an employer's perspective, misclassification of an individual as self-employed rather than as an employee is not uncommon. This misclassification can be unintentional, resulting from the difficulty in applying a complex set of rules related to employee versus independent contractor status. However, classifying someone as a contractor instead of as an employee may be an intentional strategy to avoid certain costs. Unlike employees, self-employed individuals need not be included in various fringe benefit programs (e.g., group term life insurance and retirement plans). Further, employers are not required to pay FICA and unemployment taxes (see text Section 11-4e) on compensation paid to independent contractors.

From the worker's perspective, categorization as an employee may avoid certain risks associated with self-employment that employees generally do not assume. For example, a self-employed individual assumes responsibility for employment-related tax obligations and assumes the legal responsibilities associated with performing the job. From a tax perspective, a self-employed individual is responsible for both the employee and the employer share of FICA and unemployment taxes. However, allowable business expenses of self-employed taxpayers are generally classified as deductions *for* AGI and are reported on Schedule C (Profit or Loss from Business) of Form 1040.[1] With the exception of reimbursement under an accountable plan (covered later in the chapter), expenses of employees are deductions *from* AGI. However, from 2018 through 2025, the deduction for these expenses (i.e., miscellaneous itemized deductions) is suspended. As a result, such deductions provide no tax benefit during this period.[2]

Failure to categorize an individual's work status correctly can have serious tax consequences; tax deficiencies as well as interest and penalties may result for the employer and the employee. The next section discusses those factors that are considered in the proper classification of an individual as an employee or as an independent contractor.

11-1a Factors Considered in Classification

The pivotal issue in classifying an individual as an independent contractor or an employee is whether an employer-employee relationship exists. The common law definition of an employee originated in the courts and is summarized in various IRS

---

[1] §§ 62(a)(1) and 162(a). In simple situations, a Schedule C–EZ can be used. In that case, a Schedule SE (Self-Employment Tax) also is filed.

[2] § 67(a), added by the Tax Cuts and Jobs Act (TCJA) of 2017.

BRIDGE DISCIPLINE   **Bridge to Equity or Fairness and Business Law**

Max performs services for Calico, Inc. Amy performs services for Amber, Inc. Max and Amy's work products are very similar. Yet, Max is classified as an employee, and Amy is classified as an independent contractor. Does such a legal classification produce equitable results in terms of the effects it has on Max and Amy?

In distinguishing between an employee and an independent contractor, the overriding theme of common law is that the employee is subject to the will and control of the employer as to what is to be done and how it is to be done. Put in tax law terminology, an employer has the right to control and direct the individual who performs the services, not only as to the result to be accomplished by the work but also as to the details and means by which the result is accomplished. Among the factors generally considered in determining whether this right exists are the following.

- Degree of control exercised over the details of the work.
- Provision of facilities used in the work.
- Opportunity for profit or loss.
- Right to discharge.
- Whether work is part of regular business.
- Permanency of the relationship.
- Relationship that the parties believe they are creating.
- Manner of payment (e.g., by the job or by the hour).
- Skill required.
- Offering of the services to the general public rather than to one individual or entity.
- Distinct occupation or recognized trade or calling involved.
- Custom in the trade.

pronouncements; one specifies 20 factors that can be used to determine whether a worker is a common law employee or an independent contractor (and, thus, self-employed).[3]

A common law employee-employer relationship exists when the employer has the right to specify the end result and the ways and means by which that result is to be attained.[4] This means that a worker is subject to the will and control of the employer with respect to what should be done and how it should be done. If the individual is told what to do but is allowed to determine independently how to do it, an employee-employer relationship likely does not exist.

If the business provides the following items to a worker, a common law employee-employer relationship likely exists.

- Furnishing tools or equipment and a place to work.
- Providing support services, including the hiring of assistants to help do the work.
- Making training available to provide needed job skills.
- Allowing participation in various workplace fringe benefits (e.g., accident and health plans, group life insurance, and retirement plans).
- Paying for services based on time rather than the task performed.

Alternatively, independent contractors are more likely to have unreimbursed business expenses, a significant investment in tools and work facilities, and less permanency in their business relationships. Independent contractors, moreover, anticipate a profit from their work, make their services available in a marketplace, and are likely to be paid a flat fee on a per-job basis.

In resolving employment status, each case is tested on its own merits; generally, the right to control the means and methods of accomplishment is the definitive test. Generally, physicians, attorneys, dentists, contractors, subcontractors, and others who offer services to the public are not classified as employees.

In-depth coverage can be found on this book's companion website: www.cengage.com   **1** DIGGING DEEPER

---

[3]Rev.Rul. 87–41, 1987–1 C.B. 296. Also see IRS Publication 1779 (*Independent Contractor or Employee*).

[4]Reg. § 31.3401(c)–1(b).

The Big Picture

EXAMPLE 1

Return to the facts of *The Big Picture* on p. 11-1. Mark is a consultant whose major client accounts for 60% of his billings. He does the routine consulting work at the client's request. He is paid a monthly retainer in addition to amounts charged for extra work. Mark is an independent contractor. Even though most of his income comes from one client, he still has the right to determine *how* the end result of his work is attained.

The Big Picture

EXAMPLE 2

Return to the facts of *The Big Picture* on p. 11-1. Ellen is a recent MBA graduate hired by Mark to assist him in the performance of services for the client mentioned in Example 1. Ellen is under Mark's supervision; he reviews her work and pays her an hourly fee. Ellen is considered an employee of Mark.

 DIGGING DEEPER 2   **In-depth coverage can be found on this book's companion website: www.cengage.com**

TAX PLANNING STRATEGIES   Self-Employed Individuals

FRAMEWORK FOCUS: DEDUCTIONS

Strategy: Maximize Deductible Amounts.

Some taxpayers, such as real estate agents and consultants, might be classified as either employees or independent contractors. These taxpayers should consider all factors and not automatically assume that one status is preferable to the other.

It is advantageous to deduct one's business expenses *for* AGI. However, an independent contractor may incur additional expenses such as local gross receipts taxes, license fees, franchise fees, personal property taxes, and occupation taxes. Record-keeping and filing requirements can also be quite burdensome.

One of the most expensive considerations is the self-employment tax imposed on independent contractors and other self-employed individuals. Such individuals are required to pay twice the amount of Social Security and Medicare taxes that are imposed on an employee with the same amount of earned income (wages). Even though a deduction *for* AGI is allowed for one-half of the self-employment tax paid, an employee and an independent contractor are not in the same tax position where equal amounts are earned. This discussion continues in text Section 11-4b.

LO.2

State and explain the exclusions from income available to employees who receive fringe benefits.

11-2 EXCLUSIONS AVAILABLE TO EMPLOYEES

Several gross income exclusions that are available to *all taxpayers* were discussed in Chapter 4; these include interest income on obligations of state and local governments, life insurance proceeds, and income from discharge of indebtedness. Other exclusions, available only to *individuals*, were discussed in Chapter 10; these include gifts and inheritances, scholarships, and compensation for injuries and sickness.

Another class of exclusions available only to *employees* is referred to as qualified fringe benefits. The popularity of fringe benefits is attributable to the fact that the cost of such benefits is deductible by employers and excludible from income by employees. The next sections discuss several of the most popular fringe benefits available to employees.

Cardinal Corporation, which has a marginal tax rate of 21%, provides health insurance coverage to employees at a cost of $1,000 per employee. Because Cardinal can deduct the health insurance premiums paid to provide this coverage, the net cost to the corporation is $790 per employee ($1,000 cost − $210 tax savings). The employee excludes the value of this fringe benefit, so there is no tax cost to the employee.

The average employee of Cardinal Corporation is in the 12% bracket. If Cardinal did not provide the health insurance coverage and the employee paid a $1,000 premium, the employee would use after-tax dollars to acquire the coverage. The employee then must earn $1,136 to pay for $1,000 of coverage [$1,136 wages − ($1,136 × 12% tax)]. The after-tax cost to the corporation of $1,136 in wages is $897 ($1,136 wages − $239 corporate tax savings). Thus, the cost of health insurance coverage is $107 less per employee ($897 − $790) if it is a qualified fringe benefit, because the insurance is both deductible by the corporation and excludible by the employee.

EXAMPLE 3

11-2a **Employer-Sponsored Accident and Health Plans**

Congress encourages employers to provide employees, retired former employees, and their dependents with accident and health benefits, disability insurance, and long-term care plans. The *premiums* are deductible by the employer and are excluded from the employee's gross income.[5] Although § 105(a) provides the general rule that the employee has includible income when he or she collects the insurance *benefits*, two exceptions are provided.

Section 105(b) generally excludes payments received for medical care of the employee, spouse, and dependents. However, if the payments are for expenses that do not meet the Code's definition of medical care,[6] the amount received is included in gross income. In addition, the taxpayer includes in gross income any amounts received for medical expenses that were deducted by the taxpayer on a prior return.

In 2018, Tab's employer-sponsored health insurance plan paid $4,000 for hair transplants that did not meet the Code's definition of medical care. As a result, Tab includes $4,000 in his gross income in 2018.

EXAMPLE 4

Section 105(c) excludes payments for the permanent loss or the loss of the use of a member or function of the body or the permanent disfigurement of the employee, the spouse, or a dependent. However, payments that are a substitute for salary (e.g., related to the period of time absent from work) are included in income.

Jill loses an eye in an automobile accident unrelated to her work. As a result of the accident, Jill incurs $2,000 of medical expenses, which she deducts on her return. She collects $10,000 from an accident insurance policy carried by her employer. The benefits are paid according to a schedule of amounts that varies with the part of the body injured (e.g., $10,000 for loss of an eye and $20,000 for loss of a hand).

Because the payment is for loss of a *member or function of the body*, the $10,000 is excluded from Jill's gross income. Jill was absent from work for a week as a result of the accident. Her employer also provides her with insurance for the loss of income due to illness or injury. Jill collects $500, which is included in her gross income.

EXAMPLE 5

11-2b **Medical Reimbursement Plans**

In lieu of providing an employee with insurance coverage for hospital and medical expenses, the employer may agree to reimburse the employee for these expenses. The amounts received through the insurance coverage (insured plan benefits) are excluded from gross income (as previously discussed).

---

[5]§ 106, Reg. § 1.106–1, and Rev.Rul. 82–196, 1982–2 C.B. 53.   [6]See text Section 10-4a for an additional discussion of medical care.

The media frequently report on challenges facing senior citizens. Organizations such as the AARP effectively lobby for the rights of senior citizens through direct lobbying in Washington and through grassroots efforts throughout the country. With the "graying of America," these concerns and lobbying efforts are likely to be magnified.

The Internal Revenue Code contains a number of provisions that are "senior citizen friendly." Among these are the following.

• Exclusion from gross income, except for taxpayers above certain income levels, of Social Security benefits (§ 86).

• Exclusion from gross income of certain life insurance proceeds paid on account of death (§ 101).

• Exclusion from gross income of medical insurance premiums and benefits (§§ 105 and 106).

• Limited exclusion from gross income of gain on the sale of a principal residence (§ 121).

• Limited exclusion from gross income of long-term care insurance premiums and benefits (§ 7702B).

• Tax-deferred treatment of retirement plans (§§ 401–436).

Insurance companies that issue this type of policy usually require a broad coverage of employees. An alternative is to have a plan that is not funded with insurance (a self-insured arrangement). Under a self-insured plan, the employer reimburses employees directly for any medical expenses. The benefits received under a self-insured plan can be excluded from the employee's gross income if the plan does not discriminate in favor of highly compensated employees.[7]

There is an alternative means of accomplishing a medical reimbursement plan. The employer can purchase a medical insurance plan with a high deductible (e.g., the employee is responsible for the first $2,600 of the family's medical expenses) and then make contributions to the employee's **Health Savings Account (HSA)**.[8] The employer can make contributions each month up to the maximum contribution of 100 percent of the deductible amount. Under a high-deductible plan, the monthly deductible amount is limited to one-twelfth of $3,450 for self-only coverage; for an individual with family coverage, the monthly deductible amount is limited to one-twelfth of $6,900.

Withdrawals from the HSA must be used to reimburse the employee for the medical expenses paid by the employee that are not covered under the high-deductible plan. The employee is not taxed on the employer's contributions to the HSA, the earnings on the funds in the account, or the withdrawals made for medical expenses.[9]

11-2c Long-Term Care Insurance Benefits

Generally, long-term care insurance, which covers expenses such as the cost of care in a nursing home, is treated the same as accident and health insurance benefits. Thus, the employee does not recognize gross income when the employer pays the premiums. An individual who purchases his or her own policy can exclude the benefits from gross income. However, statutory limitations (indexed for inflation) exist for the following amounts.

• Premiums paid by the employer.

• Benefits collected under the employer's plan.

• Benefits collected from the individual's policy.

---

[7]§ 105(h). Also see § 106 and Rev.Rul. 61–146, 1961–2 C.B. 25. Employers should make sure that such reimbursement plans fall within the requirements of the Affordable Care Act to avoid an excise tax. See § 4980D, Notice 2013–54, 2013–40 I.R.B. 287, and Notice 2015–17, 2015–10 I.R.B. 845.

[8]§§ 106(d) and 223. See additional coverage in text Section 10-4a.

[9]§§ 106(d), 223(b), and 223(d). The amounts for 2017 were $3,400 and $6,750.

The employer or insurance company generally provides the employee with information about the amount of his or her taxable benefits. The maximum amount excluded is reduced by any amount received from other third parties (e.g., Medicare, Medicaid).[10]

EXAMPLE 6

Hazel, who suffers from Alzheimer's disease, is a patient in a nursing home for the last 30 days of 2018. While in the nursing home, she incurs total costs of $7,600. Medicare pays $3,500 of the costs. Hazel receives $7,600 from her long-term care insurance policy, which pays her while she is in the facility.

The amount Hazel may exclude is calculated as follows.

Greater of:		
2018 statutory amount ($360 per day × 30 days)	$10,800	
Actual cost of the care	7,600	$10,800
Less: Amount received from Medicare		(3,500)
Amount of exclusion		$ 7,300

Therefore, Hazel must include $300 ($7,600 − $7,300) of the long-term care benefits received in her gross income.

11-2d Meals and Lodging Furnished for the Convenience of the Employer

Under the following conditions, the value of meals and lodging provided to the employee and the employee's spouse and dependents is excluded from gross income.[11]

- The meals and/or lodging are *furnished by the employer*, on the employer's *business premises*, for the *convenience of the employer*. The Tax Cuts and Jobs Act (TCJA) of 2017 reduces the tax benefit to the employer for meals it provides to employees for the employer's convenience. From 2018 through 2025, the employer may only deduct 50 percent of the cost of the meals provided (rather than 100 percent). After 2025, employers may not claim a deduction for these meals. However, if the employer continues to provide such meals, their value remains as an exclusion for the employees.

- In the case of lodging, the *employee is required* to accept the lodging as a condition of employment.

Furnished by the Employer

The courts have raised two questions with regard to the *furnished by the employer* requirement.

- Who is considered an *employee*?
- What is meant by *furnished*?

The IRS and some courts have reasoned that because a partner is not an employee, the exclusion does not apply to a partner. However, the Tax Court and the Fifth Circuit Court of Appeals have ruled in favor of the taxpayer on this issue.[12]

The Supreme Court held that a *cash meal allowance* was ineligible for the exclusion because the employer did not actually furnish the meals.[13] Similarly, one court denied

---

[10]§ 7702B and § 213(d)(10).

[11]§ 119(a). The value of meals and lodging also is excluded from FICA and FUTA tax. *Rowan Companies, Inc. v. U.S.*, 81–1 USTC ¶9479, 48 AFTR 2d 81–5115, 101 S.Ct. 2288 (USSC, 1981).

[12]Rev.Rul. 80, 1953–1 C.B. 62; *Comm. v. Doak*, 56–2 USTC ¶9708, 49 AFTR 1491, 234 F.2d 704 (CA–4, 1956); but see *G. A. Papineau*, 16 T.C. 130 (1951);

Armstrong v. Phinney, 68–1 USTC ¶9355, 21 AFTR 2d 1260, 394 F.2d 661 (CA–5, 1968).

[13]*Comm. v. Kowalski*, 77–2 USTC ¶9748, 40 AFTR 2d 77–6128, 98 S.Ct. 315 (USSC, 1977).

the exclusion where the employer paid for the food and supplied the cooking facilities but the employee prepared the meal.[14]

On the Employer's Business Premises

The *on the employer's business premises* requirement, applicable to both meals and lodging, has resulted in much litigation. The Regulations define business premises as simply "the place of employment of the employee."[15] Thus, the Sixth Circuit Court of Appeals held that a residence, owned by the employer and occupied by an employee, located two blocks from the motel that the employee managed was not part of the business premises.[16] However, the Tax Court considered an employer-owned house located across the street from the hotel that was managed by the taxpayer to be on the business premises of the employer.[17]

Perhaps these two cases can be reconciled by comparing the distance from the lodging facilities to the place where the employer's business was conducted. Apparently, the closer the lodging is to the business operations, the more likely the convenience of the employer is served.

For the Convenience of the Employer

The *convenience of the employer* test is intended to focus on the employer's motivation for furnishing the meals and lodging rather than on the benefits received by the employee. If the employer furnishes the meals and lodging primarily to enable the employee to perform his or her duties properly, it does not matter that the employee considers these benefits to be a part of his or her compensation.

The Regulations give the following examples in which the tests for excluding meals are satisfied.[18]

- A restaurant requires its service staff to eat their meals on the premises during the busy lunch and breakfast hours.
- A bank furnishes meals on the premises for its tellers, to limit the time the employees are away from their booths during busy times.
- A worker is employed at a construction site in a remote part of Alaska. The employer must furnish meals and lodging due to the inaccessibility of other facilities.

Required as a Condition of Employment

The *employee is required to accept* test applies only to lodging. If the employee's use of the housing would serve the convenience of the employer but the employee is not required to use the housing, the exclusion is not available.

EXAMPLE 7

VEP, a utilities company, has all of its service personnel on 24-hour call for emergencies. The company encourages its employees to live near the plant so that they can respond quickly to emergency calls. Company-owned housing is available rent-free. Only 10 of the employees live in company housing because it is not perceived as suitable for families.

VEP employees are not required to use the company-provided housing. Therefore, the employees who live in company housing must include its value in gross income.

In addition, if the employee has the option of accepting a benefit of cash or lodging, the employer-required test is not satisfied.

---

[14]*Tougher v. Comm.*, 71–1 USTC ¶9398, 27 AFTR 2d 71–1301, 441 F.2d 1148 (CA–9, 1971).

[15]Reg. § 1.119–1(c)(1).

[16]*Comm. v. Anderson*, 67–1 USTC ¶9136, 19 AFTR 2d 318, 371 F.2d 59 (CA–6, 1966).

[17]*J. B. Lindeman*, 60 T.C. 609 (1973).

[18]Reg. § 1.119–1(f).

Khalid is the manager of a large apartment complex. The employer requires Khalid to live on the premises but does not charge him rent. The rental value of his apartment is $9,600 a year. Although Khalid considers the rent-free housing a significant benefit, he is not required to include the value of the housing in his gross income.

EXAMPLE 8

Other housing exclusions are available for certain employees of educational institutions, ministers of the gospel, and military personnel.

11-2e **Group Term Life Insurance**

An employee can claim a limited exclusion for group term life insurance benefits that are provided by the employer. The premiums on the first $50,000 of group term life insurance protection are excludible from the employee's and former employee's gross income.

The benefits of this exclusion are available only to employees. Proprietors and partners are not considered employees. Moreover, only a broad-scale coverage of employees satisfies the group requirement (e.g., shareholder-employees would not constitute a qualified group). The exclusion applies only to term insurance (protection for a period of time but with no cash surrender value) and not to ordinary life insurance (lifetime protection plus a cash surrender value that can be drawn upon before death).

As mentioned previously, the exclusion applies to the first $50,000 of group term life insurance protection. For each $1,000 of coverage in excess of $50,000, the employee must include the amounts indicated in Exhibit 11.1 in gross income.[19]

In-depth coverage can be found on this book's companion website: www.cengage.com | **3 DIGGING DEEPER**

Finch Corporation provides its employees with a group term life insurance policy with coverage equal to the employee's annual salary. Keith, age 52, is president of the corporation and receives an annual salary of $350,000. Keith must include $828 in gross income from the insurance protection for the year.

$$\frac{\$350,000 - \$50,000}{\$1,000} \times \$.23 \times 12\,\text{months} = \$828$$

EXAMPLE 9

If the plan discriminates in favor of certain key employees (e.g., officers), the key employees are not eligible for the exclusion.[20] In such a case, the key employees include in gross income the *greater* of actual premiums paid by the employer or the amount calculated from the Uniform Premiums table in Exhibit 11.1. The other (i.e., non-key) employees still are eligible for the $50,000 exclusion and use the Uniform Premiums table to compute the income from excess insurance protection.

11-2f **Qualified Tuition Reduction Plans**

Employees (including retired and disabled former employees) of nonprofit educational institutions can exclude from gross income a tuition waiver that is provided pursuant to a qualified tuition reduction plan. The exclusion applies to tuition reductions granted to the employee, the employee's spouse, and the employee's dependent children.[21]

---

[19]Reg. § 1.79–3(d)(2).
[20]§ 79(d).

[21]§ 117(d).

EXHIBIT 11.1	Uniform Premiums for $1,000 of Group Term Life Insurance Protection

Attained Age on Last Day of Employee's Tax Year	Cost of $1,000 of Protection for a One-Month Period*
Under 25	$ .05
25–29	.06
30–34	.08
35–39	.09
40–44	.10
45–49	.15
50–54	.23
55–59	.43
60–64	.66
65–69	1.27
70 and above	2.06

*Reg. § 1.79–3, effective for coverage after June 30, 1999.

11-2g Other Employee Fringe Benefits

Certain other fringe benefits available to employees also are excluded from gross income.

- The employee does not include in gross income the value of child and dependent care services paid for by the employer and incurred to enable the employee to work. The exclusion cannot exceed $5,000 per year ($2,500 if married and filing separately). For a married couple, the annual exclusion cannot exceed the earned income of the spouse who has the lesser amount of gross income. For an unmarried taxpayer, the exclusion cannot exceed the taxpayer's earned income.[22]

- The value of the use of a gym or other athletic facilities by employees, their spouses, and their dependent children is excluded from an employee's gross income. The facilities must be on the employer's premises, and substantially all of the use of the facilities must be by employees and their family members.[23]

- When an employee's personal account is credited with frequent flyer miles after taking a trip that the employer paid for, no gross income is recognized.

- A scholarship recipient may exclude from gross income the amount used for tuition and related expenses (fees, books, supplies, and equipment required for courses), provided the conditions of the grant do not require that the funds be used for other purposes.[24]

EXAMPLE 10

Kelly receives a scholarship of $9,500 from State University to be used to pursue a bachelor's degree. She spends $4,000 on tuition, $3,000 on books and supplies, and $2,500 for room and board. Kelly may exclude $7,000 ($4,000 + $3,000) from gross income. The $2,500 spent for room and board is included in Kelly's gross income.

---

[22]§ 129. The exclusion applies to the same types of expenses that, if paid by the employee (and not reimbursed by the employer), would be eligible for the credit for child and dependent care expenses; see text Section 10-5c.

[23]§ 132(j)(4).
[24]§ 117(b).

- Qualified employer-provided educational assistance (tuition, fees, books, and supplies) at the undergraduate and graduate levels is excludible from gross income. The exclusion does not cover meals, lodging, transportation costs, and educational payments for courses involving sports, games, or hobbies. The exclusion is subject to an annual statutory ceiling of $5,250 per employee.[25]

- The employee can exclude from gross income up to $13,810 of expenses incurred to adopt a child, where the adoption expenses are paid or reimbursed by the employer under a qualified adoption assistance program.[26] For 2018, the exclusion is phased out as adjusted gross income increases from $207,140 to $247,140.

11-2h Cafeteria Plans

Generally, if an employee is offered a choice between cash and some other form of compensation, the employee is deemed to have received the cash, even when the noncash option is elected. Thus, the employee recognizes gross income regardless of the option chosen.

An exception to this constructive receipt treatment is provided under the cafeteria plan rules. Under such a plan, the employee can choose between cash and nontaxable benefits (e.g., group term life insurance, health and accident protection, child care). If the employee chooses the otherwise nontaxable benefits, the cafeteria plan rules allow the benefits to be excluded from the employee's gross income.[27]

Cafeteria plans provide flexibility in tailoring the employee pay package to fit individual needs. Some employees (usually the younger group) prefer cash, while others (usually the older group) will opt for the fringe benefit program. However, long-term care insurance cannot be part of a cafeteria plan. Thus, an employer that wants to provide long-term care benefits must provide such benefits separately from the cafeteria plan.[28]

EXAMPLE 11

Hawk Corporation offers its employees (on a nondiscriminatory basis) a choice of any one or all of the following benefits.

Benefit	Cost
Group term life insurance	$ 200
Hospitalization insurance for family members	2,400
Child care payments	1,800
	$4,400

If a benefit is not selected, the employee receives cash equal to the cost of the benefit. Kay, a Hawk employee, has a spouse who works for another employer that provides hospitalization insurance but no child care payments. Kay elects to receive the group term life insurance, the child care payments, and $2,400 of cash. Only the $2,400 is included in Kay's gross income.

11-2i Flexible Spending Plans

Flexible spending plans operate much like cafeteria plans. Under these plans, the employee accepts lower cash compensation (as much as $2,650) in return for the employer's agreement to pay certain costs without the employee recognizing gross income. For example, assume that the employer's health insurance policy does not cover dental expenses. The employee could estimate his or her dental expenses for the upcoming year and agree to a salary reduction equal to the estimated dental expenses. The employer then pays or reimburses the employee for the actual dental

---

[25]§ 127.

[26]§ 137. A credit relating to the expenditures of the parents also is available under § 23, as discussed in text Section 10-5a.

[27]§ 125.

[28]§ 125(f).

expenses incurred, up to the amount of the salary reduction. If the employee's actual dental expenses are less than the reduction in cash compensation, the employee cannot recover the difference. Hence, these plans often are referred to as *use or lose* plans. To avoid forfeiture of unpaid amounts, the employee can take a payment up through March 15 of the following year. As is the case for cafeteria plans, flexible spending plans cannot be used to pay long-term care insurance premiums.

Concept Summary 11.1 reviews the exclusions discussed to this point in the chapter.

Concept Summary 11.1

Employee Fringe Benefits

Type of Benefit	Exclusion
Accident, health, and long-term care insurance and medical reimbursement (§§ 105 and 106)	Insurance premiums paid by the employer and benefits collected by the employee
High-deductible health insurance and contributions to employee's Health Savings Account (§§ 106 and 223)	Employer premiums on high-deductible medical insurance plus contributions to Health Savings Account (statutory limits, indexed for inflation)
Meals and lodging furnished for the convenience of the employer (§ 119)	Value of meals and lodging on the employer's premises
Group term life insurance (§ 79)	Premiums on up to $50,000 of protection
Qualified tuition reduction [§ 117(d)]	Value of tuition waiver
Child care provided by the employer or reimbursement for employee's cost (§ 129)	Services provided or reimbursement of expenses up to $5,000 a year
Athletic facilities on the employer's premises (§ 132)	Value of services
Educational assistance for tuition, fees, books, and supplies (§ 127)	Limited to $5,250 annually
Adoption assistance (§ 137)	Expenses up to $13,810 annually, subject to AGI phaseout
Flexible spending plans (§ 125)	Limited to $2,650 annually

11-2j General Classes of Excluded Benefits

An employer can confer numerous forms and types of economic benefits to its employees. Under the all-inclusive concept of income, the benefits are taxable unless one of the provisions previously discussed specifically excludes the item from gross income. The amount of the resulting gross income is the fair market value of the benefit. This reasoning can lead to results that are unsatisfactory, as illustrated in the following example.

EXAMPLE 12

Ryan is employed in New York as a ticket clerk for Trans National Airlines. He has a sick mother in Miami, Florida, but Ryan has no money for plane tickets. Trans National offers daily flights from New York to Miami that often leave with empty seats. The cost of a round-trip ticket is $400. If Trans National allows Ryan to fly without charge to Miami, under the general gross income rules, Ryan recognizes income equal to the value of a ticket.

Because Congress believed that taxing fringe benefits often yielded harsh results, it established seven broad classes of nontaxable employee benefits. The value of these employer-provided benefits is excluded from the employee's gross income under certain circumstances.[29]

- No-additional-cost services.
- Qualified employee discounts.

---

[29]See, generally, § 132.

- Working condition fringes.
- *De minimis* fringes.
- Qualified transportation fringes.
- Qualified moving expense reimbursements.
- Qualified retirement planning services.

The circumstances that result in the exclusion of these benefits from gross income are discussed next.

No-Additional-Cost Services

The circumstances of Example 12 illustrate the rationale for the <mark>no-additional-cost service</mark> fringe benefit. The value of the services received is excluded from an employee's gross income if all of the following conditions are satisfied.

- The employee receives services, as opposed to property.
- The employer does not incur substantial additional costs, including forgone revenue, in providing the services to the employee.
- The services are offered to customers in the ordinary course of the business in which the employee works.[30]

EXAMPLE 13

In Example 12, although the airplane may burn slightly more fuel because Ryan is on board and Ryan may receive the same meal or snacks as paying customers, the additional costs to the airline would not be substantial. Thus, the trip could qualify as a no-additional-cost service and the value of the flight would be excluded from Ryan's gross income.

On the other hand, assume that Ryan is given a reserved seat on a flight that is frequently full. The employer would be forgoing revenue to allow Ryan to fly. This forgone revenue would be a substantial additional cost, and the benefit would be included in Ryan's gross income.

In-depth coverage can be found on this book's companion website: www.cengage.com

4 DIGGING DEEPER

The no-additional-cost exclusion extends to the employee's spouse and dependent children and to retired and disabled former employees.[31] However, the exclusion is not extended to highly compensated employees unless the benefit is available on a nondiscriminatory basis to all employees.

Qualified Employee Discounts

When the employer sells goods or services (other than no-additional-cost benefits just discussed) to the employee for a price that is less than the price charged to regular customers, the employee recognizes gross income equal to the discount. However, a <mark>qualified employee discount</mark> can be excluded from the gross income of the employee under the following conditions and limitations.

- The exclusion is not available for discounted sales of real property (e.g., a house) or for personal property of the type commonly held for investment (e.g., common stock).
- The property or services must be from the same line of business in which the employee works.
- In the case of *property*, the exclusion is limited to the *gross profit component* of the price to customers.
- In the case of *services*, the exclusion is limited to 20 percent of the customer price.

---

[30]Reg. § 1.132–2.

[31]Reg. § 1.132–1(b).

Silver Corporation, which operates a department store, sells a television to its employee Kylie for $300. The regular customer price is $500, and the gross profit rate is 25%. Silver also sells Kylie a service contract for $120. The regular customer price for the contract is $150.

Customer price for property	$ 500	
Less: Gross profit (25%)	(125)	
Employee price	(300)	
Excess discount		$75
Customer price for service contract	$ 150	
Less: 20% maximum exclusion	(30)	
Employee price	(120)	
Excess discount		0
Total gross income recognized by Kylie		$75

The exclusion applies to employees, an employee's spouse and dependent children, an employee's surviving spouse, and retired and disabled former employees.

Working Condition Fringes

Generally, an employee may exclude from gross income the cost of property or services provided by the employer if the employee could deduct the cost of those items if he or she had actually paid for them. These benefits are called ==working condition fringes==.

Mitch is a CPA employed by an accounting firm. The employer pays Mitch's annual dues to professional organizations. Mitch is not required to include the payment of the dues in gross income; if he had paid the dues, he would deduct the amount as an employee business expense (as discussed later in this chapter).

In many cases, this exclusion merely avoids reporting income and an offsetting deduction. Unlike the other fringe benefits discussed previously, working condition fringes can be made available on a discriminatory basis and still qualify for the exclusion.

De Minimis Fringes

As the term suggests, ==*de minimis* fringe benefits== are so small in amount that accounting for them is impractical. Examples of *de minimis* fringes include the following.

- Occasional personal use of a company copying machine, occasional company cocktail parties or picnics for employees, occasional supper money or taxi fare for employees because of overtime work, and certain holiday gifts of property with a low fair market value are excluded.

- The value of meals consumed in a subsidized eating facility (e.g., an employees' cafeteria) operated by the employer is excluded if the facility is located on or near the employer's business premises, if the facility's revenue equals or exceeds direct operating costs, and if nondiscrimination requirements are met.

When taxpayers venture beyond established norms, there is obviously room for disagreement as to what is *de minimis*. According to the IRS, cash or gift cards never are considered *de minimis*.[32]

Generally, the value of personal use of an employer-provided cell phone is excluded if the device is provided primarily for business reasons, such as to enable the employee to be in contact with clients when the employee is away from the office.

---

[32]TAM 200437030 and IRS Publication 15-B, *Employer's Tax Guide to Fringe Benefits*.

Qualified Transportation Fringes

The intent of the exclusion for ==qualified transportation fringes== is to encourage employees to use mass transit for commuting to and from work. Qualified transportation fringes include the following.

1. Transportation in a commuter highway vehicle, like a dedicated bus or van, between the employee's residence and the place of employment.
2. A transit pass.
3. Qualified parking.

Statutory dollar limits are placed on the amount of the exclusion. Categories (1) and (2) above are combined for purposes of applying the limit. For 2018, the inflation adjusted limit for categories (1) and (2) combined, as well as for category (3), is $260 per month ($255 in 2017).

Qualified parking includes the following.

- Parking provided to an employee on or near the employer's business premises.

- Parking provided to an employee on or near a location from which the employee commutes to work via mass transit, in a commuter highway vehicle, or in a carpool.

Qualified transportation fringes may be provided directly by the employer or may be in the form of cash reimbursements.

Gray Corporation's offices are located in the center of a large city. The company pays for parking spaces to be used by the company officers. Emma, a vice president, receives $300 of such benefits each month during 2018. The parking space rental qualifies as a qualified transportation fringe. Of the $300 benefit received each month, $260 is excludible from gross income. The balance of $40 is included in Emma's gross income. The same result would occur if Emma paid for the parking and was reimbursed by her employer.

The TCJA of 2017 prohibits employers from deducting qualified transportation fringe benefits provided to employees [§ 274(a)(4)]. However, if the employer provides the benefit, the employee may exclude the amount from gross income, within the limits stated above.

Qualified Moving Expense Reimbursements

Prior to enactment of the TCJA of 2017, qualified moving expenses reimbursed or paid by the employer were excludible from gross income. A qualified moving expense was defined as an expense that would be deductible under § 217. For 2018 through 2025, the moving expense exclusion only applies to members of the Armed Forces on active duty.

Qualified Retirement Planning Services

Qualified retirement planning services include any retirement planning advice or information that an employer who maintains a qualified retirement plan provides to an employee or the employee's spouse. This exclusion is intended to motivate more employers to provide retirement planning services to their employees.

Nondiscrimination Provisions

For no-additional-cost services, qualified employee discounts, and qualified retirement planning services that are discriminatory in favor of *highly compensated employees*, exclusion treatment is denied. However, non-highly compensated employees can exclude the value of these benefits from gross income.[33]

---

[33]§§ 132(j)(1) and 132(m)(2).

EXAMPLE 17

Dove Company's officers are allowed to purchase goods from the company at a 25% discount. All other employees are allowed only a 15% discount. The company's gross profit margin on these goods is 30%. Because the officers receive more favorable discounts, the plan is discriminatory in favor of the officers. With regard to all other employees, the discount is "qualified" because it is available to all employees (other than the officers who receive a more favorable discount) and the discount is less than the company's gross profit.

Peggy, an officer in the company, purchased goods from the company for $750 when the price charged to customers was $1,000. Peggy reports $250 in gross income because the plan is discriminatory.

Mason, an employee of the company who is not an officer, purchased goods for $850 when the customer price was $1,000. Mason is not required to recognize gross income because he received a qualified employee discount.

De minimis fringe benefits (except for subsidized eating facilities), the working condition fringe benefits, and the qualified transportation fringe can be provided on a discriminatory basis.

A review of employee fringe benefits is set forth in Concept Summary 11.2.

DIGGING DEEPER 5   **In-depth coverage can be found on this book's companion website: www.cengage.com**

Concept Summary 11.2

General Classes of Fringe Benefits

Benefit	Description and Examples	Coverage Allowed	Effect of Discrimination
1. No-additional-cost services	The employee takes advantage of the employer's excess capacity (e.g., free passes for airline employees).	Current, retired, and disabled employees; their spouses and dependent children; spouses of deceased employees. Partners are treated as employees.	No exclusion for highly compensated employees.
2. Qualified discounts on goods	The employee is allowed a discount no greater than the gross profit margin on goods sold to customers.	Same as (1).	Same as (1).
3. Qualified discounts on services	The employee is allowed a discount (maximum of 20%) on services the employer offers to customers.	Same as (1).	Same as (1).
4. Working condition fringes	Expenses paid by the employer that would be deductible if paid by the employee (e.g., a mechanic's tools). Includes auto salesperson's use of a car held for sale.	Current employees, partners, directors, and independent contractors.	No effect.
5. *De minimis* items	Expenses so immaterial that accounting for them is not warranted (e.g., occasional supper money, personal use of the copy machine).	Any recipient of a fringe benefit.	No effect.
6. Qualified transportation fringes	Transportation benefits provided by the employer to employees, including a transit pass and qualified parking.	Current employees.	No effect.
7. Qualified moving expense reimbursements	Qualified moving expenses that are paid or reimbursed by the employer.	From 2018–2025, members of the Armed Forces on active duty only.	No effect.
8. Qualified retirement planning services	Qualified retirement planning services that are provided by the employer.	Current employees and spouses.	Same as (1).

11-2k **Foreign Earned Income**

For individual taxpayers, the United States employs a worldwide tax system. Under a worldwide system, a U.S. citizen generally is subject to U.S. income tax on all income earned, regardless of the income's geographic origin. Thus, under such a system, a U.S. citizen who earns income in another country could experience double taxation: the same income would be taxed in the United States and in the other country.

Out of a sense of fairness, and so as not to discourage U.S. citizens from working abroad, Congress has provided alternative forms of relief from taxes on foreign earned income. The taxpayer can elect *either* (1) to include the foreign income in his or her taxable income and then claim a credit for foreign taxes paid or (2) to exclude the foreign earnings from his or her U.S. gross income (the **foreign earned income exclusion**).[34] The foreign tax credit option is discussed in text Section 17-1i, but most taxpayers choose the exclusion.

Foreign earned income consists of the earnings from the individual's personal services rendered in a foreign country (other than as an employee of the U.S. government). Such an employee often is referred to as an "expatriate" or "expat." To qualify for the exclusion, the taxpayer must be either of the following.

- A bona fide resident of the foreign country (or countries).
- Present in a foreign country (or countries) for at least 330 days during any 12 consecutive months.

The following rules apply in calculating the exclusion and tax owed.

- The exclusion must be computed on a daily basis when the exclusion period straddles two years.
- The tax on the income in excess of the excluded amount is calculated at the marginal rate that would apply without the exclusion (i.e., as though the excluded income were included in taxable income).

EXAMPLE 18

Sandra's trip to and from a foreign country in connection with her work encompassed the following dates.

Arrived in Foreign Country	Returned to the United States
March 10, 2017	February 15, 2018

During the 12 consecutive months ending on March 10, 2018, Sandra was present in the foreign country for at least 330 days (365 days less 13 days in February and 10 days in March 2018). Therefore, all income earned in the foreign country through March 10, 2018, is eligible for the exclusion.

The exclusion is limited to an indexed amount of $103,900 for 2018 ($102,100 in 2017). For married persons, both of whom have foreign earned income, the exclusion is computed separately for each person. If all of the days in the tax year are not qualifying days (i.e., days present in the other country), the taxpayer must compute the maximum exclusion on a daily basis ($103,900 divided by the number of days in the entire year and multiplied by the number of qualifying days).

Calculating the Exclusion and Tax

EXAMPLE 19

Keith qualifies for the foreign earned income exclusion. He was present in France for all of 2018. Keith's salary for 2018 is $120,000. Because all of the days in 2018 are qualifying days, Keith can exclude $103,900 of his $120,000 salary.

Assume instead that only 342 days were qualifying days. Keith's exclusion is computed as follows.

$$\$103{,}900 \text{ maximum exclusion} \times \frac{342 \text{ days outside the U.S.}}{365 \text{ days in the year}} = \$97{,}353 \text{ exclusion allowed}$$

---

[34]§ 911(a).

LO.3

Apply the rules for computing deductible expenses of work, including transportation, travel, moving, education, and entertainment expenses.

11-3 EXPENSES RELATING TO TIME AT WORK

In general, as discussed in Chapter 5, business expenses that are ordinary and necessary are deductible in the calculation of taxable income. However, this general rule does not mean that all work-related expenses will be deductible by all taxpayers without limit.

First, an individual's classification as an employee or an independent contractor affects how business expenses are deducted in the calculation of taxable income. Unreimbursed business expenses incurred by an employee are categorized as miscellaneous itemized deductions. Such expenses are deductible only to the extent they exceed a 2%-of-AGI floor. *However*, from 2018 to 2025, the TCJA of 2017 suspends the deduction for miscellaneous itemized deductions. As a result, the only employee business expenses that are currently deductible are those that are reimbursed by an employer (and these expenses, once reimbursed, have no effect on an employee's taxable income).

In contrast, business expenses incurred by an independent contractor are deductible *for* AGI. Thus, such expenses are not limited by an AGI floor. While the TCJA of 2017 did change the tax treatment of some types of business expenses, the TCJA did not suspend the deduction for expenses incurred by an independent contractor.

Second, irrespective of whether business expenses are incurred by an employee or independent contractor, certain business expenses are limited by tax law provisions beyond the "ordinary and necessary" requirement.

The calculation of the deduction for a variety of business expenses is discussed next.

11-3a Transportation Expenses

Deductible, unreimbursed employment-related transportation expenses include only the cost of transporting the taxpayer from one place to another in the course of employment when the taxpayer is not away from home in travel status. Such costs include taxi fares, automobile expenses, tolls, and parking.

Commuting Expenses

Commuting between home and one's place of employment is a personal, nondeductible expense. The fact that one person drives 30 miles to work and another person walks six blocks is of no significance.[35] However, the expenses of getting from one job to another job or from one workstation to another workstation are deductible transportation expenses rather than nondeductible commuting expenses.

DIGGING DEEPER 6   **In-depth coverage can be found on this book's companion website: www.cengage.com**

---

[35]*U.S. v. Tauferner*, 69–1 USTC ¶9241, 23 AFTR 2d 69–1025, 407 F.2d 243 (CA–10, 1969).

In the current year, Cynthia holds two jobs, a full-time job with Blue Corporation and a part-time job with Wren Corporation. Cynthia customarily leaves home at 7:30 A.M. and drives 30 miles to the Blue plant, where she works until 5:00 P.M. After dinner at a nearby café, Cynthia drives 20 miles to Wren and works from 7:00 to 11:00 P.M. Cynthia is eligible to deduct commuting expenses based on 20 miles (the distance between jobs).

Instead, assume that Cynthia has an office in the home that qualifies as a principal place of business. In this circumstance, the transportation between home and various work locations is not a deductible commuting expense.

Computation of Automobile Expenses

A taxpayer has two choices in computing deductible automobile expenses. The first alternative is to use the actual operating cost, which includes depreciation (see text Section 5-7), fuel, oil, repairs, licenses, and insurance costs. Records must be kept that document the automobile's use for personal and business purposes. Only the percentage allocable to business transportation and travel is allowed as a deduction.

The second alternative is the **automatic mileage method**, also called the standard mileage method. For 2018, the deduction is based on 54.5 cents per mile for business miles (53.5 cents for 2017).[36] Parking fees and tolls are allowed in addition to expenses computed using the automatic mileage method.

Generally, a taxpayer may elect either method for any particular year. However, the following restrictions apply to the standard mileage method:

- The vehicle is owned or leased by the taxpayer.
- The vehicle is not used for hire (e.g., taxicab).
- If five or more vehicles are in use (for business purposes) at the *same* time (not alternately), a taxpayer may not use the automatic mileage method.
- A taxpayer may not switch to the automatic mileage method if MACRS depreciation or the election to expense under § 179 has been used.

In-depth coverage can be found on this book's companion website: www.cengage.com	**7** DIGGING DEEPER

11-3b Travel Expenses

A deduction is allowed for **travel expenses** related to a taxpayer's work. Travel expenses are more broadly defined in the Code than are transportation expenses. Travel expenses include transportation expenses and meals and lodging while away from home in the pursuit of a trade or business. Meals cannot be lavish or extravagant. Deductible travel expenses also include reasonable laundry and incidental expenses. However, a deduction for meals and lodging is available only if the taxpayer is away from his or her tax home, as discussed next.

In-depth coverage can be found on this book's companion website: www.cengage.com	**8** DIGGING DEEPER

Away-from-Home Requirement

The crucial test for the deductibility of travel expenses is whether the taxpayer is away from home overnight. "Overnight" need not be a 24-hour period, but it must be a period substantially longer than an ordinary day's work and must require rest, sleep, or a relief-from-work period.[37] Thus, a one-day business trip is not considered travel for tax purposes, and meals and lodging for such a trip are not deductible.

---

[36]Notice 2018–3, 2018–2 I.R.B. 285 and Rev.Proc. 2010–51, 2010–51 I.R.B. 883.

[37]*U.S. v. Correll*, 68–1 USTC ¶9101, 20 AFTR 2d 5845, 88 S.Ct. 445 (USSC, 1967); Rev.Rul. 75–168, 1975–1 C.B. 58.

Temporary Assignments

The taxpayer must be away from home for a temporary period. If the taxpayer is reassigned to a new location for an indefinite period of time, that new location becomes his or her tax home. Temporary indicates that the assignment's termination is expected within a reasonably short period of time. The position of the IRS is that the tax home is the business location of the taxpayer. Thus, travel expenses are not deductible if a taxpayer is reassigned for an indefinite period and does not move his or her place of residence to the new location.

Temporary Becomes Permanent

EXAMPLE 22

Malcolm maintains a consulting practice in Los Angeles. Due to new client responsibilities, Malcolm decided to open a new office in San Diego. Malcolm worked out of the new office for three months to train a new manager and to assist in setting up the new office. He tried commuting from his home in Los Angeles for a week and decided that he could not continue driving several hours a day. He rented an apartment in San Diego, where he lived during the week. He spent weekends with his wife and children at their home in Los Angeles.

Malcolm's rent, meals, laundry, incidentals, and automobile expenses in San Diego are deductible. To the extent that Malcolm's transportation expense related to his weekend trips home exceeds what his cost of meals and lodging would have been, the excess is personal and nondeductible.

EXAMPLE 23

Assume that in the previous example, Malcom decided that he was the best person to manage the new office in San Diego and so decided to move there permanently. His wife and children continued to live in Los Angeles until the end of the school year. Malcolm is no longer "away from home" because the assignment is not temporary. His travel expenses are not deductible.

To curtail controversy in this area, the Code specifies that a taxpayer "shall not be treated as temporarily away from home during any period of employment if such period exceeds 1 year."[38]

DIGGING DEEPER 9   **In-depth coverage can be found on this book's companion website: www.cengage.com**

Determining the Tax Home

Under ordinary circumstances, determining the location of a taxpayer's tax home does not present a problem. The tax home is the area in which the taxpayer works; when the taxpayer has more than one place of employment, the tax home is determined by considering the time spent, the level of activity involved, and the income earned at each job.

It is possible for a taxpayer never to be away from his or her tax home. In other words, the tax home follows the taxpayer. Under such circumstances, all meals and lodging remain personal and are not deductible.

EXAMPLE 24

Jim is single and works full-time as a long-haul truck driver. He lists his mother's home as his address and stays there during holidays. However, he contributes nothing toward its maintenance. Because Jim has no regular place of duty or place where he regularly lives, his tax home is where he works (i.e., on the road). As an itinerant (transient), he is never away from home, and all of his meals and lodging while on the road are personal and not deductible.

The result reached in Example 24 is justified on the grounds that there is no duplication of living expenses in the case of itinerant taxpayers.[39]

---

[38] § 162(a).

[39] Rev.Rul. 73–539, 1973–2 C.B. 37 and *James O. Henderson*, 70 TCM 1407, T.C.Memo. 1995–559, *aff'd* by 98–1 USTC ¶50,375, 81 AFTR 2d 98–1748, 143 F.3d 497 (CA–9, 1998).

Combined Business and Pleasure Travel

Deductible travel expenses need not be incurred in the performance of specific work functions. Travel expenses incurred to attend a professional convention are deductible if attendance is connected with the taxpayer's trade or business. For example, a lawyer could deduct travel expenses incurred to attend a meeting of the American Bar Association.

To limit the possibility of a taxpayer claiming a tax deduction for what is essentially a personal vacation, several provisions have been enacted to restrict deductions associated with combined business and pleasure trips. If the business/pleasure trip is from one point in the United States to another point in the United States (*domestic travel*), the transportation expenses are deductible only if the trip is primarily for business.[40] Meals, lodging, and other expenses are allocated between business and personal days. If the trip is primarily for pleasure, no transportation expenses qualify as a deduction.

In-depth coverage can be found on this book's companion website: www.cengage.com **10** DIGGING DEEPER

EXAMPLE 25

In the current year, Hana travels from Seattle to New York primarily for business. She spends five days conducting business and three days sightseeing and attending shows. Her plane and taxi fare amounts to $1,160. Her meals amount to $200 per day, and lodging and incidental expenses are $350 per day.

Hana can deduct the transportation expenses of $1,160 because the trip is primarily for business (five days of business versus three days of sightseeing). Deductible meals are limited to five days and are subject to the 50% cutback (discussed later in the chapter) for a total of $500 [5 days × ($200 × 50%)], and lodging and incidental expenses are limited to $1,750 (5 days × $350).

When the trip is outside the United States (*foreign travel*), different rules apply.[41] Transportation expenses must be allocated between business and personal days *unless* (1) the taxpayer is away from home for seven days or less or (2) less than 25 percent of the time was for personal purposes. No allocation is required if the taxpayer has no substantial control over arrangements for the trip or the desire for a vacation is not a major factor in taking the trip. If the trip is primarily for pleasure, no transportation charges are deductible. Days devoted to travel are considered business days. Weekends, legal holidays, and intervening days are considered business days, provided that both the preceding and succeeding days were business days.

In-depth coverage can be found on this book's companion website: www.cengage.com **11** DIGGING DEEPER

EXAMPLE 26

In the current year, Robert takes a trip from New York to Japan primarily for business purposes. He is away from home from June 10 through June 19. He spends three days vacationing and seven days (including two travel days) conducting business. His airfare is $4,000, his meals amount to $200 per day, and lodging and incidental expenses are $300 per day.

Because Robert is away from home for more than seven days and more than 25% of his time is devoted to personal travel, only 70% (7 days business/10 days total) of the transportation is deductible. His potential deductions are computed as follows.

continued

---

[40]Reg. § 1.162–2(b)(1).

[41]§ 274(c) and Reg. § 1.274–4. For purposes of the seven-days-or-less exception, the departure travel day is not counted.

Transportation (70% × $4,000)		$2,800
Lodging ($300 × 7)		2,100
Meals ($200 × 7)	$1,400	
Less: 50% cutback (discussed later in this chapter)	(700)	700
Total deductions		$5,600

If Robert was gone the same period of time but spent only two (rather than three) days vacationing, no allocation of transportation would be required. Because the pleasure portion of the trip was less than 25% of the total, all of the airfare would qualify for the travel deduction.

The foreign travel rules do not operate to bar a deduction to an employer if the expense is *compensatory* in nature. For example, the value of a trip to Rome won by a top salesperson is included in the gross income of the employee and is fully deductible by the employer.

11-3c Moving Expenses

The TCJA of 2017 suspended the deduction for moving expenses from 2018 through 2025. However, during this period, the moving expense deduction is retained for members of the Armed Forces (or their spouse or dependents) on active duty who move because of a military order that relates to a permanent change of station.[42] The rules providing for exclusions of amounts attributable to in-kind moving and storage expenses (and reimbursements or allowances for these expenses) also remain in place for these individuals.

TAX PLANNING STRATEGIES Transportation and Travel Expenses

FRAMEWORK FOCUS: DEDUCTIONS

Strategy: Maximize Deductible Amounts.

Detailed records of all transportation and travel expenses should be kept. Because the automatic (standard) mileage allowance often is modest in amount, a new, expensive automobile used primarily for business may generate a larger expense based on actual cost. The election to expense some or all of the cost of the automobile under the immediate expensing provisions or § 179, MACRS depreciation, insurance, repairs and maintenance, automobile club dues, and other related costs may result in automobile expenses greater than the automatic mileage allowance.

Additionally, if a taxpayer wants to sightsee or vacation on a business trip, it may be beneficial to schedule business on both a Friday and a Monday to turn the weekend into business days for allocation purposes. It is especially crucial to schedule appropriate business days when overseas travel is involved.

11-3d Education Expenses

Education expenses can be deducted as ordinary and necessary business expenses, provided the expenses are incurred to either:

- Meet specific employer requirements or legal requirements to keep his or her job; or
- Maintain or improve existing skills required in the present job.

Education expenses are not deductible if the education is for either of the following purposes (except as discussed in text Section 11-3e).

- To meet the minimum educational standards for qualification in the taxpayer's existing job; or
- To qualify the taxpayer for a new trade or business.[43]

---

[42]§ 217(k).

[43]Reg. §§ 1.162–5(b)(2) and (3).

Thus, fees incurred for professional exams (the bar exam, for example) and fees for review courses (such as a CPA review course) generally are not deductible.[44] If the education incidentally results in a promotion or raise, the deduction is allowed as long as the education maintained and improved existing skills and did not qualify the person for a new trade or business.

A change in duties does not by itself make the education expense nondeductible (i.e., if the worker's new duties involve the same general work). For example, a practicing dentist's education expenses incurred to become an orthodontist are deductible.[45]

Employer or Legal Requirements to Keep a Job

Taxpayers can deduct education expenses if additional courses are required by the employer or are imposed by law. For example, some states require a minimum of a bachelor's degree plus additional courses to retain a teaching job, while others require teachers to make satisfactory progress toward a master's degree to keep their positions. If the required education is the minimum degree required for the job, no deduction is allowed.

Expenses incurred for education required by law for various professions (e.g., medicine, law, and accounting) also qualify for a deduction.

In-depth coverage can be found on this book's companion website: www.cengage.com	**12** DIGGING DEEPER

Maintaining or Improving Existing Skills

The "maintaining or improving existing skills" requirement in the Code has been difficult for both taxpayers and the courts to interpret. For example, a business consultant may be permitted to deduct the costs of obtaining an advanced degree on the grounds the advanced management education is undertaken to maintain and improve existing management skills. The consultant can also deduct the costs of specialized, nondegree management courses that are taken to maintain or improve existing skills. However, expenses incurred by an accountant to obtain a law degree are not deductible, because the education constitutes training for a new trade or business.[46]

TAX PLANNING STRATEGIES Education Expenses

FRAMEWORK FOCUS: DEDUCTIONS

Strategy: Maximize Deductible Amounts.

Education expenses are treated as nondeductible personal items unless the individual is employed or is engaged in a trade or business. A temporary leave of absence for further education is one way to ensure that the taxpayer still is treated as being engaged in a trade or business. An individual was permitted to deduct education expenses even though he resigned from his job, returned to school full-time for two years, and accepted another job in the same field upon graduation. The court held that the student had merely suspended active participation in his field.[47]

If the time out of the field is too long, education expense deductions are disallowed. For example, a teacher who left the field for four years to raise her child and curtailed her employment searches and writing activities was denied a deduction for education expenses. She was no longer actively engaged in the trade or business of being an educator.[48]

---

[44]Reg. § 1.212–1(f) and Rev.Rul. 69–292, 1969–1 C.B. 84.

[45]Rev.Rul. 74–78, 1974–1 C.B. 44.

[46]Reg. § 1.162–5(b)(3)(ii), Example (1).

[47]*Stephen G. Sherman*, 36 TCM 1191, T.C.Memo. 1977–301.

[48]*Brian C. Mulherin*, 42 TCM 834, T.C.Memo. 1981–454; *George A. Baist*, 56 TCM 778, T.C.Memo. 1988–554.

Allowable Expenses

Education expenses include books and supplies, tuition, transportation (e.g., from the office to night school), and travel (e.g., meals and lodging while away from home at an executive education training program).

EXAMPLE 27

Sherry, who holds a bachelor of education degree, is a secondary education teacher in the Charlotte school system. The school board recently raised its education requirement for new teachers from four years of college training to five. A grandfather clause allows teachers with only four years of college to continue to qualify if they show satisfactory progress toward a graduate degree.

Sherry enrolls at the University of North Carolina–Charlotte and completes two graduate courses. Her unreimbursed expenses for this purpose are as follows.

Books and tuition	$3,600
Lodging while in travel status (June–August)	2,150
Meals while in travel status	1,100
Laundry while in travel status	220
Transportation	900

Sherry's education expense deduction is computed as follows.

Books and tuition	$3,600
Lodging	2,150
Meals less 50% cutback (discussed later in this chapter)	550
Laundry	220
Transportation	900
Potential deduction	$7,420

11-3e Deduction for Qualified Tuition and Related Expenses

One of the major shortcomings of the education deduction, discussed previously, is that it is unavailable for taxpayers obtaining a basic skill (i.e., to meet the minimum standards required for the taxpayer's current job). This shortcoming has been partly resolved with the **deduction for qualified tuition and related expenses**.

A deduction *for* AGI is allowed for qualified tuition and related expenses involving higher education (i.e., postsecondary). The deduction is the lesser of the qualifying amount spent or the maximum amount allowed by § 222. The amount of the deduction depends on the taxpayer's modified AGI (MAGI) and filing status (as shown in Exhibit 11.2).[49]

EXHIBIT 11.2	Limitations for Qualified Tuition Deduction	
Filing Status	**Modified AGI**	**Maximum Deduction Allowed**
Single	$65,000 or less	$4,000
	More than $65,000 and less than or equal to $80,000	$2,000
	More than $80,000	None
Married	$130,000 or less	$4,000
	More than $130,000 and less than or equal to $160,000	$2,000
	More than $160,000	None

---

[49]MAGI is defined in § 222(b)(2)(C). Examples of modifications made to AGI include adding back to regular AGI the foreign earned income exclusion and using the AGI amount after the deduction for student loan interest. See IRS Publication 970 (*Tax Benefits for Education*).

The § 222 limitations are not indexed for inflation.[50] Various additional aspects of the targeted higher education tuition deduction are summarized as follows.

- *Qualified tuition and related expenses* include whatever is required for enrollment at the institution. Usually, student activity fees, books, and room and board are not included.[51]
- The expense need not be employment-related, although it can be.
- The deduction is available for a taxpayer's spouse or anyone who can be claimed as a dependent and is an eligible student.
- The deduction is not available for married persons who file separate returns.
- To avoid a "double benefit," the deduction must be coordinated with other education provisions (e.g., American Opportunity and lifetime learning credits, as discussed in text Section 10-5d).
- No deduction is allowed for a taxpayer who qualifies as another's dependent.[52]

Tina is single and a full-time employee of a CPA firm. During the current year, she attends law school at night and incurs the following expenses: $4,200 for tuition and $340 for books and supplies. Presuming that she satisfies the MAGI limitation (see Exhibit 11.2), she can claim $4,000 as a deduction *for* AGI.

Could Tina deduct the $540 not allowed under § 222 ($200 tuition in excess of $4,000 + $340 for books and supplies) as an education expense? She could not, because obtaining a law degree leads to a new trade or business.

EXAMPLE 28

The deduction for qualified tuition and related expenses is claimed by completing Form 8917 (Tuition and Fees Deduction). The form should be attached to Form 1040 (or Form 1040-A). In addition, the taxpayer must have received a Form 1098–T (Tuition Statement) from a higher education institution to claim the deduction.

Another deduction item relating to education is the limited deduction of interest on student loans; see text Section 10-4c.[53]

11-3f Entertainment Expenses

Many businesses incur entertainment and meal expenses. While such expenses can help build business activity, a personal element also is involved in these activities. Prior to 2018, 50 percent of entertainment and meal expenses were allowed as a deduction provided the expenses were *directly related to* or *associated with* the active conduct of the taxpayer's business. Entertainment expenses have long been subject to scrutiny, by both Congress and the IRS. The complexity of the various rules, the compliance costs, and the revenue to be generated from disallowing such expenses led Congress to make a significant change in the law via the TCJA of 2017.

Beginning in 2018, no deduction is allowed with respect to:

1. An activity generally considered to be entertainment, amusement, or recreation;
2. Membership dues with respect to any club organized for business, pleasure, recreation, or other social purposes; or
3. A facility or portion thereof used in connection with any of the above items.

Taxpayers still may generally deduct 50 percent of the food and beverage expenses associated with operating their trade or business (e.g., meals consumed by employees during work travel).[54]

[50]Section 222 expired on December 31, 2017, but could be extended by Congress.

[51]Section 222(d) refers to § 25A(f), which addresses the American Opportunity and lifetime learning credits. Student activity fees and prescribed course-related books may be allowed if they are required for enrollment.

[52]§ 222(c).
[53]§ 221.
[54]§ 274.

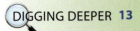

DIGGING DEEPER 13 | **In-depth coverage can be found on this book's companion website: www.cengage.com**

TAX PLANNING STRATEGIES   Meal Expenses

FRAMEWORK FOCUS: DEDUCTIONS

Strategy: Maximize Deductible Amounts.

Proper documentation of meal expenses is essential because of the strict record-keeping requirements that must be met. For example, documentation that consists solely of credit card receipts and canceled checks may be inadequate to substantiate the business purpose and business relationship.[55] Taxpayers should maintain detailed records of amounts, time, place, business purpose, and business relationships. A credit card receipt details the place, date, and amount of the expense. A notation made on the receipt of the names of the person(s) attending, the business relationship, and the topic of discussion should be sufficient.

Exceptions to the 50 Percent Rule

The 50 percent rule has a number of exceptions.[56] One exception covers the situation where the full value of the meals is included in the compensation of the employee (or independent contractor). Expenses directly related to business meetings of employees also are not subject to the 50 percent rule (and are fully deductible). A similar exception applies to employer-paid recreational activities for employees (e.g., the annual holiday party or spring picnic). In addition, businesses that have retreats and/or other off-site training events are generally allowed to deduct 100 percent of the meals provided to participants at those sites.[57]

EXAMPLE 29

Myrtle wins an all-expense-paid trip to Europe for selling the most insurance for her company during the year. Her employer treats this trip as additional compensation to Myrtle. The 50 percent rule does not limit the employer's deduction for the expenses of the trip.

Business Meals

A business meal is deductible only if all of the following are true.[58]

- The meal is business related.
- The expense is reasonable (i.e., not lavish or extravagant).
- The taxpayer (or an employee) is present at the meal.

Business Meals

EXAMPLE 30

Lance Smith has submitted a proposed consulting contract to a local business. He invites the two business owners to dinner to discuss the contract and pays for the meal, during which Lance answers questions about the proposed contract. Lance can deduct 50% of this qualified business meal.

EXAMPLE 31

Assume the same facts as Example 30, except that Lance buys dinner for the two business owners but does not attend the dinner. No deduction is allowed.

---

[55]*Kenneth W. Guenther,* 54 TCM 382, T.C.Memo. 1987–440.
[56]§§ 274(e) and (n).

[57]*Jacobs,* 148 T.C. No. 4 (6/26/17).
[58]§ 274(k).

The cost of a business meal with a business associate or customer is not deductible unless business is discussed before, during, or after the meal. If, however, the taxpayer is in travel status, his or her meal can be deducted, subject to the 50 percent rule.

Lacy travels to San Francisco for a business convention. She pays for dinner with three colleagues and is not reimbursed by her employer. They do not discuss business. She can deduct 50% of the cost of her meal. However, she cannot deduct the cost of her colleagues' meals.

EXAMPLE 32

Business Gifts

Although not subject to the 50 percent limit on meals, business gifts are deductible only to the extent of $25 per donee per year.[59] Gifts costing $4 or less (e.g., pens with the employee's or company's name on them) or promotional materials are not subject to the $25 limit. In addition, incidental costs such as engraving of jewelry and nominal charges for gift-wrapping, mailing, and delivery are not included in the cost of the gift in applying the limitation. Gifts to superiors and employers are not deductible. Records must be maintained to substantiate business gifts.

11-3g **Other Expenses of Work**

In addition to those expenses discussed previously, the Code provides for the deduction of a number of other job-related expenses. The home office deduction and educator expenses are discussed in this section.

Office in the Home

Employees and self-employed individuals are not allowed a deduction for **office in the home expenses** unless a portion of the residence is used *exclusively and on a regular basis* as either:

- The principal place of business for any trade or business of the taxpayer, or
- A place of business used by clients, patients, or customers.

Employees must meet an additional test: the use must be for the convenience of the employer rather than merely being "appropriate and helpful."[60] Remember that from 2018 through 2025, employees are not allowed to deduct expenses related to an office in the home as these expenses are miscellaneous itemized deductions.

The precise meaning of "principal place of business" has been the subject of considerable debate between taxpayers and the IRS.[61] The term *principal place of business* includes a place of business that satisfies both of the following requirements.[62]

- The office is used by the taxpayer to conduct administrative or management activities of a trade or business.
- There is no other fixed location of the trade or business where the taxpayer conducts these activities.

Dr. Sunder is a self-employed anesthesiologist. During the year, he spends 30 to 35 hours per week administering anesthesia and postoperative care to patients in three hospitals, none of which provides him with an office. He also spends two or three hours per day in a room in his home that he uses exclusively as an office. Dr. Sunder does not meet patients there, but he performs a variety of tasks related to his medical practice (e.g., contacting surgeons, bookkeeping, and reading medical journals).

A deduction for this office in the home is allowed because Dr. Sunder conducts administrative or management activities there, and he has no other fixed location where these activities can be carried out.

EXAMPLE 33

---

[59]274(b)(1). Multiple gifts to members of the same customer's family are consolidated (so there will be only one $25 deduction allowed).

[60]§ 280A(c)(1).

[61]See the restrictive interpretation arrived at in *Comm. v. Soliman*, 93–1 USTC ¶50,014, 71 AFTR 2d 93–463, 113 S.Ct. 701 (USSC, 1993).

[62]§ 280A(c)(1).

The exclusive use requirement means that a specific part of the home must be used solely for business purposes. A deduction, if permitted, requires an allocation of total expenses of operating the home between business and personal use based on floor space or number of rooms.

DIGGING DEEPER 14 | **In-depth coverage can be found on this book's companion website: www.cengage.com**

Even if the taxpayer meets the above requirements, the allowable home office expenses cannot exceed the gross income from the business less all other business expenses attributable to the activity. That is, the home office deduction cannot create a loss. Furthermore, the home office expenses that are allowed as itemized deductions anyway (e.g., mortgage interest and real estate taxes) must be deducted first.

While home office expenses of an employee are categorized as miscellaneous itemized deductions, the home office expenses of a self-employed individual are deductible *for* AGI. Any disallowed home office expenses are carried forward and used in future years, subject to the same limitations.

EXAMPLE

34

Patrick is a certified public accountant employed by a regional CPA firm as a tax manager. He operates a separate business in which he refinishes furniture in his home. For this business, he uses two rooms in the basement of his home exclusively and regularly. The floor space of the two rooms is 240 square feet, which constitutes 10% of the total floor space of his 2,400-square-foot residence. Gross income from the business totals $8,000. Expenses of the business (other than home office expenses) are $6,500. Patrick incurs the following home office expenses.

Real property taxes on residence	$ 4,000
Interest expense on residence	7,500
Operating expenses of residence (including homeowners insurance)	2,000
Depreciation on residence (based on 10% business use)	350

Patrick's deductions are determined as follows.

Business income		$ 8,000
Less: Other business expenses		(6,500)
Net income from the business (before the office in the home deduction)		$ 1,500
Less: Allocable taxes ($4,000 × 10%)	$400	
Allocable interest ($7,500 × 10%)	750	(1,150)
Subtotal		$ 350
Less: Allocable operating expenses of the residence ($2,000 × 10%)		(200)
Subtotal		$ 150
Less: Allocable MACRS depreciation ($350, limited to remaining income)		(150)
Remaining home office expenses		$ –0–

Patrick now holds a carryover deduction of $200 (the unused excess MACRS depreciation). Because he is self-employed, the allocable taxes and interest ($1,150), the other deductible office expenses ($200 + $150), and $6,500 of other business expenses are deductible *for* AGI.

Educator Expenses

Many teachers pay for professional development courses or purchase school supplies for classroom use for which they are not reimbursed by their employer. Such expenses could be considered miscellaneous itemized deductions. However, the deduction for those amounts is currently suspended.

An additional provision applies to elementary and secondary school teachers that provides modest relief. Eligible educators must work at least 900 hours during a school year as a teacher, an instructor, a counselor, a principal, or an aide. If they meet these requirements, teachers may deduct the costs they incur for books, supplies, professional development courses, computer equipment and related software and services, other equipment, and supplementary materials they use in the classroom. The annual ceiling on this *for* AGI deduction is $250.[63]

11-3h Classification of Employee Expenses

The classification of employee expenses depends on whether they are reimbursed by the employer under an accountable plan. If such expenses are reimbursed, then neither the reimbursement nor the expense is reported by the employee. In effect, this result is equivalent to reporting the reimbursement as income and treating the expenses as deductions *for* AGI.[64] Alternatively, if the expenses are reimbursed under a nonaccountable plan or are not reimbursed at all, they are classified as deductions *from* AGI and are currently nondeductible miscellaneous itemized deductions.

Accountable Plans

An accountable plan requires the employee to satisfy these two requirements.

- Substantiate the expenses. An employee provides an adequate accounting by submitting a record (e.g., completing an employer-provided travel expense reimbursement form), with receipts and other substantiation, to the employer.[65]
- Return any excess reimbursement or allowance. An "excess reimbursement or allowance" is any amount the employee does not adequately account for as an ordinary and necessary business expense.

The law provides that no deduction is allowed for any travel, entertainment, business gift, or listed property (automobiles and computers) expenditure unless properly substantiated by adequate records. The records should contain the following information:[66]

- The amount of the expense.
- The time and place of travel or entertainment (or date of gift).
- The business purpose of the expense.
- The business relationship of the taxpayer to the person entertained (or receiving the gift).

As a result, the taxpayer must keep records (e.g., in a calendar or by other means) to document these expenses. Documentary evidence such as an itemized receipt is required to support any expenditure for lodging while traveling away from home and for any other expenditure of $75 or more. If a taxpayer fails to keep adequate records, a written or oral statement of the exact details of the expense will be required, along with other corroborating evidence.[67]

In-depth coverage can be found on this book's companion website: www.cengage.com — **15 DIGGING DEEPER**

Nonaccountable Plans

A **nonaccountable plan** is a plan in which an adequate accounting or return of excess amounts, or both, is not required. All expense reimbursements are reported in full as

[63]§ 62(a)(2)(D).
[64]§ 62(a)(2).
[65]Reg. § 1.162–17(b)(4).
[66]§ 274(d).
[67]Reg. § 1.274–5T(c)(3).

wages on the employee's Form W–2. Any allowable expenses, to the extent they are deductible, are deductible in the same manner as unreimbursed expenses.

If an employer offers an accountable plan and requires employees to return excess reimbursements or allowances, but an employee fails to follow the rules of the plan, the expenses and reimbursements are subject to nonaccountable plan treatment.

Unreimbursed Employee Expenses

Unreimbursed employee business expenses (including 50 percent of any meals) are treated as miscellaneous itemized deductions. Such expenses are not deductible from 2018 through 2025. If the employee could have received, but did not seek, reimbursement for whatever reason, none of the employment-related expenses are deductible.

DIGGING DEEPER 16   **In-depth coverage can be found on this book's companion website: www.cengage.com**

LO.5

Understand the opportunities available to build wealth through Individual Retirement Accounts.

11-3i **Contributions to Individual Retirement Accounts**

Traditional and Roth Individual Retirement Accounts, or IRAs, are commonly used to provide individual savings for retirement. They can be simple to create and maintain. The tax rules that govern deductible contributions, taxable distributions, age requirements, and possible penalties for early withdrawals or excess contributions are discussed in the following section.

Traditional IRAs

An individual can contribute to a traditional **Individual Retirement Account (IRA)** assuming that the person (or spouse) has earned income and is under age 70½. These contributions may be deductible, depending upon income level and access to another work-related retirement plan. For 2018, the contribution ceiling is the lesser of $5,500 (or $11,000 for spousal IRAs) or 100 percent of compensation.[68] An individual who attains the age of 50 by the end of the tax year can make an additional "catch-up" IRA contribution of up to $1,000 annually.

If the taxpayer is an active participant in a qualified plan, the traditional IRA deduction limitation is phased out *proportionately* between certain AGI ranges, as shown in Exhibit 11.3.[69] If AGI is above the phaseout range, no IRA deduction is allowed.

AGI is calculated taking into account any passive activity losses and taxable Social Security benefits and ignoring any foreign income exclusion, savings bonds interest exclusion, and the IRA deduction itself. As long as the deduction is not completely phased out, the allowable IRA deduction cannot be less than $200.

EXHIBIT 11.3	**Phaseout of Traditional IRA Deduction of an Active Participant in 2018**	
AGI, Filing Status	**Phaseout Begins***	**Phaseout Ends***
Single and head of household	$ 63,000	$ 73,000
Married, filing joint return	101,000	121,000
Married, filing separate return	–0–	10,000

*These AGI amounts are indexed annually for inflation.

---

[68]§§ 219(b)(1) and (c)(2). The limit may be adjusted annually for inflation in $500 increments.   [69]§ 219(g).

IRA Deduction Calculation

Dan, who is single, reports compensation income of $69,000 in 2018. He is an active participant in his employer's qualified retirement plan. Dan contributes $5,500 to a traditional IRA. The deductible amount is reduced from $5,500 by $3,300 because of the phaseout mechanism (see Exhibit 11.3).

$$\frac{\$350,000 - \$50,000}{\$1,000} \times \$.23 \times 12\,\text{months} = 828$$

Therefore, of the $5,500 contribution, Dan can deduct only $2,200 ($5,500 − $3,300).

EXAMPLE 35

Bonnie, an unmarried individual, is an active participant in her employer's qualified retirement plan in 2018. With an AGI of $72,800, Bonnie's IRA deduction limit would be $110 {$5,500 − [($72,800 − $63,000)/$10,000 × $5,500]}. However, she is allowed a $200 IRA deduction.

EXAMPLE 36

An individual is not considered an active participant in a qualified plan merely because the individual's spouse is an active participant in such a plan for any part of a plan year. Thus, even when filing jointly, the nonparticipating individual may take a full $5,500 deduction regardless of the participation status of his or her spouse, unless the couple has AGI above $189,000. A deduction phaseout begins at AGI of $189,000 and ends at $199,000 (phaseout over the $10,000 range), rather than beginning and ending at the phaseout amounts in Exhibit 11.3.[70]

Nell is covered by a qualified employer retirement plan at work. Her husband, Nick, is not an active participant in a qualified plan. If Nell and Nick's combined AGI is $135,000, Nell cannot make a deductible IRA contribution because she exceeds the income threshold for an active participant. However, because Nick is not an active participant and their combined AGI does not exceed $189,000, he can make a fully deductible contribution of $5,500 to an IRA.

EXAMPLE 37

To the extent an individual is ineligible to make a deductible contribution to an IRA, *nondeductible contributions* can be made to separate accounts. The nondeductible contributions are subject to the same dollar limits as deductible contributions ($5,500 of earned income, $11,000 for a spousal IRA). Income in the account accumulates tax-free until distributed. Where nondeductible contributions are made, only the account earnings are taxed upon distribution, because the account basis equals the contributions made by the taxpayer.

Roth IRAs

A Roth IRA is a *nondeductible* alternative to the traditional deductible IRA. Earnings inside a Roth IRA are not taxable, and all qualified distributions from a Roth IRA are tax-free.[71]

The maximum allowable annual contribution to a Roth IRA for 2018 is the lesser of $5,500 ($11,000 for spousal IRAs) or 100 percent of the individual's compensation for the year. Contributions to a Roth IRA must be made by the due date (excluding extensions) of the taxpayer's tax return. Contributions to a Roth IRA (unlike a traditional IRA) may continue beyond age 70½ so long as the person generates compensation income and is not barred by the AGI limits.

A taxpayer can make tax-free withdrawals from a Roth IRA after an initial five-year holding period if any of the following requirements are satisfied.

---

[70] § 219(g)(7).   [71] § 408A.

- The distribution is made on or after the date on which the participant attains age 59½.
- The distribution is made to a beneficiary (or the participant's estate) on or after the participant's death.
- The participant becomes disabled.
- The distribution is used for qualified first-time homebuyer's expenses (maximum $10,000).

Edith establishes a Roth IRA at age 42 and contributes $5,000 per year for 20 years. The account is now worth $149,400, consisting of $100,000 of nondeductible contributions and $49,400 in accumulated earnings that have not been taxed. Edith may withdraw the $149,400 tax-free from the Roth IRA because she is over age 59½ and has met the five-year holding period requirement.

If the taxpayer receives a distribution from a Roth IRA and does not satisfy the aforementioned requirements, some of the distribution may constitute gross income. If the distribution represents a return of capital, it is not taxable. Conversely, if the distribution represents a payout of earnings, it is taxable. Under the ordering rules for Roth IRAs, distributions are treated as first made from contributions (return of capital).

Assume the same facts as in the previous example, except that Edith is only age 50 and receives a distribution of $55,000. Because her basis for the Roth IRA is $100,000 (contributions made), the distribution is tax-free, and her basis in the account is reduced to $45,000 ($100,000 − $55,000).

Contributions to Roth IRAs are subject to income limits. In 2018, the maximum annual contribution of $5,500 is phased out beginning at AGI of $120,000 for single taxpayers and $189,000 for married couples who file a joint return. The phaseout range is $10,000 for married taxpayers filing jointly and $15,000 for single taxpayers. For a married taxpayer filing separately, the phaseout begins with AGI of $0 and is phased out over a $10,000 range.

Bev, who is single, would like to contribute $5,500 to her Roth IRA. Her AGI is $130,000. As a result, her contribution is limited to $1,833 ($5,500 − $3,667), calculated as follows.

$$\frac{\$10,000}{\$15,000} \times \$5,500 = \$3,667 \text{ reduction}$$

Rollovers and Conversions

Often when employees change jobs, they do not want to leave their retirement savings with their former employer. As a result, retirement savings in a qualified plan may be directly transferred from that plan to an IRA or may be "rolled over" into an IRA. Amounts that are directly transferred to another plan are not included in the owner's gross income. Rollover distributions will not be included in gross income as long as the funds received are transferred to an IRA within 60 days of receipt.[72]

In addition, a traditional IRA may be rolled over or converted to a Roth IRA. The tax consequences depend on whether the contributions made to the traditional IRA were deductible or nondeductible. If deductible contributions were made, the basis for the IRA is zero. Thus, the entire amount of the rollover or conversion is included in gross income. If nondeductible contributions were made, the basis for the IRA is equal to

---

[72]§ 402(c)(3).

the sum of the contributions. Thus, only the IRA earnings included in the rollover or conversion are included in gross income.

See Concept Summary 11.3 for an overview of some of the primary differences between traditional and Roth IRAs.

Concept Summary 11.3

Traditional IRAs and Roth IRAs Compared

	Traditional IRA	Roth IRA
Maximum annual contribution	$5,500 or 100% of compensation, pretax dollars.	$5,500 or 100% of compensation, after-tax dollars.
Maximum annual deduction limit	$5,500 or 100% of compensation.	No deduction.
Tax benefits	Tax-deferred growth of earnings.	Tax-free growth of earnings.
Taxation of withdrawals in retirement	Deductible contributions and earnings taxed as ordinary income.	Contributions and earnings withdrawn tax-free.
Taxation of withdrawals prior to retirement	10% penalty on withdrawals before 59½, except for withdrawals to pay certain medical expenses, qualified education expenses, or qualified first-time homebuyer expenses.	10% penalty on earnings withdrawn before age 59½. No penalty on contributions withdrawn after five years or if the distribution is used to pay qualified first-time homebuyer's expenses.
Timing of contribution	Grace period up to due date of tax return (not including extensions).	Grace period up to due date of tax return (not including extensions).

11-4 INDIVIDUALS AS PROPRIETORS

State and explain the tax provisions applicable to proprietors.

A sole proprietorship is *not* a taxable entity separate from the individual who owns the proprietorship. The owner reports the results of business operations of the proprietorship on Schedule C of Form 1040. The net profit or loss reported on the Schedule C is then transferred to the first page of the Form 1040. The proprietor reports all of the net profit or net loss from the business, irrespective of the amount actually withdrawn from the proprietorship during the year.

Income and expenses of the proprietorship retain their character when reported by the proprietor. For example, ordinary income of the proprietorship is treated as ordinary income when reported by the proprietor, and capital gain of the proprietorship is treated as capital gain when reported by the proprietor.

EXAMPLE 41

George is the sole proprietor of George's Bicycle Shop. Gross income of the business is $200,000, and operating expenses are $110,000. George also sells a capital asset held by the business for a $10,000 long-term capital gain. During the year, he withdraws $60,000 cash from the business for living expenses.

George reports the operating income and expenses of the business on Schedule C, resulting in net profit (ordinary income) of $90,000 ($200,000 − $110,000). Even though he only withdrew $60,000 cash from the business, George reports all of the $90,000 net profit from the business on Form 1040. He also reports a $10,000 long-term capital gain on his personal tax return (Schedule D of Form 1040).

11-4a Accounting Periods and Methods

Proprietors may choose among various accounting methods, just as other business entities do (refer to Chapters 4 and 5). The cash method is commonly used by proprietorships that provide services, while the accrual or hybrid method generally is required if inventory is a material income-producing factor of the business.

The accounting period rules for proprietorships generally are much simpler than those for partnerships and S corporations. Because a proprietorship is not an entity separate from the proprietor, the proprietorship must use the same tax year-end as the proprietor. This does not preclude the use of a fiscal year for a proprietorship, but most proprietorships use the calendar year.

11-4b Income and Deductions of a Proprietorship

The broad definition of gross income in § 61(a) applies equally to individuals and business entities, including proprietorships, corporations, and partnerships. Thus, asset inflows into a proprietorship are to be treated as income unless a Code section provides for an exclusion from income (e.g., interest on state and local bonds, appreciation on investments). Refer to Chapter 4 for a detailed discussion of gross income.

The provisions that govern business deductions also are general and not entity-specific. The § 162 requirement that trade or business expenses be *ordinary and necessary* (refer to text Section 5-1) applies to proprietorships as well as corporations, partnerships, and other business entities. However, certain specific deductions are available only to self-employed taxpayers. These deductions are addressed next.

Health Insurance Premiums

A self-employed taxpayer may deduct *for* AGI any insurance premiums paid for medical coverage.[73] The deduction is allowed for premiums paid on behalf of the taxpayer, the taxpayer's spouse, and dependents of the taxpayer. The deduction is not allowed to a taxpayer who is eligible to participate in a subsidized health plan maintained by any employer of the taxpayer or of the taxpayer's spouse.

This deduction is reported in the Adjusted Gross Income section of Form 1040 rather than on Schedule C. Premiums paid for medical coverage of the *employees* of a self-employed taxpayer are deductible as business expenses on Schedule C, however.

EXAMPLE 42

Ellen, a sole proprietor of a restaurant, has two dependent children. This year, she paid health insurance premiums of $8,800 for her own coverage and $8,000 for coverage of her two children. Ellen can claim health insurance premiums of $16,800 as a deduction *for* AGI.

Self-Employment Tax

The tax on self-employment income is levied to provide Social Security and Medicare benefits (old age, survivors, and disability insurance and hospital insurance) for self-employed individuals. Individuals with net earnings of $400 or more from self-employment are subject to the self-employment tax.[74] For 2018, the combined self-employment (SE) tax rate is 15.3 percent (12.4 percent for Social Security and 2.9 percent for Medicare) and the tax is computed on self-employment earnings up to $128,400. This amount is adjusted annually for inflation.

Net SE earnings include gross income from a trade or business less allowable trade or business deductions, plus the taxpayer's distributive share of any business-related partnership income or loss, and any net income from rendering personal services as an independent contractor.[75]

In computing the tax, net SE earnings are reduced by 7.65 percent (to 92.35 percent of the total), to reflect a deduction for the "employer's half" of the total 15.3 percent tax. Self-employed taxpayers are allowed a deduction *for* AGI equal to one-half of the self-employment tax liability.[76]

If an individual who is self-employed also receives wages subject to the FICA tax from working as an employee of another organization, the amount of the Social

---

[73]§ 162(l).

[74]§ 6017.

[75]§ 1402(a)(12).

[76]§ 164(f).

Security portion on which the self-employment tax is computed is reduced. However, a combination of FICA wages and self-employment earnings will not reduce the Medicare component of the self-employment tax, as there is no ceiling on this component of the tax.

Computing Self-Employment Taxes

EXAMPLE 43

In 2018, Kelly recorded $86,000 of net earnings from a data imaging services business that she owns. During the year, she also received wages of $54,000 as an employee of a small accounting firm. The amount of Kelly's self-employment income subject to the Social Security tax (12.4%) is $74,400 ($128,400 − $54,000), producing a tax of $9,226 ($74,400 × 12.4%); note that $74,400 is less than Kelly's net SE income ($86,000 × .9235 = $79,421), so the smaller amount is used.

All of Kelly's net self-employment income ($79,421) is subject to the 2.9% Medicare portion of the self-employment tax. Thus, Kelly's Medicare tax on this income is $2,303 ($79,421 × 2.9%).

EXAMPLE 44

Continue with the facts in the previous example. If Kelly's wages from working at the accounting firm were only $30,000, then her ceiling for Social Security taxation would be $98,400 ($128,400 − $30,000). Because her net self-employment income ($79,421) is less than this amount, Kelly would compute her self-employment tax on the full amount of the $79,421 net SE income.

11-4c Retirement Plans for Self-Employed Individuals

Individual Retirement Accounts (discussed earlier in this chapter) are available to both employees and self-employed individuals. Other options for self-employed individuals include, but are not limited to, H.R. 10 (Keogh) plans and SIMPLE plans, both of which are discussed next.

Keogh Plans

Self-employed individuals (e.g., partners and sole proprietors) can establish and receive qualified retirement benefits under **Keogh plans** (also known as H.R. 10 plans). Self-employed individuals who establish Keogh plans for themselves also must cover their *employees* under the plan.

Keogh investments can include a variety of funding vehicles, such as mutual funds, annuities, real estate shares, certificates of deposit, debt instruments, commodities, securities, and personal properties. When an individual decides to make all investment decisions for the plan's holdings, a *self-directed retirement plan* is established. Investment in most collectibles (e.g., coins or art) is not allowed in a self-directed plan.

A Keogh plan may be either a *defined contribution* plan or a *defined benefit* plan. In a defined contribution plan, the amount that can be contributed each year is subject to limitations. Retirement benefits depend on the amount contributed and the amount earned by the plan. In a defined benefit plan, the amount of retirement income is fixed and is determined on the basis of the employee's compensation while working, the number of years in the plan, and age upon retirement. Contributions are derived actuarially, to provide the benefits that are needed when withdrawals are made.

A self-employed individual may annually contribute the smaller of $55,000 (in 2018) or 100 percent of earned income to a *defined contribution* Keogh plan.[77] However, if the defined contribution plan is a profit sharing plan or stock bonus plan, a 25 percent deduction limit applies. Under a *defined benefit* Keogh plan, the annual benefit payable to an employee is limited to the smaller of $220,000 (in 2018) or 100 percent of the employee's average compensation for the three highest years of employment.[78]

---

[77]§ 415(c)(1).   [78]§ 415(b)(1). The amount is indexed annually.

Earned income refers to net earnings from self-employment.[79] Net earnings from self-employment is defined as the gross income derived by an individual from any trade or business carried on by that individual, less appropriate deductions, plus the distributive share of income or loss from a partnership.[80] Earned income is reduced by contributions to a Keogh plan on the individual's behalf and by 50 percent of any self-employment tax.[81]

EXAMPLE 45

Pat, a partner, reports earned income of $150,000 in 2018 (after the deduction for one-half of self-employment tax, but before any Keogh contribution). The maximum contribution Pat may make to a defined contribution Keogh plan is $55,000, the lesser of $150,000 or $55,000.

TAX PLANNING STRATEGIES   Important Dates Related to IRAs and Keogh Plans

FRAMEWORK FOCUS: DEDUCTIONS

Strategy: Accelerate Recognition of Deductions to Achieve Tax Deferral.

A Keogh or IRA participant may make a deductible contribution for a tax year up to the due date for filing the individual's tax return for that tax year. A Keogh plan must have been *established* by the end of the *prior* tax year (e.g., December 31, 2018) to obtain a deduction on the 2018 income tax return. The contribution must be made by April 15, 2019, to be deductible for 2018.

SIMPLE Plans

Employers with 100 or fewer employees who do not maintain another qualified retirement plan may establish a *savings incentive match plan for employees* (SIMPLE plan).[82] The plan can be in the form of a § 401(k) plan or an IRA. A SIMPLE § 401(k) plan is not subject to the nondiscrimination rules that apply to § 401(k) plans.

All employees who received at least $5,000 in compensation from the employer during any two preceding years and who reasonably expect to receive at least $5,000 in compensation during the current year must be eligible to participate in the plan. The decision to participate is up to the employee. A *self-employed individual* also may establish a SIMPLE plan.

The contributions made by the employee (a salary reduction is made) must be expressed as a percentage of compensation rather than as a fixed dollar amount. The SIMPLE plan must not permit the elective employee contribution for the year to exceed $12,500 (in 2018).[83] The SIMPLE elective deferral limit is increased under a "catch-up" provision for employees age 50 and over. The amount is $3,000 in 2018 and is indexed for inflation in $500 increments.

Generally, the employer must either match elective employee contributions up to 3 percent of the employee's compensation or provide nonmatching contributions of 2 percent of compensation for each eligible employee. Thus, for an employee under age 50, the maximum amount that may be contributed to the plan for 2018 is $20,750 [$12,500 employee contributions + $8,250 ($275,000 compensation ceiling × 3%) employer match].

No other contributions may be made to the plan other than the employee elective contribution and the required employer matching contribution (or nonmatching contribution under the 2 percent rule). All contributions are fully vested. An employer is required to make the required matching or nonmatching contributions to a SIMPLE

---

[79]§ 401(c)(2).
[80]§ 1402(a).
[81]§§ 401(c)(2)(A)(v) and 164(f).

[82]§ 408(p).
[83]§ 408(p)(2)(E)(i).

§ 401(k) plan once it is established, whereas an employer's contributions to a traditional § 401(k) plan generally may be discretionary.

An employer's deduction for contributions to a SIMPLE § 401(k) plan is limited to the greater of 25 percent of the compensation paid or accrued or the amount the employer is required to contribute to the plan. An employer is allowed a deduction for matching contributions only if the contributions are made by the due date (including extensions) for the employer's tax return.

Contributions to a SIMPLE plan are excludible from the employee's gross income, and the SIMPLE plan itself is tax-exempt. A new SIMPLE plan must be established by October 1 of a calendar tax year, unless the employer's business is established after October 1.

TAX PLANNING STRATEGIES Factors Affecting Retirement Plan Choices

FRAMEWORK FOCUS: DEDUCTIONS

Strategy: Maximize Deductible Amounts.

An IRA might not be the best retirement plan option for many self-employed taxpayers. The maximum amount that can be deducted is $5,500 per year ($11,000 for a spousal plan), which may be too low to fund an adequate level of retirement income for the employee. Other options such as Keogh plans and SIMPLE plans allow larger contributions and larger deductions.

However, a self-employed individual who establishes either a Keogh or a SIMPLE plan is required to cover most employees of the business under such plans. This can result in substantial expenditures, not only for the required contributions but also for expenses of administering the plan. An advantage of an IRA is that coverage of employees is not required.

11-4d Deduction for Qualified Business Income

The deduction for qualified business income (QBI) became a part of the Internal Revenue Code as a result of the TCJA of 2017.[84] The rationale for the deduction relates to the TCJA's reduction of the corporate tax rate to 21 percent. The following discussion, in which the single level of tax paid by businesses operating in noncorporate form is compared to the double taxation experienced by businesses operating in corporate form, illustrates the rationale for the deduction for QBI.

Assume that a corporation has $100 of taxable income in 2018. If that corporation distributed all of its after-tax profit as a dividend to individual shareholders, the maximum combined (corporate and individual) tax rate on that $100 would be approximately 37 percent. That is, after paying Federal income taxes of $21, the corporation would distribute the remaining $79 to shareholders as a dividend. For an individual shareholder in the highest tax bracket, such a dividend would be taxed at a maximum rate of 20 percent. Thus, the shareholder would pay $16 in Federal income tax as a result of the receipt of the distribution. The remaining after-tax income equals $63. This means that a combined 37 percent in Federal income taxes was paid on the corporation's business income.[85]

If that same $100 was earned in 2018 by sole proprietorship of a taxpayer in the highest income tax bracket, the income would also be taxed at a maximum rate of 37 percent.[86] Thus, without the deduction for QBI, the (historic) tax benefit of operating in noncorporate form would have been eliminated by the TCJA of 2017. In other words, Congress enacted the deduction for QBI to maintain the tax advantage of operating in noncorporate form that existed prior to the TCJA.

---

[84]§ 199A, Tax Cuts and Jobs Act (TCJA) 2017, Pub. L. 115–97, § 11012.

[85]37% = [($21 corporate tax + $16 tax on dividends)/$100 corporate taxable income]. For ease of explanation, the presence of shareholders other than individuals is ignored in the example.

[86]For ease of explanation, taxes other than the individual income tax such as the 3.8% Medicare tax are ignored in the example.

Generally, the deduction for QBI is equal to 20 percent of a noncorporate entity's qualified business income. By allowing a 20 percent deduction, the maximum post-TCJA tax rate on noncorporate business income is approximately 30, rather than 37, percent, all else equal. Using the numbers in the previously described scenario, if the sole proprietor's $100 taxable income represented the business's QBI, then taxable income would be reduced by a $20 QBI deduction. The sole proprietor would pay tax on the remaining $80 of taxable income at a 37 percent maximum individual tax, resulting in Federal income tax of $30. All else equal, the TCJA retains the tax advantage to operating in noncorporate form. (As illustrated by the scenarios above, the advantage is approximately 8 percent.)

This section begins by discussing the general rules for and key terms in the calculation of the deduction for QBI. The limitations that apply with respect to high-income taxpayers and service businesses are discussed after the general provisions.

General Rule

Generally, § 199A permits an individual to deduct 20 percent of the qualified business income generated by a sole proprietorship.[87] More precisely, the deduction is the lesser of:

1. 20 percent of QBI, or
2. 20 percent of modified taxable income.[88]

The general rule includes a number of terms that require definition and clarification.

Qualified business income, referenced in part (1) of the general rule, is defined as the ordinary income less the ordinary deductions a taxpayer reports from a "qualified trade or business." An individual taxpayer's QBI also includes the distributive share of QBI from each partnership or S corporation interest held by the taxpayer.

Qualified business income does not include certain types of investment income, such as:

- Capital gains or capital losses;
- Dividends;
- Interest income (unless "properly allocable" to a trade or business, such as lending); or
- Certain other investment items.

Additionally, qualified business income does not include:

- "Reasonable compensation" paid to the taxpayer by a qualified trade or business; or
- Guaranteed payments made to a partner for services rendered.[89]

As noted in the definition of QBI, in order to qualify for the deduction, the taxpayer's QBI must be earned in a "qualified trade or business" (QTB). (The term "qualified" appears in a variety of contexts in § 199A.) At the most basic level, such a business is conducted by the taxpayer in the United States.[90] For taxpayers who fall below the taxable income thresholds specified in § 199A ($315,000 for married taxpayers filing jointly; $157,500 for all other taxpayers), a QTB is defined broadly. Such a business includes any trade or business other than providing services as an employee.[91]

Irrespective of the amount calculated in part (1), part (2) of the general rule provides that the § 199A deduction cannot exceed 20 percent of the taxpayer's modified taxable

---

[87]§ 199A(a). Note that the deduction is also available for QBI generated by a partnership or an S corporation.

[88]If the taxpayer has more than one qualified trade or business, the QBI deduction is determined for each business independently [§ 199A(b)(1)(A)]. These then are combined [into the "combined qualified business income amount" of § 199A(a)(1)(A)] and compared to the modified taxable income limitation in part (2) of the general rule.

[89]§ 199A(c)(4).

[90]§ 199A(c)(3)(A). As a result, foreign trade or business income does not qualify for the deduction. Certain Puerto Rico activities qualify for the deduction.

[91]§ 199A(d)(1).

income. Modified taxable income is taxable income *before* the deduction for qualified business income, reduced by any net capital gain. In computing modified taxable income, the term *net capital gain* includes both a net capital gain plus any qualified dividend income.[92]

Finally, the QBI deduction is a deduction *from* AGI. The deduction is the last deduction taken in determining an individual's taxable income.[93] Further, the deduction is available whether a taxpayer uses the standard deduction or itemizes deductions.[94] Examples 46, 47, and 48 illustrate the basic calculation of the QBI deduction.

Basic QBI Deduction Computation

EXAMPLE 46

Sanjay, a married taxpayer, operates a candy store as a sole proprietor. The business has no employees; Sanjay provides all services to customers. In 2018, the net income of Sanjay's business [as reported on Schedule C (Form 1040)] is $210,000. Sanjay's AGI is $274,000, which includes wages earned by his spouse, but no other income. He and his spouse take the standard deduction ($24,000). Sanjay's modified taxable income is $250,000 ($274,000 − $24,000).

Sanjay's QBI deduction is $42,000, the lesser of:

1. 20% of qualified business income ($42,000; $210,000 × 20%); or
2. 20% of modified taxable income ($50,000; $250,000 × 20%).

As a result, Sanjay's taxable income in 2018 is $208,000 {$250,000 of taxable income before the QBI deduction less the $42,000 QBI deduction [the lesser of the amounts calculated in (1) and (2)]}.

EXAMPLE 47

Assume that Abby is a single taxpayer who does not itemize deductions and operates a sole proprietorship. During 2018, her business generates $140,000 of business income, $40,000 of deductible business expenses, and $2,000 of interest income from her business deposits. She has no other sources of income. Abby's AGI is $102,000.

Abby has $100,000 of qualified business income ($140,000 − $40,000); the interest income does not qualify as QBI. Her modified taxable income is $90,000 ($102,000 AGI − $12,000 standard deduction).

Abby's QBI deduction is $18,000, the lesser of:

1. 20% of qualified business income ($20,000; $100,000 × 20%); or
2. 20% of modified taxable income ($18,000; $90,000 × 20%).

As a result, Abby's taxable income in 2018 is $72,000 {$90,000 of taxable income before the QBI deduction less the $18,000 QBI deduction [the lesser of the amounts calculated in (1) and (2)]}.

EXAMPLE 48

Assume the same facts as in the previous example, except that Abby has $2,000 of *qualified dividend income* rather than interest income in 2018. Abby's AGI remains $102,000, and her taxable income before the QBI deduction remains $90,000 ($102,000 AGI − $12,000 standard deduction).

Abby's modified taxable income is now $88,000 [$90,000 taxable income before the QBI deduction less $2,000 of "net capital gain" (the qualified dividend income)].

Abby's QBI deduction is $17,600, the lesser of:

1. 20% of qualified business income ($20,000; $100,000 × 20%); or
2. 20% of modified taxable income ($17,600; $88,000 × 20%).

As a result, Abby's taxable income in 2018 is $72,400 {$90,000 of taxable income before the QBI deduction less the $17,600 QBI deduction [the lesser of the amounts calculated in (1) and (2)]}.

---

[92]§§ 199A(a) and (e). § 199A relies on the definition of "net capital gain" in § 1(h).

[93]See TCJA § 11011(b), the last sentence of § 62(a), and § 63(b)(3).

[94]§ 63(d)(3).

The deduction for QBI must be determined separately for each qualified trade or business. These independent calculations are combined into the "qualified business income amount" which is then compared to the taxpayer's modified taxable income amount.

Limitations on the QBI Deduction

There are *three limitations* on the QBI deduction. An overall limitation based on modified taxable income [part (2) of the general rule, discussed previously] applies to all taxpayers. A second limitation is in place for high-income taxpayers, and a third limitation applies to certain types of service businesses of high-income taxpayers.

As discussed previously, the second and third limitations only apply when taxable income before the QBI deduction exceeds $315,000 (married taxpayers filing a joint return) or $157,500 (all other taxpayers). Once these thresholds are reached, § 199A imposes two *independent* limitations.

1. *Limitation based on wages and capital investment.* Section 199A imposes a cap on the QBI deduction, based on the percentage of the W–2 wages paid by the business (i.e., wages paid to its employees) *or* based on a smaller percentage of W–2 wages paid and a percentage of the cost of its depreciable property used to produce QBI.[95]
2. *Limitation for "specified services" businesses.* The QBI deduction generally is not available for income earned from "specified service" businesses.[96] "Specified service" businesses include physicians, dentists, attorneys, accountants, consultants, investment advisers, entertainers, and athletes (among others), but not engineers and architects.

Note that these limitations, where applicable, are compared with the overall limitation (based on modified taxable income) to determine the taxpayer's deduction for QBI.

Limitation Based on Wages and Capital Investment

This limitation, which applies once a taxpayer's income exceeds those thresholds mentioned previously, limits the 20 percent QBI deduction to the *greater of*:

1. 50 percent of the "W–2 wages" paid by the QTB, or
2. 25 percent of the "W–2 wages" paid by the QTB plus 2.5 percent of the taxpayer's share of the unadjusted basis (immediately after acquisition) of all tangible depreciable property (including real estate) used in the QTB as long as such property has not been fully depreciated prior to the close of the taxable year.

"W–2 wages" include the total amount of wages subject to income tax withholding, compensation paid into qualified retirement accounts, and certain other forms of deferred compensation paid to the employees of the business.[97] For labor-intensive businesses, 50 percent of the W–2 wages paid by the business will likely be the cap that limits the QBI deduction.

W–2 Wages Limit

EXAMPLE 49

Simone, a married taxpayer, operates a business as a sole proprietor. In 2018, the business has one employee, who is paid $80,000. Assume that the business has no depreciable property. During 2018, the net income of Simone's business [as reported on Schedule C (Form 1040)] is $230,000 and her modified taxable income is $250,000 (this is also her taxable income before the QBI deduction).

Since Simone's taxable income before the QBI deduction is below the income threshold for married taxpayers filing a joint return ($315,000), the W–2/Capital Investment Limitation does not apply. As a result, Simone's QBI deduction is $46,000, the lesser of:

1. 20% of qualified business income ($46,000; $230,000 × 20%); or
2. 20% of modified taxable income ($50,000; $250,000 × 20%).

---

[95] § 199A(b)(2)(B).

[96] § 199A(d)(2).

[97] §§ 199A(b)(3)(B) and (d)(3).

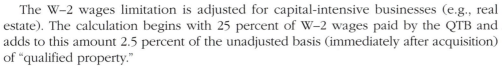

W–2 Wages Limit

Assume the same facts as in the previous example, except that the net income from Simone's proprietorship is $500,000 and her modified taxable income is $600,000 (this is also her taxable income before the QBI deduction).

EXAMPLE 50

Since Simone's taxable income before the QBI deduction exceeds $415,000, her QBI deduction is $40,000, the lesser of:

1. 20% of qualified business income ($100,000; $500,000 × 20%); or
2. 50% of W–2 wages ($40,000; $80,000 × 50%)

And *no more than*:

3. 20% of modified taxable income ($120,000; $600,000 × 20%).

The W–2 wages limitation is adjusted for capital-intensive businesses (e.g., real estate). The calculation begins with 25 percent of W–2 wages paid by the QTB and adds to this amount 2.5 percent of the unadjusted basis (immediately after acquisition) of "qualified property."

Qualified property includes depreciable tangible property—real or personal—that is used by the QTB during the year and whose "depreciable period" has not ended before the end of the taxable year. As a result, land and intangible assets are not qualified property. Additionally, given the broad-based changes to MACRS made by the TCJA of 2017—allowing taxpayers to immediately expense the cost of most property other than real estate—the "depreciable period" for "qualified property" under § 199A is a minimum of 10 years.[98]

Tom and Eileen are married and file a joint return. In 2018, their taxable income before the QBI deduction is $500,000 (this is also their modified taxable income). Tom records $400,000 in QBI from a restaurant that Tom owns as a sole proprietorship. Tom employed four individuals (cook, bartender, and wait staff) during the year and paid them $150,000 in W–2 wages in total. Tom owns the building in which the restaurant is located. He bought the building (and its furniture and fixtures) four years ago for $600,000, and the land then was worth $100,000; thus, the unadjusted acquisition basis (purchase price less the value of the land) of the building, furniture, and fixtures was $500,000.

EXAMPLE 51

As their taxable income before the QBI deduction exceeds the $415,000 threshold, the W–2 Wages/ Capital Investment Limit is applicable. Their QBI deduction is $75,000, computed as follows.

1. 20% of qualified business income ($400,000 × 20%)		$ 80,000
2. But no more than the *greater of*:		
• 50% of W–2 wages ($150,000 × 50%), or		$ 75,000
• 25% of W–2 wages ($150,000 × 25%) plus	$37,500	
2.5% of the unadjusted basis of qualified		
property ($500,000 × 2.5%)	12,500	$ 50,000
And *no more than*:		
3. 20% of modified taxable income ($500,000 × 20%)		$100,000

---

[98] § 199A(b)(6).

Many owners of pass-through businesses, especially landlords, have no employees. As a result, the 25 percent of W–2 wages plus 2.5 percent of the unadjusted basis of qualified property limit is most likely to affect them.

EXAMPLE 52

Jiaxiu, a single taxpayer, owns a five-unit apartment building that he purchased five years ago. His unadjusted basis in the building (purchase price less the value of the land) is $500,000. His taxable income before the QBI deduction is $250,000 in 2018 (this is also his modified taxable income). He has no employees in his business, and his QBI is $220,000.

As his taxable income before the QBI deduction exceeds the $207,500 threshold, the W–2 Wages/Capital Investment Limit is applicable. His QBI deduction is $12,500, computed as follows.

1. 20% of qualified business income ($220,000 × 20%)		$44,000
2. But no more than the *greater of*:		
• 50% of W–2 wages ($0 × 50%), or		$ –0–
• 25% of W–2 wages ($0 × 25%) plus	$ –0–	
2.5% of the unadjusted basis of qualified property ($500,000 × 2.5%)	12,500	$12,500
And *no more than*:		
3. 20% of modified taxable income ($250,000 × 20%)		$50,000

In Examples 51 and 52, the taxpayers are either below the taxable income threshold or at least $100,000 over the taxable income threshold. Between these ranges, the W–2 Wages/Capital Investment Limit is phased in. More precisely, this limitation does not apply to taxpayers with taxable income (before the QBI deduction) less than the threshold amount ($315,000 for married taxpayers filing jointly; $157,500 for all others). The limit does apply to taxpayers whose taxable income (before the QBI deduction) exceeds the threshold amount by more than $100,000 (married filing jointly) or $50,000 (all other taxpayers). If, however, the taxpayer's taxable income before the QBI deduction is between these two amounts *and the W–2 Wages/Capital Investment portion of the QBI limits the taxpayer's QBI deduction*, the W–2 Wages/Capital Investment limit is phased in. The calculation of the phase-in is not discussed in this chapter, though it is included in Concept Summary 11.4.

Limitation for "Specified Services" Businesses

For high-income taxpayers, § 199A excludes any "specified service trade or business" from the definition of a qualified trade or business.[99] A specified service trade or business includes those involving:

- The performance of services in fields including health, law, accounting, actuarial science, performing arts, consulting, athletics, financial services, and brokerage services, but not architecture and engineering;

- Services consisting of investing and investment management, trading or dealing in securities, partnership interests, or commodities; and

- Any trades or business where the business's principal asset is the reputation of one or more of its employees or owners.

---

[99]§§ 199A(d)(1)(A) and (d)(2); see also § 1202(e)(3)(A).

Concept Summary 11.4

An Overview of the Qualified Business Income Deduction

<u>How to Use the Concept Summary:</u> **First**, identify all qualified trades or businesses (QTB) of the taxpayer and the related qualified business income (QBI). **Then** for each QTB, move through the flowchart to determine the QBI amount for each QTB. Once this process is complete, combine all of the QBI amounts (this is the "combined qualified business income amount"). **Finally**, apply the *overall limitation* (based on modified taxable income). The QBI deduction is the *lesser of*:

1. The combined "qualified business income (QBI) amount," or
2. 20% of modified taxable income.*

* Modified taxable income is taxable income *before* the QBI deduction, less any "net capital gain" (including any qualified dividend income).

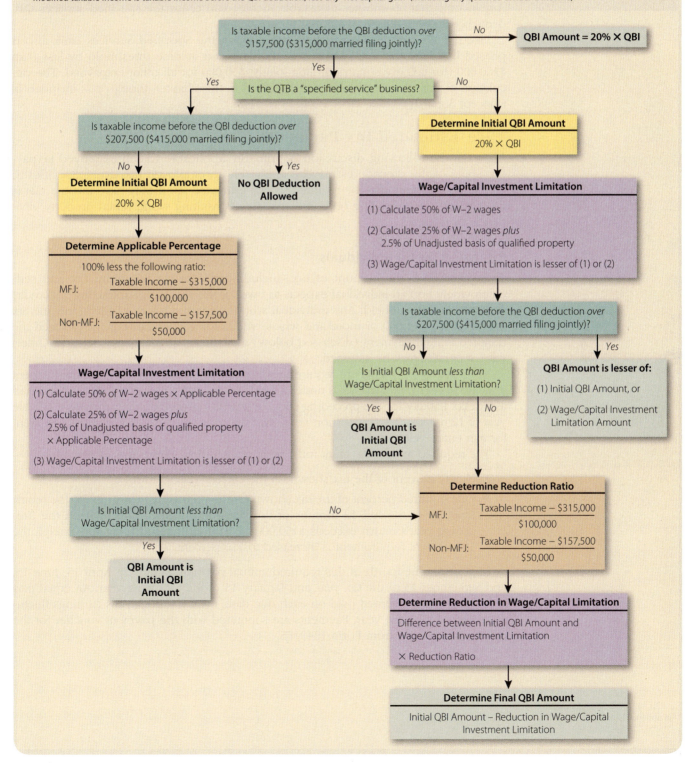

EXAMPLE 53

In Example 46, Sanjay operated a sole proprietorship that generated QBI of $210,000 and he was able to claim a QBI deduction of $42,000.

However, if Sanjay's spouse had a salary of $300,000 (instead of $64,000), he cannot claim a QBI deduction since the couple's taxable income before the QBI deduction exceeds $415,000 [$210,000 (QBI) + $300,000 (spouse's wages) − $24,000 (standard deduction) = $486,000]. The *income of Sanjay's spouse* triggered the limitation.

Example 53 illustrates an important fact. The QBI deduction phaseout for a specified services business is based on *taxable income* before the QBI deduction (*not* on QBI). *Any* income that contributes to taxable income can cause the specified services QBI deduction to be reduced.

Like the W–2 Wages/Capital Investment Limit, the Specified Services Limit also is phased in where the taxpayer is over the specified income threshhold by less than $100,000 (for taxpayers married filing jointly, $50,000 for all other taxpayers). The calculation of this phase-in is also not discussed in this chapter, though it is included in Concept Summary 11.4.

11-4e Estimated Tax Payments

Although the following discussion is primarily applicable to self-employed taxpayers, some of the procedures may be applicable to employed taxpayers. Specifically, employed taxpayers may be required to pay estimated tax if they have income that is not subject to withholding (e.g., income from consulting work, rental property, dividends, or interest).

Estimated Tax for Individuals

Estimated tax is the amount of tax (including alternative minimum tax and self-employment tax) an individual expects to owe for the year after subtracting tax credits and income tax withheld. Any individual who is expected to owe Federal income tax for the year of $1,000 or more and whose withholding does not equal or exceed the required annual payment (discussed below) must make quarterly payments.[100] Otherwise, a penalty may be assessed.

No quarterly payments are required and no penalty will apply on an underpayment if the taxpayer's estimated tax is under $1,000. No penalty will apply if the taxpayer had a zero tax liability for the preceding tax year *and* the preceding tax year was a taxable year of 12 months (i.e., not a short year) *and* the taxpayer was a U.S. citizen or resident for that entire year.

The required annual payment must be computed first. This is the smaller of:

- Ninety percent of the tax shown on the current year's return; or
- One hundred percent of the tax shown on the preceding year's return (the return must cover the full 12 months of the preceding year). If the AGI on the preceding year's return exceeds $150,000 ($75,000 if married filing separately), the 100 percent requirement is increased to 110 percent.

In general, one-fourth of this required annual payment is due on April 15, June 15, and September 15 of the tax year and January 15 of the following year. An equal part of withholding is deemed paid on each due date, even if a taxpayer's earnings fluctuate widely during the year. Payments are submitted with the payment voucher for the appropriate quarter from Form 1040–ES.

---

[100]§§ 6654(c)(1) and 6654(e)(1).

Penalty on Underpayments

A nondeductible penalty is imposed on the amount of underpayment of estimated tax. The rate for this penalty is adjusted quarterly to reflect changes in market interest rates.[101]

Marta made the following payments of estimated tax for 2018 and had no income tax withheld.

April 17, 2018	$1,400
June 15, 2018	2,300
September 17, 2018	1,500
January 15, 2019	1,800

Marta's actual tax for 2018 is $8,000, and her tax in 2017 was $10,000. Therefore, each installment should have been at least $1,800 [($8,000 × 90%) × 25%]. Of the payment on June 15, $400 will be credited to the unpaid balance of the first quarterly installment due on April 17,[102] thereby effectively stopping the underpayment penalty for the first quarter. Of the remaining $1,900 payment on June 15, $100 is credited to the September 17 payment, resulting in this third quarterly payment being $200 short. Then $200 of the January 15, 2019 payment is credited to the September 17 shortfall, ending the underpayment period for that amount. The January 15, 2019 installment is now underpaid by $200, and a penalty will apply from January 15, 2019, to April 16, 2019 (unless some tax is paid sooner).

In summary, Marta's underpayments for each quarter are as follows.

1st installment due	$400 from April 17 to June 15, 2018
2nd installment due	Paid in full
3rd installment due	$200 from September 17, 2018, to January 15, 2019
4th installment due	$200 from January 15 to April 16, 2019

If a possible underpayment of estimated tax is indicated, Form 2210 is filed to compute the penalty due or to justify that no penalty applies.

11-5 **HOBBY LOSSES**

Expenses incurred by a self-employed taxpayer are deductible only if the taxpayer can show that the activity was entered into for the purpose of making a profit.[103]

Certain activities can have attributes that make it difficult to determine if the primary motivation for the activity is to make a profit or is for personal pleasure. Examples include raising horses and operating a farm that is also used as a weekend residence. While personal losses are not deductible, losses attributable to profit-seeking activities may be deducted and used to offset a taxpayer's other income. Activities that have both personal and profit-seeking motives are classified as hobbies, and the tax law limits the deductibility of hobby losses.

The income and deductions from a hobby are reported separately on the tax return. Hobby income always is reported as *other income* on page 1 of Form 1040. The reporting of deductions is discussed below.

11-5a **General Rules**

If an individual can show that an activity has been conducted with the intent to earn a profit, losses from the activity are fully deductible (and reported, along with any income, on Schedule C). The hobby loss rules apply only if the activity is not engaged in for profit. Hobby expenses are deductible only to the extent of hobby income.[104]

---

[101]§ 6654(b)(2).

[102]Payments are credited to unpaid installments in the order in which the installments are required to be paid. § 6654(b)(3).

[103]Reg. § 1.183–1(a).

[104]§ 183(b)(2).

The Regulations stipulate that the following nine factors should be considered in determining whether an activity is profit-seeking or a hobby.[105]

- Whether the activity is conducted in a businesslike manner.
- The expertise of the taxpayers or their advisers.
- The time and effort expended.
- The expectation that the assets of the activity will appreciate in value.
- The taxpayer's previous success in conducting similar activities.
- The history of income or losses from the activity.
- The relationship of profits earned to losses incurred.
- The financial status of the taxpayer (e.g., if the taxpayer does not have substantial amounts of other income, this may indicate that the activity is engaged in for profit).
- Elements of personal pleasure or recreation in the activity.

The presence or absence of a factor is not by itself determinative of whether the activity is profit-seeking or is a hobby. Rather, the decision is a subjective one that is based on an analysis of the facts and circumstances.

11-5b Presumptive Rule of Profit-Seeking

The Code provides a rebuttable presumption that an activity is profit-seeking if the activity shows a profit in at least three of the previous five tax years.[106] If the activity involves horses, a profit in at least two of the previous seven tax years meets the presumptive rule. If these profitability tests are met, the activity is presumed to be a trade or business rather than a personal hobby. In this situation, the IRS bears the burden of proving that the activity is personal rather than trade- or business-related. On the other hand, if the three-year test (two for horses) is not met, then the activity is presumed to be a hobby and the taxpayer has the burden to prove that it is profit-seeking.

EXAMPLE 55

Camille and Walter are married taxpayers who enjoy a busy lifestyle. Camille, who is an executive for a large corporation, is paid a salary of $800,000. Walter is a collector of antiques. Several years ago, he opened an antique shop in a local shopping center, and he spends most of his time buying and selling antiques. He occasionally earns a small profit from this activity, but more frequently incurs substantial losses.

If Walter's losses are business-related, they are fully deductible against Camille's salary income on a joint return. In resolving this issue, consider the following.

- Initially determine whether Walter's antique activity has met the three-out-of-five years profit test.

- If the presumption is not met, the activity may nevertheless qualify as a business if Walter can show that the intent is to engage in a profit-seeking activity. It is not necessary to show actual profits.

- Attempt to fit the operation within the nine criteria prescribed in the Regulations listed previously.

---

[105]Reg. §§ 1.183–2(b)(1) through (9).　　　　[106]§ 183(d).

11-5c **The Deductible Amount**

If an activity is deemed to be a hobby, the expenses are deductible only to the extent of the gross income from the hobby. These expenses are deducted in the following order.

1. Amounts deductible under other Code sections without regard to the nature of the activity, such as property taxes and home mortgage interest.
2. Amounts deductible under other Code sections as if the activity had been engaged in for profit, but only if those amounts do not affect adjusted basis. Examples include maintenance, utilities, and supplies.
3. Amounts that affect adjusted basis and would be deductible under other Code sections if the activity had been engaged in for profit.[107] Examples include depreciation, amortization, and depletion.

Before 2018, the last two categories of deductions were deductible *from* AGI as miscellaneous itemized deductions (to the extent they exceeded 2 percent of AGI).[108] From 2018 through 2025, miscellaneous itemized deductions are not deductible. Since property taxes and mortgage interest are deductible even without hobby income, the net effect is that the taxpayer is taxed on all of the income from the hobby. The hobby income is reported on page 1 of Form 1040. If the taxpayer uses the standard deduction rather than itemizing, the hobby loss deductions generate no tax benefit.

EXAMPLE 56

Jim, the vice president of an oil company, reports AGI of $80,000. He decides to pursue painting in his spare time. He uses a home studio, comprising 10% of the home's square footage. During the current year, Jim incurs the following expenses.

Frames	$ 1,800
Art supplies	900
Fees paid to models	4,000
Home studio expenses	
Total home property taxes	2,000
Total home mortgage interest	10,000
Total home maintenance and utilities	4,600
Calculated depreciation on 10% of home	500

During the year, Jim sold paintings for a total of $8,660. If the activity is held to be a hobby, Jim is allowed deductions computed as follows.

Gross income	$ 8,660
Deduct: Property taxes and mortgage interest (10% of $12,000)	(1,200)
Net income	$ 7,460

Jim includes the $8,660 of income in AGI, making his AGI $88,660. The taxes and interest are itemized deductions, deductible in full. The remaining $7,460 of expenses are miscellaneous itemized deductions, which are currently not deductible. Because the property taxes and home mortgage interest are deductible even without the hobby, Jim is taxed on the $8,660 of income from his hobby.

---

[107]Reg. § 1.183–1(b)(1).

[108]Reg. § 1.67–1T(a)(1)(iv) and Rev.Rul. 75–14, 1975–1 C.B. 90.

REFOCUS ON THE BIG PICTURE

SELF-EMPLOYED VERSUS EMPLOYEE—WHAT'S THE DIFFERENCE?

Mark may deduct the ordinary and necessary business expenses incurred by his proprietorship. This includes the $18,000 for rent and utilities; the $12,000 paid to his part-time assistant; and the $40,000 paid to Ellen for consulting work. The $8,000 paid for equipment can be depreciated or may qualify for an immediate deduction. As a self-employed taxpayer, Mark may deduct the $3,000 of health insurance premiums paid, but only if he is not eligible to participate in the subsidized health plan maintained by Mary's employer. On the other hand, Mark cannot deduct the premiums of $500 paid for his life insurance policy.

Mark may want to consider contributing to his own IRA or establishing a Keogh plan or SIMPLE plan to allow for greater retirement contributions. Mark should be aware that in addition to paying income tax on the net income earned by his business, he also owes self-employment tax at a combined rate of 15.3 percent, but he can claim an income tax deduction for half of the self-employment tax paid.

While Mary will owe income tax on her $85,000 salary, the health insurance premiums of $3,000 and group term life insurance premiums paid by her employer qualify as tax-free fringe benefits. In addition, as long as Mary is required to substantiate her travel expenses as part of an accountable plan, none of the travel-related reimbursements need to be included in her gross income. Because Mary is not covered by a qualified retirement plan at work, she can deduct the entire contribution made to her traditional IRA.

While the $500 of employee business expenses is technically deductible, the deduction for these expenses is currently suspended by the TCJA of 2017. While Mary is not subject to self-employment tax, she still incurred a 7.65 percent payroll tax related to Social Security and Medicare. Her employer paid an additional 7.65 percent.

What If?

Mark is considering moving his office into a vacant room in their home. Can Mark deduct expenses associated with his home office?

As a self-employed individual, Mark can deduct the costs of a home office, as long as the office is used exclusively and on a regular basis as either the principal place of business or a place of business used by his clients and customers. Deductible expenses would include a portion of mortgage interest and property taxes paid on the home; a portion of utilities, repairs and maintenance, and other household expenses; and depreciation on the business portion of the home.

ISTOCK.COM/NEUSTOCKIMAGES

Suggested Readings

William H. Byrnes and Robert Bloink, "Pass-Through Tax Planning to Boost New QBI Deduction Value," *thinkadvisor.com*, April 9, 2018.

Jeffrey Gramlich and Kimberly Houser, "Marijuana Business and Sec. 280E: Potential Pitfalls for Clients and Advisers," *The Tax Adviser*, July 2015.

Melanie James, "When Are Commuting Costs Deductible?" *Practical Tax Strategies*, November 2014.

Annette Nellen, Caroline Bruckner, and Jennifer Brown, "Taxes and the Growing Gig Workforce: What to Know," *Journal of Taxation*, June 2018.

Ronald R. Rubenfield, "Tax Strategies for Classifying Employment: Employee v. Independent Contractor," *Journal of Taxation*, November 2017.

Richard Toolson, "The Health Savings Account as a Smart Savings Option for Retirement," *TAXES—The Tax Magazine*, December 2014.

Key Terms

Accountable plan, 11-2

Automatic mileage method, 11-19

Cafeteria plans, 11-11

De minimis fringe benefits, 11-14

Deduction for qualified tuition and related expenses, 11-24

Education expenses, 11-22

Entertainment expenses, 11-25

Estimated tax, 11-44

Flexible spending plans, 11-11

Foreign earned income exclusion, 11-17

Health Savings Account (HSA), 11-6

Hobby losses, 11-45

Independent contractor, 11-2

Individual Retirement Account (IRA), 11-30

Keogh plans, 11-35

No-additional-cost service, 11-13

Nonaccountable plan, 11-29

Office in the home expenses, 11-27

Qualified business income, 11-37

Qualified employee discount, 11-13

Qualified transportation fringes, 11-15

Self-employment tax, 11-4

Transportation expenses, 11-18

Travel expenses, 11-19

Working condition fringes, 11-14

Computational Exercises

1. **LO.2** Valentino is a patient in a nursing home for 45 days in 2018. While in the nursing home, he incurs total costs of $13,500. Medicare pays $8,000 of the costs. Valentino receives $15,000 from his long-term care insurance policy, which pays while he is in the facility. Assume that the daily Federal statutory amount for Valentino is $360. Of the $15,000, what amount may Valentino exclude from his gross income?

2. **LO.2** Mio was transferred from New York to Germany. He lived and worked in Germany for 340 days in 2018. Mio's salary for 2018 is $190,000. What is Mio's foreign earned income exclusion? (In your computation, round any division to four decimal places before converting to a percentage. For example, .473938 would be rounded to 47.39%.)

3. **LO.6** In 2018, Meghann Carlson, a single taxpayer, has QBI of $110,000 and modified taxable income of $78,000 (this is also her taxable income before the QBI deduction). Given this information, what is Meghann's QBI deduction?

4. **LO.3** Fred, who is self employed, travels from Denver to Miami primarily on business. He spends five days conducting business and two days sightseeing. His expenses are $400 (airfare), $150 per day (meals), and $300 per night (lodging). What are Fred's deductible expenses?

5. **LO.3** Brenda, who is self employed, travels from Chicago to Barcelona (Spain) on business. She is gone for 10 days (including 2 days of travel), during which time she spends 5 days conducting business and 3 days sightseeing. Her expenses are $1,500 (airfare), $200 per day (meals), and $400 per night (lodging). Because Brenda stayed with relatives while sightseeing, she paid for only 5 nights of lodging.
   What is Brenda's deduction for:
   a. Airfare?
   b. Meals?
   c. Lodging?

6. **LO.3** Samantha recently was employed by an accounting firm. During the year, she spends $2,500 for a CPA exam review course and begins working on a law degree in night school. Her law school expenses were $4,200 for tuition and $450 for books (which are not a requirement for enrollment in the course). Assuming no reimbursement, how much can Samantha deduct for the:
   a. CPA exam review course?
   b. Law school expenses?

7. **LO.3** In 2018, Robert entertains four key clients and their spouses at a nightclub. Business discussions occurred over dinner and prior to the entertainment beginning. Expenses were $200 (limo charge), $120 (cover charge), $700 (drinks and dinner), and $140 (tips to servers). If Robert is self-employed, how much can he deduct for this event?

8. **LO.3** In 2018, the CEO of Crimson, Inc., entertains seven clients at a skybox in Memorial Stadium for an athletic event. Substantive business discussions occurred at various times during the event.

   The box costs $2,000 per event and seats 10 people. (The cost of a regular seat at Memorial ranges from $55 to $100.) Refreshments served during the event cost $700. How much of these costs may Crimson deduct?

9. **LO.6** In 2018, Miranda records net earnings from self-employment of $146,000. She reports no other gross income. Determine the amount of Miranda's self-employment tax and her *for* AGI income tax deduction.

10. **LO.5** Myers, who is single, reports compensation income of $70,000 in 2018. He is an active participant in his employer's qualified retirement plan. Myers contributes $5,500 to a traditional IRA. Of the $5,500 contribution, how much can Myers deduct? See Exhibit 11.3, Phaseout of Traditional IRA Deduction of an Active Participant in 2018.

11. **LO.5** Meredith, who is single, would like to contribute $5,500 to her Roth IRA. What is the maximum amount that Meredith can contribute if her AGI is $121,000?

Problems

12. **LO.1** Mason performs various home repair services for Isabella. In determining whether Mason is an employee or an independent contractor, comment on the relevance of each of the factors listed below.
    a. Mason performs services only for Isabella and does not work for anyone else.
    b. Mason sets his own work schedule.
    c. Mason reports his job-related expenses on a Schedule C.
    d. Mason obtained his job skills from Isabella's training program.
    e. Mason performs the services at Isabella's business location.
    f. Mason is paid based on time worked rather than on task performed.

13. **LO.2** Rex, age 55, is an officer of Blue Company, which provides him with the following nondiscriminatory fringe benefits in 2018.
    • Hospitalization insurance premiums for Rex and his dependents. The cost of the coverage for Rex is $2,900 per year, and the additional cost for his dependents is $3,800 per year. The plan applies a $2,000 deductible, but his employer contributed $1,500 to Rex's Health Savings Account (HSA). Rex withdrew only $800 from the HSA, and the account earned $50 of interest during the year.
    • Insurance premiums of $840 for salary continuation payments. Under the plan, Rex will receive his regular salary in the event he is unable to work due to illness. Rex collected $4,500 on the policy to replace lost wages while he was ill during the year.
    • Rex is a part-time student working on his bachelor's degree in engineering. His employer reimbursed his $5,200 tuition under a plan available to all full-time employees.
    Determine the amounts that Rex must include in gross income.

Decision Making 14. **LO.2** Casey is in the 12% marginal tax bracket, and Jean is in the 35% marginal tax bracket. Their employer is experiencing financial difficulties and cannot continue to pay for the company's health insurance plan. The annual premiums are approximately $8,000 per employee.

The employer has proposed to either (1) require the employee to pay the premiums or (2) reduce each employee's pay by $10,000 per year with the employer paying the premium. Which option is less objectionable to Casey, and which is less objectionable to Jean?

15. **LO.2** Belinda spent the last 60 days of 2018 in a nursing home. The cost of the services provided to her was $18,000 ($300 per day). Medicare paid $8,500 toward the cost of her stay. Belinda also received $5,500 of benefits under a long-term care insurance policy she had purchased. What is the effect of each of these items on Belinda's gross income?

16. **LO.2** Does the taxpayer recognize gross income in the following situations? Explain.

a. Ava is an office associate at a large insurance company. She is permitted to leave the premises for her lunch, but she usually eats in the company's cafeteria because it is quick and she is on a tight schedule. On average, she pays $2 for a lunch that would cost $12 at a restaurant; it cost her employer $10 to prepare. However, if the prices in the cafeteria were not so low and the food was not so delicious, she would probably bring her own lunch at a cost of $3 per day.

b. Scott is an executive for an international corporation located in New York City. Often he works late, taking telephone calls from the company's European branch. Scott often stays in a company-owned condominium when he has a late-night work session. The condominium is across the street from the company office and has the technology needed to communicate with employees and customers throughout the world.

c. Ira recently moved to take a new job. For the first month on the new job, Ira was searching for a home to purchase or rent. During this time, his employer permitted Ira to live in an apartment that the company maintains for customers during the buying season. The month that Ira occupied the apartment was not during the buying season, however, and the apartment would not otherwise have been occupied.

17. **LO.2** Tim is the vice president of western operations for Maroon Oil Company and is stationed in San Francisco. He is required to live in an employer-owned home, which is three blocks from his company office. The company-provided home is equipped with high-speed internet access and several telephone lines. Tim receives telephone calls and e-mails that require immediate attention any time of day or night because the company's business is spread all over the world. A full-time administrative assistant resides in the house to assist Tim with the urgent business matters.

Tim often uses the home for entertaining customers, suppliers, and employees. The fair market value of comparable housing is $9,000 per month. Tim also is provided with free parking at his company's office, a value of $350 per month. Calculate the amount associated with the company-provided housing and free parking that Tim must include in his gross income for 2018.

18. **LO.1, 4** Finch Construction Company provides the carpenters it employs with all required tools. However, the company believes that this practice has led to some employees not taking care of the tools, and to the mysterious disappearance of some of the tools.

Communications

The company is considering requiring all of its employees to provide their own tools. Each employee's salary would be increased by $1,500 to compensate for the additional cost. Write a letter to Finch's management, explaining the tax consequences of this plan to the carpenters. Finch's address is 300 Harbor Drive, Vermillion, SD 57069.

Decision Making   19.   **LO.2** Rosa's employer has instituted a flexible benefits program. Rosa will use the plan to pay for her daughter's dental expenses and other medical expenses that are not covered by health insurance. Rosa is in the 24% marginal tax bracket and estimates that the medical and dental expenses not covered by health insurance will be within the range of $4,000 to $5,000. Her employer's plan permits her to set aside as much as $5,000 in the flexible benefits account. Rosa does not itemize her deductions.

    a.   Rosa puts $4,000 in her flexible benefits account, and her actual expenses are $5,000. What is her cost of underestimating the expenses?

    b.   Rosa puts $5,000 in her flexible benefits account, and her actual expenses are only $4,000. What is her cost of overestimating her expenses?

    c.   What is Rosa's cost of underfunding as compared with the cost of overfunding the flexible benefits account?

    d.   Does your answer in part (c) suggest that Rosa should fund the account closer to the low end or to the high end of her estimates?

20.   **LO.2** Sparrow Corporation would like you to review its employee fringe benefits program with regard to the tax consequences of the plan for the company's president (Polly), who is also the majority shareholder.

    a.   Sparrow offers a qualified retirement plan. The company pays the cost of employees attending a retirement planning seminar. The employee must be within 10 years of retirement, and the cost of the seminar is $1,500 per attendee.

    b.   The company owns a parking garage that is used by customers, employees, and the general public. Only the general public is required to pay for parking. The charge to the general public for Polly's parking for the year would have been $3,600 (a $300 monthly rate).

    c.   All employees are allowed to use the company's fixed charge long-distance telephone services as long as the privilege is not abused. Although no one has kept track of the actual calls, Polly's use of the telephone had a value (what she would have paid on her personal telephone) of approximately $600 for the year.

    d.   The company owns a condominium at the beach, which it uses to entertain customers. Employees are allowed to use the facility without charge when the company has no scheduled events. Polly used the facility 10 days during the year. The dates of Polly's personal use had a rental value of $1,000.

    e.   Sparrow operates in the household moving business. Employees are allowed to ship goods without charge whenever there is excess space on a truck. Polly purchased a dining room suite for her daughter. Company trucks delivered the furniture to the daughter. Normal freight charges would have been $750.

    f.   The company has a storage facility for household goods. Officers are allowed a 20% discount on charges for storing their goods. All other employees are allowed a 10% discount. Polly's discounts for the year totaled $900.

21.   **LO.2** Ted works for Azure Motors, an automobile dealership. All employees can buy a car at the company's cost plus 2%. The company does not charge employees the $300 dealer preparation fee that nonemployees must pay. Ted purchased an automobile for $29,580 ($29,000 + $580). The company's cost was $29,000. The price for a nonemployee would have been $33,900 ($33,600 + $300 preparation fee). What is Ted's gross income from the purchase of the automobile?

Critical Thinking   22.   **LO.2** Several of Egret Company's employees have asked the company to create a hiking trail that employees could use during their lunch hours. The company owns vacant land that is being held for future expansion, but would have to spend approximately $50,000 if it were to make a trail. Nonemployees would be allowed to use the facility as part of the company's effort to build strong community support. What are the relevant tax issues for the employees?

23. **LO.2** Bluebird, Inc., does not provide its employees with any tax-exempt fringe benefits. The company is considering adopting a hospital and medical benefits insurance plan that will cost approximately $9,000 per employee. To adopt this plan, the company may need to reduce salaries and/or lower future salary increases. Bluebird is in the 25% (combined Federal and state rates) bracket.

    Bluebird also is responsible for matching the Social Security and Medicare taxes withheld on employees' salaries (at the full 7.65% rate). The hospital and medical benefits insurance plan will not be subject to the Social Security and Medicare taxes, and the company is not eligible for the small business credit for health insurance. The employees generally fall into two marginal tax rate groups, specifically:

Income Tax	Social Security and Medicare Tax	Total
.12	.0765	.1965
.24	.0145	.2545

    The company has asked you to assist in its financial planning for the hospital and medical benefits insurance plan by computing the following.

    a. How much taxable compensation is the equivalent of $9,000 of exempt compensation for each of the two classes of employees?
    b. What is the company's after-tax cost of the taxable compensation computed in part (a)?
    c. What is the company's after-tax cost of the exempt compensation?
    d. Briefly explain your conclusions from the preceding analysis.

24. **LO.2** George is a U.S. citizen who is employed by Hawk Enterprises, a global company. Beginning on June 1, 2018, George began working in London. He worked there until January 31, 2019, when he transferred to Paris. He worked in Paris the remainder of 2019. His salary for the first five months of 2018 was $100,000, and it was earned in the United States. His salary for the remainder of 2018 was $175,000, and it was earned in London.

    George's 2019 salary from Hawk was $300,000, with part being earned in London and part being earned in Paris. What is George's gross income in 2018 and 2019 (assume that the 2019 indexed amount is the same as the 2018 indexed amount)?

25. **LO.3** During the current year, Paul, the vice president of a bank, made gifts in the following amounts.

To Sarah (Paul's personal assistant) at Christmas	$36
To Darryl (a key client)—$3 was for gift wrapping	53
To Darryl's wife (a homemaker) on her birthday	20
To Veronica (Paul's boss) at Christmas	30

    In addition, on professional assistants' day, Paul takes Sarah to lunch at a cost of $82. Presuming that Paul has adequate substantiation and is not reimbursed, how much can he deduct?

26. **LO.3** Kristen, an independent management consultant, is based in Atlanta. During March and April of 2018, she is contracted by a national hardware chain to help implement revised human resource policies in Jackson (Mississippi) temporarily. During this period, Kristen flies to Jackson on Sunday night, spends the week at the district office, and returns home to Atlanta on Friday afternoon. The cost of returning home is $550, while the cost of spending the weekend in Jackson would have been $490.

    a. Presuming no reimbursement for these expenses, how much, if any, of these weekend expenses may Kristen deduct?
    b. Would your answer in part (a) change if the amounts involved were reversed (i.e., the trip home cost $490; staying in Jackson would have been $550)? Explain.

27. **LO.3** In June of this year, Dr. and Mrs. Bret Spencer traveled to Denver to attend a three-day conference sponsored by the American Society of Implant Dentistry. Bret, a self-employed practicing oral surgeon, participated in scheduled technical sessions dealing with the latest developments in surgical procedures. On two days, Mrs. Spencer attended group meetings where various aspects of family tax planning were discussed. On the other day, she went sightseeing. Mrs. Spencer does not work for her husband, but she does their tax returns and handles the family investments. Expenses incurred in connection with the conference are summarized as follows.

Airfare (two tickets)	$2,000
Lodging (single and double occupancy are the same rate—$250 each day)	750
Meals ($200 × 3 days)*	600
Conference registration fee (includes $120 for Family Tax Planning sessions)	620
Car rental	300

*Split equally between Dr. and Mrs. Spencer.

How much, if any, of these expenses can the Spencers deduct?

28. **LO.3** On Thursday, Justin flies from Baltimore (his home office) to Cadiz (Spain). He conducts business on Friday and Tuesday; vacations on Saturday, Sunday, and Monday (a legal holiday in Spain); and returns to Baltimore on Thursday. Justin was scheduled to return home on Wednesday, but all flights were canceled due to bad weather. Therefore, he spent Wednesday watching floor shows at a local casino.

   a. For tax purposes, what portion of Justin's trip is regarded as being for business?

   b. Suppose Monday had not been a legal holiday. Would this change your answer to part (a)? Explain.

   c. Under either part (a) or (b), how much of Justin's airfare qualifies as a deductible business expense?

Ethics and Equity   29. **LO.3** Veronica is a key employee of Perdiz Corporation, an aerospace engineering concern located in Seattle. Perdiz would like to establish an office on the east coast of Florida and wants Veronica to be in charge of the branch. Veronica is hesitant about making the move because she fears she will have to sell her residence in Seattle at a loss. Perdiz buys the house from Veronica for $420,000, its cost to her. She has owned and occupied the house as her principal residence for eight years. One year later, Perdiz resells the property for $370,000.

   Nothing regarding the sale of the residence is ever reflected on Veronica's income tax returns. Perdiz absorbs all of Veronica's moving expenses. As an ethical tax professional, do you have any qualms as to the way these matters have been handled for income tax purposes? Explain.

30. **LO.3, 4** Christine is a full-time teacher of the fourth grade at Vireo Academy. During the current year, she spends $1,400 for classroom supplies. On the submission of adequate substantiation, Vireo reimburses her for $500 of these expenses—the maximum reimbursement allowed for supplies under school policy. [The reimbursement is not shown as income (Box 1) of Form W–2 given to Christine by Vireo.] What are the income tax consequences of the $1,400 if Christine:

   a. Itemizes her deductions *from* AGI?

   b. Chooses the standard deduction?

Critical Thinking   31. **LO.3** Elijah is employed as a full-time high school teacher. The school district for which he works recently instituted a policy requiring all of its teachers to start working on a master's degree. Pursuant to this new rule, Elijah spent most of the summer of 2018 taking graduate courses at an out-of-town university. His expenses include:

Tuition	$6,600
Books and course materials	1,500
Lodging	1,700
Meals	2,200
Laundry and dry cleaning	200
Campus parking	300

In addition, Elijah drove his personal automobile 2,200 miles in connection with the education. He uses the automatic mileage method.

a. How much, if any, of these expenses might qualify as a deduction *for* AGI?

b. How much, if any, of these expenses might qualify as a deduction *from* AGI?

32. **LO.3** In each of the following independent situations, determine how much, if any, qualifies as a deduction *for* AGI under § 222 (targeted tuition and related expenses).   **Critical Thinking**

a. Lily is single and is employed as an architect. During 2018, she spent $4,100 in tuition to attend law school at night. Her MAGI is $64,000.

b. Liam is single and is employed as a pharmacist. During 2018, he spent $2,400 ($2,100 for tuition and $300 for books) to take a course in herbal supplements at a local university. His MAGI is $81,000.

c. Hailey is married and is employed as a bookkeeper. She spends $5,200 for tuition and $900 for books and supplies to pursue a bachelor's degree in accounting. Her MAGI is $40,000 on the separate return that she files.

d. John spends $6,500 of his savings for tuition to attend Carmine State College. John is claimed as a dependent by his parents.

33. **LO.6** Ashley (a single taxpayer) is the owner of ABC LLC. The LLC (a sole proprietorship) reports QBI of $900,000 and is not a "specified services" business. ABC paid total W–2 wages of $300,000, and the total unadjusted basis of property held by ABC is $30,000. Ashley's taxable income before the QBI deduction is $740,000 (this is also her modified taxable income). What is Ashley's QBI deduction for 2018?   **Decision Making**

34. **LO.5** Janet, age 29, is unmarried and is an active participant in a qualified retirement plan. Her modified AGI is $65,000 in 2018.

a. Calculate the amount Janet can contribute to a traditional IRA and the amount she can deduct.

b. Assume instead that Janet is a participant in a SIMPLE IRA and that she elects to contribute 4% of her compensation to the account, while her employer contributes 3%. What amount will be contributed for 2018? What amount will be vested?

35. **LO.5** Carri and Dane, ages 34 and 32, respectively, have been married for 11 years, and both are active participants in employer-qualified retirement plans. Their total AGI in 2018 is $192,000, and they earn salaries of $87,000 and $95,000, respectively. What amount may Carri and Dane:

a. Contribute to regular IRAs?

b. Deduct for their contributions in part (a)?

c. Contribute to Roth IRAs?

d. Deduct for their contributions in part (c)?

36. **LO.6** In 2018, Susan's sole proprietorship earns $300,000 of self-employment net income (after the deduction for one-half of self-employment tax). Calculate the maximum amount Susan can deduct for contributions to a defined contribution Keogh plan.

37. **LO.6** Harvey is a self-employed accountant with earned income from the business of $120,000 (after the deduction for one-half of his self-employment tax). He has a profit sharing plan (e.g., defined contribution Keogh plan). What is the maximum amount Harvey can contribute to his retirement plan in 2018?

38. **LO.7** Alex, who is single, conducts an activity this year that is classified as a hobby. The activity produces the following revenues and expenses.

Revenue	$18,000
Property taxes	3,000
Materials and supplies	4,500
Utilities	2,000
Advertising	5,000
Insurance	750
Depreciation	4,000

Without regard to this activity, Alex's AGI is $42,000. Determine the amount of gross income that Alex must report, the amount of the expenses he is permitted to deduct, and his taxable income from the hobby.

Comprehensive Tax Return Problems

Critical Thinking

1. Beth R. Jordan lives at 2322 Skyview Road, Mesa, AZ 85201. She is a tax accountant with Mesa Manufacturing Company, 1203 Western Avenue, Mesa, AZ 85201 (employer identification number 11-1111111). She also writes computer software programs for tax practitioners and has a part-time tax practice. Beth is single and has no dependents. Beth's birthday is July 4, 1972, and her Social Security number is 123-45-6789. She wants to contribute $3 to the Presidential Election Campaign Fund.

   The following information is shown on Beth's Wage and Tax Statement (Form W–2) for 2018.

Line	Description	Amount
1	Wages, tips, other compensation	$65,000.00
2	Federal income tax withheld	10,500.00
3	Social Security wages	65,000.00
4	Social Security tax withheld	4,030.00
5	Medicare wages and tips	65,000.00
6	Medicare tax withheld	942.50
15	State	Arizona
16	State wages, tips, etc.	65,000.00
17	State income tax withheld	1,954.00

During the year, Beth received interest of $1,300 from Arizona Federal Savings and Loan and $400 from Arizona State Bank. Each financial institution reported the interest income on a Form 1099–INT. She received qualified dividends of $800 from Blue Corporation, $750 from Green Corporation, and $650 from Orange Corporation. Each corporation reported Beth's dividend payments on a Form 1099–DIV.

Beth received a $1,100 income tax refund from the state of Arizona on April 29, 2018. On her 2017 Federal income tax return, she reported total itemized deductions of $8,200, which included $2,200 of state income tax withheld by her employer.

Fees earned from her part-time tax practice in 2018 totaled $3,800. She paid $600 to have the tax returns processed by a computerized tax return service.

On February 8, 2018, Beth bought 500 shares of Gray Corporation common stock for $17.60 a share. On September 12, 2018, she sold the stock for $14 a share.

Beth bought a used sports utility vehicle for $6,000 on June 5, 2018. She purchased the vehicle from her brother-in-law, who was unemployed and was in need of cash. On November 2, 2018, she sold the vehicle to a friend for $6,500.

On January 2, 2018, Beth acquired 100 shares of Blue Corporation common stock for $30 a share. She sold the stock on December 19, 2018, for $55 a share.

During the year, Beth records revenues of $16,000 from the sale of a software program she developed. She incurred the following expenditures in connection with her software development business.

Cost of personal computer	$7,000
Cost of printer	2,000
Furniture	3,000
Supplies	650
Fee paid to computer consultant	3,500

Beth elected to expense the maximum portion of the cost of the computer, printer, and furniture allowed under the provisions of § 179. These items were placed in service on January 15, 2018, and used 100% in her business.

Although Mesa suggested that Beth attend a convention on current developments in corporate taxation, Beth was not reimbursed for the travel expenses of $1,420 she incurred in attending. The $1,420 included $200 for meals.

During the year, Beth paid $300 for prescription medicines and $2,875 for medical bills. Medical insurance premiums were paid for her by her employer, covering her for the entire year.

Beth paid real property taxes of $1,766 on her home. Interest on her home mortgage (Valley National Bank) was $3,845, and interest to credit card companies was $320. Beth contributed $2,080 to various charities during the year. Professional dues and subscriptions totaled $350. Beth paid estimated Federal income taxes of $1,000.

Part 1—Tax Computation

Compute the net tax payable or refund due for Beth R. Jordan for 2018. If you use tax forms for your solution, you will need Forms 1040, 2106-EZ, and 4562 and Schedules A, B, C, D, and SE.

Part 2—Tax Planning

Beth is anticipating significant changes in her life in 2019, and she has asked you to estimate her taxable income and tax liability for 2019. She just received word that she has been qualified to adopt a 2-year-old daughter. Beth expects that the adoption will be finalized in 2019 and that she will incur approximately $2,000 of adoption expenses. In addition, she expects to incur approximately $3,500 of child and dependent care expenses relating to the care of her new daughter, which will enable her to keep her job at Mesa Manufacturing Company.

However, with the additional demands on her time because of her daughter, she has decided to discontinue her two part-time jobs (i.e., the part-time tax practice and her software business), and she will cease making estimated income tax payments. In your computations, assume that all other income and expenditures will remain at approximately the same levels as in 2018. Use 2018 standard deduction amounts and Tax Rate Schedules in your analysis.

2. David R. and Ella M. Cole (ages 39 and 38, respectively) are husband and wife who live at 1820 Elk Avenue, Denver, CO 80202. David is a self-employed consultant, specializing in retail management and Ella is a dental hygienist for a chain of dental clinics.

   Communications

   Critical Thinking

   Decision Making

   • David earned consulting fees of $145,000 in 2018. He maintains his own office and pays for all business expenses. The Coles are adequately covered by the medical plan provided by Ella's employer, but have chosen not to participate in its § 401(k) retirement plan.

David's employment-related expenses for 2018 are summarized below.

Airfare	$8,800
Lodging	5,000
Meals (during travel status)	4,800
Entertainment	3,600
Ground transportation (e.g., limos, rental cars, and taxis)	800
Business gifts	900
Office supplies (includes postage, overnight delivery, and copying)	1,500

The entertainment involved taking clients to sporting and musical events and providing food before, during, or after those events. The business gifts consisted of $50 gift certificates to a national restaurant. These were sent by David during the Christmas holidays to 18 of his major clients.

In addition, David drove his 2016 Ford Expedition 11,000 miles for business and 3,000 for personal use during 2018. He purchased the Expedition on August 15, 2015; David always has used the automatic (standard) mileage method for tax purposes. Parking and tolls relating to business use total $340 in 2018.

- When the Coles purchased their present residence in April 2015, they devoted 450 of the 3,000 square feet of living space to an office for David. The property cost $440,000 ($40,000 of which is attributable to the land) and has since appreciated in value. Expenses relating to the residence in 2018 (except for mortgage interest and property taxes; see below) are reported as follows.

Insurance	$2,600
Repairs and maintenance	900
Utilities	4,700
Painting office area; area rugs and plants (in the office)	1,800

In terms of depreciation, the Coles use the MACRS percentage tables applicable to 39-year nonresidential real property. As to depreciable personalty (e.g., office furniture), David tries to avoid capitalization and uses whatever method provides the fastest deduction for tax purposes.

- Ella works at a variety of offices as a substitute for whichever hygienist is ill or on vacation or when one of the clinics is particularly busy (e.g., prior to the beginning of the school year). Besides her transportation, she must provide and maintain her own uniforms. Her expenses for 2018 appear below.

Uniforms	$690
State and city occupational licenses	380
Professional journals and membership dues in the American Dental Hygiene Association	340
Correspondence study course (taken online) dealing with teeth whitening procedures	420

Ella's salary for the year is $42,000, and her Form W–2 for the year shows income tax withholdings of $5,000 (Federal) and $1,000 (state) and the proper amount of Social Security and Medicare taxes.

- In addition to those items already mentioned, the Coles had the following receipts during 2018.

Interest income—		
State of Colorado general purpose bonds	$2,500	
IBM bonds	800	
Wells Fargo Bank	1,200	$ 4,500
Federal income tax refund for year 2017		510
Life insurance proceeds paid by Eagle Assurance Corporation		200,000
Inheritance of savings account from Sarah Cole		50,000
Sales proceeds from two ATVs		9,000

For several years, the Coles household has included David's divorced mother, Sarah, who has been claimed as their dependent. In late December 2017, Sarah unexpectedly died in her sleep. Unknown to Ella and David, Sarah owned a life insurance policy and a savings account (with David as the designated beneficiary of each).

In 2017, the Coles purchased two ATVs for $14,000. After several near mishaps, they decided that the sport was too dangerous. In 2018, they sold the ATVs to their neighbor.

- Additional expenditures for 2018 include the following.

Funeral expenses for Sarah		$ 4,500
Taxes—		
Real property taxes on personal residence	$6,400	
Colorado state income tax due (paid in April 2018 for tax year 2017)	310	6,710
Mortgage interest on personal residence (Rocky Mountain Bank)		6,600
Paid church pledge		2,400
Contributions to traditional IRAs for Ella and David ($5,500 + $5,500)		11,000

In 2016, the Coles made quarterly estimated tax payments of $6,000 (Federal) and $500 (state) for a total of $24,000 (Federal) and $2,000 (state).

Part 1—Tax Computation

Using the appropriate forms and schedules, compute David and Ella's joint Federal income tax for 2018. Disregard the alternative minimum tax (AMT) and various education credits. Relevant Social Security numbers are:

David Cole	123-45-6788
Ella Cole	123-45-6787

The Coles do not want to contribute to the Presidential Election Campaign Fund. They want any overpayment of tax refunded to them and *not* applied toward next year's tax liability. Note that David will have a self-employment tax liability.

Part 2—Follow-Up Advice

Ella has always wanted to pursue a career in nursing. To this end, she has earned a substantial number of college credits on a part-time basis. With Sarah no longer requiring home care, Ella believes that she now can complete her degree by attending college on a full-time basis.

David would like to know how Ella's plans will affect their income tax position. Specifically, he wants to know:

- How much Federal income tax they will save if Ella quits her job.
- Any tax benefits that might be available from the cost of the education.

Write a letter to David, addressing these concerns. In making your projections, assume that David's salary and expenses remain the same. Disregard any consideration of the educational tax credits (i.e., American Opportunity and lifetime learning).

BRIDGE DISCIPLINE

1. Justin performs services for Partridge, Inc., and receives compensation of $85,000 for the year. Determine the tax consequences of Social Security and Medicare on Justin's take-home pay if:
   a. Justin is classified as an employee of Partridge.
   b. Justin is classified as an independent contractor.

2. The Code contains provisions that are "friendly" to specific groups of taxpayers. Among these are the following.
   • Senior citizens.
   • Married taxpayers.
   • Employed taxpayers.
   • Taxpayers with children.
   • Self-employed taxpayers.

   Provide justification for the special treatment for each of the above groups, and give an example of such special treatment for each group.

Research Problems

THOMSON REUTERS
CHECKPOINT™

Note: Solutions to the Research Problems can be prepared by using the Thomson Reuters Checkpoint™ online tax research database, which accompanies this textbook. Solutions can also be prepared by using research materials found in a typical tax library.

Communications

Research Problem 1. Your client, Jasper, is an employee of a defense contractor and was assigned to work on a military base in Australia. As a condition of his employment, he was required to live in housing that was provided to military personnel. The housing provided was a condominium located in a civilian neighborhood that was 20 miles from the military base where he performed his services.

The employer paid over $6,000 of rent while Jasper was living there. He would like to know whether the value of the housing can be excluded from his gross income. Jasper read an article that indicated that employees who are required to live in a "camp" in a foreign country can exclude the cost of the housing from gross income. Send an e-mail to your instructor summarizing your findings.

Communications
Critical Thinking

Research Problem 2. Rick Beam has been an independent sales representative for various textile manufacturers for many years. His products consist of soft goods such as tablecloths, curtains, and drapes. Rick's customers are clothing store chains, department stores, and smaller specialty stores. The employees of these companies who are responsible for purchasing merchandise are known as buyers. These companies generally prohibit their buyers from accepting gifts from manufacturers' sales representatives.

Each year, Rick gives cash gifts (never more than $25) to most of the buyers who are his customers. Generally, he cashes a large check in November and gives the money personally to the buyers around Christmas. Rick says, "This is one of the ways that I maintain my relationship with my buyers." He maintains adequate substantiation of all of the gifts.

Rick's deductions for these gifts have been disallowed by the IRS based on § 162(c)(2). Rick is confused and comes to you, a CPA, for advice.

a. Write a letter to Rick concerning his tax position on this issue. Rick's address is 948 Octavia Street, Baton Rouge, LA 70821.

b. Prepare a memo for your files supporting the advice you have given.

Research Problem 3. Aaron, a resident of Minnesota, has been a driver for Green Delivery Service for the past six years. For this purpose, he leases a truck from Green, and his compensation is based on a percentage of the income resulting from his pickup and delivery services. Green allows its drivers to choose their 10-hour shifts and does not exercise any control on how these services are carried out (e.g., the route to be taken or the order in which parcels are delivered or picked up). Under Green's operating agreement with its drivers, Green can terminate the arrangement after 30 days' notice. In practice, however, Green allows its truckers to quit immediately without giving advance notice. The agreement also labels the drivers as independent contractors.

Critical Thinking

Green maintains no health or retirement plans for its drivers, and each year it reports their income by issuing Forms 1099–MISC (and not Forms W–2). Green requires its drivers to maintain a commercial driver's license and be in good standing with the state highway law enforcement division.

Citing the employment tax Regulations in §§ 31.3121(d)–1(c)(2) and 31.3306(i)–1(b), an IRS agent contends that Aaron is an independent contractor and, therefore, is subject to the self-employment tax. Based on *Peno Trucking, Inc.* (93 TCM 1027, T.C.Memo. 2007–66), Aaron disagrees and contends that he is an employee (i.e., not self-employed). Who is correct? Why?

Use internet tax resources to address the following questions. Look for reliable websites and blogs of the IRS and other government agencies, media outlets, businesses, tax professionals, academics, think tanks, and political outlets.

Research Problem 4. Jacob Patterson cannot make a fully deductible $5,500 IRA contribution because his AGI exceeds the phaseout range. Instead, he makes a $3,500 nondeductible IRA contribution to his traditional IRA. Determine how Jacob reports this on his tax return, and complete the appropriate form that he should attach to his Form 1040.

Research Problem 5. Sarah was contemplating making a contribution to her traditional IRA in 2017. She determined she would contribute $5,000 in December 2017, but forgot about making the contribution until she was preparing her 2017 tax return in February 2018. Use the website of any well-known IRA provider (e.g., Fidelity, Vanguard, T. Rowe Price) to determine if Sarah can make a deductible 2017 contribution to her IRA after the tax year has ended.

Becker CPA Review Questions

1. Linda is an employee of JRH Corporation. Which of the following is included in Linda's gross income?

   a. Premiums paid by JRH Corporation for a group term life insurance policy for $50,000 of coverage for Linda.

   b. $1,000 of tuition paid by JRH Corporation to State University for Linda's master's degree program.

   c. A $2,000 trip given to Linda by JRH Corporation for meeting sales goals.

   d. $1,200 paid by JRH Corporation for an annual parking pass for Linda.

2. Bob and Nancy are married and file a joint return. They are both under age 50 and employed, with wages of $50,000 each. Their total AGI is $110,000. Neither of them is an active participant in a qualified plan. What is the maximum traditional IRA deduction they can take for the current year?

   a. $0

   b. $5,500

   c. $7,700

   d. $11,000

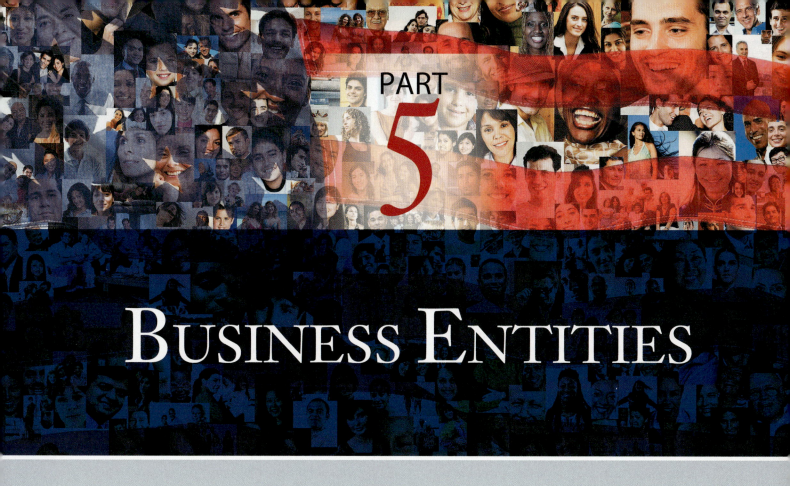

PART 5

BUSINESS ENTITIES

CHAPTER **12**
Corporations: Organization, Capital Structure, and Operating Rules

CHAPTER **13**
Corporations: Earnings & Profits and Distributions

CHAPTER **14**
Partnerships and Limited Liability Entities

CHAPTER **15**
S Corporations

Part 5 focuses on the tax effects of common legal forms with which to conduct business. The discussion includes an analysis of the life cycle of a business, from formation, to the taxation of business activities, through the termination of the entity. The specific business entities covered are the C corporation, the S corporation, the partnership, and the LLC. Rules also are reviewed as to the Federal income tax treatment of distributions from a C corporation, and special provisions for noncorporate businesses.

Corporations: Organization, Capital Structure, and Operating Rules

LEARNING OBJECTIVES: *After completing Chapter 12, you should be able to:*

LO.1 Identify major tax and nontax considerations associated with the corporate form of business.

LO.2 Explain the tax consequences of incorporating and transferring assets to controlled corporations.

LO.3 Describe the special rules that apply when a corporation assumes a shareholder's liability.

LO.4 Identify the basis issues relevant to the shareholder and the corporation.

LO.5 Explain the tax aspects of the capital structure of a corporation.

LO.6 Characterize the tax differences between debt and equity investments.

LO.7 List and apply the tax rules unique to corporations.

LO.8 Compute the corporate income tax.

LO.9 Explain the rules unique to computing the tax of related corporations.

LO.10 Describe the reporting process for corporations.

CHAPTER OUTLINE

12-1 An Introduction to Corporate Tax, 12-2
    12-1a Double Taxation of Corporate Income, 12-2
    12-1b Comparison of Corporations and Other Forms of Doing Business, 12-3
    12-1c Nontax Considerations, 12-6
    12-1d Limited Liability Companies, 12-7
    12-1e Entity Classification, 12-7

12-2 Organization of and Transfers to Controlled Corporations, 12-8
    12-2a Section 351 Rationale and General Rules, 12-8
    12-2b Transfer of Property, 12-10
    12-2c Stock, 12-11
    12-2d Control of the Corporation, 12-12
    12-2e Assumption of Liabilities—§ 357, 12-15
    12-2f Basis Determination and Other Issues, 12-20
    12-2g Recapture Considerations, 12-24

12-3 Capital Structure of a Corporation, 12-25
    12-3a Capital Contributions, 12-25
    12-3b Debt in the Capital Structure, 12-26

12-4 Corporate Operations, 12-28
    12-4a Deductions Available Only to Corporations, 12-28
    12-4b Business Interest Expense Limitation, 12-31
    12-4c Determining the Corporate Income Tax Liability, 12-34
    12-4d Controlled Groups, 12-34

12-5 Procedural Matters, 12-35
    12-5a Filing Requirements for Corporations, 12-35
    12-5b Estimated Tax Payments, 12-36
    12-5c Schedule M–1—Reconciliation of Income (Loss) per Books with Income per Return, 12-36
    12-5d Schedule M–2—Analysis of Unappropriated Retained Earnings per Books, 12-38
    12-5e Schedule M–3—Net Income (Loss) Reconciliation for Corporations with Total Assets of $10 Million or More, 12-38
    12-5f Effect of Taxes on Financial Statements, 12-39

TAX TALK *Taxes owing to the Government … are the price that business has to pay for protection and security.* —BENJAMIN N. CARDOZO

Taxation of Dividends

Double taxation stems, in part, from the nondeductibility of a C corporation's dividend distributions. This gives shareholders of a closely held corporation an incentive to try to convert dividend distributions into tax deductible expenses. A common way to do this is to increase compensation to shareholder-employees. However, the IRS scrutinizes compensation and other economic transactions (e.g., loans, leases, and sales) between shareholders and closely held corporations to ensure that payments are reasonable in amount.[2]

To reduce the severity of double taxation, Congress reduced the tax rate applicable to the dividend income of individuals. Qualified dividend income is taxed at the same preferential rate as long-term capital gains—20 percent, 15 percent, or 0 percent. Most commonly, the 15 percent rate applies. However, the 20 percent rate applies to high-income taxpayers and the 0 percent rate applies to lower-income taxpayers.[3]

12-1b Comparison of Corporations and Other Forms of Doing Business

When comparing C corporations to other business forms, there are a number of factors to consider, including:

- Tax rates;
- Character of business income;
- Business losses;
- Employment taxes; and
- State taxes.

Each of these is discussed below.[4]

Tax Rates As noted earlier, a flat rate of 21 percent applies to corporate taxable income for taxable years beginning after 2017. Before the enactment of the Tax Cuts and Jobs Act (TCJA) of 2017, the marginal tax rates for corporations ranged from 15 percent to 39 percent (see Exhibit 12.1).

---

[2]See Chapter 13 for a discussion of constructive dividends.

[3]In addition, a 3.8 percent additional tax applies to net investment income in excess of modified adjusted gross income of $200,000 ($250,000 if married filing jointly), thus increasing the double taxation of dividend income for high-income taxpayers.

[4]Chapter 18 presents a detailed comparison of sole proprietorships, partnerships, S corporations, and C corporations as forms of doing business.

EXHIBIT 2.1	Corporate Income Tax Rates for Taxable Years Beginning Before 2018

Taxable Income		Tax Is:	Of the Amount Over—
Over—	**But Not Over—**		
$ 0	$ 50,000	15%	$ 0
50,000	75,000	$ 7,500 + 25%	50,000
75,000	100,000	13,750 + 34%	75,000
100,000	335,000	22,250 + 39%	100,000
335,000	10,000,000	113,900 + 34%	335,000
10,000,000	15,000,000	3,400,000 + 35%	10,000,000
15,000,000	18,333,333	5,150,000 + 38%	15,000,000
18,333,333	—	35%	0

Note: Personal Service Corporations (PSCs) are taxed at a flat rate of 35%.

In contrast to the flat corporate rate, individuals face marginal tax rates that range from 10 percent to 37 percent. In some cases, taxes will be greater in the corporate form (as in Example 1). However, the corporate form of doing business presents tax savings opportunities when the applicable corporate marginal rate is *lower* than the applicable individual marginal rate. The post-2017 flat 21 percent corporate rate significantly increases the likelihood of these tax savings opportunities, especially for corporations that pay little or no dividends.

EXAMPLE 3

Susanna, an individual taxpayer in the 37% marginal tax rate bracket, can generate $100,000 of additional taxable income in the current year. If the income is taxed to Susanna, the associated tax is $37,000 ($100,000 × 37%).

If, however, Susanna can shift the income to a newly created corporation, the corporate tax is $21,000. The lower corporate marginal tax rates result in a tax *savings* of $16,000 ($37,000 − $21,000).

Any attempt to take advantage of the difference between the corporate and individual marginal tax rates also must consider the effect of double taxation. When the preferential rate for dividend income is considered, however, tax savings opportunities still exist.

TAX FACT   Corporations' Reporting Responsibilities

Like individuals, corporations are required to report their taxable income and other financial information to the IRS on an annual basis. The forms used depend on the type and size of the corporation. Based on projections, the IRS expects to receive approximately 6.9 million corporate income tax returns during the 2017 filing season.

Interestingly, nearly 79 percent of C and S corporations are expected to submit their returns electronically.

Type of Corporation	Form	Percentage
C corporation	1120	25.1%
C corporation	Others	5.1
S corporation	1120S	69.8
		100.0%

Source: Fiscal Year Return Projections for the United States: 2015–2022, IRS, Publication 6292, Spring 2015 Update, Table 1.

Assume in Example 3 that the corporation distributes all of its after-tax earnings to Susanna as a dividend. The dividend results in income tax of $15,800 [($100,000 − $21,000) × 20%] to Susanna.

Thus, even when the double taxation effect is considered, the combined tax burden of $36,800 ($21,000 paid by the corporation + $15,800 paid by the shareholder) represents an income tax *savings* of $200 when compared to the $37,000 of tax that results from taxing the $100,000 of income at Susanna's 37% marginal rate. The present value of these tax savings increases if the corporation distributes only part of its earnings as dividends.

Examples 3 and 4 ignore other tax issues that taxpayers must consider in selecting the proper form of doing business, but they illustrate potential tax savings that taxpayers can achieve by taking advantage of tax rate differentials.

Character of Business Income Unlike other forms of business, the tax attributes of income and expense items of a C corporation do not pass through the corporate entity to the shareholders. As a result, if the business is expected to generate tax-favored income (e.g., tax-exempt income or long-term capital gains), it may be better to choose a different business form.

Business Losses C corporation losses are treated differently than losses of other business forms. Proprietorships, partnerships, and S corporations allow their owners to deduct losses from these entities, subject to limits. In contrast, a C corporation retains its losses for use against its own future income. Therefore, if losses are anticipated, it may be better to choose a business form other than a C corporation.

Franco plans to start a business this year. He expects that the business will incur operating losses for the first three years and then become highly profitable. Franco decides to operate as an S corporation during the loss period because the losses will flow through and be deductible on his personal return. When the business becomes profitable, he intends to switch to C corporation status.

Employment Taxes The net income of a proprietorship is subject to the self-employment tax (15.3 percent), as are some partnership allocations of income to partners. Alternatively, wages paid to a shareholder-employee of a corporation (C or S) are subject to payroll taxes. The combined corporation-employee payroll tax burden must be compared with the self-employment tax in the proprietorship and partnership business forms. This analysis should include the benefit of the deduction available to a corporation for payroll taxes paid, as well as the deduction available to an individual for one-half of the self-employment taxes paid.

State Taxes At the entity level, state corporate income taxes and/or franchise taxes apply to corporations. Some states impose a corporate income tax or franchise tax on

BRIDGE DISCIPLINE Bridge to Finance

Investment brokers and promoters often try to entice individuals to invest their disposable income in ventures designed to produce handsome returns. In most situations, the type of business entity in which the funds are invested takes the form of a "flow-through" entity, such as a limited partnership. Such investment ventures rarely operate as regular corporations.

A limited partnership is the favored investment vehicle for several reasons. One of the most significant reasons is that the investors who become limited partners are protected from ex-posure to unlimited liability. In addition, any operating losses of the entity (which may be expected in the venture's early years) flow through to the partners and, as a result, may provide an immediate tax benefit on the partners' returns. Another major advantage of the partnership form, in contrast to the corporate form, is that the business earnings are subject to only one level of tax—at the partner or investor level. If the investments were housed in a corporation, a tax would be levied first on the corporate earnings and then at the investor level when the corporation makes distributions to the shareholders.

all business forms (including partnerships and S corporations). If a business will be operating in multiple states, state taxes become more important (Chapter 16 discusses the taxation of multistate corporations). At the owner level, the income of sole proprietorships, S corporations, and partnerships (along with dividend distributions) is subject to state individual income taxation.

The tax attributes of the various forms of business entities are compared in Concept Summary 12.1.

12-1c Nontax Considerations

Nontax considerations may outweigh tax considerations and lead owners to conclude that they should operate a business as a corporation. Here are some of the more important *nontax considerations*:

- Sole proprietors and general partners in partnerships face the danger of *unlimited liability*. That is, business creditors can file claims against the assets of the business *and* the *personal* assets of proprietors or general partners. State corporate law protects the personal assets of shareholders.

Concept Summary 12.1

Tax Treatment of Business Forms Compared

	Sole Proprietorships	Partnerships	S Corporations	Regular (C) Corporations
Entity tax return	None	Form 1065	Form 1120S	Form 1120
Taxation of entity income	No separate entity-level income tax. Proprietorship's income and expenses are reported on owner's Form 1040 (Schedule C). Character of entity income and expenses retained at owner level.	No separate entity-level income tax. Partnership's income and expenses are allocated and reported (on Schedule K–1) to partners who report these items on their returns (e.g., Form 1040 for individual partners). Character of entity income and expenses retained at partner level.	Generally, no separate entity-level income tax. S corporation's income and expenses are allocated and reported (Schedule K–1) to shareholders who report these items on their returns (e.g., Form 1040 for individual shareholders). Character of entity income and expenses retained at shareholder level.	Corporate income tax applies at a flat 21% rate.
Taxation of withdrawals/ distributions from entity	Withdrawals by owner are not subject to separate tax.	Distributions to partners are generally not subject to separate tax.	Distributions to shareholders are generally not subject to separate tax.	Character of entity income and expenses not retained at shareholder level. Instead, distributions to shareholders are generally taxed as dividend income. Preferential tax rates (0%/15%/20%) apply to qualified dividends.
Employment taxes	Schedule C income subject to self-employment tax.	Some partnership allocations subject to self-employment tax.	Compensation paid to shareholder/employees subject to payroll taxes. Shareholder's allocated portion of entity income not subject to self-employment tax.	Compensation paid to shareholder/employees subject to payroll taxes.

- The corporate form of business provides a vehicle for *raising capital* through widespread stock ownership. Most major businesses in the United States are operated as corporations.

- Shares of stock in a corporation are *freely transferable*; a partner's sale of his or her partnership interest must be approved by the other partners.

- A corporation continues to exist if shareholders die or sell their stock. In contrast, death or withdrawal of a partner may terminate the existing partnership and cause financial difficulties that result in dissolution of the entity. Thus, *continuity of life* is a distinct advantage of the corporate form.

- Corporations have *centralized management*. All management responsibility is assigned to a board of directors, which appoints officers to carry out the corporation's business. Partnerships often have decentralized management, in which every partner has a right to participate in the organization's business decisions. Limited partnerships, though, may have centralized management.

12-1d Limited Liability Companies

The limited liability company (LLC) is a business form that blends some corporate form advantages into a flow-through entity. All 50 states and the District of Columbia have passed laws that allow LLCs, and thousands of companies have chosen LLC status. As with a corporation, operating as an LLC allows its owners (called "members") to avoid unlimited liability, which is a primary *nontax* consideration in choosing a business form. The tax advantage of LLCs is that qualifying businesses may be treated as proprietorship or partnership for tax purposes, thereby avoiding the problem of double taxation associated with regular corporations.[5]

12-1e Entity Classification

There is a long history of taxpayers and the IRS disagreeing about taxing a business as a corporation or as a partnership. To ease this problem, the Treasury Department issued check-the-box Regulations.[6] The Regulations enable taxpayers to choose the tax status of a business entity without regard to its corporate (or noncorporate) characteristics. These rules simplified tax administration considerably and eliminated much of the litigation that arose under prior law.

Under the check-the-box Regulations, an unincorporated entity with *more than one* owner is, by default, classified as a partnership. An unincorporated entity with *only one* owner is, by default, classified as a disregarded entity, which the Regulations treat as a sole proprietorship for an individual owner or as a branch or a division of a corporate owner. If the entity wants to use its default status, it simply files the appropriate tax return. If a taxpayer wants to use a different status or change its status, it does so by "checking a box" on Form 8832. Thus, an LLC (single or multi-member) can choose to be taxed as a C corporation and, if it otherwise qualifies, even elect S corporation status.[7] Although an LLC does not typically pay Federal income taxes, LLCs must report and pay employment and excise taxes.

In-depth coverage can be found on this book's companion website: www.cengage.com   **1** DIGGING DEEPER

---

[5]Some states allow an LLC to have centralized management, but not continuity of life or free transferability of interests. Other states allow LLCs to adopt any or all of the corporate characteristics of centralized management, continuity of life, and free transferability of interests. The comparison of business entities in Chapter 18 includes a discussion of LLCs.

[6]Reg. §§ 301.7701–1 through −4, and −7.

[7]The status election is not available to entities that are incorporated under state law or to entities that are required to be taxed as corporations under Federal law (e.g., certain publicly traded partnerships). State law does not treat LLCs as corporations, so they default to either partnership or proprietorship status.

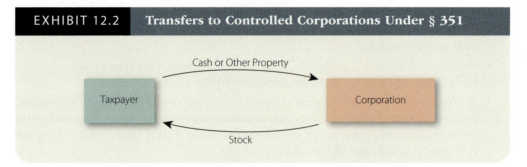

EXHIBIT 12.2   **Transfers to Controlled Corporations Under § 351**

Cash or Other Property

Taxpayer → Corporation

Stock

LO.2

Explain the tax consequences of incorporating and transferring assets to controlled corporations.

12-2 ORGANIZATION OF AND TRANSFERS TO CONTROLLED CORPORATIONS

Property transactions normally produce tax consequences if a gain or loss is realized. As a result, unless special provisions in the Code apply, a transfer of property to a corporation in exchange for stock is a taxable transaction. The amount of gain or loss is measured by the difference between the fair market value of the stock received and the tax basis of the property transferred.

12-2a Section 351 Rationale and General Rules

In contrast to the typical result of full gain or loss recognition, the Code permits non-recognition of gain or loss in limited circumstances. For example, with both § 1031 (like-kind exchanges—see Chapter 7) and § 351 (transfers of property to controlled corporations), gain or loss is postponed until a substantive change in the taxpayer's investment occurs (e.g., a sale of property or ownership shares to outsiders). When a taxpayer exchanges some of his or her property for other property of a like kind, § 1031 provides that gain (or loss) realized on the exchange is not recognized because a substantive change in the taxpayer's investment has not occurred. The deferral of gain or loss is accomplished by calculating a substituted basis for the like-kind property received. With this substituted basis, the realized gain or loss associated with the property given up is ultimately recognized when the property received in the exchange is sold.

In a similar fashion and as illustrated in Exhibit 12.2, § 351, which deals with transfers to *controlled corporations* (defined later in the chapter), provides that gain or loss is not recognized upon the transfer of property to a corporation in exchange for its own stock. For example, when a business is incorporated, the owner's economic status remains the same; only the *form* of the investment has changed. The investment in the business assets carries over to an investment in corporate stock. When only stock in the corporation is received, the shareholder is hardly in a position to pay a tax on any realized gain. Thus, this approach is justified under the *wherewithal to pay concept* discussed in Chapter 1. As noted later, however, when the taxpayer receives property other than stock (i.e., cash or other "boot") from the corporation, some or all of the realized gain is recognized.

A further justification for the nonrecognition of gain or loss provisions under § 351 is that Congress believes tax rules should not impede the exercise of sound business judgment (e.g., choice of entity form of conducting business). That is, Congress wanted to eliminate a tax disincentive to form corporations that would exist if shareholders paid tax when forming a corporation.

EXAMPLE 6

Ron is considering incorporating his sole proprietorship. He is concerned about his personal liability for the obligations of the business. Ron realizes that if he incorporates, depending on state law, he will be liable only for the debts of the business that he has personally guaranteed. If Ron incorporates his business, the following assets will be transferred to the corporation:

continued

	Tax Basis	Fair Market Value
Cash	$ 10,000	$ 10,000
Furniture and fixtures	20,000	60,000
Land and building	240,000	300,000
	$270,000	$370,000

In exchange, Ron will receive stock in the newly formed corporation worth $370,000. Without the nonrecognition provisions of § 351, Ron would recognize a taxable gain of $100,000 ($370,000 − $270,000) on the transfer. Under § 351, however, Ron does not recognize any gain because his economic status has not changed. Ron's investment in the assets of his sole proprietorship ($270,000) carries over to his investment in the incorporated business, which is now represented by his ownership of stock in the corporation. As a result, § 351 provides for tax neutrality on the initial incorporation of Ron's sole proprietorship.

In a manner similar to a like-kind exchange, if a taxpayer transfers property to a corporation and receives "boot" (money or property other than stock), § 351(b) requires gain recognition to the extent of the lesser of the gain realized or the boot received (the amount of money and the fair market value of other property received). Gain is characterized (e.g., ordinary, capital) according to the type of asset transferred.[8] Loss on a § 351 transaction is never recognized. The nonrecognition of gain or loss is accompanied by a substituted basis in the shareholder's stock.[9] The major shareholder consequences of a taxable property transaction versus one that is tax deferred are identified in Concept Summary 12.2.

Concept Summary 12.2

Shareholder Consequences: Taxable Corporate Formation versus Tax-Deferred § 351 Transaction

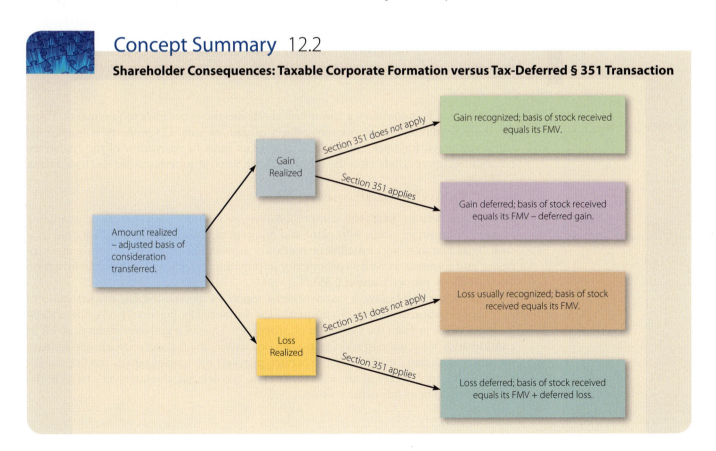

---

[8]Rev.Rul. 68–55, 1968–1 C.B. 140.

[9]§ 358(a). See the discussion preceding Example 27.

EXAMPLE 7

Abby and Bill form White Corporation. Abby transfers equipment with an adjusted basis of $30,000 and a fair market value of $60,000 for 50% of White's stock. Bill transfers equipment with an adjusted basis of $70,000 and a fair market value of $60,000 for the remaining 50% of the stock. The transfers qualify under § 351.

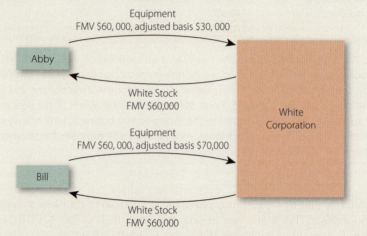

Abby has a deferred gain of $30,000, and Bill has a deferred loss of $10,000. Both have a substituted basis in the stock of White Corporation. Abby has a basis of $30,000 in her stock, and Bill has a basis of $70,000 in his stock. Therefore, if either Abby or Bill later disposes of the White stock in a taxable transaction (e.g., a sale), this deferred gain/loss will then be fully recognized—a $30,000 gain to Abby and a $10,000 loss to Bill.

Alternatively, if Abby and Bill each had received White stock worth $50,000 and cash of $10,000, Abby would recognize a gain but Bill would not recognize a loss. Specifically, Abby would recognize $10,000 of the $30,000 realized gain because she receives boot of $10,000, while Bill's receipt of boot would not trigger the loss recognition (i.e., recognition of loss never occurs in a § 351 transaction). Additional discussion of gain/loss recognition and the basis of stock received appears later in the chapter.

Section 351 is *mandatory* if a transaction satisfies the provision's requirements. There are three requirements for nonrecognition of gain or loss: (1) *property* is transferred (2) in exchange for *stock* and (3) the transferors must be in *control* of the transferee corporation immediately after the transfer. These three requirements are discussed next.

12-2b   Transfer of Property

Section 351 defines property comprehensively to include any physical or intangible assets. For example, along with plant and equipment, unrealized receivables held by a cash basis taxpayer and installment notes are considered property.[10] Proprietary processes and formulas as well as proprietary information in such as a patentable invention also qualify as property under § 351.[11]

As demonstrated below, a taxpayer must report as income the fair market value of any consideration received as compensation for services because § 351 specifically excludes services from the definition of property.[12] Thus, if a taxpayer receives stock as consideration for rendering services to the corporation, the taxpayer recognizes ordinary income. In this case, the income the service provider recognizes equals the fair market value of the stock received. Because there is no tax deferral, the taxpayer's basis in the stock received is its fair market value.

[10]*Hempt Brothers, Inc. v. U.S.*, 74–1 USTC ¶9188, 33 AFTR 2d 74–570, 490 F.2d 1172 (CA–3, 1974), and Reg. § 1.453–9(c)(2).

[11]Rev.Rul. 64–56, 1964–1 C.B. 133; Rev.Rul. 71–564, 1971–2 C.B. 179.

[12]§§ 61 and 83 generally tax service income when the service provider receives unrestricted compensation for providing the services.

Ann and Bob form Brown Corporation and transfer the following consideration:

EXAMPLE
8

	Consideration Transferred		
	Basis to Transferor	Fair Market Value	Number of Shares Issued
From Ann:			
Personal services rendered to Brown Corporation	$ –0–	$20,000	200
From Bob:			
Installment note receivable	5,000	40,000	
Inventory	10,000	30,000	800
Proprietary process	–0–	10,000	

The value of each share in Brown Corporation is $100.[13] Ann has ordinary income of $20,000 on the transfer because services do not qualify as "property." She has a basis of $20,000 in her 200 shares of stock in Brown (i.e., the law treats Ann as purchasing the Brown stock by rendering services). Bob recognizes no gain on the transfer because all of the consideration he transferred to Brown qualifies as "property" and he has "control" of Brown after the transfer. (See the discussion concerning control on the next page.) Bob has a substituted basis of $15,000 in the Brown stock.

As mentioned earlier, if property is transferred to a corporation in exchange for any property other than stock, the property received constitutes boot. The boot is taxable to the transferor-shareholder to the extent of any realized gain.[14]

12-2c **Stock**

Shareholder nonrecognition of gain occurs only when the shareholder receives stock. Stock includes common and most preferred. However, the Regulations state that the term *stock* does not include stock rights and stock warrants.[15] In addition, it does not include "nonqualified preferred stock," which possesses many of the attributes of debt.[16]

As a result, any corporate debt or **securities** (i.e., long-term debt such as bonds) are treated as boot because they do not qualify as stock. Therefore, shareholder receipt of debt in exchange for the transfer of appreciated property to a controlled corporation can cause gain recognition.

The Big Picture

EXAMPLE
9

Return to the facts of *The Big Picture* on p. 12-1. Assume that the proposed transaction qualifies under § 351, but Amber decides to receive some corporate debt along with the stock.

If Amber receives Garden stock worth $900,000 and Garden debt of $100,000 in exchange for the property transferred, Amber realizes a gain of $600,000 [$1,000,000 (value of consideration received) − $400,000 (basis in the transferred property)]. However, because the transaction qualifies under § 351, Amber recognizes only $100,000 of gain because the $100,000 of Garden debt is boot. Amber defers the remaining $500,000 realized gain.

In-depth coverage can be found on this book's companion website: **www.cengage.com**   **2** DIGGING DEEPER

---

[13]The value of closely held stock normally is presumed to be equal to the value of the property transferred.

[14]§ 351(b).

[15]Reg. § 1.351–1(a)(1)(ii).

[16]§ 351(g). Examples of nonqualified preferred stock include preferred stock that is redeemable within 20 years of issuance and whose dividend rate is based on factors other than corporate performance. See also Reg. § 1.351–1(a)(1)(ii).

12-2d **Control of the Corporation**

For a transaction to qualify as nontaxable under § 351, the transferor(s) of the property must be in `control` of the corporation immediately after the exchange. That is, the person or persons transferring *property* must have at least an 80 percent stock ownership in the corporation, resulting in the entity being a controlled corporation. The property transferors must own stock possessing at least 80 percent of the total combined voting power of all classes of stock entitled to vote *and* at least 80 percent of the total *number* of shares of all other classes of stock.[17]

Control Immediately after the Transfer

Control after the exchange can apply to a single person or to several taxpayers if they are all parties to an integrated transaction. To satisfy the timing requirement, the Regulations provide that when more than one person is involved, the exchange does not necessarily require simultaneous exchanges by two or more persons. The Regulations do, however, require that the rights of the parties (i.e., those transferring property to the corporation) be previously set out and determined. Also, the agreement to transfer property should be executed "with an expedition consistent with orderly procedure," and the transfers should occur close together in time.[18]

The Point at Which Control Is Determined

EXAMPLE 10

Jack exchanges property with a basis of $60,000 and a fair market value of $100,000 for 70% of the stock of Gray Corporation. The other 30% is owned by Jane, who acquired it several years ago. The fair market value of Jack's stock is $100,000.

Jack recognizes a taxable gain of $40,000 on the transfer because he does not have control immediately after the exchange and his transaction cannot be integrated with Jane's for purposes of the control requirement.

EXAMPLE 11

Lana, Leo, and Lori incorporate their respective businesses by forming Green Corporation. Lana exchanges her property for 300 shares in Green on January 7, 2017. Leo exchanges his property for 400 shares in Green on January 14, 2017, and Lori exchanges her property for 300 shares in Green on March 5, 2017.

The three exchanges are part of a prearranged plan, so the control requirement is met. The nonrecognition provisions of § 351 apply to all of the exchanges.

Once control has been achieved, it is not necessarily lost if, shortly after the transaction, stock received by shareholders in a § 351 exchange is sold or given to persons who are not parties to the exchange.[19]

EXAMPLE 12

Mark and Carl form Black Corporation. They transfer appreciated property to the corporation with each receiving 50 shares of Black stock. Shortly after the formation, Mark gives 25 shares to his son.

Because Mark was not committed to making the gift, he is considered to own his original shares of Black Corporation stock and, along with Carl, to control Black Corporation "immediately after the exchange." The requirements of § 351 are met, and neither Mark nor Carl is taxed on the exchange.

A different result might materialize if a plan for the ultimate disposition of the stock existed *before* the exchange.

---

[17]§ 368(c). Nonqualified preferred stock is treated as stock, not boot, for purposes of this control test.

[18]Reg. § 1.351–1(a)(1).

[19]*Wilgard Realty Co. v. Comm.*, 42–1 USTC ¶9452, 29 AFTR 325, 127 F.2d 514 (CA–2, 1942).

Assume the same facts as in Example 12, except that Mark immediately gives 25 shares to a business associate pursuant to a plan to satisfy an outstanding obligation.

In this case, the formation of Black would be taxable to Mark and Carl because of their lack of control (i.e., Mark and Carl, the property transferors, would have owned only 75% of the stock).

EXAMPLE 13

TAX PLANNING STRATEGIES   Utilizing § 351

FRAMEWORK FOCUS: INCOME AND EXCLUSIONS

Strategy: Avoid Income Recognition.

When using § 351, ensure that all parties transferring property (including cash) collectively receive control of the corporation. Simultaneous transfers are not necessary, but a long period of time between transfers makes the transaction vulnerable to taxation if the transfers are not properly documented as part of a single plan. To do this, the parties should document and preserve evidence of their intentions. Also, it is helpful to have some reasonable explanation for any delay in the transfers.

To meet the requirements of § 351, mere momentary control on the part of the transferor may not suffice if loss of control is compelled by a prearranged agreement.[20]

EXAMPLE 14

For many years, Todd operated a business as a sole proprietor employing Linda as manager. To dissuade Linda from quitting and going out on her own, Todd promised her a 30% interest in the business. To fulfill this promise, Todd transferred the business to newly formed Green Corporation in return for all of its stock. Immediately thereafter, Todd transfers 30% of the stock to Linda. As a consequence, he fails to meet the 80% control requirement.

Section 351 probably does not apply to Todd's transfer to Green Corporation. It appears that Todd was under an obligation to relinquish control. If this preexisting obligation exists, § 351 will not be available to Todd because, as the sole property transferor, he does not have 80% control of Green Corporation. If there is no obligation and the loss of control was voluntary on Todd's part, momentary control would suffice.[21]

Later transfers of property to an existing corporation must satisfy the 80 percent control requirement to avoid gain recognition. For these later transfers, a transferor's interest does not count toward control if the value of stock received is relatively small compared with the value of stock already owned. Further, the primary purpose of the transfer may not be to qualify other transferors for § 351 treatment.[22] (For a complete discussion of this issue, see "Transfers to Existing Corporations" on p. 12-15.)

Transfers for Property and Services

Section 351 treatment is lost if stock is transferred to persons who did not contribute property, causing those who did to lack control immediately after the exchange.

The Big Picture

EXAMPLE 15

Return to the facts of *The Big Picture* on p. 12-1. Assume that Amber transfers her $1,000,000 of property to Garden, Inc., and receives 50% of its stock. Jimmy receives the other 50% of the stock for services rendered (worth $1,000,000).

Both Amber and Jimmy report income from the transfers. Jimmy has ordinary income of $1,000,000 because he does not exchange property for stock. Amber has a taxable gain of $600,000 [$1,000,000 (fair market value of the stock in Garden) − $400,000 (basis in the transferred property)]. As the sole transferor of property, she receives only 50% of Garden's stock.

---

[20]Rev.Rul. 54–96, 1954–1 C.B. 111.

[21]Compare *Fahs v. Florida Machine and Foundry Co.*, 48–2 USTC ¶9329, 36 AFTR 1161, 168 F.2d 957 (CA–5, 1948), with *John C. O'Connor*, 16 TCM

213, T.C.Memo. 1957–50, *aff'd* in 58–2 USTC ¶9913, 2 AFTR 2d 6011, 260 F.2d 358 (CA–6, 1958).

[22]Reg. § 1.351–1(a)(1)(ii).

As noted earlier, a person receiving stock in exchange for services and for property transferred is taxed on the stock value related to those services but not on the stock issued for property. In addition, such a person can still be treated as a "property transferor" and in such a case, all stock received by the person transferring both property and services is counted in determining whether the transferors acquired control of the corporation.[23]

The Big Picture

EXAMPLE 16

Assume the same facts as in Example 15, except that Jimmy transfers property worth $800,000 (basis of $260,000) in addition to services rendered to Garden, Inc. (valued at $200,000).

Now Jimmy becomes a part of the control group. Amber and Jimmy, as property transferors, together receive 100% of the corporation's stock. Consequently, § 351 applies to the exchanges. Amber recognizes no gain. Jimmy recognizes no gain on the transfer of the property, but he recognizes ordinary income equal to the value of the shares issued for services rendered. Thus, Jimmy recognizes $200,000 of ordinary income currently.

Transfers for Services and Nominal Property

Note that to be part of the group meeting the 80 percent control test, the person contributing services must transfer property having more than a "relatively small value" compared with the value of services performed. Section 351 will not apply when a small amount of property is transferred and the primary purpose of the transfer is to qualify the transaction under § 351 for concurrent transferors.[24] The IRS generally requires that before a transferor who receives stock for both property and services can be included in the control group, the value of the property transferred must be at least 10 percent of the value of the services provided.

Determining Control Group Membership When Services Are Rendered

EXAMPLE 17

Ava and Rick form Grouse Corporation. Ava transfers land (worth $100,000, basis of $20,000) for 50% of the stock in Grouse. Rick transfers equipment (worth $50,000, adjusted basis of $10,000) and provides services worth $50,000 for 50% of the stock.

Because the value of the property Rick transfers is not small relative to the value of the services he renders, his stock in Grouse Corporation is counted in determining control for purposes of § 351; thus, the transferors own 100% of the stock in Grouse. In addition, all of Rick's stock, not just the shares received for the equipment, is counted in determining control.

As a result, Ava does not recognize gain on the transfer of the land. Rick, however, must recognize income of $50,000 on the transfer of services. Even though the transfer of the equipment qualifies under § 351, his transfer of services for stock does not.

EXAMPLE 18

Assume the same facts as in Example 17, except that the value of Rick's property is $2,000 and the value of his services is $98,000.

In this situation, the value of the property is small relative to the value of the services (and well below the 10% threshold provided by the IRS); therefore, Rick will not be considered a property transferor. Consequently, the control requirement is not met and the transaction is fully taxable to both Ava and Rick. None of Rick's stock is counted in determining control because the property he transfers has a nominal value in comparison to the value of the services he renders.

As a result, Ava recognizes $80,000 of gain on the transfer of the land. She has a basis of $100,000 in her Grouse stock. Rick must recognize income of $98,000 on the transfer for services rendered, and any realized gain or loss is recognized on the property transferred. Rick also has a $100,000 basis in his Grouse stock.

---

[23]Reg. § 1.351–1(a)(2), Ex. 3.   [24]Reg. § 1.351–1(a)(1)(ii).

Transfers to Existing Corporations

Once a corporation is in operation, § 351 also applies to any later transfers of property for stock by either new or existing shareholders.

> **EXAMPLE**
> **19**
>
> Sam and Beth formed Blue Corporation three years ago. Both Sam and Beth transferred appreciated property to Blue in exchange for 500 shares each in the corporation. The original transfers qualified under § 351, and neither Sam nor Beth recognized income on the exchange. In the current year, Sam transfers property (worth $100,000, adjusted basis of $5,000) for 500 additional Blue shares.
>
> Sam has a taxable gain of $95,000 on the transfer. The exchange does not qualify under § 351 because Sam does not have 80% control of Blue Corporation immediately after the transfer; he owns 1,000 shares of the 1,500 shares outstanding, or a 66⅔% interest.

If current shareholders transfer property with a small value relative to the value of stock already owned, a special rule applies (similar to the nominal property rule noted for service contributors). In particular, if the purpose of the transfer is to qualify a transaction under § 351, the ownership of the current shareholders does not count toward control. Thus, in the preceding example, if Beth had contributed $200 for one share of stock at the time of Sam's contribution, Beth's ownership would not count toward the 80 percent control requirement and Sam would still have had a taxable exchange.

12-2e **Assumption of Liabilities—§ 357**

LO.3

Describe the special rules that apply when a corporation assumes a shareholder's liability.

Without a provision to the contrary, the transfer of mortgaged property to a controlled corporation could require recognition of gain by the transferor if the corporation took over the mortgage. Liabilities assumed by the other party are considered the equivalent of cash and treated as boot received. This would be consistent with the treatment given in like-kind exchanges under § 1031. Section 357(a) provides, however, that when the acquiring corporation assumes a liability in a § 351 transaction, the liability is not treated as boot received for gain recognition purposes. Nevertheless, liabilities assumed by the transferee corporation are treated as boot in determining the basis of the stock received. As a result, the basis of the stock received is reduced by the liabilities assumed by the corporation.

> **The Big Picture**
>
> **EXAMPLE**
> **20**
>
> Return to the facts of *The Big Picture* on p. 12-1. Assume that you learn that Amber's husband, Jimmy, becomes disinterested in becoming a stockholder in Garden, Inc., and that Amber's building is subject to a liability of $70,000 that Garden assumes. Consequently, Amber receives 100% of the Garden stock and is relieved of the $70,000 liability in exchange for property with an adjusted basis of $400,000 and fair market value of $1,000,000.
>
> The exchange is tax-free under § 351 because the release of a liability is not treated as boot under § 357(a). However, the basis to Amber of the Garden stock is $330,000 [$400,000 (basis of property transferred) − $70,000 (amount of the liability assumed by Garden)].

GLOBAL TAX ISSUES   Does § 351 Cover the Incorporation of a Foreign Business?

When a taxpayer wants to incorporate a business overseas by moving assets across U.S. borders, the deferral mechanism of § 351 applies in certain situations, but not in others. In general, § 351 is available to defer gain recognition when starting up a new corporation outside the United States unless so-called tainted assets are involved. Under § 367, tainted assets, which include assets such as inventory and accounts receivable, are treated as having been sold by the taxpayer prior to the corporate formation; therefore, their transfer results in the current recognition of gain. The presence of tainted assets triggers gain because Congress does not want taxpayers to be able to shift the gain outside U.S. jurisdiction. The gain recognized is ordinary or capital depending on the nature of the asset involved.

The general rule of § 357(a) has two exceptions: (1) § 357(b) provides that if the principal purpose of the assumption of the liabilities is to avoid tax *or* if there is no bona fide business purpose behind the exchange, the liabilities are treated as boot; (2) § 357(c) provides that if the sum of the liabilities exceeds the adjusted basis of the properties transferred, the excess is taxable gain.

Exception (1): Tax Avoidance or No Bona Fide Business Purpose

Satisfying the bona fide business purpose under § 357(b) is not difficult if the liabilities are incurred in connection with the transferor's normal course of conducting a trade or business. But the bona fide business purpose requirement can cause difficulty if the liability is taken out shortly before the property is transferred and the proceeds are utilized for personal purposes.[25] This type of situation is analogous to a cash distribution by the corporation, which is taxed as boot.

Dan transfers real estate (basis of $140,000 and fair market value of $190,000) to a controlled corporation in return for stock in the corporation. Shortly before the transfer, Dan mortgages the real estate and uses the $20,000 of proceeds to meet personal obligations. Thus, along with the real estate, the mortgage is transferred to the corporation. In this case, the assumption of the mortgage lacks a bona fide business purpose. Consequently, the release of the liability is treated as boot received, and Dan has a taxable gain on the transfer of $20,000, computed as follows:[26]

Stock	$ 170,000
Release of liability—treated as boot	20,000
Total amount realized	$ 190,000
Less: Basis of real estate	(140,000)
Realized gain	$ 50,000
Recognized gain	$ 20,000

The effect of the application of § 357(b) is to taint *all* liabilities transferred, even if *some* are supported by a bona fide business purpose.

Tim, an accrual basis taxpayer, incorporates his sole proprietorship. Among the liabilities transferred to the new corporation are trade accounts payable of $100,000 and a credit card bill of $5,000. Tim had used the credit card to purchase an anniversary gift for his wife. Under these circumstances, the *entire* $105,000 of liabilities is boot and triggers the recognition of gain to the extent gain is realized.

Exception (2): Liabilities in Excess of Basis

Section 357(c) states that if the total shareholder's liabilities assumed *exceeds* the total of the adjusted bases of the properties transferred by that shareholder, the excess is taxable gain. Without this provision, if liabilities exceed the basis in the property exchanged, a taxpayer would have a negative basis in the stock received in the controlled corporation.[27] Section 357(c) precludes the negative basis possibility by treating the excess over basis as gain to the transferor.

---

[25]See, for example, *Campbell, Jr. v. Wheeler*, 65–1 USTC ¶9294, 15 AFTR 2d 578, 342 F.2d 837 (CA–5, 1965).

[26]§ 351(b).

[27]*Jack L. Easson*, 33 T.C. 963 (1960), *rev'd* in 61–2 USTC ¶9654, 8 AFTR 2d 5448, 294 F.2d 653 (CA–9, 1961).

Andre transfers land and equipment with adjusted bases of $350,000 and $50,000, respectively, to a newly formed corporation in exchange for 100% of the stock. The corporation assumes $500,000 of liabilities on the transferred land.

Without § 357(c), Andre's basis in the stock of the new corporation would be negative $100,000 [$400,000 (bases of properties transferred) + $0 (gain recognized) − $0 (boot received) − $500,000 (liabilities assumed)].

Section 357(c), however, causes Andre to recognize gain of $100,000 ($500,000 liabilities assumed − $400,000 bases of assets transferred). As a result, the stock has a zero basis in Andre's hands, determined as follows:

Bases in the properties transferred ($350,000 + $50,000)	$ 400,000
Plus: Gain recognized	100,000
Less: Boot received	(–0–)
Less: Liabilities assumed	(500,000)
Basis in the stock received	$ –0–

As a result, Andre recognizes $100,000 of gain and avoids a negative stock basis. Note that this result does not depend on the value of the contributed land and equipment. Andre would recognize $100,000 of gain under § 357(c) even if he realized a loss on the exchange.

EXAMPLE 23

The definition of liabilities under § 357(c) excludes obligations that would have been deductible to the transferor had those obligations been paid before the transfer. Thus, accounts payable of a cash basis taxpayer that give rise to a deduction are not considered liabilities for purposes of § 357(c). In addition, they are not considered in the computation of the shareholder's stock basis.

Tina, a cash basis taxpayer, incorporates her sole proprietorship. In return for all of the stock of the new corporation, she transfers the following items:

	Adjusted Basis	Fair Market Value
Cash	$10,000	$10,000
Unrealized accounts receivable (amounts due to Tina but not yet received by her)	–0–	40,000
Trade accounts payable	–0–	30,000
Note payable	5,000	5,000

Unrealized accounts receivable and trade accounts payable have a zero basis. Under the cash method of accounting, no income is recognized until the receivables are collected and no deduction materializes until the payables are satisfied. The note payable has a basis because it was issued for consideration received.

In this situation, the trade accounts payable are disregarded for gain recognition purposes and for the determination of Tina's stock basis. Thus, because the balance of the note payable does not exceed the basis of the assets transferred, Tina does not have a problem of liabilities in excess of basis (i.e., the note payable of $5,000 does not exceed the aggregate basis in the cash and accounts receivable of $10,000).

EXAMPLE 24

If §§ 357(b) and (c) both apply to the same transfer, § 357(b) dominates.[28] This could be significant because § 357(b) does not automatically create gain on the transfer, as does § 357(c). Instead, it merely converts the liability to boot. That is, § 357(b) will result in recognized gain only if there is a realized gain, while § 357(c) will always result in gain even if the overall transaction results in a realized loss.

Concept Summary 12.3 summarizes the tax rules that apply when liabilities are transferred in property transactions, including the special rules that apply in § 351 transactions.

---

[28]§ 357(c)(2)(A).

EXAMPLE
25

Chris owns land with a basis of $100,000 and a fair market value of $1 million. The land is subject to a mortgage of $300,000. One month prior to transferring the land to Robin Corporation, Chris borrows an additional $200,000 for personal purposes and gives the lender a second mortgage on the land. Therefore, upon the incorporation, Robin Corporation issues stock worth $500,000 to Chris and assumes the mortgages on the land.

Both § 357(b) and § 357(c) apply to the transfer. The mortgages on the property exceed the basis of the property. Thus, Chris has a gain of $400,000 under § 357(c). Chris borrowed $200,000 just prior to the transfer and used the loan proceeds for personal purposes. Under § 357(b), Chris has boot of $500,000 in the amount of the liabilities, which triggers $500,000 of recognized gain. Note that *all* of the liabilities are treated as boot, not just the "tainted" $200,000 liability.

	§ 357(b) Result	§ 357(c) Result
Amount realized:		
Robin Corporation stock	$ 500,000	$ 500,000
Release of mortgage on land	300,000	300,000
Release of second mortgage—personal purposes	200,000	200,000
Total amount realized	$1,000,000	$1,000,000
Basis of land	(100,000)	(100,000)
Realized gain	$ 900,000	$ 900,000
Gain recognized under § 357(b) ($300,000 + $200,000)	$ 500,000	
Gain recognized under § 357(c) [($300,000 + $200,000) − $100,000]		$ 400,000

Unfortunately for Chris, the relatively more onerous rule of § 357(b) dominates over § 357(c), requiring Chris to recognize a $500,000 gain.

Concept Summary 12.3

Tax Consequences of Liability Assumption

General rule: § 1001	If Red Corporation takes property subject to Taxpayer's liability or assumes Taxpayer's liability, Taxpayer is treated as having received cash due to the debt relief. Therefore, if the liability is $20,000, Taxpayer is treated as receiving Red stock of $80,000 and cash of $20,000 in a fully taxable transaction. Gain realized and recognized is $60,000.
Special rule in a § 351 transaction: § 357(a)	Assume the same facts as above, except that the transfer is a § 351 transaction. Taxpayer is not treated as receiving cash of $20,000 for gain recognition purposes (the debt relief is *not* treated as boot). Therefore, gain recognition is avoided. The debt relief will, however, reduce the Taxpayer's basis in Red Corporation stock.
Exception to § 351 transaction rule— Tax avoidance or no bona fide business purpose: § 357(b)	Assume the same facts as above, except that the transfer is a § 351 transaction and the liability does *not* have a business purpose. Taxpayer is treated as receiving cash of $20,000 for gain recognition purposes (the debt relief *is* treated as boot). Therefore, $20,000 of the realized gain is recognized.
Exception to § 351 transaction rule— Liabilities in excess of basis: § 357(c)	Assume the same facts as above, except that the transfer is a § 351 transaction, the liability is $45,000, the Red stock is worth $55,000, and § 357(b) does not apply. Taxpayer recognizes a $5,000 gain (excess of $45,000 liability over $40,000 property basis).

TAX PLANNING STRATEGIES   Avoiding § 351

FRAMEWORK FOCUS: TAX RATE

Strategy: Shift Net Income from High-Bracket Years to Low-Bracket Years.
Control the Character of Income and Deductions.

Section 351(a) provides for the nonrecognition of gain on transfers to controlled corporations. As such, it is often regarded as a relief provision favoring taxpayers. In some situations, however, avoiding § 351(a) may produce a more advantageous tax result. The transferors might prefer to recognize gain on the transfer of property if the tax cost is low. For example, they may be in low tax brackets, or the gain may be a capital gain that could be neutralized by available capital losses. Recognizing gain will also lead to a stepped-up basis in the transferred property in the corporation.

Another reason a particular transferor might want to avoid § 351 concerns possible loss recognition. Recall that § 351 refers to the nonrecognition of both gains and losses. Section 351(b)(2) specifically states: "No loss to such recipient shall be recognized." A transferor who wants to recognize loss has several alternatives:

- Sell the property to the corporation for its stock. The IRS could attempt to collapse the "sale," however, by taking the approach that the transfer really falls under an earlier § 351(a) contribution.[29]

- Sell the property to the corporation for other property or boot. Because the transferor receives no stock, § 351 is inapplicable.

- Transfer the property to the corporation in return for securities or nonqualified preferred stock. Recall that § 351 does not apply to a transferor who receives securities or nonqualified preferred stock. In both this and the previous alternatives, watch for the possible disallowance of the loss under the related-party rules.

Suppose loss property is to be transferred to the corporation and no loss is recognized by the transferor due to § 351(a). This could present an interesting problem in terms of assessing the economic realities involved.

EXAMPLE
26

Iris and Ivan form Wren Corporation with the following investments: property by Iris (basis of $40,000 and fair market value of $50,000) and property by Ivan (basis of $60,000 and fair market value of $50,000). Each receives 50% of the Wren stock. Has Ivan acted wisely in settling for only 50% of the stock?

At first, it would appear so because Iris and Ivan each invested property of the same value ($50,000). But what about tax considerations? By applying the general carryover basis rules, the corporation now has a basis of $40,000 in Iris's property and $60,000 in Ivan's property. In essence, Iris has shifted a possible $10,000 gain to the corporation, while Ivan has transferred a $10,000 potential loss. Thus, an equitable allocation of the Wren stock would call for Ivan to receive a greater percentage interest than Iris would receive.

This issue is further complicated by the special basis adjustment required when a shareholder such as Ivan contributes property with a built-in loss to a corporation. (See the discussion of this basis adjustment for loss property in the next section.) In this situation, if Wren is to take a carryover basis in Ivan's property, Ivan must reduce his stock basis by the $10,000 built-in loss. This reduced stock basis, of course, could lead to a greater tax burden on Ivan when he sells the Wren stock. This may suggest additional support for Ivan having a greater percentage interest than Iris has.

---

[29]*U.S. v. Hertwig,* 68–2 USTC ¶9495, 22 AFTR 2d 5249, 398 F.2d 452
(CA–5, 1968).

EXHIBIT 12.3	Shareholder's Basis of Stock Received in Exchange for Property

Adjusted basis of property transferred	$xx,xxx
Plus: Gain recognized	xxx
Minus: Boot received (including any liabilities transferred)	(xxx)
Minus: Adjustment for loss property (if elected)	(xxx)
Equals: Basis of stock received	$xx,xxx

LO.4

Identify the basis issues relevant to the shareholder and the corporation.

12-2f Basis Determination and Other Issues

Recall that § 351(a) postpones gain or loss recognition until the taxpayer's investment changes substantively. It is the basis rules described below that result in gain or loss postponement until the shareholder disposes of the stock.

Basis of Stock to Shareholder

For a taxpayer transferring property to a corporation in a § 351 transaction, the basis of *stock* received in the transaction is the same as the basis the taxpayer had in the property transferred, increased by any gain recognized on the exchange of property and decreased by boot received. For basis purposes, boot received includes liabilities transferred by the shareholder to the corporation. Also note that if the shareholder receives *other property* (i.e., boot) along with the stock, that property takes a basis equal to its fair market value.[30] In Exhibit 12.3, the reference to gain recognized does not consider any income resulting from the performance of personal services.

Basis of Property to Corporation

The basis of property received by the corporation generally is the basis of the exchanged property in the hands of the transferor increased by the amount of any gain recognized on the transfer by the transferor-shareholder.[31] Examples 27 and 28 illustrate these basis rules.

EXAMPLE 27

Maria and Ned form Brown Corporation. Maria transfers land (basis of $30,000 and fair market value of $70,000); Ned invests cash ($60,000). They each receive 50 shares in Brown Corporation, worth $1,200 per share, but Maria also receives $10,000 of cash from Brown. The transfers of property, the realized and recognized gain on the transfers, and the basis of the stock in Brown Corporation to Maria and Ned are as follows:

	A	B	C	D	E	F
	Basis of Property Transferred	FMV of Stock Received	Boot Received	Realized Gain (B + C − A)	Recognized Gain (Lesser of C or D)	Basis of Stock in Brown (A − C + E)
From Maria:						
Land	$30,000	$60,000	$10,000	$40,000	$10,000	$30,000
From Ned:						
Cash	60,000	60,000	–0–	–0–	–0–	60,000

Brown Corporation has a basis of $40,000 in the land (Maria's basis of $30,000 plus her recognized gain of $10,000).

---

[30]§ 358(a). Recall from earlier discussions that the basis of stock received for services equals its fair market value.

[31]§ 362(a).

EXHIBIT 12.4	**Corporation's Basis in Property Received**

Adjusted basis of property transferred	$xx,xxx
Plus: Gain recognized by transferor-shareholder	xxx
Minus: Adjustment for loss property (if required)	(xxx)
Equals: Basis of property to corporation	$xx,xxx

EXAMPLE 28

Assume the same facts as in Example 27, except that Maria's basis in the land is $68,000 (instead of $30,000). Because recognized gain cannot exceed realized gain, the transfer generates only $2,000 of gain to Maria. The realized and recognized gain and the basis of the stock in Brown Corporation to Maria are as follows:

	A	B	C	D	E	F
	Basis of Property Transferred	**FMV of Stock Received**	**Boot Received**	**Realized Gain (B + C − A)**	**Recognized Gain (Lesser of C or D)**	**Basis of Stock in Brown (A − C + E)**
Land	$68,000	$60,000	$10,000	$2,000	$2,000	$60,000

Brown's basis in the land is $70,000 ($68,000 basis to Maria + $2,000 gain recognized by Maria).

Exhibit 12.4 summarizes the basis calculation for property received by a corporation. Concept Summary 12.4 shows the shareholder and corporate consequences of a transfer of property to a corporation for stock, with and without the application of § 351. The facts applicable to shareholder Maria's transfer in Example 27 are used to illustrate the differences between the transaction being tax-deferred and taxable.

Concept Summary 12.4

Tax Consequences to the Shareholders and Corporation: With and Without the Application of § 351 (Based on the Facts of Example 27)

	With § 351			Without § 351		
Shareholder	**Gain/Loss Recognized**	**Stock Basis**	**Other Property Basis**	**Gain/Loss Recognized**	**Stock Basis**	**Other Property Basis**
Maria	Realized gain recognized to extent of boot received; loss not recognized.	Substituted (see Exhibit 12.3).	FMV	All realized gain or loss recognized.	FMV	FMV
	$10,000	$30,000	$10,000	$40,000	$60,000	$10,000

	With § 351		Without § 351	
Corporation	**Gain/Loss Recognized**	**Property Basis**	**Gain/Loss Recognized**	**Property Basis**
Brown	No gain or loss recognized on the transfer of corporate stock for property.	Carryover (see Exhibit 12.4).	No gain or loss recognized on the transfer of corporate stock for property.	FMV
	$0	$40,000	$0	$70,000

Note that the benefit to Maria of deferring $30,000 of gain under § 351 comes with a cost: her stock basis is $30,000 (rather than $60,000), and the corporation's basis in the property received is $40,000 (rather than $70,000).

Basis Adjustment for Loss Property

A corporation's basis for property received in a § 351 transaction is carried over from the shareholder. As a result, the corporation's basis has no correlation to the property's fair market value. However, in certain situations when **built-in loss property** is contributed to a corporation, the aggregate basis of the assets transferred by a shareholder exceeds their fair market value. When this built-in loss situation exists, an anti-loss duplication rule requires the basis in the loss properties to be stepped down by allocating the built-in loss proportionately among the assets.[32] This basis adjustment is necessary to prevent the parties from obtaining a double benefit from the losses involved. That is, this rule prevents a high shareholder stock basis *and* a high corporate asset basis. The next two examples illustrate this rule.

EXAMPLE 29

In a transaction qualifying under § 351, Charles transfers the following assets to Gold Corporation in exchange for all of its stock:

	Tax Basis	Fair Market Value	Built-In Gain/(Loss)
Equipment	$100,000	$ 90,000	($10,000)
Land	200,000	230,000	30,000
Building	150,000	100,000	(50,000)
	$450,000	$420,000	($30,000)

Charles's stock basis is $450,000 [$450,000 (basis of the property transferred) + $0 (gain recognized) − $0 (boot received)]. However, Gold must reduce its basis for the loss assets transferred by the net built-in loss ($30,000) in proportion to each asset's share of the loss.

	Unadjusted Tax Basis	Adjustment	Adjusted Tax Basis
Equipment	$100,000	($ 5,000)*	$ 95,000
Land	200,000		200,000
Building	150,000	(25,000)**	125,000
	$450,000	($ 30,000)	$420,000

* $\frac{\$10,000 \text{ (loss attributable to equipment)}}{\$60,000 \text{ (total built-in loss)}} \times \$30,000 \text{ (net built-in loss)} = \$5,000$ (adjustment to basis in equipment).

** $\frac{\$50,000 \text{ (loss attributable to building)}}{\$60,000 \text{ (total built-in loss)}} \times \$30,000 \text{ (net built-in loss)} = \$25,000$ (adjustment to basis in building).

Note the end result of Example 29:

- Charles still has a built-in loss in his stock basis. As a result, if he sells the Gold Corporation stock, he will recognize a loss of $30,000 [$420,000 (selling price based on presumed value of the stock) − $450,000 (basis in the stock)].

- Gold Corporation can no longer recognize a loss on the sale of *all* of its assets [$420,000 (selling price based on value of assets) − $420,000 (adjusted basis in assets) = $0 (gain or loss)].

In the event a corporation is subject to the built-in loss adjustment, an alternative approach is available. If both the shareholder and the corporation elect, the basis reduction can be made to the shareholder's stock rather than to the corporation's property.

EXAMPLE 30

Assume the same facts as in the previous example. If Charles and Gold elect, Charles can reduce his stock basis to $420,000 ($450,000 − $30,000). As a result, Gold's aggregate basis in the assets is $450,000. If Charles has no intention of selling his stock, this election could be desirable as it benefits Gold by giving the corporation a higher depreciable basis in the equipment and building.

---

[32]§ 362(e)(2). This adjustment is determined separately with respect to each property transferor. This adjustment also is required in the case of a contribution to capital by a shareholder.

Note the end result of Example 30:

- Charles has no built-in loss. As a result, if he sells the Gold Corporation stock, he will recognize no gain or loss [$420,000 (presumed value of the stock) − $420,000 (basis in the stock)].

- Gold Corporation has a built-in loss. As a result, if it sells *all* of its assets [$420,000 (selling price based on value of assets) − $450,000 (basis in assets)], it recognizes a loss of $30,000.

Consequently, as shown in the two previous examples, the built-in loss adjustment places the loss with either the shareholder or the corporation but not both.

Stock Issued for Services Rendered

A corporation's transfer of its stock for property is not a taxable exchange.[33] A transfer of shares for services is also not a taxable transaction to a corporation.[34] But another issue arises: Can a corporation deduct as a business expense the fair market value of the stock it issues in consideration of services? Yes, unless the services are such that the payment is characterized as a capital expenditure.[35]

The Big Picture

EXAMPLE 31

Return to the facts of *The Big Picture* on p. 12-1. Amber transfers her $1,000,000 of property to Garden, Inc., and receives 50% of the stock. In addition, assume that Jimmy transfers property worth $800,000 (basis of $260,000) and agrees to serve as manager of the corporation for one year (services worth $200,000) for 50% of the stock.

Amber's and Jimmy's transfers qualify under § 351. Neither Amber nor Jimmy is taxed on the transfer of his or her property. However, Jimmy has income of $200,000, the value of the services he will render to Garden, Inc. Garden has a basis of $260,000 in the property it acquired from Jimmy, and it may claim a compensation expense deduction under § 162 for $200,000. Jimmy's stock basis is $460,000 [$260,000 (basis of property transferred) + $200,000 (income recognized for services rendered)].

The Big Picture

EXAMPLE 32

Assume in the preceding example that Jimmy receives the Garden stock as consideration for the appreciated property and for providing legal services in organizing the corporation. The value of Jimmy's legal services is $200,000.

Jimmy has no gain on the transfer of the property but has income of $200,000 for the value of the services rendered. Garden, Inc., has a basis of $260,000 in the property it acquired from Jimmy and must capitalize the $200,000 as an organizational expenditure. Jimmy's stock basis is $460,000 [$260,000 (basis of property transferred) + $200,000 (income recognized for services rendered)].

Holding Period for Shareholder and Transferee Corporation

The shareholder's holding period for stock received for a capital asset or for § 1231 property includes the holding period of the property transferred to the corporation. The holding period of the property is *tacked on* to the holding period of the stock. The holding period for stock received for any other property (e.g., inventory) begins on the day after the exchange. The transferee corporation's holding period for property acquired in a § 351 transfer is the holding period of the transferor-shareholder regardless of the character of the property to the transferor. For instance, whether the property transferred is an ordinary asset (e.g., inventory), a § 1231 asset, or a capital asset, the corporation's holding period is the same as the transferor's.[36]

---

[33]§ 1032.
[34]Reg. § 1.1032–1(a).

[35]Rev.Rul. 62–217, 1962–2 C.B. 59, modified by Rev.Rul. 74–503, 1974–2 C.B. 117.
[36]§§ 1223(1) and (2).

12-2g **Recapture Considerations**

In a § 351 nontaxable transfer (no boot involved) to a controlled corporation, the depreciation recapture rules do not apply.[37] Instead, any recapture potential of the property carries over to the corporation as it steps into the shoes of the transferor-shareholder for purposes of basis determination. However, to the extent gain is recognized, the recapture rules apply.

EXAMPLE 33

Paul transfers equipment (adjusted basis of $30,000, original cost of $120,000, and fair market value of $100,000) to a controlled corporation in return for stock. If Paul had sold the equipment, it would have yielded a gain of $70,000, all of which would have been treated as ordinary income under the § 1245 depreciation recapture rules.

If the transfer comes within § 351, Paul has no recognized gain and no depreciation to recapture. If the corporation later disposes of the equipment in a taxable transaction, it must take into account the § 1245 recapture potential originating with Paul. So, for example, if the corporation were to sell the asset shortly after incorporation for $100,000, all of the $70,000 gain recognized would be given ordinary treatment because of the depreciation recapture rules.

Alternatively, if Paul had received boot of $60,000 on the transfer, all of the recognized gain would have been recaptured as ordinary income. The remaining $30,000 ($90,000 − $60,000) of recapture potential would have carried over to the corporation.

TAX PLANNING STRATEGIES   Other Considerations When Incorporating a Business

FRAMEWORK FOCUS: TAX RATE

Strategy: Control the Character of Income and Deductions.
Shift Net Income from High-Bracket Taxpayers to Low-Bracket Taxpayers.

FRAMEWORK FOCUS: DEDUCTIONS

Strategy: Maximize Deductible Amounts.

FRAMEWORK FOCUS: INCOME AND EXCLUSIONS

Strategy: Avoid Income Recognition.

When a business is incorporated, the organizers must determine which assets and liabilities should be transferred to the corporation. A transfer of assets that produce passive income (rents, royalties, dividends, and interest) can cause the corporation to be a personal holding company in a tax year when operating income is low. Thus, the corporation could be subject to the personal holding company penalty tax (see the discussion in Chapter 13).

A transfer of the accounts payable of a cash basis taxpayer may prevent the organizer from taking a tax deduction if the accounts are paid by the corporation. Therefore, the parties should decide who will receive the greatest benefit from the deduction and then plan accordingly.

Leasing property to the corporation may be a more attractive alternative than transferring ownership. Leasing provides the taxpayer with the opportunity of withdrawing money from the corporation in a deductible form without the payment being characterized as a nondeductible dividend. If the property is donated to a family member in a lower tax bracket, the lease income can be shifted as well. If the depreciation and other deductions available in connection with the property are larger than the lease income, a high-tax-rate taxpayer could retain the property until the income exceeds the deductions.

continued

---

[37]§§ 1245(b)(3) and 1250(d)(3).

The Big Picture

EXAMPLE
34

Return to the facts of *The Big Picture* on p. 12-1. If Amber decides to retain the $50,000 of cash basis accounts receivable rather than transfer them to the newly formed Garden, Inc., she will recognize $50,000 of ordinary income upon their collection.

Alternatively, if the receivables are transferred to Garden as the facts suggest, the corporation will recognize the ordinary income as the receivables are collected. However, a subsequent corporate distribution to Amber of the cash collected could be subject to double taxation as a dividend (see Chapter 13 for further discussion). Given the alternatives available, Amber needs to evaluate which approach is better for the parties involved.

Another way to shift income to other taxpayers is by the use of corporate debt. Shareholder debt in a corporation can be given to family members with low marginal tax rates. This technique also shifts income without a loss of control of the corporation.

12-3 CAPITAL STRUCTURE OF A CORPORATION

LO.5

Explain the tax aspects of the capital structure of a corporation.

When forming or expanding a corporation, the transaction can be financed with capital contributions or debt proceeds or a combination of the two. Evaluating the relative advantages and disadvantages of these two basic elements in the capital structure of a corporation can involve various considerations, including the tax aspects of each.

12-3a Capital Contributions

When money or property is received in exchange for capital stock (including treasury stock), the corporation does not recognize any gain or loss.[38] Also, it does not include in gross income any shareholders' contributions of money or property to the capital of the corporation or through voluntary pro rata transfers. This is the case even though there is no increase in the number of outstanding shares of stock of the corporation. The payments represent an additional price paid for the shares held by the shareholders (increasing their stock basis) and are treated as additions to the operating capital of the corporation.[39]

Contributions by nonshareholders, such as land contributed to a corporation by a civic group or a governmental group to induce the corporation to locate in a particular community, are not treated as capital contributions and so the corporation must include them in its gross income. In addition, property transferred to a corporation by a nonshareholder in exchange for goods or services rendered is taxable income to the corporation.[40]

EXAMPLE
35

A cable television company charges its customers an initial fee to hook up to a new cable system installed in the area. These payments are used to finance the total cost of constructing the cable company's infrastructure. The customers will make monthly payments for the cable service.

The initial payments are used for capital expenditures, but they represent payments for services to be rendered by the cable company. As such, they are taxable income and not contributions to capital by nonshareholders.

The basis of property received by a corporation from a shareholder as a **capital contribution** equals the basis of the property in the hands of the shareholder, although the basis may be subject to a downward adjustment when loss property is contributed.

---

[38]§ 1032.

[39]§ 118 and Reg. § 1.118–1.

[40]Reg. § 1.118–1. See also *Teleservice Co. of Wyoming Valley*, 27 T.C. 722 (1957), *aff'd* in 58–1 USTC ¶9383, 1 AFTR 2d 1249, 254 F.2d 105 (CA–3, 1958), *cert. den.* 78 S.Ct. 1360 (USSC, 1958).

The basis of property transferred to a corporation by a nonshareholder as a contribution to capital is zero. Any taxable contributions result in a fair market value basis for the property contributed.

EXAMPLE 36

A city donates land worth $400,000 to Teal Corporation as an inducement for Teal to locate in the city. In addition, the city has agreed to reduce the standard real estate tax rate for Teal by 50% on newly constructed property in the city.

The receipt of the land produces $400,000 of gross income to Teal and, as a result, the land's basis to the corporation is $400,000. However, the real estate tax abatement is not considered a contribution and it is not taxable to Teal.

LO.6

Characterize the tax differences between debt and equity investments.

12-3b **Debt in the Capital Structure**

Various tax and nontax considerations are relevant when developing the capital structure of a corporation. The relative amounts of debt and equity and their characteristics are of primary importance.

Advantages of Debt

Significant tax differences exist between debt and equity in the capital structure, and shareholders must be aware of these differences. The advantages of issuing long-term debt are numerous. Interest on debt is deductible by the corporation, while dividend payments are not.[41] Further, the shareholders are not taxed on debt repayments unless the repayments exceed basis. An investment in stock usually cannot be withdrawn tax-free as long as a corporation has earnings and profits. Withdrawals will be deemed to be taxable dividends to the extent of earnings and profits of the distributing corporation. (The concept of earnings and profits is discussed in Chapter 13.)

Another distinction between debt and equity relates to the taxation of dividend and interest income. Dividend income on equity holdings is taxed to individual investors at the low capital gains rates, while interest income on debt is taxed at the higher ordinary income rates.

EXAMPLE 37

Wade transfers cash of $100,000 to a newly formed corporation for 100% of the stock. In the first year of operations, the corporation has net income of $40,000. If the corporation distributes $7,500 to Wade, the distribution is a taxable dividend with no corresponding deduction to the corporation.

Assume, instead, that Wade transfers to the corporation cash of $50,000 for stock. In addition, he lends the corporation $50,000. The note is payable in equal annual installments of $5,000 and bears interest at the rate of 5%. At the end of the year, the corporation pays Wade interest of $2,500 ($50,000 × 5%) and a note repayment of $5,000. The interest payment is taxable to Wade and a deductible expense to the corporation. The $5,000 principal repayment on the loan is neither taxed to Wade nor deductible by the corporation. Based on the tax rates as noted, the after-tax impact to Wade and the corporation under each alternative is illustrated below.

	If the Distribution Is	
	$7,500 Dividend	**$5,000 Note Repayment and $2,500 Interest**
After-tax benefit to Wade*		
[$7,500 × (1 − 15%)]	$6,375	
{$5,000 + [$2,500 × (1 − 35%)]}		$6,625
After-tax cost to corporation**		
No deduction to corporation	$7,500	
{$5,000 + [$2,500 × (1 − 35%)]}		$6,625

*Assumes that Wade's dividend income is taxed at the 15% capital gains rate and that his interest income is taxed at the 35% ordinary income rate.

**Assumes that the corporation is in the 35% marginal tax bracket.

---

[41]However, § 163(j) limits business interest deductions to business interest income plus 30% of taxable income (see discussion that follows).

Reclassification of Debt as Equity (Thin Capitalization Problem)

In situations where the corporation is said to be thinly capitalized, the IRS contends that debt is an equity interest and denies the corporation the tax advantages of debt financing. **Thin capitalization** occurs when shareholder debt is high relative to shareholder equity. If a debt instrument has too many features of stock, it may be treated as a form of stock by the IRS. As a result, the principal and interest payments are considered dividends. Section 385 authorizes the IRS to characterize corporate debt wholly as equity or as part debt and part equity. In the current environment, however, the IRS may be less inclined to raise the thin capitalization issue because the conversion of interest income to dividend income would produce a tax benefit to individual investors.

For the most part, the principles used to classify debt as equity developed in connection with closely held corporations, where the holders of the debt are often shareholders. The rules have often proved inadequate for dealing with large, publicly traded corporations.

Section 385 lists several factors that *may* be used to determine whether a debtor-creditor relationship or a shareholder-corporation relationship exists. Also, § 385 authorizes the Treasury to prescribe Regulations that provide more definite guidelines for determining when debt should be reclassified as equity. For years, however, definitive Treasury Regulations have not been available to provide guidance in this area. As a result, taxpayers have had to rely on numerous judicial decisions to determine whether a true debtor-creditor relationship exists.

In October 2016, the Treasury released much-anticipated final and temporary Regulations under § 385. Generally, the new Regulations target certain "earnings stripping" transactions and related-party loans and are applicable to tax years ending on or after January 19, 2017. However, portions of the Regulations apply only to debt instruments issued on or after January 1, 2018. According to some tax professionals, these rules have left other important questions unanswered. As a result, the long line of judicial decisions establishing key guidelines and principles is likely to have continuing relevance.[42]

The courts have identified the following factors to be considered when classifying a security as debt or equity:

- Whether the debt instrument is in proper form. An open account advance is more easily characterized as a contribution to capital than a loan evidenced by a properly written note executed by the shareholder.[43]

- Whether the debt instrument bears a reasonable rate of interest and has a definite maturity date. When a shareholder advance does not provide for interest, the return expected is that inherent in an equity interest (e.g., a share of the profits or an increase in the value of the shares).[44] Likewise, a lender unrelated to the corporation will usually be unwilling to commit funds to the corporation for an indefinite period of time (i.e., no definite due date).

- Whether the debt is paid on a timely basis. A lender's failure to insist upon timely repayment (or satisfactory renegotiation) indicates that the return sought does not depend upon interest income and the repayment of principal.

- Whether payment is contingent on earnings. A lender ordinarily will not advance funds that are likely to be repaid only if the venture is successful.

- Whether the debt is subordinated to other liabilities. Subordination tends to eliminate a significant characteristic of the creditor-debtor relationship. Creditors should have the right to share with other general creditors in the event of the corporation's dissolution or liquidation. Subordination also destroys another basic attribute of creditor status—the power to demand payment at a fixed maturity date.[45]

---

[42]See recently issued final and temporary Reg. §§ 1.385–1 to –4T (T.D. 9790).

[43]*Estate of Mixon, Jr. v. U.S.*, 72–2 USTC ¶9537, 30 AFTR 2d 72–5094, 464 F.2d 394 (CA–5, 1972).

[44]*Slappey Drive Industrial Park v. U.S.*, 77–2 USTC ¶9696, 40 AFTR 2d 77–5940, 561 F.2d 572 (CA–5, 1977).

[45]*Fin Hay Realty Co. v. U.S.*, 68–2 USTC ¶9438, 22 AFTR 2d 5004, 398 F.2d 694 (CA–3, 1968).

- Whether holdings of debt and stock are proportionate (e.g., each shareholder owns the same percentages of debt and stock). When debt and equity obligations are held in the same proportion, shareholders are, apart from tax considerations, indifferent as to whether corporate distributions are in the form of interest or dividends.

- Whether funds loaned to the corporation are used to finance initial operations or capital asset acquisitions. Funds used to finance initial operations or to acquire capital assets the corporation needs to operate are generally obtained through equity investments.

- Whether the corporation has a high ratio of shareholder debt to shareholder equity. Thin capitalization indicates that the corporation lacks reserves to pay interest and principal on debt when corporate income is insufficient to meet current needs.[46] In determining a corporation's debt-equity ratio, courts look at the relation of the debt both to the book value of the corporation's assets and to their actual fair market value.[47]

12-4 CORPORATE OPERATIONS

LO.7

List and apply the tax rules unique to corporations.

The rules related to gross income, deductions, and losses discussed in previous chapters of this text generally apply to corporations. However, corporations face unique limitations such as the 10 percent of taxable income limitation for charitable contributions and the limitation allowing corporate capital losses to be deductible only against capital gains. In addition, corporations can deduct certain items not generally available to other entities. This section discusses these special deductions and other rules regarding the determination of the corporate income tax liability.

12-4a Deductions Available Only to Corporations

Certain deductions are specific to corporate taxpayers. These provisions include the dividends received deduction and the organizational expenditures deduction.

Dividends Received Deduction

The purpose of the **dividends received deduction** is to mitigate multiple taxation of corporate income. Without the deduction, dividends paid between corporations could be subject to several levels of tax. For example, if Corporation A pays Corporation B a dividend and B passes the dividend on to its shareholders, the dividend is taxed at three levels: Corporation A, Corporation B, and Corporation B's shareholders. The dividends received deduction alleviates this inequity by reducing or eliminating the dividend income taxable to corporations.

As Exhibit 12.5 illustrates, the amount of the dividends received deduction depends on the percentage of ownership (voting power and value) the recipient corporate shareholder holds in a *domestic corporation* making the dividend distribution.[48]

The dividends received deduction cannot exceed the taxable income limitation. This limitation is equal to the corporation's taxable income multiplied by the same percentage. Thus, if a corporate shareholder owns less than 20 percent of the stock in the distributing corporation, the dividends received deduction is limited to 50 percent of taxable income. For this purpose, taxable income is computed without regard to the

---

[46]A court held that a debt-equity ratio of approximately 14.6:1 was not excessive. See *Tomlinson v. 1661 Corp.*, 67–1 USTC ¶9438, 19 AFTR 2d 1413, 377 F.2d 291 (CA–5, 1967). A 26:1 ratio was found acceptable in *Delta Plastics, Inc.*, 85 TCM 940, T.C.Memo. 2003–54.

[47]In *Bauer v. Comm.*, 84–2 USTC ¶9996, 55 AFTR 2d 85–433, 748 F.2d 1365 (CA–9, 1984), a debt-equity ratio of 92:1 resulted when book value was

used. But the ratio ranged from 2:1 to 8:1 when equity included both paid-in capital and accumulated earnings.

[48]§ 243(a). Dividends from foreign corporations generally do not qualify for a dividends received deduction. But see § 245.

EXHIBIT 12.5	Dividends Received Deduction	

Percentage of Ownership by Corporate Shareholder	Deduction Percentage
Less than 20%	50%
20% or more (but less than 80%)	65%
80% or more*	100%

*The payor corporation must be a member of an affiliated group with the recipient corporation.

net operating loss (NOL) deduction, the dividends received deduction, and any capital loss carryback. However, the taxable income limitation does not apply if the corporation has an NOL for the current taxable year.[49]

The following steps are useful in the computation of the deduction:

1. Multiply the dividends received by the deduction percentage (See Exhibit 12.5.).
2. Multiply the taxable income by the same deduction percentage.
3. The deduction is limited to the lesser of Step 1 or Step 2, unless deducting the amount derived in Step 1 results in an NOL. If it does, the amount derived in Step 1 is used. This is referred to as the *NOL rule*.

Red, White, and Blue Corporations, three unrelated calendar year corporations, report the following information for the year:

EXAMPLE 38

	Red Corporation	White Corporation	Blue Corporation
Gross income from operations	$ 400,000	$ 320,000	$ 230,000
Expenses from operations	(340,000)	(340,000)	(340,000)
Dividends received from domestic corporations (less than 20% ownership)	200,000	200,000	200,000
Taxable income before the dividends received deduction	$ 260,000	$ 180,000	$ 90,000

In determining the dividends received deduction, use the three-step procedure described above.

	Red	White	Blue
Step 1 (50% × $200,000)	$100,000	$100,000	$100,000
Step 2			
50% × $260,000 (taxable income)	$130,000		
50% × $180,000 (taxable income)		$ 90,000	
50% × $90,000 (taxable income)			$ 45,000
Step 3			
Lesser of Step 1 or Step 2	$100,000	$ 90,000	
Step 1 amount results in an NOL			$100,000

White Corporation is subject to the 50% of taxable income limitation (Step 2). The NOL rule does not apply because subtracting $100,000 (Step 1) from $180,000 (taxable income before the dividends received deduction) does not yield a negative figure. Blue Corporation qualifies under the NOL rule because subtracting $100,000 (Step 1) from $90,000 (taxable income before the dividends received deduction) yields a negative figure.

In summary, each corporation has a dividends received deduction for the year as follows: $100,000 for Red Corporation, $90,000 for White Corporation, and $100,000 for Blue Corporation.

[49]Further, the limitation does not apply in the case of the 100% deduction available to members of an affiliated group. § 246(b)(2).

No dividends received deduction is allowed unless the corporation has held the stock for more than 45 days.[50] This restriction was enacted to close a tax loophole involving dividends on stock that is held only briefly. When stock is purchased shortly before a dividend record date and soon thereafter sold ex-dividend, a capital loss corresponding to the amount of the dividend often results (ignoring other market valuation changes). If the dividends received deduction was allowed in such cases, the capital loss resulting from the stock sale would exceed the taxable portion of the related dividend income.

EXAMPLE 39

On October 1, 2018, Pink Corporation declares a $1 per share dividend for shareholders of record as of November 1, 2018, and payable on December 1, 2018. Black Corporation purchases 10,000 shares of Pink stock on October 28, 2018, for $25,000 and sells those 10,000 shares ex-dividend on November 4, 2018, for $15,000. (This example assumes no fluctuation in the market price of the Pink stock other than from paying the dividend.) The sale results in a short-term capital loss of $10,000 ($15,000 amount realized − $25,000 basis). On December 1, Black receives a $10,000 dividend from Pink.

Without the holding period restriction, Black Corporation would recognize a $10,000 deduction (subject to the capital loss limitation) but only $5,000 of income [$10,000 dividend − $5,000 dividends received deduction ($10,000 × 50%)], or a $5,000 net loss. However, because Black did not hold the Pink stock for more than 45 days, no dividends received deduction is allowed.

DIGGING DEEPER 3   In-depth coverage can be found on this book's companion website: www.cengage.com

Organizational Expenditures Deduction

Expenses incurred in connection with the organization of a corporation normally are capitalized because they benefit the corporation during its life. But over what period should organizational expenses be amortized? If a useful life cannot be determined, no deduction is allowed. Congress enacted § 248 to solve this problem.

Under § 248, a corporation may *elect* to deduct the first $5,000 of **organizational expenditures** and amortize any remaining expenditures over the 180-month period beginning with the month in which the corporation begins business.[51] Section 248 also requires corporations to reduce the immediate deduction dollar for dollar when total expenditures exceed $50,000. Organizational expenditures include:

- Legal and accounting services related to organizing the corporation (e.g., drafting the corporate charter and bylaws, minutes of organizational meetings, and terms of original stock certificates).

- Expenses of temporary directors and of organizational meetings of directors or shareholders.

- Fees paid to the state of incorporation.

Expenditures that *do not qualify* as organizational expenditures include those connected with issuing or selling shares of stock or other securities (e.g., commissions, professional fees, and printing costs) or with transferring assets to a corporation. These expenditures reduce the amount of capital raised and are not deductible.

---

[50]The stock must be held more than 45 days during the 91-day period beginning on the date that is 45 days before the ex-dividend date (or in the case of preferred stock, more than 90 days during the 181-day period beginning on the date that is 90 days before the ex-dividend date). § 246(c).

[51]The month in which a corporation begins business may not be immediately apparent. Ordinarily, a corporation begins business when it starts the business operations for which it was organized. Reg. § 1.248–1(d). For a similar problem in the Subchapter S area, see Chapter 15.

Stork Corporation (a calendar year C corporation) began business on July 1 of the current year and incurred $52,000 of organizational expenditures. Stork wants to expense as much of these expenditures as possible, electing to amortize any amount it cannot expense. Stork's current-year deduction is $4,633, determined as follows:

Immediate expense [$5,000 − ($52,000 − $50,000)]	$3,000
Amortization [($52,000 − $3,000) ÷ 180] × 6 months in tax year	1,633
Total	$4,633

To qualify for the election, the expenditure must be *incurred* before the end of the tax year in which the corporation begins business. In this regard, the corporation's method of accounting is of no consequence. Thus, an expense incurred by a cash basis corporation in its first tax year qualifies even though the expense is not paid until a subsequent year.

A corporation is deemed to have made the election to deduct and amortize organizational expenditures for the taxable year in which it begins business. A corporation can forgo the election by capitalizing its organizational expenditures on a timely filed return for its first taxable year. In that case, the corporation deducts the capitalized organizational costs when it ceases to do business and liquidates.

Black Corporation, an accrual basis, calendar year taxpayer, was formed and began operations on April 1, 2018. The following expenses were incurred during its first year of operations (April 1– December 31, 2018):

Expenses of temporary directors and of organizational meetings	$15,500
Fee paid to the state of incorporation	2,000
Accounting services incident to organization	18,000
Legal services for drafting the corporate charter and bylaws	32,000
Expenses incident to the printing and sale of stock certificates	48,000

Black Corporation elects to amortize the $67,500 of organizational costs under § 248. Because of the dollar cap (i.e., dollar-for-dollar reduction for amounts in excess of $50,000), none of the $5,000 expensing allowance is available. The monthly amortization is $375 [($15,500 + $2,000 + $18,000 + $32,000) ÷ 180 months], and $3,375 ($375 × 9 months) is deductible for tax year 2018.

Note that the $48,000 of expenses incident to the printing and sale of stock certificates does not qualify for the election. Black Corporation must capitalize these expenses as a reduction of paid-in capital.

Organizational expenditures differ from *startup expenditures*.[52] Startup expenditures include various investigation expenses involved in entering a new business (e.g., travel, market surveys, financial audits, and legal fees) and operating expenses such as rent and payroll that are incurred by a corporation before it actually begins to produce any gross income. Taxpayers can elect to deduct startup expenditures in the same manner as organizational expenditures. So, up to $5,000 can be immediately deducted (subject to the phaseout) and any remaining amounts amortized over a period of 180 months. The same rules that apply to the deemed election (and an election to forgo the deduction and amortization) for organizational expenditures also apply to startup expenditures.

12-4b Business Interest Expense Limitation

The TCJA of 2017 includes a limitation on the deduction for business interest that applies to all taxpayers for tax years beginning after 2017.[53] Business interest is interest paid or accrued on trade or business debt. Although the limitation applies to all businesses, the

---

[52]§ 195.

[53]§ 163(j).

TAX PLANNING STRATEGIES   Organizational Expenditures

FRAMEWORK FOCUS: DEDUCTIONS

Strategy: Maximize Deductible Amounts.

To qualify for the 180-month amortization procedure of § 248, only organizational expenditures incurred in the first taxable year of the corporation can be considered. This rule could prove to be an unfortunate trap for corporations formed late in the year.

EXAMPLE 42

Thrush Corporation is formed in December 2018. Qualified organizational expenditures are incurred as follows: $62,000 in December 2018 and $30,000 in January 2019. If Thrush uses the calendar year for tax purposes, only $62,000 of the organizational expenditures qualify for amortization.

One solution to the problem posed by this example may be for Thrush Corporation to adopt a fiscal year that ends on or beyond January 31. All organizational expenditures will then have been incurred before the close of the first tax year. Alternatively, the corporation could wait until January 2019 to be formed.

rules are most likely to affect large corporations and flow-through entities due to relief provided to smaller businesses.

Under § 163(j), the deduction for business interest for any year is limited to the sum of:

1. The taxpayer's *business interest income* for the year,
2. 30 percent of the taxpayer's *adjusted taxable income* for the year, and
3. The taxpayer's *floor plan financing interest* for the year.

Any business interest deduction disallowed by reason of the limitation is treated as business interest paid or accrued in the succeeding tax year. The carryforward period is unlimited.

The business interest deduction limitation does not apply to certain small businesses.[54] In general, the small business exception applies to taxpayers with average gross receipts for the prior three-year period of $25 million or less.

Business Interest Income

"Business interest income" is the amount of interest income includible in gross income for the year which is related to a trade or business. According to the TCJA of 2017 Conference Report, a corporation typically will have neither investment interest income nor investment interest expense; instead, all interest income and interest expense of a corporation is assumed to be part of the corporation's trade or business.[55]

Adjusted Taxable Income

"Adjusted taxable income"[56] is taxable income computed without regard to:

1. Any nonbusiness income, gain, deduction, or loss;
2. Any business interest or business interest income;
3. Any net operating loss (NOL) deduction;
4. Any deduction for qualified business income (§ 199A); and
5. Any deduction allowable for depreciation, amortization, or depletion.[57]

---

[54]§ 163(j)(3).

[55]TCJA of 2017 Joint Explanatory Statement, p. 288. The Joint Explanatory Statement relies on the rationale that since § 163(d)—the investment interest expense limitation—does not apply to corporations, then any interest income and interest expense should be related to the corporation's trade or business activities (not investment activities).

[56]§ 163(j)(8)(A).

[57]The depreciation, amortization, and depletion adjustment only applies to taxable years beginning before January 1, 2022; § 163(j)(8)(A)(v).

The TCJA of 2017 authorizes the Treasury Department and the IRS to provide other adjustments to the computation of adjusted taxable income.[58] The 30 percent of adjusted taxable income amount cannot be less than zero.[59]

Floor Plan Financing Interest

Virtually all auto dealers acquire their inventory via debt (known as "floor plan" financing), with the debt being secured by the inventory. Interest on this debt ("floor plan financing interest") is deductible without limitation.

Business Interest Expense Limitation

In the current year, Tangerine Corporation, a calendar year C corporation, has $5 million of adjusted taxable income, $75,000 of business interest income, zero floor plan financing interest, and $600,000 of business interest expense.

Tangerine's business interest deduction limitation is $1,575,000 [$75,000 (business interest income) + $1.5 million (30% × $5 million adjusted taxable income)]. As a result, Tangerine can deduct all $600,000 of its business interest expense.

EXAMPLE 43

Assume the same facts as in Example 43, except that Tangerine has $2 million of business interest expense. Here, the deduction for business interest is limited to $1,575,000, and the disallowed amount of $425,000 ($2 million − $1,575,000) is carried forward to next year and treated as business interest in that year.

If Tangerine satisfies the small business exception (i.e., had average gross receipts for the prior three-year period of $25 million or less), the limitation on business interest does not apply and the entire $2 million of business interest is deductible in the current year.

EXAMPLE 44

In the current year, Eagle Corporation, a calendar year C corporation, has ($1 million) of adjusted taxable income, $40,000 of business interest income, zero floor plan financing interest, and $100,000 of business interest expense.

Eagle's business interest deduction limitation is $40,000 [$40,000 (business interest income) + $0 (30% × adjusted taxable income amount, but not less than zero)]. As a result, Eagle's current-year deduction for business interest is limited to $40,000, and the disallowed amount of $60,000 ($100,000 − $40,000) is carried forward to next year and treated as business interest in that year.

If Eagle satisfies the small business exception (i.e., had average gross receipts for the prior three-year period of $25 million or less), the limitation on business interest does not apply and the entire $100,000 of business interest is deductible in the current year.

EXAMPLE 45

Other Rules

Flow-Through Entities In the case of a partnership or S corporation, the business interest deduction limitation applies at the entity level. The general carryforward rule for disallowed business interest does not apply to partnerships (or S corporations); rather, a partner (or S corporation shareholder) can deduct the disallowed interest under a special carryforward rule. A partner's (or S corporation shareholder's) adjusted taxable income is determined without regard to the partner's (or shareholder's) distributive share of the partnership's (or S corporation's) items of income, gain, deduction, or loss.[60]

---

[58]§ 163(j)(8)(B).

[59]§ 163(j)(1), flush language.

[60]§ 163(j)(4).

Trade or Business The term "trade or business" does not include performing services as an employee.[61] As a result, an individual cannot include W–2 wages in adjusted taxable income for purposes of computing the interest deduction limitation. The term also does not include certain real property trades or businesses and certain farming businesses.

LO.8

Compute the corporate income tax.

12-4c Determining the Corporate Income Tax Liability

Corporate income tax rates have fluctuated over the years. The current top statutory corporate income tax rate was reduced from 46 percent to 35 percent over 25 years ago. Current U.S. corporate income tax rates are a flat rate of 21 percent for tax years beginning after 2017 (including for PSCs).

The Big Picture

EXAMPLE 46

Return to the facts of *The Big Picture* on p. 12-1. Assume that Amber incorporates her business as a calendar year C corporation, and that it has taxable income of $51,500. The corporation's income tax liability is $10,815 ($51,500 × 21%).

LO.9

Explain the rules unique to computing the tax of related corporations.

12-4d Controlled Groups

A controlled group of corporations includes parent-subsidiary groups, brother-sister groups, combined groups, and certain insurance companies. Parent-subsidiary controlled groups are discussed in the following section.

Parent-Subsidiary Controlled Group

A **parent-subsidiary controlled group** consists of one or more *chains* of corporations connected through stock ownership with a common parent corporation. The ownership connection can be established through either a *voting power test* or a *value test*. The voting power test requires ownership of stock possessing at least 80 percent of the total voting power of all classes of stock entitled to vote. The value test requires ownership of at least 80 percent of the total value of all shares of all classes of stock of each of the corporations, except the parent corporation, by one or more of the other corporations.[62]

EXAMPLE 47

Aqua Corporation owns 80% of White Corporation. Aqua and White Corporations are members of a parent-subsidiary controlled group. Aqua is the parent corporation, and White is the subsidiary.

The parent-subsidiary relationship described in Example 47 is easy to recognize because Aqua Corporation is the direct owner of White Corporation. Real-world business organizations are often more complex, sometimes including numerous corporations with chains of ownership connecting them. In these complex corporate structures, determining whether the controlled group classification is appropriate becomes more difficult. The ownership requirements can be met through direct ownership (refer to Example 47) or through indirect ownership, as illustrated in the following example.

EXAMPLE 48

Red Corporation owns 80% of the voting stock of White Corporation, and White Corporation owns 80% of the voting stock of Blue Corporation.

Red, White, and Blue Corporations constitute a controlled group in which Red is the common parent and White and Blue are subsidiaries. This parent-subsidiary relationship is diagrammed in Exhibit 12.6. The same result would occur if Red Corporation, rather than White Corporation, owned the Blue Corporation stock.

---

[61]§ 163(j)(7).   [62]§ 1563(a)(1).

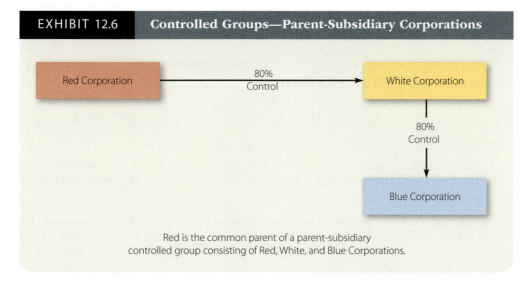

| EXHIBIT 12.6 | Controlled Groups—Parent-Subsidiary Corporations |

Red is the common parent of a parent-subsidiary
controlled group consisting of Red, White, and Blue Corporations.

In-depth coverage can be found on this book's companion website: www.cengage.com   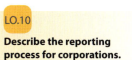 **4** DIGGING DEEPER

Application of § 482

Congress has recognized that a parent corporation has the power to shift income among its subsidiaries. Likewise, shareholders who control other related groups of corporations can shift income and deductions among the related corporations.

When the true taxable income of a subsidiary or other related corporation has been understated or overstated, the IRS can reallocate the income and deductions of the related corporations under § 482. Section 482 permits the IRS to allocate gross income, deductions, and credits between any two or more organizations, trades, or businesses that are owned or controlled by the same interests. This is appropriate when the allocation is necessary to prevent avoidance of taxes or to reflect income correctly. Controlled groups of corporations, especially multinational corporations, are particularly vulnerable to § 482.

12-5 PROCEDURAL MATTERS

LO.10

Describe the reporting process for corporations.

This section covers various aspects of the corporate income tax return, including filing requirements, estimated tax payments, and special disclosure schedules on the return.

12-5a Filing Requirements for Corporations

A corporation must file a Federal income tax return (Form 1120) whether or not it has taxable income. A corporation that was not in existence throughout an entire annual accounting period must file a return for the portion of the year during which it was in existence. In addition, a corporation must file a return even though it has ceased to do business if it has valuable claims for which it will bring suit. A corporation is relieved of filing income tax returns only when it ceases to do business and retains no assets.[63]

The due date for Form 1120 is on or before the fifteenth day of the fourth month following the close of a corporation's tax year.[64] Corporations with assets of $10 million or more generally must file electronically. A C corporation, other than a personal

---

[63]§ 6012(a)(2) and Reg. § 1.6012–2(a).

[64]§ 6072(a). Previously, the due date was the fifteenth day of the third month following the close of the corporation's tax year. In general, the new due date is effective for tax years beginning after 2015.

service corporation, can use either a calendar year or a fiscal year to report its taxable income. The tax year of the shareholders has no effect on the corporation's tax year.

12-5b Estimated Tax Payments

A corporation must make payments of estimated tax unless its tax liability can reasonably be expected to be less than $500. The required annual payment is the *lesser* of:

- 100 percent of the corporation's tax for the current year, or
- 100 percent of the tax for the preceding year (if that was a 12-month tax year, the return filed showed a tax liability, and the corporation involved is not a *large corporation*).

Estimated payments can be made in four installments due on or before the fifteenth day of the fourth month, the sixth month, the ninth month, and the twelfth month of the corporate taxable year.[65] The full amount of the unpaid tax is due on the due date of the return without regard to extensions. A corporation failing to pay its required estimated tax payments will be subjected to a nondeductible penalty on the amount by which the installments are less than the tax due.

12-5c Schedule M–1—Reconciliation of Income (Loss) per Books with Income per Return

Schedule M–1 of Form 1120 is a schedule that *reconciles* financial accounting net income or loss with taxable income reported on the corporation's income tax return by listing the corporation's book-tax differences. Schedule M–1 is used by corporations with less than $10 million of total assets.

The starting point on Schedule M–1 is net income (loss) per books. Additions and subtractions are entered for items that affect financial accounting net income and taxable income differently. The following items are entered as *additions* to financial accounting income (see lines 2 through 5 of Schedule M–1):

- Federal income tax expense per books (deducted in computing net income per books but not deductible in computing taxable income).
- The excess of capital losses over capital gains (deducted for financial accounting purposes but not deductible by corporations for income tax purposes).
- Income that is reported in the current year for tax purposes but is not reported in computing net income per books (e.g., prepaid income).
- Various expenses that reduce net income per books but are not deducted in computing taxable income (e.g., charitable contributions in excess of the 10 percent ceiling applicable to corporations).

The following *subtractions* are entered on lines 7 and 8 of Schedule M–1.

- Income reported for financial accounting purposes but not included in taxable income (e.g., tax-exempt interest).
- Deductions taken on the tax return but not expensed in computing net income per books (e.g., tax depreciation in excess of financial accounting depreciation).

The result is taxable income (before the NOL deduction and the dividends received deduction). Concept Summary 12.5 provides a conceptual diagram of Schedule M–1.

---

[65]§ 6655. If the due date falls on a Saturday, Sunday, or legal holiday, the due date is the next business day. See § 6655(g)(2) for the definition of a *large corporation*.

Concept Summary 12.5

Conceptual Diagram of Schedule M–1 (Form 1120)

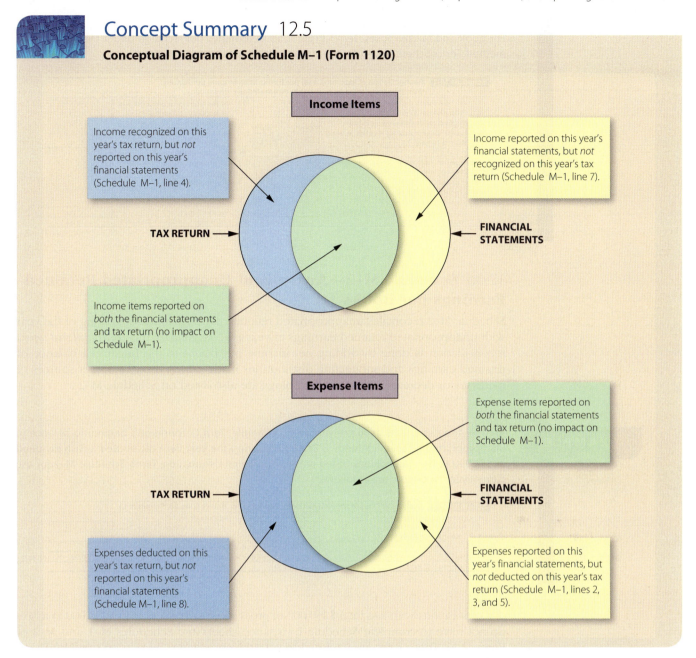

Income Items

Income recognized on this year's tax return, but *not* reported on this year's financial statements (Schedule M–1, line 4).

Income reported on this year's financial statements, but *not* recognized on this year's tax return (Schedule M–1, line 7).

TAX RETURN →

← FINANCIAL STATEMENTS

Income items reported on *both* the financial statements and tax return (no impact on Schedule M–1).

Expense Items

Expense items reported on *both* the financial statements and tax return (no impact on Schedule M–1).

TAX RETURN →

← FINANCIAL STATEMENTS

Expenses deducted on this year's tax return, but *not* reported on this year's financial statements (Schedule M–1, line 8).

Expenses reported on this year's financial statements, but *not* deducted on this year's tax return (Schedule M–1, lines 2, 3, and 5).

EXAMPLE 49

During the current year, Tern Corporation had the following transactions:

Net income per books (after tax)	$89,400
Taxable income	50,000
Federal income tax expense per books	10,500
Interest income from tax-exempt bonds	5,000
Interest paid on loan, the proceeds of which were used to purchase the tax-exempt bonds	500
Life insurance proceeds received as a result of the death of a key employee	50,000
Premiums paid on key employee life insurance policy	2,600
Excess of capital losses over capital gains	2,000

continued

For book and tax purposes, Tern Corporation determines depreciation under the straight-line method. Tern's Schedule M–1 for the current year is constructed as follows:

Schedule M-1	Reconciliation of Income (Loss) per Books With Income per Return					
	Note: The corporation may be required to file Schedule M-3 (see instructions).					
1	Net income (loss) per books	89,400		7	Income recorded on books this year not included on this return (itemize):	
2	Federal income tax per books	10,500			Tax-exempt interest $ 5,000	
3	Excess of capital losses over capital gains .	2,000			Life insurance proceeds on key	
4	Income subject to tax not recorded on books this year (itemize): _____				employee _____ $50,000	55,000
	_____			8	Deductions on this return not charged against book income this year (itemize):	
5	Expenses recorded on books this year not deducted on this return (itemize):					
a	Depreciation . . . . $ _____			a	Depreciation . . $ _____	
b	Charitable contributions . $ _____			b	Charitable contributions $ _____	
c	Travel and entertainment . $ _____				_____	
	Prem.–life ins. $2,600; Int.–tax-exempt bonds $500	3,100		9	Add lines 7 and 8	55,000
6	Add lines 1 through 5	105,000		10	Income (page 1, line 28)—line 6 less line 9	50,000

12-5d Schedule M–2—Analysis of Unappropriated Retained Earnings per Books

Schedule M–2 reconciles unappropriated retained earnings at the beginning of the year with unappropriated retained earnings at year-end. In general, this *financial statement* reconciliation is done by adding net income per books to the beginning balance of retained earnings and subtracting distributions made during the year. Other sources of increases or decreases in retained earnings are also listed on Schedule M–2.

EXAMPLE 50

Assume the same facts as in the preceding example. Tern Corporation's beginning balance in unappropriated retained earnings is $125,000. During the year, Tern distributed a cash dividend of $30,000 to its shareholders. Based on this additional information, Tern's Schedule M–2 for the current year is constructed as follows:

Schedule M-2	Analysis of Unappropriated Retained Earnings per Books (Line 25, Schedule L)					
1	Balance at beginning of year	125,000		5	Distributions: a Cash	30,000
2	Net income (loss) per books	89,400			b Stock	
3	Other increases (itemize): _____				c Property . . .	
	_____			6	Other decreases (itemize):	
	_____			7	Add lines 5 and 6	30,000
4	Add lines 1, 2, and 3	214,400		8	Balance at end of year (line 4 less line 7)	184,400

Corporations with less than $250,000 of gross receipts and less than $250,000 in assets do not have to complete Schedule L (balance sheet) and Schedules M–1 and M–2 of Form 1120. These rules are intended to ease the compliance burden on small business.

DIGGING DEEPER 5   **In-depth coverage can be found on this book's companion website: www.cengage.com**

12-5e Schedule M–3—Net Income (Loss) Reconciliation for Corporations with Total Assets of $10 Million or More

Corporate taxpayers with total assets of $10 million or more are required to report much greater detail relative to differences between income (loss) reported for financial accounting purposes and income (loss) reported for tax purposes. This expanded reconciliation of book and taxable income (loss) is reported on `Schedule M–3`.[66]

---

[66]Corporations that are not required to file Schedule M–3 may do so voluntarily. Any corporation that files Schedule M–3 is not allowed to file Schedule M–1. Corporations (and partnerships) with $10 million to $50 million of total assets may elect to file Schedule M–1 in lieu of Schedule M–3, Parts II and III. Electing entities must still file Schedule M–3, Part I (lines 1–12). Entities with less than $10 million of assets that voluntarily file Schedule M–3 also may elect the reduced Schedule M–3 filing requirements.

BRIDGE DISCIPLINE **Bridge to Financial Accounting**

Measures of corporate income for financial reporting and income tax purposes differ because the objectives of these measures differ. Income measures for financial reporting purposes are intended to help various stakeholders have a clear view of the corporation's financial position and operational results. Income measures for Federal income tax purposes, on the other hand, must comply with the relevant provisions of the Internal Revenue Code. The tax law is intended not only to raise revenues to fund government operations but also to reflect the objectives of government fiscal policy.

As a consequence of these differing objectives, revenue and expense measurements used to determine taxable income may differ from those used in financial reporting. In most cases, differences between book and tax measurements are temporary in nature. Two such temporary differences relate to the different methods of calculating depreciation expense and the limits placed on the deductibility of net capital losses for tax purposes. Permanent differences between book and tax income, such as the dividends received deduction and the domestic production activities deduction, also may exist.

Accounting standards for reporting income tax expenses and liabilities require that the tax impact of *temporary* differences be recognized currently in the financial statements. Because many temporary differences allow a firm to postpone its tax payments to later years, the financial statements must show the amount of the expense that is paid currently and that portion that is to be paid in a later period. The portion of the taxes to be paid in a later period is shown as a liability for such future income taxes. The liability for future income taxes is referred to as a deferred income tax liability.

See Chapter 3 for a complete discussion of this topic.

Schedule M–3 is a response, at least in part, to financial reporting scandals such as Enron and WorldCom. One objective of Schedule M–3 is to create greater transparency between corporate financial statements and tax returns. Another objective is to identify corporations that engage in aggressive tax practices by requiring that transactions that create book-tax differences be disclosed on corporate tax returns.

Total assets for purposes of the $10 million test and the income and expense amounts required by Schedule M–3 are determined from the taxpayer's financial reports. If the taxpayer files Form 10–K with the Securities and Exchange Commission (SEC), that statement is used. If no 10–K is filed, information from another financial source is used, in the following order: certified (audited) financial statements, prepared financial statements, or the taxpayer's books and records.

In-depth coverage can be found on this book's companion website: **www.cengage.com**   **6, 7** DIGGING DEEPER

12-5f **Effect of Taxes on Financial Statements**

Given the differences between taxable income and net income per books, what effect do these differences have on an entity's financial statements? How are income tax accruals arrived at and reported for accounting purposes? What other types of disclosures regarding present and potential tax liabilities are required to satisfy the accounting standards? Recall that Chapter 3 discussed answers to these and other questions at length.

A corporation with total assets of $10 million or more must file Schedule UTP (Uncertain Tax Position Statement) with its Form 1120. In general, a corporation must report tax positions taken on a current or prior year's Federal income tax return and for which the corporation recorded a reserve for Federal income tax in its audited financial statements (or for which the corporation recorded no reserve because of an expectation to litigate). Financial reporting of tax positions is discussed in Chapter 3.

GROWING INTO THE CORPORATE FORM

Amber, the sole property transferor, must acquire at least 80 percent of the stock issued by Garden, Inc., for the transaction to qualify for tax-deferred treatment under § 351. Otherwise, she will recognize $600,000 of taxable gain as a result of the transfer. As a corollary, Jimmy must not receive more than 20 percent of Garden's stock in exchange for services (see Example 15). Even if the requirements of § 351 are met, any debt issued by the corporation will be treated as boot and will result in at least some gain recognition to Amber (see Example 9). Therefore, Amber must evaluate the cost of recognizing gain now versus the benefit of Garden obtaining an interest deduction later.

What If?

Can the § 351 transaction be modified to further reduce personal and business tax costs, both at the time of formation and in the future? Several strategies may be worth considering:

- Have Jimmy transfer some property along with the services rendered to Garden, Inc. As long as Jimmy transfers property with more than a relatively small value compared to the value of services performed, Jimmy will be considered part of the control group. This would allow Amber to own less than 80 percent of the new corporation and still have the transaction qualify under § 351.

- Instead of having Garden issue debt on formation, Amber might withhold certain assets. For example, if the building is not transferred, it can be leased to the corporation. The resulting rent payment would mitigate the double taxation problem by reducing Garden's taxable income via a rent deduction (but would increase Amber's taxable income).

KURHAN/SHUTTERSTOCK.COM

Suggested Readings

Wei-Chih Chiang and Jianjn Du, "The Debt-Equity Debate in the Castle Harbour Case," *Practical Tax Strategies*, March 2013.

Ed Decker, "Why Am I Here?—Changing Times Necessitate Revisiting Prior Entity Choice Decisions," *Business Entities*, September/October 2015.

David B. Friedel and Yaw O. Awuah, "Sec. 351 Control Requirement: Opportunities and Pitfalls," *The Tax Adviser*, July 2014.

Janel Greiman and Thomas J. Nash, "Did Averting Fiscal Cliff Allow C Corporations to Overtake Passthroughs?," *Practical Tax Strategies*, August 2013.

Jeffrey L. Rubinger and Nadia E. Kruler, "Service Applies Substance Over Form Doctrine to Disallow Dividends-Received Deduction," *Journal of Taxation*, July 2013.

Edward J. Schnee and W. Eugene Seago, "Taxing the Transfer of Debts Between Debtors and Creditors," *The Tax Adviser*, July 2012.

Key Terms

Built-in loss property, 12-22

C corporations, 12-2

Capital contribution, 12-25

Check-the-box Regulations, 12-7

Control, 12-12

Disregarded entity, 12-7

Dividends received deduction, 12-28

Limited liability company (LLC), 12-7

Limited partnerships, 12-7

Organizational expenditures, 12-30

Parent-subsidiary controlled group, 12-34

Property, 12-10

Regular corporations, 12-2

S corporations, 12-2

Schedule M–1, 12-36

Schedule M–3, 12-38

Securities, 12-11

Thin capitalization, 12-27

Computational Exercises

1. **LO.2** Marie and Ethan form Roundtree Corporation with the transfer of the following. Marie performs personal services for the corporation with a fair market value of $80,000 in exchange for 400 shares of stock. Ethan contributes an installment note receivable (basis $25,000; fair market value $30,000), land (basis $50,000; fair market value $170,000), and inventory (basis $100,000; fair market value $120,000) in exchange for 1,600 shares. Determine Marie and Ethan's current income, gain, or loss; calculate the basis that each takes in the Roundtree stock.

2. **LO.2** Grady exchanges qualified property, basis of $12,000 and fair market value of $18,000, for 60% of the stock of Eadie Corporation. The other 40% of the stock is owned by Pedro, who acquired it five years ago. Calculate Grady 's current income, gain, or loss and the basis he takes in his shares of Eadie stock as a result of this transaction.

3. **LO.3** Jocelyn contributes land with a basis of $60,000 and fair market value of $90,000 and inventory with a basis of $5,000 and fair market value of $8,000 in exchange for 100% of Zion Corporation stock. The land is subject to a $15,000 mortgage. Determine Jocelyn's recognized gain or loss and the basis in the Zion stock received.

4. **LO.3** Martin transfers real estate with an adjusted basis of $260,000 and fair market value of $350,000 to a newly formed corporation in exchange for 100% of the stock. The corporation assumes the liability on the transferred real estate in the amount of $300,000. Determine Martin's recognized gain on the transfer and the basis for his stock.

5. **LO.4** Yvonne and Simon form Ion Corporation. Yvonne transfers equipment (basis of $110,000 and fair market value of $165,000). Simon invests $130,000 of cash. They each receive 100 shares in Ion Corporation, worth $130,000, but Yvonne also receives $35,000 of cash from Ion. Calculate Ion Corporation's basis in the equipment. In addition, determine Yvonne and Simon's basis in the Ion stock.

6. **LO.6** Chaz transfers cash of $60,000 to a newly formed corporation for 100% of the stock. In its initial year, the corporation has net income of $15,000. The income is credited to the earnings and profits account of the corporation. The corporation distributes $5,000 to Chaz.

   a. How do Chaz and the corporation treat the $5,000 distribution?

   b. Assume, instead, that Chaz transfers to the corporation cash of $30,000 for stock and cash of $30,000 for a note of the same amount. The note is payable in equal annual installments of $3,000 each (beginning at the end of the corporation's initial year of operations) and bears interest at the rate of 6%. At the end of the year, the corporation pays an amount to meet this obligation (i.e., the annual $3,000 principal payment plus the interest due). Determine the total amount of the payment and its tax treatment to Chaz and the corporation.

7. **LO.7** Crane and Loon Corporations, two unrelated C corporations, have the following transactions for the current year:

	Crane	Loon
Gross income from operations	$180,000	$300,000
Expenses from operations	255,000	310,000
Dividends received from domestic corporations (15% ownership)	100,000	230,000

   a. Compute the dividends received deduction for Crane Corporation.
   b. Compute the dividends received deduction for Loon Corporation.

8. **LO.7** Cherry Corporation, a calendar year C corporation, is formed and begins business on April 1, 2018. In connection with its formation, Cherry incurs organizational expenditures of $54,000. Determine Cherry Corporation's deduction for organizational expenditures for 2018.

9. **LO.8** Compute the income tax liability for each of the following unrelated calendar year C corporations.

   a. In 2017, Darter Corporation has taxable income of $68,000.
   b. In 2017, Owl Corporation has taxable income of $10,800,000.
   c. In 2018, Toucan Corporation has taxable income of $170,000.

Problems

10. **LO.1** Janice is the sole owner of Catbird Company. In the current year, Catbird had operating income of $100,000, a long-term capital gain of $15,000, and a charitable contribution of $5,000. Janice withdrew $70,000 of profit from Catbird. How should Janice report this information on her individual tax return if Catbird Company is:

    a. An LLC?
    b. An S corporation?
    c. A C corporation?

11. **LO.1** Can a sole proprietor form as a single-member limited liability company (LLC)? If so, how would such an LLC be taxed?

12. **LO.1** In the current year, Riflebird Company had operating income of $220,000, operating expenses of $175,000, and a long-term capital loss of $10,000. How do Riflebird Company and Roger, the sole owner of Riflebird, report this information on their respective Federal income tax returns for the current year under the following assumptions?

    a. Riflebird Company is a proprietorship (Roger did not make any withdrawals from the business).
    b. Riflebird Company is a C corporation (no dividends were paid during the year).

13. **LO.1** Ellie and Linda are equal owners in Otter Enterprises, a calendar year business. During the current year, Otter Enterprises has $320,000 of gross income and $210,000 of operating expenses. In addition, Otter has a long-term capital gain of $15,000 and makes distributions to Ellie and Linda of $25,000 each. Discuss the impact of this information on the taxable income of Otter, Ellie, and Linda if Otter is:

    a. A partnership.
    b. An S corporation.
    c. A C corporation.

14. **LO.1** In the current year, Azure Company has $350,000 of net operating income before deducting any compensation or other payments to its sole owner, Sasha. In addition, Azure has interest on municipal bonds of $25,000. Sasha has significant income from other sources and is in the 37% marginal tax bracket. Based on this information, determine the income tax consequences to Azure Company and to Sasha during the year for each of the following independent situations. (Ignore the 3.8% Medicare surtax on net investment income.)

    a. Azure is a C corporation and pays no dividends or salary to Sasha.

    b. Azure is a C corporation and distributes $75,000 of dividends to Sasha.

    c. Azure is a C corporation and pays $75,000 of salary to Sasha.

    d. Azure is a sole proprietorship, and Sasha withdraws $0.

    e. Azure is a sole proprietorship, and Sasha withdraws $75,000.

15. **LO.2** Sarah incorporates her small business but does not transfer the machinery and equipment used by the business to the corporation. Instead, the machinery and equipment are leased to the corporation for an annual rent. What tax reasons might Sarah have for not transferring the machinery and equipment to the corporation when the business was incorporated? Suppose Sarah tells you that some of her friends lease equipment to their corporations. Why might that be a poor tax planning idea in 2018?   Critical Thinking

16. **LO.2, 4** Seth, Pete, Cara, and Jen form Kingfisher Corporation with the following consideration:

	Consideration Transferred		
	Basis to Transferor	Fair Market Value	Number of Shares Issued
From Seth—			
Inventory	$30,000	$96,000	30*
From Pete—			
Equipment ($30,000 of depreciation			
taken by Pete in prior years)	45,000	99,000	30**
From Cara—			
Proprietary process	15,000	90,000	30
From Jen—			
Cash	30,000	30,000	10

  *Seth receives $6,000 in cash in addition to the 30 shares.
  **Pete receives $9,000 in cash in addition to the 30 shares.

Assume that the value of each share of Kingfisher stock is $3,000. As to these transactions, provide the following information:

a. Seth's recognized gain or loss. Identify the nature of any such gain or loss.

b. Seth's basis in the Kingfisher Corporation stock.

c. Kingfisher Corporation's basis in the inventory.

d. Pete's recognized gain or loss. Identify the nature of any such gain or loss.

e. Pete's basis in the Kingfisher Corporation stock.

f. Kingfisher Corporation's basis in the equipment.

g. Cara's recognized gain or loss.

h. Cara's basis in the Kingfisher Corporation stock.

i. Kingfisher Corporation's basis in the proprietary process.

j. Jen's recognized gain or loss.

k. Jen's basis in the Kingfisher stock.

l. During discussions relating to the formation of Kingfisher, Seth mentions that he may be interested in either (1) just selling all of his inventory in the current year for its fair market value of $96,000 or (2) proceeding with his involvement in Kingfisher's formation as shown above but followed by a sale of his stock five years later for $90,000. What would be the tax cost of these alternative plans, stated in present value terms? Referring to Appendix F, assume a discount rate of 6%. Further, assume that Seth's marginal income tax rate is 35% and his capital gains rate is 15%.

m. Prepare your solution to part (l) using spreadsheet software such as Microsoft Excel.

17. **LO.2, 4** Tom and Gail form Owl Corporation with the following consideration:

	Consideration Transferred		
	---	---	---
	Basis to Transferor	Fair Market Value	Number of Shares Issued
From Tom—			
Cash	$ 50,000	$ 50,000	
Installment note	240,000	350,000	40
From Gail—			
Inventory	$ 60,000	$ 50,000	
Equipment	125,000	250,000	
Patentable invention	15,000	300,000	60

The installment note has a face amount of $350,000 and was acquired last year from the sale of land held for investment purposes (adjusted basis of $240,000). As to these transactions, provide the following information:

a. Tom's recognized gain or loss.

b. Tom's basis in the Owl Corporation stock.

c. Owl Corporation's basis in the installment note.

d. Gail's recognized gain or loss.

e. Gail's basis in the Owl Corporation stock.

f. Owl Corporation's basis in the inventory, equipment, and patentable invention.

g. How would your answers to the preceding questions change if Tom received common stock and Gail received preferred stock?

h. How would your answers change if Gail was a partnership?

i. Gail is considering an alternative to the plan as presented above. She is considering selling the inventory to an unrelated third party for $50,000 in the current year instead of contributing it to Owl. After the sale, she will transfer the $50,000 sales proceeds along with the equipment and patentable invention to Owl for 60 shares of Owl stock. Whether or not she pursues the alternative, she plans to sell her Owl stock in six years for an anticipated sales price of $700,000. In present value terms and assuming she later sells her Owl stock, determine the tax cost of (1) contributing the property as originally planned, or (2) pursuing the alternative she has identified. Referring to Appendix F, assume a discount rate of 6%. Further, assume Gail's marginal income tax rate is 32% and her capital gains rate is 15%.

Decision Making 18. **LO.2** Luciana, Jon, and Clyde incorporate their respective businesses and form Starling Corporation. On March 1 of the current year, Luciana exchanges her property (basis of $50,000 and value of $150,000) for 150 shares in Starling Corporation. On April 15, Jon exchanges his property (basis of $70,000 and value of $500,000) for 500 shares in Starling. On May 10, Clyde transfers his property (basis of $90,000 and value of $350,000) for 350 shares in Starling.

a.   If the three exchanges are part of a prearranged plan, what gain will each of the parties recognize on the exchanges?

b.   Assume that Luciana and Jon exchanged their property for stock four years ago, while Clyde transfers his property for 350 shares in the current year. Clyde's transfer is not part of a prearranged plan with Luciana and Jon to incorporate their businesses. What gain will Clyde recognize on the transfer?

c.   Returning to the original facts, if the property that Clyde contributes has a basis of $490,000 (instead of $90,000), how might the parties otherwise structure the transaction?

19. **LO.2** Dan and Patricia form Crane Corporation. Dan transfers land (worth $200,000, basis of $60,000) for 50% of the stock in Crane. Patricia transfers machinery (worth $150,000, adjusted basis of $30,000) and provides services worth ($50,000) for 50% of the stock.   *Critical Thinking*

a.   Will the transfers qualify under § 351? Explain.

b.   What are the tax consequences to Dan and Patricia?

c.   What is Crane Corporation's basis in the land and the machinery?

20. **LO.2** John organized Toucan Corporation 10 years ago. He contributed property worth $1 million (basis of $200,000) for 2,000 shares of stock in Toucan (representing 100% ownership). John later gave each of his children, Julie and Rachel, 500 shares of the stock. In the current year, John transfers property worth $350,000 (basis of $170,000) to Toucan for 1,000 more of its shares. What gain, if any, will John recognize on the transfer?

21. **LO.2** Rhonda owns 50% of the stock of Peach Corporation. She and the other 50% shareholder, Rachel, have decided that additional contributions of capital are needed if Peach is to remain successful in its competitive industry. The two shareholders have agreed that Rhonda will contribute assets having a value of $200,000 (adjusted basis of $15,000) in exchange for additional shares of stock. After the transaction, Rhonda will hold 75% of Peach Corporation and Rachel's interest will fall to 25%.   *Decision Making*

Communications

a.   What gain is realized on the transaction? How much of the gain will be recognized?

b.   Rhonda is not satisfied with the transaction as proposed. How will the consequences change if Rachel agrees to transfer $1,000 of cash in exchange for additional stock? In this case, Rhonda would own slightly less than 75% of Peach, and Rachel's interest would be slightly more than 25%.

c.   If Rhonda still is not satisfied with the result, what should be done to avoid any gain recognition?

d.   Summarize your solution in an e-mail, and send it to your instructor.

22. **LO.2, 3, 4** Adam transfers property with an adjusted basis of $50,000 (fair market value of $400,000) to Swift Corporation for 90% of the stock. The property is subject to a liability of $60,000, which Swift assumes.

a.   What is the basis of the Swift stock to Adam?

b.   What is the basis of the property to Swift Corporation?

23. **LO.2, 3, 4** Allie forms Broadbill Corporation by transferring land (basis of $125,000, fair market value of $775,000), which is subject to a mortgage of $375,000. One month prior to incorporating Broadbill, Allie borrows $100,000 for personal reasons and gives the lender a second mortgage on the land. Broadbill Corporation issues stock worth $300,000 to Allie and assumes the mortgages on the land.

a.   What are the tax consequences to Allie and to Broadbill Corporation?

b.   How would the tax consequences to Allie differ if she had not borrowed the $100,000?

Decision Making

24. **LO.2, 4** Rafael transfers the following assets to Crane Corporation in exchange for all of its stock. (Assume that neither Rafael nor Crane plans to make any special tax elections at the time of incorporation.)

Assets	Rafael's Adjusted Basis	Fair Market Value
Inventory	$ 60,000	$100,000
Equipment	150,000	105,000
Shelving	80,000	65,000

a.   What is Rafael's recognized gain or loss?

b.   What is Rafael's basis in the stock?

c.   What is Crane's basis in the inventory, equipment, and shelving?

d.   If Rafael has no intentions of selling his Crane stock for at least 15 years, what action would you recommend that Rafael and Crane Corporation consider? How does this change the previous answers?

25. **LO.2, 3, 4** Kesha, a sole proprietor, is engaged in a cash basis service business. In the current year, she incorporates the business to form Kiwi Corporation. She transfers assets with a basis of $500,000 (fair market value of $1.2 million), a bank loan of $450,000 (which Kiwi assumes), and $80,000 in trade payables in return for all of Kiwi's stock. What are the tax consequences of the incorporation of the business?

Critical Thinking

26. **LO.2** Nancy and her daughter, Kathleen, have been working together in a cattery called "The Perfect Cat." Nancy formed the business several years ago as a sole proprietorship, and it has been very successful. Assets currently have a fair market value of $450,000 and a basis of $180,000. On the advice of their tax accountant, Nancy decides to incorporate "The Perfect Cat." Because of Kathleen's participation, Nancy would like her to receive shares in the corporation. What are the relevant tax issues?

Ethics and Equity

27. **LO.2** Early in the year, Charles, Lane, and Tami form the Harrier Corporation for the express purpose of developing a shopping center. All parties are experienced contractors, and they transfer various business assets (e.g., building materials, land) to Harrier in exchange for all of its stock. Three months after it is formed, Harrier purchases two cranes from Lane for their fair market value of $400,000 by issuing four annual installment notes of $100,000 each. Because the adjusted basis of the cranes is $550,000, Lane plans to recognize a § 1231 loss of $150,000 in the year of the sale. Does Lane have any potential income tax problem with this plan? Explain.

28. **LO.2, 4** Alice and Jane form Osprey Corporation. Alice transfers property, basis of $25,000 and fair market value of $200,000, for 50 shares in Osprey Corporation. Jane transfers property, basis of $50,000 and fair market value of $165,000, and agrees to serve as manager of Osprey for one year; in return, Jane receives 50 shares in Osprey. The value of Jane's services to Osprey is $35,000.

a.   What gain or income will Alice and Jane recognize on the exchange?

b.   What basis will Osprey Corporation have in the property transferred by Alice and Jane? How should Osprey treat the value of the services that Jane renders?

29. **LO.2, 4** Assume in Problem 28 that Jane receives the 50 shares of Osprey Corporation stock in consideration for the appreciated property and for the provision of accounting services in organizing the corporation. The value of Jane's services is $35,000.

a.   What gain or income does Jane recognize?

b.   What is Osprey Corporation's basis in the property transferred by Jane? How should Osprey treat the value of the services that Jane renders?

30. **LO.2, 4** In January of the current year, Wanda transferred machinery worth $200,000 (adjusted basis of $30,000) to a controlled corporation, Oriole, Inc. The

transfer qualified under § 351. Wanda had deducted $165,000 of depreciation on the machinery while it was used in her proprietorship. Later during the year, Oriole sells the machinery for $190,000. What are the tax consequences to Wanda and to Oriole on the sale of the machinery?

31. **LO.5** Red Corporation wants to set up a manufacturing facility in a midwestern state. After considerable negotiations with a small town in Ohio, Red accepts the following offer: land (fair market value of $3 million) and cash of $1 million.

    a.   How much gain or income, if any, must Red Corporation recognize?

    b.   What basis will Red Corporation have in the land?

    c.   Assume that in addition to the facts given, the small town offers to reduce the established property tax rate by 40% on new assets acquired by Red during the two-year period after locating in the town. What are the Federal income tax consequences of the property tax abatement?

32. **LO.6** Emily Patrick (36 Paradise Road, Northampton, MA 01060) formed Teal Corporation a number of years ago with an investment of $200,000 of cash, for which she received $20,000 in stock and $180,000 in bonds bearing interest of 8% and maturing in nine years. Several years later, Emily lent the corporation an additional $50,000 on open account. In the current year, Teal Corporation becomes insolvent and is declared bankrupt. During the corporation's existence, Emily was paid an annual salary of $60,000. Write a letter to Emily in which you explain how she should treat her losses for tax purposes.

Critical Thinking

Communications

33. **LO.7** In each of the following independent situations, determine the dividends received deduction for the calendar year C corporation. The corporate share-holders own less than 20% of the stock in the corporations paying the dividends.

	Almond Corporation	Banana Corporation	Cherry Corporation
Income from operations	$ 700,000	$ 800,000	$ 900,000
Expenses from operations	(600,000)	(860,000)	(910,000)
Qualifying dividends	100,000	100,000	100,000

34. **LO.7** Gull Corporation, a cash method, calendar year C corporation, was formed and began business on November 1, 2018. Gull incurred the following expenses during its first year of operations (November 1, 2018–December 31, 2018):

Expenses of temporary directors and organizational meetings	$21,000
Fee paid to state of incorporation	3,000
Expenses for printing and sale of stock certificates	11,000
Legal services for drafting the corporate charter and bylaws (not paid until January 2019)	19,000

    a.   Assuming that Gull Corporation elects under § 248 to expense and amortize organizational expenditures, what amount may be deducted in 2018?

    b.   Assume the same facts as above, except that the amount paid for the legal services was $28,000 (instead of $19,000). What amount may be deducted as organizational expenditures in 2018?

35. **LO.7** Egret Corporation, a calendar year C corporation, was formed on March 6, 2018, and opened for business on July 1, 2018. After its formation but prior to opening for business, Egret incurred the following expenditures:

Accounting	$ 7,000
Advertising	14,500
Employee payroll	11,000
Rent	8,000
Utilities	1,000

What is the maximum amount of these expenditures that Egret can deduct in 2018?

36. **LO.8** a. In each of the following *independent* situations, determine the corporation's income tax liability. Assume that all corporations use a calendar year for tax purposes and that the tax year involved is 2017.

	Taxable Income
Purple Corporation	$ 65,000
Azul Corporation	290,000
Pink Corporation	12,350,000
Turquoise Corporation	19,000,000
Teal Corporation (a personal service corporation)	130,000

b. Using Microsoft Excel (or a similar software program), create a spreadsheet template that incorporates the 2017 corporate tax rate schedule and can be used to calculate the tax at any given amount of taxable income.

Digging Deeper   37. **LO.9** The outstanding stock in Red, Blue, and Green Corporations, each of which has only one class of stock, is owned by the following unrelated individuals:

	Corporations		
Shareholders	**Red**	**Blue**	**Green**
Marrin	20%	10%	30%
Murray	10%	50%	20%
Moses	50%	30%	35%

a. Determine whether Red, Blue, and Green Corporations constitute a brother-sister controlled group.

b. Assume that Murray does not own stock in any of the corporations. Would a brother-sister controlled group exist? Explain.

38. **LO.10** Emerald Corporation, a calendar year and accrual method taxpayer, provides the following information and asks you to prepare Schedule M–1 for 2018:

Net income per books (after-tax)	$268,200
Federal income tax per books	31,500
Tax-exempt interest income	15,000
Life insurance proceeds received as a result of death of corporate president	150,000
Interest on loan to purchase tax-exempt bonds	1,500
Excess of capital losses over capital gains	6,000
Premiums paid on life insurance policy on life of Emerald's president	7,800

39. **LO.10** The following information for 2018 relates to Sparrow Corporation, a calendar year, accrual method taxpayer.

Net income per books (after-tax)	$205,050
Federal income tax per books	55,650
Tax-exempt interest income	4,500
MACRS depreciation in excess of straight-line depreciation used for financial accounting purposes	7,200
Excess of capital loss over capital gains	9,400
Nondeductible meals and entertainment	5,500
Interest on loan to purchase tax-exempt bonds	1,100

Based on the above information, use Schedule M–1 of Form 1120, which is available on the IRS website, to determine Sparrow's taxable income for 2018.

Digging Deeper   40. **LO.10** In the current year, Woodpecker, Inc., a C corporation with $8.5 million in assets, deducted amortization of $40,000 on its financial statements and $55,000 on its Federal tax return. Is Woodpecker required to file Schedule M–3? If a Schedule M–3 is filed by Woodpecker, how is the difference in amortization amounts treated on that schedule?

41. **LO.10** Dove Corporation, a calendar year C corporation, had the following informa- Critical Thinking
tion for 2018:

Net income per books (after-tax)	$386,250
Taxable income	120,000
Federal income tax per books	25,200
Cash dividend distributions	150,000
Unappropriated retained earnings as of January 1, 2018	796,010

Based on the above information, use Schedule M–2 of Form 1120 (see Example 50 in the text) to determine Dove's unappropriated retained earnings balance as of December 31, 2018.

42. **LO.10** In the current year, Pelican, Inc., incurs $50,000 of nondeductible fines Digging Deeper
and penalties. Its depreciation expense is $245,000 for financial statement purposes and $310,000 for tax purposes. How is this information reported on Schedule M–3?

43. **LO.10** In January 2018, Pelican, Inc., established an allowance for uncollectible Digging Deeper
accounts (bad debt reserve) of $70,000 on its books and increased the allowance by $120,000 during the year. As a result of a client's bankruptcy, Pelican, Inc., decreased the allowance by $60,000 in November 2018. Pelican, Inc., deducted the $190,000 of increases to the allowance on its 2018 income statement, but was not allowed to deduct that amount on its tax return. On its 2018 tax return, the corporation was allowed to deduct the $60,000 actual loss sustained because of its client's bankruptcy. On its financial statements, Pelican, Inc., treated the $190,000 increase in the bad debt reserve as an expense that gave rise to a temporary difference. On its 2018 tax return, Pelican, Inc., took a $60,000 deduction for bad debt expense. How is this information reported on Schedule M–3?

Comprehensive Tax Return Problem

1. On November 1, 2008, Janet Morton and Kim Wong formed Pet Kingdom, Inc., to sell pets and pet supplies. Pertinent information regarding Pet Kingdom is summarized as follows.

   • Pet Kingdom's business address is 1010 Northwest Parkway, Dallas, TX 75225; its telephone number is (214) 555-2211; and its e-mail address is petkingdom@pki.com.

   • The employer identification number is 11-1111111, and the principal business activity code is 453910.

   • Janet and Kim each own 50% of the common stock; Janet is president and Kim is vice president of the company. No other class of stock is authorized.

   • Both Janet and Kim are full-time employees of Pet Kingdom. Janet's Social Security number is 123-45-6789, and Kim's Social Security number is 987-65-4321.

   • Pet Kingdom is an accrual method, calendar year taxpayer. Inventories are determined using FIFO and the lower of cost or market method. Pet Kingdom uses the straight-line method of depreciation for book purposes and accelerated depreciation (MACRS) for tax purposes.

   • During 2018, the corporation distributed cash dividends of $250,000.

Pet Kingdom's financial statements for 2018 are shown below.

Income Statement

Income

Gross sales		$ 5,750,000
Sales returns and allowances		(200,000)
Net sales		$ 5,550,000
Cost of goods sold		(2,300,000)
Gross profit		$ 3,250,000
Dividends received from stock investments in less-than-20%-owned U.S. corporations		43,750
Interest income:		
State bonds	$ 15,000	
Certificates of deposit	20,000	35,000
Total income		$ 3,328,750

Expenses

Salaries—officers:			
Janet Morton	$262,500		
Kim Wong	262,500	$525,000	
Salaries—clerical and sales		725,000	
Taxes (state, local, and payroll)		238,000	
Repairs and maintenance		140,000	
Interest expense:			
Loan to purchase state bonds	$ 9,000		
Other business loans	207,000	216,000	
Advertising		58,000	
Rental expense		109,000	
Depreciation*		106,000	
Charitable contributions		38,000	
Employee benefit programs		60,000	
Premiums on term life insurance policies on lives of Janet Morton and Kim Wong; Pet Kingdom is the designated beneficiary		40,000	
Total expenses			(2,255,000)
Net income before taxes			$ 1,073,750
Federal income tax			(221,734)
Net income per books			$ 852,016

*Depreciation for tax purposes is $136,000. You are not provided enough detailed data to complete a Form 4562 (depreciation). If you solve this problem using Intuit ProConnect, enter the amount of depreciation on line 20 of Form 1120.

Balance Sheet

Assets	January 1, 2018	December 31, 2018
Cash	$ 1,200,000	$ 1,039,461
Trade notes and accounts receivable	2,062,500	2,147,000
Inventories	2,750,000	3,030,000
Stock investment	1,125,000	1,125,000
State bonds	375,000	375,000
Certificates of deposit	400,000	400,000
Prepaid Federal tax	–0–	2,266
Buildings and other depreciable assets	5,455,000	5,455,000
Accumulated depreciation	(606,000)	(712,000)
Land	812,500	812,500
Other assets	140,000	128,500
Total assets	$13,714,000	$13,802,727

continued

Liabilities and Equity	January 1, 2018	December 31, 2018
Accounts payable	$ 2,284,000	$ 1,840,711
Other current liabilities	175,000	155,000
Mortgages	4,625,000	4,575,000
Capital stock	2,500,000	2,500,000
Retained earnings	4,130,000	4,732,016
Total liabilities and equity	$13,714,000	$13,802,727

During 2018, Pet Kingdom made estimated tax payments of $56,000 each quarter to the IRS. Prepare a Form 1120 for Pet Kingdom for tax year 2018 (if the final 2018 Form 1120 is not available, see if a draft 2018 Form 1120 is available on the IRS website).

BRIDGE DISCIPLINE

1. Charles is planning to invest $10,000 in a venture whose management is undecided as to whether it should be structured as a regular corporation or as a partnership. Charles will hold a 10% interest in the entity. Determine the treatment to Charles if the entity is a corporation and if it is a partnership. Charles is in the 37% marginal tax bracket. Also, assume that the passive activity rules do not apply to Charles.

    a. If the entity incurs an $80,000 operating loss in year 1, what is Charles's cash outflow if the entity is a corporation? A partnership? Do not consider the 3.8% additional tax on net investment income in the analysis.

    b. In year 2, the entity earns operating income of $200,000 and makes no distributions to any of the owners. What is the Federal income tax burden on Charles if the investment is a corporation? A partnership?

    c. In year 3, the entity earns operating income of $200,000 and distributes all of that year's after-tax proceeds to the owners. What amount of cash is available to Charles if the entity operates as a corporation (assume that any distribution is a qualified dividend)? A partnership?

2. On your review of the books and records of Ridge Corporation, you note the following information pertaining to its tax provision:

Net income per books	$615,100
Book income tax expense	144,900
Dividends received deduction	70,000
Capital gains	50,000
Capital losses	(60,000)
MACRS depreciation	80,000
Book depreciation	65,000

    a. Calculate Ridge's taxable income and Federal income tax liability for the year.

    b. Calculate Ridge's deferred income tax liability.

Research Problems

Note: Solutions to the Research Problems can be prepared by using the Thomson Reuters Checkpoint™ online tax research database, which accompanies this textbook. Solutions can also be prepared by using research materials found in a typical tax library.

Research Problem 1. Tim is a real estate broker who specializes in commercial real estate. Although he usually buys and sells on behalf of others, he also maintains a portfolio of property of his own. He holds this property, mainly unimproved land, either as an investment or for sale to others.

In early 2016, Irene and Al contact Tim regarding a tract of land located just outside the city limits. Tim bought the property, which is known as the Moore farm, several years ago for $600,000. At that time, no one knew that it was located on a geological fault line. Irene, a well-known architect, and Al, a building contractor, want Tim to join them in developing the property for residential use. They are aware of the fault line but believe that they can circumvent the problem by using newly developed design and construction technology. Because of the geological flaw, however, they regard the Moore farm as being worth only $450,000. Their intent is to organize a corporation to build the housing project, and each party will receive stock commensurate to the property or services contributed.

After consulting his tax adviser, Tim agrees to join the venture if certain modifications to the proposed arrangement are made. The transfer of the land would be structured as a sale to the corporation. Instead of receiving stock, Tim would receive a note from the corporation. The note would be interest-bearing and be due in five years. The maturity value of the note would be $450,000—the amount that even Tim concedes is the fair market value of the Moore farm.

What income tax consequences ensue from Tim's suggested approach? Compare this result with what would happen if Tim merely transferred the Moore farm in return for stock in the new corporation.

Communications

Research Problem 2. A new client, John Dobson, recently formed John's Premium Steakhouse, Inc., to operate a new restaurant. The restaurant will be a first-time business venture for John, who recently retired after 30 years of military service. John transferred cash to the corporation in exchange for 100% of its stock, and the corporation is considering leasing a building and restaurant equipment. John has asked you for guidance on the tax treatment of various expenses (e.g., licensing, training, advertising) he expects the corporation to incur during the restaurant's pre-opening period. Research the tax treatment of startup expenditures, including the point at which a business begins for purposes of determining what expenses are included. Prepare a memo for the client files, describing the results of your research.

Partial list of research aids:
§ 195.
Reg. § 1.195–1.

Decision Making

Communications

Research Problem 3. Lynn Jones, Shawn, Walt, and Donna are trying to decide whether they should organize a corporation and transfer their shares of stock in several corporations to this new corporation. All of their shares are listed on the New York Stock Exchange and are readily marketable. Lynn would transfer shares in Brown Corporation, Shawn would transfer stock in Rust Corporation, Walt would transfer stock in White Corporation, and Donna would transfer stock in several corporations. The stock would be held by the newly formed corporation for investment purposes. Lynn asks you, her tax adviser, whether she would have gain on the transfer of her substantially appreciated shares in Brown Corporation if she transferred the shares to a newly formed corporation. Your input will be critical as they make their decision. Prepare a letter to your client, Lynn Jones, and a memo for the firm's files. Lynn's address is 1540 Maxwell Avenue, Highland, KY 41099.

Use internet tax resources to address the following questions. Look for reliable websites and blogs of the IRS and other government agencies, media outlets, businesses, tax professionals, academics, think tanks, and political outlets.

Research Problem 4. On November 21, 2013, Max Baucus, Chairman of the Senate Finance Committee, released a proposal to change several provisions related to the taxation of business income including, but not limited to, that earned by corporations. The proposal deals primarily with cost recovery and tax accounting methods. Many of the proposed changes are similar to ones contained in House Ways and Means Committee Chairman Dave Camp's small business tax reform discussion draft released earlier in the year. Locate the staff discussion draft of Chairman Baucus's proposal, and prepare a PowerPoint presentation of no more than five slides highlighting the major reforms contained in the proposal.

Communications

Research Problem 5. Limited liability company (LLC) status has become a popular form of operating a business in the United States. Investigate how the growth of LLC status has affected the relative number of new businesses that have chosen to operate as corporations.

Becker CPA Review Questions

1. Gearty and Olinto organized The Worthington Corp., which issued voting common stock with a fair market value of $240,000. They each transferred property in exchange for stock as follows:

Property		Adjusted Basis	Fair Market Value	Percentage of The Worthington Corp. Stock Acquired
Gearty	Building	$80,000	$164,000	60%
Olinto	Land	10,000	96,000	40%

The building was subject to a $20,000 mortgage that was assumed by The Worthington Corp. What was The Worthington Corp.'s basis in the building?

a. $60,000
b. $80,000
c. $144,000
d. $104,000

2. Gearty and Olinto organized The Worthington Corp., which issued voting common stock with a fair market value of $240,000. They each transferred property in exchange for stock as follows:

Property		Adjusted Basis	Fair Market Value	Percentage of The Worthington Corp. Stock Acquired
Gearty	Building	$80,000	$164,000	60%
Olinto	Land	10,000	96,000	40%

The building was subject to a $20,000 mortgage that was assumed by The Worthington Corp. What amount of gain did Gearty recognize on the exchange?

a. $0
b. $20,000
c. $84,000
d. $104,000

3. Ron, David, and Mary formed Widget, Inc. Ron and David each received 40% of the stock, and Mary received the remaining 20%. Ron contributed land with an FMV of $70,000 and an adjusted basis of $20,000. The corporation also assumed a $30,000 liability on the property. David contributed land with an FMV of $30,000 and an adjusted basis of $15,000. David also contributed $10,000 in cash. Mary received her stock for services rendered. She normally would bill $20,000 for these services. What is Mary's basis in the corporate stock received?

   a. $0

   b. $10,000

   c. $15,000

   d. $20,000

4. In the current year, Acorn, Inc., had the following items of income and expense:

Sales	$500,000
Cost of sales	250,000
Dividends received	25,000

   The dividends were received from a corporation of which Acorn owns 30%. In Acorn's current-year corporate income tax return, what amount should be reported as income before special deductions?

   a. $525,000

   b. $505,000

   c. $275,000

   d. $250,000

5. Hirsch, Incorporated, is a calendar year corporation that has had revenues of less than $500,000 since inception. In 2017, Hirsch had a net operating loss that was able to be used in full via a carryback to 2016. For 2018, Hirsch expects to have taxable income of $100,000. How will Hirsch avoid a penalty for underpayment of estimated Federal taxes in the current year?

   a. Hirsch must pay 100% of the tax shown on its 2018 return via estimated taxes to avoid an underpayment penalty.

   b. Hirsch must pay the amount of taxes owed on its 2017 return via estimated taxes to avoid an underpayment penalty.

   c. Hirsch must pay 90% of the tax shown on its 2018 return via estimated taxes to avoid an underpayment penalty.

   d. Hirsch may pay the lower of the amount of taxes owed in 2017 or 100% of the tax shown on the return for 2018 via estimated taxes to avoid an underpayment penalty.

Corporations: Earnings & Profits and Distributions

LEARNING OBJECTIVES: *After completing Chapter 13, you should be able to:*

LO.1 Explain the role that earnings and profits play in determining the tax treatment of distributions.

LO.2 Compute a corporation's earnings and profits (E & P).

LO.3 Apply the rules for assigning earnings and profits to distributions.

LO.4 Evaluate the tax effects of noncash dividends on the recipient shareholder and the corporation making the distribution.

LO.5 Identify the nature and treatment of constructive dividends.

LO.6 Distinguish between taxable and nontaxable stock dividends.

LO.7 Discuss the tax treatment of stock redemptions and corporate liquidations.

CHAPTER OUTLINE

13-1 Corporate Distributions—Overview, 13-2

13-2 Earnings and Profits (E & P), 13-2
13-2a Computation of E & P, 13-3
13-2b Summary of E & P Adjustments, 13-7
13-2c Allocating E & P to Distributions, 13-7

13-3 Noncash Dividends, 13-13
13-3a Noncash Dividends—Effect on the Shareholder, 13-14
13-3b Noncash Dividends—Effect on the Corporation, 13-14

13-4 Constructive Dividends, 13-16
13-4a Types of Constructive Dividends, 13-17
13-4b Tax Treatment of Constructive Dividends, 13-18

13-5 Stock Dividends, 13-21

13-6 Stock Redemptions, 13-22

13-7 Corporate Liquidations, 13-24
13-7a The Liquidation Process, 13-24
13-7b Liquidating and Nonliquidating Distributions Compared, 13-24

13-8 Restrictions on Corporate Accumulations, 13-25

TAX TALK *The relative stability of profits after taxes is evidence that the corporation profits tax is, in effect, almost entirely shifted; the government simply uses the corporation as a tax collector.* —K. E. BOULDING

ALEXANDER RATHS/SHUTTERSTOCK.COM

TAXING CORPORATE DISTRIBUTIONS

Plainwell Ice Cream Corporation, a premium ice cream manufacturer, has had a very profitable year. To share its profits with its two shareholders, Waffle Cone Corporation and Luis, it distributes cash of $200,000 to Cone and real estate worth $300,000 (adjusted basis of $20,000) to Luis, a married individual filing a joint return. The real estate is subject to a mortgage of $100,000, which Luis assumes. The distribution is made on December 31, Plainwell's year-end.

Plainwell experienced both good and bad years in the past. More often than not, however, it has lost money. Despite this year's banner profits, Plainwell's GAAP-based balance sheet indicates a year-end deficit in retained earnings. Consequently, for financial reporting purposes, the distribution of cash and land is treated as a liquidating distribution, resulting in a reduction of Plainwell's paid-in capital account.

The tax consequences of the distributions to Plainwell and its shareholders depend on a variety of factors that are not directly related to the financial reporting treatment. Identify these factors, and explain the tax effects of the distributions to both the entity and its two shareholders.

Read the chapter and formulate your response.

Generally, a corporation cannot deduct distributions made to its shareholders. In contrast, shareholders may be required to treat distributions as fully subject to tax, a nontaxable recovery of capital, or capital gain.

Because distributions provide no deduction to the paying corporation and often require income recognition by the shareholders, corporate income seemingly is subject to a double income tax (i.e., at both the corporate and shareholder levels). Because of the possibility of a double income tax when dealing with corporations, the tax treatment of distributions often raises issues such as the following.

- The availability of earnings to be distributed.
- The basis of the shareholder's stock.
- The character of the property being distributed.
- Whether the shareholder gives up ownership in return for the distribution.
- Whether the distribution is liquidating or nonliquidating.

13-1 CORPORATE DISTRIBUTIONS—OVERVIEW

LO.1

Explain the role that earnings and profits play in determining the tax treatment of distributions.

To the extent that a distribution is made from corporate earnings and profits (E & P), the shareholder receives a **dividend**, usually taxed in a preferential manner.[1] Generally, corporate distributions are presumed to be paid out of E & P (discussed in text Section 13-2a) and are treated as dividend income, *unless* the parties to the transaction can show otherwise.

The portion of a corporate distribution that is not taxed as a dividend (because of insufficient E & P) is nontaxable to the extent of the shareholder's basis in the stock. The stock basis is reduced accordingly. The excess of the distribution over the shareholder's basis is treated as a gain from the sale or exchange of the stock.[2]

EXAMPLE 1

At the beginning of the year, Amber Corporation (a calendar year taxpayer) holds accumulated E & P of $30,000. The corporation reports no current E & P. During the year, the corporation distributes $40,000 to its *equal* shareholders, Bob and Bonnie (i.e., each receives $20,000). Only $30,000 of the $40,000 distribution is a taxable dividend.

Suppose Bob's basis in his stock is $8,000, while Bonnie's basis is $4,000. Under these conditions, Bob recognizes a taxable dividend of $15,000 and reduces the basis of his stock from $8,000 to $3,000. The $20,000 Bonnie receives from Amber Corporation is accounted for as follows.

- Taxable dividend of $15,000.
- Reduction in stock basis from $4,000 to zero.
- Taxable gain of $1,000.

13-2 EARNINGS AND PROFITS (E & P)

The notion of **earnings and profits** is similar in many respects to the financial accounting concept of retained earnings. Both are measures of the firm's accumulated capital. However, these two concepts differ in a fundamental way. The computation of retained earnings is based on financial accounting rules, while E & P is determined using rules specified in the tax law.

Congress has not provided a specific definition of *earnings and profits* in the Internal Revenue Code. Rather, it has provided adjustments that are made to a corporation's taxable income to arrive at E & P. The Treasury (through regulations), the IRS (through rulings), and the courts (through case law) have provided additional guidance. All of these rules must be taken into account when calculating E & P.

---

[1] §§ 301(c)(1) and 316(a). Corporate shareholders can claim a dividends received deduction. See text Section 12–4a. Others typically pay a tax on dividends at a maximum 15% or 20% rate.

[2] § 301(c).

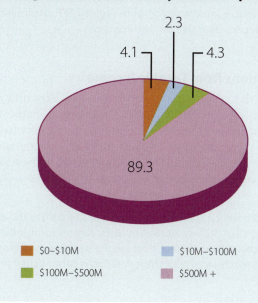

E & P is a measure of the dividend-paying capacity of a corporation (i.e., a measure of *economic income*). As a result, when a corporation makes a distribution to a shareholder, E & P identifies the maximum amount of dividend income shareholders must recognize as a result of a distribution by the corporation. As a result, the effect of a specific transaction on the E & P account often can be determined by considering whether the transaction increases or decreases the corporation's ability to pay a dividend.

13-2a Computation of E & P

Earnings and profits is computed by applying a series of adjustments to a C corporation's taxable income, providing a measure of the corporation's dividend-paying capacity (or economic income).[3] In general, E & P determinations are applied in the same manner for cash and accrual basis taxpayers.

Accumulated E & P is fixed as of the beginning of the tax year; it is the sum of the undistributed earnings of the entity since the later of its incorporation date or February 28, 1913. **Current E & P** is that portion of E & P attributable to the current tax year's operations. It is computed by using the corporation's Federal taxable income and then applying a series of adjustments to more closely approximate the cash flow of the entity.[4]

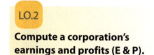

Compute a corporation's earnings and profits (E & P).

Additions to Taxable Income

To determine current E & P, one must add certain previously excluded income items back to taxable income. Included among these positive adjustments are interest income on municipal bonds, excluded life insurance proceeds (in excess of cash surrender value), and Federal income tax refunds from taxes paid in prior years.

---

[3]Reg. § 1.312–6(a).

[4]Section 312 describes many of the adjustments to taxable income necessary to determine E & P. Regulation § 1.312–6 addresses the effect of accounting methods on E & P.

The dividends received deduction is added back to taxable income to determine E & P; this item does not decrease the corporation's assets. This amount is added back to taxable income because it does not impair the corporation's ability to pay dividends: this is a deduction that does not reduce E & P.

Eagle Corporation paid $120,000 of Federal income taxes this year. Eagle also received $6,000 of tax-exempt interest income from State X bonds.

The Federal income taxes are subtracted from taxable income to compute Eagle's E & P because this amount is not available for distribution to shareholders. In contrast, the tax-exempt interest is added to taxable income to compute Eagle's E & P; the interest is not part of taxable income but it represents funds available for distribution.

Subtractions from Taxable Income

Some of the corporation's nondeductible expenditures are subtracted from taxable income to arrive at current E & P. These negative adjustments include the nondeductible portion of business meals and entertainment expenses; related-party losses; expenses incurred to produce tax-exempt income; Federal income taxes paid; nondeductible key employee life insurance premiums (net of increases in cash surrender value); and nondeductible fines, penalties, and lobbying costs.

Joseph Corporation sells property (basis of $10,000) to its sole shareholder for $8,000. Because of the related-party loss disallowance rules, Joseph cannot deduct the $2,000 loss in computing its taxable income. Nonetheless, because the overall economic effect of the transaction is a decrease in Joseph's assets by $2,000, the loss reduces current E & P for the year of the sale.

Timing Adjustments

Some E & P adjustments shift the effect of a transaction from the year of its inclusion in or deduction from taxable income to the year in which it has an economic effect on the corporation. Charitable contribution carryovers, net operating loss carryovers, and capital loss carryovers all give rise to this kind of adjustment.

During 2018, Raven Corporation makes charitable contributions, $12,000 of which cannot be deducted in arriving at its taxable income for the year because of the 10% of taxable income limitation. Consequently, the $12,000 is carried forward to 2019 and available for deduction in that year.

The excess charitable contribution reduces Raven's 2018 current E & P by $12,000 and increases its current E & P for 2019, when the deduction is allowed, by a like amount. Raven paid cash to the charity in 2018, thereby reducing its dividend-paying capacity. For 2019, the charitable contribution carryover reduces Raven's taxable income for that year (the starting point for computing E & P), but no cash outlay was made in that year; the payment is reversed as it already has been taken into account in determining 2018 current E & P.

Gains and losses from property transactions generally affect the determination of E & P only to the extent they are recognized for tax purposes. As a result, gains and losses deferred under the like-kind exchange provision and gains deferred under the involuntary conversion gains do not affect E & P until recognized, and no timing adjustment is required for these items.

Accounting Method Adjustments

Some E & P adjustments arise because the accounting methods used for determining E & P generally are more conservative than those allowed for calculating taxable income. For example, the installment method is not permitted for E & P purposes even though, in some cases, it is allowed when computing taxable income. Accordingly, an adjustment is required for the deferred gain attributable to sales of property made during the year under the installment method. Specifically, all principal payments are treated as having been received in the year of sale.[5]

In 2018, Cardinal Corporation, a calendar year taxpayer, sells unimproved real estate (basis of $20,000) for $100,000. Under the terms of the sale, a 4% interest rate applies, and payments of principal are scheduled to be $60,000 in 2019 and $40,000 in 2020. Cardinal does not elect out of the installment method.

Because Cardinal's 2018 taxable income will not reflect any of the gain from the sale, the corporation must make an $80,000 positive adjustment for that year (the deferred gain from the sale) in computing current E & P. Then negative E & P adjustments are required in 2019 and 2020 (i.e., when the deferred gain is recognized under the installment method).

Treatment of the gain for regular tax and E & P purposes by Cardinal is summarized as follows.

Tax Year	Regular Tax	E & P Treatment	E & P Adjustment
2018	$ –0–	$80,000	+$80,000
2019	48,000*	–0–	−48,000
2020	32,000	–0–	−32,000

*$80,000 gain × $60,000 principal received this year/$100,000 total principal to be received.

A similar analysis can be used for most of the timing and accounting method adjustments.

The alternative depreciation system (ADS) is used in computing E & P.[6] This method requires straight-line depreciation with a half-year convention, over a recovery period equal to the Asset Depreciation Range (ADR) midpoint life.[7] If MACRS cost recovery is used for income tax purposes, a positive or negative adjustment equal to the difference between MACRS and ADS must be made each year. Finally, no additional first-year (bonus) depreciation is allowed under the ADS.[8]

Likewise, when assets are sold, an additional adjustment to taxable income is required to account for the difference in gain or loss resulting from the difference in income tax basis and E & P basis.[9] The adjustments arising from depreciation are illustrated in the following example.

EXAMPLE 6

On January 2, 2018, White Corporation purchased equipment with an ADR midpoint life of 10 years for $30,000. The equipment was then depreciated over its 7-year MACRS class life. No § 179 or additional first-year depreciation was claimed. The asset was sold on July 2, 2020, for $27,000. For purposes of determining taxable income and E & P, cost recovery claimed on the equipment is summarized below.

Year	Cost Recovery Computation	MACRS	ADS	E & P Adjustment
2018	$30,000 × 14.29%	$ 4,287		
	$30,000 ÷ 10-year ADR recovery period × ½ (half-year for first year of service)		$1,500	$2,787
2019	$30,000 × 24.49%	7,347		
	$30,000 ÷ 10-year ADR recovery period		3,000	4,347
2020	$30,000 × 17.49% × ½ (half-year for year of disposal)	2,624		
	$30,000 ÷ 10-year ADR recovery period × ½ (half-year for year of disposal)		1,500	1,124
Total cost recovery		$14,258	$6,000	$8,258

continued

---

[5] § 312(n)(5).

[6] § 312(k)(3)(A).

[7] See § 168(g)(2). The ADR midpoint life for most assets is set out in Rev.Proc. 87–56, 1987–2 C.B. 674. The recovery period is five years for automobiles and light-duty trucks and 40 years for real property. For assets with no class life, the recovery period is 12 years.

[8] § 168(k)(2). Under the MACRS provisions, additional first-year (bonus) cost recovery is available for certain assets placed in service from 2008 through 2026. See text Section 5-8g.

[9] § 312(f)(1).

Each year, White Corporation increases its taxable income by the adjustment amount indicated above to determine E & P. In addition, when computing 2020 E & P, White reduces taxable income by $8,258 to account for the excess gain recognized for income tax purposes.

	Income Tax	E & P
Amount realized	$ 27,000	$ 27,000
Adjusted basis for income tax ($30,000 cost − $14,258 MACRS)	(15,742)	
Adjusted basis for E & P ($30,000 cost − $6,000 ADS)		(24,000)
Gain on sale	$ 11,258	$ 3,000
Adjustment amount ($3,000 − $11,258)	($ 8,258)	

In addition to more conservative depreciation methods, the E & P rules impose limitations on the deductibility of § 179 expense.[10] Specifically, this expense is deducted over a period of five years for E & P purposes (20 percent per year). Therefore, in any year that § 179 is elected, 80 percent of the resulting expense is added back to taxable income to determine current E & P. In each of the following four years, a subtraction from taxable income equal to 20 percent of the § 179 expense is made.

EXAMPLE

7

On January 2, 2014, LarsonCo placed in service a five-year depreciable asset. The acquisition price of the asset was $50,000, and LarsonCo claimed a § 179 deduction for the full amount. Treatment of the § 179 amounts for regular tax and E & P purposes is summarized as follows.

Tax Year	Regular Tax	E & P Treatment	E & P Adjustment
2014	$50,000	$10,000	+$40,000
2015	–0–	10,000	−10,000
2016	–0–	10,000	−10,000
2017	–0–	10,000	−10,000
2018	–0–	10,000	−10,000

The E & P rules also require specific accounting methods in various situations, making adjustments necessary when certain methods are used for income tax purposes. For example:

- E & P requires cost depletion rather than percentage depletion.
- When accounting for long-term contracts, E & P rules require the percentage of completion method rather than the completed contract method.
- E & P does not allow for the amortization of organizational expenses; any such expense deducted when computing taxable income must be added back.
- The E & P computation requires an adjustment for changes in the LIFO recapture amount (the excess of FIFO over LIFO inventory value) during the year. Increases in the LIFO recapture amount are added to taxable income and decreases are subtracted, to the extent of prior-year increases.
- E & P rules also specify that intangible drilling costs and mine exploration and development costs be amortized over a period of 60 months and 120 months, respectively.[11]

---

[10]§ 312(k)(3)(B).

[11]§ 312(n).

13-2b **Summary of E & P Adjustments**

E & P serves as a measure of the earnings of the corporation that are available for distribution as taxable dividends to the shareholders. Current E & P is determined by making a series of adjustments to the corporation's taxable income. These adjustments are reviewed in Concept Summary 13.1.

EXAMPLE 8

Crimson Corporation (a calendar year, accrual basis taxpayer) reports taxable income of $429,000 in 2019. In addition, it provides the following information.

Federal income tax liability paid	$ 90,090
Tax-exempt interest income	6,250
Business meal expenses (total)	10,000
Entertainment expenses	3,000
Premiums paid on key employee life insurance*	8,500
Life insurance proceeds from key employee life insurance policy*	250,000
Excess of capital losses over capital gains	22,000
MACRS cost recovery deduction	82,000
E & P depreciation (straight-line depreciation using ADS)	64,000
Section 179 expense elected and deducted during 2016 for regular tax purposes	120,000
Dividends received from domestic corporations (less than 20% owned)	35,000

*Term policy; no cash surrender value.

Crimson sold property using the installment method during 2017. The property was sold for $120,000 and had an $84,000 adjusted basis when sold. During 2019, Crimson received a $30,000 payment on the installment note.

Crimson did not claim any § 179 expense for 2019. Compute Crimson's current E & P.

Taxable income	$ 429,000
Federal income tax liability paid	(90,090)
Tax-exempt interest income	6,250
Disallowed portion of business meal expenses	(5,000)
Entertainment expenses	(3,000)
Life insurance premiums paid	(8,500)
Proceeds from life insurance policy	250,000
Excess capital losses	(22,000)
Excess of MACRS cost recovery over E & P (ADS) depreciation	18,000**
Allowable portion of 2016 § 179 expenses (20% × $120,000)	(24,000)
Dividends received deduction (50% × $35,000)	17,500
Installment sale gain	(9,000)***
Current E & P	$ 559,160

**$82,000 MACRS − $64,000 ADS
***[($120,000 sales price − $84,000 adjusted basis) ÷ $120,000 sales price] × $30,000 payment received

13-2c **Allocating E & P to Distributions**

When a positive balance exists in both the current and accumulated E & P accounts, corporate distributions are deemed to be made first from current E & P and then from accumulated E & P.

When more than one distribution is made during the year and total distributions exceed the amount of current E & P, it becomes necessary to allocate current and accumulated E & P to each distribution made during the year. First, dollars of current E & P are applied using the following formula.

LO.3

Apply the rules for assigning earnings and profits to distributions.

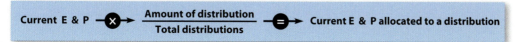

Current E & P ⊗ → $\dfrac{\text{Amount of distribution}}{\text{Total distributions}}$ ⊜ → Current E & P allocated to a distribution

Then accumulated E & P is applied in chronological order, beginning with the earliest distribution. This allocation is important if any shareholder sells stock during the year.

Concept Summary 13.1

Computing E & P

Transaction	Adjustment to Taxable Income to Determine Current E & P	
	Addition	**Subtraction**
Tax-exempt income	X	
Dividends received deduction	X	
Collection of proceeds from insurance policy on life of corporate employee (in excess of cash surrender value)	X	
Deferred gain on installment sale (all of the gain is added to E & P in year of sale)	X	
Future recognition of installment sale gross profit		X
Excess capital loss		X
Excess charitable contribution (over 10% limitation) in year incurred		X
Deduction of charitable contribution, NOL, or capital loss carryovers in succeeding taxable years (increase E & P because deduction reduces taxable income while E & P was reduced in a prior year)	X	
Federal income taxes paid		X
Federal income tax refund	X	
Loss on sale between related parties		X
Nondeductible fines, penalties, lobbying costs, meals, and entertainment		X
Payment of premiums on insurance policy on life of corporate employee (in excess of increase in cash surrender value of policy)		X
Realized gain (not recognized) on an involuntary conversion	No effect	
Realized gain or loss (not recognized) on a like-kind exchange	No effect	
Excess percentage depletion (only cost depletion can reduce E & P)	X	
Accelerated depreciation (E & P is reduced only by straight-line, units-of-production, or machine hours depreciation)	X	X
Additional first-year (bonus) depreciation	X	
§ 179 expense in year elected (80%)	X	
§ 179 expense in four years following election (20% each year)		X
Increase (decrease) in LIFO recapture amount	X	X
Intangible drilling costs deducted currently (reduce E & P in future years by amortizing costs over 60 months)	X	
Mine exploration and development costs (reduce E & P in future years by amortizing costs over 120 months)	X	

EXAMPLE 9

On January 1 of the current year, Black Corporation holds accumulated E & P of $10,000. Current E & P for the year amounts to $30,000, earned evenly throughout the year. Megan and Matt are the sole *equal* shareholders of Black from January 1 to July 31.

On August 1, Megan sells all of her stock to Helen. Black makes two distributions to shareholders during the year: $40,000 to Megan and Matt ($20,000 to each) on July 1 and $40,000 to Matt and Helen ($20,000 to each) on December 1. Current and accumulated E & P are applied to the two distributions as follows.

continued

	Source of Distribution		
	Current E & P	**Accumulated E & P**	**Return of Capital**
July 1 distribution ($40,000)	$15,000	$10,000	$15,000
December 1 distribution ($40,000)	15,000	–0–	25,000

Because 50% of the total distributions are made on July 1 and December 1, respectively, one-half of current E & P is assigned to each of the two distributions. Accumulated E & P is applied in chronological order, so the entire amount attaches to the July 1 distribution. The tax consequences to the shareholders follow.

	Shareholder		
	Megan	**Matt**	**Helen**
July distribution ($40,000)			
Dividend income—			
From current E & P ($15,000)	$ 7,500	$ 7,500	$ –0–
From accumulated E & P ($10,000)	5,000	5,000	–0–
Return of capital ($15,000)	7,500	7,500	–0–
December distribution ($40,000)			
Dividend income—			
From current E & P ($15,000)	–0–	7,500	7,500
From accumulated E & P ($0)	–0–	–0–	–0–
Return of capital ($25,000)	–0–	12,500	12,500
Total distribution	$20,000	$40,000	$20,000
Total dividend income	$12,500	$20,000	$ 7,500
Nontaxable return of capital (assuming sufficient basis in the stock investment)	$ 7,500	$20,000	$12,500

Because the balance in the accumulated E & P account is exhausted when it is applied to the July 1 distribution, Megan has more dividend income than Helen does, even though both receive equal distributions during the year. In addition, each shareholder's basis is reduced by the nontaxable return of capital; any excess over basis results in taxable gain.

When the tax years of the corporation and its shareholders are not the same, it may be impossible to determine the amount of current E & P on a timely basis. For example, if shareholders use a calendar year and the corporation uses a fiscal year, current E & P may not be known until after the shareholders' tax returns have been filed. To address this timing issue, the allocation rules presume that current E & P is sufficient to cover every distribution made during the year until the parties can show otherwise.

EXAMPLE 10

Green Corporation uses a June 30 fiscal year for tax purposes. Carol, Green's only shareholder, uses a calendar year. On July 1, 2018, Green has a zero balance in its accumulated E & P account. For fiscal year 2018–2019, the corporation incurs a $5,000 deficit in current E & P. On August 1, 2018, Green distributed $10,000 to Carol. The distribution is dividend income to Carol and is reported when she files her income tax return for the 2018 calendar year, on or before April 15, 2019.

Because Carol cannot prove until June 30, 2019, at the earliest, that the corporation has generated a deficit in current E & P for the fiscal year, she must assume that the $10,000 distribution is fully drawn from a positive current E & P. Thus, she includes the $10,000 as dividend income on her 2018 Form 1040.

When Carol learns of the deficit, she can file an amended return for 2018 showing the $10,000 as a nontaxable return of capital. Alternatively, Carol can file for an extension for her 2018 return while she awaits Green Corporation's fiscal year-end.

Additional difficulties arise when either the current or the accumulated E & P account has a deficit balance. In particular, when current E & P is positive and accumulated E & P has a deficit balance, accumulated E & P is *not* netted against current E & P. Instead, the distribution is deemed to be a taxable dividend to the extent of the positive current E & P balance.

The Big Picture

EXAMPLE 11

Return to the facts of *The Big Picture* on p. 13-1. Recall that Plainwell Ice Cream Corporation recorded a deficit in GAAP-based retained earnings at the start of the year and record profits during the year. Assume that these financial results translate into an $800,000 deficit in accumulated E & P at the start of the year and current E & P of $600,000. In addition, for purposes of this example, assume that there is no mortgage on the real estate.

In this case, current E & P would exceed the total cash and property distributed to the shareholders. The distributions are treated as taxable dividends; they are deemed to be paid from current E & P even though Plainwell's accumulated E & P still is negative at the end of the year.

In contrast to the previous rule, when a deficit exists in current E & P and a positive balance exists in accumulated E & P, the accounts are netted at the date of distribution. If the resulting balance is zero or negative, the distribution is a return of capital. If a positive balance results, the distribution is a dividend to the extent of the balance. Any loss in current E & P is deemed to accrue ratably throughout the year unless the parties can show otherwise. Various E & P rules are indicated in Concept Summary 13.2.

EXAMPLE 12

At the beginning of the current year, Gray Corporation (a calendar year taxpayer) holds accumulated E & P of $10,000. During the year, the corporation incurs a $15,000 deficit in current E & P that accrues ratably. On July 1, Gray distributes $6,000 in cash to Singh, its sole shareholder.

To determine how much of the $6,000 cash distribution represents dividend income to Singh, the balances of both accumulated and current E & P as of July 1 are determined and netted. This occurs because of the deficit in current E & P.

| | Source of Distribution | |
	Current E & P	Accumulated E & P
January 1		$10,000
July 1 (½ of $15,000 deficit in current E & P)	($7,500)	2,500

The balance in E & P just before the July 1 distribution is $2,500. Thus, of the $6,000 distribution, $2,500 is taxed as a dividend, and $3,500 represents a nontaxable return of capital. After the distribution, Singh's stock basis is $4,000 ($7,500 − $3,500).

Assume instead that Gray's current E & P deficit amounts to $30,000, and that Singh's stock basis is $5,000.

| | Source of Distribution | |
	Current E & P	Accumulated E & P
January 1		$10,000
July 1 (½ of $30,000 current E & P deficit)	($15,000)	(5,000)

The balance in E & P just before the July 1 distribution is ($5,000). As a result, there is zero dividend income. The distribution first is treated as a return of capital (to the extent of Singh's stock basis) and then as a taxable gain. Now, Singh's basis is reduced to zero, and he reports a taxable capital gain of $1,000.

BRIDGE DISCIPLINE Bridge to Finance

Investors often have tried to read the dividend policies of a corporation as indicators of the strength of the entity: constant dividend payments indicated a stable financial structure for the corporation, while dividend increases were a predictor of good times and triggered stock price increases. Reductions in historic dividend payment patterns foreshadowed financial difficulties and often caused a quick and sizable drop in share price.

Nobel Prize winners Merton Miller, University of Chicago, and Franco Modigliani, MIT, saw things differently. They viewed dividends as a remnant of various financing sources available to the corporation: if it was cheaper to finance future growth by retaining profits and decreasing or eliminating dividend payments, so be it. The entity must reduce its cost of capital wherever possible, and under this interpretation, a dividend decrease might indicate the internal financial strength of the corporation. Conversely, the payment of a dividend reduces the capital available to the entity, thereby forcing the entity to finance its operations and growth from some third-party source and risking future weakness if the cost of that capital increases.

Miller and Modigliani found that stock price and dividend policy were unrelated, and that changes in dividend patterns should not affect the capitalized value of the business. Even with lower tax rates on dividends, few shareholders complain that the typical growth stock rarely pays dividends. Nevertheless, shares of companies that pay dividends outperform those that don't pay dividends.

TAX PLANNING STRATEGIES Corporate Distributions

FRAMEWORK FOCUS: INCOME AND EXCLUSIONS

Strategy: Avoid Income Recognition.

Concerning the discussion of corporate distributions, the following points are pertinent.

- Because E & P is used to determine a shareholder's dividend income, its periodic determination is essential to corporate planning. Thus, an E & P account should be established and maintained, particularly if the possibility exists that a corporate distribution might be a return of capital.

- Accumulated E & P is the sum of all past years' current E & P. Because there is no statute of limitations on the computation of E & P, the IRS can redetermine a corporation's current E & P for a tax year long ago. Such a change affects accumulated E & P and has a direct effect on the taxability of current distributions to shareholders.

- Distributions can be planned to avoid or minimize dividend exposure.

EXAMPLE 13

Flicker Corporation holds accumulated E & P of $100,000 as of January 1 of the current year. During the year, it expects to generate earnings from operations of $80,000 and to sell an asset for a loss of $100,000. Thus, it anticipates a current E & P deficit of $20,000. Flicker also expects to make a cash distribution of $60,000 during the year.

A tax-effective approach by Flicker would be to recognize the loss as soon as possible and immediately thereafter make the cash distribution to the shareholders. Suppose these two steps take place on January 1. Because the current E & P now shows a deficit, the accumulated E & P account must be brought up to date (refer to Example 12). Thus, at the time of the distribution, the combined E & P balance is zero [$100,000 (beginning balance in accumulated E & P) − $100,000 (existing deficit in current E & P)], and the $60,000 distribution to the shareholders constitutes a return of capital. Current deficits are deemed to accrue pro rata throughout the year unless the parties can prove otherwise; here, they can.

continued

EXAMPLE

14

After several unprofitable years, Darter Corporation has a deficit in accumulated E & P of $100,000 as of January 1, 2018. Starting in 2018, Darter expects to generate annual E & P of $50,000 for the next four years and would like to distribute this amount to its shareholders. The corporation's cash position (for dividend purposes) will correspond to the current E & P generated. Compare the following possibilities; Darter shareholders are indifferent between the two alternatives.

1. On December 31 of 2018, 2019, 2020, and 2021, Darter Corporation distributes cash of $50,000.
2. On December 31 of 2019 and 2021, Darter Corporation distributes cash of $100,000.

The two alternatives are illustrated as follows.

Year	Accumulated E & P (First of Year)	Current E & P	Distribution	Amount of Dividend
		Alternative 1		
2018	($100,000)	$50,000	$ 50,000	$50,000
2019	(100,000)	50,000	50,000	50,000
2020	(100,000)	50,000	50,000	50,000
2021	(100,000)	50,000	50,000	50,000
		Alternative 2		
2018	($100,000)	$50,000	$ –0–	$ –0–
2019	(50,000)	50,000	100,000	50,000
2020	(50,000)	50,000	–0–	–0–
2021	–0–	50,000	100,000	50,000

Alternative 1 produces $200,000 of dividend income because each $50,000 distribution is fully paid from current E & P. Alternative 2, however, produces only $100,000 of dividend income to the shareholders. The remaining $100,000 is a return of capital. Why?

When Darter made its first distribution of $100,000 on December 31, 2019, it had a deficit of $50,000 in accumulated E & P (the original deficit of $100,000 is reduced by the $50,000 of current E & P from 2018). Consequently, the $100,000 distribution yields a $50,000 dividend (the current E & P for 2019), and $50,000 is treated as a return of capital. As of January 1, 2020, Darter's accumulated E & P now has a deficit balance of $50,000, because a distribution cannot increase a deficit in E & P. Adding the remaining $50,000 of current E & P from 2018, the balance as of January 1, 2021, is zero. Thus, the second distribution of $100,000 made on December 31, 2021, also yields $50,000 of dividends (the current E & P for 2021) and a $50,000 return of capital.

By adjusting the distribution schedule only slightly, Darter shareholders cut in half their gross income from the payments.

Concept Summary 13.2

Allocating E & P to Distributions

Current E & P at Time of Distribution	Accumulated E & P at Time of Distribution	Outcome	Illustration
Positive	Positive	Current E & P is applied first to distributions on a pro rata basis; then accumulated E & P is applied (as necessary) in chronological order beginning with the earliest distribution.	Example 9
		Unless the parties can show otherwise, it is presumed that current E & P covers all distributions.	Example 10
Positive	Deficit	Current and accumulated E & P are *not* netted. Distributions are dividends to the extent of current E & P. If the distribution exceeds the current E & P, the excess first reduces the stock basis to zero, and then it generates a taxable gain.	Example 11
Deficit	Positive	Current and accumulated E & P are netted. Any loss in current E & P is deemed to accrue ratably throughout the year, unless the corporation can show otherwise.	
		(1) If *positive:* Distribution is a dividend to the extent of the balance. If the distribution exceeds the net E & P, the excess first reduces the stock basis to zero, and then generates a taxable gain.	Example 12
		(2) If *negative:* Distribution is treated as a return of capital, first reducing the stock basis to zero, then generating taxable gain.	Example 12
Deficit	Deficit	Entire distribution is treated as a return of capital, first reducing the basis of the stock to zero, then generating taxable gain.	

13-3 NONCASH DIVIDENDS

LO.4

Evaluate the tax effects of noncash dividends on the recipient shareholder and the corporation making the distribution.

The previous discussion assumed that all distributions by a corporation to its shareholders are in the form of cash. Although most corporate distributions are paid in cash, a corporation may distribute a noncash, or **property dividend** for various reasons. For example, the shareholders may want a particular asset that is held by the corporation. Alternatively, a corporation that is strapped for cash may want to distribute a dividend to its shareholders.

BRIDGE DISCIPLINE   Bridge to Investments

Most investors look to the stocks of utilities, real estate investment trusts, and tobacco companies as the source of steady dividend payments. Alternatively, an investor could put together an effective portfolio using only stocks and mutual funds that regularly produce higher dividend yields.

Dividends can be important to the investor because:

- They may be attractive in a tax-sheltered account, like a § 401(k) plan, such that the tax inefficiency ("double taxation") of the dividends is not recognized immediately by the investor.

- Generally, a dividend-paying company is a profitable company, and corporate profits often are hard to come by.

- Earning and reinvesting dividends is an easy way to put into place an investment policy of dollar-cost averaging, a technique that forces the investor to buy more shares when prices are low and fewer shares when prices are high. Dollar-cost averaging often implements a contrarian investment strategy.

Distributions of noncash assets are treated for tax purposes the same as distributions of cash, except for effects attributable to any difference between the basis and the fair market value of the distributed property. Distributions of property with a basis that differs from fair market value raise several tax questions.

- For the shareholder:
  - What is the amount of the distribution?
  - What is the basis of the property in the shareholder's hands?
- For the corporation:
  - Is a gain or loss recognized as a result of the distribution?
  - What is the effect of the distribution on E & P?

13-3a   Noncash Dividends—Effect on the Shareholder

When a corporation distributes property rather than cash to a shareholder, the amount distributed is measured by the fair market value of the property on the date of distribution.[12] As with a cash distribution, the portion of a property distribution covered by existing E & P is a dividend, and any excess is treated as a return of capital. If the fair market value of the property distributed exceeds the corporation's E & P and the shareholder's stock basis, a capital gain usually results.

The amount distributed is reduced (but not below zero) by any liabilities to which the distributed property is subject immediately before and after the distribution, and by any liabilities of the corporation assumed by the shareholder. The basis in the distributed property to the shareholder is the fair market value of the property on the date of the distribution.

The Big Picture

EXAMPLE 15

Return to the facts of *The Big Picture* on p. 13-1. Plainwell Ice Cream Corporation distributed property with a $300,000 fair market value and $20,000 adjusted basis to Luis, one of its shareholders. The property was subject to a $100,000 mortgage, which Luis assumed. As a result, Luis reports a distribution of $200,000 [$300,000 (fair market value) − $100,000 (liability)], which is taxed as a dividend. The basis of the property to Luis is $300,000, its fair market value.

EXAMPLE 16

Red Corporation owns 10% of Tan Corporation. Tan holds ample E & P to cover any distributions made during the year. One distribution made to Red consists of a vacant lot with a basis of $50,000 and a fair market value of $30,000. Red recognizes dividend income of $30,000 (before the dividends received deduction), and its basis in the lot becomes $30,000.

Distributing property that has depreciated in value as a property dividend may reflect poor income tax planning. Note what happens in Example 16. Basis of $20,000 disappears due to the loss (Tan's basis $50,000, fair market value $30,000). As an alternative, if Tan Corporation sells the lot, it can use the $20,000 loss to reduce its taxable income for the year. Then Tan can distribute the $30,000 cash proceeds to its shareholders.

13-3b   Noncash Dividends—Effect on the Corporation

Recognition of Gain or Loss

All distributions of appreciated property trigger a recognized gain to the distributing corporation.[13] In effect, a corporation that distributes appreciated property is treated as if it had sold the property to the shareholder for its fair market value. However, the distributing corporation does *not* recognize any realized loss on the distributed property.

---

[12]§ 301.   [13]§ 311.

The Big Picture

Return to the facts of *The Big Picture* on p. 13-1. Plainwell Ice Cream Corporation distributed property with a fair market value of $300,000 and an adjusted basis of $20,000 to Luis, one of its shareholders. As a result, Plainwell recognizes a $280,000 gain on the distribution.

EXAMPLE 17

Siesta Corporation distributes land with a basis of $30,000 and a fair market value of $10,000. Siesta does not recognize a loss on the distribution.

EXAMPLE 18

If the distributed property is subject to a liability in excess of basis or the shareholder assumes the liability, a special rule applies. For purposes of determining gain on the distribution, the fair market value of the property is treated as being at least the amount of the liability.[14]

Assume that the land in Example 18 is subject to a liability of $35,000, which is assumed by the shareholder who receives the land. The corporation recognizes gain of $5,000 on the distribution ($35,000 liability − $30,000 basis in the land).

EXAMPLE 19

Effect of Corporate Distributions on E & P

Corporate distributions reduce E & P by the amount of money distributed and by the greater of the fair market value or the adjusted basis of property distributed, less the amount of any liability on the property.[15] E & P is increased by gain recognized when appreciated property is distributed as a property dividend.

Effects of Noncash Distributions

Crimson Corporation distributes property (basis $10,000 and fair market value $20,000) to Brenda, its shareholder. Crimson recognizes a $10,000 gain, which is added to its E & P. E & P then is reduced by $20,000, the fair market value of the distributed property. Brenda reports dividend income of $20,000 (presuming sufficient E & P from other events).

EXAMPLE 20

Assume the same facts as in Example 20, except that the property's adjusted basis to Crimson is $25,000. Crimson's E & P is reduced by $25,000, the property's adjusted basis, which is greater than the property's fair market value. Brenda reports dividend income of $20,000 (the fair market value of the property received).

EXAMPLE 21

Assume the same facts as in Example 21, except that the property is subject to a liability of $6,000, which Brenda assumes. E & P now is reduced by $19,000 [$25,000 (adjusted basis) − $6,000 (liability)]. Brenda records a dividend of $14,000 [$20,000 (amount of the distribution) − $6,000 (liability)], and her basis in the property is $20,000, its fair market value.

EXAMPLE 22

Under no circumstances can a distribution, whether cash or property, either generate a deficit in E & P or add to a deficit in E & P. Deficits can arise only through recognized corporate losses.

---

[14]§ 311(b)(2).

[15]§§ 312(a), (b), and (c).

BRIDGE DISCIPLINE **Bridge to Finance**

The double taxation of corporate income always has been controversial. Arguably, taxing dividends twice creates several undesirable economic distortions, including:

- An incentive to invest in noncorporate rather than corporate entities.

- An incentive for corporations to finance operations with debt rather than with equity because interest payments are deductible. Notably, this behavior increases the vulnerability of corporations in economic downturns.

- An incentive for corporations to retain earnings and structure distributions of profits to avoid the double tax.

Collectively, these distortions may raise the cost of capital for corporate investments. In addition, elimination of the double tax would make the United States more competitive globally, as the taxing systems of a majority of U.S. trading partners assess only one tax on corporate income.

While many support a reduced or zero tax rate on dividends, others contend that the double tax should remain in place, to rein in the concentration of economic power held by publicly traded corporations. Those favoring retention of the double tax also note that the benefits of reduced tax rates on dividends flow disproportionately to the wealthy.

EXAMPLE

23

Teal Corporation holds accumulated E & P of $10,000 at the beginning of the current tax year. During the year, it records current E & P of $15,000. At the end of the year, it distributes cash of $30,000 to its sole shareholder, Walter. Walter's basis in his Teal shares is $18,000.

Teal's E & P at the end of the year is reduced to zero by the dividend distribution. The remaining $5,000 of the distribution to Walter cannot generate a deficit in E & P; it is a nontaxable return of capital and reduces the basis in Walter's shares. Walter's stock basis now is $13,000.

Source of Distribution	Effects
Current E & P	($15,000)
Accumulated E & P	(10,000)
Return of capital	5,000

 DIGGING DEEPER **1**   **In-depth coverage can be found on this book's companion website: www.cengage.com**

LO.5

Identify the nature and treatment of constructive dividends.

13-4 **CONSTRUCTIVE DIVIDENDS**

Any measurable economic benefit conveyed by a corporation to its shareholders can be treated as a dividend for Federal income tax purposes even though it is not declared or designated as a dividend by the entity's board of directors. A so-called **constructive dividend** typically is not issued pro rata to all shareholders.[16] Nor must the distribution satisfy the requirements of a dividend as set forth by applicable state law. Instead, a constructive dividend is strictly a creation of the Federal income tax law.

Constructive dividends usually arise in the context of closely held corporations. Here the dealings between the parties are less structured, and frequently, formalities are not preserved.

The constructive dividend might be seen as a substitute for actual distributions. Usually, it is intended to accomplish some tax objective not available through the direct payment of dividends. The shareholders may be attempting to distribute corporate profits in a form, such as compensation, that is deductible to the corporation. Alternatively, the shareholders may be seeking benefits for themselves while avoiding the recognition of income.

---

[16]See *Lengsfield v. Comm.*, 57–1 USTC ¶9437, 50 AFTR 1683, 241 F.2d 508 (CA–5, 1957).

Not all constructive dividends are deliberate attempts to avoid formal dividends; many are entered into inadvertently. An awareness of the various constructive dividend situations is essential to protect the parties from unanticipated, undesirable tax consequences.

13-4a Types of Constructive Dividends

The most frequently encountered types of constructive dividends are summarized below and on the following pages.

Shareholder Use of Corporate-Owned Property

A constructive dividend can occur when a shareholder uses the corporation's property for personal purposes at no cost. Personal use of corporate-owned automobiles, airplanes, yachts, lake property, and entertainment facilities is commonplace in some closely held corporations. The shareholder recognizes dividend income to the extent of the fair rental value of the property for the period of its personal use.[17]

Bargain Sale of Corporate Property to a Shareholder

Shareholders often purchase property from a corporation at a cost below the fair market value of the property. These bargain sales produce dividend income to the extent that the property's fair market value on the date of sale differs from the amount the shareholder paid for the property.[18]

Bargain Rental of Corporate Property

A bargain rental of corporate property by a shareholder also produces dividend income. Here the measure of the constructive dividend is the excess of the property's fair rental value over the rent actually paid.

Payments for the Benefit of a Shareholder

If a corporation pays a shareholder's personal expenses, the payment is treated as a constructive dividend. The obligation involved need not be legally binding on the shareholder; it may, in fact, be motivated by a moral or charitable purpose.[19] Forgiveness of shareholder indebtedness by the corporation also constitutes a constructive dividend.[20] Excessive rentals paid by a corporation for the use of shareholder property create a constructive dividend equal to the amount paid in excess of the fair rental value.

Unreasonable Compensation

A salary payment to a shareholder-employee that is determined to be **unreasonable compensation** frequently is treated as a constructive dividend. As a consequence, it is not deductible by the corporation. In determining the reasonableness of salary payments, the following factors have been considered by the courts and the IRS.

- The employee's qualifications.
- A comparison of salaries with dividend distributions.
- The prevailing rates of compensation for comparable positions in comparable business concerns.
- The nature and scope of the employee's work.
- The size and complexity of the business.
- A comparison of salaries paid with both gross and net income.

---

[17]*Daniel L.Reeves*, 94 TCM 287, T.C.Memo. 2007–273.
[18]Reg. § 1.301–1(j).

[19]*Montgomery Engineering Co. v. U.S.*, 64–2 USTC ¶9618, 13 AFTR 2d 1747, 230 F.Supp. 838 (D.Ct. N.J., 1964), *aff'd* in 65–1 USTC ¶9368, 15 AFTR 2d 746, 344 F.2d 996 (CA–3, 1965).
[20]Reg. § 1.301–1(m).

GLOBAL TAX ISSUES   A Worldwide View of Dividends

From an international perspective, U.S. double taxation of dividends is unusual. Most developed countries have adopted a policy of *corporate integration*, which imposes a single tax on corporate profits.

Corporate integration takes several forms. One popular approach is to impose a tax at the corporate level, but allow shareholders to claim a credit for corporate-level taxes paid when dividends are received. A second alternative is to allow a corporate-level deduction for dividends paid to shareholders. A third approach is to allow shareholders to exclude corporate dividends from income.

Facing tradeoffs between equity and the economic distortions introduced by double taxation and the prevalence of corporate integration throughout the world, U.S. tax law continues to struggle with the issue of how corporate distributions should be taxed.

- The taxpayer's salary policy toward all employees.

- For small corporations with a limited number of officers, the amount of compensation paid to the employee in question in previous years.

- For large corporations, whether a "reasonable investor," acting in the best interests of the entity, would have agreed to the level of compensation paid.[21]

Loans to Shareholders

Advances to shareholders that are not bona fide loans usually are reclassified as constructive dividends. Whether an advance qualifies as a bona fide loan is a question of fact to be determined in light of the particular circumstances. Factors considered in determining whether the advance is a bona fide loan include the following.[22]

- Whether the advance is on open account or is evidenced by a written instrument.

- Whether the shareholder furnished collateral or other security for the advance.

- How long the advance has been outstanding.

- Whether any repayments have been made.

- The shareholder's ability to repay the advance.

- The shareholder's use of the funds (e.g., payment of routine bills versus nonrecurring, extraordinary expenses).

- The regularity of the advances.

- The dividend-paying history of the corporation.

13-4b Tax Treatment of Constructive Dividends

For tax purposes, constructive distributions are treated like cash distributions.[23] Thus, a corporate shareholder is entitled to the dividends received deduction (refer to text Section 12-4a). The constructive distribution constitutes dividend income only to the extent of the corporation's current and accumulated E & P.[24]

DIGGING DEEPER 2   **In-depth coverage can be found on this book's companion website: www.cengage.com**

[21]*Mayson Manufacturing Co. v. Comm.*, 49–2 USTC ¶9467, 38 AFTR 1028, 178 F.2d 115 (CA–6, 1949) and *Alpha Medical v. Comm.*, 99–1 USTC ¶50,461, 83 AFTR 2d 99–697, 172 F.3d 942 (CA–6, 1999).

[22]*Fin Hay Realty Co. v. U.S.*, 68–2 USTC ¶9438, 22 AFTR 2d 5004, 398 F.2d 694 (CA–3, 1968).

[23]*Simon v. Comm.*, 57–2 USTC ¶9989, 52 AFTR 698, 248 F.2d 869 (CA–8, 1957).

[24]*DiZenzo v. Comm.*, 65–2 USTC ¶9518, 16 AFTR 2d 5107, 348 F.2d 122 (CA–2, 1965).

TAX PLANNING STRATEGIES Constructive Dividends

FRAMEWORK FOCUS: INCOME AND EXCLUSIONS

Strategy: Avoid Income Recognition.

Tax planning can be particularly effective in avoiding constructive dividend situations. Shareholders should try to structure their dealings with the corporation on an arm's length basis. For example, reasonable rent should be paid for the use of corporate property, and a fair price should be paid for its purchase. The parties should make every effort to support the amount involved with appraisal data or market information obtained from reliable sources at or near the time of the transaction.

Dealings between shareholders and a closely held corporation should be as formal as possible. In the case of loans to shareholders, for example, the parties should provide for an adequate rate of interest and written evidence of the debt. Shareholders also should establish and follow a realistic repayment schedule.

If shareholders want to distribute corporate profits in a form deductible to the corporation, a balanced mix of the possible alternatives lessens the risk of constructive dividend treatment. Rent for the use of shareholder property, interest on amounts borrowed from shareholders, or salaries for services rendered by shareholders are all feasible substitutes for dividend distributions.

Much can be done to protect against the disallowance of unreasonable compensation. Example 24 is an illustration, all too common in a family corporation, of what *not* to do.

> **EXAMPLE 24**
>
> Bob Cole wholly owns Eagle Corporation. Corporate employees and their annual salaries include Rebecca, Bob's wife ($120,000); Sam, Bob's son ($80,000); Bob ($640,000); and Wong, an unrelated longtime friend ($320,000). The operation of Eagle is shared about equally between Bob and Wong. Rebecca performed significant services for Eagle during its formative years but now merely attends the annual meeting of the board of directors. Sam is a full-time student and occasionally signs papers for the corporation in his capacity as treasurer.
>
> Eagle has not made a cash distribution for 10 years, although it holds substantial accumulated E & P. Rebecca, Sam, and Bob run the risk of a finding of unreasonable compensation, based on the following factors.
>
> - Rebecca's salary is vulnerable unless proof is available that some or all of her $120,000 annual salary is payment for services rendered to the corporation in prior years and that she was underpaid for those years.[25]
>
> - Sam's salary also is vulnerable; he does not appear to earn the $80,000 paid to him by the corporation. Although neither Sam nor Rebecca is a shareholder, each one's relationship to Bob is enough of a tie-in to raise the unreasonable compensation issue.
>
> - Bob's salary could be challenged by the IRS. Why is Bob receiving $320,000 more than Wong, when it appears that they share equally in the operation of the corporation?
>
> - The fact that Eagle has not distributed any cash over the past 10 years, even though it is capable of doing so, also may increase the likelihood of constructive dividend treatment.

What could have been done to improve the tax position of the parties in Example 24? Rebecca and Sam are not entitled to a significant salary, as neither seems to be performing any services for the corporation. Bob probably should reduce his compensation to correspond to that paid to Ed. He then can attempt to distribute corporate earnings to himself in some other form.

continued

---

[25]See, for example, *R. J. Nicoll Co.*, 59 T.C. 37 (1972).

Paying some dividends to Bob also might help to alleviate the problems raised in Example 24. The IRS has been successful in denying a deduction for salary paid to a shareholder-employee, even when the payment was reasonable, in a situation where the corporation had not distributed any dividends.[26] Most courts, however, have not denied deductions for compensation solely because a dividend was not paid. A better approach is to compare an employee's compensation with the level of compensation prevalent in the particular industry.

The corporation can substitute *indirect* compensation for Bob by paying expenses that benefit him personally but are nevertheless deductible to the corporation. For example, premiums paid by the corporation for sickness, accident, and hospitalization insurance for Bob are deductible to the corporation and generally nontaxable to him.[27] Any payments under the policy are not taxable to Bob unless they exceed his medical expenses.[28]

The corporation also can pay for travel and entertainment expenses incurred by Bob on behalf of the corporation. If these expenditures are primarily for the benefit of the corporation, Bob recognizes no taxable income, and the corporation claims a deduction.[29] The tax treatment of these benefits is discussed in more detail in text Section 11-2.

When testing for reasonableness, the IRS looks at the total compensation package, including indirect compensation payments to a shareholder-employee.

What Is the Employee's Compensation?

EXAMPLE 25

Cora, the president and sole shareholder of Willet Corporation, is paid an annual salary of $400,000 by the corporation. She would like to draw funds from the corporation but is concerned that additional salary payments might cause the IRS to contend that her salary is unreasonable.

Cora does not want Willet to pay any dividends. She also wants to donate $50,000 to her alma mater to establish scholarships for needy students. Willet Corporation could make the contribution on its president's behalf. The payment clearly benefits Cora, but the amount of the contribution is not taxed to her.[30] Willet claims a charitable contribution deduction for the payment.

EXAMPLE 26

Assume in Example 25 that Cora has made an individual pledge to the university to provide $50,000 for scholarships for needy students. Willet Corporation satisfies Cora's pledge by paying the $50,000 to the university. The $50,000 will be taxed to Cora. In this context, the $50,000 payment to the university may be treated as *indirect* compensation to Cora.[31]

In determining whether Cora's salary is unreasonable, both the *direct* payment of her $400,000 salary and the *indirect* $50,000 payment are considered. Cora's total compensation package is $450,000. Cora may be eligible for a charitable contribution deduction (see text Section 10-4d).

Certain activities can combine both business and personal dimensions (e.g., a business trip to Hawaii). A country club membership can generate both business and personal use. Such items can be attractive as forms of indirect compensation, but disentangling the business and personal use of business assets can be a challenge.

---

[26]*McCandless Tile Service v. U.S.*, 70–1 USTC ¶9284, 25 AFTR 2d 70–870, 422 F.2d 1336 (Ct.Cls., 1970). The court in *McCandless* concluded that a return on equity of 15% of net profits was reasonable.

[27]Reg. § 1.162–10.

[28]The medical reimbursement plan must meet certain nondiscrimination requirements. § 105(h)(2).

[29]Reg. § 1.62–2(c)(4).

[30]*Henry J. Knott*, 67 T.C. 681 (1977).

[31]*Schalk Chemical Co. v. Comm.*, 62–1 USTC ¶9496, 9 AFTR 2d 1579, 304 F.2d 48 (CA–9, 1962).

Ultimately, whether a constructive dividend exists when indirect compensation is used often depends on the employer's policies and related documentation substantiating some business justification for the usage. Many companies have policies that allow for the "limited personal use" of certain corporate assets (such as computers, telephones, mobile devices, copy machines, conference rooms, and vehicles). This "limited personal use" exception is normally provided as long as the use is occasional, is not for outside employment, does not result in excessive costs, and does not interfere with work responsibilities.

13-5 STOCK DIVIDENDS

LO.6

Distinguish between taxable and nontaxable stock dividends.

On occasion, a C corporation issues a dividend in the form of its own stock (i.e., instead of using cash or other property). This may occur because the entity is short of cash or because it wants to dispose of some treasury stock that it holds. A **stock dividend** is triggered by a board directive. Stock dividends are rare events; about 2 percent of all C corporation distributions during a typical tax year involve the corporation's own shares.

As a general rule, stock dividends are excluded from income if they are pro rata distributions of stock or stock rights paid on common stock.[32] However, there are exceptions to this general rule.

In-depth coverage can be found on this book's companion website: www.cengage.com   **3   DIGGING DEEPER**

If a stock dividend is not taxable, the corporation's E & P is not reduced.[33] If a stock dividend is taxable, the distributing corporation treats the distribution in the same manner as any other taxable distribution.

If a stock dividend is taxable, the shareholder's basis of the newly received shares is fair market value and the holding period starts on the date of receipt. If a stock dividend is not taxable, the basis of the stock on which the dividend is distributed is reallocated.[34]

If the dividend shares are identical to these formerly held shares, basis in the old stock is reallocated by dividing the taxpayer's cost in the old stock by the total number of shares. If the dividend stock is not identical to the underlying shares (e.g., a stock dividend of preferred on common), basis is determined by allocating the basis of the formerly held shares between the old and new stock according to the fair market value of each. The holding period includes the holding period of the previously held stock.[35]

Stock Dividends

Gail bought 1,000 shares of common stock two years ago for $10,000. In the current tax year, Gail receives 10 shares of common stock as a nontaxable stock dividend. To determine Gail's basis in the new shares, the existing basis of $10,000 is divided by 1,010 (the number of shares outstanding after the distribution). Consequently, each share of stock now has a basis of $9.90 instead of the pre-dividend $10 basis.

EXAMPLE 27

Assume instead that Gail received a nontaxable preferred stock dividend of 100 shares. The preferred stock has a fair market value of $1,000, and the common stock, on which the preferred is distributed, has a fair market value of $19,000. After the receipt of the stock dividend, the basis of the common stock is $9,500, and the basis of the preferred is $500, computed as follows.

continued

EXAMPLE 28

---

[32]Companies often issue stock dividends or authorize stock splits to keep the stock price in an affordable range. Stock splits do not change the total value of an investment. For example, 100 shares at $100 will become 200 shares at $50 after the split. However, some studies show that a stock split often leads to an upward price trend over the year following the split.

[33]§ 312(d)(1).

[34]§ 307(a).

[35]§ 1223(5).

Fair market value of common	$19,000	
Fair market value of preferred	1,000	
	$20,000	
Basis of common: $\frac{19}{20} \times \$10,000$	$ 9,500	
Basis of preferred: $\frac{1}{20} \times \$10,000$	$ 500	

 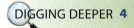 DIGGING DEEPER 4 | **In-depth coverage can be found on this book's companion website: www.cengage.com**

LO.7

Discuss the tax treatment of stock redemptions and corporate liquidations.

13-6 STOCK REDEMPTIONS

Many investors are tempted to use a "no dividends" strategy in working with a healthy corporation whose accumulated profits and market value continue to rise over time.

EXAMPLE

29

Sally invests $100,000 in the new Cream Corporation. Cream is successful in generating operating profits, and it reinvests its accumulated profits in the business rather than paying dividends. Fifteen years later, Sally's shares are worth $300,000, and her share of Cream's E & P exceeds $1 million. Sally sells the shares for a $200,000 long-term capital gain, taxed at a rate of only 20%. By selling her stock to a third party, Sally can reduce the sales proceeds by her stock basis, resulting in a significant tax savings to her, at no detriment to Cream.

A similar strategy would seem to work where several shareholders can act in concert. Using a **stock redemption** to carry out this strategy, the corporation buys back shares from its shareholders in a market transaction. Stock redemptions occur for numerous reasons, including the following.

- To acquire the holdings of a retiring or deceased shareholder.
- To carry out a property settlement related to a divorce.
- To increase the per-share price of the stock as it trades in a market.
- To implement a business succession plan (e.g., using a buy-sell agreement to transfer shares from one generation of shareholders to a younger one).

BRIDGE DISCIPLINE Bridge to Finance

Stock buybacks are popular among U.S. corporations as a means to manipulate share prices. If a buyback is executed properly, all shareholders retain their respective levels of control over the entity, but because fewer shares now are available on the market, an artificial increase in share price occurs. Often, the market temporarily "overcorrects" for the buyback, probably because of the publicity the transaction attracts in the press, and the corporation's total capitalized value actually increases.

Most stock buybacks result in dividend income to the shareholders. Stock redemptions of this type generally do not qualify for capital gain/loss treatment under the tax law. Thus, parties must measure the costs associated with an effective distribution of retained earnings in this way. If dividend income is subject to a favorable tax rate or if the corporate owner of the redeemed shares qualifies for the dividends received deduction, there are few impediments to the plans for the buyback.

Some analysts see an increase in stock buyback activity as a sign of an increasingly healthy economy. A combination of large corporate cash balances and low market interest rates, and significant cuts in effective income tax rates, also can accelerate the buyback market.

GLOBAL TAX ISSUES **Non-U.S. Shareholders Prefer Capital Gain Treatment in Stock Redemptions**

As a general rule, non-U.S. shareholders of U.S. corporations are subject to U.S. income tax on dividend income but not on capital gains. In some situations, a nonresident alien or business entity is taxed on a capital gain from the disposition of stock in a U.S. corporation, but only if the stock was effectively connected with the conduct of a U.S. trade or business of the individual. See text Section 16-2b.

Whether a stock redemption qualifies for capital gain treatment therefore takes on added significance for non-U.S. shareholders. If one of the qualifying stock redemption rules can be satisfied, the non-U.S. shareholder typically will avoid U.S. income tax on the transaction. If, instead, dividend income is the result, a 30 percent withholding tax typically applies.

Stock redemptions generally result in dividend income for the shareholder whose stock is redeemed, rather than a capital gain or loss, unless the shareholder surrenders significant control in the entity as a result of the redemption. Capital gain/loss treatment largely is restricted to stock buybacks where either:

- All of the shareholder's stock is redeemed.[36]
- After the redemption, the investor is a minority shareholder and owns less than 80 percent of the interest owned in the corporation before the redemption.[37]

In-depth coverage can be found on this book's companion website: www.cengage.com   **5 DIGGING DEEPER**

In measuring the investor's stock holdings before and after the redemption, shares owned by related taxpayers also are counted.[38]

In-depth coverage can be found on this book's companion website: www.cengage.com   **6 DIGGING DEEPER**

EXAMPLE 30

Mike and Cheryl are husband and wife, and each owns 100 shares in Mauve Corporation, the total of all of Mauve's outstanding stock. Mauve's operations have produced a sizable aggregated operating profit over the years, such that its E & P exceeds $5 million. Mike and Cheryl have realized appreciation of $600,000 on their original investment of $100,000 each, and they would like to enjoy some of the cash that Mauve has accumulated during their holding period.

At Mike's request, instead of paying a dividend, Mauve buys back one-half of Mike's shares for $350,000. This seems to produce a $300,000 long-term capital gain [$350,000 (sales proceeds) − $50,000 (basis in 50 shares of Mauve stock)], but it results in a $350,000 dividend for Mike, as the redemption did not reduce the control of Mauve that Mike and Cheryl can exercise.

When the transaction is treated as a dividend, the investor's basis in the redeemed shares *does not disappear*; rather, it attaches to any remaining shares that he or she owns. Corporate E & P is reduced by the amount of any recognized dividend.

Stock redemptions also can result in capital gain/loss treatment when the shareholder dies or when the corporation downsizes.[39] Other tax consequences for the redeeming corporation are summarized as follows.

- If noncash property is used to acquire the redeemed shares, the corporation recognizes any realized gain (but not loss) on the distributed assets.[40]
- When the shareholder is taxed as having received a capital gain, E & P of the redeeming corporation *disappears* to the extent of the percentage of shares redeemed relative to the shares outstanding before the buyback.[41]

---

[36]§ 302(b)(3).

[37]§ 302(b)(2).

[38]Section 318 is used for this purpose.

[39]For example, see §§ 302(b)(4) and 303.

[40]§ 311.

[41]The E & P reduction cannot exceed the amount of the redemption proceeds. § 312(n)(7).

Strategy: Control the Character of Income and Deductions.

Stock redemptions offer several possibilities for tax planning.

- Usually, a stock redemption triggers dividend treatment. A preferential tax rate on dividend income reduces some of the adverse consequences of a nonqualified stock redemption for noncorporate shareholders.

- Dividend treatment for a stock redemption may be preferable to a redemption that produces a capital gain if the distributing corporation has little or no E & P or where the distributee-shareholder is another C corporation. In the latter situation, dividend treatment may be preferred due to the availability of the dividends received deduction.

- Stock redemptions are particularly well suited for purchasing the interest of a retiring or deceased shareholder. Rather than the remaining shareholders buying the stock of the retiring or deceased shareholder, corporate funds are used to redeem the stock from the retiring shareholder or from the decedent shareholder's estate. The ability to use the corporation's funds to buy out a shareholder's interest also can be advantageous in property settlements between divorcing taxpayers.

13-7 **CORPORATE LIQUIDATIONS**

When a corporation makes a nonliquidating distribution (e.g., a cash dividend or a stock redemption), the entity typically continues as a going concern. With a complete liquidation, however, corporate existence terminates, as does the shareholder's ownership interest. A complete liquidation, like a qualifying stock redemption, produces capital gain/loss treatment to the *shareholder*. However, the tax effects of a liquidation to the *corporation* vary somewhat from those of a redemption. Gain/loss treatment is the general rule for the liquidating corporation, although some losses are disallowed.

13-7a **The Liquidation Process**

Shareholders may decide to liquidate a corporation for one or more reasons, including the following.

- The corporate business has been unsuccessful.

- The shareholders want to acquire the corporation's assets.

- Another person or entity wants to purchase the corporation's assets. The purchaser may buy the shareholders' stock and then liquidate the corporation to acquire the assets. Alternatively, the purchaser may buy the assets directly from the corporation. After the assets are sold, the corporation distributes the sales proceeds to its shareholders and liquidates.

A **corporate liquidation** exists when a corporation ceases to be a going concern. The corporation continues solely to wind up its affairs, pay debts, and distribute any remaining assets to its shareholders. Legal dissolution under state law is not required for a liquidation to be complete for tax purposes. A liquidation can exist even if the corporation retains a nominal amount of assets to pay remaining debts and preserve legal status.[42]

13-7b **Liquidating and Nonliquidating Distributions Compared**

As noted previously, a *nonliquidating* property distribution, whether in the form of a dividend or a stock redemption, triggers gain (but not loss) to the distributing corporation. For the shareholder, the receipt of cash or property produces dividend income to the extent of the corporation's E & P or, in the case of a qualifying stock redemption, results in a capital gain or loss.

---

[42]Reg. § 1.332–2(c).

However, a complete liquidation produces different tax consequences to the liquidating corporation.[43] With certain exceptions, a liquidating corporation recognizes gain *and* loss upon the distribution of its assets. Thus, a liquidation usually results in income tax for both the corporation and the shareholders; this can be seen as a form of double taxation.

EXAMPLE 31

Goose Corporation, with an E & P balance of $40,000, makes a cash distribution of $50,000 to one of its shareholders. The shareholder's basis in the Goose stock is $24,000. If the distribution is not a qualifying stock redemption or in complete liquidation, the shareholder recognizes dividend income of $40,000 (the amount of Goose's E & P) and treats the remaining $10,000 of the distribution as a return of capital (i.e., stock basis is reduced to $14,000).

If the distribution is a qualifying stock redemption or is pursuant to a complete liquidation, the shareholder recognizes a capital gain of $26,000 ($50,000 distribution − $24,000 stock basis).

In-depth coverage can be found on this book's companion website: www.cengage.com   **7 DIGGING DEEPER**

TAX PLANNING STRATEGIES Corporate Liquidations

FRAMEWORK FOCUS: TAX RATES

Strategy: Avoid Double Taxation.

Usually, distributions in liquidation are taxed at both the corporate level and the shareholder level. When a corporation liquidates, it can, as a general rule, deduct losses on assets that have depreciated in value. These assets should not be distributed in the form of a property dividend or stock redemption, because losses are not recognized on nonliquidating distributions.

Shareholders faced with large prospective gains in a liquidation may consider shifting part or all of that gain to other taxpayers. One approach is to donate the liquidating corporation's stock to charity, producing a deduction equal to the stock's fair market value.

Alternatively, the stock may be transferred by gift to family members. Some or all of the later capital gain on liquidation could be taxed at the reduced tax rate on long-term capital gains. However, possible gift tax issues on the stock transfer must be considered (see text Section 1-2d). Effective planning for stock transfers in the context of a liquidation therefore is crucial in arriving at the desired tax result.

13-8 RESTRICTIONS ON CORPORATE ACCUMULATIONS

Two provisions of the Code are designed to prevent corporations and their shareholders from avoiding the double tax on dividend distributions. Both provisions impose a penalty tax on undistributed income retained by the corporation. The rules underlying these provisions are complex and beyond the scope of this text. However, a brief description is provided as an introduction.

The *accumulated earnings tax*[44] imposes a 20 percent tax on the current year's corporate earnings that have been accumulated without a reasonable business need. The burden of proving what constitutes a reasonable need is borne by the taxpayer. In determining the excessive accumulated income, most businesses are allowed a $250,000 minimum exemption. Thus, most corporations can accumulate $250,000 in earnings over a series of years without fear of an accumulated earnings tax. Beyond the exemption amount, a C corporation's earnings can be accumulated, without incurring the penalty tax, for:

---

[43]§ 331.   [44]§§ 531–537.

- Working capital needs (e.g., to purchase inventory or pay salaries and taxes),
- Retirement of debt incurred in connection with the business,
- Investment or loans to suppliers or customers (if necessary to maintain the corporation's business), or
- Realistic business contingencies, including lawsuits or self-insurance.

The *personal holding company (PHC) tax*[45] acts to discourage the sheltering of gross income in corporations owned by individuals who are subject to high marginal income tax rates. The PHC tax is applied at a 20 percent rate; in any tax year, the IRS cannot impose both the PHC tax and the accumulated earnings tax on the same corporation. Generally, an entity is considered a PHC and may be subject to the tax if:

- More than 50 percent of the value of the outstanding stock was owned by five or fewer individuals at any time during the last half of the year, and
- A substantial portion (60 percent or more) of the corporation's income is comprised of dividends, interest, rents, royalties, or certain personal service income.

REFOCUS ON THE BIG PICTURE

TAXING CORPORATE DISTRIBUTIONS

A number of factors affect the tax treatment of Plainwell Ice Cream Corporation's distributions. The amount of current and accumulated E & P (which differs from the financial reporting concept of retained earnings) partially determines the tax effect on the shareholders. Given that Plainwell had a highly profitable year, it is possible that current E & P equals or exceeds the amount of the distributions. If so, they are dividends to the shareholders rather than a return of capital.

Waffle Cone Corporation receives $200,000 of dividend income that is mostly offset by the dividends received deduction. The amount of the offsetting deduction depends on the ownership percentage that Waffle Cone holds in Plainwell. In this situation, Waffle Cone likely would qualify for a dividends received deduction of $130,000 ($200,000 × 65%). Luis reports $200,000 of dividend income (i.e., $300,000 value of the real estate less the $100,000 mortgage). Assuming that Plainwell is a U.S. corporation and that Luis has held his stock for the entire year, the distribution is a qualified dividend. As a result, the dividend is subject to reduced income tax rates. Luis's basis in the real estate is its fair market value at distribution, or $300,000.

From Plainwell's perspective, the distribution of the appreciated property triggers a recognized gain, equal to $280,000 ($300,000 fair market value less $20,000 adjusted basis). While the gain increases Plainwell's E & P, the distributions to the shareholders reduce it by $200,000 for the cash and $200,000 for the real estate ($300,000 fair market value reduced by the $100,000 mortgage).

What If?

What if the balance of current E & P is less than the combined value of the cash and real estate distributed to the shareholders? Current E & P is applied pro rata to the cash and the real estate. Because the amounts received by the two shareholders are equal ($200,000 each), the current E & P applied is taxed as a dividend and is treated as described above.

To the extent the distributions are not paid from current E & P, accumulated E & P is applied in a pro rata fashion (both distributions were made on December 31). However, if Plainwell reports a deficit in accumulated E & P, the remaining amounts distributed to the two shareholders are first a tax-free recovery of stock basis, and any excess is taxed as a sale of the stock (probably classified as capital gain).

---

[45]§§ 541–547.

Suggested Readings

Julie Allen, et al., "The Forgotten Impact of Accounting Methods When Computing E & P," *Corporate Taxation*, September/October 2010.

Matt Egan, "Are Stock Buybacks Deepening America's Inequality?", **money.cnn.com**, March 5, 2018.

Albert B. Ellentuck, "Case Study: How Corporate Dividends are Taxed," **tinyurl.com/ellentuckdivs**, September 1, 2014.

Key Terms

Accumulated E & P, 13-3

Constructive dividend, 13-16

Corporate liquidation, 13-24

Current E & P, 13-3

Dividend, 13-2

Earnings and profits, 13-2

Property dividend, 13-13

Stock dividend, 13-21

Stock redemption, 13-22

Unreasonable compensation, 13-17

Computational Exercises

1. **LO.1** At the beginning of the year, Myrna Corporation (a calendar year taxpayer) holds E & P of $32,000. The corporation generates no additional E & P during the year. On December 31, the corporation distributes $50,000 to its sole shareholder, Abby, whose stock basis is $10,000. How does the Federal income tax law treat this distribution?

2. **LO.3** On January 1 of the current year, Rhondell Corporation holds accumulated E & P of $13,000. Current E & P for the year is $84,000, earned evenly throughout the year. Elizabeth and Jonathan are the sole equal shareholders of Rhondell from January 1 to April 30. On May 1, Elizabeth sells all of her stock to Marshall.

   Rhondell makes two distributions to shareholders during the year, as indicated below. Analyze the distributions by completing the table that follows. Assume that the shareholders have sufficient basis in their stock for any amount that is treated as return of capital.

Total Distribution	From Current E & P	From Accumulated E & P	Return of Capital
April 30, $42,000 cash	_____	_____	_____
December 31, $58,000 cash	_____	_____	_____

3. **LO.5** Global Corporation distributed property with an $850,000 fair market value and a $415,000 adjusted basis to Kang, one of its shareholders. The property was subject to a $230,000 mortgage, which Kang assumed. Global's accumulated E & P totals $3 million.

   What is the amount of Kang's dividend income on the distribution? What is Kang's basis in the property received?

4. **LO.5** Fargo Corporation holds $5 million in accumulated E & P. It distributes to Leilei, one of its shareholders, land worth $310,000; basis of the land to Fargo is $260,000. Determine the Federal income tax consequences of the distribution to Fargo.

5. **LO.7** During the current year, Gnatcatcher, Inc. (E & P of $1 million), distributed $200,000 each to Brandi and Yuen in redemption of some of their Gnatcatcher stock. The two shareholders are not related; they acquired their shares five years ago. Brandi and Yuen are in the 32% income tax bracket, and each had a $45,000 basis in her redeemed stock.

   a. Assume that the distribution to Brandi is a qualifying stock redemption. Determine Brandi's tax liability on the distribution.

   b. Assume that the distribution to Yuen is a nonqualified stock redemption. Determine Yuen's tax liability on the distribution.

6. **LO.7** Rosalie owns 50% of the outstanding stock of Salmon Corporation. In a qualifying stock redemption, Salmon distributes $80,000 to Rosalie in exchange for one-half of her shares, which have a basis of $100,000. Compute Rosalie's recognized loss, if any, on the redemption.

Digging Deeper   7. **LO.7** Derk owns 250 shares of stock in Rose Corporation. The remaining 750 shares of Rose are owned as follows: 150 by Derk's daughter Rosalie, 200 by Derk's aunt Penelope, and 400 by a partnership in which Derk holds an 80% interest. Determine the number of shares that Derk owns (directly and indirectly) in Rose Corporation.

8. **LO.7** Caramel Corporation has 5,000 shares of stock outstanding. In a qualifying stock redemption, Caramel distributes $145,000 in exchange for 1,000 of its shares. At the time of the redemption, Caramel has recorded paid-in capital of $800,000 and E & P of $300,000. Calculate the reduction to Caramel's E & P as a result of the distribution.

Problems

9. **LO.1, 3** At the start of the current year, Blue Corporation (a calendar year taxpayer) holds accumulated E & P of $100,000. Blue's current E & P is $60,000. At the end of the year, it distributes $200,000 ($100,000 each) to its equal shareholders, Pam and Jon. Their basis in the stock is $11,000 for Pam and $26,000 for Jon. How is the distribution treated for tax purposes?

10. **LO.2** Cardinal Corporation, a calendar year taxpayer, receives dividend income of $250,000 from a corporation in which it holds a 10% interest. Cardinal also receives interest income of $35,000 from municipal bonds. (The municipality used the proceeds from the bond issue to construct a public library.) Cardinal borrowed funds to purchase the municipal bonds and pays $20,000 of interest on the loan. Excluding these three items, Cardinal's taxable income is $500,000, on which it paid Federal income tax of $131,250 during the year.

    a. What is Cardinal's taxable income after these items are taken into account?

    b. What is Cardinal's accumulated E & P at the end of the tax year if its beginning E & P balance was $150,000?

11. **LO.2** Compute current E & P for Sparrow Corporation (a calendar year, accrual basis taxpayer). Sparrow reported the following transactions during 2018, its second year of operation.

Taxable income	$330,000
Federal income tax liability paid	69,300
Tax-exempt interest income	5,000
Business meal expenses (total)	3,000
Premiums paid on key employee life insurance	3,500
Increase in cash surrender value attributable to life insurance premiums	700
Proceeds from key employee life insurance policy	130,000
Cash surrender value of life insurance policy at distribution	20,000

Excess of capital losses over capital gains	$ 13,000
MACRS deduction	26,000
Straight-line depreciation using ADS lives	16,000
Section 179 expense elected during 2017	25,000
Dividends received from domestic corporations (less than 20% owned)	35,000

- Sparrow uses the LIFO inventory method, and its LIFO recapture amount increased by $10,000 during 2018.
- Sparrow sold some property on installments during 2017. The property was sold for $40,000 and had an adjusted basis then of $32,000. During 2018, Sparrow received a $15,000 payment on the installment sale.

12. **LO.1, 2, 3** On September 30, Silver Corporation, a calendar year taxpayer, sold a parcel of land (basis of $400,000) for a $1 million note. The note is payable in five installments, with the first payment due next year. Because Silver did not elect out of the installment method, none of the $600,000 gain is taxed this year.

     Silver Corporation had a $300,000 deficit in accumulated E & P at the beginning of the year. Before considering the effect of the land sale, Silver had a deficit in current E & P of $50,000.

     Javiera, the sole shareholder of Silver, has a basis of $200,000 in her stock. If Silver distributes $900,000 to Javiera on December 31, how much gross income must she report for Federal income tax purposes?

13. **LO.2** In determining Blue Corporation's current E & P for the current tax year, how should taxable income be adjusted as a result of the following transactions?
    a. A capital loss carryover from one year ago, fully used this year.
    b. Nondeductible business meal expenses.
    c. Interest income on municipal bonds.
    d. Nondeductible lobbying expenses.
    e. Loss on a sale between related parties.
    f. Federal income tax refund from last year's return, received this year.

14. **LO.1, 3** Sparrow Corporation is a calendar year taxpayer. At the beginning of the   Critical Thinking
    current year, Sparrow holds accumulated E & P of $33,000. The corporation incurs a deficit in current E & P of $46,000 that accrues ratably throughout the year. On June 30, Sparrow distributes $20,000 to its sole shareholder, Libby. If Libby's stock has a basis of $4,000, how is she taxed on the distribution?

15. **LO.1, 3** Complete the following schedule for each case. Unless otherwise indicated, assume that the shareholders have ample basis in the stock investment. All taxpayers use a calendar tax year.

	Accumulated E & P Beginning of Year	Current E & P	Cash Distributions (All on Last Day of Year)	Dividend Income	Return of Capital
a.	($200,000)	$ 70,000	$130,000	_____	_____
b.	150,000	(120,000)	210,000	_____	_____
c.	90,000	70,000	150,000	_____	_____
d.	120,000	(60,000)	130,000	_____	_____
e.	Sames as (d), except that the distribution of $130,000 is made on June 30.			_____	_____

16. **LO.1, 3** Larry, the sole shareholder of Brown Corporation, sold his stock to Ed on July 30 for $270,000. Larry's basis in the stock was $200,000 at the beginning of the year. Brown had accumulated E & P of $120,000 on January 1 and

current E & P of $240,000. During the year, Brown made the following distributions: $450,000 cash to Larry on July 1 and $150,000 cash to Ed on December 30. How will Larry and Ed be taxed on the distributions? How much gain will Larry recognize on the sale of his stock to Ed?

Critical Thinking   17. **LO.1, 2** In each of the following independent situations, indicate the effect on tax-able income and E & P, stating the amount of any increase (or decrease) in each as a result of the transaction. Assume that E & P has already been increased by taxable income.

Transaction	Taxable Income Increase (Decrease)	E & P Increase (Decrease)
a. Realized gain of $80,000 on involuntary conversion of building ($10,000 of gain is recognized).	_____	_____
b. Mining exploration costs incurred on May 1 of current year; $24,000 is deductible from current-year taxable income.	_____	_____
c. Sale of equipment to unrelated third party for $240,000; basis is $120,000 (no election out of installment method; no payments are received in current year).	_____	_____
d. Dividends of $20,000 received from 5% owned corporation, together with dividends received deduction (assume that the taxable income limit does not apply).	_____	_____
e. Additional first-year (bonus) depreciation of $45,000 claimed in current year.	_____	_____
f. Section 179 expense deduction of $25,000 in current year.	_____	_____
g. Continue with the facts of (f) for the next tax year.	_____	_____
h. MACRS depreciation of $80,000. ADS depreciation would have been $90,000.	_____	_____
i. Federal income taxes of $80,000 paid in current year.	_____	_____

18. **LO.2** Penguin Corporation (a cash basis, calendar year taxpayer) recorded the following income and expenses in the current year.

Income from services	$400,000
Salaries paid to employees	70,000
Tax-exempt interest income	24,000
Dividends from a corporation in which Penguin holds a 12% interest	40,000
Short-term capital loss on the sale of stock	17,000
Estimated Federal income taxes paid	110,000

Penguin purchased 7-year MACRS property in the current year for $80,000; it did not claim any § 179 or additional first-year depreciation. The property has a 10-year ADR midpoint life. Determine Penguin's taxable income and current E & P.

19. **LO.1, 3** At the beginning of the year, Teal Corporation held accumulated E & P of $210,000. On March 30, Teal sold an asset at a loss of $200,000. For the cal-endar year, Teal incurred a deficit in current E & P of $305,000, which includes the loss on the sale of the asset. If Teal made a distribution of $50,000 to its sole share-holder on April 1, how is the shareholder taxed? Her basis in the stock was $72,000.

20. **LO.1, 3** Green Corporation (a calendar year taxpayer) had a deficit in accumulated E & P of $250,000 at the beginning of the current year. Its net profit for the

period January 1 through July 30 was $300,000, but its E & P for the entire taxable year was only $40,000. If Green made a distribution of $60,000 to its sole share-holder on August 1, how will the shareholder be taxed?

21. **LO.1, 3** Black Corporation and Tom each own 50% of Tan Corporation's common stock. On January 1, Tan holds a deficit in accumulated E & P of $200,000. Its current E & P is $90,000. During the year, Tan makes cash distributions of $40,000 each to Black and Tom.

    a.   How are the two shareholders taxed on the distribution?

    b.   What is Tan's accumulated E & P at the end of the year?

22. **LO.1, 4** Heather, an individual, owns all of the outstanding stock in Silver Corpora-tion. Heather purchased her stock in Silver nine years ago, and her basis is $56,000. At the beginning of this year, the corporation has $76,000 of accumulated E & P and no current E & P (before considering the effect of the distributions as noted below). What are the tax consequences to Heather (amount and type of income and basis in property received) and Silver Corporation (gain or loss and effect on E & P) in each of the following situations?   *Critical Thinking*

    a.   Silver distributes land to Heather. The land was held as an investment and has a fair market value of $54,000 and an adjusted basis of $42,000.

    b.   Assume that Silver has no current or accumulated E & P prior to the distribution. How would your answer to part (a) change?

    c.   Assume that the land distributed in part (a) is subject to a $46,000 mortgage (which Heather assumes). How would your answer change?

    d.   Assume that the land has a fair market value of $54,000 and an adjusted basis of $62,000 on the date of the distribution. How would your answer to part (a) change?

23. **LO.1, 4** Lime Corporation, with E & P of $500,000, distributes land (worth $300,000, adjusted basis of $350,000) to Harry, its sole shareholder. The land is sub-ject to a liability of $120,000, which Harry assumes. What are the tax consequences to Lime and to Harry?

24. **LO.4** Raven Corporation owns three machines that it uses in its business. It no lon-ger needs two of these machines and is considering distributing them to its two shareholders as a property dividend. The machines have a fair market value of $20,000 each. The basis of each machine is as follows: A, $27,000; B, $20,000; and C, $12,000. Raven has asked you for advice. What do you recommend?   *Decision Making*

25. **LO.1, 2, 3, 4** Cerulean Corporation has two equal shareholders, Marco and Avery. Marco acquired his Cerulean stock three years ago by transferring property worth $700,000, basis of $300,000, for 70 shares of the stock. Avery acquired 70 shares in Cerulean Corporation two years ago by transferring property worth $660,000, basis of $110,000. Cerulean's accumulated E & P as of January 1 of the current year is $350,000.   *Critical Thinking*

    On March 1 of the current year, the corporation distributed to Marco property worth $120,000, basis to Cerulean of $50,000. It distributed cash of $220,000 to Avery. On July 1 of the current year, Avery sold her stock to Harpreet for $820,000. On December 1 of the current year, Cerulean distributed cash of $90,000 each to Harpreet and Marco. What are the tax issues?

26. **LO.1, 2, 4** Petrel Corporation has accumulated E & P of $85,000 at the beginning of the year. Its current-year taxable income is $320,000. On December 31, Petrel distributed business property (land, fair market value $140,000, adjusted basis $290,000) to Juan, its sole shareholder. Juan assumes a $70,000 liability on the property.   *Decision Making* *Critical Thinking*

    Included in the determination of Petrel's current taxable income is $16,000 of income recognized from an installment sale in a previous year. In addition, the corporation incurred a Federal income tax liability of $67,200, paid life insurance premiums of $4,500, and received term life insurance proceeds of $150,000 on the death of an officer.

   a.   What is Juan's gross income from the distribution?

   b.   What is Petrel's E & P after the property distribution?

   c.   What is Juan's tax basis in the property received?

   d.   How would your answers to parts (a) and (b) change if Petrel had sold the property at its fair market value, used $70,000 of the proceeds to pay off the liability, and distributed the remaining cash and any tax savings to Juan?

Critical Thinking   27.   **LO.5** Parrot Corporation is a closely held company with accumulated E & P of $300,000 and current E & P of $350,000. Tom and Jerry are brothers; each owns a 50% share in Parrot, and they share management responsibilities equally. What are the tax consequences of each of the following independent transactions involving Parrot, Tom, and Jerry? How does each transaction affect Parrot's E & P?

   a.   Parrot sells an office building (adjusted basis of $350,000; fair market value of $300,000) to Tom for $275,000.

   b.   Parrot lends Jerry $250,000 on March 31 of this year. The loan is evidenced by a note that is payable on demand. No interest is charged on the loan (the current applicable Federal interest rate is 3%).

   c.   Parrot owns an airplane that it leases to others for a specified rental rate. Tom and Jerry also use the airplane for personal use and pay no rent. During the year, Tom used the airplane for 120 hours, and Jerry used it for 160 hours. The rental value of the airplane is $350 per hour, and its maintenance costs average $80 per hour.

   d.   Tom leases equipment to Parrot for $20,000 per year. The same equipment can be leased from another company for $9,000 per year.

Decision Making   28.   **LO.5** Rover Corporation would like to transfer excess cash to its sole shareholder, Aleshia, who is also an employee. Aleshia is in the 24% tax bracket, and Rover is in the 21% bracket.

Because Aleshia's contribution to Rover's profit is substantial, Rover believes that a $25,000 bonus in the current year is reasonable compensation and should be deductible in full. However, Rover is considering paying Aleshia a $25,000 dividend because Aleshia's tax rate on dividends is lower than the corporate tax rate on compensation. Is Rover correct in believing that a dividend is the better choice? Why or why not?

Digging Deeper
Communications   29.   **LO.6** Your client, Raptor Corporation, declares a dividend permitting its common shareholders to elect to receive 9 shares of cumulative preferred stock or 3 additional shares of Raptor common stock for every 10 shares of common stock held. Raptor has only common stock outstanding (fair market value of $45 per share). One shareholder elects to receive preferred stock, while the remaining shareholders choose the common stock.

Raptor asks you whether the shareholders recognize any gross income on the receipt of the stock. Prepare a letter to Raptor or a memo for the tax research file regarding this matter. Raptor's address is 1812 S. Camino Seco, Tucson, AZ 85710.

Digging Deeper   30.   **LO.6** Ken purchased 10,000 shares of Gold Corporation common stock six years ago for $160,000. In the current year, Ken received a preferred stock dividend of 800 shares, while the other holders of common stock received a common stock dividend. The preferred stock that Ken received is worth $80,000, and his common stock has a fair market value of $240,000.

Gold holds ample E & P to cover any distributions made during the year. What is Ken's basis in the preferred and common stock after the dividend is received? When does his holding period commence for the preferred stock?

31. **LO.6** Denim Corporation declares a nontaxable dividend payable in rights to subscribe to common stock. One right and $60 entitle the holder to subscribe to
one share of stock. One right is issued for every two shares of stock owned. At the
date of distribution of the rights, the market value of the stock is $110 per share,
and the market value of the rights is $55 each. Lauren owns 300 shares of stock that
she purchased two years ago for $9,000. Lauren receives 150 rights, of which she
exercises 105 to purchase 105 additional shares. She sells the remaining 45 rights
for $2,475. What are the tax consequences of this transaction to Lauren?

Digging Deeper

32. **LO.6** Jacob Corcoran bought 10,000 shares of Grebe Corporation stock two years
ago for $24,000. Last year, Jacob received a nontaxable stock dividend of 2,000
shares in Grebe. In the current tax year, Jacob sold all of the stock received as a
dividend for $18,000. Prepare a letter to Jacob or a memo for the tax research file
describing the tax consequences of the stock sale. Jacob's address is 925 Arapahoe
Street, Boulder, CO 80304.

Digging Deeper

Communications

33. **LO.7** Joseph and Erica, husband and wife, jointly own all of the stock in Velvet Corporation. The two are currently involved in divorce proceedings, and pursuant to
those negotiations, they have agreed that only one of them will remain a shareholder
in Velvet after the divorce. Because Erica has been more involved in Velvet's management and operations over the years, the parties have agreed that Joseph's ownership
should be acquired by either Erica or Velvet. What issues should be considered in
determining whether Erica or Velvet should acquire Joseph's shares in the corporation?

Critical Thinking

34. **LO.1, 7** Julio is in the 32% tax bracket. He acquired 2,000 shares of stock in Gray
Corporation seven years ago at a cost of $50 per share. In the current year,
Julio received a payment of $150,000 from Gray Corporation in exchange for 1,000 of
his shares in Gray. Gray has E & P of $1 million. What tax liability would Julio incur on
the payment in each of the following situations? Assume that Julio has no capital losses.

    a. The stock redemption qualifies for sale or exchange treatment.

    b. The stock redemption does not qualify for sale or exchange treatment.

35. **LO.1, 7** How would your answer to Problem 34 differ if Julio were a corporate
shareholder rather than an individual shareholder and the stock ownership
in Gray Corporation represented a 25% interest?

36. **LO.1, 7** Assume in Problem 34 that Julio takes a capital loss carryover of $50,000
into the current tax year. Julio records no other capital gain transactions
during the year. What amount of the capital loss may Julio deduct in the current
year in the following situations?

    a. The payment from Gray Corporation is a qualifying stock redemption for tax
purposes.

    b. The payment from Gray is a nonqualified stock redemption for tax purposes.

    c. If Julio had the flexibility to structure the transaction as described in either part
(a) or (b), which form would he choose?

Decision Making

37. **LO.1, 7** How would your answer to parts (a) and (b) of Problem 36 differ if Julio
were a corporate shareholder (in the 34% tax bracket) rather than an individual shareholder and the stock ownership in Gray Corporation represented a 25%
interest?

38. **LO.8** Silver Corporation has 2,000 shares of common stock outstanding. Howard
owns 600 shares, Howard's grandfather owns 300 shares, Howard's mother
owns 300 shares, and Howard's son owns 100 shares. In addition, Maroon Corporation owns 500 shares. Howard owns 70% of the stock of Maroon.

    a. Applying the stock attribution rules, how many shares does Howard own in
Silver?

    b. Assume that Howard owns only 40% of the stock in Maroon. How many shares
does Howard own, directly and indirectly, in Silver?

Digging Deeper

c.   Assume the same facts as in part (a) above, but in addition, Howard owns a 25% interest in the Yellow Partnership. Yellow owns 200 shares in Silver. How many shares does Howard own, directly and indirectly, in Silver?

Digging Deeper   39.   **LO.7**   Shonda owns 1,000 of the 1,500 shares outstanding in Rook Corporation (E & P of $1 million). Shonda paid $50 per share for the stock seven years ago. The remaining stock in Rook is owned by unrelated individuals. What are the tax consequences to Shonda in the following independent situations?

a.   Rook redeems 450 shares of Shonda's stock for $225,000.

b.   Rook redeems 600 shares of Shonda's stock for $300,000.

Digging Deeper   40.   **LO.7**   Broadbill Corporation (E & P of $650,000) has 1,000 shares of common stock outstanding. The shares are owned by the following individuals: Tammy, 300 shares; Yvette, 400 shares; and Jeremy, 300 shares. Each of the shareholders paid $50 per share for the Broadbill stock four years ago.

In the current year, Broadbill distributes $75,000 to Tammy in redemption of 150 of her shares. Determine the tax consequences of the redemption to Tammy and to Broadbill under the following independent circumstances.

a.   Tammy and Jeremy are grandmother and grandson.

b.   The three shareholders are siblings.

Digging Deeper   41.   **LO.7**   For the last 11 years, Lime Corporation has owned and operated four different trades or businesses. Lime also owns stock in several corporations that it purchased for investment purposes.

The stock of Lime is held equally by Sultan, an individual, and by Turquoise Corporation. Sultan and Turquoise each own 1,000 shares in Lime, purchased 9 years ago at a cost of $200 per share.

Determine whether either of the following independent transactions qualify as partial liquidations under § 302(b)(4). In each transaction, determine the tax consequences to Lime, to Turquoise, and to Sultan. Lime holds E & P of $2.1 million on the date of the distribution. Lime redeems 250 shares from each shareholder.

a.   Lime sells one of its business lines (basis $500,000, fair market value $700,000) and distributes the proceeds equally to Sultan and Turquoise.

b.   Lime equally distributes stock (basis $425,000, fair market value $700,000) that it holds in other corporations to Sultan and Turquoise.

Digging Deeper   42.   **LO.7**   Dove Corporation (E & P of $800,000) has 1,000 shares of stock outstanding. The shares are owned as follows: Julia, 600 shares; Maxine (Julia's sister), 300 shares; and Janine (Julia's daughter), 100 shares. Dove owns land (basis $300,000, fair market value $260,000) that it purchased as an investment seven years ago.

Dove distributes the land to Julia in exchange for all of her shares in the corporation. Julia had a basis of $275,000 in the shares. What are the tax consequences for both Dove and Julia if the distribution is:

a.   A qualifying stock redemption?

b.   A liquidating distribution?

Critical Thinking   43.   **LO.5**   Pink Corporation has several employees. Their names and salaries are listed below.

Judy	$470,000
Holly (Judy's daughter)	100,000
Terry (Judy's son)	100,000
John (an unrelated third party)	320,000

Holly and Terry are the only shareholders of Pink. Judy and John share equally in the management of the company's operations. Holly and Terry are both full-time college students at a university 200 miles away. Pink has substantial E & P and never has distributed a dividend. Discuss any income tax issues related to Pink's salary arrangement.

BRIDGE DISCIPLINE

1. Find the audited financial statements of five major U.S. corporations, each in a different operating industry (e.g., manufacturing, energy, financial services, health care).
    a. Compute the total return on each corporation's stock for the past two years.
    b. Compute the dividend yield of the stock for the past two years.

2. Find a report involving the buyback of common stock by a publicly traded U.S. corporation. In no more than four PowerPoint slides, summarize the transaction, and discuss the tax and finance motivations for the redemption presented in the article.   Communications

3. A dividend is declared by the corporation's board of directors, and it is paid to each shareholder in an equal fashion. Evaluate this statement from an accounting and Federal income tax standpoint. Summarize your position in no more than four PowerPoint slides in preparation for a presentation to your classmates in Business Law I.   Communications

Research Problems

Note: Solutions to the Research Problems can be prepared by using the Thomson Reuters Checkpoint™ online tax research database, which accompanies this textbook. Solutions can also be prepared by using research materials found in a typical tax library.

THOMSON REUTERS
CHECKPOINT™

Research Problem 1. Kenny Merinoff and his son, John, own all of the outstanding   Communications
stock of Flamingo Corporation. John and Kenny are officers in the corporation and, together with their uncle, Ira, comprise the entire board of directors. Flamingo uses the cash method of accounting and adopted a calendar year-end.

In late 2010, the board of directors adopted the following legally enforceable resolution (agreed to in writing by each of the officers).

> Salary payments made to an officer of the corporation that are disallowed in whole or in part as a deductible expense for Federal income tax purposes shall be reimbursed by such officer to the corporation to the full extent of the disallowance. It shall be the duty of the board of directors to enforce the collection of each such amount.

In 2016, Flamingo paid Kenny $800,000 in compensation. John received $650,000. As part of an audit in late 2017, the IRS found the compensation of both officers to be excessive. It disallowed deductions for $400,000 of the payment to Kenny and $350,000 of the payment to John. The IRS recharacterized the disallowed payments as constructive dividends. Complying with the resolution by the board of directors, both Kenny and John repaid the disallowed compensation to Flamingo Corporation in 2018.

John and Kenny have asked you to determine how their repayments are treated for Federal income tax purposes. John still is working as a highly compensated executive for Flamingo, while Kenny is retired and living off of his savings. Prepare a memo for your firm's tax research files describing the results of your review.

Partial list of research aids:
§ 1341.
Vincent E. Oswald, 49 T.C. 645 (1968).

Research Problem 2. Your client, White Corporation, has done well since its formation 20 years ago. This year, it recognized a $50 million capital gain from the sale of a subsidiary. White's CEO has contacted you to discuss a proposed transaction to reduce the tax on the capital gain. Under the proposal, White will purchase all of the common stock in Purple Corporation for $200 million. Purple is a profitable corporation that has $63 million in cash and marketable securities, $137 million in operating assets, and approximately $280 million in E & P.

After its acquisition, Purple will distribute $50 million in cash and marketable securities to White. Due to the 100% dividends received deduction, no taxable income results to White from the dividend. White then will resell Purple for $150 million.

The subsequent sale of Purple generates a $50 million capital loss [$150 million (sale price) − $200 million (stock basis)]. The loss from the stock sale can then be used to offset the preexisting $50 million capital gain. Will the proposed plan work? Why or why not?

Partial list of research aids:
§ 1059.

Communications   **Research Problem 3.** Emerald Corporation must change its method of accounting for Federal income tax purposes. The change will require that an adjustment to income be made over three tax periods. Jonas, the sole shareholder of Emerald, wants to better understand the implications of this adjustment for E & P purposes, as he anticipates a distribution from Emerald in the current year. Prepare a memo for your firm's files describing the results of your research.

Partial list of research aids:
§ 481(a).
Rev.Proc. 97–27, 1997–1 C.B. 680.

Use internet tax resources to address the following questions. Look for reliable websites and blogs of the IRS and other government agencies, media outlets, businesses, tax professionals, academics, think tanks, and political outlets.

Research Problem 4. In July 2014, Windstream Corp. (Nasdaq: WIN), a Fortune 500 and S&P 500 company, made an announcement regarding the taxation of a recent distribution. It also made a projection regarding the anticipated tax consequences of future distributions.

Locate articles or press releases regarding Windstream's announcement and related distribution. What might have led Windstream to make the announcement? What implications might the information contained in the announcement have had for investors' expectations regarding the company's future earnings? On what might the predictions regarding the taxation of future distributions have been based?

Communications   **Research Problem 5.** Write an e-mail query to two tax consultants who practice in your state. Ask each for an example or two of a constructive dividend that a client recently paid. Give your instructor copies of your query and the responses you receive.

Communications   **Research Problem 6.** Publicly traded corporations reacquire their own shares for various reasons. Through the use of a tender offer, a corporation can purchase a substantial percentage of the company's stock. Prepare an outline discussing (1) why publicly traded corporations reacquire their own shares and (2) how the tender offer process works for both corporations and shareholders. E-mail your outline to your professor.

1. On January 1, year 5, Olinto Corp., an accrual basis, calendar year C corporation, had $35,000 in accumulated earnings and profits. For year 5, Olinto had current earnings and profits of $15,000 and made two $40,000 cash distributions to its share-holders, one in April and one in September of year 5. What amount of the year 5 distributions is classified as dividend income to Olinto's shareholders?

   a. $15,000

   b. $35,000

   c. $50,000

   d. $80,000

2. Fox Corp. owned 2,000 shares of Duffy Corp. stock that it bought in year 0 for $9 per share. In year 8, when the fair market value of the Duffy stock was $20 per share, Fox distributed this stock to a noncorporate shareholder. Fox's recognized gain on this distribution was:

   a. $40,000

   b. $22,000

   c. $18,000

   d. $0

3. Ridge Corp., a calendar year C corporation, made a nonliquidating cash distribu-tion to its shareholders of $1,000,000 with respect to its stock. At that time, Ridge's current and accumulated earnings and profits totaled $750,000 and its total paid-in capital for tax purposes was $10,000,000. Ridge had no corporate shareholders. Ridge's cash distribution:

   I.   Was taxable as $750,000 in dividend income to its shareholders.
   II. Reduced its shareholders' adjusted bases in Ridge stock by $250,000.

   a. I only

   b. II only

   c. Both I and II

   d. Neither I nor II

4. Jane is the sole shareholder of Buttons, Inc. Buttons has a deficit of $60,000 in accu-mulated earnings and profits (E & P) at the beginning of the current year. Current E & P is $35,000. If Buttons pays out a cash distribution to Jane during the current year of $50,000, how much is a taxable dividend to Jane?

   a. $0

   b. $35,000

   c. $50,000

   d. $85,000

5. Jane is the sole shareholder of Buttons, Inc. Buttons has accumulated earnings and profits (E & P) of $65,000 at the beginning of the current year. The current E & P is $35,000. Buttons pays out a property distribution to Jane during the current year with an FMV of $150,000 and an adjusted basis of $130,000. How much is a taxable dividend to Jane?

   a. $35,000

   b. $100,000

   c. $120,000

   d. $150,000

CHAPTER

14

Partnerships and Limited Liability Entities

LEARNING OBJECTIVES: *After completing Chapter 14, you should be able to:*

LO.1 Identify governing principles and theories of partnership taxation.

LO.2 Apply the tax rules regarding the formation of a partnership with cash and property contributions.

LO.3 Determine the tax treatment of expenditures of a newly formed partnership and identify elections available to the partnership.

LO.4 Calculate partnership taxable income and describe how partnership items affect a partner's income tax liability.

LO.5 Determine a partner's basis in the partnership interest.

LO.6 Apply the tax law's limitations on deducting partnership losses.

LO.7 Apply the tax laws regarding transactions between a partner and the partnership.

LO.8 Explain how LLPs and LLCs differ and list the tax advantages and disadvantages of using an LLC.

CHAPTER OUTLINE

14-1 Overview of Partnership Taxation, 14-2
    14-1a Forms of Doing Business—Federal Tax Consequences, 14-2
    14-1b Definition of a Partnership, 14-3
    14-1c Partnership Taxation and Reporting, 14-4
    14-1d Partner's Ownership Interest in a Partnership, 14-6

14-2 Formation of a Partnership: Tax Effects, 14-8
    14-2a Gain or Loss on Contributions to the Partnership, 14-8
    14-2b Exceptions to Nonrecognition, 14-9
    14-2c Tax Issues Related to Contributed Property, 14-11
    14-2d Inside and Outside Bases, 14-12
    14-2e Tax Accounting Elections, 14-12
    14-2f Initial Costs of a Partnership, 14-13

14-3 Operations of the Partnership, 14-15
    14-3a Schedules K and K–1, 14-15

    14-3b Partnership Allocations, 14-18
    14-3c Basis of a Partnership Interest, 14-20
    14-3d Partner's Basis, Gain, and Loss, 14-23
    14-3e Loss Limitations, 14-25

14-4 Transactions between Partner and Partnership, 14-28
    14-4a Guaranteed Payments, 14-29
    14-4b Other Transactions between a Partner and a Partnership, 14-30
    14-4c Partners as Employees, 14-30

14-5 Limited Liability Companies, 14-32
    14-5a Taxation of LLCs, 14-32
    14-5b Advantages of an LLC, 14-32
    14-5c Disadvantages of an LLC, 14-33

14-6 Summary, 14-34

TAX TALK *If you are truly serious about preparing your child for the future, don't teach him to subtract—teach him to deduct.* —FRAN LEBOWITZ

THE BIG PICTURE

THE TAX CONSEQUENCES OF PARTNERSHIP FORMATION AND OPERATIONS

For 15 years, Maria has owned and operated a seaside bakery and café called The Beachsider. Each morning, customers line up on the boardwalk in front of the building and enjoy fresh coffee and croissants while waiting for a table. "The building is too small," Maria commented to her landlord, Kyle. "Is there any way we can expand?" The Beachsider is one of several older buildings on 3 acres of a 10-acre parcel that Kyle inherited 30 years ago. The remaining 7 acres are undeveloped.

Kyle and Maria talked to Josh, a real estate developer, and he proposed an expansion to The Beachsider and upgrades to the other buildings. The improvements would preserve the character of the original retail center, and the remaining acreage would be available for future expansion. Kyle and Maria were impressed with Josh's vision and excited about the plans to upgrade the property and expand Maria's business.

The parties agreed to form a partnership to own and operate The Beachsider and to improve and lease the other buildings. Josh summarized the plan as follows: "Kyle and Maria will each contribute one-half of the capital we need. Kyle's real estate is valued at about $2 million. Maria's bakery equipment and the café furnishings are valued at about $500,000. The improvements will cost about $1.5 million, which Maria has agreed to contribute to the partnership."

Josh continued, "You have agreed that I do not need to contribute any capital to the partnership. I will oversee the construction, and when it is complete, I will vest in a 5 percent interest in the partnership's capital. On an ongoing basis, I will oversee the partnership's operations in exchange for a fixed salary and 20 percent of the partnership's ongoing profits. The construction is estimated to be completed in June of this year, and my capital interest is estimated to be valued at $200,000 at that time."

What are the tax consequences if the trio forms Beachside Properties as a limited liability company (LLC) to own and operate the retail center? What issues might arise later in the life of the entity?

Read the chapter and formulate your response.

Much of the new business in today's world of commerce is conducted through what the Internal Revenue Code would classify as *partnerships*. As evidence of their popularity, approximately 4 million partnership tax returns are filed with the IRS annually.

Whether termed a *joint venture* or some other designation, a partnership is formed when individuals or separate business entities get together for the specific purpose of earning profits by jointly operating a trade or business. For example, a group can limit its goals to a specific list of agreed-to projects or to a given time period, or businesses can work together without altering any of their underlying capital structures. In many service professions, such as law, medicine, and accounting, state laws prohibit the owners from using a corporation to limit their liability to clients or patients; there, the partnership form prevails.

LO.1

Identify governing principles and theories of partnership taxation.

14-1 OVERVIEW OF PARTNERSHIP TAXATION

There are several types of partnership entities, each suited for different situations. Partnerships are used in almost every imaginable industry, and their popularity among business owners continues to rise.

The tax law addressing the transactions of partners and partnerships is found in Subchapter K of the Internal Revenue Code. These provisions comprise only a few short pages in the Code, however. Most of the details of partnership tax law have evolved through extensive Regulations and a healthy number of court cases.

14-1a Forms of Doing Business—Federal Tax Consequences

This chapter and the next chapter analyze business forms that offer certain advantages over C corporations. These entities are partnerships and S corporations, which are called *flow-through* or *pass-through* entities because the owners of the trade or business elect to avoid treating the enterprise as a separate taxable entity. Instead, the owners are taxed on a proportionate share of the firm's taxable income, which "flows through" to them at the end of each of its taxable years, regardless of the amount of cash or property distributions the owners receive during the year. The entity serves as an information provider to the IRS and its owners with respect to the proportionate allocation of income, while the tax liability falls directly on the owners for their share of the partnership's income.

A partnership may be especially advantageous in many cases. A partnership's income is subject to only a single level of taxation, whereas C corporation income can be subject to *double taxation*. Corporate income is taxed at the entity level at rates up to 21 percent. Any after-tax corporate income that is distributed to the entity's owners may be taxed again as a dividend at the owner level.

In addition, the entity offers certain planning opportunities not available to other business structures. Both C and S corporations are subject to rigorous allocation and distribution requirements (generally, each allocation or distribution is proportionate to the ownership interest of the shareholder). A partnership, though, may adjust its allocations of income and cash flow among the partners each year according to their needs, as long as certain standards are met. Any previously unrealized income (such as appreciation of corporate assets) of a C corporation is recognized at the entity level when the corporation liquidates, but a partnership generally may liquidate tax-free. Finally, many states impose reporting and licensing requirements on corporate entities, including S corporations. These include franchise or capital stock tax returns that may require annual assessments and costly professional preparation assistance. Partnerships, on the other hand, often have no reporting requirements beyond Federal and state informational tax returns.

Although partnerships may avoid many of the income tax and reporting burdens faced by other entities, they are subject to all other taxes in the same manner as any other business. Thus, the partnership files returns and pays the outstanding amount of pertinent sales taxes, property taxes, and payroll taxes.

Partnership Flow-Throughs

Assume the same facts as in Example 1, except that the partnership realizes a taxable loss of $100,000. Adam's $40,000 proportionate share of the loss flows through to him from the partnership, and he can deduct the loss. (Note: Loss limitation rules discussed later in the chapter may result in some or all of this loss being deducted by Adam in a later year.)

Separately Stated Items

Many items of partnership income, expense, gain, or loss retain their tax identity as they flow through to the partners. These **separately stated items** include those items that may affect any two partners' tax liability computations differently.[6] For example, the § 179 expense of a partnership is separately stated because one partner might be able to deduct his or her share of the expense completely, while another's deduction might be limited.

Separately stated items include recognized gains and losses from property transactions, dividend income, immediately expensed tangible personal property (§ 179), and expenditures that individual partners would treat as itemized deductions (e.g., charitable contributions).

Items that are not separately stated, because all partners treat them the same on their income tax returns, are aggregated and form the *ordinary income* of the partnership. Thus, profits from product sales, advertising expenses, and depreciation recapture amounts are combined to form the entity's ordinary income. This amount then is allocated among the partners and flows through to their tax returns. The ordinary income that flows through to a general partner, as well as any salary-like guaranteed payments (discussed in text Section 14-4a) received, usually is subject to self-employment tax, as well as Federal income tax.[7]

Beth is a 25% partner in the BR Partnership, a manufacturer of solar energy panels. The cash basis entity collected sales income of $60,000 and incurred $15,000 in business expenses. In addition, it sold a corporate bond for a $9,000 long-term capital gain. Finally, the partnership made a $1,000 contribution to the local Performing Arts Fund. The fund is a qualifying charity. BR and all of its partners use a calendar tax year.

Beth is allocated ordinary taxable income of $11,250 [($60,000 − $15,000) × 25%] from the partnership. She also reports her allocated share of the entity's long-term capital gain ($2,250) and charitable contributions ($250).

The partnership ordinary income increases Beth's gross income, and is subject to both income and self-employment taxes. Beth's share of BR's capital gain and charitable contribution are combined with her other similar activities for the year as though she had incurred them herself. These items could be treated differently on the tax returns of the various partners (e.g., because a partner may be subject to a percentage limitation on charitable contribution deductions), so they are not included in the computation of ordinary partnership income. Instead, the items flow through to the partners separately.

Tax Reporting Rules

Even though it is not a taxpaying entity, the partnership files an information tax return, Form 1065. This return is due by the fifteenth day of the third month following the end of the tax year. For a calendar year partnership, this deadline is March 15 (not April 15). An automatic six-month extension is available (to September 15 for a calendar year partnership) for filing the Form 1065.

As part of the Form 1065, the partnership prepares a Schedule K–1 for each partner that shows that partner's share of partnership items. Each partner receives a copy of Schedule K–1 for use in preparing the respective partner's tax return.

---

[6]§ 703(a)(1).

[7]§ 1402(a).

The partnership incurs a penalty if it fails to file a timely (by the extended due date) Form 1065. The penalty is $195 per month times the numbers of partners, up to a maximum of 12 months.

Look at Form 1065 at **irs.gov**, and refer to it during the following discussion. The ordinary income and expense items generated by the partnership's trade or business activities are netted to produce a single income or loss amount. The partnership reports this ordinary income or loss from its trade or business activities on Form 1065, page 1. Schedule K (page 4 of Form 1065) accumulates all items that must be separately reported to the partners, including net trade or business income or loss (from page 1). The amounts on Schedule K are allocated among and reported by the partners on each owner's Schedule K–1.

EXAMPLE 4

The BR Partnership in Example 3 reports its $60,000 of sales income on Form 1065, page 1, line 1. The $15,000 of business expenses are reported in the appropriate amounts on page 1, line 2 or lines 9–20. Partnership ordinary income of $45,000 is shown on page 1, line 22, and on Schedule K, line 1. The $9,000 capital gain and the $1,000 charitable contribution are reported only on Schedule K, on lines 9a and 13a, respectively.

Beth receives a Schedule K–1 from the partnership that shows her shares of partnership ordinary income of $11,250, long-term capital gain of $2,250, and charitable contributions of $250 on lines 1, 9a, and 13 (Code A), respectively.

She combines these amounts with similar items from other sources on her personal tax return. For example, if she has a $5,000 long-term capital loss from a stock transaction during the year, her overall net capital loss is $2,750. She then evaluates this net amount to determine the amount she may deduct on her Form 1040.

The partnership reconciles book income with its tax return data on Schedule M–1 or Schedule M–3. This reconciliation is similar to the book-tax reconciliation prepared by a C corporation, as discussed in text Sections 3-1d and 12-5.

Schedule M–3 generally is required in lieu of Schedule M–1 if the partnership owns $10 million or more in assets at the end of the year or it reports gross receipts of at least $35 million. The net taxable income calculated on the Analysis of Net Income (Loss) schedule should agree with the reconciled taxable income on Schedule M–1 or Schedule M–3. Schedule L shows an accounting-basis balance sheet, and Schedule M–2 reconciles partners' beginning and ending capital accounts.

14-1d Partner's Ownership Interest in a Partnership

Each partner typically owns both a **capital interest** and a **profits (loss) interest** in the partnership. A capital interest is measured by a partner's **capital sharing ratio**, which is the partner's percentage ownership of the capital of the partnership. A partner's capital interest can be determined in several ways. The most widely accepted method measures the capital interest as the percentage of net asset value (asset value remaining after payment of all partnership liabilities) a partner would receive upon immediate liquidation of the partnership.

A profits (loss) interest relates to the partner's percentage allocation of current partnership operating results. **Profit and loss sharing ratios** usually are specified in the partnership agreement. They are used to determine each partner's allocation of partnership ordinary taxable income (loss) and separately stated items.[8] The partnership can change its profit and loss allocations at any time by amending the partnership agreement.

---

[8]§ 704(a).

BRIDGE DISCIPLINE **Bridge to Business Law**

Although a written partnership agreement is not required by most U.S. states, many rules governing the tax consequences to partners and their partnerships refer to such an agreement. Remember that a partner's distributive share of income, gain, loss, deduction, or credit is determined in accordance with the partnership agreement. Consequently, if taxpayers operating a business in partnership form want a measure of certainty as to the tax consequences of their activities, a carefully drafted partnership agreement is crucial.

An agreement that sets forth the obligations, rights, and powers of the partners should prove invaluable in settling controversies among them and provide some degree of certainty as to the tax consequences of the partners' actions.

The partnership agreement may provide for a **special allocation** of certain items to specified partners, or it may allocate items in a different proportion from the general profit and loss sharing ratios. These items are reported separately to the partner receiving the allocation. For a special allocation to be recognized for tax purposes, it also must produce nontax economic consequences to the partners receiving the allocation.[9]

Partnership Special Allocations

When the George-Helen Partnership was formed, George contributed cash and Helen contributed some City of Boise bonds that she had held for investment purposes. The partnership agreement allocates all of the tax-exempt interest income from the bonds ($15,000 this year) to Helen as an inducement for her to remain a partner.

This is an acceptable special allocation for income tax purposes; it reflects the differing economic circumstances that underlie the partners' contributions to the capital of the entity. Because Helen would have received the tax-exempt income if she had not joined the partnership, she can retain the tax-favored treatment via the special allocation.

EXAMPLE 5

Assume the same facts as in Example 5. Three years after it was formed, the George-Helen Partnership purchased some City of Butte bonds. The municipal bond interest income of $15,000 flows through to the partners as a separately stated item, so it retains its tax-exempt status.

The partnership agreement allocates all of this income to George because he is subject to a higher marginal income tax rate than is Helen. The partnership then allocates $15,000 more of the partnership's ordinary income to Helen than to George. These allocations are not effective for income tax purposes because they have no purpose other than a reduction of the partners' combined income tax liability.

EXAMPLE 6

A partner has a **basis in the partnership interest**, just as he or she would have a tax basis in any asset owned. When income flows through to a partner from the partnership, the partner's basis in the partnership interest increases accordingly. When a loss flows through to a partner, the interest basis is reduced.[10] A partner's basis is important when determining the treatment of distributions from the partnership to the partner, establishing the deductibility of partnership losses, and calculating gain or loss on the disposition of the partnership interest.

The Philly Clinic (Philly) contributes $20,000 of cash to acquire a 30% capital and profits interest in the Red Robin LLC. In its first year of operations, the LLC earns ordinary income of $40,000 and makes no distributions to its members. Philly's initial basis is the $20,000 it paid for the interest. Philly recognizes ordinary income of $12,000 (30% interest × $40,000 ordinary income) and increases its basis in Red Robin by the same amount, to $32,000.

---

[9]§ 704(b).   [10]§§ 705, 722, and 723.

The Code provides for increases and decreases in a partner's basis so that the income or loss from partnership operations is taxed only once. In Example 7, if Philly sold its interest at the end of the first year for $32,000, it would recognize no gain or loss. If the Code did not provide for an adjustment to the owner's basis for flow-through amounts, Philly's basis still would be $20,000. In that case, Philly would recognize a gain of $12,000 in addition to being taxed on its $12,000 share of the flow-through income from Red Robin.

DIGGING DEEPER 1   In-depth coverage can be found on this book's companion website: **www.cengage.com**

LO.2

Apply the tax rules regarding the formation of a partnership with cash and property contributions.

14-2 FORMATION OF A PARTNERSHIP: TAX EFFECTS

14-2a Gain or Loss on Contributions to the Partnership

When a taxpayer transfers property to an entity in exchange for valuable consideration, a taxable exchange usually results. Typically, both the taxpayer and the entity realize and recognize gain or loss on the exchange. The gain or loss recognized by the transferor is the difference between the fair market value of the consideration received and the adjusted basis of the property transferred.[11]

As a general rule, however, neither the partner nor the partnership recognizes the gain or loss that is realized when a partner contributes property to a partnership in exchange for a partnership interest. Instead, recognition of any realized gain or loss is deferred under § 721.[12] These rules apply whenever an owner makes a contribution to the capital of the partnership or LLC, not just when the entity is formed.

There are two reasons for this nonrecognition treatment. First, forming a partnership allows investors to combine their assets toward greater economic goals than could be achieved separately. Only the form of ownership, rather than the amount owned by each investor, has changed. Requiring that gain be recognized on such transfers would make the formation of some partnerships economically unfeasible. Second, because the partnership interest received is typically not a liquid asset, the partner may not be able to generate the cash with which to pay the tax. Thus, deferral of the gain recognizes the economic realities of the business world and follows the wherewithal to pay principle. This treatment is similar to the treatment of assets transferred to a controlled corporation.[13]

Creating a Partnership

EXAMPLE

8

In exchange for a 60% profits and loss interest worth $60,000, Alicia transfers two assets to the Wren LLC on the day the entity is created. She contributes cash of $40,000 and retail display equipment (basis to her as a sole proprietor, $8,000; fair market value, $20,000). Because an exchange has occurred between two parties, Alicia *realizes* a $12,000 gain on this transaction. The gain realized is the fair market value of the LLC interest of $60,000 less the basis of the assets that Alicia surrendered to the entity [$40,000 (cash) + $8,000 (equipment)].

Under § 721, Alicia *does not recognize* the $12,000 realized gain in the year of contribution. Alicia might not have had sufficient cash if she had been required to pay tax on the $12,000 gain. All that she received from the entity was an illiquid LLC interest; she received no cash with which to pay any resulting tax liability.

---

[11]§§ 1001(a) and (c).   [13]§ 351.

[12]§ 721.

Creating a Partnership

Assume the same facts as in Example 8, except that the equipment Alicia contributes to the LLC has an adjusted basis of $25,000. She has incurred a $5,000 *realized* loss [$60,000 − ($40,000 + $25,000)], but she cannot deduct the loss. Realized losses, as well as realized gains, are deferred by § 721.

Unless it was essential that the entity receive Alicia's display equipment rather than similar equipment purchased from an outside supplier, Alicia should have considered selling the equipment to a third party. This would have allowed her to deduct a $5,000 loss in the year of the sale. Alicia then could have contributed $60,000 of cash (including the proceeds from the sale) for her interest in the entity, and Wren would have had funds to purchase similar equipment.

EXAMPLE 9

Five years after Wren (Examples 8 and 9) was created, Alicia contributes another piece of equipment to the entity. This property has a basis of $35,000 and a fair market value of $50,000. Alicia will be able to defer the recognition of the $15,000 realized gain. Section 721 is effective *whenever* an owner makes a contribution to the capital of the partnership or LLC, not just when the entity is formed.

EXAMPLE 10

Concept Summary 14.1

Partnership/LLC Taxation: Tax Reporting

1. Compared with a C corporation, a partnership may offer some advantages, including a single level of taxation, the availability of certain planning opportunities, and simplified administration and reporting.

2. Entities treated as a partnership for tax purposes include general partnerships, limited partnerships, limited liability companies (LLCs), and limited liability partnerships (LLPs).

3. Partnership income and losses flow through to the partners and are reported on the partners' tax returns. The partnership reports ordinary income or loss as well as *separately stated items* to the partners. Under certain conditions, items may be *specially allocated* to specified partners.

4. The partnership files Form 1065 as an information return and prepares a Schedule K–1 to report each partner's share of income and deductions.

14-2b **Exceptions to Nonrecognition**

Contributions to the capital of a partnership or limited liability entity sometimes trigger recognized gain or loss. Realized gain or loss may be recognized when:

- Appreciated stocks are contributed to an investment partnership, or
- The transaction is essentially a disguised sale or exchange of properties, or
- The partnership interest is received in exchange for services rendered to the partnership by the partner.[14]

Investment Partnership

If the transfer consists of appreciated stocks and securities and the partnership is an investment partnership, it is possible that the contributing partner will recognize the inherent realized gain at the time of the contribution.[15] This rule prevents investors from using the partnership form to diversify their investment portfolios on a tax-free basis.

Disguised Exchange

If a transaction is essentially a taxable exchange of properties, tax on the gain is not deferred under the nonrecognition provisions of § 721.[16]

---

[14]§ 721(b). A few other exceptions to § 721 treatment also exist.
[15]§ 721(b).
[16]Reg. § 1.731–1(c)(3).

EXAMPLE 11

Sara owns land, and Bob owns stock. Sara would like to have Bob's stock, and Bob wants Sara's land. If Sara and Bob both contribute their property to newly formed SB Partnership in exchange for interests in the partnership, the tax on the transaction appears to be deferred under § 721. The tax on a subsequent distribution by the partnership of the land to Bob and the stock to Sara also appears to be deferred under partnership distribution rules.

Not so! Tax law disregards the passage of the properties through the partnership and holds, instead, that Sara and Bob exchanged the land and stock directly. Thus, the transaction is treated as any other taxable exchange.

Disguised Sale

Immediate gain recognition also occurs in the context of a **disguised sale** of property or of a partnership interest. A disguised sale occurs when a partner contributes property to a partnership and soon thereafter receives a distribution from the partnership. This distribution could be viewed as a payment by the partnership for purchase of the property.[17]

EXAMPLE 12

Kim transfers property to the existing KLM Partnership. The property has an adjusted basis of $10,000 and a fair market value of $30,000. Two weeks later, the partnership distributes $30,000 of cash to Kim. Lacking an exception under the distribution rules, the $30,000 of cash received would not be taxable to Kim if the basis for her partnership interest prior to the distribution was greater than the amount distributed.

However, the transaction appears to be a disguised purchase-sale transaction, rather than an asset contribution and distribution. Therefore, Kim recognizes gain of $20,000 on transfer of the property, and the partnership is deemed to have purchased the property for $30,000.

A disguised sale or exchange is presumed to exist when a contribution by one partner is followed within two years by a specified distribution to him or her from the partnership.

Services

Another exception to the nonrecognition provision of § 721 occurs when a partner receives a capital interest in the partnership as compensation for services rendered to the partnership. This is not a tax-deferred transaction because services are not treated as "property" that can be transferred to a partnership on a tax-free basis. Instead, the partner performing the services recognizes ordinary compensation income equal to the fair market value of the partnership interest received.[18]

The partnership may deduct the amount included in the *service partner's* income if the services are of a deductible nature. If the services are not deductible by the partnership, they are capitalized. For example, architectural plans created by a partner are capitalized into the basis of a structure built with those plans. Alternatively, day-to-day management services performed by a partner for the partnership usually are deductible by the partnership.

EXAMPLE 13

Bill, Carol, and Dave form the BCD Partnership, with each receiving a one-third capital and profits interest in the entity. Dave receives his one-third interest as compensation for the accounting and tax planning services he rendered to the partnership. The value of a one-third capital interest in the partnership (for each of the parties) is $20,000.

The partnership deducts $20,000 for Dave's services in computing ordinary income. Dave recognizes $20,000 of compensation income, and he takes a $20,000 basis in his partnership interest. The same result would occur if the partnership had paid Dave $20,000 for his services and he immediately contributed that amount to the entity for a one-third ownership interest.

---

[17]§ 707(a)(2)(B).   [18]§ 83(a).

In-depth coverage can be found on this book's companion website: www.cengage.com

14-2c Tax Issues Related to Contributed Property

When a partner makes a tax-deferred contribution of an asset to the capital of a partnership, the entity assigns a *carryover basis* to the property.[19] The partnership's basis in the asset (the asset's "inside basis") is equal to the basis the partner held in the property prior to its transfer to the partnership. The partner's basis in the new partnership interest (the owner's "outside basis") equals the prior basis in the contributed asset. The tax term for this basis concept is *substituted basis*. Thus, two assets are created out of one when a partnership is formed, namely, the property in the hands of the new entity and the new asset (the partnership interest) in the hands of the partner. Both assets are assigned a basis that is derived from the partner's basis in the contributed property.

The holding period of a partner's ownership interest includes that of the contributed property when the property was a § 1231 asset or capital asset in the partner's hands. When other assets, including cash, are contributed, the holding period starts on the day the interest is acquired.

EXAMPLE 14

On June 1, José transfers property to the JKL LLC in exchange for a one-third interest in the entity. The property has an adjusted basis to José of $10,000 and a fair market value of $30,000. José incurs a $20,000 realized gain on the exchange ($30,000 − $10,000), but he does not recognize any of the gain. Jose's basis for his interest in JKL is the amount necessary to recognize the $20,000 deferred gain if his interest later is sold for its $30,000 fair market value. This amount, $10,000, is the substituted basis.

The basis of the property contributed to JKL is the amount necessary to allow for the recognition of the $20,000 deferred gain if the property later is sold for its $30,000 fair market value. This amount, also $10,000, is the carryover basis.

The holding period for the contributed asset also carries over to the entity. Thus, JKL's holding period for the asset includes the period during which José owned the asset individually.

Depreciation Method and Period

If depreciable property is contributed to the partnership, the partnership usually is required to use the same cost recovery method and life as had been used by the partner. The partnership merely "steps into the shoes" of the partner and continues the same cost recovery calculations.

Intangible Assets

If a partner contributes an existing intangible asset to the partnership, the partnership generally will "step into the shoes" of the partner in determining future amortization deductions. Section 197 intangible assets are amortized over 15 years and include purchased goodwill, going-concern value, information systems, customer- or supplier-related intangible assets, patents, licenses obtained from a governmental unit, franchises, trademarks, covenants not to compete, and other items.

---

[19]§ 723.

Receivables, Inventory, and Built-In Losses

To prevent ordinary income from being converted into capital gain, gain or loss is treated as ordinary when the partnership disposes of either of the following.[20]

- Contributed receivables that were unrealized in the contributing partner's hands at the contribution date. Such receivables include the right to receive payment for goods or services.
- Contributed property that was inventory in the contributor's hands on the contribution date, if the partnership disposes of the property within *five years of the contribution*. For this purpose, inventory includes all tangible property except capital and real or depreciable business assets.

A similar rule is designed to prevent a capital loss from being converted into an ordinary loss. Under the rule, if contributed property is disposed of at a loss and the property had a "built-in" capital loss on the contribution date, the loss is treated as a capital loss if the partnership disposes of the property *within five years of the contribution*. The capital loss is limited to the "built-in" loss on the date of contribution.[21]

The Big Picture

EXAMPLE 15

Return to the facts of *The Big Picture* on p. 14-1. Recall that Kyle, Maria, and Josh decide to structure their venture as an LLC. Assume that Kyle has a basis of $600,000 in the $2 million of real estate he contributed, and that Maria has a $0 basis in the bakery equipment and the café furnishings.

When Beachside Properties LLC is formed, no tax results for the LLC or for Kyle or Maria. Kyle does not recognize his $1.4 million realized gain, nor does Maria recognize her $500,000 realized gain.

Kyle takes a substituted basis of $600,000 for his interest, and Maria takes a substituted basis of $1.5 million ($1.5 million for contributed cash + $0 for contributed property). Beachside Properties assumes a carryover basis of $600,000 for the real estate contributed by Kyle and $0 for the property contributed by Maria. To the extent that the buildings and other land improvements are depreciable, the LLC "steps into Kyle's shoes" in calculating depreciation deductions.

When Josh vests in his 5% capital interest in the LLC, the $200,000 value of the interest is taxable to him, because it is a capital interest received in exchange for services. Beachside Properties probably will capitalize this amount because it relates to construction activities. Josh's 20% share of the future profits of the LLC are taxed to him as they flow through from the LLC.

14-2d Inside and Outside Bases

Reference has been made previously to the partnership's inside basis and the partners' outside basis. **Inside basis** refers to the adjusted basis of each partnership asset, as determined from the partnership's tax accounts. **Outside basis** represents each partner's basis in the partnership interest. Each partner "owns" a share of the partnership's inside basis for all of its assets, and all partners should maintain a record of their respective outside bases.

LO.3
Determine the tax treatment of expenditures of a newly formed partnership and identify elections available to the partnership.

14-2e Tax Accounting Elections

Numerous tax accounting elections must be made when a new partnership is formed. These elections are formal decisions on how a particular transaction or tax attribute should be handled. Most of these elections must be made by the partnership rather than

---

[20]§ 724. For this purpose, § 724(d)(2) waives the holding period requirement in defining § 1231 property.

[21]§ 724(c).

Concept Summary 14.2

Partnership Formation and Basis Computation

1. Generally, partners or partnerships do not recognize gain or loss when property is contributed in exchange for capital interests.

2. Partners take a substituted basis in the partnership interest (*outside basis*) equal to the basis of the property contributed to the partnership.

3. The partnership takes a carryover basis in assets received (*inside basis*) equal to the partner's basis in those assets.

4. The partnership's holding period for contributed property may include the contributing partner's holding period.

5. Income or gain is recognized by a contributing partner when services are contributed or when the capital contribution is a disguised sale or exchange.

6. Special rules may apply when the partnership disposes of contributed receivables, inventory, or loss assets.

by the partners individually.[22] For example, the *partnership* makes the elections involving the following tax accounting items.

- Inventory methods.
- Tax year and accounting method (cash, accrual, or hybrid).
- Cost recovery methods and assumptions.
- Immediate cost recovery deductions for certain tangible personal property.
- Amounts and treatment (i.e., deduction or credit) of research and experimentation costs.
- Amortization of organizational costs and amortization period.

Each partner is bound by the decisions made by the partnership relative to these items. If the partnership fails to make an election, a partner cannot make the election individually.

Although most elections are made by the partnership, each *partner* separately makes a specific election for the following relatively narrow tax accounting issues.

- Whether to take a deduction or a credit for taxes paid to foreign countries.
- Whether to claim the cost or percentage depletion method for oil and gas wells.

14-2f Initial Costs of a Partnership

In its initial stages, a partnership incurs expenses relating to some or all of the following: forming the partnership (organizational costs), admitting partners to the partnership, marketing and selling partnership units to prospective partners (**syndication costs**), acquiring assets, starting business operations (startup costs), negotiating contracts, and dealing with other items.

Many of these expenditures are not currently deductible. However, the Code permits a deduction or ratable (straight-line) amortization of "organizational" and "startup" costs. Costs incurred to acquire tangible assets are included in the initial basis of the acquired assets, leading to depreciation deductions. "Syndication costs" may be neither amortized nor deducted.[23]

---

[22]§ 703(b).   [23]§ 709(a).

Organizational Costs

<mark>Organizational costs</mark> are incurred incident to the creation of the partnership and are capital in nature. Such costs include accounting and legal fees associated with the partnership formation.[24] Costs incurred for the following purposes are *not* organizational costs.

- Acquiring assets for the partnership.
- Transferring assets to the partnership.
- Admitting partners, other than at formation.
- Removing partners, other than at formation.
- Negotiating operating contracts.

For Federal income tax purposes, a partnership may deduct up to $5,000 of organizational costs in the year in which it begins business. This amount is reduced, however, by organizational costs that exceed $50,000. Any organizational costs that cannot be deducted under this provision are amortizable over 180 months beginning with the month in which the partnership begins business.

The election to deduct organizational costs is made by entering the proper amounts on the first partnership return. Lacking such a computation, no deduction or amortization of the organizational costs is allowed until the entity is liquidated.

EXAMPLE 16

The Bluejay LLC, which was formed on March 1, incurs $52,000 in organizational costs. Bluejay uses a calendar tax year. On its first tax return for the period March–December, Bluejay can deduct $5,722 for these items. This deduction is the sum of:

- $5,000 reduced by the $2,000 ($52,000 − $50,000) amount by which the organizational costs exceed $50,000 = $3,000.
- $2,722 ($49,000 × 10/180) amortization of the remaining $49,000 ($52,000 − $3,000) of organizational costs for 10 months.

If Bluejay had failed to make a proper election to deduct or amortize the organizational costs, none of these costs would have been deductible until the entity liquidated.

Startup Costs

Operating costs that are incurred after the entity is formed but before it begins business are known as startup costs. Like organizational costs, startup costs are capitalized and may be immediately expensed and/or amortized.[25] Such costs include marketing surveys prior to conducting business, pre-operating advertising expenses, costs of establishing an accounting system, and salaries paid to executives and employees before the start of business.

For Federal income tax purposes, startup costs follow the same rules as organization costs. A partnership may deduct up to $5,000 of startup costs in the year in which it begins business. This amount is reduced, however, by the startup costs that exceed $50,000.

Costs that are not deductible under this provision are amortizable over 180 months beginning with the month in which the partnership begins business. If the deduction for startup costs is not claimed, no deduction or amortization of the startup costs is allowed until the entity is liquidated.

DIGGING DEEPER 3   In-depth coverage can be found on this book's companion website: **www.cengage.com**

---

[24]§ 709(b)(2).   [25]§ 195.

14-3 OPERATIONS OF THE PARTNERSHIP

LO.4

Calculate partnership taxable income and describe how partnership items affect a partner's income tax liability.

A key consideration in the taxation of partnerships is that a variety of entities can be partners and each may be affected differently by the partnership's operations. In particular, any combination of individuals, corporations, trusts, estates, or other partnerships may be partners. Furthermore, at the end of each year, every partner receives a share of the partnership's income, deductions, credits, and alternative minimum tax (AMT) preferences and adjustments.[26]

These flow-through items ultimately may be reported and taxed on a wide variety of income tax returns [e.g., Forms 1040 (Individuals), 1041 (Fiduciaries), 1120 (C corporations), and 1120S (S corporations)], each facing different limitations and rules. Thus, the ultimate tax treatment of partnership operations is directly affected by how the partnership reports its operating results.

14-3a Schedules K and K–1

A partnership measures and reports two kinds of income: separately stated items and nonseparately stated ordinary (business) income. A separately stated item is any item with tax attributes that could affect partners differently. Separately stated items are segregated and reported separately on the partnership's Schedule K and each partner's Schedule K–1. All other (nonseparately stated) income and expenses are reported as income from operations on page 1 of the partnership's Form 1065; the net amount then is allocated to the partners on Schedules K and K–1. Items passed through separately include the following.[27]

- Net short-term and net long-term capital gains or losses.
- Section 1231 gains and losses.
- Charitable contributions.
- Portfolio income items (qualified and ordinary dividends, interest, and royalties).
- Expenses related to portfolio income.
- Immediately expensed tangible personal property (§ 179).
- Disallowed business interest expense.[28]
- AMT preference and adjustment items.
- Self-employment income.[29]
- Passive activity items (e.g., rental real estate income or loss).
- Intangible drilling and development costs.[30]
- General business tax credits.[31]

A partnership is not allowed to claim the following deductions.

- Net operating loss (NOL).
- Dividends received deduction.
- Items that are allowed only to individuals, such as standard deductions.

---

[26]§ 702(a).
[27]§ 702(b).
[28]§ 163(j).

[29]§ 1402(a).
[30]See text Section 5-10a.
[31]E.g., §§ 38–52.

The Big Picture

EXAMPLE
17

Return to the facts of *The Big Picture* on p. 14-1. In its second year of operations, Beachside Properties LLC reports income and expenses from operating the café as well as rent income and expenses from leasing the other buildings. Beachside's activities are summarized as follows.

Sales revenue	$2,000,000
Cost of sales	800,000
W–2 wages paid to employees	500,000
Cost recovery deductions	91,984
Utilities, supplies, and other expenses	128,016
Taxes and licenses (including payroll taxes)	60,000
Contribution to charity	6,000
Short-term capital gain	12,000
Net income from rental real estate	300,000
Qualified dividends received	4,000
Tax-exempt income (bond interest)	2,100
Alternative minimum tax (AMT) adjustment (cost recovery)	18,224
Payment of medical expenses on behalf of Kyle	4,000
Net operating loss (NOL) from last year's operations	250,000
Cash distribution to Maria	20,000

Refer to Form 1065 at **irs.gov**. Beachside's ordinary income is determined and reported on the partnership return as follows.

Nonseparately Stated Items (Ordinary Income)	
Sales revenue	$2,000,000
Cost of sales	(800,000)
W–2 wages paid to employees	(500,000)
Cost recovery deductions	(91,984)
Utilities, supplies, and other expenses	(128,016)
Taxes and licenses (including payroll taxes)	(60,000)
Ordinary income [Form 1065, page 1, line 22, and Form 1065, page 4 (Schedule K), line 1]	$ 420,000

Beachside's separately stated income and deduction items are:

Separately Stated Income and Deductions (Schedule K)	
Net income from rental real estate (line 2)	$ 300,000
Qualified dividends received (line 6b)	4,000
Short-term capital gain (line 8)	12,000
Contribution to charity (line 13a)	(6,000)

Beachside is not allowed a deduction for payment of Kyle's medical expenses. This payment probably is handled as a distribution to Kyle, who may report it as a medical expense on his Form 1040, Schedule A in determining itemized deductions.

Maria's distribution is not deducted by Beachside. That amount instead reduces Maria's basis in her LLC interest.

The AMT adjustment is not a separate component of Beachside's ordinary income. It is reported to Beachside's members so that they can properly calculate any AMT liability of their own.

Beachside reports the following additional information the members may utilize in preparing their own income tax returns.

continued

Beachside reported an operating loss last year. The LLC could not deduct that loss; instead, the loss was passed through to the LLC members last year. Partnerships and LLCs do not incur net operating loss carryforwards.

Additional Information (Schedule K)	
AMT adjustment—cost recovery (line 17a)	$18,224
Tax-exempt income—bond interest (line 18a)	2,100
Distributions (line 19a)	24,000
Investment income (line 20a)	4,000

The LLC members' pass-through income represents net earnings (loss) from self-employment and is reported on line 14a.

The Big Picture

EXAMPLE 18

Continue with the facts in Example 17, but now consider the entity's book-tax reconciliation. Beachside Properties LLC must prepare the Analysis of Net Income (Loss) and Schedule M–1 on Form 1065, page 5. In preparing these schedules, the LLC combines the ordinary income of $420,000 and the four separately stated income and deduction amounts in Example 17 to arrive at "net income" of $730,000. This amount is shown on line 1 of the Analysis of Net Income (Loss) and is the amount to which book income is reconciled on Schedule M–1, line 9.

The Big Picture

EXAMPLE 19

Assume the same facts as in Example 17, but now consider the effect of the LLC's operations on one of its members. Maria, a 40% owner, will receive a Schedule K–1 from Beachside Properties, on which she is allocated a 40% share of ordinary income and separately stated items. Thus, on her Form 1040, Maria includes $168,000 of ordinary income, a $2,400 charitable contribution, a $4,800 short-term capital gain, $120,000 of passive activity rent income, and $1,600 of qualified dividend income. Maria's Schedule K–1 also reports the $20,000 cash distribution received.

Maria discloses her $840 share of tax-exempt interest on the first page of Form 1040. In determining her AMT liability (if any), Maria will take into account a $7,290 positive adjustment ($18,224 × 40%).

In-depth coverage can be found on this book's companion website: www.cengage.com

4 DIGGING DEEPER

Distributions, Withdrawals

Asset distributions and withdrawals by partners during the year do not affect the partnership's income determination.[32] These items usually are treated as made on the last day of the partnership's tax year. Such distributions reduce the partner's outside basis in the entity by the amount of the cash received, or by the inside basis of the asset to the entity, but not below zero. The entity's inside basis in assets is similarly reduced. The partner usually assigns to the received property a basis equal to the entity's inside basis in the distributed asset.

---

[32]§ 731(a).

EXAMPLE 20

Bueno Company is a partner in the BB Partnership. The basis in Bueno's partnership interest is $10,000. The partnership distributes $3,000 cash to Bueno at the end of the year. Bueno does not recognize any gain on the distribution. It reduces its basis in BB by $3,000 (the amount of the distribution) to $7,000. Bueno's basis in the cash received is $3,000, and the partnership's inside basis for its assets is reduced by the $3,000 of cash distributed.

BB also distributes to Bueno a plot of land worth $5,000, with a $2,000 basis to BB. Neither BB nor Bueno recognizes a gain from this distribution. Bueno assigns the land a $2,000 basis, and it reduces its basis in BB by the same amount.

The result in Example 20 arises whether or not a similar distribution is made to other partners. In a partnership, all partners need not receive a pro rata distribution at the same time, as long as capital account balances are maintained appropriately.

 DIGGING DEEPER 5   In-depth coverage can be found on this book's companion website: www.cengage.com

14-3b Partnership Allocations

After ordinary income, separately stated items, and other related information are determined at the partnership level, those amounts are allocated among the partners and reported on their tax returns. Allocations are made as required by the partnership agreement, using the profit and loss sharing ratios agreed to by the owners.

Concept Summary 14.3

Tax Reporting of Partnership Activities

Item	Partnership Level (Form 1065)	Partner Level (Schedule K–1)
1. Compute partnership ordinary income.	Page 1, line 22. Schedule K, line 1.	Line 1. Each partner's share is passed through for separate reporting. Each partner's basis is increased.
2. Compute partnership ordinary loss.	Page 1, line 22. Schedule K, line 1.	Line 1. Each partner's share is passed through for separate reporting. Each partner's basis is decreased. The amount of a partner's loss deduction may be limited. Losses that may not be deducted are carried forward for use in future years.
3. Separately reported income and deduction items such as portfolio income, capital gain and loss, AMT and foreign tax items, and § 179 deductions.	Schedule K, various lines.	Various lines. Each partner's share of each item is passed through for separate reporting.
4. Net earnings from self-employment.	Schedule K, line 14a, Code A.	Line 14, Code A.

Alternatively, two key special allocation rules also can affect a partner's Schedule K–1 results.[33]

Economic Effect

The partnership agreement can provide that any partner may share capital, profits, and losses in ratios that are tailored to their needs.[34] For example, a partner could have a 25 percent capital sharing ratio, yet be allocated 30 percent of the profits and 20 percent of the losses of the partnership, or, as in Examples 5 and 6, a partner could be allocated a specific amount or items of income, deduction, gain, or loss. Such special allocations are permissible if they meet the **economic effect test**.[35] The economic effect rules prevent partners from shifting income and loss items merely to reduce current income taxes. The rules also ensure that a partner bears the economic burden of a loss or deduction allocation and receives the economic benefit of an income or gain allocation.

In-depth coverage can be found on this book's companion website: **www.cengage.com**	**6 DIGGING DEEPER**

Precontribution Gain or Loss

Certain income, gain, loss, and deductions relative to contributed property may not be allocated under the economic effect rules.[36] Instead, **precontribution gain or loss** is allocated among the partners to take into account the variation between the basis of the property and its fair market value on the date of contribution.[37] For nondepreciable property, this means that *built-in* gain or loss on the date of contribution is allocated to the contributing partner when the property eventually is disposed of by the partnership in a taxable transaction.

The Big Picture

EXAMPLE 21

Return to the facts of *The Big Picture* on p. 14-1. When Beachside Properties LLC was formed, among other items, Kyle contributed land (value of $800,000 and basis of $600,000) and buildings (value of $1,200,000 and basis of $0). Maria contributed equipment and furnishings (value of $500,000 and basis of $0).

For book purposes, Beachside records the land and other properties at their fair market values. For tax purposes, the LLC takes carryover bases in the properties. The LLC must keep track of the differences between the basis in each property and the value at the contribution date. If any of this property is sold, the gain is allocated to the contributing partner to the extent of any previously unrecognized built-in gain.

For example, if Beachside sells the land contributed by Kyle for $1.1 million, the gain is calculated and allocated as follows.

	Book	Tax
Amount realized	$1,100,000	$1,100,000
Less: Adjusted basis	(800,000)	(600,000)
Gain realized	$ 300,000	$ 500,000
Built-in gain allocated solely to Kyle	(–0–)	(200,000)
Remaining gain (allocated among members)	$ 300,000	$ 300,000

For Federal income tax purposes, Kyle recognizes $320,000 of the gain [($300,000 × 40%) + $200,000], Maria recognizes $120,000 ($300,000 × 40%), and Josh recognizes $60,000 ($300,000 × 20%).

---

[33]The Code requires or allows certain other allocations not discussed here.

[34]§ 704(a).

[35]Reg. § 1.704–1(b).

[36]§ 704(b).

[37]§ 704(c)(1)(A).

Qualified Business Income Deduction

A special deduction generally allows owners of flow-through entities including partners to claim a deduction from income equal to 20 percent of the income that is allocated to them from the entity.[38] If the owner's taxable income from all sources is less than certain thresholds ($315,000 for taxpayers filing joint returns and $157,500 for all other returns), the deduction is calculated as 20 percent of qualified business income (QBI). QBI includes the ordinary net income from the pass-through entity, including rental income. However, QBI does not include other separately stated items of income, gain, or loss.

Hugh is a single taxpayer. He owns a 25% interest in HG Partnership. The partnership records ordinary net income of $600,000. Hugh's share of partnership ordinary net income is $150,000. His share of W–2 wages paid by HG Partnership is $50,000, and his share of the unadjusted basis of qualified property is $400,000. The partnership is his sole source of income. Hugh's tentative § 199A deduction is $30,000 ($150,000 × 20%).

If the owner's taxable income exceeds the appropriate threshold, the allowable deduction may be reduced. In this case, the § 199A deduction is the lesser of the 20 percent QBI deduction or the greater of 50 percent of W–2 wages paid by the business or 25 percent of the W–2 wages plus 2.5 percent of unadjusted basis of tangible depreciable property. The limitation phases in over $100,000 of taxable income for taxpayers filing joint returns and $50,000 for all other returns. An additional limitation applies if the income is from qualified services. In this instance, if the taxpayer's income exceeds the appropriate threshold the taxpayer gets no deduction.

Continue with the facts of Example 22. Now assume that Hugh's taxable income from all sources is $250,000. In this case, taxable income from all sources exceeds the threshold, so Hugh's QBI deduction may be reduced. Hugh's QBI deduction would be $25,000: the lesser of (1) 20% of QBI or (2) the greater of 50% of allocated W–2 wages or 25% of allocated W–2 wages plus 2.5% of unadjusted basis of tangible depreciable property.

1. 20% of QBI ($150,000 × 20%)		$30,000
2. Greater of		
a. 50% of W–2 wages ($50,000 × 50%)	$25,000	
b. 25% of W–2 wages plus 2.5% of unadjusted basis of depreciable property [($50,000 × 25%) + ($400,000 × 2.5%)]	$22,500	
		$25,000

LO.5

Determine a partner's basis in the partnership interest.

14-3c Basis of a Partnership Interest

A partner's basis in the partnership interest is important for determining the treatment of distributions from the partnership to the partner, establishing the deductibility of partnership losses, and calculating gain or loss on the partner's disposition of the partnership interest.

A partner's basis is not reflected anywhere on the Schedule K–1. Instead, each partner maintains a personal record of the basis in the partnership interest.

Initial Basis in the Partnership Interest

A partner's basis in a newly formed partnership usually equals (1) the adjusted basis in any cash or other property contributed to the partnership plus (2) the fair market value of any services the partner performed for the partnership (i.e., the amount of ordinary income reported by the partner for services rendered to the partnership).

[38]§ 199A.

BRIDGE DISCIPLINE **Bridge to Financial Accounting**

The equivalent in financial accounting to the partner's income tax basis in his or her partnership interest is the **capital account**. A partner's ending balance in the capital account is not required to be the same as his or her basis in the partnership interest. Just as the tax and accounting bases of a specific asset may differ, a partner's capital account and basis in the partnership interest usually are not equal.

Whereas asset contributions and most distributions from the partnership do not create financial accounting income, the capital account is "written up or down" to aggregate fair market value when the entity is formed. For most partnerships with simple financial transactions, *changes* to the capital account parallel closely the annual changes to the partner's basis in the partnership. Basis in one's partnership interest cannot be a negative number, but the capital account can become negative.

Oddly, the Schedules K–1 for the partners require an accounting for their capital accounts, but there is no required reconciliation for the partner's tax basis on the Schedule K–1. As a result, the tax adviser may find that a new partnership client has poor records with respect to the basis amounts of the partners, and a reconstruction must take place so that future computations will be correct.[39]

A partnership interest also can be acquired after the partnership has been formed. The method of acquisition controls how the partner's initial basis is computed. If the partnership interest is purchased from another partner, the purchasing partner's basis is the amount paid (cost basis) for the partnership interest. The basis of a partnership interest acquired by gift is the donor's basis for the interest plus, in certain cases, some or all of the transfer (gift) tax paid by the donor. The basis of a partnership interest acquired through inheritance generally is the fair market value of the interest on the date the partner dies.

Basis Adjustments Due to Entity Operations

After the partnership begins its activities, or after a new partner is admitted to the partnership, the partner's basis is adjusted for numerous items. The following operating results *increase* a partner's basis.

- The partner's proportionate share of partnership income (including capital gains and tax-exempt income).
- The partner's proportionate share of any increase in partnership liabilities.

The following operating results *decrease* the partner's basis in the partnership.

- The partner's proportionate share of partnership deductions and losses (including capital losses).
- The partner's proportionate share of nondeductible expenses.
- The partner's proportionate share of any reduction in partnership liabilities.[40]

Under no circumstances can a partner's basis in the partnership's interest be reduced below zero.

Increasing the basis for the partner's share of partnership taxable income is logical, because the partner already has been taxed on the income. By increasing the partner's basis, the partner is not taxed again on the income when he or she sells the interest or receives a distribution from the partnership.

It also is logical that tax-exempt income should increase the partner's basis. If the income is tax-exempt in the current period, it should not contribute to the recognition of gain when the partner either sells the interest or receives a distribution from the partnership. Decreasing the basis for the partner's share of deductible losses, deductions, and noncapitalizable, nondeductible expenditures is done for the same reasons.

---

[39]Sometimes, lacking adequate information with which to make this computation, the capital account is used for this purpose, because it is "close enough" and forms a good surrogate for the partner's basis in the partnership.

[40]§§ 705 and 752.

TAX FACT What Do Partnerships Do?

Partnerships report over $26 trillion in assets on their Form 1065 balance sheets. The partnership form seems to be especially popular for businesses operating in the financial services and real estate industries. Manufacturing assets tend not to be found as frequently in these entities.

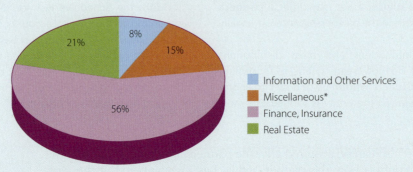

Assets of Partnerships, by Industry

- 8% Information and Other Services
- 15% Miscellaneous*
- 56% Finance, Insurance
- 21% Real Estate

*Includes aggregated amounts from the agriculture, health care, construction, manufacturing, wholesale and retail trade, education, and arts and entertainment sectors.

EXAMPLE 24

Yuri is a one-third member in the XYZ LLC. His proportionate share of operations during the current year consists of $20,000 of ordinary taxable income and $10,000 of tax-exempt income. None of the income is distributed to Yuri.

The basis of Yuri's LLC interest before adjusting for his share of income is $35,000, and the fair market value of the interest before considering the income items is $50,000.

The unrealized gain inherent in Yuri's investment in XYZ is $15,000 ($50,000 − $35,000). Yuri's proportionate share of the income items should increase the fair market value of the interest to $80,000 ($50,000 + $20,000 + $10,000). When the basis of Yuri's interest is increased to $65,000 ($35,000 + $20,000 + $10,000), the unrealized gain inherent in Yuri's investment remains at $15,000.

Thus, $20,000 of ordinary taxable income is taxed to Yuri this year and should not be taxed again when Yuri either sells his interest or receives a distribution. Similarly, the tax-exempt income is exempt this year and should not increase Yuri's gain when he either sells his interest or receives a distribution from XYZ.

Partnership Liabilities

A partner's basis includes the partner's share of partnership debt.[41] Partnership debt includes most debt that is considered a liability under financial accounting rules. However, partnership debt for this purpose does *not* include the accounts payable of a cash basis partnership and certain contingent liabilities.

Partnership debt is classified as either recourse or nonrecourse.[42] For **recourse debt**, the partnership or at least one of the partners is personally liable. This liability can exist, for example, through the operation of state law or through personal guarantees that a partner makes to the creditor. If the entity defaults on the loan, the lender can pursue the other assets of the borrower, including personal use property.

For **nonrecourse debt**, no partner is personally liable. Lenders of nonrecourse debt generally require that collateral be pledged against the loan. Upon default, the lender can claim only the collateral, not the partners' personal assets.

---

[41] § 752.

[42] Reg. § 1.752–1(a). All of the debts of an LLC generally are treated as nonrecourse debt for its members, because it is the entity, and not the members, that is ultimately liable for repayment.

Liabilities and Partnership Interest Basis

The Bay Partnership financed its asset acquisitions with debt. If the partnership defaults on the debt, the lender can place a lien on the partners' salaries and personal assets. This constitutes recourse debt.

EXAMPLE 25

The Tray LLC financed its asset acquisitions with debt. If the entity defaults on the debt, the lender can repossess the equipment purchased with the loan proceeds. This constitutes non-recourse debt.

EXAMPLE 26

A partner's share of entity-level debt usually increases as a result of increases in outstanding partnership debt. This increase is treated as a cash contribution and creates additional basis in the partnership for the partner, against which flow-through losses can be deducted.

Jim and Becky contribute property to form the JB Partnership. Jim contributes cash of $30,000. Becky contributes land with a basis and fair market value of $45,000, subject to a liability of $15,000. The partnership borrows $50,000 to finance construction of a building on the contributed land. At the end of the first year, the accrual basis partnership owes $3,500 in trade accounts payable to various vendors. No other operating activities occurred. If Jim and Becky share equally in liabilities, the partners' bases in their partnership interests are determined as follows.

EXAMPLE 27

Jim's Basis		Becky's Basis	
Contributed cash	$30,000	Basis in contributed land	$ 45,000
		Less: Debt assumed by partnership	(15,000)
Share of debt on land (assumed by partnership)	7,500	Share of debt on land (assumed by partnership)	7,500
Share of construction loan	25,000	Share of construction loan	25,000
Share of trade accounts payable	1,750	Share of trade accounts payable	1,750
Basis, end of year 1	$64,250	Basis, end of year 1	$ 64,250

A decrease in a partner's share of partnership debt is treated as a cash distribution and decreases the partner's basis, because distributions are taken into consideration before any current-year losses from the partnership. This ordering procedure limits the partner's ability to deduct current-year flow-through losses.

In-depth coverage can be found on this book's companion website: **www.cengage.com**    **7** DIGGING DEEPER

14-3d **Partner's Basis, Gain, and Loss**

The partner's basis in an ownership interest also is affected by (1) postacquisition contributions of cash or property to the partnership and (2) postacquisition distributions of cash or property from the partnership.

Ed is a one-third member in ERM LLC. On January 1, Ed's basis in his interest was $50,000. The calendar year, accrual basis entity generated ordinary taxable income of $210,000. It also received $60,000 of tax-exempt interest income from City of Buffalo bonds. It paid $3,000 in nondeductible fines and penalties.

EXAMPLE 28

continued

On July 1, Ed contributed $20,000 cash and a computer (zero basis to him) to ERM. Ed's monthly cash draw from the LLC is $3,000; this is not a guaranteed payment. The only entity liabilities are trade accounts payable. On January 1, the trade accounts payable totaled $45,000; this account balance was $21,000 on December 31. Ed's shares of the entity's liabilities is one-third for basis purposes.

Ed's basis in the LLC on December 31 is $115,000, computed as follows.

Beginning basis in the LLC interest	$ 50,000
Share of ordinary income	70,000
Share of tax-exempt income	20,000
Share of nondeductible fines and penalties	(1,000)
Ed's basis in noncash capital contribution (computer)	–0–
Additional cash contributions	20,000
Capital withdrawal ($3,000 per month)	(36,000)
Share of net decrease in ERM liabilities [⅓ × ($45,000 − $21,000)]	(8,000)
Ending basis in the LLC interest	$115,000

If Ed withdraws cash of $115,000 from ERM the next year, the withdrawal is tax-free to him and reduces his basis to zero. The distribution is tax-free because Ed has recognized his share of net income throughout his association with the entity via the annual flow-through of his share of the ERM income and expense items to his personal tax return.

If Ed receives a $20,000 cash withdrawal of his share of the municipal bond interest income, that amount retains its nontaxable character; his basis was increased when ERM received the interest income.

Noncash Distributions

When a distribution involves something other than cash, the recipient partner (1) reduces the basis in the partnership interest and (2) assigns a basis to the asset received, both by the amount of the inside basis of the distributed asset. When cash and another asset are distributed at the same time, the partner first accounts for the cash received.

Loss never is recognized when a partnership makes a distribution other than possibly in its own liquidation. A partner recognizes gain only when receiving *cash* in an amount in excess of the basis in the partnership interest.

Distributions of Noncash Assets

Pert Corporation has a $100,000 basis in the PQR Partnership. Pert receives a distribution from PQR in the form of a plot of land (basis to PQR of $40,000, fair market value of $50,000). Pert does not recognize gain from the distribution. Pert's basis in the land is $40,000 (i.e., a carryover basis), and its basis in PQR now is $60,000 ($100,000 − $40,000).

Pert Corporation has a $100,000 basis in the PQR Partnership. Pert receives a distribution from PQR in the form of a plot of land (basis to PQR of $40,000, fair market value of $50,000) and $75,000 of cash.

Pert does not recognize any gain from the distribution because the cash received ($75,000) does not exceed Pert's partnership basis ($100,000). Pert's basis in the land is $25,000, the basis in PQR remaining after accounting for the cash ($100,000 partnership basis − $75,000 cash = $25,000 basis assigned to land). Pert's basis in the partnership now is zero ($25,000 basis after accounting for the cash − $25,000 assigned to the land).

Distributions of Noncash Assets

Pert Corporation has a $100,000 basis in the PQR Partnership. Pert receives a distribution from PQR in the form of a plot of land (basis to PQR of $40,000, fair market value of $50,000) and $125,000 of cash. Pert recognizes $25,000 of gain from the distribution ($125,000 cash received − $100,000 basis in PQR). Pert's basis in the land is $0, as there is no basis in PQR remaining after accounting for the cash. Pert's basis in the partnership also is zero.

EXAMPLE 31

Capital Changes

When a partnership interest is sold, exchanged, or retired, the partner must compute the basis as of the date the transaction occurs. The partner recognizes gain or loss on the disposition of the partnership interest, and this usually is a capital gain or loss. Income "bunching" may occur if the partner recognizes the pass-through of operating income in the same tax year during which the sale of the interest occurs. To the extent the partner is allocated a share of ordinary income items (i.e., "hot assets") that have yet to be recognized by the partnership, some of the capital gain is converted to ordinary income.[43]

Hot Assets

When its basis in the TUV Partnership is $100,000, taking into account all earnings to date and the sale-date liabilities of the partnership, Kurt Corporation sells its interest in the entity to Gloria for $120,000. At the time of the sale, Kurt's share of the built-in gain in TUV's hot assets is $8,000. Kurt recognizes $8,000 of ordinary income and $12,000 of capital gain (i.e., the total gain of $20,000 is comprised of $8,000 of ordinary income and $12,000 of capital gain).

EXAMPLE 32

When its basis in the TUV Partnership is $100,000, taking into account all earnings to date and the sale-date liabilities of the partnership, Kurt Corporation sells its interest in the entity to Gloria for $120,000. At the time of the sale, Kurt's share of the built-in gain in TUV's hot assets is $28,000. Kurt recognizes $28,000 of ordinary income and $8,000 of capital loss (i.e., the total gain of $20,000 is comprised of $28,000 of ordinary income and $8,000 of capital loss).

EXAMPLE 33

14-3e **Loss Limitations**

Partnership losses flow through to the partners for use on their tax returns. However, the amount and nature of the partner's deductible losses may be limited. When limitations apply, all or some of the losses are suspended and carried forward until the rules allow them to be used. Only then can the losses decrease the partner's tax liability.

LO.6

Apply the tax law's limitations on deducting partnership losses.

Different limitations may apply to partnership losses that are passed through to a partner. The first allows the deduction of *losses* only to the extent the partner has a positive basis in the partnership interest. The tax basis in the entity cannot be reduced below zero.

Losses that are deductible under this basis limitation may then be subject to the *at-risk* limitations. Losses are deductible under this provision only to the extent the partner is at risk for the partnership interest. Any losses that survive this second limitation may be subject to a third limitation, the *passive activity loss* rules. If a loss passes the three limitations, a noncorporate partner must consider whether the excess business loss limitation might apply. Only losses that make it through all of these applicable limitations are eligible to be deducted on the partner's tax return.

---

[43]Partnership items that hold unrecognized ordinary income are known as *hot assets*. Hot assets include the unrealized receivables of a cash basis partnership and a broadly defined concept of inventory. §§ 751(a) and (d).

EXAMPLE 34

Meg is a 50% member in MQ Telecomm Services LLC. On January 1, Meg's basis in her LLC interest is $50,000, and her at-risk amount is $35,000. Her share of losses from MQ for the year is $60,000, all of which is a passive activity loss. Meg owns another investment that generated $25,000 of passive activity income during the year. Meg can deduct $25,000 of the MQ losses on her Form 1040.

Applicable Provision	Deductible Loss	Suspended Loss
Basis limitation	$50,000	$10,000
At-risk limitation	35,000	15,000
Passive activity loss limitation	25,000	10,000
Excess business loss limitation	25,000	10,000

Meg can deduct only $50,000 under the basis limitation rule. Of this $50,000, only $35,000 is deductible under the at-risk limitation. Under the passive activity loss limitation, passive activity losses can only be deducted against passive activity income. The loss is less than the excess business loss threshold described later, so no further limitations apply. Thus, Meg can deduct only $25,000 on her return. The remaining $35,000 of losses is suspended.

Basis Limitation

A partner may deduct losses and deductions from the partnership only to the extent of the partner's basis in the partnership.[44] Items that cannot be deducted because of this rule are suspended and carried forward (never back) for use against future increases in the partner's basis. Such increases might result from additional capital contributions, from sharing in additional partnership debts, or from future partnership income. The suspended loss can be carried forward for an unlimited term.

EXAMPLE 35

Carol and Dan do business as the CD Partnership, sharing profits and losses equally. All parties use the calendar year. At the start of the current year, the basis of Carol's partnership interest is $25,000. The partnership sustains an operating loss of $80,000 in the current year. Only $25,000 of Carol's $40,000 allocable share of the partnership loss can be deducted under the basis limitation. As a result, the basis of Carol's partnership interest is zero as of January 1 of the following year, and Carol must carry forward the remaining $15,000 of partnership losses.

Now assume that CD earns a profit of $70,000 for the next calendar year. Carol reports net partnership income of $20,000 ($35,000 share of income − $15,000 carryforward loss). The basis of Carol's partnership interest becomes $20,000.

Concept Summary 14.4 later in the chapter shows that contributions to capital, partnership income items, and distributions from the partnership are taken into account before loss items. This *losses last* rule can produce some unusual results in taxation of partnership distributions and deductibility of losses.

TAX PLANNING STRATEGIES   **Make Your Own Tax Shelter**

FRAMEWORK FOCUS: DEDUCTIONS

Strategy: Maximize Deductible Amounts.

In Example 35, Carol's entire $40,000 share of the current-year partnership loss could have been deducted under the basis limitation in the current year if she had contributed an additional $15,000 or more to the entity's capital by December 31 of the first tax year. Alternatively, if the partnership had incurred additional debt by the end of the first tax year, Carol's basis might have been increased to permit some or all of the loss to be deducted in that year.

Thus, if partnership losses are projected for a given year, careful tax planning can ensure their deductibility under the basis limitation. Note, however, that the effects of the at-risk and passive activity limitations as discussed on the next page also must be considered.

---

[44]§ 704(d).

The Basis Limitation on Losses

EXAMPLE 36

The Ellen-Glenn Partnership is owned equally by two partners: Ellen and the Glenn Hospital. At the beginning of the year, Ellen's basis in her partnership interest is $0. Her share of partnership income is $12,000 for the year, and she receives a $10,000 distribution from the partnership.

Under the basis adjustment ordering rules of Concept Summary 14.4, as shown on the next page, Ellen's basis first is increased by the $12,000 of partnership income; then it is decreased by her $10,000 distribution. She reports her $12,000 share of partnership taxable income on her personal tax return. Her basis in the partnership at the end of the year is $2,000 ($0 beginning basis + $12,000 income − $10,000 distribution).

EXAMPLE 37

Assume the same facts as in Example 36, except that Ellen's share of partnership operating results is a $12,000 loss instead of $12,000 of income. She again receives a $10,000 distribution.

A distribution of cash in excess of basis in the partnership interest results in a gain to the distributee partner to the extent of the excess. Ellen's distribution is considered before the deductibility of the loss is evaluated under the basis limitation.

Therefore, Ellen recognizes gain on the $10,000 distribution because she has a $0 basis in her partnership interest. Unfortunately for Ellen, the operating loss cannot be deducted under the basis limitation rule because Ellen still holds a $0 basis in her partnership interest. The loss is suspended, and Ellen carries it forward to a future tax year.

At-Risk Limitation

Under the at-risk rules (see text Section 6-6), a partner's deductions for certain pass-through losses are limited to amounts that are economically invested in the partnership. Invested amounts include the cash and the adjusted basis of property contributed by the partner and the partner's share of partnership earnings that has not been distributed.[45]

Losses that are not deductible under the at-risk rules are suspended and carried forward indefinitely. When a positive at-risk amount arises in a future tax year, the suspended loss is allowed.

When some or all of the partners are personally liable for partnership recourse debt, that debt is included in the basis of the partnership for those partners. Usually, those partners also include the debt in their amount at risk.

No partner, however, carries any financial risk on nonrecourse debt. Therefore, as a general rule, partners cannot include nonrecourse debt in their amount at risk even though that debt is included in the basis of their partnership interest. This rule has an important exception, however. Real estate nonrecourse financing provided by a bank, retirement plan, or similar party or by a Federal, state, or local government generally is deemed to be at risk.[46] Such debt is termed **qualified nonrecourse financing**.

Losses and At-Risk Amounts

EXAMPLE 38

Kelly invests $5,000 in the Kelly Green Limited Partnership as a 5% general partner. Shortly thereafter, the partnership acquires the master recording of a well-known vocalist for $250,000 ($50,000 from the partnership and $200,000 secured from a local bank via *recourse* debt). Kelly's share of the recourse debt is $10,000, and her basis in the interest is $15,000 ($5,000 cash investment + $10,000 debt share).

Because the debt is recourse, Kelly's at-risk amount also is $15,000. Kelly's share of partnership losses in the first year of operations is $11,000. Kelly can deduct the full $11,000 of partnership losses under both the basis and the at-risk limitations because this amount is less than both her outside basis and at-risk amount.

---

[45]§ 465(a).

[46]§ 465(b)(6).

Losses and At-Risk Amounts

EXAMPLE
39

Assume the same facts as in Example 38, except that the bank loan is nonrecourse. Kelly's basis in the partnership interest still is $15,000, but she can deduct only $5,000 of the flow-through loss. The amount she has at risk in the partnership does not include the nonrecourse debt. (The debt does not relate to real estate, so it cannot be qualified nonrecourse debt.)

The $6,000 suspended loss ($11,000 loss pass-through − $5,000 deduction) is deducted in a future tax year when a positive at-risk amount exists. This might occur because the entity has generated an undistributed net profit, or due to a capital contribution by Kelly.

Passive Activity Rules

Partnership losses also may be disallowed under the passive activity rules. Recall from text Section 6-7 that an activity is considered passive if the taxpayer (in this case, a partner) does not materially participate or if the activity is considered a rental activity.

Losses from passive partnership activities are aggregated by each partner with his or her other passive activity income and losses. Passive activity losses generally are deducted only to the extent they offset passive activity income. Any excess passive activity loss is suspended and carried forward to future years. The passive activity limitation applies after the owner's basis and at-risk limitations.

Limitation on the Deduction of Excess Business Losses

Another provision limits the total amount of net business losses that can be deducted by an active owner. The rule limits the maximum loss to $500,000 for married filing joint tax returns and $250,000 for all other tax returns. Any loss in excess of these amounts can be carried forward indefinitely.[47]

Concept Summary 14.4

Partner's Basis in Partnership Interest

Basis generally is adjusted in the following order.

Initial basis: Amount paid for partnership interest, or gift or inherited basis (including share of partnership debt).

+ Partner's subsequent asset contributions and allocable debt increases.

+ Partner's share of the partnership's:
  - Income items.
  - Tax-exempt income items.
  - Excess of depletion deductions over adjusted basis of property subject to depletion.

− Partner's distributions and withdrawals and allocable debt decreases.

− Partner's share of the partnership's:
  - Separately stated deductions.
  - Nondeductible items not chargeable to a capital account.
  - Special depletion deduction for oil and gas wells.
  - Loss items.

The basis of a partner's interest never can be negative.

Entity-level liabilities, and thus a partner's basis in the partnership, may change from day to day, but the partner's basis generally needs to be computed only once or twice a year.

LO.7

Apply the tax laws regarding transactions between a partner and the partnership.

14-4 TRANSACTIONS BETWEEN PARTNER AND PARTNERSHIP

Many types of transactions occur between a partnership and its partners. A partner may contribute property to the partnership, perform services for the partnership, or receive distributions from the partnership. A partner may borrow money from or lend money to the partnership. Property may be bought and sold between a partner and

[47]§ 461(l).

the partnership. Several of these transactions were discussed earlier in the chapter. The remaining types of partner-partnership transactions are the focus of this section.

14-4a Guaranteed Payments

A **guaranteed payment** is a payment for services performed by the partner or for the use of the partner's capital. The payment is not determined by reference to partnership income. Guaranteed payments usually are expressed as a fixed-dollar amount or as a percentage of capital the partner has invested in the partnership. Whether the partnership deducts or capitalizes the guaranteed payment depends on the nature of the payment.

Donna, Deepak, and Diane formed the accrual basis DDD Partnership. DDD and each of the partners are calendar year taxpayers. According to the partnership agreement, Donna is to manage the partnership and receive a $21,000 distribution from the entity every year, payable in 12 monthly installments. Deepak is to receive an amount that is equal to 8% of his capital account, as it is computed by the firm's accountant at the beginning of the year, payable in 12 monthly installments. Diane is DDD's advertising specialist. She withdraws 4% of the partnership's net income for personal use. Donna and Deepak receive guaranteed payments from the partnership, but Diane does not.

EXAMPLE
40

Guaranteed payments resemble the salary or interest payments of other businesses and receive somewhat similar income tax treatment. In contrast to the provision that usually applies to withdrawals of assets by partners from their partnerships, guaranteed payments are deductible (or capitalized) by the entity. Deductible guaranteed payments, like any other deductible expense of a partnership, can create an ordinary loss for the entity.

The partner's guaranteed payment is reported as a separately stated item on Schedules K and K–1. The partner uses this information (in lieu of a Form W–2 or 1099) to report the income on the partner's tax return. Partners receiving a guaranteed payment report ordinary income and treat it as paid on the last day of the entity's tax year.

Guaranteed Payments: Income and Deductions

Continue with the situation introduced in Example 40. For calendar year 2019, Donna receives the $21,000 as provided by the partnership agreement, Deepak's guaranteed payment is $17,000, and Diane withdraws $20,000 under the personal expenditures clause. Before considering these amounts, the partnership's ordinary income for the year is $650,000.

DDD can deduct its payments to Donna and Deepak, so the final amount of its ordinary income is $612,000 ($650,000 − $21,000 − $17,000). Thus, each of the equal partners is allocated $204,000 of ordinary partnership income ($612,000 ÷ 3). In addition, Donna reports the $21,000 guaranteed payment as gross income, and Deepak includes the $17,000 guaranteed payment in his gross income.

Diane's partnership draw is a distribution from her interest basis and is not taxed separately to her.

EXAMPLE
41

Assume the same facts as in Example 41, except that the partnership uses a "natural business" tax year that ends on March 31, 2020. Thus, even though Donna received 9 of her 12 payments for fiscal 2020 in the 2019 calendar year, all of Donna's guaranteed payments are taxable to her in 2020. Similarly, all of Deepak's guaranteed payments are taxable to him in 2020, rather than when they are received.

The deduction for, and the gross income from, guaranteed payments is allowed on the same date that all of the other income and expense items relative to the partnership are allocated to the partners (i.e., on the last day of the entity's tax year).

EXAMPLE
42

14-4b Other Transactions between a Partner and a Partnership

Many common transactions between a partner and the partnership are treated as if the partner were an outsider, dealing with the partnership at arm's length. Loan transactions, rental payments, and sales of property between the partner and the partnership generally are treated in this manner.

The Eastside Co-op, a one-third partner in the ABC Partnership, owns a tract of land the partnership wants to purchase. The land has a fair market value of $30,000 and a basis to Eastside of $17,000. If Eastside sells the land to ABC, Eastside recognizes a $13,000 gain on the sale, and ABC takes a $30,000 cost basis in the land. If the land has a fair market value of $10,000 on the sale date, Eastside recognizes a $7,000 loss.

DIGGING DEEPER **8** | In-depth coverage can be found on this book's companion website: **www.cengage.com**

Sales of Property

No loss is recognized on a sale of property between a person and a partnership when the person owns, directly or indirectly, more than 50 percent of partnership capital or profits.[48] The disallowed loss may not vanish entirely, however. If the person later sells the property at a gain, the disallowed loss reduces the gain that would otherwise be recognized.

Barry sells land (basis, $30,000; fair market value, $45,000) to the BCD LLC, of which he owns a 60% capital interest. BCD pays him only $20,000 for the land. Barry cannot deduct his $10,000 realized loss. Barry and the LLC are related parties, and the loss is disallowed.

When BCD sells the land to an outsider at a later date, it receives a sales price of $44,000. The entity can offset the recognition of its $24,000 realized gain on the subsequent sale ($44,000 sales proceeds − $20,000 basis) by the amount of the $10,000 prior disallowed loss ($20,000 − $30,000). Thus, BCD recognizes a $14,000 gain on its sale of the land.

Using a similar rationale, any gain that is realized on a sale or exchange between a partner and a partnership in which the partner owns a capital or profits interest of more than 50 percent is recognized as ordinary income, unless the asset is a capital asset to both the seller and the purchaser.[49]

The Kent School purchases some land (basis, $30,000; fair market value, $45,000) for $45,000 from the JJ Realty LLC, in which Kent owns a 90% profits interest. The land was a capital asset to JJ. If Kent holds the land as a capital asset, JJ recognizes a $15,000 capital gain. However, if the school also is a land developer and the property is not a capital asset to it, JJ recognizes $15,000 of ordinary income from the sale, even though it held the property as a capital asset.

14-4c Partners as Employees

A partner does not qualify as an employee under Federal tax law, specifically for purposes of payroll taxes (e.g., FICA or FUTA). Moreover, because a partner is not an employee, the partnership cannot deduct its payments for the partner's fringe benefits,[50] and the partner reports as gross income the value of the fringe benefits received. Nonetheless, a general partner's share of ordinary partnership income and guaranteed payments for services generally are classified as Federal self-employment (SE) income.

---

[48] 707(b).

[49] § 707(b)(2).

[50] § 3401(a).

The partner pays an SE tax in addition to the Federal income tax on pass-through items, and the additional Medicare taxes also may apply. The combination of these tax obligations can become expensive. Tax liabilities on SE income of a partner include:

- A 12.4 percent tax on the first $127,200 for 2017 and $128,400 for 2018 of SE income, for the individual's account in the FICA retirement system.

- A 2.9 percent tax on all SE income, to support the Medicare system.

TAX PLANNING STRATEGIES Transactions between Partners and Partnerships

FRAMEWORK FOCUS: DEDUCTIONS

Strategy: Maximize Deductible Amounts.

To ensure that no negative tax results occur, partners should be careful when engaging in transactions with the partnership. A partner who owns a majority of the partnership generally should not sell property at a loss to the partnership because the loss is disallowed. Similarly, a majority partner should not sell a capital asset to the partnership at a gain if the asset is to be used by the partnership as other than a capital asset. The gain on this transaction is taxed as ordinary income to the selling partner rather than as capital gain.

As an alternative to selling property to a partnership, a partner may lease it to the partnership. The partner recognizes rent income, and the partnership has a rent deduction. A partner who needs more cash immediately can sell the property to an outside third party; then the third party can lease the property to the partnership for a fair rental.

A partner who is an individual may be subject to additional taxes that support the Federal Medicare system, on flow-through items from the entity. Certain upper-income taxpayers must pay:

- A .9 percent tax on SE income,[51] and

- A 3.8 percent tax on flow-through net investment income (NII), including interest and dividend income, passive/portfolio income, and capital gains. NII does not include tax-exempt interest income, but it does include the share of pass-through operating income for a passive or limited partner.[52]

In-depth coverage can be found on this book's companion website: www.cengage.com   **9 DIGGING DEEPER**

Concept Summary 14.5

Partner-Partnership Transactions

1. Partners can transact business with their partnerships in a non-partner capacity. These transactions include the sale and exchange of property, rentals, and loans of funds.

2. A payment to a partner may be classified as a guaranteed payment if it is for services or use of the partner's capital and is not based on partnership income. A guaranteed payment usually is deductible by the partnership and is included in the partner's income on the last day of the partnership's tax year.

3. Losses are disallowed between a partner or related party and a partnership when the partner or related party owns more than a 50% interest in the partnership's capital or profits.

4. Income from a related-party sale is treated as ordinary income if the property is not a capital asset to both the transferor and the transferee.

5. Partners are not employees of their partnership, so the entity cannot deduct payments for partner fringe benefits, nor need it withhold or pay any payroll tax for payments to partners.

6. A partner may be subject to self-employment and the additional Medicare taxes on guaranteed payments received, and on a distributive share of flow-through income.

---

[51]§ 1401(b)(2)(A). Form 8959 is used to compute this tax.   [52]§ 1411. Form 8960 is used to compute this tax.

LO.8

Explain how LLPs and LLCs differ and list the tax advantages and disadvantages of using an LLC.

14-5 LIMITED LIABILITY COMPANIES

The *limited liability company (LLC)* combines partnership taxation with limited personal liability for all owners of the entity. All states and the District of Columbia have passed legislation permitting the establishment of LLCs. The following sections explain the taxation, advantages, and disadvantages of using LLCs.

14-5a Taxation of LLCs

A properly structured LLC can elect to be treated as a partnership for income tax purposes. Because LLC members are not personally liable for the debts of the entity, the LLC effectively is treated as a limited partnership with no general partners. This treatment may result in an unusual application of partnership taxation rules.

The IRS has not specifically ruled on most aspects of LLC taxation, but the following comments explain how an LLC member would be taxed, assuming that the LLC has elected to be treated as a partnership.

- Formation of a new LLC is treated in the same manner as formation of a partnership. Generally, no gain or loss is recognized by the LLC member or the LLC, the member takes a substituted basis in the LLC interest, and the LLC takes a carryover basis in the assets it receives.
- An LLC's income and losses are allocated proportionately. Special allocations are permitted, as long as they are supported by a nontax economic effect.
- An LLC member contributing property with built-in gains can be subject to tax on certain distributions within seven years of the contribution.
- A loss must meet the basis, at-risk, and passive activity loss requirements to be currently deductible. Because debt of an LLC is considered nonrecourse to each of the members, it is not included in the at-risk limitation unless it is "qualified nonrecourse financing."
- The initial accounting period and accounting method elections are available to an LLC.
- Property takes a carryover or substituted basis when distributed from an LLC.

14-5b Advantages of an LLC

An LLC offers certain advantages over a limited partnership.

- Generally, none of the members of an LLC is personally liable for the entity's debts. In contrast, general partners in a limited partnership have personal liability for partnership recourse debts.
- Limited partners cannot participate in the management of a partnership. All owners of an LLC have the legal right to participate in the entity's management.

An LLC also offers certain advantages over an S corporation (see Chapter 15), including the following.

- An LLC can have an unlimited number of owners, while an S corporation is limited to 100 shareholders.
- Any taxpayers, including corporations, nonresident aliens, other partnerships, and trusts, can be owners of an LLC. S corporation shares can be held only by specified parties.
- The transfer of property to an LLC in exchange for an ownership interest in the entity is governed by partnership tax provisions rather than corporate tax provisions. Thus, the transfers need not satisfy the 80 percent control requirement needed for tax-free treatment under the corporate tax statutes (see text Section 12-2d).

- The S corporation taxes on built-in gains and investment income do not apply to LLCs.

- An owner's basis in an LLC includes the owner's share of almost all LLC liabilities under the law. Only certain entity liabilities are included in the S corporation shareholder's basis.

- An LLC may make special allocations, whereas S corporations must allocate income, loss, etc., only on a per-share/per-day basis.

14-5c Disadvantages of an LLC

Only a limited body of case law interprets the various state statutes, so the application of specific provisions in a specific state may be uncertain. An additional uncertainty for LLCs that operate in more than one jurisdiction pertains to which state's law will prevail and how it will be applied.

Among other factors, statutes differ from state to state as to the type of business an LLC can conduct—primarily the extent to which a service-providing firm can operate as an LLC. Special rules also may apply where the LLC has only one member.

Despite these uncertainties and limitations, LLCs are being formed at increasing rates, and the ranks of multistate LLCs also are rising quickly.

Concept Summary 14.6

Advantages and Disadvantages of the Partnership Form

The partnership form may be attractive when one or more of the following factors is present.

- The entity is generating net taxable losses and/or valuable tax credits, which will be of use to the owners.

- The owners want to avoid complex corporate administrative and filing requirements.

- The owners want to make special allocations of certain income or deduction items that are not possible under the C or S corporation forms.

- Other means of reducing the effects of the double taxation of corporate business income (e.g., compensation to owners, interest, and rental payments) have been exhausted.

- The entity does not generate material amounts of tax preference and adjustment items, which increase the AMT liabilities of its owners.

- The entity is generating net passive activity income, which its owners can use to claim immediate deductions for net passive activity losses they have generated from other sources.

- The owners hold adequate bases in their ownership interests to facilitate the deduction of flow-through losses and the assignment of an adequate basis to assets distributed in kind to the owners.

The partnership form may be less attractive when one or more of the following factors is present.

- The tax paid by the owners on the entity's income is greater than that payable by the entity as a C corporation, and the income is not expected to be distributed soon. (If earnings are distributed by a C corporation, double taxation would likely occur.)

- The entity is generating net taxable income without distributing any cash to the owners. The owners may not have sufficient cash with which to pay the tax on the entity's earnings.

- The type of income the entity is generating (e.g., business and portfolio income) is not as attractive to its owners as net passive activity income would be, because the owners could offset net passive activity income by the net passive activity losses they have generated on their own.

- The entity is in a high-exposure business, and the owners want protection from personal liability. An LLC or LLP structure may be available, however, to limit personal liability.

- The owners want to reduce exposure to Federal self-employment and additional Medicare taxes.

14-6 **SUMMARY**

Partnerships and LLCs are popular among business owners; there are more than twice as many partnerships and limited liability entities as there are C corporations subject to Federal income tax law. This may be partly because formation of the entity is relatively simple and tax-free. The Code places very few restrictions on who can be a partner. Partnerships are especially attractive when operating losses are anticipated or when marginal rates that would apply to partnership income are less than those that would be paid by a C corporation. Partnerships do not offer the limited liability of a corporate entity, but the use of limited partnerships, LLCs, and LLPs can offer some protection to the owners.

Partnerships are tax-reporting, not taxpaying, entities. Distributive shares of ordinary income and separately stated items are taxed to the partners on the last day of the tax year. Special allocations and guaranteed payments are allowed and offer partners the ability to tailor the cash-flow and taxable amounts that are distributed by the entity to its owners. Deductions for flow-through losses may be limited by the related-party, passive activity, excess business loss, and at-risk rules, as well as by the partner's basis in the partnership. The flexibility of the partnership rules makes this form continually attractive to new businesses, especially in a global setting.

REFOCUS ON THE BIG PICTURE

THE TAX CONSEQUENCES OF PARTNERSHIP FORMATION AND OPERATIONS

RODERICK PAUL WALKER/ALAMY STOCK PHOTO

After considering the various types of partnerships, Kyle, Maria, and Josh decided to form Beachside Properties as an LLC. Upon formation of the entity, there was no gain or loss recognized by the LLC or any of its members (see Example 15). Beachside Properties computes its income as shown in Example 17 and allocates the income as illustrated in Example 19. The LLC's income affects the members' bases and capital accounts. An important consideration for the LLC members is whether their distributive shares and guaranteed payments will be treated as self-employment income.

What If?

What happens in the future when the LLC members decide to expand or renovate Beachside's facilities? At that time, the existing members can contribute additional funds, the entity can receive capital from new members, or the entity can borrow money. A partnership or limited liability entity is not subject to the 80 percent control requirement applicable to the formation of a corporation and subsequent transfers to it. Therefore, new investors can contribute cash or other property in exchange for interests in the entity—and the transaction will qualify for tax-deferred treatment.

Suggested Readings

Susan L. Megaard and Michael M. Megaard, "Reducing Self-Employment Taxes on Owners of LLPs and LLCs," *Business Entities*, March/April 2012.

Darla Mercado, "One Way to Play the New Tax Law: Start an LLC," ***cnbc.com***, January 25, 2018.

Eric J. Toder, "Tax Reform and Small Business," ***taxpolicycenter.org***, April 15, 2015.

Key Terms

Basis in the partnership interest, 14-7

Capital account, 14-21

Capital interest, 14-6

Capital sharing ratio, 14-6

Disguised sale, 14-10

Economic effect test, 14-19

General partnership, 14-3

Guaranteed payment, 14-29

Inside basis, 14-12

Limited liability company (LLC), 14-4

Limited liability partnership (LLP), 14-4

Limited partnership, 14-3

Nonrecourse debt, 14-22

Organizational costs, 14-14

Outside basis, 14-12

Precontribution gain or loss, 14-19

Profit and loss sharing ratios, 14-6

Profits (loss) interest, 14-6

Qualified nonrecourse financing, 14-27

Recourse debt, 14-22

Separately stated items, 14-5

Special allocation, 14-7

Syndication costs, 14-13

Computational Exercises

1. **LO.4** Enerico contributes $100,000 cash in exchange for a 40% interest in the calendar year ABC LLC. This year, ABC generates $80,000 of ordinary taxable income. Enerico withdraws $10,000 cash from the partnership at the end of the tax year.

   a. Compute Enerico's gross income from ABC's ordinary income for the tax year.

   b. Compute Enerico's gross income from the LLC's cash distribution.

2. **LO.2** Henrietta transfers cash of $75,000 and equipment with a fair market value of $25,000 (basis to her as a sole proprietor, $10,000) in exchange for a 40% profit and loss interest worth $100,000 in the XYZ Partnership.

   a. Compute Henrietta's realized and recognized gains from the asset transfers.

   b. Compute Henrietta's basis in her interest in XYZ.

   c. What is XYZ's basis in the equipment that it now holds?

3. **LO.2** Wozniacki and Wilcox form Jewel LLC, with each investor receiving a one-half interest in the capital and profits of the LLC. Wozniacki receives his one-half interest as compensation for tax planning services that he rendered prior to the formation of the LLC. Wilcox contributes $50,000 cash. The value of a one-half capital interest in the LLC (for each of the parties) is $50,000.

   a. Compute Wozniacki's realized and recognized gain from joining Jewel.

   b. Compute Wozniacki's basis in his interest in Jewel.

   c. How does Jewel treat the services that Wozniacki has rendered?

4. **LO.5** At the beginning of the tax year, Barnaby's basis in the BBB Partnership was $50,000, including his $5,000 share of partnership debt. At the end of the tax year, his share of the entity's debt was $8,000.

   Barnaby's share of BBB's ordinary income for the year was $20,000, and he received cash distributions totaling $12,000. In addition, his share of the partnership's tax-exempt income was $1,000. Determine Barnaby's basis at the end of the tax year.

5. **LO.3** Candlewood LLC began its business on September 1; it uses a calendar tax and accounting year. Candlewood incurred $6,500 in legal fees for drafting the LLC's operating agreement and $3,000 in accounting fees for tax advice of an organizational nature, for a total of $9,500 of organizational costs.

   Candlewood also incurred $30,000 of preopening advertising expenses and $24,500 of salaries and training costs for new employees before opening for business, for a total of $54,500 of startup costs. The LLC desires to take the largest deduction available for these costs. Compute Candlewood's deductions for the first year of its operations for:

   a. Organizational expenses.

   b. Startup expenses.

6. **LO.4** Franco owns a 60% interest in the Dulera LLC. On December 31 of the current tax year, his basis in the LLC interest is $128,000. The fair market value of the interest is $140,000. Dulera then distributes to Franco $30,000 cash and equipment with an adjusted basis of $5,000 and a fair market value of $8,000.

   a.   Compute Franco's basis in Dulera after the distribution.

   b.   Compute Franco's basis in the equipment that he received from Dulera.

Digging Deeper   7. **LO.4** When Bruno's basis in his interest in the MNO LLC is $150,000, he receives cash of $55,000, a proportionate share of inventory, and land in a distribution that liquidates MNO and his interest in the LLC. The inventory has a basis to the entity of $45,000 and a fair market value of $48,000. The land's basis is $70,000, and its fair market value is $60,000. Compute Bruno's recognized gain or loss from the liquidating distribution, and his tax basis in the inventory and land.

Problems

Critical Thinking   8. **LO.2** Janda and Kelsey contributed $1 million each to the JKL LLC in exchange for 45% capital and profits interests in the entity. Lilli will contribute no cash, but has agreed to manage the LLC's business operations in exchange for an $80,000 annual salary and a 10% interest in the LLC's capital and profits (valued at $200,000). What are the consequences of the entity formation and Lilli's compensation arrangement to the LLC members? To the LLC itself?

9. **LO.2** Emma and Laine form the equal EL Partnership. Emma contributes cash of $100,000. Laine contributes property with an adjusted basis of $40,000 and a fair market value of $100,000.

   a.   How much gain, if any, must Emma recognize on the transfer? Must Laine recognize any gain? If so, how much?

   b.   What is Emma's basis in her partnership interest?

   c.   What is Laine's basis in her partnership interest?

   d.   What basis does the partnership take in the property transferred by Laine?

Decision Making   10. **LO.2** Kenisha and Shawna form the equal KS LLC with a cash contribution of $360,000 from Kenisha and a property contribution (adjusted basis of $380,000, fair market value of $360,000) from Shawna.

   a.   How much gain or loss, if any, does Shawna realize on the transfer? Does Shawna recognize any gain or loss? If so, how much?

   b.   What is Kenisha's basis in her LLC interest?

   c.   What is Shawna's basis in her LLC interest?

   d.   What basis does the LLC take in the property transferred by Shawna?

   e.   Are there more effective ways to structure the formation? Explain.

11. **LO.2** Liz and John formed the equal LJ Partnership on January 1 of the current year. Liz contributed $80,000 of cash and land with a fair market value of $90,000 and an adjusted basis of $75,000. John contributed equipment with a fair market value of $170,000 and an adjusted basis of $20,000. John previously used the equipment in his sole proprietorship.

   a.   How much gain or loss will Liz, John, and LJ realize?

   b.   How much gain or loss will Liz, John, and LJ recognize?

   c.   What bases will Liz and John take in their partnership interests?

   d.   What bases will LJ take in the assets it receives?

   e.   How will LJ depreciate any assets it receives from the partners?

12. **LO.2, 5** Sam and Drew are equal members of the SD LLC, formed on June 1 of the current year. Sam contributed land that he inherited from his uncle Garza in 2009. Garza had purchased the land in 1984 for $30,000. The land was worth

$100,000 when Garza died. The fair market value of the land was $200,000 at the date it was contributed to SD.

Drew has significant experience developing real estate. After SD is formed, he will prepare a plan for developing the property and secure zoning approvals for the LLC. Drew usually would bill a third party $50,000 for these efforts. Drew also will contribute $150,000 of cash in exchange for his 50% interest in SD. The value of Drew's 50% interest is $200,000.

a. How much gain or income does Sam recognize on his contribution of the land to SD? What is the character of any gain or income recognized?

b. What basis does Sam take in his LLC interest?

c. How much gain or income will Drew recognize on the formation of SD? What is the character of any gain or income recognized?

d. What basis will Drew take in his LLC interest?

13. **LO.2** Continue with the facts presented in Problem 12. At the end of the first year, SD distributes $100,000 cash to Sam. No distribution is made to Drew.

a. How does Sam treat the payment?

b. How much income or gain would Sam recognize as a result of the distribution?

c. Under general tax rules, what basis would SD take in the land Sam contributed?

14. **LO.3** On July 1 of the current year, the R&R Partnership was formed as a limited partnership to operate a bed-and-breakfast inn. The partnership paid $3,000 in legal fees for drafting the partnership agreement and $5,000 for accounting fees related to organizing the entity. It also paid $10,000 in syndication costs to locate and secure investments from limited partners.

In addition, before opening the inn for business, the entity paid $15,500 for advertising and $36,000 in costs related to an open house just before the grand opening of the property. The partnership opened the inn for business on October 1.

a. How are these expenses classified?

b. How much may the partnership deduct in its initial year of operations?

c. How are costs treated that are not deducted currently?

15. **LO.2, 4** Phoebe and Parker are equal members of Phoenix Investors LLC. They are real estate investors who formed the entity several years ago with equal cash contributions. Phoenix then purchased a parcel of land.

On January 1 of the current year, to acquire a one-third interest in the entity, Reece contributed to Phoenix some land she had held for investment. Reece purchased the land five years ago for $75,000; its fair market value at the contribution date was $90,000. No special allocation agreements were in effect before or after Reece was admitted to the LLC. Phoenix holds all land for investment.

Immediately before Reece's property contribution, the Phoenix balance sheet was as follows.

	Basis	FMV		Basis	FMV
Land	$30,000	$180,000	Phoebe, capital	$15,000	$ 90,000
			Parker, capital	15,000	90,000
	$30,000	$180,000		$30,000	$180,000

a. At the contribution date, what is Reece's basis in her interest in Phoenix?

b. When does the LLC's holding period begin for the contributed land?

c. On June 30 of the current year, the LLC sold the land contributed by Reece for $90,000. How much is the recognized gain or loss? How is it allocated among the LLC members?

d. Prepare a balance sheet reflecting basis and fair market value for the entity immediately after the land sale. No other transactions occurred during the year.

16. **LO.4, 5** Amy and Mitchell share equally in the profits, losses, and capital of the accrual basis AM Products LLC. Amy is the managing member of the LLC (treated as a general partner) and is a U.S. citizen. At the beginning of the current tax year, Amy's capital account has a balance of $300,000, and the LLC has recourse debts of $200,000 payable to unrelated parties. All partnership recourse debt is shared equally between the partners.

The following information about AM's operations for the current year is obtained from the entity's records.

Ordinary income	$ 900,000
W–2 wages to employees	200,000
Depreciation expense	300,000
Interest income from P & G bond	4,000
Long-term capital loss	6,000
Short-term capital gain	12,000
Charitable contribution	4,000
Cash distribution to Amy	20,000
Unadjusted basis of partnership depreciable property	1,600,000

Year-end LLC debt payable to unrelated parties is $140,000. If all transactions are reflected in her beginning capital and basis in the same manner:

  a. What is Amy's basis in her LLC interest at the beginning of the year?

  b. What is Amy's basis in her LLC interest at the end of the current year?

17. **LO.4, 5** Assume the same facts as in Problem 16. What income, gains, losses, and deductions does Amy report on her income tax return? Based on the information provided, what other calculations is she required to make?

18. **LO.4, 5** Continue with the same facts of Problem 16. Consider Amy's tax-basis capital account.

  a. What is Amy's capital account at the beginning of the year?

  b. What is Amy's capital account at the end of the year?

  c. How do the capital account balances differ from her basis amounts in Problem 16?

Digging Deeper 19. **LO.3** Cerulean, Inc., Coral, Inc., and Crimson, Inc., form the Three Cs Partnership on January 1 of the current year. Cerulean is a 50% partner, and Crimson and Coral are 25% partners. For reporting purposes, Crimson uses a fiscal year with an October 31 year-end, Coral uses the calendar year, and Cerulean uses a fiscal year with a February 28/29 year-end. What is the required tax year for Three Cs under the least aggregate deferral method?

20. **LO.2, 4, 5** The JM Partnership was formed to acquire land and subdivide it as residential housing lots. On March 1, 2018, Jessica contributed land valued at $600,000 to the partnership in exchange for a 50% interest. She had purchased the land in 2010 for $420,000 and held it for investment purposes (capital asset). The partnership holds the land as inventory.

On the same date, Matt contributed land valued at $600,000 that he had purchased in 2008 for $720,000. He became a 50% owner. Matt is a real estate developer, but he held this land personally for investment purposes. The partnership holds this land as inventory.

In 2019, the partnership sells the land contributed by Jessica for $620,000. In 2020, the partnership sells the real estate contributed by Matt for $580,000.

  a. What is each partner's initial basis in his or her partnership interest?

  b. What is the amount of gain or loss recognized on the sale of the land contributed by Jessica? What is the character of this gain or loss?

  c. What is the amount of gain or loss recognized on the sale of the land contributed by Matt? What is the character of this gain or loss?

  d. How would your answer in part (c) change if the property were sold in 2025?

21. **LO.2, 5** Lee, Brad, and Rick form the LBR Partnership on January 1 of the current year. In return for a 25% interest, Lee transfers property (basis of $15,000, fair market value of $17,500) subject to a nonrecourse liability of $10,000. The liability is assumed by the partnership. Brad transfers property (basis of $16,000, fair market value of $7,500) for a 25% interest, and Rick transfers cash of $15,000 for the remaining 50% interest.

    a. How much gain must Lee recognize on the transfer?

    b. What is Lee's basis in his interest in the partnership?

    c. How much loss may Brad recognize on the transfer?

    d. What is Brad's basis in his interest in the partnership?

    e. What is Rick's basis in his interest in the partnership?

    f. What basis does the LBR Partnership take in the property transferred by Lee?

    g. What is the partnership's basis in the property transferred by Brad?

22. **LO.2, 5** Assume the same facts as in Problem 21, except that the property contrib-   *Digging Deeper*
    uted by Lee has a fair market value of $27,500 and is subject to a nonre-
    course mortgage of $20,000.

    a. What is Lee's basis in his partnership interest?

    b. How much gain must Lee recognize on the transfer?

    c. What is Brad's basis in his partnership interest?

    d. What is Rick's basis in his partnership interest?

    e. What basis does the LBR Partnership take in the property transferred by Lee?

23. **LO.5, 6** The BCD Partnership plans to distribute cash of $20,000 to partner Barb at   *Critical Thinking*
    the end of the tax year. The partnership reported a loss for the year, and   *Decision Making*
    Barb's share of the loss is $10,000. Barb holds a basis of $15,000 in the partnership
    interest, including her share of partnership liabilities. The partnership expects to
    report substantial income in future years.

    a. How does Barb calculate the ending basis in the BCD Partnership interest?

    b. How much gain or loss must Barb report for the tax year due to the distribution?

    c. Will the deduction for any of the $10,000 loss be suspended? Why or why not?

    d. Could any planning opportunities be used to minimize the tax ramifications of
        the distribution? Explain.

24. **LO.2, 3** The Pelican Partnership was formed on August 1 of the current year and
    admitted Morlan and Merriman as equal partners on that date. The partners
    both contributed $300,000 of cash to establish a children's clothing store in the local
    mall. The partners spent August and September buying inventory, equipment, sup-
    plies, and advertising for their "Grand Opening" on October 1. The partnership will
    use the accrual method of accounting. The following are some of the costs incurred
    during Pelican's first year of operations. Pelican uses a calendar tax year.

Legal fees to form partnership	$ 8,000
Advertising for "Grand Opening"	18,000
Advertising after opening	30,000
Consulting fees for establishing accounting system	20,000
Rent, at $2,000 per month	10,000
Utilities, at $1,000 per month	5,000
Salaries to salesclerks (beginning in October)	50,000
Payments to Morlan and Merriman for services ($6,000 per month each for three months)	36,000
Tax return preparation expense	12,000

In addition, on October 1, Pelican purchased all of the assets of Granny Newcombs, Inc. Of the total purchase price for these assets, $200,000 was allocated to the Granny Newcombs trade name and logo.

Determine how each of the listed costs is treated by Pelican, and identify the period over which the costs can be deducted, if any.

25. **LO.2** Bill and Mary filed a joint Federal income tax return this year. Mary owns a 30% interest in MAJIC Partnership, a women's dress boutique. Mary's share of the partnership's net income is $280,000. Her shares of the partnership's W–2 wages and unadjusted basis of depreciable property are $100,000 and $300,000, respectively.

    a.   What is Bill and Mary's maximum QBI deduction if their total taxable income is $300,000?

    b.   What is the maximum QBI deduction if Bill and Mary's total taxable income is $450,000?

    c.   What is the maximum QBI deduction if MAJIC's income was from qualified services and Bill and Mary's total taxable income was $450,000?

26. **LO.7** Four GRRLs Partnership is owned by four unrelated friends. Lacy holds a 40% interest; each of the others owns 20%. Lacy sells investment property to the partnership for its fair market value of $200,000. Her tax basis in the property was $250,000.

    a.   How much loss, if any, may Lacy recognize?

    b.   If Four GRRLs later sells the property for $260,000, how much gain must it recognize?

    c.   How would your answers in parts (a) and (b) change if Lacy owned a 60% interest in the partnership?

    d.   If Lacy's basis in the investment property was $120,000 (instead of $250,000) and she was a 60% partner, how much, if any, gain would she recognize on the sale of the property to Four GRRLs? How is it characterized?

27. **LO.7** Burgundy, Inc., and Violet Gomez are equal partners in the calendar year BV LLC. Burgundy uses a fiscal year ending April 30, and Violet uses a calendar year. Burgundy receives an annual guaranteed payment of $100,000 for use of capital contributed by Burgundy. BV's taxable income (after deducting the payment to Burgundy) is $80,000 for 2018 and $90,000 for 2019.

    a.   How much income from BV must Burgundy report for its tax year ending April 30, 2019?

    b.   How much income from BV must Violet report for her tax year ending December 31, 2019?

Digging Deeper   28. **LO.4, 7** Mona and Denise, mother and daughter, operate a local restaurant as an LLC. The MD LLC earned a profit of $200,000 in the current year. Denise's equal LLC interest was acquired by gift from Mona. Assume that capital is a material income-producing factor and that Mona manages the day-to-day operations of the restaurant without any help from Denise. Reasonable compensation for Mona's services is $50,000.

    a.   How much of the MD income is allocated to Mona?

    b.   What is the maximum amount of LLC income that can be allocated to Denise?

    c.   Assuming that Denise is 15 years old, has no other income, and is claimed as a dependent by Mona, how is Denise's income from the restaurant taxed?

Digging Deeper   29. **LO.5** In each of the following independent cases in which the partnership owns no hot assets, indicate the following. All of the partners received proportionate distributions.

    • Whether the partner recognizes gain or loss.

    • Whether the partnership recognizes gain or loss.

    • The partner's adjusted basis for the property distributed.

    • The partner's outside basis in the partnership after the distribution.

a. Kim receives $20,000 of cash in partial liquidation of her interest in the partnership. Kim's outside basis for her partnership interest immediately before the distribution is $3,000.

b. Kourtni receives $40,000 of cash and land with a $30,000 inside basis to the partnership (value $50,000) in partial liquidation of her interest. Kourtni's outside basis for her partnership interest immediately before the distribution is $80,000.

c. Assume the same facts as in part (b), except that Kourtni's outside basis for her partnership interest immediately before the distribution is $60,000.

d. Klois receives $50,000 of cash and inventory with a basis of $30,000 and a fair market value of $50,000 in partial liquidation of her partnership interest. Her basis was $90,000 before the distribution.

30. **LO.4, 5, 7** At the beginning of the tax year, Melodie's basis in the MIP LLC was $60,000, including Melodie's $40,000 share of the LLC's liabilities. At the end of the year, MIP distributed to Melodie cash of $10,000 and inventory (basis of $6,000, fair market value of $10,000). MIP repaid all of its liabilities by the end of the year.

    Digging Deeper

a. If this is a proportionate current distribution, what is the tax effect of the distribution to Melodie and MIP? After the distribution, what is Melodie's basis in the inventory and in her MIP interest?

b. Would your answers to part (a) change if this had been a proportionate liquidating distribution? Explain.

31. **LO.2, 4, 5** Suzy contributed assets valued at $360,000 (basis of $200,000) in exchange for her 40% interest in Suz-Anna GP (a general partnership in which both partners are active owners). Anna contributed land and a building valued at $640,000 (basis of $380,000) in exchange for the remaining 60% interest. Anna's property was encumbered by qualified nonrecourse financing of $100,000, which was assumed by the partnership.

    Digging Deeper

The partnership reports the following income and expenses for the current tax year.

Sales	$560,000
Utilities, salaries, depreciation, other operating expenses	360,000
Short-term capital gain	10,000
Tax-exempt interest income	4,000
Charitable contributions (cash)	8,000
Distribution to Suzy	10,000
Distribution to Anna	20,000

At the end of the year, Suz-Anna held recourse debt of $100,000 for partnership accounts payable and qualified nonrecourse financing of $200,000.

a. What is Suzy's basis in Suz-Anna after formation of the partnership? Anna's basis?

b. What income and separately stated items does Suz-Anna report on Suzy's Schedule K–1? What income deductions and taxes does Suzy report on her tax return?

c. All partnership debts are shared proportionately. At the end of the tax year, what are Suzy's basis and amount at risk in her partnership interest?

32. **LO.2, 4, 5, 8** Continue with the facts presented in Problem 31, except that Suz-Anna was formed as an LLC instead of a general partnership.

    Digging Deeper
    Critical Thinking

a. How would Suz-Anna's ending liabilities be treated?

b. How would Suzy's basis and amount at risk be different? Explain.

Ethics and Equity

Communications

33. **LO.4** The Sparrow Partnership plans to distribute $200,000 cash to its partners at the end of the year. Marjorie is a 40% partner and would receive $80,000. Her basis in the partnership is only $10,000, however, so she would recognize a $70,000 gain if she receives the proposed cash distribution.

Marjorie has asked Sparrow instead to purchase a parcel of land that she has found, on which she will build her retirement residence. The partnership then will distribute that land to her. Under the partnership distribution rules, Marjorie would take a $10,000 basis in the land worth $80,000. Her basis in the partnership would be reduced to $0, but recognition of the $70,000 gain is deferred.

Do you think this is an appropriate transaction? Explain your conclusion in an e-mail to your instructor.

Comprehensive Tax Return Problem

1. Ryan Ross (111-11-1112), Oscar Omega (222-22-2222), Clark Carey (333-33-3333), and Kim Kardigan (444-44-4444) are equal active members in ROCK the Ages LLC. ROCK serves as agent and manager for prominent musicians in the Los Angeles area. The LLC's Federal ID number is 55-5555555. It uses the cash basis and a calendar tax year, and it began operations on January 1, 2004. Its current address is 6102 Wilshire Boulevard, Suite 2100, Los Angeles, CA 90036.

   ROCK was the force behind such music icons as Rhiannon, Burgundy Six, Elena Gomez, Tyler Quick, Queen Bey, and Bruno Mercury, and it has had a very profitable year. The following information was taken from the LLC's income statement for the current year.

Revenues	
Fees and commissions	$4,800,000
Taxable interest income from bank deposits	1,600
Tax-exempt interest	3,200
Net gains on stock sales	4,000
Total revenues	$4,808,800

Expenses	
Advertising and public relations	$ 380,000
Charitable contributions	28,000
Section 179 expense	20,000
Employee W–2 wages	1,000,000
Guaranteed payment (services), Ryan Ross, office manager	800,000
Guaranteed payment (services), other members	600,000
Entertainment, subject to 50% disallowance	200,000
Travel	320,000
Legal and accounting fees	132,000
Office rentals paid	80,000
Interest expense on line of credit for operations	10,000
Insurance premiums	52,000
Office expense	200,000
Payroll taxes	92,000
Utilities	54,800
Total expenses	$3,968,800

During the past few years, ROCK has taken advantage of bonus depreciation and § 179 deductions and fully remodeled the premises and upgraded its leasehold improvements. This year, ROCK wrapped up its remodeling with the purchase of $20,000 of office furniture, for which it will claim a § 179 deduction. ROCK uses the same cost recovery methods for both tax and financial purposes. There is no depreciation adjustment for alternative minimum tax purposes.

ROCK invests much of its excess cash in non-dividend-paying growth stocks and tax-exempt securities. During the year, the LLC sold two securities. On June 15, ROCK purchased 1,000 shares of Tech, Inc. stock for $100,000; it sold those shares on December 15, for $80,000. On March 15 of last year, ROCK purchased 2,000 shares of BioLabs, Inc. stock for $136,000; it sold those shares for $160,000 on December 15 of the current year. These transactions were reported to the IRS on Forms 1099–B; ROCK's basis in these shares was reported on the form.

Net income per books for the current year is $840,000. On January 1, the members' capital accounts equaled $200,000 each. No additional capital contributions were made during the year. In addition to their guaranteed payments, each member withdrew $250,000 cash during the year.

ROCK's book balance sheet as of December 31 of this year is as follows.

	Beginning	Ending
Cash	$ 444,000	$??
Tax-exempt securities	120,000	120,000
Marketable securities	436,000	300,000
Leasehold improvements, furniture, and equipment	960,000	980,000
Accumulated depreciation	(960,000)	(980,000)
Total assets	$1,000,000	$??
Line of credit for operations	$ 200,000	$160,000
Capital, Ross	200,000	??
Capital, Omega	200,000	??
Capital, Carey	200,000	??
Capital, Kardigan	200,000	??
Total liabilities and capital	$1,000,000	$??

All debt is shared equally by the members. Each member has personally guaranteed the debt of the LLC. All of the owners are active in ROCK's operations.

The appropriate business code for the entity is 711410. For the Form 1065 page 5 Analysis of Net Income, put all amounts in cell 2(b)(ii). The LLC's Form 1065 was prepared by Ryan Ross and sent to the Ogden, UT, IRS Service Center.

a. Prepare pages 1, 4, and 5 of a Form 1065 for ROCK the Ages LLC. Use tax-basis data in completing Schedules L and M–2. Include any information the LLC members might need including information for § 199A calculation. Use 2018 tax rules. If available use 2018 tax forms.

b. If you are using tax return preparation software, prepare Form 4562 and Schedule D.

c. Prepare Schedule K–1 for Ryan Ross, 15520 W. Earlson Street, Pacific Palisades, CA 90272.

BRIDGE DISCIPLINE

1. What is the function of a partner's capital account under the rules of generally accepted accounting principles (GAAP)? What is the partner's initial balance in the capital account? How and when does the capital account increase and decrease? What is the GAAP treatment of distributions to a partner?

2. Jim Dunn, Amy Lauersen, and Tony Packard have agreed to form a partnership. In return for a 30% capital interest, Dunn transferred machinery (basis $268,000, fair market value $400,000) subject to a liability of $100,000. The liability was assumed by the partnership. Lauersen transferred land (basis $450,000, fair market value $300,000) for a 30% capital interest. Packard transferred cash of $400,000 for the remaining 40% interest. Compute the initial values of Dunn's:
   a. Basis in his partnership interest for tax purposes.
   b. Capital account for financial reporting purposes.

3. To what extent are the personal assets of a general partner, limited partner, or member of an LLC subject to (a) contractual liability claims, such as trade accounts payable, and (b) malpractice claims against the entity? Answer the question for partners or members in a general partnership, an LLP, a nonprofessional LLC, and a limited partnership.

Research Problems

THOMSON REUTERS
CHECKPOINT™

Note: Solutions to the Research Problems can be prepared by using the Thomson Reuters Checkpoint™ online tax research database, which accompanies this textbook. Solutions can also be prepared by using research materials found in a typical tax library.

Research Problem 1. Fredstone Consolidated, Inc., and Gradison Enterprises, Inc., are both real estate developers. Each entity owns a 50% general partner interest in Realty Partners, GP, a general partnership.

Fredstone and Gradison each contributed $15,000 to form the partnership. The partnership uses the $30,000 contributed by the partners and a recourse loan of $100,000 obtained from an unrelated third-party lender to acquire $130,000 of rental properties. (All amounts are in thousands.)

The partners believe that they will generate extensive tax losses in the first year due to depreciation expense and initial cash-flow requirements. Fredstone and Gradison agreed to share losses equally. To make sure that the losses can be allocated as intended, they included a provision in the partnership agreement requiring each partner to restore any deficit balance in their partnership capital account upon liquidation of the partnership.

Fredstone also was willing to include a provision that requires it to make up any deficit balance within 90 days of liquidation of the partnership. This provision does not apply to Gradison; instead, it must restore any deficit balance in its capital account within three years following liquidation of the partnership. No interest accrues on the deferred restoration payment.

Can Realty allocate the $100,000 recourse debt equally to the two partners, so that they can deduct their respective shares of partnership losses? Explain.

Research Problem 2. Barney Chang and Aldrin, Inc., a domestic C corporation, have decided to form BA LLC. The new entity will produce a product that Barney recently developed and patented. Barney and Aldrin each will own a 50% capital and profits interest in the LLC. Barney is a calendar year taxpayer, while Aldrin is taxed using a June 30 fiscal year-end. BA does not have a "natural business year" and elects to be taxed as a partnership.

Digging Deeper

a. Determine the taxable year of the LLC under the Code and Regulations.

b. Two years after formation of BA, Barney sells half of his interest (25%) to Aldrin. Can BA retain the taxable year determined in part (a)? Why or why not?

Use internet tax resources to address the following questions. Look for reliable websites and blogs of the IRS and other government agencies, media outlets, businesses, tax professionals, academics, think tanks, and political outlets.

Research Problem 3. Find an article posted by a law firm that comments on pitfalls to avoid in drafting partnership agreements. Ideally, use the home page of a firm that has offices in your state. Summarize the posting in no more than four PowerPoint slides, and send your file to your instructor.

Communications

Research Problem 4. Find a blog that concentrates on the taxation of partners and partnerships. Post a message defining the terms *inside basis* and *outside basis* and illustrating why the distinction between them is important. Respond to any replies you receive. Print your message and one or two of the replies.

Communications

Research Problem 5. Determine the statutory tax treatment in your state of a one-member LLC. Write an e-mail to your professor comparing this rule with Federal tax law.

Communications

Research Problem 6. Construct a graph that shows the increases in the numbers of LLCs and LLPs filing Federal tax returns for five-year periods beginning with 1970. Explain any trends in the data that you identify. Send your report as an e-mail to your instructor.

Communications

Becker CPA Review Questions

1. Gray is a 50% partner in Fabco Partnership. Gray's tax basis in Fabco on January 1, year 4, was $5,000. Fabco made no distributions to the partners during year 4 and recorded the following.

Ordinary income	$20,000
Tax-exempt income	8,000
Portfolio income	4,000

What is Gray's tax basis in Fabco on December 31, year 4?

a. $21,000   c. $12,000

b. $16,000   d. $10,000

2. Nick, Chris, Stacey, and Mike are each 25% partners in Liberty Partnership, a general partnership. During the current year, the partnership had revenues of $300,000 and nonseparately allocated business expenses of $100,000, including a guaranteed payment of $30,000 to Nick for services rendered. Liberty also recorded interest income

of $10,000 and charitable contributions of $16,000. With regard to activity in the partnership, what should Stacey report on her income tax return for the current year?

	Ordinary Income	Interest Income	Charitable Contributions
a.	$200,000	$10,000	$16,000
b.	80,000	2,500	4,000
c.	57,500	2,500	4,000
d.	50,000	2,500	4,000

3. Duffy Associates is a partnership engaged in real estate development. Olinto, a civil engineer, billed Duffy $40,000 in the current year for consulting services rendered. In full settlement of this invoice, Olinto accepted a $15,000 cash payment plus the following.

	Fair Market Value	Carrying Amount on Duffy's Books
10% partnership interest in Duffy	$10,000	N/A
Automobile	7,000	$3,000

What amount should Olinto, a cash basis taxpayer, report in his current-year return as income for the services rendered to Duffy?

a. $15,000

b. $28,000

c. $32,000

d. $40,000

4. At the inception of a partnership, Black acquires a 50% interest in Decorators Partnership by contributing property with an adjusted basis of $250,000. Black recognizes a gain if:

I. The fair market value of the contributed property exceeds its adjusted basis.

II. The property is encumbered by a mortgage with a balance of $100,000.

a. I only

b. II only

c. Both I and II

d. Neither I nor II

5. When a partner's share of partnership liabilities increases, that partner's basis in the partnership interest:

a. Increases by the partner's share of the liabilities.

b. Decreases by the partner's share of the liabilities.

c. Decreases, but not to less than zero.

d. Is not affected.

6. A reduction of a partner's share of partnership liabilities will have what effect on the partner's basis in the partnership interest?

a. There is no effect on partnership basis.

b. The same result (basis reduction and/or gain recognition) as if the partner received a distribution of that same amount of cash.

c. A reduction of the partner's basis by the amount of the partner's share of liability reduction, without regard to the amount of the partner's basis before the liability share reduction.

d. An increase in the partner's basis by the amount of the partner's share of liability reduction, without regard to the amount of the partner's basis before the liability share reduction.

7. Peter, a 25% partner in Gold & Stein Partnership, received a $20,000 guaranteed payment in the current year for deductible services rendered to the partnership. Guaranteed payments were not made to any other partner. Gold & Stein's current-year partnership income consisted of:

Net business income before guaranteed payments	$80,000
Net long-term capital gains	10,000

What amount of income should Peter report from Gold & Stein Partnership on his current-year tax return?

a. $37,500

b. $27,500

c. $22,500

d. $20,000

8. Hart's adjusted basis of his interest in a partnership was $30,000. He received a nonliquidating distribution of $24,000 cash plus a parcel of land with a fair market value and partnership basis of $9,000. Hart's basis for the land is:

a. $9,000

b. $6,000

c. $3,000

d. $0

LEARNING OBJECTIVES: *After completing Chapter 15, you should be able to:*

LO.1 Explain the tax effects associated with S corporation status.

LO.2 Identify corporations that qualify for the S election.

LO.3 Explain how to make and terminate an S election.

LO.4 Compute nonseparately stated income and allocate income, deductions, and credits to shareholders.

LO.5 Determine how distributions to S corporation shareholders are taxed.

LO.6 Calculate a shareholder's basis in S corporation stock.

LO.7 Explain the tax effects of losses on S shareholders.

LO.8 Compute the entity-level taxes on S corporations.

CHAPTER OUTLINE

15-1 An Overview of S Corporations, 15-2

15-2 Qualifying for S Corporation Status, 15-3
15-2a Definition of a Small Business Corporation, 15-3
15-2b Making the Election, 15-6
15-2c Shareholder Consent, 15-7
15-2d Loss of the Election, 15-7

15-3 Operational Rules, 15-10
15-3a Computation of Taxable Income, 15-10
15-3b Qualified Business Income Deduction, 15-12
15-3c Allocation of Income and Loss, 15-13
15-3d Tax Treatment of Distributions to Shareholders, 15-14

15-3e Tax Treatment of Noncash Distributions by the Corporation, 15-19
15-3f Shareholder's Basis in S Stock, 15-21
15-3g Treatment of Losses, 15-23
15-3h Limitation on the Deduction of Excess Business Losses, 15-25
15-3i Other Operational Rules, 15-26

15-4 Entity-Level Taxes, 15-27
15-4a Tax on Pre-Election Built-In Gain, 15-27
15-4b Passive Investment Income Penalty Tax, 15-29

15-5 Summary, 15-30

TAX TALK *In levying taxes and in shearing sheep it is well to stop when you get down to the skin.* —AUSTIN O'MALLEY

CONVERTING A C CORPORATION TO AN S CORPORATION

Fowle, Inc., has been operating as a C corporation for a number of years, consistently earning taxable income of less than $100,000 per year. The company has accumulated its earnings for a variety of business needs and has not paid dividends to date. Thus, the corporation has been able to take advantage of lower C corporation tax rates and has avoided double taxation problems so far.

Fowle receives some tax-exempt income, generates a small amount of passive income, and holds about $200,000 of C corporation earnings and profits. The company's sole owner, David, currently draws a salary of $92,000. Fowle has issued two classes of stock, voting common and nonvoting preferred.

The company now is facing increased competition as a result of cheaper imports from China. David expects very large operating losses for the next few years. David would like to know if there is a way that he can deduct the anticipated losses.

Read the chapter and formulate your response.

LO.1

Explain the tax effects associated with S corporation status.

An individual establishing a business has a number of choices as to the form of business entity under which to operate. Chapters 12 and 13 outline many of the rules, advantages, and disadvantages of operating as a regular C corporation. Chapter 14 discusses the partnership entity, as well as the limited liability company (LLC) and limited liability partnership (LLP) forms.

Another alternative, the **S corporation**, provides many of the benefits of partnership taxation and at the same time gives the owners limited liability protection from creditors. The S corporation rules, which are contained in **Subchapter S** of the Internal Revenue Code (§§ 1361–1379), were enacted to allow flexibility in the entity choice that businesspeople face. Thus, S status combines the legal environment of C corporations with taxation similar to that applying to partnerships. S corporation status is obtained through an election by a *qualifying* corporation with the consent of its shareholders.

15-1 AN OVERVIEW OF S CORPORATIONS

S corporations (like C corporations) are organized under state law. Other than for income tax purposes, they are recognized as separate legal entities and generally provide shareholders with the same liability protection available to C corporations. As a rule, where the S corporation provisions are silent, C corporation rules apply.

The S corporation rules should be seen as supplementary to the Federal income tax rules for all C corporations (see Chapters 12 and 13) and to those for partnerships and limited liability entities (contained in Code Subchapter K; see Chapter 14). Some provisions apply only to electing S corporations (addressed throughout this chapter), but S corporations also must apply certain tax rules of Code Subchapters C and K.

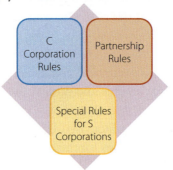

Today, the choice of a flow-through entity for a closely held business often is between an S corporation (a Federal tax entity) and an LLC (a state tax entity). Both are flow-through entities for Federal income tax purposes and provide limited liability for the owners under nontax state law. In the typical year, over 4 million S corporations file Federal income tax returns, and filings are received from over 2 million LLCs.

As the following examples illustrate, S corporations can be advantageous even when the individual tax rate exceeds the corporate tax rate.

S Corporation Advantages

An S corporation earns $300,000, and all after-tax income is distributed currently. The marginal individual tax rate applicable to the entity's shareholders is 37% for ordinary income and 20% for dividend income (ignoring the 3.8% investment income tax). Assume that the corporate tax rate is 21%, and the S corporation shareholders receive the full 20% qualified business income deduction (see text Section 15-3b). The entity's available after-tax earnings, compared with those of a similar C corporation, are computed below.

continued

	C Corporation	S Corporation
Earnings	$300,000	$300,000
Less: Corporate income tax	(63,000)	(–0–)
Amount available for distribution	$237,000	$300,000
Less: Income tax at owner level	(47,400)*	(88,800)**
Available after-tax earnings	$189,600	$211,200

*$237,000 × 20% dividend income tax rate.
**($300,000 − $60,000 qualified business income deduction) × 37%.

The S corporation generates an extra $21,600 of after-tax earnings ($211,200 − $189,600) when compared with a similar C corporation. The C corporation might be able to reduce this disadvantage by paying out its earnings as deductible compensation, rents, or interest to its owners. In addition, tax at the owner level is deferred or avoided by not distributing after-tax earnings.

EXAMPLE 2

A new corporation elects S status and incurs a net operating loss (NOL) of $300,000. The shareholders may use their proportionate shares of the NOL to offset other taxable income in the current year, providing an immediate tax savings. In contrast, a newly formed C corporation is required to carry the NOL forward and receives no tax benefit in the current year. Hence, an S corporation can accelerate the use of NOL deductions and thereby provide a greater present value for the tax savings generated by the loss.

15-2 QUALIFYING FOR S CORPORATION STATUS

LO.2
Identify corporations that qualify for the S election.

There are certain conditions that a corporation must meet before S corporation status is available.

15-2a Definition of a Small Business Corporation

To achieve S corporation status, a corporation *first* must qualify as a <mark>small business corporation</mark>. A small business corporation:

- Is a *domestic* corporation (incorporated and organized in the United States).
- Is eligible to elect S corporation status.
- Issues only one class of stock.

BRIDGE DISCIPLINE **Bridge to Business Law**

An S corporation is a corporation for all purposes other than its Federal and state income tax law treatment. The entity registers as a corporation with the secretary of state of the state of its incorporation. It issues shares and may hold some treasury stock. Dealings in its own stock are not taxable to the S corporation.

The corporation itself is attractive as a form of business ownership because it offers limited liability to all shareholders from the claims of customers, employees, and others. This is not the case for any type of partnership, where there always is at least one general partner bearing the ultimate personal liability for the operations of the entity. Forming an entity as an S corporation facilitates the raising of capital for the business, as an infinite number of shares can be divided in any way imaginable, so as to pass income and deductions, gains, losses, and credits through to the owners, assuming that the

fairly generous "type of shareholder" requirements continue to be met.

An S corporation must comply with all licensing and registration requirements of its home state under the rules applicable to corporate entities. Some states levy privilege taxes on the right to do business in the corporate form, and the S corporation typically is not exempted from this tax.

Because an S corporation is a separate legal entity from its owners, shareholders can be treated as employees and receive qualified retirement and fringe benefits under the Code, as well as unemployment and worker's compensation protection through the corporation. Some limitations apply to the deductibility of the shareholders' fringe benefits, though.

The tax fiction of the S corporation is attractive to investors, as demonstrated by the fact that about two-thirds of all U.S. corporations have an S election in effect.

- Is limited to a maximum of 100 shareholders.
- Has only individuals, estates, and certain trusts and exempt organizations as shareholders.
- Has no nonresident alien shareholders.

In addition to non-U.S. corporations, S status is also not permitted for certain banks or insurance companies. S corporations are permitted to have wholly owned C and S corporation subsidiaries.[1] No maximum or minimum dollar sales or capitalization restrictions apply to S corporations.

TAX PLANNING STRATEGIES   When to Elect S Corporation Status

FRAMEWORK FOCUS: DEDUCTIONS

Strategy: Maximize Deductible Amounts.

FRAMEWORK FOCUS: TAX RATE

Strategy: Shift Net Income from High-Bracket Taxpayers to Low-Bracket Taxpayers.
Shift Net Income from High-Tax Jurisdictions to Low-Tax Jurisdictions.

A number of considerations will affect a decision to make an S election.

- If shareholders have high marginal income tax rates relative to C corporation rates, avoid an S election.
- If current and future corporate losses are anticipated, S corporation status is advisable.
- If a C corporation holds an NOL carryover from prior years, the losses cannot be used in an S corporation year.

- There may be tax advantages to the S shareholder who receives a flow-through of passive activity income.
- Some states treat S corporations as C corporations and apply a corporate income tax to them.
- Tax-exempt income at the S level does not lose its special tax treatment for shareholders.
- An S corporation avoids the corporate personal holding company tax and accumulated earnings tax.

One Class of Stock

A small business corporation may have only one class of stock issued and outstanding.[2] This restriction permits differences in voting rights, but not differences in distribution or liquidation rights.[3] Thus, two classes of common stock that are identical, except that one class is voting and the other is nonvoting, are treated as a single class of stock for S corporation purposes.

In contrast, voting common stock and voting preferred stock (with a preference on dividends) are treated as two classes of stock. Authorized and unissued stock or treasury stock of another class does not disqualify the corporation. Likewise, unexercised stock options, phantom stock, stock appreciation rights, warrants, and convertible debentures usually do not constitute a second class of stock.[4]

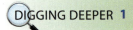 DIGGING DEEPER 1   **In-depth coverage can be found on this book's companion website: www.cengage.com**

Although the one-class-of-stock requirement seems straightforward, it is possible for debt to be reclassified as stock, resulting in an unexpected loss of S corporation status.[5] To mitigate concern over possible reclassification of debt as a second class of stock, the law provides a set of *safe harbor* provisions. Neither straight debt[6] nor short-term advances[7] constitute a second class of stock.

---

[1]Other eligibility rules exist. § 1361(b).
[2]§ 1361(b)(1)(D).
[3]§ 1361(c)(4).
[4]Reg. § 1.1361–1(l)(1).

[5]Refer to the discussion of debt-versus-equity classification in Chapter 12.
[6]§ 1361(c)(5)(A).
[7]Reg. § 1.1361–1(l)(1).

TAX FACT The Business of S Corporations

S corporations file more than 4 million tax returns every year, concentrated in the services and financial industries.

S Corporation Returns Filed (%), 2013 Tax Year

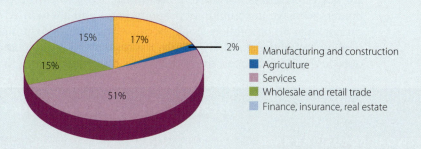

- 17% Manufacturing and construction
- 2% Agriculture
- 51% Services
- 15% Wholesale and retail trade
- 15% Finance, insurance, real estate

The Big Picture

Return to the facts of *The Big Picture* on p. 15-1. Fowle, Inc., could elect to be an S corporation, except that one class of stock is voting common and the other class is nonvoting preferred. If S status is desired, a recapitalization of the Fowle stock is required, perhaps issuing nonvoting common in place of the preferred stock, which would satisfy the one-class-of-stock requirement.

EXAMPLE 3

In-depth coverage can be found on this book's companion website: **www.cengage.com**

2 DIGGING DEEPER

Shareholder Limitations

An S corporation is limited to 100 shareholders. However, several exceptions allow the number of shareholders to exceed 100. For instance, if shares of stock are owned jointly by two individuals, they generally are treated as separate shareholders. However, a group of family members (e.g., ancestors, descendants, spouses, and former spouses) of the investor can be counted as one shareholder for purposes of determining the number of shareholders.[8]

Fred and Wilma (husband and wife) jointly own 10 shares in Oriole, Inc., an S corporation, with the remaining 90 shares outstanding owned by 99 other shareholders. Fred and Wilma are divorced. Both before and after the divorce, the 100-shareholder limit is met, and Oriole can qualify as a small business corporation.

EXAMPLE 4

S corporation shareholders may be individuals, estates, or certain trusts and exempt organizations.[9] This limitation prevents partnerships, corporations, most LLCs, LLPs, and most IRAs from owning S corporation stock. Without this rule, partnerships and corporate shareholders could easily circumvent the 100-shareholder limitation.

[8] §§ 1361(c)(1)(A)(ii) and (B)(i). TD 9422, 2008–42 I.R.B. 898 provides a definition of who is a family member.

[9] § 1361(b)(1)(B). A one-member LLC typically is an eligible S shareholder.

EXAMPLE 5

Paul and 200 other individuals want to form an S corporation. Paul reasons that if the group forms a partnership, the partnership can then form an S corporation and act as a single shareholder, thereby avoiding the 100-shareholder rule. Paul's plan will not work, because partnerships cannot own stock in an S corporation.

Nonresident aliens cannot own stock in an S corporation.[10] Thus, individuals who are not U.S. citizens *must live in the United States* to own S corporation stock. Shareholders who live in community property states and are married to a nonresident alien[11] cannot own S corporation stock, because the nonresident alien spouse is treated as owning half of the stock.[12] Similarly, if a resident alien shareholder permanently moves outside the United States, the S election is terminated.

TAX PLANNING STRATEGIES   Beating the 100-Shareholder Limit

FRAMEWORK FOCUS: TAX RATE

Strategy: Avoid Double Taxation.

Although partnerships and corporations cannot own small business corporation stock, S corporations themselves can be partners in a partnership or shareholders in a corporation. In this way, the 100-shareholder requirement can be bypassed in a limited sense. For example, if two S corporations, both with 80 shareholders, form a partnership, the shareholders of both corporations can enjoy the limited liability conferred by S corporation status and a single level of tax on the resulting profits, even though there are 160 shareholders involved.

LO.3

Explain how to make and terminate an S election.

15-2b Making the Election

To become an S corporation, the entity must file a valid election with the IRS. The election is made on Form 2553. For the election to be valid, all shareholders must consent. For S corporation status to apply in the current tax year, the election must be filed either in the previous year or on or before the fifteenth day of the third month of the current year.[13]

The Big Picture

EXAMPLE 6

Return to the facts of *The Big Picture* on p. 15-1. Suppose that in 2018, David decides to elect that Fowle, Inc., become an S corporation beginning January 1, 2019. Fowle's S election can be made at any time in 2018 or by March 15, 2019. An election after March 15, 2019, will not be effective until the 2020 calendar tax year.

Even if the 2½-month deadline is met, an S election is not valid unless the corporation qualifies as a small business corporation for the *entire* tax year. Otherwise, the election is effective for the following tax year.

A corporation that does not yet exist cannot make an S corporation election.[14] A new corporation's 2½-month election period begins at the earliest of any of the following events.

- When the corporation has shareholders.
- When it acquires assets.
- When it begins doing business.[15]

[10]§ 1362(b)(1)(C).

[11]Assets acquired by a married couple are generally considered community property in these states: Alaska (by election), Arizona, California, Idaho, Louisiana, Nevada, New Mexico, Texas, Washington, and Wisconsin.

[12]See *Ward v. U.S.*, 81–2 USTC ¶9674, 48 AFTR 2d 81–5942, 661 F.2d 226 (Ct. Cls., 1981), where the court found that the stock was owned as community property. Because the taxpayer-shareholder (a U.S. citizen) was married to a citizen and resident of Mexico, the nonresident alien prohibition was violated. If the taxpayer-shareholder had held the stock as separate property, the S election would have been valid.

[13]§ 1362(b). Extensions of time to file Form 2553 may be possible in certain situations; see Rev.Proc. 2007–62, 2007–41 I.R.B. 786.

[14]See, for example, *T.H. Campbell & Bros., Inc.*, 34 TCM 695, T.C.Memo. 1975–149; Ltr.Rul. 8807070.

[15]Reg. § 1.1372–2(b)(1). Also see, for example, *Nick A. Artukovich*, 61 T.C. 100 (1973).

15-2c **Shareholder Consent**

A qualifying election requires the consent of all of the corporation's shareholders.[16] Consent must be in writing, and it generally must be filed by the election deadline. Both husband and wife must consent if they own their stock jointly (as joint tenants, tenants in common, tenants by the entirety, or community property).[17] In certain circumstances (e.g., a shareholder is out of the country when the consent form is due), one may receive an extension of time to file a consent. For current-year S elections, any person who was a shareholder during any part of the year must sign the consent.

TAX PLANNING STRATEGIES **Making a Proper Election**

FRAMEWORK FOCUS: TAX RATE

Strategy: Avoid Double Taxation.

- Because S corporation status is *elected*, strict compliance with the requirements is demanded by both the IRS and the courts. Any failure to meet a condition in the law may lead to loss of the S election and raise the specter of double tax.

- Make sure that all shareholders timely file a proper consent. If any doubt exists concerning the shareholder status of an individual, it would be wise to request that he or she sign a

consent anyway.[18] Missing consents are fatal to the election, whereas there is no problem with submitting too many consents.

- Make sure the election is timely and properly filed. Either deliver the election to an IRS office in person or send it by certified or registered mail or via a major overnight delivery service. The date used to determine timeliness is the postmark date, not the date the IRS receives the election.

In-depth coverage can be found on this book's companion website: www.cengage.com   **3** DIGGING DEEPER

15-2d **Loss of the Election**

An S election remains in force until it is revoked or lost. Election or consent forms are not required for future years. However, an S election can terminate if any of the following occurs.[19]

- Shareholders owning a majority of shares (voting and nonvoting) voluntarily revoke the election.
- A new shareholder owning more than one-half of the stock affirmatively refuses to consent to the election.
- The corporation no longer qualifies as a small business corporation.
- The corporation does not meet the passive investment income limitation.

Voluntary Revocation

A **voluntary revocation** of the S election requires the consent of shareholders owning a majority of shares on the day the revocation is to be made.[20] A revocation filed up to and including the fifteenth day of the third month of the tax year is effective for the entire tax year, unless a later date is specified. Similarly, unless an effective date is specified, a revocation made after the first 2½ months of the current tax year is effective for the following tax year.

---

[16]§ 1362(a)(2).

[17]Rev.Rul. 60–183, 1960–1 C.B. 625; *William Pestcoe*, 40 T.C. 195 (1963); Reg. § 1.1362–6(b)(3)(iii). This rule likely also applies to all family members who are being treated as one shareholder.

[18]See *William B. Wilson*, 34 TCM 463, T.C.Memo. 1975–92.

[19]§ 1362(d).

[20]§ 1362(d)(1)(B).

EXAMPLE 7

The shareholders of Petunia Corporation, a calendar year S corporation, voluntarily revoke the S election on January 5 of the current year (not a leap year). They do not specify a future effective date in the revocation. If the revocation is properly executed and timely filed, Petunia will be a C corporation for the entire current tax year. If the revocation is not made until June, Petunia remains an S corporation this year and becomes a C corporation at the beginning of the next year.

A corporation can revoke its S status *prospectively* by specifying a future date when the revocation is to be effective. A revocation that designates a future effective date splits the corporation's tax year into a short S corporation year and a short C corporation year. The day on which the revocation occurs is treated as the first day of the C corporation year. The corporation allocates income or loss for the entire year on a pro rata basis using the number of days in each short year.

EXAMPLE 8

Assume the same facts as in the preceding example, except that Petunia designates July 1 as the revocation date. Accordingly, June 30 is the last day of the S corporation's tax year. The C corporation's tax year runs from July 1 to December 31 of the current year. Income or loss for the 12-month period is allocated between the two short years (i.e., 184/365 to the C corporation year).

Rather than allocating on a pro rata basis, the corporation can elect to compute the actual income or loss attributable to the two short years. This election requires the consent of everyone who was a shareholder at any time during the S corporation's short year and everyone who owns stock on the first day of the C corporation's year.[21]

EXAMPLE 9

Assume the same facts as in the preceding example, except that all of Petunia's shareholders consent to allocate the income or loss to the two short years based on its actual realization. Assume further that Petunia experiences a total loss of $102,000, of which $72,000 is incurred in the first half of the year, and only $30,000 is allocated to the C corporation year.

Loss of S Corporation Status

If an S corporation fails to qualify as a small business corporation at any time after the election has become effective, its status as an S corporation ends. The termination occurs on the day the corporation ceases to be a small business corporation.[22] Thus, if the corporation ever has more than 100 shareholders, a second class of stock, or a nonqualifying shareholder, or it otherwise fails to meet the definition of a small business corporation, the S election is terminated immediately.

EXAMPLE 10

Peony Corporation has been a calendar year S corporation for three years. On August 13, one of its 100 shareholders sells *some* of her stock to an outsider. Peony now has 101 shareholders, and it ceases to be a small business corporation. Peony is an S corporation through August 12 and a C corporation from August 13 to December 31.

Passive Investment Income Limitation

The Code provides a **passive investment income (PII)** limitation for S corporations that previously were C corporations or for S corporations that have merged with C corporations. If an S corporation holds C corporation earnings and profits (E & P) and it generates passive investment income in excess of 25 percent of its gross receipts for three consecutive tax years, the S election is terminated as of the beginning of the fourth year.[23]

[21]§ 1362(e)(3).
[22]§ 1362(d)(2)(B).
[23]§ 1362(d)(3)(A)(ii).

For 2017, 2018, and 2019, Chrysanthemum Corporation, a calendar year S corporation, derived passive investment income in excess of 25% of its gross receipts. If Chrysanthemum holds accumulated E & P from years in which it was a C corporation, its S election is terminated as of January 1, 2020.

EXAMPLE 11

PII includes dividends, interest, rents, gains and losses from sales of capital assets, and royalties net of investment deductions. Rents are not considered PII if the corporation renders significant personal services to the occupant.

Violet Corporation owns and operates an apartment building. The corporation provides utilities for the building, maintains the lobby, and furnishes trash collection for tenants. These activities are not considered significant personal services, so any rent income earned by the corporation will be considered PII.

Alternatively, if Violet also provides maid services to its tenants (personal services beyond what normally would be expected from a landlord in an apartment building), the rent income would no longer be PII.

EXAMPLE 12

Reelection after Termination

After an S election has been terminated, the corporation must wait five years before reelecting S corporation status. The five-year waiting period is waived if:

- There is a more-than-50% change in ownership of the corporation after the first year for which the termination is applicable, or
- The event causing the termination was not reasonably within the control of the S corporation or its majority shareholders.

Conditions that a corporation must meet before S corporation status is available are illustrated in Exhibit 15.1.

TAX PLANNING STRATEGIES Preserving the S Election

FRAMEWORK FOCUS: TAX RATE

Strategy: Avoid Double Taxation.

Unexpected loss of S corporation status can be costly to a corporation and its shareholders. Given the complexity of the rules facing these entities, constant vigilance is necessary to preserve the S election.

- As a starting point, the corporation's management and shareholders should be made aware of the various transactions that can lead to the loss of an election.

- Prevent violations of the small business corporation limitations. Because most such violations result from transfers

of stock, the corporation and its shareholders should consider adopting a set of stock transfer restrictions.

A carefully designed set of restrictions could prevent sale of stock to nonqualifying entities or violation of the 100-shareholder rule. Similarly, stock could be repurchased by the corporation under a buy-sell agreement upon the death of a shareholder, thereby preventing nonqualifying trusts from becoming shareholders.[24]

---

[24]Most such agreements do not create a second class of stock. Rev.Rul. 85–161, 1985–2 C.B. 191; *Portage Plastics Co. v. U.S.*, 72–2 USTC ¶9567, 30 AFTR 2d 72–5229, 470 F.2d 308 (CA–7, 1973).

EXHIBIT 15.1	Conditions Required to Elect S Corporation Status

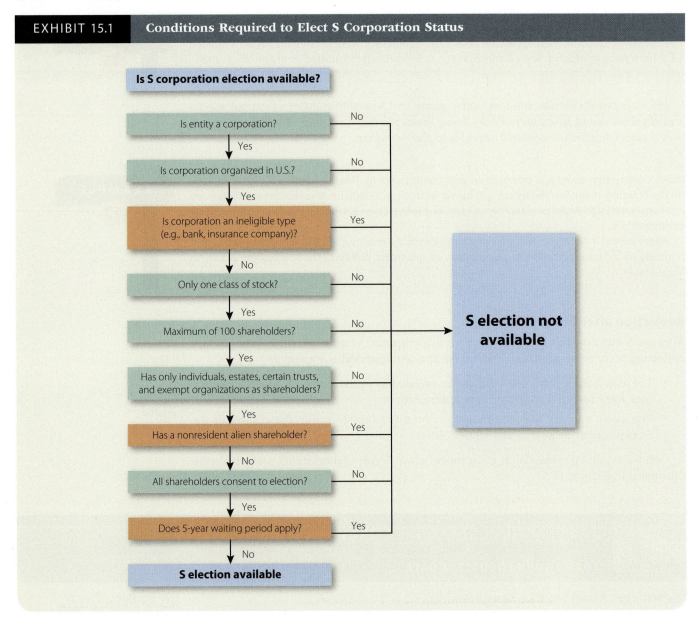

15-3 OPERATIONAL RULES

LO.4

Compute nonseparately stated income and allocate income, deductions, and credits to shareholders.

S corporations are treated much like partnerships for tax purposes. Each year, the S corporation determines nonseparately stated income or loss and separately stated income, deductions, and credits. These items are taxed only once, as they pass through to shareholders without incurring a corporate-level income tax. All items are allocated to each shareholder based on average ownership of stock throughout the year.[25] The *flow-through* of each item of income, deduction, and credit from the corporation to the shareholder is illustrated in Exhibit 15.2.

15-3a Computation of Taxable Income

An S corporation's taxable income or loss is determined in a manner similar to the tax rules that apply to partnerships, except that S corporations recognize gains (but not losses) on distributions of appreciated property to shareholders.[26] With a few exceptions,

---

[25]§§ 1366(a), (b), and (c).   [26]§ 1363(b).

EXHIBIT 15.2	Flow-Through of Items of Income and Loss to S Corporation Shareholders

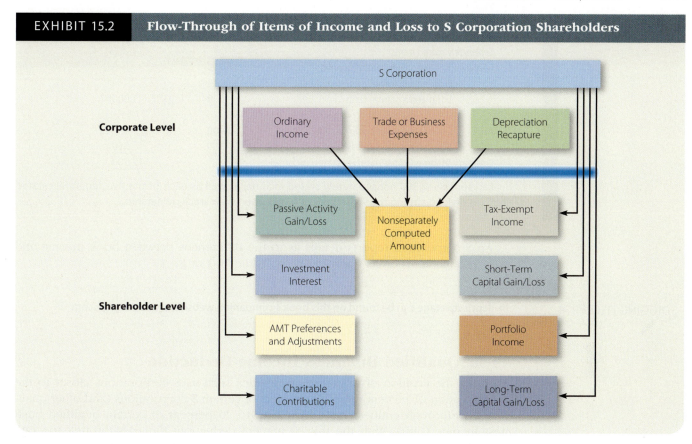

S corporations generally make tax accounting and other elections at the corporate level.[27] Other special provisions affecting only the computation of C corporation income, such as the dividends received deduction, do not extend to S corporations.[28]

In general, S corporation items are divided into (1) nonseparately stated income or loss and (2) separately stated income, losses, deductions, and credits that could uniquely affect the tax liability of any shareholder in a different manner, depending on other factors in the shareholder's tax situation. In essence, nonseparately stated items are aggregated into an undifferentiated amount that constitutes S corporation ordinary income or loss.

EXAMPLE 13

The following is the income statement for Larkspur, Inc., an S corporation.

Sales		$ 40,000
Less: Cost of goods sold		(23,000)
Gross profit on sales		$ 17,000
Less: Interest expense	$1,200	
Charitable contributions	400	
Advertising expenses	1,500	
Other operating expenses	2,000	(5,100)
Book income from operations		$ 11,900
Add: Tax-exempt interest income	$ 300	
Dividend income	200	
Long-term capital gain	500	1,000
Less: Short-term capital loss		(150)
Net income per books		$ 12,750

Larkspur's ordinary income (i.e., S corporation nonseparately stated income) is calculated as follows, using net income for book purposes as the starting point.

continued

---

[27]Certain elections are made at the shareholder level (e.g., the choice between a foreign tax deduction or credit; see Chapter 16).

[28]§ 703(a)(2).

Net income per books		$12,750
Separately stated items		
Remove: Tax-exempt interest income	$300	
Dividend income	200	
Long-term capital gain	500	(1,000)
Add: Charitable contributions	$400	
Short-term capital loss	150	550
Ordinary income (nonseparately stated income)		$12,300

Larkspur's $12,300 nonseparately stated income, as well as each of the five separately stated items, is divided among the shareholders based upon their stock ownership.

An S corporation reports details as to the differences between book income and pass-through items on its Form 1120S, Schedule M–1 or M–3.

DIGGING DEEPER 4 **In-depth coverage can be found on this book's companion website: www.cengage.com**

15-3b Qualified Business Income Deduction

To bring the taxation of flow-through entities such as S corporations closer to the C corporation 21 percent rate, shareholders of certain S corporations (and other qualified flow-through entities) may deduct up to 20 percent of certain qualified business income (QBI). With the full 20 percent deduction, the pass-through top rate is 29.6 percent (.80 × .37), ignoring payroll and other taxes. Income earned by a C corporation that is distributed after-tax as a dividend to the shareholders may be subject to a maximum Federal income tax rate of 39.8 percent [.21 + (.79 × .238)], which includes the 3.8 percent investment income tax rate.

The **qualified business income deduction (QBID)** is based on the following formula:

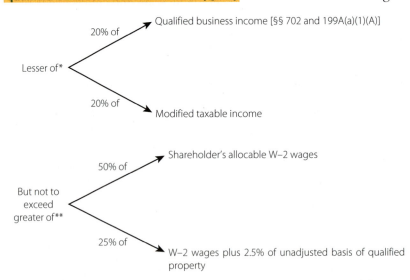

*Deduction limited for certain specified service-type S corporations where taxable income exceeds $157,500 (single; phased out at $207,500) and $315,000 (joint; phased out at $415,000). The phaseout percentage is the ratio of the excess over the threshold amount to $50,000 for individual taxpayers or $100,000 if married filing jointly.
**Does not apply if taxable income is equal to or less than $157,500 (single; phased out at $207,500) or $315,000 (joint; phased out at $415,000).

There are some important limitations on the QBID. The deduction is the smaller of 20 percent of qualified business income or modified taxable income, reduced by net capital gains.[29] Taxable income for this purpose is computed without considering the

---
[29]§ 199A(a).

QBID. QBI does not include any service-related income paid by the S corporation, including reasonable compensation paid to the S corporation shareholder.[30]

QBI is the net amount of domestic qualified items of income, gains, deductions, and losses in the determination of taxable income with respect to the S shareholders qualified businesses. In case of a qualified business loss in one year, the loss can be carried over to the next year to reduce QBI (but not below zero). Further, QBI does not include certain investment-type gains, deductions, or losses.

The W–2 wages limitation is the greater of (1) 50 percent of wages paid by the S corporation or (2) the sum of 25 percent of the W–2 wages plus 2.5 percent of the unadjusted basis (determined immediately after purchase) of all depreciable property.[31] An S corporation's W–2 wages are the sum of wages paid subject to withholding, elective deferrals, and deferred compensation (including wages paid to S corporation owners).

QBI Deduction

EXAMPLE 14

Fran is a single taxpayer. She owns a 25% interest in Flower Inc., which is an S corporation. Flower has ordinary net income of $600,000. Fran's share of S corporation ordinary net income is $150,000. Her share of W–2 wages paid by Flower is $50,000, and her share of the unadjusted basis of qualified property is $400,000. Income from the partnership is her sole source of income. Fran's tentative § 199A deduction would be $30,000 ($150,000 × 20%).

EXAMPLE 15

From Example 14, assume Fran's taxable income from all sources is $300,000. In this case, her taxable income from all sources exceeds the $207,500 threshold. As a result, Fran must determine her QBI deduction including the W–2 wages/capital investment limitation.

Fran's QBI deduction is $25,000, computed as follows:

1. 20% of QBI ($150,000 × 20%)			$30,000
2. Greater of:			
a. 50% of W–2 wages ($50,000 × 50%), or		$25,000	
b. 25% of W–2 wages plus 2.5% of unadjusted basis of depreciable property ($50,000 × 25% + $400,000 × 2.5%)		$22,500	$25,000

15-3c **Allocation of Income and Loss**

Each shareholder is allocated a pro rata portion of nonseparately stated income or loss and all separately stated items. The pro rata allocation method assigns an equal amount of each of the S items to each day of the year.[32] If a shareholder's stock holding changes during the year, this allocation assigns the shareholder a pro rata share of each item for each day the stock is owned. On the date of transfer, the transferor is considered to own the stock.[33]

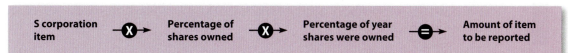

S corporation item ⊗→ Percentage of shares owned ⊗→ Percentage of year shares were owned ═→ Amount of item to be reported

EXAMPLE 16

Pat, a shareholder, owned 10% of Larkspur's stock (from Example 13) for 100 days and 12% for the remaining 265 days. Using the required per-day allocation method, Pat's share of the S corporation ordinary income is $1,409, the total of $12,300 × [10% × (100/365)] plus $12,300 × [12% × (265/365)]. All of Pat's Schedule K–1 totals flow through to the corresponding lines on his individual income tax return (Form 1040).

---

[30]§ 199A(e)(5)(A).

[31]§ 199A(b)(2)(B)(ii). For more detail, see D. L. Crumbley and J. R. Hasselback, "Attractiveness of S Corporations After 2017," *Tax Notes*, February 26, 2018.

[32]§§ 1366(a)(1) and 1377(a)(1).

[33]Reg. § 1.1377–1(a)(2)(ii).

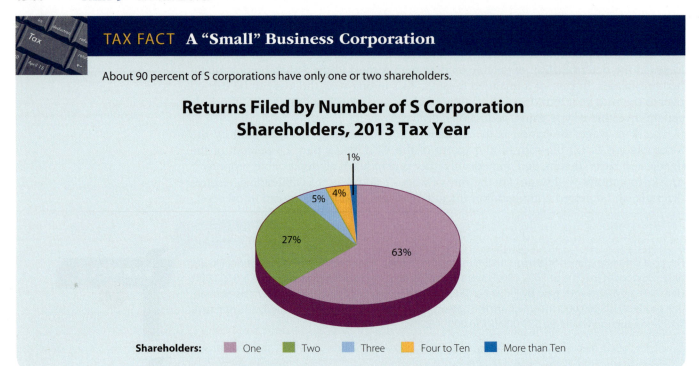

TAX FACT   A "Small" Business Corporation

About 90 percent of S corporations have only one or two shareholders.

Returns Filed by Number of S Corporation Shareholders, 2013 Tax Year

1%
4%
5%
27%
63%

Shareholders: ■ One   ■ Two   ■ Three   ■ Four to Ten   ■ More than Ten

The Short-Year Election

If a shareholder's interest is completely terminated during the tax year by a sale or by a disposition following death, all shareholders owning stock during the year and the corporation may elect to treat the S taxable year as two taxable years. The first year ends on the date of the termination. Under this election, there is an interim closing of the books, and the shareholders report their shares of the S corporation items as they occurred during the short tax year.[34]

The short-year election provides an opportunity to shift income, losses, and credits among shareholders (e.g., items that have a clearly identifiable date of occurrence). The election is desirable in circumstances where more loss can be allocated to taxpayers with higher marginal tax rates.

EXAMPLE 17

Alicia, the owner of all of the shares of an S corporation, transfers her stock to Cindy halfway through the tax year. There is a $100,000 NOL for the entire tax year, but $30,000 of the loss occurs during the first half of the year. Without a short-year election, $50,000 of the loss is allocated to Alicia and $50,000 is allocated to Cindy.

If the corporation makes the short-year election, Cindy is allocated $70,000 of the loss. In this case, the sales price of the stock probably would be increased to recognize the tax benefits being transferred from Alicia to Cindy.

DIGGING DEEPER 5   In-depth coverage can be found on this book's companion website: **www.cengage.com**

LO.5

Determine how distributions to S corporation shareholders are taxed.

15-3d Tax Treatment of Distributions to Shareholders

S corporations do not generate E & P while the S election is in effect. Indeed, all profits are taxed in the year earned, as though they were distributed on a pro rata basis to the shareholders. Thus, distributions from S corporations do not constitute dividends in the traditional sense—there is no corporate E & P to distribute.

---

[34]§ 1377(a)(2).

TAX PLANNING STRATEGIES Salary Structure

FRAMEWORK FOCUS: TAX RATE

Strategy: Shift Net Income from High-Bracket Taxpayers to Low-Bracket Taxpayers.
Avoid Double Taxation.

The amount of any salary paid to a shareholder-employee of an S corporation can have varying tax consequences and should be considered carefully. Larger amounts might be advantageous if the maximum contribution allowed under the employee's retirement plan has not been reached. Smaller amounts may be beneficial if the parties are trying to shift taxable income to lower-bracket shareholders, reduce payroll taxes, curtail a reduction of Social Security benefits, or restrict losses that do not pass through because of the basis limitation.

A strategy of decreasing compensation and correspondingly increasing distributions to shareholder-employees often results in substantial savings in employment taxes. However, a shareholder of an S corporation cannot always perform substantial services and arrange to receive distributions rather than compensation so that the corporation may avoid paying employment taxes. The shareholder may be deemed an employee, and any distributions will be recharacterized as wages subject to FICA and FUTA taxes.[35] For planning purposes, some level of compensation should be paid to all shareholder-employees to avoid any recharacterization of distributions as deductible salaries—especially in personal service corporations.[36]

The qualified business income (QBI) deduction rules (§ 199A) complicate the issue of salary versus distribution as wages paid to an S corporation shareholder are included in W–2 wages when computing the QBI limitation. However, the 20 percent QBI deduction is only allowed for business income allocated to the shareholder and does not include the shareholder's wages from the S corporation.

It is possible, however, for S corporations to have an accumulated E & P (AEP) account. This can occur when:

- The S corporation was previously a C corporation, or
- A C corporation with its own AEP merged into the S corporation.

Distributions from S corporations are measured as the cash received plus the fair market value of any other distributed property. The tax treatment of distributions differs, depending upon whether the S corporation holds AEP. Concept Summary 15.1 outlines the taxation of distributions.

S Corporation with No AEP

If the S corporation holds no AEP, the distribution is a tax-free recovery of capital to the extent it does not exceed the basis of the shareholder's stock. When the amount of the distribution exceeds the stock basis, the excess is treated as a gain from the sale or exchange of property (capital gain in most cases). The vast majority of S corporations fall into this favorable category.

Hyacinth, Inc., a calendar year S corporation, holds no AEP. During the year, Juan, an individual shareholder of the corporation, receives a cash distribution of $12,200 from Hyacinth. Juan's basis in his stock is $9,700. Juan recognizes a capital gain of $2,500, the excess of the distribution over the stock basis ($12,200 − $9,700). The remaining $9,700 is tax-free, but it reduces Juan's basis in his stock to zero.

EXAMPLE
18

---

[35]Rev. Rul. 74–44, 1974–1 C.B. 287; *Spicer Accounting, Inc. v. U.S.*, 91–1 USTC ¶50,103, 66 AFTR 2d 90–5806, 918 F.2d 90 (CA–9, 1990); *Radtke v. U.S.*, 90–1 USTC ¶50,113, 65 AFTR 2d 90–1155, 895 F.2d 1196 (CA–7, 1990); *Joseph M. Grey Public Accountant, P.C.*, 119 T.C. 121 (2002); *David E. Watson, P.C. v. U.S.*, 2010–1 USTC ¶50,444, 105 AFTR 2d 2010–2624, 714 F.

Supp.2d 954 (D.C. S.IA). The IRS uses salary surveys and other statistical methods to determine the appropriate compensation level. *McAlary Ltd.*, T.C. Summary Opinion 2013–62.

[36]FS-2008-25, Wage Compensation for S Corporation Officers, August 2008.

Concept Summary 15.1

Distributions from an S Corporation

Where Earnings and Profits Exist	Where No Earnings and Profits Exist
1. Distributions are tax-free to the extent of the accumulated adjustments account (AAA).*	
2. Distributions from accumulated E & P (AEP) constitute dividend income.†	
3. Distributions are tax-free to the extent of the other adjustments account (OAA).*	
4. Any residual distribution is nontaxable to the extent of the shareholder's basis in stock.*	1. Distributions are nontaxable to the extent of shareholder's basis in stock.*
5. Excess is treated as gain from a sale or exchange of stock (capital gain in virtually all cases).	2. Excess is treated as gain from a sale or exchange of stock (capital gain in virtually all cases).

*The distribution reduces the shareholder's stock basis. A shareholder's stock basis serves as the upper limit on the amount that may be received tax-free.
†The AAA bypass election is available to pay out AEP before reducing the AAA [§ 1368 (e)(3)].

S Corporation with AEP

A more complex set of rules applies to S corporations that hold AEP. These rules treat distributions of pre-election (C corporation) and post-election (S corporation) earnings differently. Distributions of AEP are taxed as dividends and do not reduce stock basis, while distributions of previously taxed S corporation earnings are tax-free to the extent of the shareholder's basis in the stock.

Distributions are deemed to be first from previously taxed, undistributed earnings of the S corporation. These distributions are tax-free and are determined by reference to a special account, the **accumulated adjustments account (AAA)**.[37] Next, AEP is distributed as taxable dividends (i.e., as payments from AEP). After AEP is depleted, tax-free distributions are made from the **other adjustments account (OAA)**, as discussed below. Remaining amounts of the distribution are received tax-free until the shareholder's stock basis reaches zero,[38] with any excess being treated typically as capital gain.

Ordering Rules for Distributions

 EXAMPLE 19

Short, a calendar year S corporation, distributes $1,300 of cash to its only shareholder, Otis, on December 31. Otis's basis in his stock is $1,400, AAA is $500, and Short has $750 of AEP before the distribution.

The first $500 of the distribution is a tax-free recovery of basis from the AAA. The next $750 is a taxable dividend distribution from AEP. The remaining $50 of cash is a tax-free recovery of basis. Immediately after the distribution, Short records a zero balance in AAA and AEP. Otis's stock basis now is $850.

	Corporate AAA	Corporate AEP	Otis's Stock Basis
Beginning balance	$ 500	$ 750	$1,400
Distribution from AAA	(500)		(500)
Distribution from AEP		(750)	
Distribution from stock basis			(50)
Ending balance	$–0–	$–0–	$ 850

---

[37]For S corporations in existence prior to 1983, an account similar to the AAA was used. This account, called *previously taxed income* (PTI), can be distributed in cash tax-free to shareholders after AAA has been distributed. See §§ 1368(c)(1) and (e)(1).

[38]§ 1368(c).

Ordering Rules for Distributions

Assume the same facts as in the preceding example. The next year, Short's income totals zero. It distributes $1,000 to Otis. Of the distribution, $850 is a tax-free recovery of the stock basis, and $150 is taxed to Otis as a capital gain.

EXAMPLE 20

With the consent of all of its shareholders, an S corporation can elect to have a distribution treated as if it first were made from AEP rather than from the AAA. This mechanism is known as an AAA bypass election . This election may be desirable when making distributions to move the entity to the no-AEP system of accounting for distributions, at a maximum tax cost of 20 percent of the AEP (i.e., the maximum income tax rate applied to dividends for most shareholders).

Rotor, an S corporation, has $1,000 of AEP and a balance of $10,000 in the AAA. An AAA bypass election for Rotor's next shareholder distribution would eliminate the need to track the AAA and would greatly simplify the accounting for future distributions. The cost for this simplification is the tax on $1,000 of dividend income.

EXAMPLE 21

Accumulated Adjustments Account

The AAA is the cumulative total of undistributed nonseparately and separately stated income and deduction items for the S corporation. The AAA provides a mechanism to ensure that earnings of an S corporation are taxed only once. Changes to the AAA are reported annually in Schedule M–2 on page 4 of the Form 1120S.

The initial AAA balance is zero when an S election is made. AAA then is computed at the end of each tax year rather than at the time of a distribution. The ending balance in the AAA account is calculated first by adding to the beginning balance any current nonseparately computed income and positive separately stated items (except tax-exempt income). The next step is to reduce the balance by any distributions from AAA. The last step is to reduce the balance by any other negative items.

AAA is applied to the distributions made during the year on a pro rata basis (in a fashion similar to the application of current E & P, discussed in Chapter 13). The determination of AAA is summarized in Exhibit 15.3.

Although adjustments to AAA and stock basis adjustments are similar, there are some important differences between the two amounts. In particular,

- The AAA is not affected by tax-exempt income and related expenses.
- The AAA can have a negative balance. All losses decrease the AAA balance, even those in excess of the shareholder's basis. However, distributions may not make the AAA negative or increase a negative balance in the account.
- Every shareholder has a proportionate interest in the AAA, regardless of the amount of his or her stock basis.[39] In fact, AAA is a corporate account, so there is no connection between the amount and any specific shareholder.[40] Thus, the benefits of AAA can be shifted from one shareholder to another. For example, when an S corporation shareholder sells stock to another party, any AAA balance on the purchase date can be distributed tax-free to the purchaser.

Other Adjustments Account

The OAA tracks the entity's net items that affect basis but not the AAA, such as tax-exempt income and any related nondeductible expenses. Distributions from this account are tax-free.

---

[39]§ 1368(c).　　　　　　　　　　　[40]§ 1368(e)(1)(A).

EXHIBIT 15.3	Adjustments to the Corporate AAA

Increase by:

1. Schedule K income items other than tax-exempt income.
2. Nonseparately computed income.

Decrease by:

3. Distribution(s) from AAA (but not below zero).
4. Negative Schedule K items other than distributions (e.g., losses, deductions).

Schedule M–2

Page 4 of the Form 1120S includes Schedule M–2, a reconciliation of beginning and ending balances in the AAA and OAA accounts. Most tax professionals recommend that the Schedule M–2 be kept current even if the entity has retained no AEP, so that if future events require the use of these amounts, they need not be reconstructed after the fact.

EXAMPLE 22

Poinsettia, an S corporation, records the following items.

AAA, beginning of year	$ 8,500
OAA, beginning of year	–0–
Ordinary income	25,000
Tax-exempt interest income	4,000
Key employee life insurance proceeds received	5,000
Payroll penalty expense	2,000
Charitable contributions	3,000
Unreasonable compensation	5,000
Premiums on key employee life insurance	2,100
Distributions to shareholders	16,000

Poinsettia's Schedule M–2 appears as follows.

Schedule M-2	Analysis of Accumulated Adjustments Account, Other Adjustments Account, and Shareholders' Undistributed Taxable Income Previously Taxed (see instructions)		
		(a) Accumulated adjustments account	**(b)** Other adjustments account	**(c)** Shareholders' undistributed taxable income previously taxed
1	Balance at beginning of tax year	8,500	0	
2	Ordinary income from page 1, line 21 . . .	25,000		
3	Other additions		9,000**	
4	Loss from page 1, line 21	( )		
5	Other reductions	(10,000*)	(2,100)	
6	Combine lines 1 through 5	23,500	6,900	
7	Distributions other than dividend distributions	16,000		
8	Balance at end of tax year. Subtract line 7 from line 6	7,500	6,900	

*$2,000 (payroll penalty) + $3,000 (charitable contributions) + $5,000 (unreasonable compensation).
**$4,000 (tax-exempt interest income) + $5,000 (life insurance proceeds).

Effect of Terminating the S Election

As a result of the reduced C corporation tax rate after 2017, there is the expectation that some S corporations will terminate the S election and convert to C corporation status. Normally, distributions to shareholders from a C corporation are taxed as dividends to the extent of E & P. However, any distribution of *cash* by a C corporation to shareholders during a one-year period[41] following an S election termination receives special treatment. Such a distribution is treated as a tax-free recovery of stock basis to the extent that it does not exceed the AAA.[42] Because *only* cash distributions reduce the AAA during this *post-election termination period*, a corporation should not make property distributions during this time. Instead, the entity should sell property and distribute the proceeds to shareholders.

---

[41]§ 1377(b).

[42]§ 1371(e).

TAX PLANNING STRATEGIES The Accumulated Adjustments Account

FRAMEWORK FOCUS: TAX RATE

Strategy: Avoid Double Taxation.

The AAA is needed to determine the tax treatment of distributions from S corporations with AEP *and* distributions made during the post-termination election period. Therefore, it is important for all S corporations (even those with no AEP) to maintain a current AAA (and OAA) balance. Without an accurate AAA balance, distributions could needlessly be classified as taxable dividends. Alternatively, it will be costly to reconstruct the AAA after the S election terminates.

Distributions should be made when AAA is positive. If future years bring operating losses, AAA is reduced and shareholder exposure to AEP and taxable dividends increases.

The Big Picture

EXAMPLE 23

Return to the facts of *The Big Picture* on p. 15-1. Assume that Fowle has operated as an S corporation for many years and that the entity turned profitable once it mastered the pricing methods of its import markets. Then David decides to terminate the S election as of the end of the year. On December 31 of that year, Fowle's AAA balance totals $1.3 million.

David can receive a nontaxable distribution of cash during the next year, to the full extent of the entity's AAA balance. Any cash distributions received during the next year reduce the basis of David's Fowle stock, but not below zero.

15-3e Tax Treatment of Noncash Distributions by the Corporation

An S corporation recognizes a gain on any distribution of appreciated property as if the asset were sold to the shareholder at its fair market value.[43] The corporate gain is passed through to the shareholders, and the asset's basis to the receiving shareholder is stepped up to fair market value. The character of the gain—capital gain or ordinary income—depends upon the type of asset being distributed.

The S corporation does not recognize a loss when distributing assets that are worth less than their basis. As with gain property, the shareholder's basis is equal to the asset's fair market value. Thus, the potential loss is postponed until the shareholder sells the stock of the S corporation. Because loss property receives a step-down in basis without any loss recognition by the S corporation, distributions of loss property should be avoided. See Concept Summary 15.2.

Noncash Distributions by an S Corporation

EXAMPLE 24

Yarrow, Inc., an S corporation for 12 years, distributes to Xiang, one of its shareholders, a tract of land held as an investment. The land was purchased for $22,000 many years ago and currently is worth $82,000. Yarrow recognizes a capital gain of $60,000, which increases the AAA by $60,000. The gain flows through proportionately to all of Yarrow's shareholders and is taxed to them.

This tax-free noncash distribution reduces AAA and Xiang's S stock basis by $82,000 (fair market value). The tax consequences are the same for appreciated property whether (a) it is distributed to shareholders and they dispose of it or (b) the corporation sells the property and distributes the proceeds to its shareholders.

---

[43]§ 311(b).

Concept Summary 15.2

Consequences of Noncash Distributions

	Appreciated Property	Depreciated Property
S corporation	Realized gain is recognized by the corporation, which passes it through to the shareholders. This gain increases a shareholder's stock basis, generating a basis in the property equal to FMV. On the distribution, the shareholder's stock basis is reduced by the FMV of the property (but not below zero).	Realized loss is not recognized. The shareholder takes an FMV basis in the property, and stock basis is reduced by the same amount. AAA is reduced by the amount of the unrecognized loss.
C corporation	Realized gain is recognized under § 311(b) and increases E & P (net of tax). The shareholder reports a taxable dividend to the extent of corporate E & P, equal to the property's FMV (reduced by any liabilities assumed). The shareholder takes a basis in the asset equal to its FMV.	Realized loss is not recognized. The shareholder takes an FMV basis in the property.
Partnership	No gain is recognized by the partnership or partner. The partner takes a carryover basis in the asset, but the asset basis is limited to the partner's basis in the partnership.	Realized loss is not recognized. The partner takes a carryover basis in the asset, but the asset basis is limited to the partner's basis in the partnership.

Noncash Distributions by an S Corporation

EXAMPLE 25

Continue with the facts of Example 24. If the land had been purchased for $82,000 and was currently worth $22,000, Xiang would take a $22,000 basis in the land. The $60,000 realized loss is not recognized at the corporate level. The loss does reduce Yarrow's AAA, though not an attractive result for Yarrow shareholders. However, if the S corporation sells the asset to an unrelated party, it does recognize the loss and reduces AAA.

EXAMPLE 26

Assume the same facts as in Examples 24 and 25, except that Yarrow is a C corporation (E & P balance of $1 million) or a partnership. Assume that Xiang's basis before the distribution in her corporate stock or partnership interest is $100,000, and ignore any corporate-level taxes. Compare the results.

	Appreciated Property		
	S Corporation	C Corporation	Partnership
Entity gain/loss	$60,000	$60,000	$ –0–
Owner's gain/loss/dividend	60,000	82,000	–0–
Owner's basis in land	82,000	82,000	22,000

	Property That Has Declined in Value		
	S Corporation	C Corporation	Partnership
Entity gain/loss	$ –0–	$ –0–	$ –0–
Owner's gain/loss/dividend	–0–	22,000	–0–
Owner's basis in land	22,000	22,000	82,000

15-3f **Shareholder's Basis in S Stock**

The calculation of the initial tax basis of stock in an S corporation is similar to that for the basis of stock in a C corporation and depends upon the manner in which the shares are acquired (e.g., gift, inheritance, purchase, exchange under § 351). Once the initial tax basis is determined, various transactions during the life of the corporation affect the shareholder's basis in the stock. Although each shareholder is required to compute his or her own basis in the S shares, neither Form 1120S nor Schedule K–1 provides a place for tracking this amount.

A shareholder's basis is increased by stock purchases and capital contributions. Operations during the year cause the following additional upward adjustments to basis.[44]

- Nonseparately computed income.
- Separately stated income items (e.g., tax-exempt income).

Basis then is reduced by distributions not reported as income by the shareholder (e.g., an AAA distribution). Next, the following items reduce basis (but not below zero).

- Nondeductible expenses of the corporation (e.g., fines, penalties, and illegal kickbacks).
- Nonseparately computed loss.
- Separately stated loss and deduction items.

As under the partnership rules, basis first is increased by income items; then it is decreased by distributions and finally by losses.[45] In most cases, this *losses last* rule is advantageous to the S shareholder.

EXAMPLE 27

In its first year of operation, Iris, Inc., a calendar year S corporation, earns income of $2,000. Before accounting for the entity's operating results, assume the stock basis of Iris's sole shareholder, Marty, is zero. Therefore, Marty's stock basis is increased to $2,000. On February 2 in its second year of operation, Iris distributes $2,000 to Marty. During the remainder of the second year, the corporation incurs a $2,000 loss.

Under the S corporation ordering rules, the $2,000 distribution is tax-free AAA to Marty. The distribution is accounted for before the loss. The $2,000 loss is suspended until Marty generates additional stock basis (e.g., from capital contributions or future entity profits).

A shareholder's basis in S corporation stock never is reduced below zero. Once stock basis reaches zero, any additional basis reductions (losses or deductions, but *not* distributions) decrease the shareholder's basis in loans made to the S corporation (but not below zero). Any excess of losses or deductions over both stock and loan bases is not deductible in the current year. Thus, until additional basis is created due to capital contributions or flow-through income, the loss deductions are suspended.

When there is a capital contribution or an item of flow-through income after both stock and loan bases have been reduced to zero, basis first is restored to the shareholder loans, up to the original principal amount.[46] Then, basis in the stock is restored. A distribution in excess of stock basis does not reduce any debt basis. If a loss and a distribution occur in the same year, the loss reduces the stock basis *after* the distribution.

---

[44]§ 1367(a).
[45]Reg. § 1.1367–1(f).

[46]§ 1367(b)(2); Reg. § 1.1367–2(e).

EXAMPLE

28

Stacey, a sole shareholder, holds a $7,000 stock basis and a $2,000 basis in a loan that she made to Romulus, a calendar year S corporation with zero AEP. At the beginning of the year, the corporation's AAA and OAA balances are zero. Ordinary income for the year is $8,200. During the year, the corporation also received $2,000 of tax-exempt interest income.

Cash of $17,300 is distributed to Stacey on November 15. As a result, Stacey recognizes only a $100 capital gain.

	Corporate AAA	Corporate OAA	Stacey's Stock Basis	Stacey's Loan Basis
Beginning balance	$ –0–	$ –0–	$ 7,000	$2,000
Ordinary income	8,200		8,200	
Tax-exempt income		2,000	2,000	
Subtotal	$ 8,200	$ 2,000	$17,200	$2,000
Distribution ($17,300)				
From AAA	(8,200)		(8,200)	
From OAA		(2,000)	(2,000)	
From stock basis			(7,000)	
Ending balance	$ –0–	$ –0–	$ –0–	$2,000
Distribution in excess of stock basis (capital gain)			$ 100	

Pass-through losses can reduce loan basis, but distributions do not. Stock basis cannot be reduced below zero, so the $100 excess distribution does not reduce Stacey's loan basis.

The basis rules for S corporation stock are similar to the rules for determining a partner's basis in a partnership interest. However, a partner's basis in the partnership interest includes the partner's direct investment plus a *ratable share* of partnership liabilities.[47] If a partnership borrows from a partner, the partner receives a basis increase as if the partnership had borrowed from an unrelated third party.[48]

In contrast, corporate borrowing has no effect on the stock basis of an S corporation shareholder. The fact that a shareholder has guaranteed a loan made to the corporation by a third party has no effect on the shareholder's loan basis, unless payments actually have been made as a result of that guarantee. Direct loans from a shareholder to the S corporation have a tax basis only for the shareholder making the loan.

If a loan's basis has been reduced and is not restored, income is recognized when the corporation repays the loan. If the corporation issued a note as evidence of the debt, repayment constitutes an amount received in exchange for a capital asset and the amount that exceeds the shareholder's basis is capital gain.[49] However, if the loan is made on open account, the repayment constitutes ordinary income to the extent it exceeds the shareholder's basis in the loan. Thus, a written note should be provided to avoid the ordinary income implications of an open account.

The Big Picture

EXAMPLE

29

Return to the facts of *The Big Picture* on p. 15-1. Assume that Fowle has made an S election. At the beginning of 2018, David's basis in his Fowle stock was $90,000. During the year, he made a $40,000 loan to the corporation, using a written debt instrument and market interest rates.

Fowle generated a $93,000 taxable loss for 2018. Thus, at the beginning of 2019, David's stock basis was zero, and the basis in his loan to Fowle was $37,000.

Fowle repaid the loan in full on March 1, 2019. David recognizes a $3,000 capital gain as a result of the repayment.

---

[47]§ 752(a).

[48]Reg. § 1.752–1(e).

[49]*Joe M. Smith*, 48 T.C. 872 (1967), *aff'd* and *rev'd* in 70–1 USTC ¶9327, 25 AFTR 2d 70–936, 424 F.2d 219 (CA–9, 1970); Rev.Rul. 64–162, 1964–1

C.B. 304. An open account loan is treated as evidenced by a note if the shareholder's net payable at the end of the tax year exceeds $25,000. Reg. § 1.1367–2.

In-depth coverage can be found on this book's companion website: www.cengage.com

6 DIGGING DEEPER

TAX PLANNING STRATEGIES Working with Suspended Losses

FRAMEWORK FOCUS: INCOME AND EXCLUSION

Strategy: Avoid Income Recognition.

Distributions made to shareholders with suspended losses usually create capital gain income because there is no stock basis to offset. Typically, distributions should be deferred until the shareholder creates stock basis in some form. In this way, no gross income is recognized until the suspended losses are fully used.

The Big Picture

Continue with the facts of Example 29, except that Fowle's loss cannot be deducted by David because he has a zero basis in both the stock and debt of the entity. David purchases $5,000 of additional stock in Fowle. David gets an immediate deduction for his investment, due to his $93,000 in suspended losses. Alternatively, if Fowle shows a $5,000 profit for the year, David pays no tax on the flow-through income, as it is offset by the suspended losses.

However, if Fowle distributes $5,000 to David in 2019 without earning any profit for the year, and prior to any capital contribution by him, David recognizes a $5,000 capital gain, because the distribution exceeds the zero stock basis.

EXAMPLE
30

15-3g **Treatment of Losses**

Net Operating Loss

One major advantage of an S election is the ability to pass through net operating losses (NOLs) of the corporation directly to the shareholders. A shareholder can deduct an NOL for the year in which the S corporation's tax year ends. The corporation does not deduct the NOL. A shareholder's basis in the stock is reduced by any NOL pass-through, but not below zero. The entity's AAA is reduced by the same deductible amount.[50]

Deductions for an S corporation's pass-throughs (e.g., NOL, capital loss, and charitable contributions) cannot exceed a shareholder's stock basis *plus* the basis of any loans made by the shareholder to the corporation.[51] A shareholder is entitled to carry forward a loss pass-through to the extent the loss for the year exceeds basis. Any loss carried forward may be deducted *only* by the *same* shareholder if and when the basis in the stock of or loans to the corporation is restored.[52]

LO.7

Explain the tax effects of losses on S shareholders.

---

[50]§§ 1368(a)(1)(A) and (e)(1)(A).

[51]See *Donald J. Sauvigne*, 30 TCM 123, T.C.Memo. 1971–30.

[52]§ 1366(d).

Ginny owns 10% of the stock of Pilot, a calendar year S corporation. Her basis in the shares is $10,000 at the beginning of year 1. The indicated events are accounted for under the S corporation rules as follows.

Tax Year	Event	Tax Consequences
1	Ginny's share of Pilot's operating loss is $15,000.	Ginny deducts $10,000. Her stock basis is reduced to zero. She has a $5,000 suspended loss.
2	Ginny's share of Pilot's operating loss is $4,000.	No current deduction allowed for the loss, as Ginny has no stock basis to offset. Her suspended loss is now $9,000.
3	Ginny's share of Pilot's operating loss is $7,000. She purchases an additional $10,000 of stock from Pilot.	The purchase creates $10,000 of stock basis. Ginny deducts $10,000—the current $7,000 loss and $3,000 of the suspended loss. Stock basis again is zero, and the new suspended loss is $6,000.
4	Ginny sells all of her Pilot shares to Christina on January 1.	The $6,000 suspended loss disappears—it cannot be transferred to Christina.

Concept Summary 15.3 provides a summary of the treatment of S corporation losses.

Concept Summary 15.3

Treatment of S Corporation Losses

Step 1.   Allocate total loss to the shareholder on a daily basis, based upon stock ownership.

Step 2.   If the shareholder's loss exceeds his or her stock basis, apply any excess to the basis of corporate indebtedness to the shareholder. Loss allocations do not reduce stock or loan basis below zero.

Step 3.   Where a flow-through loss exceeds the stock and loan basis, any excess is suspended and carried over to succeeding tax years.

Step 4.   In succeeding tax years, any net increase in basis restores the debt basis first, up to its original amount.

Step 5.   Once debt basis is restored, any remaining net increase restores stock basis.

If the S election terminates, any suspended loss carryover may be deducted during the post-termination period to the extent of the stock basis at the end of this period. Any loss remaining at the end of this period is lost forever.

TAX PLANNING STRATEGIES Loss Considerations

FRAMEWORK FOCUS: DEDUCTIONS

Strategy: Maximize Deductible Amounts.

A net loss in excess of tax basis may be carried forward and deducted only by the same shareholder in succeeding years. Thus, before disposing of the stock, a shareholder should increase stock/loan basis to flow through the loss. The next shareholder cannot acquire the loss carryover.

The NOL provisions create a need for sound tax planning during the last election year and the post-termination transition period. If it appears that the S corporation is going to sustain an NOL or use up any loss carryover, each shareholder's basis should be analyzed to determine whether it can absorb the owner's share of the loss. If basis is insufficient to absorb the loss, further investments should be considered before the end of the post-termination period. Such investments can be accomplished through additional stock purchases from the corporation or from other shareholders to increase basis.

continued

A calendar year C corporation records a $20,000 NOL during the previous year. The corporation makes a valid S election for the current year and incurs another $20,000 NOL. At all times during the current year, the stock of the corporation was owned by the same 10 shareholders, each of whom owned 10% of the stock.

Tim, one of the shareholders, holds a stock basis of $1,800 at the beginning of the current year. None of the C corporation NOL may be carried forward into the S year. Although Tim's share of the S corporation NOL is $2,000, his deduction for the loss is limited to $1,800 with a $200 carryover to the next year.

At-Risk Rules

As discussed in Chapters 6 and 14, S corporation shareholders, like partners, are limited in the amount of loss they may deduct by their "at-risk" amounts.

An at-risk amount is determined separately for each shareholder. A shareholder usually is considered at risk with respect to an activity to the extent of cash and the adjusted basis of other property contributed to the electing corporation, any amount borrowed for use in the activity for which the taxpayer has personal liability for payment from personal assets, and the net fair market value of personal assets that secure nonrecourse borrowing.

Any losses that are suspended under the at-risk rules are carried forward to future tax years. The S stock basis limitations and at-risk limitations are applied before the passive activity limitations (see below).

Carl has a basis of $35,000 in his S corporation stock. He takes a $15,000 nonrecourse loan from a local bank and lends the proceeds to the S corporation. Carl now has a stock basis of $35,000 and a loan basis of $15,000.

Carl's share of this year's S corporation loss is $40,000. Due to the at-risk rules, he can deduct only $35,000 of S corporation losses, reducing his S corporation stock basis to zero.

Passive Activity Losses and Credits

S corporations are not directly subject to the passive activity limits, but corporate rental activities are inherently passive, and other activities of an S corporation may be passive unless the shareholder(s) materially participate(s) in operating the business.

If the corporate activity involves rentals or the shareholders do not materially participate, the shareholders can apply these losses or credits only against income from other passive activities. An S shareholder's stock basis is reduced by passive activity losses that flow through to the shareholder, even though the shareholder may not be entitled to a current deduction due to the passive activity loss limitations.

Passive activity gains and income flow through to the shareholder as investment income, and this income is subject to the additional Medicare tax (see Chapter 9).

15-3h Limitation on the Deduction of Excess Business Losses

A fourth limitation applies to the deduction of business losses of pass-through entities. Section 461(l) limits the total amount of net business losses that can be deducted from an active owner's tax return. The new rule limits the maximum loss to $500,000 for married filing joint tax returns and $250,000 for all other tax returns. Any loss in excess of these amounts can be carried forward indefinitely. This limitation applies after the rules for stock basis, at-risk, and passive activity losses are applied.

15-3i **Other Operational Rules**

Several other points may be made about the possible effects of various Code provisions on S corporations.

- An S corporation must make estimated tax payments with respect to any recognized built-in gain and excess passive investment income tax (discussed next).

- Any family member who renders services or furnishes capital to an S corporation must be paid reasonable compensation. Otherwise, the IRS can make adjustments to reflect the value of the services or capital. This rule may make it more difficult for related parties to shift S corporation taxable income to children or other family members.

- The flow-through of S items to a shareholder is not self-employment income and is not subject to the self-employment tax.[53] Compensation for services rendered to an S corporation is, however, subject to FICA taxes for the employee-shareholder, but it is not considered wages for purposes of the 20 percent QBI deduction. This treatment of earned income of S corporations is attractive compared to the treatment of a proprietorship or a partnership, whose income is taxed as self-employment income to the owners.

- A number of qualified fringe benefits, which typically are received by employees on a tax-free basis, are subject to Federal income tax when received by a more-than-2% shareholder-employee of an S corporation. These benefits include the value of group term life insurance, medical insurance, and meals and lodging furnished for the convenience of the employer. These items are treated as wages and are subject to most payroll taxes. The employee can deduct medical insurance premiums on his or her Form 1040.

- An S corporation is liable for a penalty if it does not file its Form 1120S on a timely basis. The penalty is $195 per month times the number of S shareholders, for up to 12 months.[54]

- An accrual basis S corporation uses the cash method of accounting for purposes of deducting business expenses and interest owed to a cash basis related party.[55] Thus, the timing of the shareholder's income and the corporate deduction must match.

- The S election is not recognized by the District of Columbia and several states, including Connecticut, Michigan, and Tennessee. Thus, some or all of the entity's income may be subject to a state-level income tax.

- An S corporation may issue § 1244 stock to its shareholders to obtain ordinary loss treatment (see Chapter 8).

- Loss deductions may be disallowed due to a lack of a profit motive. If the activities at the corporate level are not profit-motivated, the losses may be disallowed under the hobby loss rules (see Chapter 11).[56]

BRIDGE DISCIPLINE **Bridge to Public Finance**

Proceeds from the Federal self-employment tax are used by the Federal government to fund retirement and health care entitlements. Any shortfalls in these funds mean that the following may occur.

- Citizens needing retirement annuities and/or health care services will receive less than is needed. This may not be a desirable result in a moral or ethical sense, as life will be more difficult than it otherwise might be for those of modest means.

- Retirement income and health care services must be funded from general revenues, meaning almost exclusively funds from the Federal income tax. This represents a mismatch of payor and payee, an income redistribution result that would not be attractive to some. In a zero-sum sense, benefits of this sort reduce funding for other budgetary needs of the Federal government (e.g., for defense, transportation, or research).

---

[53]Rev.Rul. 59–221, 1959–1 C.B. 225.

[54]§ 6699. The penalty is waived if the entity can show reasonable cause for the failure to file.

[55]§ 267(b).

[56]§ 183; *Michael J. Houston*, 69 TCM 2360, T.C.Memo. 1995–159; *Mario G. De Mendoza, III*, 68 TCM 42, T.C.Memo. 1994–314.

15-4 ENTITY-LEVEL TAXES

LO.8

Compute the entity-level taxes on S corporations.

Normally, an S corporation does *not* pay any Federal income tax, because all items flow through to the shareholders. But an S corporation that previously was a C corporation may be required to pay a built-in gains tax, a LIFO recapture tax, a general business credit recapture, or a passive investment income tax.

15-4a Tax on Pre-Election Built-In Gain

Without the built-in gains tax, it would be possible to avoid the corporate double tax on a disposition of appreciated property by electing S corporation status.

> **EXAMPLE 34**
>
> Zinnia, Inc., a C corporation, owns a single asset with a basis of $100,000 and a fair market value of $500,000. If Zinnia sells this asset and distributes the cash to its shareholders, there are two levels of tax, one at the corporate level and one at the shareholder level. Alternatively, if Zinnia distributes the asset to its shareholders as a dividend, a double tax still results.
>
> In an attempt to avoid the double tax, Zinnia elects S corporation status. It then sells the asset and distributes the proceeds to shareholders. Without the built-in gains tax, the gain would be taxed only once, at the shareholder level. The distribution of the sales proceeds would be a tax-free reduction of the stock basis and the AAA. However, the built-in gains tax ensures that Zinnia would not avoid the double tax. (See Example 35.)

The built-in gains tax generally applies to C corporations that convert to S status. It is a *corporate-level* tax on any built-in gain recognized when the S corporation disposes of an asset in a taxable disposition within five calendar years after the date on which the S election took effect.[57]

General Rules

The base for the built-in gains tax includes any unrealized gain on appreciated assets (e.g., real estate, cash basis receivables, goodwill) held by a corporation on the day it elects S status. The highest corporate tax rate (currently 21 percent) is applied to the unrealized gain when any of the assets are sold. Any gain from the sale (net of the built-in gains tax)[58] also passes through as a taxable gain to shareholders.

> **EXAMPLE 35**
>
> Assume the same facts as in the preceding example. A corporate-level built-in gains tax must be paid by Zinnia if it sells the asset after electing S status. Upon sale of the asset, Zinnia owes a tax of $84,000 ($400,000 × 21%). In addition, Zinnia's shareholders report a $316,000 taxable flow-through gain ($400,000 − $84,000). The built-in gains tax effectively imposes a double tax on Zinnia and its shareholders, as would have been the case had Zinnia remained a C corporation.

In-depth coverage can be found on this book's companion website: www.cengage.com

7 DIGGING DEEPER

The amount of built-in gain recognized in any year is limited to an *as if* taxable income for the year, computed as if the corporation were a C corporation. Any built-in gain that escapes taxation due to the taxable income limitation is carried forward and recognized in future tax years. Thus, a corporation can defer a built-in gain tax liability if it has a low or negative taxable income.

---

[57]§ 1374(d)(7)(B). [58]§ 1366(f)(2).

EXAMPLE 36

Vinca, an S corporation, recognizes $400,000 of built-in gains during the year. Had Vinca been a C corporation, its taxable income would have been $300,000. Thus, the amount of built-in gain subject to tax is $300,000. The excess built-in gain of $100,000 is carried forward and taxed in the next year (assuming adequate C corporation taxable income in that year).

There is no statutory limit on the carryforward period, but the gain would effectively expire at the end of the built-in gain recognition period.[59]

An S corporation can offset built-in gains with unexpired NOLs or capital losses from C corporation years.

EXAMPLE 37

Yowler, an S corporation, reports a built-in gain of $100,000 and taxable income of $90,000. Yowler holds a $12,000 NOL carryforward and an $8,000 capital loss carryforward from C corporation years prior to its S election. Yowler also has a business credit carryforward of $4,000. Yowler's built-in gains tax liability is calculated as follows.

Lesser of taxable income or built-in gain	$ 90,000
Less: NOL carryforward from C year	(12,000)
Capital loss carryforward from C year	(8,000)
Tax base	$ 70,000
Highest corporate income tax rate	× .21
Tentative tax	$ 14,700
Less: Business credit carryforward from C year	(4,000)
Built-in gains tax liability	$ 10,700

The $10,000 realized (but not taxed) built-in gain in excess of taxable income is carried forward to the next year, as long as the next year is within the built-in gain recognition period.

TAX PLANNING STRATEGIES   Managing the Built-In Gains Tax

FRAMEWORK FOCUS: INCOME AND EXCLUSION

Strategy: Avoid Income Recognition.
Postpone Recognition of Income to Achieve Tax Deferral.

Although limitations exist on contributions of loss property to the corporation before S status is elected, it still is possible for a corporation to minimize built-in gains and maximize built-in losses prior to the S election. A cash basis S corporation can accomplish this by reducing receivables, accelerating payables, and accruing compensation costs.

To further reduce or defer the tax, the corporation may take advantage of the taxable income limitation by shifting income and deductions to minimize taxable income in years when built-in gain is recognized. Although the postponed built-in gain is carried forward to future years, the time value of money makes the postponement beneficial. For example, paying compensation to shareholder-employees in place of a distribution creates a deduction that reduces taxable income and postpones the built-in gains tax.

Built-in *loss* property may be sold in the same year built-in gain property is sold to reduce or eliminate the built-in gains tax. Generally, the taxpayer should sell built-in loss property in a year when an equivalent amount of built-in gain property is sold. Otherwise, the built-in loss could be wasted.

EXAMPLE 38

Tulip, Inc., an S corporation, holds a built-in gain of $110,000 and reports current taxable income of $120,000 before payment of salaries to its shareholders. If Tulip pays at least $120,000 in salaries to the shareholders (rather than making a distribution), its taxable income drops to zero and the built-in gains tax is postponed. Thus, Tulip may want to keep its salaries higher, to postpone the built-in gains tax in future years and reap a benefit from the time value of money. Of course, paying the salaries may increase the associated payroll tax liabilities.

---

[59]§ 1374(d)(7); Notice 90–27, 1990–1 C.B. 336.

LIFO Recapture Tax

When a C corporation uses the FIFO method for its last year before making the S election, any built-in gain is recognized and taxed as the inventory is sold. A LIFO-basis corporation would not recognize this gain unless the corporation invaded the LIFO layer during the built-in gains tax period. To preclude a deferral of gain recognition by a C corporation that elects S status, any LIFO recapture amount at the time of the S election is subject to a corporate-level tax.

The taxable LIFO recapture amount equals the excess of the inventory's value under FIFO over the LIFO value. The resulting tax, determined by including the LIFO recapture amount in the last C corporation tax return, is payable in four equal installments, with the first payment due on or before the due date for the corporate return for the last C corporation year (without regard to any extensions). The remaining three installments are paid on or before the due dates of the succeeding corporate returns. No interest is due if payments are made by the due dates, and no estimated taxes are due on the four tax installments. No refund is allowed if the LIFO value is higher than the FIFO value.

> **EXAMPLE 39**
>
> Daffodil Corporation converts from a C corporation to an S corporation at the beginning of the year. Daffodil used the LIFO inventory method and held an ending LIFO inventory of $110,000 (FIFO value of $190,000) before the S election. Daffodil's marginal tax rate on its final C corporation tax return is 21%.
>
> Daffodil adds the $80,000 LIFO recapture amount to its C corporation taxable income, resulting in an increased tax liability of $16,800 ($80,000 × 21%). Daffodil pays one-fourth of the tax ($4,200) with its final C corporation tax return. The three succeeding installments of $4,200 each are paid with Daffodil's first three S corporation tax returns.

15-4b Passive Investment Income Penalty Tax

A tax is imposed on the excess passive income of S corporations that possess AEP from C corporation years. The tax rate is the highest corporate income tax rate for the year (currently 21 percent). The rate is applied to excess net passive income (ENPI), which is determined using the following formula.

Passive investment income (PII) includes gross receipts derived from royalties, rents, dividends, interest, and annuities. Only the net gain from the disposition of capital assets is taken into account in computing PII gross receipts.[60] Net passive income is PII reduced by any deductions directly connected with the production of that income. Any PII tax reduces the gross income that flows through to the shareholders.

---

[60]§§ 1362(d)(3)(B) and (C).

Total assets controlled by S corporations make up a significant part of the economy. The 4.2 million S corporations that file Federal tax returns, representing over 7 million shareholders, employ $3.6 trillion in assets in their investments and operations.

Here are some more data about the S corporation sector.

- Trade or business income accounts for over 85 percent of all S corporation net income.
- About 70 percent of all S corporations report a positive amount of gross income.
- About 60 percent of all S corporations report business gross receipts of $250,000 or less.

The excess net passive income (ENPI) cannot exceed a hypothetical C corporate taxable income for the year, before considering special C corporation deductions (e.g., the dividends received deduction) or an NOL carryover.[61]

EXAMPLE 40

Lilac Corporation, an electing S corporation, records gross receipts totaling $264,000 (of which $110,000 is PII). Expenditures directly connected to the production of the PII total $30,000. Therefore, Lilac reports net PII of $80,000 ($110,000 − $30,000), and its PII exceeds 25% of its gross receipts by $44,000 [$110,000 PII − (25% × $264,000)]. Excess net passive income (ENPI) is $32,000, calculated as follows.

$$\text{ENPI} = \frac{\$44,000}{\$110,000} \times \$80,000 = \$32,000$$

Lilac's PII tax is $6,720 ($32,000 × 21%).

TAX PLANNING STRATEGIES   Avoid PII Pitfalls

FRAMEWORK FOCUS: TAX RATE

Strategy: Avoid Double Taxation.

Watch for a possible violation of the PII limitation. Avoid a consecutive third year with excess passive income when the corporation has accumulated E & P from C corporation years. In this connection, assets that produce passive income (e.g., stocks and bonds, certain rental assets) might be retained by the shareholders in their individual capacities and kept out of the corporation.

DIGGING DEEPER 8   In-depth coverage can be found on this book's companion website: **www.cengage.com**

15-5 **SUMMARY**

The S corporation rules are elective and can be used to benefit a number of owners of small businesses.

- When the business is profitable, the S corporation election removes the threat of double taxation on corporate profits.
- When the business is generating losses, deductions for allocable losses are immediately available to the shareholders.

---

[61]§§ 1374(d)(4) and 1375(a) and (b).

About 70 percent of all U.S. corporations operate under the S rules. Flow-through income is taxed to the shareholders, who increase basis in their corporate stock accordingly. In this manner, subsequent distributions to shareholders can be made tax-free. Flow-through losses reduce stock and debt basis, but loss deductions are suspended when basis reaches zero. Flow-through items that could be treated differently by various shareholders are separately stated on Schedule K–1 of the Form 1120S.

The S rules are designed for the closely held business with a simple capital structure. Eligibility rules are not oppressive, and they do not include any limitations on the corporation's capitalization value, sales, number or distribution of employees, or other operating measures. Accounting for an S corporation's shareholder distributions can be complex, though, and maintenance of S status must be monitored on an ongoing basis.

Corporate-level taxes seldom are assessed on S corporations, but they guard against abuses of the S rules, such as shifting appreciated assets from higher C corporation rates to lower individual rates (the built-in gains tax) or doing the same with investment assets (the tax on excessive PII).

REFOCUS ON THE BIG PICTURE

CONVERTING A C CORPORATION TO AN S CORPORATION

As long as Fowle, Inc., is a C corporation, David cannot deduct on his individual tax return the losses the business incurs. However, the corporation can carry any net operating losses (NOLs) back and claim refunds for prior taxes paid and carry any remaining NOLs forward to reduce taxes paid if the company becomes profitable again.

If David wants to deduct the losses on his individual return, the corporation should make an S election or possibly become an LLC. Assuming that Fowle meets the one class of stock requirement, an S election may be appropriate. The election should be made before any losses are incurred because any regular corporate NOLs do not flow through to an S shareholder.

Fowle should make a timely election on Form 2553, and David must consent to the election in writing. For the S election to be effective this year, it should be made on or before the fifteenth day of the third month of the current year.

The S corporation's tax-exempt interest income flows through to David. The entity may want to reconsider its salary and fringe benefits levels for David, so as to minimize the creation of a payroll tax burden, and to manage the restrictions on deductions for fringe benefits provided to an S shareholder. Fowle's tax-exempt interest can be distributed to David tax-free only after all of the entity's AEP has been accounted for.

What If?

What if David expects the loss years to be followed by increased profitability as the company shifts some of its manufacturing to other countries with cheaper labor and material costs? In this case, David expects that the corporation will make significant distributions to him. How might this affect David's decision about whether the corporation should make an S election?

David should be aware of several rules that may result in income tax being paid by the S corporation or by him as the shareholder. First, distributions from an S corporation may be treated as taxable dividends to a shareholder to the extent the S corporation has earnings and profits dating to its years as a C corporation. While distributions are deemed to be made first from accumulated net S corporation earnings (i.e., the balance in AAA), distributions in excess of that amount may be treated as a taxable dividend, being paid from AEP (accumulated E & P).

continued

In addition, David should be aware that an S corporation that has been a C corporation in the past may be required to pay a built-in gains tax or LIFO recapture tax. The base for the built-in gains tax includes any unrealized gain on appreciated assets held by Fowle, Inc., on the day the company becomes an S corporation. The Federal corporate income tax rate is applied to the unrealized gains when any of the assets are sold within a specified number of years. If Fowle uses the LIFO inventory method, any LIFO recapture amount at the time of the S election also is subject to a corporate-level tax.

Suggested Readings

"Benefits of Using an S Corporation for Trading," **forbes.com**, May 13, 2014.

"Forming an S Corporation to Reduce Self-Employment Taxes," **www.mymoneyblog.com**.

John R. Cooper, "Appraisal Considerations in C to S Conversions," *Practical Tax Strategies*, November 2015.

Tony Nitti, "S Corporation Shareholder Compensation: How Much Is Enough?" *The Tax Adviser*, August 2011.

Ryan H. Pace, "Debunking the Notion That S Corporations Are Taxed 'Just Like' Partnerships," *Business Entities*, July/August 2007.

Key Terms

AAA bypass election, 15-17

Accumulated adjustments account (AAA), 15-16

Built-in gains tax, 15-27

Other adjustments account (OAA), 15-16

Passive investment income (PII), 15-8

Qualified business income deduction (QBID), 15-12

S corporation, 15-2

Small business corporation, 15-3

Subchapter S, 15-2

Voluntary revocation, 15-7

Computational Exercises

1. **LO.4** Dion, an S shareholder, owned 20% of MeadowBrook's stock for 292 days and 25% for the remaining 73 days in the year. Using the per-day allocation method, compute Dion's share of the following S corporation items.

	Schedule K Totals	Dion's Schedule K–1 Totals
Ordinary income	$60,000	_____
Tax-exempt interest	1,000	_____
Charitable contributions	3,400	_____

2. **LO.4, 6** Greiner, Inc., a calendar year S corporation, holds no AEP. During the year, Chad, an individual shareholder, receives a $30,000 cash distribution from Greiner. Prior to the distribution, Chad's basis in his Greiner stock is $25,000.

   a.   Determine Chad's ordinary income and capital gain, if any, from the distribution.

   b.   What is the basis of Chad's Greiner stock after accounting for the distribution?

3. **LO.5, 6** Holbrook, a calendar year S corporation, distributes $15,000 cash to its only shareholder, Cody, on December 31. Cody's basis in his stock is $20,000, Holbrook's AAA balance is $8,000, and Holbrook holds $2,500 AEP before the distribution. Complete the chart below.

	Distribution from Account	Effect on Stock Basis	Balance after Distribution
From AAA account			
From AEP account			
From Cody's stock basis			

4. **LO.5** Ten years ago, Vogel, Inc., an S corporation, purchased a plot of investment land for $45,000. This year, Vogel distributed the land, now worth $120,000, to Jamari, its majority shareholder.

   a. Determine the effects of the distribution on the gross income of Vogel and Jamari and on Vogel's AAA balance.

   b. How would your responses change if the land had been purchased for $120,000 and now was worth $45,000?

5. **LO.7** Kaiwan, Inc., a calendar year S corporation, is partly owned by Sharrod, whose beginning stock basis is $32,000. During the year, Sharrod's share of a Kaiwan long-term capital gain (LTCG) is $5,000, and his share of an ordinary loss is $18,000. Sharrod then receives a $20,000 cash distribution. Compute the following.

   a. Sharrod's deductible loss.

   b. Sharrod's suspended loss.

   c. Sharrod's new basis in the Kaiwan stock.

Problems

6. **LO.2** Which of the following can be a shareholder of an S corporation?

   a. Resident alien.

   b. Partnership.

   c. IRA.

   d. C corporation.

7. **LO.2** Isaac and 121 of his close friends want to form an S corporation. Isaac reasons that if he and his friends form a partnership, the partnership then can establish an S corporation and act as a single shareholder, thereby avoiding the 100 shareholder rule. Will Isaac's plan work? Why or why not?

8. **LO.2** Joey lives in North Carolina, a common law state. He is a shareholder in an S corporation. If he marries a nonresident alien, will the S election terminate? Would your answer change if he lived in Louisiana? Explain.

9. **LO.3** On March 2, 2018, the two 50% shareholders of a calendar year corporation decide to elect S status. One of the shareholders, Terry, purchased her stock from a previous shareholder (a nonresident alien) on January 18, 2018. Identify any potential problems for Terry or the corporation.   *Critical Thinking*

10. **LO.5, 6** Scott Tierney owns 21% of an S corporation. He is confused with respect to the amounts of the corporate AAA and his stock basis. Write a memo to the tax research file, identifying the key differences between AAA and an S shareholder's stock basis.   *Communications*

11. **LO.6** For each of the following independent statements, indicate whether the transaction will increase (+), decrease (−), or have no effect (*NE*) on the basis of a shareholder's stock in an S corporation.

   a. Expenses related to tax-exempt income.

   b. Short-term capital gain.

   c. Nonseparately computed loss.

   d. Section 1231 gain.

   e. Depletion *not* in excess of basis.

   f. Separately computed income.

   g. Nontaxable return-of-capital distribution by the corporation.

   h. Advertising expenses.

   i. Business gifts in excess of $25.

   j. Depreciation recapture income.

   k. Dividends received by the S corporation from an investment in ExxonMobil stock.

   l. LIFO recapture tax paid.

   m. Long-term capital loss.

   n. Cash distribution to shareholder out of AAA.

Critical Thinking 12. **LO.6, 7** Junie's share of her S corporation's net operating loss is $50,000, but her stock basis is only $30,000. Point out the Federal income tax consequences that Junie must face.

13. **LO.5, 6** Mary is a shareholder in CarrollCo, a calendar year S corporation. At the beginning of the year, her stock basis is $10,000, her share of the AAA is $2,000, and her share of corporate AEP is $6,000. At the end of the year, Mary receives a $6,000 cash distribution from CarrollCo.

   Mary's share of S corporation items includes a $2,000 long-term capital gain and a $10,000 ordinary loss. Determine the effects of these events on Mary's share of CarrollCo's AAA, on CarrollCo's AEP, and on Mary's stock basis.

14. **LO.4** The profit and loss statement of Kitsch Ltd., an S corporation, shows $100,000 book income. Kitsch is owned equally by four shareholders. From supplemental data, you obtain the following information about items that are included in book income.

Selling expenses	($21,200)
Tax-exempt interest income	3,000
Dividends received	9,000
§ 1231 gain	7,000
Depreciation recapture income	11,000
Net income from passive real estate rentals	5,000
Long-term capital loss	(6,000)
Salary paid to owners (each)	(12,000)
Cost of goods sold	(91,000)

   a. Compute Kitsch's nonseparately stated income or loss for the tax year.

   b. What would be the share of this year's nonseparately stated income or loss items for James Billings, one of the Kitsch shareholders?

15. **LO.4** Maul, Inc., a calendar year S corporation, incurred the following items.

Tax-exempt interest income	$ 7,000
Sales	140,000
Depreciation recapture income	12,000
Long-term capital gain	20,000
§ 1231 gain	7,000
Cost of goods sold	(42,000)
Administrative expenses	(15,000)
Depreciation expense (MACRS)	(17,000)
Charitable contributions	(7,000)

a.   Calculate Maul's nonseparately computed income or loss.

b.   If Carl is a 40% shareholder of Maul, what is Carl's share of Maul's long-term capital gain?

16. **LO.4** Zebra, Inc., a calendar year S corporation, incurred the following items this year. Sammy is a 40% Zebra shareholder throughout the year.

Operating income	$100,000
Cost of goods sold	(40,000)
Depreciation expense (MACRS)	(10,000)
Administrative expenses	(5,000)
§ 1231 gain	21,000
Depreciation recapture income	25,000
Short-term capital loss from stock sale	(6,000)
Long-term capital loss from stock sale	(4,000)
Long-term capital gain from stock sale	15,000
Charitable contributions	(4,500)

a.   Calculate Sammy's share of Zebra's nonseparately computed income or loss.

b.   Calculate Sammy's share of any Zebra long-term capital gain, if any.

17. **LO.4** On January 1, Bobby and Alicia own equally all of the stock of an electing S corporation called Prairie Dirt Delight. The company has a $60,000 loss for the year (not a leap year). On the 219th day of the year, Bobby sells his half of the stock to his son, Bubba. How much of the $60,000 loss, if any, is allocated to Bubba?

18. **LO.4, 5** McLin, Inc., a calendar year S corporation, holds $90,000 of AEP. Tobias, the sole McLin shareholder, has an $80,000 basis in his stock with a zero balance in the AAA.   **Decision Making**

a.   Determine the tax aspects if a $90,000 salary is paid to Tobias. Ignore the QBI deduction.

b.   Same as part (a), except that Tobias receives a cash distribution of $90,000 from AEP.

19. **LO.4, 5** Tiger, Inc., a calendar year S corporation, is owned equally by four shareholders: Ann, Becky, Chris, and David. Tiger owns investment land that was purchased for $160,000 four years ago. On September 14, when the land is worth $240,000, it is distributed to David. Assuming that David's basis in his S corporation stock is $270,000 on the distribution date, discuss any Federal income tax ramifications. Ignore the QBI deduction.

20. **LO.4, 5, 6** Spence, Inc., a calendar year S corporation, generates an ordinary loss   **Communications** of $110,000 and makes a distribution of $140,000 to its sole shareholder, Storm Nelson. Nelson's stock basis and AAA at the beginning of the year both total $200,000. Write a memo to your senior manager, Aaron McMullin, discussing the tax treatment of Spence's activities.

21. **LO.5** Polly has been the sole shareholder of a calendar year S corporation since its inception. Polly's stock basis is $15,500, and she receives a distribution of $19,000. Corporate-level accounts indicate a $6,000 balance in AAA and a $500 balance in AEP. How is Polly taxed on the distribution? What is her stock basis after the distribution?

Communications   22. **LO.4, 7** Sweetie, a calendar year S corporation, reports an ordinary loss of $80,000 and a capital loss of $20,000. Mei Freiberg owns 30% of the corporate stock and holds a $24,000 basis in the stock. Determine the amounts of the ordinary loss and capital loss, if any, that flow through to Freiberg. Prepare a memo for the tax research files explaining your computations.

23. **LO.4, 5, 6** Valence Corporation's Form 1120S shows ordinary income of $88,000 for the year. Daniel owns 40% of the Valence stock throughout the year. The following information is obtained from the corporate records.

Salary paid to Daniel	($40,000)
Tax-exempt interest income	5,000
Charitable contributions	(6,000)
Dividends received from a non-U.S. corporation	5,000
Long-term capital loss	(6,000)
Depreciation recapture income	11,000
Refund of prior-year state income taxes	5,000
Cost of goods sold	(80,000)
Short-term capital loss	(7,000)
Administrative expenses	(18,000)
Short-term capital gain	14,000
Selling expenses	(11,000)
Daniel's beginning stock basis	32,000
Daniel's additional stock purchases	9,000
Beginning AAA	45,000
Daniel's loan to corporation	20,000

a. Compute Valence's book income or loss.
b. Compute Daniel's ending stock basis.
c. Calculate ending corporate AAA.

24. **LO.5** If the beginning balance in Swan, Inc.'s OAA is $6,700 and the following transactions occur, what is Swan's ending OAA balance?

Depreciation recapture income	$ 21,600
Payroll tax penalty	(4,200)
Tax-exempt interest income	4,012
Nontaxable life insurance proceeds	100,000
Life insurance premiums paid (nondeductible)	(3,007)

25. **LO.5, 6** Cougar, Inc., is a calendar year S corporation. Cougar's Form 1120S shows nonseparately stated ordinary income of $80,000 for the year. Johnny owns 40% of the Cougar stock throughout the year. The following information is obtained from Cougar's corporate records.

Tax-exempt interest income	$ 3,000
Salary paid to Johnny	(52,000)
Charitable contributions	(6,000)
Dividends received from a non-U.S. corporation	5,000
Short-term capital loss	(6,000)
Depreciation recapture income	11,000
Refund of prior state income taxes	5,000
Cost of goods sold	(72,000)

Long-term capital loss	($ 7,000)
Administrative expenses	(18,000)
Long-term capital gain	14,000
Selling expenses	(11,000)
Johnny's beginning stock basis	32,000
Johnny's additional stock purchases	9,000
Beginning AAA	31,000
Johnny's loan to corporation	20,000

a. Compute Cougar's book income or loss.

b. Compute Johnny's ending stock basis.

c. Calculate Cougar's ending AAA balance.

26. **LO.6** Maple, Inc., is an S corporation with a single shareholder, Bob Maple. Bob   *Critical Thinking*
believes that his stock basis in the entity is $50,000, but he has lost some of
the records to substantiate this amount. Maple reports an ordinary loss for the year
of $80,000. What are the Federal income tax aspects to consider?

27. **LO.6, 7** Orange, Inc., a calendar year corporation in Clemson, South Carolina, elects   *Critical Thinking*
S corporation status for 2018. The company generated a $74,000 NOL in
2017 and another NOL of $43,000 in 2018.

Orange stock always is owned by the same four shareholders, each owning 25%
of the stock. Pete, one of the shareholders, holds a $6,020 basis in this Orange stock
at the beginning of 2018. Identify the Federal income tax issues that Pete faces.

28. **LO.7** Samuel Reese sold 1,000 shares of his stock in Maroon, Inc., an S corporation.   *Critical Thinking*
He sold the stock for $15,700 after he had owned it for six years. Samuel had
paid $141,250 for the stock, which was issued under § 1244. Samuel is married and
separately owns the 1,000 shares. Determine the appropriate Federal income tax
treatment of any gain or loss on the stock sale.

29. **LO.7** Blue is the owner of all of the shares of Blue Bell, an S corporation. Blue is   *Critical Thinking*
considering receiving a salary of $110,000 from the business. She will pay the   *Decision Making*
7.65% FICA taxes on the salary, and the S corporation will pay the same amount of
FICA tax. If Blue reduces her salary to $50,000 and takes an additional $60,000 as a
cash distribution from AAA, how would her Federal income tax liabilities change?

30. **LO.1** One of your clients, Texas, Inc., is considering electing S status. Both of   *Critical Thinking*
Texas's equal shareholders paid $30,000 for their stock. As of the beginning   *Decision Making*
of 2018, Texas's Subchapter C NOL carryforward is $110,000. Its taxable income
projections for the next few years are as follows. Will you counsel Texas to make
the S election in 2018? Explain.

2018	$40,000
2019	25,000
2020	25,000
2021	25,000

31. **LO.6, 7** C&C Properties is an S corporation that owns two rental real estate   *Critical Thinking*
undertakings: Carrot Plaza and Cantaloupe Place. Each property produces
an annual $10,000 operating loss. C&C's Schedule K aggregates the results of the
two locations into one number.

Dan and Marta, C&C's two equal shareholders, each hold a $7,000 stock basis in
C&C as of the beginning of the year. Marta actively participates in the Cantaloupe
location, but not at Carrot. Dan actively participates at neither location. Determine
the amount of the available loss pass-throughs for both shareholders.

Comprehensive Tax Return Problem

1. John Parsons (123-45-6781) and George Smith (123-45-6782) are 70% and 30% owners, respectively, of Premium, Inc. (11-1111111), a candy company located at 1005 16th Street, Cut and Shoot, TX 77303. Premium's S election was made on January 15, 2010, its date of incorporation. The following information was taken from the company's 2017 income statement. Premium's book income for the year was $704,574.

Interest income	$ 100,000
Gross sales receipts	2,410,000
Beginning inventory	9,607
Direct labor	(203,102)
Direct materials purchased	(278,143)
Direct other costs	(249,356)
Ending inventory	3,467
Salaries and wages	(442,103)
Officers' salaries ($75,000 each to Parsons and Smith)	(150,000)
Repairs	(206,106)
Depreciation expense, tax and book	(15,254)
Interest expense	(35,222)
Rent expense (operating)	(40,000)
Taxes	(65,101)
Charitable contributions (cash)	(20,000)
Advertising expenses	(20,000)
Payroll penalties	(15,000)
Other deductions	(59,899)

A 2017 comparative balance sheet appears below.

	January 1	December 31
Cash	$ 47,840	$?
Accounts receivable	93,100	123,104
Inventories	9,607	3,467
Prepaid expenses	8,333	17,582
Building and equipment	138,203	185,348
Accumulated depreciation	(84,235)	(?)
Land	2,000	2,000
Total assets	$214,848	$844,422
Accounts payable	$ 42,500	$ 72,300
Notes payable (less than 1 year)	4,500	2,100
Notes payable (more than 1 year)	26,700	24,300
Capital stock	30,000	30,000
Retained earnings	111,148	?
Total liabilities and capital	$214,848	$844,422

Premium's accounting firm provides the following additional information.

Cash distributions to shareholders	$100,000
Beginning balance, accumulated adjustments account	$111,148

Using the preceding information, prepare a Form 1120S and Schedule K–1s for John Parsons and George Smith, both of whom live at 5607 20th Street, Cut and Shoot, TX 77303. Do not complete Forms 1125-A, 1125-E, and 4562. If any information is missing, make realistic assumptions.

BRIDGE DISCIPLINE

1. Using an online research service, determine whether your state:
   a. Allows flow-through treatment for Federal S corporations.
   b. Requires any state-specific form to elect or elect out of S treatment at the state level.
   c. Places any additional withholding tax burdens on out-of-state U.S. shareholders or on non-U.S. shareholders of an S corporation.
   d. Requires any additional information disclosures or compliance deadlines for S corporations operating in the state *other than* to the revenue department (e.g., a report that must be filed with the secretary of state).
   e. Accepts "composite" or "block" income tax returns.

2. Using no more than five slides, at least two of which include a chart or graphic to illustrate your observations, prepare a presentation for your fellow students at the annual Pay It Forward conference at the university student union. In your talk, discuss the societal implications of the rule that excludes from the self-employment tax any flow-through income (other than salary and wages) that is assigned to a shareholder in an S corporation, while taxing that of the owners of a partnership or an LLC.

Communications

Research Problems

Note: Solutions to the Research Problems can be prepared by using the Thomson Reuters Checkpoint™ online tax research database, which accompanies this textbook. Solutions can also be prepared by using research materials found in a typical tax library.

THOMSON REUTERS
CHECKPOINT™

Research Problem 1. Alice owns 100% of Medical Data, a C corporation, and 100% of Your Realtors, an S corporation. She worked full-time for Medical Data (i.e., she materially participated in the entity), but Alice did not materially participate in Your Realtors. For several tax years, Your Realtors leased real estate to Medical Data.

Decision Making

Alice reported these rental amounts as passive activity income on her Schedule E, and she offset that income against passive activity losses from other entities. The IRS reclassified this rental income as nonpassive income under Reg. § 1.469–2(f)(6). Who is right? Does § 469 apply to S corporations? Elaborate.

Research Problem 2. Sean Moon is president, secretary, treasurer, sole director, and sole shareholder of Streetz, an S corporation real estate company. He manages all aspects of the company's operations, and he is the only person working at the company that holds a real estate broker's license. Sean works 12-hour days and takes few days off. Corporate records indicate the following.

Year	Gross Receipts	Net Income
2017	$376,453	$122,605
2018	405,244	161,660
2019	518,189	231,454

Sean and his wife, Kim, filed joint Federal income tax returns, but they did not report any wages or salaries on their returns. During 2019, Sean transferred $240,000 from Streetz to his personal account.

You are an expert witness for the IRS. Identify the items that you would present to the U.S. Tax Court with respect to the amount of Sean's compensation that is subject to employment taxes and any other taxes due for 2019 (especially the additional Medicare net investment income tax). *Hint*: This is a reasonable compensation issue.

Use internet tax resources to address the following questions. Look for reliable web-sites and blogs of the IRS and other government agencies, media outlets, businesses, tax professionals, academics, think tanks, and political outlets.

Communications   **Research Problem 3.** Prepare a graph of the growth in the number of S corporation returns filed. Obtain data for these years: 1980, 1985, 1990, 1995, 2000, 2005, and 2010. In a note to your instructor, explain the trends that you found in S returns filed.

Communications   **Research Problem 4.** Summarize the trends in court decisions concerning salaries paid to shareholders of small S corporations. Title your essay "S Corporation Salaries: Too Much or Too Little?" Send your essay in an e-mail to your instructor.

Becker CPA Review Questions

1. Village Corp., a calendar year corporation, began business in year 1. Village made a valid S corporation election on December 5, year 4, with the unanimous consent of its shareholders. The eligibility requirements for S status continued to be met throughout year 5. On what date did Village's S status become effective?

    a. January 1, year 4
    b. January 1, year 5
    c. December 5, year 4
    d. December 5, year 5

2. Fox Corp., an S corporation, had an ordinary loss of $36,500 for the year ended December 31, year 2. At January 1, year 2, Duffy owned 50% of Fox's stock. Duffy held the stock for 40 days in year 2 before selling the entire 50% interest to an unrelated third party. Duffy's basis for the stock was $10,000. Duffy was a full-time employee of Fox until the stock was sold. Duffy's share of Fox's loss was:

    a. $0
    b. $2,000
    c. $10,000
    d. $18,250

3. An S corporation has 30,000 shares of voting common stock and 20,000 shares of nonvoting common stock issued and outstanding. The S election can be revoked vol-untarily with the consent of the shareholders holding, on the day of the revocation, the following number of outstanding shares.

	Shares of Voting Stock	Shares of Nonvoting Stock
a.	0	20,000
b.	7,500	5,000
c.	10,000	16,000
d.	20,000	0

4. The Haas Corp., a calendar year S corporation, has two equal shareholders. For the year ended December 31, year 6, Haas had net income of $60,000, which included $50,000 from operations and $10,000 from investment interest income. There were no other transactions that year. Each shareholder's basis in the stock of Haas will increase by:

    a. $50,000
    b. $30,000
    c. $25,000
    d. $0

5. Zinco Corp. was a calendar year S corporation. Zinco's S status terminated on April 1, year 6, when Case Corp. became a shareholder. During year 6 (365-day calendar year), Zinco had nonseparately computed income of $310,250. If no election was made by Zinco, what amount of the income, if any, was allocated to the S short year for year 6?

    a. $233,750

    b. $155,125

    c. $76,500

    d. $0

6. The Matthew Corporation, an S corporation, is equally owned by three shareholders—Emily, Alejandra, and Kristina. The corporation is on the calendar year basis for tax and financial purposes. On April 1 of the current year, Emily sold her one-third interest in the Matthew Corporation equally to the other two shareholders. For the current year, the corporation had nonseparately stated ordinary income of $900,000. For the current year, how much ordinary income should be allocated to Kristina on her Schedule K–1?

    a. $25,000

    b. $75,000

    c. $337,500

    d. $412,500

7. After a corporation's status as an S corporation is revoked or terminated, how many years is the corporation required to wait before making a new S election, in the absence of IRS consent to an earlier election?

    a. 1

    b. 3

    c. 5

    d. 10

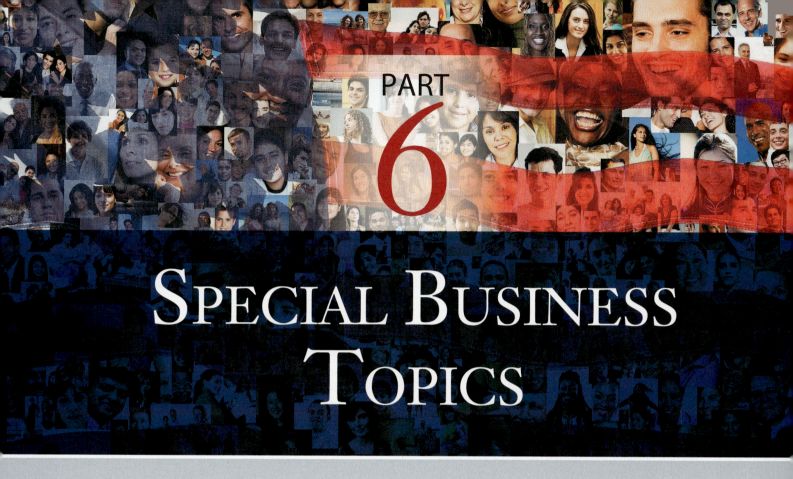

PART 6

SPECIAL BUSINESS TOPICS

CHAPTER **16**
Multijurisdictional Taxation

CHAPTER **17**
Business Tax Credits and the Alternative Minimum Tax

CHAPTER **18**
Comparative Forms of Doing Business

Part 6 covers several topics that are relevant to all types of taxpayers. Business entities operate in both the international and state arenas. Therefore, multijurisdictional taxation is addressed from the perspective of both a multinational business and a multistate business. A review then follows of tax credits allowed to reduce the Federal income tax liability on business income and the application of the AMT to individual taxpayers. Part 6 concludes with a comparative analysis of the different types of business entities discussed throughout the text.

Multijurisdictional Taxation

LEARNING OBJECTIVES: *After completing Chapter 16, you should be able to:*

LO.1 Discuss the computational and compliance issues that arise when a taxpayer operates in more than one taxing jurisdiction.

LO.2 Identify the sources of tax law applicable to a taxpayer operating in more than one country.

LO.3 Outline the U.S. tax effects related to the offshore operations of a U.S. taxpayer.

LO.4 Describe the tax effects related to the U.S. operations of a non-U.S. taxpayer.

LO.5 Identify the sources of tax law applicable to a taxpayer operating in more than one U.S. state.

LO.6 Apply principles designed to compute state taxable income for a taxpayer operating in more than one U.S. state.

LO.7 Synthesize key aspects of international and multistate tax systems to identify common rules and issues taxpayers face in both systems.

CHAPTER OUTLINE

16-1 The Multijurisdictional Taxpayer, 16-2

16-2 U.S. Taxation of Multinational Transactions, 16-2
16-2a Sources of Law, 16-4
16-2b Tax Issues, 16-5

16-3 Crossing State Lines: State and Local Income Taxation in the United States, 16-17
16-3a Sources of Law, 16-18
16-3b Tax Issues, 16-19

16-4 Common Challenges, 16-25
16-4a Authority to Tax, 16-25
16-4b Division of Income, 16-26
16-4c Transfer Pricing, 16-26
16-4d Tax Havens, 16-27
16-4e Interjurisdictional Agreements, 16-28

TAX TALK *Don't tax you, don't tax me; tax the fellow behind the tree.* —U.S. SEN. RUSSELL B. LONG

Don't tax you, don't tax me; tax the companies across the sea. —U.S. REP. DAN ROSTENKOWSKI

THE BIG PICTURE

GOING INTERNATIONAL

VoiceCo, a domestic corporation, designs, manufactures, and sells specialty microphones for use in theaters. All of its activities take place in Florida, although it ships products to customers all over the United States. When it received inquiries about its products from foreign customers, VoiceCo decided to test the foreign market and placed ads in foreign trade journals. Soon it was taking orders from non-U.S. customers.

VoiceCo is concerned about its potential foreign income tax exposure. Although it has no assets or employees in the foreign jurisdictions, it now is involved in international commerce. Is VoiceCo subject to income taxes in foreign countries? Must it pay U.S. income taxes on the profits from its foreign sales? What if VoiceCo pays taxes to other countries? Does it receive any benefit from these payments on its U.S. tax return?

Later, VoiceCo established a manufacturing plant in Ireland to meet the European demand for its products. VoiceCo incorporated the Irish operation as a controlled foreign corporation (CFC) named VoiceCo-Ireland. How does U.S. corporate income tax law affect these events?

Read the chapter and formulate your response.

One of the tax planning principles that has been discussed throughout this text relates to the use of favorable tax jurisdictions—moving income into lower-taxed districts and deductions into higher-taxed ones. Many individuals dream of moving all of their income and wealth to a tax-friendly state or a proverbial island in the tropics, never to be taxed again. This chapter examines the temptations that attract taxpayers to this idea and various ways in which this goal can and cannot be accomplished.

16-1 THE MULTIJURISDICTIONAL TAXPAYER

LO.1

Discuss the computational and compliance issues that arise when a taxpayer operates in more than one taxing jurisdiction.

Companies large and small must deal with the consequences of earning income through activities in different jurisdictions. A small business may have its center of operations in a single city but have customers in many states and countries. Consider the typical U.S. multinational corporation. Its assets, employees, customers, suppliers, lenders, and owners are located in numerous locations, crossing city, county, state, national, and "virtual" borders.

EXAMPLE 1

RobotCo, a corporation created and organized in Delaware, produces and sells robotic manufacturing equipment for the auto industry. It holds its valuable patents and intangible property in Delaware and Bermuda. The company has manufacturing operations in Ireland, Singapore, Germany, Texas, and New Jersey. It operates distribution centers in Canada, the United Kingdom, Germany, Hong Kong, Texas, New Jersey, Georgia, California, Illinois, and Arizona. RobotCo's sales force spends time in Europe, Asia, Mexico, Canada, and almost every state in the union. RobotCo's engineers likewise provide technical service to customers wherever they may be located. RobotCo also maintains a substantial web presence.

RobotCo must determine its potential exposure to tax in each of these jurisdictions. Such exposure usually is based on RobotCo's nexus (or economic connection) to the various locations. Unfortunately for all concerned, each of these taxing jurisdictions uses a different taxing system and methods, imposes taxes under differing structures, and even defines the tax base differently. How does RobotCo divide its income among the various jurisdictions that want a piece of its tax dollars, determine its tax costs, mitigate any potential double taxation, and file the appropriate returns with this diverse set of taxing authorities? Such questions and more must be addressed by modern-day businesses.

Thousands of state and local jurisdictions are involved in the taxation of interstate transactions through income, property, sales, or other taxes. State and local taxes make up over one-third of all taxes collected in the United States. Global trade also represents a major portion of the U.S. economy. In a recent year, U.S. exports of goods and services amounted to $2.2 trillion, with imports reaching $2.7 trillion. Hundreds of countries and many more political subdivisions participated in the taxation of these transactions. These interstate and international trade flows, along with cross-state and cross-country investments, create significant Federal, state, and local tax consequences for both U.S. and foreign entities.

16-2 U.S. TAXATION OF MULTINATIONAL TRANSACTIONS

Cross-border transactions create the need for special tax considerations for both the United States and its trading partners. From a U.S. perspective, international tax laws should promote the global competitiveness of U.S. enterprises and at the same time protect the tax revenue base of the United States. These two objectives sometimes conflict, however. The need to deal with both objectives contributes to the complexity of the rules governing the U.S. taxation of cross-border transactions.

BRIDGE DISCIPLINE **Bridge to International Law**

Many provisions of the U.S. tax law relating to international transactions are thinly disguised extensions of a principle of international law—the ability of sovereign countries to protect the safety and privacy of their citizens abroad.

For instance, U.S. tax auditors often have difficulty obtaining or reviewing the documentation supporting deductions claimed by U.S. taxpayers operating overseas. Banking, credit card, and other records that are available (in the course of business or forcibly by summons) for strictly U.S. transactions are not available once those same transactions cross national borders.

How could the U.S. tax base include rental and royalty income of a U.S. investor operating through a corporation in another country when property ownership and taxation records are not available for substantiation or audit outside the country of the investment? Perhaps this explains why the U.S. tax base typically excludes such items.

Conversely, when the taxing agencies of multiple countries are allowed by law to trade among themselves information about business operations and taxpayers, the fairness and completeness of the taxing process may improve. But such lengthening of the reach of the taxing authorities results from diplomatic negotiations among the countries, not from the passage of legislation.

U.S. persons engage in activities outside the United States for many different reasons. Consider two U.S. corporations that have established sales subsidiaries in foreign countries. Dedalus, Inc., operates in Germany, a high-tax country, because customers demand local attention from sales agents. Mulligan, Inc., operates in the Cayman Islands, a tax haven country, simply to shift income outside the United States. U.S. tax law must fairly address both situations with the same law.

EXAMPLE 2

U.S. multinational taxpayers—and tax professionals—must understand the Federal tax rules related to international business, so that the effects of these rules can be incorporated into their overall tax plans. Generally, this involves reducing the exposure to double taxation of business profits, locating cash and other assets where they will be the most productive, and decreasing the present value of tax liabilities (for example, by accelerating losses and deductions, deferring taxable income recognition, and taking advantage of favorable tax rules where possible).

U.S. international tax provisions are concerned primarily with two types of potential taxpayers: U.S. persons earning income from outside the United States, and non-U.S. persons earning income from inside the United States.[1] U.S. persons earning income only from within the country do not create any international tax issues and are taxed under the purely domestic provisions of the Internal Revenue Code. Non-U.S. persons earning income from outside the United States are not within the taxing jurisdiction of the United States (unless this income is somehow directly connected to U.S. operations).

The U.S. taxation of international transactions can be organized in terms of "outbound" and "inbound" taxation. **Outbound taxation** refers to the U.S. taxation of foreign-source income earned by U.S. taxpayers. **Inbound taxation** refers to the U.S. taxation of U.S.-source income earned by foreign taxpayers. Exhibit 16.1 illustrates these concepts.

U.S. taxpayers often "internationalize" gradually over time. A U.S. business may operate on a strictly domestic basis for several years, then explore offshore markets by exporting its products abroad, and later license its products to a foreign manufacturer or enter into a joint venture with a foreign partner. If its forays into non-U.S. markets are successful, the U.S. business may create a foreign subsidiary and move a portion of its operations abroad by establishing a sales or manufacturing facility.

---

[1]The term *person* includes an individual, corporation, partnership, trust, estate, or association. § 7701(a)(1). The terms *domestic* and *foreign* are defined in §§ 7701(a)(4) and (5).

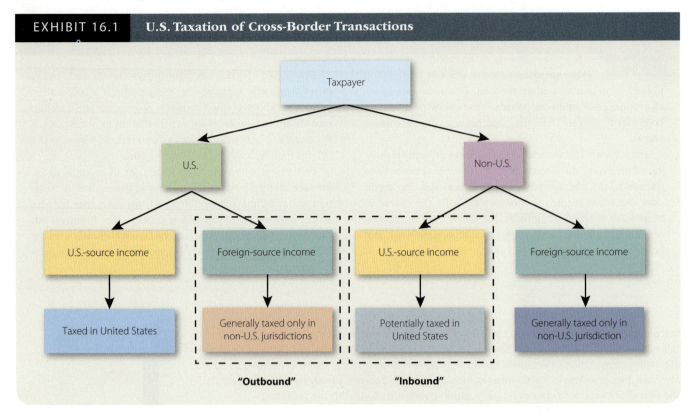

EXHIBIT 16.1 **U.S. Taxation of Cross-Border Transactions**

Both U.S. and offshore entities generally move into international markets in this manner. In this timeline, each step generates increasingly significant international income tax consequences. Exhibit 16.2 shows a typical timeline for "going global."

 DIGGING DEEPER 1   In-depth coverage can be found on this book's companion website: **www.cengage.com**

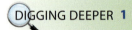

Identify the sources of tax law applicable to a taxpayer operating in more than one country.

16-2a Sources of Law

U.S. individuals and companies operating across national borders are subject to the laws of every jurisdiction in which they operate or invest. Accordingly, the source of law depends on the nature of a taxpayer's connection with a particular country.

For U.S. persons, the Internal Revenue Code addresses the tax consequences of earning income anywhere in the world. However, U.S. persons also must comply with the local tax law of the other nations in which they operate.

EXHIBIT 16.2 **Global Activities Timeline**

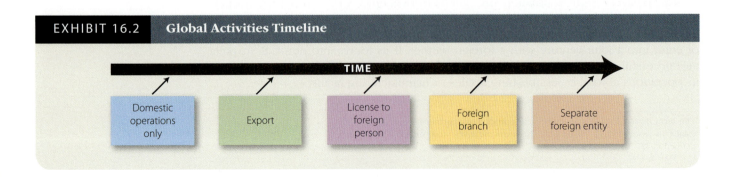

For non-U.S. persons, U.S. statutory law is relevant to income they earn that is connected to U.S. income-producing activities, whether those activities involve a passive investment or an active trade or business. Whether non-U.S. persons also are subject to potential tax in their home countries on their U.S. income depends on their own local tax law.

It is difficult for the United States (or any country) to craft local tax laws that equitably address all of the potential issues that arise when two countries attempt to tax the same income. Furthermore, any uncertainty as to tax consequences can be an impediment to global business investment. Consequently, countries enter into **income tax treaties** with each other to provide more certainty to taxpayers.

Tax treaties are the result of specific negotiations with a treaty partner, so each treaty is unique. Nevertheless, all tax treaties are organized in the same way and address similar issues. For example, all treaties include provisions regarding the taxation of investment income, business profits from a **permanent establishment (PE)**, personal service income, and exceptions for certain persons (e.g., athletes, entertainers, students, and teachers).

Permanent establishment (PE) is an important concept that is defined in all income tax treaties. A person has a PE within a country when its activities within that country rise beyond a minimal level. Tax treaties outline the activities that create a PE, including an office, plant, or other fixed place of business. Treaties also specify certain activities that do not create a PE (e.g., a temporary construction project). Once a person has a PE within a country, the business profits associated with the PE become subject to tax in that country.

EXAMPLE 3

Amelia, Inc., a U.S. corporation, sells boating supplies to customers in the United States and Canada. Amelia has no assets in Canada. All Canadian sales transactions are conducted via the internet or telephone from Amelia's Florida office. Because Amelia does not have any assets in Canada or conduct any activities within Canada, it does not have a Canadian PE. Consequently, Canada does not impose an income tax on the profit associated with Amelia's Canadian sales. However, if Amelia opens a sales office in Canada, a PE will exist, and Canada will tax the profits associated with the PE.

Although the United States has entered into almost 70 income tax treaties, many jurisdictions where U.S. taxpayers operate are not covered by a treaty. Where there is no tax treaty, the more subjective test of whether a person is "engaged in a trade or business" within a country replaces the PE determination. Both the PE concept and the engaged in a trade or business concept are closely related to the determination of whether a person has *nexus* within a jurisdiction for state and local tax purposes (discussed later in this chapter).

16-2b Tax Issues

LO.3

Outline the U.S. tax effects related to the offshore operations of a U.S. taxpayer.

Authority to Tax

The United States taxes the *worldwide* income of U.S. taxpayers.[2] The United States claims the right to tax all of a U.S. person's income because of the protection of U.S. law provided to a person connected to the United States through citizenship, residency, or place of organization. Because non-U.S. governments also may tax some of the U.S. person's income when it is earned within the other country's borders, U.S. taxpayers may be subjected to double taxation.

There are two broad methods of taxing cross-border income. Under the *territorial* approach, a country simply exempts from tax the income derived from sources outside

---

[2]Gross income for a U.S. person includes all income from whatever source derived. "Source" in this context means not only type of income (e.g., wages or interest) but also geographic source (e.g., the United States or Belgium). § 61.

TAX FACT   U.S. Income Tax Treaties in Force

The United States has entered into income tax treaties with the following nations.

Armenia	France	Lithuania	South Africa
Australia	Georgia	Luxembourg	Spain
Austria	Germany	Malta	Sri Lanka
Azerbaijan	Greece	Mexico	Sweden
Bangladesh	Hungary	Moldova	Switzerland
Barbados	Iceland	Morocco	Tajikistan
Belarus	India	Netherlands	Thailand
Belgium	Indonesia	New Zealand	Trinidad
Bulgaria	Ireland	Norway	Tunisia
Canada	Israel	Pakistan	Turkey
China	Italy	Philippines	Turkmenistan
Cyprus	Jamaica	Poland	Ukraine
Czech Republic	Japan	Portugal	United Kingdom
Denmark	Kazakhstan	Romania	Uzbekistan
Egypt	Korea	Russia	Venezuela
Estonia	Kyrgyzstan	Slovak Republic	
Finland	Latvia	Slovenia	

its borders. Most European and Asian countries have adopted this approach.[3] The second approach is to tax the *worldwide* income of all domestic persons and then provide a **foreign tax credit (FTC)** against home country taxes for taxes paid to other countries on the same income. When the foreign tax credit is available, the United States allows its taxpayers to reduce their U.S. tax liability by some or all of the foreign income taxes paid on income earned outside the United States.

EXAMPLE 4

Gator Enterprises, Inc., a U.S. corporation, operates a manufacturing branch in Italy because of customer demand there, local availability of raw materials, and the high cost of shipping finished goods. This branch income is taxed in the United States as part of Gator's worldwide income, but it also is taxed in Italy. Without the availability of a foreign tax credit to mitigate this double taxation, Gator Enterprises would suffer an excessive tax burden and could not compete with local Italian companies.

The United States uses the territorial approach in taxing non-U.S. persons. Such inbound taxpayers generally are subject to tax only on income earned within U.S. borders.

EXAMPLE 5

Purdie, Ltd., a corporation based in the United Kingdom, operates in the United States. Although it is not a U.S. person, Purdie is taxed in the United States on its U.S.-source business income. If Purdie, Ltd., could operate free of U.S. tax, its U.S.-based competitors would face a serious disadvantage.

---

[3]In some cases, countries allow the territorial exemption from home country taxation only if the income has been subject to tax in another country. Other countries, however, exempt such income even if no source country tax is imposed.

The United States now offers a form of territorial taxation to U.S. corporations, as a political response designed to increase the competitiveness of U.S. businesses in the global marketplace. A 100% dividends received deduction is available when a non-U.S. subsidiary remits profits earned overseas to its U.S. parent as a dividend. Structurally, the worldwide taxation approach remains as the chief means by which U.S. persons are taxed on multinational income, but this deduction allows the U.S. corporation some movement toward a territorial system, and it encourages the repatriation of current earnings to the United States by many corporations.

Other pertinent changes enacted as part of the Tax Cuts and Jobs Act (TCJA) of 2017 were designed to:

- provide incentives for U.S. businesses to locate jobs in the United States, and to repatriate overseas profits to the United States, and
- prevent U.S. entities from shifting taxable income outside the United States into low-tax-rate countries.

Income Sourcing

Determining the source of net income is a critical component in calculating the U.S. tax consequences to both U.S. and foreign persons. The sourcing rules are used in computing the foreign tax credit (discussed later in the chapter) and in determining the Federal income tax base for non-U.S. persons.

A number of specific provisions contained in §§ 861 through 865 address the income-sourcing rules for all types of income, including interest, dividends, rents, royalties, services, and sales of assets. Generally, the sourcing rules assign income to a geographic source based on the location where the economic activity producing the income took place. In some cases, this relationship is clear, and in others, the connection is more obscure.

Sourcing Rules

Wickless, Inc., a U.S. corporation, provides scuba diving lessons to customers in Florida and in the Bahamas. These services are sourced based on the place where the activity is performed. The services performed in Florida are U.S.-source income, and those performed in the Bahamas are foreign-source income.

EXAMPLE 6

Brown, Inc., a U.S. corporation, receives dividend income from Takeda Corporation, a Japanese corporation, based on its ownership of Takeda common stock. Brown purchased the stock in the United States and receives all payments in the United States. At first glance, it appears that all of the activities related to earning the dividend income take place in the United States. Nevertheless, the dividend income is treated as foreign source because it is paid by a non-U.S. corporation.[4]

EXAMPLE 7

In addition to sourcing income, the U.S. rules require taxpayers to assign deductions to U.S.- or foreign-source categories. Deductions that are directly related to an activity or property first are allocated to classes of income to which they directly relate (e.g., sales, services, rentals). Then the deductions are apportioned between the U.S. and foreign groupings using a reasonable basis (e.g., revenue, gross profit, assets, units sold, time spent). If a deduction is not definitely related to any class of gross income, the deduction is first assigned to all classes of gross income and then apportioned between U.S.- and foreign-source income.

Many deductions may be allocated and apportioned based on any reasonable method the taxpayer chooses.[5] However, the U.S. tax rules impose a specific method for certain types of deductions, including interest and research and experimentation expenses. Interest expense is allocated and apportioned based on the theory that borrowed money can be raised and spent in any country, without being earmarked to any specific

---

[4]Section 861(a)(2) establishes that only dividends from domestic corporations are U.S.-source income.

[5]Reg. § 1.861–8.

TAX FACT   Where Do We Stand?

Drastic reductions in marginal business income tax rates have rippled through the world. Even perpetually high-tax countries such as Sweden and the United Kingdom have cut back marginal tax rate structures to remain competitive, and often they have changed the tax base to match similar revisions of the U.S. tax law.

As a result of this dramatic evolution in international tax rates, the average marginal business income tax rate in developed countries now lies between 25 and 30 percent, down from perhaps 50 percent in the 1960s. These numbers do not take into account, though, the dependence of many U.S. trading partners on transaction taxes, such as the value added tax and wealth-based taxes, which make difficult an apples-to-apples comparison of rates alone.

The provisions of the TCJA of 2017 made significant reductions in U.S. Federal tax rates, and the United States now may be seen as closer to the global average in corporate tax rates. As a result of the tax rate cut by the United States, though, other countries may continue to reduce their pertinent tax rates further below the worldwide average.

Top Statutory Corporate Income Tax Rates for Selected Countries	
Bermuda	0.0%
France	34.4%
Germany	30.0%
Ireland	12.5%
Japan	30.0%
Mexico	30.0%
Sweden	22.0%
United Kingdom	19.0%
United States, through 2017	39.0%
United States, after 2017	25.8%

Note: The above rates include additional taxes on corporate taxable income levied by states, cities, provinces, cantons, and other smaller jurisdictions. Deductions, exemptions, and credits can reduce an entity's effective tax rate below the top statutory rate.

location or use (i.e., it is *fungible*). For example, if a taxpayer borrows to support its manufacturing activity, this frees up other funds for use to support its investment activities, regardless of where the borrowing and spending actually occurred. Accordingly, interest expense is allocated and apportioned to all activities and property of the taxpayer. Taxpayers must allocate and apportion interest expense on the basis of asset location, using the tax book value of the assets.

The Big Picture

EXAMPLE 8

Return to the facts of *The Big Picture* on p. 16-1. Assume that VoiceCo makes an overseas investment and generates $2 million of gross income and a $50,000 expense, all related to its microphone manufacturing and sales. The expense is allocated and apportioned on the basis of gross income.

	Gross Income			Apportionment	
	Foreign	U.S.	Allocation	Foreign	U.S.
Sales	$1,000,000	$500,000	$37,500*	$25,000	$12,500**
Manufacturing	400,000	100,000	12,500	10,000	2,500***
Totals			$50,000	$35,000	$15,000

   * $50,000 × ($1,500,000/$2,000,000) = $37,500.
  ** $37,500 × ($500,000/$1,500,000) = $12,500.
*** $12,500 × ($100,000/$500,000) = $2,500.

If VoiceCo could show that $45,000 of the expense was directly related to its sales income, the $45,000 would be allocated directly to that class of gross income, with the remainder allocated and apportioned between U.S. and foreign sources ratably.

		Apportionment	
	Allocation	Foreign	U.S.
Sales	$45,000	$30,000	$15,000
Manufacturing	5,000	4,000	1,000
Totals	$50,000	$34,000	$16,000

TAX PLANNING STRATEGIES Sourcing Income from Sales of Inventory

FRAMEWORK FOCUS: TAX RATE

Strategy: Control the Character of Income and Deductions.

Generally, income from the sale of personal property is sourced according to the residence of the seller under § 865. Several important exceptions exist for inventory. Income from the sale of purchased inventory is sourced in the country in which the sale takes place under the "title passage" rule. This rule provides the taxpayer with flexibility regarding the sourcing of income and deductions, and it allows for the creation of zero-taxed foreign-source income.

USCo, a domestic corporation, purchases inventory for resale from unrelated parties and sells the inventory to customers in the United States and Brazil. If title on the Brazilian sales passes in the United States (i.e., risks of loss shift to the Brazilian customers at the shipping point), the inventory income is U.S. source. If title passes outside the United States (e.g., at the customer's warehouse in Brazil), the inventory income is foreign source.

Although the Code identifies the income item as foreign source, this income likely is not subject to any Brazilian tax because USCo has no employees, assets, or activities in Brazil. Although the income is subject to U.S. tax in either case (as it represents taxable income to a U.S. person), in the latter case, USCo has generated foreign-source income with no corresponding foreign income tax. This will prove useful in managing USCo's ability to use foreign tax credits, as discussed next.

When a taxpayer both produces and sells inventory, the income is sourced to the country of production.

The Big Picture

EXAMPLE 9

Return to the facts of *The Big Picture* on p. 16-1. Assume that VoiceCo makes an overseas investment and generates both U.S.-source and foreign-source gross income for the current year. VoiceCo's assets (measured at tax book value) are as follows.

Assets generating U.S.-source income	$18,000,000
Assets generating foreign-source income	5,000,000
Total VoiceCo assets	$23,000,000

VoiceCo incurs interest expense of $800,000 for the current year. Interest expense is apportioned to foreign-source income as follows.

$$\frac{\$5,000,000 \,(\text{foreign assets})}{\$23,000,000 \,(\text{total assets})} \times \$800,000 \,(\text{interest expense}) = \$173,913$$

Foreign Tax Credit

The United States retains the right to tax its citizens and residents on their worldwide taxable income. To reduce the possibility of double taxation, Congress created the foreign tax credit (FTC).

A qualified taxpayer is allowed a tax credit for foreign income taxes paid or accrued. All of the taxes paid by the taxpayer to various countries on its operations are combined to compute the FTC. The credit is a dollar-for-dollar reduction of U.S. income tax liability.

EXAMPLE 10

Caulkin Tools, Inc., a U.S. corporation, operates a branch operation in Largo from which it earns taxable income of $750,000 for the current year. Caulkin pays income tax of $100,000 on these earnings to the Largo tax authorities. Caulkin also includes the $750,000 in gross income for U.S. tax purposes.

Before considering the FTC, Caulkin owes $157,500 in U.S. income taxes on this foreign-source income. Thus, total taxes on the $750,000 could equal $257,500 ($100,000 + $157,500), a 34% effective rate.

But Caulkin takes an FTC of $100,000 against its U.S. tax liability on the foreign-source income. Caulkin's total taxes on the $750,000 now are $157,500 ($100,000 + $57,500), a 21% effective rate.

The FTC is elective for the tax year. Lacking an election to take the FTC, a deduction is claimed for foreign taxes paid or incurred. One cannot take a credit and a deduction for the same foreign income taxes, and in most situations, the FTC is more valuable to the taxpayer.

FTC Limits   The United States does not grant an FTC for all foreign taxes paid, and there are limits on the amount of foreign taxes that can be taken as a credit. First, only foreign *income* taxes are potentially creditable. Second, the FTC allowed in any tax year is limited to the U.S. tax imposed on the foreign-source income included on the U.S. tax return.[6] Thus, taxpayers are allowed a credit for the lesser of the foreign income taxes paid or accrued or the following limitation.

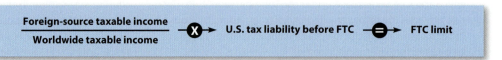

$$\frac{\text{Foreign-source taxable income}}{\text{Worldwide taxable income}} \quad \boxed{\times} \quad \text{U.S. tax liability before FTC} \quad \boxed{=} \quad \text{FTC limit}$$

Worldwide taxable income is the total taxable income reported on the taxpayer's U.S. tax return. Any potential FTCs disallowed because of the FTC limitation may be carried back 1 year or forward 10 years, subject to the FTC limits in those tax years.

EXAMPLE

11

Lassaline, Inc., a domestic corporation, invests in the bonds of non-U.S. corporations. Lassaline's worldwide taxable income for the tax year is $1.2 million, consisting of $1 million of profits from U.S. sales and $200,000 of interest income from foreign sources. Foreign taxes of $90,000 were withheld on these interest payments.

Lassaline's U.S. tax before the FTC is $252,000. Its FTC is limited to $42,000 [($200,000/ $1,200,000) × $252,000]. Thus, Lassaline's net U.S. tax liability is $210,000 after allowing the $42,000 FTC. The remaining $48,000 of FTCs ($90,000 − $42,000) may be carried back or forward.

TAX PLANNING STRATEGIES   Utilizing the Foreign Tax Credit

FRAMEWORK FOCUS: TAX CREDITS

Strategy: Maximize Tax Credits.

The FTC limitation can prevent the total amount of foreign taxes paid in high-tax jurisdictions from being credited against U.S. income tax liabilities. Taxpayers can overcome this problem by using the sourcing rules to:

- Generate **income** items that are **foreign-source**, so as to maximize net foreign-source income, the numerator of the FTC fraction.

- Realize **deduction** items as **U.S.-source**, so as to minimize any reduction in net foreign-source income, the numerator of the FTC fraction.

A U.S. taxpayer's ability to use FTCs is directly related to its level of foreign-source income relative to its total taxable income. To the extent a U.S. taxpayer can keep the average tax rate on its foreign-source income at or below the U.S. tax rate on such income, the foreign taxes will be fully creditable. Consequently, combining high- and low-tax foreign-source income is an important planning objective.

---

[6]Sections 901 and 903 provide definitions of creditable foreign taxes. Section 904 contains the FTC limitation rules.

EXAMPLE

12

Compare the following scenarios where Genius, a U.S. corporation, incurs FTC situations that differ depending on its ability to mix high- and low-taxed income. In the first scenario, Genius earns only $500,000 of highly taxed foreign-source income. In the second scenario, it also generates $100,000 of low-taxed foreign-source income.

	Only Highly Taxed Income	With Low-Taxed Income
Foreign-source income	$500,000	$600,000
Foreign taxes	275,000	280,000
U.S.-source income	700,000	700,000
U.S. taxes (21%)	252,000	273,000
FTC limitation	105,000*	126,000**

* ($500,000/$1,200,000) × $252,000 = $105,000.
** ($600,000/$1,300,000) × $273,000 = $126,000.

When the low-taxed income is added, Genius's actual foreign taxes increase by only $5,000 ($280,000 versus $275,000), but its FTC limitation increases by $21,000 (from $105,000 to $126,000). The ability to "cross-credit" high- and low-taxed foreign income is available, though, only when all of the foreign-source income is classified in the same income basket, as discussed next.

To limit the ability of U.S. taxpayers to cross-credit foreign taxes, the FTC rules provide for several **separate foreign tax credit income categories** (or baskets), including those for passive (investment) and general operating income. In any tax year, taxpayers are allowed to credit the lesser of foreign income taxes paid or accrued or the FTC limit only *within each separate basket*. The separate FTC limitation categories for different types of income each use this same basic FTC limitation formula. The baskets affect the amount of FTC that can be taken, by generally segregating income subject to a high level of foreign tax from lower-taxed foreign income.

EXAMPLE

13

BenCo, Inc., a U.S. corporation, operates a foreign branch in Adagio that earns taxable income of $1.5 million from manufacturing operations and $600,000 from passive activities. BenCo pays Adagio income taxes of $600,000 (40%) and $100,000 (16⅔%), respectively, on this foreign-source income.

The corporation earns $4 million of U.S.-source taxable income, resulting in worldwide taxable income of $6.1 million. BenCo's U.S. taxes before the FTC are $1,281,000 (at 21%). The following table illustrates the effect of the separate limitation baskets on cross-crediting.

Separate Foreign Income Category	Net Taxable Amount	Foreign Taxes	U.S. Tax before FTC at 21%	FTC Allowed with Separate Limits
General	$1,500,000	$600,000	$315,000	$315,000
Passive	600,000	100,000	126,000	100,000
Total	$2,100,000	$700,000	$441,000	$415,000

Without the separate limitation provisions, the FTC would be the lesser of (1) $700,000 foreign taxes or (2) $441,000 share of U.S. tax [($2,100,000/$6,100,000) × $1,281,000]. The "basket" provisions reduce the FTC by $285,000 ($700,000 versus $415,000). In this way, the foreign-source income taxed at the foreign tax rate of 40% cannot be aggregated with foreign-source income taxed at only 16⅔%.

Controlled Foreign Corporations

To minimize current U.S. tax liability, taxpayers often attempt to shift the income-generating activity to a foreign entity, often in a low-tax-rate country. For example, a U.S. person can create a foreign holding company to own the stock of foreign operating affiliates or intangible assets, such as patents and trademarks. A non-U.S. corporation also can be used to accumulate income from sales or service activities by acting as an intermediary between the U.S. corporation and an offshore customer. The subsidiary would be used to purchase goods from the U.S. parent or domestic affiliates and then resell the goods to overseas customers or provide services on behalf of the U.S. parent or affiliates.

In some cases, the use of intermediate overseas subsidiaries is based on a substantive business purpose. In other cases, they are employed only to reduce the present value of income tax costs. Because of this potential for abuse, Congress has enacted various provisions to limit the use of income-shifting techniques.

The most important of these provisions are those affecting **controlled foreign corporations (CFCs)**. Subpart F of the Code provides that certain types of "tainted" income generated by CFCs are included in current-year gross income by the U.S. shareholders, without regard to actual distributions. U.S. shareholders must include in gross income their pro rata share of **Subpart F income**. This rule applies to U.S. shareholders who own stock in the corporation on the last day of the tax year or on the last day the foreign corporation is a CFC. Subpart F and CFC rules thus create an immediate "flow through" of taxable income from the foreign subsidiary to its U.S. shareholders.

EXAMPLE 14

Jordan, Ltd., a calendar year foreign corporation, is a CFC for the entire tax year. Taylor, Inc., a U.S. corporation, owns 60% of Jordan's one class of stock for the entire year. Jordan earned $100,000 of Subpart F income for the year and makes no actual distributions during the year. Taylor, a calendar year taxpayer, includes $60,000 in gross income as a constructive dividend for the tax year.

To the extent Jordan has paid any foreign income taxes, Taylor may claim an indirect foreign tax credit for the portion of the foreign taxes related to the $60,000 constructive dividend.

What Is a CFC?   A CFC is any non-U.S. corporation in which more than 50 percent of the total combined voting power of all classes of voting stock, or the total value of the stock of the corporation, is owned by U.S. shareholders on any day during the taxable year of the foreign corporation. The offshore subsidiaries of most multinational U.S. parent corporations are CFCs. About 100,000 CFCs exist, largely in the United Kingdom, Canada, China, Mexico, Germany, and the Netherlands.

For the purposes of determining whether a foreign corporation is a CFC, a **U.S. shareholder** is a U.S. person who owns, or is considered to own, 10 percent or more of the total combined voting power of all classes of voting stock of the foreign corporation. Stock owned directly, indirectly, and constructively is counted. Indirect ownership involves stock held through a foreign entity, such as a foreign corporation, foreign partnership, or foreign trust. This stock is considered to be actually owned proportionately by the shareholders, partners, or beneficiaries.

Subpart F Income A U.S. shareholder of a CFC does not necessarily lose the ability to defer U.S. taxation of income earned by the CFC. Only certain income earned by the CFC triggers immediate U.S. taxation as a constructive dividend. This tainted income, often referred to as *Subpart F income,* can be characterized as income that is easily shifted or has little or no economic connection with the CFC's country of incorporation. Examples include:

- Passive/portfolio income such as interest, dividends, rents, and royalties.
- Sales income where neither the manufacturing activity nor the customer base is in the CFC's country and either the property supplier or the customer is related to the CFC.
- Service income where the CFC is providing services on behalf of its U.S. owners outside the CFC's country.

Subpart F Income

EXAMPLE 15

Collins, Inc., a domestic corporation, sells $1 million of its products to customers in Europe. All manufacturing and sales activities take place in the United States. Collins has no employees, assets, or operations in Europe and thus is not subject to income tax in any European jurisdiction.

Collins reported the following tax consequences from these inventory sales.

Sales revenue	$1,000,000
Cost of goods sold	(600,000)
Net income	$ 400,000
U.S. tax at 21%	$ 84,000

Assume that Collins instead creates a wholly owned foreign subsidiary in the Cayman Islands, where no income taxes are imposed on corporate income. Collins then sells the inventory to the subsidiary at an intercompany transfer price of $700,000, and the subsidiary sells the inventory to the ultimate European customers for $1 million. The subsidiary does not further process the inventory and is only minimally involved in the sales function, as Collins's employees arrange the transactions with the ultimate customers. In essence, the sale to the subsidiary can be seen as a "paper" transaction.

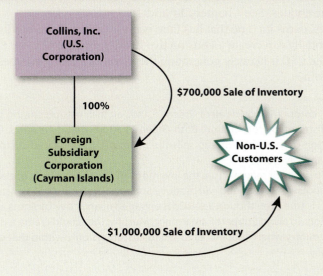

continued

If there were no tax law restrictions, this structure would create the following tax consequences.

	Collins, Inc.	Foreign Subsidiary
Sales revenue	$ 700,000	$1,000,000
Cost of goods sold	(600,000)	(700,000)
Net income	$ 100,000	$ 300,000
U.S. tax at 21%	$ 21,000	
Foreign tax at 0%		$ –0–

Because the Cayman subsidiary is not engaged in a U.S. trade or business, it is not subject to any U.S. tax on its income. Thus, at first glance, it appears that using the foreign subsidiary significantly reduces Collins's current tax cost from $84,000 to $21,000.

However, Collins will find this strategy attacked by the U.S. taxing authorities on two fronts, either of which results in the loss of all or most of the tax savings.

First, the IRS may use the transfer pricing rules of § 482 to claim that the $700,000 intercompany transfer price between Collins and its subsidiary is not a correct ==arm's length price==. The IRS may claim that the transfer price should be $1 million because the subsidiary does not add any value to the inventory through further processing or sales activities and all of the risks of the transaction are borne by Collins. With this transfer pricing adjustment, Collins will record a $400,000 profit from the sales and the same $84,000 tax cost as if it had not used the foreign subsidiary as an intermediary.

Second, under the Subpart F rules, the subsidiary's $300,000 income creates a constructive dividend for Collins, thus producing a $63,000 tax cost ($300,000 × 21%). Combined with its original $21,000 tax, Collins's total tax cost for the sales is $84,000 ($21,000 + $63,000), and the use of the foreign subsidiary does not achieve any tax savings.

EXAMPLE 16

Assume that, in Example 15, Collins's foreign subsidiary instead was incorporated in Ireland, where the tax rate on such sales income is 12.5%. The subsidiary purchases raw materials from Collins and performs substantial manufacturing activity in Ireland before selling the inventory to customers in Hong Kong.

In this case, the sales income is not Subpart F income. Because of the substantial activity provided by the Ireland subsidiary, there is economic substance to the non-U.S. entity that generates the income.

The fact that the Irish subsidiary pays a substantially lower tax rate than the U.S. parent does not by itself trigger a constructive dividend. However, Collins must still document the appropriateness of its intercompany transfer price on raw material sales to its Irish subsidiary.

Subpart F Income—Summary The Subpart F and CFC rules create an immediate flow-through of Federal taxable income, regardless of whether distributions are made to the U.S. shareholder. This is similar to the income treatment of partnerships, S corporations, and similar entities. See Chapters 14 and 15.

Any time a CFC earns income that has little economic connection to its local country, the income potentially can create a constructive dividend to the CFC's U.S. shareholders. Alternatively, if the CFC is actively generating the income, it likely escapes the definition of Subpart F income.

EXAMPLE 17

Murphy, Inc., a U.S. corporation owns all of GreenCo, Ltd., an Irish manufacturing corporation, and SwissCo, a Swiss distribution corporation. Both GreenCo and SwissCo are CFCs. GreenCo sells its inventory production to SwissCo. SwissCo sells the inventory to unrelated customers located in Switzerland, Italy, and Germany.

Because SwissCo does not manufacture the inventory and acquires it from a related supplier, any sales to customers outside Switzerland will produce Subpart F income and a constructive dividend to Murphy, Inc. This is true even though SwissCo is engaged in an active business and is not merely a "paper" corporation. To avoid Subpart F treatment, Murphy, Inc., could create a distribution company within each country where it operates to sell to customers only within that country.

Additional Tax for Base Erosion The Code provides another sanction for large C corporations that appear to shift "too much" taxable income to other countries where a lower income tax rate may be available. The *base erosion anti-abuse* provision applies to U.S. and non-U.S. corporations with average annual gross receipts of at least $500 million for the prior three tax years.

An alternative tax computation applies to the entity when "excessive" deductible royalties, management fees, and similar payments are made to a related (25 percent ownership) non-U.S. person; such payments often are used to shift taxable income to the country where the payment is received. If these base erosion items total at least 3 percent of total deductible payments for the year, the entity pays a Federal corporate income tax equal to the *greater of* the corporation's regular tax liability, or:

> 10% ─**X**→ Taxable income (after adding back the base erosion items)

The base erosion tax is similar in nature to provisions adopted in the last decade by other developed countries that want to keep the income tax base indicative of where multinational profits are earned. The provisions effectively act as a minimum tax to keep a taxpayer from unduly reducing its U.S. taxable income to zero (or close to it), by using income-shifting deductions and other devices with a related party.

The tax sometimes is called the "BEAT," or the base erosion anti-abuse tax. Base erosion items do not include those related to cost of goods sold and other active trade or business expenses, like salaries, or those where a withholding tax already applies. The 10 percent tax rate is 5 percent for the 2018 tax year and 12.5 percent after 2025.

Special Tax Rate for Intangible Income

The U.S. tax law provides an extra incentive for domestic C corporations to generate taxable income overseas in the form of intangible income. A lower tax rate (effectively 13.125 percent) applies to income from intangible assets that the U.S. entity employs overseas. The discounted tax rate is meant to encourage U.S. C corporations to conduct international business that leverages U.S. expertise (especially in technological fields) in profitable operations around the world. The lower tax rate may have a significant effect on how domestic C corporations position their assets and personnel in various countries, including the possibility of net job losses for the United States.

The special tax rate does not apply to the sale of goods or services, or to income that otherwise is taxed under Subpart F. The base for the lower tax rate, sometimes known as foreign-derived intangible income (FDII), is limited to the entity's foreign-source taxable income for the year.

Inbound Issues

Generally, only the U.S.-source income of nonresident alien individuals and foreign corporations is subject to U.S. taxation. This reflects the reach of the U.S. tax jurisdiction. This constraint, however, does not prevent the United States from also taxing the foreign-source income of nonresident alien individuals and foreign corporations when that income is effectively connected with the conduct of a U.S. trade or business.

A **nonresident alien (NRA)** is an individual who is not a citizen or resident of the United States. *Citizenship* is determined under the immigration and naturalization laws of the United States. A person is treated as a *resident* of the United States for income tax purposes if he or she meets either the green card test or the substantial presence test. If either of these tests is met for the calendar year, the individual is deemed a U.S. resident for the year.

Two important definitions determine the U.S. tax consequences to non-U.S. persons with U.S.-source income: "the conduct of a U.S. trade or business" and "**effectively connected income**." Specifically, for a foreign person's noninvestment income to be subject to U.S. taxation, the non-U.S. person must be considered engaged in a U.S. trade or business and must earn income effectively connected with that business.

LO.4

Describe the tax effects related to the U.S. operations of a non-U.S. taxpayer.

General criteria for determining whether a U.S. trade or business exists include the location of production activities, management, distribution activities, and other business functions. The Code does not explicitly define a U.S. trade or business, but case law has described the concept as activities carried on in the United States that are regular, substantial, and continuous.

Once a non-U.S. person is considered engaged in a U.S. trade or business, all U.S.-source income other than investment and capital gain income is considered effectively connected to that trade or business and is therefore subject to U.S. taxation. Effectively connected income is taxed at the same rates that apply to U.S. persons, and deductions for expenses attributable to that income are allowed.

Certain U.S.-source income that is *not* effectively connected with the conduct of a U.S. trade or business is subject to a flat 30 percent tax. This income includes dividends; certain interest; rents; royalties; certain compensation; premiums; annuities; and other income of this type. This tax generally is levied by a withholding mechanism that requires the payors of the income to withhold 30 percent of gross amounts (or a lower rate as established by a treaty). This method improves the collectability of Federal taxes from nonresidents and non-U.S. corporations.

EXAMPLE 18

Robert, a citizen and resident of New Zealand, produces wine for export. During the current year, Robert earns $500,000 from exporting wine to unrelated wholesalers in the United States. The title to the wine passes to the U.S. wholesalers in New York. Robert has no offices or employees in the United States. The income from the wine sales is U.S.-source income, but because Robert is not engaged in a U.S. trade or business, the income is not subject to taxation in the United States.

Robert begins operating a hot dog cart in New York City. This activity constitutes a U.S. trade or business. Consequently, all U.S.-source income other than investment income is taxed in the United States as income effectively connected with a U.S. trade or business. Thus, both the hot dog cart profits and the $500,000 in wine income are taxed in the United States.

Several exceptions exempt non-U.S. persons from U.S. taxation on their U.S. investment income that is not connected with a U.S. business. For example, certain U.S.-sourced portfolio debt investments and capital gains (other than gains on U.S. real property investments) are exempt from U.S. tax for most non-U.S. investors. Gains from investments in U.S. real property usually are subject to U.S. income taxation. Concept Summary 16.1 summarizes the U.S. income taxation of non-U.S. persons.

DIGGING DEEPER 3   In-depth coverage can be found on this book's companion website: **www.cengage.com**

Concept Summary 16.1

U.S. Income Tax Treatment of a Non-U.S. Person's Income*

Type of Income	Tax Rate
U.S.-source investment income	Generally 30% withholding on gross amount (or lower treaty rate) with certain limited exceptions.
U.S.-source income effectively connected with a U.S. trade or business	Regular individual or corporate rates applied against net income (after deductions).
Gain on U.S. real property (direct or indirect ownership)	Taxed as if effectively connected to a U.S. trade or business.
Capital gains (other than on U.S. real property) not effectively connected to a U.S. trade or business	Foreign corporation: Not subject to U.S. tax. Individual: Generally not taxed but may be subject to a 30% U.S. tax if taxpayer is physically present in the United States for 183 days or more in a taxable year.
Foreign-source business income	Generally not subject to U.S. taxation unless attributable to a U.S. office or fixed place of business.

*Subject to change under treaty provisions.

16-3 CROSSING STATE LINES: STATE AND LOCAL INCOME TAXATION IN THE UNITED STATES

Few taxpayers sell goods and services solely in the U.S. state in which they are based. Sales in other states are attractive for a variety of business reasons, including the expansion of market share and the achievement of economies of scale. By extending its operations into other states, a firm may be able to lower its labor and distribution costs, obtain additional sources of long-term debt and equity, and perhaps find a more favorable tax climate.

Many of the same issues discussed earlier in the chapter concerning international operations are encountered when a multistate operation is in place. Both international and multistate operations raise basic questions such as where did the transaction occur and who is liable for the collection of the tax.

FINANCIAL DISCLOSURE INSIGHTS   Tax Rates in Non-U.S. Jurisdictions

When Congress changes the U.S. tax law, it seldom applies tax rate changes retroactively or prospectively—the rate changes usually are applicable on the date the tax bill is effective. Other countries do not always enact tax law changes in this way. Sometimes a country will adopt a schedule of tax rate increases or decreases to go into effect over a period of years.

Tax legislation of this sort can have an important effect on the U.S. taxpayer's effective tax rate as computed in the footnotes to the financial statements. When another country adopts prospective tax rate changes, an increase or decrease in the effective tax rate is reported with respect to the deferred tax accounts for GAAP purposes. Specifically,

the effective tax rate decreases when a tax rate cut is scheduled in a country that does business with the U.S. party, and the rate increases when a tax rate increase is adopted for future tax years. In the last three decades, most developed countries have been cutting business income tax rates.

A recent effective tax rate computation for Berkshire Hathaway showed a decrease of about 1 percentage point due to scheduled tax rate cuts in Germany and the United Kingdom. Allied Healthcare Products showed a similar adjustment of about 2 percentage points. In contrast, the effective tax rate increased by about 1 percentage point for American Travellers Life Insurance Company.

TAX FACT   State Tax Revenue Sources

The corporate income tax accounts for only a small portion of total tax revenues of the states. Each year, over $1.8 trillion in taxes are collected by the states (i.e., more than $5,000 per U.S. individual). Property taxes typically are collected by cities, counties, and other local-level jurisdictions.

Licenses, other 6%
Property 2%
Corporate income 6%
Sales/use 47%
Individual income 39%

However, as state and local income taxation has evolved in the United States, differences in terminology, definitions, and scope of the tax have arisen. In addition, the sheer number of income taxing districts at the state and local levels makes an encounter with the state and local income tax laws of the United States a challenging experience.

16-3a Sources of Law

LO.5

Identify the sources of tax law applicable to a taxpayer operating in more than one U.S. state.

Think of how complicated a tax professional's work would be if there were several hundred different Internal Revenue Codes, each with its own Regulations, rulings, and court decisions. That description is hardly an exaggeration of the state and local income tax law faced by a taxpayer operating in more than one jurisdiction. Unless a firm's salable goods or services are designed, made, and sold strictly within one taxing jurisdiction, the multistate regime comes into effect.

Almost every U.S. state taxes the recognized income of proprietors, corporations, and other entities that have a presence in the state.[7] All of those states have constitutional provisions allowing an income tax and aggregated legislation defining the tax base, specifying when the tax is due and from whom, and otherwise administering the tax. A separate revenue department interprets the law and administers the annual taxing process.

Every one of these systems is distinct and different in multiple ways—the name and location of the chief tax official, the definitions of what is taxable and deductible and what is not, the due dates and filing requirements applicable to the tax, and the taxpayer-friendliness of the audit and appeals system.

Income taxes are levied by states, cities, counties, villages, commuter districts, school districts, stadium boards, and numerous other bodies that have been granted such taxing authority by their states. By one estimate, a business taxpayer might possibly be exposed to over 1,000 different income taxing jurisdictions in the United States at the state and local levels. Politicians often think they can gain economic development advantages over neighboring states by granting special tax breaks—"Locate your assembly plant here, and we'll exempt one-half of your employees' wages from the state income tax." Economic development goals, as well as fluctuating needs to either increase or decrease tax revenues, mean that state and local tax laws are constantly changing.

[7]Some states tax the investment income of individuals, but those taxes are not addressed in this chapter. Nevada, South Dakota, Washington, and Wyoming do not have a corporate income tax. Washington uses a business and occupation tax; several states impose a tax on the gross receipts (not on the net income) of a business.

The Federal government has mostly stayed out of the fray and not attempted to force states and localities to use a single common tax formula and administrative organization. Only in **Public Law 86–272** (P.L. 86–272) has Congress attempted to bring order to the multistate income tax process. This 1959 pro-interstate commerce provision exempts from state and local taxation a sale of tangible personal property where the only contact with the state is the **solicitation** activity of the taxpayer.

Still, the states have taken some steps to coordinate their activities. Several groups of states exchange information as to the seller and purchase price for cross-border sales so that income and sales/use tax obligations can be computed and collected properly. A few states have reciprocity arrangements with their neighbors to straighten out the complications that can arise when an employee lives in one jurisdiction but works in another.

Harry works at the Illinois plant of Big Corporation, but he lives in Iowa. His wages are subject to Iowa tax. If Illinois and Iowa had a reciprocity agreement in place, either (1) Big would collect and remit income tax at Iowa's rates and remit the tax to the Iowa revenue department or (2) Big would collect Illinois tax, and that state would keep the withholdings paid, in full satisfaction of Harry's Iowa tax obligations for the year.

EXAMPLE 19

About half of the states are members of the **Multistate Tax Commission (MTC)**, a body that proposes legislation to the states and localities and issues its own regulations and informational materials. A majority of the non-MTC members also follow the agency's rules virtually without exception. The Uniform Division of Income for Tax Purposes Act (UDITPA) is made available to states and localities interested in a coherent set of income assignment rules, and it forms the basis for the income tax statutes in most of the MTC member states.

The MTC, which provides very specific formulas and definitions to be used in computing state taxable income, is as close as the states have come so far to a multilateral tax treaty process. If all states and localities followed all of the MTC rules, taxpayers would be unable to gain any "border advantages" or disadvantages. But political concerns likely will keep this coordinated result from ever happening.

16-3b Tax Issues

The key issues facing a state or locality in drafting and implementing an income tax model are the same as those facing the international tax community. The results of the deliberative process, though, have produced somewhat different sets of rules and terminology.

Authority to Tax

A business is taxable in the state in which it is resident, organized, or incorporated. Tax liabilities also arise in other jurisdictions where **nexus** exists; that is, a sufficient presence in the other state has been established on an ongoing basis. Such presence might come about because the corporation was organized there, the proprietor lives there, an in-state customer made a purchase, or the business employed people or equipment within the borders of the state. The precise activities that create nexus vary from jurisdiction to jurisdiction, although most of the taxing states follow the broad rules of P.L. 86–272 and the regulations of the MTC.[8]

[8]Income and sales/use tax regimes use different nexus standards. Generally, it has been "easier" to establish nexus for sales/use tax purposes; most states have a separate set of rules to determine the taxability of income or a transaction. U.S. Supreme Court cases apply a "physical presence" test for the sales/use tax, a somewhat stricter test than the income tax nexus rules of the MTC, but this requirement is under challenge. This chapter concentrates on income tax nexus provisions.

When a taxpayer operates in more than one state, total taxable income for the year is split among the jurisdictions in which the operations take place. Portions of the total income amount are assigned to each of the business locations, so several tax returns and payments will be due. For a taxpayer considering an expansion of operations, the tax adviser can make an important contribution in helping to decide with which state(s) nexus will be created.

The nexus rules of state/local taxation serve much the same function as do the permanent establishment provisions of international taxation. The PE standards are based in the language of the applicable tax treaty and interpretive court decisions. They look for real estate holdings and manufacturing equipment. Permanent establishment is found when an office in the host country participates significantly in the making of a sales or service contract.

DIGGING DEEPER 4 | In-depth coverage can be found on this book's companion website: **www.cengage.com**

LO.6

Apply principles designed to compute state taxable income for a taxpayer operating in more than one U.S. state.

Income Sourcing

The multistate business, like its international counterpart, must divide the taxable income generated for the year among the states in which it operates. Then tax liability is computed for the states in which nexus has been established. The computational template illustrated in Exhibit 16.3 indicates how most states derive their shares of the entity's aggregate taxable income. Usually, the starting point for this computation is Federal taxable income.

State modification items come about because each state creates its own tax base in the legislative process, and some of the rules adopted may differ from those used in the Internal Revenue Code. The modification items reflect such differences in the tax base. For example, modifications might be created to reflect the following differences between state and Federal taxable income.

- The state might allow a different cost recovery schedule.
- The state might tax interest income from its own bonds or from those of other states.
- The state might allow a deduction for Federal income taxes paid.

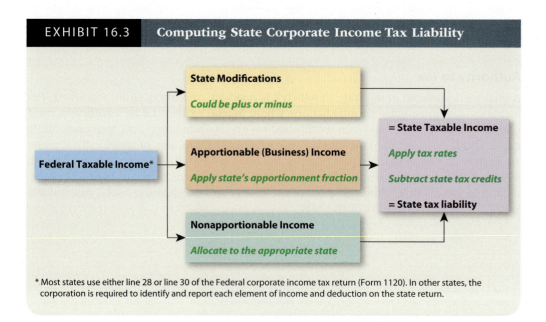

EXHIBIT 16.3   **Computing State Corporate Income Tax Liability**

State Modifications

Could be plus or minus

Federal Taxable Income*

Apportionable (Business) Income

Apply state's apportionment fraction

Nonapportionable Income

Allocate to the appropriate state

= State Taxable Income

Apply tax rates

Subtract state tax credits

= State tax liability

* Most states use either line 28 or line 30 of the Federal corporate income tax return (Form 1120). In other states, the corporation is required to identify and report each element of income and deduction on the state return.

TAX PLANNING STRATEGIES   Nexus: To Have or Have Not

FRAMEWORK FOCUS: TAX RATE

Strategy: Shift Net Income from High-Tax Jurisdictions to Low-Tax Jurisdictions.

Most taxpayers try to avoid establishing nexus in a new state, for example, by providing a sales representative with a cash auto allowance rather than a company car, by restricting the location of inventory to only a few states, or by limiting a salesperson's activities to those that are protected by the solicitation standard of P.L. 86–272. This effort to avoid nexus stems in part from the additional compliance burden that falls upon the taxpayer when a new set of income tax returns, information forms, and deadlines must be dealt with in the new state.

Another concern is that the marginal tax rate that applies to the net taxable income generated by the taxpayer may increase. Such a tax increase occurs, of course, only when the applicable tax rate in the new state is higher than the rate that would apply in the home state. If a business already is based in a tax-friendly state such as Florida or Texas or in a no-tax state such as Nevada, its aggregate tax liability is sure to increase.

Still, nexus is not necessarily a bad thing. Consider what happens if a business based in California, Massachusetts, Illinois, or another high-tax jurisdiction purposely creates nexus in a low- or no-tax state. If the new state applies a lower marginal rate than is available in the home state or offers special exemptions or exclusions that match the tax-payer's operations, the aggregate tax bill can decrease. Then the planning efforts include determining which activities will *create* nexus in the new jurisdiction and meeting or maintaining that standard.

For instance, an entertainer based in Manhattan is subject to the high income taxes of New York City and New York State. By establishing a permanent office in Tennessee, nexus will be created, and some portion of the taxpayer's income will be subject to taxation there, instead of New York. These are permanent savings, accruing immediately to after-tax income and the share price of the stock of the taxpayer.

- The state might disallow a deduction for payment of its own income taxes.
- The state might allow a net operating loss (NOL) deduction only for losses generated in the state.
- The state's NOL deduction might reflect different carryover periods than Federal law allows.

State tax modifications are made even if the taxpayer operates only in its home state.

Allocation and Apportionment   The next step in computing state taxable income is to **allocate** items of nonbusiness income and loss to the states in which such items are derived. For instance, a Kansas entity might recognize some net income from the rental of a Missouri office building to a tenant. The net rental amount is in Federal taxable income, but it must appear only and fully in Missouri taxable income. So by means of the modification process, the rents are removed from the taxable income for both states and then added back into Missouri taxable income. The allocation process is very much like the income-sourcing procedures employed in international taxation.

HammerCo reports $400,000 in taxable income for the year from its sales operations based exclusively in Mississippi and Arkansas. HammerCo recognized net rent income of $60,000 from a building it owns in Mississippi. It earned $20,000 in interest income from Arkansas bonds. This amount is excluded from Federal taxable income, and it is taxed under Mississippi law, but not by Arkansas. HammerCo also claimed a Federal NOL carryforward of $75,000 from a prior period. Mississippi follows Federal law for NOLs, but Arkansas does not allow such carryovers. Thus, Federal taxable income totals $385,000 ($400,000 + $60,000 − $75,000).

EXAMPLE

20

continued

HammerCo's modifications to determine the state tax base, after starting with Federal taxable income, are as follows.

Mississippi		Arkansas	
Amount	**Modification**	**Amount**	**Modification**
− $60,000	Total nonbusiness income	− $60,000	Total nonbusiness income
+ $20,000	Municipal bond interest income	+ $75,000	Remove Federal NOL deduction
+ $60,000	Net rent income from Mississippi rentals		

The business income of the taxpayer is **apportioned** among the states in which it operates. The apportionment percentage for the state is multiplied times the apportionable income of the taxpayer to measure the extent of the taxpayer's exposure to the state's income tax. The application of the apportionment percentage is illustrated in Exhibit 16.3.

Most states apply an apportionment procedure involving three factors, each meant to estimate the taxpayer's relative activities in the state.

- The **sales factor** = In-state sales/total sales.
- The **payroll factor** = In-state payroll/total payroll.
- The **property factor** = In-state property/total property.

The state's apportionment percentage is the average of these three factors. This three-factor apportionment can be traced to the earliest days of state income taxation. Today, most states require or allow the taxpayer to add additional weight to the sales factor, believing it to be the most accurate and measurable reflection of the taxpayer's in-state activities. It is common to "double-weight" the sales factor. Many states use a sales-factor-only apportionment procedure.

EXAMPLE 21

LinkCo, Inc., operates in two states. It reports the following results for the year. LinkCo's apportionment percentages for both states are computed as shown. Amounts are stated in millions of dollars.

	State A	State B	Totals
Sales	$30	$20	$50
Payroll	40	20	60
Property	45	5	50
Sales factor	$30/$50 = .6	$20/$50 = .4	
Payroll factor	$40/$60 = .67	$20/$60 = .33	
Property factor	$45/$50 = .9	$5/$50 = .1	
Apportionment percentage	(.6 + .67 + .9) ÷ 3 = .72	(.4 + .33 + .1) ÷ 3 = .28	

Note that 100% of LinkCo's income is apportioned between the two states: 72% to State A and 28% to State B.

Now assume that State A double-weights the sales factor. LinkCo's apportionment percentages are computed as follows.

	State A	State B	Totals
Sales	$30	$20	$50
Payroll	40	20	60
Property	45	5	50
Sales factor	$30/$50 = .6	$20/$50 = .4	
Payroll factor	$40/$60 = .67	$20/$60 = .33	
Property factor	$45/$50 = .9	$5/$50 = .1	
Apportionment percentage	(.6 + .6 + .67 + .9) ÷ 4 = .69	(.4 + .33 + .1) ÷ 3 = .28	

continued

State B's apportionment computations are not affected by A's double-weighting of the sales factor. The percentages now do not total 100%. The effect of the special weighting is to reduce LinkCo's tax liability in A. This is likely LinkCo's "home state" given the location of its personnel and plant and equipment.

Finally, assume that State B uses a "sales-factor-only" weighting. The A apportionment percentage is .69, and the B percentage is .4. Now the apportionment percentages *exceed* 100%.

Most states follow the regulations of the MTC and the outline of the UDITPA in defining and applying the apportionment factors. But because the states do not follow identical rules in the makeup of the factors, the apportionment percentages seldom total precisely to 100 percent of Federal taxable income. Some other aspects of the three-factor approach include the following.

- Sales are assigned using the tax accounting methods of the taxpayer. Sales are assigned using the "ultimate destination" concept; that is, a sale is usually assigned to the state of the purchaser.

- If a sale is made into a state with no income tax or a state with which the taxpayer has not established nexus, tax is likely escaped. But over a third of the states apply a **throwback rule** that causes the sale to be sourced to the state of the seller (i.e., by overriding the "ultimate destination" rule).

- Payroll is assigned to the state in which the employee's services primarily are performed. Payroll includes wages, bonuses, commissions, and taxable fringe benefits. Some states exclude officer compensation because it can distort the computations. Some states exclude contributions to a § 401(k) plan.

- The property factor uses an average historical cost basis, net of accumulated depreciation. Idle property is ignored, but construction in progress is included. Property in transit is assigned to the state of its presumed destination.

- Property leased but not owned by the taxpayer is included in the property factor at eight times the annual rentals paid.

Many states use specialized apportionment percentages for industries whose sales and asset profile is not properly reflected in the traditional three-factor formula. For instance, the airline industry might divide its income based on passenger-miles beginning and ending in the state. Truckers might be able to divide taxable income among the states based on in-state vehicle-trips or tons-per-day. Communications companies might use the in-state miles of cable or number of wireless devices to make up an apportionment formula.

In-depth coverage can be found on this book's companion website: www.cengage.com   **5 DIGGING DEEPER**

The Unitary Theory   About 30 states use or allow a **unitary approach** in computing the apportionment factors. Conglomerates are required, or can elect, to base their computations on the data for all of their affiliated corporations, not just the legal entities that do business with the state. Affiliates included under the unitary theory share a majority ownership with a parent or group of shareholders. They also often share data processing, sales force, and marketing resources.

The *combined return* that the unitary business files includes much more data than might be expected on a separate-entity basis, but the taxing jurisdictions often believe that the unitary figures offer a more accurate reflection of the taxpayer's activity within the state and that, therefore, a more accurate tax liability can be derived.

FINANCIAL DISCLOSURE INSIGHTS   State/Local Taxes and the Tax Expense

In applying GAAP principles for a business entity, state and local tax expenses are found in several places in the taxpayer's financial reports. In the tax footnote, the state/local tax costs often are reported in dollar and/or percentage terms, in both current and deferred components. The following are examples of state/local tax expenses that were reported in a recent year.

	Current State/Local Tax Expense ($ million)	Deferred State/Local Tax Expense ($ million)
Eli Lilly	($125)	$ 6
Wal-Mart	495	51
Amazon	208	(31)
Ford Motor	12	225

Corporations also report permanent book-tax differences in determining the effective tax rate for the reporting period. In a recent year, Berkshire Hathaway reported that state/local permanent book-tax differences reduced its effective income tax rate by about 2 percentage points. Ford Motor reported a similar rate reduction, but Ryder Systems's effective tax rate increased by about 5 percentage points for the year due to such permanent book-tax differences.

EXAMPLE

22

Kipp Industries is a holding company for three subsidiaries: GrapeCo operating in California, PotatoCo operating in Idaho, and BratCo operating in Germany. Only GrapeCo has nexus with California. But because California is a unitary state, the California apportionment percentage is computed also using PotatoCo and BratCo data.

DIGGING DEEPER 6   In-depth coverage can be found on this book's companion website: **www.cengage.com**

Concept Summary 16.2 sets out some of the key issues in corporate multistate income taxation.

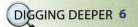

Concept Summary 16.2

Corporate Multistate Income Taxation

1. A taxpayer is subject to income tax in the state in which it resides or is organized.

2. A taxpayer is subject to income tax in states where it has a business presence and enjoys the resources of the host state in conducting its operations.

3. A multistate taxpayer must divide its aggregate taxable income for the year among the states in which it conducts business.

4. Nonbusiness income is allocated to the state in which it is generated.

5. Business income is apportioned among the states in which the taxpayer has nexus.

6. Apportionment usually is conducted using a formula based on the relative sales, employment, and asset holdings in the various states.

7. The sales factor uses a destination test, while the payroll and property factors use a source test.

8. Most states weight the sales factor higher than the other apportionment factors.

9. Some states apply a special apportionment formula for certain industries when the traditional three-factor formula could distort the income division procedure in some way.

10. About 30 states employ the unitary theory in deriving the apportionment factors, using the data from a group of corporations to compute the apportionment formula. Other states allow or require a consolidated return from a conglomerate.

TAX PLANNING STRATEGIES Where Should My Income Go?

FRAMEWORK FOCUS: TAX RATE

Strategy: Shift Net Income from High-Tax Jurisdictions to Low-Tax Jurisdictions.

Every state defines its apportionment factors in a slightly different manner. The multistate taxpayer needs to keep track of these differences and place activities in the state that will serve them best.

Planning with the sales factor includes a detailed analysis of the destination point of the product shipments for the year, especially when the firm has customers in low- and no-tax states. The property factor should include only assets that are used in the taxpayer's trade or business, not the investment, leasing, or research functions. Permanently idle property is excluded from the property factor as well. The payroll factor can be manipulated by hiring independent contractors to carry out certain sales and distribution work or by relocating highly paid managers to low-tax states.

By setting up an investment holding company in a no- or low-tax state such as Delaware or Nevada and transferring income-producing securities and intangible assets to that entity, significant tax reductions can be obtained. When the net investment income is paid back to the parent corporation, the dividends received deduction eliminates the tax liability there.

Use of the unitary system does not always result in a tax increase, although the additional record-keeping burden of operating in a unitary state cannot be understated. If the affiliates make available less profitable operations or a presence in low- or no-tax states or countries, the current tax liability may be reduced. The record-keeping burden can be reduced if the taxpayer makes a **waters'-edge election**, which allows it to include only affiliate data from within the boundaries of the United States.

Return to the facts of Example 22. If Kipp Industries files a waters'-edge election, the unitary group that files a California income tax return can be limited to GrapeCo and PotatoCo since BratCo operates outside the United States.

EXAMPLE
23

16-4 COMMON CHALLENGES

LO.7

Synthesize key aspects of international and multistate tax systems to identify common rules and issues taxpayers face in both systems.

Practical and policy issues facing the U.S. states, developed countries, and the taxpayers operating in all of them show a great degree of similarity between the multistate and international tax regimes. Terminology may differ, and the evolution of tax solutions may take radically different paths, but the key issues that face the multijurisdictional community are at once challenging and rewarding.

16-4a Authority to Tax

The old-economy orientation of the nexus and permanent establishment rules presents great difficulty in today's economy, as jurisdictions attempt to describe the income and sales/use tax base fairly. An electronic presence also exploits the resources of the host country and should trigger a tax in the visited jurisdiction. Mathematically, the apportionment and sourcing rules should result in only a modest tax liability in the host jurisdiction, but it is improper to maintain that no presence exists and no tax should be paid in the context of a toll-free telephone number or internet sale.

But perhaps the notion of *physical presence* is becoming less important over time, and the level of resource usage in the host jurisdiction also is declining. For example, just-in-time manufacturing and purchasing strategies reduce the need for warehousing by some taxpayers. Human capital can be dispersed through telecommuting, video conferencing,

Multijurisdictional companies operate across state and country borders. The transfer price used by a company can have a significant effect on the amount of profits subject to taxation within a particular taxing jurisdiction. Companies face other concerns when establishing transfer pricing policies. For example, the internal determination of how a division of the company is performing may be based on transfer pricing between related entities within the global group. Furthermore, the compensation of the managers within those divisions may be tied directly to divisional performance.

If an intercompany price is set in a manner that optimizes the global tax position, a separate cost accounting policy may be required to determine an entity's profitability for purposes of compensating employees. Tax advisers often face resistance from operations managers when suggesting improved transfer pricing methods, because such improvements often change the traditional division of profits among different parts of the business.

and project rotation using work-group software that provides acceptable levels of data security. As future business activities will become almost exclusively wireless, perhaps the standard of presence will diminish, as the buyer and the seller are both "everywhere."

16-4b Division of Income

The multistate apportionment procedure could use an overhaul. The fact that a majority of states change the weighting of the sales factor indicates that some other income division method might better serve taxpayers and governments. Three-factor apportionment was designed for an age of traveling sales representatives and sales of built, grown, and manufactured goods. Sales reps were assigned territories they could drive through on short notice, so they usually lived close to their customer base. In that case, the sales and payroll factors could be highly redundant.

Today, with communication and distribution systems more highly developed, the sales factor appears incrementally to be the preferred income-sourcing device; this resembles a customer-based sourcing rule. Sales of goods and services should be assigned based on a destination test so that the transaction is assigned to the state of the purchaser.

The three-factor formula further breaks down for income derived from specialized industries, as evidenced by the special computational methods allowed by many states. Perhaps the economy is so specialized today that income simply cannot be assigned by the use of one simple formula. Nonetheless, more uniformity among the states as to definitions and computational rules for the factors would be welcome.

The U.S. Treasury has held hearings in the last decade concerning the adoption of an apportionment approach to the sourcing of international taxable income. Although formulary apportionment would represent a more reliable and predictable method of dividing multinational income and deduction amounts, the data collection burden that such a system would create may be too much to expect from most of the trading partners in the short term.

16-4c Transfer Pricing

The transfer pricing system used in international trade requires the taxpayer to keep a database of comparable prices and transactions, even though often no such comparability exists. Especially when dealing with proprietary goods and design, it may be impossible to find comparable goods and, therefore, an acceptable transfer price for them. One solution to this situation would be to allow additional definitions of comparable goods, or of ranges of acceptable transfer prices, perhaps subjected to audit on a

BRIDGE DISCIPLINE **Bridge to Economic Development and Political Science**

The tax professional occasionally is in a position to negotiate with a state or city taxing jurisdiction to garner tax relief for a client as an incentive to locate a plant or distribution center in that geographic area. In times when construction budgets are high and interstate competition is fierce to attract or retain businesses that are making location decisions, such tax concessions can be significant.

For instance, to encourage a business to build a large distribution center in the area, community leaders might be agreeable to:

- Paying for roads, sewer, water, and other improvements through taxpayer bonds;

- Reducing property taxes by 50 percent for the first 10 years of the center's operations; and

- Permanently excluding any distribution-related vehicles and equipment from the personal property tax.

An incentive-granting community provides the concessions even though the influx of new workers will place a great strain on public school facilities and likely necessitate improvements in traffic patterns and other infrastructure.

Consider the position of a large employer that has been located in the area for more than 50 years. By how much should it be willing to absorb the tax increases that result when economic development concessions are used to attract new, perhaps temporary, businesses to the area? Should the employer challenge the constitutionality of the grant of such sizable tax breaks to some, but not all, business taxpayers in the jurisdiction? Should higher "impact fees" be assessed on new developments?

Does your analysis change if the new business competes with the longtime resident for sales? For employees? For political power?

rotating five-year basis. The use of advance pricing agreements further allows a greater degree of control by the governments in data collection and analysis, ideally prior to the undertaking of the sales or manufacturing transactions. The anti-base-erosion tax might restrict these arrangements.

In-depth coverage can be found on this book's companion website: www.cengage.com   **7 DIGGING DEEPER**

16-4d Tax Havens

When taxpayers perceive effective tax rates as too high, planning usually includes seeking out a **tax haven**. If income-producing securities or profitable service operations can be moved to another jurisdiction, ideally one with significantly lower marginal tax rates on that type of income, permanent tax savings can be achieved. A tax haven usually has adopted rules that allow taxpayers to establish residency with a minimal presence, and the jurisdiction provides little or no cooperation in international exchanges of tax and financial information. The Bahamas, Monaco, and Panama, among other countries, often are seen as tax havens.

When a government witnesses a loss of its tax base due to the transfer of assets and income out of the jurisdiction, anti-tax-haven legislation is discussed, but it seldom is effective. The U.S. international tax regime shows several distinct attempts to find and tax income moved offshore, but those taxes collect only nominal revenues in the typical tax year. Income-shifting devices currently used by multistate taxpayers have been attacked by the states in various ways, but legislators hesitate to be too aggressive, probably out of fear of the state being branded "anti-business."

Perhaps a separate set of nexus rules could be created to address the most portable types of income, such as that from interest and dividends. But this difficult problem likely needs a multilateral solution, which is unlikely to be found in the short term among states and countries, each with unique revenue shortfalls and political profiles.

16-4e **Interjurisdictional Agreements**

Treaties are documents that address many issues other than the taxable income computation. They involve several players within the governmental structure, and they take several years to draft and adopt. Tax treaties involving the United States are only bilateral, meaning that it is difficult to anticipate and coordinate the interaction of several treaties as they apply to a single taxpayer.

At the multistate level, the Federal government has been slow to take up issues involving a synchronization of the income tax systems used by the states. Although this reluctance may be partly for strictly constitutional reasons, it exists largely because of the difficulties presented by the lack of uniformity among the states' tax laws and enforcement efforts.

But the future must hold a greater degree of cooperation among various taxing jurisdictions, at least in the trading of information and the coordination of enforcement efforts. The United States must create additional treaties or information-sharing agreements with countries in South America and Africa. And the future of the European Union probably holds a series of revised agreements addressing tax issues with U.S. entities that relocate intangible assets overseas and that move administrative operations offshore to avoid the U.S. concept of worldwide taxation.

Sharing data, while still respecting the confidentiality needs of the taxpayer and requirements of the governments, represents a technologically sound method of collecting taxes in today's multijurisdictional economy.

REFOCUS ON THE BIG PICTURE

GOING INTERNATIONAL

Income earned from non-U.S. sales is taxed currently to VoiceCo in the United States, under the worldwide approach to cross-border income taxation. If VoiceCo receives Subpart F income from its Irish subsidiary, current income taxation results, but VoiceCo can claim foreign tax credits, which help alleviate the double taxation that would otherwise result. Or if the subsidiary pays a dividend to the parent, a 100 percent dividends received deduction may be available, thereby exempting the dividend from current U.S. income taxation.

What If?

VoiceCo is considering building a new manufacturing facility in another state in the United States. How will VoiceCo's expansion decision be affected by state tax considerations? In making the decision to expand, VoiceCo should consider a variety of state tax issues, including whether the state imposes a corporate income tax at all and, if so, whether the state requires unitary reporting. Other relevant issues affecting the tax calculation in the state include what apportionment formula is used by the state, whether the state has a throwback rule, and whether the state will offer tax incentives for the relocation.

Suggested Readings

Jason W. Klimek, "A Big Data Approach to Formulary Apportionment," *Corporate Taxation*, May/June 2014.

Albena Peters, "Controlled Foreign Corporation Rules in the United States, Canada, and Germany," *Corporate Taxation*, March/April 2012.

Kyle Pomerleau, et. al., "International Tax Competitiveness Index," *Tax Foundation*, October 2017.

Jon P. Skavlern and Alyssa R. Schmitz, "Managing Sales and Use Tax Risk Through a Policy and Procedure Review," *The Tax Adviser*, October 2016.

Key Terms

Allocate, 16-21

Apportioned, 16-22

Arm's length price, 16-14

Controlled foreign corporations (CFCs), 16-12

Effectively connected income, 16-15

Foreign tax credit, 16-6

Inbound taxation, 16-3

Income tax treaties, 16-5

Multistate Tax Commission (MTC), 16-19

Nexus, 16-19

Nonresident alien (NRA), 16-15

Outbound taxation, 16-3

Payroll factor, 16-22

Permanent establishment (PE), 16-5

Property factor, 16-22

Public Law 86–272, 16-19

Sales factor, 16-22

Separate foreign tax credit income categories, 16-11

Solicitation, 16-19

Subpart F income, 16-12

Tax haven, 16-27

Throwback rule, 16-23

Unitary approach, 16-23

U.S. shareholder, 16-12

Waters'-edge election, 16-25

Computational Exercises

1. **LO.3** Cordero, Inc., is a calendar year taxpayer and a CFC for the entire tax year. Yancy Company, a U.S. corporation, owns 75% of Cordero's one class of stock for the entire year. Cordero's Subpart F income for the year is $450,000, and no distributions were made to the parent. Determine Yancy's gross income from the Subpart F constructive dividend from Cordero.

2. **LO.3** Enders, Inc., a domestic corporation, reports $290,000 total taxable income for the year, consisting of $208,800 in U.S.-source business profits and $81,200 of income from foreign investment securities. Overseas tax authorities withheld $24,000 in income taxes on the investment income. Enders's U.S. tax before the FTC is $60,900.

   a. Compute Enders's foreign tax credit for the year.

   b. Express your answer as a Microsoft Excel formula.

3. **LO.6** Castle Corporation conducts business and has nexus in States A, B, and C. All of the states use a three-equal-factors apportionment formula, with the factors evenly weighted. Castle generates $555,000 apportionable income and $75,000 allocable income related to State C activities. Castle's sales, payroll, and property are divided evenly among the three states. Compute taxable income for:

   a. State A.

   b. State B.

   c. State C.

4. **LO.6** Fillon operates manufacturing facilities in States A and B. Fillon has nexus with both states; apportionment factors are .70 for A and .30 for B. Taxable income for the year totaled $150,000, with a $200,000 A profit and a $50,000 B loss. Calculate taxable income for the year for:

   a. State A.

   b. State B.

5. **LO.6** Beckett Corporation has nexus with States A and B. Apportionable income for the year totals $800,000. Beckett's apportionment factors for the year use the following data. Compute Beckett's B taxable income for the year; B uses a three-factor apportionment formula, with a double-weighted sales factor.

	State A	State B	Totals
Sales	$960,000	$640,000	$1,600,000
Property	180,000	–0–	180,000
Payroll	220,000	–0–	220,000

6. **LO.6** Vogel Corporation owns two subsidiaries. Song, located in State A, generated $500,000 taxable income this year. Bird, located in State B, generated a $100,000 loss for the period.

   a. Determine Song's taxable income in States A and B, assuming that the subsidiaries constitute independent corporations under the tax law.

   b. How does your answer change if the companies constitute a unitary business?

Problems

7. **LO.3** BlueCo, a domestic corporation, incorporates GreenCo, a new wholly owned entity in Germany. Under both German and U.S. legal principles, this entity is a corporation. BlueCo faces a 21% U.S. tax rate.

   GreenCo earns $1,500,000 in net profits from its German manufacturing activities, and GreenCo makes no dividend distributions to BlueCo. How much Federal income tax will BlueCo pay for the current year as a result of GreenCo's earnings, assuming that it incurs no deemed dividend under Subpart F?

8. **LO.3** Evaluate this statement: It is unfair that the United States taxes some of its citizens and residents on their worldwide income.

9. **LO.3** Describe the different approaches used by countries to tax the earnings of their citizens and residents generated outside the borders of the country.

10. **LO.3** Chock, a U.S. corporation, purchases inventory for resale from distributors within the United States and resells this inventory at a $1 million profit to customers outside the United States. Title to the goods passes outside the United States. What is the source of Chock's inventory sales income?

11. **LO.3** Willa, a U.S. corporation, owns the rights to a patent related to a medical device. Willa licenses the rights to use the patent to IrishCo, which uses the patent in its manufacturing facility located in Ireland. What is the source of the $1 million royalty income received by Willa from IrishCo for the use of the patent?

12. **LO.3** USCo incurred $100,000 in interest expense for the current year. The tax book value of USCo's assets generating foreign-source income is $5 million. The tax book value of USCo's assets generating U.S.-source income is $45 million. How much of the interest expense is allocated and apportioned to foreign-source income?

13. **LO.3** QuinnCo could not claim all of the income taxes it paid to Japan as a foreign tax credit (FTC) this year. What computational limit probably kept QuinnCo from taking its full FTC? Explain.

14. **LO.3** FoldIt, a U.S. business, paid income taxes to Mexico relative to profitable sales of shipping boxes it made in that country. Can it claim a deduction for these taxes in computing U.S. taxable income? A tax credit? Both? Explain.

15. **LO.3** ABC, Inc., a domestic corporation, reports $50 million of taxable income, including $15 million of foreign-source taxable income from services rendered, on which ABC paid $2.5 million in foreign income taxes. The U.S. tax rate is 21%. What is ABC's foreign tax credit?

16. **LO.3** Fleming, Inc., a domestic corporation, operates in both Canada and the United States. This year, the business generated taxable income of $400,000 from foreign sources and $300,000 from U.S. sources. All of Fleming's foreign-source income is in the general limitation basket. Fleming's total worldwide taxable income is $700,000. Fleming pays Canadian taxes of $152,000. What is Fleming's allowed FTC for the tax year? Assume a 21% U.S. income tax rate.

17. **LO.3** Drake, Inc., a U.S. corporation, operates a branch sales office in Turkey. During the current year, Drake earned $500,000 in taxable income from U.S. sources and $100,000 in taxable income from sources in Turkey. Drake paid $40,000 in income taxes to Turkey. All of the income is characterized as general limitation income. Compute Drake's U.S. income tax liability after consideration of any foreign tax credit. Drake's U.S. tax rate is 21%.

18. **LO.3** Crank, Inc., a U.S. corporation, operates a branch sales office in Ghana. During the current year, Crank earned $200,000 in taxable income from U.S. sources and $50,000 in taxable income from sources in Ghana. Crank paid $5,000 in income taxes to Ghana. All of the income is characterized as general limitation income. Compute Crank's U.S. income tax liability after consideration of any foreign tax credit. Crank's U.S. tax rate is 21%.

19. **LO.3** Night, Inc., a domestic corporation, earned $300,000 from foreign manufacturing activities on which it paid $36,000 of foreign income taxes. Night's foreign sales income is taxed at a 50% foreign tax rate. Both sales and manufacturing income are assigned to the general limitation basket. What amount of foreign sales income can Night earn without generating any excess FTCs for the current year? Assume a 21% U.S. rate. **Decision Making**

20. **LO.3** Orion, Inc., a U.S. corporation, reports foreign-source income and pays foreign taxes for the tax year as follows.

	Income	Taxes
Passive basket	$150,000	$ 13,000
General basket	300,000	150,000

Orion's worldwide taxable income is $600,000, and U.S. taxes before the FTC are $126,000 (assume a 21% rate). What is Orion's U.S. tax liability after the FTC?

21. **LO.3** Discuss the policy reasons for the existence of the Subpart F rules. Give two examples of Subpart F income. **Critical Thinking**

22. **LO.3** USCo owns 65% of the voting stock of LandCo, a Country X corporation. Terra, an unrelated Country Y corporation, owns the other 35% of LandCo. LandCo owns 100% of the voting stock of OceanCo, a Country Z corporation. Assuming that USCo is a U.S. shareholder, do LandCo and OceanCo meet the definition of a CFC? Explain.

23. **LO.3** Is a foreign corporation owned equally by 100 unrelated U.S. citizens considered to be a controlled foreign corporation (CFC)? Explain.

24. **LO.3** Hart Enterprises, a domestic corporation, owns 100% of OK, Ltd., an Irish corporation. OK's gross income for the year is $10 million. Determine whether any of the following transactions produce Subpart F gross income for the current year.

 a. OK earned $600,000 from sales of products purchased from Hart and sold to customers outside Ireland.

 b. OK earned $1 million from sales of products purchased from Hart and sold to customers in Ireland.

 c. OK earned $400,000 from sales of products purchased from unrelated suppliers and sold to customers in Germany.

 d. OK purchased raw materials from Hart, used these materials to manufacture finished goods, and sold these goods to customers in Italy. OK earned $300,000 from these sales.

 e. OK earned $50,000 in dividend income from Canada and Mexico passive investments.

25. **LO.3** HiramCo, a U.S. entity, operates a manufacturing business in both Mexico and Costa Rica, and it holds its investment portfolio in Sweden. How many foreign tax credit computations must HiramCo make? Be specific, and use the term *basket* in your answer.

26. **LO.4** Give a simple answer to Andre's question: "If I move to the United States, how will the Federal government tax my widget sales and capital gains?" Andre will be living in New York City, where state and local taxes are very high. Ignore the effects of tax treaties in your answer.

27. **LO.4** Evaluate the following statement: Non-U.S. persons never are subject to U.S. taxation on U.S.-source investment income, so long as they are not engaged in a U.S. trade or business.

Communications 28. **LO.3, 4** Write a memo for the tax research file on the difference between "inbound" and "outbound" activities in the context of U.S. taxation of international income.

29. **LO.3** Warwick, Inc., a U.S. corporation, owns 100% of NewGrass, Ltd., a foreign corporation. NewGrass earns only general limitation income. During the current year, NewGrass paid Warwick a $10,000 dividend. The deemed-paid foreign tax credit associated with this dividend is $3,000. The foreign jurisdiction requires a withholding tax of 10%, so Warwick received only $9,000 in cash as a result of the dividend. What is Warwick's total U.S. gross income reported as a result of the cash dividend?

30. **LO.5** Evaluate this statement: A state can tax only its resident individuals and the corporations and partnerships that are organized in-state.

Critical Thinking 31. **LO.5** You are working with the top management of one of your clients in selecting
Communications the U.S. location for a new manufacturing operation. Craft a plan for the CEO to use in discussions with the economic development representatives of each of the top candidate states. In no more than three PowerPoint slides, list some of the tax incentives the CEO should request from a particular state during the bilateral negotiations between the parties. Your list should be both creative and aggressive in its requests.

Decision Making 32. **LO.5** Considering only the aggregate state income tax liability, how should Norris, who sells widgets from its domicile State A, deploy its sales force? The states that entail the taxpayer's entire customer base use the following flat income tax rates.

State A	5%
State B	3
State C	6
State D	0

33. **LO.5** Continue to consider the case of the taxpayer in Problem 34. Is it acceptable **Ethics and Equity** to you if Norris purposely shifts its sales force among the states to reduce its tax liabilities? In your response, first explain the tax-related motivations of the taxpayer in this regard.

34. **LO.6** Compute state taxable income for HippCo, Inc. Its Federal taxable income for the year is $1 million. Its operations are confined to Oregon and Montana. HippCo generates only business and interest income for the year.

    • Federal cost recovery deductions totaled $200,000. Montana used this amount, but Oregon allowed only $120,000.

    • Interest income of $25,000 from Oregon bonds was excluded from Federal taxable income. Oregon taxes all municipal bond income, while Montana taxes all such interest except that from its own bonds.

    • Interest income from Treasury bonds that was recognized on the Federal return came to $11,000. Neither state taxes such income.

35. **LO.6** Continue with the facts of Problem 36. Using the format of Exhibit 16.3, compute state taxable income for HippCo, assuming also that the taxpayer recognized $225,000 of net rent income during the year from a warehouse building in Montana. Federal taxable income still is $1 million.

36. **LO.6** PinkCo, Inc., operates in two states, both of which equally weight the three apportionment factors. PinkCo reports the following results for the year. Compute the apportionment percentage for both states. Amounts are stated in millions of dollars.

	State A	State B	Totals
Sales	$25	$ 75	$100
Payroll	20	30	50
Property	0	100	100

37. **LO.6** Repeat the computations of Problem 38, but now assume that State B uses a double-weighted sales factor in its apportionment formula.

38. **LO.6** Repeat the computations of Problem 38, but now assume that State A is a sales-factor-only state and that State B uses the following weights: sales .70, payroll .15, and property .15.

39. **LO.6** State A enjoys a prosperous economy, with high real estate values and **Critical Thinking** compensation levels. State B's economy has seen better days—property values are depressed, and unemployment is higher than in other states. Most consumer goods are priced at about 10% less in B as compared with prices in A. Both A and B apply unitary income taxation on businesses that operate in-state. Does unitary taxation distort the assignment of taxable income between A and B? Explain.

40. **LO.6** Hernandez, which has been an S corporation since inception, is subject to **Digging Deeper** tax in States Y and Z. On Schedule K of its Federal Form 1120S, Hernandez **Communications** reported ordinary income of $500,000 from its business, taxable interest income of $10,000, capital loss of $30,000, and $40,000 of dividend income from a corporation in which it owns 30%.

    Both states apportion income by use of a three-factor formula that equally weights sales, payroll, and the average cost of property; both states treat interest and dividends as business income. In addition, both Y and Z follow Federal provisions with respect to the determination of corporate taxable income. Y recognizes S status, but Z does not.

    Based on the following information, write a memo to the shareholders of Hernandez, detailing the amount of taxable income on which Hernandez will pay tax in Y and Z. Hernandez corporate offices are located at 5678 Alabaster Circle, Bowling Green, KY 42103.

	State Y	State Z
Sales	$1,000,000	$800,000
Property (average cost)	500,000	100,000
Payroll	800,000	200,000

Critical Thinking   41. **LO.6** Prepare a PowerPoint presentation (maximum of six slides) entitled "Plan-

Communications   ning Principles for Our Multistate Clients." The slides will be used to lead a 20-minute discussion with colleagues in the corporate tax department. Keep the outline general, but assume that your colleagues already work with clients operating in at least 15 states. Address only income tax issues.

Critical Thinking   42. **LO.3, 7** Miha Ohua is the CFO of a U.S. company that has operations in Europe

Communications   and Asia. The company has several manufacturing subsidiaries in low-tax foreign countries where the tax rate averages 6%. These subsidiaries purchase raw materials used in the production process from related subsidiaries located in countries where the tax rate averages 33%.

Miha is considering establishing a transfer price for the raw materials so that the higher-tax subsidiaries charge a low price for the raw materials. In this way, little of the profit is left in these subsidiaries, and most of the profits end up in the low-tax subsidiaries. This approach might reduce the U.S. company's overall global tax rate. Write a memo to Miha, outlining the issues with this plan.

BRIDGE DISCIPLINE

1. What type of information-sharing agreements does the IRS have with the revenue agency of the Bahamas? Canada? Germany? Israel? Argentina?

Communications   2. Write a paper of no more than two pages discussing the treatment of state and local taxes that is found in the text of U.S. income tax treaties with two other countries.

Communications   3. Several U.S. states finance their operations without the benefit of a corporate income tax. Prepare five to seven PowerPoint slides, and make a presentation to your school's Accounting Club. In your presentation, discuss the public economic and policy effects of using nontraditional revenue sources to fund state operating and infrastructure projects. Compare the taxing and expenditure process used in your state with at least two of these jurisdictions: Alaska; Hawaii; Michigan; Texas; Washington, D.C.; and Washington State.

Critical Thinking   4. The trend in state income taxation is to move to an apportionment formula that places extra weight on the sales factor. Several states now use sales-factor-only apportionment. Explain why this development is attractive to the taxing states.

Note: Solutions to the Research Problems can be prepared by using the Thomson Reuters Checkpoint™ online tax research database, which accompanies this textbook. Solutions can also be prepared by using research materials found in a typical tax library.

THOMSON REUTERS
CHECKPOINT™

Research Problem 1. Jerry Jeff Keen, the CFO of Boots Unlimited, a Texas corporation, has come to you regarding a potential restructuring of business operations. Boots long has manufactured its western boots in plants in Texas and Oklahoma.

Communications
Critical Thinking

Recently, Boots has explored the possibility of setting up a manufacturing subsidiary in Ireland, where manufacturing profits are taxed at 10%. Jerry Jeff sees this as a great idea, given that the alternative is to continue all manufacturing in the United States, where profits are taxed at 21%. Boots plans to continue all of the cutting, sizing, and hand tooling of leather in its U.S. plants. This material will be shipped to Ireland for final assembly, with the finished product shipped to retail outlets all over Europe and Asia. Your initial concern is whether the income generated by the Irish subsidiary is Subpart F income. Address this issue in a research memo, along with any planning suggestions.

Partial list of research aids:
§ 954(d).
Reg. § 1.954–3(a).
Bausch & Lomb, 71 TCM 2031, T.C.Memo. 1996–57.

Research Problem 2. Polly Ling is a successful professional golfer. She is a resident of a country that does not have a tax treaty with the United States. Ling plays matches around the world, about one-half of which are in the United States. Ling's reputation is without blemish; in fact, she is known as being exceedingly honest and upright, and many articles discuss how she is a role model for young golfers due to her tenacious and successful playing style and her favorable character traits. Every year, she reports the most penalty strokes on herself among the participants in women's matches, and this is seen as reinforcing her image as an honest and respectful competitor.

This combination of quality play and laudable reputation has brought many riches to Ling. She comes to you with several Federal income tax questions. She knows that as a non-U.S. resident, any of her winnings from tournament play that occurs in the United States are subject to U.S. income taxation. But what about each of the following items? How does U.S. tax law affect Ling? Apply the sourcing rules in this regard, and determine whether the graduated U.S. Federal income tax rate schedules apply.

- Endorsement income from YourGolf, for wearing clothing during matches with its logo prominently displayed. Ling must play in at least 10 tournaments per year that are televised around the world. She also must participate in photo sessions and in blogs and tweets associated with the tournaments. Payment to Ling is structured as a flat fee, with bonuses paid if she finishes in the top five competitors for each match. This is known as an *on-court endorsement*.

- Endorsement income from GolfZone, for letting the company use her likeness in a video game that simulates golf tournaments among known golfers and other players that the (usually middle-aged men and women) gamers identify. In this way, the gamer seems to be playing against Ling on famous golf courses. Two-thirds of all dollar sales of the game licenses are to U.S. customers.

- Endorsement income from Eliteness, for appearing in print and internet ads that feature Ling wearing the company's high-end watches. One-fifth of all dollar sales of the watches are to U.S. customers. The latter two items are known as *off-court endorsements*.

Use internet tax resources to address the following questions. Look for reliable web-sites and blogs of the IRS and other government agencies, media outlets, businesses, tax professionals, academics, think tanks, and political outlets.

Research Problem 3. Supervise and Wager Company produces consumer goods that are distributed and sold primarily in North America, Europe, and Asia. The business includes a U.S. parent company, S&W, Inc., and separate operating subsidiaries in each region in which the company conducts significant business.

The company's board is considering a structural reorganization to reduce the global tax costs. Options include reorganizing the parent company in either Bermuda or Ireland. Under any option, current shareholders will contribute their stock in the U.S. parent company in return for an equivalent amount of stock in the new parent. The U.S. parent will be liquidated, and the new corporation then will be the sole shareholder of the operating subsidiaries.

a. What might S&W be trying to achieve with the proposed organizational restructuring?

b. What insight can you provide regarding the immediate and longer-term tax consequences of the reorganization? *Hint*: Use the word *inversion* in your search term.

Research Problem 4. Make a list of five countries with which the United States does *not* have in force a bilateral income tax treaty.

Communications   **Research Problem 5.** For your analysis, choose 10 countries, one of which is the United States. Create a table showing whether each country applies a worldwide or territorial approach to international income taxation. Then list the country's top income tax rate on business profits. Send a copy of this table to your instructor.

Communications   **Research Problem 6.** Locate data on the size of the international economy, including data on international trade, foreign direct investment of U.S. firms, and investments in the United States by foreign firms. Useful websites include **www.census.gov** and **www.bea.gov**. Prepare an analysis of these data for a three-year period, using spreadsheet and graphing software, and e-mail your findings to your instructor.

Communications   **Research Problem 7.** Read the "tax footnote" of five publicly traded U.S. corporations. Find the effective state/local income tax rates of each. Create a PowerPoint presentation (maximum of five slides) for your instructor, summarizing the search and reporting your findings.

Research Problem 8. Identify three states considered to be in the same economic region as your own.

a. For each of the three states and your own state, answer the following questions, creating a table with your answers. Answers to most can be found at the website **www.taxadmin.org**.

i. What is the overall tax burden per capita, and where does it rank among all states?

ii. What is the overall tax burden as a percentage of personal income, and where does it rank among all states?

iii. From what source(s) does it raise most of its revenues (e.g., sales/use tax, highway tolls)?

iv. What is the highest marginal tax rate on corporate income?

v. What is its apportionment formula, including factors and weights?

b. What advice or insight might you provide to your state legislature regarding your state's tax system, based on your findings for part (a)?

1. Olinto, Inc., reports taxable income (before special deductions and net operating loss deduction) of $92,000. Included in that amount is $12,000 interest and dividends income. Forty percent of Olinto's property, payroll, and sales are in its home state. What amount of this taxable income will be taxed by Olinto, Inc.'s home state?

   a. $12,000

   b. $36,800

   c. $44,000

   d. $90,000

2. In which of the following cases will Federal law prohibit a state from imposing a tax on net income?

   a. The business has a retail outlet store in the state.

   b. The business has its corporate headquarters in the state and generates sales from there.

   c. Orders are taken within the state, accepted at corporate headquarters outside of the state, and shipped from a location outside of the state.

   d. Orders are taken within the state, accepted at corporate headquarters outside of the state, and shipped from a location inside the state.

Business Tax Credits and the Alternative Minimum Tax

CHAPTER OUTLINE

17-1 Business-Related Tax Credit Provisions, 17-2

    17-1a General Business Credit, 17-2

    17-1b Tax Credit for Rehabilitation Expenditures, 17-4

    17-1c Work Opportunity Tax Credit, 17-5

    17-1d Research Activities Credit, 17-6

    17-1e Energy Credits, 17-8

    17-1f Disabled Access Credit, 17-8

    17-1g Credit for Small Employer Pension Plan Startup Costs, 17-9

    17-1h Credit for Employer-Provided Child Care, 17-9

    17-1i Foreign Tax Credit, 17-10

    17-1j Small Employer Health Insurance Credit, 17-11

    17-1k Credit for Employer-Provided Family and Medical Leave, 17-11

17-2 Individual Alternative Minimum Tax, 17-13

    17-2a Alternative Minimum Taxable Income (AMTI), 17-13

    17-2b AMT Formula: Other Components, 17-15

    17-2c AMT Adjustments, 17-16

    17-2d AMT Preferences, 17-28

    17-2e Illustration of the AMT Computation, 17-30

    17-2f AMT Credit, 17-31

17-3 Corporate Alternative Minimum Tax, 17-33

TAX TALK *A government which robs Peter to pay Paul can always count on the support of Paul.* —GEORGE BERNARD SHAW

ISTOCKPHOTO.COM/MONKEY BUSINESS IMAGES

Dealing With Tax Credits and the AMT

Mike, the CEO of Progress Corporation, is committed to helping revitalize the crumbling downtown area in his hometown. The area has experienced high unemployment as companies have left for the suburbs, and Mike is considering expanding his business and purchasing an old office building in a historic section of downtown. The building, a certified historic structure, will require substantial renovations, and Mike has heard that there are tax credits that might help reduce his costs. He would also like to hire inner-city workers and help working families by providing on-site child care. He is interested in learning whether his company might take advantage of any other tax credits offered by the Federal government that might reduce his costs.

Read the chapter and formulate your response.

Explain the difference in the use of credits and deductions as a Federal tax policy tool.

Federal tax law often serves other purposes besides merely raising revenue for the government. Evidence of equity, social, and economic considerations is found throughout the tax law, including in the area of <mark>tax credits</mark>. Congress has generally used tax credits to promote social or economic objectives or to work toward greater tax equity among different types of taxpayers. For example, the disabled access credit was enacted to accomplish a social objective: to encourage taxpayers to renovate older buildings so that they would be accessible to the disabled and be in compliance with the Americans with Disabilities Act. The foreign tax credit has as its chief purpose the economic and equity objectives of mitigating the burden of multiple taxation on a single stream of income that is generated in more than one country.

A tax credit is much different than an income tax deduction. Income tax deductions reduce a taxpayer's tax base; tax credits reduce a taxpayer's tax liability. The tax benefit received from a tax deduction depends on the tax rate; a tax credit is not affected by the tax rate of the taxpayer.

Assume that Congress wants to encourage a certain type of expenditure. One way to accomplish this objective is to allow a tax credit of 25% for these expenditures. Another way is to allow an itemized deduction for the expenditures. Assume that Abby's tax rate is 15% and Bill's tax rate is 35% and that each itemizes deductions. In addition, assume that Carmen does not incur enough qualifying expenditures to itemize deductions. The following tax benefits are available to each taxpayer for a $1,000 expenditure.

	Abby	Bill	Carmen
Tax benefit if a 25% credit is allowed	$250	$250	$250
Tax benefit if an itemized deduction is allowed	150	350	–0–

As these results indicate, tax credits provide benefits on a more equitable basis than do tax deductions—all three taxpayers reduce their tax liabilities by the same amount. Equally apparent is that the deduction approach in this case benefits only taxpayers who itemize deductions, while the credit approach benefits all taxpayers who make the specified expenditure.

In order to prevent taxpayers with high income from completely avoiding a Federal income tax liability, the alternative minimum tax (AMT) was introduced in 1969 and has since been amended on multiple occasions. The corporate AMT was repealed for tax years beginning after 2017. The purpose of the individual AMT is to require taxpayers that have more economic profits than their regular taxable income reflects to pay additional income taxes.

Apply various business-related tax credits.

17-1 BUSINESS-RELATED TAX CREDIT PROVISIONS

Congress has generally used tax credits to achieve social or economic objectives or to promote equity among different types of taxpayers. This section of the chapter describes the operation of the general business credit along with the most common types of credits that affect a business.

17-1a General Business Credit

The <mark>general business credit</mark> is comprised of a number of other credits, each of which is computed separately under its own set of rules. The general business credit combines these credits into one amount to limit the annual credit that can be used to offset a taxpayer's income tax liability.

TAX FACT Business Tax Credits

The amount of business tax credits claimed by corporations fluctuates significantly based on the type of credit. The amount of each credit for 2013 varies from a low of $232,000 to over $100,000,000,000.

Credit Type	Amount of Credits (reported in thousands of dollars)
Foreign tax credit	$118,279,104
Research activities credit	11,427,529
Low-income housing credit	8,485,643
Disabled access credit	346
Renewable electricity production credit	784,804
Credit for contributions for small employer pension plan startup costs	232
Credit for employer provided childcare facilities and services	16,767
Biodiesel and renewable diesel fuels credit	16,786
Work-opportunity credit	1,194,524
Small employer health insurance premiums credit	105,046

Source: IRS Tax Statistics.

Two special rules apply to the general business credit. First, any unused credit is carried back 1 year, then forward 20 years. Second, for any tax year, the general business credit is limited to the taxpayer's *net income tax* reduced by the greater of:[1]

- The *tentative minimum tax* [see the discussion of the alternative minimum tax (AMT) later in this chapter].
- 25 percent of *net regular tax liability* that exceeds $25,000.[2]

Net regular tax liability is the regular tax liability reduced by certain nonrefundable credits (e.g., foreign tax credit).

> **EXAMPLE 2**
>
> Tanager Corporation's general business credit for the current year is $70,000. Tanager's net income tax is $150,000, tentative minimum tax is $130,000, and net regular tax liability is $150,000. Tanager has no other tax credits. The general business credit allowed for the tax year is computed as follows.
>
> | | |
> |---|---|
> | Net income tax | $ 150,000 |
> | Less: The greater of— | |
> | • $130,000 (tentative minimum tax) | |
> | • $31,250 [25% × ($150,000 − $25,000)] | (130,000) |
> | Amount of general business credit allowed for tax year | $ 20,000 |
>
> Tanager then has $50,000 ($70,000 − $20,000) of unused general business credits that may be carried back or forward.

Treatment of Unused General Business Credits

Unused general business credits are initially carried back one year and reduce the tax liability of that year. Thus, the taxpayer may receive a tax refund as a result of the carryback. Any remaining unused credits are then carried forward 20 years.[3]

---

[1] § 38(c). This rule works to keep the general business credit from completely eliminating the tax liability for many taxpayers.

[2] § 38(c)(3)(B). The $25,000 amount is apportioned among the members of a controlled group.

[3] § 39(a)(1).

A FIFO method is applied to the carryback, carryovers, and utilization of credits earned during a particular year. When the oldest credits are used first, the FIFO method minimizes the potential for loss of a general business credit benefit due to the expiration of credit carryovers and generally works to the taxpayer's benefit.

EXAMPLE 3

This example illustrates the use of general business credit carryovers for the taxpayer's 2018 tax year.

General business credit carryovers (unused in prior tax years)			
2015		$ 4,000	
2016		6,000	
2017		2,000	
Total carryovers		$12,000	
2018 general business credit			$ 40,000
Total credit allowed in 2018 (based on tax liability)		$50,000	
Less: Carryovers used			
2015		(4,000)	
2016		(6,000)	
2017		(2,000)	
Remaining credit allowed in 2018		$38,000	
2018 general business credit used			(38,000)
2018 unused amount carried forward to 2019			$ 2,000

Each component of the general business credit is determined separately under its own set of rules. Some of the more important credits that make up the general business credit are explained here in the order listed in Exhibit 17.1.

17-1b Tax Credit for Rehabilitation Expenditures

The **rehabilitation expenditures credit** is intended to discourage businesses from moving from economically distressed areas (e.g., an inner city) to outlying locations and to encourage the preservation of historic structures. The credit is 20 percent of qualified rehabilitation expenditures related to a certified historic structure (either residential or nonresidential).[4] The 20 percent credit is taken ratably over a five-year period starting with the year the rehabilitated building is placed in service. Taxpayers who claim the rehabilitation credit must reduce the basis of the rehabilitated building by the credit allowed.[5]

EXHIBIT 17.1	Principal Components of the General Business Credit

The general business credit combines (but is not limited to) the following.

- Tax credit for rehabilitation expenditures
- Work opportunity tax credit
- Research activities credit
- Various energy credits
- Low-income housing credit
- Disabled access credit
- Credit for small employer pension plan startup costs
- Credit for employer-provided child care

---

[4] § 47. In years prior to 2018, a separate 10% rehabilitation credit was allowed for *noncertified* historic structures placed in service before 1936. The Tax Cuts and Jobs Act (TCJA) of 2017 repealed this credit beginning in 2018.

[5] § 50(c).

BRIDGE DISCIPLINE **Bridge to Finance**

When calculating the cash-flow benefit of particular tax attributes and making a decision based on this analysis, an inappropriate decision can be made unless present value analysis is incorporated into the calculation.

The general business credit and the related carryback and carryover provisions can be used to illustrate the cash-flow impact.

Blonde, Inc.'s general business credit for 2018 is $400,000. However, the amount that may be used to reduce the current-year tax liability is only $280,000. None can be used in 2017 (the carryback year), so the $120,000 is carried forward. The $120,000 of unused general business credit is expected to offset Blonde's future tax liability as follows.

2019	$20,000
2020	40,000
2021	60,000

It appears that the cash-flow benefit to Blonde is $400,000. In nominal dollars, this result is correct. However, when the present value concept is applied, the cash-flow benefit is only $376,280 (assuming that Blonde's discount rate is 4 percent).

2018	$280,000 × 1.000	=	$280,000
2019	20,000 × .9615	=	19,230
2020	40,000 × .9246	=	36,984
2021	60,000 × .8890	=	53,340
			$389,554

The carryforward period for the general business credit is 20 years. Using a 4 percent discount rate, one dollar in 20 years is worth about 46 cents ($1 × .4564) today. So taxpayers should use the general business credit to offset tax liability as rapidly as possible.

The Big Picture

EXAMPLE 4

Return to the facts of *The Big Picture* on p. 17-1. Assume that Progress spends $60,000 to rehabilitate the office building (adjusted basis of $40,000).

Progress is allowed a credit of $12,000 (20% × $60,000) for rehabilitation expenditures. The credit is spread over five years ($2,400 per year). The corporation then increases the basis of the building by $48,000 [$60,000 (rehabilitation expenditures) − $12,000 (credit allowed)].

To qualify for the credit, buildings must be substantially rehabilitated. A building has been *substantially rehabilitated* if qualified rehabilitation expenditures exceed the *greater of*:

- The adjusted basis of the property before the rehabilitation expenditures, or
- $5,000.

Qualified rehabilitation expenditures do not include the cost of acquiring a building, the cost of facilities related to a building (such as a parking lot), and the cost of enlarging an existing building. Stringent rules apply concerning the retention of the building's original internal and external walls.

17-1c **Work Opportunity Tax Credit**

The **work opportunity tax credit** [6] was enacted to encourage employers to hire individuals from a variety of targeted and economically disadvantaged groups. Examples include long-term unemployed individuals (those unemployed for at least 27 weeks), qualified ex-felons, high-risk youths, food stamp recipients, veterans, summer youth employees, and long-term family assistance recipients.

Computation of the Work Opportunity Tax Credit: General

The credit generally is equal to 40 percent of the first $6,000 of wages (per eligible employee) for the first 12 months of employment. The credit is not available for wages paid to an employee after the *first year* of employment. If the employee's first year

---

[6] § 51. The credit is available for qualifying employees who start work before 2020.

overlaps two of the employer's tax years, however, the employer may take the credit over two tax years. If the credit is claimed, the employer's tax deduction for wages is reduced by the amount of the credit.

To qualify an employer for the 40 percent credit, the employee must (1) be certified by a designated local agency as being a member of one of the targeted groups and (2) have completed at least 400 hours of service to the employer. If an employee meets the first condition but not the second, the credit is reduced to 25 percent, provided the employee has completed a minimum of 120 hours of service to the employer.

DIGGING DEEPER **1**   **In-depth coverage can be found on this book's companion website: www.cengage.com**

The Big Picture

EXAMPLE 5

Return to the facts of *The Big Picture* on p. 17-1. In January 2018, Progress Corporation hires four individuals who are certified to be members of a qualifying targeted group. Each employee works 1,000 hours and is paid wages of $8,000 during the year.

Progress's work opportunity credit is $9,600 [($6,000 × 40%) × 4 employees]. If the tax credit is taken, Progress reduces its deduction for wages paid by $9,600. No credit is available for wages paid to these employees after their first year of employment.

EXAMPLE 6

On June 1, 2018, Maria, a calendar year taxpayer, hires Joe, a member of a certified group, and obtains the required certification to qualify Maria for the work opportunity credit. During his seven months of work in 2018, Joe is paid $3,500 for 500 hours of work. Maria is allowed a credit of $1,400 ($3,500 × 40%) for 2018.

Joe continues to work for Maria in 2019 and is paid $7,000 through May 31, 2019. Because up to $6,000 of first-year wages are eligible for the credit, Maria is also allowed a 40% credit on $2,500 [$6,000 − $3,500 (wages paid in 2018)] of 2019 wages paid. The credit is $1,000 ($2,500 × 40%). None of Joe's wages paid after May 31, 2019, the end of the first year of Joe's employment, are eligible for the credit.

17-1d **Research Activities Credit**

To encourage business-related research and development (R & D) in the U.S. business community, a credit is allowed for certain qualifying expenditures paid or incurred by a taxpayer. The **research activities credit** is the *sum* of three components: (1) an incremental research activities credit, (2) a basic research credit, and (3) an energy research credit.[7]

Incremental Research Activities Credit

The incremental research activities credit applies at a 20 percent rate to the *excess* of qualified research expenses for the taxable year (the credit year) over a base amount.[8] Determining the *base amount* involves a relatively complex series of computations meant to approximate recent historical levels of research activity by the taxpayer. Thus, the credit is allowed only for increases in research expenses.

In general, *research expenditures* qualify if the research relates to discovering technological information that is intended for use in the development of a new or improved business component of the taxpayer. If the research is performed in-house (by the

---

[7]§ 41. A qualified startup company (less than $5 million in gross receipts) can offset the credit against its payroll tax liability.

[8]In lieu of determining the incremental research credit as described here, a taxpayer may elect to calculate the credit using an alternative simplified credit procedure. See §§ 41(c)(4) and (5).

taxpayer or its employees), all of the expenses qualify. If the research is contracted to others outside the taxpayer's business, only 65 percent of the amount paid qualifies for the credit.[9]

Bobwhite Company incurs the following research expenditures.

In-house wages, supplies, computer time	$135,000
Payment to Cutting Edge Scientific (a contractor)	100,000

Bobwhite's qualified research expenditures are $200,000 [$135,000 + ($100,000 × 65%)]. If the base amount is $100,000, the incremental research activities credit is $20,000 [($200,000 − $100,000) × 20%].

The research incremental credit is *not* allowed for:[10]

- Research conducted once commercial production begins.
- Surveys and studies such as market research, testing, or routine data collection.
- Research conducted *outside* the United States (other than research undertaken in Puerto Rico or U.S. possessions).
- Research in the social sciences, arts, or humanities.

In addition to qualifying for the research credit, research expenditures also can be *expensed* in the year incurred. One of three options must be chosen by the taxpayer:[11]

1. Use the full credit and reduce the expense deduction for research expenses by 100 percent of the credit, or
2. Retain the full expense deduction and reduce the credit by the product of the full credit times the maximum corporate tax rate (35 percent), or
3. Use the full credit, *capitalize* the research expenses and *amortize* them over 60 months or more.[12]

EXAMPLE 8

Assume the same facts as in Example 7, which shows that the potential incremental research activities credit is $20,000. In the current year, the amounts Bobwhite can deduct and the credit amount under each of the three choices are computed as follows.

	Credit Amount	Deduction Amount
• Full credit and reduced deduction		
$20,000 − $0	$20,000	
$200,000 − $20,000		$180,000
• Reduced credit and full deduction		
$20,000 − [(100% × $20,000) × 35%]	13,000	
$200,000 − $0		200,000
• Full credit and capitalize and elect to amortize costs over 60 months		
$20,000 − $0	20,000	
($200,000/60) × 12		40,000

The value of the deduction depends on Bobwhite's marginal tax rates.

---

[9]§ 41(b)(3)(A). In the case of payments to a qualified research consortium, § 41(b)(3)(A) provides that 75% of the amount paid qualifies for the credit. In contrast, for amounts paid to an energy research consortium, § 41(b)(3)(D) allows the full amount to qualify for the credit.

[10]§ 41(d).

[11]§§ 174 and 280C(c). Recall the discussion of rules for deducting research and experimental expenditures in Chapter 5.

[12]In this case, the amount capitalized and subject to amortization is reduced by the full amount of the credit *only* if the credit exceeds the amount allowable as a deduction.

Basic Research Credit

Corporations (other than S corporations or personal service corporations) are allowed an additional 20 percent credit for basic research expenditures incurred, in *excess* of a base amount.[13] *Basic research* is defined generally as any original investigation for the advancement of scientific knowledge not having a specific commercial objective. Basic research conducted outside the United States and in the social sciences, arts, or humanities does not qualify.

Energy Research Credit

This component of the research credit encourages taxpayers to support a specific type of exempt organization conducting energy research (called an energy research consortium). The credit is equal to 20 percent of payments made to these organizations.

17-1e Energy Credits

The Internal Revenue Code contains a variety of **energy credits** for businesses and individuals to encourage the conservation of natural resources and the development of energy sources other than oil and gas. The primary goals of the tax provisions are to improve energy-related infrastructure and encourage higher levels of energy conservation. Credit amounts and expiration dates differ for the various provisions.

Some of the more widely applicable provisions include credits for:

- Businesses that buy fuel cell and microturbine power plants.
- Taxpayers who purchase alternative power motor vehicles and refueling property.

17-1f Disabled Access Credit

The **disabled access credit** is designed to encourage eligible small businesses to make their facilities more accessible to disabled individuals. The credit, created as part of the Americans with Disabilities Act of 1990, is calculated at the rate of 50 percent of the eligible expenditures that exceed $250 but do not exceed $10,250. As a result, the maximum credit is $5,000 ($10,000 × 50%).[14]

An *eligible small business* is a business that during the previous year either had gross receipts of $1 million or less or had no more than 30 full-time employees. A sole proprietorship, a partnership, a regular corporation, or an S corporation can qualify as such an entity.

Eligible expenditures include any reasonable and necessary amounts that are paid or incurred to make older buildings accessible (only buildings first placed in service before November 6, 1990, qualify). Qualifying projects include installing ramps, widening doorways, and adding raised markings on elevator control buttons. Costs to assist hearing- or visually-impaired employees or customers who interact with the business also qualify. These costs can include both personnel (e.g., an interpreter) or equipment (e.g, audio or visual equipment or modifications to existing equipment).

The property's tax basis is reduced by the amount of the credit.

EXAMPLE 9

This year, Red, Inc., an eligible small business, makes $11,000 of capital improvements to a building that had been placed in service in June 1990. The improvements make Red's business more accessible to the disabled and are eligible expenditures for purposes of the disabled access credit.

The amount of the credit is $5,000 [($10,250 maximum − $250 floor) × 50%]. Although $11,000 of eligible expenditures are incurred, only $10,000 qualifies for the credit. The capital improvements have a depreciable basis of $6,000 [$11,000 (cost) − $5,000 (amount of the credit)].

---

[13]§ 41(e).   [14]§ 44.

17-1g Credit for Small Employer Pension Plan Startup Costs

Small businesses are entitled to a nonrefundable credit for administrative costs associated with establishing and maintaining certain qualified retirement plans.[15] While these costs (e.g., payroll system changes, retirement-related education programs, and consulting fees) are deductible as ordinary and necessary business expenses, the credit lowers the after-tax cost of establishing a qualified retirement program and encourages eligible employers to offer retirement plans for their employees.

The **credit for small employer pension plan startup costs** is 50 percent of qualified startup costs. An eligible employer is one with fewer than 100 employees who have earned at least $5,000 of compensation. The maximum credit is $500 (based on a maximum $1,000 of qualifying expenses), and the deduction for the startup costs incurred is reduced by the amount of the credit. The credit can be claimed for qualifying costs incurred in each of the three years beginning with the tax year in which the retirement plan becomes effective (maximum total credit of $1,500).

> **EXAMPLE 10**
>
> Maple Company decides to establish a qualified retirement plan for its employees. In the process, it pays consulting fees of $1,200 to a firm that will provide educational seminars to Maple's employees and will assist the payroll department in making necessary changes to the payroll system.
>
> Maple may claim a credit for the pension plan startup costs of $500 ($1,200 of qualifying costs, limited to $1,000 × 50%), and its deduction for these expenses is reduced to $700 ($1,200 − $500).

17-1h Credit for Employer-Provided Child Care

An employer's expenses to provide for the care of employee's children is a deductible business expense. Alternatively, employers may claim a credit for providing child care facilities to their employees during normal working hours.[16]

The **credit for employer-provided child care**, limited annually to $150,000, is composed of the aggregate of two components: 25 percent of qualified child care expenses and 10 percent of qualified child care resource and referral services. *Qualified child care expenses* include the costs of acquiring, constructing, rehabilitating, expanding, and operating a child care facility. *Child care resource and referral services* include amounts paid or incurred under a contract to provide child care resource and referral services to an employee.

Any qualifying expenses otherwise deductible by the taxpayer are reduced by the amount of the credit. In addition, the taxpayer's basis for any property acquired or constructed and used for qualifying purposes is reduced by the amount of the credit. If within 10 years of being placed in service a child care facility ceases to be used for a qualified use, the taxpayer recaptures a portion of the credit previously claimed.[17]

> **The Big Picture**
>
> **EXAMPLE 11**
>
> Return to the facts of *The Big Picture* on p. 17-1. During the year, Progress Corporation constructs a child care facility for $400,000 to be used by its employees who have preschool-aged children in need of child care services while their parents are at work. In addition, Progress incurs salary costs for child care workers and other administrative costs associated with the facility of $100,000 during the year.
>
> As a result, Progress's credit for employer-provided child care is $125,000 [($400,000 + $100,000) × 25%]. Correspondingly, the basis of the facility is reduced to $300,000 ($400,000 − $100,000), and the deduction for salaries and administrative costs is reduced to $75,000 ($100,000 − $25,000).

In-depth coverage can be found on this book's companion website: **www.cengage.com**   **2** DIGGING DEEPER

---

[15]§ 45E.
[16]§ 45F.
[17]§ 45F(d).

GLOBAL TAX ISSUES   **Sourcing Income in Cyberspace—Getting It Right When Calculating the Foreign Tax Credit**

The overall limitation on the foreign tax credit plays a critical role in restricting the amount of the credit available to a taxpayer. In the overall limitation formula, the taxpayer must characterize the year's taxable income as either earned (or sourced) inside or outside the United States. As a general rule, a relatively greater percentage of foreign-source income in the formula leads to a larger foreign tax credit. But classifying income as either foreign or U.S. source is not always a simple matter.

The existing income-sourcing rules were developed long before the existence of the internet, and taxing authorities are finding it challenging to apply these rules to internet transactions. Where does a sale take place when the web server is in Scotland, the seller is in India, and the customer is in Illinois? Where is a service performed when all activities take place over the internet? These questions and more must be answered by the United States and its trading partners as the internet economy grows in size and importance.

17-1i Foreign Tax Credit

Income and loss from the export, licensing, and branch operations of a U.S. person are taxed under the worldwide system of business taxation. If the non-U.S country also imposes an income tax on such income, the possibility of double taxation arises. Problems associated with double taxation include the stacking of tax rates for the various countries upon each other, resulting in high effective tax rates on the dual-taxed income, and the harmonization of the tax rules of the various countries to the taxpayer's detriment.

Concerns involving double taxation most often are addressed through language in applicable tax treaties, ideally assigning taxable income to only one of the countries involved, and through tax credits and exemptions in the taxpayer's home country. The United States long has allowed a **foreign tax credit (FTC)** for this purpose, typically for use when the dual-taxed transaction occurs in a non-treaty country.[18] The FTC is an annual taxpayer election; lacking an FTC election, the tax payments are claimed as deductions against gross income.

The FTC is allowed against the taxpayer's regular tax liability, such that only the non-U.S. tax obligation is paid on the dual-taxed income. The FTC is limited, though, to the U.S. tax that would be incurred on the income amount. Thus, the credit equals the *lesser of* (1) the foreign tax actually paid or (2) the following amount:[19]

$$\frac{\text{Foreign-source taxable income}}{\text{Total (worldwide) taxable income}} \quad \boxed{\text{X}} \rightarrow \text{U.S. tax before FTC}$$

Where a foreign tax payment is not allowed as a current-year credit under the *lesser of* rule, the disallowed amount is allowed in another tax year as a carryover. FTCs are carried back 1 year and forward 10 years. FTC carryovers tend to occur when the effective tax rate that applies to the dual-taxed income is lower in the United States than it is in the other country.

---

[18]The credit is allowed via § 27, but the qualifications and calculation procedure for the FTC are contained in §§ 901-908. Although taxpayer can claim a deduction for the foreign taxes paid, instead of a credit, in most instances, the credit is advantageous since it is a direct offset against the tax liability.

[19]§ 904.

BlueCo, a U.S. corporation, manufactures and sells most of its products in the United States. It also conducts some business in the European Union through various branches. During the current year, BlueCo reports taxable income of $700,000, of which $500,000 is U.S.-source and $200,000 is foreign-source. Foreign income taxes paid amounted to $45,000. BlueCo's U.S. income tax liability is $147,000. What is its allowable foreign tax credit?

(1)	Foreign taxes paid	$45,000
(2)	U.S. tax associated with dual-taxed income	
	$\dfrac{\$200{,}000\,(\text{Foreign-source TI})}{\$700{,}000\,(\text{Total TI})} \times \$147{,}000\,(\text{U.S. tax})$	$42,000
(3)	FTC allowed [lesser of (1) or (2)]	$42,000
(4)	FTC carryforward [(1) − (2), but not below $0]	$ 3,000

17-1j Small Employer Health Insurance Credit

Under the Affordable Care Act (ACA), a tax credit is available to a qualified small employer for nonelective contributions to purchase health insurance for its employees.[20] The insurance must be purchased through a Small Business Health Options Program (SHOP) Marketplace established as part of the ACA. The credit is available only for two consecutive tax years.

To qualify for the credit in 2018, the employer must have no more than 25 full-time equivalent employees whose annual full-time wages average no more than $53,200 ($52,400 in 2017). The employer must pay at least half the cost of the health insurance premiums.[21] The credit is 50 percent of the health insurance premiums paid. It is subject to a phaseout if the employer has more than 10 full-time equivalent employees and/or has annual full-time wages that average more than $26,600 ($26,200 in 2017).[22]

17-1k Credit for Employer-Provided Family and Medical Leave

Employers can claim a general business credit equal to 12.5 percent of the wages paid to qualifying employees while they are on family and medical leave.[23] To claim the **credit for employer-provided family and medical leave**, employers must pay a minimum of 50 percent of the wages normally paid to an employee during the leave. If the wages paid during the leave *exceed* 50 percent of normal wages, the credit is increased by .25 percentage point for each percentage point above 50 percent. For example, if the employer pays 60 percent of the usual wages, then the credit is 15 percent [12.5 percent + (0.25 × 10)].

The credit is capped at 25 percent of wages paid (this would be allowed if the employer paid 100 percent of the employee's wages during the leave). The credit is limited to 12 weeks of leave per employee during any taxable year.

An employer must have a written policy in place that allows all qualifying full-time employees no less than two weeks of annual paid family and medical leave (non-full-time employees must be offered leave on a pro rata basis). Wages paid as vacation leave, personal leave, or other medical or sick leave are not considered to be family and medical leave. The credit applies to wages paid in taxable years beginning after 2017 and before 2020.

Concept Summary 17.1 provides an overview of the tax credits discussed in this chapter.

---

[20] § 45R.

[21] §§ 45R(d)(1) and (4). The wage amount is indexed for inflation each year.

[22] § 45R(c). The credit percentage for tax-exempt employers is 35%.

[23] § 45S, added by the TCJA of 2017. "Family and medical leave" is as defined by the Family and Medical Leave Act of 1993.

Concept Summary 17.1

Tax Credits

Credit	Computation	Comments
General business (§ 38)	May not exceed net income tax minus the greater of tentative minimum tax or 25% of net regular tax liability that exceeds $25,000.	Components include tax credit for rehabilitation expenditures, work opportunity tax credit, research activities credit, low-income housing credit, disabled access credit, credit for small employer pension plan startup costs, and credit for employer-provided child care. Unused credit may be carried back 1 year and forward 20 years. FIFO method applies to carrybacks, carryovers, and credits earned during current year.
Rehabilitation expenditures (§ 47)	Qualifying investment times rehabilitation percentage; rate for certified historic structures is 20%.	Part of general business credit and therefore subject to same carryback, carryover, and FIFO rules. Purpose is to discourage businesses from moving from economically distressed areas to new locations.
Work opportunity (§ 51)	Credit is limited to 40% of the first $6,000 of wages paid to each eligible employee.	Part of the general business credit and therefore subject to the same carryback, carryover, and FIFO rules. Purpose is to encourage employment of members of economically disadvantaged groups.
Research activities (§ 41)	Incremental credit is 20% of excess of computation-year expenditures over a base amount. Basic research credit is allowed to certain corporations for 20% of cash payments to qualified organizations that exceed a specially calculated base amount. An energy research credit is allowed for 20% of qualifying payments made to an energy research consortium.	Part of general business credit and therefore subject to same carryback, carryover, and FIFO rules. Purpose is to encourage high-tech and energy research in the United States.
Low-income housing (§ 42)	Appropriate rate times eligible basis (portion of project attributable to low-income units).	Part of general business credit and therefore subject to same carryback, carryover, and FIFO rules. Recapture may apply. Purpose is to encourage construction of housing for low-income individuals. Credit is available each year for 10 years.
Energy credits	Various items to encourage individuals and businesses to "go green."	Part of general business credit and therefore subject to same carryback, carryover, and FIFO rules.
Disabled access (§ 44)	Credit is 50% of eligible access expenditures that exceed $250 but do not exceed $10,250. Maximum credit is $5,000.	Part of general business credit and therefore subject to same carryback, carryover, and FIFO rules. Purpose is to encourage small businesses to become more accessible to disabled individuals. Available only to eligible small businesses.
Credit for small employer pension plan startup costs (§ 45E)	The credit equals 50% of qualified startup costs incurred by eligible employers. Maximum annual credit is $500. Deduction for related expenses is reduced by the amount of the credit.	Part of general business credit and therefore subject to same carryback, carryover, and FIFO rules. Purpose is to encourage small employers to establish qualified retirement plans for their employees.
Credit for employer-provided child care (§ 45F)	Credit is equal to 25% of qualified child care expenses plus 10% of qualified expenses for child care resource and referral services. Maximum credit is $150,000. Deduction for related expenses or basis must be reduced by the amount of the credit.	Part of general business credit and therefore subject to same carryback, carryover, and FIFO rules. Purpose is to encourage employers to provide child care for their employees' children during normal working hours.
Foreign tax (§ 27)	Foreign taxable income/total worldwide taxable income × U.S. tax = Overall limitation. Lesser of foreign taxes imposed or overall limitation.	Unused credits may be carried back 1 year and forward 10 years. Purpose is to reduce double taxation of foreign income.

continued

Tax Credits—(Continued)

Credit	Computation	Comments
Small Employer Health Insurance Credit (§ 45R)	The credit is 50% of the health insurance premiums paid (subject to a phaseout).	To qualify for the credit, the employer must have no more than 25 full-time equivalent employees whose annual full-time wages average no more than $53,200 (2018).
Credit for employer-provided family and medical leave (§ 45S)	Credit is equal to 12.5% of wages paid to qualifying employees while they are on family and medical leave (limited to 12 weeks per employee per year). Employers must pay a minimum of 50% of the wages normally paid; if wages paid during the leave *exceed* 50% of normal wages, the credit is increased by .25% for each percentage point above 50% to a maximum credit of 25%.	Nonrefundable credit. Part of general business credit and therefore subject to same carryback, carryover, and FIFO rules. Purpose is to encourage employers to provide leave to their employees for family and medical purposes (e.g,, birth of a child; care for a sick child, spouse, or parent).

17-2 **INDIVIDUAL ALTERNATIVE MINIMUM TAX**

LO.3

Explain the rationale for the alternative minimum tax (AMT).

The tax law has always contained incentives intended to influence the economic and social behavior of taxpayers. Some taxpayers were able to take advantage of enough of these incentives to significantly minimize or entirely avoid any Federal income tax liability. Although these taxpayers were legally minimizing their tax liabilities, Congress became concerned about the inequity that resulted when taxpayers with substantial economic incomes could avoid paying income tax.[24] To attempt to alleviate this inequity, the **alternative minimum tax (AMT)** was enacted. The goal of the AMT is to ensure that all taxpayers with more than modest economic incomes pay some minimum amount of tax. In the tax years prior to the Tax Cuts and Jobs Act (TCJA) of 2017, approximately 4 million individual taxpayers indicated a positive AMT liability on their Form 1040, raising more than $25 billion in revenue for the U.S. Treasury annually. The changes made by the TCJA will reduce the number of taxpayers in AMT significantly; the impact of these changes on AMT revenue generated remains to be seen.

The AMT applies to individuals, trusts, and estates. While the calculations involved are similar for all taxpayers subject to the AMT, certain components of the AMT formula are unique to specific entities. The focus of this section of the chapter is on the individual AMT.

In theory all individual taxpayers subject to the Federal income tax are subject to the AMT. Whether a taxpayer has an AMT liability depends on a number of factors, including the taxpayer's income, geographic location, and family situation as well as the exclusions, deductions, and credits utilized in the calculation of his or her regular Federal income tax liability. The first part of this section of the chapter presents a detailed discussion of the individual AMT; the TCJA's repeal of the corporate AMT is briefly addressed at the end of this section.

17-2a **Alternative Minimum Taxable Income (AMTI)**

LO.4

Present and explain the formula for computing the AMT for individuals.

The tax base used to determine AMT liability is referred to as the **alternative minimum taxable income (AMTI)** amount (Exhibit 17.2). The calculation of AMTI does not follow the direct approach taken in the calculation of a taxpayer's regular taxable income.[25] Rather than having a taxpayer recalculate the components of his or her individual income tax formula using a different set of AMT rules, the calculation of AMTI *begins*

---

[24]Joint Committee on Taxation, *General Explanation of the Tax Reform Act of 1986 ("Blue Book"),* (JCS-10-87) May 4, 1987, pp. 432–433.

[25]A "direct approach" means that in calculating regular taxable income, gross income is reduced by deductions to arrive at taxable income.

with regular taxable income as shown in Exhibit 17.2. In other words, the AMT calculation requires a taxpayer to reconcile taxable income to AMTI, thus taking an indirect approach to the calculation.

Part of the reason for this indirect approach may be that many items of income and expense are treated the same way for both regular income tax and AMT purposes. For example, a taxpayer's salary is included in computing taxable income and is also included in AMTI. Some itemized deductions, such as charitable contributions and medical expenses, also are allowed for both regular income tax and AMT purposes.

While many amounts are left unchanged, the tax law provides that some income and expense items are treated differently for regular income tax and AMT purposes. In some cases, the income or expense amount is reconsidered in aggregate. For example, interest income on bonds issued by state, county, and local governments is excluded in computing taxable income. However, if such bonds are private activity bonds, the interest income earned is included in AMTI.

In other cases, the income or expense item is included in both the regular income tax and AMT computations, but the amount differs. For example, the completed contract method can be used to report income from some long-term contracts for regular income tax purposes, but the percentage of completion method is required for AMT purposes. Thus, in the tax year, the amount of income from the contract included in taxable income will differ from the amount included in AMTI. Similarly, passive activity losses, to the extent of passive income, are deductible in calculating both taxable income and AMTI, but the AMT passive loss may differ from the regular tax passive loss as a result of other AMT provisions.[26]

As shown in Exhibit 17.2, differences between regular tax and AMT income and expense amounts are categorized as either adjustments or preferences. Most adjustments relate to timing differences that arise because of different regular income tax and AMT treatment. Adjustments that are caused by timing differences will eventually reverse; positive adjustments will be offset by negative adjustments in the future and vice versa.[27]

Depreciation provides a good example of a timing difference. In general, AMT depreciation methods are slower than regular tax depreciation methods. Initially then, there will be less depreciation for AMT purposes than for regular tax purposes. This difference will result in positive timing differences until AMT depreciation is larger than regular tax depreciation, when the timing difference will become negative. However, over time, the same amount of depreciation will be deducted for regular tax and AMT purposes because the asset's basis for regular tax and AMT depreciation is the same.

EXHIBIT 17.2	Alternative Minimum Tax Formula for Individuals

Taxable income (increased by any standard deduction taken)

Plus or minus: Adjustments

Plus: Preferences

Equals: Alternative minimum taxable income (AMTI)

Minus: Exemption

Equals: Alternative minimum tax (AMT) base

Multiplied by: 26% or 28% rate

Equals: Tentative minimum tax before foreign tax credit

Minus: AMT foreign tax credit

Equals: Tentative minimum tax (TMT)

Minus: Regular tax liability (less any foreign tax credit)

Equals: AMT (if TMT > regular tax liability)

---

[26]§ 58(b).   [27]§ 56.

In contrast, in the reconciliation of taxable income to AMTI, preference items will always serve to increase the starting point of the AMTI calculation.[28] Certain deductions and exclusions allowed to taxpayers for regular income tax purposes provide significant tax savings. AMT preferences are designed to take back all or part of the tax benefit derived as a result of the use of these deductions and exclusions. This is why preference items serve only to increase the taxable income amount that is the starting point of the AMTI calculation. The effect of adding back these preference items is to disallow them for AMT purposes. Examples of preferences include percentage depletion in excess of the property's adjusted basis and excess intangible drilling costs. Both adjustments and preferences are discussed in more detail later in the chapter.

17-2b **AMT Formula: Other Components**

Calculating AMTI is the first step in the determination of whether a taxpayer will have an alternative minimum tax liability. To complete the AMT calculation, as shown in Exhibit 17.2, the exemption, rates, credit, and regular tax liability must all be considered.

Exemption Amount

After calculating AMTI, the taxpayer determines the AMT **exemption amount**. Tax law provides for exemption amounts in both the regular tax and AMT liability calculations. The exemption amounts for AMT are higher than the exemption amounts for regular tax liability purposes. Thus, taxpayers with minimal positive adjustments or preferences will avoid being subject to the AMT as a result of the exemption.

The initial exemption amounts for 2018 are listed below.[29] The annual exemption is phased out at a rate of 25 cents on the dollar when AMTI exceeds certain amounts (see Example 13). These amounts are tied to the taxpayer's filing status.

Status	Exemption	Phaseout Begins at	Phaseout Ends at
Married, joint	$109,400	$1,000,000	$1,437,600
Single or head of household	70,300	500,000	781,200
Married, separate	54,700	500,000	718,800

Once AMTI equals the end of the phaseout range, a taxpayer's exemption amount will equal zero. Example 13 explains the calculation of the phaseout of the AMT exemption.

Harry, who is single, records AMTI of $680,000 for the year. His $70,300 initial exemption amount is reduced by $45,000 [($680,000 − $500,000) × 25% phaseout rate]. Harry's AMT exemption is $25,300 ($70,300 exemption − $45,000 reduction).

EXAMPLE
13

AMT Liability

After the exemption is calculated, a taxpayer's AMT liability can be determined. As shown in Exhibit 17.2, AMTI less the exemption equals the AMT base. This base amount is multiplied by the tax rate and reduced by any credits that are allowed, resulting in the tentative minimum tax (TMT).

The relationship between the regular tax liability and the TMT is key to the AMT calculation. If the regular tax liability exceeds the TMT, the taxpayer's AMT liability is zero. However, if the TMT exceeds the regular tax liability, the excess is the taxpayer's AMT liability. Technically, the AMT is a surtax; both tax law and the Form 6251 categorize any excess of TMT over the taxpayer's regular tax liability as the AMT

[28]§ 57.

[29]The exemption amounts are indexed annually for inflation. § 55(d)(4).

amount.[30] For practical purposes, the taxpayer pays whichever tax liability is greater—that calculated using the regular income tax rules or that calculated using the AMT rules.

A graduated, two-tier AMT rate schedule applies in calculating the TMT. A 26 percent rate applies on an AMT base up to $191,100 ($95,550 for married, filing separately); a 28 percent rate applies to that base amount and above.[31] Any net capital gain or qualified dividend income included in the AMT base is taxed at the favorable tax rates for such amounts rather than at the AMT statutory rates.

EXAMPLE 14

Anna, an unmarried individual, has regular taxable income of $450,000. Anna itemizes deductions; she has positive adjustments of $70,000 and preferences of $65,000. Anna's regular tax liability for 2018 is $133,190. Her AMT in 2018 is calculated as follows.

Taxable income	$450,000
Plus: Adjustments	70,000
Plus: Preferences	65,000
Equals: AMTI	$585,000
Minus: AMT exemption ($70,300 − $21,250)	49,050
Equals: AMT base	$535,950
TMT [($191,100 × 26%) + ($535,950 − $191,100) × 28%]	$146,244
Minus: Regular tax liability	133,190
Equals: AMT	$ 13,054

Anna will pay the IRS a total of $146,244, consisting of her regular tax liability of $133,190 plus her AMT of $13,054.

Credits against regular tax liability are allowed to some taxpayers depending on their economic circumstances or the type of business activity in which they engage. Personal nonrefundable credits (e.g., Adoption Credit, Lifetime Learning Credit, and Saver's Credit) can offset any AMT liability as well as any regular tax liability.[32]

EXAMPLE 15

Michael has total personal nonrefundable credits of $11,000, regular tax liability of $133,000, and tentative minimum tax of $126,000. The entire $11,000 credit is available to offset Michael's $133,000 tax liability.

17-2c **AMT Adjustments**

LO.5

Identify the adjustments made in calculating AMTI.

As discussed previously, adjustments relate to timing differences that arise because of differences in how an item is treated for regular income tax and AMT purposes. As a result, it is necessary to determine the amount of an adjustment and whether the adjustment is positive or negative.

Remember that the AMTI calculation begins with the regular taxable income amount before any standard deduction taken by the taxpayer. Where the regular tax and AMT treatment of a deduction (or an item of expense) differ, the direction of the adjustment is determined as follows.

Regular tax deduction	**>**	AMT deduction	**=**	Positive AMT adjustment
Regular tax deduction	**<**	AMT deduction	**=**	Negative AMT adjustment

---

[30]§ 55(a).

[31]§§ 55(b)(1)(A) and (d)(4)(B).

[32]§ 26(a)(2).

Conversely, the direction of an adjustment attributable to an income (or revenue) item can be determined as follows.

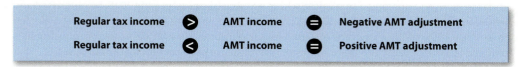

The remainder of this section discusses specific AMT adjustments.

Depreciation of Real Property

For regular income tax purposes, real property is depreciated using the straight-line method. The cost of residential real property is recovered over 27.5 years, and the cost of all other real property is recovered over 39 years.[33] Whether an AMT adjustment is required for real property depreciation depends on when the property was placed in service.

For real property placed in service after 1986 (MACRS property) and before 1999, AMT depreciation is computed using the straight-line method, but the longer alternative depreciation system (ADS) recovery period is used. For real property placed in service after 1998, no AMT adjustment is required.[34] After 1998, real property depreciation is the same for both AMT and regular tax purposes. In other words, because straight-line depreciation and the same recovery period are used for both regular tax and AMT purposes, no AMT adjustment is necessary.

Depreciation of Personal Property

While the TCJA did not substantially change the provisions that govern the calculation of regular tax depreciation, it increased the amount that could be immediately expensed and expanded the definition of property eligible for such expensing. Changes to these immediate expensing provisions (also known as bonus depreciation or additional first-year depreciation) decreased the need for AMT depreciation adjustments for tangible personal property. The expanded definition of property eligible for such expensing included in the TCJA of 2017 will further reduce the need for such adjustments.

As discussed in text Section 5-7g, until December 31, 2022, taxpayers are eligible to expense immediately 100 percent of the cost of qualified property placed in service for regular tax purposes. In general, qualified property is broadly defined to include property with a recovery period of 20 years or less, software amortized over 36 months, water-utility property, qualified films, television and live theatrical productions, certain self-constructed assets, and plants and vines bearing fruits and nuts. The TCJA also broadened the definition of property eligible for full expensing by eliminating the requirement that the original use of property must begin with the taxpayer; in other words, used property is now eligible for full expensing.[35]

With respect to the AMT, a depreciation adjustment is not required when the cost of an asset is expensed under the immediate expensing provisions.[36] This is true both in the year the asset is placed in service and in all succeeding years in which the asset is depreciated for regular tax purposes (which would occur where the immediate expensing percentage is less than 100 percent). Additionally, a taxpayer may elect not to expense the cost of an asset for regular tax purposes. However, as long as the asset was *eligible for* such expensing, no AMT depreciation adjustment is required, again, either in the year placed in service or in any succeeding year.[37] As a result of these provisions and the applicability of expensing to used property, the AMT depreciation amount for most tangible personal property is the same as the regular tax depreciation amount of such property. The following examples illustrate these ideas.

---

[33]The 39-year life generally applies to nonresidential real property placed in service on or after May 13, 1993.

[34]§ 56(a)(1)(A).

[35]§ 168(k).

[36]§ 168(k)(2)(G).

[37]Rev.Proc. 2017–33, 2017–19 I.R.B. 1236, § 4.04.

Full Expensing and AMT Depreciation

EXAMPLE 16

Emerson owns and operates a small after-school tutoring business. In early 2018, he purchased and placed in service furniture costing $18,000. Rather than depreciate the furniture, Emerson elected to expense 100% of the cost of the furniture for tax purposes. No AMT depreciation adjustment is required in 2018 because the office furniture was fully expensed for regular tax purposes.

EXAMPLE 17

Assume the same facts as in Example 16, except that Emerson elected to depreciate the furniture for regular tax purposes rather than immediately expense the cost. He believes that his business will be more profitable in the future and would like to ensure that he has tax deductions available to offset this future income.

In 2018, Emerson's regular tax depreciation deduction for the furniture is $2,572 ($18,000 × .1429). Even though the furniture is being depreciated for regular tax purposes, no AMT depreciation adjustment is needed because the property was *eligible* for full expensing.

Where AMT depreciation adjustments will be required (e.g., for public utility property and certain property owned by car dealerships ineligible for full expensing), the amount and direction of the adjustment is driven by a difference in the accelerated-depreciation percentage for regular tax and AMT purposes. For personal property, the GDS recovery period and convention (see text Section 5-8d) are used to calculate regular tax depreciation as well as AMT depreciation. However, where the depreciation deduction for regular tax purposes is calculated using the 200 percent declining-balance method, AMT depreciation is calculated using the 150 percent declining-balance method.[38] (See Exhibit 5.8 in Chapter 5.) Example 18 illustrates the adjustment calculation.

EXAMPLE 18

Sawyer placed an $8,000 asset ineligible for full expensing in service in year 1. The MACRS recovery period for such an asset is three years. Annual regular tax (using 200% declining balance) and AMT depreciation (using 150% declining balance) amounts are as follows.

Tax Year	Regular Income Tax Deduction	AMT Deduction	AMT Adjustment
1	$2,666	$2,000	$ 666
2	3,556	3,000	556
3	1,185	2,000	(815)
4	593	1,000	(407)

As is shown in Example 18, the same conventions are used for regular tax and AMT depreciation. Thus, the asset is fully depreciated over four years for both regular tax and AMT purposes, because the same recovery period and the half-year convention are applied in both calculations. The AMT depreciation deduction is initially smaller because of the lesser declining balance percentage used for AMT purposes. As a result, the adjustments in year 1 and year 2 are positive; taxable income is increased by these amounts to arrive at the AMT depreciation amount. In the last two years of the asset's life, the AMT adjustments are negative. Taxable income will be decreased by these amounts to arrive at the AMT depreciation amount. In total, the same amount of depreciation is taken for both regular tax and AMT purposes.

All personal property is taken into consideration in computing one net AMT depreciation adjustment, regardless of the date placed in service. Using this netting process, the AMT adjustment for a tax year is the difference between the total regular tax depreciation for all personal property and the total depreciation computed for that property for AMT purposes. The same principles that apply in Example 18 apply in aggregate.

---

[38]§ 56(a)(1)(A)(ii).

Pollution Control Facilities

To encourage private industry to abate pollution, tax law provides beneficial amortization provisions for certified pollution control facilities in lieu of depreciation. For regular income tax purposes, a taxpayer may elect to amortize the cost of certified facilities over 60 months. For AMT purposes, such an election is not allowed. Instead, the cost of certified pollution control facilities is recovered through depreciation.

For facilities placed in service after 1998, depreciation for AMT purposes is calculated using the straight-line method over the recovery period that would be used for regular tax (MACRS) purposes.[39] The adjustment for AMTI is equal to the difference between the regular tax amortization deduction and the AMT depreciation amount. The adjustment may be positive or negative.

Circulation Expenditures

Circulation expenditures are expenses incurred to establish, maintain, or increase the circulation of a newspaper, a magazine, or another periodical. For regular income tax purposes, circulation expenditures, other than those the taxpayer elects to charge to a capital account, may be expensed in the year incurred.[40] For AMT purposes, circulation expenditures are not deductible in the year incurred. In computing AMTI, these expenditures must be capitalized and amortized ratably over the three-year period beginning in the year the expenditures were made.[41]

The AMT adjustment for circulation expenditures is calculated by comparing the amount expensed for regular income tax purposes with the amount that can be amortized for AMT purposes. In general, in the year the circulation expenditures are incurred, the adjustment will be positive; more circulation expenditures are deducted for regular tax purposes than are allowed for AMT purposes. In the second and third years, the adjustment will be negative; a deduction is allowed for AMT purposes that was taken in the first year for regular tax purposes.

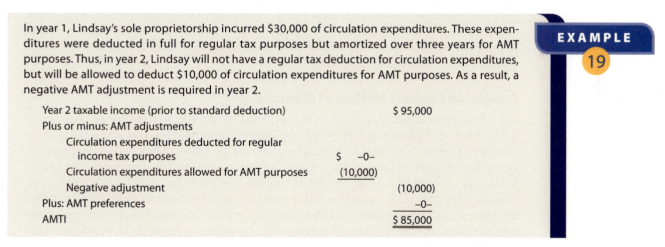

EXAMPLE 19

In year 1, Lindsay's sole proprietorship incurred $30,000 of circulation expenditures. These expenditures were deducted in full for regular tax purposes but amortized over three years for AMT purposes. Thus, in year 2, Lindsay will not have a regular tax deduction for circulation expenditures, but will be allowed to deduct $10,000 of circulation expenditures for AMT purposes. As a result, a negative AMT adjustment is required in year 2.

Year 2 taxable income (prior to standard deduction)		$ 95,000
Plus or minus: AMT adjustments		
Circulation expenditures deducted for regular income tax purposes	$ –0–	
Circulation expenditures allowed for AMT purposes	(10,000)	
Negative adjustment		(10,000)
Plus: AMT preferences		–0–
AMTI		$ 85,000

In Example 19, the allowable AMT deduction is $10,000 more than the allowable regular income tax deduction. Therefore, AMTI is $10,000 less than taxable income. This result is obtained by making a negative AMT adjustment of $10,000.

A taxpayer can avoid an AMT adjustment for circulation expenditures by electing to write off the expenditures over a three-year period for regular income tax purposes.[42]

Expenditures Requiring 10-Year Write-Off for AMT Purposes

Certain expenditures that may be deducted in the year incurred for regular income tax purposes must be written off over a 10-year period for AMT purposes. These rules apply to (1) mine exploration and development costs and (2) research and experimental expenditures.

---

[39]§ 56(a)(5).
[40]§ 173(a).
[41]§ 56(b)(2).
[42]§ 59(e)(2)(A).

In computing taxable income, taxpayers are allowed to deduct expenditures paid or incurred during the taxable year for exploration (ascertaining the existence, location, extent, or quality of a deposit or mineral) and for development of a mine or other natural deposit, other than an oil or gas well.[43] Mine development expenditures are expenses paid or incurred after the existence of ores and minerals in commercially marketable quantities has been discovered.

For AMT purposes, however, mine exploration and development costs must be capitalized and amortized ratably over a 10-year period.[44] Although circulation expenditures are recoverable over a three-year period for AMT purposes, the calculation of the adjustment for mine exploration and development costs is similar in spirit to that for circulation expenditures. The AMT adjustment is calculated by comparing the amount of mine exploration and development costs expensed (if any) for regular tax purposes with the amount amortized for AMT purposes. In general, the adjustment will be positive in the year these expenses are incurred and negative thereafter.

EXAMPLE 20

This year, Audrey incurs $150,000 of mine exploration expenditures and deducts this amount for regular income tax purposes. For AMT purposes, these mine exploration expenditures must be amortized over a 10-year period. Audrey makes a positive adjustment for AMTI of $135,000 ($150,000 allowed for regular income tax − $15,000 for AMT) for this year (i.e., the year in which the expenses were incurred). For AMT purposes, in each of the next nine years, Audrey makes a negative adjustment of $15,000 ($0 allowed for regular income tax − $15,000 for AMT).

To avoid the AMT adjustments for mine exploration and development costs, a taxpayer may elect to write off the expenditures over a 10-year period for regular income tax purposes.[45]

Similarly, for regular tax purposes, rather than capitalize the costs of research and experimentation, a taxpayer can choose to deduct those costs in the year incurred. For AMT purposes, such costs must be amortized over a 10-year period. As a result, the calculation of the adjustment for research and experimental expenditures is similar to the mine development and exploration costs adjustment and similar in spirit to the adjustment for circulation expenditures.

Completed Contract Method of Accounting

For a long-term contract, taxpayers are required to use the percentage of completion method for AMT purposes.[46] However, in limited circumstances, taxpayers can use the completed contract method for regular income tax purposes. Thus, where the percentage of completion method is not used for regular tax purposes, a taxpayer recognizes a different amount of income for regular income tax purposes than for AMT purposes. The resulting AMT adjustment is equal to the difference between income reported under the percentage of completion method and the amount reported using the completed contract method. The adjustment can be either positive or negative, depending on the amount of income recognized under the different methods.

Similar to many of the other adjustments discussed previously, a taxpayer can avoid an AMT adjustment on long-term contracts by using the percentage of completion method for regular income tax purposes rather than the completed contract method.

Incentive Stock Options

Like other compensatory options, **incentive stock options (ISOs)** are granted by employers to motivate employees to work harder to increase the value of the company. In return, employees should benefit from the increased compensation that a higher stock price brings.

---

[43]§§ 617(a) and 616(a).

[44]§ 56(a)(2).

[45]§§ 59(e)(2)(D) and (E).

[46]§ 56(a)(3).

At the time an ISO is granted, the option typically has a zero value. As a result, no gross income is recognized at the date of grant for regular tax purposes, and no adjustment is required for AMT purposes. If the value of the stock increases during the option period, the employee can obtain shares at a favorable price by exercising the option. For regular tax purposes, the exercise of an ISO does not increase taxable income.[47] However, for AMT purposes, the excess of the fair market value of the stock over the exercise price (the *spread* or the *bargain element*) is treated as an adjustment in the taxable year in which the option is exercised.[48]

In January 2018, Manuel exercised an ISO that had been granted by his employer, Gold Corporation, in March 2014. Manuel acquired 1,000 shares of Gold stock for the exercise price of $20 per share. The fair market value of the stock at the date of exercise was $50 per share. The transaction does not affect regular taxable income in either 2014 or 2018. For AMT purposes, Manuel records a positive adjustment of $30,000 ($50,000 fair market value − $20,000 exercise price) for 2018.

As a result of this adjustment, the regular income tax basis of the stock acquired through the exercise of ISOs is different from the AMT basis. The regular income tax basis of the stock is equal to its cost, the exercise price of the option, whereas the AMT basis is equal to the fair market value of the stock on the date the option is exercised. Consequently, the amount of any gain or loss upon disposition of the stock will likely differ for regular income tax and AMT purposes.

Assume the same facts as in the previous example and that Manuel sells the stock acquired with the option for $60,000 in December 2019. His gain for regular income tax purposes is $40,000 ($60,000 amount realized − $20,000 regular income tax basis). For AMT purposes, the gain is $10,000 ($60,000 amount realized − $50,000 AMT basis). Therefore, Manuel will make a negative $30,000 adjustment in computing AMT in 2019. Because the gain on sale was larger for regular tax purposes, the gain reflected in taxable income is decreased by $30,000 ($40,000 regular income tax gain − $10,000 AMT gain) to reflect the $10,000 AMT gain. Note that this $30,000 negative adjustment upon disposition offsets the $30,000 positive adjustment made in the year of exercise.

An employee may be restricted as to when he or she can dispose of stock acquired with an ISO. In other words, the stock acquired with the option may not be freely transferable until some specified period has passed. If there were some restriction, then the employee would not make the AMT adjustment until the stock was freely transferable.

In January 2017, Manuel exercised an ISO that had been granted by his employer, Gold Corporation, in March 2014. Manuel acquired 1,000 shares of Gold stock for the exercise price of $20 per share, when the fair market value of the stock was $50 per share. The stock became freely transferable in February 2018, when the fair market value was $55 per share. For AMT purposes, Manuel will make a positive adjustment of $30,000 ($50,000 fair market value − $20,000 exercise price) in 2018. The option contract does not affect regular taxable income in any tax year.

Finally, if the taxpayer exercises the ISO and disposes of the stock in the same tax year, otherwise known as a disqualifying disposition, compensation income is reported for regular tax purposes, which means that an AMT adjustment is not required for that option exercise.

---

[47]§ 421(a).   [48]§ 56(b)(3).

Adjusted Gain or Loss

When property is sold or disposed of during the year, gain or loss reported for regular income tax purposes may differ from gain or loss determined for AMT purposes. This difference occurs because the adjusted basis of the property for AMT purposes must reflect any current and prior AMT adjustments for the following.[49]

- Depreciation.
- Circulation expenditures.
- Research and experimental expenditures.
- Mine exploration and development costs.
- Certified pollution control facility amortization.

Remember that the AMT calculation begins with regular taxable income. Thus, any gain or loss adjustment should reflect the difference between the regular tax and AMT gain or loss amount. A negative gain or loss adjustment is required if:

- Any gain for AMT purposes is less than the gain for regular income tax purposes,
- Any loss for AMT purposes is more than the loss for regular income tax purposes, or
- A loss is computed for AMT purposes and a gain is computed for regular income tax purposes.

Where the relationship between the regular tax and the AMT amount is reversed, the AMT gain or loss adjustment is positive.

EXAMPLE 24

Sawyer sells the asset he placed in service in year 1 (Example 18) on September 1 of year 3 for $12,500. In the year of sale, two AMT adjustments result: the depreciation adjustment for year 3 and any gain (or loss) adjustment resulting from the sale.

The regular income tax depreciation for year 3 is $593 [$8,000 cost × 14.81% (Chapter 5, Exibit 5.4) × .5]. AMT depreciation for that year is $1,000 [$8,000 × 25% (Chapter 5, Exhibit 5.8) × .5]. Sawyer's negative AMT adjustment for year 3, reflecting the additional depreciation for AMT purposes, is $407 ($593 regular income tax depreciation − $1,000 AMT depreciation).

In computing gain (or loss) as a result of the sale, the adjusted basis in the asset is different for regular income tax and AMT purposes because of depreciation. The adjusted basis for each purpose is determined as follows.

	Regular Income Tax	AMT
Cost	$ 8,000	$ 8,000
Less: Depreciation for prior tax years (see Example 18)	(6,222)	(5,000)
Depreciation for year 3 (see prior paragraph)	(593)	(1,000)
Adjusted basis	$ 1,185	$ 2,000

Having determined the adjusted basis, the recognized gain for regular tax and AMT purposes is calculated as follows.

	Regular Income Tax	AMT
Amount realized	$12,500	$12,500
Adjusted basis	(1,185)	(2,000)
Recognized gain	$11,315	$10,500

Because the regular income tax gain is greater than the AMT gain on the sale of the asset, Sawyer incurs a negative AMT adjustment of $815 ($11,315 regular income tax gain − $10,500 AMT gain). Note that this negative adjustment offsets the prior and current-year adjustments for depreciation.

---

[49]§ 56(a)(6).

Passive Activity Losses

Losses on passive activities are not deductible in computing either regular taxable income or AMTI. However, the rules for computing taxable income differ from the rules for computing AMTI. It follows, then, that the rules for computing such a loss for regular income tax purposes differ from the AMT rules for computing such a loss. For example, where a passive activity involves circulation expenditures, if the amount of such expenditures differs for regular tax and AMT purposes, the amount of loss disallowed for AMT purposes will be larger or smaller than the loss disallowed for regular tax purposes. Therefore, any *passive activity* loss computed for regular income tax purposes may differ from the passive activity loss computed for AMT purposes.[50]

Matt acquired two passive activities this year. He received net passive income of $10,000 from Activity A and had no AMT adjustments or preferences in connection with the activity. Activity B produced gross income of $27,000 and operating expenses (not affected by AMT adjustments or preferences) of $19,000. In the current year, Matt claimed $30,000 of circulation expenditures related to Activity B. As a result, for AMT purposes, a positive $20,000 adjustment for circulation expenditures would be required for Activity B. In addition, Matt deducted $10,000 of percentage depletion in excess of basis (an AMT preference) for Activity B. The following comparison illustrates the differences in the computation of the passive activity loss for regular income tax and AMT purposes for Activity B.

	Regular Income Tax	AMT
Gross income	$ 27,000	$ 27,000
Deductions		
Operating expenses	(19,000)	(19,000)
Circulation expenditures	(30,000)	(10,000)
Depletion	(10,000)	–0–
Passive activity loss	($ 32,000)	($ 2,000)

Because of the $20,000 adjustment for circulation expenditures and the preference for depletion (see the discussion of AMT preferences later in the chapter), the regular income tax passive activity loss of $32,000 for Activity B is reduced, resulting in a passive activity loss of $2,000 for AMT purposes.

For regular income tax purposes, Matt would offset the $10,000 of net passive income from Activity A with $10,000 of the passive loss from Activity B. For AMT purposes, he would offset the $10,000 of net passive income from Activity A with the $2,000 passive loss allowed from Activity B, resulting in passive activity income of $8,000. Thus, in computing AMTI, Matt makes a positive passive activity loss adjustment of $8,000 [$10,000 (passive activity loss allowed for regular income tax) − $2,000 (passive activity loss allowed for AMT)].

To avoid duplication, the AMT adjustment for circulation expenditures and the AMT preference for depletion are *not* reported separately. They are accounted for in determining the passive activity loss adjustment. Also note that differences in regular tax and AMT passive activity loss amounts in the current year will affect the amount of suspended passive activity losses carried forward to future tax years.

Assume the same facts as in the previous example. For regular income tax purposes, Matt reports a suspended passive activity loss of $22,000 [$32,000 (amount of loss) − $10,000 (loss used this year)]. This suspended passive activity loss can offset passive activity income in the future, or it can offset active or portfolio income when Matt disposes of the loss activity. For AMT purposes, Matt's suspended passive activity loss is $0 [$2,000 (amount of loss) − $2,000 (amount used this year)].

---

[50]See text Section 11-3.

Alternative Tax Net Operating Loss Deduction

In computing taxable income, taxpayers can deduct net operating losses (NOLs) created in prior years. While the NOL deduction is allowed for AMT purposes, the regular income tax NOL must be modified to compute AMTI correctly.

The starting point in computing the **alternative tax NOL deduction (ATNOLD)** is the NOL computed for regular income tax purposes. The regular income tax NOL is modified for AMT adjustments and tax preferences to arrive at the ATNOLD. Preferences and adjustment items that have benefited the taxpayer in computing the regular income tax NOL (in other words, the adjustments and preferences that have increased the regular tax NOL) are added back, thereby reducing or eliminating the NOL for AMT purposes.[51]

In 2018, Max incurred a regular tax NOL of $400,000. In 2017, Matt incurred mine exploration and development expenditures of $100,000; no additional expenditures were incurred in 2018. For AMT purposes, in 2018, Matt will expense (make a negative AMT adjustment of) $10,000 related to the 2017 expenditures. Max's deductions also include tax preferences of $80,000. His ATNOLD carryforward to 2019 is $310,000 [$400,000 regular income tax NOL − $80,000 tax preferences deducted in computing the NOL − $10,000 mine exploration and development costs adjustment].

In Example 27, if the regular income tax NOL was allowed in full for AMT purposes, the $80,000 in tax preference items would have the effect of reducing AMTI in the year (or years) the 2018 NOL was utilized. Given that this amount was disallowed in the calculation of AMTI, such an outcome is contradictory to the purpose of the AMT.

Finally, in keeping with the goal of ensuring that taxpayers with economic income pay some minimum amount of tax, a ceiling exists on the amount of the ATNOLD that can be deducted. The deduction is limited to 90 percent of AMTI (before the ATNOLD) in the year to which the NOL is carried forward.[52]

EXAMPLE 28

Assume the same facts as in the previous example, except that Max's AMTI (before the ATNOLD) in 2019 is $190,000. Therefore, of the $310,000 ATNOLD carried forward to 2019 from 2018, only $171,000 ($190,000 × 90%) can be used in recalculating the 2019 AMT. The unused $139,000 of 2018 ATNOLD will next be carried to 2020 for use in recalculating that year's AMT.

A taxpayer who has an ATNOLD that is carried forward to another year must use the ATNOLD against AMTI in that year, even if the taxpayer is not subject to the AMT. This can result in the loss of an ATNOLD, even when the taxpayer does not have an AMT liability.

Emily's ATNOLD for 2019 (carried over from 2018) is $10,000. AMTI in 2019, before considering the ATNOLD, is $25,000. If Emily's regular income tax liability exceeds her TMT, the AMT does not apply. Nevertheless, Emily's ATNOLD of $10,000 is "used up" in 2019 and is not available for carryover to a later year.

The TCJA of 2017 changed the carryover provisions for regular income tax NOLs on a "going forward" basis. NOLs generated in 2018 and thereafter cannot be carried back, but they are carried forward indefinitely. However, such NOLs can offset, at most, 80 percent of taxable income (prior to the NOL deduction) in any carryforward year.

These changes do not apply to NOLs generated prior to 2018. Such NOLs can be carried back 2 years and forward 20 years. For pre-2018 NOLs, the taxpayer may elect

[51]§ 56(a)(4).

[52]§ 56(d)(1)(A)(i)(II).

to forgo the 2-year carryback. Additionally, the NOL deduction is not limited to a percentage of taxable income.

In general, the ATNOLD provisions mirror those in place for the related, regular tax NOL provisions in the tax year generated. Thus, AMT NOLs generated in 2018 (and after) cannot be carried back; such NOLs may only be carried forward. Pre-2018 AMT NOLs can be carried back 2 years and forward 20 years. If the election to forgo the 2-year carryback is made for regular tax purposes, the election also applies for AMT purposes. Finally, whether generated prior to, in, or after 2018, the ATNOLD is limited to 90 percent of AMTI prior to the AMT NOL deduction.

Itemized Deductions

Most of the itemized deductions that are allowed for regular income tax purposes are allowed for AMT purposes. As discussed below, for AMT purposes, the itemized deductions for certain taxes as well as interest expense require adjustment.

Taxes Any state and local sales, income, or property taxes (up to $10,000) deducted by an individual taxpayer in the calculation of regular taxable income are not allowed as a deduction in computing AMTI.[53] Thus, a positive AMT adjustment equal to the amount of such taxes deducted (up to $10,000) is required.

Also remember that under the tax benefit rule, a tax refund is included in regular taxable income to the extent the taxpayer obtained a tax benefit by deducting the tax in a prior year. If the taxpayer's gross income includes the recovery of any tax deducted as an itemized deduction for regular income tax purposes, a negative AMT adjustment in the amount of the recovery is allowed for AMTI purposes.[54] For example, state income taxes can be deducted for regular income tax purposes but cannot be deducted in computing AMTI. Because of this, any refund of such taxes from a prior year that would be included in the calculation of regular taxable income is not included in AMTI.

EXAMPLE 30

Joann, age 35, is a resident of Minnesota. In 2017, her Federal taxable income included an itemized deduction of $4,200 for Minnesota income taxes. In February 2018, Joann received a Federal income tax refund of $5,800 and a Minnesota income tax refund of $600.

In 2018, Joann makes a negative AMT adjustment of $600 for the state tax refund. The $600 refund is included in 2018 regular taxable income because the deduction for state taxes reduced her prior year Federal income tax liability. However, the $600 refund is excluded from her 2018 AMTI because the deduction for state taxes was not allowed for AMT purposes.

Joann's Federal income tax refund does not create an AMT adjustment, as Federal income taxes are not deducted in the calculation of regular taxable income or AMTI.

Interest in General In computing regular taxable income, taxpayers who itemize deductions can deduct qualified residence interest, and they can deduct investment interest to the extent of net investment income.

The AMT deduction allowed for interest expense includes only qualified housing interest[55] and investment interest,[56] to the extent of net investment income included in AMTI (as compared to regular taxable income). Any interest deducted in calculating regular taxable income that is not permitted in calculating AMTI is treated as a positive adjustment. The AMT adjustments for these amounts are discussed below.

Housing Interest Under current regular income tax rules, taxpayers who itemize deductions can deduct *qualified residence interest* on up to two residences. The deduction is limited to interest on acquisition indebtedness up to $750,000 ($350,000 for

---

[53]§ 56(b)(1)(A).
[54]§ 56(b)(1)(D).

[55]§ 56(b)(1)(C)(i).
[56]§ 56(b)(1)(C)(iii).

married taxpayers filing separately).[57] Acquisition indebtedness is debt that is incurred in acquiring, constructing, or substantially improving a qualified residence of the taxpayer and is secured by the residence.

The mortgage interest deduction for AMT purposes is limited to *qualified housing interest* rather than *qualified residence interest*. Qualified housing interest includes only interest incurred to acquire, construct, or substantially improve the taxpayer's principal residence and one other qualified dwelling used for personal purposes.

When additional mortgage interest is incurred (e.g., a mortgage refinancing), interest paid is deductible as qualified housing interest for AMT purposes only if:

- The proceeds are used to acquire or substantially improve a qualified residence,
- Interest on the prior loan was qualified housing interest, and
- The amount of the loan is not increased.

Prior to the TCJA of 2017, interest on home equity loans was the most likely cause of an AMT adjustment for mortgage interest. That is, where a taxpayer took on a home equity loan that was not used to construct or substantially improve the taxpayer's principal residence, such interest was not considered *qualified housing interest* and, as a result, was not deductible in the calculation of AMTI. However, the TCJA suspended the deduction for home equity interest. Thus, post-TCJA, an AMT adjustment for mortgage interest would only arise where interest was incurred on a second residence that was not used for personal purposes (e.g., a vacation rental property). In such situations, a positive AMT adjustment is required in the amount of the difference between qualified *residence* interest allowed as an itemized deduction for regular income tax purposes and qualified *housing* interest allowed in the calculation of AMTI.

Investment Interest Investment interest is deductible for regular income tax purposes and for AMT purposes to the extent of qualified net investment income.

However, because the categorization of interest as investment interest may differ for regular tax and AMT purposes, an adjustment is required if the amount of investment interest deductible for regular income tax purposes differs from the amount deductible for AMT purposes. For example, an adjustment will arise if proceeds from a home equity loan are used to purchase investments. Interest on a home equity loan is not deductible as qualified residence interest for regular income tax purposes. For AMT purposes, however, interest on a home equity loan is deductible as investment interest expense if proceeds from the loan are used for investment purposes.

---

[57]§ 163(h)(3)(F). For loans entered into prior to December 15, 2017, the $1,000,000 ($500,000 for married taxpayers filing separately) pre-TCJA of 2017 acquisition indebtedness limits apply.

To determine the AMT adjustment for investment interest expense, it is necessary to compute the investment interest expense deduction for both regular income tax and AMT purposes.

EXAMPLE 31

Tom earned $20,000 interest income from corporate bonds and $5,000 dividends from preferred stock. He reported the following amounts of investment income for regular income tax and AMT purposes.

	Regular Income Tax	AMT
Corporate bond interest	$20,000	$20,000
Preferred stock dividends	5,000	5,000
Net investment income	$25,000	$25,000

Tom incurred investment interest expense of $10,000 related to the corporate bonds. He also incurred $4,000 interest on a home equity loan, the proceeds of which were used to purchase preferred stock. For regular income tax purposes, this $4,000 is not deductible as qualified residence interest. His *investment* interest expense for regular income tax and AMT purposes is computed below.

	Regular Income Tax	AMT
To carry corporate bonds	$10,000	$10,000
On home equity loan to carry preferred stock	–0–	4,000
Total investment interest expense	$10,000	$14,000

Investment interest expense is deductible to the extent of net investment income. Because the amount deductible for regular income tax purposes ($10,000) differs from the amount deductible for AMT purposes ($14,000), an AMT adjustment is required. The adjustment is computed as follows.

AMT deduction for investment interest expense	$ 14,000
Regular income tax deduction for investment interest expense	(10,000)
Negative AMT adjustment	$ 4,000

As discussed subsequently in text Section 17-3d, the interest on private activity bonds usually is a tax preference for AMT purposes. Such interest can also affect the calculation of the AMT investment interest deduction in that it is included in the calculation of net investment income.

Medical Expenses The regular tax medical expense deduction provisions generally apply to the AMT. Prior to the TCJA of 2017, for taxpayers under 65, medical expenses were deductible only to the extent they exceeded 10% of AGI for regular tax and AMT purposes. Thus, no AMT adjustment for medical expenses was required for such taxpayers. However, taxpayers at least age 65 were eligible for a 7.5%-of-AGI limit for regular tax purposes. Thus, these taxpayers were required to make an AMT adjustment for medical expenses equal to the difference between the 10%- and 7.5%-of-AGI limits.

As a result of the TCJA, for 2017 and 2018, all taxpayers, irrespective of age, can deduct medical expenses to the extent these expenses exceed 7.5% of AGI for both regular tax and AMT purposes. Beginning in 2019, medical expenses will be subject to the 10% floor for all taxpayers, irrespective of age, for both regular tax and AMT purposes. Thus, post-TCJA, no AMT adjustment for medical expenses is required.[58]

Computations and Elections Unlike some other AMT adjustments, a taxpayer cannot mitigate the effect of the itemized deduction adjustments by electing to treat the amounts in the same way for regular income tax and AMT purposes. Also note that a taxpayer who elects the standard deduction for regular tax purposes cannot claim itemized deductions for AMT purposes.[59]

---

[58]§§ 213(f)(2) and 56(b)(1)(B).   [59]SCA 200103073.

Other Adjustments

The standard deduction is not allowed in the calculation of AMTI. Thus, the standard deduction also gives rise to an AMT adjustment.[60] However, this adjustment enters the AMTI calculation indirectly by adjusting the taxable income amount that begins the AMTI calculation. If a taxpayer itemizes deductions, then the starting point for the AMTI calculation is adjusted gross income (AGI) less itemized deductions. If, instead, a taxpayer takes the standard deduction, the starting point for the AMTI calculation is AGI. Thus, any standard deduction amount taken in the calculation of regular taxable income is accounted for by adjusting the starting point of the AMTI calculation. As discussed earlier in the chapter, a separate exemption (see Exemption Amount) is allowed for AMT purposes.

EXAMPLE 32

Michael is single and has no dependents. He earned a salary of $225,000 in 2018, and his itemized deductions are less than the $12,000 standard deduction. Based on this information, Michael's taxable income for 2018 is $213,000 ($225,000 − $12,000 standard deduction). However, Michael's taxable income starting point for the AMTI calculation would be $225,000, as the adjustment for the standard deduction is made to the taxable income amount that starts the AMTI calculation. Any remaining adjustments (or preferences, discussed below) are made in the AMTI calculation.

Concept Summary 17.2 summarizes the key points related to AMT adjustments.

Concept Summary 17.2

Summary of AMT Adjustment Provisions

1. Adjustments that reflect *timing differences* can be either positive or negative.

2. Apart from adjustments related to itemized deductions, many adjustments *can be avoided* if the taxpayer adopts the same tax treatment for regular tax purposes as is required for AMT purposes.

3. *Not all* itemized deductions trigger adjustments.

4. Where an asset is eligible for full expensing or an asset is fully expensed in the year placed in service, *no depreciation adjustment* is required for the asset either in that year or in subsequent years in which depreciation is claimed.

5. The adjustment for the standard deduction *enters the AMT calculation indirectly* by adjusting the taxable income amount that begins the AMTI computation.

LO.6

Identify the preferences that are included in calculating AMTI.

17-2d AMT Preferences

Unlike adjustments, which can be positive or negative, AMT **preferences** always are positive. In other words, preferences are added back to taxable income in the calculation of AMTI. The following section discusses AMT preferences.

Percentage Depletion

Congress enacted the percentage depletion rules to provide taxpayers with incentives to invest in the development of certain natural resources. Percentage depletion is computed by multiplying a rate specified in the Code by the gross income from the property.[61] The rate is based on the type of mineral involved. Generally, the basis of the property is reduced by the amount of depletion taken until the basis reaches zero. However, because percentage depletion is based on gross income, rather than the investment in the property, taxpayers are allowed to continue taking percentage depletion deductions even after the basis of the property reaches zero. Thus, over the life of the property, depletion deductions may greatly exceed the cost of the property.

---

[60]§ 56(b)(1)(E).   [61]§ 613(a).

The percentage depletion preference is equal to the excess of the regular income tax deduction for percentage depletion over the adjusted basis of the property at the end of the taxable year.[62] Note that the end-of-year basis is determined without regard to the depletion deduction for the taxable year. This preference is calculated separately for each mineral property owned by the taxpayer.[63] As a result, a taxpayer cannot use basis in one property to reduce the preference for excess depletion on another property.

Kim owns a mineral property that qualifies for a 22% depletion rate. The basis of the property at the beginning of the year, prior to any current-year depletion deduction, is $10,000. Gross income from the property for the year is $100,000. For regular income tax purposes, Kim's percentage depletion deduction (assume that it is not limited by taxable income from the property) is $22,000. For AMT purposes, Kim has a tax preference of $12,000 ($22,000 – $10,000).

Intangible Drilling Costs

In computing regular taxable income, taxpayers can deduct certain intangible drilling and development costs in the year incurred, although such costs are normally capital in nature. The deduction is allowed for costs incurred in connection with oil and gas wells and geothermal wells.

For AMT purposes, excess intangible drilling costs (IDC) for the year are treated as a preference.[64] The excess IDC preference is computed as follows.

IDC expensed in the year incurred
Minus: Deduction if IDC were capitalized and amortized over 10 years
Equals: Excess of IDC expense over amortization
Minus: 65% of net oil and gas or geothermal income
Equals: Preference amount

The IDC preference is computed separately for oil and gas wells and geothermal wells.

Ben incurred IDC of $50,000 during the year and elected to expense that amount for regular tax purposes. His net oil and gas income for the year was $60,000. Currently, Ben has no income from geothermal wells. Ben's preference for IDC is $6,000 [($50,000 IDC − $5,000 amortization) − (65% × $60,000 income)].

A taxpayer can avoid the preference for IDC by electing to write off the expenditures over a 10-year period for regular income tax purposes.

Interest on Private Activity Bonds

Like interest income earned on other municipal bonds, income from private activity bonds is not included in taxable income, and expenses related to carrying such bonds are not deductible for regular income tax purposes. However, interest on private activity bonds is considered a preference in computing AMTI. As a result, expenses incurred in carrying the bonds are offset against the interest income in computing the preference amount.[65] Interest on private activity bonds issued in 2009 and 2010 is not treated as a preference.

In general, **private activity bonds** are bonds issued by states or municipalities where more than 10 percent of the proceeds are used for private business use.[66] For example, a bond whose proceeds are used to construct a factory that is leased to a private business at a favorable rate is a private activity bond.

---

[62] § 57(a)(1). The preference does not include percentage depletion on oil and gas wells of independent producers or royalty owners, as defined in § 613A(c).

[63] § 614(a).

[64] § 57(a)(2).

[65] § 57(a)(5).

[66] § 141.

TAX PLANNING STRATEGIES Avoiding Preferences and Adjustments

FRAMEWORK FOCUS: TAX RATE

Strategy: Control the Character of Income and Deductions.

One strategic approach to managing AMT liabilities is to avoid preference and adjustment amounts where possible.

- A taxpayer who expects to be subject to the AMT should not invest in private activity bonds unless doing so makes good investment sense. Any AMT triggered by interest on private activity bonds reduces the yield on an investment in such bonds.

- A taxpayer could be better off taking itemized deductions even when those deductions are less than the standard deduction if the itemized deductions do not require AMT adjustments. For example, a taxpayer with itemized deductions comprised of charitable contributions (that

were less than the standard deduction) would not make an AMT adjustment for such contributions, but would be required to make an adjustment for the standard deduction, which could potentially put the taxpayer into AMT.

- Neither property taxes nor real estate taxes are deductible for AMT if they are categorized as itemized deductions. However, taxes deductible as a part of business operations or rental activities are allowed for AMT purposes. Therefore, a taxpayer who could qualify for a home-office deduction would be able to deduct a portion of his or her home's real estate taxes as business expenses rather than as an itemized deduction.

The vast majority of tax-exempt bonds issued by states and municipalities are not classified as private activity bonds. Therefore, the interest income from such bonds does not regularly create a preference for AMT purposes.

EXAMPLE 35

In the current year, Lindsay earned $8,300 of interest income, comprised of the following amounts.

10-year Treasury bond (issued in 2013)	$4,000
10-year municipal bond (issued in 2014)	2,500
10-year private activity bond (issued in 2016)	1,800

All of the bonds were purchased on their issuance date. Lindsay's preference for interest is $1,800, the interest on the private activity bond. Treasury bond interest is included in both regular taxable income and AMTI; the interest from the non-private activity municipal bond is not included in either regular taxable income or AMTI.

Exclusion for Certain Small Business Stock

Gain on the sale of certain small business stock is excluded from gross income for regular income tax purposes if that stock was acquired after September 28, 2010.[67]

For AMT purposes, for years in which the 100 percent exclusion applies for regular tax purposes, the exclusion does not create an AMT preference.[68]

LO.7

Compute the AMT.

17-2e Illustration of the AMT Computation

The computation of the AMT is illustrated in the following example. Because the 2018 Form 6251 was not available at the time of printing, the AMT form is not included in the chapter.

---

[67]§ 1202(a)(4). Different percentages for the excluded gain applied prior to this date.

[68]§§ 57(a)(7) and 1202(a)(4)(C).

Molly Seims, who is single and age 56 and resides in Houston, Texas, had taxable income for 2018 as follows.

Salary		$292,000
Interest		18,000
Adjusted gross income		$310,000
Less itemized deductions:		
Medical expenses (do not exceed 7.5% of AGI)	$ 0	
State income taxes	9,500	
Interest[a]		
Home mortgage (for qualified housing)	20,000*	
Investment interest	6,300*	
Charitable contributions (cash)	15,000*	
Casualty loss ($48,000 − 10% of $310,000 AGI)[b]	17,000*	(67,800)
Taxable income		$242,200

[a]In this illustration, all interest is deductible in computing AMTI. Qualified housing interest is deductible without adjustment. Investment interest ($6,300) is deductible to the extent of net investment income included in AMTI. The $18,000 of interest income is treated as net investment income for regular tax and for AMT purposes.
[b]The casualty loss is the result of flooding that occurred in a Federally declared disaster area in Houston. Per § 165(h)(A), such losses are deductible subject to the $100 floor and the 10%-of-AGI limit. The $48,000 loss amount is after the $100 floor.

Deductions marked with an asterisk are allowed for AMT purposes. Thus, an adjustment is required for state income taxes; the remaining itemized deductions are allowed in calculating both regular taxable income and AMT.

In addition, Molly earned $40,000 of interest income on private activity bonds issued in 2014. She also exercised ISOs in 2018. The option spread (the difference between the exercise price and the fair market value on the date of exercise) was $35,000. Molly's regular tax liability in 2018 is $60,460. AMTI is computed as follows.

Taxable income	$242,200
Plus: Adjustments	
State income taxes	9,500
Incentive stock options	35,000
Plus: Preference (interest on private activity bonds)	40,000
Equals: AMTI	$326,700
Minus: AMT exemption	(70,300)
Equals: Minimum tax base	$256,400
TMT [($191,100 × 26%) + ($65,300 × 28%)]	$ 67,970
Minus: Regular tax liability	(60,460)
Equals: AMT	$ 7,510

17-2f **AMT Credit**

LO.8

Describe and illustrate the role of the AMT credit in the alternative minimum tax structure.

As was illustrated in several of the examples in this chapter, timing differences that give rise to AMT adjustments eventually reverse. To provide equity for taxpayers, a tax credit is created in a year in which a taxpayer pays AMT as a result of these timing differences.[69]

This credit, known as the ==alternative minimum tax credit==, is created only by the AMT liability that results from timing differences.[70] A credit is not created or increased by AMT exclusions, which create permanent differences between the regular income tax liability and the AMT. These AMT exclusions include the following amounts.

- The standard deduction.
- Itemized deductions not allowable for AMT purposes, including state and local taxes and certain interest expense.

---

[69]§ 53.   [70]S. Rep. No. 99–313 (PL 99–514), p. 536.

TAX PLANNING STRATEGIES Other AMT Planning Strategies

FRAMEWORK FOCUS: TAX RATE

Strategy: Control the Character of Income and Deductions.

A potential AMT liability can be reduced by decreasing adjusted gross income (AGI). Certain contributions to qualified retirement savings plans are excluded from gross income, which would result in a decreased AGI amount. Where a taxpayer participates in a § 401(k), § 457(b) plan, or SIMPLE IRA plan, the maximum allowable salary deferral contributions to such a plan would reduce AGI, which is beneficial for both regular tax and AMT purposes as well as for retirement planning.

While the lower tax rates for long-term capital gains apply for both regular tax and AMT purposes, such long-term capital gains increase AGI and AMTI, and these income items could reduce the amount of the AMT exemption available to a taxpayer. In a year for which a taxpayer expects to be subject to the AMT, the taxpayer should evaluate how the recognition of long-term capital gains affects AMTI and consider, where possible, whether the recognition of such gains should be deferred to a future year.

- Excess percentage depletion.
- Tax-exempt interest on private activity bonds.

EXAMPLE 37

Patrick, who is single, has zero taxable income for 2018. He also has positive timing adjustments of $600,000 and AMT exclusions of $300,000. Because of the amount of his AMTI, the exemption is phased out completely and his AMT base is $900,000. Patrick's TMT is $248,178 [($191,100 × 26%) + ($708,900 × 28%)].

To determine the amount of AMT credit to carry over, the AMT must be recomputed to reflect only the effect of timing differences, as shown in Example 38.

EXAMPLE 38

Assume the same facts as in the previous example. If there had been no positive timing adjustments for the year, Patrick's AMT base would have been $229,700 ($300,000 AMTI considering only exclusions − $70,300 exemption) and his TMT would have been $60,494 [($191,100 × 26%) + ($38,600 × 28%)]. Patrick may carry over an AMT credit of $187,684 ($248,178 actual TMT − $60,494 TMT considering only exclusions) to 2019 and subsequent years.

Where a taxpayer has an AMT credit, the credit can be utilized only in a year in which the taxpayer is not subject to the AMT. In addition, as demonstrated in the following example, the amount of the credit that can be used is equal to the excess of the taxpayer's regular tax liability over his or her tentative minimum tax liability. Finally, while the AMT credit cannot be carried back, the credit can be carried forward indefinitely.

EXAMPLE 39

Amber holds a $11,600 AMT credit from 2014. In 2018, prior to consideration of the AMT credit, Amber's regular tax liability is $60,000 and her tentative minimum tax is $54,000. In this situation, Amber can use $6,000 of the AMT credit from 2014 to reduce her 2018 regular tax liability. Thus, Amber's tax liability in 2018 is $54,000. The remaining $5,600 AMT credit is carried forward to future tax years.

Key points related to AMT preferences are summarized in Concept Summary 17.3. A broader summary of AMT adjustments and preferences for individual taxpayers is included in Concept Summary 17.4.

Concept Summary 17.3

Summary of AMT Preference Provisions

1. Preferences are *always* positive in amount. A preference reflects a permanent difference between the regular tax and the AMT treatment of an amount.

2. With the exception of the IDC preference, preferences *cannot be avoided* by adopting the same tax treatment for regular tax and AMT purposes. In general, preferences can be avoided by not engaging in the activity that causes the preference, which may not be economically rational.

3. On occasion, Congress changes the tax code to stimulate economic activity. To the extent that an AMT preference could hinder this economic goal, the *preference may also be modified* (e.g., private activity bond interest, small business stock gain).

Concept Summary 17.4

AMT Adjustments and Preferences for Individuals

Adjustments	Positive	Negative	Both*
Adjusted gain or loss on property dispositions			X
Alternative tax NOL deduction (ATNOLD)			X
Circulation expenditures			X
Completed contract method			X
Depreciation of personal property			X
Depreciation of real property			X
Incentive stock options	X**		
Itemized deductions:			
Private activity bond interest that is AMT investment interest		X	
Property tax on personalty	X		
Property tax on realty	X		
Qualified residence interest that is AMT investment interest		X	
Qualified residence interest that is not qualified housing interest	X		
State income taxes	X		
Tax benefit rule for state income tax refund		X	
Mine exploration and development costs			X
Passive activity losses			X
Pollution control facilities			X
Research and experimental expenditures			X
Standard deduction	X		
Preferences			
Intangible drilling costs	X		
Percentage depletion in excess of adjusted basis	X		
Private activity bond interest income	X***		

*Timing differences.
**While the adjustment is positive, the AMT basis for the stock acquired is increased by the amount of the positive adjustment.
***Interest on private activity bonds issued after 2008 and before 2011 is not treated as a tax preference.

17-3 CORPORATE ALTERNATIVE MINIMUM TAX

Historically, C corporations were required to calculate and pay AMT in a manner similar to individuals.

In its original version of the TCJA of 2017, the House of Representatives eliminated the corporate AMT. The Senate's original version of the bill preserved the corporate

AMT in order to offset tax revenue expected to be lost as a result of other provisions in its version of the TCJA.

The concern with retaining the corporate AMT was that it could reduce or eliminate the benefit of the reduced regular corporate income tax rate. Unlike the individual TMT calculation, tax credits apart from the foreign tax credit were not allowed in the calculation of a corporation's TMT. Policymakers were concerned that with the reduced regular corporate income tax rate, more corporations would find themselves in AMT and, as such, would lose the benefit of these credits, especially the R&D credit. As a result, the retention of the corporate AMT could have reduced the economic benefits that policymakers expected the TCJA to generate.

The TCJA eliminates the corporate AMT for tax years beginning after 2017.

REFOCUS ON THE BIG PICTURE

DEALING WITH TAX CREDITS AND THE AMT

Tax credits are used by the Federal government to promote certain social and economic objectives. Credits are dollar-for-dollar reductions in tax liability. While tax credits may have strict qualification requirements, taking advantage of available credits may significantly reduce a business's tax liability. Progress Corporation qualifies for a 20 percent tax credit for rehabilitating a certified historic building (see Example 4). In addition, Progress hires workers from economically disadvantaged groups, so it qualifies for the work opportunity tax credit (see Example 6).

The company also qualifies for the credit for employer-provided child care, equal to 25 percent of qualified child care expenses (see Example 12). Mike and his CPA might also want to explore taking advantage of the disabled access credit, which is designed to encourage small businesses to make their facilities accessible to disabled individuals.

What If?

Mike has heard horror stories about the alternative minimum tax (AMT) and is concerned about its potential impact. Is Mike's concern warranted?

For tax years beginning after 2017 the corporate AMT has been repealed. So Mike should not have concerns with it. The AMT for individual taxpayers is still in existence, but as long as Progress Corporation is a regular corporation, its operations will not cause Mike to be subject to the individual AMT. If Progress Corporation should make an S election in the future, then the flow-through tax items to Mike could potentially impact the likelihood that he is subject to the individual AMT.

ISTOCKPHOTO.COM/MONKEY BUSINESS IMAGES

Suggested Readings

Yair Holtzman, "U.S. Research and Development Tax Credit," *CPA Journal*, October 2017.

Thomas Horan and Margaret Horan, "Strategies for Reducing the Alternative Minimum Tax Liability," *The CPA Journal*, March 2013.

Kreig D. Mitchell, "The R&D Tax Credit for Start-Up Companies," *Practical Tax Strategies*, February 2012.

Jeanne Sahadi, "Why You Probably Won't Have to Pay the AMT Again," http://money.cnn.com/2018/01/18/pf/taxes/2018-amt-exemption-increase/index.html, January 18, 2018.

Kris Siolka, "A Closer Look at AMT: Common Adjustments and Preferences," *Taxpro Monthly*, July 2014.

S. Wayne Swilley, "Long-Term Contracts and AMT," *Journal of Accountancy*, December 2017.

Key Terms

Adjustments, 17-16

Alternative minimum tax (AMT), 17-13

Alternative minimum tax credit, 17-31

Alternative minimum taxable income (AMTI), 17-13

Alternative tax NOL deduction (ATNOLD), 17-24

Credit for employer-provided child care, 17-9

Credit for employer-provided family and medical leave, 17-11

Credit for small employer pension plan startup costs, 17-9

Disabled access credit, 17-8

Energy credits, 17-8

Exemption amount, 17-15

Foreign tax credit (FTC), 17-10

General business credit, 17-2

Incentive stock options (ISOs), 17-20

Preferences, 17-28

Private activity bonds, 17-29

Rehabilitation expenditures credit, 17-4

Research activities credit, 17-6

Tax credits, 17-2

Work opportunity tax credit, 17-5

Computational Exercises

1. **LO.2** Carlson's general business credit for the current year is $84,000. His net income tax is $190,000, tentative minimum tax is $175,000, and net regular tax liability is $185,000. He has no other tax credits. Determine the amount of Carlson's general business credit for the year.

2. **LO.2** Emily spent $135,000 to rehabilitate a certified historic building (adjusted basis of $90,000) that originally had been placed in service in 1935. What is Emily's rehabilitation expenditures tax credit?

3. **LO.2** During 2018, Lincoln Company hires seven individuals who are certified to be members of a qualifying targeted group. Each employee works in excess of 600 hours and is paid wages of $7,500 during the year. Determine the amount of Lincoln's work opportunity credit.

4. **LO.2** Alison incurs the following research expenditures.

In-house wages	$60,000
In-house supplies	5,000
Payment to ABC, Inc., for research	80,000

    a. Determine the amount of qualified research expenditures.
    b. Assuming that the base amount is $50,000, determine Alison's incremental research activities credit.

5. **LO.3** In March 2018, Serengeti exercised an ISO that had been granted by his employer, Thunder Corporation, in December 2015. Serengeti acquired 5,000 shares of Thunder stock for the exercise price of $65 per share. The fair market value of the stock at the date of exercise was $90 per share.

    What is Serengeti's 2015 AMT adjustment related to the ISO? What is the 2018 adjustment?

6. **LO.5** Brennen sold a machine used in his sole proprietorship for $180,000. The machine was purchased eight years ago for $340,000. Depreciation up to the date of the sale for regular income tax purposes was $210,000 and $190,000 for AMT purposes.

    What, if any, AMT adjustment arises as a result of the sale of the machine? Assume that bonus depreciation was not claimed on the machine.

7. **LO.5** Pineview Company, a single member LLC, placed a $5,000 asset that is ineligible for full expensing in service on June 1, 2018. The asset has a three-year MACRS class life; no bonus depreciation was taken on this asset. Complete the

table below by providing the AMT adjustment, and indicate whether the adjustment increases or decreases taxable income.

Year	Tax Deduction	AMT Deduction	AMT Adjustment	Increases or Decreases
2018	$1,667	$1,250	_____	_____
2019	2,222	1,875	_____	_____
2020	740	1,250	_____	_____
2021	371	625	_____	_____

8. **LO.6** Dimitri owns a gold mine that qualifies for a 15% percentage depletion rate. The basis of the property at the beginning of the year, prior to any current-year depletion deduction, is $21,000. Gross income from the property for the year is $200,000, and taxable income before depletion is $65,000.

What is Dimitri's AMT depletion preference?

Problems

9. **LO.2** Adelyn has a tentative general business credit of $42,000 for the current year. Her net regular tax liability before the general business credit is $107,000, and her tentative minimum tax is $88,000. Compute Adelyn's allowable general business credit for the year.

10. **LO.2** Oak Corporation holds the following general business credit carryovers.

2014	$ 5,000
2015	15,000
2016	6,000
2017	19,000
Total carryovers	$45,000

If the general business credit generated by activities during 2018 equals $36,000 and the total credit allowed during the current year is $60,000 (based on tax liability), what amounts of the current general business credit and carryovers are utilized against the 2018 income tax liability? What is the amount of the unused credit carried forward to 2019?

11. **LO.2** In January 2017, Iris Corporation purchased and placed in service a certified historic structure building that houses retail businesses. The cost was $300,000, of which $25,000 applied to the land. In modernizing the facility, Iris Corporation incurred $312,000 of renovation costs of the type that qualify for the rehabilitation credit. These improvements were placed in service in October 2018.

a. Compute Iris Corporation's rehabilitation tax credit for 2018.

b. Calculate the cost recovery deductions for the building and the renovation costs for 2018.

Decision Making

Communications

12. **LO.2** In the current year, Paul Chaing (4522 Fargo Street, Geneva, IL 60134) acquires a qualifying historic structure for $350,000 (excluding the cost of the land) and plans to substantially rehabilitate the structure. He is planning to spend either $320,000 or $380,000 on rehabilitation expenditures.

Write a letter to Paul and a memo for the tax files explaining, for the two alternative expenditures, (1) the computation that determines the rehabilitation expenditures tax credit available to Paul, (2) the effect of the credit on Paul's adjusted basis in the property, and (3) the cash-flow differences as a result of the tax consequences related to his expenditure choice.

13. **LO.2** The tax credit for rehabilitation expenditures is available to help offset the   **Ethics and Equity**
costs related to substantially rehabilitating certain buildings. The credit is cal-
culated on the rehabilitation expenditures incurred and not on the acquisition cost
of the building itself.

    You are a developer who buys, sells, and does construction work on real estate in
the inner city of your metropolitan area. A potential customer approaches you about
acquiring one of your buildings that easily could qualify for the 20% rehabilitation
credit on historic structures. The stated sales price of the structure is $100,000 (based
on appraisals ranging from $80,000 to $120,000), and the rehabilitation expenditures,
if the job is done correctly, would be about $150,000.

    Your business has been slow recently due to the sluggish real estate market in
your area, and the potential customer makes the following proposal: if you reduce
the sales price of the building to $75,000, he will pay you $175,000 to perform the
rehabilitation work. Although the buyer's total expenditures would be the same, he
would benefit from this approach by obtaining a larger tax credit ($25,000 increased
rehabilitation costs × 20% = $5,000).

    It has been a long time since you have sold any of your real estate. How will
you respond?

14. **LO.2** Green Corporation hires six individuals on January 4, 2018, all of whom
qualify for the work opportunity credit. Three of these individuals receive
wages of $8,500 during 2018, and each individual works more than 400 hours dur-
ing the year. The other three individuals each work 300 hours and receive wages of
$5,000 during the year.

  a. Calculate the amount of Green's work opportunity credit for 2018.

  b. If Green pays total wages of $140,000 to its employees during the year, how
much of this amount is deductible in 2018 assuming that the work opportunity
credit is taken?

15. **LO.2** Tom, a calendar year taxpayer, informs you that during the year, he incurs   **Decision Making**
expenditures of $40,000 that qualify for the incremental research activities
credit. In addition, it is determined that his base amount for the year is $32,800.

  a. Determine Tom's incremental research activities credit for the year.

  b. Tom is in the 24% tax bracket. Determine which approach to the research
expenditures and the research activities credit (other than capitalization and
subsequent amortization) would provide the greater tax benefit to Tom.

16. **LO.2** Ahmed Zinna (16 Southside Drive, Charlotte, NC 28204), one of your clients,   **Communications**
owns two retail establishments in downtown Charlotte and has come to you
seeking advice concerning the tax consequences of complying with the Americans
with Disabilities Act. He understands that he needs to install various features at his
stores (e.g., ramps, doorways, and restrooms that are handicapped-accessible) to
make them more accessible to disabled individuals. He asks whether any tax credits
will be available to help offset the cost of the necessary changes. He estimates the
cost of the planned changes to his facilities as follows.

Location	Projected Cost
Calvin Street	$22,000
Stowe Avenue	8,500

He reminds you that the Calvin Street store was constructed in 2004, while the
Stowe Avenue store is in a building that was constructed in 1947. Ahmed operates
his business as a sole proprietorship and has approximately eight employees at
each location. Write a letter to Ahmed in which you summarize your conclusions
concerning the tax consequences of the proposed capital improvements.

17. **LO.2** Blue Sky, Inc., a U.S. corporation, is a manufacturing concern that sells most of its products in the United States. It also conducts some business in the European Union through various branches. During the current year, Blue Sky reports taxable income of $700,000, of which $500,000 is U.S.-sourced and $200,000 is foreign-sourced. Foreign income taxes paid amounted to $38,000. Blue Sky's U.S. income tax liability is $147,000. What is its U.S. income tax liability net of the allowable foreign tax credit?

18. **LO.4** Use the following data to calculate Chiara's AMT base in 2018.

Taxable income	$248,000
Positive AMT adjustments	73,000
Negative AMT adjustments	25,000
Preferences	30,000

Chiara will itemize deductions and will file as a single taxpayer.

19. **LO.6** Falcon has a sole proprietorship that owns a silver mine that she purchased several years ago for $925,000. The adjusted basis at the beginning of the year is $400,000. For the year, Falcon deducts depletion of $700,000 (greater of cost depletion of $290,000 or percentage depletion of $700,000) for regular income tax purposes.
    a. Calculate Falcon's AMT preference.
    b. Calculate Falcon's adjusted basis for regular income tax purposes.
    c. Calculate Falcon's adjusted basis for AMT purposes.

Decision Making
Communications

20. **LO.5** In March 2018, Helen Carlon acquired used equipment for her business at a cost of $300,000. The equipment is five-year property for regular tax depreciation purposes.
    a. If Helen depreciates the equipment using the method that will produce the greatest deduction for 2018 for regular income tax purposes, what is the amount of the AMT adjustment?
    b. Draft a letter to Helen regarding the choice of depreciation methods. Helen's address is 500 Monticello Avenue, Glendale, AZ 85306.

21. **LO.5** David is the sole proprietor of a real estate construction business. He uses the completed contract method on a particular contract that requires 16 months to complete. The contract is for $500,000, with estimated costs of $300,000. At the end of 2017, $180,000 of costs had been incurred. The contract is completed in 2018, with the total cost being $295,000. Determine the amount of adjustments for AMT purposes for 2017 and 2018.

Ethics and Equity

22. **LO.5** Allie, who was an accounting major in college, is the owner of a medium-size construction limited liability company. She prepares the company's Schedule C each year. Due to reporting a home construction contract using the completed contract method, the corporation is subject to the AMT in 2018. Allie files her 2018 tax return in early February 2019. Her total tax liability is $58,000 ($53,000 regular income tax liability + $5,000 AMT). Assume that Allie is in the 37% tax bracket.

In early March, Allie reads an article on minimizing income taxes. Based on this article, she decides that it would be beneficial for the company to report the home construction contract using the percentage of completion method on its 2018 return. Although this will increase her 2018 income tax liability, it will minimize the total income tax liability over the two-year construction period. Therefore, Allie files an amended return on March 14, 2019. Evaluate Allie's actions from both a tax avoidance and an ethical perspective.

23. **LO.5** Buford sells an apartment building for $720,000. His adjusted basis is $500,000 for regular income tax purposes and $550,000 for AMT purposes. Calculate Buford's:
    a. Gain for regular income tax purposes.
    b. Gain for AMT purposes.
    c. AMT adjustment, if any.

24. **LO.5** Lilia is going to be subject to the AMT in 2018. She owns an investment build-   Issue ID
    ing and is considering disposing of it and investing in other realty. Based on an appraisal of the building's value, the realized gain would be $85,000.
    Two individuals have indicated an interest in buying the building, Ed and Abby. Ed has offered to purchase the building from Lilia with a December 29, 2018 clos-ing date. Ed wants to close the transaction in 2018 because he will receive certain beneficial tax consequences only if the transaction is closed prior to 2019. Abby has offered to purchase the building with a January 2, 2019 closing date.
    The adjusted basis of the building is $95,000 greater for AMT, purposes than for the regular income tax. Lilia expects to be in the 37% regular income tax bracket.
    What are the relevant Federal income tax issues that Lilia faces in making her decision?

25. **LO.5** Flicker, a single member LLC, acquired a passive activity this year. Gross income from operations of the activity was $160,000. Operating expenses, not including depreciation, were $122,000. Regular income tax depreciation of $49,750 was computed under MACRS. AMT depreciation, computed using the ADS, was $41,000. Compute Flicker's passive activity loss deduction and passive activity loss suspended for regular income tax purposes. Then determine the same amounts for AMT purposes.

26. **LO.5** Sammy and Monica, both age 67, incur and pay medical expenses in excess of insurance reimbursements during the year as follows.

For Sammy	$16,000
For Monica (spouse)	4,000
For Chuck (son)	2,500
For Carter (Monica's father)	5,000

Sammy and Monica's 2018 AGI is $130,000. They file a joint return. Chuck and Carter are Sammy and Monica's dependents.
    a. What is Sammy and Monica's medical expense deduction for regular income tax purposes?
    b. What is Sammy and Monica's AMT adjustment for medical expenses?

27. **LO.5** Wolfgang, who is age 33, records AGI of $125,000. He incurs the following itemized deductions for 2018.

Medical expenses [$15,000 − (7.5% × $125,000)]	$ 5,625
State income taxes	4,200
Charitable contributions	5,000
Home mortgage interest on his personal residence	6,000
	$20,825

    a. Calculate Wolfgang's itemized deductions for AMT purposes.
    b. What is the total amount of his AMT adjustments from these items?

28. **LO.6** Walter, who is single, owns a personal residence in the city. He also owns a cabin near a ski resort in the mountains. He uses the cabin as a vacation home. In the current year, he borrowed $60,000 on a home equity loan and used the proceeds to reduce credit card obligations and other debt. During the year, he paid the following amounts of interest.

On his personal residence	$16,000
On the cabin	7,000
On the home equity loan	2,500
On credit card obligations	1,500
On the purchase of an SUV	1,350

What amount, if any, must Walter recognize as an AMT adjustment?

29. **LO.4, 5, 6** Determine whether each of the following transactions is a preference (P), is an adjustment (A), or is not applicable (NA) for purposes of the AMT.
   a. Depletion in excess of basis.
   b. Accelerated depreciation on property.
   c. Charitable contributions of cash.
   d. State income taxes.
   e. Untaxed appreciation on property donated to charity.
   f. 2% miscellaneous itemized deductions.

30. **LO.7** Gabriel, age 40, and Emma, age 33, are married with two dependents. They recorded AGI of $250,000 in 2018 that included net investment income of $3,000 and gambling winnings of $2,500.

   The couple incurred the following expenses during the year (all of which resulted in itemized deductions for regular income tax purposes).

Medical expenses (before 7.5%-of-AGI floor)	$12,000
State income taxes	5,800
Real estate tax	9,100
Interest on personal residence	18,600
Interest on home equity loan (proceeds were used to remodel the couple's kitchen)	9,800
Investment interest expense	4,500
Charitable contribution (cash)	14,200

   a. What is Gabriel and Emma's AMT adjustment for itemized deductions in 2018? Is it positive or negative?
   b. Gabriel and Emma also earned interest of $5,000 on private activity bonds that were issued in 2014. They borrowed money to buy these bonds and paid interest of $3,900 on the loan. Determine the effect on AMTI.

31. **LO.7** Chuck is single, has no dependents, and does not itemize deductions. In 2018, he reports taxable income of $320,000. His tax preferences total $51,000. What is Chuck's AMTI for 2018?

32. **LO.7** Included in Alice's regular taxable income and in her AMT base is a $300,000 capital gain on the sale of stock she owned for three years. Alice is in the 20% tax bracket for net capital gains for regular income tax purposes.
   a. What rate should Alice use in calculating her tentative AMT?
   b. What is Alice's AMT adjustment?

33. **LO.7** In the current year, Dylan earned taxable and tax-exempt interest from the following investments.

Investment	Interest Income
10-year municipal bond (issued in 2009)	$1,300
10-year private activity bond (issued in 2010)	1,600
10-year Treasury bond (issued in 2014)	2,000
10-year private activity bond (issued in 2016)	900
Savings account	1,100

Dylan purchased all of the bonds on their issuance date. In addition, Dylan borrowed funds with which to purchase the 2010 private activity bond and incurred interest expense of $350 on that loan in the current year.

a. How much interest income will Dylan recognize for regular tax purposes in the current year?

b. What is her current-year AMT preference or adjustment for interest?

34. **LO.7** Jane and Robert Brown are married and have eight children, all of whom are eligible to be claimed as the couple's dependents. Robert earns $196,000 working as a senior manager in a public accounting firm, and Jane earns $78,000 as a second-grade teacher. Given their large family, they live in a frugal manner. The Browns maintain a large garden and some fruit trees from which they get most of their produce, and the children take family and consumer science classes so that they can help make the family's clothing.

The Browns record no gross income other than their salaries (all of their investment income is earned from qualified retirement savings), and their itemized deductions are less than the standard deduction. In addition, they incur no additional adjustments or preferences for AMT purposes.

a. What is the couple's 2018 regular tax liability?

b. What is the couple's 2018 AMT?

c. Express the calculation of the couple's AMT for 2018 as an Excel formula. Place any parameter that could change annually in a separate cell, and incorporate the cell references into the formula.

35. **LO.7** Pat is 40, is single, and has no dependents. She received a salary of $390,000 in 2018. She earned interest income of $11,000, dividend income of $15,000, gambling winnings of $14,000, and interest income from private activity bonds (issued in 2015) of $40,000. The dividends are not qualified dividends. The following additional information is relevant.

Medical expenses (before 7.5%-of-AGI floor)	$12,000
State income taxes	8,100
Real estate taxes	4,000
Mortgage interest on residence	13,100
Investment interest expense	3,800
Gambling losses	5,100

Compute Pat's tentative minimum tax for 2018.

36. **LO.7** Renee and Sanjeev Patel, who are married, reported taxable income of $1,008,000 for 2018. They incurred positive AMT adjustments of $75,000 and tax preference items of $67,500. The couple itemizes their deductions.

a. Compute the Patels' AMTI for 2018.

b. Compute their tentative minimum tax for 2018.

BRIDGE DISCIPLINE

1. Balm, Inc., has a general business credit for 2018 of $90,000. Balm's regular income tax liability before credits is $140,000, and its tentative AMT is $132,000.

   Calculate the amount of general business credit Balm can use in 2018, and calculate its general business credit carryback and carryforward, if any.

2. Cooper Partnership, a calendar year partnership, made qualifying rehabilitation expenditures to a building that it has used in its business for eight years. These improvements were placed in service on January 5, 2017. The amount of the rehabilitation expenditures credit was $40,000.

   Cooper is negotiating to sell the building in either December 2018 or January 2019. The sales price will be $600,000, and the recognized gain will be $100,000. Provide support for the CFO's position that Cooper should delay the sale until 2019.

3. For many years, Saul's sole proprietorship and his related Form 1040 have had a number of AMT tax preferences and AMT adjustments. He has made the AMT calculation each year, but the calculated amount always has been $0. Saul's regular taxable income and the AMT adjustments and preferences for 2018 are the same as for last year. Yet, he must pay AMT this year. Explain how this could happen.

Research Problems

Note: Solutions to the Research Problems can be prepared by using the Thomson Reuters Checkpoint™ online tax research database, which accompanies this textbook. Solutions can also be prepared by using research materials found in a typical tax library.

Research Problem 1. During a recent Sunday afternoon excursion, Miriam, an admirer of early twentieth-century architecture, discovers a 1920s-era house in the countryside outside Mobile, Alabama. She wants not only to purchase and renovate this particular house but also to move the structure into Mobile so that her community can enjoy its architectural features.

Being aware of the availability of the tax credit for rehabilitation expenditures, she wants to maximize her use of the provision, if it is available in this case, once the renovation work begins in Mobile. However, Miriam also informs you that she will pursue the purchase, relocation, and renovation of the house only if the tax credit is available.

Comment on Miriam's decision and on whether any renovation expenditures incurred will qualify for the tax credit for rehabilitation expenditures.

Partial list of research aids:
George S. Nalle III v. Comm., 72 AFTR 2d 93–5705, 997 F.2d 1134, 93–2 USTC ¶50,468 (CA–5, 1993).

Communications   **Research Problem 2.** Your ophthalmologist, Dr. Hunter Francis (55 Wheatland Drive, Hampton, CT 06247), has been very pleased with the growth of his practice in the 15 years he has been in business. This growth has resulted, at least in part, because he has aggressively marketed his services and tried to accommodate clients with various needs.

This year, Dr. Francis purchased a sophisticated piece of equipment that enables him to diagnose persons with mental handicaps, hearing impairments, and physical disabilities without having to go through a series of questions. In addition, he can treat his patients who are not disabled more accurately and efficiently by using this equipment.

Since purchasing the machine this year for $9,500, Dr. Francis has used it on many occasions. Unfortunately, he has not been able to attract any patients with disabilities, even though previously he referred such people to other ophthalmologists who owned the necessary equipment. Therefore, the primary purpose for acquiring the equipment (i.e., to attract patients with disabilities) has not been realized, but he has put it to good use in treating other patients. Write a letter to Dr. Francis explaining whether he may claim the disabled access credit for this acquisition.

Research Problem 3. Teal Company, a single member LLC, owns two warehouses that were placed in service before 1987. This year, accelerated depreciation on Warehouse A is $36,000 (straight-line depreciation would have been $30,000). On Warehouse B, accelerated depreciation was $16,000 (straight-line depreciation would have been $20,000). What is the amount of Teal's AMT tax preference for excess depreciation?

Use internet tax resources to address the following questions. Look for reliable websites and blogs of the IRS and other government agencies, media outlets, businesses, tax professionals, academics, think tanks, and political outlets.

Research Problem 4. The foreign tax credit is especially valuable when a U.S. business earns income in a country whose income tax rates exceed those of the United States. List five countries whose tax rates on business income exceed those of the United States and five where the corresponding U.S. rates are higher.

Research Problem 5. In an e-mail to your instructor, outline an AMT planning opportunity not mentioned in the chapter. In the e-mail, discuss the feasibility of the suggested planning opportunity.

Becker CPA Review Questions

1. Anthony entered into a long-term construction contract in year 3. The total profit of the contract is $80,000 and does not change over the life of the contract. The contract will be completed in year 5. The contract is 20% and 70% complete at the end of years 3 and 4, respectively. What is the alternative minimum tax adjustment required in year 4?

   a. $16,000

   b. $40,000

   c. $56,000

   d. $80,000

2. How is the alternative minimum tax credit applied in the calculation of the tentative minimum tax (TMT)?

   a. It is carried forward indefinitely and applied to regular tax only.

   b. It is carried back five years and applied to regular tax only.

   c. It is carried forward indefinitely and can be applied to regular tax or AMT.

   d. It is carried forward five years and applied to regular tax only.

3. Carol reports taxable income of $48,000. Included in that calculation are the following items.

Real estate taxes on her home	$2,000
Mortgage interest on acquisition indebtedness	1,200
Charitable contribution	550

Carol also had excluded municipal bond interest income of $8,000, $3,000 of which was deemed to be private activity bond interest. What are Carol's total alternative minimum tax (AMT) adjustments?

a. $1,200

c. $3,000

b. $2,000

d. $6,750

4. Which of the following statements is most correct?

a. Tax preference items for the alternative minimum tax are always added back to regular taxable income.

b. Itemized deductions that are added back to regular taxable income for the alternative minimum tax are preference items.

c. Tax preference items for the alternative minimum tax can be an increase or decrease to regular taxable income.

d. All taxpayers are able to deduct the full exemption in the calculation of the alternative minimum tax.

Comparative Forms of Doing Business

LEARNING OBJECTIVES: *After completing Chapter 18, you should be able to:*

LO.1 Identify the principal legal and tax forms for conducting a business.

LO.2 Apply nontax factors in the choice among alternative organizational forms.

LO.3 Contrast the conduit and entity approaches to legal organizational forms.

LO.4 Identify the influence of the conduit and entity perspectives on the tax treatment of an entity's operations, including the possibility of the double taxation of business income.

LO.5 Identify techniques for avoiding double taxation.

LO.6 Analyze the effects of the disposition of a business on the owners and the entity for each organizational form.

CHAPTER OUTLINE

18-1 Alternative Organizational Forms in which Business May Be Conducted, 18-2

18-2 Nontax Factors Affecting the Choice of Business Form, 18-2
18-2a Limited Liability, 18-3
18-2b Other Factors, 18-3
18-2c Capital Formation, 18-4

18-3 The Conduit and Entity Perspectives of Legal Business Forms, 18-4
18-3a Effect on the Taxation of Business Operations, 18-5
18-3b Effect on the Ability to Specially Allocate Income among Owners, 18-6
18-3c Effect on the Tax Treatment of Capital Contributions, 18-7
18-3d Effect on the Basis of an Ownership Interest, 18-7
18-3e Effect on the Application of the At-Risk and Passive Activity Loss Rules, 18-8
18-3f Effect on the Tax Treatment of Distributions, 18-10
18-3g Effect on Other Taxes, 18-10

18-4 Minimizing Double Taxation, 18-11
18-4a Making Deductible Distributions, 18-11
18-4b Deferring Distributions, 18-13
18-4c Making Return-of-Capital Distributions, 18-13
18-4d Electing S Corporation Status, 18-14

18-5 Disposing of a Business, 18-15
18-5a Sole Proprietorships, 18-15
18-5b Partnerships and Limited Liability Companies, 18-16
18-5c C Corporations, 18-17
18-5d S Corporations, 18-18

18-6 Converting to Another Business Form, 18-20
18-6a Sole Proprietorship, 18-20
18-6b C Corporation, 18-20
18-6c Partnership, 18-21

18-7 Overall Comparison of Business Forms, 18-21

TAX TALK *[My firm] had a rule—at least it seemed to be a rule—that everybody that came had to spend at least a year working on taxes. The general rationale for the rule as I could understand it was that taxes were so important to everything that you do, whatever the kind of case you are handling, you have to know something about the tax consequences of things.* —CHARLES A. HORSKY

FUSE/GETTY IMAGES

CHOOSING A BUSINESS FORM AND OTHER INVESTMENTS

Bill and George are going to start a new business and have come to you for advice on the most appropriate organizational form for the business. They have narrowed the choice to a C corporation, an S corporation, or an LLC, but they would like you to advise them as to the primary advantages and disadvantages of the different forms. They have an adequate amount in savings to finance the business initially. Limited liability is a significant concern as is limiting the amount of taxes paid. Bill and George anticipate that the company will lose money in the first two years of operation. After that, however, they expect to earn $200,000 in before-tax profit and distribute any after-tax profit to the owners. Bill and George are both single, and both are subject to a 24 percent marginal tax rate.

George also is considering investing $10,000 in a limited partnership. As a way of leveraging the risks and rewards associated with his investments, Bill earlier had acquired a 30 percent interest in a boutique retail coffee franchise outlet. Bill now is considering selling this investment, which has experienced rapid appreciation. Because he is considering cashing out the gain, he needs to know the adjusted basis of his ownership interest.

Read the chapter and formulate your response.

A variety of factors, both tax and nontax, can affect the choice of the legal form in which a business is conducted. The form that is most appropriate at one point in the life of a business and its owners may not be the most appropriate at a later time. This chapter provides the basis for comparing and contrasting the tax consequences of several business decisions across different types of tax and legal business forms. Understanding the comparative tax consequences of those decisions and being able to apply them effectively to specific fact patterns will facilitate effective tax planning, including the initial choice of an organizational form in which to conduct a business.

18-1 ALTERNATIVE ORGANIZATIONAL FORMS IN WHICH BUSINESS MAY BE CONDUCTED

LO.1

Identify the principal legal and tax forms for conducting a business.

The principal legal forms in which to conduct a business are the sole proprietorship, partnership, limited liability company, and corporation. The specific legal attributes of each of these organizational forms, including their relations to their owners and non-owners, are determined by the laws of the state in which they are organized.

These same forms generally are recognized for Federal income tax purposes as well, with the tax treatment of a business and its activities determined by the legal form in which the business is conducted. However, three major exceptions exist. First, the "check-the-box" Regulations provide for LLCs generally to be either disregarded or treated as partnerships for tax purposes, depending on the number of owners. An LLC with only one owner is a disregarded entity for tax purposes, treated as a sole proprietorship if the owner is an individual or as a division of a corporate owner. An LLC with more than one owner is treated as a partnership.

Second, the same Regulations allow most unincorporated entities to *elect* to be treated as corporations for Federal income tax purposes.[1] Therefore, an entity may be taxed as a corporation even though it is not organized as such under state law. Finally, a corporation may elect to be treated as an S corporation for tax purposes.[2] The income of an S corporation is taxed similarly to that of a partnership. However, the designation has no effect on the corporation for state law purposes: it is relevant only for tax purposes.

Approximately 6 million corporations file U.S. income tax returns every year, with about 4.5 million of these choosing to be taxed under Subchapter S. About 3.5 million partnership returns are filed every year, with over 65 percent of those being filed by LLCs. More than 23 million individual returns report sole proprietorship business or farming activities in a typical tax year.

18-2 NONTAX FACTORS AFFECTING THE CHOICE OF BUSINESS FORM

LO.2

Apply nontax factors in the choice among alternative organizational forms.

Taxes are only one of many factors to consider when making a business decision, including the choice of the legal form in which to conduct the business. Above all, any business decision should make economic sense.

The Big Picture

EXAMPLE 1

Return to the facts of *The Big Picture* on p. 18-1. George is considering investing $10,000 in a limited partnership. The partnership is expected to generate losses for two years before generating any profits. George projects that he will be able to deduct his share of the losses up to his $10,000 capital contribution within the next two years. Because George's marginal tax rate is 24%, the investment will produce tax savings of $2,400 ($10,000 × 24%).

However, there is a substantial risk that George will not recover any of his original investment. If this occurs, his negative cash flow from the investment in the limited partnership is $7,600 ($10,000 − $2,400). The tax savings cannot make up for the loss of the investment itself. George must decide whether the investment makes economic sense.

---

[1]Reg. §§ 301.7701–1 through –4, and –6.   [2]§§ 1361 and 1362. See Chapter 15.

18-2a Limited Liability

As an entity separate and distinct from its shareholders, a corporation is liable for its own debts under state law. A shareholder cannot be held liable for the debts or actions of the corporation. Therefore, a shareholder's liability resulting from investing in a corporation is limited to his or her investment. This protection from personal liability is the most frequently cited advantage of the corporate form.

Ed, Fran, and Gabriella each invest $25,000 for all of the stock of Brown Corporation. Brown obtains creditor financing of $100,000. Brown later becomes the defendant in a personal injury suit resulting from an accident involving one of its delivery trucks. The court awards a judgment of $2.5 million to the plaintiff. The award exceeds Brown's insurance coverage by $1.5 million. Even though the judgment may result in Brown's bankruptcy, the shareholders have no personal liability for the unpaid corporate debts.

Limited liability is not available to the shareholders of all corporations. For example, many states do not limit the liability of certain professionals (e.g., accountants, attorneys, architects, and physicians) who incorporate their practices.

Even when state law provides for limited liability, the shareholders of small corporations may be forced, in effect, to forgo this benefit. For example, a corporation may be unable to obtain external financing (e.g., a bank loan) at reasonable interest rates unless the shareholders personally guarantee the loan.

Certain partnerships may also offer their owners liability protection. For example, a limited partnership provides limited liability, but only to its limited partners. Like shareholders in a corporation, a limited partner's liability is limited to the amount of their investment in the entity. However, limited partnerships are generally required to have at least one general partner. A general partner's liability for partnership debts is unlimited.

HIJ is a limited partnership. Hazel, the general partner, invests $250,000 in HIJ. Iris and Jane, the limited partners, each invest $50,000. While the potential loss for Iris and Jane is limited to the $50,000 each has invested, Hazel's liability for any debts HIJ incurs is unlimited.

In-depth coverage can be found on this book's companion website: **www.cengage.com**   **1 DIGGING DEEPER**

Like a corporation, an LLC provides liability protection to all of its owners. This protection, coupled with the ability to be taxed as a partnership, is the most frequently cited benefit of an LLC. However, as discussed below, other potentially desirable corporate characteristics often are missing from LLCs (e.g., under state law, an LLC may lack unlimited life or the transferability of ownership interests may be limited). Limited liability partnerships (LLPs) also provide liability protection to all of their owners, but only for liabilities arising from the negligence or wrongdoing (i.e., "torts") of the other owners. This makes LLPs a popular organizational form for professional service firms (e.g., accountants, architects, attorneys). However, partners in an LLP are not protected from the entity's contractual liabilities.

18-2b Other Factors

Other nontax factors may be significant in selecting an organization form. For example, in addition to limited liability, the corporation generally is characterized by unlimited life (i.e., the corporation's existence is unaffected by a change in its ownership), separation of ownership and management, and the free transferability of interests. One or more of these characteristics is usually absent in other business forms.

18-2c **Capital Formation**

The combination of liability exposure with other nontax factors may significantly affect an entity's ability to raise capital. For example, a sole proprietorship offers the proprietor no protection against the venture's liabilities and limits its available capital to that which can be provided, or raised, by the proprietor. A partnership has a greater opportunity to raise funds through the pooling of owner resources. However, general partners remain subject to any liabilities generated by the business.

EXAMPLE 4

Adam and Beth decide to form a partnership, AB. Adam contributes cash of $200,000, and Beth contributes land with an adjusted basis of $60,000 and a fair market value of $200,000. The partnership plans to construct an apartment building at a cost of $800,000. AB borrows $700,000 to construct the apartment building. AB has acquired a total of $1.1 million of financing, more than either Adam or Beth may have been able to acquire on their own. However, if Adam and Beth are general partners, they both are responsible for all of the liabilities of AB.

A limited partnership offers greater potential to raise capital than does a general partnership because a limited partnership can secure funds from investors (i.e., limited partners) without exposing them to the liabilities related to the venture or involving them in the management of the business.

EXAMPLE 5

Carol and Dave form a limited partnership, CD. Carol contributes cash of $200,000, and Dave contributes land with an adjusted basis of $60,000 and a fair market value of $200,000. The partnership is going to construct a shopping center at a cost of $5 million. Included in this cost is the purchase price of $800,000 for land adjacent to that contributed by Dave. Thirty limited partnership interests are sold for $100,000 each to raise $3 million. CD then borrows another $2 million from a third party.

Each limited partner is liable only for the $100,000 they invest, even if CD is unable to repay the loan. As general partners, Carol and Dave are liable for repayment of the third-party loan as well as any other debts incurred by CD.

Of the different business entities, the corporate form offers the greatest ease and potential for obtaining owner financing, because it can offer investors a combination of liability protection and liquidity that other business forms cannot. The ultimate examples of this form are the large public companies that are listed on the stock exchanges.

LO.3

Contrast the conduit and entity approaches to legal organizational forms.

18-3 **THE CONDUIT AND ENTITY PERSPECTIVES OF LEGAL BUSINESS FORMS**

All business forms other than the sole proprietorship are artificial entities. Their legal rights and responsibilities, including their relations to their owners as well as other parties, are defined under state law.

State law generally uses one of two perspectives when defining the rights and responsibilities of a business entity. In its simplest form, the conduit, or aggregate, perspective treats the business as simply an aggregation of its owners joined together in an agency relationship. Under the strictest interpretation of the ==conduit perspective==, the business has no existence separate from its owners. Conversely, the ==entity perspective== considers the business as separate and distinct from its owners, with its own rights and responsibilities.

The rights and responsibilities afforded to corporations consistently reflect the entity perspective, with the corporation able to contract with other parties and responsible for its own debts. Shareholders have neither the right to directly manage the corporation, nor are they liable for its debts.

The approach to partnerships, including LLCs, is less consistent. Partnerships more often reflect the aggregate approach to an entity. For example, general partners have the right to participate directly in the management of a partnership, as well as to bind the partnership to contracts. It follows then that general partners are liable for the debts arising from the partnership's activities and contractual obligations. Furthermore, a significant change in ownership may result in the dissolution of the partnership. However, partnerships also reflect the entity perspective in several respects. For example, a partnership's income is determined separately from that of its owners. The liability protection afforded to limited partners and LLC members also is consistent with the entity perspective.

As discussed below, the taxation of business entities follows from the legal approach taken to each.

18-3a Effect on the Taxation of Business Operations

The view of the corporation as an entity separate from its owners leads to it also being considered a separate taxable entity, legally responsible for the income tax on the income it earns. As the corporation's shareholders, taxpayers distinct from the corporation, are taxed on this income when it is distributed, the income generated by a corporation is subject to double taxation before it is available for use by shareholders. This potential for double taxation frequently is cited as the major disadvantage of the corporate form, although several techniques, discussed below, can mitigate or eliminate the burden of double taxation.

Conversely, the sole proprietorship and partnership, including the LLC, are not considered taxpayers separate and distinct from their owners and, therefore, are subject to neither the regular income tax nor the AMT. Rather, the owners of these entities are directly and immediately responsible for any tax on the income these entities generate (i.e., these entities are "flow-through" entities, as their income flows through to their owners for tax purposes). Therefore, the income generated by proprietorships and partnerships is taxed only once before it is available for use by owners, escaping double taxation. Further, the income, gains, losses, etc., generated by sole proprietorships and

LO.4

Identify the influence of the conduit and entity perspectives on the tax treatment of an entity's operations, including the possibility of the double taxation of business income.

GLOBAL TAX ISSUES **Do Corporations Pay Taxes?**

A disadvantage of being a C corporation is the potential for double taxation. This potential disappears, however, if the taxable income of the corporation is zero or negative.

A Government Accountability Office (GAO) study indicates that for the period 1996–2000, more than 60 percent of U.S. corporations did not owe or pay any Federal income taxes. Neither did 70 percent of foreign-owned corporations doing business in the United States. By 2003, corporate tax receipts

had fallen to 7.4 percent of overall Federal receipts, the lowest percentage since 1983.

Another GAO study released in early 2009 found that 83 of the largest publicly traded corporations maintain subsidiaries in 50 tax havens. Senator Carl Levin (who requested the GAO study), along with Senator Byron Dorgan (now retired), concluded that "too many corporations are finagling ways to dodge paying Uncle Sam, despite the benefits they receive from doing business in this country."

partnerships retain their character when recognized by the entity's owners. This can be beneficial (e.g., capital gains recognized by the entity may continue to receive preferential treatment) or disadvantageous (e.g., preference items generated by the entity may trigger the AMT) for a partner in a partnership relative to a shareholder of a corporation. Finally, as discussed further below, the conduit perspective also eliminates the owner's ability to defer the recognition of this income.

S corporations provide an opportunity for certain corporations and their shareholders to avoid double taxation while retaining corporate status and, therefore, the nontax benefits of corporate status. However, as discussed in text Section 15-2a, the tax law limits the number and type of shareholders a corporation may have and still be eligible for S status.

In addition to subjecting an entity's income to double taxation, the choice to conduct a business in the corporate form also makes it ineligible for the qualified business income (QBI) deduction[3]. Individuals, estates, and trusts are eligible for a deduction of up to 20 percent of their domestic business income, including income flowing through to them from a sole proprietorship, partnership (including an LLC taxed as a partnership), or S corporation. Certain limitations apply.

EXAMPLE 6

Sarah, a single taxpayer, owns a car wash business. The business generates $200,000 of income annually before considering $50,000 of compensation paid to Sarah. Sarah has a marginal tax rate of 22%. If Sarah incorporated the business, it would generate a total of $200,000 of taxable income annually, $150,000 taxable to the corporation and $50,000 to Sarah, with a combined tax liability of $42,500 [(150,000 × 21% = $31,500) + ($50,000 × .22 = $11,000)].

Assume instead that Sarah chose to run her business as an LLC. Her taxable income from the business after the QBI deduction would be $170,000 [$50,000 + .8($200,000 − $50,000)], resulting in a tax liability of $37,400 and a Federal income tax savings of $5,100. However, if Sarah incorporated the business and the corporation immediately distributed its $118,500 of after-tax income ($150,000 taxable income less the $31,500 corporate tax paid) to Sarah, her Federal income tax would increase by $17,775 ($118,500 × 15%), meaning that the tax savings of operating as an LLC is $22,875.

18-3b Effect on the Ability to Specially Allocate Income among Owners

Business entities may have several reasons to attribute certain income and expenses to specific owners, including the following.

- A desire to share profits and losses in a proportion different from that of their capital contributions (e.g., based on relative contributions to the generation of those profits or losses).
- A desire to share profits and losses differently from year to year.
- A desire to allocate a built-in gain or loss on contributed property to the contributing owner.

Partnerships and LLCs can allocate taxable income, gains, losses, etc., among their owners in any way they desire as long as the economic consequences follow that same allocation (i.e., as long as the allocation has a *substantial economic effect*). In fact, a special allocation generally is required when a partnership sells property originally contributed by a partner, if the property had a built-in gain or loss at the time of the contribution.

Conversely, the right of shareholders to corporate income is legally determined by their stock ownership. Corporations and their shareholders may be able to achieve results similar to those produced with special allocations by making payments to owners (e.g., salary payments, lease rental payments, and interest payments) and by

---

[3]§ 199A.

using different classes of stock (e.g., preferred and common). However, C corporations cannot directly allocate taxable income, gains, losses, etc., among their owners, as partnerships and LLCs can.

Although the income generated by S corporations generally is taxed in a manner similar to that generated by partnerships, S corporations still are corporations, with the owners' right to income determined by their stock ownership. Special allocations of income, therefore, can be made only through payments to S shareholders.

In-depth coverage can be found on this book's companion website: **www.cengage.com**

2 DIGGING DEEPER

EXAMPLE

7

Khalid contributes land with an adjusted basis of $10,000 and a fair market value of $50,000 for a 50% ownership interest in Maple Company. At the same time, Tracy contributes cash of $50,000 for the remaining 50% ownership interest. Because Maple is unable to obtain the desired zoning for the property, it subsequently sells the land for $50,000.

Khalid has a realized gain of $40,000 ($50,000 − $10,000) and a recognized gain of $0 resulting from the contribution. His basis in his ownership interest in Maple is $10,000, and Maple takes a basis in the land of $10,000. Maple realizes and recognizes a gain of $40,000 ($50,000 − $10,000) when it sells the land.

If Maple is a corporation, the appreciation of the land attributable to the time it was owned by Khalid becomes part of the corporation's taxable income, the resulting tax is paid by the corporation, and the tax burden is indirectly shared equally by both shareholders. There is no way by which the corporation can allocate the recognized gain, and the related tax burden, directly to Khalid.

If Maple is a partnership, the entire $40,000 recognized gain on the sale is allocated to Khalid, regardless of his profits or equity interest. Note that although S corporations are taxed similarly to partnerships, the S corporation provisions do not allow special allocations. If the entity were an S corporation, Khalid and Tracy would each include $20,000 of the recognized gain in their taxable income.

18-3c **Effect on the Tax Treatment of Capital Contributions**

Because of the conduit approach generally taken with partnerships, § 721 generally requires that no gain or loss be recognized when a partner contributes property to a partnership in exchange for a partnership interest. Section 721 protects contributions associated with the formation of the partnership as well as all subsequent contributions. The partnership takes a carryover basis in the contributed property, and the partners have a carryover basis in their partnership interests.[4]

Conversely, because of the entity approach applied to corporations, the transfer of property to a corporation in exchange for its stock is more likely to be a taxable event. Although meeting the control requirement of § 351 may allow shareholders who contribute appreciated property to the corporation to avoid immediate recognition of gain, the control requirement increases the likelihood of gain recognition, especially on contributions made after the corporation's formation. When no gain or loss must be recognized, both the corporate property and the shareholders' stock take a carryover basis.[5]

18-3d **Effect on the Basis of an Ownership Interest**

As alluded to above, because the contribution of property to a partnership or an LLC in exchange for an ownership interest is not a taxable event under § 721, the owner's initial basis for the ownership interest carries over from the contributed property. The same is true of contributions to C and S corporations if the 80 percent control requirement of § 351 is satisfied. If the control requirement is not satisfied, any realized gain or loss

---

[4]Refer to the pertinent discussion in text Section 14-2.

[5]Refer to the pertinent discussion in text Section 12-2f.

TAX FACT **Profitability of Partnerships**

Since 1980, the number of partnership income tax returns has more than doubled (i.e., from 1.4 million returns to 3.4 million returns). The beneficial tax treatment of LLCs is expected to cause this trend to continue. While the partnership provides a tax shelter opportunity by passing losses through to the partner, a majority of partnerships are profitable.

	1985	1990	1995	2000	2010	2014
% of returns with profit	53%	56%	63%	60%	50%	56%
% of returns with losses	47%	44%	37%	40%	50%	44%

Source: IRS Tax Stats.

on a contribution of property to a corporation is recognized by the shareholder, and the investor's stock basis is equal to the fair market value of the contributed property.

In a partnership or an LLC, because the owner directly and immediately recognizes his or her allocable share of the income, gains, losses, etc., of the entity, those items also affect the owner's basis in the entity interest. Likewise, the owner's basis is increased by the owner's share of the amount by which the entity's liabilities increase and is decreased by the owner's share of the amount by which the entity's liabilities decrease. Accordingly, the owner's basis in the ownership interest changes continuously.[6] Conversely, because the income of a shareholder in a C corporation is unaffected by the corporation's operations, the shareholder's basis in his or her stock is not affected by corporate income, gain, loss, etc. Similarly, because the shareholder of a C corporation is not responsible for any of the corporation's liabilities, those liabilities have no effect on the basis of the shareholder's stock.

The treatment of an S corporation shareholder falls between that of the partner and the C corporation shareholder. Because the shareholder directly and immediately recognizes the income, gains, losses, etc., of an S corporation, an S corporation shareholder's stock basis is affected by the owner's share of those items. However, because S corporation shareholders are not responsible for the corporation's liabilities, the shareholder's stock basis is not affected by the corporation's liabilities.

The Big Picture

EXAMPLE 8

Return to the facts of *The Big Picture* on p. 18-1. Bill contributed cash of $100,000 to an entity for a 30% ownership interest in the franchise. Assume that the entity borrowed $50,000 and repaid $20,000 of this amount by the end of the taxable year. The profits for the year are $90,000.

If the entity is a partnership or LLC, Bill's basis at the end of the period is $136,000 ($100,000 investment + $9,000 share of net liability increase + $27,000 share of profits). If the entity is a C corporation, Bill's stock basis is $100,000 ($100,000 original investment). If the corporation is an S corporation, Bill's stock basis is $127,000 ($100,000 + $27,000).

18-3e Effect on the Application of the At-Risk and Passive Activity Loss Rules

The at-risk and passive activity loss rules prevent certain taxpayers from recognizing losses that might otherwise be available to them. The at-risk rules prevent affected taxpayers from recognizing losses for which they are not at a risk of economic loss. The passive activity loss rules generally allow affected taxpayers to recognize losses from passive activities only to offset income from passive activities.

The at-risk and passive activity loss rules apply to individuals and closely held C corporations. The passive activity loss rules apply to personal service corporations

---

[6]§§ 705 and 752.

as well. Although neither set of rules applies to flow-through entities directly, the rules are especially relevant to the individual owners of these entities who may not be at risk for all of the losses that may pass through to them from the entity, or who may not actively participate in the entity's activities. See text Sections 6-6 and 6-7 for a detailed discussion.

The at-risk rules are particularly relevant to partners who may have nonrecourse debt included in the basis of their partnership interest (see discussion in text Section 14-3e). Note that, in spite of partners being able to include nonrecourse debt in the basis of their partnership interest, the at-risk rules will prevent partners from being able to recognize any more losses than if the entity had been organized as an S corporation.

However, as partnership recourse debt may also be included in a partner's basis in the partnership interest, taxpayers organizing as a partnership rather than as an S corporation may allow business owners to recognize more losses that may be generated by a pass-through entity. Of course, this will expose the owners to a greater risk of economic loss. Recall that an important exception to the at-risk rules allows taxpayers, including partners in partnerships, to be considered at-risk for qualified nonrecourse debt. This allows taxpayers to recognize losses from real estate activities even though they may not be at risk.

EXAMPLE 9

Walt is the general partner and Ira and Vera are the limited partners in the WIV limited partnership. Walt contributes land with an adjusted basis of $40,000 and a fair market value of $50,000 for his partnership interest, and Ira and Vera each contribute cash of $100,000 for their partnership interests. They agree to share profits and losses in proportion to their capital contributions.

To finance construction of an apartment building, the partnership obtains $600,000 of nonrecourse financing (not qualified nonrecourse financing; see text Section 14-3e), pledging the land and building as collateral on the loan. Each partner's basis for the partnership interest is computed as follows.

	Walt	Ira	Vera
Contribution	$ 40,000	$100,000	$100,000
Share of nonrecourse debt	200,000	200,000	200,000
Basis	$240,000	$300,000	$300,000

Without the at-risk rules, Ira and Vera could recognize losses up to $300,000 each even though they invested only $100,000 and have no personal liability for the nonrecourse debt. However, the at-risk rules limit loss recognition to the at-risk basis, which is $100,000 each for Ira and Vera.

The at-risk rules also affect the general partner. Because Walt is not at risk for the nonrecourse debt, his at-risk basis is $40,000.

If, instead, the entity were an S corporation and Walt received 20% of the stock and Ira and Vera each received 40%, the basis for their stock would be computed as follows.

	Walt	Ira	Vera
Contribution	$40,000	$100,000	$100,000
Share of nonrecourse debt	–0–	–0–	–0–
Basis	$40,000	$100,000	$100,000

Notice that the at-risk rules prevent any nonrecourse debt included in basis of a partner's interest from increasing the ability to recognize losses over what would be available if the owners had organized as an S corporation. Whether WIV had organized as a partnership or an S corporation, Walt would be able only to recognize losses up to $40,000, while Ira and Vera would only be able to recognize losses up to $100,000.

If the debt were recourse debt, however, it would be included in the at-risk basis of Walt's partnership interest, allowing him to recognize losses up to $640,000 ($40,000 contribution + $600,000 partnership recourse debt). It would not, however, affect the basis of his stock if WIV had organized as an S corporation.

The passive activity loss rules generally allow individuals and personal service corporations to recognize losses from passive activities only to offset income from passive activities. The passive activity losses of a closely held corporation, however, also can be used to offset active income.

Neither the at-risk nor the passive activity loss rules apply to C corporations that are not closely held. A closely held corporation is one in which five or fewer individuals own more than 50 percent of the value of its outstanding stock. Therefore, C corporations that are not closely held can recognize losses for which they may not be at risk as well as from activities in which they do not materially participate.

As noted above, the passive activity loss rules also apply to personal service corporations. A corporation is classified as a *personal service corporation* if the following requirements are satisfied.[7]

- The principal activity of the corporation is the performance of personal services.
- The services are substantially performed by owner-employees.
- Owner-employees own more than 10 percent in value of the stock of the corporation.

Because the conduit concept applies to partnerships, S corporations, and limited liability entities, passive activity income and losses are separately stated at the entity level and are passed through to the owners with their passive character maintained.

18-3f Effect on the Tax Treatment of Distributions

The application of the conduit perspective to partnerships, including LLCs, results in distributions being generally tax-free. The distribution triggers no gain or loss for the partnership, while the owners treat it as a recovery of capital. The application of the entity perspective to corporations produces the opposite result. Distributions of appreciated property by a C corporation are taxed immediately to the corporation, while the owners generally recognize any distribution as a taxable dividend to the extent of the corporation's earnings and profits.

A combination entity/conduit approach applies to property distributions from S corporations. The entity perspective generally applicable to corporations leads to the recognition of gain by the corporation for any appreciation attributable to the distributed property.[8] However, despite the distribution itself representing a recovery of capital to the shareholder, the conduit concept leads to any gain recognized by the corporation being taxable at the shareholder level.

EXAMPLE 10

Tan, an S corporation, is equally owned by Leif and Matt. Tan distributes two parcels of land to Leif and Matt. Tan has a basis of $10,000 for each parcel. Each parcel has a fair market value of $15,000. The distribution results in a $10,000 ($30,000 − $20,000) recognized gain for Tan. Leif and Matt each report $5,000 of the gain on their individual income tax returns.

18-3g Effect on Other Taxes

The choice of organizational form will have state and local, as well as Federal, income tax consequences. Although the state tax consequences often are similar to the Federal results, this may not always be the case.

The S corporation provides a good illustration of this point. Not all states recognize the Federal S election. Therefore, although the income, gains, losses, etc., from S corporations and partnerships may affect their owners' Federal taxable incomes and tax liabilities similarly, the same may not be true with respect to their state taxable income and tax liability. Rather, the items recognized by S corporations may be taxable directly to the corporation with no change in its owners' state taxable incomes or tax liabilities until distributed.

Income taxes are not the only taxes affected by the choice of organizational form. For example, the taxes imposed by the Federal Insurance Contributions Act (i.e., FICA) are assessed on most earned income of individuals, including that of business owners.

---

[7]§ 469, derived from the definition in § 269A.   [8]§ 311(b).

FICA taxes include assessments to fund Social Security and Medicare and are imposed on individuals at rates of 6.2% and 1.45% of earned income, respectively.[9] Employers typically withhold these taxes from employees' wages. However, employers are responsible for matching the amounts paid by employees, resulting in taxes equal to 15.3% of the employee's earned income. However, the Social Security tax is imposed on only the first $128,400 of wages in 2018.

Business owners who organize as sole proprietorships are required to pay both the employer's and employee's share of the tax in the form of the self-employment tax. As the proprietor has no "wages," the tax is imposed on his or her self-employment income, generally the income earned by the business, subject to the same limitations. A general partner in a partnership is treated similarly, with the partner's share of the partnership's aggregate income subject to the tax.

However, other organizational forms may offer their owners an opportunity to reduce their FICA taxes. For example, although the wages paid to a shareholder of an S corporation are subject to FICA tax, a shareholder's share of the corporation's aggregate income is not.

EXAMPLE 11

Wayne and Irving are starting a new business venture. Each will own one-half of the company. Wayne will be paid $50,000 annually to provide personal services to the venture, while Irving is solely an investor. It is estimated that after the $50,000 paid to Wayne, the venture will generate $80,000 of income. That income will be reinvested in the venture for the foreseeable future. The income subject to FICA taxes will be:

	Wayne	**Irving**
If organized as a general partnership	$50,000 + ½ ($80,000) = $90,000	$40,000
If organized as a C corporation	$50,000	$0
If organized as an S corporation	$50,000	$0

As this table shows, an S corporation has an incentive not to pay wages to its owners. The IRS, therefore, may be interested in whether an S corporation pays adequate compensation to its owners.[10]

18-4 MINIMIZING DOUBLE TAXATION

LO.5
Identify techniques for avoiding double taxation.

As explained earlier, only income earned in the corporate form is potentially subject to double taxation. However, two features of the tax law help mitigate the double taxation of income earned by corporations. First, corporate income is subject to a flat tax rate of 21 percent, much lower than the top rate that can be faced by individuals. Second, the lower tax rates that apply to dividends reduce the burden of double taxation on all qualified dividends. Together, these lower rates prevent the effective tax rate on income earned by corporations from exceeding approximately 37% $[1-(1-.21)(1-.20)]$, the top marginal rate faced by individuals. However, the double taxation of corporate income still may result in an effective tax rate higher than what might be faced by income earned in other organizational forms. For example, a business owner with a marginal tax rate of 24% might face an effective rate of approximately 33% $[1-(1-.21)$ $(1-.15)]$ on business income earned through a corporation.

Several other planning techniques also are available for further reducing, or eliminating, the second layer of taxation.

18-4a Making Deductible Distributions

The double taxation of corporate income typically is triggered by the payment of dividends by the corporation to its shareholders. As distributions of corporate income, dividends are taxable to shareholders but are not deductible by the corporation. However, if distributions can be made to shareholders in their capacity other than as shareholders, the distributions may be deductible by the corporation. Although the payment may increase

---

[9]These amounts are indexed annually.

[10]This issue has been the subject of a series of court cases brought by the Treasury.

the rate at which the distribution is taxed at the individual shareholder level (e.g., from 20 to 37 percent for a shareholder in the top marginal bracket), it will save 21 percent tax at the corporate level. Common examples of such deductible distributions include:

- Salary payments to shareholder-employees.
- Lease or rental payments to shareholder-lessors.
- Interest payments to shareholder-creditors.

Recognizing the potential for abuse, the IRS scrutinizes these types of distributions carefully. For example, all three types of distribution are evaluated for *reasonableness*.[11] In addition, shareholder loans that lack a sufficient number of the characteristics usually associated with debt may be reclassified as equity.[12] IRS success with either approach raises the specter of double taxation. The recharacterization of shareholder debt as equity can have especially negative consequences for the shareholder as the repayment of the "debt" itself, as well as the related "interest," will be treated as a taxable dividend rather than a recovery of capital.

Using Deductible Distributions to Avoid Double Taxation

EXAMPLE 12

Donna owns all the stock of Green Corporation and is the chief executive officer. Green's taxable income before salary payments to Donna is as follows.

Year 1	Year 2	Year 3
$80,000	$50,000	$250,000

Donna receives a monthly salary of $3,000. In December of each year, Donna reviews the operations for the year and determines the year-end bonus she is to receive. Donna's yearly bonuses are as follows.

Year 1	Year 2	Year 3
$44,000	$14,000	$214,000

The apparent purpose of Green's bonus program is to reduce the corporate taxable income to zero and thereby avoid double taxation. Assuming Donna's marginal tax rate was 24%, the total tax on the year 3 income distributed as a bonus would be $51,360 ($214,000 × .24).

However, the IRS would likely find the bonus to be unreasonable compensation and, therefore, nondeductible by the corporation. Rather, the distribution would be considered a constructive dividend. In this case, the total tax on the income distributed as a dividend would be $70,299 {[$214,000 × .21] + [214,000 × (1−.21) × .15]}.

EXAMPLE 13

Tom and Vicki each contribute $20,000 to TV Corporation in return for all of its stock. In addition, they each lend $80,000 to TV, evidenced by notes payable by the corporation to Tom and Vicki.

The notes provide the opportunity for the corporation to make payments of $6,400 each year to both Tom and Vicki. Although the annual interest payments are taxable to Tom and Vicki, they are deductible by the corporation, escaping double taxation. At the time of repayment in 10 years, neither Tom nor Vicki recognizes gross income from the repayment of the notes; the $80,000 amount realized is equal to the basis for the note of $80,000.

If the notes lack sufficient characteristics typically associated with debt (e.g., they lack a reasonable interest rate or penalty for failure to make timely payments) and the IRS succeeded in reclassifying them as equity, Tom and Vicki still would recognize annual gross income of $6,400, but the interest would be reclassified as dividend income. Although the dividends may be taxable to Tom and Vicki at a lower rate than would be interest income, the tax due on the dividend nonetheless

continued

[11]§ 162(a)(1). *Mayson Manufacturing Co. v. Comm.*, 49–2 USTC ¶9467, 38 AFTR 1028, 178 F.2d 115 (CA–6, 1949); *Harolds Club v. Comm.*, 65–1 USTC ¶9198, 15 AFTR 2d 241, 340 F.2d 861 (CA–9, 1965).

[12]§ 385; Rev.Rul. 83–98, 1983–2 C.B. 40; *Bauer v. Comm.*, 84–2 USTC ¶9996, 55 AFTR 2d 85–433, 748 F.2d 1365 (CA–9, 1984).

would trigger double taxation, as the distribution no longer would be deductible by the corporation. To make matters worse, the repayment of the notes in 10 years would no longer qualify as a recovery of capital, resulting in additional dividend income for Tom and Vicki.

Note, however, that recharacterizing a distribution to a shareholder as a deductible expense may not always result in a reduction in taxes. Given the lower tax rate faced by corporations and the rate reduction available to individuals for qualified dividends, the double taxation of corporate income may actually reduce overall taxes.

Return to the facts of Example 12. Assume that Donna's marginal tax rate was 35% rather than 24%. The total tax due on the year 3 income distributed as a bonus would increase to $74,900 ($214,000 × .35). However, if the income were distributed as a dividend, the total tax would remain $70,299 {[$214,000 × .21] + [214,000 × (1 − .21) × .15]}. In this case, the lower tax rates on corporate income and dividends relative to Donna's marginal tax rate on her ordinary income result in the dividend triggering less overall tax, despite subjecting the distributed income to double taxation.

EXAMPLE 14

18-4b Deferring Distributions

Double taxation is not triggered unless the corporation makes (actual or deemed) distributions to the shareholders. Deferring distributions to shareholders can postpone the second layer of taxation on corporate earnings, reducing the net present value of the tax.

Further tax savings are available if the distributions are delayed until a shareholder's death. Note that any earnings retained by the corporation will increase the value of its stock. Under the basis step-up rule, the basis of the stock for the shareholder's beneficiaries will be its fair market value, including the value due to the undistributed income at the date of the shareholder's death. The increased basis will allow the beneficiaries to dispose of the stock with the corporate earnings accrued, while the decedent who held the stock never is subject to Federal income tax at the individual level.

In-depth coverage can be found on this book's companion website: **www.cengage.com**   **3 DIGGING DEEPER**

18-4c Making Return-of-Capital Distributions

The exposure to double taxation can be reduced if corporate distributions to shareholders can qualify as a recovery of capital rather than as a dividend. This can occur if distributions are made when the corporation's earnings and profits (E & P) are low or negative (see discussion in text Section 13-2). The stock redemption and liquidation provisions offer another opportunity to avoid dividend treatment. Under these rules, a distribution may be treated as a sale of the shareholder's stock. Although any gain on such a sale would be taxed at the

TAX FACT Income Tax Returns Filed by Business Entities

Type of Taxpayer	Tax Returns Filed (millions)			
	1980	**1990**	**2000**	**2014**
Individual	93.1	112.3	126.9	148.1
Partnership	1.4	1.8	2.1	3.6
C corporation	2.1	2.3	2.2	1.8
S corporation	.5	1.5	2.8	4.5

Source: IRS *Tax Stats.*

The increase in the popularity of LLCs has led to a notable increase in the number of partnership returns filed since 1980. However, despite the tax and nontax advantages offered by LLCs, the number of S corporation returns has increased proportionately more than has the number of partnership returns over the same period.

Corporations such as Coca-Cola, IBM, Micro-soft, Walmart, and ExxonMobil are major players not only in their industries but also in the world economy. However, some people also are attracted to "mom-and-pop stores," which cumulatively play a major role in the economy.

In recognition of the important role of small businesses and the competitive disadvantages that often result from their size, Congress has provided small businesses with tax benefits that are not available to larger business entities. Included among such benefits are the following.

- § 179 – immediate expensing for tangible personal property.
- § 1045 – deferral of gain for qualified small business stock.

- § 1202 – partial exclusion of gain for certain small business stock.
- § 1244 – ordinary loss treatment on the sale of certain small business stock.

Each of these provisions defines "small" differently. Sometimes, however, the term "small" may be interpreted inappropriately by taxpayers. The classic example is the small business corporation of Subchapter S. Although many assume that S corporations must be "small," some S corporations hold billions of dollars of assets. They are "small" chiefly in the sense that the number of shareholders cannot exceed 100 unrelated shareholders.

same rate as a dividend would be, the amount of the distribution representing a recovery of capital would escape current income taxation altogether. Further, a final distribution that is less than the shareholder's basis in the stock triggers recognition of a capital loss.[13]

18-4d Electing S Corporation Status

Electing S corporation status generally eliminates double taxation.[14] Several factors should be considered when making this election.

- Are all of the shareholders willing to consent to the election?
- Can the qualification requirements for S status be satisfied at the time of the election?
- Can the S corporation requirements continue to be satisfied?
- For what period will the conditions that make the election beneficial continue to prevail?
- Will the corporate distribution policy create wherewithal to pay problems at the shareholder level?

EXAMPLE 15

Emerald Corporation commenced business in January 2017. The two shareholders, Diego and Jaime, are both in the 28% combined state and Federal income tax bracket. The following operating results are projected for the first five years of operations.

2017	2018	2019	2020	2021
($50,000)	$400,000	$600,000	$800,000	$1,000,000

The corporation plans to expand rapidly. Therefore, no distributions to shareholders are anticipated. In addition, beginning in 2018, preferred stock will be offered to a substantial number of investors to help finance the expansion.

If the S corporation election is made for 2017, the $50,000 loss can be passed through to Diego and Jaime. The loss will generate a positive cash-flow effect of $14,000 ($50,000 × 28%). Assume that the S election is either revoked or involuntarily terminated at the beginning of 2018 as a result of the issuance of the preferred stock. The C corporation tax liability for 2018 is $136,000 ($400,000 × 34%).

If the S corporation election is not made for 2017, the $50,000 loss is a net operating loss. The amount can be carried forward to reduce the 2018 corporate taxable income to $350,000 ($400,000 − $50,000). The resultant tax liability is $119,000 ($350,000 × 34%).

continued

---

[13]See § 302 and text Section 13-7.

[14]Recall the text Section 15-4 discussions of the taxes on an S corporation's built-in gains, LIFO recapture, and investment income. These taxes ensure that income earned before a corporation elects S corporation status remains subject to double taxation in certain circumstances.

Should the S corporation election be made for just the one-year period? The answer is unclear. With an assumed after-tax rate of return to Diego and Jaime of 10%, the value of the $14,000 one year hence is $15,400 ($14,000 × 110%). Even considering the time value of money, the combined corporation-shareholder negative cash-flow effect of $120,600 ($136,000 − $15,400) in the case of an S election is not significantly different from the $119,000 corporate tax liability that would result for a C corporation.

18-5 DISPOSING OF A BUSINESS

LO.6

Analyze the effects of the disposition of a business on the owners and the entity for each organizational form.

A key factor in evaluating the tax consequences of a business disposition is whether the disposition is viewed as the sale of an ownership interest in the business or as a sale of the underlying assets used in the business. Generally, the tax consequences are more favorable to the seller if the transaction is treated as a sale of the ownership interest. Conversely, the purchaser will prefer that the transaction be treated as a purchase of the individual assets, as this results in a higher basis in those assets. This difference in the preferences of the parties may influence the price paid by the seller.

18-5a Sole Proprietorships

Because a sole proprietorship is not recognized as an entity separate and distinct from its owner, the sale of a sole proprietorship is treated as the sale of individual assets. Thus, gains and losses must be calculated separately for each asset. Classification as capital gain or ordinary income depends on the nature and holding period of the individual assets. Ordinary income property such as inventory will result in ordinary gains and losses. Section 1231 property such as land, buildings, and machinery used in the business will produce § 1231 gains and losses (subject to depreciation recapture under §§ 1245 and 1250). Capital assets such as investment land and stocks qualify for capital gain or loss treatment.

If the amount realized exceeds the fair market value of the identifiable assets sold, the excess is treated as goodwill, which generates capital gain for the seller. If instead the excess payment is allocated to a covenant not to compete, the related gain is classified as ordinary income rather than capital gain. Both goodwill and covenants are amortized by the purchaser over a 15-year statutory period.[15]

Seth, who is in the 35% tax bracket, sells his sole proprietorship to Wilma for $600,000. The identifiable assets are as follows.

EXAMPLE

	Adjusted Basis	Fair Market Value
Inventory	$ 20,000	$ 25,000
Accounts receivable	40,000	40,000
Machinery and equipment*	125,000	150,000
Buildings**	175,000	250,000
Land	40,000	100,000
	$400,000	$565,000

*Potential § 1245 recapture of $50,000.
**Potential § 1250 recapture of $20,000.

continued

---

[15]§ 197.

The sale produces the following results for Seth.

	Gain (Loss)	Ordinary Income	§ 1231 Gain	Capital Gain
Inventory	$ 5,000	$ 5,000		
Accounts receivable	–0–			
Machinery and equipment	25,000	25,000		
Buildings	75,000	20,000	$ 55,000	
Land	60,000		60,000	
Goodwill	35,000			$35,000
	$200,000	$50,000	$115,000	$35,000

If the sale is structured this way, Wilma can amortize the $35,000 paid for goodwill over a 15-year period. If instead Wilma paid the $35,000 to Seth for a covenant not to compete for a period of seven years, Seth's $35,000 gain would be taxed to him as ordinary income. If the legal classification of the payment has no nontax consequences for Wilma, in exchange for treating the payment as a goodwill payment, she should negotiate for a price reduction that reflects Seth's benefit from the lower capital gains tax.

18-5b Partnerships and Limited Liability Companies

The sale of a partnership or LLC can be structured as the sale of assets or as the sale of an ownership interest. If the transaction takes the form of an asset sale, it is treated the same as for a sole proprietorship (described previously).

The sale of an ownership interest generally is treated as the sale of a capital asset. Therefore, structuring a transaction as a sale of an ownership interest may be preferable to structuring it as a sale of the partnership assets. However, this benefit is severely curtailed by the need to recognize gain related to appreciation of many of the partnership's ordinary income-producing assets as ordinary gain, even on the sale of an ownership interest.[16]

From a buyer's perspective, the tax consequences are not affected by the form of the transaction. If the transaction is an asset purchase, the basis for the assets equals the amount paid. If a buyer intends to continue to operate as an LLC or a partnership, the assets can be contributed to the entity under § 721. Therefore, the owner's basis in the entity interest is equal to the purchase price for the assets. Likewise, if ownership interests are purchased, the purchaser's basis in the interest is the price paid. The partnership's basis for the assets is the purchase price because the original partnership was terminated.[17]

A problem may arise when a taxpayer purchases a partnership or LLC interest (rather than the entire business) from another owner. In such a case, the amount paid for the interest may not be equal to the new owner's share of the entity's basis in its assets. Put another way, the basis of the assets inside the entity may not reflect the amount paid for them by the new owner. To help prevent this problem, the entity may make an election to adjust its basis in its assets to reflect the amount paid by the new owner. This basis adjustment is allocable entirely to the new owner, ensuring the new owner can recover the (indirect) cost of the underlying assets.

EXAMPLE 17

Roz buys a one-third interest in the RST Partnership for $50,000 (i.e., Roz's outside basis is $50,000). All of the entity's assets are depreciable, and their basis to the partnership (i.e., their inside basis) is $90,000. If a § 754 election is in effect, the partnership can step up the basis of its depreciable assets by $20,000, the difference between Roz's outside basis and Roz's share of the inside basis amounts [$50,000 − (1/3 × $90,000)]. All of the "new" asset basis is allocated to Roz.

---

[16]§ 751.   [17]§ 708(b)(1)(B).

TAX PLANNING STRATEGIES Selling Stock or Assets

FRAMEWORK FOCUS: TAX RATE

Strategy: Avoid Double Taxation.

Structuring the transfer of a business as a stock sale may produce detrimental tax results for the purchaser. As Example 18 illustrates, the basis of the corporation's assets is not affected by a stock sale. If the fair market value of the stock exceeds the corporation's adjusted basis for its assets, the purchaser is denied the opportunity to step up the basis of the assets to reflect the amount in effect paid for them through the stock acquisition—no § 754 election is available for C corporations.

An asset sale resolves the purchaser's problem of not being able to step up the basis of the assets to their fair market value. The basis for each asset is its purchase price. Then the purchaser may transfer the property to a corporation in a § 351 transaction. However, an asset sale may not be attractive to the seller.

If an asset sale is used, the seller of the business can be either the corporation or its shareholders. If the seller is the corporation, the corporation sells the business (the assets), pays any debts not transferred, and makes a liquidating distribution to the shareholders. If the sellers are the shareholders, the corporation pays any debts that will not be transferred and makes a liquidating distribution to the shareholders; then the shareholders sell the business.

Regardless of the approach used for an asset sale, double taxation occurs. The corporation is either taxed on the actual sale of the assets or it is taxed as if it had sold the assets when it makes the liquidating distribution to the shareholders. The shareholders are taxed when they receive cash or assets distributed in kind by the corporation.

From the perspective of the seller, the ideal form of the transaction is a stock sale. Conversely, from the purchaser's perspective, the ideal form is an asset purchase. Thus, a conflict exists between the buyer's and the seller's objectives regarding the form of the transaction. Therefore, the bargaining ability of the seller and the purchaser to structure the sale as a stock sale or an asset sale, respectively, is critical.

Such an election, once made, is binding on the entity and applies to all subsequent exchanges of ownership interests. Therefore, while it may benefit a new owner if the entity's assets have appreciated prior to the acquisition date, creating a positive basis adjustment for the acquiring owner, it may be detrimental to a future acquirer if assets are depreciated at the time of acquisition, resulting in a negative basis adjustment for the new owner.[18]

18-5c C Corporations

The sale of a business held by a C corporation can be structured as either an asset sale or a stock sale. The stock sale has the dual advantage to the seller of being less complex both as a legal transaction and as a tax transaction. It also has the advantage of providing a way to avoid double taxation. Finally, any gain or loss on the sale of the stock is treated as a capital gain or loss to the shareholder.

Jane and Zina each own 50% of the stock of Purple Corporation. They have owned the business for 10 years. Jane's basis in her stock is $40,000, and Zina's basis in her stock is $60,000. They agree to sell the stock to Rex for $300,000. Jane recognizes a long-term capital gain of $110,000 ($150,000 − $40,000), and Zina recognizes a long-term capital gain of $90,000 ($150,000 − $60,000). Rex takes a basis in his stock of $300,000. Purple's basis in its assets does not change as a result of the stock sale.

EXAMPLE
18

Conversely, the purchaser will prefer that the transaction be structured as a sale of the individual assets, assuming those assets have a fair market value in excess of their basis to the corporation. This allows the purchaser to increase the basis of the assets to their fair market value.

---

[18]§§ 743 and 754.

EXAMPLE 19

Returning to the previous example, assume that Purple's assets have a fair market value of $300,000 but an adjusted basis to Purple of $100,000. If the transaction is structured as an asset sale rather than a stock sale, Rex will take a basis of $300,000 in his acquired assets. However, Purple will recognize a gain of $200,000 ($300,000 − $100,000) in addition to the gain recognized by Jane and Zina on the liquidation of Purple.

18-5d S Corporations

Because the S corporation is a corporation under state law, it is subject to the provisions for a C corporation discussed in the prior section. An asset sale at the corporate level or a liquidating distribution of assets produces gain or loss recognition at the corporate level. However, under the conduit concept applicable to the S corporation, the recognized gain or loss is passed through to the shareholders. Therefore, double taxation is avoided directly for a stock sale (because only the shareholder is involved) and indirectly for an asset sale (because the conduit perspective ignores the involvement of the corporation).[19] However, an asset sale still is more likely to generate ordinary income than is a sale of S corporation stock.

Concept Summary 18.1 reviews the tax consequences of business dispositions.

Concept Summary 18.1

Tax Treatment of Disposition of a Business

Form of Entity	Form of Transaction	Tax Consequences	
		Seller	**Buyer**
Sole proprietorship	Sale of individual assets.	Gain or loss is calculated separately for the individual assets. Classification as capital or ordinary depends on the nature and holding period of the individual assets. If amount realized exceeds the fair market value of the identifiable assets, the excess is allocated to goodwill (except to the extent identified with a covenant not to compete), which is a capital asset.	Basis for individual assets is the allocated cost. The buyer is neutral regarding the classification of any amount paid over the fair market value of the identifiable assets, because both goodwill and noncompete covenants are amortized over a 15-year statutory period.
	Sale of the business.	Treated as a sale of the individual assets (as above).	Treated as a purchase of the individual assets (as above).
Partnership and limited liability company	Sale of individual assets.	Treatment is the same as for the sole proprietorship.	Treatment is the same as for the sole proprietorship. If the intent is to operate in partnership form, the assets can be contributed to a partnership under § 721.
	Sale of ownership interest.	Entity interest is treated as the sale of a capital asset [subject to ordinary income potential for any gain attributable to ordinary income-producing ("hot") assets].	Basis for new owner's ownership interest is the cost. The new entity's basis for the assets is also the pertinent cost (i.e., contributed to the entity under § 721) because the original entity will have terminated.

continued

---

[19]Double taxation might seem to be avoided by making an S corporation election prior to the liquidation of a C corporation, but the built-in gains tax eliminates this opportunity; taxation occurs at the corporate level, and double taxation results. See text Section 15-4a.

Tax Treatment of Disposition of a Business—(Continued)

Form of Entity	Form of Transaction	Tax Consequences	
		Seller	**Buyer**
C corporation	Sale of corporate assets by corporation (i.e., corporation sells assets, pays debts, and makes liquidating distribution to the shareholders).	Double taxation occurs. Corporation is taxed on the sale of the assets with the gain or loss determination and the classification as capital or ordinary treated the same as for the sole proprietorship. Shareholders calculate gain or loss as the difference between the stock basis and the amount received from the corporation in the liquidating distribution. Capital gain or loss usually results, because stock typically is a capital asset.	Basis for individual assets is the allocated cost. If the intent is to operate in corporate form, the assets can be contributed to a corporation in a tax-deferred manner under § 351.
	Sale of corporate assets by the shareholders (i.e., corporation pays debts and makes liquidating distribution to the shareholders).	Double taxation occurs. At the time of the liquidating distribution to the shareholders, the corporation is taxed as if it had sold the assets. Shareholders calculate gain or loss as the difference between the stock basis and the fair market value of the assets received from the corporation in the liquidating distribution. Capital gain or loss usually results, because stock typically is a capital asset.	Same as corporate asset sale.
	Sale of corporate stock.	Double taxation is avoided. Because the corporation is not a party to the transaction, there are no tax consequences at the corporate level. Shareholders calculate gain or loss as the difference between the stock basis and the amount received for the stock. Capital gain or loss usually results, because stock typically is a capital asset.	Basis for the stock is its cost. The basis for the corporate assets is not affected by the stock purchase.
S corporation	Sale of corporate assets by corporation.	Recognition occurs at the corporate level on the sale of the assets, with the gain or loss determination and the classification as capital or ordinary treated the same as for the sole proprietorship. Conduit concept applicable to the S corporation results in the recognized amount being taxed at the shareholder level. Double taxation associated with the asset sale is avoided because any gain or loss on the sale is recognized directly by the shareholders, increasing or decreasing their basis in the stock. Shareholders calculate gain or loss as the difference between the stock basis and the amount received from the corporation in the liquidating distribution. Capital gain or loss usually results, because stock typically is a capital asset.	Basis for individual assets is the allocated cost. If the intent is to operate in corporate form (i.e., as an S corporation), the assets can be contributed to a corporation in a tax-deferred manner under § 351.

continued

Tax Treatment of Disposition of a Business—(Continued)

Form of Entity	Form of Transaction	Tax Consequences	
		Seller	Buyer
S corporation *(continued)*	Sale of corporate assets by the shareholders.	At the time of the liquidating distribution to the shareholders, recognition occurs at the corporation level as if the corporation had sold the assets. The resulting tax consequences for the shareholders and the corporation are the same as for the sale of corporate assets by the S corporation.	Same as corporate asset sale by the S corporation.
	Sale of corporate stock.	Same as the treatment for the sale of stock of a C corporation.	Same as the treatment for the purchase of stock of a C corporation.

18-6 CONVERTING TO ANOTHER BUSINESS FORM

As the owners' tax and nontax goals change, they may decide to change the organizational form in which the business is conducted. This raises three primary issues.

- Does the conversion result in the recognition of gain or loss?
- What is the basis of the owners' interests in the new entity?
- What is the basis of the assets held by the new entity?

18-6a Sole Proprietorship

The conversion of a sole proprietorship into another entity form can be achieved without any recognition of gain or loss at the entity or owner level. This result occurs regardless of the choice of the new entity form.[20]

Given the conduit approach taken for sole proprietorships, the liquidation of a proprietorship triggers no immediate income tax consequences. If the proprietorship converts into a partnership or an LLC, the owner's basis in the ownership interest carries over from the contributed property.[21] Similarly, if the proprietorship converts into a corporation, the shareholder's basis for the stock received carries over from the shareholder's basis in the contributed property.[22] After a conversion, the entity takes a carryover basis for its assets.[23] As discussed below, a newly formed corporation then may elect S status if the owner desires.

18-6b C Corporation

A C corporation can convert into any of the following entity forms.

- Sole proprietorship.
- Partnership or LLC.
- S corporation.

---

[20]§§ 351(a) and 721(a).

[21]§ 722.

[22]§ 358(a).

[23]§§ 352(a) and 723.

Converting to an S corporation merely requires the election of S status.[24] As discussed in text Section 15-2a, the S election can be made only if all shareholders consent to the election and if the S corporation qualification requirements are satisfied.[25] These qualification requirements become maintenance requirements that must be met to retain the S election.

The election of S status has no immediate income tax consequences for the corporation or its shareholders. No gains or losses are recognized, and the bases of the shareholders' stock and the corporation's assets all are unchanged. However, an S corporation's prior status as a C corporation may trigger a corporate-level tax on the built-in gains related to assets the corporation held at the time it converted.

Conversely, if a C corporation converts into a sole proprietorship, a partnership, or an LLC, the corporation must be liquidated. This produces the following tax consequences.

- Recognition of gain or loss at the corporate level related to the assets held by the corporation.[26]
- Recognition of gain or loss at the shareholder level related to the stock held by the shareholders.[27]
- Fair market value basis for the assets distributed in liquidation.[28]

After liquidation, the C corporation's former shareholders contribute the assets to the new entity. The tax consequences to the owners and to the entity are the same as those discussed earlier.

18-6c **Partnership**

A partnership or an LLC can convert into a corporation. The corporation may then elect S status, if the owners desire, with no immediate income tax consequences.

The owners can transfer their interests to the corporation in exchange for the stock of the entity. Because the transfer likely satisfies the § 351 requirements, any realized gain or loss is not recognized.[29] If, however, the 80 percent control requirement is not satisfied, the realized gain or loss is recognized by the owners.[30]

Assuming that the § 351 requirements for nonrecognition are satisfied, the following tax results occur.

- The basis of the stock to the shareholders is a carryover basis.[31]
- The basis of the assets to the corporation is a carryover basis.[32]

18-7 **OVERALL COMPARISON OF BUSINESS FORMS**

Concept Summary 18.2 provides a detailed comparison of the tax consequences of the choice among the most common forms of doing business.

---

[24]§ 1362(a).

[25]§§ 1361(a), 1361(b), and 1362(a)(2).

[26]§ 336(a).

[27]§ 331(a).

[28]§ 334(a).

[29]§ 351(a).

[30]§ 368(c).

[31]§ 358(a).

[32]§ 362(a).

Concept Summary 18.2

Tax Attributes of Different Forms of Doing Business
(Assume That Partners and Shareholders Are All Individuals)

	Sole Proprietorship	Partnership/Limited Liability Company	S Corporation	C Corporation
Restrictions on type or number of owners	One owner. The owner must be an individual.	Must have at least two owners.	Only individuals, estates, certain trusts, and certain tax-exempt entities can be owners. Maximum number of shareholders limited to 100.*	None, except some states require a minimum of two shareholders.
Incidence of tax	Sole proprietorship's income and deductions are included in the proprietor's taxable income, reported on Schedule C of the individual's Form 1040. A separate Schedule C is prepared for each business.	Entity not subject to Federal income tax. Owners in their separate capacity subject to tax on their distributive share of income. Entity files Form 1065.	Except for certain built-in gains and passive investment income when earnings and profits are present from C corporation tax years, entity not subject to Federal income tax. S corporation files Form 1120S. Shareholders are subject to tax on income attributable to their stock ownership.	Income subject to double taxation. Entity subject to tax, and shareholder subject to tax on any corporate dividends received. Corporation files Form 1120.
Highest tax rate (before additional Medicare taxes)	37% at individual level.	37% at owner level.	37% at shareholder level.	21% at corporate level; 20%/15%/0% on qualified dividends at shareholder level.
Qualified business income deduction (§ 199A)	Applicable.	Applicable. Eligible partners (noncorporate) need data from the entity to compute the deduction amount.	Applicable. Eligible shareholders need data from the entity to compute the deduction amount.	Deduction not available to C corporations.
Contribution of property to the entity	Not a taxable transaction.	Generally not a taxable transaction.	Taxable transaction unless the § 351 requirements are satisfied.	Taxable transaction unless the § 351 requirements are satisfied.
Choice of tax year	Same tax year as owner.	Selection generally restricted to coincide with tax year of owners.	Generally restricted to a calendar year.	Unrestricted selection allowed at time of filing first tax return.
Timing of taxation	Based on owner's tax year.	Owners report their share of income in their tax year within which the entity's tax year ends. Owners in their separate capacities are subject to payment of estimated taxes.	Shareholders report their shares of income in their tax year within which the corporation's tax year ends. Shareholders may be subject to payment of estimated taxes.	Corporation subject to tax at close of its tax year. May be subject to payment of estimated taxes. Dividends are subject to tax at the shareholder level in the tax year received.

* Spouses and family members can be treated as one shareholder.

continued

Tax Attributes of Different Forms of Doing Business—(Continued)

	Sole Proprietorship	Partnership/Limited Liability Company	S Corporation	C Corporation
Basis for allocating income/losses to owners	Not applicable (only one owner).	Profit and loss sharing agreement. Cash basis items of cash basis entities are allocated on a daily basis. Other entity items are allocated after considering varying interests of owners. Special allocations are available if they have substantial economic effect.	Pro rata share based on stock ownership. Shareholder's pro rata share is determined on a daily basis, according to the number of shares of stock held on each day of the corporation's tax year. Special allocations are not available.	Not applicable.
Character of income/losses taxed to owners	Retains source characteristics.	Conduit—retains source characteristics.	Conduit—retains source characteristics.	All source characteristics are lost when income is distributed to owners.
Limitation on losses deductible by owners	Investment in business assets plus prior income.	Owner's investment plus share of liabilities and prior income.	Shareholder's investment plus loans made by shareholder to corporation and owner's share of prior income.	Not applicable.
Subject to at-risk rules?	Yes, at the owner level. Indefinite carryover of excess loss.	Yes, at the owner level. Indefinite carryover of excess loss.	Yes, at the shareholder level. Indefinite carryover of excess loss.	Yes, for closely held corporations. Indefinite carryover of excess loss.
Subject to passive activity loss rules?	Yes, at the owner level. Indefinite carryover of excess loss.	Yes, at the owner level. Indefinite carryover of excess loss.	Yes, at the shareholder level. Indefinite carryover of excess loss.	Yes, for closely held corporations and personal service corporations. Indefinite carryover of excess loss.
Subject to limitation on excess business losses [§ 461(l)]?	Yes, at the owner level.	Yes, at the owner level (unless partner is a corporation).	Yes, at the shareholder level.	No. Limitation does not apply to corporate taxpayers.
Nonliquidating distributions to owners	Not taxable.	Not taxable unless money received exceeds recipient owner's basis in entity interest. Existence of § 751 assets may cause recognition of ordinary income.	Generally not taxable unless the distribution exceeds the shareholder's AAA or stock basis. Existence of accumulated earnings and profits could cause some distributions to be dividends.	Taxable in year of receipt to extent of earnings and profits or if exceeds basis in stock. Corporation may be subject to penalty tax on unreasonable accumulations.
Net capital gains (before additional Medicare taxes)	Taxed at owner level.	Conduit—owners must account for their respective shares. Taxed at owner level.	Conduit, with certain exceptions (a possible penalty tax)—shareholders must account for their respective shares. Tax treatment determined at shareholder level.	Taxed at corporate rate of 21%. No other benefits.

continued

Tax Attributes of Different Forms of Doing Business—(Continued)

	Sole Proprietorship	Partnership/Limited Liability Company	S Corporation	C Corporation
Net capital losses	Only $3,000 of capital losses can be offset each tax year against ordinary income. Indefinite carryover.	Conduit—owners must account for their respective shares. Tax treatment determined at owner level.	Conduit—shareholders must account for their respective shares. Tax treatment determined at shareholder level.	Carried back three years and carried forward five years. Deductible only to offset other entity capital gains.
§ 1231 gains and losses	Taxable or deductible at owner level. Five-year lookback rule for § 1231 losses.	Conduit—owners must account for their respective shares. Tax treatment determined at owner level.	Conduit—shareholders must account for their respective shares. Tax treatment determined at shareholder level.	Taxable or deductible at corporate level only. Five-year lookback rule for § 1231 losses.
Deduction for fringe benefits to owners	None.	None unless included in a guaranteed payment.	None unless a 2% or less shareholder.	Available within antidiscrimination rules.
Foreign tax credits	Available at owner level.	Conduit—tax payments passed through to owners.	Generally conduit—tax payments passed through to shareholders.	Available at corporate level only.
§ 1244 treatment of loss on sale of interest	Not applicable.	Not applicable.	Available.	Available.
Basis treatment of entity liabilities	Not applicable.	Includible in interest basis.	Not includible in stock basis.	Not includible in stock basis.
Effect of liquidation/ redemption/ reorganization on basis of entity assets	Not applicable.	Usually carried over from entity to owner.	Taxable step-up to fair market value.	Taxable step-up to fair market value.
Sale of ownership interest	Treated as the sale of individual assets. Classification of recognized gain or loss depends on the nature of the individual assets.	Treated as the sale of an entity interest. Recognized gain or loss is classified as capital, although appreciated inventory and receivables are subject to ordinary income treatment.	Treated as the sale of corporate stock. Recognized gain is classified as capital gain. Recognized loss is classified as capital loss, subject to ordinary loss treatment under § 1244.	Treated as the sale of corporate stock. Recognized gain is classified as capital gain. Recognized loss is classified as capital loss, subject to ordinary loss treatment under § 1244.
Distribution of appreciated property	Not taxable.	No recognition at the entity level.	Gain recognition at the corporate level to the extent of the appreciation. Conduit—amount of recognized gain is passed through to shareholders.	Taxable at the corporate level to the extent of any realized appreciation.

continued

Tax Attributes of Different Forms of Doing Business—(Continued)

	Sole Proprietorship	Partnership/Limited Liability Company	S Corporation	C Corporation
Splitting of income among family members	Not applicable (only one owner).	Difficult—IRS will not recognize a family member as an owner unless certain requirements are met.	Rather easy—gift of stock will transfer tax on a pro rata share of income to the donee. However, IRS can make adjustments to reflect adequate compensation for services.	Same as an S corporation, except that donees will be subject to tax only on earnings distributed to them. Other than unreasonable compensation, IRS generally cannot make adjustments to reflect adequate compensation for services and capital.
Organizational and startup costs	Startup expenditures are eligible for $5,000 limited expensing (subject to phaseout) with any balance amortized over 180 months.	Organizational and startup expenditures each are eligible for $5,000 limited expensing (subject to phaseout) with any balance amortized over 180 months.	Same as partnership.	Same as partnership.
Charitable contributions	Various limitations apply at owner level.	Conduit—owners are subject to deduction limitations in their own capacities.	Conduit—shareholders are subject to deduction limitations in their own capacities.	Limited to 10% of taxable income before certain deductions.
Alternative minimum tax	Applies at owner level. AMT rates are 26% and 28%.	Applies at the owner level rather than at the entity level. AMT preferences and adjustments are passed through from the entity to the owners.	Applies at the shareholder level rather than at the corporate level. AMT preferences and adjustments are passed through from the S corporation to the shareholders.	C corporations are not subject to AMT.

REFOCUS ON THE BIG PICTURE

CHOOSING A BUSINESS FORM AND OTHER INVESTMENTS

Conducting their business as a C corporation, an S corporation, or an LLC would meet Bill and George's objectives of providing limited liability. From a tax perspective, both the S corporation and the LLC would allow the early-year losses to be passed through to the owners. This cannot be achieved with a C corporation, in which the losses are trapped until future years when the company is profitable. Once the entity turns profitable, the tax consequences are as follows.

- As a C corporation, the entity would pay income tax of $42,000 on taxable earnings of $200,000. If the remaining after-tax earnings of $158,000 are distributed equally to Bill and George (each owner would receive a taxable dividend of $79,000), each shareholder pays an additional income tax of $11,850 ($79,000 × 15%).

continued

FUSE/GETTY IMAGES

The combined entity/owner tax liability is $65,700, resulting in after-tax cash flows of $134,300.

- If the entity is operated as an S corporation or an LLC, no tax is paid at the entity level. Further, Bill and George may each be eligible for the 20 percent qualified business income deduction at the individual level. However, the income will be taxed as ordinary income at the owner level, resulting in each owner paying $19,200 ($80,000 × 24%) income tax. The combined entity/owner tax liability is $38,400, resulting in after-tax cash flows of $161,600.

It appears that either the S corporation or the LLC meets Bill and George's objectives of having limited liability and minimizing tax liability. The LLC form offers an additional advantage in that an LLC need not satisfy the numerous statutory qualification requirements to elect and maintain S corporation status. However, based on the facts in this situation, it is unlikely that satisfying the requirements would create any difficulty for Bill and George. Further, an LLC might result in a portion of any gains recognized when the business is sold or liquidated being characterized as ordinary.

The results of George's investing in a limited partnership appear in Example 1. While beneficial tax results are expected to occur, George needs to be aware of the economic risk of losing his $10,000 investment.

For Bill, the recognized gain on the sale of his investment in the retail coffee franchise outlet is dependent on that entity's form. If the franchise were a pass-through entity, the recognized gain would be different than if the entity were a C corporation: entity profits increase the owner's interest basis in a pass-through entity, whereas entity profits have no effect on a shareholder's basis in C corporation stock.

What If?

Assume that the $200,000 of anticipated business profits could be paid to Bill and George as reasonable salaries. This would allow the owners to escape double taxation, even if organized as a C corporation.

Assume instead that Bill and George decide to expand the business and reinvest the annual $200,000 before-tax earnings instead of paying out dividends to the owners. If the business is organized as a C corporation, it can accumulate the earnings—as long as the company can show that it has reasonable business needs—and avoid the additional tax that is paid by Bill and George when the company makes taxable dividend distributions. Although the entity-level tax of $42,000 still must be paid, after-tax cash flows increase to $158,000. While the S corporation or LLC with after-tax cash flows of $161,600 still would be preferred in this situation, the double tax problem of the C corporation can be reduced with effective planning.

Suggested Readings

Stewart Karlinsky and Hughlene Burton, "Dis-Incorporation of the American Business Model," *ATA Journal of Legal Tax Research*, Spring 2016.

Roger A. McEowen, "Form C Corporation—The New Vogue in Business Structure?" *Law Professors Blog*, February 26, 2018.

Ruth Simon, "Pass-Through Businesses are Rethinking Their Status," *Wall Street Journal*, February 22, 2018.

Michael A. Yuhas and Richard Harris, "The Retiring LLC Member: Sale Versus Liquidation," *Journal of Taxation*, January 2016.

Key Terms

Conduit perspective, 18-5

Entity perspective, 18-5

Computational Exercises

1. **LO.4** Roscoe contributes a personal use asset, adjusted basis $15,000 and fair market value $28,000, to a new business in which he is an owner. Determine Roscoe's recognized gain on the transfer, and the basis of the asset to the business, if the new operation is a:

   a. Sole proprietorship.

   b. Partnership, where Roscoe holds a 10% interest.

   c. Corporation, where Roscoe holds a 25% interest and all shareholders contribute assets for stock in the transaction.

2. **LO.4** Mira and Lemma are equal owners of a business entity. Each contributed $25,000 cash to the business. Then the entity acquired a $100,000 loan from a bank. This year, operating profits totaled $30,000. Determine Lemma's basis in her interest at the end of the tax year, assuming that the entity is:

   a. A partnership.

   b. A C corporation.

   c. An S corporation.

3. **LO.4** Castle and Dave formed an S corporation; Castle owns 75% of the outstanding shares, and Dave owns the rest. When the entity's AAA balance is $1 million, it distributes an asset to each shareholder; the basis of each asset to the corporation is $45,000. Castle's asset is worth $90,000, and Dave's is worth $50,000.

   a. How much gain, if any, does the the corporation recognize as a result of the distribution?

   b. By how much, if any, does the distribution increase Dave's gross income?

   c. By how much, if any, does the distribution increase Castle's gross income?

Problems

4. **LO.2** Sea Green Enterprises reports the following assets and liabilities on its balance sheet.

	Net Book Value	Fair Market Value
Assets	$600,000	$925,000
Liabilities	200,000	200,000

Sea Green has just lost a product liability suit with damages of $10 million being awarded to the plaintiff. Although Sea Green will appeal the judgment, legal counsel indicates that the judgment is highly unlikely to be overturned by the appellate court. The product liability insurance carried by Sea Green includes a payout ceiling of $6 million. For how much of the judgment is the entity and its owners liable if Sea Green is:

   a. A sole proprietorship?

   b. A partnership or an LLC?

   c. A C corporation?

   d. An S corporation?

5. **LO.3** With which of the two perspectives to business forms, conduit or entity, is each of the following most consistent?

    a. Limited liability for the entity's owners.

    b. Unlimited life for the entity.

    c. The ability of owners to participate directly in the management of the entity.

    d. The ability of owners to transfer assets to the entity without recognizing gain or loss.

    e. The payment of a wage from the entity to an owner who provides services to the entity.

    f. The inclusion of entity debt in the basis of an owner's interest in the entity.

Decision Making

Communications

6. **LO.2, 4** Amy and Jeff Barnes will operate their florist shop as a partnership or as an S corporation. After paying salaries of $100,000 to each of the owners, the shop's annual earnings are projected to be about $150,000. The earnings are to be invested in the growth of the business. Write a letter to Amy and Jeff, advising them of which of the two entity forms they should select. Their mailing address is 5700 Richmond Highway, Alexandria, VA 22301.

Decision Making

7. **LO.3, 4** Gerald is an entrepreneur who likes to be actively involved in his business ventures. He is going to invest $500,000 in a business that he projects will produce a tax loss of approximately $125,000 per year in the short run. However, Gerald is confident that, once consumers become aware of the new product being sold by the business and the quality of the service it provides, the business will generate a profit of at least $200,000 per year. Gerald generates substantial other income (from both business ventures and investment activities) each year. Advise Gerald on the business form he should select for the short run. He will be the sole owner of the business.

Decision Making

8. **LO.2, 3, 4** Duke and Jacquie Coleman, married filing jointly, will establish a manufacturing business. The couple anticipates that the business will be profitable immediately due to a patent that Jacquie holds; profits for the first year will be about $300,000 and will increase at a rate of about 20% per year for the foreseeable future. Advise the Colemans as to the form of business entity that they should select. The Colemans are in the 37% Federal income tax bracket.

Decision Making

9. **LO.4** Plum Corporation will begin operations on January 1. Earnings for the next five years are projected to be relatively stable at about $80,000 per year. The shareholders of Plum are in the 32% tax bracket. Evaluate whether Plum should operate as a C corporation or as an S corporation given the following assumptions.

    a. Plum will reinvest its after-tax earnings in the growth of the company.

    b. Plum will distribute its after-tax earnings each year to its shareholders.

10. **LO.3, 4** Mabel and Alan, who are in the 32% tax bracket, recently acquired a fast-food franchise. Both of them will work in the business and receive a salary of $175,000. They anticipate that the annual profits of the business, after deducting salaries, will be approximately $450,000. The entity will distribute only enough cash each year to Mabel and Alan to cover their Federal income taxes associated with any flow-through income from the franchise. Any remaining profits will be reinvested in the business.

    a. What amount will the entity distribute if the franchise operates as a C corporation?

    b. What amount will the entity distribute if the franchise operates as an S corporation?

    c. What will be the amount of the combined entity/owner tax liability in parts (a) and (b)?

11. **LO.3, 4** Owl is a closely held corporation owned by eight shareholders (each has 12.5% of the stock). Its taxable income for the most recent year was $6,250,000. Owl's financial records also provides the following information.

Positive AMT adjustments	$ 600,000
Negative AMT adjustments	(30,000)
Tax preferences	5,000,000
Retained earnings	900,000
Accumulated E & P	2,000,000

   a.   Calculate Owl's Federal income tax liability if it is a C corporation.

   b.   Calculate Owl's Federal income tax liability if it is an S corporation.

   c.   How would your answers in parts (a) and (b) change if Owl was not closely held (e.g., 5,000 shareholders with no shareholder owning more than 2% of the stock)?

12. **LO.4** Using the legend provided, indicate which form of business entity each of the following characteristics describes. Some of the characteristics may apply to more than one form of business entity.

Legend

P = Applies to partnership and LLC
S = Applies to S corporation
C = Applies to C corporation

---

   a.   Basis for an ownership interest is increased by an investment by the owner.

   b.   Basis for an ownership interest is decreased by a distribution to the owner.

   c.   Basis for an ownership interest is increased by entity profits.

   d.   Basis for an ownership interest is decreased by entity losses.

   e.   Basis for an ownership interest is increased as the entity's liabilities increase.

   f.   Basis for an ownership interest is decreased as the entity's liabilities decrease.

13. **LO.4** Phillip and Evans form a business entity. Each contributes the following   Decision Making
property.

	Phillip	Evans
Cash	$600,000	
Land		$600,000*

*Fair market value. Evans's adjusted basis is $200,000.

   Three months later, the entity sells the land for $652,000 because of unexpected zoning problems. The proceeds are to be applied toward the purchase of another parcel of land, to be used for real estate development. Determine the Federal income tax consequences to the entity and to the owners upon both the formation and the later sale of the land. Perform your analysis assuming that the entity is:

   a.   A partnership.

   b.   An S corporation.

   c.   A C corporation.

14. **LO.4** Amy, Becky, and Chau form a business entity with each contributing the following.

	Adjusted Basis	Fair Market Value
Amy: Cash	$100,000	$100,000
Becky: Land	60,000	120,000
Chau: Services		50,000

Their ownership percentages will be as follows.

Amy	40%
Becky	40%
Chau	20%

Becky's land has a $20,000 mortgage that is assumed by the entity. Chau is an attorney who receives her ownership interest in exchange for legal services. Determine the recognized gain to the owners, the basis for their ownership interests, and the entity's basis for its assets if the entity is organized as:

a.   A partnership.

b.   A C corporation.

c.   An S corporation.

15. **LO.4** Emmy contributes $40,000 to MeldCo in exchange for a 30% ownership interest. During the first year of operations, MeldCo earns a profit of $200,000. At the end of that year, MeldCo holds liabilities of $75,000. Calculate Emmy's basis for her ownership interest if the entity is:

a.   A C corporation.

b.   An S corporation.

c.   A partnership.

16. **LO.4** ListCo reports the following income for the current tax year.

Operations	$92,000
Tax-exempt interest income	19,000
Long-term capital gain	60,000

ListCo holds earnings and profits (AAA for an S corporation) of $900,000 at the beginning of the year. Then ListCo distributes $200,000 in total to the owners.

a.   Calculate the taxable income if ListCo is (1) a C corporation and (2) an S corporation.

b.   Determine the effect of the distribution on the shareholders if ListCo is (1) a C corporation and (2) an S corporation.

Ethics and Equity   17. **LO.4** For many years, Sophie has owned and operated several apartment buildings. In 2012, upon the advice of her attorney, Sophie transferred the apartment buildings to a newly created corporation. Her main reason for incorporating the business was to achieve the legal protection of limited liability.

Every year since 2012, Sophie has prepared and filed a Form 1120 for the corporation. No corporate income tax has been paid because, after the deduction of various expenses (including Sophie's "management fee"), the corporation reports zero taxable income.

This year, Sophie decides that filing Form 1120 is a waste of time and serves no useful purpose. Instead, she plans to report all of the financial activities of the apartment business on her own individual Form 1040.

Comment on the propriety of what Sophie plans to do.

18. **LO.4** The Coffee Company engages in the following transactions during the taxable year.

- Sells stock held for three years as an investment for $30,000 (adjusted basis of $20,000).
- Sells land used in the business for $65,000. The land has been used as a parking lot and originally cost $40,000.
- Receives tax-exempt interest on municipal bonds of $5,000.
- Receives dividends on IBM stock of $80,000.

Describe the effect of these transactions on the entity and its owners if the entity is organized as:

a. A partnership.

b. A C corporation.

c. An S corporation.

19. **LO.4** Swift Corporation agreed to redeem some of the shares of two of its share-holders. It distributed land (basis $55,000 and fair market value $120,000) to Sam in exchange for part of his stock. Sam's basis in the redeemed stock was $25,000. Swift also distributed $240,000 cash to Allison in exchange for part of her stock. Allison's basis in the redeemed stock was $40,000. As a result of the redemptions, Sam's interest in the corporation declined from 20% to 15%, and Allison's interest declined from 70% to 60%.

Determine the tax consequences to Swift, Sam, and Allison if Swift is:

a. A C corporation.

b. An S corporation.

20. **LO.4** Indigo, Inc., a personal service corporation, incurs the following income and losses.

Active income	$325,000
Portfolio income	49,000
Passive activity loss	333,000

a. Calculate Indigo's taxable income.

b. Assume that instead of being a personal service corporation, Indigo is a closely held C corporation. Calculate Indigo's taxable income.

c. Would the answer in part (b) change if the passive loss was $320,000 rather than $333,000? Explain.

21. **LO.4** Rosa contributes $50,000 to FlipCo in exchange for a 10% ownership interest. Rosa materially participates in FlipCo's business.

FlipCo incurs a loss of $900,000 for the current tax year. Entity liabilities at the end of the year are $700,000. Of this amount, $150,000 is for recourse debt, and $550,000 is for nonrecourse debt.

a. Assume that FlipCo is a partnership. How much of Rosa's share of the loss can she deduct for the year on her individual tax return? What is Rosa's basis for her partnership interest at the end of the year?

b. Assume that FlipCo is a C corporation. How much of Rosa's share of the loss can she deduct for the year on her individual tax return? What is Rosa's basis for her stock at the end of the year?

22. **LO.4** Bishop contributes undeveloped land to a business entity in January for a 40% ownership interest. Bishop's basis for the land is $140,000, and the fair market value is $600,000. The business entity was formed three years ago by Petula and Rene, who have equal ownership. The entity is successful in getting the land rezoned from agricultural to residential use, but the owners decide to sell the land so that the entity can invest in another project.

In August, the land is sold for $650,000. Determine the tax consequences of the sale of the undeveloped land for the business entity and the three owners if the entity is organized as:

a. A C corporation.

b. An S corporation.

c. A partnership.

d. An LLC.

23. **LO.4** Jo and Velma are equal owners of JV Company. Jo invests $500,000 cash in the venture. Velma contributes land and a building (basis to her of $125,000, fair market value of $500,000). The entity then borrows $250,000 cash using recourse financing and $100,000 using nonrecourse financing.

   a. Determine each owner's basis in their ownership interest and their amount at risk, assuming that the venture is a general partnership.

   b. Determine each owner's basis in their ownership interest and their amount at risk, assuming the venture is an S corporation.

24. **LO.4** Megan owns 55% and Vern owns 45% of a business entity. The owners would like to share profits (55% for Megan and 45% for Vern) and losses (80% for Vern and 20% for Megan) differently if possible. Determine the tax consequences if the entity has a tax loss of $160,000 and is organized as:

   a. A partnership.

   b. A C corporation.

   c. An S corporation.

25. **LO.4** Sanjay contributes land to a business entity in January of the current year for a 30% ownership interest. Sanjay's basis for the land is $60,000, and the fair market value is $100,000. The business entity was formed three years ago by Polly and Rita, who have equal ownership. The entity is unsuccessful in getting the land rezoned from agricultural to residential. In October of the current year, the land is sold for $110,000.

   Determine the tax consequences of the sale of the land for the entity and its owners if the entity is organized as:

   a. A C corporation.

   b. An S corporation.

   c. A partnership.

Ethics and Equity

Digging Deeper

26. **LO.5** Heron Corporation has been in operation for 10 years. Since Heron's creation, all of its stock has been owned by Andy, who initially invested $200,000 in the corporation. Heron has been successful far beyond Andy's expectations, and the current fair market value of the stock is $10 million. While he has been paid a salary of $200,000 per year by the corporation, all of Heron's earnings have been reinvested in the growth of the corporation.

   Heron currently is being audited by the IRS. One of the issues raised by the IRS agent is the possibility of the assessment of the accumulated earnings tax. Andy is not concerned about this issue because he believes Heron can easily justify the accumulations based on its past rapid expansion by opening new outlets. The expansion program is fully documented in the minutes of Heron's board of directors. Andy has provided this information to the IRS agent.

   Two years ago, Andy decided that he would curtail any further expansion into new markets by Heron. In his opinion, further expansion would exceed his ability to manage the corporation effectively. Because the tax year under audit is three years in the past, Andy sees no reason to provide the IRS agent with this information.

   Heron will continue its policy of no dividend payments into the foreseeable future. Andy believes that if the accumulated earnings issue is satisfactorily resolved on this audit, it probably will not be raised again on any subsequent audits. Thus, double taxation in the form of the tax on dividends at the shareholder level or the accumulated earnings tax at the corporate level can be avoided.

   What is Heron's responsibility to disclose to the IRS agent the expected change in its growth strategy? Are Andy's beliefs regarding future accumulated earnings tax issues realistic? Explain.

Critical Thinking

27. **LO.5** Turtle, a C corporation, reports taxable income of $200,000 before paying salaries to the two equal shareholder-employees, Britney and Alan. Turtle follows a policy of distributing all after-tax earnings to the shareholders.

a. Determine the tax consequences for Turtle, Britney, and Alan if the corporation pays salaries as follows. Britney and Alan have no other sources of income.

Option 1		Option 2	
Britney	$50,000	Britney	$100,000
Alan	50,000	Alan	100,000

b. Which option would you recommend? Explain.

28. **LO.5** Parrott, Inc., a C corporation, is owned by Abner (60%) and Deanna (40%). Abner is the president, and Deanna is the vice president for sales. Parrott, Abner, and Deanna are cash basis taxpayers. Late in the year, Parrott encounters working capital difficulties. Therefore, Abner loans the corporation $810,000 and Deanna loans the corporation $540,000. Each loan uses a 5% note that is due in five years with interest payable annually. Abner and Deanna are both in the 24% marginal tax bracket.

   a. Determine the tax consequences to Parrott, Abner, and Deanna if the notes are classified as debt.

   b. Determine the tax consequences to Parrott, Abner, and Deanna if the notes are classified as equity.

29. **LO.5** Laurie Gladin owns land and a building that she has been using in her sole proprietorship. She is going to incorporate her sole proprietorship as a C corporation. Laurie must decide whether to contribute the land and building to the corporation or to lease them to the corporation. The net income of the sole proprietorship for the past five years has averaged $250,000. Advise Laurie on the tax consequences. Summarize your analysis in a memo for the tax research file.

Decision Making

Communications

30. **LO.5** Marci and Jennifer each own 50% of the stock of Lavender, a C corporation. After each of them is paid a "reasonable" salary of $150,000, the taxable income of Lavender typically is about $800,000.

   The corporation is about to purchase a $2 million shopping mall ($1,500,000 allocated to the building and $500,000 allocated to the land). The mall will be rented to tenants at a net rental rate (including rental commissions, depreciation, etc.) of $600,000 annually. Marci and Jennifer will contribute $1 million each to the corporation to provide the cash required for the acquisition.

   Their CPA has suggested that Marci and Jennifer purchase the shopping mall as individuals and lease it to Lavender for a fair rental of $400,000. Both Marci and Jennifer are in the 32% tax bracket. The acquisition will occur on January 2 next year. Determine whether the shopping mall should be acquired by Lavender or by Marci and Jennifer in accordance with their CPA's recommendation. Depreciation on the shopping mall for the year is $37,000.

Decision Making

31. **LO.5** Since Garnet Corporation was formed five years ago, its stock has been held as follows: 525 shares by Frank and 175 shares by Grace. Their basis in the stock is $350,000 for Frank and $150,000 for Grace. As part of a stock redemption, Garnet redeems 125 of Frank's shares for $175,000 and 125 of Grace's shares for $175,000.

   a. What are the tax consequences of the stock redemption to Frank and Grace?

   b. How would the tax consequences to Frank and Grace be different if, instead of the redemption, they each sell 125 shares to Chuck (an unrelated party)?

   c. What factors should influence their decision on whether to redeem or sell the 250 shares of stock?

Decision Making

32. **LO.5** Oscar created Lavender Corporation four years ago. The C corporation has paid Oscar as president a salary of $200,000 each year. Annual earnings after taxes approximate $700,000 each year. Lavender has not paid any dividends, nor

Critical Thinking

does it intend to do so in the future. Instead, Oscar wants his heirs to receive the stock with a step-up in stock basis when he dies. Identify the relevant tax issues.

Critical Thinking   33. **LO.5** Tammy and Willy own 40% of the stock of Roadrunner, an S corporation. The other 60% is owned by 99 other shareholders, all of whom are single and unrelated. Tammy and Willy have agreed to a divorce and are in the process of negotiating a property settlement. Identify the relevant tax issues for Tammy and Willy.

Decision Making   34. **LO.5** Clay Corporation has been an S corporation since its incorporation 10 years ago. During the first three years of operations, it incurred total losses of $250,000. Since then, Clay has generated earnings of approximately $180,000 each year. None of the earnings have been distributed to the three equal shareholders, Claire, Lynn, and Todd, because the corporation has been in an expansion mode.

At the beginning of this year, Claire sells her stock to Nell for $400,000. Nell has reservations about the utility of the S election. Therefore, Lynn, Todd, and Nell are discussing whether the election should be continued. They expect the earnings to remain at approximately $180,000 each year. However, because they perceive that the company's expansion period is over and Clay has adequate working capital, they may start distributing the earnings to the shareholders. All of the shareholders are in the 32% tax bracket.

Advise the three shareholders as to whether Clay's S election should be maintained.

35. **LO.6** Emily and Freda are negotiating with George to purchase the business he operates as Pelican, Inc. The assets of Pelican, Inc., a C corporation, are recorded as follows.

Asset	Basis	FMV
Cash	$ 20,000	$ 20,000
Accounts receivable	50,000	50,000
Inventory	100,000	110,000
Furniture and fixtures	150,000	170,000*
Building	200,000	250,000**
Land	40,000	150,000

*Potential depreciation recapture is $45,000.
**The straight-line method was used to depreciate the building. Accumulated depreciation is $340,000.

George's basis for the Pelican stock is $560,000. George is subject to a 32% marginal tax rate.

a.   Emily and Freda purchase the *stock* of Pelican from George for $908,000. Determine the tax consequences to Emily and Freda, Pelican, and George.

b.   Emily and Freda purchase the *assets* from Pelican for $908,000. Determine the tax consequences to Emily and Freda, Pelican, and George.

c.   The purchase price is $550,000 because the fair market value of the building is $150,000 and the fair market value of the land is $50,000. No amount is assigned to goodwill. Emily and Freda purchase the *stock* of Pelican from George. Determine the tax consequences to Emily and Freda, Pelican, and George.

Decision Making   36. **LO.6** Linda is the owner of a sole proprietorship. The entity has the following assets.

Asset	Basis	FMV
Cash	$10,000	$10,000
Accounts receivable	–0–	25,000
Office furniture and fixtures*	15,000	17,000
Building**	75,000	90,000
Land	60,000	80,000

*Potential depreciation recapture is $5,000.
**The straight-line method has been used to depreciate the building.

Linda sells the business for $260,000 to Juan.

a. Determine the tax consequences to Linda, including the classification of any recognized gain or loss.

b. Determine the tax consequences to Juan.

c. Advise Juan on how the purchase agreement could be modified to produce more beneficial tax consequences for him. *Hint*: Consider the use of a covenant not to compete.

37. **LO.6** Gail and Harry own the GH Partnership. They have conducted the business as a partnership for 10 years. The bases for their partnership interests are as follows.   Decision Making

Gail	Harry
$100,000	$150,000

GH Partnership holds the following assets.

Asset	Basis	FMV
Cash	$ 10,000	$ 10,000
Accounts receivable	30,000	28,000
Inventory	25,000	26,000
Building*	100,000	150,000
Land	250,000	400,000

*The straight-line method has been used to depreciate the building. Accumulated depreciation is $70,000.

Gail and Harry sell their partnership interests to Keith and Liz for $307,000 each.

a. Determine the tax consequences of the sale to Gail, Harry, and GH Partnership.

b. From a tax perspective, should it matter to Keith and Liz whether they purchase Gail and Harry's partnership interests or the partnership assets from GH Partnership? Explain.

38. **LO.6** Hector and Walt are purchasing the Copper Partnership from Jan and Gail for $700,000; Hector and Walt will be equal partners. During the negotiations, Jan and Gail succeeded in having the transaction structured as the purchase of the partnership rather than as a purchase of the individual assets. The adjusted basis of the individual assets of Copper is $580,000.   Decision Making

a. What are Hector's and Walt's bases for their partnership interests (i.e., outside bases)?

b. What is Copper's adjusted basis for its assets after the transaction? Would an optional adjustment-to-basis election be helpful? Why or why not?

39. **LO.6** Vladimir owns all of the stock of Ruby Corporation. The fair market value of the stock (and Ruby's assets) is about four times his adjusted basis for the stock. Vladimir is negotiating with an investor group for the sale of the corporation. Identify the relevant tax issues for Vladimir.   Critical Thinking

40. **LO.6** Maurice Allred is going to purchase either the stock or the assets of Jewel Corporation. All of the Jewel stock is owned by Charley. Maurice and Charley agree that Jewel is worth $700,000. The tax basis for Jewel's assets is $500,000.   Decision Making   Communications

Write a letter to Maurice, advising him on whether he should negotiate to purchase the stock or the assets. Prepare a memo for the tax research file on this matter. Maurice's address is 100 Aspen Green, Chattanooga, TN 37403.

41. **LO.2, 3, 4, 5, 6** Using the legend provided, indicate which form of business entity each of the following characteristics describes. Some of the characteristics may apply to more than one form of business entity.

Legend

SP = Applies to sole proprietorship
P = Applies to partnership
L = Applies to LLC
S = Applies to S corporation
C = Applies to C corporation
N = Applies to none

---

a. Has limited liability.

b. Greatest ability to raise capital.

c. Subject to double taxation.

d. Limit on types and number of shareholders.

e. Has unlimited liability.

f. Sale of the business can be subject to double taxation.

g. Contribution of property to the entity in exchange for an ownership interest can result in the nonrecognition of realized gain.

h. Profits and losses affect the basis for an ownership interest.

i. Entity liabilities affect the basis for an ownership interest.

j. Distributions of earnings are taxed as dividend income to the owners.

k. Total invested capital cannot exceed $1 million.

l. AAA is an account that relates to this entity.

BRIDGE DISCIPLINE

1. Parchment, Inc., is created with the following asset and liability contributions. Jake and Fran each receive 100 shares of Parchment common stock.

Shareholder	Assets	Basis	Fair Market Value
Jake	Cash	$100,000	$100,000
Fran	Land	40,000	120,000*

*The land is subject to a mortgage of $20,000 that Parchment assumes.

   a. Prepare a financial accounting balance sheet for Parchment. Discuss the relevance of conduit theory and entity theory in the creation of Parchment.

   b. Prepare a tax balance sheet for Parchment. Discuss the relevance of conduit theory and entity theory in the creation of Parchment.

   c. Assume that Parchment sells the land for $150,000 four months after Parchment was created. Discuss the effect of the sale on the financial accounting statements and the related income tax computations.

2. Assume that Parchment in (1) elects S corporation status at the time of its creation. Respond to parts (a), (b), and (c).

3. Assume that Parchment in (1) is a general partnership rather than a corporation. Respond to parts (a), (b), and (c). Would your answer change if Parchment were an LLC that "checked the box" to be taxed as a partnership? Explain.

Research Problems

Note: Solutions to the Research Problems can be prepared by using the Thomson Reuters Checkpoint™ online tax research database, which accompanies this textbook. Solutions can also be prepared by using research materials found in a typical tax library.

THOMSON REUTERS
CHECKPOINT™

Research Problem 1. The Turnaround LLC was formed several years ago. It incurred losses for several years, reducing many of its members' bases in their interests to zero. However, the business recently obtained some new and promising contracts, and there is an expectation of profits in the coming years.

Decision Making

Turnaround then admitted several new members, who each made capital contributions for their interests. The new owners anticipate that it will be necessary to reinvest any profits back into the business for some time. As there no longer will be losses to pass through and any double taxation of profits will be delayed for some time, the owners of Turnaround are considering converting the business to a C corporation.

The business controls the following assets. There is no § 754 election in effect.

	Fair Market Value	Adjusted Basis
Cash	$ 500,000	$500,000
PP&E	500,000	500,000
Customer contracts	1,000,000	–0–

The original owners of Turnaround now hold a 50% capital and profits interest. They have come to you for advice regarding the potential tax consequences of the conversion for them, as well as for the new corporation.

Partial list of research aids:
Rev.Rul. 70–239, 1970–1 C.B. 74.
Rev.Rul. 84–111, 1984–2 C.B. 88.
Rev.Rul. 2004–59, 2004–24 I.R.B 1050.
Treas. Reg. § 301.7701–3(g)(i).

Research Problem 2. Crane is a partner in the Cardinal Partnership. A dispute arose with the partnership regarding Crane's share of current earnings. The partnership contends that the amount is $75,000, while Crane believes his share is $100,000.

Crane ceased being a partner on November 1. As a result of the dispute, the partnership distributed only $75,000 to Crane. It placed the disputed $25,000 in escrow. However, Crane's Schedule K–1 from the partnership included the full $100,000. Crane believes that the K–1 should include only the $75,000 that is not in dispute. Is Crane correct? Explain.

Use internet tax resources to address the following questions. Look for reliable websites and blogs of the IRS and other government agencies, media outlets, businesses, tax professionals, academics, think tanks, and political outlets.

Research Problem 3. Find a blog posting or discussion thread with comments from tax professionals about Federal income tax consequences that occur when a business converts from an LLC to an S corporation or when a C corporation converts to a pass-through entity. Summarize the comments and suggestions that you find in these discussions in a one-page memo to your instructor.

Communications

Research Problem 4. The Tax Cuts and Jobs Act (TCJA) of 2017 made changes in how business entities are taxed. Find an article written by a tax practitioner that discusses how the TCJA of 2017 changes choice of entity considerations. In a paper you send to your instructor, summarize the article, and explain how the changes are relevant to (a) a retail clothing business and (b) a CPA firm.

Communications

Critical Thinking

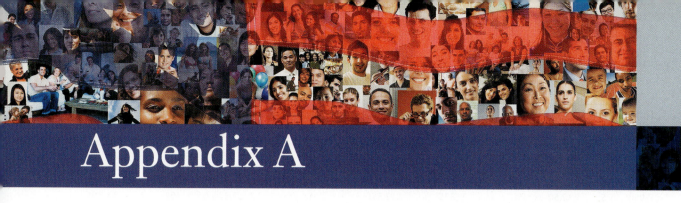

Appendix A

Tax Rate Schedules and Tables

Income Tax Rates—Individuals   A-2

Income Tax Rates—Estates and Trusts   A-3

Income Tax Rates—C Corporations, 2018 and after   A-3

Unified Transfer Tax Rates (For Gifts Made and for Deaths after 2012)   A-4

The 2017 Tax Tables and 2017 Sales Tax Tables can be accessed at the IRS website: **www.irs.gov/forms-instructions**. The 2018 Tax Tables and 2018 Sales Tax Tables will be available on that website toward the end of 2018.

2017 Tax Rate Schedules

Single—Schedule X

If taxable income is: Over—	But not over—	The tax is:	of the amount over—
$ 0	$ 9,325	.........10%	$ 0
9,325	37,950	$ 932.50 + 15%	9,325
37,950	91,900	5,226.25 + 25%	37,950
91,900	191,650	18,713.75 + 28%	91,900
191,650	416,700	46,643.75 + 33%	191,650
416,700	418,400	120,910.25 + 35%	416,700
418,400	....	121,505.25 + 39.6%	418,400

Head of household—Schedule Z

If taxable income is: Over—	But not over—	The tax is:	of the amount over—
$ 0	$ 13,350	.........10%	$ 0
13,350	50,800	$ 1,335.00 + 15%	13,350
50,800	131,200	6,952.50 + 25%	50,800
131,200	212,500	27,052.50 + 28%	131,200
212,500	416,700	49,816.50 + 33%	212,500
416,700	444,550	117,202.50 + 35%	416,700
444,550	....	126,950.00 + 39.6%	444,550

Married filing jointly or Qualifying widow(er)—Schedule Y–1

If taxable income is: Over—	But not over—	The tax is:	of the amount over—
$ 0	$ 18,650	.........10%	$ 0
18,650	75,900	$ 1,865.00 + 15%	18,650
75,900	153,100	10,452.50 + 25%	75,900
153,100	233,350	29,752.50 + 28%	153,100
233,350	416,700	52,222.50 + 33%	233,350
416,700	470,700	112,728.00 + 35%	416,700
470,700	....	131,628.00 + 39.6%	470,700

Married filing separately—Schedule Y–2

If taxable income is: Over—	But not over—	The tax is:	of the amount over—
$ 0	$ 9,325	.........10%	$ 0
9,325	37,950	$ 932.50 + 15%	9,325
37,950	76,550	5,226.25 + 25%	37,950
76,550	116,675	14,876.25 + 28%	76,550
116,675	208,350	26,111.25 + 33%	116,675
208,350	235,350	56,364.00 + 35%	208,350
235,350	....	65,814.00 + 39.6%	235,350

2018 Tax Rate Schedules

Single—Schedule X

If taxable income is: Over—	But not over—	The tax is:	of the amount over—
$ 0	$ 9,525	.........10%	$ 0
9,525	38,700	$ 952.50 + 12%	9,525
38,700	82,500	4,453.50 + 22%	38,700
82,500	157,500	14,089.50 + 24%	82,500
157,500	200,000	32,089.50 + 32%	157,500
200,000	500,000	45,689.50 + 35%	200,000
500,000	....	150,689.50 + 37%	500,000

Head of household—Schedule Z

If taxable income is: Over—	But not over—	The tax is:	of the amount over—
$ 0	$ 13,600	.........10%	$ 0
13,600	51,800	$ 1,360.00 + 12%	13,600
51,800	82,500	5,944.00 + 22%	51,800
82,500	157,500	12,698.00 + 24%	82,500
157,500	200,000	30,698.00 + 32%	157,500
200,000	500,000	44,298.00 + 35%	200,000
500,000	....	149,298.00 + 37%	500,000

Married filing jointly or Qualifying widow(er)—Schedule Y–1

If taxable income is: Over—	But not over—	The tax is:	of the amount over—
$ 0	$ 19,050	.........10%	$ 0
19,050	77,400	$ 1,905.00 + 12%	19,050
77,400	165,000	8,907.00 + 22%	77,400
165,000	315,000	28,179.00 + 24%	165,000
315,000	400,000	64,179.00 + 32%	315,000
400,000	600,000	91,379.00 + 35%	400,000
600,000	....	161,379.00 + 37%	600,000

Married filing separately—Schedule Y–2

If taxable income is: Over—	But not over—	The tax is:	of the amount over—
$ 0	$ 9,525	.........10%	$ 0
9,525	38,700	$ 952.50 + 12%	9,525
38,700	82,500	4,453.50 + 22%	38,700
82,500	157,500	14,089.50 + 24%	82,500
157,500	200,000	32,089.50 + 32%	157,500
200,000	300,000	45,689.50 + 35%	200,000
300,000	....	80,689.50 + 37%	300,000

Income Tax Rates—Estates and Trusts

Tax Year 2017

Taxable Income		The Tax Is:	Of the Amount
Over—	But not Over—		Over—
$ 0	$ 2,550	15%	$ 0
2,550	6,000	$ 382.50 + 25%	2,550
6,000	9,150	1,245.00 + 28%	6,000
9,150	12,500	2,127.00 + 33%	9,150
12,500	....	3,232.50 + 39.6%	12,500

Tax Year 2018

Taxable Income		The Tax Is:	Of the Amount
Over—	But not Over—		Over—
$ 0	$ 2,550	10%	$ 0
2,550	9,150	$ 255.00 + 24%	2,550
9,150	12,500	1,839.00 + 35%	9,150
12,500	....	3,011.50 + 37%	12,500

Income Tax Rates—C Corporations, 2018 and after

For all income levels, the tax rate is 21%.

Unified Transfer Tax Rates

For Gifts Made and for Deaths after 2012

If the Amount with Respect to Which the Tentative Tax to Be Computed Is:	The Tentative Tax Is:
Not over $10,000	18 percent of such amount.
Over $10,000 but not over $20,000	$1,800, plus 20 percent of the excess of such amount over $10,000.
Over $20,000 but not over $40,000	$3,800, plus 22 percent of the excess of such amount over $20,000.
Over $40,000 but not over $60,000	$8,200, plus 24 percent of the excess of such amount over $40,000.
Over $60,000 but not over $80,000	$13,000, plus 26 percent of the excess of such amount over $60,000.
Over $80,000 but not over $100,000	$18,200, plus 28 percent of the excess of such amount over $80,000.
Over $100,000 but not over $150,000	$23,800, plus 30 percent of the excess of such amount over $100,000.
Over $150,000 but not over $250,000	$38,800, plus 32 percent of the excess of such amount over $150,000.
Over $250,000 but not over $500,000	$70,800, plus 34 percent of the excess of such amount over $250,000.
Over $500,000 but not over $750,000	$155,800, plus 37 percent of the excess of such amount over $500,000.
Over $750,000 but not over $1,000,000	$248,300, plus 39 percent of the excess of such amount over $750,000.
Over $1,000,000	$345,800, plus 40 percent of the excess of such amount over $1,000,000.

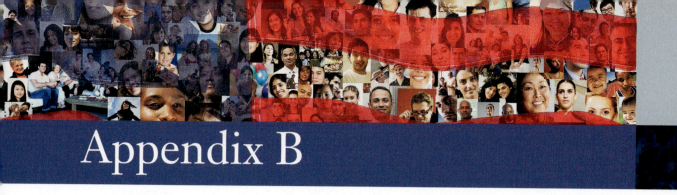

Appendix B

Tax Forms

The IRS tax forms mentioned in this text can be found at the IRS website at **www.irs.gov/forms-instructions**. At the time of publication of this 2019 edition textbook, the forms for 2018 reflecting changes made by the Tax Cuts and Jobs Act (TCJA) of 2017 were not yet released.

A few months before the individual filing season begins in January, the IRS typically releases draft tax forms. The primary purpose of making these available to the public before the forms are finalized is to allow interested parties an opportunity to provide comments to the IRS. Draft IRS tax forms can be found at **apps.irs.gov/app/picklist/list/ draftTaxForms.html**.

In addition to reviewing and using the IRS tax forms in your study of taxation, also consider reviewing the comparable forms from the tax agency in your state (usually called the Department of Revenue). A list of state tax agency links is available at **www.aicpa.org/research/externallinks/ taxesstatesdepartmentsofrevenue.html**. This can help you see some of the differences between Federal and state income tax rules, as well as similarities.

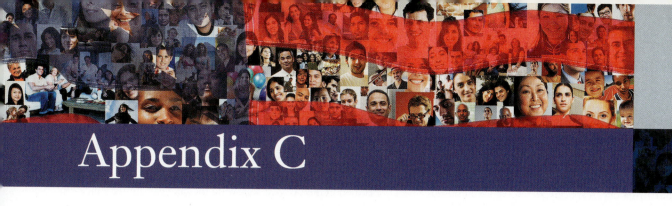

Appendix C

Glossary

The key terms in this glossary have been defined to reflect their conventional use in the field of taxation. The definitions may therefore be incomplete for other purposes.

A

AAA bypass election. In the context of a distribution by an S corporation, an election made by the entity to designate that the distribution is first from accumulated earnings and profits (AEP) and only then from the accumulated adjustments account (AAA).

Abandoned spouse. The abandoned spouse provision enables a married taxpayer with a dependent child whose spouse did not live in the taxpayer's home during the last six months of the tax year to file as a head of household rather than as married filing separately.

Accelerated cost recovery system (ACRS). A method in which the cost of tangible property is recovered (depreciated) over a prescribed period of time. This depreciation approach disregards salvage value, imposes a period of cost recovery that depends upon the classification of the asset into one of various recovery periods, and prescribes the applicable percentage of cost that can be deducted each year. A modified system is currently the default cost recovery method; it is referred to as MACRS. § 168.

Accelerated death benefits. The amount received from a life insurance policy by the insured who is terminally ill or chronically ill. Any realized gain may be excluded from the gross income of the insured if the policy is surrendered to the insurer or is sold to a licensed viatical settlement provider. § 101(g).

Acceleration rule. Treatment of an intercompany transaction on a consolidated return, when a sold asset leaves the group.

Accident and health benefits. Employee fringe benefits provided by employers through the payment of health and accident insurance premiums or the establishment of employer-funded medical reimbursement plans. Employers generally are entitled to a deduction for such payments, whereas employees generally exclude such fringe benefits from gross income. §§ 105 and 106.

Accident and health insurance benefits. See *accident and health benefits.*

Accountable plan. A type of expense reimbursement plan that requires an employee to render an adequate accounting to the employer and return any excess reimbursement or allowance. If the expense qualifies, it will be treated as a deduction *for* AGI.

Accounting income. The accountant's concept of income is generally based upon the realization principle. Financial accounting income may differ from taxable income (e.g., accelerated depreciation might be used for Federal income tax and straight-line depreciation for financial accounting purposes). Differences are included in a reconciliation of taxable and accounting income on Schedule M–1 or Schedule M–3 of Form 1120 for corporations.

Accounting method. The method under which income and expenses are determined for tax purposes. Important accounting methods include the cash basis and the accrual basis. Special methods are available for the reporting of gain on installment sales, recognition of income on construction projects (the completed contract and percentage of completion methods), and the valuation of inventories (last-in, first-out and first-in, first-out). §§ 446–474.

Accounting period. The period of time, usually a year, used by a taxpayer for the determination of tax liability. Unless a fiscal year is chosen, taxpayers must determine and pay their income tax liability by using the calendar year (January 1 through December 31) as the period of measurement. An example of a fiscal year is July 1 through June 30. A change in accounting period (e.g., from a calendar year to a fiscal year) generally requires the consent of the IRS. Usually, taxpayers are free to select either an initial calendar or a fiscal year without the consent of the IRS. §§ 441–444.

Accrual method. A method of accounting that recognizes expenses as incurred and income as earned. In contrast to the cash basis of accounting, expenses need not be paid to be deductible, nor need income be received to be taxable. § 446(c)(2).

Accumulated adjustments account (AAA). An account that aggregates an S corporation's post-1982 income, loss, and deductions for the tax year (including nontaxable income and nondeductible losses and expenses). After the year-end income and expense adjustments are made, the account is reduced by distributions made during the tax year.

Accumulated E & P. See *accumulated earnings and profits (AEP).*

Accumulated earnings and profits (AEP). Net undistributed tax-basis earnings of a corporation aggregated from March 1, 1913, to the end of the prior tax year. Used to determine the amount of dividend income associated with a distribution to shareholders. § 316 and Reg. § 1.316–2.

Accumulated earnings tax. A special 20 percent tax imposed on C corporations that accumulate (rather than distribute) their earnings beyond the reasonable needs of the business. The accumulated earnings tax and related interest are imposed on accumulated taxable income in addition to the corporate income tax. §§ 531–537.

Accuracy-related penalties. Major civil taxpayer penalties relating to the accuracy of tax return data, including misstatements stemming from taxpayer negligence and improper valuation of income and deductions, are coordinated under this umbrella term. The penalty usually equals 20 percent of the understated tax liability.

Acquiescence. Agreement by the IRS on the results reached in certain judicial decisions; sometimes abbreviated *Acq.* or *A.*

Acquisition indebtedness. Debt incurred in acquiring, constructing, or substantially improving a qualified residence of the taxpayer. The interest on such loans is deductible as qualified residence interest. However, interest on such debt is deductible only on the portion of the indebtedness that does not exceed $750,000 ($1 million for debt incurred before December 15, 2017). § 163(h)(3).

Active income. Wages, salary, commissions, bonuses, profits from a trade or business in which the taxpayer is a material participant, gain on the sale or other disposition of assets used in an active trade or business, and income from intangible property if the taxpayer's personal efforts significantly contributed to the creation of the property. The passive activity loss rules require classification of income and losses into three categories with active income being one of them.

Ad valorem taxes. A tax imposed on the value of property. The most common ad valorem tax is that imposed by states, counties, and cities on real estate. Ad valorem taxes can be imposed on personal property as well.

Additional first-year depreciation. In general, this provision provides for an additional cost recovery deduction of 100 percent for qualified property acquired and placed in service after September 27, 2017, and before January 1, 2027. (The bonus depreciation percentage is reduced by 20 percent for each tax year after 2022.) Qualified property includes most types of new and used property other than buildings. The taxpayer can elect to forgo this bonus depreciation. Different rules applied between 2008 and September 28, 2017.

Adjusted basis. The cost or other basis of property reduced by depreciation allowed or allowable and increased by capital improvements. Other special adjustments are provided in § 1016 and the related Regulations.

Adjustments. In calculating AMTI, certain adjustments are added to or deducted from taxable income. These adjustments generally reflect timing differences. § 56.

Adoption expenses credit. A provision intended to assist taxpayers who incur nonrecurring costs directly associated with the adoption process, such as legal costs, social service review costs, and transportation costs. Up to $13,840 of costs incurred to adopt an eligible child qualify for the credit (unique rules apply when adopting a special needs child). A taxpayer may claim the credit in the year qualifying expenses are paid or incurred if the expenses are paid during or after the year in which the adoption is finalized. For qualifying expenses paid or incurred in a tax year prior to the year the adoption is finalized, the credit must be claimed in the tax year following the tax year during which the expenses are paid or incurred. § 23.

Affiliated group. A parent-subsidiary group of corporations that is eligible to elect to file on a consolidated basis. Eighty percent ownership of the voting power and value of all of the corporations must be achieved every day of the tax year, and an identifiable parent corporation must exist (i.e., it must own at least 80 percent of another group member without applying attribution rules).

Aggregate (or conduit) concept. A perspective taken towards a venture that regards the venture as an aggregation of its owners joined together in an agency relationship rather than as a separate entity. For tax purposes, this results in the income of the venture being taxable directly to its owners. For example, items of income and expense, capital gains and losses, tax credits, etc., realized by a partnership pass through the partnership (a conduit) and are subject to taxation at the partner level. Also, in an S corporation, certain items pass through and are reported on the returns of the shareholders. See also *entity concept.*

Alimony and separate maintenance payments. Alimony deductions result from the payment of a legal obligation arising from the termination of a marital relationship. Payments designated as alimony generally are included in the gross income of the recipient and are deductible *for* AGI by the payor. For divorce or separation instruments executed after December 31, 2018, alimony is neither gross income for the recipient nor deductible by the payor.

Alimony recapture. The amount of alimony that previously has been included in the gross income of the recipient and deducted by the payor that now is deducted by the recipient and included in the gross income of the payor as the result of front-loading. § 71(f).

All events test. As applied to the recognition of income, the all events test requires that income of an accrual basis taxpayer be recognized when (1) all events have occurred that fix the taxpayer's right to receive the income and (2) the amount can be determined with reasonable accuracy. The TCJA of 2017 added a rule at § 451(b) requiring an accrual method taxpayer to include amounts in income no later than for financial reporting purposes other than for special rules such as the installment method. As applied to the recognition of expenses, the all events test prevents the recognition of a deduction by an accrual basis taxpayer until all the events have occurred that fix the taxpayer's related obligation. This can be contrasted with GAAP under which a fixed or legal obligation is not required before an expense is recognized. Reg. §§ 1.446–1(c)(1)(ii) and 1.461–1(a)(2).

Allocate. The assignment of income for various tax purposes. A multistate corporation's nonbusiness income usually is allocated to the state where the nonbusiness assets are located; it is not apportioned with the rest of the entity's income. The income and expense items of an estate or a trust are allocated between income and corpus components.

Specific items of income, expense, gain, loss, and credit can be allocated to specific partners if a substantial economic nontax purpose for the allocation is established.

Alternate valuation date. Property passing from a decedent by death may be valued for estate tax purposes as of the date of death or the alternate valuation date. The alternate valuation date is six months after the date of death or the date the property is disposed of by the estate, whichever comes first. To use the alternate valuation date, the executor or administrator of the estate must make an affirmative election. Election of the alternate valuation date is not available unless it decreases the amount of the gross estate and reduces the estate tax liability.

Alternative depreciation system (ADS). A cost recovery system in which the cost or other initial basis of an asset is recovered using the straight-line method over recovery periods similar to those used in MACRS. The alternative system must be used in certain instances and can be elected in other instances. § 168(g).

Alternative minimum tax (AMT). The AMT is calculated as a percentage of alternative minimum taxable income (AMTI). AMTI generally starts with the taxpayer's taxable income, prior to any standard deduction taken. To this amount, the taxpayer (1) adds designated preference items (e.g., tax-exempt interest income on private activity bonds), (2) makes other specified adjustments (e.g., to reflect a slower cost recovery method), (3) adjusts certain AMT itemized deductions for individuals (e.g., interest incurred on housing), and (4) subtracts an exemption amount. The taxpayer must pay the greater of the resulting AMT or the regular income tax (reduced by all allowable tax credits). AMT preferences and adjustments are assigned to partners, LLC members, and S corporation shareholders. The AMT does not apply to C corporations for tax years beginning after 2017.

Alternative minimum tax credit. AMT liability can result from timing differences that give rise to positive adjustments in calculating AMTI. To provide equity for the taxpayer when these timing differences reverse, the regular tax liability may be reduced by a tax credit for a prior year's minimum tax liability attributable to timing differences. § 53.

Alternative minimum taxable income (AMTI). The base (prior to deducting the exemption amount) for computing a taxpayer's alternative minimum tax. This consists of the taxable income for the year modified for AMT adjustments and AMT preferences. § 55(b)(2).

Alternative tax. An option that is allowed in computing the tax on net capital gain. For noncorporate taxpayers, the rate is usually 15 percent (but is 25 percent for unrecaptured § 1250 gain and 28 percent for collectibles). However, the alternative tax rate is 0 percent (rather than 15 percent) for lower-income taxpayers (e.g., taxable income of $77,200 or less for married persons filing jointly). Certain high-income taxpayers (e.g., taxable income of more than $479,000 for married persons filing jointly) have an alternative tax rate of 20 percent. § 1(h).

Alternative tax NOL deduction (ATNOLD). In calculating the AMT, the taxpayer is allowed to deduct NOL carryovers and carrybacks. The AMT NOL amount is referred to as the ATNOLD. The regular income tax NOL is modified for AMT adjustments and preferences to produce the ATNOLD. § 56(d).

American Opportunity credit. This credit replaces the HOPE scholarship credit for years after 2008 and applies for qualifying expenses for the first four years of postsecondary education. Qualified expenses include tuition and related expenses and books and other course materials. Room and board are ineligible for the credit. The maximum credit available per student is $2,500 (100 percent of the first $2,000 of qualified expenses and 25 percent of the next $2,000 of qualified expenses). Eligible students include the taxpayer, taxpayer's spouse, and taxpayer's dependents. To qualify for the credit, a student must take at least one-half of the full-time course load for at least one academic term at a qualifying educational institution. The credit is phased out for higher-income taxpayers. § 25A.

Amortization. The tax deduction for the cost or other basis of an intangible asset over the asset's estimated useful life. Examples of amortizable intangibles include patents, copyrights, and leasehold interests. Most purchased intangible assets (e.g., goodwill) can be amortized for income tax purposes over a 15-year period.

Amount realized. The amount received by a taxpayer upon the sale or exchange of property. Amount realized is the sum of the cash and the fair market value of any property or services received by the taxpayer plus any related debt assumed by the buyer. Determining the amount realized is the starting point for arriving at realized gain or loss. § 1001(b).

Annual exclusion. In computing the taxable gifts for the year, each donor excludes the first $15,000 (for 2018) of a gift to each donee. Usually, the annual exclusion is not available for gifts of future interests. § 2503(b).

Annuity. A fixed sum of money payable to a person at specified times for a specified period of time or for life. If the party making the payment (i.e., the obligor) is regularly engaged in this type of business (e.g., an insurance company), the arrangement is classified as a commercial annuity. A so-called private annuity involves an obligor that is not regularly engaged in selling annuities (e.g., a charity or family member).

Apportion. The assignment of the business income of a multistate corporation to specific states for income taxation. Usually, the apportionment procedure accounts for the property, payroll, and sales activity levels of the various states, and a proportionate assignment of the entity's total income is made using a three-factor apportionment formula. These activities indicate the commercial domicile of the corporation relative to that income. Some states exclude nonbusiness income from the apportionment procedure; they allocate nonbusiness income to the states where the nonbusiness assets are located.

Appreciated inventory. In partnership taxation, appreciated inventory is a hot asset, and a partner's share of its ordinary income potential must be allocated. If a partner sells an interest in the partnership, ordinary income is recognized to the extent of the partner's share in the partnership's inventory and unrealized receivables. The definition of "inventory" here is broad enough to include any accounts receivable, including unrealized receivables.

Arm's length. See *arm's length price*.

Arm's length price. The standard under which unrelated parties would determine an exchange price for a transaction. Suppose, for example, Cardinal Corporation sells property to its sole shareholder for $10,000. In testing whether the $10,000 is an "arm's length" price, one would ascertain the price that would have been negotiated between the corporation and an unrelated party in a bargained exchange.

ASC 740. Under Generally Accepted Accounting Principles, the rules for the financial reporting of the tax expense of an enterprise. Permanent differences affect the enterprise's effective tax rate. Temporary differences create a deferred tax asset or a deferred tax liability on the balance sheet.

ASC 740-10. An interpretation by the Financial Accounting Standards Board. When an uncertain tax return position exists, this interpretation is used to determine the financial reporting treatment, if any, for the taxpayer. If it is more likely than not (i.e., a greater than 50 percent probability) that the uncertain return position will be sustained (e.g., by the courts) on its technical merits, it must be reported on the financial statements. The amount to be reported then is computed based on the probabilities of the outcome of the technical review and the amounts at which the dispute would be resolved. If the more-likely-than-not test is failed, no current financial disclosure of the results of the return position is required.

Asset use test. In the context of a corporate reorganization, a means by which to determine if the continuity of business enterprise requirement is met. The acquiring corporation must continue to use the target entity's assets in the acquiror's business going forward; if this is not the case, the requirement is failed.

Assignment of income. A taxpayer attempts to avoid the recognition of income by assigning to another the property that generates the income. Such a procedure will not avoid income recognition by the taxpayer making the assignment if the income was earned at the point of the transfer. In this case, the income is taxed to the person who earns it.

At-risk limitation. Generally, a taxpayer can deduct losses related to a trade or business, S corporation, partnership, or investment asset only to the extent of the at-risk amount. The taxpayer has an amount at risk in a business or investment venture to the extent that personal assets have been subjected to the risks of the business. Typically, the taxpayer's at-risk amount includes (1) the amount of money or other property that the investor contributed to the venture for the investment, (2) the amount of any of the entity's liabilities for which the taxpayer personally is liable and that relate to the investment, and (3) an allocable share of nonrecourse debts incurred by the venture from third parties in arm's length transactions for real estate investments.

Attribution. Under certain circumstances, the tax law applies attribution (constructive ownership) rules to assign to one taxpayer the ownership interest of another taxpayer. If, for example, the stock of Gold Corporation is held 60 percent by Marsha and 40 percent by Sidney, Marsha may be deemed to own 100 percent of Gold Corporation if Marsha and Sidney are mother and child. In that case, the stock owned by Sidney is attributed to Marsha. Stated differently, Marsha has a 60 percent direct and a 40 percent indirect interest in Gold Corporation. It can also be said that Marsha is the constructive owner of Sidney's interest.

Automatic mileage method. Automobile expenses are generally deductible only to the extent the automobile is used in business or for the production of income. Personal commuting expenses are not deductible. The taxpayer may deduct actual expenses (including depreciation and insurance), or the standard (automatic) mileage rate may be used (54.5 cents per mile for 2018 and 53.5 cents per mile for 2017). Automobile expenses incurred for medical purposes are deductible to the extent of actual out-of-pocket expenses or at the rate of 18 cents per mile for 2018 and 17 cents per mile for 2017. For charitable activities, the rate is 14 cents per mile.

B

Bad debt. A deduction is permitted if a business account receivable subsequently becomes partially or completely worthless, providing the income arising from the debt previously was included in income. Available methods are the specific charge-off method and the reserve method. However, except for certain financial institutions, TRA of 1986 repealed the use of the reserve method for 1987 and thereafter. If the reserve method is used, partially or totally worthless accounts are charged to the reserve. A nonbusiness bad debt deduction is allowed as a short-term capital loss if the loan did not arise in connection with the creditor's trade or business activities. Loans between related parties (family members) generally are classified as nonbusiness. § 166.

Balance sheet approach. The process under ASC 740 (SFAS 109) by which an entity's deferred tax expense or deferred tax benefit is determined as a result of the reporting period's changes in the balance sheet's deferred tax asset and deferred tax liability accounts.

Basis in partnership interest. The acquisition cost of the partner's ownership interest in the partnership. Includes purchase price and associated debt acquired from other partners and in the course of the entity's trade or business.

Benchmarking. The tax professional's use of two or more entities' effective tax rates and deferred tax balance sheet accounts. Used chiefly to compare the effectiveness of the entities' tax planning techniques and to suggest future tax-motivated courses of action.

Blockage rule. A factor to be considered in valuing a large block of corporate stock. Application of this rule generally justifies a discount in the asset's fair market value, because the disposition of a large amount of stock at any one time may depress the value of the shares in the marketplace.

Boot. Cash or property of a type not included in the definition of a tax-deferred exchange. The receipt of boot causes an otherwise tax-deferred transfer to become immediately taxable to the extent of the lesser of the fair market value of the boot or the realized gain on the transfer. For example, see transfers to controlled corporations under § 351(b), reorganizations under § 368, and like-kind exchanges under § 1031(b).

Built-in gains tax. A penalty tax designed to discourage a shift of the incidence of taxation on unrealized gains from a C corporation to its shareholders, via an S election. Under this provision, any recognized gain during the first 10 (or 7 or 5) years of S status generates a corporate-level tax on a base not to exceed the aggregate untaxed built-in gains brought into the S corporation upon its election from C corporation taxable years.

Built-in loss property. Property contributed to a corporation under § 351 or as a contribution to capital that has a basis in excess of its fair market value. An adjustment is necessary to step down the basis of the property to its fair market value. The adjustment prevents the corporation and the contributing shareholder from obtaining a double tax benefit. The corporation allocates the adjustment proportionately among the assets with the built-in loss. As an alternative to the corporate adjustment, the shareholder may elect to reduce the basis in the stock.

Business bad debt. A tax deduction allowed for obligations obtained in connection with a trade or business that have become either partially or completely worthless. In contrast to nonbusiness bad debts, business bad debts are deductible as business expenses. § 166.

Business purpose. A justifiable business reason for carrying out a transaction. Mere tax avoidance is not an acceptable business purpose. The presence of a business purpose is crucial in the area of corporate reorganizations and certain liquidations.

Buy-sell agreement. An arrangement, particularly appropriate in the case of a closely held corporation or a partnership, whereby the surviving owners (shareholders or partners) or the entity agrees to purchase the interest of a withdrawing owner. The buy-sell agreement provides for an orderly disposition of an interest in a business and may aid in setting the value of the interest for estate tax purposes.

Bypass amount. The amount that can be transferred by gift or at death free of any unified transfer tax. For 2018, the bypass amount is $11.18 million for estate tax and 11.18 million for gift tax.

Bypass election. In the context of a distribution by an S corporation, an election made by the entity to designate that the distribution is first from accumulated earnings and profits and only then from the accumulated adjustments account (AAA).

C

C corporation. A separate taxable entity subject to the rules of Subchapter C of the Code. This business form may create a double taxation effect relative to its shareholders. The entity is subject to the regular corporate tax and a number of penalty taxes at the Federal level.

Cafeteria benefit plans. See *cafeteria plan*.

Cafeteria plan. An employee benefit plan under which an employee is allowed to select from among a variety of employer-provided fringe benefits. Some of the benefits may be taxable, and some may be statutory nontaxable benefits (e.g., health and accident insurance and group term life insurance). The employee is taxed only on the taxable benefits selected. A cafeteria benefit plan is also referred to as a flexible benefit plan. § 125.

Capital account. The financial accounting analog of a partner's tax basis in the entity.

Capital account maintenance. Under the § 704(b) Regulations, partnership allocations will be respected only if capital accounts are maintained in accordance with those regulations. These so-called "§ 704(b) book capital accounts" are properly maintained if they reflect the partner's contributions and distributions of cash; increases and decreases for the fair market value of contributed/distributed property; and adjustments for the partner's share of income, gains, losses, and deductions. Certain other adjustments are also required. See also *economic effect test* and *Section 704(b) book capital accounts*.

Capital asset. Broadly speaking, all assets are capital except those specifically excluded from that definition by the Code. Major categories of noncapital assets include property held for resale in the normal course of business (inventory), trade accounts and notes receivable, and depreciable property and real estate used in a trade or business (§ 1231 assets). § 1221.

Capital contribution. Various means by which a shareholder makes additional funds available to the corporation (placed at the risk of the business), sometimes without the receipt of additional stock. If no stock is received, the contributions are added to the basis of the shareholder's existing stock investment and do not generate gross income to the corporation. § 118.

Capital gains. The gain from the sale or exchange of a capital asset.

Capital gain property. Property contributed to a charitable organization that if sold rather than contributed, would have resulted in long-term capital gain to the donor.

Capital interest. Usually, the percentage of the entity's net assets that a partner would receive on liquidation. Typically determined by the partner's capital sharing ratio.

Capital losses. The loss from the sale or exchange of a capital asset.

Capital sharing ratio. A partner's percentage ownership of the entity's capital.

Carbon tax. A tax on fossil fuels to help reduce greenhouse gas emissions.

Carried interest. A "partnership interest held in connection with performance of services," as defined under § 1061. Long-term capital gains from such an interest are reclassified as short-term capital gains (with potential ordinary income treatment) unless the underlying asset that triggered the gain had more than a three-year holding period. This provision only applies to income and gains arising from managing portfolio investments on behalf of third-party investors, including publicly traded securities, commodities, certain real estate, or options to buy/sell such assets. Section 1061 was enacted in the TCJA of 2017 in an effort to curtail an industry practice that resulted in fund managers receiving partnership profits interests in exchange for services: these "profits partners" received long-term capital gain allocations from the fund, rather than ordinary income for the services provided in managing the fund's assets. In addition to § 1061, the IRS has, from time to time, announced that it might issue regulations (under its general "anti-abuse" authority) to expand the scope of the carried interest rules.

Cash balance plan. A hybrid form of pension plan similar in some aspects to a defined benefit plan. Such a plan is funded by the employer, and the employer bears the investment risks and rewards. But like defined contribution plans, a cash balance plan establishes allocations to individual employee accounts, and the payout for an employee depends on investment performance.

Cash method. See *cash receipts method*.

Cash receipts method. A method of accounting that reflects deductions as paid and income as received in any one tax year. However, deductions for prepaid expenses that benefit more than one tax year (e.g., prepaid rent and prepaid interest) usually are spread over the period benefited rather than deducted in the year paid. § 446(c)(1).

Casualty loss. A casualty is defined as "the complete or partial destruction of property resulting from an identifiable event of a sudden, unexpected or unusual nature" (e.g., floods, storms, fires, auto accidents). Individuals may deduct a casualty loss only if the loss is incurred in a trade or business or in a transaction entered into for profit or arises from fire, storm, shipwreck, or other casualty or from theft. Individuals usually deduct personal casualty losses as itemized deductions subject to a $100 nondeductible amount and to an annual floor equal to 10 percent of adjusted gross income that applies after the $100 per casualty floor has been applied. Special rules are provided for the netting of certain casualty gains and losses. For tax years beginning after 2017 (and before 2026), personal casualty losses are limited to those sustained in an area designated as a disaster area by the President of the United States.

Charitable contribution. Contributions made to qualified nonprofit organizations. Taxpayers, regardless of their accounting method, are generally allowed to deduct (subject to various restrictions and limitations) contributions in the year of payment. Accrual basis corporations may accrue contributions at year-end if payment is properly authorized before the end of the year and payment is made within three and one-half months after the end of the year. § 170.

Check-the-box Regulations. By using the check-the-box rules prudently, an entity can select the most attractive tax results offered by the Code, without being bound by legal forms. By default, an unincorporated entity with more than one owner is taxed as a partnership; an unincorporated entity with one owner is a disregarded entity, taxed as a sole proprietorship or corporate division. No action is necessary by the taxpayer if the legal form or default status is desired. Form 8832 is used to "check a box" and change the tax status. Not available if the entity is incorporated under state law.

Child tax credit. A tax credit based solely on the number of qualifying children under age 17. The maximum credit available is $2,000 per qualifying child. (In addition, a $500 non-refundable credit is available for qualifying dependents other than qualifying children.) A qualifying child must be claimed as a dependent on a parent's tax return to qualify for the credit. Taxpayers who qualify for the child tax credit may also qualify for a supplemental credit. The supplemental credit is treated as a component of the earned income credit and is therefore refundable. The credit is phased out for higher-income taxpayers. § 24. See also *dependent tax credit*.

Circuit Court of Appeals. Any of 13 Federal courts that consider tax matters appealed from the U.S. Tax Court, a U.S. District Court, or the U.S. Court of Federal Claims. Appeal from a U.S. Court of Appeals is to the U.S. Supreme Court by Certiorari.

Circular 230. A portion of the Federal tax Regulations that describes the levels of conduct at which a tax preparer must operate. Circular 230 dictates, for instance, that a tax preparer may not charge an unconscionable fee or delay the execution of a tax audit with inappropriate delays. Circular 230 requires that there be a reasonable basis for a tax return position and that no frivolous returns be filed.

Citator. A tax research resource that presents the judicial history of a court case and traces the subsequent references to the case. When these references include the citing cases' evaluations of the cited case's precedents, the research can obtain some measure of the efficacy and reliability of the original holding.

Claim of right doctrine. A judicially imposed doctrine applicable to both cash and accrual basis taxpayers that holds that an amount is includible in income upon actual or constructive receipt if the taxpayer has an unrestricted claim to the payment. For the tax treatment of amounts repaid when previously included in income under the claim of right doctrine, see § 1341.

Closely held C corporation. A regular corporation (i.e., the S election is not in effect) for which more than 50 percent of the value of its outstanding stock is owned, directly or indirectly, by five or fewer individuals at any time during the tax year. The term is relevant in identifying C corporations that are subject to the passive activity loss provisions. § 469.

Closely held corporation. A corporation where stock ownership is not widely dispersed. Rather, a few shareholders are in control of corporate policy and are in a position to benefit personally from that policy.

Closing agreement. In a tax dispute, the parties sign a closing agreement to spell out the terms under which the matters are settled. The agreement is binding on both the Service and the taxpayer.

Collectibles. A special type of capital asset, the gain from which is taxed at a maximum rate of 28 percent if the holding period is more than one year. Examples include art, rugs, antiques, gems, metals, stamps, some coins and bullion, and alcoholic beverages held for investment.

Combined return. In multistate taxation, a group of unitary corporations may elect or be required to file an income tax return that includes operating results for all of the affiliates, not just those with nexus in the state. Thus, apportionment data is reported for the group's worldwide or water's-edge operations.

Community property. Louisiana, Texas, New Mexico, Arizona, California, Washington, Idaho, Nevada, and Wisconsin have community property systems. Alaska residents can elect community property status for assets. The rest of the states are common law property jurisdictions. The difference between common law and community property systems centers around the property rights possessed by married persons. In a common law system, each spouse owns whatever he or she earns. Under a community property system, one-half of the earnings of each spouse is considered owned by the other spouse. Assume, for example, that Jeff and Alice are husband and wife and that their only income is the $50,000 annual salary Jeff receives. If they live in New York (a common law state), the $50,000 salary belongs to Jeff. If, however, they live in Texas (a community property state), the $50,000 salary is owned one-half each by Jeff and Alice.

Compensatory damages. Damages received or paid by the taxpayer can be classified as compensatory damages or as punitive damages. Compensatory damages are paid to compensate one for harm caused by another. Compensatory damages received on account of physical injuries are excludible from the recipient's gross income.

Complete termination redemption. Sale or exchange treatment is available relative to this type of redemption. The shareholder must retire all of his or her outstanding shares in the corporation (ignoring family attribution rules) and cannot hold an interest, other than that of a creditor, for the 10 years following the redemption. § 302(b)(3).

Completed contract method. A method of reporting gain or loss on certain long-term contracts. Under this method of accounting, all gross income and expenses are recognized in the tax year in which the contract is completed. Reg. § 1.451–3.

Complex trust. Not a simple trust. Such trusts may have charitable beneficiaries, accumulate income, and distribute corpus. §§ 661–663.

Composite return. In multistate taxation, an S corporation may be allowed to file a single income tax return that assigns pass-through items to resident and nonresident shareholders. The composite or "block" return allows the entity to remit any tax that is attributable to the nonresident shareholders.

Conduit concept. A perspective taken toward a venture that regards the venture as an aggregation of its owners joined together in an agency relationship rather than as a separate entity. For tax purposes, this results in the income of the venture being taxable directly to its owners. For example, items of income and expense, capital gains and losses, tax credits, etc., realized by a partnership pass through the partnership (a conduit) and are subject to taxation at the partner level. Also, in an S corporation, certain items pass through and are reported on the returns of the shareholders.

Conduit perspective. See *conduit concept.*

Conservatism principle. The theory behind much of Generally Accepted Accounting Principles, under which assurance is provided that an entity's balance sheet assets are not overstated, nor liabilities understated. For instance, under ASC 740 (SFAS 109), a deferred tax asset is not recorded until it is more likely than not that the future tax benefit will be realized.

Consolidated returns. A procedure whereby certain affiliated corporations may file a single return, combine the tax transactions of each corporation, and arrive at a single income tax liability for the group. The election to file a consolidated return usually is binding on future years. §§ 1501–1505 and related Regulations.

Consolidation. The combination of two or more corporations into a newly created corporation. Thus, Black Corporation and White Corporation combine to form Gray Corporation. A consolidation may qualify as a nontaxable reorganization if certain conditions are satisfied. §§ 354 and 368(a)(1)(A).

Constructive dividends. A taxable benefit derived by a shareholder from his or her corporation that is not actually initiated by the board of directors as a dividend. Examples include unreasonable compensation, excessive rent payments, bargain purchases of corporate property, and shareholder use of corporate property. Constructive dividends generally are found in closely held corporations.

Constructive liquidation scenario. The means by which recourse debt is shared among partners in basis determination.

Constructive receipt. If income is unqualifiedly available although not physically in the taxpayer's possession, it still is subject to the income tax. An example is accrued interest on a savings account. Under the constructive receipt concept, the interest is taxed to a depositor in the year available, rather than the year actually withdrawn. The fact that the depositor uses the cash basis of accounting for tax purposes is irrelevant. See Reg. § 1.451–2.

Continuity of business enterprise. In a tax-favored reorganization, the acquiring corporation must continue the historic business of the target or use a significant portion of the target's assets in the new business.

Continuity of interest. In a tax-favored reorganization, a shareholder or corporation that has substantially the same investment after an exchange as before should not be taxed on the transaction. Specifically, the target shareholders must acquire an equity interest in the acquiring corporation equal in value to at least 40 percent of all the outstanding stock of the target entity.

Control. Holding a specified level of stock ownership in a corporation. For § 351, the new shareholder(s) must hold at least 80 percent of the total combined voting power of all voting classes of stock and at least 80 percent of the shares of all nonvoting classes. Other tax provisions require different levels of control to bring about desired effects, such as 50 or 100 percent.

Controlled foreign corporation (CFC). A non-U.S. corporation in which more than 50 percent of the total combined voting power of all classes of stock entitled to vote or the total value of the stock of the corporation is owned by U.S. shareholders on any day during the taxable year of the foreign corporation. For purposes of this definition, a U.S. shareholder is any U.S. person who owns, or is considered to own, 10 percent or more of the total combined voting power of all classes of voting stock of the foreign corporation. Stock owned directly, indirectly, and constructively is used in this measure. See *U.S. shareholder.*

Controlled group. Controlled groups include parent-subsidiary groups, brother-sister groups, combined groups, and certain insurance companies. Controlled groups are required to share certain elements of tax calculations (e.g., $250,000 accumulated earnings credit) or tax credits (e.g., research credit). In addition, some transactions between a controlled group might be treated differently. §§ 1561 and 1563.

Corporate liquidation. Occurs when a corporation distributes its net assets to its shareholders and ceases to be a going concern. Generally, a shareholder recognizes capital gain or loss upon the liquidation of the entity, regardless of the corporation's balance in its earnings and profits account. The liquidating corporation recognizes gain and loss on assets that it sells during the liquidation period and on assets that it distributes to shareholders in kind.

Corpus. The body or principal of a trust. Suppose, for example, Grant transfers an apartment building into a trust, income payable to Ruth for life, remainder to Shawn upon Ruth's death. Corpus of the trust is the apartment building.

Correspondence audit. An audit conducted by the IRS by the U.S. mail. Typically, the IRS writes to the taxpayer requesting the verification of a particular deduction or exemption. The remittance of copies of records or other support is requested of the taxpayer.

Cost depletion. Depletion that is calculated based on the adjusted basis of the asset. The adjusted basis is divided by the expected recoverable units to determine the depletion per unit. The depletion per unit is multiplied by the units sold during the tax year to calculate cost depletion.

Cost recovery. The system by which taxpayers are allowed to recover their investment in an asset by reducing their taxable income by the asset's cost or initial basis. Cost recovery methods include MACRS, § 179 expense, additional first-year depreciation, amortization, and depletion. §§ 168, 179, and 613.

Court of Federal Claims. A trial court (court of original jurisdiction) that decides litigation involving Federal tax matters. Appeal from this court is to the Court of Appeals for the Federal Circuit.

Court of original jurisdiction. The Federal courts are divided into courts of original jurisdiction and appellate courts. A dispute between a taxpayer and the IRS is first considered by a court of original jurisdiction (i.e., a trial court). The four Federal courts of original jurisdiction are the U.S. Tax Court, the U.S. District Court, the Court of Federal Claims, and the Small Cases Division of the U.S. Tax Court.

Coverdell education savings account (§ 530 plan). Coverdell education savings account exempts from tax the earnings on amounts placed in a qualified account for the education expenses of a named beneficiary. Contributions are limited to $2,000 per year per beneficiary, and the proceeds can be withdrawn without tax provided the funds are used to pay qualified educational expenses for primary, secondary, or higher education. (There is an annual $10,000 per student limitation on distributions for tuition expenses for primary and secondary education.) Qualified educational expenses also include certain homeschooling expenses. The account is named for the late Senator Paul Coverdell (R-GA), who sponsored the legislation in Congress. § 530.

Credit for certain retirement plan contributions. A nonrefundable credit is available based on eligible contributions of up to $2,000 to certain qualified retirement plans, such as traditional and Roth IRAs and § 401(k) plans. The benefit provided by this credit is in addition to any deduction or exclusion that otherwise is available resulting from the qualifying contribution. The amount of the credit depends on the taxpayer's AGI and filing status. § 25B.

Credit for child and dependent care expenses. A tax credit ranging from 20 percent to 35 percent of employment-related expenses (child and dependent care expenses) for amounts of up to $6,000 is available to individuals who are employed (or deemed to be employed) and maintain a household for a dependent child under age 13, disabled spouse, or disabled dependent. § 21.

Credit for employer-provided child care. A nonrefundable credit is available to employers who provide child care facilities to their employees during normal working hours. The credit, limited to $150,000, is comprised of two components. The portion of the credit for qualified child care expenses is equal to 25 percent of these expenses, while the portion of the credit for qualified child care resource and referral services is equal to 10 percent of these expenses. Any qualifying expenses otherwise deductible by the taxpayer must be reduced by the amount of the credit. In addition, the taxpayer's basis for any property used for qualifying purposes is reduced by the amount of the credit. § 45F.

Credit for employer-provided family and medical leave. A nonrefundable credit is available to employers who pay wages to employees while they are on family and medical leave. The credit is equal to 12.5% of wages paid to qualifying employees (limited to 12 weeks per employee per year). Employers must pay a minimum of 50% of the wages normally paid; if wages paid during the leave *exceed* 50% of normal wages, the credit is increased by 0.25% for each percentage point above 50% to a maximum of 25% of wages paid. § 45S.

Credit for small employer pension plan startup costs. A nonrefundable credit available to small businesses based on administrative costs associated with establishing and maintaining certain qualified plans. While such qualifying costs generally are deductible as ordinary and necessary business expenses, the availability of the credit is intended to lower the costs of starting a qualified retirement program and therefore encourage qualifying businesses to establish retirement plans for their employees. The credit is available for eligible employers at the rate of 50 percent of qualified startup costs. The maximum credit is $500 (based on a maximum $1,000 of qualifying expenses). § 45E.

Crop insurance proceeds. The proceeds received when an insured crop is destroyed. Section 451(d) permits the farmer to defer reporting the income from the insurance proceeds until the tax year following the taxable year of the destruction.

Crop method. A method of accounting for agricultural crops that are planted in one year but harvested in a subsequent year. Under this method, the costs of raising the crop are accumulated as inventory and are deducted when the income from the crop is realized.

Cross-purchase buy-sell agreement. Under this arrangement, the surviving owners of the business agree to buy out the withdrawing owner. Assume, for example, Ron and Sara are equal shareholders in Tip Corporation. Under a cross-purchase buy-sell agreement, Ron and Sara would contract to purchase the other's interest, should that person decide to withdraw from the business.

Current distribution. A payment made by a partnership to a partner when the partnership's legal existence does not cease thereafter. The partner usually assigns a basis in the distributed property that is equal to the lesser of the partner's basis in the partnership interest or the basis of the distributed asset to the partnership. The partner first assigns basis to any cash that he or she receives in the distribution. A cash distribution in excess of the partner's basis triggers a gain. The partner's remaining basis, if any, is assigned to the noncash assets according to their relative bases to the partnership.

Current E & P. Net tax-basis earnings of a corporation aggregated during the current tax year. A corporate distribution is deemed to be first from the entity's current earnings and profits and then from accumulated earnings and profits. Shareholders recognize dividend income to the extent of the earnings and profits of the corporation. A dividend results to the extent of current earnings and profits, even if there is a larger negative balance in accumulated earnings and profits.

Current tax expense. Under ASC 740 (SFAS 109), the book tax expense that relates to the current reporting period's net income and is actually payable (or creditable) to the appropriate governmental agencies for the current period. Also known as "cash tax" or "tax payable."

D

De minimis fringe. Benefits provided to employees that are too insignificant to warrant the time and effort required to account for the benefits received by each employee and the value of those benefits. Such amounts are excludible from the employee's gross income. § 132.

De minimis fringe benefits. See *de minimis fringe*.

Death benefits. A payment made by an employer to the beneficiary or beneficiaries of a deceased employee on account of the death of the employee.

Debt-financed income. Included in computations of the unrelated business income of an exempt organization, the gross income generated from debt-financed property.

Deceased spouse's unused exclusion (DSUE). In computing the Federal estate tax, the decedent uses the exclusion amount to shelter an amount of the gross estate from taxation. When the first spouse to die fails to use a portion of his/her exclusion amount, the unused portion is "portable" and becomes available to the surviving spouse. The surviving spouse can use the DSUE only of his/her last spouse to predecease.

Deduction for qualified business income. A deduction allowed for noncorporate taxpayers based on the qualified business income of a qualified trade or business. In general, the deduction is limited to the lesser of 20 percent of qualified business income, or 20 percent of taxable income before the qualified business income deduction less any net capital gain. There are *three limitations* on the deduction—an overall limitation (based on modified taxable income), another that applies to high-income taxpayers, and a third that applies to certain types of services businesses. § 199A.

Deduction for qualified tuition and related expenses. Taxpayers are allowed a deduction of up to $4,000 for higher education expenses. Certain taxpayers are not eligible for the deduction: those whose gross AGI exceeds a specified amount and those who can be claimed as a dependent by another taxpayer. These expenses are classified as a deduction *for* AGI, and they need not be employment-related. § 222.

Deductions *for* adjusted gross income. The Federal income tax is not imposed upon gross income. Rather, it is imposed upon taxable income. Congressionally identified deductions for individual taxpayers are subtracted either from gross income to arrive at adjusted gross income or from adjusted gross income to arrive at the tax base, taxable income.

Deductions *from* adjusted gross income. See *deductions for adjusted gross income*.

Deductions in respect of a decedent. Deductions accrued at the moment of death but not recognizable on the final income tax return of a decedent because of the method of accounting used. Such items are allowed as deductions on the estate tax return and on the income tax return of the estate (Form 1041) or the heir (Form 1040). An example of a deduction in respect of a decedent is interest expense accrued to the date of death by a cash basis debtor.

Deferred compensation. Compensation that will be taxed when received or upon the removal of certain restrictions on receipt and not when earned. Contributions by an employer to a qualified pension or profit sharing plan on behalf of an employee are an example. The contributions will not be taxed to the employee until the funds are made available or distributed to the employee (e.g., upon retirement).

Deferred tax asset. Under ASC 740, an asset recorded on the balance sheet to reflect the future tax benefits related to a transaction or activity which has already been reflected in the financial statements. A deferred tax asset is often the result of the deferral of a deduction or the acceleration of income for tax purposes relative to Generally Accepted Accounting Principles.

Deferred tax benefit. Under ASC 740, a reduction in the book tax expense that relates to the current reporting period's net income but will not be realized until a future reporting period. Creates or adds to the entity's deferred tax asset balance sheet account. For instance, the carryforward of a net operating loss is a deferred tax benefit.

Deferred tax expense. Under ASC 740, a book tax expense that relates to the current reporting period's net income but will not be realized until a future reporting period. Creates or adds to the entity's deferred tax liability balance sheet account. For instance, a deferred tax expense is created when tax depreciation deductions for the period are "accelerated" and exceed the corresponding book depreciation expense.

Deferred tax liability. Under ASC 740, a liability recorded on the balance sheet to reflect the future tax costs of a transaction or activity which has already been reflected in the financial statements. A deferred tax liability is often the result of the deferral of the recognition of income or the acceleration of a deduction for tax purposes relative to Generally Accepted Accounting Principles.

Defined benefit plan. Qualified plans can be dichotomized into defined benefit plans and defined contribution plans. Under a defined benefit plan, a formula defines the benefits employees are to receive. The formula usually includes years of service, employee compensation, and some stated percentage. The employer must make annual contributions based on actuarial computations that will be sufficient to pay the vested retirement benefits.

Defined contribution pension plan. Qualified plans can be dichotomized into defined benefit plans and defined contribution plans. Under a defined contribution plan, a separate account is maintained for each covered employee. The employee's benefits under the plan are based solely on (1) the amount contributed and (2) income from the fund that accrues to the employee's account. The plan defines the amount the employer is required to contribute (e.g., a flat dollar amount, an amount based on a special formula, or an amount equal to a certain percentage of compensation).

Dependency exemption. See *personal and dependency exemptions.*

Dependent tax credit. For 2018 through 2025, the TCJA of 2017 replaces the dependency exemption with a $500 non-refundable credit. This credit can be claimed for dependents who are not a qualifying child and are citizens or residents of the United States.

Depletion. The process by which the cost or other basis of a natural resource (e.g., an oil or gas interest) is recovered upon extraction and sale of the resource. The two ways to determine the depletion allowance are the cost and percentage (or statutory) methods. Under cost depletion, each unit of production sold is assigned a portion of the cost or other basis of the interest. This is determined by dividing the cost or other basis by the total units expected to be recovered. Under percentage (or statutory) depletion, the tax law provides a special percentage factor for different types of minerals and other natural resources. This percentage is multiplied by the gross income from the interest to arrive at the depletion allowance. §§ 613 and 613A.

Depreciation. The system by which a taxpayer allocates for financial reporting purposes the cost of an asset to periods benefited by the asset.

Determination letter. Upon the request of a taxpayer, the IRS will comment on the tax status of a completed transaction. Determination letters frequently are used to determine whether a retirement or profit sharing plan qualifies under the Code and to determine the tax-exempt status of certain nonprofit organizations.

Disabled access credit. A tax credit designed to encourage small businesses to make their facilities more accessible to disabled individuals. The credit is equal to 50 percent of the eligible expenditures that exceed $250 but do not exceed $10,250. Thus, the maximum amount for the credit is $5,000. The adjusted basis for depreciation is reduced by the amount of the credit. To qualify, the facility must have been placed in service before November 6, 1990. § 44.

Disaster area losses. A casualty sustained in an area designated as a disaster area by the President of the United States. In such an event, the disaster loss may be treated as having occurred in the taxable year immediately preceding the year in which the disaster actually occurred. Thus, immediate tax benefits are provided to victims of a disaster. § 165(i).

Disclaimer. Rejections, refusals, or renunciations of claims, powers, or property. Section 2518 sets forth the conditions required to avoid gift tax consequences as the result of a disclaimer.

Disguised sale. When a partner contributes property to the entity and soon thereafter receives a distribution from the partnership, the transactions are collapsed and the distribution is seen as a purchase of the asset by the partnership. § 707(a)(2)(B).

Disproportionate distribution. A distribution from a partnership to one or more of its partners in which at least one partner's interest in partnership hot assets is increased or decreased. For example, a distribution of cash to one partner and hot assets to another changes both partners' interest in hot assets and is disproportionate. The intent of rules for taxation of disproportionate distributions is to ensure that each partner eventually recognizes his or her proportionate share of partnership ordinary income.

Disproportionate redemption. Sale or exchange treatment is available relative to this type of redemption. After the exchange, the shareholder owns less than 80 percent of his or her pre-redemption interest in the corporation and only a minority interest in the entity. § 302(b)(2).

Disregarded entity. The Federal income tax treatment of business income usually follows the legal form of the taxpayer (i.e., an individual's sole proprietorship is reported on the Form 1040); a C corporation's taxable income is computed on Form 1120. The check-the-box Regulations are used if the unincorporated taxpayer wants to use a different tax regime. Under these rules, a disregarded entity is taxed as an individual or a corporate division; other tax regimes are not available. For instance, a one-member limited liability company is a disregarded entity.

Distributable net income (DNI). The measure that determines the nature and amount of the distributions from estates and trusts that the beneficiaries must include in income. DNI also limits the amount that estates and trusts can claim as a deduction for such distributions. § 643(a).

District Court. See *Federal District Court.*

Dividend. A nondeductible distribution to the shareholders of a corporation. A dividend constitutes gross income to the recipient if it is paid from the current or accumulated earnings and profits of the corporation.

Dividends received deduction. A deduction allowed a shareholder that is a corporation for dividends received from a domestic corporation. The deduction usually is 50 percent of the dividends received, but it could be 65 or 100 percent depending upon the ownership percentage held by the recipient corporation. §§ 243–246.

Divisive reorganization. A "Type D" spin-off, split-off, or split-up reorganization in which the original corporation divides its active business (in existence for at least five years) assets among two or more corporations. The stock received by the original corporation shareholders must be at least 80 percent of the other corporations.

Dock sales. A purchaser uses its owned or rented vehicles to take possession of the product at the seller's shipping dock. In most states, the sale is apportioned to the operating state of the purchaser, rather than the seller. See also *apportion* and *sales factor.*

Dollar-value LIFO. An inventory technique that focuses on the dollars invested in the inventory rather than the particular items on hand each period. Each inventory item is assigned to a pool. A pool is a collection of similar items and is treated as a separate inventory. At the end of the period, each pool is valued in terms of prices at the time LIFO was adopted (base period prices), whether or not the particular items were actually on hand in the year LIFO was adopted, to compare with current prices to determine if there has been an increase or decrease in inventories.

E

Earned income credit. A tax credit designed to provide assistance to certain low-income individuals who generally have a qualifying child. This is a refundable credit. To receive the most beneficial treatment, the taxpayer must have qualifying children. However, it is possible to qualify for the credit without having a child. See the text chapter on credits for the computation procedure required in order to determine the amount of the credit allowed.

Earnings and profits (E & P). Measures the economic capacity of a corporation to make a distribution to shareholders that is not a return of capital. Such a distribution results in dividend income to the shareholders to the extent of the corporation's current and accumulated earnings and profits.

Economic effect test. Requirements that must be met before a special allocation may be used by a partnership. The premise behind the test is that each partner who receives an allocation of income or loss from a partnership bears the economic benefit or burden of the allocation.

Economic income. The change in the taxpayer's net worth, as measured in terms of market values, plus the value of the assets the taxpayer consumed during the year. Because of the impracticality of this income model, it is not used for tax purposes.

Economic performance test. One of the requirements that must be satisfied for an accrual basis taxpayer to deduct an expense. Economic performance occurs when property or services are provided to the taxpayer, or in the case in which the taxpayer is required to provide property or services, whenever the property or services are actually provided by the taxpayer.

Education expenses. Employees may deduct education expenses that are incurred either (1) to maintain or improve existing job-related skills or (2) to meet the express requirements of the employer or the requirements imposed by law to retain employment status. The expenses are not deductible if the education is required to meet the minimum educational standards for the taxpayer's job or if the education qualifies the individual for a new trade or business. Reg. § 1.162–5.

Educational savings bonds. U.S. Series EE bonds whose proceeds are used for qualified higher educational expenses for the taxpayer, the taxpayer's spouse, or a dependent. The interest may be excluded from gross income, provided the taxpayer's adjusted gross income does not exceed certain amounts. § 135.

Effective tax rate. The financial statements for an entity include several footnotes, one of which reconciles the expected (statutory) income tax rate (e.g., 21 percent for a C corporation) with the effective tax rate (i.e., total tax expense as a percentage of book income). The reconciliation often is done in dollar and/or percentage terms.

Effectively connected income. Income of a nonresident alien or foreign corporation that is attributable to the operation of a U.S. trade or business under either the asset-use or the business-activities test.

E-file. The electronic filing of a tax return. The filing is either direct or indirect. As to direct, the taxpayer goes online using a computer and tax return preparation software. Indirect filing occurs when a taxpayer utilizes an authorized IRS e-file provider. The provider often is the tax return preparer.

E-filing. See *e-file*.

Employment taxes. Taxes that an employer must pay on account of its employees. Employment taxes include FICA (Federal Insurance Contributions Act) and FUTA (Federal Unemployment Tax Act) taxes. Employment taxes are paid to the IRS in addition to income tax withholdings at specified intervals. Such taxes can be levied on the employees, the employer, or both.

Energy credits. See *energy tax credits*.

Energy tax credits. Various tax credits are available to those who invest in certain energy property. The purpose of the credit is to create incentives for conservation and to develop alternative energy sources.

Enrolled agents (EAs). A tax practitioner who has gained admission to practice before the IRS by passing an IRS examination and maintaining a required level of continuing professional education.

Entertainment expenses. Expenses that are deductible only if they are directly related to or associated with a trade or business. Various restrictions and documentation requirements have been imposed upon the deductibility of entertainment expenses to prevent abuses by taxpayers. The TCJA of 2017 repealed the deduction for entertainment expenses paid or incurred after 2017. § 274.

Entity accounting income. Entity accounting income is not identical to the taxable income of a trust or estate, nor is it determined in the same manner as the entity's financial accounting income would be. The trust document or will determines whether certain income, expenses, gains, or losses are allocated to the corpus of the entity or to the entity's income beneficiaries. Only the items that are allocated to the income beneficiaries are included in entity accounting income.

Entity buy-sell agreement. An arrangement whereby the entity is to purchase a withdrawing owner's interest. When the entity is a corporation, the agreement generally involves a stock redemption on the part of the withdrawing shareholder. See also *buy-sell agreement* and *cross-purchase buy-sell agreement*.

Entity concept. A perspective taken toward a venture that regards the venture as an entity separate and distinct from its owners. For tax purposes, this results in the venture being directly responsible for the tax on the income it generates. The entity perspective taken toward C corporations results in the double taxation of income distributed to the corporation's owners.

Entity perspective. See *entity concept*.

Equity method. Under Generally Accepted Accounting Principles, the method of financial reporting for the operations of a subsidiary when the parent corporation owns between 20 and 50 percent of the subsidiary's stock. Creates a book-tax difference, as the two entities' operating results are combined for book purposes, but a Federal income tax consolidated return cannot be filed.

Estate tax. A tax imposed on the right to transfer property by death. Thus, an estate tax is levied on the decedent's estate and not on the heir receiving the property.

Estimated tax. The amount of tax (including alternative minimum tax and self-employment tax) a taxpayer expects to owe for the year after subtracting tax credits and income tax withheld. The estimated tax must be paid in installments at designated intervals (e.g., for the individual taxpayer, by April 15, June 15, September 15, and January 15 of the following year).

Excess business loss. The excess of aggregate deductions of the taxpayer attributable to trades or businesses of the taxpayer over the sum of aggregate gross income or gain of the taxpayer plus a threshold amount. In 2018, the threshold amount is $250,000 ($500,000 in the case of a married taxpayer filing a joint return). The threshold amount is adjusted for inflation each year. This loss limitation applies to taxpayers other than C corporations and applies after the passive activity loss limitation of § 469. § 461(l).

Excess lobbying expenditures. An excise tax is applied on otherwise tax-exempt organizations with respect to the excess of total lobbying expenditures over grass roots lobbying expenditures for the year.

Excess loss account. When a subsidiary has generated more historical losses than its parent has invested in the entity, the parent's basis in the subsidiary is zero, and the parent records additional losses in an excess loss account. This treatment allows the parent to continue to deduct losses of the subsidiary, even where no basis reduction is possible, while avoiding the need to show a negative stock basis on various financial records. If the subsidiary stock is sold while an excess loss account exists, capital gain income usually is recognized to the extent of the balance in the account.

Excise taxes. A tax on the manufacture, sale, or use of goods; on the carrying on of an occupation or activity; or on the transfer of property. Thus, the Federal estate and gift taxes are, theoretically, excise taxes.

Exclusion amount. The value of assets that is exempt from transfer tax due to the credit allowed for gifts or transfers by death. For gifts and deaths in 2018, the exclusion amount is $11.18 million. An exclusion amount unused by a deceased spouse may be used by the surviving spouse. See also *exemption equivalent amount*.

Exempt organizations. An organization that is either partially or completely exempt from Federal income taxation. § 501.

Exemption amount. An amount deducted from alternative minimum taxable income to determine the alternative minimum tax base. The exemption amount is phased out when AMTI exceeds specified threshold amounts. § 55(d).

Exemption equivalent. The maximum value of assets that can be transferred to another party without incurring any Federal gift or estate tax because of the application of the unified tax credit. See also *exemption equivalent amount*.

Exemption equivalent amount. The nontaxable amount (in 2018, $11.18 million for gift tax and estate tax) that is the equivalent of the unified transfer tax credit allowed.

F

Fair market value. The amount at which property would change hands between a willing buyer and a willing seller, neither being under any compulsion to buy or to sell and both having reasonable knowledge of the relevant facts. Reg. §§ 1.1001–1(a) and 20.2031–1(b).

Farm price method. A method of accounting for agricultural crops. The inventory of crops is valued at its market price less the estimated cost of disposition (e.g., freight and selling expense).

Federal District Court. A trial court for purposes of litigating Federal tax matters. It is the only trial court in which a jury trial can be obtained.

Feeder organization. An entity that carries on a trade or business for the benefit of an exempt organization. However, such a relationship does not result in the feeder organization itself being tax-exempt. § 502.

FICA tax. An abbreviation that stands for Federal Insurance Contributions Act, commonly referred to as the Social Security tax. The FICA tax is comprised of the Social Security tax (old age, survivors, and disability insurance) and the Medicare tax (hospital insurance) and is imposed on both employers and employees. The employer is responsible for withholding from the employee's wages the Social Security tax at a rate of 6.2 percent on a maximum wage base and the Medicare tax at a rate of 1.45 percent (no maximum wage base). The maximum Social Security wage base for 2018 is $128,400 and for 2017 is $127,200.

Fiduciary. One who holds a legal obligation to act on another's behalf. A *trustee* and an *executor* take fiduciary relationships relative to the *grantor* and the *decedent*, respectively. The fiduciary is assigned specific duties by the principal party (e.g., to file tax returns, manage assets, satisfy debt and other obligations, and to make investment decisions). The fiduciary often possesses specialized knowledge and experience. A fiduciary must avoid conflicts of interest in which the principal's goals are compromised in some way.

Field audit. An audit conducted by the IRS on the business premises of the taxpayer or in the office of the tax practitioner representing the taxpayer.

Filing status. Individual taxpayers are placed in one of five filing statuses each year (single, married filing jointly, married filing separately, surviving spouse, or head of household). Marital status and household support are key determinants. Filing status is used to determine the taxpayer's filing requirements, standard deduction, eligibility for certain deductions and credits, and tax liability.

Final Regulations. The U.S. Treasury Department Regulations (abbreviated Reg.) represent the position of the IRS as to how the Internal Revenue Code is to be interpreted. Their purpose is to provide taxpayers and IRS personnel with rules of general and specific application to the various provisions of the tax law. Regulations are published in the *Federal Register* and in all tax services.

Financial Accounting Standards Board (FASB). See *Generally Accepted Accounting Principles (GAAP)*.

Financial transaction tax. A tax imposed on some type of financial transaction, such as stock sales.

Fiscal year. A 12-month period ending on the last day of a month other than December. In certain circumstances, a taxpayer is permitted to elect a fiscal year instead of being required to use a calendar year.

Flat tax. A form of consumption tax designed to alleviate the regressivity of a value added tax (VAT). It is imposed on individuals and businesses at the same single (flat) rate.

Flexible spending plans. An employee benefit plan that allows the employee to take a reduction in salary in exchange for the employer paying benefits that can be provided by the employer without the employee being required to recognize income (e.g., medical and child care benefits). Contributions to a flexible spending plan are limited to $2,650 for 2018.

Flow-through entity. The entity is a tax reporter rather than a taxpayer. The owners are subject to tax. Examples are partnerships, S corporations, and limited liability companies.

Foreign earned income exclusion. The Code allows exclusions for earned income generated outside the United States to alleviate any tax base and rate disparities among countries. In addition, the exclusion is allowed for housing expenditures incurred by the taxpayer's employer with respect to the non-U.S. assignment, and self-employed individuals can deduct foreign housing expenses incurred in a trade or business. The exclusion is limited to $104,100 per year for 2018 ($102,100 in 2017). § 911.

Foreign Investment in Real Property Tax Act (FIRPTA). Under the Foreign Investment in Real Property Tax Act, gains or losses realized by nonresident aliens and non-U.S. corporations on the disposition of U.S. real estate creates U.S. source income and are subject to U.S. income tax.

Foreign tax credit (FTC). A U.S. citizen or resident who incurs or pays income taxes to a foreign country on income subject to U.S. tax may be able to claim some of these taxes as a credit against the U.S. income tax. §§ 27 and 901–905.

Franchise. An agreement that gives the transferee the right to distribute, sell, or provide goods, services, or facilities within a specified area. The cost of obtaining a franchise may be amortized over a statutory period of 15 years. In general, the franchisor's gain on the sale of franchise rights is an ordinary gain because the franchisor retains a significant power, right, or continuing interest in the subject of the franchise. §§ 197 and 1253.

Franchise tax. A tax levied on the right to do business in a state as a corporation. Although income considerations may come into play, the tax usually is based on the capitalization of the corporation.

Fraud. Tax fraud falls into two categories: civil and criminal. Under civil fraud, the IRS may impose as a penalty an amount equal to as much as 75 percent of the underpayment [§ 6651(f)]. Fines and/or imprisonment are prescribed for conviction of various types of criminal tax fraud (§§ 7201–7207). Both civil and criminal fraud involve a specific intent on the part of the taxpayer to evade the tax; mere negligence is not enough. Criminal fraud requires the additional element of willfulness (i.e., done deliberately and with evil purpose). In practice, it becomes difficult to distinguish between the degree of intent necessary to support criminal, rather than civil, fraud. In either situation, the IRS has the burden of proof to show the taxpayer committed fraud.

Fringe benefits. Compensation or other benefit received by an employee that is not in the form of cash. Some fringe benefits (e.g., accident and health plans, group term life insurance) may be excluded from the employee's gross income and therefore are not subject to the Federal income tax.

Fruit and tree metaphor. The courts have held that an individual who earns income from property or services cannot assign that income to another. For example, a father cannot assign his earnings from commissions to his child and escape income tax on those amounts.

Functional currency. The currency of the economic environment in which the taxpayer carries on most of its activities and in which the taxpayer transacts most of its business.

FUTA tax. An employment tax levied on employers. Jointly administered by the Federal and state governments, the tax provides funding for unemployment benefits. FUTA applies at a rate of 6.0 percent on the first $7,000 of covered wages paid during the year for each employee in 2018. The Federal government allows a credit for FUTA paid (or allowed under a merit rating system) to the state. The credit cannot exceed 5.4 percent of the covered wages.

Future interest. An interest that will come into being at some future time. It is distinguished from a present interest, which already exists. Assume that Dan transfers securities to a newly created trust. Under the terms of the trust instrument, income from the securities is to be paid each year to Wilma for her life, with the securities passing to Sam upon Wilma's death. Wilma has a present interest in the trust because she is entitled to current income distributions. Sam has a future interest because he must wait for Wilma's death to benefit from the trust. The annual exclusion of $15,000 (in 2018) is not allowed for a gift of a future interest. § 2503(b).

G

General business credit. The summation of various nonrefundable business credits, including the tax credit for rehabilitation expenditures, business energy credit, work opportunity credit, research activities credit, low-income housing credit, and disabled access credit. The amount of general business credit that can be used to reduce the tax liability is limited to the taxpayer's net income tax reduced by the greater of (1) the tentative minimum tax or (2) 25 percent of the net regular tax liability that exceeds $25,000. Unused general business credits can be carried back one year and forward 20 years. § 38.

General partners. A partner who is fully liable in an individual capacity for the debts owed by the partnership to third parties. A general partner's liability is not limited to the investment in the partnership. See also *limited partners*.

General partnership (GP). A partnership that is owned by one or more general partners. Creditors of a general partnership can collect amounts owed them from both the partnership assets and the assets of the partners individually.

Generally Accepted Accounting Principles (GAAP). Guidelines relating to how to construct the financial statements of enterprises doing business in the United States. Promulgated chiefly by the Financial Accounting Standards Board (FASB).

Gift tax. A tax imposed on the transfer of property by gift. The tax is imposed upon the donor of a gift and is based on the fair market value of the property on the date of the gift.

Golden parachute payments. A severance payment to employees that meets the following requirements: (1) the payment is contingent on a change of ownership of a corporation through a stock or asset acquisition and (2) the aggregate present value of the payment equals or exceeds three times the employee's average annual compensation. To the extent the severance payment meets these conditions, a deduction is disallowed to the employer for the excess of the payment over a statutory base amount (a five-year average of compensation if the taxpayer was an employee for the entire five-year period). In addition, a 20 percent excise tax is imposed on the employee who receives the excess severance pay. §§ 280G and 4999.

Goodwill. The reputation and built-up business of a company. For accounting purposes, goodwill has no basis unless it is purchased. In the purchase of a business, goodwill generally is the difference between the purchase price and the fair market value of the assets acquired. The intangible asset goodwill can be amortized for tax purposes over a 15-year period. § 197 and Reg. § 1.167(a)–3.

Grantor. A transferor of property. The creator of a trust is usually referred to as the grantor of the entity.

Grantor trust. A trust under which the grantor retains control over the income or corpus (or both) to such an extent that he or she is treated as the owner of the property and its income for income tax purposes. Income from a grantor trust is taxable to the grantor and not to the beneficiary who receives it. §§ 671–679.

Grass roots expenditures. Exempt organizations are prohibited from engaging in political activities, but spending incurred to influence the opinions of the general public relative to specific legislation is permitted by the law.

Gross estate. The property owned or previously transferred by a decedent that is subject to the Federal estate tax. The gross estate can be distinguished from the probate estate, which is property actually subject to administration by the administrator or executor of an estate. §§ 2031–2046.

Gross income. Income subject to the Federal income tax. Gross income does not include all economic income. That is, certain exclusions are allowed (e.g., interest on municipal bonds). For a manufacturing or merchandising business, gross income usually means gross profit (gross sales or gross receipts less cost of goods sold). § 61 and Reg. § 1.61–3(a).

Group term life insurance. Life insurance coverage provided by an employer for a group of employees. Such insurance is renewable on a year-to-year basis, and typically no cash surrender value is built up. The premiums paid by the employer on the insurance are not taxed to the employees on coverage of up to $50,000 per person. § 79 and Reg. § 1.79–1(b).

Guaranteed payments. Payments made by a partnership to a partner for services rendered or for the use of capital to the extent the payments are determined without regard to the income of the partnership. The payments are treated as though they were made to a nonpartner and thus are deducted by the entity. A guaranteed payment might be subject to self-employment tax (guaranteed payment for services) or net-investment income tax (guaranteed payment for capital). In addition, a guaranteed payment for capital might be eligible for the qualified business income deduction, but a guaranteed payment for services is not.

H

H.R. 10 (Keogh) plans. See *Keogh plans*.

Half-year convention. A cost recovery convention that assumes that property is placed in service at mid-year and thus provides for a half-year's cost recovery for that year.

Head of household. An unmarried individual who maintains a household for another and satisfies certain conditions set forth in § 2(b). This status enables the taxpayer to use a set of income tax rates that are lower than those applicable to other unmarried individuals but higher than those applicable to surviving spouses and married persons filing a joint return.

Health Savings Account (HSA). A medical savings account created in legislation enacted in December 2003 that is designed to replace and expand Archer Medical Savings Accounts.

Highly compensated employee. The employee group is generally divided into two categories for fringe benefit (including pension and profit sharing plans) purposes. These are (1) highly compensated employees and (2) non-highly compensated employees. For most fringe benefits, if the fringe benefit plan discriminates in favor of highly compensated employees, it will not be a qualified plan with respect, at a minimum, to the highly compensated employees.

Historic business test. In a corporate reorganization, a means by which to determine if the continuity of business enterprise requirement is met. The acquiring corporation must continue to operate the target entity's existing business(es) going forward; if this is not the case, the requirement is failed.

Hobby losses. Losses from an activity not engaged in for profit. The Code restricts the amount of losses that an individual can deduct for hobby activities so that these transactions cannot be used to offset income from other sources. The TCJA of 2017 suspended the deduction of hobby expenses for tax years after 2017 (and through 2025). § 183.

Holding period. The period of time during which property has been held for income tax purposes. The holding period is significant in determining whether gain or loss from the sale or exchange of a capital asset is long or short term. § 1223.

Home equity loans. Loans that utilize the personal residence of the taxpayer as security. The interest on such loans is deductible as qualified residence interest. However, interest is deductible only on the portion of the loan that does not exceed the lesser of (1) the fair market value of the residence, reduced by the acquisition indebtedness, or (2) $100,000 ($50,000 for married persons filing separate returns). A major benefit of a home equity loan is that there are no tracing rules regarding the use of the loan proceeds. The TCJA of 2017 suspended the deduction of interest on home equity indebtedness for tax years after 2017 (and through 2025). § 163(h)(3).

Hot assets. Unrealized receivables and substantially appreciated inventory under § 751. When hot assets are present, the sale of a partnership interest or the disproportionate distribution of the assets can cause ordinary income to be recognized.

Hybrid method. A combination of the accrual and cash methods of accounting. That is, the taxpayer may account for some items of income on the accrual method (e.g., sales and cost of goods sold) and other items (e.g., interest income) on the cash method.

I

Imputed interest. For certain long-term sales of property, under §§ 483 and 1274 the IRS can convert some of the gain from the sale into interest income if the contract does not provide for a minimum rate of interest to be paid by the purchaser. The seller recognizes less long-term capital gain and more ordinary income (interest income). Imputed interest rules also apply on certain below-market loans under § 7872.

Inbound taxation. U.S. tax effects when a non-U.S. person begins an investment or business activity in the United States.

Incentive stock options (ISOs). A type of stock option that receives favorable tax treatment. If various qualification requirements can be satisfied, stock option grants do not create taxable income for the recipient. However, the spread (the excess of the fair market value at the date of exercise over the option price) is a tax preference item for purposes of the alternative minimum tax. The gain on disposition of the stock resulting from the exercise of the stock option will be classified as long-term capital gain if certain holding period requirements are met (the employee must not dispose of the stock within two years after the option is granted or within one year after acquiring the stock). § 422.

Income. For tax purposes, an increase in wealth that has been realized.

Income in respect of a decedent (IRD). Income earned by a decedent at the time of death but not reportable on the final income tax return because of the method of accounting that appropriately is utilized. Such income is included in the gross estate and is taxed to the eventual recipient (either the estate or heirs). The recipient is, however, allowed an income tax deduction for the estate tax attributable to the income. § 691.

Income tax provision. Under ASC 740, a synonym for the book tax expense of an entity for the financial reporting period. Following the "matching principle," all book tax expense that relates to the net income for the reporting period is reported on that period's financial statements, including not only the current tax expense but also any deferred tax expense and deferred tax benefit.

Income tax treaties. See *tax treaties*.

Independent contractor. A self-employed person as distinguished from one who is employed as an employee.

Indexation. A procedure whereby adjustments are made by the IRS to key tax components (e.g., standard deduction, tax brackets, personal and dependency exemptions) to reflect inflation. The adjustments usually are made annually and are based on the change in the consumer price index.

Individual Retirement Account (IRA). A type of retirement plan to which an individual with earned income can contribute a statutory maximum of $5,500 in 2018. IRAs can be classified as traditional IRAs or Roth IRAs. With a traditional IRA, an individual can contribute and deduct a maximum of $5,500 per tax year in 2018. The deduction is a deduction *for* AGI. However, if the individual is an active participant in another qualified retirement plan, the deduction is phased out proportionally between certain AGI ranges (note that the phaseout limits the amount of the deduction and not the amount of the contribution). With a Roth IRA, an individual can contribute a maximum of $5,500 per tax year in 2018. No deduction is permitted. However, if a five-year holding period requirement is satisfied and if the distribution is a qualified distribution, the taxpayer can make tax-free withdrawals from a Roth IRA. The maximum annual contribution is phased out proportionally between certain AGI ranges. §§ 219 and 408A.

Individual Shared Responsibility Payment (ISRP). A mandate or penalty tax that individuals owe starting in 2014 for any month in which they do not have health coverage and do not qualify for an exemption. This mandate was created as part of the Affordable Care Act to encourage individuals to obtain health care coverage. If owed, the penalty is the greater of a "flat dollar amount" or a percentage of household income less the filing threshold. For 2018, the flat dollar amount is $695 and the percent applied to household income is 2.5 percent. For a family, the flat dollar amount cannot exceed three times the flat dollar amount. The overall cap on the penalty is the national average cost of a bronze level plan (this amount is published by the IRS). Worksheets for computing the penalty are included in the instructions to Form 8965 (Health Coverage Exemptions). For months beginning after 2018, the penalty is zero. § 5000A.

Inheritance tax. A tax imposed on the right to receive property from a decedent. Thus, theoretically, an inheritance tax is imposed on the heir. The Federal estate tax is imposed on the estate.

Inside basis. A partnership's basis in the assets it owns.

Installment method. A method of accounting enabling certain taxpayers to spread the recognition of gain on the sale of property over the collection period. Under this procedure, the seller arrives at the gain to be recognized by computing the gross profit percentage from the sale (the gain divided by the contract price) and applying it to each payment received. § 453.

Intangible drilling and development costs (IDCs). Taxpayers may elect to expense or capitalize (subject to amortization) intangible drilling and development costs. However, ordinary income recapture provisions apply to oil and gas properties on a sale or other disposition if the expense method is elected. §§ 263(c) and 1254(a).

Intermediate sanctions. The IRS can assess excise taxes on disqualified persons and organization management associated with so-called public charities engaging in excess benefit transactions. An excess benefit transaction is one in which a disqualified person engages in a non-fair market value transaction with the exempt organization or receives unreasonable compensation. Prior to the idea of intermediate sanctions, the only option available to the IRS was to revoke the organization's exempt status.

International Accounting Standards Board (IASB). The body that promulgates International Financial Reporting Standards (IFRS). Based in London, representing accounting standard setting bodies in over 100 countries, the IASB develops accounting standards that can serve as the basis for harmonizing conflicting reporting standards among nations.

International Financial Reporting Standards (IFRS). Produced by the International Accounting Standards Board (IASB), guidelines developed since 2001 as to revenue recognition, accounting for business combinations, and a conceptual framework for financial reporting. IFRS provisions are designed so that they can be used by all entities, regardless of where they are based or conduct business. IFRS have gained widespread acceptance throughout the world, and the SEC is considering how to require U.S. entities to use IFRS in addition to, or in lieu of, the accounting rules of the Financial Accounting Standards Board.

Interpretive Regulations. A Regulation issued by the Treasury Department that purports to explain the meaning of a particular Code Section. An interpretive Regulation is given less deference than a legislative Regulation.

Inventory. Under § 1221(a)(1), a taxpayer's stock in trade or property held for resale. For partnership tax purposes, inventory is defined in § 751(d) as inventory (per the above definition) or any partnership asset other than capital or § 1231 assets. See also *appreciated inventory.*

Investment income. Consisting of virtually the same elements as portfolio income, a measure by which to justify a deduction for interest on investment indebtedness.

Investment interest. Payment for the use of funds used to acquire assets that produce investment income. The deduction for investment interest is limited to net investment income for the tax year.

Investor loss. Losses on stock and securities. If stocks and bonds are capital assets in the hands of the holder, a capital loss materializes as of the last day of the taxable year in which the stocks or bonds become worthless. Under certain circumstances involving stocks and bonds of affiliated corporations, an ordinary loss is permitted upon worthlessness.

Involuntary conversion. The loss or destruction of property through theft, casualty, or condemnation. Gain realized on an involuntary conversion can, at the taxpayer's election, be deferred for Federal income tax purposes if the owner reinvests the proceeds within a prescribed period of time in property that is similar or related in service or use. § 1033.

Itemized deductions. Personal expenditures allowed by the Code as deductions from adjusted gross income. Examples include certain medical expenses, interest on home mortgages, state income taxes, and charitable contributions. Itemized deductions are reported on Schedule A of Form 1040.

J

Joint tenants. Two or more persons having undivided ownership of property with the right of survivorship. Right of survivorship gives the surviving owner full ownership of the property. Suppose Bob and Tami are joint tenants of a tract of land. Upon Bob's death, Tami becomes the sole owner of the property. For the estate tax consequences upon the death of a joint tenant, see § 2040.

K

Keogh plans. Retirement plans available to self-employed taxpayers. They are also referred to as H.R. 10 plans. Under such plans, a taxpayer may deduct each year up to 100 percent of net earnings from self-employment or $55,000

for 2018, whichever is less. If the plan is a profit sharing plan, the percentage is 25 percent.

Kiddie tax. Passive income, such as interest and dividends, that is recognized by a child under age 19 (or under age 24 if a full-time student) is taxed according to the brackets applicable to estates and trusts, generally to the extent the income exceeds $2,100 for 2018. The additional tax is assessed regardless of the source of the income or the income's underlying property. § 1(g).

L

Least aggregate deferral method. An algorithm set forth in the Regulations to determine the tax year for a partnership or an S corporation with owners whose tax years differ. The tax year selected is the one that produces the least aggregate deferral of income for the owners.

Least aggregate deferral rule. See *least aggregate deferral method.*

Legislative Regulations. Some Code Sections give the Secretary of the Treasury or his delegate the authority to prescribe Regulations to carry out the details of administration or to otherwise complete the operating rules. Regulations issued pursuant to this type of authority truly possess the force and effect of law. In effect, Congress is almost delegating its legislative powers to the Treasury Department.

Lessee. One who rents property from another. In the case of real estate, the lessee is also known as the tenant.

Lessor. One who rents property to another. In the case of real estate, the lessor is also known as the landlord.

Letter ruling. The written response of the IRS to a taxpayer's request for interpretation of the revenue laws with respect to a proposed transaction (e.g., concerning the tax-free status of a reorganization). Not to be relied on as precedent by other than the party who requested the ruling.

Liabilities in excess of basis. On the contribution of capital to a corporation, an investor recognizes gain on the exchange to the extent contributed assets carry liabilities with a face amount in excess of the tax basis of the contributed assets. This rule keeps the investor from holding the investment asset received with a negative basis. § 357(c).

Life insurance proceeds. A specified sum (the face value or maturity value of the policy) paid to the designated beneficiary of the policy by the life insurance company upon the death of the insured.

Lifetime learning credit. A tax credit for qualifying expenses for taxpayers pursuing education beyond the first two years of postsecondary education. Individuals who are completing their last two years of undergraduate studies, pursuing graduate or professional degrees, or otherwise seeking new job skills or maintaining existing job skills are all eligible for the credit. Eligible individuals include the taxpayer, taxpayer's spouse, and taxpayer's dependents. The maximum credit is 20 percent of the first $10,000 of qualifying expenses and is computed per taxpayer. The credit is phased out for higher-income taxpayers. § 25A.

Like-kind exchanges. An exchange of real property held for productive use in a trade or business or for investment for other investment or trade or business real property. Unless non-like-kind property (boot) is received, the exchange is fully tax-deferred. § 1031.

Limited liability company (LLC). A legal entity in which all owners are protected from the entity's debts but which may lack other characteristics of a corporation (i.e., centralized management, unlimited life, free transferability of interests). LLCs are treated as partnerships (or disregarded entities if they have only one owner) for tax purposes.

Limited liability partnership (LLP). A legal entity allowed by many of the states, where a general partnership registers with the state as an LLP. All partners are at risk with respect to any contractual liabilities of the entity as well as any liabilities arising from their own malpractice or torts or those of their subordinates. However, all partners are protected from any liabilities resulting from the malpractice or torts of other partners.

Limited partners. A partner whose liability to third-party creditors of the partnership is limited to the amounts invested in the partnership. See also *general partners* and *limited partnership (LP)*.

Limited partnership (LP). A partnership in which some of the partners are limited partners. At least one of the partners in a limited partnership must be a general partner.

Liquidating distribution. A distribution by a partnership that is in complete liquidation of the entity's trade or business activities or in complete liquidation of a partner's interest in the partnership. A liquidating distribution is generally a tax-deferred transaction if it is proportionate with respect to the partnership's hot assets. In a proportionate liquidating distribution, the partnership recognizes no gain or loss. The partner only recognizes gain if the distributed cash (and cash equivalents, such as debt relief or certain marketable securities) exceeds the partner's basis in the partnership. The partner recognizes a loss if *only* cash and hot assets are distributed and their combined inside (partnership) basis is less than the partner's basis in the partnership interest. In any case where no gain or loss is recognized, the partner's basis in the partnership interest is fully assigned to the basis of the assets received in the distribution.

Listed property. Property that includes (1) any passenger automobile; (2) any other property used as a means of transportation; (3) any property of a type generally used for purposes of entertainment, recreation, or amusement; and (4) any other property of a type specified in the Regulations. If listed property is predominantly used for business, the taxpayer is allowed to use the statutory percentage method of cost recovery. Otherwise, the straight-line cost recovery method must be used. § 280F.

Lobbying expenditures. An expenditure made for the purpose of influencing legislation. Such payments can result in the loss of the exempt status of, and the imposition of Federal income tax on, an exempt organization. Lobby expenditures are not deductible.

Long-term care insurance. Insurance that helps pay the cost of care when the insured is unable to care for himself or herself. Such insurance is generally thought of as insurance against the cost of an aged person entering a nursing home. The employer can provide the insurance, and the premiums may be excluded from the employee's gross income. § 7702B.

Long-term contract. A building, installation, construction, or manufacturing contract that is entered into but not completed within the same tax year. A manufacturing contract is a long-term contract only if the contract is to manufacture (1) a unique item not normally carried in finished goods inventory or (2) items that normally require more than 12 calendar months to complete. The two available methods to account for long-term contracts are the percentage of completion method and the completed contract method. The completed contract method can be used only in limited circumstances. § 460.

Long-term nonpersonal use capital assets. Includes investment property with a long-term holding period. Such property disposed of by casualty or theft may receive § 1231 treatment.

Long-term tax-exempt rate. Used in deriving the yearly limitation on net operating loss and other tax benefits that carry over from the target to the acquiring when there is a more than 50-percentage-point ownership change (by value). The highest of the Federal long-term interest rates in effect for any of the last three months. § 382.

Lower of cost or market (replacement cost). An elective inventory method, whereby the taxpayer may value inventories at the lower of the taxpayer's actual cost or the current replacement cost of the goods. This method cannot be used in conjunction with the LIFO inventory method.

Low-income housing credit. Beneficial treatment to owners of low-income housing is provided in the form of a tax credit. The calculated credit is claimed in the year the building is placed in service and in the following nine years. § 42.

Lump-sum distribution. Payment of the entire amount due at one time rather than in installments. Such distributions often occur from qualified pension or profit sharing plans upon the retirement or death of a covered employee. The recipient of a lump-sum distribution may recognize both long-term capital gain and ordinary income upon the receipt of the distribution. The ordinary income portion may be subject to a special 10-year income averaging provision. § 402(e).

M

Majority interest partners. Partners who have more than a 50 percent interest in partnership profits and capital, counting only those partners who have the same taxable year. The term is of significance in determining the appropriate taxable year of a partnership. § 706(b).

Marital deduction. A deduction allowed against the taxable estate or taxable gifts upon the transfer of property from one spouse to another.

Marriage penalty. The additional tax liability that results for a married couple when compared with what their tax liability would be if they were not married and filed separate returns.

Matching rule. Treatment of an intercompany transaction on a consolidated return, when a sold asset remains within the group.

Material participation. If an individual taxpayer materially participates in a nonrental trade or business activity, any loss from that activity is treated as an active loss that can be offset against active income. Material participation is achieved by meeting any one of seven tests provided in the Regulations. § 469(h).

Meaningful reduction test. A decrease in the shareholder's voting control. Used to determine whether a stock redemption qualifies for sale or exchange treatment.

Medical expenses. Medical expenses of an individual, a spouse, and dependents are allowed as an itemized deduction to the extent such amounts (less insurance reimbursements) exceed 7.5 percent (10 percent for tax years beginning after 2018) of adjusted gross income. § 213.

Merger. The absorption of one corporation by another with the corporation being absorbed losing its legal identity. Flow Corporation is merged into Jobs Corporation, and the shareholders of Flow receive stock in Jobs in exchange for their stock in Flow. After the merger, Flow ceases to exist as a separate legal entity. If a merger meets certain conditions, it is not currently taxable to the parties involved. § 368(a)(1).

Mid-month convention. A cost recovery convention that assumes that property is placed in service in the middle of the month that it is actually placed in service.

Mid-quarter convention. A cost recovery convention that assumes that property placed in service during the year is placed in service at the middle of the quarter in which it is actually placed in service. The mid-quarter convention applies if more than 40 percent of the value of property (other than eligible real estate) is placed in service during the last quarter of the year.

Miscellaneous itemized deductions. A special category of itemized deductions that includes expenses such as professional dues, tax return preparation fees, job-hunting costs, unreimbursed employee business expenses, and certain investment expenses. Such expenses are deductible only to the extent they exceed 2 percent of adjusted gross income. The TCJA of 2017 suspended the deduction for these items for 2018 through 2025. § 67.

Modified accelerated cost recovery system (MACRS). A method in which the cost of tangible property is recovered over a prescribed period of time. Enacted by the Economic Recovery Tax Act (ERTA) of 1981 and substantially modified by the Tax Reform Act (TRA) of 1986, the method disregards salvage value, imposes a period of cost recovery that depends upon the classification of the asset into one of various recovery periods, and prescribes the applicable percentage of cost that can be deducted each year. § 168.

Multiple support agreement. To qualify for a dependency exemption, the support test must be satisfied. This requires that over 50 percent of the support of the potential dependent be provided by the taxpayer. Where no one person provides more than 50 percent of the support, a multiple support agreement enables a taxpayer to still qualify for the dependency exemption. Any person who contributed more than 10 percent of the support is entitled to claim the exemption if each person in the group who contributed more than 10 percent files a written consent (Form 2120). Each person who is a party to the multiple support agreement must meet all of the other requirements for claiming the dependency exemption. § 152(c).

Multistate Tax Commission (MTC). A regulatory body of the states that develops operating rules and regulations for the implementation of the UDITPA and other provisions that assign the total taxable income of a multistate corporation to specific states.

N

National sales tax. Intended as a replacement for the current Federal income tax. Unlike a value added tax (VAT), which is levied on the manufacturer, it would be imposed on the consumer upon the final sale of goods and services. To reduce regressivity, individuals would receive a rebate to offset a portion of the tax.

Negligence. Failure to exercise the reasonable or ordinary degree of care of a prudent person in a situation that results in harm or damage to another. A penalty is assessed on taxpayers who exhibit negligence or intentional disregard of rules and Regulations with respect to the underpayment of certain taxes.

Net capital gain (NCG). The excess of the net long-term capital gain for the tax year over the net short-term capital loss. The net capital gain of an individual taxpayer is eligible for the alternative tax. § 1222(11).

Net capital loss (NCL). The excess of the losses from sales or exchanges of capital assets over the gains from sales or exchanges of such assets. Up to $3,000 per year of the net capital loss may be deductible by noncorporate taxpayers against ordinary income. The excess net capital loss carries over to future tax years. For corporate taxpayers, the net capital loss cannot be offset against ordinary income, but it can be carried back three years and forward five years to offset net capital gains. §§ 1211, 1212, and 1221(10).

Net investment income. The excess of investment income over investment expenses. Investment expenses are those deductible expenses directly connected with the production of investment income. Investment expenses do not include investment interest. The deduction for investment interest for the tax year is limited to net investment income. § 163(d).

Net operating loss (NOL). To mitigate the effect of the annual accounting period concept, § 172 allows taxpayers to use an excess loss of one year as a deduction for certain past or future years. In this regard, a carryback period of two (or more) years and a carryforward period of 20 years are allowed for NOLs generated before 2018. There is no carryback period and an indefinite carryforward period for NOLs arising in tax years beginning after 2017, and such NOLs are subject to an 80 percent of taxable income limitation in any carryforward year.

Nexus. The degree of activity that must be present before a taxing jurisdiction has the right to impose a tax on an out-of-state entity. The rules for income tax nexus are not the same as for sales tax nexus.

Ninety-day (90-day) letter. This notice is sent to a taxpayer upon request, upon the expiration of the 30-day letter, or upon exhaustion by the taxpayer of his or her administrative remedies before the IRS. The notice gives the taxpayer 90 days in which to file a petition with the U.S. Tax Court.

If a petition is not filed, the IRS will demand payment of the assessed deficiency. §§ 6211–6216.

No-additional-cost service. Services the employer may provide the employee at no additional cost to the employer. Generally, the benefit is the ability to utilize the employer's excess capacity (e.g., vacant seats on an airliner). Such amounts are excludible from the recipient's gross income.

Nonaccountable plan. An expense reimbursement plan that does not have an accountability feature. The result is that employee expenses are not deductible.

Nonacquiescence. Disagreement by the IRS on the result reached in certain judicial decisions. *Nonacq.* or *NA*.

Nonbusiness bad debt. A bad debt loss that is not incurred in connection with a creditor's trade or business. The loss is classified as a short-term capital loss and is allowed only in the year the debt becomes entirely worthless. In addition to family loans, many investor losses are nonbusiness bad debts. § 166(d).

Nonqualified deferred compensation (NQDC). Compensation arrangements that are frequently offered to executives. Such plans may include stock options and restricted stock, for example. Often, an executive may defer the recognition of taxable income. The employer, however, does not receive a tax deduction until the employee is required to include the compensation in income.

Nonqualified stock option (NQSO). A type of stock option that does not satisfy the statutory requirements of an incentive stock option. If the NQSO has a readily ascertainable fair market value (e.g., the option is traded on an established exchange), the value of the option must be included in the employee's gross income at the date of the grant. Otherwise, the employee does not recognize income at the grant date. Instead, ordinary income is recognized in the year of exercise of the option.

Nonrecourse debt. Debt secured by the property that it is used to purchase. The purchaser of the property is not personally liable for the debt upon default. Rather, the creditor's recourse is to repossess the related property. Nonrecourse debt generally does not increase the purchaser's at-risk amount.

Nonrefundable credits. A credit that is not paid if it exceeds the taxpayer's tax liability. Some nonrefundable credits qualify for carryback and carryover treatment.

Nonresident alien (NRA). An individual who is neither a citizen nor a resident of the United States. Citizenship is determined under the immigration and naturalization laws of the United States. Residency is determined under § 7701(b) of the Internal Revenue Code.

Nontaxable exchange. A transaction in which realized gains or losses are not recognized. The recognition of gain or loss is postponed (deferred) until the property received in the nontaxable exchange is subsequently disposed of in a taxable transaction. Examples are § 1031 like-kind exchanges and § 1033 involuntary conversions.

Not essentially equivalent redemption. Sale or exchange treatment is given to this type of redemption. Although various safe-harbor tests are failed, the nature of the redemption is such that dividend treatment is avoided, because it represents a meaningful reduction in the shareholder's interest in the corporation. § 302(b)(1).

Occupational fee. A tax imposed on various trades or businesses. A license fee that enables a taxpayer to engage in a particular occupation.

Occupational taxes. See *occupational fee.*

Offer in compromise. A settlement agreement offered by the IRS in a tax dispute, especially where there is doubt as to the collectibility of the full deficiency. Offers in compromise can include installment payment schedules as well as reductions in the tax and penalties owed by the taxpayer.

Office audit. An audit conducted by the IRS in the agent's office.

Office in the home expenses. Employment and business-related expenses attributable to the use of a residence (e.g., den or office) are allowed only if the portion of the residence is exclusively used on a regular basis as a principal place of business of the taxpayer or as a place of business that is used by patients, clients, or customers. In computing the office in the home expenses, a taxpayer can use either the regular method or simplified method. As a general rule, the regular method requires more effort and recordkeeping but results in a larger deduction. Office in home expenses incurred by an employee are not deductible. § 280A.

One-year rule for prepaid expenses. Taxpayers who use the cash method are required to use the accrual method for deducting certain prepaid expenses (i.e., must capitalize the item and can deduct only when used). If a prepayment will not be consumed or expire by the end of the tax year following the year of payment, the prepayment must be capitalized and prorated over the benefit period. Conversely, if the prepayment will be consumed by the end of the tax year following the year of payment, it can be expensed when paid. To obtain the current deduction under the one-year rule, the payment must be a required payment rather than a voluntary payment.

Operating agreement. The governing document of a limited liability company. This document is similar in structure, function, and purpose to a partnership agreement.

Optional adjustment election. See *Section 754 election.*

Options. The sale or exchange of an option to buy or sell property results in capital gain or loss if the property is a capital asset. Generally, the closing of an option transaction results in short-term capital gain or loss to the writer of the call and the purchaser of the call option. § 1234.

Ordinary and necessary. Two tests for the deductibility of expenses incurred or paid in connection with a trade or business; for the production or collection of income; for the management, conservation, or maintenance of property held for the production of income; or in connection with the determination, collection, or refund of any tax. An expense is ordinary if it is common and accepted in the general industry or type of activity in which the taxpayer is engaged. An expense is necessary if it is appropriate and helpful in furthering the taxpayer's business or income-producing activity. §§ 162(a) and 212.

Ordinary income property. Property contributed to a charitable organization that, if sold rather than contributed, would have resulted in other than long-term capital gain to the donor (i.e., ordinary income property and short-term capital gain property). Examples are inventory and capital assets held for less than the long-term holding period. A contribution of ordinary income property must generally be valued at its fair market value less the gain, if any, that would have been realized if sold.

Organizational costs. See *organizational expenditures.*

Organizational expenditures. Expenditures related to the creation of a corporation or partnership. Common organizational expenditures include legal and accounting fees and state incorporation payments. Organizational expenditures exclude those incurred to obtain capital (underwriting fees) or assets (subject to cost recovery). Such expenditures incurred by the end of the entity's first year are eligible for a $5,000 limited expensing (subject to phaseout) and an amortization of the balance over 180 months. §§ 248 and 709(b).

Original issue discount (OID). The difference between the issue price of a debt obligation (e.g., a corporate bond) and the maturity value of the obligation when the issue price is less than the maturity value. OID represents interest and must be amortized over the life of the debt obligation using the effective interest method. The difference is not considered to be original issue discount for tax purposes when it is less than one-fourth of 1 percent of the redemption price at maturity multiplied by the number of years to maturity. §§ 1272 and 1273(a)(3).

Other adjustments account (OAA). Used in the context of a distribution from an S corporation. The net accumulation of the entity's exempt income (e.g., municipal bond interest).

Other property. In a corporate reorganization, any property in the exchange that is not stock or securities, such as cash or land. This amount constitutes boot. This treatment is similar to that in a like-kind exchange.

Outbound taxation. U.S. tax effects when a U.S. person begins an investment or business activity outside the United States.

Outside basis. A partner's basis in his or her partnership interest.

Ownership change. An event that triggers a § 382 limitation for the acquiring corporation.

P

Parent-subsidiary controlled group. A controlled or affiliated group of corporations where at least one corporation is at least 80 percent owned by one or more of the others. The affiliated group definition is more difficult to meet.

Partial liquidation. A stock redemption where noncorporate shareholders are permitted sale or exchange treatment. In certain cases, an active business must have existed for at least five years. Only a portion of the outstanding stock in the entity is retired. §§ 302(b)(4) and (e).

Partnership. For income tax purposes, a partnership includes a syndicate, group, pool, or joint venture as well as ordinary partnerships. In an ordinary partnership, two or more parties combine capital and/or services to carry on a business for profit as co-owners. § 7701(a)(2).

Partnership agreement. The governing document of a partnership. A partnership agreement should describe the rights and obligations of the partners; the allocation of entity income, deductions, and cash flows; initial and future capital contribution requirements; conditions for terminating the partnership; and other matters.

Passive activity loss. Any loss from (1) activities in which the taxpayer does not materially participate or (2) rental activities (subject to certain exceptions). Net passive losses cannot be used to offset income from nonpassive sources. Rather, they are suspended until the taxpayer either generates net passive income (and a deduction of such losses is allowed) or disposes of the underlying property (at which time the loss deductions are allowed in full). One relief provision allows landlords who actively participate in the rental activities to deduct up to $25,000 of passive losses annually. However, a phaseout of the $25,000 amount commences when the landlord's AGI exceeds $100,000. Another relief provision applies for material participation in a real estate trade or business.

Passive investment company. A means by which a multistate corporation can reduce the overall effective tax rate by isolating investment income in a low- or no-tax state.

Passive investment income (PII). Gross receipts from royalties, certain rents, dividends, interest, annuities, and gains from the sale or exchange of stock and securities. When earnings and profits (E & P) also exists, if the passive investment income of an S corporation exceeds 25 percent of the corporation's gross receipts for three consecutive years, S status is lost.

Pass-through entity. A form of business structure for which the income and other tax items are attributed directly to the owners and generally no separate tax is levied upon the entity itself. Examples include sole proprietorships, partnerships, and S corporations. Also referred to as a flowthrough entity.

Patent. An intangible asset that may be amortized over a statutory 15-year period as a § 197 intangible. The sale of a patent usually results in favorable long-term capital gain treatment. §§ 197 and 1235.

Payroll factor. The proportion of a multistate corporation's total payroll that is traceable to a specific state. Used in determining the taxable income that is to be apportioned to that state.

Pension plan. A type of deferred compensation arrangement that provides for systematic payments of definitely determinable retirement benefits to employees who meet the requirements set forth in the plan.

Percentage depletion. Depletion based on a statutory percentage applied to the gross income from the property. The taxpayer deducts the greater of cost depletion or percentage depletion. § 613.

Percentage of completion method. A method of reporting gain or loss on certain long-term contracts. Under this method of accounting, the gross contract price is included in income as the contract is completed. Reg. § 1.451–3.

Permanent and total disability. A person is considered permanently and totally disabled if he or she is unable to engage in any substantial gainful activity due to a physical or mental impairment. In addition, this impairment must be one that can be expected to result in death or that has lasted or can be expected to last for a continuous period of not less than 12 months. The taxpayer generally must provide the IRS with a physician's statement documenting this condition.

Permanent differences. Under ASC 740, tax-related items that appear in the entity's financial statements or its tax return but not both. For instance, interest income from a municipal bond is a permanent book-tax difference.

Permanent establishment (PE). A level of business activity, as defined under an income tax treaty, that subjects the taxpayer to taxation in a country other than that in which the taxpayer is based. Often evidenced by the presence of a plant, an office, or other fixed place of business. Inventory storage and temporary activities do not rise to the level of a PE. PE is the treaty's equivalent to nexus.

Personal and dependency exemptions. The tax law provides an exemption for each individual taxpayer and an additional exemption for the taxpayer's spouse if a joint return is filed. An individual may also claim a dependency exemption for each dependent, provided certain tests are met. Beginning in 2018, however, the TCJA of 2017 suspended the deduction for exemptions through 2025.

Personal exemptions. See *personal and dependency exemptions.*

Personal holding company (PHC) tax. A penalty tax imposed on certain closely held corporations with excessive investment income. Assessed at a 20 percent tax rate on personal holding company income, reduced by dividends paid and other adjustments. § 541.

Personal residence. If a residence has been owned and used by the taxpayer as the principal residence for at least two years during the five-year period ending on the date of sale, up to $250,000 of realized gain is excluded from gross income. For a married couple filing a joint return, the $250,000 is increased to $500,000 if either spouse satisfies the ownership requirement and both spouses satisfy the use requirement. § 121.

Personal service corporation (PSC). A corporation whose principal activity is the performance of personal services (e.g., health, law, engineering, architecture, accounting, actuarial science, performing arts, or consulting) and where such services are substantially performed by the employee-owners.

Personalty. All property that is not attached to real estate (realty) and is movable. Examples of personalty are machinery, automobiles, clothing, household furnishings, and personal effects.

Points. Loan origination fees that may be deductible as interest by a buyer of property. A seller of property who pays points reduces the selling price by the amount of the points paid for the buyer. While the seller is not permitted to deduct this amount as interest, the buyer may do so.

Portfolio income. Income from interest, dividends, rentals, royalties, capital gains, or other investment sources. Net passive losses cannot be used to offset net portfolio income.

Precedents. A previously decided court decision that is recognized as authority for the disposition of future decisions.

Precontribution gain or loss. Partnerships allow for a variety of special allocations of gain or loss among the partners, but gain or loss that is "built in" on an asset contributed to the partnership is assigned specifically to the contributing partner. § 704(c)(1)(A).

Preferences. In calculating alternative minimum taxable income (AMTI), certain preference items are added to the taxable income starting point of the AMT calculation. AMT preferences generally reflect amounts allowed in the calculation of regular taxable income but not in the calculation of AMTI. For instance, interest income from certain state and local bonds (i.e., private activity bonds) may be an AMT preference item.

Preferred stock bailout. A process where a shareholder used the issuance and sale, or later redemption, of a preferred stock dividend to obtain long-term capital gains, without any loss of voting control over the corporation. In effect, the shareholder received corporate profits without suffering the consequences of dividend income treatment. This procedure led Congress to enact § 306, which, if applicable, converts the prior long-term capital gain on the sale or redemption of the tainted stock to dividend income.

Premium Tax Credit (PTC). A tax credit that is refundable and available in advance of filing a return for the year. The PTC serves to reduce the cost of health coverage obtained on the Marketplace (Exchange). A PTC is available to individuals who purchase coverage on the Exchange and have household income equal to or greater than 100 percent of the Federal poverty line (FPL) and no greater than 400 percent of the FPL. Also, an individual must not have been able to obtain affordable coverage from his or her employer. If obtained in advance, the PTC is given to the insurance provider to lower the monthly premium cost to the individual. The PTC is reconciled on Form 8962 (Premium Tax Credit) filed with Form 1040 or 1040-A (not Form 1040-EZ). Individuals who obtain insurance through the Marketplace receive Form 1095-A (Health Insurance Marketplace Statement) by January 31 of the following year. This form provides information necessary to claim or reconcile the PTC, including the monthly cost of premiums and the amount of PTC received in advance each month. § 36B.

Previously taxed income (PTI). Under prior law, the undistributed taxable income of an S corporation was taxed to the shareholders as of the last day of the corporation's tax year and usually could be withdrawn by the shareholders without tax consequences at some later point in time. The role of PTI has been taken over by the accumulated adjustments account. See also *accumulated adjustments account (AAA).*

Principal partner. A partner with a 5 percent or greater interest in partnership capital or profits. § 706(b)(3).

Private activity bonds. Interest on state and local bonds is excludible from gross income. Certain such bonds are labeled private activity bonds. Although the interest on such bonds is excludible for regular income tax purposes, it is treated as a tax preference in calculating the AMT. §§ 57(a)(5) and 103.

Private foundations. An exempt organization that is subject to additional statutory restrictions on its activities and on contributions made to it. Excise taxes may be levied on certain prohibited transactions, and the Code places more stringent restrictions on the deductibility of contributions to private foundations. § 509.

Probate costs. The costs incurred in administering a decedent's estate.

Probate estate. The property of a decedent that is subject to administration by the executor or administrator of an estate.

Procedural Regulations. A Regulation issued by the Treasury Department that is a housekeeping-type instruction indicating information that taxpayers should provide the IRS as well as information about the internal management and conduct of the IRS itself.

Profit and loss sharing ratios. Specified in the partnership agreement and used to determine each partner's allocation of ordinary taxable income and separately stated items. Profits and losses can be shared in different ratios. The ratios can be changed by amending the partnership agreement or by using a special allocation. § 704(a).

Profit sharing plan. A deferred compensation plan established and maintained by an employer to provide for employee participation in the company's profits. Contributions are paid from the employer's current or accumulated profits to a trustee. Separate accounts are maintained for each participant employee. The plan must provide a definite, predetermined formula for allocating the contributions among the participants. It also must include a definite, predetermined formula for distributing the accumulated funds after a fixed number of years, on the attainment of a stated age, or on the occurrence of certain events such as illness, layoff, or retirement.

Profits (loss) interest. The extent of a partner's entitlement to an allocation of the partnership's operating results. This interest is measured by the profit and loss sharing ratios.

Property. Assets defined in the broadest legal sense. Property includes the unrealized receivables of a cash basis taxpayer, but not services rendered. § 351.

Property dividend. Generally treated in the same manner as a cash distribution, measured by the fair market value of the property on the date of distribution. Distribution of appreciated property causes the distributing C or S corporation to recognize gain. The distributing corporation does not recognize loss on property that has depreciated in value.

Property factor. The proportion of a multistate corporation's total property that is traceable to a specific state. Used in determining the taxable income that is to be apportioned to that state.

Proportionate distribution. A distribution in which the partners' interests in hot assets does not change. This can happen, for instance, when no hot assets are distributed (e.g., a proportionate cash distribution) or when each partner in a partnership receives a pro rata share of hot assets being distributed. For example, a distribution of $10,000 of hot assets equally to two 50 percent partners is a proportionate distribution.

Proposed Regulations. A Regulation issued by the Treasury Department in proposed, rather than final, form. The interval between the proposal of a Regulation and its finalization permits taxpayers and other interested parties to comment on the propriety of the proposal.

Proprietorship. A business entity for which there is a single owner. The net profit of the entity is reported on the owner's Federal income tax return (Schedule C of Form 1040).

Public Law 86–272. A congressional limit on the ability of the state to force a multistate corporation to assign taxable income to that state. Under P.L. 86–272, where orders for tangible personal property are both filled and delivered outside the state, the entity must establish more than the mere solicitation of such orders before any income can be apportioned to the state.

Punitive damages. Damages received or paid by the taxpayer can be classified as compensatory damages or as punitive damages. Punitive damages are those awarded to punish the defendant for gross negligence or the intentional infliction of harm. Such damages are includible in gross income. § 104.

Q

QBI deduction. See *deduction for qualified business income*.

Qualified ABLE program. A state program that allows funds to be set aside for the benefit of an individual who became disabled or blind before age 26. Cash may be put into the fund annually up to the annual gift tax exclusion amount. Distributions to the designated beneficiary are not taxable provided they do not exceed qualified disability expenses for the year. § 529A.

Qualified business income (QBI). For purposes of the qualified business income deduction, it is the ordinary income less ordinary deductions a taxpayer earns from a qualified trade or business conducted in the United States by the taxpayer. It also includes the distributive share of these amounts from each partnership or S corporation interest held by the taxpayer. It does not include certain types of investment income (e.g., capital gains or losses and dividends), "reasonable compensation" paid to a taxpayer with respect to any qualified trade or business, or guaranteed payments made to a partner for services rendered. § 199A(c).

Qualified business income deduction (QBID). See *deduction for qualified business income*.

Qualified business unit (QBU). A subsidiary, branch, or other business entity that conducts business using a currency other than the U.S. dollar.

Qualified dividend income (QDI). See *qualified dividends*.

Qualified dividends. Distributions made by domestic (and certain non-U.S.) corporations to noncorporate shareholders that are subject to tax at the same rates as those applicable to net long-term capital gains (i.e., 0 percent, 15 percent, or 20 percent). The 20 percent rate applies to certain high-income taxpayers. The dividend must be paid out of earnings and profits, and the shareholders must meet certain holding period requirements as to the stock. §§ 1(h)(1) and (11).

Qualified employee discount. Discounts offered employees on merchandise or services that the employer ordinarily sells or provides to customers. The discounts must be generally available to all employees. In the case of property, the discount cannot exceed the employer's gross profit (the sales price cannot be less than the employer's cost). In the case of services, the discounts cannot exceed 20 percent of the normal sales price. § 132.

Qualified improvement property. Any improvement to an interior portion of nonresidential real property made after the property is placed in service, including leasehold improvements.

Qualified joint venture. At the election of the taxpayers, certain joint ventures between spouses can avoid partnership classification. Known as a qualified joint venture, the spouses generally report their share of the business activities from the venture as sole proprietors (using two

Schedule C forms). This would be reported on Schedule E if the venture relates to a rental property. § 761(f).

Qualified nonrecourse financing. Debt issued on realty by a bank, retirement plan, or governmental agency. Included in the at-risk amount by the investor. § 465(b)(6).

Qualified real property business indebtedness. Indebtedness that was incurred or assumed by the taxpayer in connection with real property used in a trade or business and is secured by such real property. The taxpayer must not be a C corporation. For qualified real property business indebtedness, the taxpayer may elect to exclude some or all of the income realized from cancellation of debt on qualified real property. If the election is made, the basis of the property must be reduced by the amount excluded. The amount excluded cannot be greater than the excess of the principal amount of the outstanding debt over the fair market value (net of any other debt outstanding on the property) of the property securing the debt. § 108(c).

Qualified residence interest. A term relevant in determining the amount of interest expense the individual taxpayer may deduct as an itemized deduction for what otherwise would be disallowed as a component of personal interest (consumer interest). Qualified residence interest consists of interest paid on qualified residences (principal residence and one other residence) of the taxpayer. Debt that qualifies as qualified residence interest is limited to $1 million of debt to acquire, construct, or substantially improve qualified residences (acquisition indebtedness). For acquisition indebtedness incurred after December 15, 2017, the limit is reduced to $750,000. § 163(h)(3).

Qualified small business corporation. For purposes of computing an exclusion upon the sale of qualified small business stock, a C corporation that has aggregate gross assets not exceeding $50 million and that is conducting an active trade or business. § 1202.

Qualified small business stock. Stock in a qualified small business corporation, purchased as part of an original issue after August 10, 1993. The shareholder may exclude from gross income 100 (or 50 or 75) percent of the realized gain on the sale of the stock if he or she held the stock for more than five years. The exclusion percentage depends on when the stock was acquired. § 1202.

Qualified terminable interest property (QTIP). Generally, the marital deduction (for gift and estate tax purposes) is not available if the interest transferred will terminate upon the death of the transferee spouse and pass to someone else. Thus, if Jim (the husband) places property in trust, life estate to Mary (the wife), and remainder to their children upon Mary's death, this is a terminable interest that will not provide Jim (or Jim's estate) with a marital deduction. If, however, the transfer in trust is treated as qualified terminable interest property (the QTIP election is made), the terminable interest restriction is waived and the marital deduction becomes available. In exchange for this deduction, the surviving spouse's gross estate must include the value of the QTIP election assets, even though he or she has no control over the ultimate disposition of the asset. Terminable interest property qualifies for this election if the donee (or heir) is the only beneficiary of the asset during his or her lifetime and receives income distributions relative to the property at least annually. For gifts, the donor spouse is the one who makes the QTIP election. For property transferred by death, the executor of the estate of the deceased spouse makes the election. §§ 2056(b)(7) and 2523(f).

Qualified trade or business. Used in determining the deduction for qualified business income (§ 199A). In general, it includes any trade or business other than providing services as an employee. In addition, a "specified services trade or business" is not a qualified trade or business. § 199A(d)(1)(B).

Qualified transportation fringes. Transportation benefits provided by the employer to the employee. If these benefits are reimbursed by the employer, they are excludible from gross income by the employee, but not deductible by the employer after 2017. Such benefits include (1) transportation in a commuter highway vehicle between the employee's residence and the place of employment, (2) a transit pass, and (3) qualified parking. Qualified transportation fringes are excludible from the employee's gross income to the extent categories (1) and (2) above do not exceed $260 per month in 2018 and category (3) does not exceed $260 per month in 2018. These amounts are indexed annually for inflation. § 132.

Qualified tuition program (§ 529 plan). A program that allows college tuition to be prepaid for a beneficiary. When amounts in the plan are used, nothing is included in gross income provided they are used for qualified higher education expenses. § 529.

Qualifying child. An individual who, as to the taxpayer, satisfies the relationship, abode, and age tests. To be claimed as a dependent, such individual must also meet the citizenship and joint return tests and not be self-supporting. §§ 152(a)(1) and (c).

Qualifying relative. An individual who, as to the taxpayer, satisfies the relationship, gross income, support, citizenship, and joint return tests. Such an individual can be claimed as a dependent of the taxpayer. §§ 152(a)(2) and (d).

R

Rate reconciliation. Under Generally Accepted Accounting Principles, a footnote to the financial statements often includes a table that accounts for differences in the statutory income tax rate that applies to the entity (e.g., 21 percent) and the higher or lower effective tax rate that the entity realized for the reporting period. The rate reconciliation includes only permanent differences between the book tax expense and the entity's income tax provision. The rate reconciliation table often is expressed in dollar and/or percentage terms.

Realized gain. See *realized gain or loss*.

Realized gain or loss. The difference between the amount realized upon the sale or other disposition of property and the adjusted basis of the property. § 1001.

Realized loss. See *realized gain or loss*.

Realty. Real estate.

Reasonable cause. Relief from taxpayer and preparer penalties often is allowed where reasonable cause is found for the taxpayer's actions. For example, reasonable cause for the late filing of a tax return might be a flood that damaged the taxpayer's record-keeping systems and made a timely completion of the return difficult.

Reasonable needs of the business. A means of avoiding the penalty tax on an unreasonable accumulation of earnings. In determining the base for this tax (accumulated taxable income), § 535 allows a deduction for "such part of earnings and profits for the taxable year as are retained for the reasonable needs of the business." § 537.

Reasonableness. See *reasonableness requirement.*

Reasonableness requirement. The Code includes a reasonableness requirement with respect to the deduction of salaries and other compensation for services. The courts have expanded this requirement to all business expenses, ruling that an expense must be reasonable in order to be ordinary and necessary. What constitutes reasonableness is a question of fact. If an expense is unreasonable, the amount that is classified as unreasonable is not allowed as a deduction. The question of reasonableness generally arises with respect to closely held corporations where there is no separation of ownership and management. § 162(a)(1).

Recapitalization. A "Type E" reorganization, constituting a major change in the character and amount of outstanding equity of a corporation. Tax-free exchanges are stock for stock, bonds for bonds, and bonds for stock. For example, common stock exchanged for preferred stock can qualify as a tax-free "Type E" reorganization.

Recognized gain. See *recognized gain or loss.*

Recognized gain or loss. The portion of realized gain or loss subject to income taxation.

Recognized loss. See *recognized gain or loss.*

Recourse debt. Debt for which the lender may both foreclose on the property and assess a guarantor for any payments due under the loan. A lender also may make a claim against the assets of any general partner in a partnership to which debt is issued, without regard to whether the partner has guaranteed the debt.

Recovery of capital doctrine. When a taxable sale or exchange occurs, the seller may be permitted to recover his or her investment (or other adjusted basis) in the property before gain or loss is recognized.

Redemption to pay death taxes. Sale or exchange treatment is available relative to this type of stock redemption, to the extent of the proceeds up to the total amount paid by the estate or heir for estate/inheritance taxes and administration expenses. The stock value must exceed 35 percent of the value of the decedent's adjusted gross estate. In meeting this test, shareholdings in corporations where the decedent held at least 20 percent of the outstanding shares are combined. § 303.

Refundable credits. A credit that is paid to the taxpayer even if the amount of the credit (or credits) exceeds the taxpayer's tax liability.

Regular corporations. See *C corporation.*

Rehabilitation expenditures credit. A credit that is based on expenditures incurred to rehabilitate industrial and commercial buildings and certified historic structures. The credit is intended to discourage businesses from moving from older, economically distressed areas to newer locations and to encourage the preservation of historic structures. § 47.

Related party. Various Code Sections define related parties and often include a variety of persons within this (usually detrimental) category. Generally, related parties are accorded different tax treatment from that applicable to other taxpayers who enter into similar transactions. For instance, realized losses that are generated between related parties are not recognized in the year of the loss. However, these deferred losses can be used to offset recognized gains that occur upon the subsequent sale of the asset to a nonrelated party. Other uses of a related-party definition include the conversion of gain upon the sale of a depreciable asset into all ordinary income (§ 1239) and the identification of constructive ownership of stock relative to corporate distributions, redemptions, liquidations, reorganizations, and compensation.

Related-party transactions. The tax law places restrictions upon the recognition of gains and losses between related parties because of the potential for abuse. For example, restrictions are placed on the deduction of losses from the sale or exchange of property between related parties. In addition, under certain circumstances, related-party gains that would otherwise be classified as capital gain are classified as ordinary income. §§ 267, 707(b), and 1239.

Rental activity. Any activity where payments are received principally for the use of tangible property is a rental activity. Temporary Regulations provide that in certain circumstances, activities involving rentals of real and personal property are not to be treated as rental activities. The Temporary Regulations list six exceptions.

Reorganization. Any corporate restructuring, including when one corporation acquires another, a single corporation divides into two or more entities, a corporation makes a substantial change in its capital structure, a corporation undertakes a change in its legal name or domicile, or a corporation goes through a bankruptcy proceeding and continues to exist. The exchange of stock and other securities in a corporate reorganization can be effected favorably for tax purposes if certain statutory requirements are followed strictly. Tax consequences include the nonrecognition of any gain that is realized by the shareholders except to the extent of boot received. § 368.

Report of Foreign Bank and Financial Accounts (FBAR). FinCEN Form 114, Report of Foreign Bank and Financial Accounts (FBAR), must be filed by individuals and some businesses if they have foreign bank, brokerage or similar accounts where at any time during the calendar year the aggregate balance exceeds $10,000. The form is filed electronically with the U.S. Department of the Treasury and is due by April 15 with an automatic extension to October 15. Significant penalties apply for failure to file the FBAR. The form is not attached to the income tax return (it is separately filed), but any interest earned by the foreign accounts is generally included in the account holder's U.S. taxable income.

Required taxable year. A partnership or limited liability company must use a required tax year as its tax accounting period, or one of three allowable alternative tax year-ends. If there is a common tax year used by owners holding a majority of the entity's capital or profits interests or if the same year end is used by all "principal partners" (partners who hold 5 percent or more of the capital or profits interests), then that tax year-end is used by the entity. If neither of the first tests results in an allowable year-end (e.g., because there is no majority partner or because the principal partners do not have the same tax year), then the partnership uses the least aggregate deferral method to determine its tax year.

Research activities credit. A tax credit whose purpose is to encourage research and development. It consists of three components: the incremental research activities credit, the basic research credit, and the energy credit. The incremental research activities credit is equal to 20 percent of the excess qualified research expenditures over the base amount. The basic research credit is equal to 20 percent of the excess of basic research payments over the base amount. § 41.

Research and experimental expenditures. Costs incurred to develop a product or process for which there exists uncertainty regarding its viability. The Code provides three alternatives for the tax treatment of research and experimentation expenditures. They may be expensed in the year paid or incurred, deferred subject to amortization, or capitalized. If the taxpayer does not elect to expense such costs or to defer them subject to amortization (over 60 months), the expenditures must be capitalized. § 174. In general, research and experimentation expenditures paid or incurred after 2021 must be capitalized and amortized over a five-year period. Some of these expenditures may also qualify the taxpayer for the credit for increasing research activities. § 41.

Reserve method. A method of accounting whereby an allowance is permitted for estimated uncollectible accounts. Actual write-offs are charged to the reserve, and recoveries of amounts previously written off are credited to the reserve. The Code permits only certain financial institutions to use the reserve method. § 166.

Residential rental real estate. Buildings for which at least 80 percent of the gross rents are from dwelling units (e.g., an apartment building). This type of building is distinguished from nonresidential (commercial or industrial) buildings in applying the recapture of depreciation provisions. The term also is relevant in distinguishing between buildings that are eligible for a 27.5-year life versus a 39-year life for MACRS purposes. Generally, residential buildings receive preferential treatment.

Restricted property plan. An arrangement whereby an employer transfers property (usually stock) to an employee at a bargain price (for less than the fair market value). If the transfer is accompanied by a substantial risk of forfeiture and the property is not transferable, no compensation results to the employee until the restrictions disappear. An example of a substantial risk of forfeiture would be a requirement that the employee return the property if his or her employment is terminated within a specified period of time. § 83.

Revenue Agent's Report (RAR). A Revenue Agent's Report (RAR) reflects any adjustments made by the agent as a result of an audit of the taxpayer. The RAR is mailed to the taxpayer along with the 30-day letter, which outlines the appellate procedures available to the taxpayer.

Revenue neutrality. A description that characterizes tax legislation when it neither increases nor decreases the total revenue collected by the taxing jurisdiction. Thus, any tax revenue losses are offset by tax revenue gains.

Revenue Procedures. A matter of procedural importance to both taxpayers and the IRS concerning the administration of the tax laws is issued as a Revenue Procedure (abbreviated Rev.Proc.). A Revenue Procedure is published in an *Internal Revenue Bulletin* (I.R.B.).

Revenue Rulings. A Revenue Ruling (abbreviated Rev.Rul.) is issued by the National Office of the IRS to express an official interpretation of the tax law as applied to specific transactions. It is more limited in application than a Regulation. A Revenue Ruling is published in an *Internal Revenue Bulletin* (I.R.B.).

Reversionary interest. The trust property that reverts to the grantor after the expiration of an intervening income interest. Assume that Phil places real estate in trust with income to Junior for 11 years and that upon the expiration of this term, the property returns to Phil. Under these circumstances, Phil holds a reversionary interest in the property. A reversionary interest is the same as a remainder interest, except that, in the latter case, the property passes to someone other than the original owner (e.g., the grantor of a trust) upon the expiration of the intervening interest.

Roth IRA. See *Individual Retirement Account (IRA)*.

S

S corporation. The designation for a corporation that elects to be taxed similarly to a partnership. See also *Subchapter S*.

Sale or exchange. A requirement for the recognition of capital gain or loss. Generally, the seller of property must receive money or relief from debt to have sold the property. An exchange involves the transfer of property for other property. Thus, collection of a debt is neither a sale nor an exchange. The term *sale or exchange* is not defined by the Code.

Sales factor. The proportion of a multistate corporation's total sales that is traceable to a specific state. Used in determining the taxable income that is to be apportioned to that state.

Sales tax. A state- or local-level tax on the retail sale of specified property. Generally, the purchaser pays the tax, but the seller collects it, as an agent for the government. Various taxing jurisdictions allow exemptions for purchases of specific items, including certain food, services, and manufacturing equipment. If the purchaser and seller are in different states, a use tax usually applies.

Schedule K–1. A tax information form prepared for each partner in a partnership, each shareholder of an S corporation, and some beneficiaries of certain trusts. The Schedule K–1 reports the owner's share of the entity's ordinary income or loss from operations as well as the owner's share of separately stated items.

Schedule M–1. On the Form 1120, a reconciliation of book net income with Federal taxable income. Accounts for temporary and permanent differences in the two computations, such as depreciation differences, exempt income, and nondeductible items. On Forms 1120S and 1065, the Schedule M–1 reconciles book income with the owners' aggregate ordinary taxable income.

Schedule M–3. An *expanded* reconciliation of book net income with Federal taxable income (see *Schedule M–1*).

Required of C and S corporations and partnerships/LLCs with total assets of $10 million or more.

Scholarship. Scholarships are generally excluded from the gross income of the recipient unless the payments are a disguised form of compensation for services rendered. However, the Code imposes restrictions on the exclusion. The recipient must be a degree candidate. The excluded amount is limited to amounts used for tuition, fees, books, supplies, and equipment required for courses of instruction. Amounts received for room and board are not eligible for the exclusion. § 117.

Section 121 exclusion. If a residence has been owned and used by the taxpayer as the principal residence for at least two years during the five-year period ending on the date of sale, up to $250,000 of realized gain is excluded from gross income. For a married couple filing a joint return, the $250,000 is increased to $500,000 if either spouse satisfies the ownership requirement and both spouses satisfy the use requirement.

Section 179 expensing. The ability to deduct the cost of qualified property in the year the property is placed in service rather than over the asset's useful life or cost recovery period. The annual ceiling on the deduction is $1 million in 2018 ($510,000 in 2017). However, the deduction is reduced dollar for dollar when § 179 property placed in service during the taxable year exceeds $2,500,000 ($2,030,000 in 2017). In addition, the amount expensed under § 179 cannot exceed the aggregate amount of taxable income derived from the conduct of any trade or business by the taxpayer.

Section 179 expensing election. See *Section 179 expensing*.

Section 338 election. When a corporation acquires at least 80 percent of a subsidiary within a 12-month period, it can elect to treat the acquisition of such stock as an asset purchase. The acquiring corporation's basis in the subsidiary's assets then is the cost of the stock. The subsidiary is deemed to have sold its assets for an amount equal to the grossed-up basis in its stock.

Section 382 limitation. When one corporation acquires another, the acquiring corporation's ability to use the loss and credit carryovers of the target may be limited by this anti-abuse provision. For instance, the maximum NOL deduction available to the acquiring is the value of the target when acquired times the long-term tax-exempt interest rate on that date.

Section 401(k) plan. A cash or deferred arrangement plan that allows participants to elect to receive up to $18,500 in 2018 in cash (taxed currently) or to have a contribution made on their behalf to a profit sharing or stock bonus plan (excludible from gross income). The plan may also be in the form of a salary reduction agreement between the participant and the employer.

Section 704(b) book capital accounts. Capital accounts calculated as described under Reg. § 1.704–1(b)(2)(iv). All partnerships must maintain § 704(b) book capital accounts for the partners with the intent that final liquidating distributions are in accordance with these capital account balances. Partnership allocations will not be accepted unless they are properly reflected in the partners' § 704(b) book capital accounts. These capital accounts are a hybrid of book and tax accounting methods. They reflect contributions and distributions of property at their fair market values, but the capital accounts are otherwise generally increased by the partnership's tax-basis income and decreased by tax-basis deductions (as reported on the partner's Schedule K–1). Liabilities are only reflected in these capital accounts to the extent the partnership assumes a partner's liability [reduces that partner's § 704(b) book capital account] or a partner assumes a partnership liability [increases that partner's § 704(b) book capital account]. See also *capital account maintenance* and *economic effect test*.

Section 754 election. An election that may be made by a partnership to adjust the basis of partnership assets to reflect a purchasing partner's outside basis in interest or to reflect a gain, loss, or basis adjustment of a partner receiving a distribution from a partnership. The intent of the election is to maintain the equivalence between outside and inside basis for that partner. Once the election is made, the partnership must make basis adjustments for all future transactions, unless the IRS consents to revoke the election.

Section 1231 gains and losses. If the combined gains and losses from the taxable dispositions of § 1231 assets plus the net gain from business involuntary conversions (of both § 1231 assets and long-term capital assets) is a gain, the gains and losses are treated as long-term capital gains and losses. In arriving at § 1231 gains, however, the depreciation recapture provisions (e.g., § 1245) are applied first to produce ordinary income. If the net result of the combination is a loss, the gains and losses from § 1231 assets are treated as ordinary gains and losses. § 1231(a).

Section 1231 lookback. For gain to be classified as § 1231 gain, the gain must survive the § 1231 lookback. To the extent of nonrecaptured § 1231 losses for the five prior tax years, the gain is classified as ordinary income. § 1231(c).

Section 1231 property. Depreciable assets and real estate used in trade or business and held for the required long-term holding period. § 1231(b).

Section 1244 stock. Stock issued under § 1244 by qualifying small business corporations. If § 1244 stock becomes worthless, the shareholders may claim an ordinary loss rather than the usual capital loss, within statutory limitations.

Section 1245 property. Property that is subject to the recapture of depreciation under § 1245. For a definition of § 1245 property, see § 1245(a)(3).

Section 1245 recapture. Upon a taxable disposition of § 1245 property, all depreciation claimed on the property is recaptured as ordinary income (but not to exceed any recognized gain from the disposition).

Section 1250 property. Real estate that is subject to the recapture of depreciation under § 1250. For a definition of § 1250 property, see § 1250(c).

Section 1250 recapture. Upon a taxable disposition of § 1250 property, accelerated depreciation or cost recovery claimed on the property may be recaptured as ordinary income.

Securities. Stock, debt, and other financial assets. To the extent securities other than the stock of the transferee corporation are received in a § 351 exchange, the new shareholder recognizes a gain. For purposes of corporate reorganizations, securities are generally debt with terms longer than 10 years. To the extent stock and securities are transferred in a corporate reorganization under § 368, no gain or loss is recognized.

Self-employment tax. A tax of 12.4 percent is levied on individuals with net earnings from self-employment (up to $128,400 in 2018) to provide Social Security benefits (i.e., the old age, survivors, and disability insurance portion) for such individuals. In addition, a tax of 2.9 percent is levied on individuals with net earnings from self-employment (with no statutory ceiling) to provide Medicare benefits (i.e., the hospital insurance portion) for such individuals. If a self-employed individual also receives wages from an employer that are subject to FICA, the self-employment tax will be reduced. A partial deduction is allowed in calculating the self-employment tax. Individuals with net earnings of $400 or more from self-employment are subject to this tax. §§ 1401 and 1402.

Separate foreign tax credit income categories. The foreign tax credit of a taxpayer is computed for each of several types of income sources, as specified by the Code to limit the results of tax planning. FTC income "baskets" include general and passive. The FTC for the year is the sum of the credits as computed within all of the taxpayer's separate FTC baskets used for the tax year.

Separate return limitation year (SRLY). A series of rules limits the amount of an acquired corporation's net operating loss carryforwards that can be used by the acquiror. Generally, a consolidated return can include the acquiree's net operating loss carryforward only to the extent of the lesser of the subsidiary's (1) current-year or (2) cumulative positive contribution to consolidated taxable income.

Separately stated items. Any item of a partnership or an S corporation that might be taxed differently to any two owners of the entity. These amounts are not included in the ordinary income of the entity, but are instead reported separately to the owners; tax consequences are determined at the owner level.

Severance taxes. A tax imposed upon the extraction of natural resources.

Short period. See *short taxable year.*

Short sale. A sale that occurs when a taxpayer sells borrowed property (usually stock) and repays the lender with substantially identical property either held on the date of the short sale or purchased after the sale. No gain or loss is recognized until the short sale is closed, and such gain or loss is generally short term. § 1233.

Short taxable year. A tax year that is less than 12 months. A short taxable year may occur in the initial reporting period, in the final tax year, or when the taxpayer changes tax years.

Significant participation activity. Seven tests determine whether an individual has achieved material participation in an activity, one of which is based on more than 500 hours of participation in significant participation activities. A significant participation activity is one in which the individual's participation exceeds 100 hours during the year. Temp.Reg. § 1.469–5T.

Simple trust. Trusts that are not complex trusts. Such trusts may not have a charitable beneficiary, accumulate income, or distribute corpus.

Simplified employee pension (SEP) plans. An employer may make contributions to an employee's IRA in amounts not exceeding the lesser of 15 percent of compensation or $55,000 per individual in 2018. These employer-sponsored simplified employee pensions are permitted only if the contributions are nondiscriminatory and are made on behalf of all employees who have attained age 21 and have worked for the employer during at least three of the five preceding calendar years. § 219(b).

Small business corporation. A corporation that satisfies the definition of § 1361(b), § 1244(c), or both. Satisfaction of § 1361(b) permits an S election, and satisfaction of § 1244 enables the shareholders of the corporation to claim an ordinary loss on the worthlessness of stock.

Small business stock (§ 1244 stock). See *Section 1244 stock.*

Small Cases Division. A division within the U.S. Tax Court where jurisdiction is limited to claims of $50,000 or less. There is no appeal from this court.

Solicitation. A level of activity brought about by the taxpayer within a specific state. Under Public Law 86-272, certain types of solicitation activities do not create nexus with the state. Exceeding mere solicitation, though, creates nexus.

Special allocation. Any amount for which an agreement exists among the partners of a partnership outlining the method used for spreading the item among the partners.

Special use value. Permits the executor of an estate to value, for estate tax purposes, real estate used in a farming activity or in connection with a closely held business at its current use value rather than at its most suitable or optimal use value. Under this option, a farm is valued for farming purposes even though, for example, the property might have a higher potential value as a shopping center. For the executor of an estate to elect special use valuation, the conditions of § 2032A must be satisfied.

Specific charge-off method. A method of accounting for bad debts in which a deduction is permitted only when an account becomes partially or completely worthless.

Specified service trade or business. For purposes of the deduction for qualified business income, a specified service trade or business includes those involving the performance of services in certain fields, including health, law, accounting, actuarial science, performing arts, consulting, athletics, financial services, and brokerage services; services consisting of investing and investment management, trading or dealing in securities, partnership interests, or commodities; and any trade or business where the business's principal asset is the reputation of one or more of its employees or owners. § 199A(d)(2).

Spin-off. A type of reorganization where, for example, Apple Corporation transfers some assets to Core Corporation in exchange for Core stock representing control. Apple then distributes the Core stock to its shareholders.

Split-off. A type of reorganization where, for example, Apple Corporation transfers some assets to Core Corporation in exchange for Core stock representing control. Apple then distributes the Core stock to its shareholders in exchange for some of their Apple stock. Not all shareholders need to exchange stock.

Split-up. A type of reorganization where, for example, Firefly Corporation transfers some assets to Fire Corporation and the remainder to Fly Corporation. In return, Firefly receives enough Fire and Fly stock representing control of each corporation. Firefly then distributes the Fire and Fly stock to its shareholders in return for all of their Firefly stock. Firefly then liquidates, and its shareholders now have control of Fire and Fly.

Sprinkling trust. When a trustee has the discretion to either distribute or accumulate the entity accounting income of the trust and to distribute it among the trust's income beneficiaries in varying magnitudes. The trustee can "sprinkle" the income of the trust.

Standard deduction. The individual taxpayer can either itemize deductions or take the standard deduction. The amount of the standard deduction depends on the taxpayer's filing status (single, head of household, married filing jointly, surviving spouse, or married filing separately). For 2018, the amount of the standard deduction ranges from $12,000 (for single) to $24,000 (for married, filing jointly). Additional standard deductions of either $1,300 (for married taxpayers) or $1,600 (for single taxpayers) are available if the taxpayer is blind or age 65 or over. Limitations exist on the amount of the standard deduction of a taxpayer who is another taxpayer's dependent. The standard deduction amounts are adjusted for inflation each year. § 63(c).

Startup expenditures. Expenditures paid or incurred prior to the beginning of the business that would have been deductible as an ordinary and necessary business expense if business operations had begun. Examples of such expenditures include advertising; salaries and wages; travel and other expenses incurred in lining up prospective distributors, suppliers, or customers; and salaries and fees to executives, consultants, and professional service providers. A taxpayer will immediately expense the first $5,000 (subject to phaseout) of startup expenditures and amortize the balance over a period of 180 months, unless the taxpayer elects not to do so.

Statute of limitations. Provisions of the law that specify the maximum period of time in which action may be taken concerning a past event. Code §§ 6501–6504 contain the limitation periods applicable to the IRS for additional assessments, and §§ 6511–6515 relate to refund claims by taxpayers.

Statutory employees. Statutory employees are considered self-employed independent contractors for purposes of reporting income and expenses on their tax returns. Generally, a statutory employee must meet three tests:

- It is understood from a service contract that the services will be performed by the person.

- The person does not have a substantial investment in facilities (other than transportation used to perform the services).

- The services involve a continuing relationship with the person for whom they are performed.

For further information on statutory employees, see Circular E, *Employer's Tax Guide* (IRS Publication 15).

Step down. See *step-down in basis.*

Step transaction. Disregarding one or more transactions to arrive at the final result. Assume, for example, Beta Corporation creates Alpha Corporation by transferring assets desired by Beta's sole shareholder, Carl. Carl then causes Alpha to liquidate to obtain the assets. Under these circumstances, the IRS may contend that the creation and liquidation of Alpha be disregarded. What really happened was a dividend distribution from Beta to Carl.

Step up. See *step-up in basis.*

Step-down in basis. A reduction in the tax basis of property. See also *step-up in basis.*

Step-up in basis. An increase in the income tax basis of property. In an estate context, a step-up in basis occurs when a decedent dies owning appreciated property. Since the estate or heir acquires a basis in the property equal to the property's fair market value on the date of death (or alternate valuation date if available and elected), any appreciation is not subject to the income tax. Thus, a step-up in basis is the result, with no immediate income tax consequences. In the partnership context, a step-up arises when a § 754 election is in effect and when one of several transactions arises: (1) a partner purchases a partnership interest for an amount that exceeds the partner's share of the partnership's inside basis, (2) the partner recognizes a gain on a distribution of cash from the partnership, or (3) the partnership takes a basis in a partnership property that is less than the partnership's basis in that asset. In the opposite situations (e.g., loss recognition), a step-down can arise. See also *step-down in basis.*

Stock bonus plan. A type of deferred compensation plan in which the employer establishes and maintains the plan and contributes employer stock to the plan for the benefit of employees. The contributions need not be dependent on the employer's profits. Any benefits of the plan are distributable in the form of employer stock, except that distributable fractional shares may be paid in cash.

Stock dividend. Not taxable if pro rata distributions of stock or stock rights on common stock. Section 305 governs the taxability of stock dividends and sets out five exceptions to the general rule that stock dividends are nontaxable.

Stock option. The right to purchase a stated number of shares of stock from a corporation at a certain price within a specified period of time. §§ 421 and 422.

Stock redemption. A corporation buys back its own stock from a specified shareholder. Typically, the corporation recognizes any realized gain on the noncash assets that it uses to effect a redemption, and the shareholder obtains a capital gain or loss upon receipt of the purchase price.

Stock rights. Assets that convey to the holder the power to purchase corporate stock at a specified price, often for a limited period of time. Stock rights received may be taxed as a distribution of earnings and profits. After the right is exercised, the basis of the acquired share includes the investor's purchase price or gross income, if any, to obtain the right. Disposition of the right also can be taxable.

Subchapter S. Sections 1361–1379 of the Internal Revenue Code. An elective provision permitting certain small business corporations (§ 1361) and their shareholders (§ 1362) to elect to be treated for income tax purposes in accordance with the operating rules of §§ 1363–1379. However, some S corporations usually avoid the corporate income tax, and corporate losses can be claimed by the shareholders.

Subpart F income. Certain types of income earned by a controlled foreign corporation that are included in U.S. gross income by U.S. shareholders of such an entity as they are generated, not when they are repatriated.

Substance over form. A standard used when one must ascertain the true reality of what has occurred. Suppose, for example, a father sells stock to his daughter for $1,000. If the stock is really worth $50,000 at the time of the transfer, the substance of the transaction is probably a gift to her of $49,000.

Substantial authority. Taxpayer and tax preparer understatement penalties are waived where substantial authority existed for the disputed position taken on the return.

Substantial basis reduction. Arises when the partnership makes a distribution to a partner and the distributee partner recognizes a loss (or has a basis increase for the distributed assets) of at least $250,000. (The second situation would arise when the basis of the assets the partner receives must be stepped up to absorb all remaining partnership interest basis.) If there is a substantial basis reduction, the partnership is required to make a downward adjustment to the basis of its assets, even if the partnership does not have a § 754 election in effect. This adjustment is treated as a § 754 adjustment related to a distribution and so is allocated to the basis of all remaining partnership assets (except for cash). See also *substantial built-in loss* and *§ 754 election*.

Substantial built-in loss. Arises when a partner sells a partnership interest and the selling partner recognizes a loss on the sale of at least $250,000. In addition, a substantial built-in loss arises if the selling partner would be allocated more than a $250,000 loss if all partnership assets were sold (after considering special allocations). If there is a substantial built-in loss, the partnership is required to make a downward adjustment in the basis of its assets, even if the partnership does not have a § 754 election in effect. This adjustment is treated as a § 754 adjustment related to a sale of a partnership interest and so is allocated to the purchasing partner. See also *substantial basis reduction* and *§ 754 election*.

Substantial risk of forfeiture (SRF). A term that is associated with a restricted property plan. Generally, an employee who receives property (e.g., stock of the employer-corporation) from the employer at a bargain price or at no cost must include the bargain element in gross income. However, the employee currently does not have to do so if there is a substantial risk of forfeiture. A substantial risk of forfeiture exists if a person's rights to full enjoyment of property are conditioned upon the future performance, or the refraining from the performance, of substantial services by the individual. § 83.

Sunset provision. A provision attached to new tax legislation that will cause such legislation to expire at a specified date. Sunset provisions are attached to tax cut bills for long-term budgetary reasons to make their effect temporary. Once the sunset provision comes into play, the tax cut is rescinded and former law is reinstated. An example of a sunset provision is contained in the Tax Relief Reconciliation Act of 2001 that related to the estate tax. After the estate tax was phased out in 2010, a sunset provision called for the reinstatement of the estate tax as of January 1, 2011.

Supreme Court. See *U.S. Supreme Court*.

Surviving spouse. When a husband or wife predeceases the other spouse, the survivor is known as a surviving spouse. Under certain conditions, a surviving spouse may be entitled to use the income tax rates in § 1(a) (those applicable to married persons filing a joint return) for the two years after the year of death of his or her spouse. § 2(a).

Syndication costs. Incurred in promoting and marketing partnership interests for sale to investors. Examples include legal and accounting fees, printing costs for prospectus and placement documents, and state registration fees. These items are capitalized by the partnership as incurred, with no amortization thereof allowed.

T

Tax avoidance. The minimization of one's tax liability by taking advantage of legally available tax planning opportunities. Tax avoidance can be contrasted with tax evasion, which entails the reduction of tax liability by illegal means.

Tax benefit rule. A provision that limits the recognition of income from the recovery of an expense or a loss properly deducted in a prior tax year to the amount of the deduction that generated a tax saving. Assume that last year Gary had medical expenses of $4,000 and adjusted gross income of $30,000. Because of the AGI limitation, Gary could deduct only $1,000 of these expenses [$4,000 − (10% × $30,000)]. If this year Gary is reimbursed in full by his insurance company for the $4,000 of expenses, the tax benefit rule limits the amount of income from the reimbursement to $1,000 (the amount previously deducted with a tax saving).

Tax Court. See *U.S. Tax Court*.

Tax credit for the elderly or disabled. An elderly (age 65 and over) or disabled taxpayer may receive a tax credit amounting to 15 percent of $5,000 ($7,500 for qualified married individuals filing jointly). This amount is reduced by Social Security benefits, excluded pension benefits, and one-half of the taxpayer's adjusted gross income in excess of $7,500 ($10,000 for married taxpayers filing jointly). § 22.

Tax credits. Amounts that directly reduce a taxpayer's tax liability. The tax benefit received from a tax credit is not dependent on the taxpayer's marginal tax rate, whereas the benefit of a tax deduction or exclusion is dependent on the taxpayer's tax bracket.

Tax evasion. The reduction of taxes by the use of subterfuge or fraud or other nonlegal means. For example, a cash basis taxpayer tries to increase his or her charitable contribution deduction by prepaying next year's church pledge with a pre-dated check issued in the following year.

Tax haven. A country in which either locally sourced income or residents of the country are subject to a low rate of taxation.

Tax preparer. One who prepares tax returns for compensation. A tax preparer must register with the IRS and receive a special ID number to practice before the IRS and represent taxpayers before the agency in tax audit actions. The conduct of a tax preparer is regulated under Circular 230. Tax preparers also are subject to penalties for inappropriate conduct when working in the tax profession.

Tax Rate Schedules. Rate schedules that are used by upper-income taxpayers and those not permitted to use the tax table. Separate rate schedules are provided for married individuals filing jointly, heads of households, single taxpayers, estates and trusts, and married individuals filing separate returns. § 1.

Tax research. The method used to determine the best available solution to a situation that possesses tax consequences. Both tax and nontax factors are considered.

Tax shelters. The typical tax shelter generated large losses in the early years of the activity. Investors would offset these losses against other types of income and therefore avoid paying income taxes on this income. These tax shelter investments could then be sold after a few years and produce capital gain income, which is taxed at a lower rate compared to ordinary income. The passive activity loss rules and the at-risk rules now limit tax shelter deductions.

Tax Table. A table that is provided for taxpayers with less than $100,000 of taxable income. Separate columns are provided for single taxpayers, married taxpayers filing jointly, heads of households, and married taxpayers filing separately. § 3.

Tax treaties. An agreement between the U.S. Department of State and another country designed to alleviate double taxation of income and asset transfers and to share administrative information useful to tax agencies in both countries. The United States has income tax treaties with almost 70 countries and transfer tax treaties with about 20.

Taxable estate. The taxable estate is the gross estate of a decedent reduced by the deductions allowed by §§ 2053–2057 (e.g., administration expenses, marital and charitable deductions). The taxable estate is subject to the unified transfer tax at death. § 2051.

Taxable gift. The amount of a gift that is subject to the unified transfer tax. Thus, a taxable gift has been adjusted by the annual exclusion and other appropriate deductions (e.g., marital and charitable). § 2053.

Taxable year. The annual period over which income is measured for income tax purposes. Most individuals use a calendar year, but many businesses use a fiscal year based on the natural business year. Certain entities, including S corporations, have a required taxable year. §§ 441, 706, and 1378.

Technical Advice Memoranda (TAM). TAMs are issued by the IRS in response to questions raised by IRS field personnel during audits. They deal with completed rather than proposed transactions and are often requested for questions related to exempt organizations and employee plans.

Temporary differences. Under ASC 740 (SFAS 109), tax-related items that appear in the entity's financial statements and its tax return, but in different time periods. For instance, doubtful accounts receivable often create a temporary book-tax difference, as a bad debt reserve is used to compute an expense for financial reporting purposes, but a bad debt often is deductible only under the specific write-off rule for tax purposes, and the difference observed for the current period creates a temporary difference.

Temporary Regulations. A Regulation issued by the Treasury Department in temporary form. When speed is critical, the Treasury Department issues Temporary Regulations that take effect immediately. These Regulations have the same authoritative value as Final Regulations and may be cited as precedent for three years. Temporary Regulations are also issued as proposed Regulations.

Tenants by the entirety. Essentially, a joint tenancy between husband and wife.

Tenants in common. A form of ownership where each tenant (owner) holds an undivided interest in property. Unlike a joint tenancy or a tenancy by the entirety, the interest of a tenant in common does not terminate upon that individual's death (there is no right of survivorship). Assume that Tim and Cindy acquire real estate as equal tenants in common. Upon Tim's death, his one-half interest in the property passes to his estate or heirs, not automatically to Cindy.

Terminable interests. An interest in property that terminates upon the death of the holder or upon the occurrence of some other specified event. The transfer of a terminable interest by one spouse to the other may not qualify for the marital deduction. §§ 2056(b) and 2523(b).

Theft losses. A loss from larceny, embezzlement, or robbery. It does not include misplacement of items.

Thin capitalization. When debt owed by a corporation to the shareholders becomes too large in relation to the corporation's capital structure (i.e., stock and shareholder equity), the IRS may contend that the corporation is thinly capitalized. In effect, some or all of the debt is reclassified as equity. The immediate result is to disallow any interest deduction to the corporation on the reclassified debt. To the extent of the corporation's earnings and profits, interest payments and loan repayments on the reclassified debt are treated as dividends to the shareholders.

Thirty-day (30-day) letter. A letter that accompanies an RAR (Revenue Agent's Report) issued as a result of an IRS audit of a taxpayer (or the rejection of a taxpayer's claim for refund). The letter outlines the taxpayer's appeal procedure before the IRS. If the taxpayer does not request any such procedures within the 30-day period, the IRS issues a statutory notice of deficiency (the 90-day letter).

Throwback rule. If there is no income tax in the state to which a sale otherwise would be apportioned, the sale essentially is exempt from state income tax, even though the seller is domiciled in a state that levies an income tax. Nonetheless, if the seller's state has adopted a throwback rule, the sale is attributed to the seller's state and the transaction is subjected to a state-level tax.

Traditional IRA. See *Individual Retirement Account (IRA)*.

Transfer pricing. The process of setting internal prices for transfers of goods and services among related taxpayers. For example, what price should be used when Subsidiary purchases management services from Parent? The IRS can adjust transfer prices when it can show that the taxpayers were attempting to avoid tax by, for example, shifting losses, deductions, or credits from low-tax to high-tax entities or jurisdictions.

Transportation expenses. Expenses that include the cost of transporting the self-employed taxpayer (or employee) from one place to another in the course of business when the taxpayer is not in travel status. For tax years beginning after 2017 and before 2026, only reimbursed transportation expenses are deductible by employees. Commuting expenses are not deductible.

Travel expenses. Expenses that include meals (generally subject to a 50 percent disallowance) and lodging and transportation expenses while away from home in the pursuit of a trade or business (including that of an employee). For tax years beginning after 2017 and before 2026, only reimbursed travel expenses are deductible by employees.

Treaty shopping. An international investor attempts to use the favorable aspects of a tax treaty to his or her advantage, often elevating the form of the transaction over its substance (e.g., by establishing only a nominal presence in the country offering the favorable treaty terms).

U

UDITPA. The Uniform Division of Income for Tax Purposes Act has been adopted in some form by many of the states. The Act develops criteria by which the total taxable income of a multistate corporation can be assigned to specific states.

Unclaimed property. A U.S. state may have the right to acquire property that has been made available to an individual or legal entity for a fixed period of time, where the claimant has not taken possession of the property after a notice period. Examples of such property that a state could acquire are an uncashed payroll check or an unused gift card.

Unearned income. Income received but not yet earned. Normally, such income is taxed when received, even for accrual basis taxpayers.

Unified transfer tax. Rates applicable to transfers by gift and death made after 1976. § 2001(c).

Unified transfer tax credit. A credit allowed against any unified transfer tax. §§ 2010 and 2505.

Uniform capitalization (UNICAP) rules. Under § 263A, the Regulations provide a set of rules that all taxpayers (regardless of the particular industry) can use to determine the items of cost (and means of allocating those costs) that must be capitalized with respect to the production of tangible property. Small businesses, defined as those with average annual gross receipts in the prior three-year period of $25 million or less, that are not a tax shelter, are not required to use the UNICAP rules.

Unitary approach. See *unitary theory*.

Unitary theory. Sales, property, and payroll of related corporations are combined for nexus and apportionment purposes, and the worldwide income of the unitary entity is apportioned to the state. Subsidiaries and other affiliated corporations found to be part of the corporation's unitary business (because they are subject to overlapping ownership, operation, or management) are included in the apportionment procedure. This approach can be limited if a water's-edge election is in effect.

Unit-livestock-price method. A method of accounting for the cost of livestock. The livestock are valued using a standard cost of raising an animal with the characteristics of the animals on hand to the same age as those animals.

Unrealized receivables. Amounts earned by a cash basis taxpayer but not yet received. Because of the method of accounting used by the taxpayer, these amounts have a zero income tax basis. When unrealized receivables are distributed to a partner, they generally convert a transaction from nontaxable to taxable or an otherwise capital gain to ordinary income (i.e., as a "hot asset").

Unreasonable compensation. A deduction is allowed for "reasonable" salaries or other compensation for personal services actually rendered. The issue of unreasonable compensation usually is limited to closely held corporations, where the motivation is to pay out profits in some form that is deductible to the corporation. To the extent compensation is "excessive" ("unreasonable"), the distribution could be treated as a dividend, such that no deduction is allowed.

Unreasonable position. A tax preparer penalty is assessed regarding the understatement of a client's tax liability due to a tax return position that is found to be too aggressive. The penalty is avoided if there is substantial authority for the position or if the position is disclosed adequately on the tax return. The penalty equals the greater of $1,000 or one-half of the tax preparer's fee that is traceable to the aggressive position.

Unrecaptured § 1250 gain. Gain from the sale of depreciable real estate held more than one year. The gain is equal to or less than the depreciation taken on such property and is reduced by § 1245 and § 1250 gain.

Unrelated business income (UBI). Income recognized by an exempt organization that is generated from activities not related to the exempt purpose of the entity. For instance, the gift shop located in a hospital may generate unrelated business income. §§ 511 and 512.

Unrelated business income tax (UBIT). Levied on the unrelated business income of an exempt organization.

U.S. Court of Federal Claims. A trial court (court of original jurisdiction) that decides litigation involving Federal tax matters. Appeal from this court is to the Court of Appeals for the Federal Circuit.

U.S. shareholder. For purposes of classification of an entity as a controlled foreign corporation, a U.S. person who owns, or is considered to own, 10 percent or more of the total combined voting power of all classes of voting stock of a foreign corporation. Stock owned directly, indirectly, and constructively is counted for this purpose.

U.S. Supreme Court. The highest appellate court or the court of last resort in the Federal court system and in most states. Only a small number of tax decisions of the U.S. Courts of Appeal are reviewed by the U.S. Supreme Court under its certiorari procedure. The Supreme Court usually grants certiorari to resolve a conflict among the Courts of Appeal (e.g., two or more appellate courts have assumed opposing positions on a particular issue) or when the tax issue is extremely important (e.g., size of the revenue loss to the Federal government).

U.S. Tax Court. One of four trial courts of original jurisdiction that decides litigation involving Federal income, death, or gift taxes. It is the only trial court where the taxpayer must not first pay the deficiency assessed by the IRS. The Tax Court will not have jurisdiction over a case unless a statutory notice of deficiency (90-day letter) has been issued by the IRS and the taxpayer files the petition for hearing within the time prescribed.

U.S. trade or business. A set of activities that is carried on in a regular, continuous, and substantial manner. A non-U.S. taxpayer is subject to U.S. tax on the taxable income that is effectively connected with a U.S. trade or business.

Use tax. A use tax is designed to complement the sales tax. The use tax has two purposes: to prevent consumers from evading sales tax by purchasing goods outside the state for instate use and to provide an equitable sales environment between in-state and out-of-state retailers. Purchasers of taxable goods or services who were not charged sales tax because the seller did not have a physical presence in the state, owe use tax on the purchase.

V

Vacation homes. The Code places restrictions upon taxpayers who rent their residences or vacation homes for part of the tax year. The restrictions may result in a scaling down of expense deductions for the taxpayers. § 280A.

Valuation allowance. Under ASC 740 (SFAS 109), a tax-related item is reported for book purposes only when it is more likely than not that the item actually will be realized. When the "more likely than not" test is failed, a contra-asset account is created to offset some or all of the related deferred tax asset. For instance, if the entity projects that it will not be able to use all of its net operating loss carryforward due to a lack of future taxable income, a valuation allowance is created to reduce the net deferred tax asset that corresponds to the carryforward. If income projections later change and it appears that the carryforward will be used, the valuation allowance is reversed or "released." Creation of a valuation allowance usually increases the current tax expense and thereby reduces current book income, and its release often increases book income in the later reporting period.

Value added tax (VAT). A national sales tax that taxes the increment in value as goods move through the production process. A VAT is much used in the majority of countries but has not yet been incorporated as part of the U.S. Federal tax structure.

Vesting requirements. A qualified deferred compensation arrangement must satisfy a vesting requirement. Under this provision, an employee's right to accrued plan benefits derived from employer contributions must be nonforfeitable in accordance with one of two vesting time period schedules (or two required alternate vesting schedules for certain employer matching contributions).

Voluntary revocation. The owners of a majority of shares in an S corporation elect to terminate the S status of the entity as of a specified date. The day on which the revocation is effective is the first day of the corporation's C tax year.

W

W–2 Wages/Capital Investment Limit. A limitation on the deduction for qualified business income that caps the deduction at the greater of (1) 50 percent of the wages paid by a qualified trade or business or (2) 25 percent of the wages paid by the qualified trade or business plus 2.5 percent of the taxpayer's share of the unadjusted basis of property used in the business that has not been fully depreciated prior to the close of the taxable year. § 199A(b)(2)(B).

Wash sale. A loss from the sale of stock or securities that is disallowed because the taxpayer, within 30 days before or after the sale, has acquired stock or securities substantially identical to those sold. § 1091.

Waters' edge. A limitation on the worldwide scope of the unitary theory. If a corporate waters'-edge election is in effect, the state can consider in the apportionment procedure only the activities that occur within the boundaries of the United States.

Waters'-edge election. See *waters' edge*.

Wherewithal to pay. This concept recognizes the inequity of taxing a transaction when the taxpayer lacks the means with which to pay the tax. Under it, there is a correlation between the imposition of the tax and the ability to pay the tax. It is particularly suited to situations in which the taxpayer's economic position has not changed significantly as a result of the transaction.

Whistleblower Program. An IRS initiative that offers special rewards to informants who provide evidence regarding tax evasion activities of businesses or high-income individuals. More than $2 million of tax, interest, and penalty must be at stake. The reward can reach 30 percent of the tax recovery that is attributable to the whistleblower's information.

Withholding allowances. The number of withholding allowances serves as the basis for determining the amount of income taxes withheld from an employee's salary or wages. The more withholding allowances claimed, the less income tax withheld by an employer. An employee may claim withholding allowances for personal exemptions for self and spouse (unless claimed as a dependent of another person), dependency exemptions, and special withholding allowances.

Work opportunity tax credit. Employers are allowed a tax credit equal to 40 percent of the first $6,000 of wages (per eligible employee) for the first year of employment. Eligible employees include certain hard-to-employ individuals (e.g., qualified ex-felons, high-risk youth, food stamp recipients, and veterans). The employer's deduction for wages is reduced by the amount of the credit taken. For qualified summer youth employees, the 40 percent rate is applied to the first $3,000 of qualified wages.

Working condition fringes. A type of fringe benefit received by the employee that is excludible from the employee's gross income. It consists of property or services provided (paid or reimbursed) by the employer for which the employee could take a tax deduction if the employee had paid for them. § 132.

Worthless securities. A loss (usually capital) is allowed for a security that becomes worthless during the year. The loss is deemed to have occurred on the last day of the year. Special rules apply to securities of affiliated companies and small business stock. § 165.

Writ of Certiorari. Appeal from a U.S. Court of Appeals to the U.S. Supreme Court is by Writ of Certiorari. The Supreme Court need not accept the appeal, and it usually does not (*cert. den.*) unless a conflict exists among the lower courts that must be resolved or a constitutional issue is involved.

Appendix D-1

Table of Code Sections Cited

I.R.C. Sec.	This Work Page	I.R.C. Sec.	This Work Page
1	2-5, 2-6, 9-21	25A(f)	11-25
1(g)	10-30	25A(i)(3)	10-30
1(g)(2)	9-24	26(a)(2)	17-16
1(h)	4-19, 11-39	27	17-10, 17-12
1(h)(11)	4-15	32	10-31
1(h)(11)(C)(i)	4-15	32(i)	10-31
1(h)(11)(C)(ii)	4-15	36B	10-33, 10-47
2	2-5, 2-6, 2-7	38	17-12
2(a)	2-5, 9-18	38–52	14-15
2(a)(1)(A)	2-5, 2-6	38(c)	17-3
2(b)	9-18	38(c)(3)(B)	17-3
3	2-5	39(a)(1)	17-3
4	2-5	41	5-16, 17-6, 17-12
5	2-5	41(b)(3)(A)	17-7
6	2-5	41(b)(3)(D)	17-7
6(a)(4)	17-24	41(c)(4)	17-6
6(b)(1)(D)	17-25	41(c)(5)	17-6
6(d)(1)(A)(i)(II)	17-24	41(d)	17-7
7	2-2, 2-5	41(e)	17-8
8	2-2, 2-5	42	17-12
9	2-5	44	17-8, 17-12
10	2-2, 2-5	45E	17-9, 17-12
11	2-5, 18-14	45F	17-9
12	2-5	45F(d)	17-9
12(d)	2-6	45R	17-11, 17-13
15(a)	12-2	45R(c)	17-11
17(d)	11-12	45R(d)(1)	17-11
21	10-28	45R(d)(4)	17-11
21(d)	10-29	45S	17-11, 17-13
22(e)(3)	9-10	47	17-4, 17-12
23	10-27, 11-11	50(c)	17-4
24	10-28	51	17-5, 17-12
24(a)	10-28	53	17-31
24(b)	10-28	55(a)	17-16
24(h)(4)(B)	9-15	55(b)(1)(A)	17-16
25A	10-30	55(d)(4)	17-15

I.R.C. Sec.	This Work Page
55(d)(4)(B)	17-16
56	17-13
56(a)(1)(A)	17-17
56(a)(1)(A)(ii)	17-18
56(a)(2)	17-20
56(a)(3)	17-20
56(a)(4)	17-24
56(a)(5)	17-19
56(a)(6)	17-22
56(b)(1)(A)	17-25
56(b)(1)(B)	17-27
56(b)(1)(C)(i)	17-25
56(b)(1)(C)(iii)	17-25
56(b)(1)(E)	17-28
56(b)(2)	17-19
56(b)(3)	17-21
56(d)(1)(A)(i)(II)	17-24
57	17-15
57(a)(1)	17-29
57(a)(2)	17-29
57(a)(5)	17-29
57(a)(7)	17-30
58(b)	17-13
59(e)	5-16
59(e)(2)(A)	17-19
59(e)(2)(D)	17-20
59(e)(2)(E)	17-20
61	2-29, 4-2, 4-3, 12-10, 16-5
61(a)	1-23, 9-3, 11-34
61(a)(3)	7-7
61(a)(12)	4-23
61(a)(13)	2-35
62	9-4
62(a)	11-39
62(a)(1)	6-10, 11-2
62(a)(2)	11-29
62(a)(2)(D)	11-29
63(b)(3)	11-39
63(c)(1)	9-7
63(c)(5)	9-8
63(d)(3)	11-39
67	10-25
67(a)	11-2
71	10-3
71–90	4-17
71(c)(2)	10-5
71(c)(3)	10-5
74	10-5
74(b)	10-5
74(c)	10-5
79	11-12
79(d)	11-9
83	12-10
83(a)	14-10
85	10-5
86	10-6, 11-6
101	4-18, 11-6
101–140	10-2
101–150	4-17

I.R.C. Sec.	This Work Page
101(a)(2)	4-22
102	4-17, 10-6
102(c)	10-6
103	4-17, 5-13
103(a)	4-20
104(a)(1)	10-10
104(a)(2)	10-9
104(a)(3)	10-10
105	11-6, 11-12
105(a)	11-5
105(b)	11-5
105(c)	11-5
105(h)	11-6
105(h)(2)	13-20
106	11-5, 11-6, 11-12
106(d)	11-6
108	4-18, 4-23
108(a)(1)(D)	4-24
108(b)	4-24
108(e)(5)	4-25
108(e)(6)	4-25
108(f)	4-25
109	4-18, 4-28, 7-18
111(a)	4-25
117	4-17
117(a)	10-7
117(b)	10-8, 11-10
117(d)	10-7, 11-9
118	12-25
119	11-12
119(a)	11-7
121	7-31, 10-18, 11-6
125	11-11, 11-12
125(f)	11-11
127	11-11, 11-12
129	11-10, 11-12
132	11-12
132(j)(1)	11-15
132(j)(4)	11-10
132(m)(2)	11-15
135	10-10
137	11-11, 11-12
139	10-6
141	17-29
152	9-9
152(b)(2)	9-15
152(b)(3)	9-15
152(c)	9-9
152(c)(4)	9-10
152(d)	9-11
152(d)(2)(H)	9-11
152(d)(3)	9-11, 9-13
152(e)(2)	9-14
152(e)(5)	9-14
152(f)(2)	9-9
152(f)(3)	9-11
152(f)(5)	9-10
152(f)(6)	9-9
161(a)	5-2

I.R.C. Sec.	This Work Page
162	5-3, 5-11, 5-12, 5-18, 11-34
162(a)	5-2, 5-60, 11-2, 11-20
162(a)(1)	18-12
162(c)	5-8
162(c)(2)	11-60
162(e)	5-9
162(f)	5-8, 5-60
162(f)(1)	5-8
162(g)	5-8
162(l)	11-34
162(m)	5-10
163(d)	12-32
163(d)(1)	10-17
163(h)(3)	10-18
163(h)(3)(E)(i)	10-19
163(h)(3)(E)(ii)	10-19
163(h)(3)(F)	17-26
163(h)(3)(F)(i)(I)	10-19
163(j)	5-14, 5-40, 12-26, 12-31, 12-32, 14-15
163(j)(1)	12-33
163(j)(3)	12-32
163(j)(4)	12-33
163(j)(7)	12-34
163(j)(8)(A)	12-32
163(j)(8)(A)(v)	12-32
163(j)(8)(B)	12-33
164	10-15
164(b)(6)	10-15
164(f)	11-34, 11-36
165	10-25
165(a)	7-7
165(c)(3)	6-11
165(g)	6-5
165(g)(1)	8-7
165(h)	6-11
165(h)(3)	6-11
165(h)(4)(E)	6-10
165(h)(5)(B)	6-11
165(h)(A)	17-31
165(i)	6-8
166(a)	6-3
167	7-18, 8-30
168	7-18, 8-30
168(b)	5-28
168(b)(5)	5-27
168(c)	5-28
168(d)(1)	5-28
168(d)(3)	5-26
168(d)(4)(A)	5-24
168(e)	5-24, 5-28
168(e)(6)	5-27
168(g)	5-40
168(g)(2)	13-5
168(k)	5-32, 8-30, 17-17
168(k)(2)	13-5
168(k)(2)(D)	5-35
168(k)(2)(F)	5-36
168(k)(2)(G)	17-17
170	5-18, 10-21

I.R.C. Sec.	This Work Page
170(a)(2)	5-19
170(b)	5-21
170(b)(1)(C)(iii)	10-24
170(b)(1)(G)(iii)(II)	10-24
170(c)	5-18, 10-21
170(d)	5-21, 10-25
170(e)(1)(A)	8-35
170(e)(1)(B)	8-35
170(f)	10-22
170(i)	10-22
170(j)	10-22
170(l)	10-22
171(c)	7-6
172	6-14
173(a)	17-19
174	5-15, 5-16, 17-7
174(a)(2)	5-17
174(b)(2)	5-15, 5-16
174(c)	5-15
179	5-29, 5-30, 5-31, 5-32, 5-33, 5-34, 5-35, 5-37, 5-49, 5-51, 5-56, 5-57, 5-58, 5-59, 5-60, 5-61, 5-62, 7-5, 7-18, 8-30, 8-32, 11-19, 11-22, 11-57, 13-6, 13-7, 13-8, 13-29, 13-30, 14-5, 14-15, 14-18, 14-42, 14-43, 17-36, 18-14
179(b)(6)	5-37
179(f)	5-50
183	15-26
183(b)(2)	11-45
183(d)	11-46
195	12-31, 12-52, 14-14
195(b)	5-11
197	3-5, 5-41, 8-30, 8-32, 18-15
197(a)	5-41
199A	11-37, 11-38, 11-39, 11-40, 11-41, 11-42, 12-32, 14-20, 18-22
199A(a)	11-38, 11-39, 15-12
199A(a)(1)(A)	11-38, 15-12
199A(b)(1)(A)	11-38
199A(b)(2)(B)	11-40
199A(b)(2)(B)(ii)	15-13
199A(b)(3)(B)	11-40
199A(b)(6)	11-41
199A(c)(3)(A)	11-38
199A(c)(4)	11-38
199A(d)(1)	11-38
199A(d)(1)(A)	11-42
199A(d)(2)	11-40, 11-42
199A(d)(3)	11-40
199A(e)	11-39
199A(e)(5)(A)	15-13
211	2-5
212	5-13, 10-11
212(1)	2-5
213(d)(1)(A)	10-12
213(d)(10)	11-7
213(f)	10-11
213(f)(2)	17-27
215	10-3

I.R.C. Sec.	This Work Page
217	11-15
217(k)	11-22
219(b)(1)	11-30
219(c)(2)	11-30
219(g)	11-30
219(g)(7)	11-31
221	10-17, 11-25
221(b)(2)(C)	10-17
222	11-25
222(b)(2)(C)	11-24
222(c)	11-25
222(d)	11-25
223	10-13, 11-6, 11-12
223(b)	11-6
223(b)(2)	10-14
223(c)(2)	10-14
223(d)	10-14, 11-6
223(f)	10-14
241	2-5
243(a)	12-28
245	12-28
246(b)(2)	12-29
246(c)	12-30
248	12-30, 12-32, 12-47
262	8-14, 10-25
263A(i)	4-8
265	5-13
265(a)(2)	10-20
267	2-23, 5-6, 5-7, 5-12, 5-52, 7-14, 7-15, 8-14
267(a)	2-18, 2-23, 2-24
267(a)(1)	2-18, 5-12, 7-8
267(b)	2-18, 7-14, 15-26
267(b)(2)	2-18, 2-23
267(c)	2-18
267(c)(2)	2-23, 2-24
267(c)(4)	2-18, 2-24
269A	18-10
274	5-40, 11-25
274(a)(4)	11-15
274(b)(1)	11-27
274(c)	11-21
274(d)	5-40, 11-29
274(e)	5-15, 11-26
274(i)	5-40
274(j)	10-5
274(k)	5-14, 11-26
274(n)	5-14, 5-15, 11-26
275	10-15
276	5-9
280A	10-18
280A through 280H	2-5
280A(c)(1)	11-27
280C(c)	17-7
280E	5-9
280F	5-35
280F(a)(1)	5-36
280F(b)(2)	5-38
280F(b)(3)	5-36
280F(d)(1)	5-37

I.R.C. Sec.	This Work Page
280F(d)(4)	5-35
280F(d)(5)	5-36
291	8-34
291(a)(1)	8-33
301	13-14
301(c)	13-2
301(c)(1)	13-2
302	18-13
302(b)(2)	13-23
302(b)(3)	13-23
302(b)(4)	13-23, 13-34
303	13-23
305(a)	7-10
307(a)	7-10, 13-21
311	13-14, 13-23
311(b)	15-19, 15-20, 18-10
311(b)(2)	13-15
312	13-3
312(a)	13-15
312(b)	13-15
312(c)	13-15
312(d)(1)	13-21
312(f)(1)	13-5
312(k)(3)(A)	13-5
312(k)(3)(B)	13-6
312(n)	13-6
312(n)(5)	13-5
312(n)(7)	13-23
316(a)	13-2
318	13-23
331	13-25
331(a)	18-21
332	8-35
334(a)	18-21
336(a)	18-21
351	2-7, 7-31, 8-35, 12-8–12-10, 12-12, 12-13, 12-14, 12-15, 12-18, 12-19, 12-20, 12-21, 12-22, 12-23, 12-24, 12-40, 12-47, 14-8, 15-21, 18-7, 18-17, 18-19, 18-21, 18-22
351(a)	12-19, 12-20, 18-20, 18-21
351(b)	12-9, 12-11, 12-16
351(b)(2)	12-19
351(g)	12-11
352(a)	18-20
357	12-15–12-18
357(a)	12-15, 12-16, 12-18
357(b)	12-16, 12-17, 12-18
357(c)	12-16, 12-17, 12-18
357(c)(2)(A)	12-17
358(a)	12-9, 12-20, 18-20, 18-21
362(a)	12-20, 18-21
362(e)(2)	12-22
367	12-15
367(b)(2)	15-21
368(c)	12-12, 18-21
385	12-27, 18-12
401	16-23
401–436	11-6
401(c)(2)	11-36

I.R.C. Sec.	This Work Page
401(c)(2)(A)(v)	11-36
401(k)	10-3, 11-36, 11-37, 11-57, 13-13, 17-32
402(c)(3)	11-32
408(m)	8-17
408(p)	11-36
408(p)(2)(E)(i)	11-36
408A	11-31
415(b)(1)	11-35
415(c)(1)	11-35
421(a)	17-21
441	4-6
446(a)	5-4
446(b)	4-7, 5-4
446(e)	5-4
448	4-8
448(c)	5-14
448(d)(2)(A)	6-21
451(b)	4-8
451(c)	4-12
453	4-7
457(b)	17-32
460	4-7
461(g)(1)	10-20
461(g)(2)	10-19
461(h)	5-5
461(l)	6-32, 14-28, 15-25
461(l)(3)	6-32
461(l)(3)(A)(i)	6-33
461(l)(4)(A)	6-32
465(a)	14-27
465(b)(1)	6-16
465(b)(6)	6-16, 14-27
465(e)	6-16
469	6-32, 15-39, 18-10
469(a)	6-21
469(b)	6-19
469(c)(2)	6-24
469(c)(7)	6-27
469(c)(7)(B)	6-28
469(d)(2)	6-20
469(f)	6-20
469(g)(2)	6-29
469(h)(2)	6-24
469(h)(5)	6-24
469(i)	6-28
469(i)(6)	6-28
469(j)(5)	6-28
469(j)(6)	6-30
469(j)(8)	6-24
471(c)	4-7, 4-8
474	2-28
481(a)	13-36
482	12-35, 16-14
509	5-20
531–537	13-25
541–547	13-26
585	6-2
611(a)	5-43
612	5-42
613(a)	5-43, 17-28
613A	5-43
613A(c)	17-29
614(a)	17-29
616(a)	17-20
617(a)	17-20
643(a)(2)	2-35
691	10-25
701	14-4
702	14-4
702(a)	14-15
702(b)	14-15
703(a)(1)	14-5
703(a)(2)	15-11
703(b)	14-13
704(a)	14-6, 14-19
704(b)	14-7, 14-19
704(c)(1)(A)	14-19
704(d)	14-26
705	14-7, 14-21, 18-8
707	2-23, 7-14
707(a)(2)(B)	14-10
707(b)	14-30
707(b)(2)	14-30
708(a)	2-35
708(b)(1)(B)	18-16
709(a)	14-13
709(b)(2)	14-14
721	7-31, 8-35, 14-8, 14-9, 14-10, 18-7, 18-16, 18-18, 18-20
721(a)	18-20
721(b)	14-9
722	14-7, 18-20
723	14-7, 14-11, 18-20
724	14-12
724(c)	14-12
724(d)(2)	14-12
731(a)	14-17
742	4-21
743	18-17
751	18-16, 18-23
751(a)	14-25
751(d)	14-25
752	14-21, 14-22, 18-8
752(a)	15-22
754	18-16, 18-17
761(a)	14-3
861(a)(2)	16-7
861 through 865	16-7
865	16-7
901	16-10
901–908	17-10
902	16-10
903	16-10
904	16-10, 17-10
911(a)	11-17
954(d)	16-35
1001	12-18
1001(a)	7-2, 14-8

I.R.C. Sec.	This Work Page
1001(b)	7-3
1001(c)	7-7, 14-8
1011	7-13
1011(a)	7-4
1012	7-9
1014	7-42
1014(a)	7-13
1015(a)	7-11
1015(d)(6)	7-12
1016(a)	7-4
1016(a)(2)	7-5
1016(a)(4)	7-6
1016(a)(5)	7-6
1017	4-23
1022	7-13
1031	7-20, 7-22, 7-23, 7-27, 7-31, 7-32, 7-33, 7-39, 7-41, 7-42, 8-36, 8-39, 12-8, 12-15
1031(a)	7-20
1031(a)(3)	7-22
1032	12-23, 12-25
1033	7-25, 7-26, 7-27, 7-29, 7-30, 7-40, 8-25
1033(a)	7-27
1033(a)(2)(A)	7-29
1033(a)(2)(B)	7-28
1033(b)	7-29
1033(g)(4)	7-28
1041	10-4
1045	18-14
1045(a)	8-22
1059	13-36
1060	7-10
1091	2-23, 7-15
1091(a)	2-24, 7-15
1091(b)	7-15
1091(d)	7-15
1202	18-14
1202(a)	8-21
1202(a)(4)	17-30
1202(a)(4)(C)	17-30
1202(e)(3)(A)	11-42
1211	4-20
1211(b)	8-16
1211(b)(1)	8-20
1212	4-20
1212(a)(1)	8-23
1221	8–6, 8-31, 8-46
1221(a)	8-3
1221(a)(2)	8-23
1221(b)(3)	8-3
1222	8-13
1222(1)	2-5
1222(3)	8-13
1222(11)	11-39
1223	8-13
1223(1)	7-24, 12-23
1223(2)	7-12, 12-23
1223(4)	7-15
1223(5)	7-10, 13-21

I.R.C. Sec.	This Work Page
1223(11)	7-14
1231	5-19, 7-24, 8-1, 8-2, 8-4, 8-12, 8-13, 8-23, 8-24, 8-25, 8-26, 8-27, 8-28, 8-29, 8-30, 8-31, 8-32, 8-34, 8-35, 8-36, 8-37, 8-43, 8-44, 8-47, 12-23, 12-46, 14-11, 14-12, 14-15, 15-34, 18-15, 18-24
1231(b)(1)	8-28
1231(c)	8-28
1233	7-29, 8-14
1234(a)	8-7
1234(b)(1)	8-8
1234A	8-7
1235	8-9
1237	8-6, 8-38, 8-40, 8-46
1241	8-12
1244	6-5, 6-6, 6-33, 6-34, 6-36, 8-7, 15-26, 15-37, 18-14, 18-24
1245	8-2, 8-11, 8-12, 8-24, 8-29, 8-30, 8-31, 8-32, 8-33, 8-34, 8-35, 8-36, 8-37, 8-39, 8-45, 8-47, 18-15
1245(b)(1)	8-34
1245(b)(2)	8-35
1245(b)(3)	8-35, 12-24
1250	8-2, 8-18, 8-19, 8-20, 8-24, 8-29, 8-30, 8-31, 8-32, 8-33, 8-34, 8-36, 8-37, 8-47, 18-15
1250(d)(1)	8-34
1250(d)(2)	8-35
1250(d)(3)	8-35, 12-24
1253	8-10
1253(b)(1)	8-10
1259	8-15
1271	8-7
1272(a)(2)	4-11
1272(a)(3)	4-11
1273(a)	4-11
1341	13-35
1361	18-2
1361–1379	15-2
1361(a)	18-21
1361(b)	18-21
1361(b)(1)(B)	15-5
1361(b)(1)(D)	15-4
1361(c)(1)(A)(ii)	15-5
1361(c)(1)(B)(i)	15-5
1361(c)(4)	15-4
1361(c)(5)(A)	15-4
1362	18-2
1362(a)	18-21
1362(a)(2)	15-7, 18-21
1362(b)	15-6
1362(b)(1)(C)	15-6
1362(d)	15-7
1362(d)(1)(B)	15-7
1362(d)(2)(B)	15-8
1362(d)(3)(A)(ii)	15-8
1362(d)(3)(B)	15-29
1362(d)(3)(C)	15-29

I.R.C. Sec.	This Work Page
1362(e)(3)	15-8
1363(b)	15-10
1366(a)	15-10
1366(a)(1)	15-13
1366(b)	15-10
1366(c)	15-10
1366(d)	15-23
1366(f)(2)	15-27
1367(a)	15-21
1367(b)(2)	15-22
1368(a)(1)(A)	15-23
1368(c)	15-16, 15-17
1368(c)(1)	15-16
1368(e)(1)	15-16
1368(e)(1)(A)	15-17, 15-23
1368(e)(3)	15-16
1371(a)	2-35
1371(e)	15-18
1374(d)(4)	15-30
1374(d)(7)	15-28
1374(d)(7)(B)	15-27
1375(a)	15-30
1375(b)	15-30
1377(a)(1)	15-13
1377(a)(2)	15-13
1377(b)	15-18
1401(b)(2)(A)	14-31
1402(a)	11-36, 14-5, 14-15
1402(a)(12)	11-34
1411	14-31
1501–1504	3-3
1563(a)(1)	12-34
2010	1-12
2032(a)(1)	7-14
2032(c)	7-14
2503(a)	2-35
2503(g)(2)(A)	2-35
2505	1-12
3401(a)	14-30
3402	9-22
4942	5-20
4980D	11-6

I.R.C. Sec.	This Work Page
5000A	10-32
6012(a)(1)	9-20
6012(a)(2)	12-35
6013(a)(1)	9-19
6013(g)	9-19
6017	11-34
6072(a)	9-29, 12-35
6110(c)	2-8
6654	9-22
6654(b)(2)	11-45
6654(b)(3)	11-45
6654(c)(1)	11-44
6654(e)(1)	11-44
6655	12-36
6655(g)(2)	12-36
6662	2-9, 2-23
6699	15-26
6712(a)	2-6
7463(b)	2-36
7701(a)(1)	16-3
7701(a)(2)	14-3
7701(a)(4)	16-3
7701(a)(5)	16-3
7702B	11-6, 11-7
7703(b)	9-20
7805	2-7
7805(a)	2-7
7805(e)	2-7
7852(d)	2-6
7872	4-39
7872(a)(1)	4-26
7872(b)(2)	4-26
7872(c)	4-27
7872(c)(1)(D)	4-27
7872(c)(1)(E)	4-27
7872(c)(2)	4-27
7872(c)(3)	4-27
7872(d)	4-27
7872(d)(1)(B)	4-28
7872(f)(2)	4-26
11011(b)	11-39
11012	11-37

Appendix D-2

Table of Regulations Cited

Temporary Treasury Regulations

Temp.Reg. Sec.	This Work Page
1.67–1T(a)(1)(iv)	11-47
1.101–7T	4-22
1.152–4T	9-14
1.162–1T(d)	5-18
1.274–5T(c)(3)	11-29
1.280F–6T(e)	5-36
1.385–1 to –4T	12-27
1.469–1T(e)(3)	6-25
1.469–1T(g)(3)(i)(A)	6-24
1.469–1T(g)(3)(i)(B)	6-24
1.469–5T(a)	6-23
1.469–5T(e)(3)(ii)	6-24
1.469–5T(f)(3)	6-24
1.956–2T	2-30

Proposed Treasury Regulations

Prop. Reg. Sec.	This Work Page
1.2	2-7
1.117–6(b)(2)	10-8
1.117–6(c)(3)(i)	10-7
1.152–1(a)(2)	9-15
1.469–5	6-24

Treasury Regulations

Reg. Sec.	This Work Page
1.2	2-7
1.61–1(a)	4-5
1.61–2(d)(2)(i)	7-9
1.61–3(a)	5-9
1.61–6(a)	7-7, 7-10
1.61–8(b)	8-12
1.61–9(c)	4-16
1.62–2(c)(4)	13-20
1.72–7(c)(1)	4-22
1.79–3	11-10

Treasury Regulations

Reg. Sec.	This Work Page
1.79–3(d)(2)	11-9
1.106–1	11-5
1.117–2(a)	10-7
1.118–1	12-25
1.119–1(c)(1)	11-8
1.119–1(f)	11-8
1.132–1(b)	11-13
1.132–2	11-13
1.162–2(b)(1)	11-21
1.162–5(b)(2)	11-22
1.162–5(b)(3)	11-22
1.162–5(b)(3)(ii)	11-23
1.162–8	5-3
1.162–10	13-20
1.162–17(b)(4)	11-29
1.162–21(b)	5-60
1.165–1	6-42
1.165–1(a)	7-7
1.165–1(d)(2)	6-9
1.165–1(d)(2)(i)	6-7
1.165–7(a)(2)(ii)	6-10
1.165–8(a)(2)	6-9
1.165–8(d)	6-9
1.165–9(b)(2)	7-17
1.166–1(e)	6-2
1.167(g)–1	7-13, 7-17
1.170A–4(b)(1)	8-35
1.170A–4A(b)(2)(ii)(C)	2-36
1.170A–10	10-25
1.174–2	5-15
1.183–1(a)	11-45
1.183–1(b)(1)	11-47
1.183–2(b)(1) through (9)	11-46
1.195–1	12-52
1.212–1(f)	11-23
1.213–1(e)(1)(iii)	10-13
1.248–1(d)	12-30
1.263(a)–4(f)	5-7
1.263(a)–4(f)(6)	5-7

Treasury Regulations

Reg. Sec.	This Work Page
1.267(b)–1(b)(1)	2-23
1.274–4	11-21
1.280F–7(a)	5-39
1.301–1(j)	7-9, 13-17
1.301–1(m)	13-17
1.312–6	13-3
1.312–6(a)	13-3
1.332–2(c)	13-24
1.351–1(a)(1)	12-12
1.351–1(a)(1)(ii)	12-11, 12-13, 12-14
1.351–1(a)(2)	2-7, 12-14
1.408–10(b)	8-17
1.441–1	4-6
1.446–1(a)(2)	5-4
1.446–1(a)(3)	4-7
1.446–1(c)(1)(i)	4-7
1.446–1(c)(2)(i)	4-7
1.451–1(a)	4-8
1.451–2	4-7
1.451–2(a)	4-10
1.451–2(b)	4-10
1.451–5	4-12
1.451–5(b)	4-12
1.451–5(c)	4-12
1.453–9(c)(2)	12-10
1.461–1(a)	5-5
1.461–4(g)(6)	5-18
1.469–2(f)(6)	15-39
1.469–4	6-22
1.469–4(c)(3)	6-22
1.469–4(d)	6-22
1.469–4(f)	6-22
1.469–9	6-28
1.672(b)–1	2-36
1.704–1(b)	14-19
1.731–1(c)(3)	14-9
1.752–1(a)	14-22
1.752–1(e)	15-22
1.861–8	16-7
1.954–3(a)	16-35
1.1001–1(a)	7-2
1.1001–1(b)	7-3
1.1001–1(c)(1)	7-2
1.1002–1(a)	7-7
1.1002–1(c)	7-19
1.1011–1	7-4, 7-13
1.1012–1(a)	7-9
1.1012–1(c)(1)	7-9
1.1015–1(a)(1)	7-11
1.1015–1(a)(3)	7-11
1.1015–5(c)(2)	7-12
1.1015–5(c)(5)	7-12
1.1016–1	7-4
1.1016–3(a)(1)(i)	7-5

Treasury Regulations

Reg. Sec.	This Work Page
1.1016–5(a)	7-6
1.1016–5(b)	7-6
1.1016–6(a)	7-5
1.1031(a)–1(a)	7-20
1.1031(a)–1(b)	7-20
1.1031(d)–2	7-25
1.1032–1(a)	12-23
1.1033(a)–1	7-27
1.1033(a)–1(a)	7-27
1.1033(a)–2(a)	7-27
1.1033(a)–2(c)(1)	7-29
1.1033(a)–2(c)(3)	7-28
1.1091–1(a)	7-15
1.1091–1(c)	7-15
1.1091–1(f)	7-15
1.1091–2(a)	7-15
1.1221–1(b)	8-12
1.1223–1(a)	7-24
1.1223–1(b)	7-12
1.1223–1(d)	7-15
1.1223–1(e)	7-10
1.1234–1(a)(1)	8-7
1.1235–2(b)(1)	8-9
1.1241–1(a)	8-12
1.1245–2(a)(4)	7-24, 8-35
1.1245–2(c)(2)	8-35
1.1245–4(a)(1)	8-34
1.1245–4(c)	8-35
1.1250–2(d)(1)	7-24, 8-35
1.1250–2(d)(3)	8-35
1.1250–3(a)(1)	8-34
1.1250–3(c)	8-35
1.1361–1(l)(1)	15-4
1.1362–6(b)(3)(iii)	15-7
1.1367–1(f)	15-21
1.1367–2	15-22
1.1367–2(e)	15-21
1.1372–2(b)(1)	15-4
1.1377–1(a)(2)(ii)	15-7
1.6012–2(a)	12-35
1.6081–4	9-29
1.6661–3(b)(2)	2-23
20.2031–7(f)	2-36
31.3121(d)–1(c)(2)	11-61
31.3306(i)–1(b)	11-61
31.3401(c)–1(b)	11-3
301.7216–2(c)(2)	1-29
301.7701–1 to –3	14-3
301.7701–1 through –4	12-7, 18-2
301.7701–1 through –6	18-2
301.7701–1 through –7	12-7
301.7701–1 through 24	12-7
301.7701–1 through 27	12-7
301.7701–3(g)(i)	18-37

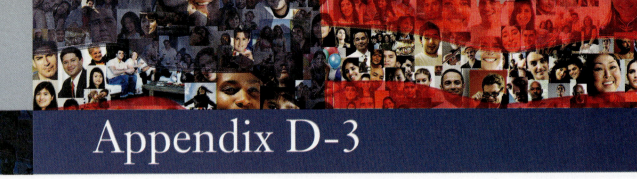

Appendix D-3

Table of Revenue Procedures and Revenue Rulings Cited

Revenue Procedures

Rev. Proc.	This Work Page
87–54	10-5
87–56	5-24, 13-5
87–57	5-47, 5-48
97–27	13-36
2004–34	3-5, 4-12
2010–51	11-19
2014–21	5-36
2014-34	4-12
2016–24	10-32
2017–21	10-33
2017–33	17-17
2017–36	10-33
2018–3	2-8

Revenue Rulings

Rev. Rul.	This Work Page
54–96	12-13
56–60	7-14
56–406	7-15
57–374	10-5
57–418	5-11
58–142	5-18
59–44	2-23, 2-24
59–86	7-12
59–221	15-26
60–183	15-7
61	4-4
61–146	11-6
62–217	12-23
63–221	7-27
63–232	6-7
64–56	12-10
64–162	15-22
66–7	8-13
68–55	12-9
68–291	7-7

Revenue Rulings

Rev. Rul.	This Work Page
69–188	10-19
69–292	11-23
70–40	5-18
70–239	18-37
70–466	7-28
71–190	10-16
71–564	12-10
72–312	4-14
72–592	6-7
73–539	11-20
74–44	15-15
74–78	11-23
74–503	12-23
75–14	11-47
75–168	11-19
75–448	10-8
77–263	10-7
77–414	7-7
78–39	5-5
79–379	4-16
80	11-7
80–52	4-10
80–335	5-5
82–74	7-27
82–196	11-5
82–202	4-23
82–208	10-16
83–98	18-12
84–111	18-37
85–161	15-9
87–22	10-19
87–41	11-3
2004–59	18-37
2009–34	2-33
2012–15	2-30
2013–17	9-17
2017–16	2-8

Appendix E

Table of Cases Cited

A

Allen, Mary Francis, 6-9
Alpha Medical v. Comm., 13-18
Anderson, Comm. v., 11-8
Anton, M. G., 4-16
Apollo Computer, Inc. v. U.S., 2-16
Aragona, Frank, Trust, 6-28
Armantrout, Richard T., 10-8
Armstrong v. Phinney, 11-7
Arrigoni v. Comm., 6-43
Artukovich, Nick A., 15-6
Ashtabula Bow Socket Co., 2-33
Augustus v. Comm., 2-20

B

Baist, George A., 11-23
Balistrieri, Joseph P., 7-27
Bauer v. Comm., 12-28, 18-12
Bausch & Lomb, 16-35
BB&T Corp., 2-33
Bedell v. Comm., 4-7
Bell, Kay, 4-30
Bernal, Kathryn, 2-36
Bhalla, C. P., 10-7
Bingler v. Johnson, 10-7
Bolker, Joseph R., 2-33
Bright v. U.S., 4-8
Brody, Clifford L. and Barbara J. DeClerk, 6-43
Brown v. Helvering, 4-8
Burnet v. Sanford and Brooks, 4-9

C

Campbell, Jr. v. Wheeler, 12-16
Cesarini v. U.S., 4-4
Choate Construction Co., 2-33
Comm. v. (see opposing party)
Commissioner v. Newman, 1-22

Correll, U.S. v., 11-19
Cowden v. Comm., 4-11
Crane v. Comm., 7-3

D

Daly, D. R., Estate of, 4-21, 10-6
Davis, U.S. v., 7-4, 10-4
De Mendoza, III, Mario G., 15-26
de Werff, Cheryl L., 10-42
Delman, Estate of v. Comm., 4-23
Delta Plastics, Inc., 12-28
Deputy v. DuPont, 5-2
DiZenzo v. Comm., 13-18
Doak, Comm. v., 11-7
Donruss Co., The, U.S. v., 2-16
Duberstein, Comm. v., 10-6, 10-21

E

Easson, Jack L., 12-16
English, Jesse W. and Betty J., 8-46
Estate of (see name of party)

F

F. W. Woolworth Co., 2-7
Fagan, Charles Edward, 2-15
Fahs v. Florida Machine and Foundry Co., 12-13
Fay v. Helvering, 6-7
Fin Hay Realty Co. v. U.S., 12-27, 13-18
Fischer, L. M., 4-9
Frank, Morton, 5-11

G

Generes, U.S. v., 6-43
George S. Nalle III v. Comm., 17-42
Glenshaw Glass Co., Comm. v., 4-4, 9-3
Golsen, Jack E., 2-13

Green, Thomas J. Jr., 2-36
Grey, Joseph M., Public Accountant, P.C., 15-15
Gribauskas, Estate of v. Comm., 2-16
Guenther, Kenneth W., 11-26

H

Harolds Club v. Comm., 18-12
Hawkins, C. A., 10-9
Heininger, Comm. v., 5-2
Helvering v. (see opposing party)
Hempt Brothers, Inc. v. U.S., 12-10
Henderson, James O., 11-20
Hertwig, U.S. v., 12-19
Higgins v. Comm., 2-36
Hillsboro National Bank v. Comm., 5-5
Houston, Michael J., 15-26
Hughes, Nick R., 2-15

J

Jacobs, 11-26
Jacobson, Comm. v., 4-24
James v. U.S., 4-2
Johnson v. Comm., 10-5

K

Kahler, Charles F., 4-8
Keator, Todd D., 4-30
Kennedy, Jr. v. Comm., 5-3
Kieselbach v. Comm., 4-20
Kirby Lumber Co., U.S. v., 4-23
Kluger Associates, Inc., 7-9
Knott, Henry J., 13-20
Kowalski, Comm. v., 11-7

L

Landfield Finance Co. v. U.S., 4-21
Lengsfield v. Comm., 13-16
Lincoln Electric Co., Comm. v., 5-3
Lindeman, J. B., 11-8
Loco Realty Co. v. Comm., 7-28
Lucas v. North Texas Lumber Co., 4-8
Lucas v. Ox Fibre Brush Co., 2-33
Lynch v. Turrish, 7-2

M

Magneson, 2-33
Malat v. Riddell, 8-3

Mantell, John, 4-11
Marshman, Comm. v., 7-4
Martinez, Estate of, 2-15
Mayson Manufacturing Co. v. Comm., 13-18, 18-12
McAlary Ltd., 15-15
McCandless Tile Service v. U.S., 13-20
McWilliams v. Comm., 7-15
Merchants Loan and Trust Co. v. Smietanka, 4-3
Miller, Harris M., 2-7
Mitchell, Maria Antionette Walton, 2-36
Mixon, Jr., Estate of v. U.S., 12-27
Montgomery Engineering Co. v. U.S., 13-17
Mulherin, Brian C., 11-23

N

National Federation of Independent Business v. Sebelius, 10-32
Nico, Severino R., Jr., 2-21
North American Oil Consolidated Co. v. Burnet, 4-9

O

O'Connor, John C., 12-13
O'Malley v. Ames, 7-4
Oregon Mesabi Corporation, 6-42
Oswald, Vincent E., 13-35

P

Page v. Rhode Island Trust Co., 5-4
Pahl v. Comm., 2-36
Papineau, G. A., 11-7
Pauli, Karl, 2-14
Peno Trucking, Inc., 11-61
Pestcoe, William, 15-7
Pollock v. Farmer's Loan & Trust Co., 4-20
Portage Plastics Co. v. U.S., 15-9

R

R. J. Nicoll Co., 13-19
Radtke v. U.S., 15-15
Rapoport, Herbert M., Estate of, 6-43
Ray, John and Rochelle, 2-33
Reeves, Daniel L., 13-17
Riach v. Frank, 10-13
Robertson v. U.S., 10-6
Rogers, U.S. v., 6-7
Rosenberg v. Comm., 6-7
Rowan Companies, Inc. v. U.S., 11-7
Rubenfield, Ronald R., 11-48

S

Sargent v. Comm., 4-13
Sauvigne, Donald J., 15-23
Schalk Chemical Co. v. Comm., 13-20
Schuster's Express, Inc., 2-33
Selig, Bruce, 5-60
Sherman, Stephen G., 11-23
Shopmaker v. U.S., 6-7
Simon v. Comm., 13-18
Slappey Drive Industrial Park v. U.S., 12-27
Snow v. Comm., 5-16
Soliman, Comm. v., 11-27
Solomon, S. L., 6-7
South Carolina v. Baker III, 4-20
Spicer Accounting, Inc. v. U.S., 15-15
Strauss, Julia A., 4-7
Sullivan, Comm. v., 5-9
Sundby, Dale H., 6-43

T

T.H. Campbell & Bros., Inc., 15-6
Talen v. U.S., 2-36
Tank Truck Rentals, Inc. v. Comm., 5-8
Tanner, Douglas H., 5-18
Tauferner v. U.S., 11-18
Teleservice Co. of Wyoming Valley, 12-25
Terrell, 2-35
Thor Power Tool Co. v. Comm., 4-5
Tomerlin, James O., Trust, 2-7
Tomlinson v. 1661 Corp., 12-28

Tougher v. Comm., 11-8
Turner v. U.S., 2-15, 2-16

U

U.S. Trust Co. of New York v. Anderson, 4-20
United Draperies, Inc. v. Comm., 2-32
United States v. (see opposing party)

V

Veterinary Surgical Consultants PC, 2-36
Vichich, Nadine L., 2-14
Villamena, Vincenzo, 4-30

W

Ward, Dwight A., 5-11
Ward v. U.S., 15-6
Watson, David E., P.C. v. U.S., 15-15
Welch v. Helvering, 5-3
Wilgard Realty Co. v. Comm., 12-12
Wilson, William B., 15-7
Windsor, U.S. v., 9-17

Y

Yeagle Drywall Co., 2-36
York v. Comm., 5-11

Z

Zaninovich v. Comm., 5-5

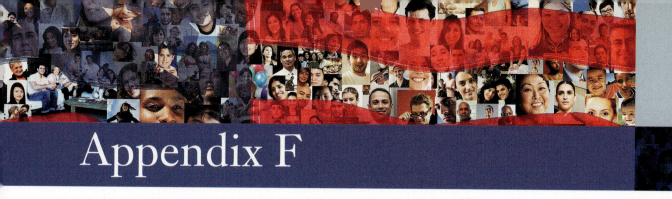

Appendix F

Present Value and Future Value Tables

Present Value of $1   F-2

Present Value of an Ordinary Annuity of $1   F-2

Future Value of $1   F-3

Future Value of an Ordinary Annuity of $1   F-3

Present Value of $1

N/R	1%	2%	3%	4%	5%	6%	7%	8%	9%	10%	11%	12%
1	0.9901	0.9804	0.9709	0.9615	0.9524	0.9434	0.9346	0.9259	0.9174	0.9091	0.9009	0.8929
2	0.9803	0.9612	0.9426	0.9246	0.9070	0.8900	0.8734	0.8573	0.8417	0.8264	0.8116	0.7972
3	0.9706	0.9423	0.9151	0.8890	0.8638	0.8396	0.8163	0.7938	0.7722	0.7513	0.7312	0.7118
4	0.9610	0.9238	0.8885	0.8548	0.8227	0.7921	0.7629	0.7350	0.7084	0.6830	0.6587	0.6355
5	0.9515	0.9057	0.8626	0.8219	0.7835	0.7473	0.7130	0.6806	0.6499	0.6209	0.5935	0.5674
6	0.9420	0.8880	0.8375	0.7903	0.7462	0.7050	0.6663	0.6302	0.5963	0.5645	0.5346	0.5066
7	0.9327	0.8706	0.8131	0.7599	0.7107	0.6651	0.6227	0.5835	0.5470	0.5132	0.4817	0.4523
8	0.9235	0.8535	0.7894	0.7307	0.6768	0.6274	0.5820	0.5403	0.5019	0.4665	0.4339	0.4039
9	0.9143	0.8368	0.7664	0.7026	0.6446	0.5919	0.5439	0.5002	0.4604	0.4241	0.3909	0.3606
10	0.9053	0.8203	0.7441	0.6756	0.6139	0.5584	0.5083	0.4632	0.4224	0.3855	0.3522	0.3220
11	0.8963	0.8043	0.7224	0.6496	0.5847	0.5268	0.4751	0.4289	0.3875	0.3505	0.3173	0.2875
12	0.8874	0.7885	0.7014	0.6246	0.5568	0.4970	0.4440	0.3971	0.3555	0.3186	0.2858	0.2567
13	0.8787	0.7730	0.6810	0.6006	0.5303	0.4688	0.4150	0.3677	0.3262	0.2897	0.2575	0.2292
14	0.8700	0.7579	0.6611	0.5775	0.5051	0.4423	0.3878	0.3405	0.2992	0.2633	0.2320	0.2046
15	0.8613	0.7430	0.6419	0.5553	0.4810	0.4173	0.3624	0.3152	0.2745	0.2394	0.2090	0.1827
16	0.8528	0.7284	0.6232	0.5339	0.4581	0.3936	0.3387	0.2919	0.2519	0.2176	0.1883	0.1631
17	0.8444	0.7142	0.6050	0.5134	0.4363	0.3714	0.3166	0.2703	0.2311	0.1978	0.1696	0.1456
18	0.8360	0.7002	0.5874	0.4936	0.4155	0.3503	0.2959	0.2502	0.2120	0.1799	0.1528	0.1300
19	0.8277	0.6864	0.5703	0.4746	0.3957	0.3305	0.2765	0.2317	0.1945	0.1635	0.1377	0.1161
20	0.8195	0.6730	0.5537	0.4564	0.3769	0.3118	0.2584	0.2145	0.1784	0.1486	0.1240	0.1037

Present Value of an Ordinary Annuity of $1

N/R	1%	2%	3%	4%	5%	6%	7%	8%	9%	10%	11%	12%
1	0.9901	0.9804	0.9709	0.9615	0.9524	0.9434	0.9346	0.9259	0.9174	0.9091	0.9009	0.8929
2	1.9704	1.9416	1.9135	1.8861	1.8594	1.8334	1.8080	1.7833	1.7591	1.7355	1.7125	1.6901
3	2.9410	2.8839	2.8286	2.7751	2.7232	2.6730	2.6243	2.5771	2.5313	2.4869	2.4437	2.4018
4	3.9020	3.8077	3.7171	3.6299	3.5460	3.4651	3.3872	3.3121	3.2397	3.1699	3.1024	3.0373
5	4.8534	4.7135	4.5797	4.4518	4.3295	4.2124	4.1002	3.9927	3.8897	3.7908	3.6959	3.6048
6	5.7955	5.6014	5.4172	5.2421	5.0757	4.9173	4.7665	4.6229	4.4859	4.3553	4.2305	4.1114
7	6.7282	6.4720	6.2303	6.0021	5.7864	5.5824	5.3893	5.2064	5.0330	4.8684	4.7122	4.5638
8	7.6517	7.3255	7.0197	6.7327	6.4632	6.2098	5.9713	5.7466	5.5348	5.3349	5.1461	4.9676
9	8.5660	8.1622	7.7861	7.4353	7.1078	6.8017	6.5152	6.2469	5.9952	5.7590	5.5370	5.3282
10	9.4713	8.9826	8.5302	8.1109	7.7217	7.3601	7.0236	6.7101	6.4177	6.1446	5.8892	5.6502
11	10.3676	9.7868	9.2526	8.7605	8.3064	7.8869	7.4987	7.1390	6.8052	6.4951	6.2065	5.9377
12	11.2551	10.5753	9.9540	9.3851	8.8633	8.3838	7.9427	7.5361	7.1607	6.8137	6.4924	6.1944
13	12.1337	11.3484	10.6350	9.9856	9.3936	8.8527	8.3577	7.9038	7.4869	7.1034	6.7499	6.4235
14	13.0037	12.1062	11.2961	10.5631	9.8986	9.2950	8.7455	8.2442	7.7862	7.3667	6.9819	6.6282
15	13.8651	12.8493	11.9379	11.1184	10.3797	9.7122	9.1079	8.5595	8.0607	7.6061	7.1909	6.8109
16	14.7179	13.5777	12.5611	11.6523	10.8378	10.1059	9.4466	8.8514	8.3126	7.8237	7.3792	6.9740
17	15.5623	14.2919	13.1661	12.1657	11.2741	10.4773	9.7632	9.1216	8.5436	8.0216	7.5488	7.1196
18	16.3983	14.9920	13.7535	12.6593	11.6896	10.8276	10.0591	9.3719	8.7556	8.2014	7.7016	7.2497
19	17.2260	15.6785	14.3238	13.1339	12.0853	11.1581	10.3356	9.6036	8.9501	8.3649	7.8393	7.3658
20	18.0456	16.3514	14.8775	13.5903	12.4622	11.4699	10.5940	9.8181	9.1285	8.5136	7.9633	7.4694

Future Value of $1

N/R	1%	2%	3%	4%	5%	6%	7%	8%	9%	10%	11%	12%
1	1.0100	1.0200	1.0300	1.0400	1.0500	1.0600	1.0700	1.0800	1.0900	1.1000	1.1100	1.1200
2	1.0201	1.0404	1.0609	1.0816	1.1025	1.1236	1.1449	1.1664	1.1881	1.2100	1.2321	1.2544
3	1.0303	1.0612	1.0927	1.1249	1.1576	1.1910	1.2250	1.2597	1.2950	1.3310	1.3676	1.4049
4	1.0406	1.0824	1.1255	1.1699	1.2155	1.2625	1.3108	1.3605	1.4116	1.4641	1.5181	1.5735
5	1.0510	1.1041	1.1593	1.2167	1.2763	1.3382	1.4026	1.4693	1.5386	1.6105	1.6851	1.7623
6	1.0615	1.1262	1.1941	1.2653	1.3401	1.4185	1.5007	1.5869	1.6771	1.7716	1.8704	1.9738
7	1.0721	1.1487	1.2299	1.3159	1.4071	1.5036	1.6058	1.7138	1.8280	1.9487	2.0762	2.2107
8	1.0829	1.1717	1.2668	1.3686	1.4775	1.5938	1.7182	1.8509	1.9926	2.1436	2.3045	2.4760
9	1.0937	1.1951	1.3048	1.4233	1.5513	1.6895	1.8385	1.9990	2.1719	2.3579	2.5580	2.7731
10	1.1046	1.2190	1.3439	1.4802	1.6289	1.7908	1.9672	2.1589	2.3674	2.5937	2.8394	3.1058
11	1.1157	1.2434	1.3842	1.5395	1.7103	1.8983	2.1049	2.3316	2.5804	2.8531	3.1518	3.4785
12	1.1268	1.2682	1.4258	1.6010	1.7959	2.0122	2.2522	2.5182	2.8127	3.1384	3.4985	3.8960
13	1.1381	1.2936	1.4685	1.6651	1.8856	2.1329	2.4098	2.7196	3.0658	3.4523	3.8833	4.3635
14	1.1495	1.3195	1.5126	1.7317	1.9799	2.2609	2.5785	2.9372	3.3417	3.7975	4.3104	4.8871
15	1.1610	1.3459	1.5580	1.8009	2.0789	2.3966	2.7590	3.1722	3.6425	4.1772	4.7846	5.4736
16	1.1726	1.3728	1.6047	1.8730	2.1829	2.5404	2.9522	3.4259	3.9703	4.5950	5.3109	6.1304
17	1.1843	1.4002	1.6528	1.9479	2.2920	2.6928	3.1588	3.7000	4.3276	5.0545	5.8951	6.8660
18	1.1961	1.4282	1.7024	2.0258	2.4066	2.8543	3.3799	3.9960	4.7171	5.5599	6.5436	7.6900
19	1.2081	1.4568	1.7535	2.1068	2.5270	3.0256	3.6165	4.3157	5.1417	6.1159	7.2633	8.6128
20	1.2202	1.4859	1.8061	2.1911	2.6533	3.2071	3.8697	4.6610	5.6044	6.7275	8.0623	9.6463

Future Value of an Ordinary Annuity of $1

N/R	1%	2%	3%	4%	5%	6%	7%	8%	9%	10%	11%	12%
1	1.0000	1.0000	1.0000	1.0000	1.0000	1.0000	1.0000	1.0000	1.0000	1.0000	1.0000	1.0000
2	2.0100	2.0200	2.0300	2.0400	2.0500	2.0600	2.0700	2.0800	2.0900	2.1000	2.1100	2.1200
3	3.0301	3.0604	3.0909	3.1216	3.1525	3.1836	3.2149	3.2464	3.2781	3.3100	3.3421	3.3744
4	4.0604	4.1216	4.1836	4.2465	4.3101	4.3746	4.4399	4.5061	4.5731	4.6410	4.7097	4.7793
5	5.1010	5.2040	5.3091	5.4163	5.5256	5.6371	5.7507	5.8666	5.9847	6.1051	6.2278	6.3528
6	6.1520	6.3081	6.4684	6.6330	6.8019	6.9753	7.1533	7.3359	7.5233	7.7156	7.9129	8.1152
7	7.2135	7.4343	7.6625	7.8983	8.1420	8.3938	8.6540	8.9228	9.2004	9.4872	9.7833	10.0890
8	8.2857	8.5830	8.8923	9.2142	9.5491	9.8975	10.2598	10.6366	11.0285	11.4359	11.8594	12.2997
9	9.3685	9.7546	10.1591	10.5828	11.0266	11.4913	11.9780	12.4876	13.0210	13.5795	14.1640	14.7757
10	10.4622	10.9497	11.4639	12.0061	12.5779	13.1808	13.8164	14.4866	15.1929	15.9374	16.7220	17.5487
11	11.5668	12.1687	12.8078	13.4864	14.2068	14.9716	15.7836	16.6455	17.5603	18.5312	19.5614	20.6546
12	12.6825	13.4121	14.1920	15.0258	15.9171	16.8699	17.8885	18.9771	20.1407	21.3843	22.7132	24.1331
13	13.8093	14.6803	15.6178	16.6268	17.7130	18.8821	20.1406	21.4953	22.9534	24.5227	26.2116	28.0291
14	14.9474	15.9739	17.0863	18.2919	19.5986	21.0151	22.5505	24.2149	26.0192	27.9750	30.0949	32.3926
15	16.0969	17.2934	18.5989	20.0236	21.5786	23.2760	25.1290	27.1521	29.3609	31.7725	34.4054	37.2797
16	17.2579	18.6393	20.1569	21.8245	23.6575	25.6725	27.8881	30.3243	33.0034	35.9497	39.1899	42.7533
17	18.4304	20.0121	21.7616	23.6975	25.8404	28.2129	30.8402	33.7502	36.9737	40.5447	44.5008	48.8837
18	19.6147	21.4123	23.4144	25.6454	28.1324	30.9057	33.9990	37.4502	41.3013	45.5992	50.3959	55.7497
19	20.8109	22.8406	25.1169	27.6712	30.5390	33.7600	37.3790	41.4463	46.0185	51.1591	56.9395	63.4397
20	22.0190	24.2974	26.8704	29.7781	33.0660	36.7856	40.9955	45.7620	51.1601	57.2750	64.2028	72.0524

Appendix G

Tax Formulas

Tax Rate Schedules	G-2
Tax Formula for Individuals	G-3
Basic Standard Deduction Amounts	G-3
Amount of Each Additional Standard Deduction	G-3
Personal and Dependency Exemption	G-3
AMT Formula for Individuals	G-4
AMT Exemption and Phaseout for Individuals	G-4
Income Tax Rates—Estates and Trusts	G-5
Income Tax Rates—C Corporations, 2018 and after	G-5
Tax Formula for Corporate Taxpayers	G-5

2017 Tax Rate Schedules

Single—Schedule X

If taxable income is: Over—	But not over—	The tax is:	of the amount over—
$ 0	$ 9,325	........10%	$ 0
9,325	37,950	$ 932.50 + 15%	9,325
37,950	91,900	5,226.25 + 25%	37,950
91,900	191,650	18,713.75 + 28%	91,900
191,650	416,700	46,643.75 + 33%	191,650
416,700	418,400	120,910.25 + 35%	416,700
418,400	....	121,505.25 + 39.6%	418,400

Head of household—Schedule Z

If taxable income is: Over—	But not over—	The tax is:	of the amount over—
$ 0	$ 13,350	........10%	$ 0
13,350	50,800	$ 1,335.00 + 15%	13,350
50,800	131,200	6,952.50 + 25%	50,800
131,200	212,500	27,052.50 + 28%	131,200
212,500	416,700	49,816.50 + 33%	212,500
416,700	444,550	117,202.50 + 35%	416,700
444,550	....	126,950.00 + 39.6%	444,550

Married filing jointly or Qualifying widow(er)—Schedule Y–1

If taxable income is: Over—	But not over—	The tax is:	of the amount over—
$ 0	$ 18,650	........10%	$ 0
18,650	75,900	$ 1,865.00 + 15%	18,650
75,900	153,100	10,452.50 + 25%	75,900
153,100	233,350	29,752.50 + 28%	153,100
233,350	416,700	52,222.50 + 33%	233,350
416,700	470,700	112,728.00 + 35%	416,700
470,700	....	131,628.00 + 39.6%	470,700

Married filing separately—Schedule Y–2

If taxable income is: Over—	But not over—	The tax is:	of the amount over—
$ 0	$ 9,325	........10%	$ 0
9,325	37,950	$ 932.50 + 15%	9,325
37,950	76,550	5,226.25 + 25%	37,950
76,550	116,675	14,876.25 + 28%	76,550
116,675	208,350	26,111.25 + 33%	116,675
208,350	235,350	56,364.00 + 35%	208,350
235,350	....	65,814.00 + 39.6%	235,350

2018 Tax Rate Schedules

Single—Schedule X

If taxable income is: Over—	But not over—	The tax is:	of the amount over—
$ 0	$ 9,525	........10%	$ 0
9,525	38,700	$ 952.50 + 12%	9,525
38,700	82,500	4,453.50 + 22%	38,700
82,500	157,500	14,089.50 + 24%	82,500
157,500	200,000	32,089.50 + 32%	157,500
200,000	500,000	45,689.50 + 35%	200,000
500,000	....	150,689.50 + 37%	500,000

Head of household—Schedule Z

If taxable income is: Over—	But not over—	The tax is:	of the amount over—
$ 0	$ 13,600	........10%	$ 0
13,600	51,800	$ 1,360.00 + 12%	13,600
51,800	82,500	5,944.00 + 22%	51,800
82,500	157,500	12,698.00 + 24%	82,500
157,500	200,000	30,698.00 + 32%	157,500
200,000	500,000	44,298.00 + 35%	200,000
500,000	....	149,298.00 + 37%	500,000

Married filing jointly or Qualifying widow(er)—Schedule Y–1

If taxable income is: Over—	But not over—	The tax is:	of the amount over—
$ 0	$ 19,050	........10%	$ 0
19,050	77,400	$ 1,905.00 + 12%	19,050
77,400	165,000	8,907.00 + 22%	77,400
165,000	315,000	28,179.00 + 24%	165,000
315,000	400,000	64,179.00 + 32%	315,000
400,000	600,000	91,379.00 + 35%	400,000
600,000	....	161,379.00 + 37%	600,000

Married filing separately—Schedule Y–2

If taxable income is: Over—	But not over—	The tax is:	of the amount over—
$ 0	$ 9,525	........10%	$ 0
9,525	38,700	$ 952.50 + 12%	9,525
38,700	82,500	4,453.50 + 22%	38,700
82,500	157,500	14,089.50 + 24%	82,500
157,500	200,000	32,089.50 + 32%	157,500
200,000	300,000	45,689.50 + 35%	200,000
300,000	....	80,689.50 + 37%	300,000

Tax Formula for Individuals

Income (broadly defined)...	$xx,xxx
Less: Exclusions..	(x,xxx)
Gross income..	$xx,xxx
Less: Deductions *for* adjusted gross income......................................	(x,xxx)
Adjusted gross income..	$xx,xxx
Less: The greater of—	
Total itemized deductions	
or standard deduction..	(x,xxx)
Less: Personal and dependency exemptions*.....................................	(x,xxx)
Deduction for qualified business income**...................................	(x,xxx)
Taxable income..	$xx,xxx
Tax on taxable income..	$ x,xxx
Less: Tax credits (including Federal income tax	
withheld and prepaid)..	(xxx)
Tax due (or refund)..	$ xxx

*Exemption deductions are not allowed from 2018 through 2025.
**Only applies from 2018 through 2025.

Basic Standard Deduction Amounts

Filing Status	2017	2018
Single	$ 6,350	$12,000
Married, filing jointly	12,700	24,000
Surviving spouse	12,700	24,000
Head of household	9,350	18,000
Married, filing separately	6,350	12,000

Amount of Each Additional Standard Deduction

Filing Status	2017	2018
Single	$1,550	$1,600
Married, filing jointly	1,250	1,300
Surviving spouse	1,250	1,300
Head of household	1,550	1,600
Married, filing separately	1,250	1,300

Personal and Dependency Exemption

2017	2018*
$4,050	$4,150

*Note: Exemption deductions have been
suspended from 2018 through 2025.

AMT Formula for Individuals

Taxable income (increased by any standard deduction taken)

Plus or minus: Adjustments

Plus: Preferences

Equals: Alternative minimum taxable income (AMTI)

Minus: Exemption

Equals: Alternative minimum tax (AMT) base

Multiplied by: 26% or 28% rate

Equals: Tentative minimum tax before foreign tax credit

Minus: AMT foreign tax credit

Equals: Tentative minimum tax (TMT)

Minus: Regular tax liability (less any foreign tax credit)

Equals: AMT (if TMT > regular tax liability)

2017 AMT Exemption and Phaseout for Individuals

Filing Status	Exemption	Phaseout	
		Begins at	**Ends at**
Married, filing jointly	$84,500	$160,900	$498,900
Single or Head of household	54,300	120,700	337,900
Married, filing separately	42,250	80,450	249,450

2018 AMT Exemption and Phaseout for Individuals

Filing Status	Exemption	Phaseout	
		Begins at	**Ends at**
Married, filing jointly	$109,400	$1,000,000	$1,437,600
Single or Head of household	70,300	500,000	781,200
Married, filing separately	54,700	500,000	718,800

Income Tax Rates—Estates and Trusts

Tax Year 2018

Taxable Income		The Tax Is:	Of the Amount Over—
Over—	But not Over—		
$ 0	$ 2,550	10%	$ 0
2,550	9,150	$ 255.00 + 24%	2,550
9,150	12,500	1,839.00 + 35%	9,150
12,500	....	3,011.50 + 37%	12,500

Income Tax Rates—C Corporations, 2018 and after

For all income levels, the tax rate is 21%.

Tax Formula for Corporate Taxpayers

Income (from whatever source)...............................	$ xxx,xxx
Less: Exclusions from gross income........................	− xx,xxx
Gross Income...	$ xxx,xxx
Less: Deductions...	− xx,xxx
Taxable Income..	$ xxx,xxx
Tax rate...	× 21%
Gross Tax...	$ xx,xxx
Less: Tax credits and prepayments.........................	− x,xxx
Tax Due (or refund)..	$ xx,xxx

Index

A

AAA bypass election, **15**:17
Abandoned spouse rules, **9**:19–20
Accelerated cost recovery system (ACRS), **5**:22
Accident and health insurance benefits, **10**:10
Accident and health plans, employer-sponsored, **11**:5
Accountable plan, **11**:2, **11**:29
Accounting
　and tax concepts of income, comparison of, **4**:5
　ASC 740-10, Accounting for Uncertainty in Income Taxes, **3**:18–20
　flow of data, **3**:3
　for income taxes in international standards, **3**:10
　income, **4**:4
Accounting methods, **4**:6–10
　adjustments, **13**:4–6
　prescribed by IRS, **4**:7
　proprietorship, **11**:33–34
　See also Accrual method; Cash receipts and disbursements method; Cash receipts method; Completed contract method; Hybrid method; Installment method; Percentage of completion method
Accounting periods, proprietorship, **11**:33–34
Accounts and notes receivable, definition of capital asset, **8**:3, **8**:4
Accrual basis account, collection of, **8**:4
Accrual basis corporation, **5**:19
　exception, **1**:25
Accrual basis taxpayers, special rules for, **4**:11–12
　deferral of advance payments for services, goods and certain other items, **4**:12
　prepaid income, **4**:11
Accrual method, **4**:6, **4**:8–9
　business, **6**:3
　requirements, **5**:5–6
Accrued income and expenses, **3**:4–5
Accumulated adjustments account (AAA), **15**:16, **15**:17, **15**:19
　adjustments to corporate, **15**:18
Accumulated E & P, **13**:3
　chronological order allocation of, **13**:7
　S corporation with no, **15**:15
　S corporations with, **15**:16–17

Accumulated earnings tax, **13**:25
Accuracy-related penalty, **2**:23
Acquiescence (A or Acq.), **2**:15
Acquisition indebtedness, **10**:18
Action on Decision, **2**:15
Active income, **6**:15, **6**:17
Active participant in 2018, phaseout of traditional IRA deduction of, **11**:30
Active participation, **6**:28
Ad valorem, **10**:16
　taxes, **1**:12
Additional depreciation, **8**:32
Additional first-year depreciation, **5**:32
　personal property, **17**:17
Additional Medicare Tax, **9**:27–28
Additional standard deduction, **9**:7–8
　amount of each, **9**:8
Additional tax for base erosion, **16**:15
Additional taxes for certain individuals, **9**:24–28
　alternative minimum tax, **9**:25–27
Adjusted basis, **4**:18, **7**:2, **7**:4
Adjusted gross income (AGI). *See* Deductions for AGI; Deductions from AGI
Adjusted taxable income, business interest expense limitation and, **12**:32–33
Adjustments, **17**:16
　summary of basis, **7**:17–18
　summary of E & P, **13**:7
　tax planning strategies for controlling the timing of preferences and, **17**:26
　to basis, **7**:18
Administrative pronouncements, other, **2**:9
Administrative sources of tax law, **2**:6–9
　assessing significance of other, **2**:21
　letter rulings, **2**:8–9
　other administrative pronouncements, **2**:9
　revenue rulings and revenue procedures, **2**:7–8
　treasury department regulations, **2**:7
Adoption assistance programs, employee fringe benefit, **11**:11
Adoption expenses credit, **10**:27–28
ADS. *See* Alternative depreciation system
Advance payments for services, goods and certain other items, deferral of, **4**:12
Affordable Care Act (ACA) of 2010, **9**:27, **10**:32–33
　individual shared responsibility payment, **10**:32
　premium tax credit, **10**:33
　small employer health insurance credit, **17**:11

After-tax value of the assets, **10**:3
Age 65 or over, additional standard deduction, **9**:7
Age test for qualifying child, **9**:9–10
Agent, income received by, **4**:16
Alimony
　and separate maintenance payments, **10**:3–5
　payments, deductible for AGI, **9**:5
　requirements for, **10**:4
All events text, **5**:5
Allocate, **16**:21
Allocation problems, cost basis, **7**:10
Alternate valuation amount, **7**:13
Alternative depreciation system (ADS), **5**:25, **5**:40, **13**:5
　cost recovery tables, **5**:47–48
　depreciation of real property, **17**:17
Alternative minimum tax (AMT), **9**:25–27, **17**:2, **17**:13
　corporate, **17**:33–34
　exemption, **9**:26
　individual, **17**:13–33
　　AMT formula, **9**:25, **17**:15–16, **17**:14, **17**:15–16
　　illustration of AMT computation, **17**:30–31
　liability, education tax credits, **10**:30–31
　tax rate, **9**:26–27
　TCJA and corporate, **17**:33–34
　See also AMT adjustments; AMT preferences
Alternative minimum tax credit, **9**:26, **17**:31–32
Alternative minimum taxable income (AMTI), **9**:25–26, **17**:13–15
Alternative organizational forms in which business may be conducted, **18**:2
Alternative tax NOL deduction (ATNOLD), **17**:24–25
American Federal Tax Reports (AFTR), **2**:15
American Opportunity credit, **10**:30, **11**:25
Americans with Disabilities Act of 1990, **17**:2, **17**:8
Amortizable bond premium, capital recoveries, **7**:6
Amortizable Section 197 intangible, **5**:41
Amortization, **5**:41
　intangible assets, **5**:21
　research and experimental expenditures, **5**:16–17
Amount realized, **4**:18, **7**:2, **7**:3–4

AMT adjustments, individual, **17**:16–28, **17**:33
  adjusted gain or loss, **17**:22
  alternative tax net operating loss deduction, **17**:24–25
  circulation expenditures, **17**:19
  completed contract method of accounting, **17**:20
  depreciation of personal property, **17**:17–18
  depreciation of real property, **17**:17
  expenditures requiring 10-year write-off for AMT purposes, **17**:19–20
  incentive stock options, **17**:20–21
  itemized deductions, **17**:25–27
  other adjustments, **17**:28
  passive activity losses, **17**:23
  pollution control facilities, **17**:19
  summary of provisions, **17**:28
  tax planning strategies for avoiding, **17**:30
  See also Alternative minimum tax
AMT preferences, individual, **17**:28–30, **17**:33
  exclusion for certain small business stock, **17**:30
  intangible drilling costs, **17**:29
  interest on private activity bonds, **17**:29–30
  percentage depletion, **17**:28–29
  summary of provisions, **17**:33
  tax planning strategies for avoiding, **17**:30
Analysis of Net Income (Loss) Schedule, **14**:6
Annual accounting period concept, **1**:31
Annual exclusion, gift tax, **1**:12
Antitrust law violations, **5**:8
Appeals, **2**:12
Appellant, **2**:22
Appellate courts, **2**:12–14
  other rules and strategies, **2**:13–14
  process and outcomes, **2**:12–13
  See also Courts
Appellee, **2**:22
Apportioned, **16**:22
Appreciated property, **7**:23
  determining the deduction for contributions of, by individuals, **10**:24
Appreciated securities, tax planning strategies for gifts of, **8**:17
Appropriate economic unit, **6**:22
Arm's length price, **16**:14
ASC 740, **3**:8–9, **3**:12–13
ASC 740-10, **3**:18–20
  disclosures under, **3**:19
Asset Depreciation Range (ADR), **13**:5
Assets
  allocation of, in a lump-sum purchase, **7**:10
  business fixed, **8**:4
  C corporation, disposing of as sale of, **18**:17–18
  capital, **8**:2
  choosing for immediate expensing, **5**:34
  classification and use of, **1**:14
  dispositions of personal use, **7**:8
  election to expense under Section 179, **5**:29–31
  fixed, **3**:4, **8**:23
  intangible, **3**:5, **14**:11, **5**:21
  LLCs. disposing of as sale of, **18**:16–17
  of partnerships, by industry, **14**:22

partnerships, disposing of as sale of, **18**:16–17
  personal use, **5**:22
  S corporation, disposing of as corporate level sale or liquidating distribution of, **18**:18
  Section 1231, **8**:2, **8**:23–29
  sole proprietorship, disposing of as sale of individual, **18**:15
  tainted, **12**:15
  tax planning strategies for selling, **18**:17
  transfer of to business entity, **7**:31
Assignment of income, **4**:13
Associated with business, **11**:25
Assumption of liabilities, **12**:15–18
  exceptions, **12**:16–18
Athletic facilities, employee fringe benefit, **11**:10
At-risk amount, calculation of, **6**:17
At-risk and passive activity loss limits, interaction of, **6**:26
At-risk limitation, **6**:15, **6**:16–17, **14**:25, **14**:27–28
At-risk loss rules, conduit and entity perspectives effect on application of, **18**:8–10
At-risk rules, **15**:25
Automatic mileage method, **11**:19
Automobile expenses, computation of, **11**:19
Automobiles
  change from predominantly business use, **5**:38
  inclusion amount in gross income for leased, **5**:39
  limitation for SUVs, **5**:37–38
  limits on cost recovery, **5**:36–37
  passenger, **5**:36
Automobiles and other listed property
  business and personal use of, **5**:35–40
  used predominantly in business, **5**:36
Average rate, **9**:22
Awards, prizes and, **10**:5
Away-from-home requirement, **11**:19

B

Bad debts, **6**:2–5
  business vs. nonbusiness, **6**:4
  deductions, **6**:3
  loans between related parties, **6**:5
  specific charge-off method, **6**:3–4
Balance sheet, **3**:15
  approach, **3**:9
Bankruptcy, **2**:12, **6**:3
  insolvency and, **4**:24
Bargain element, **17**:21
Bargain purchase of property, **7**:9
Bargain rental of corporate property, **13**:17
Bargain sale of corporate property to a shareholder, **13**:17
Base amount, incremental research activities credit, **17**:6
Base erosion, additional tax for, **16**:15
Bases, inside and outside, **14**:12
Basic research defined, **17**:8
Basic standard deduction, **9**:7–8
  amounts, **9**:7
Basis
  adjusted, **7**:4
  adjustments to, **7**:18

and holding period of property received, **7**:23–25
  carryover, **7**:11
  determination of cost, **7**:9–10
  election to expense assets under Section 179, effect on, **5**:31
  liabilities in excess, **12**:16–18
  stepped-down, **7**:13
  stepped-up, **7**:13
Basis adjustments
  due to entity operations, **14**:21–22
  for loss property, **12**:22–23
  summary of, **7**:17–18
Basis computation, partnership formation and, **14**:13
Basis considerations, **7**:9–18
  conversion of property from personal use to business or income-producing use, **7**:16–17
  determination of cost basis, **7**:9–10
  disallowed losses, **7**:14–16
  gift basis, **7**:11–13
  inherited property, **7**:13–14
Basis determination and other issues, **12**:20–23
Basis for depreciation, **7**:13
  converted property, **7**:17
Basis in S stock, shareholder's, **15**:21–23
Basis in the partnership interest, **14**:7
Basis limitation, **14**:26–27
Basis of a partnership interest, **14**:20–23
  partner's basis, gain and loss, **14**:23–25
  partnership liabilities, **14**:22–23
Basis of boot, **7**:23
Basis of like-kind property, **7**:23–24
Basis of ownership interest, conduit and entity perspectives effect on, **18**:7–8
Basis of property to corporation, **12**:20–21
Basis of stock to shareholder, **12**:20
BEAT (base erosion anti-abuse tax), **16**:15
Below-market loans, imputed interest on, **4**:26–28
  exceptions and limitations, **4**:27–28
Benchmarking, **3**:24–26
  analysis, uses of, **3**:26
  refining the analysis, **3**:24–25
  sustaining the tax rate, **3**:25–26
Benefit received rule, **10**:21
Benefits
  general classes of excluded, **11**:12–16
  general classes of fringe, **11**:16
Bequests and inheritances, **10**:6
Blind, additional standard deduction, **9**:7
Board of Tax Appeals, **2**:14
Bonus depreciation, **5**:32
  and Section 179, **5**:33–35
  depreciation of personal property, **17**:17
Book and tax depreciation, **5**:32
Book vs. tax income reporting, **3**:7
Book-tax differences, **1**:19, **1**:21, **3**:2–8
  different methods, **3**:4–5
  different reporting entities, **3**:2–3
  different taxes, **3**:4
  overseas operations and, **16**:12
  tax return disclosures, **3**:6–8
Book-tax expense, steps in determining, **3**:16
Book-tax income gap, **3**:9
Boot, **7**:22–23, **12**:8–9, **12**:20
  basis of, **7**:23
  giving of, **7**:22–23
  receipt of, **7**:22
  transfer of property, **12**:11

Bribes, **5**:8
Built-in gain or loss, **14**:19
Built-in gains tax, **15**:27, **15**:28
    general rules, **15**:27–28
    LIFO recapture tax, **15**:29
Built-in loss property, **12**:22
Business
    disposing of, **18**:15–20
    investigation of, **5**:11–12
    tax planning strategies for the sale of, **5**:41
    tax planning strategies when incorporating, **12**:24–25
    tax treatment of disposition, **18**:18–20
    vs. nonbusiness bad debts, **6**:4
Business activities, deductions for AGI, **1**:16
Business and personal use of automobiles and other listed property, **5**:35–40
    change from predominantly business use, **5**:38
    leased automobiles, **5**:39–40
    limitation for SUVs, **5**:37–38
    limits on cost recovery for automobiles, **5**:36–37
    substantiation requirements, **5**:40
    used predominantly in business, **5**:36
Business bad debt, **6**:4
Business cycle, economics and, **5**:35
Business debt, **6**:3
Business deductions
    common, **5**:3–4
    ordinary and necessary requirement, **5**:2–3
    overview of, **5**:2–4
    partial list of, **5**:4
    reasonableness requirement, **5**:3
Business depreciable property or real estate, as definition of capital asset, **8**:3
Business entities
    federal tax consequences, **14**:2–3
    income tax returns filed by, **18**:14
    income taxation of, **1**:19–21
    transfer of assets to, **7**:31
    See also C corporations; Closely held C corporations; Corporations; Limited liability company; Limited liability partnership; Partnership; Proprietorship; S corporations; Sole proprietorship
Business expenses
    deductible for AGI, **9**:4
    interest expense, **5**:17
    other, **5**:17–18
    Schedule C of Form 1040, **10**:20
    taxes, **5**:17–18
Business fixed assets, definition of capital asset, **8**:4
Business forms, **18**:2
    conduit and entity perspectives of legal, **18**:4–11
    converting to another, **18**:20–21
    nontax factors affecting choice of, **18**:2–4
    overall comparison of, **18**:21–25
    tax attributes of different, **18**:22–25
    tax treatment of, **12**:6
    See also C corporations; Closely held C corporations; Corporations; Limited liability company; Limited liability partnership; Partnership; Proprietorship; S corporations; Sole proprietorship
Business gifts, **11**:27

Business income
    and loss, **4**:16
    corporation character of, **12**:5
    limitations, Section 179 expensing election, **5**:30, **5**:31
    tax rates, reductions in, **16**:8
Business interest, **5**:14
    expense limitation, **12**:31–34
    income, business interest expense limitation and, **12**:32
Business law
    employee or independent contractor, **11**:3
    income tax laws, **2**:19
    partnership agreement, **14**:7
    S corporation, **15**:3
Business losses, corporations, **12**:5
Business meals, **11**:26–27
Business of S corporations, **15**:5
Business operations, conduit and entity perspectives effect on taxation of, **18**:5–6
Business property
    complete destruction of, **6**:9
    Form 4797, Sales of Business Property, **8**:36
    losses, **6**:7
    partial destruction of, **6**:9
Business supplies, definition of capital asset, **8**:3
Business tax credits, **17**:3
Business use percentage, automobiles and other listed property used predominantly in business, **5**:36
Business use personalty, **1**:14
Business use realty, **1**:14
Business-related tax credit provisions, **17**:2–13
    See also Tax credits
Buy-sell agreements, **4**:22

C

C corporations, **1**:19–20, **12**:2, **14**:2–3
    consequences of noncash distributions, **15**:20
    converting to another entity form, **18**:20–21
    decrease in tax rate, **3**:21
    disposing of, **18**:17–18, **18**:19
    Form 1120, **1**:19, **14**:15
    repeal of AMT, **3**:22
    tax attributes of, **18**:22–25
Cafeteria plans, **11**:11
Calendar year, **4**:6
Capital account, **14**:21
Capital additions, **7**:4, **7**:5
Capital assets, **8**:2, **8**:3–6
    definition of, **8**:3–5
    long-term nonpersonal use, **8**:25
    Section 1231 assets relationship to, **8**:23–24
    statutory expansions, **8**:5–6
Capital changes, partner's basis, gain and loss, **14**:25
Capital contributions, **12**:25–26
    conduit and entity perspectives effect on tax treatment of, **18**:7
Capital expenditures, medical expenses, **10**:13
Capital formation, business forms, **18**:4

Capital gain property, **5**:19, **10**:23
Capital gain treatment in the U.S. and other countries, **8**:17
Capital gains, **4**:18–20, **8**:2
    and losses of noncorporate taxpayers, tax treatment of, **8**:16–22
    for wealthy, **8**:24
    long-term gains, **8**:16–18
    netting process, **8**:19–21
    of corporate taxpayers, tax treatment of, **8**:23
    short-term gains, **8**:16
    tax planning strategies for the timing of, **8**:15
    See also Long-term capital gains; Net long-term capital gain; Net short-term capital gain; Short-term capital gains
Capital interest, **14**:6
Capital investment, QBI deduction limitation based on, **11**:40–42
Capital loss carryovers, timing adjustments, **13**:4
Capital loss deduction, **8**:19
    deductible for AGI, **9**:5
Capital losses, **4**:18–20, **8**:2, **8**:16
    netting process, **8**:19–21
    of corporate taxpayers, tax treatment of, **8**:23
    of noncorporate taxpayers, tax treatment of, **8**:16–22
    short-term, nonbusiness bad debt, **6**:4
    See also Long-term capital losses; Net long-term capital loss; Net short-term capital loss; Short-term capital losses
Capital, raising of, **12**:7
Capital recoveries, **7**:4, **7**:5–7
Capital sharing ratios, **14**:6
Capital structure of a corporation, **12**:25–28
    capital contributions, **12**:25–26
    debt in the capital structure, **12**:26–28
Carryover basis, **7**:11, **14**:11
Cash basis account, collection of, **8**:4
Cash basis taxpayers, special rules for, **4**:10–11
    amounts received under an obligation to repay, **4**:11
    constructive receipt, **4**:10–11
    original issue discount, **4**:11
Cash management, relevance of taxation to accounting and finance professionals, **1**:3
Cash meal allowance, **11**:7
Cash method requirements, **5**:4–5
Cash receipts and disbursements method, **4**:6–7
Cash receipts method, **4**:7–8
Casualties, capital recoveries, **7**:5–6
Casualty gain, **6**:9
Casualty losses, **6**:7–13
    deduction of, **6**:7–9
    deductible from AGI, **8**:27
    definition of casualty, **6**:7
    Form 4684, Casualties and Thefts, **8**:36
    individual, **6**:10–13
    loss measurement, **6**:9–10
    tax planning strategies for documentation of, **6**:8
Casualty netting, general procedure for Section 1231 computation, **8**:27
Casualty or theft and nonpersonal use capital assets, Section 1231 assets, **8**:25

CCH IntelliConnect, **2**:19

Ceiling amount, Section 179 expensing election, **5**:30

Centralized management, **12**:7

Change in form not in substance, **7**:19

Charitable contributions, **5**:18–21, **10**:21–25
  benefit received rule, **10**:21
  contribution carryovers, **10**:25, **13**:4
  contribution of services, **10**:21–22
  criteria for a gift, **10**:21
  fifty percent ceiling, **10**:24
  Form 8283, **10**:23
  limitations on deduction, **5**:21, **10**:23
  nondeductible items, **10**:22
  property contributions, **5**:19–20
  record-keeping requirements, **10**:22–23
  temporary 60 percent ceiling, **10**:24
  thirty percent ceiling, **10**:24–25
  time of deduction, **10**:22
  twenty percent ceiling, **10**:25
  valuation requirements, **10**:23

Charitable transfers, recapture potential of, **8**:35

Checkpoint, **2**:14, **2**:19

Check-the-box Regulations, **12**:7, **18**:2

Child and dependent care expenses, credit for, **10**:28–29
  calculation of, **10**:29
  earned income ceiling, **10**:29
  eligibility for, **10**:28
  eligible employment-related expenses, **10**:28

Child and dependent care services, employee fringe benefit, **11**:10

Child care resource and referral services, **17**:9

Child support, alimony and separate maintenance payments, **10**:4–5

Child tax credit, **10**:28

Children of divorced or separated parents, multiple support agreement and, **9**:14

Children, unearned income of dependent, **9**:23–24

Chronological order allocation of accumulated E & P, **13**:7

Circuit Court of Appeals, **2**:12–14

Circular 230, **1**:22

Circulation expenditures, individual AMT adjustments, **17**:19

Citator, **2**:22

Citizenship, inbound tax issues, **16**:15

Citizenship test for dependency status, **9**:15

Civil unions, filing status, **9**:17

Claim of right doctrine, **4**:9

Claims Court Reporter (Cl.Ct.), **2**:16

Client letter, **2**:25

Closely held C corporations, **6**:21–22
  conduit and entity perspectives effect on application of at-risk and passive activity loss rules, **18**:8–10

Collectibles, **8**:17

Combined return of a unitary business, **16**:23

Committee Reports, **2**:4

Commodities options, **8**:8

Commodity futures options, **8**:8

Common business deductions, **5**:3–4

Common law employee-employer relationship, **11**:3

Common law system, **1**:31–32
  married individuals, **9**:17

Community property system, **1**:31–32
  married individuals, **9**:17

Commuting expenses, **11**:18–19

Compensation
  disguised, **10**:8
  tax planning strategies for unreasonable, **5**:4
  unemployment, **10**:5
  workers', **10**:10

Compensation-related expenses, **3**:4

Compensation-related loans, imputed interest rules, **4**:27

Compensatory damages, **10**:8

Completed contract method, **4**:7
  individual AMT adjustments for, **17**:20

Compliance, relevance of taxation to accounting and finance professionals, **1**:2

Condemnation gains and losses, **8**:25

Condemnations, special rule for, **7**:28

Conduit and entity perspectives of legal business forms, **18**:4–11

Conduit perspective, **18**:5
  ability to specially allocate income among owners, **18**:6–7
  application of at-risk and passive activity loss rules, **18**:8–10
  basis of ownership interest, **18**:7–8
  other taxes, **18**:10–11
  tax treatment of capital contributions, **18**:7
  tax treatment of distributions, **18**:0
  taxation of business operations, **18**:5–6

Conference Committee, **2**:4
  example of compromise in, **2**:4

Congress, intent of, **2**:4

Congressional Budget Office (CBO), health insurance, **10**:33

Conservatism principle, **3**:12

Constructive dividend, **13**:16–21
  tax planning strategies for, **13**:19–20
  tax treatment of, **13**:18–21
  types of, **13**:17–18

Constructive ownership provisions in transactions between related parties, **5**:6–7

Constructive receipt, **4**:10–11

Constructive sale treatment, short sales, **8**:15

Contingent payments, franchises, **8**:11

Continuity of life, **12**:7

Contributed property, tax issues related to, **14**:11–12
  depreciation method and period, **14**:11
  intangible assets, **14**:11
  receivables, inventory, and built-in losses, **14**:12

Contribution carryovers, **10**:25

Contribution of services, **10**:21–22

Contributions of appreciated property by individuals, determining the deduction for, **10**:24

Control, **12**:12

Control of the corporations, **12**:12–15
  immediately after the transfer, **12**:12–13
  transfers for property and services, **12**:13–14
  transfers for services and nominal property, **12**:14
  transfers to existing corporations, **12**:15

Controlled corporations, organization of and transfers to, **12**:8–25
  assumption of liabilities—Section 357, **12**:15–18
  basis determination and other issues, **12**:20–23
  control of the corporations, **12**:12–15

general rules, **12**:8–10
  recapture considerations, **12**:24
  stock, **12**:11
  transfer of property, **12**:10–11

Controlled foreign corporations (CFCs), **16**:12–15
  defined, **16**:12–13

Controlled groups, **12**:34–35
  application of Section 482, **12**:35
  parent-subsidiary controlled group, **12**:34–35
  parent-subsidiary corporations, **12**:35

Controversy, relevance of taxation to accounting and finance professionals, **1**:3

Convenience of the employer test, **11**:8

Conversion of property from personal use to business or income-producing use, **7**:16–17

Copyrights and creative works, as definition of capital asset, **8**:3, **8**:5

Copyrights, Section 197 intangible, **5**:41

Corporate accumulations, restrictions on, **13**:25–26

Corporate distributions, **13**:2, **13**:11–12
  capital recoveries, **7**:6

Corporate income, double taxation of, **12**:2–3
  taxation of dividends, **12**:3

Corporate income tax liability, determining the, **12**:34

Corporate income tax rates for taxable yeas beginning before 2018, **12**:4

Corporate integration, **13**:18

Corporate liquidations, **13**:24–25

Corporate multistate income taxation, **16**:24

Corporate obligations, retirement of, **8**:7

Corporate operations, **12**:28–35
  controlled groups, **12**:34–35
  deductions available only to corporations, **12**:28–31
  determining the corporate income tax liability, **12**:34

Corporate tax, **12**:2–7
  comparison of corporations and other forms of doing business, **12**:3–6
  double taxation of corporate income, **12**:2–3
  entity classification, **12**:7
  limited liability companies, **12**:7
  nontax considerations, **12**:6–7

Corporate taxpayers, tax treatment of capital gains and losses of, **8**:23
  vs. individual taxpayers, revenue relevance of, **18**:4

Corporate-level tax, **15**:27

Corporations, **18**:2
  additional recapture for, **8**:33–34
  advantages of debt in the capital structure of, **12**:26
  and other forms of doing business, comparison of, **12**:3–6
  basis in property received, **12**:21
  basis of property to, **12**:20–21
  business losses, **12**:5
  capital structure of, **12**:25–28
  character of business income, **12**:5
  debt in the capital structure of, reclassification of debt as equity (thin capitalization problem), **12**:27–28
  effect of noncash dividends on, **13**:14–16
  employment taxes, **12**:5

filing requirements for, **12**:35–36
income taxation of, business interest expense limitation, **12**:31–34
material participation, **6**:24
reporting responsibilities, **12**:4
state taxes, **12**:5–6
tax consequences to, with and without the application of Section 351, **12**:21
tax rates, **12**:3–5
transfers to existing, **12**:15
Corporation-shareholder loans, imputed interest rules, **4**:27
Cosmetic surgery, medical expenses, **10**:12
Cost accounting and executive compensation, **16**:26
Cost basis, determination of, **7**:9–10
allocation problems, **7**:10
identification problems, **7**:9
Cost depletion, **5**:42–43
Cost method, **3**:2
Cost of repairs, **6**:10
Cost recovery, **5**:22
allowed or allowable, **5**:23
in general, **5**:22–24
nature of property, **5**:22–23
placed in service requirement, **5**:23
Cost recovery allowances, **5**:21–40
additional first-year depreciation, **5**:32
alternative depreciation system (ADS), **5**:40
business and personal use of automobiles and other listed property, **5**:35–40
depreciation and, **7**:5
election to expense assets (Section 179), **5**:29–31
MACRS for personal property, **5**:4–28
MACRS for real estate, **5**:28–29
modified accelerated cost recovery system (MACRS), **5**:24
using Section 179 and bonus depreciation effectively, **5**:33–35
Cost recovery basis for personal use assets converted to business or income-producing use, **5**:23–24
Cost recovery periods/classes: personalty, **5**:25
Cost recovery recapture, **5**:38
Cost recovery tables, **5**:44–48
Costs
organizational, **14**:14
startup, **14**:14
Courts
appellate, **2**:12–14
other rules and strategies, **2**:13–14
process and outcomes, **2**:12–13
Circuit courts of appeals, **2**:12
Court of Appeals, **2**:12–14
judicial citations of, **2**:15–16
Court of Federal Claims, **2**:10–16
judicial citations of, **2**:15–16
jurisdiction of, **2**:11
Court of original jurisdiction, **2**:10
District, **2**:10–16
judicial citations of, **2**:15–16
jurisdiction of, **2**:11
Federal district courts, **2**:12
influence of on tax law, **1**:32–33, **1**:34
judicial concepts relating to tax, **1**:33
judicial influence on statutory provisions, **1**:33
level of, **2**:21
Supreme Court, **2**:13
judicial citations of, **2**:16

Tax, **2**:10–16
judicial citations of, **2**:14–15
jurisdiction of, **2**:11
Small Cases Division of, **2**:10
trial, **2**:10, **2**:11–12
Covenants not to compete, Section 197 intangible, **5**:41
CPA examination, tax research on, **2**:27–28
Creative works, definition of capital asset, **8**:5
Credit, **6**:3
Credit for child and dependent care expenses, **10**:28–29
calculation of, **10**:29
earned income ceiling, **10**:29
eligibility for, **10**:28
eligible employment-related expenses, **10**:28
Credit for employer-provided child care, **17**:9, **17**:12
Credit for employer-provided family and medical leave, **17**:11, **17**:13
Credit for small employer pension plan startup costs, **17**:9, **17**:12
Creditors' gifts, income from discharge of indebtedness, **4**:24
Cross-border transactions, U.S. taxation of, **16**:4
Crossing state lines, state and local income taxation in the U.S., **16**:17–25
Current E & P, **13**:3
Current income tax expense, **1**:21
Current participation, tests based on, **6**:23
Current tax expense, **3**:9
Cyberspace, foreign tax credit and income sourced in, **17**:10

D

Daily Tax Reports, **2**:8
Damages, **10**:8–9
compensatory, **10**:8
personal injury, **10**:9
punitive, **10**:9
taxation of, **10**:9
De minimis exception of in-house expenditures, **5**:9
De minimis fringe benefits, **11**:14, **11**:16
De minimis fringes, **11**:13
De minimis items, **11**:16
Death
disposition of a passive activity by, **6**:29–30
federal estate tax, **1**:11
recapture potential of, **8**:35
state death taxes, **1**:11
taxes, **1**:10–11
Debt
advantages of, **12**:26
nonrecourse, **14**:22
qualified nonrecourse, **14**:27
recourse, **14**:22
See also Bad debts; Business debt; Nonbusiness debt
Debt distinguished from equity, **12**:26
Debt in the capital structure, **12**:26–28
advantages of, **12**:26
reclassification of debt as equity (thin capitalization problem), **12**:27–28
Debt obligation, retirement of, **8**:7
Decision
memorandum, **2**:14
regular, **2**:14

type of, **2**:21
weight of, **2**:22
Declining balance method, depreciation of personal property, **17**:18
Deductible distributions, minimizing double taxation by making, **18**:11–13
Deductible taxes, tax planning strategies for timing the payment of, **10**:17
Deduction for contributions of appreciated property by individuals, determining, **10**:24
Deduction for qualified business income, **9**:6, **11**:37–44
general rule, **11**:38–40
limitation for specified services businesses, **11**:42–44
limitations based on wages and capital investment, **11**:40–42
limitations on QBI deduction, **11**:40
Deduction for qualified tuition and related expenses, **11**:24–25
Deduction limitations, Section 179 expensing election, **5**:30–31
Deductions, **4**:3
business, **5**:2–4
character of, **1**:26
justification for denying, **5**:8
limitations on charitable contribution, **10**:23
ordinary and necessary requirement, **5**:2–3
reasonableness requirement, **5**:3
tax minimization strategies related to, **1**:24–25
tax planning strategies for shifting across time, **9**:22
tax planning strategies for the time value of, **5**:5
time of charitable contribution, **10**:22
Deductions available only to corporations, **12**:28–31
dividends received deduction, **12**:28–30
organizational expenditures deduction, **12**:30–31
Deductions for AGI, **4**:3, **9**:4–5
business activities, **1**:16
business expenses of self-employed, **11**:2
business losses of individuals, **6**:10
health insurance premiums of self-employed, **11**:34
home office expense of self-employed individual, **11**:28
interest on qualified student loans, **10**:17
qualified tuition and related expenses, **11**:24
reimbursed employee expenses under an accountable plan, **11**:29
rent or royalty property expenses, **10**:11
Section 1231 asset casualty losses, **8**:27
Section 1231 asset losses, **8**:27
self-employment tax, **11**:34
trade or business expenses, **10**:11
Deductions from AGI, **4**:3, **9**:5
casualty losses, **8**:27
employee expenses, **11**:2
itemized deductions, **1**:16, **10**:11
personal use losses of individuals, **6**:10–11
QBI deduction, **11**:39
reimbursed employee expenses under a nonaccountable plan, **11**:29
unreimbursed employee expenses, **11**:29
Deemed to be long term, **7**:14
Defendant, **2**:10

Deferral and amortization method
    of research and experimental
    expenditures, **5**:16–17
Deferral of advance payments for services,
    goods and certain other items, **4**:12
Deferred income tax expense, **1**:21
Deferred tax asset, **1**:21, **3**:9, **3**:11–12
    tax losses and, **3**:15
Deferred tax benefit, **3**:9
Deferred tax expense, **3**:9
Deferred tax liability, **1**:21, **3**:9, **3**:10, **3**:12
Deferring distributions, minimizing double
    taxation by, **18**:13
Deficiency, payment of, **2**:11–12
Defined benefit plan, **11**:35
Defined contribution plan, **11**:35
Dependency exemptions, **9**:6, **9**:9
Dependency status, **9**:9–16
    citizenship test, **9**:15
    comparison of categories for, **9**:15–16
    joint return test, **9**:15
    other rules for determining, **9**:14–15
    qualifying child, **9**:9–10
    qualifying relative, **9**:11–14
    tests for, **9**:16
    tiebreaker rules for determining, **9**:10
Dependent care expenses, credit for child
    and, **10**:28–29
    calculation of, **10**:29
    earned income ceiling, **10**:29
    eligibility for child and, **10**:28
    eligible employment-related expenses,
        10:28
Dependent tax credit, **10**:28
    nonrefundable, **10**:28
Dependents
    basic standard deduction, **9**:8
    filing requirements for, **9**:20
    medical expenses for, **10**:13
    special limitations on the standard
        deduction for, **9**:8
Depletion, **5**:41–44
    intangible drilling and development costs
        (IDC), **5**:42
    of natural resources, **5**:21
Depletion methods, **5**:42–44
    tax planning strategies for switching, **5**:44
Depreciable real estate, tax planning
    strategies for selling, **8**:34
Depreciable real property, **8**:31
Depreciated property, **7**:23
Depreciation, **5**:22
    additional first-year, **5**:32
    and cost recovery allowances, capital
        recoveries, **7**:5
    bonus, **5**:32
    method and period, **14**:11
    of personal property, individual AMT
        adjustments, **17**:17–18
    of real property, individual AMT
        adjustments, **17**:17
    on fixed assets, **3**:4
    on gift property, basis for, **7**:13
Depreciation recapture, comparison of
    Section 1245 and Section 1250, **8**:32
Determination letters, **2**:9
Dicta, **2**:22
Directly related to business, **11**:25
Disabled access credit, **17**:2, **17**:8, **17**:12
Disallowance possibilities, **5**:8–15
    business interest, **5**:14
    excessive executive compensation, **5**:10

expenses and interest related to
    tax-exempt income, **5**:13–14
expenses related to entertainment,
    recreation, or amusement, **5**:14–15
investigation of a business, **5**:11–12
other, **5**:15
political contributions and lobbying
    activities, **5**:9–10
public policy limitations, **5**:8–9
transactions between related parties,
    5:12–13
Disallowed loss transactions, special
    holding period rules, **8**:14
Disallowed losses, **7**:14–16
    related taxpayers, **7**:14–15
    wash sales, **7**:15
Disaster area losses, **6**:8–9
Discharge of indebtedness, income from,
    4:23–25
    creditors' gifts, **4**:24
    insolvency and bankruptcy, **4**:24
    qualified real property indebtedness, **4**:24
    seller cancellation, **4**:25
    shareholder cancellation, **4**:25
    student loans, **4**:25
Disclosures under ASC 740-10, **3**:19
Disguised compensation, scholarships, **10**:8
Disguised exchange, **14**:9–10
Disguised sale, **14**:10
Disposition of a business, **18**:15–20
Disposition of passive activities, **6**:29–30
Disregarded entity (DRE), **12**:7
Distributions
    allocating E & P to, **13**:7–13
    certain corporate, **7**:6
    conduit and entity perspectives effect on
        tax treatment of, **18**:10
    consequences of noncash, **15**:20
    corporate, **13**:2
    liquidating and nonliquidating compared,
        13:24–25
    minimizing double taxation, **18**:13
    Schedules K and K-1, **14**:17–18
Distributions from an S corporations, **15**:16
Distributions to shareholders, tax treatment
    of S corporation, **15**:14–19
District Court, **2**:10–16
    judicial citations of, **2**:15–16
    jurisdiction of, **2**:11
Dividends, **4**:15–16, **13**:2
    constructive, **13**:16–21
    from foreign corporation, **4**:15
    noncash, **13**:13–16
    percentage of, paid by size of corporate
        assets, **13**:3
    property, **13**:13
    stock, **13**:21–22
    taxation of, **12**:3
    worldwide view of, **13**:18
Dividends received deduction (DRD), **1**:24,
    12:28–30
    additions to taxable income, **13**:4
Divorced or separated parents, multiple
    support agreement and children of,
    9:14
Domestic corporation, **12**:28, **15**:3
Domestic partners, filing status, **9**:17
Domestic subsidiaries, **3**:3
Domestic travel, **11**:21
Double taxation, **1**:19, **1**:26–27, **15**:29
    C corporations, **14**:2
    minimizing, **18**:11–15

of corporate income, **12**:2–3
taxation of business operations, **18**:5–6
Double taxation problem
    territorial approach, **16**:5–7
    worldwide approach, **16**:5–7
Dual basis rule, **7**:11

E

E & P. *See* Earnings and profits
Earned income ceiling, credit for child and
    dependent care expenses, **10**:29
Earned income credit, **10**:31–32
    amount of, **10**:32
    eligibility requirements, **10**:31
Earnings and profits (E & P), **4**:16, **13**:2–13
    allocating to distributions, **13**:7–13
    computation of, **13**:3–6, **13**:8
    effect of corporate distributions on,
        13:15–16
    summary of adjustments, **13**:7
    timing adjustments, **13**:4
Easements, capital recoveries, **7**:7
Economic and societal needs, senior
    citizens, **11**:6
Economic considerations
    encouragement of certain activities,
        1:28–29
    encouragement of certain industries, **1**:29
    encouragement of small business, **1**:29
    tax law, **1**:33
Economic development, incentive-granting
    community, **16**:27
Economic effect of partnership allocations,
    14:19
Economic effect test, **14**:19
Economic income, **4**:3, **13**:3
Economic performance test, **5**:5
Economics
    business cycle and, **5**:35
    finance and, **4**:9, **5**:40
    investments, **10**:3
    nontaxable exchanges, **7**:24
    role of small businesses, **18**:14
Education expenses, **11**:22–24
    allowable expenses, **11**:24
    employer or legal requirements to keep a
        job, **11**:23
    maintaining or improving existing skills,
        11:23
Education tax credits, **10**:30–31
    eligible individuals, **10**:30
    income limitations and refundability,
        10:30–31
    maximum credit, **10**:30
Educational assistance, employee fringe
    benefit, **11**:11
Educational savings bonds, **10**:10–11
Educator expenses, **11**:28–29
Effective tax rate, **1**:21
    for selected Fortune 100 companies, **3**:15
Effectively connected income, **16**:15
E-file, **9**:28–29
EFTPS (Electronic Federal Tax Payment
    System), **9**:29
Eighty percent stock ownership, **12**:12
Election to expense assets under Section
    179, **5**:29–31
    deduction limitations, **5**:30–31
    effect on basis, **5**:31

Eligible expenditures, **17**:8
Eligible small business, **17**:8
Employee achievement awards, **10**:5
Employee expenses, classification of, **11**:29–30
  accountable plans, **11**:29
  nonaccountable plans, **11**:29–30
  unreimbursed expenses, **11**:30
Employee fringe benefits, **11**:12
  other, **11**:10–11
Employee vs. self-employed, **11**:2–4
  factors considered in classification, **11**:2–4
Employees
  exclusions available to, **11**:4–18
  highly compensated, **11**:15
  partners as, **14**:30–31
  required to accept test, **11**:8
  services of, **4**:13
Employer
  Form 941, Employer's Quarterly Federal Tax Return, **1**:9
  meals and lodging furnished for the convenience of, **11**:7–9
Employer-sponsored accident and health plans, **11**:5
Employment taxes, **1**:5, **1**:9–10
  corporations, **12**:5
  FICA taxes, **1**:9–10
  self-employment, Schedule SE of Form 1040, **1**:10
  self-employment taxes, **1**:10
  unemployment taxes, **1**:10
Employment-related expenses, credit for child and dependent care expenses, **10**:28
Energy credits, **17**:8, **17**:12
Energy research credit, **17**:8
Entertainment expenses, **11**:25–27
  business gifts, **11**:27
  business meals, **11**:26–27
  exceptions to the 50 percent rule, **11**:26
Entities
  and individuals, dealings between, **1**:21
  different reporting, **3**:2–3
Entity classification, **12**:7
Entity operations, basis adjustments due to, **14**:21–22
Entity perspective, **18**:5
  ability to specially allocate income among owners, **18**:6–7
  application of at-risk and passive activity loss rules, **18**:8–10
  basis of ownership interest, **18**:7–8
  of legal business forms, conduit and, **18**:4–11
  other taxes, **18**:10–11
  tax treatment of capital contributions, **18**:7
  tax treatment of distributions, **18**:10
  taxation of business operations, **18**:5–6
Entity-level taxes, **15**:27–30
  passive investment income penalty tax, **15**:29–30
  tax on pre-election built-in gain, **15**:27–29
Equity considerations
  mitigating effect of the annual accounting period concept, **1**:31
  tax law, **1**:33
  wherewithal to pay concept, **1**:30–31
Equity distinguished from debt, **12**:26
Equity method, **3**:2
Equity or fairness
  employee or independent contractor, **11**:3
  marriage penalty, **9**:18

Equity, reclassification of debt as (thin capitalization problem), **12**:27–28
Estate tax, **1**:10
Estimated tax, **11**:44
  Form 1040-ES, Estimated Tax for Individuals, **9**:23
  payments, **11**:44–45, **12**:36
  penalty on underpayments, **11**:45
Ethics of tax planning, **1**:22
Ethics, overview of, **1**:22
Excess business loss, **6**:32–33
  computing the limit, **6**:32–33
  definition and rules, **6**:32
  limitation on deduction of, **14**:28, **15**:25
Excess cost recovery, **5**:38
Excess net passive income (ENPI), **15**:29–30
Excessive executive compensation, **5**:10
Excise taxes, **1**:6
  federal, **1**:6–7
  local, **1**:7
  state, **1**:7
Exclusion treatment, exceptions to, **4**:21–22
Exclusions, **9**:3–4
  from the income tax base, **4**:2
Executive compensation, cost accounting and, **16**:26
Exemption amount, **17**:15
Exemptions
  dependency, **9**:6, **9**:9
  personal, **9**:6, **9**:9
Expenditures, research and experimental, **5**:15–17
Expense method of research and experimental expenditures, **5**:16
Expense recognition, timing of, **5**:4–7
  accrual method requirements, **5**:5–6
  cash method requirements, **5**:4–5
  expenses accrued to related parties, **5**:6–7
  prepaid expenses (12-month rule), **5**:7
Expenses
  accountable plans, classification of employee, **11**:29
  compensation-related, **3**:4
  nonaccountable plans, classification of employee, **11**:29–30
  nondeductible, **3**:5
  related to an illegal business, **5**:9
  related to entertainment, recreation, or amusement, **5**:14–15
  unreimbursed expenses, classification of employee, **11**:30
Expenses accrued to related parties, **5**:6–7
  relationships and constructive ownership, **5**:6–7
Expenses and income, accrued, **3**:4–5
Expenses and interest related to tax-exempt income, **5**:13–14
Expenses of work, **11**:18–33
  classification of employee expenses, **11**:29–30
  contributions to individual retirement accounts, **11**:30–33
  deduction for qualified tuition and related expenses, **11**:24–25
  education expenses, **11**:22–24
  educator expenses, **11**:28–29
  entertainment expenses, **11**:25–27
  moving expenses, **11**:22
  office in the home, **11**:27–28
  other, **11**:27–29

  transportation expenses, **11**:18–19
  travel expenses, **11**:19–22
Experimental expenditures
  deferral and amortization method of, **5**:16–17
  expense method of, **5**:16
  research and, **5**:15–17

F

Facts and circumstances, tests based on, **6**:23
Failure to disclose penalty, **2**:6
Fair market value, **7**:4
  of leasehold improvements when lease is terminated (Section 109), gross income exclusion, **4**:18
FASB. *See* Financial Accounting Standards Board
Federal customs duties, **1**:14
Federal district courts, **2**:12
Federal estate tax, **1**:11
  on income earned or received after death, miscellaneous itemized deductions, **10**:25
Federal excise taxes, **1**:6–7
  Form 720, **1**:7
Federal gift tax, **1**:11–12
Federal income tax, **1**:27
  basic formula for, **1**:15
  formula for individuals, **1**:16
  structure of, **1**:15–16
Federal Insurance Contribution Act. *See* FICA
Federal judicial system, **2**:10
  trial courts, **2**:11
Federal Register, **2**:7
Federal Second Series (F.2d), **2**:16
Federal Supplement Second Series (F.Supp.2d), **2**:15
Federal Supplement Series (F.Supp), **2**:15
Federal tax collections, **1**:13
Federal tax consequences of business entities, **14**:2–3
Federal Tax Coordinator, 2d, **2**:19
Federal tax law, understanding, **1**:28–33
Federal Third Series (F.3d), **2**:16
Federal Unemployment Tax Act. *See* FUTA
Fees distinguished from taxes, **10**:15
FICA, **1**:9, **18**:10
FICA tax, **1**:9–10
  Form 941, Employer's Quarterly Federal Tax Return, **1**:9
Fiduciaries, Form 1041, **14**:15
FIFO method applied to carryback, carryovers, and utilization of credits, **17**:4
Fifty percent ceiling on charitable contributions, **10**:24
50 percent rule, exceptions to, **11**:26
Filing procedures
  e-file approach, **9**:28–29
  modes of payment, **9**:29
  selecting the proper form, **9**:28
  tax return, **9**:28–29
  when and where to file, **9**:29
Filing requirements, **9**:16, **9**:20
  for corporations, **12**:35–36
  for dependents, **9**:20
  general rules, **9**:20

Filing status, **9**:16–20
  abandoned spouse rules, **9**:19–20
  head of household, **9**:18–19
  married individuals, **9**:17–18
  single taxpayers, **9**:17
Final Regulations, **2**:7
Finance
  business entities, **5**:22
  cash-flow benefit of particular tax
      attributes, **17**:5
  dividend policies, **13**:11
  double taxation of corporate income,
      13:16
  economics and, **4**:9, **5**:40
  investments, **10**:3, **12**:5
  limited partnerships or LLCs, **14**:4
  public, **15**:26
  stock buybacks, **13**:22
  wealth maximization, **6**:15
Financial accounting
  capital account, **14**:21
  for tax uncertainties, **3**:18–20
  maximizing net income, **8**:31
  measures of corporate income, **12**:39
  property transactions, **7**:7
Financial accounting income (FAI), **1**:19, **1**:21
Financial Accounting Standards Board
      (FASB), **1**:19, **2**:27, **3**:10
Financial analysis, **3**:24
Financial reporting, relevance of taxation
      to accounting and finance
      professionals, **1**:2
Financial statement footnotes, **3**:16
Financial statements
  effect of taxes on, **12**:39
  income taxes in, **3**:8–23
  tax disclosure in, **3**:15–18
Fines, **5**:8
First-in, first-out (FIFO) basis, **7**:9
Fiscal year, **4**:6
Fixed assets
  classification of, **8**:23
  depreciation on, **3**:4
Fixture, **1**:13
Flexible spending plans, **11**:11–12
Floor plan financing interest, business
      interest expense limitation and, **12**:33
Flow-through entity, **1**:20, **1**:27, **12**:5, **14**:2
  business interest expense limitation and,
      12:33
  taxation of business operations, **18**:5–6
Flow-through of items of income and loss
      to S corporation shareholders, **15**:11
Foreign Corrupt Practice Act (FCPA), **5**:8
Foreign earned income, **11**:17–18
  exclusion, **11**:17
Foreign person's income, U.S. income tax
      treatment of, **16**:17
Foreign tax credit (FTC), **16**:6, **16**:9–11,
      17:2, **17**:10–11, **17**:12
  limits, **16**:10–11
  sourcing income in cyberspace, **17**:10
Foreign travel, **11**:21
Foreign-derived intangible income (FDII),
      16:15
Form 720, Federal excise tax return, **1**:7
Form 941, Employer's Quarterly Federal Tax
      Return, **1**:9
Form 1040, U.S. Individual Income Tax
      Return, **1**:10, **1**:19, **9**:28, **11**:25, **14**:15
  Schedule A, personal use interest, **10**:20
  Schedule C, Profit or Loss from
      Business, **11**:2
Form 1040A, **9**:28, **11**:25

Form 1040-ES, Estimated Tax for
      Individuals, **9**:23
Form 1040EZ, **9**:28
Form 1041, fiduciaries, **14**:15
Form 1065, partnerships, **1**:20, **14**:5–6
Form 1095-A, Health Insurance Marketplace
      Statement, **10**:33
Form 1098-T, Tuition Statement, **10**:30, **11**:25
Form 1120, C corporation, **1**:19, **14**:15
Form 1120S, S corporations, **1**:20, **14**:15
Form 2553, S election, **15**:6
Form 4684, Casualties and Thefts, **8**:36
Form 4797, Sales of Business Property, **8**:36
Form 4868, Application for Automatic
      Extension of Time to File U.S.
      Individual Income Tax Return, **9**:29
Form 6251, **17**:15
Form 8283, Noncash Charitable
      contributions, **10**:23
Form 8453, U.S. Individual Income Tax
      Transmittal for an IRS e-file Return,
      9:29
Form 8832, **12**:7
Form 8879, IRS e-file Signature
      authorization, **9**:28
Form 8917, Tuition and Fees Deduction,
      11:25
Form 8962, Premium Tax Credit, **10**:33
Form of receipt of gross income, **4**:5–6
Form W-2, Wage and Tax Statement, **9**:22
Forms of doing business. *See* Business
      entities; Business forms
401k plan, **11**:37
Franchise payments, **8**:11
  contingent payments, **8**:11
  noncontingent payments, **8**:11
Franchise tax, **1**:14–15
Franchisee, consequences to, **8**:12
Franchises, **8**:10–11
  consequences to franchisor and
      franchisee, **8**:12
  Section 197 intangible, **5**:41
  significant power, right, or continuing
      interest, **8**:11
Franchising, **8**:10
Franchisor, consequences to, **8**:12
Frequent-flyer miles, employee fringe
      benefit, **11**:10
Fringe benefits, **11**:4
  general classes, **11**:16
  other specific employee, **11**:10–11
Fruit and tree metaphor, **4**:13
Full recapture, **8**:30
Functional use test, **7**:27, **7**:28
FUTA, **1**:8
  tax, **1**:9

G

GAAP. *See* Generally accepted accounting
      principles
Gain
  built-in, **14**:19
  capital, **8**:2
  determination of, **7**:2–8
  individual AMT adjustments, **17**:22
  long-term, **8**:16–18
  nonrecognition of, **7**:8
  precontribution, **14**:19
  realized, **7**:2–7, **7**:8
  recognition of, effect on corporation,
      13:14–15
  recognized, **7**:7–8

  short-term, **8**:16
  See also Capital gains; Realized gain;
      Recognized gain
Gain basis for converted property, **7**:17
Gain or loss on contributions to the
      partnership, **14**:8–9
Gains and losses
  casualty, **6**:12–13
  from property transactions, **4**:18–20
  tax planning strategies for matching, **8**:21
Gambling losses, miscellaneous itemized
      deductions, **10**:25
General business credit, **17**:2–4, **17**:12
  principal components of, **17**:4
  treatment of unused, **17**:3–4
General depreciation system (GDS)
      recovery period and convention,
      depreciation of personal property,
      17:18
General framework for income tax
      planning, **1**:23
General partner, **6**:24, **18**:3
  at-risk limitation, **6**:16
  material participation, **6**:24
  unlimited liability, **12**:6
General partnership, **14**:3
General sales tax, **1**:7
Generally accepted accounting principles
      (GAAP), **1**:19, **2**:27, **3**:2, **3**:8–12
Gift basis, **7**:11–13
  adjustment for gift tax, **7**:12
  basis for depreciation, **7**:13
  holding period, **7**:12–13
  rules, in general, **7**:11–12
Gift loans, imputed interest rules, **4**:27
Gift splitting, **1**:12
Gift taxes, **1**:11–12
  adjustment for, **7**:12
  federal, **1**:11–12
Gifts
  and inheritances, **10**:6–7
  business, **11**:27
  criteria for, **10**:21
  disposition of a passive activity by, **6**:30
  of appreciated securities, tax planning
      strategies for, **8**:17
  recapture potential of, **8**:34
  special holding period rules, **8**:14
  tax planning strategies for, **7**:12
Global activities timeline, **16**:4
Global tax issues
  accounting for income taxes in
      international standards, **3**:10
  capital gain treatment in the U.S. and
      other countries, **8**:17
  choose the charity wisely, **10**:23
  do corporations pay taxes, **18**:5
  does Section 351 cover the incorporation
      o a foreign business, **12**:15
  filing a joint return, **9**:19
  non-U.S. shareholders prefer capital gain
      treatment in stock redemptions,
      13:23
  outsourcing of tax return preparation, **1**:29
  overseas gun sales result in large fines, **5**:8
  sourcing income in cyberspace, **17**:10
  U.S. corporate taxes and international
      business competitiveness, **12**:3
  which foreign dividends get the
      discounted rate, **4**:15
  why is gasoline expensive, **1**:8
  worldwide view of dividends, **13**:18
Going-concern value, Section 197
      intangible, **5**:41

Golsen case, **2**:13
Goods
    deferral of advance payments for, **4**:12
    taxes on the production and sale of, **1**:6–9
Goodwill, **7**:10
    Section 197 intangible, **5**:41
    supersized, **3**:6
Government Accountability Office
    (GAO), **18**:5
Grantee
    consequences to, **8**:9
    exercise of options by, **8**:8–9
Grantor, consequences to, **8**:9
Gray areas, **2**:12
Green card test, **16**:15
Gross estate, **1**:11
Gross income, **4**:2–3, **4**:3–6, **9**:3, **10**:2
    comparison of the accounting and tax
        concepts of income, **4**:5
    concepts of income, **4**:3–5
    form of receipt, **4**:5–6
    inclusion amount for leased automobiles
        in, **5**:39
    partial list of exclusions from, **9**:4
    partial list of items, **9**:3
    receipts, **4**:6
    Section 61(a) definition of, **1**:23
    specific items of, **4**:17–29
    test, for qualifying relative, **9**:11–12
    See also Foreign earned income; Income;
        Income sources
Group term life insurance, **11**:9
    uniform premiums, **11**:10
Guaranteed payments, **14**:29
    Schedules K and K-1, **14**:29

H

H.R. 10 (Keogh) plans. *See* Keogh plans
Half-year convention, **5**:24, **13**:5
Head-of-household, **9**:18–19
Health Insurance Marketplace, **10**:33
    Form 1095-A, **10**:33
Health insurance premiums, proprietorship,
    11:34
Health Savings Accounts (HSA), **10**:13–15,
    11:6
    deductible amount, **10**:14–15
    high-deductible plans, **10**:14
    payments to are deductible for AGI, **9**:5
    tax treatment of contributions and
        distributions, **10**:14
Highly compensated employees, **11**:15
Hobby losses, **11**:45–47
    deductible amount, **11**:47
    general rules, **11**:45–46
    presumptive rule of profit-seeking, **11**:46
Holder, **8**:9
    defined, **8**:10
Holding, **2**:22
Holding period, **7**:12–13, **8**:13–15
    for shareholder and transferee
        corporation, **12**:23
    of a partner's ownership interest, **14**:11
    of new stock or securities, **7**:15
    short sales, **8**:14–15
    special holding period rules, **8**:13–14
Holding period of property, **8**:2
    inherited property, **7**:14
    received, **7**:23–25
Home equity interest, TCJA and, **17**:26
Home equity loans, **10**:18

HOPE scholarship credit. *See* American
    Opportunity Credit
House of Representatives, **2**:3–4
House Ways and Means Committee, **2**:3–4
Housing interest, itemized deductions,
    individual AMT adjustments, **17**:25–26
Hybrid method, **4**:6, **4**:9–10

I

IASB. *See* International Accounting
    Standards Board
Identification problems, cost basis, **7**:9
IFRS. *See* International Financial Reporting
    Standards
Immediate expensing, depreciation of
    personal property, **17**:17
Impairment-related work expenses,
    miscellaneous itemized deductions,
    10:25
Imputed interest income and deductions,
    effect of certain below-market
    loans, **4**:27
Imputed interest on below-market loans,
    4:26–28
    exceptions and limitations, **4**:27–28
Inbound issues, tax issues, **16**:15–16
Inbound sector, **16**:16
Inbound taxation, **16**:3
Incentive stock options (ISOs), **17**:20–21
    individual AMT adjustments, **17**:20–21
Income, **4**:2, **4**:3, **9**:3
    accounting, **4**:4
    active, **6**:15, **6**:17
    alternative minimum taxable (AMTI),
        17:13–15
    assignment of, **4**:13
    character of, **1**:26
    comparison of the accounting and tax
        concepts of, **4**:5
    computation of taxable, **15**:10–12
    concepts of, **4**:3–5
    conduit and entity perspectives effect on
        ability to specially allocate among
        owners, **18**:6–7
    division of, multijurisdictional taxation,
        16:26
    economic, **4**:3
    effectively connected, **16**:15
    financial accounting, **1**:19, **1**:21
    how much and what type, **4**:14
    nontaxable, **3**:5
    passive activity, **6**:17
    portfolio, **6**:15, **6**:17
    prepaid, **4**:11
    Section 61 broad definition of, **4**:3
    Subpart F, **16**:12, **16**:13–14
    tax minimization strategies related to,
        1:23–24
    taxable, **1**:19, **1**:21, **10**:2
    U.S. income tax treatment of a foreign
        person's, **16**:17
    windfall, **4**:4
    See also Gross income; Income sources
Income and deductions of a proprietorship,
    11:34–35
Income and expenses, accrued, **3**:4–5
Income and loss
    allocation of, **15**:13–14
    to S corporation shareholders,
        flow-through of items of, **15**:11
Income definitions, **1**:19

Income earned or received after death,
    miscellaneous itemized deduction of
    Federal estate tax on, **10**:25
Income from discharge of indebtedness,
    4:18, **4**:23–25
    creditors' gifts, **4**:24
    insolvency and bankruptcy, **4**:24
    qualified real property indebtedness, **4**:24
    seller cancellation, **4**:25
    shareholder cancellation, **4**:25
    student loans, **4**:25
Income from property, **4**:13–16
    dividends, **4**:15–16
    interest, **4**:14
Income provisions applicable to individuals,
    overview of, **10**:2
Income received by an agent, **4**:16
Income recognition, **1**:23–24
    rules, **4**:29
Income reporting, book vs. tax, **3**:7
Income shifting, tax planning strategies for,
    1:25–26, **9**:22, **16**:25
Income sources, **4**:13–16
    from property, **4**:13–16
    from sales of inventory, tax planning
        strategies, **16**:9
    in cyberspace, foreign tax credit, **17**:10
    multinational transactions, **16**:7–9
    personal services, **4**:13
    received by an agent, **4**:16
Income sourcing crossing state lines,
    16:20–24
    allocation and apportionment, **16**:21–23
    unitary theory, **16**:23–24
Income splitting option, married
    individuals, **9**:17
Income statement, **3**:15
Income tax accounting, **4**:13
Income Tax Act of 1913, **10**:6
Income tax deduction, tax credit or, **17**:2
Income tax liability, determining the
    corporate, **12**:34
Income tax planning, general framework
    for, **1**:23
Income tax provision, **3**:8
Income tax returns filed by business
    entities, **18**:14
Income tax treaties, **16**:5
    in force, U.S., **16**:6
Income taxation in the U.S., state and
    local income, crossing state lines,
    16:17–25
    sources of law, **16**:18–19
    tax issues, **16**:19–24
Income taxes, **1**:15–18
    accounting for in international
        standards, **3**:10
    federal, **1**:27
    in the financial statements, **3**:8–23
    local income taxes, **1**:17, **10**:16
    state income taxes, **1**:16–17, **10**:16
    structure of the federal income tax,
        1:15–16
Incremental research activities credit, **17**:6–7
Independent contractor, **11**:2
Individual retirement accounts (IRAs), **11**:30
    contributions to, **11**:30–33
    payments to are deductible for AGI, **9**:5
    rollovers and conversions, **11**:32–33
    Roth IRAs, **11**:31–32, **11**:33
    spousal, **11**:30, **11**:31
    tax planning strategies of important dates
        related to, **11**:36
    traditional IRAs, **11**:30–31, **11**:33

Individual shared responsibility payment (ISRP), **10**:32
  consequences of reduction, **10**:33
Individual tax credits, **10**:27–32
  adoption expenses credit, **10**:27–28
  child and dependent tax credit, **10**:28
  credit for child and dependent care expenses, **10**:28–29
  earned income credit, **10**:31–32
  See also Tax credits
Individual tax formula, **9**:2–6
Individual vs. corporate taxpayers, revenue relevance of, **18**:4
Individuals
  and entities, dealings between, **1**:21
  casualty and theft losses, **6**:10–13
  determining the deduction for contributions of appreciated property by, **10**:24
  effect on application of at-risk and passive activity loss rules, **18**:8–10
  Form 1040, **14**:15
  overview of income provisions applicable to, **10**:2
  specific exclusions applicable to, **10**:6–11
  specific inclusions applicable to, **10**:3–6
  taxes and, **1**:3–4
Individuals as proprietors, **11**:33–45
  accounting periods and methods, **11**:33–34
  deduction for qualified business income, **11**:37–44
  estimated tax payments, **11**:44–45
  health insurance premiums, **11**:34
  income and deductions of a proprietorship, **11**:34–35
  retirement plans for self-employed individuals, **11**:35–37
  self-employment tax, **11**:34–35
Inheritance tax, **1**:10
Inheritances, **10**:6–7
Inherited property, **7**:13–14
  holding period of, **7**:14
  special holding period rules, **8**:14
Inside basis, **14**:12
  in partnership interest, **14**:20–21
Insolvency and bankruptcy, **4**:24
Installment method, **4**:7
Intangible assets, **3**:5, **14**:11
Intangible drilling and development costs (IDC), **5**:42
  individual AMT preferences, **17**:29
Intangible income, special tax rate for, **16**:15
Intangible property, personalty, **1**:14
Intangible real property, **8**:31
Inter vivos gifts, **10**:6
Interest, **4**:14, **10**:17–21
  basis in the partnership, **14**:7
  capital, **14**:6
  classification of interest expense, **10**:20
  deductibility of personal, student loan, investment, and mortgage, **10**:21
  investment, **10**:17–18
  prepaid, **10**:20
  prepayment penalty, **10**:20
  profits (loss), **14**:6
  qualified residence, **10**:18–19
  tax-exempt securities, **10**:20
Interest earned, **4**:11
Interest expense
  classification of, **10**:20
  other business expenses, **5**:17
Interest in general, itemized deductions, individual AMT adjustments, **17**:25

Interest on
  certain state and local government obligations, **4**:20–21
  private activity bonds, individual AMT preferences, **17**:29–30
  qualified student loans, **10**:17
  state and local bonds (Section 103), gross income exclusion, **4**:17
Interest paid
  for services, **10**:19–20
  to related parties, **10**:20
Interest related to tax-exempt income, **5**:13–14
Interjurisdictional agreements, multijurisdictional taxation, **16**:28
Internal Revenue Bulletin (I.R.B.), **2**:7, **2**:8, **2**:9, **2**:15
Internal Revenue Code, **16**:4
  arrangement of, **2**:5
  citing of, **2**:5–6
  interpreting, **2**:20
  of 1939, **2**:2
  of 1954, **2**:2
  of 1986, **2**:2
  origin of, **2**:2
Internal Revenue Service
  accounting method prescribed by, **4**:7
  Direct Pay, **9**:29
  influence of, tax law, **1**:33, **1**:34
  IRS Letter Rulings Reports, **2**:8
  Publication 925, *Passive Activity and At-Risk Rules*, **6**:25
International Accounting Standards Board (IASB), **1**:19, **3**:10
International business competitiveness, U.S. corporate taxes and, **12**:3
International Financial Reporting Standards (IFRS), **1**:19, **3**:10
International law, international transactions, **16**:3
Interpretive Regulations, **2**:21
Inventions and processes, as definition of capital asset, **8**:3, **8**:4
Inventory
  definition of capital asset, **8**:3–4
  tax issues related to contributed property, **14**:12
Investment earnings, **4**:22
Investment income, tax planning strategies for reducing, **4**:17
Investment interest, **10**:17–18
  deductibility of, **10**:21
  itemized deductions, individual AMT adjustments, **17**:26–27
Investment partnership, **14**:9
Investment property
  complete destruction of, **6**:9
  partial destruction of, **6**:9
Investments, **13**:13
Involuntary conversions, **8**:25
  defined, **7**:27
  financial accounting, **7**:7
  gains, tax planning strategies for recognizing, **7**:30
  nonrecognition of gain, **7**:29–30
  recapture potential of, **8**:36
  replacement property, **7**:27–28, **7**:28–29
  Section 1033, **7**:25–30
IRA. *See* Individual retirement account
IRS. *See* Internal Revenue Service
Itemized deductions, **9**:5, **10**:11–27
  charitable contributions, **10**:21–25
  deductions from AGI, **1**:16, **10**:11
  individual AMT adjustments, **17**:25–27

  interest, **10**:17–21
  medical expenses, **10**:11–15
  other miscellaneous, **10**:25–26
  partial list of, **10**:11
  tax planning strategies for effective utilization of, **10**:27
  taxes, **10**:15–16

J

Joint return
  tax planning strategies for problems with, **9**:15
  Tax Rate Schedule, **9**:17
  test for dependency status, **9**:15
  worldwide approach to taxation, **9**:19
Joint venture, **14**:2
Judicial citations, **2**:14–16
Judicial concepts relating to tax, **1**:33
Judicial influence on statutory provisions, **1**:33
Judicial opinions, understanding, **2**:22
Judicial sources of the tax law, **2**:10–16
  appellate courts, **2**:12–14
  assessing significance of, **2**:21–22
  judicial citations, **2**:14–16
  trial courts, **2**:11–12
Jury trial, **2**:11

K

Keogh plans, **11**:35–36
  tax planning strategies of important dates related to, **11**:36
Kickbacks, **5**:8
Kiddie tax, **8**:17, **9**:23–24
  net unearned income, **9**:24

L

Law
  sources of in crossing state lines, **16**:18–19
  sources of in U.S. taxation of multinational transactions, **16**:4–5
Lease cancellation payments, **8**:11–12
  lessee treatment, **8**:12
  lessor treatment, **8**:12
Leased automobiles, inclusion amount in gross income, **5**:39
Leased property, improvements on, **4**:28–29
Leasehold improvements, fair market value of when lease is terminated (Section 109), gross income exclusion, **4**:18
Legislation, monitoring, **5**:10
Legislative grace, **1**:15
Legislative process, **2**:3–4
  for tax bills, **2**:3
Legislative Regulations, **2**:21
Lessee, **8**:11
  treatment, **8**:12
Lessor, **8**:11
  treatment, **8**:12
Letter rulings, **2**:8–9
Liabilities
  in excess of basis, **12**:16–18
  partnership, **14**:22–23
Liability assumption, tax consequences of, **12**:18

Life insurance proceeds, **4**:21–22
  exceptions to exclusion treatment, **4**:21–22
  received by reason of death of the insured (Section 101), gross income exclusion, **4**:17–18
Lifetime learning credit, **10**:30, **11**:25
LIFO recapture tax, **15**:29
Like-kind exchanges, **7**:20–25
  financial accounting, **7**:7
  recapture potential of, **8**:36
  Section 1031, **7**:20–25
Like-kind property, **7**:20–21
  basis of, **7**:23–24
Limitation on deduction of excess business losses, **15**:25
Limitations based on wages and capital investment, **11**:40–42
Limitations on QBI deduction, **11**:40
Limited liability, **18**:3
Limited liability company (LLC), **1**:20, **12**:7, **14**:4, **14**:32–33, **18**:2, **18**:3
  advantages of, **14**:32–33
  disadvantages of, **14**:33
  disposing of, **18**:16–17, **18**:18
  tax attributes of, **18**:22–25
  taxation of, **14**:32
Limited liability partnership (LLP), **1**:20, **14**:4, **18**:3
Limited partners, material participation, **6**:24
Limited partnerships, **12**:7, **14**:3–4
Liquidating and nonliquidating distributions compared, **13**:24–25
Liquidation process, **13**:24
Listed property, **5**:35
  business and personal use of automobiles and other, **5**:35–40
  change from predominantly business use, **5**:38
  cost recovery, **5**:39
  substantiation requirements, **5**:40
  used predominantly in business, **5**:36
LLCs. *See* Limited liability companies
Loans, below-market, **4**:26–28
Loans between related parties, **6**:5
  tax planning strategies for documentation of, **6**:8
Loans to executives prohibited, **4**:27
Loans to shareholders, **13**:18
Lobbying expenses, **5**:9–10
Local excise taxes, **1**:7
Local income taxes, **1**:17
Lodging and meals furnished for the convenience of the employer, **11**:7–9
Lodging, medical expenses for transportation, meal, and, **10**:13
Long-term capital gains (LTCG), **4**:19
Long-term capital losses (LTCL), **4**:19
Long-term care insurance benefits, **11**:6–7
Long-term gains, **8**:16–18
Long-term nonpersonal use capital assets, **8**:25
Loss
  allocation of, **15**:13–14
  built-in, **14**:19
  business debt deductible as ordinary, **6**:4
  business property, **6**:7
  capital, **8**:2, **8**:18
  casualty and theft, **6**:7–13
  casualty gain and, **6**:12–13
  determination of, **7**:2–8
  hobby, **11**:45–47
  individual AMT adjustments, **17**:22
  net operating, **3**:5
  nonrecognition of, **7**:8
  ordinary, **6**:6

precontribution, **14**:19
realized, **7**:2–7, **7**:8
recognition of, effect on corporation, **13**:14–15
recognized, **7**:7–8
small business stock, **6**:5–6
tax issues related to contributed property of built-in, **14**:12
tax planning strategies for matching gains with, **8**:21
treatment of, **15**:23–25
worthless securities, **6**:5
See also Capital losses
Loss basis for converted property, **7**:17
Loss considerations, tax planning strategies for, **15**:24–25
Loss limitations, **14**:25–28
  at-risk limitation, **14**:27–28
  basis limitation, **14**:26–27
  passive activity rules, **14**:28
Loss measurement, casualty and theft, **6**:9–10
Loss of the election, **15**:7–10
  loss of S corporation status, **15**:8
  passive investment income limitation, **15**:8–9
  reelection after termination, **15**:9
  voluntary revocation, **15**:7–8
Loss on contributions to the partnership, **14**:8–9
Loss property, basis adjustment for, **12**:22–23
Loss to S corporation shareholders, flow-through of items of income and, **15**:11
Loss transactions, disallowed, special holding period rules, **8**:14
Losses from property transactions, **4**:18–20
  capital gains and losses, **4**:18–20
Losses last rule, **15**:21
Losses of individuals, casualty and theft, **6**:10–13
  personal use property, **6**:11–12
Losses subject to at-risk and passive activity loss limitations, treatment of, **6**:27
Low-income housing credit, **17**:12
Luxury auto limitation, **5**:36

M

MACRS: class lives, methods, and conventions, **5**:24
MACRS. *See* Modified accelerated cost recovery system
Management of property held for production of income, itemized deductions, **10**:11
Marginal rate, **9**:22
Marital deduction, **1**:11, **1**:12
Marketplace. *See* Health Insurance Marketplace
Marriage penalty, **9**:18
  equity or fairness, **9**:18
Married individuals, **9**:17–18
Matching principle, **3**:8
Material participation, **6**:22–24, **6**:28
  corporations, **6**:24
  limited partners, **6**:24
  participation defined, **6**:24
  tests based on current participation, **6**:23
  tests based on facts and circumstances, **6**:23
  tests based on prior participation, **6**:22
  tests to determine, **6**:23
Meal expenses, tax planning strategies for, **11**:26
Meals and lodging furnished for the convenience of the employer, **11**:7–9

furnished by the employer, **11**:7–8
on the employer's business premises, **11**:8
required as condition of employment, **11**:8–9
Medical care, **10**:12
Medical expense deduction, tax planning strategies for the multiple support agreement and, **9**:14
Medical expenses, **10**:11–15
  capital expenditures, **10**:13
  cosmetic surgery, **10**:12
  defined, **10**:12
  examples of deductible and nondeductible, **10**:12
  for spouse and dependents, **10**:13
  health savings accounts, **10**:13–15
  itemized deductions, individual AMT adjustments, **17**:27
  nursing home care, **10**:12–13
  TCJA and, **17**:27
  transportation, meal, and lodging, **10**:13
Medical reimbursement plans, **11**:5–6
Medicare health insurance, **1**:9
Member-of-the-household requirement, multiple support agreement and, **9**:13
Memorandum decisions, **2**:14
Mid-month convention, **5**:28
Mid-quarter convention, **5**:26–27
Mining exploration and development costs, **17**:19–20
Modes of payment, **9**:29
Modified accelerated cost recovery system (MACRS), **5**:22, **5**:24
  cost recovery tables, **5**:45–47
  deductions, deferring to future years, **5**:33
  depreciation on fixed assets, **3**:4
  for personal property, **5**:24–28
  for real estate, **5**:28–29
  property, **17**:17
Modified adjusted gross income (MAGI), **10**:10
Monitoring legislation, **5**:10
More-than-50 percent test, automobiles and other listed property used predominantly in business, **5**:36
Mortgage interest, deductibility of, **10**:21
Moving expenses, **11**:22
Multijurisdictional taxation, common challenges of, **16**:25–28
  authority to tax, **16**:25–26
  division of income, **16**:26
  interjurisdictional agreements, **16**:28
  tax havens, **16**:27
  transfer pricing, **16**:26–27
Multijurisdictional taxpayer, **16**:2
Multinational transactions, U.S. taxation of, **16**:2–17
  sources of law, **16**:4–5
  tax issues, **16**:5–17
Multiple support agreement, **9**:13
  and the medical expense deduction, tax planning strategies for, **9**:14
Multistate income taxation, corporate, **16**:24
Multistate Tax Commission (MTC), **16**:19

N

Natural resources, depletion of, **5**:21
Net capital gain, **8**:19, **11**:39
  computing, **4**:19
  taxing, **4**:19–20
Net capital loss, **8**:19
  computing, **4**:19
  taxing, **4**:19–20

Net income tax, **17**:3
Net investment income, **10**:18
　tax (NIIT), **9**:27–28
Net long-term capital gain (NLTCG), **4**:19
Net long-term capital loss (NLTCL), **4**:19
Net operating loss carryovers, timing
　adjustments, **13**:4
Net operating losses (NOLs), **3**:5, **6**:13–14,
　15:23–24, **17**:24–25
　and carryovers, tax law changes, **3**:22, **17**:24
　carryforwards, **6**:14
　NOL rule, **12**:29
Net regular tax liability, **17**:3
Net short-term capital gain (NSTCG), **4**:19
Net short-term capital loss (NSTCL), **4**:19
Net taxes payable or refund due,
　computation of, **9**:22–23
Net unearned income, **9**:24
Net worth, change in as a measure of
　income (or loss), **4**:3
Nexus, **16**:19, **16**:21
No-additional-cost services, **11**:12, **11**:13,
　11:16
NOLs. *See* Net operating losses
Nominal property, transfers for, **12**:14
Nonaccountable plans, **11**:29–30
Nonacquiescence (NA or Nonacq.), **2**:15
Nonbusiness bad debt, **6**:4
Nonbusiness debt, **6**:3
Nonbusiness expenses, **10**:11
Noncash charitable contributions,
　Form 8283, **10**:23
Noncash distributions
　by the corporation, tax treatment of,
　　15:19–20
　consequences of, **15**:20
　partner's basis, gain and loss, **14**:24–25
Noncash dividends, **13**:13–16
　effect on corporation, **13**:14–16
　effect on shareholder, **13**:14
Noncontingent payments, franchises, **8**:11
Noncorporate taxpayers
　capital gains of, **8**:18
　tax treatment of capital gains and losses
　　of, **8**:16–22
Nondeductible contributions, IRA, **11**:31
Nondeductible expenses, **3**:5
Nondeductible items, charitable
　contributions, **10**:22
Nondiscrimination provisions, **11**:15–16
Nonliquidating and liquidating distributions
　compared, **13**:24–25
Nonliquidating property distribution, **13**:24
Nonpersonal use capital assets, casualty or
　theft and, Section 1231 assets, **8**:25
Nonrecaptured net Section 1231 losses, **8**:29
Nonrecognition, exceptions to, **14**:9–10
　disguised exchange, **14**:9–10
　disguised sale, **14**:10
　investment partnership, **14**:9
　services, **14**:10
Nonrecognition of gain, **7**:29–30
　conversion into money, **7**:29–30
　direct conversion, **7**:29
Nonrecognition of gain or loss, **7**:8
　dispositions of personal use assets, **7**:8
Nonrecognition provision, other, **7**:31
　sale of a principal residence—Section
　　121, **7**:31
　transfer of assets to business entity—
　　Sections 351 and 721, **7**:31
Nonrecourse debt, **14**:22
Nonresident alien (NRA), **16**:15
　shareholder limitations, **15**:6

Nontax considerations, **12**:6–7
Nontax factors of business forms, **18**:2–4
　capital formation, **18**:4
　limited liability, **18**:3
　other factors, **18**:3
Nontaxable economic benefits, **4**:9
Nontaxable exchange, **7**:19
　general concept of, **7**:19
　financial accounting, **7**:7
　special holding period rules, **8**:13
Nontaxable income, **3**:5
Nontaxable stock dividends, **7**:10
Nontaxable transactions, recapture potential
　of certain, **8**:35
Nursing home care, medical expenses,
　10:12–13

O

ObamaCare. *See* Affordable Care Act
Obligation to repay, amounts received
　under, **4**:11
Occupational taxes, **1**:15
Office in the home expenses, **11**:27–28
On the employer's business premises
　requirement, **11**:8
One-time transition tax for unrepatriated
　profits of U.S. entities, **3**:22–23
Options, **8**:7–9
　consequences to grantor and grantee, **8**:9
　exercise of by grantee, **8**:8–9
　failure to exercise, **8**:8
　sale of, **8**:7–8
Ordinary and necessary, **5**:2
　business expenses, **11**:34
　requirement, **5**:2–3
Ordinary income, **8**:16, **8**:29, **14**:5
　property, **5**:19, **10**:23
Ordinary loss, **6**:6
　business bad debt, **6**:4
Organization for Economic Cooperation
　and Development (OECD), **12**:3
Organizational costs, **14**:14
Organizational expenditures, **12**:30, **12**:32
　deduction, **12**:30–31
Original issue discount, **4**:11
Other adjustments account (OAA), **15**:16,
　15:17–18
Outbound taxation, **16**:3
Out-of-the-home expenses, child and
　dependent care expenses, **10**:28
Outside basis, **14**:12
Outsourcing of tax return preparation, **1**:29
Overseas operations and book-tax
　differences, **16**:12
Ownership interest
　conduit and entity perspectives effect on
　　basis of, **18**:7–8
　disposing of partnerships and LLCs as
　　sale of, **18**:16–17
Owner-user or owner-investor, **7**:27

P

Parent-subsidiary controlled group, **12**:34
Parker Tax Pro Library, **2**:19
Partial recapture, **8**:32
Participation
　active, **6**:28
　defined, **6**:24
　material, **6**:22–24, **6**:28

　tests based on current, **6**:23
　tests based on prior, **6**:23
Partner and partnership, transactions
　between, **14**:28–31
　guaranteed payments, **14**:29
　other transactions, **14**:30
　partners as employees, **14**:30–31
Partner's basis
　gain and loss, **14**:23–25
　in partnership interest, **14**:28
Partner's ownership interest in a
　partnership, **14**:6–8
Partner-partnership transactions, **14**:31
Partners as employees, **14**:30–31
Partnership, **1**:20, **14**:2–3, **18**:2
　assets of, by industry, **14**:22
　basis of a partnership interest,
　　partnership liabilities, **14**:22–23
　consequences of noncash distributions,
　　15:20
　converting to another entity form, **18**:21
　defined, **14**:3–4
　disposing of, **18**:16–17, **18**:18
　Form 1065, **1**:20, **14**:5–6
　initial costs of, **14**:13–14
　loss limitations, **14**:26–27, **14**:28
　operations of, **14**:15–28
　profitability of, **18**:8
　tax attributes of, **18**:22–25
　tax effects in formation of, **14**:8–14
　tax treatment of business forms
　　compared, **12**:6
　transactions between partner and,
　　14:28–31
Partnership activities, tax reporting of, **14**:18
Partnership allocations, **14**:18–20
　economic effect, **14**:19
　precontribution gain or loss, **14**:19
　qualified business income deduction, **14**:20
Partnership form, advantages and
　disadvantages of, **14**:33
Partnership formation and basis
　computation, **14**:13
Partnership interest
　basis in, **14**:7
　basis of, **14**:20–23, **14**:23–25
　initial basis in, **14**:20–21
Partnership liabilities, **14**:22–23
　ratable share of, **15**:22
Partnership operations
　distributions, **14**:17–18
　withdrawals, **14**:17–18
Partnership power, **14**:3
Partnership taxation
　and reporting, **14**:4–6
　definition of a partnership, **14**:3–4
　forms of doing business—federal tax
　　consequences, **14**:2–3
　overview of, **14**:2–8
　partner's ownership interest in a
　　partnership, **14**:6–8
　separately stated items, **14**:5
　tax reporting rules, **14**:5–6
　taxation and reporting, **14**:4–6
Partnership/LLC taxation, tax reporting, **14**:9
Passenger automobiles, **5**:36
Passive activities
　disposition of, **6**:29–30
　rules for determining, **6**:22
Passive activity income and loss, **6**:17
　carryovers of passive activity credits, **6**:20
　carryovers of suspended losses, **6**:19
　classification of, **6**:17
　impact of suspended losses, **6**:18–19

passive activity changes to active, **6**:20–21
passive activity credits, **6**:20
Passive activity loss, **6**:15
Passive activity loss limits, **6**:17–31
    classification and impact of passive
        activity income and loss, **6**:17–21
    disposition of passive activities, **6**:29–30
    interaction of at-risk and passive activity
        loss limits, **6**:26
    material participation, **6**:22–24
    rental activities, **6**:24–25
    special rules for real estate, **6**:27–29
    taxpayers subject to the passive activity
        loss rules, **6**:21–22
Passive activity loss rules, **14**:25
    conduit and entity perspectives effect on
        application of, **18**:8–10
    key issues and answers, **6**:25
    taxpayers subject to, **6**:21–22
Passive activity losses (PALs), **6**:30
    and credits, **15**:25
    individual AMT adjustments, **17**:23
    tax planning strategies for utilizing,
        6:30–31
Passive activity rules, **14**:28
Passive income and loss, general impact
    of, **6**:18
Passive income generator (PIG), **6**:30
Passive investment income (PII), **15**:8–9,
    15:29
    pitfalls, tax planning strategies to avoid,
        15:30
Passive investment income penalty tax,
    15:29–30
Pass-through entities, **14**:2
Patents, **8**:9–10
    as definition of capital asset, **8**:3
    holder defined, **8**:10
    Section 197 intangible, **5**:41
    substantial rights, **8**:9–10
Pay-as-you-go procedures, **1**:15
Payment of deficiency, **2**:11–12
Payroll factor, **16**:22
Penalties, **5**:8
    accuracy-related, **2**:23
    failure to disclose, **2**:6
    on underpayments, **11**:45
Percentage depletion, **5**:43–44
    individual AMT preferences, **17**:28–29
    rates, **5**:44
Percentage of completion method, **4**:7
Permanent differences, **3**:4
Permanent establishment (PE), **16**:5
Personal exemptions, **9**:6, **9**:9
Personal expenses, itemized deductions,
    10:11
Personal holding company (PHC)
    tax, **13**:26
Personal identification number (Self-Select
    PIN), **9**:28
Personal injury, **10**:9
Personal interest, deductibility of, **10**:21
Personal nonrefundable credits, AMT
    liability and, **17**:16
Personal property
    MACRS for, **5**:24–28
    taxes, **10**:16
Personal service corporations, **6**:21
    classification requirements, **18**:10
    conduit and entity perspectives effect on
        application of passive activity loss
        rules, **18**:8–10
Personal services, **4**:13
    of an employee, **4**:13

Personal use assets, **5**:22
    converted to business or income-
        producing use, cost recovery basis
        for, **5**:23–24
    dispositions of, **7**:8
Personal use interest, Schedule A of
    Form 1040, **10**:20
Personal use of automobiles and other
    listed property, **5**:35–40
Personal use personalty, **1**:14
Personal use property, **5**:22
    casualty and theft losses of individuals,
        6:11–12
    partial or complete destruction of, **6**:9
    special rule on insurance recovery, **6**:10
Personal use realty, **1**:14
Personal use to business or income-
    producing use, conversion of
    property from, **7**:16–17
Personalty, **1**:13, **5**:22
    business use, **1**:14
    cost recovery periods/classes, **5**:25
    personal use, **1**:14
    taxes on, **1**:14
Petitioner, **2**:10, **2**:22
Phaseout of traditional IRA deduction of an
    active participant in 2018, **11**:30
Physical personal injury or sickness, **10**:9
Placed in service requirement, cost
    recovery, **5**:23
Plaintiff, **2**:10
Planning, relevance of taxation to accounting
    and finance professionals, **1**:2
Points, **10**:19
Political considerations, **1**:31–32
    special interest legislation, **1**:31
    state and local government influences,
        1:31–32
    tax law, **1**:34
Political contributions, **5**:9
Political science
    incentive-granting community, **16**:27
    tax law, **1**:18
Pollution control facilities, individual AMT
    adjustments, **17**:19
Portfolio income, **6**:15, **6**:17
Post-election termination period, **15**:18
Precedents, **2**:10, **2**:13
Precontribution gain or loss, **14**:19
Preferences, **17**:28
    and adjustments, tax planning strategies
        for controlling the timing of, **17**:26
Premium tax credit (PTC), **10**:33
    Form 8962, Premium Tax Credit, **10**:33
Prepaid expenses (12-month rule), **5**:7
Prepaid income, **4**:11, **4**:12
Prepaid interest, **10**:20
Prepayment penalty, **10**:20
Presumptive rule of profit-seeking, **11**:46
Primary valuation amount, **7**:13
Principal place of business, **11**:27
Principal residence, sale of, **7**:31
Prior participation, tests based on, **6**:23
Private activity bonds, **17**:29
Prizes and awards, **10**:5
Procedural matters, **12**:35–39
    effect of taxes on financial statements,
        12:39
    estimated tax payments, **12**:36
    filing requirements for corporations,
        12:35–36
    Schedule M-1, reconciliation of income
        (loss) per books with income per
        return, **12**:36–38

Schedule M-2, analysis of unappropriated
    retained earnings per books, **12**:38
Schedule M-3, net income (loss)
    reconciliation for corporations with
    total assets of $10 million or more,
    12:38–39
Procedural Regulations, **2**:21
Production and sale of goods, taxes on, **1**:6–9
Production or collection of income,
    expenses related to, itemized
    deductions, **10**:11
Production-of-income percentage,
    automobiles and other listed
    property used predominantly in
    business, **5**:36
Profit and loss sharing ratios, **14**:6
Profits (loss) interest, **14**:6
Profit-seeking, presumptive rule of, hobby
    losses, **11**:46
Progressive (or graduated) rate, **9**:22
Progressive tax rate, **1**:4–5
Property, **12**:10
    appreciated or depreciated, **7**:23, **10**:24
    bargain purchase of, **7**:9
    bargain rental of corporate, **13**:17
    bargain sale of corporate to a
        shareholder, **13**:17
    basis adjustment for loss, **12**:22–23
    basis of like-kind, **7**:23–24
    business, complete or partial destruction
        of, **6**:9
    capital gain, **10**:23
    conversion from personal use to business
        or income-producing use, **7**:16–17
    definition for Section 351 purposes, **12**:10
    depreciable real, **8**:31
    excluded in Section 1231 assets, **8**:25
    Form 4797 Sales of Business, **8**:36
    holding period of, **8**:2
    included in Section 1231 assets, **8**:25
    income from, **4**:13–16
    individual AMT adjustments for
        depreciation of personal, **17**:17–18
    individual AMT adjustments for
        depreciation of real, **17**:17
    inherited, special holding period rules, **8**:14
    intangible, **1**:14, **8**:31
    investment, complete or partial
        destruction of, **6**:9
    manner of disposition, **8**:2
    nature of, **5**:22–23
    ordinary income, **10**:23
    personal use, **5**:22, **6**:9
    qualified for additional first-year
        depreciation, **5**:32
    replacement, **7**:27–28
    sale or other disposition of, **7**:2–3
    sales of, **14**:30
    shareholder use of corporate-owned, **13**:17
    tangible, **1**:14
    tax status of, **8**:2
    transfer of, **12**:10–11
    transfers for, **12**:13–14
Property acquired from a decedent. *See*
    Inherited property
Property contributions, **5**:19–20
Property dividend, **13**:13
Property factor, **16**:22
Property paced in service maximum,
    Section 179 expensing election,
    5:30–31
Property received
    basis and holding period of, **7**:23–25
    corporation's basis in, **12**:21

Property settlements, alimony and separate maintenance payments, **10**:4
Property taxes, **1**:12–14
  on personalty, **1**:14
  on realty, **1**:13
Property transactions
  financial accounting, **7**:7
  gains and losses from, **4**:18–20
Proportional tax rate, **1**:4–5
Proposed Regulations, **2**:7
Proprietorship, **1**:19
  Schedule C, Profit or Loss from Business of Form 1040, **1**:19
  See also Sole proprietorship
Prospect of full recovery, **6**:7
Public economics, **4**:20
Public finance, **15**:26
Public Law 86-272, **16**:19
Public policy, **2**:16
Public policy limitations, **5**:8–9
  expenses related to an illegal business, **5**:9
  justification for denying deductions, **5**:8
Punitive damages, **10**:9

Q

Qualified business income (QBI), **11**:37
Qualified business income deduction (QBID), **9**:6, **11**:37–44, **14**:20 **15**:12–13
  deductions from AGI, **1**:16
  overview of, **11**:43
  rules (Section 199A), **15**:15
Qualified child care expenses, **17**:9
Qualified discounts on goods, **11**:16
Qualified discounts on services, **11**:16
Qualified dividends, **4**:15
Qualified employee discounts, **11**:12, **11**:13–14
Qualified higher education expenses, **10**:10
Qualified housing interest, itemized deductions, individual AMT adjustments, **17**:26
Qualified improvement property, **5**:27
Qualified moving expense reimbursements, **11**:13, **11**:15
Qualified nonrecourse debt, **14**:27
Qualified nonrecourse financing, **6**:16
Qualified plan award, **10**:5
Qualified property, additional first-year depreciation, **5**:32
Qualified real property business indebtedness, **4**:23, **4**:24
Qualified residence defined, **10**:18
Qualified residence interest, **10**:18–19
  itemized deductions, individual AMT adjustments, **17**:25–26
Qualified retirement planning services, **11**:13, **11**:15, **11**:16
Qualified small business stock, **8**:21, **8**:17
Qualified trade or business (QTB), **11**:38
Qualified transportation fringes, **11**:13, **11**:15, **11**:16
Qualified tuition and related expenses, **11**:25
Qualified tuition reduction plans, **11**:9
  limitations for, **11**:24
Qualifying child, **9**:9–10, **10**:31
  age test, **9**:9–10
  relationship test, **9**:9
  residence test, **9**:9
  support test, **9**:10
  tiebreaker rules, **9**:10

Qualifying relative, **9**:11–14
  gross income test, **9**:11–12
  relationship test, **9**:11
  support test, **9**:12–14

R

Rate reconciliation, **3**:16–18
Ratios
  capital sharing, **14**:6
  profit and loss sharing, **14**:6
Real estate, **7**:20
  MACRS for, **5**:28–29
  professionals, **6**:27–28
  special rules for, **6**:27–29
  tax planning strategies for selling depreciable, **8**:34
  taxes, **10**:16
  See also Realty
Real property
  depreciable, **8**:31
  intangible, **8**:31
  subdivided for sale, **8**:6
Realization, **4**:26
  principle, **4**:4
Realized gain, **4**:18, **7**:2–7
  adjusted basis, **7**:4
  amount realized, **7**:3–4
  capital additions, **7**:5
  capital recoveries, **7**:5–7
  sale or other disposition of property, **7**:2–3
Realized loss, **4**:18, **7**:2–7
  adjusted basis, **7**:4
  amount realized, **7**:3–4
  capital additions, **7**:5
  capital recoveries, **7**:5–7
  sale or other disposition of property, **7**:2–3
Realty, **1**:13, **5**:22
  business use, **1**:14
  personal use, **1**:14
Reasonableness, **18**:12
Reasonableness requirement, **5**:3
Recapture considerations, **12**:24
Recapture provisions in Sections 1245 and 1250, **8**:2
Recapture, tax planning for the timing of, **8**:36
Receivables, tax issues related to contributed property, **14**:12
Recognized gain, **4**:18, **7**:7–8, **8**:2
Recognized loss, **4**:18, **7**:7–8, **8**:2
Record-keeping requirements for charitable contributions, **10**:22–23
Recourse debt, **14**:22
Reductions in marginal business income tax rates, **16**:8
Reelection after termination, **15**:9
Refund due, computation of, net taxes payable or, **9**:22–23
Regressive tax rate, **1**:5
Regular (C) corporations, tax treatment of business forms compared, **12**:6
Regular corporations, **12**:2
  See also C corporations
Regular decisions, **2**:14
Regulation and oversight, **2**:28
Rehabilitation expenditures, **17**:12
  credit, **17**:4–5
Related parties
  expenses accrued to, **5**:6–7
  for purposes of Section 267, **5**:6–7
  interest paid to, **10**:20
  loans between, **6**:5
Related taxpayers, **7**:14–15

Related-party transactions, **5**:6, **5**:12–13
  relationships and constructive ownership, **5**:6–7
  tax planning strategies for documentation of, **6**:8
Relationship test
  qualifying child, **9**:9
  qualifying relative, **9**:11
  multiple support agreement and, **9**:13
Relationships and constructive ownership in transactions between related parties, **5**:6–7
Rent or royalty property expenses
  deductions for AGI, **10**:11
  Schedule E, **10**:20
Rental activity, **6**:24–25
Rental real estate with active participation, **6**:28–29
Replacement property, **7**:27–28
  functional use test, **7**:27
  special rule for condemnations, **7**:28
  taxpayer use test, **7**:27–28
  tests, involuntary conversions, **7**:28
  time limitation on, **7**:28–29
Reporting procedures, **8**:36–37
Research activities credit, **17**:6–8, **17**:12
  basic research credit, **17**:8
  energy research credit, **17**:8
  incremental research activities credit, **17**:6–7
Research and experimental expenditures, **5**:15–17, **17**:19–20
  deferral and amortization method of, **5**:16–17
  expense method of, **5**:16
Research expenditures, **17**:6
Residence, inbound tax issues, **16**:15
Residence test for qualifying child, **9**:9
Residential rental real estate, **5**:28
Respondent, **2**:10, **2**:22
Retirement plans for self-employed individuals, **11**:35–37
  Keogh plans, **11**:35–36
  SIMPLE plans, **11**:36–37
Return-of-capital distributions, minimizing double taxation by making, **18**:13
Returns filed by number of S corporation shareholders, 2013 tax year, **15**:14
Revenue Procedures, **2**:7–8
Revenue relevance of corporate vs. individual taxpayers, **18**:4
Revenue Rulings, **2**:7–8
Revenue-neutral, **2**:19
Right of offset, **5**:12
Rollovers and conversions, IRAs, **11**:32–33
Roth IRAs, **11**:31–32
  and traditional IRAs compared, **11**:33

S

S corporation economy, **15**:30
S corporation losses, treatment of, **15**:24
S corporation returns filed (%), 2013 tax year, **15**:5
S corporation shareholders
  flow-through of items of income and loss to, **15**:11
  returns filed by number of, 2013 tax year, **15**:14
S corporation status
  conditions required to elect, **15**:10
  definition of a small business corporation, **15**:3–6

loss of the election, **15**:7–10
making the election, **15**:6
minimizing double taxation by electing, **18**:14–15
qualifying for, **15**:3–10
shareholder consent, **15**:7
tax planning strategies on when to elect, **15**:4
S corporations, **1**:20, **12**:2, **14**:2–3, **15**:2
an overview, **15**:2–3
consequences of noncash distributions, **15**:20
disposing of, **18**:18, **18**:19–20
distributions from, **15**:16
Form 1120S, **1**:20, **14**:15
operational rules, **15**:10–26
tax attributes of, **18**:22–25
tax treatment of business forms compared, **12**:6
S election
effect of terminating, **15**:18–19
Form 2553, **15**:6
tax planning strategies for, **15**:7, **15**:9
Safe harbor provisions, **15**:4
Salary structure, tax planning strategies for, **15**:15
Sale of a business, tax planning strategies for, **5**:41
Sale of a principal residence, **7**:31
Sale of goods, taxes on the production and, **1**:6–9
Sale or exchange, **8**:6–12
franchises, trademarks, and trade names, **8**:10–11
lease cancellation payments, **8**:11–12
options, **8**:7–9
patents, **8**:9–10
retirement of corporate obligations, **8**:7
worthless securities and Section 1244 stock, **8**:7
Sale or other disposition of property, **7**:2–3
Sales factor, **16**:22
Sales of property, **14**:30
Sales taxes, **1**:4
state and local, **10**:16
Same-sex marriage, filing status, **9**:17
Sarbanes-Oxley, **4**:27
Savings incentive match plan for employees. *See* SIMPLE plan
Schedule A of Form 1040, personal use interest, **10**:20
Schedule C, Profit or Loss from Business, Form 1040, **1**:19, **10**:20, **11**:2, **11**:33
Schedule E, rent or royalty expenses, **10**:20
Schedule K, partnership operations, **14**:6, **14**:15–18, **14**:29
Schedule K-1, partnership operations, **14**:5–6, **14**:15–18, **14**:29
Schedule L, partnerships, **14**:6
Schedule M-1, reconciliation of income (loss) per books with income per return**3**:6–7, **12**:36–38, **14**:6
conceptual diagram of, **12**:37
Schedule M-2, analysis of unappropriated retained earnings per books, **12**:38, **14**:6, **15**:18
Schedule M-3, net income (loss) reconciliation for corporations with total assets of $10 million or more, **3**:7, **12**:38–39, **14**:6
Schedule SE, Form 1040, **1**:10
Schedule UTP (Uncertain Tax Position Statement), **3**:7–8, **12**:39

Scholarships, **10**:7–8
disguised compensation, **10**:8
employee fringe benefit, **11**:10
general information, **10**:7–8
timing issues, **10**:8
Section 61, broad definition of gross income, **1**:23, **4**:2, **11**:34
Section 162, business deductions, **5**:2, **11**:34
Section 179 expensing election, **5**:29, **5**:33–35, **13**:6
Section 197 intangible asset, **14**:11
Section 199A deduction, **11**:38–40, **14**:20
Section 121, sale of a principal residence, **7**:31
Section 222 limitations, **11**:25
Section 248, organizational expenditures, **12**:30
Section 262, sale or exchange of personal use assets, **8**:14
Section 267, sale or exchange between related taxpayers, **7**:14–15, **8**:14
Section 274, substantiation requirements, **5**:40
Section 351, transfer of assets to business entity, **7**:31, **12**:8–10, **12**:12, **12**:13, **12**:15, **12**:19, **12**:21, **18**:7
Section 357, assumption of liabilities, **12**:15–18
Section 367, tainted assets under, **12**:15
Section 482, application of, **12**:35
Section 721, transfer of assets to business entity, **7**:31, **14**:8, **18**:7
Section 1031, like-kind exchanges, **7**:20–25, **12**:8
Section 1033, involuntary conversions, **7**:25–30
Section 1221, definition of a capital asset, **8**:3–5
Section 1231 assets, **8**:2, **8**:23–29
Section 1231 gains and losses, **8**:24
Section 1231 lookback, **8**:28–29
Section 1231 netting procedure, **8**:26, **8**:27–28
Section 1231 property, **8**:23
Section 1237, real property subdivided for sale, **8**:6
Section 1244 stock, **6**:5–6, **8**:7
Section 1245 property, **8**:30–31
Section 1245 recapture, **8**:2, **8**:29–31
exceptions to, **8**:34–36
Section 1250 property, **8**:31
Section 1250 recapture, **8**:2, **8**:31–32, **8**:33–34
exceptions to, **8**:34–36
Section 1253, franchises, trademarks, and trade names, **8**:10–11
Securities, **12**:11
dealers in, **8**:5
holding period of new, **7**:15
options, **8**:8
substantially identical, **2**:23
tax-exempt, **10**:20
Securities and Exchange Commission, regulation and oversight, **2**:28
Self-directed retirement plan, **11**:35
Self-employed individuals, **11**:2, **11**:4
employee vs., **11**:2–4
retirement plans for, **11**:35–37
Schedule C of Form 1040, **11**:2
Self-employment, Schedule SE of Form 1040, **1**:10
Self-employment tax, **1**:10, **11**:4, **11**:34–35
deductible for AGI, **9**:4
Seller cancellation, **4**:25
Senate, **2**:3–4
Senate Finance Committee, **2**:4

Separate foreign tax credit income categories, **16**:11
Separately stated items, **14**:5
Schedules K and K-1, **14**:15
Series EE savings bonds, **10**:10
Services, **14**:10
contribution of, **10**:21–22
goods and certain other items, deferral of advance payments for, **4**:12
interest paid for, **10**:19–20
no-additional-cost, **11**:13
of an employee, **4**:13
rendered, stock issued for, **12**:23
transfer of property, **12**:10
transfers for, **12**:13–14
Severance taxes, **1**:15
Shareholder
effect of noncash dividends on, **13**:14
flow-through of items of income and loss to S corporation, **15**:11
loans to, **13**:18
payments for the benefit of, **13**:17
tax consequences to, with and without the application of Section 351, **12**:21
tax treatment of distributions to, **15**:14–19
U.S., **16**:12
Shareholder cancellation, **4**:25
Shareholder consent, S corporation status, **15**:7
Shareholder consequences, taxable corporate formation vs. tax-deferred Section 351 transaction, **12**:9
Shareholder limit, tax planning strategies for, **15**:6
Shareholder limitations, **15**:5–6
Shareholder use of corporate-owned property, **13**:17
Shareholder's basis in
S stock, **15**:21–23
stock received in exchange for property, **12**:20
Shares of stock, freely transferable, **12**:7
Shifting income and deductions across time, tax planning strategies for, **9**:22
Short sales, **8**:14–15
Short-term capital gains (STCG), **4**:19
Short-term capital losses (STCL), **4**:19
nonbusiness bad debt, **6**:4
Short-term gains, **8**:16
Short-year election, **15**:14
Significant participation activity, **6**:23
SIMPLE plans, **11**:36–37
Single taxpayers, 2018 tax rate schedule for, **9**:21
Single taxpayers, **9**:17
Small business corporation, **15**:3, **15**:14
one class of stock, **15**:4–5
shareholder limitations, **15**:5–6
Small Business Health Options Program (SHOP) Marketplace, **17**:11
Small business stock (Section 1244 stock), **6**:5–6, **8**:21–22
exclusion, individual AMT preferences, **17**:30
losses, tax planning strategies for maximizing the benefits of, **6**:6
Small Cases Division of the Tax Court, **2**:10
Small employer health insurance credit, **17**:11, **17**:13
Social considerations, **1**:30
tax law, **1**:33
Social Security, **1**:9
benefits, **10**:6
Sociology, tax law, **1**:18

Sole proprietor
  Schedule C of Form 1040, **11**:33
  unlimited liability, **12**:6
Sole proprietorship, **18**:2
  converting to another entity form, **18**:20
  disposing of, **18**:15–16, **18**:18
  tax attributes of, **18**:22–25
  tax treatment of business forms
    compared, **12**:6
Solicitation, **16**:19
Special allocation, **14**:7
Special holding period rules, **8**:13–14
  disallowed loss transactions, **8**:14
  gifts, **8**:14
  inherited property, **8**:14
  nontaxable exchanges, **8**:13
Special interest legislation, **1**:31
Special rule for condemnations, **7**:28
Specific charge-off method, **6**:3–4
  tax treatment of bad debts, **6**:4
Specified services businesses, QBI limitation
    for, **11**:42–44
Spousal IRAs, **11**:30, **11**:31
Spouse and dependents, medical expenses
    for, **10**:13
Spread, **17**:21
Standard deduction, **1**:16, **9**:5, **9**:6–8
  basic amounts, **9**:7
  special limitations for dependents, **9**:8
Standard Federal Tax Reporter, **2**:19
Standard mileage method, **11**:19
Startup costs, **14**:14
Startup expenditures, **5**:11, **12**:31
State and local government influences,
    1:31–32
State and local income taxation in the U.S.,
    crossing state lines, **16**:17–25
  sources of law, **16**:18–19
  tax issues, **16**:19–24
State income tax liability, computing, **16**:20
State tax revenue sources, **16**:18
State taxes
  corporations, **12**:5–6
  death taxes, **1**:11
  excise taxes, **1**:7
  income taxes, **1**:16–17
Statutory (or nominal) rates, **9**:22
Statutory depletion, **5**:43
Statutory expansions
  dealers in securities, **8**:5
  real property subdivided for sale, **8**:6
Statutory sources of tax law, **2**:2–6
  arrangement of the code, **2**:5
  citing the code, **2**:5–6
  effect of treaties, **2**:6
  legislative process, **2**:3–4
  origin of the Internal Revenue Code, **2**:2
Statutory tax law changes
  decrease in C corporation tax rate, **3**:21
  effects of, **3**:20–23
  one-time transition tax for unrepatriated
    profits of U.S. entities, **3**:22–23
  repeal of C corporation alternative
    minimum tax, **3**:22
  treatment of net operating losses and
    carryovers, **3**:22
Stepped-down basis, **7**:13
Stepped-up basis, **7**:13
Stock, **12**:11
  disposing of C corporation as sale of,
    18:17–18
  holding period of new, **7**:15
  one class of, **15**:4–5

substantially identical, **2**:23
  tax planning strategies for selling, **18**:17
Stock buybacks, **13**:22
Stock dividends, **13**:21–22
Stock issued for services rendered, **12**:23
Stock options, **8**:8
Stock received exchange for property,
    shareholder's basis in, **12**:20
Stock redemptions, **13**:22–24
  non-U.S. shareholders prefer capital gain
    treatment in, **13**:23
Stock to shareholder, basis of, **12**:20
Straight-line depreciation, **13**:5
Straight-line election, **5**:27–28
Straight-line method
  depreciation of real property, **17**:17
  depreciation on fixed assets, **3**:4
  election of, **5**:25
  pollution control facilities, **17**:19
Student loans, **4**:25
  deductibility of interest, **10**:21
Subchapter C, Corporate Distributions and
    Adjustments, **2**:5
Subchapter K, Partners and Partnerships, **2**:5
Subchapter S, Tax Treatment of S
    Corporations and Their Shareholders,
    2:5, **15**:2
Subpart F income, **16**:12, **16**:13–14
Subsequent events, **2**:22
Substantial economic effect, **18**:6
Substantial presence test, **16**:15
Substantial rights, patents, **8**:9–10
Substantially identical, **7**:15, **8**:15
  stock or securities, **2**:23
Substantially rehabilitated, **17**:5
Substantiation requirements, **5**:40
Substituted basis, **14**:11
Sudden event, casualty loss, **6**:7
Support test for
  qualifying child, **9**:10
  qualifying relative, **9**:12–14
Supreme Court, **2**:13
  judicial citations of, **2**:16
Supreme Court Reporter (S.Ct.), **2**:16
Surviving spouse, **9**:18
Suspended losses
  carryovers of, **6**:19
  impact of, **6**:18–19
  tax planning strategies for, **15**:23
Syndication costs, **14**:13

T

Tables, cost recovery, **5**:44–48
Tainted assets, **12**:15
Tangible property, personalty, **1**:14
Tariffs, **1**:14
Tax accounting elections, **14**:12–13
Tax and book depreciation, **5**:32
Tax attributes of different forms of business,
    18:22–25
Tax avoidance, **1**:22
  or no bona fide business purpose, **12**:16
Tax bases, **1**:5–6
  territorial approach to, **3**:22
Tax benefit rule, **4**:25
Tax bills, legislative process for, **2**:3
Tax burden, **1**:5
  U.S., **1**:17
Tax compliance, **3**:23
  what form of, **9**:28

Tax concepts of income, comparison of
    accounting and, **4**:5
Tax consequences of liability assumption,
    12:18
Tax consequences to the shareholders and
    corporation with and without the
    application of Section 351, **12**:21
Tax controversy, **3**:23
Tax conventions, **2**:6
Tax Court, **2**:10–16
  http://www.ustaxcourt.gov, **2**:14
  judicial citations of, **2**:14–15
  jurisdiction of, **2**:11
Tax Court of the United States Reports (T.C.),
    2:14
Tax credit or income tax deduction, **17**:2
Tax credits, **3**:5, **9**:23, **17**:2, **17**:12–13
  business-related provisions, **17**:2–13
  child tax credit, **10**:28
  computation of work opportunity tax
    credit: general, **17**:5–6
  credit for employer-provided child care,
    17:9, **17**:12
  credit for employer-provided family and
    medical leave, **17**:11, **17**:13
  credit for small employer pension plan
    startup costs, **17**:9, **17**:12
  dependent tax credit, **10**:28
  disabled access credit, **17**:2, **17**:8, **17**:12
  energy credits, **17**:8, **17**:12
  foreign tax credit, **17**:2, **17**:10–11, **17**:12
  general business credit, **17**:2–4, **17**:12
  low-income housing credit, **17**:12
  rehabilitation expenditures credit, **17**:4–5,
    17:12
  research activities credit, **17**:6–8, **17**:12
  small employer health insurance credit,
    17:11, **17**:13
  tax minimization strategies related to, **1**:28
  work opportunity credit, **17**:5–6, **17**:12
Tax Cuts and Jobs Act (TCJA) of 2017
  accounting methods, **4**:10
  adjusted taxable income, **12**:33
  alimony and separate maintenance
    payments, **10**:3
  AMT and, **17**:13
  bonus depreciation, **5**:32
  broad-based changes to MACRS, **11**:41
  business expenses, **11**:18
  business interest expense limitation
    under, **12**:31
  child and dependent tax credits, **10**:28
  child tax credit, **2**:4
  Conference Report, **12**:32
  corporate AMT and, **17**:33–34
  corporate tax rate, **11**:37, **12**:3–5
  deductibility of business interest, **5**:14
  deductions from AGI and, **9**:5
  depreciation of personal property and, **17**:17
  entertainment expenses, **11**:25
  excess business loss limitation, **6**:32
  exemptions and, **9**:9
  home equity interest and, **17**:26
  independent contractor expenses, **11**:18
  individual shared responsibility payment,
    10:32
  international competitiveness, **12**:3
  itemized deductions, **10**:15, **10**:25–26
  meals furnished for the convenience of
    the employer, **11**:7
  medical expenses and, **17**:27
  moving expense reimbursements, **11**:15,
    11:22

NOLs carryover provisions and, **17**:24
personal and dependency exemptions, **9**:6
qualified business income, **11**:37–38
qualified residence interest and, **10**:19
standard deduction, **9**:9, **10**:26
tax issues in global marketplace, **16**:7
temporary 60 percent ceiling on charitable contributions, **10**:24
transportation fringes, **11**:15
U.S. Federal tax rates, **16**:8
Tax deductions, **9**:23, **10**:2
special, **3**:5
tax planning strategies for time value of, **5**:5
Tax deferral, **1**:24, **1**:25, **4**:9, **4**:12, **10**:17
Tax department, functions of by percent of time spent, **3**:23
Tax determination, **9**:21–24
computation of net taxes payable or refund due, **9**:22–23
Kiddie tax, **9**:23–24
tax rate schedule method, **9**:21–22
tax table method, **9**:21
unearned income of dependent children, **9**:23–24
Tax disclosures in the financial statements, **3**:15–18
balance sheet, **3**:15
financial statement footnotes, **3**:16
income statement, **3**:15
rate reconciliation, **3**:16–18
Tax evasion, **1**:22
Tax file memorandum, **2**:24
Tax formula, **4**:2–3
components of, **4**:2–3, **9**:2–6
deductions, **4**:3, **9**:4–5
determining the tax, **4**:3
exclusions, **4**:2, **9**:3–4
gross income, **4**:2–3, **9**:3
income (broadly conceived), **4**:2, **9**:3
individual, **9**:2–6
personal and dependency exemptions, **9**:6
qualified business income deduction, **9**:6
standard deduction, 9:5, **9**:6–8
taxable income, **9**:6
Tax Foundation, **12**:3
Tax Freedom Day, **1**:17
Tax haven, **16**:27
Tax home, determining for travel expenses, **11**:20
Tax issues
authority to tax, **16**:5–7
controlled foreign corporations, **16**:12–15
crossing state lines, **16**:19–24
foreign tax credit, **16**:9–11
inbound issues, **16**:15–16
income sourcing, **16**:7–9
multinational transactions, **16**:5–17
special tax rate for intangible income, **16**:15
Tax issues related to contributed property, **14**:11–12
depreciation method and period, **14**:11
intangible assets, **14**:11
receivables, inventory, and built-in losses, **14**:12
Tax law
economic considerations, **1**:28–29, **1**:33
equity considerations, **1**:30–31
influence of IRS, **1**:33, **1**:34
influence of the courts on, **1**:32–33, **1**:34
political considerations, **1**:31–32, **1**:34
primary sources of, **2**:22
revenue needs, **1**:28

secondary materials, **2**:22
social considerations, **1**:30, **1**:33
understanding the federal, **1**:28–33
Tax law equity considerations, **1**:33
Tax law sources, **2**:2–16
administrative, **2**:6–9
assessing for tax research, **2**:20–23
judicial, **2**:10–16
statutory, **2**:2–6
tax commentary, **2**:19–20
tax services, **2**:19
Tax losses and the deferred tax asset, **3**:15
Tax Management Portfolios, **2**:19
Tax minimization strategies related to
credits, **1**:28
deductions, **1**:24–25
income, **1**:23–24
tax rates, **1**:25–27
Tax Notes, **2**:8
Tax on pre-election built-in gain, **15**:27–29
general rules, **15**:27–28
LIFO recapture tax, **15**:29
Tax payments, estimated, **11**:44–45
penalty on underpayments, **11**:45
Tax planning, **3**:23
avoidance vs. evasion, **1**:22
overview of, **1**:22
Tax planning fundamentals, **1**:22–28
general framework for income tax planning, **1**:23
overview of tax planning and ethics, **1**:22
tax minimization strategies related to credits, **1**:28
tax minimization strategies related to deductions, **1**:24–25
tax minimization strategies related to income, **1**:23–24
tax minimization strategies related to tax rates, **1**:25–27
Tax planning strategies
accumulated adjustments account, **15**:19
avoid PII pitfalls, **15**:30
avoiding preferences and adjustments, **17**:30
avoiding Section 351, **12**:19
avoiding wash sales, **7**:16
beating the 100-shareholder limit, **15**:6
cash receipts method, **4**:8
constructive dividends, **13**:19–20
controlling the timing of preferences and adjustments, **17**:26
corporate distributions, **13**:11–12
corporate liquidations, **13**:25
education expenses, **11**:23
effective utilization of itemized deductions, **10**:27
factors affecting retirement plan choices, **11**:37
for documentation of related-taxpayer loans, casualty losses, and theft losses, **6**:8
for gift planning, **7**:12
gifts of appreciated securities, **8**:17
important dates related to IRAs and Keogh plans, **11**:36
income of certain children, **9**:24
income shifting, **16**:25
inherited property, **7**:14
life insurance, **4**:22
like-kind exchanges, **7**:21
loss considerations, **15**:24–25
make your own tax shelter, **14**:26
making a proper election, **15**:7
managing the built-in gains tax, **15**:28

matching gains with losses, **8**:21
maximizing the benefits of small business (Section 1244 stock) losses, **6**:6
meal expenses, **11**:26
multiple support agreement and the medical expense deduction, **9**:14
nexus, **16**:21
organizational expenditures, **12**:32
other AMT planning strategies, **17**:32
other considerations when incorporating a business, **12**:24–25
prepaid income, **4**:12
preserving the S election, **15**:9
problems with a joint return, **9**:15
recognizing involuntary conversion gains, **7**:30
releasing valuation allowances, **3**:14
salary structure, **15**:15
self-employed individuals, **11**:4
selling depreciable real estate, **8**:34
selling stock or assets, **18**:17
shifting income and deductions across time, **9**:22
sourcing income from sales of inventory, **16**:9
stock redemptions, **13**:24
structuring the sale of a business, **5**:41
switching depletion methods, **5**:44
tax savings are not always created equal, **3**:19
techniques for reducing investment income, **4**:17
time value of tax deductions, **5**:5
timing capital gains, **8**:15
timing of recapture, **8**:36
timing the payment of deductible taxes, **10**:17
transactions between partners and partnerships, **14**:31
transportation and travel expenses, **11**:22
unreasonable compensation, **5**:4
utilizing passive activity losses, **6**:30–31
utilizing Section 351, **12**:13
utilizing the foreign tax credit, **16**:10
when to elect S corporation status, **15**:4
working with suspended losses, **15**:23
Tax Rate Schedule method, **9**:21–22
for single taxpayers (2018), **9**:21
joint return, **9**:17
Tax rates, **1**:4–5
corporations, **12**:3–5
in non-U.S. jurisdictions, **16**:17
progressive, **1**:4–5
proportional, **1**:4–5
regressive, **1**:5
tax minimization strategies related to, **1**:25–27
Tax reporting of partnership activities, **14**:18
Tax reporting rules, **14**:5–6
Tax research
arriving at the solution or at alternative solutions, **2**:23
assessing tax law sources, **2**:20–23
best practices, **2**:25–26
communicating, **2**:23–25
identifying the problem, **2**:18
locating the appropriate tax law sources, **2**:18–20
on the CPA examination, **2**:27–28
process, **2**:17
refining the problem, **2**:18
updates, **2**:25
working with the tax law, **2**:17–26

Tax return disclosures, **3**:6–8
  uncertain tax positions, **3**:7–8
Tax return filing procedures, **9**:28–29
Tax return preparation, outsourcing of, **1**:29
Tax savings, tax planning strategies for, **3**:19
Tax shelters, **6**:14–15, **14**:26
Tax status of property, **8**:2
Tax system
  incidence of taxation, **1**:6
  scope of U.S., **2**:3
  structure of, **1**:4–6
Tax Table, **9**:21
Tax treatment of disposition of a business, **18**:18–20
Tax uncertainties, financial accounting for, **3**:18–20
Taxable corporate formation vs. tax-deferred Section 351 transaction, shareholder consequences, **12**:9
Taxable estate, **1**:11
Taxable income, **1**:19, **1**:21, **10**:2, **9**:6
  additions to, **13**:3–4
  computation of, **15**:10–12
  subtractions from, **13**:4
  worldwide, **3**:22
Taxable year, **4**:6
Taxation of damages, **10**:9
Taxation
  general scheme of, **8**:2
  how to study, **1**:3
  incidence of, **1**:6
  of multinational transactions, U.S., **16**:2–17
  relevance of to accounting and finance professionals, **1**:2–3
TaxCenter, **2**:19
Tax-deferred Section 351 transaction vs. taxable corporate formation, shareholder consequences, **12**:9
Taxes, **10**:15–16
  ad valorem, **1**:12
  and tax expense, state/local, **16**:24
  book-tax differences, **3**:4
  conduit and entity perspectives effect on other, **18**:10–11
  death, **1**:10–11
  deductible and nondeductible, **10**:15
  determining, **4**:3
  employment, **1**:5, **1**:9–10
  entity-level, **15**:27–30
  estate, **1**:10, **1**:11
  excise, **1**:6–7
  federal collections, **1**:13
  FICA, **1**:9–10
  franchise, **1**:14–15
  FUTA, **1**:9
  gift, **1**:11–12
  in U.S., overview of, **1**:18
  income, **1**:15–18, **10**:16
  individuals and, **1**:3–4
  inheritance, **1**:10
  itemized deductions, individual AMT adjustments, **17**:25
  occupational, **1**:15
  other business expenses, **5**:17–18
  personal property taxes, **10**:16
  property, **1**:12–14
  real estate taxes, **10**:16
  sales, **1**:4, **1**:7, **10**:16
  self-employment, **1**:10, **11**:34–35
  severance, **1**:15
  tax planning strategies for timing the payment of deductible, **10**:17

types of, **1**:6–18
  unemployment, **1**:10
  use, **1**:8
  value added tax, **1**:8–9
Taxes on personalty, **1**:14
Taxes on privileges and rights, **1**:14–15
  federal customs duties, **1**:14
  franchise taxes and occupational taxes, **1**:14–15
  severance taxes, **1**:15
Taxes on realty, **1**:13
Taxes on the production and sale of goods, **1**:6–9
  Federal excise taxes, **1**:6–7
  general sales tax, **1**:7
  local excise taxes, **1**:7
  state excise taxes, **1**:7
  use taxes, **1**:8
  value added tax (VAT), **1**:8–9
Tax-exempt income, expenses and interest related to, **5**:13–14
Tax-exempt securities, **10**:20
Tax-free transaction, **7**:19
Taxpayer
  legal residence of, **2**:21
  multijurisdictional, **16**:2
  use test, **7**:27–28
Tax-related websites, **2**:26
Technical Advice Memoranda (TAMs), **2**:9
Temporary assignments, travel expenses, **11**:20
Temporary differences, **3**:4
Temporary Regulations, **2**:7
Tentative minimum tax (TMT), **17**:3, **17**:15
Territorial approach
  double taxation problem, **16**:5–7
  to tax base, **3**:22
Theft losses, **6**:7–13
  definition of theft, **6**:9
  Form 4684 Casualties and Thefts, **8**:36
  individual, **6**:10–13
  loss measurement, **6**:9–10
  multiple losses, **6**:10
  personal use property, **6**:11–12
  tax planning strategies for documentation of, **6**:8
  timing of recognition of, **6**:9
Theft or casualty and nonpersonal use capital assets, Section 1231 assets, **8**:25
Thefts, capital recoveries, **7**:5–6
Thin capitalization, **12**:27
Thirty percent ceiling on charitable contributions, **10**:24–25
Throwback rule, **16**:23
Tiebreaker rules for
  determining dependency status, **9**:10
  qualifying child, **9**:10
Trade names, **8**:10–11
  significant power, right, or continuing interest, **8**:11
Trade or business
  business interest expense limitation and, **12**:34
  expenses, deductions for AGI, **10**:11
Trademarks, **8**:10–11
  Section 197 intangible, **5**:41
  significant power, right, or continuing interest, **8**:11
Traditional IRAs, **11**:30–31
  and Roth IRAs compared, **11**:33
  deduction of an active participant in 2018, phaseout of, **11**:30

Transfer pricing, multijurisdictional taxation, **16**:26–27
Transportation expenses, **11**:18–19, **11**:22
  commuting expenses, **11**:18–19
  computation of automobile expenses, **11**:19
Transportation, meal, and lodging, medical expenses for, **10**:13
Travel expenses, **11**:19–22
  away-from-home requirement, **11**:19
  combined business and pleasure travel, **11**:21–22
  determining the tax home, **11**:20
  temporary assignments, **11**:20
Treasury Decisions (TDs), **2**:9
Treasury department regulations, **2**:7
Treasury, regulation and oversight, **2**:28
Treasury regulation, assessing the significance of, **2**:20–21
Treaties, effect of, **2**:6
Trial court, **2**:10, **2**:11–12
  federal judicial system, **2**:11
Twenty percent ceiling on charitable contributions, **10**:25
Twenty-eight percent property, **8**:17, **8**:19–21

U

U.S. corporate taxes and international business competitiveness, **12**:3
U.S. government publications, definition of capital asset, **8**:3, **8**:5
U.S. income tax treaties in force, **16**:6
U.S. income tax treatment of foreign person's income, **16**:17
U.S. shareholder, **16**:12
U.S. tax burden, **1**:17
U.S. Tax Cases (USTC), **2**:15
U.S. tax system, scope of, **2**:3
U.S. taxation of multinational transactions, **16**:2–17
  sources of law, **16**:4–5
  tax issues, **16**:5–17
U.S. trade or business, conduct of, **16**:15
UDITPA (Uniform Division of Income for Tax Purposes Act), **16**:19
Uncertain tax positions, **3**:7–8
Unearned income, **9**:23
  of dependent children, **9**:23–24
Unemployment compensation, **10**:5
Unemployment taxes, **1**:10
Unexpected event, casualty loss, **6**:7
Uniform premiums, group term life insurance, **11**:10
Unitary approach, **16**:23
Unitary theory, income sourcing crossing state lines, **16**:23–24
United States Board of Tax Appeals Reports (B.T.A.), **2**:14
United States Reports, Lawyer's Edition (L.Ed.), **2**:16
United States Supreme Court Reports (U.S.), **2**:16
Unlimited liability, **12**:6
Unreasonable compensation, **13**:17–18
  tax planning strategies for, **5**:4
Unrecaptured Section 1250 gains, **8**:18, **8**:19–21, **8**:33

Unreimbursed employee expenses, **11**:30
Unrepatriated profits of U.S. entities,
    one-time transition tax for, **3**:22–23
Unusual event, casualty loss, **6**:7
Use or lose plans, **11**:12
Use taxes, **1**:8

V

Valuation allowance, **3**:12–14
Valuation requirements for charitable
    contributions, **10**:23
Value added tax (VAT), **1**:8–9
Value test, **12**:34
Voluntary revocation, **15**:7–8
Voting power test, **12**:34

W

Wage and Tax Statement, Form W-2, **9**:22
Wages, QBI deduction limitation based on,
    11:40–42
Wash sales, **7**:15
    rules, **7**:16
    tax planning strategies for avoiding, **7**:16
Water's edge election, **16**:25
Wherewithal to pay, **1**:30–31, **7**:19, **12**:8
Windfall income, **4**:4
Withdrawals, Schedules K and K-1,
    14:17–18
Work opportunity tax credit, **17**:5–6, **17**:12
Workers' compensation, **10**:10
Working condition fringes, **11**:13, **11**:14,
    11:16
    benefits, **11**:16

Y

Year of discovery, theft loss, **6**:9
Year of inclusion, **4**:6–12
    accounting methods, **4**:6–10
    special rules for accrual basis taxpayers,
        4:11–12
    special rules for cash basis taxpayers,
        4:10–11
    taxable year, **4**:6

Worldwide approach, double taxation
    problem, **16**:5–7
Worldwide income tax base, **4**:3
Worldwide taxable income, **3**:22
Worthless securities, **6**:5, **8**:7
Writ of Certiorari, **2**:14

AMT Formula for Individuals

Taxable income (increased by any standard deduction taken)
Plus or minus: Adjustments
Plus: Preferences
Equals: Alternative minimum taxable income (AMTI)
Minus: Exemption
Equals: Alternative minimum tax (AMT) base
Multiplied by: 26% or 28% rate
Equals: Tentative minimum tax before foreign tax credit
Minus: AMT foreign tax credit
Equals: Tentative minimum tax (TMT)
Minus: Regular tax liability (less any foreign tax credit)
Equals: AMT (if TMT > regular tax liability)

2017 AMT Exemption and Phaseout for Individuals

Filing Status	Exemption	Phaseout Begins at	Phaseout Ends at
Married, filing jointly	$84,500	$160,900	$498,900
Single or Head of household	54,300	120,700	337,900
Married, filing separately	42,250	80,450	249,450

2018 AMT Exemption and Phaseout for Individuals

Filing Status	Exemption	Phaseout Begins at	Phaseout Ends at
Married, filing jointly	$109,400	$1,000,000	$1,437,600
Single or Head of household	70,300	500,000	781,200
Married, filing separately	54,700	500,000	718,800